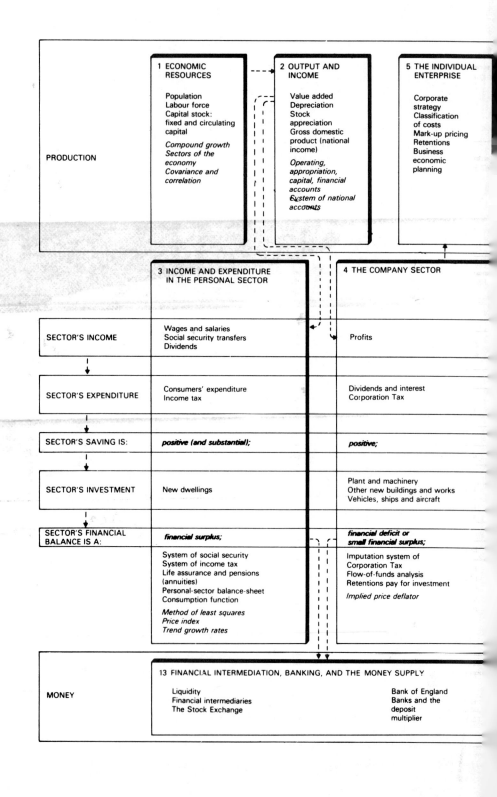

PRODUCTION

1 ECONOMIC RESOURCES

Population
Labour force
Capital stock:
fixed and circulating
capital

Compound growth
Sectors of the
economy
Covariance and
correlation

2 OUTPUT AND INCOME

Value added
Depreciation
Stock
appreciation
Gross domestic
product (national
income)

Operating,
appropriation,
capital, financial
accounts
System of national
accounts

5 THE INDIVIDUAL ENTERPRISE

Corporate
strategy
Classification
of costs
Mark-up pricing
Retentions
Business
economic
planning

---

3 INCOME AND EXPENDITURE IN THE PERSONAL SECTOR

4 THE COMPANY SECTOR

	3 Income and expenditure in the personal sector	4 The company sector
SECTOR'S INCOME	Wages and salaries Social security transfers Dividends	Profits
SECTOR'S EXPENDITURE	Consumers' expenditure Income tax	Dividends and interest Corporation Tax
SECTOR'S SAVING IS:	*positive (and substantial);*	*positive;*
SECTOR'S INVESTMENT	New dwellings	Plant and machinery Other new buildings and works Vehicles, ships and aircraft
SECTOR'S FINANCIAL BALANCE IS A:	*financial surplus;*	*financial deficit or* *small financial surplus;*

System of social security
System of income tax
Life assurance and pensions
(annuities)
Personal-sector balance-sheet
Consumption function

Method of least squares
Price index
Trend growth rates

Imputation system of
Corporation Tax
Flow-of-funds analysis
Retentions pay for investment

Implied price deflator

MONEY

13 FINANCIAL INTERMEDIATION, BANKING, AND THE MONEY SUPPLY

Liquidity
Financial intermediaries
The Stock Exchange

Bank of England
Banks and the
deposit
multiplier

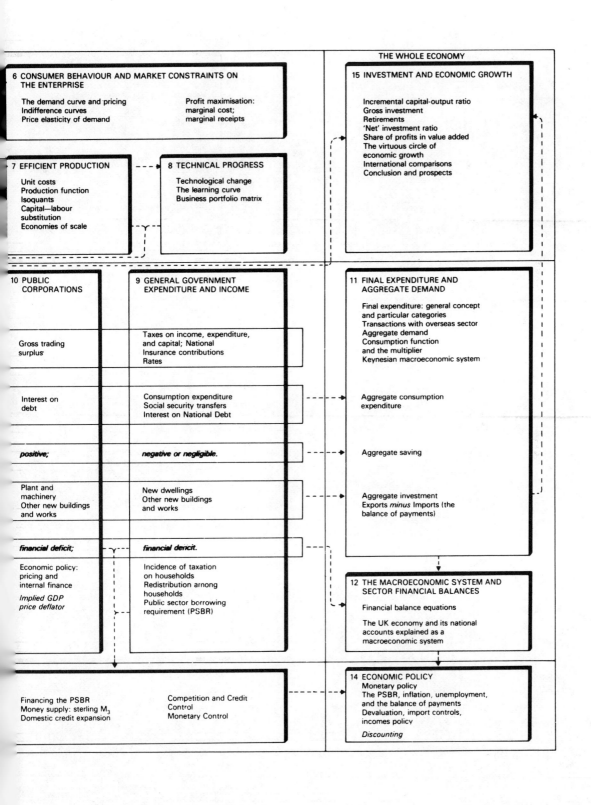

THE WHOLE ECONOMY

6 CONSUMER BEHAVIOUR AND MARKET CONSTRAINTS ON THE ENTERPRISE

The demand curve and pricing
Indifference curves
Price elasticity of demand

Profit maximisation:
marginal cost;
marginal receipts

15 INVESTMENT AND ECONOMIC GROWTH

Incremental capital-output ratio
Gross investment
Retirements
'Net' investment ratio
Share of profits in value added
The virtuous circle of
economic growth
International comparisons
Conclusion and prospects

7 EFFICIENT PRODUCTION

Unit costs
Production function
Isoquants
Capital—labour
substitution
Economies of scale

8 TECHNICAL PROGRESS

Technological change
The learning curve
Business portfolio matrix

10 PUBLIC CORPORATIONS

9 GENERAL GOVERNMENT EXPENDITURE AND INCOME

11 FINAL EXPENDITURE AND AGGREGATE DEMAND

Final expenditure: general concept
and particular categories
Transactions with overseas sector
Aggregate demand
Consumption function
and the multiplier
Keynesian macroeconomic system

Gross trading
surplus

Taxes on income, expenditure,
and capital; National
Insurance contributions
Rates

Interest on
debt

Consumption expenditure
Social security transfers
Interest on National Debt

Aggregate consumption
expenditure

positive;

negative or negligible.

Aggregate saving

Plant and
machinery
Other new buildings
and works

New dwellings
Other new buildings
and works

Aggregate investment
Exports *minus* Imports (the
balance of payments)

financial deficit;

financial deficit.

Economic policy:
pricing and
internal finance

*Implied GDP
price deflator*

Incidence of taxation
on households
Redistribution among
households
Public sector borrowing
requirement (PSBR)

12 THE MACROECONOMIC SYSTEM AND SECTOR FINANCIAL BALANCES

Financial balance equations

The UK economy and its national
accounts explained as a
macroeconomic system

14 ECONOMIC POLICY
Monetary policy
The PSBR, inflation, unemployment,
and the balance of payments
Devaluation, import controls,
incomes policy
Discounting

Financing the PSBR
Money supply: sterling M_3
Domestic credit expansion

Competition and Credit
Control
Monetary Control

INTRODUCTION TO ECONOMICS:
THEORY AND DATA

Other books by Dudley Jackson

Poverty

Unfair Dismissal: How and Why the Law Works

Do Trade Unions Cause Inflation? (with H. A. Turner and Frank Wilkinson)

INTRODUCTION TO ECONOMICS:
THEORY AND DATA

DUDLEY JACKSON

Professor of Business Economics
University of Aston Management Centre

First published 1982 by
THE MACMILLAN PRESS LTD
London and Basingstoke
Companies and representatives throughout the world

ISBN 0 333 33355 1 (hard cover)
ISBN 0 333 33357 8 (paper cover)

Filmset by Vantage Photosetting Co. Ltd, Eastleigh and London
Printed in Great Britain

To Ted and Mary

Contents

Acknowledgement

The author and publishers wish to thank the Controller of Her Majesty's Stationery Office for permission to reproduce tables from *National Income and Expenditure, Economic Trends* and *Financial Statistics*.

Chapter 1

Economic Resources

Contents

Chapter guide

Chapter 1 begins by explaining why economics must be studied with data, and the first data to be considered relate to the *economic resources* of the economy: namely, *labour* and *capital*. We look first at data on the British labour force and on the population from which the labour force is drawn. We look at the distribution of people in the economy and at the growth and fluctuations in numbers. *En route* we consider some technical matters such as: the distinction between *stocks* and *flows*; how the population and the labour force are counted; why we use a *ratio*, or '*logarithmic*', *scale* to present certain data and how such scales work; how to deal with *compound growth*; and the useful 'Rule of 70' is explained.

Second, we look at data on the *capital stock*, explaining the important distinctions between *fixed* and *circulating* capital and between 'capital' and 'financial assets'. When we consider who owns what in the capital stock, we have to understand the *sectors* of the economy (both the concept of a sector and the actual sectors into which the economy is divided). We examine how the United Kingdom's *net* and *gross* capital stock is valued.

This involves a consideration of *depreciation* and the *perpetual inventory method*, which uses data on *fixed capital formation* and *retirements*. We look at all the relevant data because it is important to see how the capital stock grows.

Finally, we look at data on labour and capital together, both as they have grown in the past century and on their distribution among industries (or 'branches') of the economy. The purpose of this is to show how capital per worker influences output per worker. In order that we may systematically analyse such influences we consider the technical issues of *scatter diagrams, covariance, standard deviations,* and *correlation*.

The chapter ends, as do all chapters, with some *Exercises* designed to give you practical training and practice in finding, using and presenting data, and in applying the concepts you have learned. Exercise 1.2 contains the First and Greatest Commandment addressed to those who use data: namely, CHECK YOUR RESULTS!

Introduction

This book is intended to explain how a modern industrial economy works. This book is concerned with *economic concepts and theory*, because the first requirement is an understanding of the structure and activities of various economic organisations, and of how they interact. We are concerned also with *data*, because the second requirement is knowledge of the statistics which measure the economic activities of organisations. The book is also an introduction to economics, in that it starts from basic concepts, assumes no previous study of either economics or statistics, and tries systematically to cover most of what a beginner student is expected to learn about economics.

What does it mean to become an economist? All of us are familiar with the idea that one can open a book and read a page of *words* and thereby gain knowledge and understanding, but few beginner students of economics are accustomed to the idea that one can similarly open a book containing statistics and read a page of *numbers*; it is even more important to do this because most of the facts relating to an economy are in the form of statistics. The amount of statistical information that is published about the United Kingdom's economy is now extremely plentiful, and it is not possible to count oneself an economist unless one has developed the ability to read and 'make sense out of' such statistical information. The student should firmly put away any idea that consulting and working with such sources of data is an advanced or a difficult thing to do, especially in this era of inexpensive electronic calculators which help with the simple arithmetic required when interpreting tables. The notes to, and exercises on, the tables in this book and the source references should be studied, because they will show you both where you can find facts for yourself and also how to interpret them.

To find the statistics for yourself and to work with them is absolutely essential to becoming an economist. Unfortunately, many students of economics (and their teachers) do not appreciate this: they do not realise that becoming an economist is like becoming an athlete or a musician or a mechanic. This textbook is like a book on the theory of running or of music or of motor-cars; while it is undoubtedly helpful to study a book on the proper way to run, or play a musical instrument or repair a car, such study will not by itself make you into a runner, musician or mechanic. In order to do that you have to get out on the track and daily train your muscles by running, or practise a musical instrument, or work with cars. Exactly the same applies in economics: you have to practise your understanding by working with economic data; and if you do not do this, you can never hope to be a trained economist – just as you could never expect to be a trained athlete, musician or mechanic if you never practised.

In learning economics and using data the first essential is to understand a (fairly large) number of descriptive and analytic concepts, starting from the simpler concepts such as the labour force, the capital stock, value added, and so on. Inevitably, therefore, a textbook must start off with a considerable chunk of *description* and straightforward learning of concepts (just as you must develop your vocabulary when learning a foreign language). This is so that you can begin to understand in concrete terms the things with which economics is concerned; only after learning these concepts and these descriptions can we get to the *analytic* aspect of economics, which is concerned with seeing how all these things fit together in a working economic system. Analysis tends to be more exciting than (boring, old) description; but it is a great weakness in the present-day teaching of economics that students are not provided with an adequate understanding of the basic descriptive concepts of economics (let alone being required to practise their understanding of those concepts by working with the data). From this it follows that their ability to describe the working of an economy remains deficient, and so their ability analytically to understand the working of an economy is, even at the end of their course, most imperfect. Clearly this is a bad state of affairs: one would rightly not have much confidence in an athlete who collapsed exhausted after fifty yards, or a musician who could not get the right notes, or a mechanic who (a) could not describe to you the basic parts of a motor car, and (b) had never worked on motor cars anyway. For example, in learning about the important economic concepts of depreciation (on fixed capital) or stock appreciation (on circulating capital) it is essential first of all to have some (descriptive) understanding of the stocks of fixed and circulating capital in the UK economy.

The first things we have to study are the nation's *economic* resources: those resources which work mainly upon *natural* resources, such as raw materials, and upon the various processed forms of materials, to produce goods and services which people will purchase. By contrast, we are not particularly concerned with natural resources as such: this is not a textbook on economic geography, one of the purposes of which is to study the occurrences of such things as coal, oil and iron-ore, or where wheat may best be grown or dairy cows kept, and so on. Of course, such natural resources are extremely important to an economy, and it helps to know about the geography of things, just as it may help to know about the technology of mining or farming, but as economists we are more concerned with the *economic* aspects of the activities whereby these natural resources are obtained and processed into the goods which people wish to consume, such as electricity (from coal) or bread (from wheat).

Since the middle of the nineteenth century, economists have divided economic resources into three categories: land, labour, and capital. These have usually been called the factors (or agents) of production. One outstanding feature of a modern *industrial* economy is that agriculture accounts for only a small share of total output. For this reason we shall not be much concerned with land, which also has the distinction, among economic resources, of being non-reproducible and therefore incapable of being extended (apart from minor qualifications, mostly in the Netherlands, where land has been reclaimed from the sea).

The important distinction between stocks and flows

A general definition of 'resource' is: a means of supplying some want, a stock or reserve upon which one can draw when necessary. In studying economics, we shall be much concerned with the distinction between *stocks* and *flows*:

1. A stock exists *at* a moment in time.
2. A flow occurs *during* a period of time.

Any reference to a flow should always mention the period during which that flow occurred; any reference to a stock should always mention the date at which the stock existed. Wealth is a stock – for example, the amount one owns *at* any given moment; income is a flow – for example, the amount one earned *during* any given period. To say that a person's income is £5,000 is meaningless unless one adds 'per year' or 'per month' – two very different situations, indeed! To say that a person's wealth is £5,000 is imprecise but not completely meaningless because the listener will generally supply the implicit 'at this moment in time'. The student of economics should always state explicitly the nature of the variable referred to.

The relevance of this distinction to labour and capital as factors of production is that labour and capital are both stocks which exist at a moment in time; from these stocks a flow of productive services is obtained during a period of time. Thus the economy has a number of workers – a stock – from which it obtains a flow of man-hours of work per annum: the productive services of labour. Likewise, the economy has a stock of capital from which is also derived a flow of productive services: for example, so many hours of machine-time per annum. In this chapter we shall be concerned mainly with stocks.

The labour force and the population

The nation's stock of workers is drawn from among the number of people living in this country. If you look at Diagram 1.1, you will see that on the night of the 25/26 April 1971 (the date of the population census), there were 55.5 million people living in the United Kingdom.* Of these, approximately 25.1 million, or forty-five out of every hundred (45

DIAGRAM 1.1 *Distribution of the population of the United Kingdom in mid-1971 (numbers in millions)*

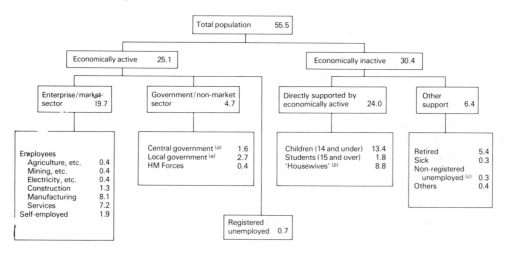

(a) Including educational and health services.
(b) Defined as economically inactive females aged 15 and over who were neither students nor retired persons.
(c) Calculated as the difference between the census unemployed and the registered unemployed.

Sources: Central Statistical Office, *Annual Abstract of Statistics, 1979 Edition* (no. 115), tables 2.4 and 6.1, pp. 11 and 154; CSO, *Social Trends*, no. 6, 1975, table 3.2, p. 82 and pp. 234–5; CSO, *National Income and Expenditure 1967–77*, table 1.11, p. 17; Department of Employment, *British Labour Statistics Year Book 1971*, tables 100 and 103, pp. 203 and 206.

*For convenience, we use the decimal point, and instead of writing 55,500,000 people, we write 55.5 *million* people; thus 0.7 million is 700,000, seven hundred thousand.

per cent) of the total population, were 'economically active', in the sense that they were either working or were out of employment (but who were registered as being available for work). The remaining 30.4 million, or 55 per cent of the total population, were 'economically inactive', in the sense that they were not working for pay and were not available for work.

Of the economically inactive, exactly half, 15.2 million, were children or students and another 8.8 million were 'housewives'. It may be assumed that all of these 24 million persons were directly supported by someone who was participating in the economy. Besides these, there were another 6.4 million persons who were supported in other ways, mostly from retirement pensions.

Our main concern is with the 25.1 million economically active people who were obtaining (or could obtain) their own and their families' livelihoods by working. Of these 25.1 million: 19.7 million were working in the enterprise/market sector of the economy; 4.7 million were working in the government/non-market sector; and 0.7 million were temporarily out of work because of unemployment. Like the economically inactive population, this last group has to be supported either from their own savings or (indirectly) by those with jobs, but as they are registered to be available for work the convention is to count them as economically active.

The word 'enterprise' in the term 'enterprise sector' is used in a broad sense to denote any undertaking which sells goods or services and whose activities are therefore not financed by compulsory levies. The distinction between the enterprise and the non-enterprise sector rests on the way in which the activity of the undertaking is paid for. If the activity is wholly or partly dependent upon some form of selling to voluntary buyers in the market, then the organisation is in the enterprise sector. If the activity is wholly independent of selling in the market and is paid for by compulsory levies upon people (such as taxes or local authority rates), then it is in the government or non-market sector.

The reason for making the distinction between the enterprise/market sector on the one hand, and the government/non-market sector on the other, is, first, that the activities of the government sector are largely supported by compulsory levies upon incomes produced in the enterprise sector. Second, to the extent that the annual expenses of government-sector activities are not covered by compulsory levies, the difference is met by government borrowing, and such borrowing has a special impact on the economy (these are both matters to which we subsequently return).

As you can see in Diagram 1.1, most of the 19.7 million persons working in the market sector are engaged as employees of enterprises. Relatively few, 1.9 million only, are listed as 'self-employed'. An employee is a person who works under a contract of employment with the employing organisation, the contract of employment being a contract *of service* in return for payment where the service is an *integral part* of the work of the employing organisation and where the manner of work is, at least to some extent, *controlled* by the employer. A self-employed person, on the other hand, works on his own account: there may be a contract *for services*, such as when an organisation reaches an agreement with a self-employed electrician to install some electrical wiring, but the electrician is not, in these circumstances, an integrated part of the organisation, nor is the way he does his work controlled by the organisation with whom he has such a contract. A self-employed person is a one-man (or one-woman) enterprise, independent of other enterprises; an employee does not have this status.

Nearly all of Britain's workers, then, are employees, and a large proportion, 10.2 million out of the 25.1 million economically active, or 41 per cent, are employees in the industrial sector of the economy, defining this sector to comprise: mining and quarrying (including, unless separately given, North Sea oil); electricity, gas, and water supplies; construction; and manufacturing. Therefore, when we speak of the British economy as an 'industrial market economy' we mean that it is an economy:

(a) where a large proportion of the economically active population derive their livelihood from work in industry, and

(b) where most of the economic activity takes place in the enterprise or market sector.

(The British economy is also referred to as a 'mixed economy' because of the importance of enterprises which are owned by the state, and we shall, in the next section, see precisely what this term means.)

   In contrast to this industrial aspect of the economy, relatively few workers are engaged in agriculture, forestry or fishing: about 0.3 million of the 1.9 million persons counted as self-employed are in fact farmers or fishermen, making a total of 0.7 million engaged in agriculture, forestry or fishing, so that in 1971 a little under 3 per cent of the economically active population in the United Kingdom derived their livelihood from agriculture, forestry or fishing.* This is, of course, a great contrast with bygone decades and with the less-developed economies of today's Third World countries. Diagram 1.2 shows the steady decline since 1841 in the proportion of Britain's economically active population engaged in agriculture, forestry and fishing (either as employees or as self-employed workers). Behind this change lies all the vast panorama of Britain's economic history and the Industrial Revolution. (I mention this because it is the reason why we concentrate on the economics of the industrial enterprise to the relative neglect of the economics of farming.)

DIAGRAM 1.2   *Percentage of the total occupied population of Great Britain who were engaged in agriculture, forestry, and fishing at successive censuses*

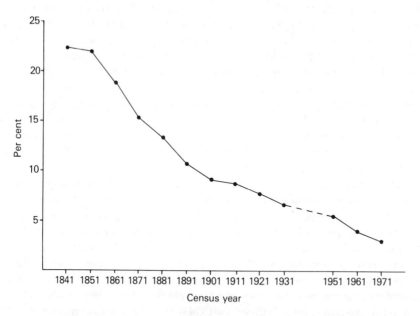

Sources: calculated from B. R. Mitchell and Phyllis Deane, *Abstract of British Historical Statistics* (Cambridge University Press, 1962) pp. 60–1; B. R. Mitchell and H. G. Jones, *Second Abstract of British Historical Statistics* (Cambridge University Press, 1971) p. 37; Office of Population Censuses and Surveys, *Census 1971: Great Britain Economic Activity*, Part II (HMSO, 1975) table 4, p. 51.

   The supply of labour is one important element in the growth of the economy. In the 125 years or so since 1851 the labour force of the United Kingdom has more than doubled from 12 million to 26 million. The figures in Table 1.1, which show these long-run changes in the United Kingdom's labour force, deserve to be studied with a little care because the labour

* 0.7 *divided by* 25.1 *equals* 0.028 or 2.8 per cent: hence 'a little under 3 per cent'.

TABLE 1.1　　*The labour force* (a) *of the United Kingdom, 1851 to 1980*

Year(b)	Total labour force (thousands)	Year(b)	Total labour force (thousands)
1851	12,050	1960	25,185
1861	13,090	1960(d)	24,586
1871	14,050	1961	24,815
1881	15,060	1962	25,060
1891	16,660	1963	25,186
1901	18,680	1964	25,370
1911	20,390	1965	25,554
1920	22,000	1966	25,650
1920(c)	20,688	1967	25,513
1921	20,120	1968	25,413
1931	21,920	1969	25,400
1938	23,580	1970	25,339
1951	23,841	1971	25,106
1952	23,925	1972	25,332
1953	24,053	1973	25,583
1954	24,346	1974(e)	25,684
1955	24,583	1975	25,909
1956	24,766	1976	26,134
1957	24,787	1977	26,305
1958	24,678	1978	26,414
1959	24,857	1979	26,419
		1980	26,314

(a) Comprising: employees in employment; employers; self-employed; HM Forces; unemployed (registered 1951–80).

(b) At census dates (generally late March/early April) 1851 to 1931 excepting 1920 and 1938 estimates; average of quarterly estimates (March, June, September, December) 1951 to 1980; unadjusted for seasonal variation.

(c) Excluding the Republic of Ireland from this year onwards.

(d) Using revised estimates of employees in employment from this year onwards (see *Department of Employment Gazette*, March 1975, pp. 193–205, and October 1975, pp. 1030–9).

(e) Using November unemployment figure to estimate December labour force.

Sources: 1851 to 1938, C. H. Feinstein, *National Income, Expenditure and Output of the United Kingdom 1855–1965* (Cambridge University Press, 1972) tables 11.8, 11.10 and 57, pp. 224, 227 and T126; Department of Employment, *British Labour Statistics Historical Abstract 1886–1968* (HMSO, 1971) table 118, p. 220; Department of Employment, *British Labour Statistics Year Book 1976* (HMSO, 1978) table 55, p. 122; *Department of Employment Gazette*, April 1979, table 101, p. 382; Department of Employment, *Employment Gazette*, September 1980, table 101, p. 1032; Department of Employment, *Employment Gazette*, January 1982, table 1.1, p. S7; note that some of these labour-force figures will be subject to revision when the results of the 1981 Census of Population become available in 1983.

force is a country's most important productive asset.* First we need to ask: what exactly is the meaning of 'labour force'? To answer this we need to know what is being counted and how the counting is done. Footnote (*a*) to the table explains very briefly the coverage of the statistics: the figures include employees in employment, their employers, the self-employed and the armed forces; everyone who was working for pay or profit. In addition it includes those who were unemployed but who were available (or looking) for work. It is

* In a table such as this, one is never going to be able to remember all the figures, so that one needs to develop a technique for 'extracting' the information in a form in which it can be remembered: for example, note that in 1851 the labour force was 12 million; by 1951 (a hundred years later) it was 24 million (in round terms); so, conveniently, the labour force had doubled in a century; by 1980, the labour force was 26 million. You could 'fix' this last figure in your mind by reflecting that 2¼ million people unemployed would then represent about 10 per cent of the labour force.

Censuses: counting the population and the labour force

How were the figures in Table 1.1 arrived at? Before 1951, we have only the decennial population census. The first population census was carried out in England, Wales and Scotland in 1801 (in Ireland in 1821) and decennially thereafter, with the exception of 1941. A population census is carried out by having trained enumerators go to every 'household' on a specific date to count the number of people living in the household, and to ascertain (at least) each person's sex, age and relationship (if any) to the head of household. Nowadays a lot more information is obtained, not only on people but also on household amenities, and because nearly every head of household is literate the census is conducted by the householder filling in a printed form which is collected, and checked, by an enumerator. The census-takers tried also to find out how people were making a living, and by 1851 they had devised a system for ascertaining and reporting who was economically active and in what occupation. So from 1851 and every ten years thereafter, we have a reliable assessment of the labour force. It is also possible to make estimates of the labour force for the years between the censuses, but these are estimates rather than actual counts and the table gives such figures only for 1920 (so that we can see the effect of the exclusion of the Republic of Ireland) and for 1938 (the year before the Second World War broke out).

From 1951 onwards we have annual counts of the labour force. By this time every working person in the United Kingdom was in the National Insurance scheme, and nearly every person (whether employed or self-employed) had a National Insurance card (on which were stamped his or her contributions and the employers' contributions, if an employee – some civil servants and Post Office workers paid contributions without using cards, but their numbers were known anyway). The cards were renewed annually, and every three months one-quarter of the cards were changed. By counting the number of cards exchanged each quarter, and by scaling up, it was possible to estimate the total labour force at four different times each year. In 1971, with the abolition of the card-stamping system (National Insurance contributions are now paid directly to the Inland Revenue along with income tax), a new system of counting the labour force had to be devised. The count is done partly through a census of employment taken in June each year* when each employer making income tax (Pay As You Earn – PAYE) returns to the Inland Revenue and employing three or more employees must fill in a form detailing the number of employees, with separate figures for males and females, full-time and part-time workers; the employer must supply separate figures for each given address (so that local and regional employment figures can be calculated) and is asked to give a brief description of the business activity at each address (so that the industrial distribution of employees can be analysed). The census excludes working proprietors and the self-employed, for whom separate estimates are made. The June census is normally confined to employers employing three or more employees, but every third year a full census is taken to include the 300,000 employers with only one or two employees. Unlike the card count, which was carried out on a sample of one-quarter of all workers four times a year, the June census is carried out on (nearly) all workers once a year, and estimates are then made (using other data and sample surveys) of the labour force at the other quarters. The census only counts employees if they were in employment in the census week; by contrast the card count

*Cuts in government expenditure mean that the employment census will now be taken once every three years.

the United Kingdom's 'economically active population'. It excludes people who made their living simply as property-owners and it does not include 'housewives'. Nor does it include the elderly who had 'retired' from the labour market; students also are excluded. It is, more or less, a measure of the supply of labour available to the economy, except that this supply can be, and has been, augmented by increases in the number of housewives going out to work.

Having established the basic data, we need to analyse the information. First of all, we included everybody with a card even if they had worked only a part of the year. Because there are quite a number of part-year workers, especially among women, the June census gives a lower estimate of employees in employment. The census of employment is, however, a count of *jobs* rather than of *persons*: a person holding two different (presumably part-time) jobs with two different employers (or PAYE pay-points) would be counted twice; this was not the case with the card count, as each person had only one card.

In 1971 both the employment census and the card count were carried out in parallel. That year was also a population census year, so we may compare the figures from all three methods of counting employees in employment. Table 1.2 shows that the card count, probably because of its inclusion of part-year workers, returned a higher count of employees than did the June employment census. In turn, probably because the employment census counts jobs rather than people, it returned a higher count of 'employees in employment' than did the April population census (however, unemployment had declined a little between April and June). The lesson to be learned from all this is that most of the statistics one sees are *estimates* with a margin of error, and that some figures are more reliable than others. The purpose of going through these (admittedly important) labour-force figures at such length is to show you that in handling any data you must be on guard. For instance in Table 1.1, it might appear that the UK labour force had fallen between 1970 and 1971, but we now know that this is more likely to be the result of the switch to a new method of counting. Even the most obvious terms must be questioned. One might think that the term 'United Kingdom' was not worth thinking about, but this is far from being the case. Up until January 1922 the United Kingdom included Southern Ireland, now the Republic of Ireland, whose independence from the United Kingdom was formally initiated in December 1921 and formally approved in December 1922. The consequence of this is that up to and including 1920 statistics for the 'United Kingdom' generally include Southern Ireland; thereafter, they exclude it. Particularly when dealing with figures on employment or earnings it is necessary to be careful about geographic coverage because many of these statistics exclude Northern Ireland. Throughout this book (and in all official statistical publications):

Great Britain = England + Wales + Scotland

United Kingdom = Great Britain + Northern Ireland

TABLE 1.2 *1971 estimates of employees in employment in Great Britain*

	Employees in employment [a] (thousands)		
	Males	Females	Total
National Insurance card count (June)	13,531	8,406	21,937
Census of employment (June)	13,424	8,224	21,648
Census of population (April)	13,340	8,150	21,490

[a] Excluding HM Forces and those in private domestic service.

Source: Department of Employment, *British Labour Statistics Year Book 1972* (HMSO, 1974) appendix I, table 1, p. 350.

should draw a graph. Diagram 1.3 shows the figures of Table 1.1 as points plotted on a scale and joined by straight lines to indicate the direction and extent of change. (Note that it would be cheating to join 1938 to 1951, because the wartime labour force did not lie on such a path.) Naturally, we expect that the labour force will grow; furthermore, we expect that it will grow at a *proportionate* or *relative* rate: that is, we do not expect it simply to expand by a constant *absolute* amount each year. In the 1850s the labour force tended to grow by about 100,000 a year but in the 1950s it tended to grow by about 150,000 a year.

DIAGRAM 1.3   *The working population of the United Kingdom, 1851 to 1980*

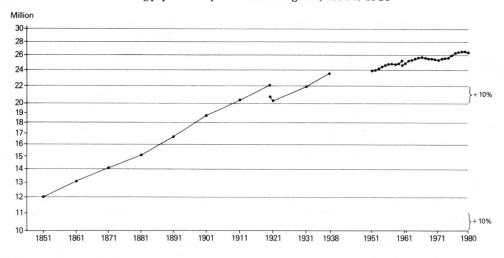

Using a ratio, or 'logarithmic', scale

Because we are concerned with the growth rate of the labour force, Diagram 1.3 is drawn on a 'logarithmic' or 'ratio' scale in the vertical direction. The years pass with even step, so the horizontal scale for years is marked on an arithmetic scale, and the graph paper on which Diagram 1.3 is drawn is called 'semi-logarithmic' paper because it has a log scale in only one direction ('double-logarithmic' paper has a log scale in both directions). Whenever you have a time series of data where growth is involved, then it is always advisable to plot the data on semi-log paper, because in this way one can readily discern changes in the rate of growth. The reason for this is as follows. An arithmetic scale uses distance (along a ruler) to represent *absolute* amounts while a logarithmic scale uses distance (along a ruler) to represent *relative* amounts. That is, along an arithmetic scale, a movement of 1cm will, wherever it occurs, represent the same absolute amount, say 10 units. Accordingly the

increase from 10 to 20 will measure 1cm as will the increase from 100 to 110. Along a logarithmic scale, a movement of 1cm will, wherever it occurs, represent the same *relative* amount, say a change of one-tenth: so the increase from 10 to 11, an increase of one-tenth, will measure 1cm, and an increase from 100 to 110 (ten times bigger in absolute amount but still only a relative increase of one-tenth) will also measure 1cm; so, too, will the increase from 20 to 22 or 50 to 55, and so on. That is why the logarithmic scale has the appearance of getting 'squashed up' as you go up the scale: the ruler distance from 1 to 2, a doubling or an increase of 100 per cent, will be the same as the ruler distance from 2 to 4 or 4 to 8, and so on. So any slackening in the *rate* of growth will show itself immediately in a flattening of the line drawn on semi-log paper. This does not happen with arithmetic-scale paper, which can give a misleadingly optimistic picture.

We are not surprised by this, because the labour force was much larger in the 1950s than in the 1850s, so the increase in the *absolute* annual increase does not mean that the labour force is growing at a faster rate.

When we plot the labour force data in this way we can see that the growth of the labour force was pretty constant right from 1851 to 1938. We can also see that in the 1950s growth was a bit slower and that in the 1960s it was very slow indeed, but that growth then picked up in the 1970s. The trend growth rates shown in Table 1.3 indicate the accuracy of our visual analysis. Clearly, we have a major puzzle on our hands: why did the rate of

TABLE 1.3   *Trend growth rates of the UK labour force*

Period	Trend growth rate (per cent per annum)
1851 to 1911	0.88
1921 to 1938	0.93
1951 to 1960	0.58
1960 to 1970	0.29
1971 to 1980	0.58

Source: calculated by fitting an exponential function to data in Table 1.1; this technique is explained towards the end of Chapter 3.

growth of the labour force slow down so much (by historical standards) in the 1950s and 1960s, and why did it then speed up again in the 1970s? And what is going to happen in the 1980s?

In order to try to answer these questions we need to look in more detail at the post-war growth of the labour force and at its projections. Unfortunately, the labour-force projections exclude Northern Ireland, so we have to look at the figures for Great Britain only. Table 1.4 shows the figures at five-year intervals. The really startling feature of Table 1.4 is the extent to which the expansion of the labour force has depended upon women workers. In the period 1951 to 1971, nine out of every ten extra workers in the economy were women,* and in the coming decades women will again provide the greater part of the expansion of the labour force. Many of these women will be coming from the ranks of Britain's housewives, who in 1971 numbered over 8 million. We are looking at an enormous social revolution, and it is no wonder, with their growing importance to the economy, that women have demanded, and are obtaining, better treatment in the labour market than that which they used customarily to receive.

In the period 1971 to 1976, nearly all the labour-force increase was caused by women moving into employment, and in the projections for 1971 to 1991 (which include estimates of the non-registered unemployed), 71 per cent of the increase in the labour force will be caused similarly. The effect of all this is that while in 1951 women constituted 32 per cent of Britain's labour force, in 1976 they constituted 38 per cent and in 1991 they will probably constitute 40 per cent. The expansion of the labour force in these successive five-year periods has been, and is projected to be, very 'jerky', especially the male labour force: in 1951 to 1956 the male labour force rose by 405,000; but in 1966 to 1971 it fell by 602,000, and in 1981 to 1986 it is projected to rise by 439,000. Obviously, the British economy now suffers severe fluctuations in the growth of its labour force, due largely, but not entirely, to fluctuations in the growth of the male labour force. Why is this so?

The annual increase in the labour force will be equal to the annual number of new entrants to the labour market *minus* the number of people who retire (or otherwise withdraw) during each year from economic activity. Data on annual retirements and other withdrawals are not readily available – nor are data on the annual number of entrants to the labour force. These entrants will be drawn from three sources:

(a) the number of people born about fifteen years previously who were leaving full-time education and entering the labour force;
(b) the number of economically inactive adults who choose to enter into paid employment; and
(c) the number of new immigrants who seek work.

* Calculated as follows:

$$\frac{8,970 - 7,441}{24,926 - 23,239} = \frac{1,529}{1,687} = 0.906 = \text{nine-tenths}$$

TABLE 1.4   *Great Britain's working population,*[a] *1951 to 1991*

June each year	Thousands					
	Stock at given date			Change (flow) between dates		
	Males	Females	Total	Males	Females	Total
Card count [b]						
1951	15,798	7,441	23,239	—	—	—
1956	16,203	7,953	24,156	405	512	917
1961	16,366	8,407	24,773	163	454	617
1966	16,558	9,027	25,585	192	620	812
1971	15,956	8,970	24,926	−602	−57	−659
Employment census						
1971	15,837	8,708	24,545	—	—	—
1976[c]	15,846	9,641	25,487	9	933	942
Projections						
1971	15,933	9,085	25,018	—	—	—
1976	15,914	9,954	25,868	−19	869	850
1981	16,164	10,570	26,734	250	616	866
1986	16,603	11,178	27,781	439	608	1,047
1991	16,868	11,401	28,269	265	223	488

[a] For the card count and the employment census, the working population comprises: employees in employment; employers and self-employed; registered wholly unemployed; and HM Forces (including those stationed overseas); the projections include, additionally to the categories just mentioned, the so-called 'unregistered unemployed' who describe themselves in censuses and surveys as looking for work even though not registered as unemployed (this particularly affects women); throughout students in full-time education are excluded.

[b] Unrevised card-count data; the revisions go back only to 1960, and there is no revised card-count data for 1971.

[c] The change in the working population between 1971 and 1976 was affected by the raising of the school-leaving age from 15 to 16 in the educational year 1972–3.

Sources: 1951 to 1961, Department of Employment, *British Labour Statistics Historical Abstract 1886–1968* (HMSO, 1971) table 122, pp. 224–5; 1966 to 1971, Department of Employment, *British Labour Statistics Year Book 1973* (HMSO, 1975) table 55, pp. 120–1; 1971 to 1976 (census), Department of Employment, *British Labour Statistics Year Book 1976* (HMSO, 1978) table 56, pp. 125–6 (this source contains some revised estimates for previous years – see appendix H in the 1975 *Year Book* – which have not been used here because they do not enable us to see the difference made by the change in 1971); 1976 to 1991, *Department of Employment Gazette*, April 1978, table 2, p. 427.

Of these three, the first source is overwhelmingly the most important, except that in wartime the number of economically inactive women entering the labour force can assume a temporary importance, and slowly in the long run women's increasing participation has boosted the supply of labour. Fortunately we do have information covering a long period on the annual number of births in Great Britain, and, making some small allowance for deaths and emigration between the ages of 0 and 15 or so, these births will, fifteen or so years later, largely determine the annual number of entrants to the labour market.

Diagram 1.4 shows the number of births registered during each year in Great Britain in the period 1855 to 1980 (from 1932 onwards, the figures relate precisely to the number of births actually occurring during the year, some births being registered in the year after they occur, but this is a minor matter). It is immediately apparent from the diagram that the First World War, the economic depression of the interwar period, and then the Second World War, have all caused the most extraordinary, and large, downward and upward movements in the annual number of births. This is not a textbook on the economic history

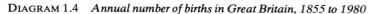

DIAGRAM 1.4   *Annual number of births in Great Britain, 1855 to 1980*

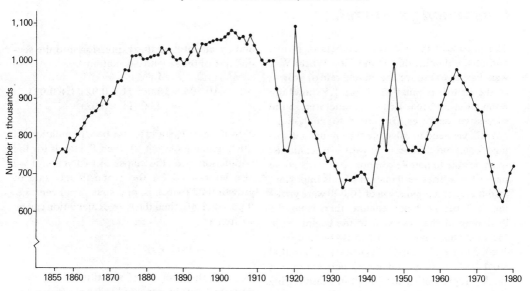

of Britain's population, so our discussion of this diagram will be necessarily brief even though the facts depicted by Diagram 1.4 are of the greatest significance for society and for the economy.

First, we should note the very large and sudden fall in the annual number of births during the First World War (which lasted from 4 August 1914 to 11 November 1918). During 1914 there were 1,002,900 births registered in Great Britain; during 1915, there were 929,200 births; and by 1918 the number had declined to 761,600, almost equal to the figure recorded sixty-two years previously in 1856. Immediately after the war, allowing time for natural events, the number of births rose very steeply to 1,094,500 during 1920, the highest number recorded in British history. One may conjecture that this occurred as families made up for births postponed during the war. But a large number of men had been killed during the war – the number may be as many as three-quarters of a million UK dead – and this meant that not only were fewer babies born during the war but also that subsequently many wives were left without husbands and many young single women were unable to get married. On top of this, unemployment was appallingly high during the interwar period: the 'best' year was 1927, when 1.4 million workers (6.8 per cent of the labour force) were unemployed in the United Kingdom; the worst year was 1932, when 3.4 million workers (15.6 per cent) were unemployed. By the interwar period, contraceptive techniques (among them the rubber sheath, used to protect the First World War troops from venereal disease) were widely known about, so we may conjecture that the economic recession led married couples to limit the number of children they had. It is plausible that these two factors – lack of husbands and fathers and reduced size of families – explain much of the very deep and prolonged interwar trough in the number of births: the lowest figure for births recorded since 1855 was in 1933 (the year following the worst year of the economic recession), when there were only 666,500 births in Great Britain. As economic conditions improved during the second half of the 1930s, the annual number of births rose slowly, interrupted by the start of the Second World War (which lasted from 3 September 1939 to 8 May 1945 – Victory in Europe Day; the Japanese formally surrendered on 2 September 1945). By the early 1940s those children born during the 'baby boom' immediately after the First World War were themselves becoming old enough to have children of their own, and the number of births rose, despite the Second World War; perhaps this was helped by the American and Commonwealth troops stationed here

Compound growth rates

The impact of the reduced numbers of births, and of the deaths, during the First World War was sharply to reduce the annual rate of growth of the British population. Table 1.5 shows the population of Great Britain enumerated at the successive censuses. In order to analyse its growth, we need to calculate the annual percentage (compound) rates of growth. An economist must be able to handle compound growth, so we pause for a brief explanation of this important arithmetic. If a population of 10,000 were growing at 2 per cent per annum, then from the beginning of the base year to the beginning of the following year it would grow by 200 from 10,000 to 10,200. That is, it grows from its initial stock of 10,000 by adding on 2 per cent of that stock – representing the (flow) increase during the year to reach the new stock level:

$$10,000 + 0.02 \times 10,000$$
$$= 10,000 (1 + 0.02)$$
$$= 10,000 (1.02) = 10,200$$

From the beginning of this year to the beginning of the following year it grows by adding on 2 per cent to this new stock of 10,200:

$$10,200 + 0.02 \times 10,200$$
$$= 10,200 (1 + 0.02)$$
$$= 10,200 (1.02) = 10,404$$

Now we may roll these two calculations into one by noting that:

$$10,200 = 10,000 (1 + 0.02)$$

and by substituting this expression into the second line of the second calculation:

$$10,404 = 10,000 (1 + 0.02)(1 + 0.02)$$
$$= 10,000 (1 + 0.02)^2$$

Now if we let P_0 stand for the base population (at the beginning of year 0), then P_2 stands for the population after the elapse of two years; if we also let r stand for the proportionate rate of growth 0.02 (which is, of course, 2 per cent: i.e. $0.02 = 2/100$), then the above calculation can be written as:

$$P_2 = P_0 (1 + r)^2$$

Because the process of substitution we have described can be repeated indefinitely, we can always reach the same general result no matter how many years elapse; and if n years elapse, then:

$$P_n = P_0 (1 + r)^n$$

This is the general expression for steady compound growth. Note that r is expressed as a proportionate rate per period (in this case, per annum) so n must represent the number of the same periods (e.g. if r were the rate of increase over six months, n would have to be the number of six-month periods elapsing). In Table 1.5 we know P_0, P_n and n (10 years in each case but 20 between 1931 and 1951) and the problem is to

during the latter part of the War! Again, we see the phenomenon of a postwar baby boom in 1946 and 1947 – presumably due to families making up for postponed children – and again we see the decline in births after that as the fewer babies born in the late 1920s and early 1930s meant there were fewer women coming into child-bearing age in the late 1940s and early 1950s. But with prosperity and full employment during the 1950s the reduction in the number of births was far less drastic than during the interwar period. The Second World War was also less costly in terms of men killed than the First World War: only (!) about 400,000 UK military personnel died. The year 1955 saw the low point in births – some 760,500 babies were born that year – and then births began to rise, presumably as the children born during the long and interrupted upswing from 1934 to 1947 began themselves to have children. This movement peaked in 1964, when there were 980,400 births and from then, until 1977, there was a steady decline in the annual number of births. This may be due partly to the decline in the number of children born during the 1948 to 1955 period – that is, to the decline in the number of parents twenty years or so later – but it may also be due to changing social attitudes in favour of smaller families,

ascertain the unknown r. Using the general expression above, first divide through by P_0 to give:

$$\frac{P_n}{P_0} = (1 + r)^n$$

then take the nth root of both sides to give:

$$\sqrt[n]{\frac{P_n}{P_0}} = 1 + r$$

(for example, the square root of P_2/P_0 equals $(1 + r)$). And, finally, therefore, subtracting 1 from both sides gives:

$$r = \sqrt[n]{\frac{P_n}{P_0}} - 1$$

By taking the nth root of P_n/P_0 and subtracting 1 the proportionate rate of growth can be calculated. This used to be quite a laborious task, but a medium-price calculator should have a key for calculating roots to any value (not simply square roots). To illustrate for the 1801 to 1811 growth rate:

$$r = \sqrt[10]{\frac{11{,}970}{10{,}501}} - 1$$

$$= \sqrt[10]{1.13989} - 1$$

$$= 1.013179 - 1$$

$$= 0.0132 \text{ (to four decimal places)}$$

TABLE 1.5 *Population of Great Britain, 1801 to 1981*

Census date	Total population (thousands)	Annual percentage growth rate
1801 9–10 March	10,501	—
1811 26–27 May	11,970	1.32
1821 27–28 May	14,092	1.65
1831 29–30 May	16,261	1.44
1841 6–7 June	18,534	1.32
1851 30–31 March	20,817	1.17
1861 7–8 April	23,128	1.06
1871 2–3 April	26,072	1.21
1881 3–4 April	29,710	1.31
1891 5–6 April	33,029	1.06
1901 31 March–1 April	37,000	1.14
1911 2–3 April	40,831	0.99
1921 19–20 June	42,769	0.46
1931 26–27 April	44,795	0.46
1951 8–9 April	48,854	0.43
1961 23–24 April	51,284	0.49
1971 25–26 April	53,979	0.51
1981 5–6 April	54,129	0.03

Sources: B. R. Mitchell and Phyllis Deane, *Abstract of British Historical Statistics* (Cambridge University Press, 1962) p. 6; B. R. Mitchell and H. G. Jones, *Second Abstract of British Historical Statistics* (Cambridge University Press, 1971) p. 3; Central Statistical Office, *Annual Abstract of Statistics 1979 Edition*, no. 115 (HMSO, 1978) table 2.1, p. 7; Office of Population Censuses and Surveys, *Census 1981: Preliminary Report England and Wales* (HMSO, 1981) table 2, p. 13 as corrected by correction slip.

possibly helped by the growing use of 'the Pill' during the second half of the 1960s and the 1970s. In 1978, however, the number of births increased, and as this is twenty-three years after the up-turn in births in 1956, we may conjecture that the girls born then are now beginning to have babies, and, as this upward trend continued in 1979 and 1980, we may expect the number of births to continue rising, probably for quite a number of years, unless the economic recession of the 1980s adversely affects family formation and family size.

Whatever the exact causes and mechanisms of the fluctuations in births, there is no getting away from the very large magnitude of these movements. If we go back fifteen years from 1951 to 1936 (choosing 15 because that was the school-leaving age), we can see that from 1936 to 1947 the number of births was rising, so that the annual number of entrants to the labour market in the period 1951 to 1962 would also have been rising and the annual increase in the working population would have been at a relatively high level.

After 1961 not only did the annual number of entrants to the labour market begin to slow down but also the numbers in higher education began to rise rapidly. In 1961–2 there were about one-quarter of a million students in full-time higher education in Great Britain

The rule of 70

During the first forty years of the nineteenth century, the population grew at about 1.4 per cent per annum. During the next seventy years to 1911 it grew a little more slowly at about 1.1 per cent per annum. Then the effect both of wartime casualties and the falling number of births considerably reduced the population growth rate to 0.46 per cent per annum. The low number of births in the 1920s and 1930s coupled with wartime deaths during the 1940s kept the growth rate low. In the 1950s and 1960s the balance between births, deaths, immigration and emigration appears to have continued to keep the population growth rate down, though it was a little higher than previously. By comparison, the growth rate of population in many Third World countries tends to be about $2\frac{1}{2}$ per cent per annum: for example, between 1963 and 1971 the population of Sri Lanka (Ceylon) grew by 2.3 per cent per annum. The difference between this sort of population growth rate and the United Kingdom's $\frac{1}{2}$ per cent per annum is enormous but not easy to understand.

A little trick worth knowing is based on the calculation that anything growing at 1 per cent per annum will double in seventy years, and, correspondingly, anything growing at 2 per cent per annum will double in half that time, thirty-five years. Therefore, if one wants to think about the effect of a growth rate, one can divide the percentage growth rate into 70 to give an estimate of the time it will take for the series to double itself. Sri Lanka's population will double in about thirty years (assuming the growth rate of 2.3 per cent is maintained), while the United Kingdom's population will take 137 years to double (on the 1960s growth rate). The contrast between doubling in thirty years and doubling in 137 years helps one to appreciate the enormous impact of what may at first sight appear to be only minor differences in growth rates. The rule: 'divide the annual percentage growth into 70' is a very helpful device (for example, when one is told that energy demand in the non-communist world grew by 4.6 per cent per annum between 1950 and 1973 – *Energy Policy: A Consultative Document,* Cmnd 7101 (HMSO, 1978) p. 7 – how long is it taking for energy demand to double?)

(universities, polytechnics, colleges of technology, etc.) but by 1971–2 this number had doubled to half a million. Furthermore, relatively large numbers of men and women born in 1901 to 1906 were reaching retirement age in the late 1960s. The combined effect of all this – falling numbers coming of working age, rising numbers entering higher education, and large numbers of retirements – led to the considerable drop in the British labour force between 1966 and 1971.

After 1971–2 the numbers in higher education more or less stopped growing and, as births had increased in the 1955–64 upswing, the annual number of entrants to the labour market began to rise. In the period to 1976 retirements were still quite high (following the relatively large number of births sixty to sixty–five years previously), so the male labour force did not then increase. In the period around 1981, however, the annual number of entrants to the labour market will reach a maximum, because of the peak in births in 1964, and this will coincide with a relatively low number of retirements (due to the small number of births during the First World War). Accordingly, during the period 1981 to 1986 the labour force will grow rather rapidly before beginning again to be affected by the falling number of births in the period 1964–77.

So we now know why the British labour force changes in such a jerky manner: Britain is still being affected by the demographic fluctuations caused by the First World War and the economic recession of the interwar period. This has many implications for the British economy: at one period the economy may be operating in conditions of very 'tight' labour markets; at other periods there will be a rapidly growing labour force which, if not matched by growth in the economy, may result in unemployment, especially among young people.

In the late 1960s the economy could make do with relatively little investment and consequent provision of fewer jobs; during the late 1980s it will be necessary to increase the rate of investment and the provision of jobs. One way and another, many of Britain's economic problems derive ultimately from these fluctuations in the number of births and their subsequent impact upon the labour force.

It is clear that the British economy now suffers instability caused by this major 'demographic cycle' during which the annual number of births may fluctuate by as much as one-third. The effects of this must be far-reaching. At one stage there will be a large wave of children progressing through the consumer market – with consequent booming demand for sweets, toys, children's clothing, school places, and so on; at other times demand for such goods will fall off and be at a low ebb. At some stages there will be a large number of young couples getting married and setting up homes, boosting the demand for new housing, furniture and appliances; and at other times the reverse will be the case. Furthermore, it seems as if this cycle will continue for many generations as the pattern of babies born to babies born during the preceding wave repeats itself.

In order to understand the interaction between population growth and labour-force growth in postwar Britain we need to examine the 'participation rates'. A 'participation rate' is defined as

the ratio of the labour force to the population from which that labour force is drawn.

In the United Kingdom people cannot legally work full-time until after their sixteenth birthday, and most men and women retire at the age at which they become eligible to draw the National Insurance retirement pension, which is 65 for men and 60 for women. Therefore, the population from which the labour force is drawn is that aged between 16 to 59/64. A participation rate which relates male workers to the appropriate male population is known as a *sex-specific* participation rate. (If the participation rate relates workers in a given age-group to the population in that same age group, it is called an *age-specific* participation rate.) Participation rates differ among men and women, and Table 1.6 shows the past and projected population of Great Britain divided, by sex, among children, those of working age, and those of retirement age. One very important result of the slow population growth rate in Britain is that the average age of the population is rising: in 1951, 13.6 per cent of the population was of retirement age; in 1991, 17.4 per cent of the population will be of retirement age.

But the main use of Table 1.6 is that, in conjunction with the figures in Table 1.4, it permits us to calculate the participation rates shown in Table 1.7. In 1951 and in 1961 the male participation rate was 100 per cent: that is, the numbers in the male labour force were equal to the numbers of males aged 15 to 64; in 1951, indeed, the labour force was a little bigger, and this must have been due to there being workers over retirement age. There are, of course, a number of youths aged over 15 in full-time education, and in 1951 and 1961 these youths were almost exactly counterbalanced by 'over-age' workers. Between 1961 and 1971 there was a steep drop in the male participation rate, and this was probably largely due to the rise in the number of youths in full-time higher education. The other important feature of Table 1.7 is the rise in the female participation rate from 47.8 per cent in 1951 to 56.5 per cent in 1971 (actual) to 71 per cent in 1991 (projected). As explained, it is this change in the female participation rate which has been responsible for most of the labour-force growth in postwar Britain.

One further aspect of the United Kingdom's labour force which we need to study is the number of those who were unemployed: that is, those who were involuntarily without jobs although they were available for work. Diagram 1.5 shows the average numbers unemployed in each year between 1855 and 1980 (the numbers before 1913 are estimates). Four features of this graph are worth noting. First, the large cyclical fluctuations in unemployment in the period 1855 to 1914, and the generally high level of unemployment, which was

TABLE 1.6   *Population of Great Britain, 1951 to 1991*

Population who are	Population in thousands [a]		
	Males	Females	Total
Children [b]			
1951	5,587.9	5,358.8	10,946.7
1961	6,109.3	5,814.4	11,923.7
1971	6,636.1	6,293.6	12,929.7
1981	6,165.6	5,832.3	11,997.9
1991	6,237.7	5,896.9	12,134.6
Working age [c]			
1951	15,674.6	15,569.0	31,243.6
1961	16,360.3	15,446.7	31,807.0
1971	16,823.7	15,413.6	32,237.3
1981	17,162.5	15,567.2	32,729.7
1991	17,821.4	16,052.9	33,874.3
Retirement age [d]			
1951	2,187.1	4,476.3	6,663.4
1961	2,316.9	5,236.7	7,553.6
1971	2,736.8	6,073.0	8,809.8
1981	3,144.7	6,450.8	9,595.5
1991	3,226.6	6,464.5	9,691.1
All ages			
1951	23,449.6	25,404.1	48,853.7
1961	24,786.5	26,497.8	51,284.3
1971	26,196.6	27,780.2	53,976.8
1981 [e]	26,472.8	27,850.3	54,323.1
1991	27,285.7	28,414.3	55,700.0

[a] As enumerated at the censuses of 1951, 1961 and 1971, and as projected for 1981 and 1991 by the Office of Population Censuses and Surveys on the mid-1975-based population; minor discrepancies of totals with enumerations/projections are due to rounding errors.

[b] 0 to 14 inclusive for 1951, 1961 and 1971; 0 to 15 inclusive for 1981 and 1991 (school-leaving age raised from 15 to 16 in 1972–3).

[c] 15 to 64 inclusive for males and 15 to 59 inclusive for females in 1951, 1961 and 1971; and 16 to 64 inclusive for males and 16 to 59 inclusive for females in 1981 and 1991 (retirement age for men being 65 and for women 60).

[d] 65 and over for males and 60 and over for females; includes age not stated category.

[e] These are projections made in 1978, and so do not exactly match the figures recorded for the 1981 census in Table 1.5.

Sources: 1951 and 1961, B. R. Mitchell and H. G. Jones, *Second Abstract of British Historical Statistics* (Cambridge University Press, 1971) p. 6; Central Statistical Office, *Annual Abstract of Statistics, 1979 Edition*, no. 115 (HMSO, 1978) table 2.4, p. 11; Office of Population Censuses and Surveys, *Population Projections Area 1975–1991*, series PP3, no. 2 (HMSO, 1978) appendix table 1, p. 14.

mostly well above half a million in any year. Second, the low levels of unemployment achieved during both the First and Second World Wars, which is hardly surprising. Third, an oft-told story, the appalling levels of unemployment which lasted throughout the interwar period. From 1921 to 1939 inclusive, unemployment was always well above one million; indeed, in only three of those nineteen years was it below one-and-a-half million. Fourth, during the period since the end of the Second World War unemployment has fluctuated much less sharply, and about much lower levels, than it used to. Until 1966 unemployment was generally below half a million, but since then it has risen to over 3 million at the beginning of 1982.

TABLE 1.7   *Labour-force participation rates, 1951 to 1991*

	Percentage of working-age population economically active		
	Males	Females	Total
1951 *(a)*	100.8	47.8	74.4
1961 *(a)*	100.0	54.4	77.9
1971 *(b)*	94.1	56.5	76.1
1981	94.2	67.9	81.7
1991	94.7	71.0	83.5

(a) Card-count data.
(b) Employment census data.

Source: calculated from Tables 1.4 and 1.6.

DIAGRAM 1.5   *Number of workers unemployed in the United Kingdom, 1851 to 1981 (June)*

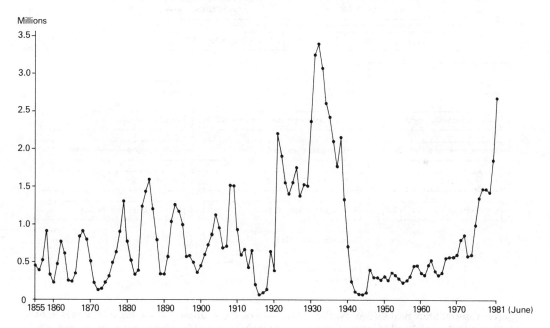

We can draw two conclusions from all this. First, by historical standards (excluding the wartime years) the utilisation of the labour force in the decades following the Second World War has (at least until 1970) been quite good: there has been nothing like the waste of manpower – of economic resources – which the economy used to suffer in the past. Second, despite this cheerful conclusion, we can see that the levels of unemployment in the United Kingdom are now much too high. This is all the less excusable as the factors determining the level of total employment, and hence the level of unemployment, are by now well known. Unemployment is, of course, a serious matter to which we shall return.

So far we have considered the distribution of, and the changes in, the stock of workers who constitute the main factor of production in the UK economy. But these workers do not work with their bare hands: all the services of labour in a 'developed' economy are considerably assisted by machinery and other equipment, and we turn now to a consideration of this factor of production, capital.

Capital

The analytic basis for describing where, and in what forms, the United Kingdom's stock of capital exists is quite simple. Consider the disposition of the stock of capital as described in Diagram 1.6. Stocks are fundamentally of two sorts: real assets, and financial assets. Real assets are real in the sense that they are 'tangible' material things, rather than pieces of paper which form claims either upon real things or upon other persons, such claims being financial assets. At the moment we are not concerned with financial assets, so they disappear from Diagram 1.6. In economics, the word 'capital' should be reserved to denote only real assets, and should not be used to mean financial assets. Real assets can be divided into two basic categories: fixed capital, and circulating capital.

DIAGRAM 1.6   *The distribution of real assets in the United Kingdom, at 31 December 1980, valued at current replacement cost in £ thousand million*

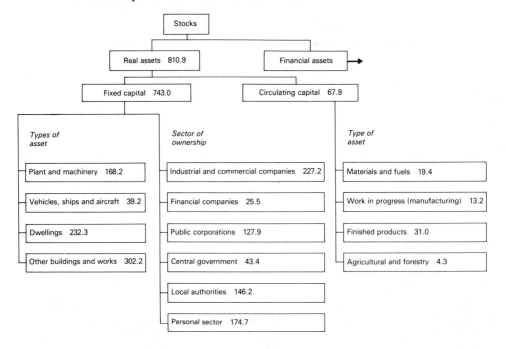

Source: Central Statistical Office, *National Income and Expenditure 1981 Edition* (HMSO), tables 11.11 and 12.1, pp. 83 and 86; these figures may be slightly revised in subsequent editions; note CSO discrepancies, due to rounding, between totals and sums of items.

It is important to understand the distinction between fixed and circulating capital because it helps to explain the two different ways of charging the customer for the cost of capital services used. The distinction goes back at least as far as Adam Smith's *Wealth of Nations* published over 200 years ago in 1776. Adam Smith based his argument on the two fundamentally different ways in which a fund of money could be employed to yield a revenue.

First, he said, it could be used to obtain goods and to sell them again with a profit, the proceeds of the sale then being used to obtain more goods for sale at a profit, and so on. You will recognise this as a description of the activities of a shopkeeper, or, more generally, a merchant. As Adam Smith said:

The goods of the merchant yield him no revenue or profit till he sells them for money, and the money yields him as little till it is again exchanged for goods. His capital is continually going from him in one shape, and returning to him in another, and it is only by means of such circulation, or successive exchanges, that it can yield him any profit. Such capitals, therefore, may very properly be called circulating capitals.

But, he said, in the second place, a fund of money could

be employed in the improvement of land, in the purchase of useful machines and instruments of trade, or in such-like things as yield a revenue or profit without changing masters, or circulating any further. Such capitals, therefore, may very properly be called fixed capitals. (*An Inquiry into the Nature and Causes of the Wealth of Nations,* book II 'Of the Nature, Accumulation, and Employment of Stock', chapter I 'Of the Division of Stock'.)

What Adam Smith's distinction amounts to is a distinction between those real assets which, during the process of production, have a once-for-all use and those which have a continuing use. This was clearly stated by John Stuart Mill, who devoted to the subject of fixed and circulating capital a whole chapter of his *Principles of Political Economy,* first published in 1848. Mill said: 'Capital which ... fulfils the whole of its office in the production in which it is engaged by a single use, is called Circulating Capital.' Mill then distinguished the other type of capital 'the efficacy of which is not exhausted by a single use ... [and] the return to which is spread over a period of corresponding duration, is called Fixed Capital.' (*Principles of Political Economy,* book I 'Production', chapter VI 'On Circulating and Fixed Capital'.)

Thus circulating capital consists of those items which have a once-for-all use; fixed capital consists of those items which have a continuing use. When the hairdresser puts shampoo on a customer's hair he uses part of his stock of circulating capital, for that shampoo cannot again be used on anyone else's hair; but when the hairdresser cuts hair with a pair of scissors, he is using an item of fixed capital, because another customer can, subsequently, have his or her hair cut with that same pair of scissors. In drawing this distinction it is of help that items of circulating capital (bottles of shampoo) are generally used up and replaced several times during the normal accounting period of one year, while items of fixed capital generally last for more than one accounting period. But use and replacement within an accounting period is not the essence of the distinction: *once-for-all use as against continuing service is the essence of the distinction.* It follows, perhaps confusingly, that the same item can be fixed or circulating capital depending on the purpose for which it is held. In a hairdresser's establishment, a pair of scissors is fixed capital; in a factory which manufactures lots and lots of pairs of scissors, a pair of scissors is an item of circulating capital because it then has only a once-for-all use so far as the factory is concerned – to be sold.

From this, you will see that land is fixed capital: the field in which wheat is grown or on which cattle are grazed can be used repeatedly. But, unlike other capital, land is not reproducible. And the same is true of underground or undersea deposits of minerals which are of course circulating capital – and non-renewable circulating capital at that! The non-reproducibility of these 'natural' capital resources of land and minerals makes them a special category, and they tend to be excluded from the economic analysis of capital: in economics, 'capital' is conventionally defined as comprising *reproducible real* assets, and so excludes land.

Stocks of both fixed and circulating capital can be classified according to (a) the type of capital, and (b) who owns it. Normally the owners of capital are grouped into different 'sectors' of the economy. The sectoral classification is based on a mixture of economic types and legal forms: for instance, in the enterprise sector of the economy, a distinction is made between private companies and the nationalised industries (called 'public corporations'). In order to give some concreteness to our discussion of the distribution of capital, let us consider the figures for the UK economy shown in Diagram 1.6. Diagram 1.6 gives, with figures for the end of 1980 (that is, at 31 December 1980), the stock of real capital in the United Kingdom valued in thousands of millions of pounds (in accordance with international usage, I shall, throughout this book, use the word 'billion' to denote a thousand million).

At the end of 1980 the United Kingdom's stock of real assets was valued at £810.9 billion. Nine-tenths, or £743 billion, of this stock of real assets was in the form of fixed capital, and about one-tenth, £67.9 billion, was in the form of circulating capital. These valuations refer not to the original prices of all the items making up the stock, but to what it would have cost in 1980 to replace each item in the condition in which it then stood (we shall return later to the question of how these valuations were arrived at – for the moment, let us take the figures on trust).

The stock of fixed capital can be divided among four main types according to the function or use of the asset. These are shown on the left-hand side of Diagram 1.6.

(1) The term 'plant and machinery' is an abbreviation for 'plant, machinery and equipment'. It covers the sorts of things most of us would automatically think of in connection with the term 'fixed capital', for example blast furnaces, steel presses, lathes, conveyor belts, electric motors, and so on. But the term has a wider coverage than this, for instance tractors, bulldozers, mobile cranes and fork-lift trucks are classified as plant and machinery. The value of the stock of plant and machinery in the United Kingdom at the end of 1980 was £168.2 billion, nearly one-quarter of the value of the total stock of fixed capital.

(2) At the end of 1980 the United Kingdom had a stock of 'vehicles, ships and aircraft' worth £39.2 billion, about 5 per cent of the total value of fixed capital. This figure includes cars which are owned by companies, but it excludes cars owned by private individuals: by convention in national accounts (and also perhaps because the information would be difficult to obtain), the value of privately owned cars is excluded from estimates of national capital stocks. (So, too, are the value of all privately owned household durable goods such as furniture, carpets, refrigerators, cookers, washing-machines, and so on – strictly speaking, these are all items of fixed capital, giving continuing use, but the benefits from their services do not form part of the marketed output of the economy. Of course, the motor-cars which are owned by a car-hire company for renting out are valued as part of the nation's stock of fixed capital, as are refrigerators and cookers belonging to a landlord in a rented dwelling.) Also excluded from the valuation of capital stocks are all items of military equipment, and this affects particularly the category of vehicles, ships and aircraft. These figures include no army lorries, no tanks, no warships and no fighter planes or bombers. This exclusion may be due partly to security reasons, but, more importantly, the purpose of military equipment is to be destroyed in battle rather than to be used in the process of production. So the exclusion is justifiable on economic grounds.

(3) An important item in the nation's stock of fixed capital is dwellings. This term covers houses, bungalows, flats and maisonettes. The stock of dwellings in the United Kingdom at the end of 1980 was worth £232.3 billion, 31 per cent of the total value of fixed capital. This valuation excludes the value of the land on which dwellings are situated.

(4) The category 'other buildings and works' forms the largest single category. The term 'other buildings' means all buildings other than dwellings; 'works' means mostly civil engineering works. So this category includes all factory buildings, warehouses, shops, offices, hotels, hospitals, schools, and works such as roads, pavements, railway track, bridges, harbours, airports, gas and water mains, and drainage systems. The total value of other buildings and works in the United Kingdom at the end of 1980 was £302.2 billion, or 41 per cent of the total value of fixed capital.

Sectors of the economy: groupings of transactors

Each and every item classified under fixed capital is owned by some organisation or person. It is therefore possible also to classify fixed capital assets according to the broad sector of ownership; Diagram 1.6 shows these sectors and the amount they owned, while Diagram 1.7 shows, in more detail, what they owned at the end of 1980. In the UK economy six types of owning entities are distinguished and are accordingly grouped into six different sectors of the economy. The concept of a sector of the economy is very important because 'the division of the economy into sectors is a primary feature of a national accounting system' (Central Statistical Office, *National Accounts Sources and Methods* (HMSO, 1968) p. 19). Throughout this book we shall be concerned with learning to understand the interactions among sectors of the economy. Therefore, we must spend a little time learning both about the concept of a sector of the economy and also about the particular sectors distinguished in the UK economy (these sectoral divisions are fairly uniformly followed in the national accounts of the industrialised market economies – as distinguished from industrialised centrally planned economies and non-industrial economies).

In a very general and abstract way, economic activity consists of transactions – dealings or pieces of business – among transactors. The concept of a transactor is rather abstract; but if each transactor has a bank account, then you can think of a transactor as being represented in the economy by that bank account. The number of transactors in an economy is exceedingly numerous and it is therefore necessary to group them together into distinct sectors. A sector of the economy is a grouping of transactors. Three basic sectors, or groups of transactors, are normally distinguished, according to their economic characteristics. Among each of these groupings, subdivisions may be made, often according to the legal status of the transactor. The three basic groupings of transactors into sectors are:

1. The enterprise sector.
2. The household sector.
3. The government sector.

Enterprises include all firms, organisations and institutions which produce or supply goods and/or services for sale at a price intended approximately to cover the cost of production or supply: in other words, the aim of an 'enterprise' is (it is hoped) to earn a profit.

Households are basically the family unit. The characteristic of a household is that it is not established primarily to earn a profit: the purposes for which it is established are fundamentally non-economic. The household unit shares this characteristic with other institutions such as charitable bodies, trade unions and sporting clubs, and these private non-profit making institutions are also included in the household sector. This inclusion makes the name 'household sector' rather inappropriate, so in the na-

DIAGRAM 1.7   *Who owned what in the United Kingdom at the end of 1980*

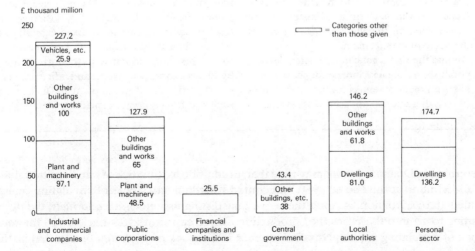

tional accounts it is called 'the personal sector'.

Finally the *government sector* comprises the 'agencies' which undertake forms of activity financed (for the most part) by compulsory levies. The services of the government are not normally sold to the community; they are mostly provided 'free of charge' and paid for by taxes.

These three basic sectors can be, and mostly are, sub-divided in several different ways, as shown in Diagram 1.7. This diagram provides a summary picture of who owned what (fixed capital only) in the United Kingdom at the end of 1980. It is a snapshot of the ownership structure of the United Kingdom's capital stock.

In the enterprise sector we have first the *industrial and commercial companies*. This sector consists of all privately-controlled corporate enterprises organised in order to make a profit on their operation. At the end of 1980 these companies owned £227.2 billion worth of fixed capital assets, or 31 per cent of total fixed capital in the United Kingdom. Industrial and commercial companies owned mostly plant and machinery and other buildings and works: that is, mainly factories or shops, etc. and their equipment.

Second, there are the *public corporations*, which are mainly the bodies managing the United Kingdom's nationalised industries: the National Coal Board, British Rail, the Central Electricity Generating Board, and so on. This sector also includes such bodies as the BBC (but not the privately controlled independent television companies), the Civil Aviation Authority, the Scottish and Welsh Development Agencies, and so on. A public corporation is distinguished from other trading bodies or enterprises by two main characteristics:

1. It is publicly controlled, to the extent that the Queen, Parliament or a Minister of the Crown appoints the whole or the majority of the board of management.
2. Despite the first legal characteristic, the corporation has financial independence of central government revenues in that its surpluses (if such there be) do not accrue as revenue to

the central government; it can therefore maintain its own financial reserves, or, conversely, can borrow on its own account.

The theory behind this type of organisation is that the organisation should be managed 'in the public interest', but that, at the same time, it should be conducted in most respects on ordinary 'business lines' and should aim to make a profit – or rather, because the word 'profit' is normally reserved for organisations in private ownership, it should aim to make a 'trading surplus', as it is officially called.

Public corporations in the United Kingdom owned £127.9 billion worth of fixed capital at the end of 1980. This represents a substantial proportion, 17 per cent, of the United Kingdom's stock of fixed capital. This explains why the UK economy is often referred to as a 'mixed economy': that is, a mixture of privately-controlled and state-controlled economic organisations. Like the industrial and commercial companies, the public corporations had most of their fixed capital in the form of either plant and machinery or other buildings and works.

Third, *financial companies* are distinguished separately, though they too are privately controlled and are organised for profit. But they derive their profit fundamentally from the financial operation of borrowing money at one rate of interest and lending it on at a higher rate of interest. The operations of financial companies are different in kind from those of industrial and commercial companies which derive their income from processing or handling goods; financial companies act mainly as intermediaries between those with money to lend and those who wish to borrow. Their operations are therefore best analysed separately. These financial companies, such as banks and building societies, own a relatively small amount of fixed capital; only £25.5 billion at the end of 1980, 3 per cent of the total. This was held partly in the form of other buildings and works – banks and office premises – and partly in the form of plant and machinery, such as office equipment and computers.*

Returning to Diagram 1.6 we may note that, in addition to the stock of fixed capital valued at £743 billion at the end of 1980, the United Kingdom had stocks of circulating capital valued at £67.9 billion. Among these, we may distinguish *materials and fuels*, the items waiting to go into the process of production. These constituted 29 per cent of the total stock of circulating capital. Next in sequence is the stock of *work in progress*: that is, the value of goods on the assembly line going through the factory at 31 December 1980. This

Fourth, the *central government* itself owns fixed capital, mostly in the form of buildings and works. The sector of the central government is quite widely defined and includes, besides all government -departments, all those organisations which have to submit each year to Parliament, or to a Minister of the Crown, statements of expenditures and revenues. This includes most hospitals but does not include universities; although universities receive most of their income indirectly from the government, they are independent in the sense that they are not required to submit statements of their expenditure and income to Parliament and in the United Kingdom the universities are in the personal sector. At the end of 1980 the central government owned 5.8 per cent of the stock of fixed capital, nearly all of it in the form of other buildings and works.

Fifth, there are the *local authorities*. Local authorities are public authorities of limited geographical scope with power to raise revenue in certain forms of local taxation. Local authorities own a large part of the stock of fixed capital: £146.2 billion, or one-fifth of the total. More than half of this, £81 billion, was owned in the form of dwellings; this arises because of the United Kingdom's history of providing publicly owned housing for lower-income families – so-called 'council housing'.

Sixth, and finally, there is the *personal sector*. Besides all individual persons, or the households into which people are grouped, this sector includes private non-profit-making bodies serving *persons*, such as trade unions, universities and most charities (private non-profit-making bodies serving *companies*, such as the Confederation of British Industries, are included in the company sector). The personal sector in the United Kingdom also includes the unincorporated enterprises such as all partnerships – for example, firms of solicitors or estate agents – and the businesses of sole traders and self-employed contractors who have not formed themselves into limited companies – for example, corner grocers, farmers, plumbers, electricians, and other craftsmen. The inclusion departs from the distinction between enterprises and households, but the problem is that it is not possible in the case of many unincorporated enterprises to separate business transactions from household transactions. For instance, if a plumber buys a spanner, is it meaningful to ask whether the spanner is being paid for out of business or household savings? The personal sector also includes the funds of the private pension schemes and of the life-assurance companies as these funds are deemed to 'belong' to the personal sector. The personal sector owned 24 per cent of the United Kingdom's stock of fixed capital at the end of 1980, over three-quarters of it in the form of dwellings. If 24 per cent seems a surprisingly small proportion in a 'property-owning' democracy, you should recall that we are talking about the direct ownership of fixed capital, not about the ownership of financial assets, such as shares, through which the personal sector 'indirectly' owns much of the capital in the company sector.

*Until about the mid-1970s, sector of ownership and sector of usership would have almost invariably been the same for most capital items. The growth since then of *leasing*, whereby a *financial* company may purchase (and own) an item of fixed capital but lease it for use by an *industrial* or *commercial* company, means that this is no longer so true. United Kingdom capital stock and capital formation statistics are reported on the basis of ownership rather than usership, and this should be borne in mind when looking at the fine details of these statistics – see Central Statistical Office, *National Income and Expenditure 1981 Edition*, pp. 130–2, and table 10.8, pp. 74–7; Central Statistical Office, *Economic Trends*, February 1982, 'Effects of leasing on statistics of manufacturing capital expenditure' by Stephen Penneck and Roy Woods, pp. 97–104; Tom Griffin, 'The stock of fixed assets in the United Kingdom: how to make the best use of the statistics', in K. D. Patterson and Kerry Schott (eds), *The Measurement of Capital Theory and Practice* (Macmillan, 1979) pp. 99–132.

amounted to £13.2 billion, or 19 per cent of the stock of circulating capital. Following this, we have the stocks of *finished products* valued at £31 billion, or 46 per cent of the total. These are mainly the goods held by wholesale and retail traders: the wholesaler buys in bulk from the factory, and so, at any one moment, will be holding goods in his warehouses. The retailer then buys in smaller quantities from the wholesaler, and at any given moment will have goods on the shelves in his shop. Last but not least, I have put the circulating capital of *agriculture and forestry* in separately because of its intrinsically different nature from the things we have so far considered in this paragraph. The circulating capital of the agricultural sector includes not only the farmers' stocks of fertiliser and feeding stuffs, but also their growing crops and livestock, while the forestry sector's stocks include the value of standing timber. Note that in neither case is the value of land included. The value of these stocks was £4.3 billion, about 6 per cent of the value of stock of circulating capital.

There are a few small problems with the classification of agricultural stocks as circulating capital, and they serve to practise our understanding of the distinction between fixed and circulating capital. Clearly it is wrong to classify all livestock as circulating capital: an animal raised for meat has a once-for-all use – to be slaughtered and so is circulating capital, but a dairy cow and an egg-laying hen constitute fixed capital because of the continuing nature of their services. Likewise, a crop of wheat is circulating capital, but an orchard of apple trees is fixed capital.

Valuing the capital stock: depreciation or 'capital consumption'

We need to ask how the figures in Diagrams 1.6 and 1.7 were arrived at. By way of preliminary explanation, I said earlier that they represented what it would cost to replace each item in the condition in which it then stood at the prices ruling at the time to which this valuation referred, all this being the meaning of the term 'net fixed capital stock at current replacement cost' – 'net' meaning 'in the condition in which it then stood', and 'current replacement cost' meaning 'valued at the prices ruling at the date to which the valuation refers'.

There are several problems here which may be explained by the use of a simple example relating to two second-hand cars, say two Minis, one built (or licensed) at the end of 1970, the other at the end of 1975 (the Minis are, of course, standing for fixed capital generally: that is, and making corresponding alterations, the Minis could be substituted by electricity power stations or any other item of fixed capital). As we have two definitions to sort out – 'net' and 'current replacement cost' – it is best if we do this one at a time, so I shall (for the moment) ignore the second part of the term by assuming that there is no inflation – that all prices of *new* goods remain the same. This enables us to concentrate simply on the meaning of 'net'. We can assume, therefore, that the Mini built at the end of 1970 cost £1,000 when new, and that the Mini built at the end of 1975 also cost £1,000 when new.

Now, the important thing that (nearly) all items of fixed capital have in common is that they have a finite life: no item of fixed capital (apart perhaps from railway cuttings) can be used for ever: sooner or later, it comes to the end of its useful life and it is then fit for nothing but the scrap-heap. Let us suppose that the useful life of an average Mini is ten years (just to keep the arithmetic simple). This means that at the end of 1980 the Mini built at the end of 1970 will be worth nothing and that at the end of 1985 the Mini built at the end of 1975 will be worth nothing; again, to keep the arithmetic simple, we are assuming that the Mini has no, or at least a negligible, scrap-value at the end of its life. This means that the price of the Mini at the end of its life is exactly nothing, £0. The important question is: what would be the price of the Mini in the intervening years? What the motorist buys when acquiring a car is not so much the car itself but the services of so many years of transport from that car. So the purchase price of a new Mini is, in effect, £1,000 for ten years' transport; obviously, £100 is the capital cost of one year's transport services (note that we are talking about the cost of equipping oneself for a year's transport – the 'capital cost' – and we are not concerned with running costs). So a Mini which has used up six years of its life and has four years to go (like the end-1970 Mini at end-1976) should be worth £400. Given that there is an informed market dealing in second-hand Minis, one could sell or buy a six-year-old Mini with four years' life left for £400 – because people will not pay a

TABLE 1.8 *Valuing the net capital stock*

| | £ | |
Item	Valued at end-1976	Valued at end-1977
Mini, built end-1970	400	300
Mini, built end-1975	900	800
Total net capital stock	1,300	1,100

capital cost of more than £100 for a year's transport services. We can now value at any point in time a stock of fixed capital consisting of two Minis. Table 1.8 shows the data.

In the absence of general inflation, it would have cost £1,300 at the end of 1976 to replace the two Minis in the condition in which they then stood; and at the end of 1977 it would have cost £1,100. If you understand this, and it is all simple common sense, we can proceed to explain the word 'net'. Comparing the first and second columns, what is happening in Table 1.8 is that each Mini is 'depreciating' at the rate of £100 a year. Depreciation is a *flow* which measures the decline, over a period such as a year, in the value of an item of fixed capital. This flow can be taken as measuring the (annual) cost in terms of using up the services of fixed capital (in this case, transport services). This is why depreciation is also known as 'capital consumption' (the term generally used in national income accounts).

(The simplest and most widely used method of calculating depreciation is to take the initial cost, or value, of the item in question (*minus* residual scrap-value, if any) and to divide this by the length of the asset's life. If this life is measured in years, we arrive by this process at the annual depreciation. That is to say, and ignoring scrap-value as an inessential complication:

$$\text{Flow of depreciation per annum} = \frac{\text{Initial cost of asset}}{\text{Length of life in years}}$$

In the case of the two Minis, the price (valuation) of a second-hand Mini is arrived at by deducting from the initial cost of the Mini the *cumulated* amount of depreciation. So, at the end of 1976, the cumulated depreciation of £600 over six years was deducted from the initial cost of the end-1970 Mini, and the cumulated £100 was deducted from the initial cost of the end-1975 Mini. The process of deducting the cumulated depreciation, when repeated at the end of 1977, gives the results seen in the last column of Table 1.8.)

The adjective 'net' is different from 'gross'. 'Gross' means entire, total, or whole; and 'net' means after any deduction. In economics, 'gross' means including, or before deductions; and 'net' means excluding, or after deductions. It is therefore advisable for economists to be explicit and specific about what is being included when 'gross' is used and about what is being excluded when 'net' is used. In economics, 'gross' and 'net' are very often, but by no means always, used to indicate the inclusion or exclusion respectively of depreciation. The gross capital stock does not take account of depreciation and is simply the total of items in the capital stock at their original cost (remember that we are assuming no inflation; if prices rise, this statement has to be amended in a way which we shall shortly consider). The net capital stock is the gross capital stock net of (i.e. *minus*) cumulated depreciation.

Table 1.9 shows how the gross and net capital stock are related by cumulated depreciation (note especially the cumulative nature of the middle three columns). You can see that the last two figures in the last column of Table 1.9 are the same as in the bottom row of Table 1.8. The reason for going through all the rigmarole of Table 1.9, apart from

TABLE 1.9   *Gross and net capital stock*

	Gross capital stock at date			Cumulated depreciation to date			Net capital stock at date		
Date	End-1970 Mini	End-1975 Mini	Total	End-1970 Mini	End-1975 Mini	Total	End-1970 Mini	End-1975 Mini	Total
End-1970	1,000	—	1,000	0	—	0	1,000	—	1,000
End-1971	1,000	—	1,000	100	—	100	900	—	900
End-1972	1,000	—	1,000	200	—	200	800	—	800
End-1973	1,000	—	1,000	300	—	300	700	—	700
End-1974	1,000	—	1,000	400	—	400	600	—	600
End-1975	1,000	1,000	2,000	500	0	500	500	1,000	1,500
End-1976	1,000	1,000	2,000	600	100	700	400	900	1,300
End-1977	1,000	1,000	2,000	700	200	900	300	800	1,100

explaining the meaning of the adjective 'net' in this context, is that, unlike Minis, for many of the items in the capital stock there is no regular second-hand market and there are no market valuations of the sort shown in Table 1.8. However, because the initial cost of each item is known and its working life can be estimated, we can arrive at essentially the same valuations by the method of deducting cumulated depreciation, as shown in Table 1.9.

By now, you ought to understand the concepts of the gross and the net capital stock. You can see (in Table 1.9) that the gross capital stock is simply the total cost at (new) purchase price of items in the capital stock. It is, in fact, the sort of concept one might use when referring to the stock of fixed capital in one's home. Furthermore, the concept of a gross stock makes economic sense, because both a new Mini and a nine-year-old Mini are capable of providing, during the forthcoming year, the same transport services (just as a new house and a fifty-year-old house are capable of providing the same accommodation services). The net capital stock represents what would be the market valuation of the stock, making allowance in that valuation for cumulated depreciation. And despite what has just been said about a new Mini and an old Mini being equivalent in terms of their ability to provide services, there is a real sense in which the owner of a new Mini is 'wealthier' than the owner of an old Mini. This is why in looking at the structure of capital ownership in the United Kingdom it was preferable to take the net capital stock.

We have now dealt with one of our problems: the distinction between *gross* and *net*. But in explaining it, we assumed price stability, and everybody knows that prices do not remain the same; they rise and go on rising, and this must affect the valuation of the capital stock. So we must now turn our attention to the meaning of 'current replacement cost'. How does inflation affect the value of the capital stock? Suppose, as shown in Table 1.10, that the price of a new Mini, which was £1,000 at the end of 1970, rises each year by £200. We thus have the price series given in the first column of Table 1.10. This rise in the price of new Minis must affect the capital cost of a year's transport services, and, still assuming a working life of ten years for a Mini, each year the capital cost of a year's transport services rises as shown in the next column (which is, of course, the first column divided by 10). Now, the economic value of a second-hand Mini is determined, as before, by the value of the number of years of transport service it will provide, and this is the capital cost of one year's transport *multiplied by* the remaining life (in years) of the Mini, as shown in the fifth and sixth columns of Table 1.10 with a total value for this net capital stock value as shown in the seventh column. In principle, this is the value of the net capital stock (comprising an end-1970 Mini and an end-1975 Mini) at current replacement cost. If, at the end of 1977,

TABLE 1.10   *Effect of inflation on the value of the net capital stock*

Date	£ Current [a] price, new Mini	Capital cost of one year's transport	Life remaining in years End-1970 Mini	Life remaining in years End-1975 Mini	Second-hand price in £: [b] 'net stock' End-1970 Mini	Second-hand price in £: [b] 'net stock' End-1975 Mini	Total	*By comparison* Net capital stock value in absence of inflation [c] £	Ratio [d]
End-1970	1,000	100	10	—	1,000	—	1,000	1,000	1.00
End-1971	1,200	120	9	—	1,080	—	1,080	900	1.20
End-1972	1,400	140	8	—	1,120	—	1,120	800	1.40
End-1973	1,600	160	7	—	1,120	—	1,120	700	1.60
End-1974	1,800	180	6	—	1,080	—	1,080	600	1.80
End-1975	2,000	200	5	10	1,000	2,000	3,000	1,500	2.00
End-1976	2,200	220	4	9	880	1,980	2,860	1,300	2.20
End-1977	2,400	240	3	8	720	1,920	2,640	1,100	2.40

[a] 'Current' refers to the date in the row heading: that is, it is 'current at date end-1970', 'current at date end-1971', and so on.

[b] Calculated as current cost of one year's transport *multiplied by* life remaining in years.

[c] From Table 1.9, which is exactly the same example but with no change in the price of a new Mini.

[d] Ratio of total value at second-hand prices when there is inflation, to net capital stock value in absence of inflation.

you had to replace those two Minis in the condition in which they then stood, it would cost you £2,640; this ought also to be the amount you would recover from an insurance company were these two Minis written off in a crash.

You ought by now to understand, in principle, the concept of the net capital stock at current replacement cost. The gross stock would also have to be similarly revalued in line with rising prices.

We now come back to the problem that there are no informed second-hand markets for all capital goods (have you bought any good second-hand railway embankments lately?), so how do the statisticians calculate the net capital stock at current replacement cost? We have seen how the statisticians could, in the absence of inflation, calculate the net capital stock by deducting cumulated depreciation from the gross capital stock. In principle, this method gives the same total as would be arrived at in an informed second-hand market. If we take this no-inflation valuation from Table 1.9 and compare it with the inflation valuation in Table 1.10 (remember that the real structure of the examples in Table 1.9 and 1.10 is exactly the same), we may calculate the ratio of the valuations as shown in the last column of Table 1.10. Now, suppose that instead of taking the price of a new Mini in £s we expressed this price in index form as a proportion of the initial price at end-1970; thus the price at end-1970 is represented by 1.00 (*equals* £1,000 ÷ £1,000); at end-1971 by 1.20 (*equals* £1,200 ÷ £1,000) at end-1972 by 1.40 (*equals* £1,400 ÷ £1,000); and so on. You will notice that this price index is exactly the same as the ratio of the net capital stock at current replacement cost to the net capital stock were there to be no inflation. This result is not accidental because we started off by 'inflating' the capital cost of a year's motoring by the price index for a new Mini, so we have simply come back full circle. However, the equivalence of the ratio in Table 1.10 to the new Mini price index does provide the statisticians with a method for calculating the net capital stock at current replacement cost, providing they have the price index (which they do). In effect, the statisticians proceed to value the gross and net capital stock as if there were no inflation. Having then reached valuations like those shown in Table 1.9, they can multiply these by a price index for capital goods (new Minis) and get valuations identical in principle to those shown in Table 1.10's seventh column.

The gross capital stock must, in any case, be valued as if there were no inflation: that is, the 'prices' or costs of the items in the gross capital stock must be at a common price – specifically, both Minis must be priced at a common price, either at £1,000 ('at 1970 prices') or at £2,000 ('at 1975 prices'). This is because if you double the number of (identical) items in the capital stock, you must double its gross valuation, either from £1,000 to £2,000 in 1975 (as happens in Table 1.9), or, if a 1975-price base is used, from £2,000 (comprising one Mini of end-1970 vintage but valued at end-1975 prices) to £4,000 (comprising two Minis – an end-1970 vintage and an end-1975 vintage – both valued at end-1975 prices). It makes no economic sense to add one Mini priced at £1,000 to another Mini priced at £2,000, because there is little meaning in saying that the total gross capital stock has trebled when the number of items in it have only doubled: the problem is that the trebling is the combined result of a *volume* change and a *price* change and we need to know which is contributing what.

So, in the national accounts for the United Kingdom, there are two tables on the capital stock, the net capital stock at current replacement cost and the gross capital stock with all items valued at common 1975 prices. The change from one year to another in the net capital stock is, of course, a mixture of price changes and 'volume' changes; but we have seen in Table 1.9 that the volume changes in the stock are, because of the effect of cumulating depreciation, rather peculiar anyway; for example, by 1975 one (perfectly serviceable) end-1970 Mini is only counted for half as much as an end-1975 Mini. So we cannot expect to get much useful information from time-series data on the net capital stock: we know that at the end of 1979 it would have cost £617.3 billion to replace the United Kingdom's capital stock, in the condition in which it then stood, at the prices then ruling; and in 1980 the same operation, at 1980 prices, would have cost £743 billion. A positive part of that increase is due to price rises, another positive part is due to there being more items in the capital stock, and a negative part is due to the increased accumulation of depreciation between 1979 and 1980. And we do not know which is contributing what. The real usefulness of the figures on net capital stock at current replacement cost is that, in any single year, they enable us to take a meaningful look at the capital structure, just as we did in Diagrams 1.6 and 1.7. As I said, there is a meaningful sense in which, in 1975, the owner of a 1970 Mini is half as 'wealthy' as is the owner of a 1975 Mini. So we can make comparisons, at a point in time, about the structure by type of asset and/or by sector of ownership of the capital stock. And that is precisely what table 11.11 in the *National Income and Expenditure* accounts does.

By contrast, we can make comparisons over time using the gross capital stock valued at common 1975 prices. Because the effects of price changes are excluded, this is exactly the measure of the 'volume' change in the capital stock, and that volume is not being affected by any 'deductions' for cumulated depreciation: double the number of Minis means double the gross valuation for the stock of Minis. So the gross stock, and changes in it, measure the productive potential: double the number of Minis means double the capacity to produce transport services, and if one taxi firm has double the valuation of a gross stock of Minis than another firm, then the former firm has double the capacity to provide taxi rides. So the information that the gross capital stock of the UK economy has risen from £399 billion in 1970 to £541.6 billion in 1980 (both at constant 1975 prices) is an important piece of information: it means that the productive capacity of the UK economy has risen by 36 per cent in ten years, or by 3.1 per cent per annum – using our 'rule of 70', we can see that, at this rate of growth, the productive capacity of the economy will double every $22\frac{1}{2}$ years.

The data on the gross capital stock in the United Kingdom enables us to look at the structure of the 'productive potential' which the gross stock of capital represents. Diagram 1.8 shows the gross stock of fixed capital divided in the first instance among the productive sectors of the economy and, in the second instance, distinguishing roads and dwellings as functionally distinct types of fixed capital. Manufacturing industry dominates the produc-

DIAGRAM 1.8   *Structure of the UK gross fixed capital stock at end-1980 (valued at 1975 prices)*

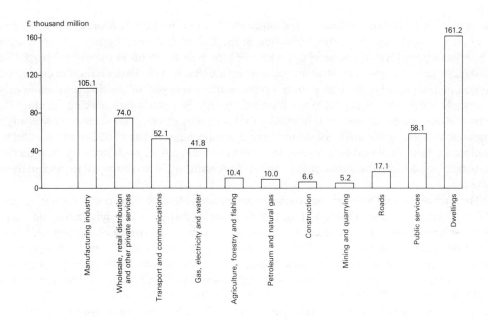

tive sector, with £105.1 billion of gross fixed capital stock at the end of 1980. The sector of distribution and other private services (including financial services) had £74 billion of gross capital stock. Transport and communications (including railway track but excluding roads) has a large proportion of the gross capital stock, as does the public utility sector of gas, electricity and water (most of this gross capital stock being electricity-generating stations and the associated network of overhead and underground cables and sub-stations). Agriculture, forestry and fishing has only a relatively small proportion of the fixed capital stock, but we must remember, first, that this excludes land, and, second, that a great deal of farmers' capital is circulating capital – animals and growing crops. The petroleum and natural-gas sector has, as everyone knows, only recently grown so big and it is now bigger than the mining and quarrying sector. Public services contain a considerable slice of the gross capital stock, mostly in the form of buildings such as offices, hospitals and schools. As we have already noted, the United Kingdom has a considerable portion of its capital stock in the form of dwellings (both publicly and privately owned) and the gross capital stock figures show this clearly.

There is a sense in which these figures on the gross capital stock are the most 'important' in the national accounts and they are next in 'importance' to the figures on the total and the working population: this is because we need to look at the fixed capital counterpart to the labour force. One could not claim to know much about an economy if one did not know the size or distribution of its labour force; and the same is true for the gross capital stock.

We know that the net capital stock equals the gross capital stock *minus* cumulated depreciation, and as the two stocks are valued at common prices at the end of 1975, we can ascertain the cumulated amount of depreciation at that date. Subtracting the net from the gross capital stock gives a figure of £140·7 billion, which is 30 per cent of the gross stock. So we can see that the cumulated depreciation is a significant proportion of the gross stock; depreciation is not something that can be ignored – it plays an important role in the economy.

The perpetual inventory method: fixed capital formation and retirements

Before going on to the combination of capital and labour in the UK economy, we need to study one more thing about the derivation of the UK capital stock figures. The examples which have been given all depend upon knowing each of the items in the capital stock and its date of construction. The student will appreciate that it is difficult enough to conduct a census of people even though people come neatly packaged in distinct and eminently countable similar units (apart from Siamese twins). But the items making up the UK capital stock are so diverse and manifold that a census of the capital stock is well-nigh impossible. Even if it were feasible to make a comprehensive list of distinct items and to count each item, it would be impossible to ascertain the age of each item. So how do the statisticians calculate the value of the capital stock without an inventory of items and their dates?

The answer is that the capital stock estimates are calculated from the known annual *flows* of expenditure on investment, or fixed capital formation. Although we may not have an inventory of factories and their machines, etc., we do know pretty accurately what was spent on factories and machines for a number of years, and knowledge of these annual flows enables us, after a lapse of years, to calculate the capital stock. For example, suppose we know that in 1970 there was an investment expenditure of £1,000 on a Mini and that in 1975 there was another flow of investment of £1,000 on another Mini.

(If the price had risen, we should have to correct for inflation, so as to make sure that we are adding items valued at a common price; if the price of Minis had doubled between 1970 and 1975, we should either halve the 1975 price – taking it all back to 1970 prices – or double the 1970 price – taking all to 1975 prices. Let us assume we do the former).

Now at end-1970 we know the gross stock of Minis comprises the £1,000 spent on Minis that year *plus* an unknown value of pre-1970 Minis; at the end of 1975 we know that the gross stock comprises £2,000-worth of Minis – that is, the 1970 investment and the 1975 investment – *plus* the unknown value of pre-1970 Minis. Now, because the working life of a Mini is 10 years, all the pre-1970 Minis must eventually 'retire' from the gross capital stock. For instance, at the beginning of 1979 the 1968 vintage Minis will have been 'retired'' and only the 1969 vintage Minis will be left as the 'unknowns'. At the beginning of 1980 the 1969 vintage Minis will be retired, and there will be left only the 1970 vintage and the 1975 vintage. So, providing we have (a) accurate information on the annual flow of capital expenditure, and (b) accurate estimates of the lives of (categories of) items on which those capital expenditures are made, then, starting with the flows in a given year, we can estimate the known capital stock at the date of the given year *plus* the item's working life in years.

If this seems a bit too complicated to understand, let us think of the capital stock as being a child's box of toys and then, at the beginning of 1970, we start counting (the value of) the toys put into the box. We have one other piece of knowledge: as each toy completes its tenth year of working life, it disappears from the box (assuming a ten-year working – or playing – life for toys). Now, by the beginning of 1980 all the unknown toys will have disappeared: the unknown toys which started their working life on Christmas day 1969 will complete their tenth year on Christmas day 1979 and will disappear. So that by the beginning of 1980 the only toys in the box will be the ones we started counting on 1 January 1970 onwards, and we know the gross (and the net) value of all those toys. Of course, during 1980, the 1970 toys will be retired and will have to be deducted from the (now known) value of the (toy) capital stock. And we shall also have to carry on adding in the 1980 expenditure on toys.

From 1980 onwards the value of the *gross* (fixed) capital stock can be calculated as:

| Gross capital stock at end of previous year | + | Gross capital formation during year | − | Retirements from capital stock during year | = | Gross capital stock at end of year |

This method of calculating the capital stock is known as the 'perpetual inventory method' – the term simply means that providing we keep a perpetual inventory (list) of the value of additions to the capital stock (of toys going into the box), then after a certain number of years we can be confident of having a reasonable estimate of the stock of fixed capital, and these estimates can then be carried forward. The change (at constant prices) in the gross stock is, as explained, a measure of the change in productive potential. The formula just given has to be applied in terms of unchanging price levels – if prices do change, then the flow of fixed capital formation has to be revalued to some common price; as explained, it makes no sense to add a new Mini priced at £2,000 to another originally priced at £1,000.

Likewise, from 1980 onwards, the *net* stock of (fixed) capital can be calculated as:

| Net capital stock at end of previous year | + | Gross capital formation during year | − | Capital consumption during year | = | Net capital stock at end of year |

The difference between gross fixed capital formation and capital consumption during the year is known as *net fixed capital formation*. Net fixed capital formation is an important flow because it measures the change in the value of fixed capital which an enterprise owns (remember that we are abstracting from inflation). Going back to Table 1.9, at the end of 1974 one owns a Mini (1970 vintage) worth £600, and this is a measure of how 'wealthy' one is (in terms of Minis). During 1975 one buys another Mini for £1,000 – this is gross fixed capital formation. However, also during 1975, the process of depreciation knocks £100 of capital consumption from the value of the 1970 Mini, so *net* fixed capital formation is £900, and at the end of 1975 one's wealth (in terms of Minis) has risen to £1,500. During 1976, one buys no new Minis, so gross fixed capital formation is zero. There is, however, capital consumption of £200 during the year (£100 on each of the two Minis), so net fixed capital formation is −£200, and at the end of 1976 one's wealth (in terms of Minis) has diminished to £1,300. However, if prices are changing, the market value of the (net) stock of fixed capital will be affected and in this case the formula just given does not apply, because there is, additionally, a revaluation effect (on the whole capital stock) to be taken into account.

The *National Income and Expenditure* accounts provide two series of data on the United Kingdom's stock of fixed capital – Table 1.11. One set of figures gives the net capital stock at current replacement cost by type of asset, each type subdivided by sector of ownership. These are the figures we used first of all to examine the 'amount' of fixed capital in the economy and the 'wealth' (in terms of fixed capital) of each sector. The other set of figures gives the gross capital stock at constant 1975 prices (the national accounts, a bit confusingly, calls it 'at 1975 replacement cost', but this must not be taken as implying 'in its (depreciated) condition') by sector of the economy, by types of asset, and a more detailed breakdown by manufacturing industry. From the point of view of the productive capacity of the capital stock it is these gross capital stock figures which are important, so we shall subsequently be considering this stock and the annual flows which affect its growth.

Table 1.12 shows, in the first two columns, the annual flow (valued at 1975 prices) of gross fixed capital formation in recent years and the flow of retirements. These 'retirements' relate to the flow of expenditure on items of fixed capital in previous years, valued at 1975 prices, which items have now reached the end of their – estimated – working lives and which (like our ten-year-old Minis) are deemed to leave the capital stock. Unlike the flow of expenditure on capital formation which is based on 'hard' countable (and counted)

TABLE 1.11   *The capital stock in the United Kingdom, 1967 to 1980*

	£ thousand million	
Year-end	Net capital stock at current replacement cost	Gross capital stock at 1975 replacement cost
1967	89.1	353.2
1968	97.6	368.0
1969	108.1	384.2
1970	122.6	399.0
1971	141.2	414.0
1972	169.0	428.8
1973	215.6	444.3
1974	275.6	459.1
1975	332.7	473.4
1976	381.7	487.4
1977	432.5	501.0
1978	504.2	514.6
1979	617.3	528.1
1980	743.0	541.6

Sources: Central Statistical Office, *National Income and Expenditure 1967–77*, tables 11.11 and 11.12, pp. 90 and 91; Central Statistical Office, *National Income and Expenditure 1979 Edition*, tables 11.11 and 11.12, pp. 88 and 89; Central Statistical Office, *National Income and Expenditure 1980 Edition*, tables 11.11 and 11.12, pp. 83 and 84; Central Statistical Office, *National Income and Expenditure 1981 Edition*, tables 11.11 and 11.12, pp. 83 and 84.

TABLE 1.12   *Growth of fixed capital stock in the United Kingdom, 1974 to 1980*

	£ million at constant 1975 prices			
Year	Gross domestic fixed capital formation [a]	Retirements [b]	Gross capital formation *less* retirements	Gross fixed capital stock, year-end
1974	20,050	5,195	14,855	459,100
1975	19,791	5,580	14,211	473,400
1976	20,016	5,964	14,052	487,400
1977	19,500	5,777	13,723	501,000
1978	20,109	6,453	13,656	514,600
1979	20,203	6,773	13,430	528,100
1980	20,087	6,520	13,567	541,600

[a] Excluding the transfer costs of land and buildings.
[b] Sometimes called 'replacement investment' – that investment necessary in a year simply to maintain the gross capital stock (or output capacity) at the same level.

Source: Central Statistical Office, *National Income and Expenditure 1981 Edition*, tables 10.7, 11.2, 11.6 and 11.12, pp. 73, 78, 80 and 84.

transactions (sales and purchases) in the markets for capital goods, the flow of retirements is the statisticians' estimate of the impact of retirements. Retirement of fixed capital is, of course, a real economic phenomenon that is taking place all the time in the economy – a commonly visible example is the demolition of 'slum' houses – but there is not much 'hard' data reported on retirements, so estimates have to be made. The procedure in the UK accounts for estimating retirements is now quite sophisticated and allows for some 'spreading' of retirements (for example, the service life of a Mini could be prolonged or foreshortened) and these estimates of retirements are likely to be quite 'reliable' in the sense of being an economically meaningful estimate of 'replacement investment' – that is, of the flow of investment which would just suffice to maintain the gross capital stock (perhaps it would be better to say: to maintain the productive capacity of the capital stock) at an unchanged level. It follows that, if gross capital formation *exceeds* retirements, then the gross capital stock (or, rather, its productive capacity) will expand. As you can calculate from Table 1.12, the excess of gross capital formation over retirements is the expansion of the gross capital stock from year-end to year-end.

We can better understand this very important process (because, after all, it is the gross capital stock which fundamentally determines our standard of living, and it is the growth of that stock which determines the increase in our standard of living) if we imagine the gross capital stock to be like a volume of water in a tank – Diagram 1.9. Into this tank there is an inflow of water which is measured over a period of time; this is the gross fixed capital formation during the year, which during 1980 was £20,087 million. But there is also an outlet pipe at the bottom of the tank, and through this there is an outflow of water – measured over the same period – representing retirements during the year; during 1980 these were £6,520 million. Whether, and to what extent, the level of water in the tank changes depends on the balance of the inflow over the outflow. In 1980 gross fixed capital formation exceeded retirements by £13,567 million, so that the stock of fixed capital rose between the end of 1979 and the end of 1980 by £13,500 million (the capital stock figures being rounded to the nearest hundred million).

The flow of retirements is a 'technically' determined flow rather than an economically determined flow. That is to say, items in the capital stock have more or less fixed working lives and, given that they were installed so many years back, when their time comes they have to retire. Analogously we might say that 'retirements' from the labour force is, by and large, an age-determined matter rather than something determined by economic forces. For this reason, we shall not be concerned with studying the magnitude of the flow of retirements from the capital stock; we simply take it as given. But the flow of gross fixed capital formation *is* economically determined by many important economic forces and

DIAGRAM 1.9 *How the stock of fixed capital changes*

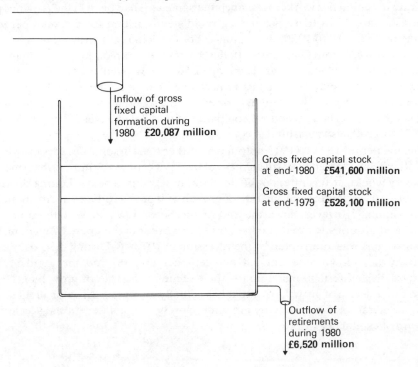

Inflow of gross
fixed capital
formation during
1980 **£20,087 million**

Gross fixed capital stock
at end-1980 **£541,600 million**

Gross fixed capital stock
at end-1979 **£528,100 million**

Outflow of
retirements
during 1980
£6,520 million

accordingly we shall be much concerned to study the magnitude of this flow. Indeed, it could be said that understanding the flow of gross fixed capital formation – understanding what influences it and what impact it has – is the main underlying preoccupation of economics.

Labour and capital

So far, we have discussed labour and capital separately. But, of course, during the process of production, labour and capital are used together: indeed, almost the whole purpose of the stock of fixed capital (excluding dwellings and civic amenities) is to provide the equipment and other requisites to assist workers during the process of production. The amount of capital equipment a worker has, on average, to assist in the work is a significant determinant of how productive that work is. It is therefore important to realise that since 1945 the United Kingdom has experienced a historically rapid rise in the stock of fixed capital, valued at constant prices, per worker in employment.

Diagram 1.10 shows this post-1945 rise in historical perspective (the data for Diagram 1.10 are given in Appendices 1.1, 1.2 and 1.3). The diagram (plotted on semi-log graph paper, for reasons already discussed, p. 10) charts the course of the 'real' value (that is, *after* adjusting for the effects of price inflation) of the gross stock of fixed capital in the United Kingdom *divided by* the total number of persons actually working in the United Kingdom (that is, the total of employees and self-employed *plus* the armed forces but excluding the unemployed). The diagram also charts 'real' output per worker in employment. The years up to 1913 include the Republic of Ireland (then Southern Ireland); the years after 1921 exclude the Republic.

Table 1.13 gives the percentage growth rates of labour force in employment, capital stock, output, capital per worker and output per worker over each of the three periods distinguished. The years between 1871 and 1913 and between 1921 and 1938 see a slow rise in the stock of fixed capital per worker: during the period 1871 to 1913 the value of the capital stock per worker rose by about 0.6 per cent a year. During the interwar period the growth rate in capital per worker was much the same as it had been in the previous period. By contrast, since 1948 there has been a rapid steady rise in fixed capital per worker: during the period 1948 to 1980, the capital–labour ratio has grown at a rate of 3 per cent a year. As you can see from Diagram 1.10, this is a far more rapid rate of growth than in the previous periods for which data are available. Later on, we shall analyse theoretically the whys, hows and consequences of this remarkable change in the annual growth rate of capital per worker in the UK economy. The economic significance of this rise in capital per worker can be appreciated when we compare the parallel changes in output per worker from 1871 to 1980, also measured at constant prices.

During the period 1871 to 1913 output per worker rose, in some decades growing faster than in others, but with an over-all increase of 0.75 per cent per annum – which means that productivity would, at this rate, double in about ninety-three years. During the interwar years, there was an increase in the rate of growth of labour productivity, to about 1.2 per cent per annum. However, since the end of the Second World War there has been a sustained and historically rapid rise in output per worker in the United Kingdom, though the upward trend was interrupted by the recession in 1974–6. During this postwar period productivity has grown at about 2.4 per cent per annum, and the rapid growth of productivity has more than made up for the decline in the rate of growth of the labour force, so that the rate of growth of output has actually increased. As we shall subsequently see, this acceleration in productivity growth is closely connected with the acceleration in the growth of capital per worker.

DIAGRAM 1.10   *Capital per worker and output per worker in the United Kingdom, 1861 to 1980*

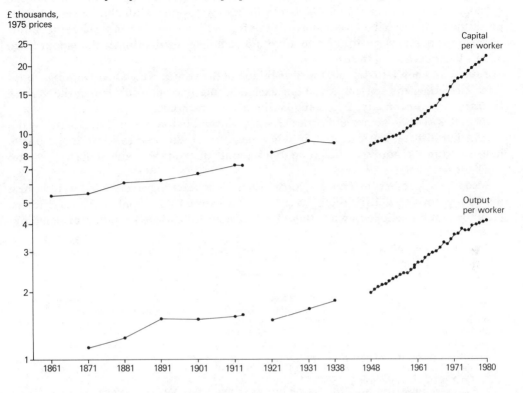

TABLE 1.13   *Trend growth rates of labour force in work, capital stock, output, capital per worker and output per worker since 1871*

	Trend growth rate, per cent per annum		
	1871 to 1913	1921 to 1938	1948 to 1980
Labour force in work	0.95	1.01	0.20
Fixed capital stock (at constant prices)	1.60	1.61	3.23
Gross domestic product at factor cost (at constant prices)	1.70	2.20	2.65
Fixed capital per worker (at constant prices)	0.64	0.60	3.03
Gross domestic product per worker (at constant prices)	0.75	1.19	2.44

Source: computed by fitting an exponential trend to data in Appendices 1.1, 1.2 and 1.3. This technique for estimating the growth rate is explained towards the end of Chapter 3.

This growth of productivity and output may not have been as fast as most UK citizens would have liked: certainly, during the post-war period other economies have been growing faster than the United Kingdom's. Nevertheless, the UK economy has, during the past three decades, been growing at a historically rapid rate, and one of the main tasks for applied economic theory is to assess and analyse this process of growth.

We have just seen that, over a period of time, more capital per worker and rising labour productivity have gone together. But it is also the case that, among the industries of the economy, differences in capital – labour ratios also go together with differences in labour productivity. It is possible to demonstrate this for 1971, the year when we have the results of the population census to provide us with a complete distribution of the labour force among the industries of the economy.

Table 1.14 shows, first of all, the distribution of the United Kingdom's working labour force (including the self-employed but excluding the unemployed) among the various industries of the economy. Two preliminaries need to be noted.

First, this division among industries is a bit arbitrary, in that it is dictated partly by the availability of data. For example, it might have been preferable to separate the textile industry from the others in the group, but separate data on the textile industry's capital stock are not published.

Second, the numbers in the work-force rather oddly refer to two dates in 1971 because the figures for Great Britain are taken from the April 1971 population census (these include the self-employed), while those for Northern Ireland are from the June employ-

TABLE 1.14   *Labour, capital and output in the industries of the UK economy (excluding dwellings and their imputed income), 1971*

Industry, or productive branch of the economy	Total work-force in employment, April–June, 1971 [a]	£ million		£	
		Gross fixed capital stock, end-1970 [b]	Gross value added during 1971 [c]	Gross fixed capital per worker	Output per worker
1. Electricity, gas and water supply	370,100	17,700	1,572	47,825	4,248
2. Coal, petroleum products, chemicals, allied industries	520,230	7,300	1,418	14,032	2,726
3. Transport and communications	1,587,120	20,900	4,097	13,169	2,581
4. Food, drink, tobacco industries	767,540	4,530	1,862	5,902	2,426
5. Mining and quarrying	394,260	2,300	642	5,834	1,628
6. Agriculture, forestry and fishing	643,550	3,600	1,435	5,594	2,230
7. Bricks, pottery, glass industries	310,660	1,660	592	5,343	1,906
8. Paper, printing, publishing industries	618,880	2,700	1,376	4,363	2,223
9. Metal manufacture and all engineering industries	4,270,150	18,310	7,775	4,288	1,821
10. Textile, leather, clothing, manufacturing industries (n.e.s.)	1,521,230	5,440	2,201	3,576	1,447
11. All private and public-sector services, inc. defence	11,014,440	36,100	21,115	3,278	1,917
12. Timber and furniture industries	307,100	590	484	1,921	1,576
13. Construction	1,711,930	2,260	3,417	1,320	1,996
Whole economy [a] [b] [c]	24,037,190	123,390	47,986	5,133	1,996

[a]   Excluding about 714,000 registered unemployed and excluding about 170,000 persons whose industry was 'inadequately described', but including the self-employed.

[b]   Excluding private and public dwellings and roads; all capital stock valued at 1970 replacement cost.

[c]   Gross of (i.e. including) depreciation, but excluding stock appreciation and excluding imputed income from ownership of dwellings; all flows valued at current (1971) prices.

n.e.s. = not elsewhere specified.

Sources: Office of Population Censuses and Surveys, *Census 1971: Great Britain, Economic Activity*, part III (10% sample) (HMSO, 1975) table 20, pp. 125–48; Department of Employment, *British Labour Statistics Year Book 1971* (HMSO, 1973) table 57, pp. 132–39; Central Statistical Office, *National Income and Expenditure 1966–76*, tables 3.2, 11.12, 11.14, pp. 14, 24, 87 and 88; Central Statistical Office, *National Income and Expenditure 1980 Edition*, tables 1.9 and 3.2, pp. 12 and 26.

ment census (these do not include the self-employed, but the proportionate effect of this omission on total UK figures will be very small).

Table 1.14 also gives, for each industry, the amount of gross fixed capital at the end of 1970 (measured in 1970 prices) and the flow of output during 1971 (measured in 1971 prices). From these three columns of figures we can calculate the final two columns showing capital per worker and output per worker. The industries are listed in descending order of capital per worker, and it is possible to see that the figures on output per worker descend more or less in line with the figures on capital per worker.

The industry of electricity, gas and water supply is outstanding in its very high capital-labour ratio. When you think of all the fixed capital that each of these three activities requires – power-generating stations and electricity-transmission lines, gas mains, and reservoirs and water mains – but the relatively small amounts of labour that are needed to keep them running, it is not surprising that this industry's capital-labour ratio should be so high. The annual flow of output per worker employed in this industry is also the highest in the economy.

Next, we have two industries – the coal and petroleum products and chemicals and allied industries, and the transport and communications industries – both of which have capital-labour ratios that are high relative to the economy-wide average capital-labour ratio; output per worker in these two industries is also well above the over-all average for the economy.

After this, the remaining industries are grouped around the over-all averages of capital and output per worker. Not surprisingly, the construction industry has the lowest amount of capital per worker, as the process of construction requires plant and machinery, but very little in the way of 'other buildings and works'. It is worth noting, in connection with the low proportion of workers engaged in agriculture, forestry and fishing, that this branch of the economy is a quite highly 'capital-intensive' industry, in that its workers have an above-average amount of fixed capital per worker, and also a flow of annual output per worker that is higher than that in most manufacturing industries.

Scatter diagram: covariance, standard deviation, and correlation

It is possible to relate labour productivity – output per worker as measured by *value added* per worker* – more systematically to capital per worker by drawing a 'scatter diagram' which plots each industry's output per worker against its capital per worker. Diagram 1.11 gives the last two columns of Table 1.14 in this form. The convention is that the dependent, or 'caused', variable is measured on the upright vertical axis (sometimes called 'the Y-axis') and the independent, or 'causing', variable is measured on the horizontal axis (sometimes called 'the X-axis'). In this case we assume that capital per worker causally affects output per worker, so we take capital per worker as the independent variable. The point in the upper right-hand corner then represents the 'co-ordinate' for the electricity, gas and water supply industry: namely, £47,825 along the X-axis and £4,248 up the Y-axis. There are thirteen points in all, each representing one of the industries in Table 1.14 (the co-

ordinate for the whole economy is *not* plotted because this does not represent a separate industry). When we plot the points in such a way, we see that there is a *tendency* for industries with a larger amount of capital per worker than other industries also to have a higher level of output per worker. This is only a broad tendency over *all* the industries, and may not apply to a few specific pairs of industries; for example, paper, printing and publishing has a *lower* capital–labour ratio than mining and quarrying but nevertheless has a *higher* productivity. Nevertheless, in most cases the positive relationship between capital per worker and output per worker holds good; by the term 'positive relationship' what we mean is that an industry with an above-average amount of capital per worker is likely also to have an above-average level of output per worker. Conversely, an industry with a below-average amount of capital per worker is likely also to have a below-average level of

*The concept of *value added* is explained in the next chapter.

output per worker. (A 'negative', or 'inverse', relationship occurs when an above-average value of a variable tends to be associated with a *below*-average value of another variable.) In this statement, the word 'average' refers to the simple, or unweighted, averages of the two columns, which are £8,957.3 for capital per worker and £2,209.6 for output per worker. If we use these averages, denoted by $\bar{X}$ and $\bar{Y}$ ('*X*-bar', '*Y*-bar') respectively, to divide the scatter diagram into four quadrants, then we see that most of the points fall into the lower-left quadrant where the co-ordinates of both capital per worker and output per worker are below average; three points fall in the upper-right quadrant where both co-ordinates are above average; and three co-ordinates (but two of them only just) fall into the upper-left quadrant where output per worker is above average but capital per worker is below average. So that, considering the whole ensemble of points, the relationship between capital per worker and output per worker is a positive one.

Statisticians have a method of measuring not simply whether the relationship is positive or negative but also the *degree* to which the relationship holds. This is done in two steps. First, we measure the 'covariance' between the two variables. The covariance is measured by taking for any *i*th observation (e.g. that for electricity,

gas and water) the difference between its capital per worker and the simple average of capital per worker, that is:

$$47,825 - 8,957.3 = (+)\,38,867.7$$

and the difference between its output per worker and the simple average of output per worker, that is:

$$4,248 - 2,209.6 = (+)\,2,038.4$$

and multiplying the two (positive) differences together:

$$(+)\,38,867.7 \times (+)\,2,038.4$$
$$= 79,227,919.7$$

You will note that the first calculation reveals that electricity, gas and water supply's capital per worker is above average (the difference is positive) and the second reveals that its output per worker is also above average; therefore when we multiply the two differences together, we get a (large) positive number.

Now if we take the observations for the construction industry we see that its capital per worker is below average, that is:

$$1,320 - 8,957.3 = -7,637.3$$

and its output per worker is also below average, that is:

$$1,996 - 2,209.6 = -213.6$$

DIAGRAM 1.11 *Output per worker and capital per worker, 1971*

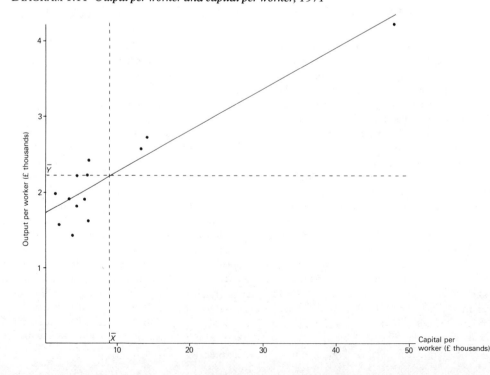

This means that when we multiply the two differences together we again get a *positive* number:

$$-7,637.3 \times (-)\,213.6 = 1,631,327.2$$

Clearly, if we add all the products of the differences for each industry together, that is:

79,227,919.7	(Electricity, gas and water)
1,631,327.2	(Construction)
$\vdots$	$\vdots$
99,204,749.0	(Total for thirteen industries)

we get a *positive* total. The average of this total is known as the *covariance* between the two variables:

$$\text{covariance} = \frac{1}{13} \times 99,204,749$$
$$= 7,631,134.5$$

In symbolic expression, if we let X stand for capital per worker and Y stand for output per worker, and we let subscript i denote an industry, the covariance is measured by taking:

$$(X_i - \bar{X}) \times (Y_i - \bar{Y})$$

and summing over all thirteen industries, and finally taking the average. The symbol for such adding is the Greek capital letter, Σ, sigma, so we can write the covariance as:

$$\frac{1}{13} \sum_{i=1}^{13} (X_i - \bar{X})(Y_i - \bar{Y})$$

and the summation says that we must calculate the product of the two differences for each i, from $i = 1$ (electricity, gas and water) to $i = 13$ (construction) and add them all up to a total and then get the average by dividing by 13. As we have seen, this covariance between capital per worker and output per worker is positive, so the relationship between the two variables is said to be a positive one. (Conversely, if an above-average X_i tends to be associated with a below-average Y_i, each of the products will be negative, the sum of the products will therefore be negative, and the covariance will be negative, demonstrating a negative or inverse relationship between the two variables.)

The problem with the covariance is that it is a number in absolute terms: that is, it is the product of two numbers in £s (in this case) multiplied, summed and averaged (in effect it is a number in £s squared). As such it is an awkward number to comprehend, so it is preferable to standardise the covariance by expressing it as a ratio to another figure of similar dimensions (£s squared). This is the second step in ascertaining the degree to which the relationship holds. This second step is performed by dividing the covariance by the product of the 'standard deviations' of the two variables.

The *standard deviation* of a variable measures the extent to which that variable deviates about its average. It is calculated as follows: first, we take the difference of each observation on a variable (capital per worker) about the simple average, for example:

$$47,825 - 8,957.3 = (+)38,867.7$$

or:

$$1,320 - 8,957.3 = -7,637.3$$

for electricity, gas and water, or construction (respectively). Then we square those differences:

$$(+)38,867.7^2 = (+)1,510,698,103$$

and:

$$-7,637.3^2 = (+)58,328,351$$

(the purpose of squaring being to make all the numbers positive). Then we sum all the squared differences:

1,510,698,103
58,328,351
$\vdots$
1,809,614,573 (Total sum of squares for thirteen industries)

then we take the average of the squared differences to find the 'variance':

$$\frac{1}{13}(1,809,614,573) = 139,201,121$$

Finally, because this is an average of a squared number, we convert back to the original units by taking the square root of this variance:

$$\sqrt[2]{139,201,121} = 11,798.4$$

This standard deviation is then a measure, in £s, of the average extent to which the thirteen observations on capital per worker vary about the simple average of capital per worker. In symbolic, or general algebraic terms, the standard deviation is computed as:

$$\sqrt[2]{\frac{1}{13} \sum_{i=1}^{13} (X_i - \bar{X})^2}$$

(In very general terms, we would substitute the letter n for the number 13, where n is the number of observations.) Using the same general formula, the standard deviation for value added per worker can likewise be computed as 696.3.

We are now in a position to ascertain the *relative* extent to which the covariance measures the *degree* of the relationship between output per worker and capital per worker. This may be done by dividing the covariance by the product of the two standard deviations. Remember that the awkwardness of the covariance lay in it being an absolute measure, in £s squared, of the relationship between the variables. Each standard deviation is measured in £s, so the product of the two is in £s squared; accordingly, the division of the covariance by the product of the standard deviations results in a purely relative number (£s squared *divided by* £s squared). This relative number is known as a 'coefficient of correlation': 'coefficient' meaning a relative number, 'correlation' meaning a degree of relationship.

In the case of the data in Table 1.14 and Diagram 1.11, the coefficient of correlation is:

$$\text{Coefficient of correlation between } X \text{ and } Y = \frac{\text{Covariance between } X \text{ and } Y}{\text{Standard deviation of } X \times \text{Standard deviation of } Y}$$

$$= \frac{(+)7,631,134.5}{11,798.4 \times 696.3}$$

$$= \frac{(+)7,631,134.5}{8,215,225.9}$$

$$= (+)0.9289$$

Now, the highest value attainable by a correlation coefficient is +1 in the case of a positive covariance (or −1 in the case of a negative covariance). This occurs only when each observation on Y is exactly convertible by some linear formula to its corresponding X value. By a linear formula, we mean either a simple proportional relationship exists, for example each Y is exactly one-quarter of the corresponding observation on X:

| Output per worker in industry i | $= 0.25 \times$ | Capital per worker in industry i |

and this relationship holds exactly for each ith observation. Or we may mean that this relationship has, in each case, the same constant term, such as 1,000, added to it:

| Output per worker in industry i | $= 1,000 + 0.25$ | Capital per worker in industry i |

and that this relationship holds exactly for each ith observation. The reason this is called a *linear* relationship is that if you make up an imaginary set of observations on capital per worker and work out the corresponding observations on output per worker, according to the formula, and then plot on a scatter diagram the resulting co-ordinates, you will get a straight line.

The coefficient of correlation which we obtained was not equal to +1, but it was not too far from it, so the value of 0.9289 indicates that there is a quite close statistical relationship between output per worker in an industry and capital per worker in that industry. In fact, the straight-line linear relationship which fits best with the set of observations in Table 1.14 and Diagram 1.11 is:

| Output per worker | $= 1,718.6 + 0.055$ | Capital per worker |

and this straight line is drawn in Diagram 1.11.

Conclusion

So we have seen that historically over the last one hundred years or so rising amounts of capital per worker in the UK economy have led to rising output per worker, and also that across the industries of the economy above-average output per worker tends to be associated with above-average capital per worker. Subsequently, we shall discuss the relationship between capital per worker and output per worker in more detail; for the moment we need only note the fact of a relationship between the two.

This first chapter has discussed the two main economic resources, or 'factors of production', in the UK economy: labour and capital. We considered the stocks of labour and capital available to the economy, and we then saw how the combined inputs of labour and capital are used to enhance the productivity of labour.

In the rest of this book, we shall be mainly concerned with the economy's stock of capital and with the processes by which this stock is increased and how such increases affect labour productivity. From an economist's viewpoint, the difference between labour and capital as factors of production is that fixed capital is a *produced means of production*. Human beings cannot similarly be produced to order; and there is the further very important socio-legal fact that human beings cannot be owned either. Our next task is to investigate the process of production and what happens to the output which is thereby produced.

Exercises

1.1 *(To practise finding data – as per the famous recipe for jugged hare which began 'First, catch your hare'.)* Update, to the latest available year, the data on the UK labour force in Table 1.1 and check whether there have been any revisions to the given data.

(*Hint:* use all the notes to Table 1.1; you need a library which takes the *Employment Gazette* or the *Monthly Digest of Statistics:* note that Table 1.1 uses the figures unadjusted for seasonal variation.)

1.2 *(To practise calculating compound growth and annual percentage changes.)* Using your updated and possibly revised figures, calculate the *annual* percentage changes (to two decimal places) in the labour force between each of the successive pair of years given in Table 1.1. Present your results clearly in a table.

(*Example*: for 1851 to 1861 (10 years) we have: $\{(13{,}090/12{,}050)\ \exp.\ \frac{1}{10}\} - 1 = 1.00831275 - 1 = 0.00831275 = 0.83$ per cent; or for 1951 to 1952 (1 year only) we have $(23{,}925/23{,}841) - 1 = 0.003523342 = 0.35$ per cent. Note the movement in the decimal point. Note the alternative way of writing an exponent, i.e.

$$(13{,}090/12{,}050)\ \exp.\ \tfrac{1}{10}\ \text{is}\ \left(\frac{13{,}090}{12{,}050}\right)^{\frac{1}{10}}$$

Note also the quick way to calculate a year-to-year percentage change: rather than work out for 1951–52 (23,925–23,841)/23,841, which involves a subtraction and a division (two operations), we simply divide the two numbers (one operation) and knock off the 1 when we write the answer down. Note also the snags at 1920 and 1960 and devise and footnote your solution to these snags.*)

To answer this question, you need a calculator with an x^y key, where y can be any number (positive or negative) including, especially, fractions – some calculators have only an x^n key where n must be an integer (a whole number) but this is insufficient: if in doubt, test before you buy.

WHEN YOU ARE FINISHED, CHECK YOUR RESULTS! This is the First and Greatest Commandment of working with data: checking entails (a) ensuring that you have correctly written down the original numbers to start with (if you were devising Table 1.1 from scratch) and, in this exercise, that you have correctly written down the updated numbers and any revised numbers, and (b) repeating all the calculations and ticking each result as right or altering it if wrong. If you have a calculator which prints out each number entered *and* the calculation performed and the answer, then you can do your checking by checking the print-out. To enjoin you to check your

*Snags of this sort often arise in practice; you must therefore develop your own skills (and self-confidence) in dealing with them; in this there is no substitute for relying on your own common sense; the vitally important thing is for you to spot the problem in the first place and then, in the second place, to give a few minutes thought to dealing with it; if you can justify your solution, then, by that fact alone, your solution is 'right'; the 'wrong' thing is not to spot the snag at all or, having spotted it, to omit doing anything systematic about it.

results is not to insult you by implying careless-ness. In Exercise 1.2 you will probably have entered forty-three numbers twice, each number containing five digits (i.e. about 430 digits) and you will have pressed the ÷ and = key forty-three times; suppose we compliment you by assuming that you work to 99 per cent accuracy (you would surely not wish to claim a superhu-man 100 per cent accuracy!); then 1 per cent of the digits entered (keys pressed) will be wrong, i.e. there would be about four incorrectly en-tered digits in your table of results. One day in your job you may be presenting some results to your boss or client/customer, and if you fail always to CHECK YOUR RESULTS there may be a (serious) mistake which may cost you very dear (you will have lost your reputation for reliabili-ty). All the figures in this book have been check-ed at least once and often twice at *every* stage from manuscript to typescript to proof, but given the number of digits in the book and the statisti-cal probability of, say, one error in each 1,000 digits (0.1 per cent), I certainly would not bet even £1 on each and every digit being correctly produced; all I can hope is that such mistakes as there must (*statistically* must) remain are not too serious!

1.3 (*To practise calculating percentages; percen-tages are proportions multiplied by 100.*) Calcu-late the percentage of women in Great Britain's working population for all the years given in Table 1.4. Present your results in a table. (*Ex-ample*: 7,441/23,239 = 0.3201945 = 32.019 per cent.)

Think about how to 'present' or lay out the table: Are you going to include the original figures or not? How many decimal places are you going to present? How are you going to explain three separate percentages for 1971?*

1.4 (*To practise presenting data visually.*) Draw a graph to illustrate your results from Exercise 1.3.

Hint: you need some graph paper; Chartwell W34G is a convenient size and scale. How are you going to handle the three 1971 percentages and the two 1976 percentages on the graph?

Some more hints: you want to demonstrate both levels at given years and also trends be-tween years. Draw up the scale, using the graph page as fully as reasonable: there are 40 years and between 0 to 40.3 per cent to be covered. Chartwell W34G has fourteen main (20mm) divisions each with ten subsidiary 2mm divisions and 9½ main divisions: in this graph it may be preferable to turn the paper sideways and mark off the years in 4mm divisions (ten years to each two main divisions; this uses up about nine of the fourteen divisions, leaving room at the left for numbering the vertical scale and room at the right for any label to the curve; the percentages can then go up the vertical scale either at 1 percentage point to 1mm or 1 percentage point to 2mm. (If you were preparing the graph for an important client, you may have to draw the graph both ways to see which 'looks' better. A 2mm =1 percentage point scale probably gives a better visual impression of the rise and flattening off.)

Dots or crosses above each given year joined by straight lines seem to me the 'best' way then to proceed (hoping, probably reasonably, that the intervening years are close to a straight-line trend). As a general rule, always start your scales at zero. Note the importance of being aware of the assumptions behind drawing the straight line. Note also that I said 'dots or crosses': the important thing is that you should, with deliber-ate and conscious choice, choose what you want – the 'wrong' thing is simply to put down, say, a dot, without thinking, 'would a cross, or a little square, "look" better?' If a cross which way should it go: × or +? Do you want to join the dots (or crosses) with a continuous straight line or a broken (dashed) straight line?

EVERYTHING YOU DO ON A GRAPH MUST BE THE RESULT OF A DELIBERATE CHOICE FROM AMONG CONSIDERED ALTERNATIVES.

1.5 (*To practise the difference between percen-tage points and percentages.*) Explain the follow-ing statement: 'The change in the percentage of women in Great Britain's labour force between 1951 and 1991 is (projected to be) 8.3 percen-tage points; it is not 8.3 per cent: the percentage

---

*This last question deals with a 'snag'. The other questions raise points about table layout; here again the 'right' answer results simply from giving the matter some considered thought; the 'wrong' answer is simply to be unaware that there is a problem of layout and presentation; some day your job – in business, advertising, television, government – may involve you in presenting facts in the form of figures to others: therefore, it is helpful if you start right now on practising how to lay out and present tables; study how I lay out tables in this book; see whether you can improve the layout (suggestions and criticism will be gratefully received by me!).

change in the percentage is 26 per cent.' (Newspaper and television reporters may make this mistake, you must not.)

1.6 *(To practise calculating percentages and presenting data again.)* Calculate the percentage of Great Britain's population who are (a) of working age, and (b) of retirement age, in the years given in Table 1.6. Present your results in a table. Draw *one* graph to illustrate your results.

1.7 *(To demonstrate that Exercise 1.6 has important economic implications, i.e. that these exercises are not simply for 'fun' but relate to the real world.)* How many persons of retirement age would there have been in 1981 if the total population were 54.3231 million but the age structure of that population were as it was in 1951? How does this hypothetical figure for persons of retirement age compare with the actual figure for 1981?

The rate of National Insurance retirement pension in November 1980 was £27.15 per week for a person aged under 80 on own insurance. At this 'price', what is the approximate annual 'cost' of the change in the age structure of the population (proportion of persons of retirement age) between 1951 and 1981?

(Note that although the increase in the percentage of persons of retirement age between 1951 and 1981 is 4.02 percentage points, this represents an increase of 29.5 per cent in the percentage itself, or in the number of pensioners due to the change in the age structure. Exercise 1.5 was not simply an exercise in pedantry!)

1.8 *(To practise your understanding of data through explanation and presentation.)* Table 1.7 gives the 'percentage of working-age population economically active'. Explain what this means and show how the percentage for 1971 was calculated (i.e. give the figures which result in the percentage). Draw a 'pie-chart' to illustrate the relationship of the numerator to the denominator. (A pie-chart or pie-diagram represents a total (the denominator) as the area of circle; constituent parts are represented by multiplying 360° by the proportions which the constituent parts bear to the total; you need a protractor and pair of compasses to do this exercise. You can see examples of pie-charts in Central Statistical Office, *Social Trends 1981 Edition*, no. 11, pp. 27, 43, 44, 135 and 207.)

1.9 *(To practise finding data.)* Update Diagram 1.4. Tabulate the quarterly flow of live births in Great Britain for the most recent past three (complete calendar) years, and draw a diagram to illustrate the table. Can you find any pattern among the quarterly figures for each year? If so, describe the pattern in words. Can you suggest any explanation for the pattern? (Have you CHECKED YOU RESULTS? Have you tabulated the figures for *Great Britain*?)

1.10 *(To practise using ratio scales.)* Using semi-logarithmic paper – or 'logarithmic one-way scales' – draw a time-series chart of the data in Table 1.5 to show the growth of the population of Great Britain. (Chartwell C5521 or C5522 is a convenient scale.) Draw on ordinary, arithmetic-scale, graph paper the same time-series chart, and compare the two curves.

1.11 *(To practise finding data.)* Update Diagram 1.5 (see Appendix 1.2).

1.12 *(To practise finding and presenting data.)* Update the figures for the fixed capital stock in Diagram 1.6. Draw a pie-chart to show the (updated) distribution of fixed capital by type of asset.

1.13 *(To practise finding data.)* Update Diagrams 1.7 and 1.8.

1.14 *(To practise your understanding of depreciation and retirements in the calculation of the gross and net capital stock.)* Work out a version of Table 1.9 on the assumption that the life of a Mini is five years (not ten).

1.15 *(To practise calculating (unweighted) averages, standard deviations, covariance, and the correlation coefficient.)* For the data of Table 1.14, verify that: (a) the unweighted average of capital per worker is £8,957.3; (b) the unweighted average of output per worker is £2,209.6; (c) the standard deviation of capital per worker is £11,798.4; (d) the standard deviation of output per worker is £696.3; (e) the covariance between capital per worker and output per worker is £7,631,134.5; and (f) the correlation coefficient of 0.9289 is the ratio between the covariance and the product of the standard deviations.

APPENDIX 1.1   *UK gross domestic product and capital stock, 1871 to 1980*

Year	Gross domestic product at factor cost, £ million			Gross capital stock, £ thousand million [b]					
	1900 factor cost	1938 factor cost	1975 prices [a]	1900 replacement cost	1938 replacement cost	1958 replacement cost	1963 replacement cost	1970 replacement cost	1975 replacement cost [c]
1861				3.81					67.4
1871	1,080		15,878.8	4.29					75.9
1881	1,238		18,201.8	5.02					88.8
1891	1,479		24,745.1	5.65					100.0
1901	1,880		27,640.8	6.82					120.7
1911	2,097		30,831.3	8.14					144.0
1913	2,201	4,080	32,360.3	8.32	14.66				147.2
1920		3,760	29,822.3		15.26				153.2
1920 [d]		3,607	28,608.7		14.66				147.2
1921		3,402	26,982.8		14.83				148.9
1931		3,980	31,567.2		17.29				173.6
1938		4,985	39,538.3		19.52	65.28			196.0
1948		5,806	46,050		20.70	68.51	70.7		205.7
1949			47,482			69.83			209.7
1950			49,039			71.42			214.5
1951			50,813			72.86	75.4		218.8
1952			50,819			74.36			223.3
1953			53,206			76.10			228.5
1954			55,131			78.02	81.1		234.3
1955			57,155			79.87			239.8
1956			58,271			81.72			245.4
1957			59,376			83.78			251.6
1958			59,089			85.80	89.7		257.6
1959			61,090			88.16	92.1		264.5
1960			63,911			90.74	95.7		274.9
1961			66,197			93.81	99.0		284.4
1962			66,815			96.83	102.1	131.6	293.3
1963			69,532			99.97	105.5	136.0	303.1
1964			73,261			103.97	109.8	141.5	315.3
1965			75,234			108.00	114.2	147.2	328.0
1966			76,821				118.8	152.0	338.7
1967			78,813				123.8	158.5	353.2
1968			82,328				129.1	165.4	368.0
1969			83,760				134.3	172.2	384.2
1970			85,484				139.6	179.3	399.0
1971			87,654				144.6	186.4	414.0
1972			88,815					193.6	428.8
1973			95,635					201.1	444.3
1974			94,905					208.6	459.1
1975			94,475					215.6	473.4
1976			97,948					221.7	487.4
1977			99,240						501.0
1978			101,869						514.6
1979			102,957						528.1
1980			101,354						541.6

[a] Italicised figures for 1871 to 1938 scaled according to Feinstein's figures (scaling gives identical proportionate changes in given series and derived series).
[b] At end of year.
[c] Italicised figures for 1861 to 1966 scaled according to other series given.
[d] This and subsequent figures exclude Southern Ireland (Eire); preceding figures include Southern Ireland.

Sources: C. H. Feinstein, *National Income, Expenditure and Output of the United Kingdom 1855–1965* gross domestic product: table 5, pp. T14–T16; capital stock: table 43, pp. T96–T98; Central Statistical Office, *Economic Trends Annual Supplement 1981 Edition*, p. 5 for gross domestic product: gross capital stock from Central Statistical Office, *National Income and Expenditure 1969*, table 63, p. 76; *National Income and Expenditure 1971*, table 65, p. 78; *National Income and Expenditure 1972*, table 64, p. 76; *National Income and Expenditure 1973*, table 64, p. 76; *National Income and Expenditure 1966–76*, table 11.12, p. 87; *National Income and Expenditure 1967–77*, table 11.12, p. 91; *National Income and Expenditure 1979 Edition*, table 11.12, p. 89; *National Income and Expenditure 1980 Edition*, table 11.12, p. 84; *National Income and Expenditure 1981 Edition*, tables 2.1 and 11.12, pp. 17 and 84.

APPENDIX 1.2   *Working population, wholly unemployed, and total in work in the United Kingdom, 1851 to 1981*

	Thousands				Thousands		
Year	Working population	Wholly unem- ployed	Total in work	Year	Working population	Wholly unem- ployed	Total in work
1851	12,050	—	12,050	1959	24,856.50	457.25	24,399.25
1861	13,090	470	12,620	1960	25,185.00	360.75	24,824.25
1871	14,050	220	13,830	1960 [d]	24,586.25	360.75	24,225.50
1881	15,060	520	14,540	1961	24,814.50	339.75	24,474.75
1891	16,660	570	16,090	1962	25,060.00	472.00	24,588.00
1901	18,680	600	18,080	1963	25,186.00	540.75	24,645.25
1911	20,390	600	19,790	1964	25,370.00	382.75	24,987.25
1913	20,740	430	20,310	1965	25,553.75	339.25	25,214.50
1920	22,000	430	21,570	1966	25,649.75	368.25	25,281.50
1920 [a]	20,688	391	20,297	1967	25,512.50	553.25	24,959.25
1921	20,120	2,210	17,910	1968	25,413.00	571.50	24,841.50
1931	21,917	3,252	18,665	1969	25,400.00	571.00	25,829.00
1938	23,582	2,164	21,418	1970	25,339.25	607.75	24,731.50
1948	23,364	300	23,064	1971	25,105.75	803.00	24,302.75
1949	23,360	270	23,090	1972	25,331.50	853.25	24,478.25
1950 [b]	23,609.67	307.33	23,302.34	1973	25,582.75	590.00	24,992.75
1951 [c]	23,840.50	256.50	23,584.00	1974 [e]	25,684.00	615.75	25,068.25
1952	23,925.00	369.25	23,555.75	1975	25,909.25	1,003.75	24,905.50
1953	24,053.25	341.25	23,712.00	1976	26,133.50	1,361.00	24,772.50
1954	24,345.75	287.00	24,058.75	1977	26,304.75	1,480.75	24,824.00
1955	24,583.25	235.50	24,347.75	1978	26,413.50	1,447.25	24,966.25
1956	24,766.25	258.50	24,507.75	1979	26,418.75	1,374.00	25,044.75
1957	24,786.50	323.00	24,463.50	1980	26,314.00	1,855.50	24,458.50
1958	24,678.25	454.50	24,223.75	1981 (June)	26,069.00	2,680.50	23,388.50

[a] This and subsequent figures exclude Southern Ireland (Eire); previous figures include Southern Ireland.

[b] Average for June, September and December.

[c] This and subsequent figures the average for March, June, September and December.

[d] Revised series. Unadjusted for seasonal variation; average of four quarters. Wholly unemployed excludes adult students.

[e] Using November unemployment as estimate for missing December figure.

Sources: 1851 to 1949: C. H. Feinstein, *National Income, Expenditure and Output of the United Kingdom 1855–1965*, pp. 224, 227, table 57, pp. T125–T126; 1950 to 1960: Department of Employment, *British Labour Statistics Historical Abstract 1886–1968*, table 118, p. 220; 1960 [d] to 1973: Department of Employment, *British Labour Statistics Year Book 1976*, table 55, p. 122; 1974: *Department of Employment Gazette*, December 1978, tables 101, 104, pp. 1422, 1426; 1975: *Department of Employment Gazette*, December 1979, table 101, p. 1278; 1976 to 1981, Department of Employment, *Employment Gazette*, December 1980, table 1.1, p. S7; Department of Employment, *Employment Gazette*, January 1982, table 1.1, p. S7.

APPENDIX 1.3   *Output per worker and capital per worker in the United Kingdom, 1861 to 1980*

Year	£ at constant 1975 prices		Year	£ at constant 1975 prices	
	GDP per worker in work	Capital stock per worker in work		GDP per worker in work	Capital stock per worker in work
1861	—	5,341	1959	2,504	10,840
1871	1,148	5,488	1960	2,575	11,074
1881	1,252	6,107	1960 [b]	2,638	11,348
1891	1,538	6,215	1961	2,705	11,620
1901	1,529	6,676	1962	2,717	11,929
1911	1,558	7,276	1963	2,821	12,299
1913	1,593	7,248	1964	2,932	12,618
1920	1,383	7,102	1965	2,984	13,008
1920 [a]	1,410	7,252	1966	3,039	13,397
1921	1,507	8,314	1967	3,158	14,151
1931	1,691	9,301	1968	3,314	14,814
1938	1,846	9,151	1969	3,243	14,875
1948	1,997	8,919	1970	3,456	16,133
1949	2,056	9,082	1971	3,607	17,035
1950	2,104	9,205	1972	3,628	17,518
1951	2,155	9,277	1973	3,827	17,777
1952	2,157	9,480	1974	3,786	18,314
1953	2,244	9,636	1975	3,793	19,008
1954	2,292	9,739	1976	3,954	19,675
1955	2,347	9,849	1977	3,998	20,182
1956	2,378	10,013	1978	4,080	20,612
1957	2,427	10,285	1979	4,111	21,086
1958	2,439	10,634	1980	4,144	22,144

[a] Excluding Eire.
[b] Revised series.

Source: calculated from Appendices 1.1 and 1.2.

Chapter 2

Output and Income

Contents

Chapter guide

Value added is one of the most basic, and most important, concepts which an economist has to learn, so this chapter explains value added at length, going from a simple 'model' economy to the real UK economy and from a simple model of an enterprise to actual enterprise accounts (of the Delta Metal Company). The production of value added and its distribution as *income* is explained. *Depreciation* appears again, this time as something which makes the difference between *gross* and *net* income.

To understand value added fully we need to understand why and how *opening* and *closing stocks* of circulating capital must be brought into the reckoning, and we must therefore also understand what *stock appreciation* is, how it should be calculated, and why it ought to be excluded from value added (and from profits). All this is explained using reasonably straightforward arithmetic models.

On the basis of a full understanding of value added, we can explain the important concept of the *national income*. We look at data on, and explain, the following relevant concepts: *gross domestic product*; *gross national product*; and *net national product* (or the 'national income' proper). The vital importance of the Central Statistical Office's *National Income and Expenditure* 'Blue Book' is explained. We see how the national output is distributed as income, and we look at data on the percentage shares of income in gross domestic product from 1855 to the present. (Some advice on reading a table and on minding your language when talking about percentages is offered.)

In order to understand the arrangement of national income and expenditure accounts, we need to follow how the accounts deal systematically with *types of account* (*operating*, *appropriation*, *capital*, and *financial* accounts) by sector of the economy. The concepts of *financial surplus* and *financial deficit* (both encompassed in the rather formidable term *'net acquisition of financial assets'*) are explained so that we may understand how the accounts fit together.

Finally, we see how the system of accounts, together with the sectors of the economy, provide a 'street map' to the Blue Book which should help you find your way around this indispensable source of data.

Introduction

A modern economy is the whole system of productive activities by which people gain their livelihoods. This chapter is concerned with the flow of output produced by the combination of the stocks of labour and capital which we considered in Chapter 1. It is important to realise from the outset the indissoluble link between production on the one hand and income distribution on the other. From the economist's viewpoint *output* is that flow stemming from production which can properly be distributed as income. Hence, in this book, the word 'output' always means *value added*, which is a subtle concept embodying this twofold aspect of production and income. Our first task is to understand this key concept of value added.

Value added

Value added is the economist's measure of the flow of output. In any enterprise the annual flow of value added is the difference between the total annual receipts from sales and the total annual cost of bought-in materials upon which the enterprise's labour and capital work. The adjective 'annual' here refers to the same accounting period of twelve months, and the statement that value added per annum is equal to sales receipts per annum *minus* cost of bought-in materials per annum is subject to some qualifications which will be explained later in the section on stock appreciation. But these qualifications are matters of detail rather than principle and for the moment we shall concentrate on the definition:

$$\frac{\text{Value}}{\text{added}} = \frac{\text{Receipts}}{\text{from sales}} - \frac{\text{Cost of bought-}}{\text{in materials}}$$

In order to understand the concept of value added more exactly, and also to begin to see what a system of productive activities comprises, let us consider the model of a simple economy set out in Table 2.1.

TABLE 2.1 *A model showing the production of value added and its distribution as income*

£ a year (flow)

Productive industry (and product)	Production of value added					Distribution of income		
	Sales receipts *minus*	Cost of bought-in materials *equals*	Value added	*identical to*	Total income *minus*	Employees' wages *equals*	Capitalists' profits (residual)
Farming (wheat)	20 *(to miller)*	0	20		20	8	12
Milling (flour)	30 *(to baker)*	20 *(from farmer)*	10		10	6	4
Woodcutting (fuel)	5 *(to baker)*	0	5		5	0	5
Baking (bread)	45 *(final sale to consumers)*	35 *(from miller and woodcutter)*	10		10	6	4
Whole economy	100	55	45		45	20	25

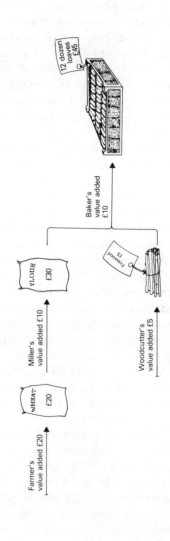

Farmer's value added £20

wHEAT £20

Miller's value added £10

FLOUR £30

Woodcutter's value added £5

Firewood £5

Baker's value added £10

12 dozen loaves £45

This economy produces the staff of life: namely, loaves of bread. The model economy has only four productive industries:* farming, milling, woodcutting, and baking. This is what we mean in economics by the word 'model': a simplified schematic representation of reality which is used to analyse the most important and relevant elements of the real world.

In this model, the economic system of production is very straightforward. Without using any materials bought from outside the farm, during the year the farmer grows wheat, all of which he sells to the miller for £20, as shown by the italics in the table. The miller grinds the wheat into flour, all of which he sells to the baker for £30, these annual receipts from sales more than covering his annual purchase of wheat from the farmer. Besides buying £30-worth of wheat annually from the miller, the baker also buys £5-worth of wood each year from the self-employed woodcutter. Using the flour as raw materials and the wood as fuel, the baker bakes loaves of bread, all of which he sells directly to consumers, thereby obtaining an annual flow of receipts from sales of £45. At this point, the bread sold 'disappears' from the process of producing value added, so the sale is called a 'final sale', or a sale to a 'final' customer, to distinguish it from the other 'intermediate' sales which are sales from one producer to another producer.

Now, in common talk, one often loosely refers to annual sales receipts as 'output', as one might say 'British Leyland's output of cars in 1979 was £2,060 million', meaning thereby that British Leyland sold £2,060 million worth of cars during 1979 (from *BL Limited Report and Accounts 1979,* p. 18). But if we stick by this meaning of 'output' we have then to say that the annual 'output' of our model economy is the sum of annual sales receipts in the four productive industries: namely, £20 *plus* £30 *plus* £5 *plus* £45 *equals* £100.

But crucially this statement does one thing wrong: it doublecounts all the various commodities being produced. First, we count the value of the wheat in the sales receipts of the farmer; next, we count the value of wheat again in the sales receipts of the miller (because these receipts cover the miller's purchases of wheat). Following on from this we doublecount the value of the flour: once in the sales receipts of the miller, and once again in the sales receipts of the baker (because, similarly, these receipts cover the cost of the flour). Likewise, the value of the wood is counted twice: once in the sales receipts of the woodcutter; and again in the sales receipts of the baker.

Furthermore, to measure 'output' by sales receipts implies another crucially wrong thing. It implies that the benefit to the economy of this activity is measured by sales receipts. Now, the economic benefit derived from an activity must correspond to the income obtained by the factors of production engaged in that activity. And it is by no means the case that the bakery workers and the owner of the bakery together derive £45 a year of income from baking. If the baker were to pay workers £40 a year as wages and keep £5 a year as profit, he would be in dead trouble, because he would not then be able to pay his bills to the miller and the woodcutter for supplying him with materials. Only after the baker has settled his bills for bought-in materials can he begin to think about paying wages and taking his profit: £35 of his £45 of sales receipts provide no benefit to him or to his employees; it must be used to pay the miller and the woodcutter. In short, the *income* derived from the activity of baking bread is confined to the value added which is produced by that activity.

So it is most important to think very carefully what one means by the word 'output'. If in any industry we deduct from the annual sales receipts the annual cost of bought-in materials to obtain the annual flow of value added, then we have a measure of that industry's output which (a) avoids doublecounting the commodities produced, and (b)

---

*Note the use of the word 'industry' to denote a branch of economic activity, e.g. in this context farming is an 'industry'. Thus 'Standard Industrial Classification' (SIC) refers to the classification of branches of economic activity.

shows the flow of income payable to factors of production engaged in that industry. If we then take the sum of value added in all industries of the economy, we obtain, without doublecounting, a measure of the total annual benefit to the economy which is derived from productive activities.

We have already stressed the importance of the link between production and distribution. The benefits derived from producing output – or value added, as we shall now call this flow – are the incomes which the factors of production thereby obtain. The total income that is derived from production is therefore also measured by value added, so that when we continue, in Table 2.1, to the distribution of value added as income, the two columns – value added and total income – are identical. Indeed, it would have been quite in order, though perhaps a little confusing, to have put these two middle columns as one column with a single heading: 'Value added/total income'. In this simple economy we assume that there are only two classes in society: workers, and people who own fixed and circulating capital – the capitalists. Thus there is a farmer who owns the fixed and circulating capital necessary for growing wheat (as well as the land on which the wheat is grown); there is a miller who owns the mill; and there is a baker who owns the bakery. Each of these employs workers under a contract of employment so that these workers are employees. The woodcutter, by contrast, is a self-employed worker working on his own account. He may have with the baker a contract *for* services, but his work is not an integral part of the activity of the bakery, and how and when he does his work is his own affair: the woodcutter is an independent contractor.

Employees, as such, receive out of value added an income which is called *wages*; capitalists, as such, receive the *remaining*, or residual, income which is called *profits*. It is a nice point as to what we should call the income of the woodcutter; it is generally classified separately as income from self-employment and, when summary details are given, income from self-employment is lumped together with profits. So in Table 2.1 the woodcutter's income appears under profits, in line with his status as an independent contractor distinct from that of the other workers who are employees. But we must not forget that this contractor's income is derived because of his own-account work and not because of his ownership or management of capital.

Value added is then divided among these classes as their income. At this early stage of the analysis, we shall treat profits as a *residual* annual flow remaining from the annual flow of value added after the employees' annual wages have been paid. That is why, in the column headings of the right-hand part of Table 2.1, I have written 'Total income *minus* Employees' wages *equals* Capitalists' profits', because that is the way the world works. It is preferable to see the equation this way round, rather than the more conventional way 'Total income *equals* Employees' wages *plus* Capitalists' profits', because this latter equation leaves one feeling rather mystified as to how, exactly, the sum of wages and profits equals total income, as if all three were independent items, which, of course, they are not. Furthermore, it is possible for profits to be negative: that is, enterprises can make losses, and this possibility is made quite explicit by the equation in Table 2.1.

Thus the farmer pays the farm's employees £8 per annum as wages. We can assume that, in accordance with long-established practice, this payment of wages is a contractually agreed amount; in fact, this is from the employee's point of view the most important part of the contract of employment. The remaining part of the flow of value added then becomes the farm's profits. (The reader who finds the sums of £8 a year in wages and £12 a year in profits a cause for amusement should multiply all the figures in the table and in the text by one thousand – I shall stick to the model's easy-to-remember numbers.) The miller pays his employees £6 a year and keeps £4 a year as the mill's profits; and the baker also pays his employees £6 a year, keeping £4 a year as the bakery's profits. The self-employed woodcutter, who cuts wood by himself and has no bought-in materials, simply keeps the whole of his annual receipts from sales of wood as his income, which is here classified under profits.

Thus in each industry the entire flow of value added is necessarily distributed as income (because profits take whatever remains after the payment from value added of wages), and the total of all incomes in the economy equals the total output of the economy (because output is being measured by value added).

To repeat (and subject to the qualifications which will be explained in the section on stock appreciation), value added is measured as the (annual) flow of sales receipts *minus* the (annual) cost of bought-in materials.

We may now clarify a little further the matter of bought-in materials. First, in the real world, we should speak of the cost of bought-in materials *and services*. Anything that an enterprise buys from another *independent* organisation is 'bought-in'; thus, if an enterprise buys some legal advice from an independent solicitor, the cost of that advice should be deducted from the enterprise's sales receipts when calculating value added. The cost of the woodcutter's wood is deducted from the sales of the bakery, because the woodcutter is an independent contractor. His sales receipts must then be reported separately. Suppose, however, that the woodcutter became an employee of the bakery, forsaking his independent status in return for a contractually agreed wage of £5 a year. The woodcutter continues to do exactly the same work as before, namely supplying the bakery with fuel, but because the woodcutter is no longer an independent enterprise, woodcutting disappears from Table 2.1 as a separate productive industry and the woodcutter's sales receipts of £5 a year also disappear. But the bakery's cost of *bought-in* materials is now reduced by £5 a year (and, correspondingly, its wage-bill is increased by £5 a year). So although the sum of sales receipts in the economy as a whole is reduced to £95 a year, the sum of the costs of bought-in materials is also reduced by £5 a year to £50, leaving total value added at the same amount, £45 a year. Value added in the woodcutting industry disappears, but value added in the baking sector is now £5 a year higher at £15 a year. This illustrates, again, why sales receipts should not be used as a measure of output, and why value added

Labour-only subcontractors

Such changes in status which alter both the total sums of sales receipts and the cost of bought-in materials and services in equal amounts are not altogether fanciful. Recently, in the UK construction industry, many employees forsook their status as employees to become independent labour-only subcontractors. These workers would then ask for a lump-sum payment in return for completing some particular task, for example building a wall. (The advantage they derived thereby was that income tax and National Insurance contributions were not deducted at source as they must be by law from an *employee's* wages. Workers 'on the lump' – as this practice came to be known – could thereby, and illegally, evade tax and National Insurance contributions. Steps have now been taken to make it more difficult, if not impossible, for such evasion to continue.) While this change of status from employees to self-employed, independent labour-only subcontractors would have increased the aggregate of sales receipts and the aggregate cost of bought-in materials and services in the economy as a whole, value added in the economy as a whole would have been unchanged. Within the construction industry itself, total value added would also have been unchanged, though its distribution among the two parts of the industry, the building contractors proper and the labour-only subcontractors, would have altered substantially. The wage-bill for the building contractors' employees would have diminished, being replaced by the cost of bought-in (labour) services, and value added in the labour-only subcontracting sector would have risen.

should be used: the change in the woodcutter's status does not alter the total flow of output in the economy. On the income side, the wodcutter's income from self-employment would disappear, being replaced by £5 under employees' wages: the bakery's value added now of £15 a year is distributed as £11 a year in wages and £4 a year in profits. Total wages are now £25 a year and total profits £20 a year so that distribution of income is altered, but not its total amount.

So value added *includes* wages and salaries. Or, put the other way round, when calculating the value added of an enterprise the wages and salaries of an enterprise's *employees* are *not* deducted from sales receipts. Or, just to put the matter into perspective, another way of saying the same thing is that value added is *not* the same as profits, because profits are equal to value added *minus* wages and salaries. (These three statements need to be clearly understood as amounting to the same assertion: a beginner student can sometimes confuse value added with profits, which is a serious failure to understand these basic economic concepts.)

Finally, we need to note that when calculating an enterprise's value added, only the receipts from sales should be counted. Suppose that the miller, having paid for some of the bakery's initial capital equipment, was thereby a part-owner of the bakery and on that account received a share of the bakery's profits. If we mistakenly included these receipts in with the receipts for the purposes of calculating the value added by milling, then that would be doublecounting. Many enterprises are in the position of being part-owners of another enterprise and receive a share of the latter's profits (a payment known as 'dividends'), but this receipt of income must not be counted as part of the recipient's value added. We should note that the word 'profits' in Table 2.1 means 'profits before payment of dividends'.

We have been exploring what the concept of value added means and why it is the economist's measure of output. In order to do this we have used a simple model; it is now time to see how the concept of value added is used in the real world.

We need first to consider the production of value added by the enterprise. In this book the noun 'enterprise' means any undertaking which sells goods or services; the term 'enterprise sector' denotes that part of the economy which is made up of enterprises.* In the UK economy there are many types of enterprises, distinguished according to their legal status. Enterprises may be self-employed individual contractors, or 'sole proprietors' (such as the woodcutter), or partnerships (such as a partnership of solicitors or estate agents), or small private limited liability companies (whose shares cannot be offered for sale to the public and whose number of shareholders may not exceed fifty), or large public limited liability companies (whose shares can be open to public subscription without limit on the number of shareholders), or the great state-owned nationalised industries. The term 'limited liability' means that the shareholder's liability for the debts of the company is limited to his or her share subscription. By contrast, the sole proprietor or partner is liable without limit for debts, and private assets, such as house and furniture, can be claimed by creditors in settlement of debts. The great advantage of the limited liability public company is that large amounts of money may be raised by issuing shares for sale to the general public, a share being an entitlement to a portion of the profits of the company, such payments being known as 'dividends'. The sums of money raised by share issues may then be used to acquire the fixed capital necessary for the undertaking. It is this advantage which has led to the predominance of the limited liability public company in the UK economy.

From an operational point of view, an enterprise is a joint combination of labour and capital to produce goods or services for sale. Any enterprise will have a certain stock of capital, fixed and circulating, and is likely also to have a stock of financial assets, such as a

---

*Note here the use of the word 'sector' to denote a classification by status of transactor.

DIAGRAM 2.1 *A model to show the working of an enterprise*

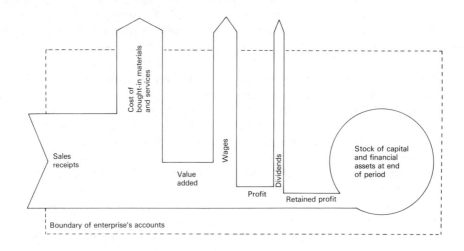

positive balance in a bank account. Most enterprises will also employ employees from whom labour services are obtained.

The basic model of how an enterprise works, from an economic point of view, is shown in Diagram 2.1. The enterprise has a stock of capital and financial assets and, together with the services of employees, labour and capital produce a flow of products (or services) which are sold and so generate a flow of receipts from sales. These receipts are shown on the left-hand side as entering the boundary of the enterprise's accounts. From this flow of sales receipts, a flow of payments is made to meet the cost of bought-in materials and services. Flows of outward payments which cross the boundary leave the enterprise's accounts, and the flow of payments for bought-in materials and services is shown accordingly. After paying for its materials, the enterprise is left with a flow of value added. From this flow of value added, the enterprise must first meet its contractual obligations to its employees: that is, it must pay its employees' wages. (In most of this book we shall take no account of the common distinction between weekly paid *wages* for operatives and monthly paid *salaries* for higher-scale employees. In our usage the word 'wages' includes salaries. Sometimes, I shall use the more comprehensive but longer term 'income from employment'. Additionally, throughout this book the term 'wages' or 'income from employment' *includes* income tax paid directly by the employer on behalf of the employee under the UK Pay As You Earn (PAYE) scheme.) After payment of wages, the enterprise is left with the residual profits (before dividends) from which it may make a payment of dividends to shareholders who provided the initial funds to acquire the necessary stocks of capital and financial assets. Any remaining flow is retained by the enterprise, and these profits after dividends (or retained profits, or retentions, as they may be called) flow into the stock of capital and financial assets. That is, retained profits may be used:

(a) to acquire more fixed capital;
(b) to acquire more circulating capital;
(c) to acquire more financial assets (at the very simplest, if there is no capital expenditure, the enterprise's bank balance will rise by the amount of its retained profits); or
(d) to acquire some mixture of all three.

Thus at the end of the accounting period the enterprise's stock of capital and financial assets may be larger than at the beginning and, because of this expansion in its capacity to produce, the subsequent flows may be larger than the previous flows: that is, the enterprise will be growing.

Diagram 2.1, then, represents the basic model for the working of an enterprise: it is a model which shows clearly how value added is produced and how it is distributed. It is also a model which begins the analysis of the process of economic growth (or stagnation, if that be the case). Having got the basic model, it is necessary to put in two important details. The first of these concerns depreciation. The second concerns stock appreciation.

Depreciation

As we noted in Chapter 1, no item of fixed capital lasts for ever; eventually all items of fixed capital need to be replaced even though some may last for a very long time. At the date of its installation or the completion of construction, an item of fixed capital will have had a certain value; at the end of its life, that value will have been reduced to a 'scrap-value', which may even be zero. Depreciation is a *flow* which measures the decline, over a period such as a year, in the value of an item of fixed capital. As has been explained in Chapter 1, this flow is taken to measure the (annual) cost in terms of 'using up' fixed capital during the process of production. This is why depreciation is sometimes called 'capital consumption'.

The simplest and most widely used method of calculating depreciation is to take the initial cost of the item in question *minus* residual scrap-value, if any, and to divide this by the length of the asset's working life. If this working life is measured in years, we arrive by this process at the annual depreciation (if in hours, we get depreciation per hour). That is to say (ignoring scrap-value as an inessential feature):

$$\frac{\text{Initial cost of asset}}{\substack{\text{Length of life} \\ \text{(in number of periods)}}} = \substack{\text{Flow of} \\ \text{depreciation} \\ \text{(per period)}}$$

There are two related economic reasons why depreciation is important. The first is to ensure that the (annual) cost of providing the services of the item in question are taken into account when the enterprise charges for its products. Otherwise the enterprise will gradually be making a free gift of capital services to its customers. The second is that neither an enterprise nor a nation can afford to spend on consumption all that it produces by way of value added. Some part of that value added must be reserved for replacing the used-up capital – for making good 'capital consumption' (as depreciation is called in the national accounts).

Whatever the basis on which depreciation is charged, it is a flow of great economic importance, because it must be taken to diminish the amount of value added which can be distributed as income. To illustrate, when the sewing lady (see over) was not charging her customers for depreciation, she imagined that her income was 30 pence an hour. Certainly her value added was 30 pence an hour; but she could not have continued in business for more than five years had she spent all that 30 pence an hour because she would not have been able to replace the sewing-machine when it came to the end of its working life. She would have been all right if she saved 5 pence out of every hour's earnings, but this would have been equivalent to valuing her labour at only 25 pence an hour: in other words, to reducing the value added which could 'properly' be distributed as income. We turn now to this question of the distribution of profits when depreciation is taken into account.

An example of depreciation

Both these points can be illustrated by a homely example. At one time, I used to have various bits and pieces of sewing done for me by a lady who did such work in her home (a self-employed person). I thought her charges were exceedingly reasonable; for instance, she would charge about half the price quoted by shops for shortening trousers or making up curtains, and her work was of meticulous quality. I once asked her how she set her charges, and she replied that she charged 30 pence per hour for her labour (this was some years ago) and added on the cost of any materials used. But, I asked, she had an expensive electric sewing-machine fully equipped with all the requisite gadgets for specialised sewing: did she charge her customers anything for the use of the machine? No, came the reply. And how much did the machine cost? All told, about £300. And how long did she think it would last? At the rate she used it, five years, because she worked the machine 'quite hard': about twenty-five hours a week for about forty-eight weeks a year. Now, twenty-five hours a week for forty-eight weeks a year for five years is a total of 6,000 hours. If we measure the sewing-machine's life at 6,000 hours, then, taking its original cost as £300, and ignoring any residual scrap-value (such as she might receive on 'trading in' the old machine for a new one), we may estimate the hourly flow of depreciation as amounting to:

$$\frac{£300}{6,000 \text{ hours}} = 5 \text{ pence per hour}$$

Therefore, the sewing lady ought additionally to charge her customers 5 pence an hour for the use of the machine; otherwise she would be making a gift, over the years, to all her customers of the value of the sewing-machine. Furthermore, if she intended to continue in business, she ought in the second instance, to put this money, amounting to £60 a year, into a savings account, so that at the end of five years she would have the money to replace the sewing-machine. In other words, she should not use the receipts from an additional 5 pence an hour depreciation charge to pay for consumption such as food or holidays. This second bit of advice is a separate matter from the first, though the question of what is to be done with the receipts clearly has a bearing on the question of how much to charge per period for capital services. In the matter of the sewing-machine, if it were expected that within the five years its price would have doubled to £600 because of inflation, then it would be commercially prudent to anticipate that inflation and, instead of charging depreciation on the initial *historic* cost of £300, she should charge depreciation at 10 pence an hour on the basis of the estimated *replacement* cost of £600.

Gross and net profits

The adjective 'gross' originally meant entire, total, or whole; the adjective 'net' meant after any deduction. More generally, the related use of these words in economics is that 'gross' means including, and 'net' means 'excluding'. It is therefore advisable always to be specific about what it is that is included when the adjective 'gross' is used, and about what is being deducted or excluded when the adjective 'net' is used. In economics, 'gross' and 'net' are very often, but by no means always, used to indicate the inclusion or exclusion respectively of depreciation, and in this book, when these adjectives are used without further qualification, this is what is meant. But there are other uses: for example, the term 'gross output' or 'gross sales receipts' is often used to refer to the flow of sales receipts gross of (including) the cost of bought-in materials and services. To illustrate from a previous example: we might have said that British Leyland's gross sales were £2,060 million in 1979; but it would be preferable to say that British Leyland's sales, gross of the cost of bought-in materials and services, were £2,060 million in 1979.

The basic model of how an enterprise works was described in Diagram 2.1. Diagram 2.2 again shows the main flows in an enterprise's accounts, now including the flow of

DIAGRAM 2.2   *A model of the working of an enterprise showing gross and net profit*

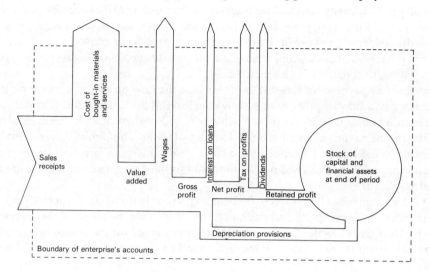

depreciation and the flow which is the tax levied upon profits: in the United Kingdom this tax is officially called 'Corporation Tax', but we shall here call it what it is, i.e. a profits tax.

In Diagram 2.2 the flow of profits remaining after the payment of wages out of value added is *gross* profit, profit before deduction of any provision to cover depreciation. To revert to the example of the sewing-machine shown earlier: if her charges to her customers were raised to 35 pence an hour, 30 pence for labour and 5 pence for depreciation, it would clearly be unfair for income tax to be levied on 35 pence an hour, because, as I have already explained, there is a real sense in which her income, or benefit, from that flow of value added was not 35 pence but 30 pence an hour. Alternatively, if she had gone on charging simply 30 pence an hour, income tax ought to have been levied on the *net* benefit derived, i.e. 25 pence an hour.

By exactly the same argument, profits tax should be levied on net profits: that is, on profits *after* the deduction of depreciation from gross profits. The flow of depreciation is accordingly shown as being deducted from the flow of gross profits. Unlike the other outflows, however, this flow does not cross the boundary of the enterprise's accounts but remains within those boundaries and eventually adds to the enterprise's stock of capital and financial assets as valued at the end of the period.

One further detail about Diagram 2.2 needs discussion: payment by the enterprise of interest on any loans it may have received. We have noted that one way for an enterprise to obtain finance is to issue shares either to a confined group of people (the private limited liability company) or to the general public (the public limited liability company), and the payments out of profits to shareholders – 'dividends' – are legally a distribution of profit. Of course, if there are no profits, there will be no dividends, and that is that.

Another way for any enterprise to obtain finance is to borrow money. When an enterprise borrows money, it issues a financial liability against itself. Such a liability comprises:

(a)   a contractual agreement to repay the loan in some agreed manner;
(b)   a contractual agreement to pay a periodic flow of interest on the loan outstanding.

If an enterprise fails to make enough money to pay interest on its loans, the creditors have the legal right to put the enterprise into liquidation and to pay themselves both the value of the loan outstanding and any interest due from the enforced sale of the enterprise's assets.

Thus the payment of interest on loans is a contracted amount, to be paid regardless of the amount of profit actually made. The payment by an enterprise of interest on a loan is therefore treated for tax purposes as a cost to the enterprise: that is, interest payments may also be deducted from gross profits before net taxable profits are arrived at. Conventionally, interest payments are deducted from gross profits, rather than treating them as part of the cost of bought-in materials and services.

Net profit after payment of interest then becomes the flow on which profits tax is levied, and accordingly a flow of profits tax is shown as leaving the enterprise's accounts at this stage. The remaining flow is net profits after tax, and part of this can be distributed as dividends (including the tax payable on dividends by the shareholder which, as in PAYE, is paid directly to the Inland Revenue by the enterprise), the remaining part being retained by the enterprise. These retained profits then add to the enterprise's stock of capital and financial assets.

Table 2.2 summarises all that has so far been explained in this chapter; you will note that the table refers to a company rather than to an enterprise, because of the payment of dividends. The table links the flows arithmetically, showing how the company's results are obtained (wherever there is a dash in the right-hand column, the arithmetic starts again).

TABLE 2.2   *The origin and distribution of the profits of a company*

	Annual flow	By, and to, whom paid
	Sales revenue	By customers to company
minus	Cost of bought-in materials and services	By company to suppliers
equals	Value added	—
minus	Wages	By company to employees
equals	Gross profits	—
minus	Depreciation	*Kept by company*
minus	Interest payments on loans	By company to creditors
equals	Net taxable profits	—
minus	Profits tax	By company to government
equals	Net profits after tax	—
minus	Dividends	By company to shareholders
equals	Retained profit	*Kept by company*

TABLE 2.3   *The value-added statement of the Delta Metal Company for the year 1974*

Annual flow	£ million
Sales	399.81
Bought-in materials and services	284.51
Value added	115.30
Applied in the following way	
To pay employees	
Wages and salaries	74.31
To pay providers of capital	
Interest on loans and other facilities	9.44
Dividends to shareholders	4.72
Outside shareholders' interests	2.87
Payable to governments	
Corporation Tax and overseas taxation	12.11
To provide for maintenance and expansion of assets	
Depreciation	6.85
Increase in retentions	5.00

Source: The Delta Metal Company Limited, *Report and Accounts 1975*, p. 24.

Table 2.3 shows the exact form of the accounts published by one UK company in 1974: the Delta Metal Company. The figures given refer to the year 4 January 1974 to 3 January 1975. During this year the sales receipts of the Delta Metal Company totalled £399.81 million. Deducting the cost of bought-in materials and services (£284.51 million) gives the company's value added of £115.30 million. Deducting from value added the payments of wages and salaries of £74.31 million gives gross profits of £40.99 million (not shown in this account). From this, the payment of interest on loans, etc. (£9.44 million) and the provision for depreciation (£6.85 million) should be deducted to give net taxable profits of £24.7 million, on which £12.11 million of taxation was levied, leaving £12.59 million as net profits after tax. Of this amount, £7.59 million was distributed to all shareholders, leaving £5 million as retained profits. Together the flow of depreciation and retained profits would provide, as Delta Metal say in their accounts, 'for the maintenance and expansion of assets'.

Stock appreciation

We have just seen why and how depreciation must be taken into account when discussing profits, and why one should always be careful to state whether profits are being considered gross or net of depreciation. But there is also a second problem in the definition of 'profits'; this arises because of the existence of stocks of circulating capital. In common terminology the word 'stocks' is used to denote circulating capital; in the USA the less confusing word 'inventories' is used. However, we shall stick by the common term, so that in context 'stocks' means stocks of circulating capital.

The problem arises because enterprises hold stocks of circulating capital in the form of materials and fuels, work in progress, and finished products. So far we have been talking of the flow of gross profits from a rather limited point of view: that is, as the difference between the annual flow of value added and the annual flow of wages and salaries, which results in the annual flow of gross profits before interest. The annual flow of value added is calculated as the annual flow of sales receipts *minus* the annual flow of costs of bought-in materials and services. This approach is adequate only if enterprises start each production period with no stocks of circulating capital and end with no stocks.

Suppose, for the sake of simplicity, that stocks are simply stocks of materials; Table 2.4 shows, in column (1), a situation of no opening or closing stocks, and you can see that 60 is a proper measure of value added. Consider now the situation depicted in column (2). The enterprise starts off with 40-worth of raw materials; during the year it uses up these materials but does not actually buy in any materials, so a zero is shown under the annual flow of bought-in materials. As sales receipts are still 100, value added, on the basis of the original (and too simple) definition, would appear to be 100; wages are 40, so profits appear to be 60; and closing stocks are 0.

Clearly, something has gone wrong in our calculation. Profits are *not* 60, nor is value added 100, because 40-worth of materials has been used up, though not bought in, during the accounting period. Provision should be made for replacing these stocks, which is why profits are not 60. So what can be done to rectify the 'wrong' answer? The method adopted by accountants is to treat stocks taken over from the preceding period as a purchase, which is a sensible solution. In this case, value added is calculated by a revised method as follows:

	Sales receipts	100
minus	Cost of bought-in materials −	0
minus	Opening stocks (treated as a purchase) −	40
equals	Value added =	60

TABLE 2.4   *Examples showing the need to calculate value added with reference to both opening and closing stocks*

	Value-added calculations				
Item	(1) Right: by accident, no opening or closing stocks	(2) Wrong: ignores opening stocks	(2a) Right: opening stocks included	(3) Wrong: ignores closing stocks	(3a) Right: opening and closing stocks included
Opening stocks	0	40	40	40	40
Sales receipts	100	100	100	100	100
Bought-in materials	40	0	0	40	40
Value added	60	100	60	20	60
Wages	40	40	40	40	40
Gross profits	20	60	20	−20	20
Closing stocks	0	0	0	40	40

(1)   Value added *equals* Sales receipts *minus* Bought-in materials.
(2)   Value added *equals* Sales receipts *minus* Bought-in materials.
(2a)   Value added *equals* Sales receipts *minus* Bought-in materials *minus* Opening stocks (right by accident, because closing stocks are zero).
(3)   Value added *equals* Sales receipts *minus* Bought-in materials *minus* Opening stocks.
(3a)   Value added *equals* Sales receipts *plus* Closing stocks *minus* Bought-in materials *minus* Opening stocks.

So we are back to a situation of value added being 60, and profits as being 20 (60 *minus* 40, shown in the corrected column (2a) of Table 2.4). This seems, and is, a much more economically meaningful result.

However, we are not clear of all problems yet. Suppose that we calculate value added by the revised method just mentioned, and that the enterprise started with stocks worth 40, during the year bought raw materials worth 40, and ended the year with stocks worth 40. Applying the revised method for calculating value added (shown in column (3) of Table 2.4) again gives a wrong answer because value added now appears to be 20: that is, 100 *minus* 40 *minus* 40 *equals* 20, and profits appear to be −20.

Yet it is clear that the enterprise is not making such a loss, because if it sold its closing stocks for 40 on the day of the end of the accounting period it would have a profit of 20. The accountant's solution to this problem is therefore to treat closing stocks handed on to the next accounting period as a sale for the accounting period which has been closed. Value added for this latter accounting period is accordingly calculated by the complete method as follows:

	Sales receipts	100
plus	Closing stocks (treated as a sale)	+ 40
minus	Cost of bought-in materials	− 40
minus	Opening stocks (treated as a purchase)	− 40
equals	Value added	= 60

So we are back to a situation of value added being 60 and profits being 20 (shown in the corrected column (3a) of Table 2.4), and this again seems, and is, the right answer.

We have just demonstrated that in order to get sensible answers when calculating value added and profits, opening and closing stocks must not be ignored but must be taken account of in the way shown immediately above. Clearly, column (1) in Table 2.4 gives the 'right' answer only by virtue of the accidental fact that opening and closing stocks are both zero, so that ignoring them does not make any difference.

However, a major problem now arises over the valuation of opening and closing stocks. For the annual flows of sales receipts, bought-in materials and wages there is no problem of valuation because money changes hands, and all that needs to be done is to record the amount of money changing hands during the year. But the opening and closing stocks do not similarly change hands: the 'purchase' of opening stocks and the 'sales' of closing stocks are *nominal* transactions (that is, transactions in name only, as opposed to actual transactions – they are 'pretend' transactions), for the purposes of getting the accounts right. Because no money changes hands, this 'purchase' and this 'sale' both have to have a valuation imputed to them. That is, the opening and closing stocks have to be 'artificially' valued at some price or other; they cannot be valued by the 'normal' process of money changing hands in a market transaction.

Suppose that during the year the price of raw materials doubles but that, in terms of real things, everything else remains the same as in column (3a) of Table 2.4. We may imagine that the enterprise buys in its materials early on in the year before prices rise, so keeping the annual cost of its bought-in materials at 40. Now, the accounting convention is that stocks are valued at the prices ruling at the date when the valuation takes place (this convention is helpful to accountants because the required data – prices currently ruling – will be to hand, and it minimises the scope for fiddling). So when the accountant assesses what the *closing* stocks are worth (these being the same *quantity* as opening stocks) he comes up with the answer 80, because he values these closing stocks in terms of the prices currently ruling at the date of the valuation; thus although the volume of stocks is the same – that is, the quantities in the closing stocks are the same as the quantities in the opening stocks – the value of the stock is now doubled. The accountant then calculates value added and profits according to his formula *and* his valuations, as follows:

	Sales receipts		100
plus	Closing stocks (at closing prices)	+	80
minus	Bought-in materials	−	40
minus	Opening stocks (at opening prices)	−	40
equals	Value added	=	100

Thus value added is now much higher than before (when it was 60), and gross profits, being equal to value added *minus* wages, now treble from 20 to 60.

Two problems arise from this calculation, or rather this valuation, of the accountant. One is a complicated issue in accountancy, and does not really concern the present book, though I shall briefly consider it. The second is a relatively simple issue of how best to calculate the national income, and this is the issue with which we are most closely concerned.

On the matter of accountancy, the profits figure of 60 is not a sensible figure for an enterprise which wishes to continue in business. Clearly, in the *next* accounting period the enterprise is going to have to spend double the amount on bought-in materials if it is to maintain the same physical level of stocks. Stocks are expensive: it costs money to buy and to hold them, and it costs money to store them properly; enterprises do not carry stocks for fun, and most enterprises carry only the minimum stocks necessary for efficient operation so that production is not disrupted by lack of materials when needed. So that it is a serious thing for an enterprise if it has to reduce the level of its stocks, and most enterprises seek to maintain a minimum level. Because it can look forward to having to spend double the amount on bought-in materials during the next accounting period (in order to maintain its physical level of stocks), the enterprise should ensure that it reserves from the profits of the previous accounting period an amount of money sufficient to do this. If it does not, it might not have enough cash to keep up its levels of stocks. The accountant might tell the enterprise that its profits are 60 but he ought also to warn the enterprise that, during the next accounting period, an additional 40 will have to be spent on buying materials, so that it would be only prudent to reserve 40 from the profits of 60 for this purpose: in other words, the firm should act as if its profits (for distribution and for spending on fixed capital, etc.) were 20, not 60; the enterprise should not act as though it could give a large distribution of profits in dividends or could use undistributed profits to pay for a large amount of fixed capital formation. If it does so, it could run short of cash with which to pay for its next period's bought-in materials. In other words, the profit figure should be calculated after charging the replacement cost of maintaining intact the physical quantity of stocks. There is also the further problem that the enterprise will be paying profits tax on profits reported as 60, rather than on distributable, 'freely available', profits of 20. In the recent period of rapid inflation this 'over-taxation' of company profits became so threatening that in November 1974 the Chancellor of the Exchequer had to grant emergency relief by deferring some tax liabilities, a practice that has since continued – thus acknowledging the problem we are here considering.

On the matter of calculating the enterprise's value added for inclusion in the national income, we need to begin by reminding ourselves that stocks include not only materials but also work in progress and stocks of finished products. Now, if the real quantity of these stocks rises, it is clear that a benefit is to be derived from such investment in circulating capital: there are more goods available to be worked on or to be sold. But if the real quantity of these items of circulating capital remains the same, while the money value goes up because of inflation, it is *not* the case that the nation derives any tangible benefit from such an appreciation in the value of (the constant volume of) stocks, and therefore this 'stock appreciation' should not be counted as part of the national output/income.

How should we calculate stock appreciation? Clearly, the problem arises because the change in the current-price valuation of stocks between two dates is a compound effect of (a) a change in the physical volume of stocks, and (b) changes in the prices of items in the stock. The problem is to remove the effect of the price change. Obviously, if we value opening and closing stocks at a common (constant) set of prices and compare the change in the current-price valuation of stocks with the change in the constant-price valuation of stocks, we shall be able to distinguish the volume-change effect from the price-change effect. Consider an example where stocks are something entirely homogeneous, like tonnes of steel (of a given quality). Suppose we start with opening stocks of 100 tonnes and opening prices of £1 per tonne; and suppose we end with closing stocks of 110 tonnes and closing prices of £2 per tonne. Suppose also that sales receipts during the year are £1,000, bought-in materials £500, and wages £400. Value added must, we know, be calculated using the complete formula:

$$\frac{\text{Value}}{\text{added}} = \frac{\text{Sales}}{\text{receipts}} + \frac{\text{Closing}}{\text{stocks}} - \frac{\text{Bought-in}}{\text{materials}} - \frac{\text{Opening}}{\text{stocks}}$$

But at what prices should opening and closing stocks be valued? We know that the accountant's method of using current prices (opening prices for opening stocks and closing prices for closing stocks) does not produce an economically appropriate figure for profits (when wages have been deducted from value added). So let us value opening and closing stocks at common prices. But which prices? Table 2.5 shows three possibilities, as well as the accountant's current-price valuation.

We could choose to value both opening and closing stocks at opening prices of £1 per tonne. The value of the physical increase in stocks would, on this valuation, be £10 (i.e. a 10-tonne increase in stocks at £1 per tonne). On the other hand, we could value both opening and closing stocks at closing prices of £2 per tonne; the value of the physical increase would then be £20. Given the sales receipts, bought-in materials and wages – these flows remain the same regardless of the method of valuing stock – we can see that the two methods imply different figures for value added, and hence for profits. The basic

TABLE 2.5 *How to calculate stock appreciation*

	£			
	Stock valuation using:			
	Opening prices, £1 per tonne (1)	Closing prices, £2 per tonne (2)	'Average' (mid-year) prices, £1.50 per tonne (3)	Current prices, £1 and £2 per tonne [a] (4)
Opening stocks (100 tonnes)	100	200	150	100
Closing stocks (110 tonnes)	110	220	165	220
Value of physical increase in stocks	10	20	15	—
Change in current-price valuation of stocks	—	—	—	120
Sales receipts	1,000	1,000	1,000	1,000
Bought-in materials	500	500	500	500
Value added [b]	510	520	515	620
Wages	300	300	300	300
Profits	210	220	215	320
Stock appreciation: Change in current-price valuation *minus* Value of physical increase in stocks	110	100	105	—

[a] Using opening prices to value opening stocks and closing prices to value closing stocks.
[b] Calculated as: Sales receipts + Closing stocks − Bought-in materials − Opening stocks.

problem is to value the benefit which is derived from the fact that the stock of steel has risen by 10 tonnes. Suppose that the increment of 10 tonnes accrued at a steady rate throughout the year: that is, 1 tonne every five weeks or so. Suppose also that the price rose steadily throughout the year, increasing by 10 pence every five weeks. Then it would be reasonable to value each increase of 1 tonne by the average price ruling during the period in which that tonne was produced; so the first extra tonne in the stockpile would be valued at £1.05 (over the first period of five weeks the price would have risen from £1.00 per tonne to £1.10 per tonne, so £1.05 is a representative price for this period); the second extra tonne would be valued at £1.15, and so on. This method of valuing each tonne as it accrues throughout the year gives the following sequence:

										Total/ average
Tonne	1st	2nd	3rd	4th	5th	6th	7th	8th	9th	10th	10
Price (£)	1.05	1.15	1.25	1.35	1.45	1.55	1.65	1.75	1.85	1.95	1.50
Value (£)	1.05	1.15	1.25	1.35	1.45	1.55	1.65	1.75	1.85	1.95	15.00

So the average price turns out to be, not surprisingly, £1.50 per tonne, and on the basis of valuing each tonne as it accrues the value of the physical increase in stocks would be £15. If prices also rise steadily throughout the year, the average price is equivalent to the price ruling at mid-year. If we take the average or mid-year price of £1.50 and value both opening and closing stocks at this price, we get the same result. Thus we can use the relatively simple method shown in column (3) of Table 2.5 to value the physical increase in stocks. Of course, if the increase in stocks or the rise in prices do not occur steadily throughout the year, the method of simply using the average price does not give the 'right' answer; but we do not have the information on the month-by-month accrual of stocks or movement of prices, and the only practicable method is to take the average price. The

Complete formulae for value added

In conclusion, therefore, you should learn, and be able to explain, the complete formula for calculating value added in an economically meaningful way:

$$\frac{\text{Value}}{\text{added}} = \frac{\text{Sales}}{\text{receipts}} + \begin{array}{l}\text{Closing stocks} \\ \text{(valued at average} \\ \text{[mid-year] prices)}\end{array}$$

$$- \frac{\text{Bought-in}}{\text{materials}} - \begin{array}{l}\text{Opening stocks} \\ \text{(valued at average} \\ \text{[mid-year] prices)}\end{array}$$

Alternatively:

$$\frac{\text{Value}}{\text{added}} = \frac{\text{Sales}}{\text{receipts}} - \frac{\text{Bought-in}}{\text{materials}}$$

$$+ \begin{array}{l}\text{Value of physical increase} \\ \text{in stocks (at average} \\ \text{[mid-year] prices)}\end{array}$$

Unfortunately, a lot of data from which the national accounts are derived are based on the accounting formula:

$$\frac{\text{Value}}{\text{added}} = \frac{\text{Sales}}{\text{receipts}} + \begin{array}{l}\text{Closing stocks} \\ \text{(valued at} \\ \text{closing prices)}\end{array}$$

$$- \frac{\text{Bought-in}}{\text{materials}} - \begin{array}{l}\text{Opening stocks} \\ \text{(valued at} \\ \text{opening prices)}\end{array}$$

In other words, in some of the national accounts tables:

$$\frac{\text{Value}}{\text{added}} = \frac{\text{Sales}}{\text{receipts}} - \frac{\text{Bought-in}}{\text{materials}}$$

$$+ \begin{array}{l}\text{Change in current-price} \\ \text{value of stocks}\end{array}$$

and these value-added or profits figures which are reported 'before providing for stock appreciation' correspond to the economically misleading figures of Table 2.5's last column. However, if we deduct stock appreciation from these (misleading) figures we get back to the economically appropriate data of column (3) of Table 2.5.

For this reason, care must always be taken not only to specify whether profits are gross or net of depreciation, but also to state whether or not profits (and value added) includes or excludes stock appreciation.

---

national accounts statisticians therefore use the average-price method to value the physical increase in stocks in the economy, and (as you can see) this produces a 'compromise' estimate of value added and profits by comparison with the methods of using either opening prices or closing prices. Now the change in the (money) value of stocks, that is, the change from opening stocks at opening prices to closing stocks at closing prices, is obviously a compound of the effects of the change in price and the change in the physical quantity of stocks:

$$\begin{array}{l}\text{Change in} \\ \text{(money) value} \\ \text{of stocks}\end{array} = \begin{array}{l}\text{Value of} \\ \text{physical increase} \\ \text{in stocks}\end{array} + \begin{array}{l}\text{Effect} \\ \text{of price} \\ \text{inflation}\end{array}$$

That is to say, we can calculate the effect of price inflation, which effect is called stock appreciation, simply by deducting the value of the physical increase in stocks from the change in the money value of stocks:

$$\begin{array}{l}\text{Stock} \\ \text{appreciation}\end{array} = \begin{array}{l}\text{Change in} \\ \text{(money) value} \\ \text{of stocks}\end{array} - \begin{array}{l}\text{Value of} \\ \text{physical increase} \\ \text{in stocks}\end{array}$$

As there are three different methods for valuing the physical increase in stocks, so there will be three different figures for stock appreciation. However, as we have selected the average-price method for valuing the physical increase in stocks because it corresponds more closely to the on-going realities of production during the year, stock appreciation will be measured as at the bottom of column (3) in Table 2.5.* Again, you can see that it appears as a 'compromise' estimate.

The national income

The national income is simply the total flow of value added (excluding stock appreciation) in all the productive industries of the economy. For the model economy shown in Table 2.1, the annual national income is obtained by taking the sum of all the figures in the value-added column. It follows from what we said previously about all value added being distributed as income that the national income can also be calculated by adding together all the incomes received by the factors of production: that is to say, national output and national income are the same flow from different aspects. How is the national product, the total flow of value added, produced in the United Kingdom, and how is it distributed as income?

Table 2.6 shows the available data on the production of value added and its distribution as income in the UK economy during 1963 (the last year when complete input–output tables – which give data on sales and on purchases – were published with the national accounts). The national income 'year' is always the calendar year from 1 January to 31 December inclusive: unless otherwise stated, all references to years are to calendar years. Table 2.6 divides productive activities among the conventional industries of the economy, except that a distinction is made between the enterprise or market sector and the non-market sector. Enterprise-sector services include: transport; communication; distributive trades (wholesale and retail); banking, insurance, other finance, and business services; and other services. Non-market-sector services include: public administration and defence; public health services; education; other local authority services; and a small amount of domestic services. Value added in this sector is measured by income from employment, because there are no sales receipts and the concept of profit is inapplicable to most public-sector services.

In the enterprise sector of the economy, value added is measured for each industry by deducting from sales receipts the cost of bought-in materials and services. Table 2.6 shows, in column (1), the total receipts from sales made by enterprises in each productive industry. These are 'over-the-counter' sales receipts and as such include any taxes on expenditure (sales taxes of all sorts) *less* subsidies on expenditure: that is, column (1) contains *market price* sales receipts. Column (2) shows the total cost of purchasing bought-in materials and services and this also includes all taxes (*less* subsidies) on those materials and services *and* the expenditure taxes levied on the industry's own sales – these expenditure taxes being regarded as payment for (government) services. Total sales receipts include receipts from export sales, and total cost of bought-in materials and services includes the cost of imported materials. In each, the difference between sales receipts and cost of bought-in materials, etc., is that industry's value added which is available to be distributed as income to the factors of production; it is thus known as value added *at factor cost* (at the cost of the factors of production). Had we not included in column (2) each industry's sales taxes the figures in that column would have been smaller, and the (larger) value added would have been value added *at market prices*; but part of this – the sales tax part – has to be paid over to the government, leaving, as before, value added (at factor cost) to be distributed as factor incomes. The value added (at factor cost) in each industry may be added up to give the total flow of value added produced within the

*That is, and applying the last equation:

$$105 = 120 - 15$$

TABLE 2.6 *The production and distribution of the United Kingdom's national income during 1963*

£ million

Productive industry	Sales receipts [a] (1)	Cost of bought-in materials, etc. [b] (2)	Value added (3)	Income from employment (4)	Gross profits, self-employment income, and rents [c] (5)
Agriculture, forestry and fishing	1,676	723	953	353	600
Mining and quarrying	1,095	362	733	582	151
Manufacturing industry	19,823	10,949	8,874	6,168	2,706
Construction	3,150	1,378	1,772	1,364	408
Electricity, gas and water	1,612	784	828	374	454
Transport and communication	3,566	1,274	2,292	1,603	689
Distributive trades	4,776	1,604	3,172	1,924	1,248
Other services	5,439	1,504	3,935	2,717	1,218
Total: enterprise/market sector	41,137	18,578	22,559	15,085	7,474
Government/non-market sector [d]	—	—	3,075	3,075	—
Total value added	—	—	25,634	18,160	7,474
'Output' from dwellings	—	—	1,135	—	1,135
Gross domestic product (at factor cost)	—	—	26,769	18,160	8,609
Net property income from abroad	—	—	394	—	394
Gross national product	—	—	27,163	18,160	9,003
Capital consumption	—	—	-2,318	—	-2,318
Net national product: 'the national income'	—	—	24,845	18,160	6,685 [e]

[a] From sales at home and abroad, including taxes on expenditure (*less* subsidies); adjusted to exclude stock appreciation; including 'output' of land and buildings (imputed to owner-occupiers or at market rents).

[b] Including imports and all taxes on expenditure *less* subsidies (that is, including expenditure taxes on sector's own sales).

[c] All value added other than income from employment.

[d] Including public administration, defence, public health and educational services, and domestic services to households but excluding 'output' from ownership of dwellings.

[e] *Net* profits.

Source: Central Statistical Office, *National Income and Expenditure 1968*, tables 1, 11, 19, pp. 3, 13, 24–5 and 102.

geographical boundaries of the United Kingdom. The total value added, sales receipts *minus* bought-in materials, in the enterprise sector of the economy during 1963 was £22,559 million.

Apart from this problem of taxes on expenditure, calculating value added in the enterprise sector of the economy presents no difficulty, and you can see, in each industry, how value added is distributed as income from employment, with the residual balance accruing as gross profits, self-employment income and rents.

However, the valuation of the 'output' produced by the government, or non-market, sector does present a difficulty because this sector receives no sales receipts. Yet it produces services which, in general, we value: for example, if the service of refuse collection were not provided by the government, it would certainly be provided by the enterprise sector, because we all need a refuse-collection service. Suppose it were the case that refuse collection was undertaken by private enterprise. There would then be no difficulty in calculating value added in this sector: sales receipts would be the charges made to householders, etc., for collecting their rubbish; there would be costs of bought-in materials (fuel for the refuse-collection vehicles); and value added produced thereby would be used to pay wages, with residual profits being taken by the refuse-collection enterprises (to cover depreciation and a net return on capital employed). This value added is then a measure of the (esteemed) benefits which the population derives from the activity of refuse collection.

Now, the essentially *institutional* arrangement in the United Kingdom, whereby refuse-collection services are (compulsorily) provided free of direct charge by local authorities which cover the costs by general rates so that there are no sales receipts (or charges) specifically apportionable to refuse collection, and so that value added cannot therefore be directly calculated for refuse collection, cannot be permitted to result in our simply ignoring these very real benefits. If we ignored these benefits in calculating the total output of an economy, then this would imply that we could increase the national income simply by abandoning refuse collection by local authorities and switching to a system of refuse collection by private enterprise. In terms of economic activity nothing would have changed; only the institutional arrangements under which that activity is carried out would have changed. Clearly, this is not economically sensible; and the corollary is, therefore, that we must count the services of local authority refuse collection as part of the output of the economy. But how to do this when there are no sales receipts from which to calculate value-added?

The answer lies in recognising that value added can also be measured by the incomes which result from an activity; because the government is a non-profit-making body, these incomes comprise simply the wages earned by the employees engaged in refuse collection. So the convention adopted by the national accounts statisticians is to value the services of the government, non-market sector at the total of employment incomes in that sector. In Table 2.6 we have, for the government sector, a total of £3,075 million in the income from employment column; that is the basic figure, and the convention is that this also measures the value added produced by that sector, and so it appears again in the value-added column. This can then be added to the £22,559 million of 'straightforward' total value added in the enterprise sector to give total value added of £25,634 million during 1963.

This total flow of £25,634 million during 1963 would be a measure of the economy's total 'output' without further ado, were it not for one further complication.

This complication mainly concerns the benefits which we all derive from dwellings, and the need to value these benefits. It cannot be doubted that we derive substantial services of shelter from the stock of dwellings in the United Kingdom. Supposing all the dwellings in the United Kingdom were owned by a commercial property company which rented dwellings out to people and which kept the dwellings in a state of good repair, just as the car-hire companies do with cars. Then there would be no problem with valuing the services from dwellings: value added in this sector would simply be the total of rents from dwellings (analogous to sales receipts in other sectors) *minus* the costs of repair and maintenance (the flow which corresponds to the costs of bought-in materials and services required in other sectors to produce the flow of sales receipts). The snag is that a large proportion of dwellings are owner-occupied so that no rents are paid; and another large proportion of dwellings are owned by local authorities and let at subsidised rents. But it is essential that some valuation be placed on the benefits derived from dwellings: these benefits make far too substantial and important a contribution to our well-being to be ignored, and we have already seen (Diagrams 1.6 and 1.8) that a large proportion of the United Kingdom's stock of fixed capital is in the form of dwellings. So the national income statisticians have to make an assessment of the value added which would be produced by dwellings were they all commercially owned; this is called an 'imputed' output, and during 1963 it was estimated to be £1,135 million. There is one other point: the flow of services from dwellings is not like a flow of services from other productive sectors, because the services of dwellings are produced simply by the mere inhabiting of the dwellings; unlike factories or shops, no *paid* labour is required to work in conjunction with the capital stock to produce the flow of services from dwellings. This puts the flow of 'output' from dwellings in a peculiar class by itself. For these reasons, the imputed 'output' from dwellings is added on separately at the end of the table. The 'output' derived from the ownership of land and buildings other than dwellings (whether resulting from the actual payment of rent for the use of property or imputed to owner-occupiers) is included in the appropriate sector's sales receipts, with expenditure on repairs and maintenance included in column (2), so that elsewhere value added includes this 'output' of property.

The total of all the flows of value added produced by all the productive sectors, together with estimated value of 'output' from dwellings, make up what is known as the *gross domestic product* of the United Kingdom. The word 'gross' means that this flow includes the total flow of depreciation during the year; the word 'domestic' means that it is the flow of total value added produced 'domestically': that is, geographically within the United Kingdom.* This flow was £26,769 million during 1963. Had we not deducted expenditure taxes from market-price sales receipts, we would have had gross domestic product at market prices, but this is not a very useful total because the inclusion of expenditure taxes doublecounts the benefits (e.g. the police force) which those taxes pay for – the wages of public-sector employees (e.g. the police) being already counted in the value added.

People and organisations resident in the United Kingdom benefit additionally by receiving income from abroad on account of property which they own in foreign countries; but they have also to pay to non-residents some of the income produced in the United Kingdom on account of property which those non-residents own in the United Kingdom. For the United Kingdom as a whole, the balance of such payments received from non-residents over payments made to non-residents – called 'net property income from abroad' ('net' here means payments from non-residents net of payments to non-residents) – is positive: during 1963 this flow amounted to £394 million, so the United Kingdom received more from non-residents than it paid out to them. If we then add this amount on to the gross *domestic* product (income produced domestically) we have the total known as the gross *national* product, which is the total gross income received by 'nationals' – strictly speaking, the residents – of the United Kingdom. (We should say 'residents' – although 'nationals' is a useful mnemonic, because, for example, the pay of an American citizen working for an American corporation in the United Kingdom and resident in the United Kingdom, is part of the United Kingdom's national income – it accrues to a person who is a

---

*The 'geographical' scope of the United Kingdom now includes the 'continental shelf' from which comes the North Sea oil and gas owned by the United Kingdom.

resident (but not a national) of the United Kingdom. However, the pay of foreign diplomatic staff resident in the United Kingdom is not included; conversely, the pay of British diplomatic staff abroad is included.) This flow of gross national product was £27,163 million during 1963. Both gross domestic product and gross national product are called 'gross' because they include the flow of depreciation, which the national income statisticians more descriptively call 'capital consumption'.

If we *deduct* the total flow of capital consumption in the United Kingdom, shown accordingly in the table with a minus sign, we derive the total of *net national product* (where 'net' signifies that the flow is net of capital used up during the process of production). More commonly, the net national product is called simply 'the national income': this is the best measure of the benefit derived by a country from its productive activities and from its (net balance of) properties owned abroad. The national income of the United Kingdom during 1963 was £24,845 million.

Table 2.6 also shows how value added in the various productive industries of the economy is distributed between wages and gross profits. Here, and throughout this book, the term 'wages' means all the benefits which employees derive from employment. Such benefits come in two distinct parts.

First, there are the sums specified to be paid to employees in their contracts of employment. These sums include both income tax and also the contributions which the employee is required to pay to the National Insurance social security scheme. If you agree to work for someone for £100 a week, then you yourself will have to bear the burden of income tax and your National Insurance contributions out of this £100 a week. However, both tax and employees' contributions to National Insurance are by law deducted at source by the employer (the deductions being paid directly to the government), so that employees' net pay, or take-home pay, is smaller than gross pay.

Second, there are the sums which employers pay on behalf of employees to the National Insurance scheme or to private pension funds. These sums are not treated as part of employees' taxable income. (The origin of the dual employee–employer contribution to National Insurance goes back to Lloyd George's 1911 National Insurance Act. Part I of the Act provided insurance against sickness for all employees: the employee paid 4*d* (old pence) per week; the employer paid 3*d* per week per employee; and the Treasury (that is, the taxpayer) paid 2*d* per week per employee – this was Lloyd George's political slogan 'ninepence for fourpence' – and from this fund sick employees could receive sick pay of 10*s* a week with free medical attention from a panel of doctors. We are now talking about the *employer's* 3*d*, or its present-day counterpart.) Increasingly, these days, employers may also pay a contribution to a private pension scheme for employees; the employee then receives a pension additional to the state retirement pension when he or she retires. These sorts of contributions paid by employers on behalf of their employees are known as 'employers' contributions' in the national accounts and they, too, form part of the total reported as 'income from employment'. So, income from employment comprises gross pay and employers' contributions.

On average, over the whole economy in 1963, income from employment, at £18,160 million, took up 71 per cent of the total of gross value added, excluding the output from dwellings and net property income from abroad. Because income from employment measures the total cost which the employer has to bear as a result of employing labour, the amount remaining from value added represents gross profits (and this also includes rent and income from self-employment). Gross profits are, as we saw earlier, the residual amount of value added remaining after the payment of wages. Accordingly, the share of gross profits, £7,474 million, in gross value added was 29 per cent in 1963, but of these gross profits, almost one-third, £2,318 million, was capital consumption. That is, this latter amount must be reserved for the replacement of capital and is not strictly available for distribution as income to the owners of capital.

TABLE 2.7   *The production and distribution of the United Kingdom's national income during 1980*

Productive industry	£ million, current prices		
	Value added [a]	Income from employment	Gross profits, self-employment income, and rents [b]
Enterprise/market sector			
Agriculture, forestry and fishing	4,296	1,665	2,631
Petroleum and natural gas	7,649	207	7,442
Other mining and quarrying	3,222	2,569	653
Manufacturing	48,060	39,656	8,404
Construction	13,025	8,048	4,977
Electricity, gas and water	5,803	2,914	2,889
Transport and communication	15,410	11,301	4,109
Distributive trades	19,328	13,173	6,155
Insurance, banking and finance	18,288	10,067	8,221
Professional, scientific and miscellaneous services	30,142	21,212	8,930
Sub-total: enterprise/market sector	165,223	110,812	54,411
Government/non-market sector			
Public administration	10,938	9,853	1,085
HM Forces	3,049	3,049	—
Public health services	6,450	6,150	300
Local authority educational services	7,609	7,219	390
Sub-total: government/non-market sector	28,046	26,271	1,775
Unadjusted total of value added	193,269	137,083	56,186
Adjustments			
Doublecounting of financial services	−9,732	—	−9,732
Residual error	−2,045	—	−2,045
Adjusted total of value added	181,492	137,083	44,409
'Output' from dwellings	11,996	—	11,996
Gross domestic product at factor cost	193,488	137,083	56,405
Net property income from abroad	−38	—	−38
Gross national product at factor cost	193,450	137,083	56,367
Capital consumption	27,045	—	27,045
National income (i.e. net national product)	166,405	137,083	29,322

[a] Excluding stock appreciation.

[b] Gross profits before depreciation but excluding stock appreciation; the figures for the government/non-market sector are imputed rentals on owner-occupied buildings ('imputed charge for capital consumption'); the very last figure in this column is *net* profits, net self-employment income and net rents.

Source: Central Statistical Office, *National Income and Expenditure 1981 Edition*, tables 1.1, 1.9 and 3.1, pp. 3, 12 and 24–6.

Table 2.7 brings the data of Table 2.6 more up to date. The data are not available for each industry's sales receipts and cost of bought-in materials and services. But it should by now be appreciated that, for the purposes of economic analysis, these figures on sales and costs are important only for the calculation of value added.

By 1980, compared with 1963 (Table 2.6), prices generally had risen nearly fivefold, so the money flows in Table 2.7 are much larger than those in Table 2.6. This does not mean that the benefit derived from economic activity had risen from £24,845 million in 1963 to £166,405 million in 1980: that is, people were not six times better off in 1980 than in 1963, but for the moment we shall simply use the flows of value added as calculated in terms of the prices ruling at the time when the flows of sales receipts and cost of bought-in materials were measured. Such flows are known as 'current-price' flows, and unless otherwise stated

The National Income and Expenditure *'Blue Book'*

Table 2.7 brings together the basic figures relating to production and distribution of value added. These figures are taken from the most important regular publication of statistics relating to the UK economy: the *National Income and Expenditure* 'Blue Book'. The term 'Blue Book' is its familiar title, or nickname, because it appears in a blue cover. The Blue Book is published each year about September. Until 1974, each Blue Book used to be called also by the year of its publication and it would contain data covering the ten years up to and including the previous year. In 1974 the title was changed to include the time period covered by most of the tables so the Blue Book published in 1974 became *National Income and Expenditure 1963–73*. Additionally, in *National Income and Expenditure 1965–75*, the system of numbering tables was changed from a single sequence to a sequence within each chapter (just like the one used in this textbook), the first number referring to a 'section' of the Blue Book, the second to the table. The 1978 publication was the last to bear the title *National Income and Expenditure 1967–77*; the following year's Blue Book was called *National Income and Expenditure 1979 Edition*, and this international standard system of naming will remain in the future. Every student of economics, at no matter what level he or she is studying, must equip himself or herself with a copy of *National Income and Expenditure*:

it is the single indispensable source of information on the working of the UK economy. The observant student will already have noticed, from the source notes to Diagrams 1.1 and 1.6 and Tables 1.11, 1.12, 1.14 and 2.6, how many of the statistics contained in this book are drawn from the Blue Book. Although it is a little difficult at first to find one's way around the Blue Book, the effort to do so will be well rewarded, and this book should help you to be able to study the Blue Book for any special purpose you might have. It will help if you try at first to see where the figures in this book came from, though here I ought to add that some figures may be slightly revised in subsequent issues of the Blue Book because of late-arriving information, so do not be puzzled if some of the figures change slightly from one Blue Book to the next.

I should like to stress that the extracts from Blue Book tables (and from other official publications such as *Financial Statistics*) given in this textbook are only one-tenth for the purpose of accompanying the text; they are nine-tenths meant as an introduction to finding your way about the original tables themselves; in other words, the full learning process intended in this textbook requires you throughout to consult the Blue Book itself as you read along (and *Financial Statistics* and other official publications, too, when mentioned).

here and in the Blue Book, all prices and valuations are in current-price terms. The value-added figures in Table 2.7 are taken from the basic table concerned with production in the Blue Book: this is table 1.9 called 'Gross domestic product by industry'. This table shows the gross value added in each productive industry of the economy (this is what is meant by the table's official title: the figures are gross because they all include depreciation but, as explained, the figures exclude stock appreciation). The Blue Book's table 1.9 is really the starting-point of it all.* I have taken the industries pretty much as they stand in the Blue Book. The figures for the government, or non-market, sector now include some small amounts of imputed rents. These amounts represent the imputed value of the 'output' derived from government-owned property (e.g. the 'output' derived from hospital buildings or school buildings) and it is similar to the 'output' imputed to owner-occupied dwellings. In the Blue Book this is called the 'imputed charge for capital consumption' because the imputed annual output/cost of, for example, a hospital building's services is best measured by the annual depreciation in that building's 'value'. As before, the 'output' derived from the ownership of dwellings is put separately in Table 2.7.

*Details on the distribution of income from value added are found in the Blue Book's table 3.1.

There are two technical complications as compared with Table 2.6. The first concerns the doublecounting of the financial sector's value added. We pointed out earlier that interest payments to the financial industry by other productive industries for loans incurred were like payments for bought-in materials and services and ought to be deducted from these other industry's value added. The information required to do this separately for each industry is not available to the national income statisticians. It would, of course, be doublecounting not to deduct these intermediate interest payments while at the same time counting the 'value added' which is produced in the financial industry by these interest payments. (The measurement of 'value added' in the financial industry is a tricky business, because banks and other financial institutions derive most of their income – with which to pay their employees and dividends to their shareholders – from the difference between the interest rates they charge on loans and the (lower) interest which they pay on deposits: the conventional definition of value added does not, therefore, apply to most financial institutions.) So while doublecounting cannot be avoided in the component figures, it can at least be avoided in the grand total by an over-all *deduction* because the aggregate figure of net interest payments is known to the statisticians.

The second complication concerns the adjustment known as the 'residual error'. This arises because the national income is measured from both the income side and the output side (output here being measured by expenditure, as will be explained in Chapter 11). In the first place, not all the data on income are available by the time the first estimate of gross domestic product is published, so the residual error tends to be revised downwards in successive Blue Books. For example, the residual error for 1978 in *National Income and Expenditure 1979 Edition* was £1,071 million, but in the *1980 Edition* the 1978 residual error was reduced to £598 million. So the residual error is partly ascribable, initially, to problems of tardy data. However, despite these revisions the residual error remains, albeit proportionately very small. This remaining error is due to the difference between the output measurement of gross domestic product and the income measurement. If the latter is smaller than the former, the residual error is regarded as a (positive) item of unrecorded income. Sometimes, however, as in 1980, it is negative. By the very nature of the residual error, we do not know where or how it arises. So it is purely arbitrary to regard it as either an understatement or an overstatement of income.

It should be remarked that both the financial adjustment and the residual error are common in Western systems of national accounts and are not peculiar to the United Kingdom.

The total of value added in the enterprise sector of the UK economy in 1980 was £165,223 million, or 91 per cent of the (adjusted) gross domestic product (the classification of the enterprise or market sector is not one you will find in the Blue Book, however; it is my own arrangement). Total value added, or, rather, incomes earned in the government or non-market sector, was £28,046 million, or 15 per cent of the gross domestic product. Together, these give an unadjusted total of value added, but we then have to adjust both downwards by 6 per cent for the doublecounting of financial services and for the residual error (which adjustments I take, a little arbitrarily, to affect gross profits, etc.). This gives an adjusted total of £181,492 million, and when we add on the imputed 'output' from dwellings of £11,996 million we have the gross domestic product at factor cost of £193,488 million. This is the basic measure of the output/income produced within the geographical boundaries of the United Kingdom. But we need also to take account of the benefit (income) which UK residents obtain on account of their ownership of property and factories abroad (net of income which the United Kingdom has to pay to non-residents on account of their ownership of property, etc., in the United Kingdom). In 1980 this net property income from abroad was −£38 million (in other words, we paid more overseas than they paid us), and it makes the gross national product equal to £193,450 million. Finally, we must deduct capital consumption of £27,045 million, to give net national product, or *the* national income, of £166,405 million. We should note that capital consumption is quite a large proportion of the gross national product: just 14 per cent; in other words, out of every £7 which the economy obtained in the form of the gross flow of value added, about £1 had to be set aside to 'pay' for the using up of capital.

Table 2.7 also shows how this value added was distributed in each industry of the economy between income from employment on the one hand and gross profits, rents and self-employment income on the other. The figures on income from employment are taken from the Blue Book's table 3.1 called 'Gross domestic product by industry and type of income'. The term 'income from employment' includes both wages and salaries (gross of income tax) and also the employers' contributions to National Insurance and to pension funds on employees' behalf; in this table you can find a detailed breakdown of income from employment into the two parts of wages and salaries, and employers' contributions. In our Table 2.7 the figures on gross profits have been calculated as the residual amount, so they include, where applicable, rents and income from self-employment. These figures on profits exclude stock appreciation, which (as has been explained) is not properly part of the benefit the nation derives from its economic activities.

Diagram 2.3 shows in summary form both the production of output and its distribution as income in the economy as well as the relationship among the various national income concepts. We start at the top and on the right with value added at market prices, and to this we have to add, as explained, the imputed 'output' of dwellings and also the 'output' from other property; in the UK accounts this is taken to be the (imputed) 'output' of government-owned and occupied buildings and the 'output' derived from ownership of farm land and buildings (valued either at the rent paid for the farm or imputed in the case of owner-occupied farms). If a factory, office or a shop is owned by an enterprise different from the one occupying it, and a rent is paid, then the output from that property is included in 'property output', but the 'output' of owner-occupied buildings other than dwellings or farms is included in that sector's value added.

DIAGRAM 2.3 *National income accounts*

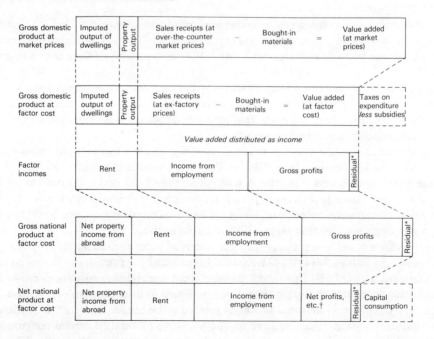

*Residual error in national accounts.
†Adjusted to exclude doublecounting of financial services.

We have to start with value added at market prices because the expenditures which take place in an economy, the record of which provides the basis for most of the national accounts figures, are valued at market prices and include the taxes on expenditure (such as VAT or the excise duty on alcohol or tobacco). This market-price value added is not generally a useful statistic because taxes on expenditure do not represent output. For example, suppose the government raised expenditure taxes and reduced income taxes; this would have the effect of raising GDP (gross domestic product) at market prices but the country would not thereby be 'better off' in the sense of having more goods and services to consume.

If we deduct from GDP at market prices the total of taxes on expenditure (*less* subsidies on expenditure: that is, treating subsidies which lower instead of raising the market price of commodities as negative expenditure taxes), then we have GDP at factor cost. This is what the total of value added would be if sales receipts were recorded at ex-factory prices before expenditure taxes are added on (together with 'output' of dwellings, etc.). Gross domestic product at factor cost measures the amount of income that is available to the economy. As shown, the income to the factors of production is distributed in three main forms.

First, the income from ownership of land and buildings is known as *rent*. In a simple case a landowner who owns a farm and rents it to a farmer receives straightforwardly an income of rent to which there is a corresponding 'output' in GDP; in a more complicated case, the owner-occupier of a dwelling has an imputed income in the form of the imputed output of the dwelling. (To illustrate, suppose we have the Jones family and the Smith family: both Mr Jones and Mr Smith receive salaries of £5,000 per annum, but Mr Jones lives in his own house (left to him by his parents) while Mr Smith rents his house from a landlord for £2,000 a year; there is a very real sense in which the Jones family are £2,000 a year 'better off' than the Smith family, and we give effect to this in the national accounts by saying that Mr Jones receives each year, in addition to his £5,000 of income from employment, an imputed income of £2,000 which is called a 'rent'.) In the UK national accounts these rents include all market rents and imputed rents to owner-occupied dwellings and owner-occupied farms; the benefit derived from other owner-occupied buildings is included in that sector's profits.

Second, there is income from employment, paid out of value added (at factor cost, because the factory does not receive the taxes on expenditure). This is gross of (including) taxes on income and also includes payments which the employer may make on employees' behalf.

Third, there is gross profits and self-employment income, including in gross profits the 'benefits' received by owner-occupied factories, offices, shops, etc. (The Jones and Smith example can be reworked to explain this for an enterprise which owns its factory building and for one which rents its factory building.)

Now, we need to note that the total of recorded income from employment and gross profits, etc., usually tends to be a little smaller than the total of value added at factor cost, and the national accounts treat this discrepancy, called the residual error, as an item of income – which I have tacked on to profits (although it may arise anywhere). The total of all these three sorts of incomes (including the residual error) is the same as GDP at factor cost; it simply shows how that output is distributed as 'benefits'.

Next we have to add on property income received from abroad net of property income paid abroad. In Tables 2.6 and 2.7 I showed this as adding to profits, but here it is best kept as a separate amount. Net property income from abroad was usually positive for the United Kingdom (but is usually negative for Third World economies), so the United Kingdom's GNP (gross national product) tended to be bigger than its GDP. Finally, we must 'deduct' – that is to say, reserve to one side – an amount of capital consumption to make good the loss during the process of production in the value of the United Kingdom's stock of fixed capital. Just like the example of the sewing lady (p. 58), we must not let

DIAGRAM 2.4   *Percentage shares in the gross national product of the United Kingdom, 1855 to 1980*

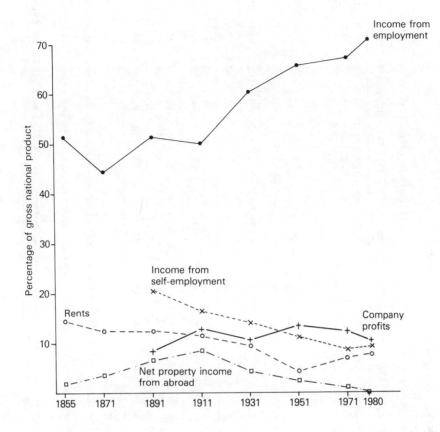

ourselves think that the 'benefits' we are deriving from production are bigger than they really are: in order to be prudent, some of the output/income must be reserved and devoted to the purpose of keeping up the stock of fixed capital.

Having learned about the concepts of national income and the types of income received, we may put the present structure of the United Kingdom's national income into a historical perspective. Table 2.8 shows the United Kingdom's national product by type of income for selected years between 1855 (the earliest year for which there is such data) and 1980. For the years up to and including 1951, these long-run income figures are given before stock appreciation, but because price inflation in the early years was very moderate, this does not matter greatly and we simply make an aggregate adjustment in 1931 and 1951; in 1971 and 1980 all the figures are after deduction of stock appreciation. Over the period as a whole, of course, the figures are affected by rising prices, so it is better to look simply at the proportionate shares in gross national product. In any case, one is never going to be able to remember the absolute figures; so the first step in 'extracting' the information is to calculate the percentage structure by income of the gross national product. Because there are a large number of percentages, one is not going to be able to remember them either, and as the 'important' things in this table are the trends, the second thing to do is to draw a graph of at least some of the trends.

Diagram 2.4 charts some of these percentages, and these trends immediately appear to be quite intriguing.

In 1855, income from employment took up just over half the gross national product; rents amounted to 14.5 per cent (about £1 in every £7) and combined income from self-employment, company profits, and the gross trading surplus of public corporations

TABLE 2.8   *Types of income received in the United Kingdom's gross national product, 1855 to 1980*

£ million (at current prices)[a]

	1855	1871	1891	1911	1931	1951	1971	1980
Income from employment [b]	328	457	705	1,065	2,382	8,501	33,481	137,083
Income from self-employment [b]	208	402	281	353	552	1,438	4,389	17,540
Gross trading profits of companies [b]	⎬	⎬	116	272	360	2,483	6,065	19,930
Gross trading surplus of public corporations and other public enterprises [b]	93	130	5	18	55	381	1,622	5,611
Rent [c]	⎬	⎬	172	243	373	564	3,501	15,369
Total domestic income (including stock appreciation up to and including 1951)	629	989	1,279	1,951	3,722	13,367	49,058	195,533
minus Stock appreciation	—	—	—	—	−63	750	n.a.	n.a.
plus Residual error	—	—	—	—	—	22	432	−2,045
Gross domestic product at factor cost	629	989	1,279	1,951	3,785	12,639	49,490	193,488
Net property income from abroad	13	39	94	177	163	342	502	−38
Gross national product	642	1,028	1,373	2,128	3,948	12,981	49,992	193,450
minus Capital consumption	47	56	66	103	290	1,129	5,109	27,045
Net national product	595	972	1,307	2,025	3,658	11,852	44,883	166,405

Percentage of gross national product

	1855	1871	1891	1911	1931	1951	1971	1980
Income from employment [b]	51.1	44.5	51.3	50.0	60.3	65.5	67.0	70.9
Income from self-employment [b]	32.4	39.1	20.5	16.6	14.0	11.1	8.8	9.1
Gross trading profits of companies [b]	⎬	⎬	8.4	12.8	9.1	19.1	12.1	10.3
Gross trading surplus of public corporations and other public enterprises [b]	14.5	12.6	0.4	0.8	1.4	2.9	3.2	2.9
Rent [c]	⎬	⎬	12.5	11.4	9.4	4.3	7.0	7.9
Total domestic income (including stock appreciation up to and including 1951)	98.0	96.2	93.2	91.7	94.3	103.0	98.1	101.1
minus Stock appreciation	—	—	—	—	−1.6	5.8	n.a.	n.a.
plus Residual error	—	—	—	—	—	0.2	0.9	−1.1
Gross domestic product at factor cost	98.0	96.2	93.2	91.7	95.9	97.4	99.0	100.0
Net property income from abroad	2.0	3.8	6.8	8.3	4.1	2.6	1.0	−0.02
Gross national product	100	100	100	100	100	100	100	100
minus Capital consumption	7.3	5.4	4.8	4.8	7.3	8.7	10.2	14.0
Net national product	92.7	94.6	95.2	95.2	92.7	91.3	89.8	86.0

n.a. means not applicable; — means not available.

[a] Including (Southern) Ireland up to 1911.

[b] Before providing for (i.e. including) stock appreciation in all figures up to and including 1951; in 1971 and 1980 stock appreciation is excluded from income figures; all figures are gross of depreciation.

[c] Before providing for depreciation; and including imputed charge for consumption of non-trading capital (mainly imputed output on government-owned and occupied buildings).

Sources: C. H. Feinstein, *National Income, Expenditure and Output of the United Kingdom 1855–1965* (Cambridge University Press, 1972) table 1, pp. T4–T6; Central Statistical Office, *National Income and Expenditure 1973*, table 1, p. 2; Central Statistical Office, *National Income and Expenditure 1981 Edition*, table 1.2, p. 5.

How to read a table

In looking at any table of data, it is necessary first of all to ask oneself: what is the 'important' thing in this table? And second, how can I best present this so that I can remember it? At the beginning of one's studies, this is a little difficult, because one may not be quite sure what one is supposed to be looking for; but as one progresses this difficulty fades away, especially as one practises such interpretation and analysis of data. One thing is certain: if you do not practise such data interpretation, you can never hope to be an economist: just as an athlete who never trained could not expect to become a proper athlete.

(the latter being state-owned enterprises but in 1855 there were only a few, such as the Royal Ordnance Factories, the Mint, and municipal water supplies; later on in the nineteenth century these would have been joined by more local authority enterprises supplying gas and public transport) amounted to 32.4 per cent. Net property income from abroad amounted to only 2 per cent of gross national product in 1855, and annual capital consumption was then estimated to be 7.3 per cent.

In 1891 the share of income from employment was 51.3 per cent – although it had dipped below its 1855 share in the intervening years – and the share of rents had declined to 12.5 per cent (and was to continue to decline for much of the twentieth century). In 1891 we can distinguish among the various forms of surpluses: the share of the profits of privately owned companies was 8.4 per cent; the share of public corporations' trading surpluses was only 0.4 per cent; and income from self-employment was 20.5 per cent. Income from self-employment covers the income of small firms, of professional persons working on their own account or in partnerships, and of sole traders.

In the eighty years following, there was a steady decline in the share of self-employment income. This must have been due partly to the relative decline of agriculture's position in the economy, partly to the tendency for people to switch from self-employment to the status of employees, and partly to the relative decline in sole trading, particularly the disappearance of the small 'corner' shop. Conversely, the share of income from employment rose to take up two-thirds of the gross national product by 1971 and nearly 71 per cent by 1980. This was partly due to the increased relative predominance of employees in the economy (both in the private and the public sector) but partly also to the rise in average incomes received by employees.

The share of company profits rose during the first half of the twentieth century, though this share declined during the depression of the 1920s and 1930s, and since 1951 the share of company profits has apparently declined from 19 per cent to about 10 per cent of gross national product. However, and this is where care with the footnotes comes in useful, we know that in 1951 profits included stock appreciation (because for that year we have no detailed data on the distribution of stock appreciation among types of income), whereas for 1971 and 1980 profits are given after stock appreciation (because the detailed data are available). So before we conclude that profits have 'collapsed' – as a journalist might put it – let us consider the possible effect of stock appreciation on company profits. How can we do this? Well the obvious thing to do is to take the 'worst' possible case and suppose that in 1951 the entire £750 million of stock appreciation arose solely in company profits; on this supposition company profits after stock appreciation would be £2,483m. *minus* £750m. *equals* £1,733m., which is 13.4 per cent of the gross national product, and this is the figure charted on Diagram 2.4. So it may be that the share of profits has not collapsed. At this

Being careful about changes in percentages

You might think that this conclusion about the importance of the change in profits' share between 1891 and 1951 is exaggerated. After all, if we take the lower figure of 13.4 per cent in 1951, and compare it with 8.4 per cent in 1891, the change appears not to be great. But changes in percentages always require careful attention, as follows. The change from 8.4 per cent to 13.4 per cent is a change of 5 *percentage points*; in relative terms, an increase of 5 percentage points on an initial percentage of 8.4 per cent represents an increase of 60 per cent in the percentage share. This is clearly a substantial increase (and is based on the lowest possible figure for the share of profits in 1951). So remember, when dealing with changes in percentages, always be careful to specify whether the change is in per-

centage points, or whether the change is the percentage change in the percentage. You will often see this mistake made in newspapers: for example, the percentage rate of unemployment (including school-leavers) in the United Kingdom was 6.1 per cent in January 1980 and 8.4 per cent in September 1980; so people said that the rate of unemployment had gone up by 2.3 per cent. This is a very wrong statement: the correct statement is either that the rate of unemployment had risen by 2.3 *percentage points* or that the rate of unemployment had risen by 38 *per cent* (2.3 over 6.1). The latter statement is of course the one which better indicates the course of events, because the actual numbers unemployed (including school-leavers) rose from 1.47 million to 2.04 million, a rise of 38 per cent.

---

stage, it is probably safest to conclude that we do not really know the answer as to what happened to profits in the postwar period.

There is another thing also to be suspicious about. Diagram 2.4 only contains *actual* points for three postwar years; the lines joining those points assume, without any further evidence, a straight-line trend between the years, and this may not be the case in practice. The moral of this is that the student, when looking at a graph, ought to ask himself or herself not only 'What does the graph show?' but also 'In what ways could this graph be misleading?' Nevertheless, the rise in company profits from 8.4 per cent of gross national product in 1891 to 19.1 per cent (or 13.4 per cent) in 1951 indicates the extent to which the limited liability company became an important vehicle for economic growth; it was these companies which were able to amass the large amounts of finance to pay for the increasingly complex and large-scale fixed-capital equipment needed in the process of production.

The other important item of income is net property income from abroad. During the second half of the nineteenth century and into the first decade of the present century, the share of net property income from abroad quadrupled from 2 per cent of gross national product in 1855 to 8.3 per cent in 1911. This was due to the large flows of investment by Britons in overseas countries – especially the USA, Canada, Australia and South Africa – during these years; already, in 1871, 7.4 per cent of gross national product was being invested abroad and by 1911 this had risen to 9.6 per cent; and this relatively large annual flow of foreign investment produced a growing return flow of income from those investments. During the First World War foreign investment by the United Kingdom declined, and although there was, in 1920 to 1923, a boom in overseas investment (net of foreign investment in the United Kingdom) thereafter net investment abroad remained small and the amount of net property income from abroad stayed constant so that its share in the (growing) gross national product declined. During the Second World War there was substantial disinvestment abroad as the United Kingdom sold assets to pay for war materials, and by 1951 the share of net property income from abroad had declined still further to 2.6 per cent, and it has since continued to decline. Some of the decline in recent years may be partly due to foreign investment in the United Kingdom, especially in North Sea oil, which after a time increases the outflow of property income paid abroad.

The need to exclude stock appreciation from the national income and from profits has been explained, but the reason for stressing this point can be appreciated if we look at stock appreciation in the company sector in relation to 'true' profits – profits excluding stock appreciation – in recent years. In 1978 the Central Statistical Office published for the first time estimates of the various items of income both before and after stock appreciation, covering the years from and including 1956, so that in Table 2.9 we can compare stock appreciation with total company profits (including stock appreciation). We can see that between 1956 and 1967 stock appreciation was only a small fraction of profits, but in 1968 it rose sharply to 9 per cent and then increased in successive steps as price inflation accelerated, until, in 1974, it amounted to no less than 41.1 per cent of company profits. In effect, this meant that firms were having to use a large and increasing proportion of their accounting 'profits' if they were simply to maintain the volume of stocks.

TABLE 2.9 *Company profits and stock appreciation, 1956 to 1980*

Year	£ million			Stock appreciation as percentage of gross profits, inc. stock appreciation	Company profits, exc. stock appreciation, as percentage of GDP [a]
	Gross trading profits of companies, inc. stock appreciation	Gross trading profits of companies, exc. stock appreciation	Stock appreciation		
1956	2,928	2,769	159	5.4	15.1
1957	3,075	2,934	141	4.6	15.1
1958	2,983	3,001	−18	−0.6	14.8
1959	3,317	3,240	77	2.3	15.2
1960	3,730	3,653	77	2.1	16.1
1961	3,639	3,518	121	3.3	14.5
1962	3,595	3,485	110	3.1	13.8
1963	4,103	3,992	111	2.7	14.8
1964	4,544	4,363	181	4.0	14.9
1965	4,741	4,517	224	4.7	14.5
1966	4,592	4,353	239	5.2	13.1
1967	4,625	4,540	85	1.8	13.0
1968	5,254	4,779	475	9.0	12.7
1969	5,668	5,092	576	10.2	12.8
1970	6,035	5,172	863	14.3	11.9
1971	6,907	6,065	842	12.2	12.3
1972	8,072	6,997	1,075	13.3	12.6
1973	10,325	8,035	2,290	22.2	12.5
1974	11,469	6,755	4,714	41.1	9.0
1975	11,961	7,678	4,283	35.8	8.1
1976	15,530	10,264	5,266	33.9	9.2
1977	19,061	15,228	3,833	20.1	12.0
1978	21,594	18,220	3,374	15.6	12.5
1979	26,776	19,779	6,997	26.1	11.9
1980	24,979	19,930	5,049	20.2	10.3

[a] Expenditure (output) based measure, i.e. includes residual error.

Sources: Central Statistical Office, *National Income and Expenditure 1967–77*, table 1.2, p. 4; Central Statistical Office, *National Income and Expenditure 1980 Edition*, table 1.2, pp. 4–5; Central Statistical Office, *National Income and Expenditure 1981 Edition*, table 1.2, pp. 4–5.

The CSO data also enable us to look at the course of company profits in the gross domestic product after 1956.

In the late 1950s and the first half of the 1960s company profits excluding stock appreciation fluctuated between 14 per cent and 16 per cent of gross domestic product (the last column of Table 2.9; note how one tries to summarise the information contained in this column; it is neither possible nor necessary to memorise and remember all the figures, but it is possible to recall the broad orders of magnitude thus: '14 to 16 per cent in the period 1956 to 1965'). In 1966 the share of profits dropped to about 13 per cent and stayed at the 12 to 13 per cent level until 1973; then in 1974, the share fell by 3.5 percentage points, or 28 per cent, before gradually recovering to about 12½ per cent in 1978, since when the share of profits has fallen still further to 10.3 per cent in 1980.

Subsequently we shall be analysing the impact of this drop in the share of company profits: the present purpose of Table 2.9 is to establish some broad description of the share of company profits in total income. Before we can go further in analysing these figures, we need to understand a bit more about the arrangement of the accounts in which such figures are presented.

Types of accounts

In the preceding sections of this chapter we saw how value added is produced and distributed as income, and we looked at some relevant figures from the *National Income and Expenditure* Blue Book. At first sight the Blue Book presents a bewildering array of tables, each with a formidable series of row headings. But the array and content of the tables is quite straightforward and easy to grasp, once the underlying structure of accounts has been understood. The purpose of this and the following sections is to explain the classification of accounts in general and the system of national accounts in particular.

The analytic basis for understanding any system of national accounts is to realise that they deal with transactions – pieces of business – between transactors. Clearly, to record separately each transaction that takes place in the UK economy during the year, even if it were possible, would not give a comprehensible set of accounts. It is obviously necessary to put transactors into groups so that we can add all their transactions together and treat them as a whole. It is also necessary to classify their transactions into a manageable number of types of transactions. Throughout the year, all the separate transactions of each type will form a flow, so we shall take these as annual flows. Let us consider first the more difficult task of classifying the annual flow of transactions.

Diagram 2.5 reproduces the flows of Diagram 2.2, which related to the working of an enterprise and which, as we subsequently saw in Table 2.6, can also be applied to the whole

DIAGRAM 2.5   *A system of accounts*

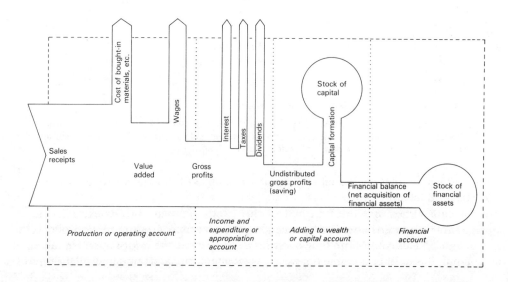

economy. The diagram shows the main flows of receipts, payments and retentions by an enterprise. Across the flows, I have drawn three dotted lines which serve to separate them into four separate sets, though each of the last three sets is connected to the preceding set.

The first set of flows shows how the gross profits of the enterprise are produced. These flows are grouped together in a production account. In the slightly more technical terminology of accounting, a production account is also called an 'operating account'. The enterprise's production account basically shows the annual receipts from sales, the annual cost of bought-in materials and services, and the payment of wages (because from the point of view of an enterprise the payment of wages is a cost of production). Sales receipts will include closing stocks (treated as a sale) and the cost of bought-in materials will include opening stocks (treated as a purchase). If these are valued at the same set of prices (average, mid-year prices), then value added and profits will exclude stock appreciation; but if the valuations of stocks are at closing and opening prices respectively (book value, or current-price value), then value added and profits will include stock appreciation.

After the deduction of wages from value added, the remaining part of the flow is gross profits, so the operating account shows how the enterprise has obtained its income of gross profits. The main purpose of a production or operating account is to show how 'income' is generated; in the case of an enterprise, gross profits are *its* income, so the operating account ends up with the flow of gross profits.

Next, we need to know how this income was spent. There are two basic forms of spending: current spending and capital spending. The adjective 'current' is a difficult word with many meanings: one of its formal dictionary *(Shorter Oxford English Dictionary)* definitions is 'running, flowing, running in time, belonging to the week, month, etc.' That is, the adjective relates in the first instance to regular, on-going, periodic receipts and outlays. But economists add a further restriction to the definition, confining the adjective 'current' to those flows which leave the enterprise's accounts to pay for services already rendered and which will not result in any future gain or benefit to the enterprise. Contrasted to this sense of 'current', there are the 'capital' flows which result in the acquisition of capital or financial assets and which do (or are expected to) provide a *future* stream of benefits to the enterprise.

Therefore, the set of accounts which comes after the production account shows how part of the income (gross profits in the case of an enterprise) goes towards meeting 'current' items, such as interest payments, taxes on profits and dividends. This account is known as an 'income and expenditure account', which is self-explanatory if we bear in mind that the expenditure flows are confined to current expenditures. More technically, the income and expenditure account is called an 'appropriation account' because it shows how income was appropriated (used up) on current items. The balance from the appropriation account represents the flow of gross saving, and this savings flow may be spent on acquiring either capital or financial assets.

It is most important to understand this definition of 'saving'. In economics, the flow of saving is defined as the (positive) balance on the income and expenditure or appropriation account, and the word 'saving' should *not* be used to refer to any flow other than this difference between total incomings to and total outgoings from the appropriation account. In the case of companies, this flow of saving may be called by the more descriptive term 'undistributed income'. Undistributed income from the appropriation account is then 'transferred' as a receipt to the capital account because in the real world this undistributed income is used to purchase items of capital. These flows of expenditure on capital are different from current expenditures because capital expenditures add to the enterprise's stock of real assets; they are expenditures which result in an expected flow of future benefits. Thus, after the appropriation account we have an adding-to-wealth account, or as it is technically known, a 'capital account'. This account shows how saving was spent on adding to the stock of real assets. Finally, any balance remaining from the capital account –

that is, any excess of capital-account receipts over capital-account expenditures – will be used to acquire financial assets, which may be as simple a matter as increasing the enterprise's credit balance in its bank deposit. This balance is now referred to as the 'financial surplus or deficit' (in previous editions of the *National Income and Expenditure* accounts it used to be called the 'net acquisition of financial assets'). Note that such an acquisition of financial assets should not be referred to as saving. It is also possible that the balance from the capital account is negative: that is, in a single period the enterprise may well spend more on acquiring real assets than it had flowing in by way of gross saving. In this case, the deficit must be made good either by borrowing or by disposing of existing stocks of financial assets. If an enterprise borrows money, it issues a financial claim against itself; if an enterprise reduces its holding of financial assets, it has a negative acquisition of financial assets. Both of these are ways of paying for, or financing, an acquisition of real assets in excess of the flow of gross savings accruing during that period. So the final account is a financing account, or, as it is called, a 'financial account'. The capital account and the financial account affect the enterprise's wealth and so both these flows are shown as flowing into a circle contained within the boundary of the enterprise's accounts. You will note that it is not strictly necessary in this system to separate out the flow of depreciation: we may simply treat the depreciation provisions and retained net profits together as one flow.

Financial surplus and financial deficit

The financial account completes the cycle of flows for one period, and you can see in Diagram 2.5 that we have drawn a situation where the flow of capital expenditure is *less* than the flow of saving, so that there is a positive residual inflow into the pool of financial assets: in other words, a positive net acquisition of financial assets. But it is possible, and indeed it quite often happens, that the flow of capital expenditure during a given period is *greater* than the flow of saving, in the way illustrated in Diagram 2.6. In this situation, the flow of expenditure on capital assets (capital formation) during the period covered by the accounts is larger than the flow of saving (the positive balance on the appropriation

DIAGRAM 2.6   *How a financial deficit (a negative net acquisition of financial assets) may arise*

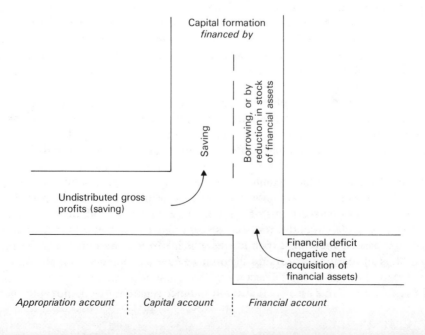

account) and the difference has to be paid for either by borrowing or by running down a pre-existing stock of financial assets (this is one of the reasons why enterprises may acquire financial assets – in anticipation of meeting a heavy bill for capital expenditure). If the balancing flow on the capital account is positive (as in Diagram 2.5), we may say that the enterprise has a 'financial surplus'; if negative (as in Diagram 2.6), then the enterprise has a 'financial deficit'.

The terminology and the algebraic signs may be a little confusing until one practises using the following:

Total income on capital account	−	Total expenditure on capital account	=	Financial balance, or net acquisition of financial assets

A positive net acquisition of financial assets	*is a*	Financial surplus
A negative net acquisition of financial assets	*is a*	Financial deficit

A financial surplus	*either* (1) increases stock of financial assets
	or (2) reduces outstanding financial liabilities (debts)
A financial deficit	*either* (1) reduces stock of financial assets
	or (2) increases outstanding financial liabilities (debts)

To increase one's outstanding financial liabilities is another way of saying that one is borrowing. Of course, it is possible for a financial deficit to result in a mixture of running down a stock of financial assets and borrowing, and this is conveniently represented as a negative net acquisition of financial assets. For example, suppose an enterprise has a flow of saving of £100 and a flow of capital expenditure of £300; it must therefore have a financial deficit of £200. Suppose it had an initial stock of financial assets of £150 and no outstanding liabilities.

Now, in the first instance let us assume the enterprise disposes of these assets and, additionally, borrows £50. The enterprise now has the finance to cover its excess of capital expenditure over saving – i.e. to cover its financial deficit. From a starting position of having £150-worth of financial assets it has gone to a closing position of having an outstanding liability of £50: a change which is encompassed by saying that the enterprise has a negative acquisition of financial assets of £200.

However, in the second instance, let us assume the enterprise does not want to run down its stock of financial assets at all. In this case it will have to borrow £200 to cover its entire financial deficit. From a starting position of having a £150-worth of financial assets it has then gone to a closing position of having £150 of financial assets *and* a financial liability of £200. Its *net* closing position is therefore outstanding assets net of financial liabilities of −£50; so that, once again, its *net* financial position has deteriorated by £200 (from +£150 to −£50).

As a third illustration, we may assume that the enterprise disposes of £100 out of its £150-worth of starting financial assets and borrows the £100 then necessary to finance the financial deficit. From a starting position of having £150 of financial assets it then goes to a closing position of having £50 of financial assets and outstanding liabilities of £100: again a *net* closing position in financial assets of −£50. In fact, whatever the enterprise does, its *net* financial asset position will deteriorate by exactly the extent of its financial deficit.

The financial account then shows either how a financial deficit was financed, or how a financial surplus was used to acquire (different types) of financial assets. The financial account is thus always the residual, balancing account which 'closes the books' on the flows for any given period.

The system of accounts

This 'residual' function of 'closing the books' is illustrated in Diagram 2.7, which shows not only which flows are allocated to which accounts but also how the 'balances' from the various accounts are 'transferred' to the account next in line. That is, in sequence:

(a)   the balance 'income' from the operating account;
(b)   the balance 'saving' from the appropriation account; and
(c)   the balance 'net acquisition of financial assets' from the capital account.

DIAGRAM 2.7   *Classification of transactions into accounts*

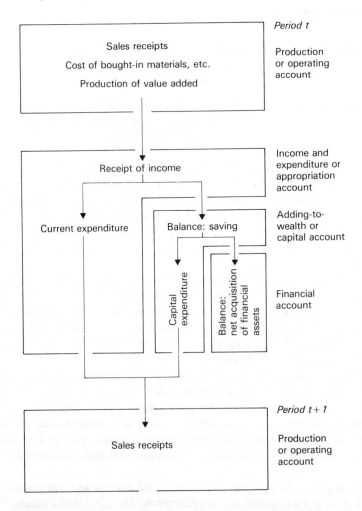

Diagram 2.7 is also adapted to show how, from the point of view of the whole economy, the periods are linked, because we may analytically think that the flows of expenditure from one period form the basis for sales receipts in the next period. (Many textbooks try to illustrate what they call the 'circular flow of income' by a circle linking the productive sector with the household sector: I have always found such circles puzzling, partly because it is seldom made clear what happens to the financial surpluses and deficits, and partly because the circle cannot show the movement from one period to the next: time is linear and not circular!)

When we switch from the accounts of an enterprise to the system of accounts for the whole economy (the 'national accounts') almost exactly the same types of accounts can be used, except that the production account is confined to value added because, from the point of view of an economy as a whole, value added is the relevant income. Correspondingly, the payment of wages appears as income in the income and expenditure account for the whole economy because this is part of the national income.

Diagram 2.7 also shows how the accounts are connected in the system of national accounts. We need especially to note how the current and capital expenditures form the link between one period and the next. In the real world, of course, these flows are circulating all the time, but it is analytically helpful if we imagine that the flows of expenditure out of the incomes distributed from value added provide the sales receipts on the basis of which the next period's flow of value added is produced. The 'circularity' of this process – from value added to income to current and capital expenditures to sales receipts and to the next period's flow of value added – is a matter of great importance, as we shall subsequently see.

Sectors of the economy

The *National Income and Expenditure* Blue Book has to concern itself not only with classifying flows of transactions into their proper accounts, but also with showing the accounts for the different groups of transactors, or the different 'sectors', of the economy. The organisation of the Blue Book depends in the first place on these sectors of the economy. We have already encountered these sectors. In the section on capital in Chapter 1 there was a lengthy description of the six types of 'organisations' which are distinguished as owning capital (real assets) in the United Kingdom, so there is no need now to repeat the basic classification at any length. However, the classification of transactors into different sectors of the economy is a little more complex than indicated by the description in Chapter 1. Diagram 2.8 shows in greater (but not complete) detail the sectors of the economy.

The fundamental classification of transactors is the threefold one between the private sector of the economy, the public sector of the economy, and the overseas or 'rest of the world' transactors. Within the UK economy a threefold distinction is made between the personal sector, the sector of corporate enterprises, and the general government sector. The personal sector comprises households and others such as the self-employed, etc. The corporate enterprise sector straddles the private and public sectors because it comprises both (private-sector) companies and (public-sector/nationalised industry) public corporations. The private-sector companies are divided, as we have seen, into industrial and commercial companies, and financial companies. The general government sector is divided between central government and local authorities. It would of course be preferable for the national accounts to distinguish separately all the transactors at the bottom of the diagram. In practice, it is not possible to separate the accounts for households from the accounts of the other transactors in the personal sector, so the personal sector is treated as a combined whole.

DIAGRAM 2.8   *Classification of transactors: the sectors of the UK economy*

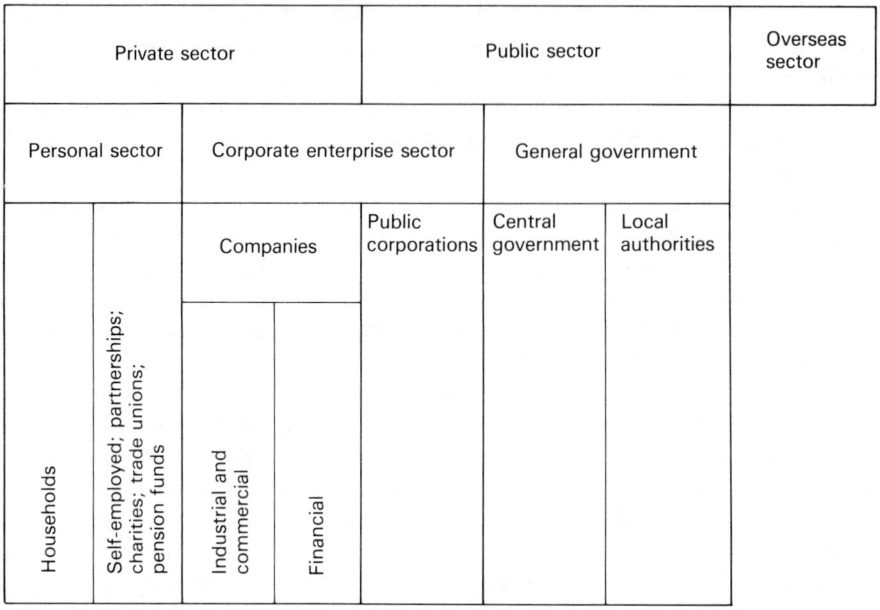

Private sector			Public sector			Overseas sector
Personal sector		Corporate enterprise sector		General government		
		Companies	Public corporations	Central government	Local authorities	
Households	Self-employed; partnerships; charities; trade unions; pension funds	Industrial and commercial	Financial			

The system of national accounts

We now have the analytic basis for understanding the arrangement of the national accounts because we can match the classification of transactors with the types of accounts. Diagram 2.9 shows how the Blue Book's main tables fit into the over-all scheme produced by the two-way classification of sectors and accounts.

The first section of the Blue Book gives the summary tables covering the whole economy: this is a combination of all the sectors of the economy. Sections 2 and 3 of the Blue Book (not shown in Diagram 2.9) give further details for the whole economy: section 2 gives the figures at 'constant prices' which make the appropriate adjustments for price inflation; section 3 gives details of outputs and inputs by industry. As shown in Diagram 2.9, section 4 contains the accounts for the personal sector; section 5 the accounts for the company sector (industrial and commercial, and financial); section 6 the accounts for the public corporations (nationalised industries); section 7 the accounts for the central government; section 8 the accounts for the local authorities. The combined accounts for central government and local authorities – the sector of general government – are shown in section 9. This combined account is useful both for seeing central and local government activities as a whole (it is also useful when making international comparisons because such aggregate figures are unaffected by countries' divisions of expenditures among central, regional and local government). There is also a combined financial account for the public sector – general government and public corporations – as a whole because the financing of public corporations' negative net acquisition of financial assets is in the last resort a central government responsibility, so it is useful to see the public-sector financial accounts over all; this is why Diagram 2.9 contains the whole public sector's financial accounts in a block. Sections 10, 11, and 12 of the Blue Book all deal with the nation's accounts for adding to wealth. Finally, section 13 covers all the various financial accounts bringing each sector's financial account into contiguity with the financial accounts for all

DIAGRAM 2.9   *The system of national accounts (with table numbers)*

Transactors: sectors of the UK economy	Transactions: type of account			
	Operating (or production) account	Appropriation (income and expenditure) account	Capital (adding to wealth) account	Financial account
United Kingdom, whole economy s. 1	1.9 / 3.1	1.1 / 1.2	1.7 (a) s.10, s.11, s.12	13.1 / 13.2
Personal sector s.4		1.3 / 4.1	4.2	13.3
Company sector s.5 — Industrial and commercial	For this account, see Input–output tables for the United Kingdom; Census of production; Census of distribution — 5.1	5.4	5.2 / 5.4	13.4
Company sector s.5 — Financial		5.5	5.5	13.5 Banking sector / 13.6 Other financial institutions
Public sector — Public corporations s.6	6.1	6.2	6.3	6.4 / 13.7
Public sector — General government s.9 — Central government s.7	9.1	7.2	9.1 / 7.3	13.10 / 13.13 / 13.12 / 7.4 / 13.8
Public sector — General government s.9 — Local authorities s.8		8.2	8.3	8.4 / 13.9
Overseas sector	For details, see United Kingdom Balance of Payments Overseas Trade Statistics of the United Kingdom		1.6	13.11

For further details on financial accounts, see Financial Statistics

(a)   Capital formation by sector and type of asset

Source: adapted from Central Statistical Office, *National Income and Expenditure 1981 Edition*, p. 139.

other sectors; this is so because one sector's borrowing is another sector's lending, so it is convenient if each sector's issuing of financial liabilities (borrowing) and acquisition of financial assets (lending) can be matched up with their corresponding figures elsewhere.

The overseas sector is only cursorily covered in the Blue Book with two brief summary tables, and there is not a separate section for this sector. This is because transactions with the overseas sector are fully covered in separate publications, especially the annual *United Kingdom Balance of Payments* and the monthly *Overseas Trade Statistics of the United Kingdom*.

Within each of these chapters of the Blue Book there is, so far as possible, the same presentation and sequence of accounts: operating; appropriation; capital; and financial. Most of the operating accounts are now published separately in the *Input-output tables for the United Kingdom* (Business Monitor PA 1004). To find the latest equivalent of this book's Table 2.6 – the United Kingdom's operating account for 1963 – one has now to consult the input–output tables. The only sector for which a complete operating account is regularly published in the Blue Book is the nationalised industry sector, and for this reason table 6.1 of the Blue Book should be carefully studied. But the tables in section 3 and table 1.9 of the Blue Book give the detailed breakdown of the production of value added by productive 'industry' of the economy: table 1.9 is indeed the starting-point of the national accounts.

Moving on from operating accounts, for all the sectors there are income and expenditure accounts, capital accounts and financial accounts, all showing how the various sectors of the economy obtained and disposed of their income, how they added to their (real) capital, and how they increased their stock of financial assets or, conversely, increased their stock of financial liabilities.

Conclusion

This chapter has explained the key concept of *value added* and the way it is produced and distributed as income to the factors of production. In order to understand value added and its related income flows, we had also to learn about depreciation and stock appreciation. We then considered the concept of *national income* starting from its simply being the sum of values added in all the productive sectors of the economy. This led on to a consideration of systems of accounts, and we should now know how and why the national income accounts for the United Kingdom are presented in the way they are.

However, this is only half the story. People obtain incomes in order to be able to spend those incomes. So our next task is to consider in more detail the expenditures out of incomes.

Exercises

2.1 *(To practise your understanding of value added.)*

(i)   Rewrite the whole of Table 2.1 on the assumption that the woodcutter becomes an employee of the baker at a wage of £5 a year.

(ii)   Expand the table of Exercise 2.1(i) to include a shop which buys bread at £45 (wholesale) from the baker and sells at £51 (retail) to the consumers, and pays the shop assistants wages of £6 (all annual flows).

(iii) Using the totals from Exercises 2.1(i) and 2.1(ii), explain why 'total sales receipts' is, in economic terms, not a useful measure of 'output', whereas total value added is.

2.2 *(To practise your understanding of value added with real data.)*

(i)   Calculate the value added of UK manufacturing industry from the following figures (all in £ million) for 1977: total sales receipts, etc. 132,030.1; total cost of bought-in materials and services (used) 88,038.1 (source of data: Department of Industry, Business Statistics Office, *Report on the Census of Production 1977 Summary Tables* (Business Monitor PA 1002), table 1, pp. 8 and 9; note that cost of materials and services (used) given here is (in the source) purchases *less* increase in stocks *plus* industrial services *plus* non-industrial services).

(ii)   The same source gives on p. 42 the following figures (all in £ million) for UK manufacturing industry in 1977: wages of operatives 15,863; salaries of all other employees 7,891.8; employers' National Insurance contributions 3,658.2. What were gross profits in UK manufacturing industry in 1977 in £ million? What were profits as a percentage of sales? As a percentage of value added?

(iii) Put the relevant numbers for UK manufacturing industry in 1977 to the first five terms on the left-hand side of Diagram 2.1 (i.e. up to and including profit).

(iv)   In Japan in 1977 total sales by manufacturing industry were ¥159,231 billion, total purchases of materials and services were ¥102,527 billion, and total wages and salaries of employees were ¥22,107 billion (source of data: United Nations, *Yearbook of Industrial Statistics 1978 Edition*, volume I, *General Industrial Statistics*, pp. 289–92). What was the share of gross profits in value added in Japan's manufacturing industry in 1977?

2.3 *(To practise your understanding of how enterprises work.)* Put the figures of Table 2.3 into Diagram 2.2 (lump dividends and outside shareholders' interests together).

2.4 *(To practise your understanding of how stocks (inventories) affect the calculation of value added.)*

(i)   The same source as for Exercise 2.2(i) gives the following figures (all in £ million) for UK manufacturing industry in 1977: sales and work done 129,483.7; increase during year in work in progress and goods on hand for sale 2,546.4 (in 2.2(i) these two were 'total sales receipts, etc.'); purchases (including industrial and non-industrial services received) 88,961.2; increase during year in stocks of materials, stores and fuels 923.1 (in 2.2(i) the former *minus* the latter was 'total cost of materials (used)'). What was UK manufacturing industry's total change in stocks (inventories) during 1977?

(ii) Fit these figures to the following equation: Sales and work done during 1977 *minus* Purchases of goods and services during 1977 *plus* Total change in stocks during 1977 *equals* Value added produced during 1977.

2.5 *(To practise your understanding of stock appreciation.)* Suppose that in Table 2.5 closing prices were £3 a tonne:

(i) Using the average-price method, what would stock appreciation then be? (Volumes of opening and closing stocks are the same as in Table 2.5.)

(ii) Using the average-price method and the same sales receipts, bought-in materials, and wages as in Table 2.5, calculate value added and profits, both excluding stock appreciation.

(iii) What would value added and profits be including stock appreciation? (That is, if we used the value-added equation with closing stocks at closing prices and opening stocks at opening prices.)

(iv) Contrast these levels of value added and profits including stock appreciation with value added and profits including stock appreciation in Table 2.5's last column (this shows the impact of a rise in the rate of inflation if stock appreciation is not excluded).

2.6 *(To practise calculating percentages again, but also to begin to look at a very serious economic problem for the United Kingdom.)*

(i) Using the data in Tables 2.6 and 2.7 calculate the percentage structure by industry of gross domestic product at factor cost in 1963 and 1980 and present your results in a table. (How are you going to deal with the snags in presentation of mining and quarrying, other services, the government sector, and adjustments?)

(ii) Bearing in mind Exercise 1.5, comment on the change between 1963 and 1980 in the share which manufacturing industry contributed to GDP. (That is, comment briefly; there is a whole book on this change;

namely Frank Blackaby (ed.), *De-industrialisation*, Heinemann/National Institute of Economic and Social Research, 1979.)

2.7 *(To practise calculating percentages again, but also to look at some interesting contrasts.)*

(i) What was the percentage share in gross domestic product at factor cost of income from employment in 1963 and in the most recent year which you can find?

(ii) In 1978, in Japan, income from employment was ¥108,084 billion and GDP at factor cost was ¥194,118 billion (source: Organisation for Economic Co-operation and Development, *National Accounts of OECD Countries 1950–1979*, Volume I, *Main Aggregates*, p. 29). What was the share of income from employment in Japan's GDP? What is the implication of this for the share of gross profits in GDP in the United Kingdom and in Japan?

2.8 *(To practise finding data.)* Update Table 2.8.

2.9 *(To practise finding data.)* Update Table 2.9.

2.10 *(To practise your knowledge of the names of accounts.)* Divide the items (and figures) of Table 2.3 between the operating account and the appropriation account. (*Hint:* see Diagrams 2.5 and 2.7.)

2.11 *(To practise finding and using data, and to extend further your understanding of value added.)* In the Central Statistical Office's *National Income and Expenditure* (the 'Blue Book'), table 6.1 gives the operating account for the public corporations (which mainly comprise the nationalised industries). Using this table and noting that taxes on expenditure are regarded as analogous to purchases of inputs, calculate the public corporations' value added for the latest available year (your answer can be checked with reference to the Blue Book's table 1.10).

2.12 *(To practise your understanding of appropriation and capital accounts and of a financial deficit.)*

(i) Draw a diagram to illustrate the public corporations' appropriation account for the latest available year. (A suitably modified version of part of Diagram 2.5 will serve, with incomes other than the gross trading surplus shown as coming from the bottom to join the gross trading surplus. The important thing is to show clearly how the balance of undistributed income ('saving') was arrived at.)

(ii)   Draw a diagram to illustrate the public corporations' capital account for the latest available year. (A suitably modified version of Diagram 2.6 will serve; capital-account receipts other than saving may be aggregated together (do not worry about the details at this stage). Likewise, aggregate all capital-account expenditure together (other than the financial surplus/deficit).)

2.13   *(To extend your knowledge of sectors.)* In the bottom boxes of Diagram 2.8, write in as many names as possible of entities known to you to be in that sector (use a big sheet of paper). Can you find at least twenty entities for each box?

2.14   *(To practise using Diagram 2.9.)* Write down from the Blue Book's contents pages a list of the exact chapter (section) headings (e.g. '1 Summary tables', '2 Expenditure and output at constant prices', and so on). Learn your list off by heart (this may sound a crazy exercise but it will help you later on). Describe what information is given in the Blue Book's table 1.9.

2.15   *(To practise using the national accounts.)* For the latest available year, fill in as many figures as you can find for the bottom three bars in Diagram 2.3. (*Hint:* you need table 1.2 in the Blue Book; cope with any negative numbers as best you can – it is exceedingly difficult to draw a negative number convincingly! Aggregate the 'imputed charge for consumption of non-trading capital' with rent, and aggregate self-employment income with gross profits and all trading surpluses.)

Chapter 3

Income and Expenditure
in the Personal Sector

Contents

Chapter guide

Having taken a bird's-eye view of the national income and expenditure accounts in the previous chapter, this chapter descends to grass-roots level to see, in economic terms, what the *personal sector* gets up to. We look at data on personal-sector income and expenditure: whence the income comes (this requires an explanation of *National Insurance* – the United Kingdom's system of social security); *consumers' expenditure*, on which the personal sector spends most of its income; and how and at what rates income is taxed. A main purpose of all this is to show the considerable extent to which the personal sector does *not* spend all its income but rather keeps a relatively large flow of *saving* (defined as the balance on the income and expenditure account).

We then look at data on the personal-sector *capital account*, but, again, the main purpose of this is to show the extent to which the personal sector does not spend its flow of saving on purchasing capital-account items but rather keeps a flow of *financial surplus* with which to acquire *financial assets*.

We examine the sorts of financial assets which the personal sector acquires, especially *national savings, government bonds, company securities* and, above all, *life assurance* and *pension funds*. These latter are the most important of the personal sector's financial assets, and they are explained through the *English Life Table* and the concept of an *annuity*. The distinction between *life insurance* and *life assurance* is explained, partly as a means of explaining why this form of asset acquisition is so popular.

We then take an over-all view of the personal-sector accounts before looking at data on the personal sector's *balance-sheet*: that is, the stocks of capital (real assets) and financial assets (paper claims) which the personal sector owns and the stocks of financial liabilities (debts) which it owes, striking the balance of all assets over all liabilities known as *net wealth*.

Most of the chapter so far will have been concerned with data (and associated concepts) which describe what the personal sector does. In the section on the *consumption function* we begin to analyse the pattern of consumers' expenditure in its relation to income. We look at both time-series and cross-section consumption functions, the latter involving an examination of the *Family Expenditure Survey*, which is an important source of basic data.

In order to follow how we obtain these actual consumption functions, we need to understand the *method of least squares*, and this is explained, using the example of the cross-section consumption function for 1979.

In order to understand how *inflation* affects consumption and income we look at the concept of a *price index*: what a price index is; how to calculate a price index; and we look at data on actual price indices in the United Kingdom since 1915, deriving data on *'real'* income and *'real'* consumers' expenditure in the United Kingdom since 1946. We estimate the *trend growth rates* of these important variables, explaining how one uses an *exponential function* and the method of least squares to calculate such growth rates.

Introduction

The previous chapter considered the meaning of 'value added' as a measure of output which is distributed as income. But people earn income so that they can spend it on acquiring the things they want. This chapter is therefore concerned with such spending. In order to analyse spending systematically we need to use the system of accounts for the specific sectors of the economy as described in the previous chapters. Through these sectoral accounts we may build up a picture of how the national income is spent, these categories of expenditure being an important element in understanding the forces which influence the size of total national output. This chapter and the next therefore proceed to examine the accounts of the private sector of the economy, describing and analysing the important features of each sector's pattern of income and expenditure.

The personal sector

We begin nearest home with the personal sector. A sector is an aggregate of transactors and, for purposes of sectoral classification, we may think of transactors as being represented by their bank accounts into and out of which all payments are received or made. In the national accounts, the personal sector represents a complicated aggregate of bank accounts because it includes households, unincorporated enterprises such as the self-employed, partnerships, sole traders, farmers, charities serving persons (churches, trade unions, universities), and finally the funds of the life assurance companies and private pension schemes which are deemed to 'belong' to the personal sector.

However, the personal sector comprises overwhelmingly the household sector, and so we shall be mainly concerned with the economics of the household sector: how it gets its income, on what it spends this income, how it is taxed, and the extent of its savings and acquisition of financial assets. One key feature of the household sector is that households (taken together in aggregate) tend always each year to have a relatively large financial surplus. This is an important *structural* feature of the household sector in all developed economies and we need therefore to examine the reasons for it and the implications for the working of the economy. But before we can get to the financial surplus we must run, in sequence, through the accounts which lead up to the financial account.

The current flows into and out of the personal sector's income and expenditure account are shown in Table 3.1. This table shows the figures for 1980 from table 4.1 of the Blue Book. One important feature of these figures is the relatively large positive balance on the income and expenditure account (that is, the excess of incomings over outgoings) known as the annual flow of personal-sector saving, which amounted in 1980 to no less than 12 per cent of total personal-sector income. But the table also contains much of descriptive interest.

Of the reported figure for personal-sector income, 68 per cent, or two-thirds, was income from employment (excluding employers' contributions to superannuation schemes). This income is basically wages and salaries, the pay of HM Forces (which is separately reported – soldiers, sailors and airforce personnel not being 'employees'), and employers' contributions to National Insurance and to pension funds. This flow is not complicated: we mentioned in Chapter 1 the extent to which the labour force was dominated by employees, and the predominance of income from employment is simply another manifestation of this.

Income from self-employment made up 9 per cent of total personal-sector income, and rents, dividends (from companies) and interest received (net of interest paid) made up another 10 per cent. National Insurance benefits (such as retirement pensions or unemployment benefits) together with other current grants from central government (such as Supplementary Benefit, student grants or redundancy payments) made up the remaining 13 per cent of total personal-sector income.

The total flow of income of the personal sector during 1980 was £200,985 million. But (see Table 2.7) the total gross national product during 1980 was only £193,450 million. How could the flow of incomes to the personal sector be £7,535 million larger than the total flow of income accruing to the economy? The anomaly arises because the £25,476 million of National Insurance benefits and other current grants are *not* part of the flow of value added/income which constitutes the gross domestic product. Rather, they are

TABLE 3.1 *Personal-sector income and expenditure account for 1980*

	£ million	Percentage of total income
Income before deduction of tax		
Income from employment [a]	137,083	68
Income from self-employment	18,394	9
Rent, dividends and net interest [b]	19,623	10
National Insurance benefits and other current grants from general government [c]	25,476	13
Miscellaneous [d]	409	—
Total personal income	200,985	100
Expenditure		
Consumers' expenditure	135,403	67
UK taxes on income (accruals) [e]	26,672	13
National Insurance contributions, Redundancy Fund contributions [f]	13,977	7
Transfers abroad (net)	290	—
Total current expenditure	176,342	88
Balance on income and expenditure account: saving [g]	24,643	12

[a] Wages and salaries of employees; pay of HM Forces; and employers' contributions to National Insurance and private pension schemes, etc.

[b] Comprising receipts of life assurance and pension funds, and other receipts (accruing directly to households).

[c] Among other things, retirement benefit, unemployment benefit, sickness benefit, etc., redundancy payment, student grants, etc.

[d] Comprising transfers to charities from companies (£46 million) and imputed charge for capital consumption of private non-profit-making bodies (£363 million) (e.g. imputed rental on buildings owned and occupied by universities).

[e] 'Accruals' means tax liabilities accruing, and this comprises (i) actual payments made to Inland Revenue during the year (£25,897 million) *plus* (ii) earmarked funds held temporarily by personal sector for eventual payment of tax liabilities (£775 million), known as 'additions to tax reserves'.

[f] Contributions by employees and by employers to National Insurance Fund, to national Health, and to the Redundancy Fund.

[g] Gross of depreciation and stock appreciation (income from self-employment includes stock appreciation) but after providing for additions to tax reserves.

Source: Central Statistical Office, *National Income and Expenditure 1981 Edition*, table 4.1, p. 28.

transfer payments out of the original value added, transfer payments being payments for which there is no corresponding return flow of services (i.e. output). The definition of a transfer income is that it is not earned by the provision of a productive service to the economy and, to make this explicit, it is sometimes called an 'unrequited transfer payment'. By contrast, a wage-earner 'requites' his payment of wages by providing his labour services for the production of value added, the appropriate meaning of 'requite' being to give or do in return for something. Such requited (income) payments are part of the national income, but unrequited (transfer) payments are not counted as part of the national income.

The economic rationale for distinguishing between the two can be seen most clearly if we contrast wages (requited income) with unemployment benefit (an unrequited transfer payment). If a large number of workers were to become unemployed but were to receive unemployment benefit at the same rate as their previous weekly wage (the unemployment benefit being paid out of taxes levied on those remaining in work), the total of personal sector 'income' – i.e. wages *plus* unemployment benefit, as reported in Table 3.1 – would not alter. Yet it is quite clear that the national output would have fallen due to the large increase in unemployment – the productive services of labour would not be fully utilised, the goods and services formerly produced by the workers now unemployed would no longer be forthcoming and the community's real standard of living would have declined. Therefore, we must exclude the transfer payments – in this case the unemployment benefit – from the national income.

Likewise, retirement pensions must be deemed to be unrequited transfer payments, because if we were suddenly to reduce the retirement age to, say, 50 for both men and women, yet pay the same amount in pensions as previously received by the newly retired in wages, then there would be a substantial fall in national output/national income, though total personal sector income would remain unchanged, so that pensions must also be excluded from the national income.

One cannot make a large sector of the employed work-force unemployed or retire them without reducing the national income; therefore, unemployment benefits and retirement pensions (and all other unrequited transfer payments) are not like other forms of income which are paid to people out of the value added to the production of which those people have contributed: that is, forms of income which are requited by that contribution. The unrequited transfer payments have no requiting, or reciprocal, return flow of productive services which are responsible for producing the value added that makes up the national output, and therefore we say 'they are not part of the national income'.

This makes the word 'income' a very tricky one in economics. It would be preferable to reserve 'income' exclusively to requited payments, but then for the personal sector the term 'income and expenditure account' would have to be changed to 'income and unrequited transfer payment and expenditure account', and we would run against common usage which generally makes no clear distinction between the two. In the rest of this book, I shall try consistently to use the term 'transfer income' when speaking of unrequited transfer payments which are not part of the national income, and shall try to use the term 'income' to refer to those incomes which are part of the national output, but on occasion the term 'income' may include transfer payments as well as (requited) incomes – such as when we talk of 'total personal-sector income'. Providing you remain aware of the ambiguity in the word 'income', this terminology should cause no undue confusion. (It is an object lesson that even apparently simple and straightforward words may refer to analytically complex things.)

To go back to the point at which we started our discussion of transfer payments: the gross national product of the United Kingdom in 1980 was £193,450 million (Table 2.7); although the personal sector received £200,985 million (Table 3.1) in total 'income', £25,476 million of this was unrequited transfer payments to households, and a further £46 million was unrequited transfers to charities (business-sector contributions to charities, included under 'miscellaneous'), so (by deduction) the requited income (resulting from contributing to the production of value added) received by the personal sector was £175,463 million in 1980, that is, the personal sector was paid 91 per cent of the gross national product. Besides ordinary wages and salaries, the requited income received by the personal sector comprised: employers' contributions to National Insurance and to private pension schemes; income from self-employment; rent, dividends and net interest (interest received from other sectors of the economy on account of loans to or deposits with those sectors net of interest paid to the other sectors on account of loans made to the personal sector by those sectors) and including the imputed (house rental) income received by owner-occupiers; the rents, dividends and net interest received by life assurance and superannuation schemes (because these funds are deemed to 'belong' to households); and, finally, there is an imputed (rental) income on the buildings owned and occupied by private non-profit-making bodies, so that if a trade union or a charity or a university owns and occupies its own office building, etc., the requisite income is imputed here (the Blue Book calls it an imputed charge for capital consumption, because if you own and occupy a building worth, say, £100,000 with a lifetime, say, of 100 years you are, in effect, deriving an annual benefit of £1,000 in the 'consumption', or depreciation, of that building).*

This requited income of £175,463 million is gross of stock appreciation as well as gross of depreciation (as noted in note *(g)* to Table 3.1) so we were being a little inaccurate in comparing it with the gross domestic product which is net of stock appreciation. However, stock appreciation affects only income from self-employment and the element of stock appreciation in self-employment income was £854 million in 1980 (calculated from table 1.2 of the Blue Book), so that personal-sector requited income net of stock appreciation was £174,609 million, or 90 per cent of the gross national product.

There is clearly no need for an explanation of why the personal sector receives this flow of requited incomes. In return for services provided – labour services or for the provision of capital – the personal sector is paid income. But why and how is there such a relatively large flow of unrequited transfer payments? The simple answer to this is that this flow forms part of the United Kingdom's 'system of social security'. In order to understand the current system of social security properly, we require not only an account of that system itself but also a bit of the historical background. Accordingly, we need to spend a few pages examining this: clearly, from the relative size of the flow (£25 billion in 1980 or 13 per cent of personal-sector income) the system of social security merits full consideration.

National Insurance (social security)

We have already mentioned (in Chapter 2) the 1911 National Insurance Act, Part I of which provided (for all employees) insurance benefits against sickness, with Part II providing (but only for some employees) insurance against unemployment under the following arrangement: in return for a weekly contribution of $2\frac{1}{2}d$ from each of the employee, the employer and the state, a workman would be guaranteed an income of 7 shillings (35p) a week during any period of unemployment but only for a maximum of fifteen weeks in any year (and each week of benefit had to be backed by five weeks of contributions).† The scheme was limited to only a few industries prone to unemployment – mainly building, shipbuilding, and some metal trades – but it was extended in 1916 to munitions workers and some other trades and at the end of the First World War to discharged servicemen. With growing unemployment, the scheme was made nearly universal for lower-paid workers in August 1920. Non-contributory 'old-age' pensions had been introduced in 1908 to pay, through the General Post Office, an income of 5 shillings (25p) a week to people over 70 with annual incomes of £21 or less.

In 1941 the government appointed an Inter-Departmental Committee on Social Insurance and Allied Services to examine the existing schemes of social security and to

---

*In the national accounts, we must not count income twice: if, as here, we regard dividends and net interest as 'requited' income for the personal sector – requited by providing the services of (finance for) capital – then we must count only *undistributed* profits, etc., as the income of the company sector. Because the national accounts statisticians prefer to count total profits (before dividend distribution) as the income of the company sector, they have then to exclude dividends, etc., from 'requited' income for the personal sector and, accordingly, treat dividends as a transfer payment. This treatment, however, is for a different reason than that for unemployment benefit or pensions (see CSO, *National Accounts Sources and Methods*, HMSO, 1968, pp. 1–2). Interest on government debt is also treated as a transfer payment by the national accounts statisticians, for the reason that payment in return for the provision of finance to the government (say, to fight the Second World War) cannot be regarded as requiting a *current* contribution to the production of value added.
†For the employees so covered, unemployment insurance was additional to the sickness insurance (covering all employees) described in Chapter 2 (p. 71).

The Beveridge Report

The rationale for Beveridge's scheme for social security is shown in Diagram 3.1. The scheme was intended to cover the whole population, so Beveridge began by dividing the population into six 'classes':

(1) employees;
(2) others gainfully occupied (e.g. the self-employed);
(3) housewives;
(4) others of working age;
(5) those below working age;
(6) those above working age.

DIAGRAM 3.1 *Beveridge's scheme for social security*

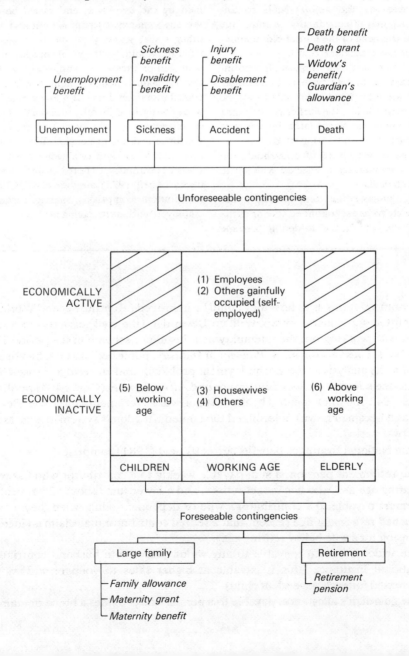

What did these 'classes' need by way of social security? The Report said (para. 300):

> The term 'social security' is used here to denote the securing of an income to take the place of earnings when they are interrupted by unemployment, sickness or accident, to provide for retirement through age, to provide against loss of support by the death of another person, and to meet exceptional expenditures such as those connected with birth, death and marriage.

Social security has, in effect, to provide against two types of contingencies.

First, there are the *unforeseeable* contingencies which may affect a family, or rather the earnings of the head of the household: unemployment, sickness, accident, death.

Second, there are the *foreseeable* contingencies based on the 'life cycle' of households: the period when the head of household will be too old to earn a living, the earlier period when the size of family may be too large, by reason of dependent children, to be supported by the income of the earning head of household, and occasional expenditures connected with birth, marriage and death.

Beveridge proposed the term 'benefit' to denote 'a weekly payment continued so long as the need lasts'; the term 'grant' to denote 'a single payment for a specific purpose'; the term 'allowance' to denote 'a weekly payment in respect of a dependant'; and the term 'retirement pension' to denote a weekly payment to those above working age. These are still the terms used. In return for a single unified weekly contribution, contributors to National Insurance should become entitled to a range of social security benefits, grants, allowances and to a retirement pension. There were to be three classes of contributors: Class 1, employees; Class 2, self-employed; and Class 3, non-employed. Class 1 contributors would pay part of the total weekly contribution themselves, with the other part paid by the employer, and would be entitled thereby to unemployment benefit and to all the other social security payments; Class 2 contributors would pay the whole of a lower weekly contribution themselves and would not be entitled to claim unemployment benefit; Class 3 contributors could pay at a lower rate still and would be entitled thereby to claim the full weekly retirement pension instead of simply getting the lower retirement pension due to a (Class 3 non-contributor) wife or a widow of a Class 1 or Class 2 contributor. (There has since been introduced (April 1975) another class (Class 4) of contributors comprising mainly certain self-employed workers receiving profits.)

---

make recommendations as to how they could be improved (after the Second World War). The committee was chaired by Sir William Beveridge (the civil servant who had been concerned with working out the unemployment insurance scheme in the period 1908 to 1911: his book *Unemployment: A Problem of Industry*, published in 1909, had been very influential in its analysis of the unemployment problem), and Beveridge himself drafted the Committee's *Report on Social Insurance and Allied Services* (Cmd 6404) published in November 1942 and implemented by the first postwar government and so the 'Beveridge Report' (as it became known) determined the United Kingdom's system of social security in the postwar period.

The main National Insurance benefits currently paid (1981) comprise:

(1)   The retirement pension, a sum payable weekly to a contributor who has reached retiring age and who has in fact retired, and a lower sum (about 62 per cent of the former) payable to a contributor's wife or dependent adult when they have both reached retirement age (except that a retired contributor may claim an increase of pension for a wife below retiring age).

(2)   The widow's benefit, payable to any widow whose late husband contributed to National Insurance (this is payable at higher rates to younger widows and is increased for each dependent child).

(3)   The guardian's allowance, payable to a person who provides a home or maintains a

child or children both of whose parents are dead and one of whose parents was a contributor.

(4) The unemployment benefit, payable to a Class 1 contributor only who is unemployed and who is capable of and available for employment; the standard unemployment benefit is increased for an adult dependant and for each dependent child.

(5) The sickness benefit, payable to a Class 1 or Class 2 contributor who is incapable of work because of illness or disablement (with increases for dependants).

(6) The invalidity benefit, payable to Class 1 or Class 2 contributors after he or she has been entitled to sickness benefit for 168 days in any period of interrupted employment or self-employment (with increases for dependants).

(7) The maternity benefit, comprising a lump-sum maternity grant payable to the wife of a contributor or to a contributor herself and a maternity allowance payable for eighteen weeks starting eleven weeks before the baby is due to a mother who has been working and has been paying full National Insurance contributions and who stays away from work to have her baby (with increases for dependants).

(8) The death grant (payable as a lump sum to the person responsible for meeting funeral expenses) on death of a contributor, his or her adult dependant or child or widow or widower.

(9) The injury benefit, payable weekly for a maximum of six months to a contributor incapable of work as a result of an industrial injury or prescribed (industrial) disease.

(10) The industrial disablement benefit, normally following a period of industrial injury benefit, payable to a contributor who is disabled by an industrial injury or industrial disease, the amount payable depending on the (medically assessed) percentage degree of disablement.

(11) The industrial death benefit, payable weekly for twenty-six weeks to the widow of a contributor who dies from an industrial accident or disease (with increases for dependants).

All these payments depend upon contributions having been paid to the National Insurance scheme*.

In addition to these National Insurance payments there are several other social security benefits. War pensions, payment of which does not depend on contributions to National Insurance, and other benefits are payable for disablement or death due to service in HM Forces (members of HM Forces being neither employees nor self-employed). Family allowances were (until 1977) payable weekly to families with *two* or more children below the age limit of compulsory school age (16) or continuing in school or college or apprenticeship (up to age 19), the amount payable depending on the number of children (in excess of the first child, but it is payable regardless of the income of the family – it is a universal benefit to which all families are entitled). In April 1977 the family allowance became payable also to families with only one dependent child and the name of the payment was then changed to 'child benefit'; the rate of child benefit in mid-November 1981 was £5.25 per week per child. Family allowances were an important part of the original Beveridge scheme because, as the Report noted (para. 411), wages 'must be based on the product of a man's labour and not on the size of his family', and this meant that many families continued to be in poverty in the twentieth century, despite the general advance in living standards, partly because of interruption or cessation of earning power (the problem which National Insurance was designed to solve) and partly because of the large size of families which could not be adequately supported by earnings. We have seen that many of

*Some of the benefits, such as the maternity grant, are due to or may become non-contributory: that is, entitlement will no longer depend on contributions having been paid.

the National Insurance benefits are paid at a rate which depends on family size, and the Report went on to observe (para. 412):

> it is dangerous to allow benefit during unemployment or disability to equal or exceed earnings during work. But, without allowances for children [i.e. family allowances payable to the families of men in work], ... this danger cannot be avoided ... the gap between income during earning and during interruption of earning should be as large as possible for every man. It cannot be kept large for men with large families, except either by making their benefit in unemployment and disability inadequate, or by giving allowances for children in time of earning and not-earning alike.

These two arguments of Beveridge's are still valid today. Additionally, it is historically interesting to note that, observing the slow rate of growth of population due to the decline of births in the interwar period (see Diagram 1.4 and Table 1.5 above), Beveridge was concerned with the long-run prospects for Britain's future (and apparently declining) population and thought that 'means of reversing the recent course of the birth rate must be found'. He hoped that family allowances would help towards this end.

Additional to the National Insurance benefits and the family allowances, Beveridge proposed that there should be a form of payment to meet any subsistence needs which might not be covered by National Insurance. These payments would depend on an examination of the means already available to the person concerned and a proof of needs – they would be 'means-tested' – and the cost would have to be met by the taxpayer: one of the principles of National Insurance – the 'insurance' part of it – was that the cost would be covered by contributions, so contributors would simply be receiving their due entitlement without any means test and could not be regarded as receiving 'charity'. But there would still remain some, only a few Beveridge thought, who would not be covered by National Insurance – for example, contributors who had paid too few contributions to be eligible for National Insurance benefits, or persons in need through causes not suitable for insurance such as desertion by the breadwinner – and, providing they could demonstrate their needs and their inadequate means to meet those needs, these persons should receive a payment known as National Assistance, but subsequently (in 1966) relabelled 'Supplementary Benefit'. Beveridge intended that National Assistance would be only a small part of social security, especially because he intended that retirement pensions and other National Insurance benefits should be fixed at a level which would ensure a reasonable standard of living. In the implementation of his scheme, however, the retirement pension and other National Insurance benefits were fixed at a low rate, partly because of the enormous cost of pensions, and many pensioners without any other supplement to their income had to claim National Assistance/Supplementary Benefit if they were to make ends meet. In practice, many pensioners and others entitled to National Insurance benefits were too proud to claim the 'charity' of National Assistance and lived in a state of poverty. The low rate of pensions meant that National Assistance/Supplementary Benefits tended to play a more important role in social security than originally intended by Beveridge. Supplementary Benefit can be claimed by any person aged 16 and over not in full-time work if his or her resources (if any and including National Insurance benefits) are less than his or her requirements (with additions for dependants). The amount of benefit payable is the amount required to bring a claimant's resources up to his or her requirements at officially prescribed rates (which also include an allowance for rent where appropriate).

So far we have been discussing the social security scheme essentially as outlined in the 1942 Beveridge Report as implemented and modified in the postwar years. There was one gap in the system which subsequently became quite an important cause of poverty. This was the problem of a family whose income from work plus family allowances was below the requirements officially recognised by National Assistance/Supplementary Benefits; this situation arose especially in the case of families with one child, these often being single-parent families where the mother went out to work but received only a low wage. In order to help wage-earners suffering this kind of poverty, the Family Income Supplement was introduced in 1971. This is a non-contributory benefit payable to a family with one or more children if the normal gross weekly income (including family allowances and any other sources of income) is less than the prescribed amount and if the head of the family is in full-time work (and so is ineligible either for National Insurance or Supplementary Benefits). The amount of Family Income Supplement payable is one-half of the difference between the family's gross weekly income and the 'prescribed amount' (depending on the number of children), subject to various maxima. The point of paying only half the difference is that this gives a wage-earner an incentive to increase his or her earnings: if the whole of the difference were payable, then any increase in earnings would simply be cancelled out by an equal corresponding reduction in benefit. For instance, when the Family Income Supplement was introduced at the end of August 1971 the 'prescribed amount' for a one-child family was £18 per week. A person earning £14 per week (including family allowances) would have been entitled to a Family Income Supplement payment of £2 per week, bringing the family income to £16 per week.* If earnings rose to £16 per week, the Family Income Supplement payment would be £1 per week, bringing the family income to £17 per week, so the family would be better off as a result of the increase in earnings. If the whole of the difference were payable, then the family income would simply remain at £18 per week, regardless of the level of earnings. Finally, in the matter of social security, we need to note that local authorities make rebates of rents payable on council housing occupied by families whose incomes are too low.

This concludes our discussion of payments made to households by way of social security. But there are two other types of payment made by the state to persons and to charities in the personal sector, and these are concerned with education.

First, because universities and certain colleges of further education are regarded as being part of the personal sector, the payments made by the central government to cover the running costs of the universities (salaries, heating and lighting, etc.) are counted as part of the personal sector's current income.

Second, any student attending university or certain colleges, and who is eligible, receives a maintenance award and payment of fees which are also part of the personal sector's income.

Table 3.2 shows the main items and amounts of these social security and other payments in 1980. First, let us consider the National Insurance payments. The biggest item is retirement pensions, totalling £10,277 million, or 40.3 per cent of the total of all payments and 71.3 per cent of payments made under the National Insurance scheme. Why is it that pensions are so relatively large in the total payment? In Table 1.6 above we saw that in 1971 there were 8.8 million people of retirement age in Great Britain (there are a further 0.2 million in Northern Ireland). Of these, 7.5 million were actually in receipt of a retirement pension – some people of retirement age continue working and in return for deferring their pension they become entitled to a larger pension (Department of Health and Social Security, *Social Security Statistics 1975* (HMSO, 1977) table 13.30, p. 88). This relatively large figure of 7.5 million in Great Britain who were receiving a pension for fifty-two weeks of the year indicates that it is the relatively large number of people of retirement age in the population – 13.6 per cent in 1951, 16.3 per cent in 1971 and about 17.7 per cent in 1981 (see Table 1.6 above) – which makes retirement pensions so large a proportion of the total.

The other National Insurance items in Table 3.2 tend to be relatively small. In 1980 total unemployment benefits were one-tenth of retirement pensions, even though 1980 was a

---

*With the introduction of child benefit in 1977, child benefit was disregarded in the FIS calculations but the prescribed amounts were reduced.

TABLE 3.2   *National Insurance benefits and other current grants paid to the personal sector in 1980*

Payments to personal sector	£ million	Percentage of total
National Insurance benefits		
Retirement pensions [a]	10,277	40.3
Widow's benefit and guardians' allowances	637	2.5
Unemployment benefit	1,097	4.3
Sickness benefit	660	2.6
Invalidity benefit	1,195	4.7
Maternity benefit	163	0.6
Death grant	17	0.1
Injury benefit	47	0.2
Disablement benefit	282	1.1
Industrial death benefit	41	0.2
Total National Insurance	14,416	56.6
Other grants		
War pensions	386	1.5
Child benefit (formerly family allowances)	2,944	11.6
Supplementary benefits	2,693	10.6
Other non-contributory benefits [b]	608	2.4
Grants to universities, colleges, etc.	1,077	4.2
Scholarships and grants (from local authorities)	861	3.4
Rent rebates and allowances (from local authorities)	232	0.9
Other central government grants to personal sector [c]	2,259	8.9
Total other grants	11,060	43.4
Total National Insurance benefits and other current grants	25,476	100

[a] Including lump-sum payments to pensioners ('Christmas bonus').
[b] Including lump-sum payments to pensioners other than those from the National Insurance Fund.
[c] Including, among other items, Family Income Supplement.

Source: Central Statistical Office, *National Income and Expenditure 1981 Edition*, tables 7.2, 7.6 and 8.2, pp. 49, 53 and 55.

year of comparatively high unemployment (by postwar standards – see Diagram 1.5 above). The other National Insurance benefits are simply listed for the sake of completeness and will not be discussed (it is, however, useful to note where these figures may be found). Among other grants, it can be seen that child benefits (formerly family allowances) are quite a substantial part of the total social security payments, as Beveridge intended they should be; their relative importance increased in 1977 when they were extended to families with one dependent child (formerly having been confined to families with two or more children). In 1980, 7.4 million families were receiving child benefit (according to Central Statistical Office, *Social Trends 1982 Edition*, no. 12, table 5.6, p. 83).

Supplementary benefits – the non-contributory, means-tested payments to those whose resources fell below the official Supplementary Benefit 'poverty line' – amounted in 1980 to £2,693 million, and their relative importance was (and always has been) far larger than Beveridge intended. According to *Social Trends*, in 1980, 3.2 million people were receiving supplementary benefits: of these 1.8 million were retirement pensioners or National Insurance widows aged 60 and over; 0.9 million were unemployed (most of these were probably not entitled to National Insurance unemployment benefit); 0.2 million were sick and disabled (again mostly without National Insurance benefit); and 0.3 million were one-parent families. The total number of people (including dependants) provided for by supplementary benefit in 1980 was no less than 5.1 million, or 9.1 per cent of the United Kingdom's population. It is obvious that inadequate National Insurance retirement and widows' pensions is still the biggest single reason as to why so many are in receipt of supplementary benefits.

The other items under other (current) grants are, again, listed for the sake of completeness, but it is, for example, interesting to note that grants to universities, etc., paid in 1980 were about the same size as the flow of unemployment benefit.

We have digressed at considerable length on the main items making up the £25,476 million transferred in 1980 as income to the personal sector in the form of National Insurance benefits and other current grants (Table 3.1). The digression is only partly justified by the relative size of the amount: 13 per cent of total personal-sector income. The major justification stems from the fact that social security is very important to those who receive it, and as there is a lot of controversy about the subject it is as well to try to keep the figures in perspective, especially as there can really be no argument against retirement pensions – indeed, only the argument that they are somewhat ungenerously on the low side. Also, the growing proportion of retired persons in the population means that the problem of ensuring adequate retirement pensions will be an ever-present one.

So we have, in 1980, a total personal-sector income including unrequited transfer payments, of £200,985 million. How was this income spent?

Consumers' expenditure

The greater part of it goes on 'consumers' expenditure'. This flow of consumers' expenditure on current goods and services in 1980 amounted to two-thirds of total personal-sector income, so it is important to know something about the composition of this flow which naturally encompassed a vast range of goods and services, as you can see in Table 3.3.

Lengthy as it is, Table 3.3 shows only the main categories of consumers' expenditure as given in the national accounts. The two biggest single categories are food (including non-alcoholic beverages), at 17.2 per cent of total consumers' expenditure, and housing, at 14.6 per cent. This latter flow includes imputed rents notionally paid by owner-occupiers (these imputed rents having also been included in income) but excludes interest paid by those owner-occupiers with mortgages (because the income side of the income and expenditure account reports interest received net of interest paid, i.e. payment of interest to building societies has already been deducted). Expenditure on consumer durables comprises expenditure on items such as motor-cars and motor-cycles, furniture and floor coverings, electrical goods (radios, television sets, hi-fi, refrigerators, washing-machines, cookers, etc.). For the household, expenditures on these goods are more in the nature of capital expenditure, because these durable goods all provide a continuing stream of services; but because these services are not the subject of further payment, the convention in national accounts is not to view the expenditures as capital formation but simply to include them with other current expenditures.

These reported expenditures will include some expenditure by foreign tourists in the United Kingdom: that is, by non-residents. For example, some of the reported expenditure on catering must be by foreign tourists and this expenditure is not being made out of UK incomes by UK residents. Because we do not have a categorisation of foreign tourists' expenditure but only a global total – that is, we know in total what foreign tourists spend, but not the separate amounts on meals, hotels, travel in the United Kingdom, etc. – we have to make a global adjustment by deducting from total reported consumers' expenditure in the United Kingdom the total of expenditure by foreign tourists in the United

TABLE 3.3   *Consumers' expenditure during 1980*

Category of expenditure	£ million	Percentage of total
Food	23,230	17.2
Alcoholic drink	10,200	7.5
Tobacco	4,867	3.6
Housing (rent, rates, maintenance, etc.)	19,722	14.6
Fuel and light	6,413	4.7
Clothing	9,908	7.3
Durable goods	12,175	9.0
Other household goods	3,596	2.7
Books, newspapers, magazines	1,896	1.4
Chemists' goods	2,109	1.6
Miscellaneous recreational goods	4,070	3.0
Other miscellaneous goods	2,571	1.9
Running costs of motor-vehicles	8,555	6.3
Travel	4,611	3.4
Communication services	2,002	1.5
Entertainment and recreational services	2,741	2.0
Domestic service	628	0.5
Catering (meals and accommodation)	7,445	5.5
Wages and salaries and other expenditure by non-profit-making bodies	2,179	1.6
Insurance	1,832	1.4
Other services and income in kind	5,556	4.1
less Expenditure by foreign tourists in the United Kingdom	−3,488	−2.6
Consumers' expenditure in the United Kingdom	132,818	98.1
Consumers' expenditure abroad	2,585	1.9
Total consumers' expenditure	135,403	100.0

Source: Central Statistical Office, *National Income and Expenditure 1981 Edition*, table 4.6, pp. 32–3.

Kingdom. This deduction gives total 'consumers' expenditure in the United Kingdom' (that is, total expenditure in the United Kingdom on consumption by UK residents); and if we add to this total the amount UK residents spend abroad on consumption (i.e. on foreign travel), we have the total known simply as 'consumers' expenditure', which amounted to £135,403 million in 1980 (full details are given in the Blue Book's table 4.6). Consumers' expenditure is thus expenditure by the personal sector (UK residents only) on goods and services (including foreign travel).

The figures relate to the acquisition of goods; for instance, if a consumer buys a car on hire purchase, and does not pay for it immediately, the whole value of the car is nevertheless included in consumers' expenditure. The estimates of consumers' expenditure include purchases of second-hand goods *less* sales of second-hand goods by the personal sector, so that transactions in second-hand goods among households does not affect the total of consumers' expenditure (apart from the dealer's margin). But the purchase of second-hand goods from other sectors of the economy (second-hand cars from car-hire firms or army-surplus stores) does affect the total.

To return to Table 3.1, households in the United Kingdom also make transfers of income abroad, and this sum is greater than the transfers of income which they receive from abroad, so the net total transferred abroad is simply reported as an item of 'expenditure' in the income and expenditure account. This item includes transfers of money abroad by missionary societies and other charitable institutions (Oxfam, Christian Aid, etc.) which are part of the personal sector.

Income tax

The other big items of personal-sector expenditure are taxes on income (£26,672 million in 1980) and National Insurance contributions (£13,977 million in 1980). Most persons pay tax at the same time as they receive their income; the tax is deducted 'at source' by the payer of income, and for wages and salaries this deduction at source is known as the Pay As You Earn (PAYE) scheme.

If we ignore the administrative complexity of the cumulative tax deductions at source and simply look at annual taxes, the structure of income tax in the United Kingdom is conditioned by two things: first, by the various allowances against income and reliefs against tax liability; and second, by the rates of taxation. Both of these are best explained by means of an example, shown in Table 3.4, for the 1980–1 tax year (which ran from 6 April 1980 to 5 April 1981).

We imagine a higher-paid employee, whose contract of employment stipulates that his pay shall be £20,000 a year. The employee is married and is therefore entitled to what is known as a 'personal allowance' at the rate for married men of £2,145 (details of these and other allowances can generally be found in one or other of the commercial booklets rushed out after each Budget – e.g. the *The Daily Mail Income Tax Guide 1980–81*). There used also to be tax allowances for each child, but these were phased out after 1977 and substituted for by (non-taxable) child benefits. He also contributes 5 per cent of his salary, £1,000 a year, to an officially approved superannuation scheme, and this too may be deducted from his gross income; this £1,000 will be supplemented by a contribution from his employer paid directly to the fund, probably of about £2,000 (the maximum contribution from employer and employee combined is 15 per cent of salary and there are also restrictions on the amount of pension payable: if the pension is related to final salary, then the annual pension for a full forty years' contributions may not exceed two-thirds of final salary). The employers' contributions to an officially approved scheme are not taken into account in assessing tax liability. The justification for all this is partly as a concession to encourage saving and partly because the contributions represent deferred income which will be taxed at the 'proper time', i.e. when the pension is paid. Note that these (private) payments are entirely distinct from the (state) payments of National Insurance contributions.

Pay As You Earn (withholding system)

The PAYE scheme was introduced in 1943 when extensions to the system of income tax – to obtain more finance for the war effort – were bringing many more (lower-paid) income earners into the 'tax net' for the first time. These lower-paid earners were accustomed to weekly budgeting out of their weekly wage, and experience during the First World War had shown that they often found it difficult to reserve savings to one side to pay a yearly (or half-yearly) tax bill. Therefore, a system had to be devised to deduct income tax at source, i.e. before the wage-earner received his or her pay; this relieved the wage-earner of the problem (and worry) of ensuring that he could meet his tax bill. The purpose of the PAYE scheme is to ensure that at the end of the tax year each taxpayer has paid exactly the right amount of tax – the tax is therefore paid on a cumulative basis. What happens is that, cumulatively, month by month for salary-earners and week by week for wage-earners, a taxpayer's gross income and allowances and taxable income (the difference between gross income and allowances) are recorded and tax is levied each month, building up cumulatively so that the total tax paid at the end of the year is the right total.

TABLE 3.4   *An example to illustrate the system of income tax in the United Kingdom in 1980–1*

	£ per annum
Gross income from employment [a]	20,000
less Married man's personal allowance (1982–3 raised £2,445)	2,145
less Employee's contributions to superannuation scheme	1,000
less Interest paid on loan to purchase the house used as the family's only or main residence [b]	2,400
equals Taxable income	14,455
Tax liability: [c] 30 per cent (basic rate) payable on first £11,250 of taxable income	3,375
40 per cent payable on the next £2,000 of taxable income	800
45 per cent on the next £3,500 of taxable income (or part thereof)	542.25
Total tax liability	4,717.25

[a] Excluding employer's contributions to National Insurance and to (private) occupational superannuation scheme.

[b] The maximum loan on which interest is tax deductible is £25,000; interest on loan to purchase a 'second house' (e.g. a holiday home) is not eligible for deduction; the interest on any loan used to *improve* the main residence is, however, also eligible for deduction. This deduction system is due to change from April 1983: a deduction will no longer be made for the individual taxpayer but, in consequence of a payment direct from the Inland Revenue to the lending institution, the taxpayer's interest payments on a house-purchase loan will be net of the tax subsidy.

[c] Tax rates in 1980–1 and 1981–2 (1982–3 bands; rates unchanged):
Basic rate   30 per cent on first £11,250 of taxable income (first £12,800)
Higher rates   40 per cent on next £2,000 of taxable income (next £2,300)
                45 per cent on next £3,500 of taxable income (next £4,000)
                50 per cent on next £5,500 of taxable income (next £6,200)
                55 per cent on next £5,500 of taxable income (next £6,200)
                60 per cent on the remainder (over £31,500)

Next we have a very important allowance – the interest payable on any loan (or loans) to purchase the house in which the family lives. In the very first Income Tax Act of 1799 (introduced by William Pitt the younger to pay for the Napoleonic wars) there was an allowance for children (on obvious grounds of social welfare) and also an allowance for interest on all debts (on the slightly less obvious, but nevertheless persuasive, grounds that as interest receivable was taxable, interest payable should be tax deductible, though nowadays only interest on loans for purchase or improvement of the family's main residence is tax deductible). As we have seen (Diagram 1.7 above), the personal sector owns a very large amount of capital in the form of dwellings, and households generally acquire their dwellings by borrowing money to pay for the dwelling and then repaying the loan in instalments and paying interest on the loan outstanding (in the United Kingdom the institutions which specialise in making such loans – properly called 'mortgages' – to households are the building societies).

The deductibility of mortgage interest is therefore an important concession, even though the maximum loan qualifying for mortgage relief is £25,000 (interest on any amount in excess of this is not deductible). There used to be a further justification for the mortgage-interest allowance because, from the time taxes were first introduced right up to 1963 households were also taxed on the imputed rental of any owner-occupied dwelling (in the example of Mr Smith and Mr Jones in Chapter 2, Mr Jones would, until 1963, have been taxed not only on his income from employment of £5,000 a year but also on his 'imputed' rental income of £2,000 a year). In 1963 the tax on imputed rental incomes was abolished (without much economic justification: it had been argued that it was wrong to tax notional as opposed to actual income and that it was inconsistent to tax house-owners on imputed (house-benefit) income but not, for example, car-owners on imputed (car-benefit) income, but neither of these arguments appears convincing). However, abolition was a politically popular move, and likewise the deductibility of mortgage interest has not been abolished because it would be politically unpopular.*

Owner-occupiers are now considerably favoured by the tax system, and the only thing that can be said in mitigation of this is that most tenants of local authority housing pay rent at less than the market value – that is, local authority tenants also enjoy subsidised housing. Paradoxically, the tax concessions to owner-occupiers may not be quite the benefit they fondly imagine themselves to be receiving because the concession makes the asset – a house – more desirable to own and so probably raises the prices of houses above the prices which would obtain in the absence of the concession. If the concession – tax-deductible interest – were withdrawn, the price of houses would probably fall, and this would inflict a hardship – a capital loss – on those who had committed themselves to buying houses at the previous higher price. Therefore, there are arguments against withdrawing the concession, even if it is not, perhaps, an economically justifiable tax concession. The effect of the tax concession can be seen if we imagine that our £20,000 p.a. taxpayer were renting a house for £2,400 a year instead of paying interest of that amount. His living expenses would remain the same but his tax bill, other things remaining the same, would rise by £1,085.25, from £4,717.25 to £5,802.50.

So that, under the UK system of income tax, the taxpayer with a mortgage may deduct the interest payment on his house-purchase loan from his gross income and thereby obtain a substantial saving in tax. Subtracting all the allowances gives the total known as 'taxable income', in our example £14,455. The tax liability is then computed on taxable income. There are several rates of taxes for successive amounts of taxable income. The first rate is called the *basic rate*, because it is levied on a wide band of income. The basic rate is 30 per cent on the first £11,250 of *taxable* income. The second and all succeeding rates are called the higher rates: levied at 40 per cent on the next £2,000 of taxable income (after the first £11,250 of taxable income); 45 per cent on the next £3,500 after that; and so on as detailed in note (*c*) to Table 3.4. The total tax liability has therefore to be calculated in successive steps in the way shown in Table 3.4 until one reaches the end of taxable income.

The total tax liability of the employee is (under the 1980–1 rates of income tax) £4,717.25. The employee's *average* rate of tax is:

$$\text{Average rate of tax} = \frac{\text{Tax paid}}{\text{Gross income}}$$
$$= \frac{4,717.25}{20,000}$$
$$= 0.236$$

so that he or she is paying 23.6 per cent of his/her income in income taxes. The marginal rate is, however, much higher than this. The marginal rate of tax is the *extra* tax paid out of any *additional* income. Suppose this person's income rose to £21,000; assuming that the employee's contribution to the superannuation scheme then rose to £1,050 (5 per cent of

---

* From April 1983, tax relief on mortgage interest is proposed to be given via a direct payment from the Inland Revenue to the lending institution, whose interest charges to the borrower will consequently be net of tax relief at the basic rate; see p. 132 below on the similar change made in 1979 for tax relief on life insurance premiums (any difference between the basic-rate tax relief and that available to higher-rate taxpayers will be taken account of when calculating income-tax liabilities – on similar lines to the 1980–1 system of providing for mortgage tax relief).

income), the total tax liability would increase to £5,144.75, and the extra tax would therefore be £427.5 on the additional £1,000 of gross income:

$$\begin{aligned} \text{Marginal rate of tax} &= \frac{\text{Extra tax}}{\text{Additional income}} \\ &= \frac{427.5}{1,000} \\ &= 0.4275 \end{aligned}$$

The total income tax liability accruing during 1980 on personal-sector income was £26,672 million. This is only 13 per cent of personal-sector income, much lower than the rates given in note (c) to Table 3.4. The reasons for this are that:

(a) the personal allowances reduce the amount of tax paid;
(b) employers' contributions (counted as part of gross income from employment in Table 3.1) are not part of taxable income;
(c) most National Insurance benefits (but not retirement pensions) and other current grants from general government are exempt from tax (but from 6 July 1982 unemployment benefit became taxable);
(d) many retirement pensioners will, because of the personal allowance, be paying very little tax anyway.

It is necessary to explain that, during the calendar year, the accrual of tax liabilities differs from taxes actually paid. The formula is:

$$\begin{aligned} \text{Accruals of tax liabilities} &= \text{Payments of tax} + \text{Additions to tax reserves} \end{aligned}$$

For the personal sector in 1980 these figures were (in £ million):

Payments of tax	25,897
Additions to tax reserves	775
Accruals of tax liabilities	26,672

This happens because some of the tax liabilities accruing during the calendar year may not be paid until the following calendar year, but the prudent taxpayer will nevertheless earmark and set aside an amount sufficient to cover the unpaid tax liability, keeping the earmarked amount as an 'addition to tax reserves'. (Companies are required by their accountants and auditors to do this.)

But it is the total accruals of tax liabilities, not actual payments of tax, which are deducted as an expenditure item in the income and expenditure account. This is done in order that we may strike a meaningful balance for personal-sector saving on the income and expenditure account. Suppose that, for some administrative reason, the Inland Revenue decided to postpone the date of collection of taxes, so reducing payments of taxes but increasing additions to tax reserves (total accruals remaining the same). If we deducted only the actual payment of taxes in the income and expenditure account, then the balance on the account (personal-sector saving) would increase. But this increase does not 'belong' to the personal sector; it is only a deferred tax liability and, strictly speaking, 'belongs' to the Inland Revenue in the sense of being ultimately payable to them. Therefore, it is not sensible to calculate the balance on the income and expenditure account by deducting only actual payments of tax. It is more realistic to deduct the total accrual of tax liabilities because then the balance remaining on the income and expenditure account is the flow of saving which 'belongs' to the personal sector.

However, if we do this, we then encounter the problem that the additions to tax reserves do enable the personal sector during the calendar year to increase (temporarily) its stock of financial assets. So, in the capital account, the additions to tax reserves have to be added back as a receipt before an accurate balance for the financial surplus may be struck. Therefore, as we shall see, additions to tax reserves re-appear as a receipt on capital account.

National Insurance and other contributions

In addition to taxes on income, the personal sector has also to pay National Insurance contributions and contributions to the National Health Service. National Insurance contributions have already been discussed;* in 1980 insured persons themselves paid £4,996 million, and their employers paid a further £7,547 million on employees' behalf (these contributions having been included in the total of income from employment), with a further £183 million in lieu of graduated contributions. Additionally, an amount is collected with all National Insurance contributions for a separate contribution to the National Health Service, which in 1980 was £1,040 million. Family allowances (now called 'child benefit') had formed one of the three planks, or 'assumptions', which Beveridge saw as supporting his National Insurance/National Assistance scheme of social security. The second assumption was a National Health Service for prevention and cure of disease and disability by medical treatment (the third assumption was the maintenance of full employment). Beveridge thought that part of the cost of such National Health Service treatment should be included in National Insurance contributions, and this is what now happens, except that access to National Health Service treatment does not depend upon contributions (as does entitlement to National Insurance benefits) but is available to everyone normally residing in the country (irrespective of age, income or nationality). National Health Service treatment is generally free of direct charge to the users, the cost being borne in small part (one-tenth) by contributions levied with National Insurance and in large part by general taxes. In 1980 these National Health Service contributions amounted to £1,040 million (total current and capital expenditure on the National Health Service being £11,444 million in that year).

Finally, all employers pay on behalf of each employee a contribution to the Redundancy Fund. This Fund was established by the Redundancy Payments Act 1965 which entitled any employee made redundant to receive from his or her employer a 'redundancy payment' (tax-free) of about one week's gross pay for every year of service with that employer (this payment to be made whether or not the employee had secured a job with another employer). Providing the employer conformed to certain requirements, he (the employer) could then obtain reimbursement of half of the redundancy payments from the Redundancy Fund (the exact proportion reimbursable has varied from time to time). The purpose of the redundancy payment is twofold: first, to compensate an employee for the loss of job; second, to encourage employers and employees to accept and co-operate in technical changes which might lead to loss of jobs. As employers make these contributions on behalf of employees, they are included in income from employment and in expenditure by (or on behalf of) the personal sector. In 1980 contributions to the Redundancy Fund totalled £211 million.

Thus total social security payments to the state by or on behalf of the personal sector totalled £13,977 million in 1980. Together with consumers' expenditure, taxes on income

*Rates of National Insurance contributions are considered further in Chapter 9.

(accruals) and net transfers abroad, the total current expenditure of the personal sector in 1980 was £176,342 million. Given its total 'income' of £200,985 million, the personal sector thus had a balance of £24,643 million of income over expenditure on current account, and this balance is known as personal-sector saving. We can see that this saving is a quite substantial proportion, 12 per cent, of personal-sector income. This balance is then carried forward to the capital account in the way explained in Diagrams 2.5 and 2.7. This substantial flow of saving is the result of all the 20 million or so households in the United Kingdom trying successfully to live 'well within their means' so that they can acquire capital assets (houses) on the one hand and financial assets on the other. In order to see how they did this we need to turn to the personal-sector capital account.

Personal-sector capital account

As explained in Chapter 2, the capital account is an 'adding-to-wealth' account. It shows the flow of resources which enables a sector to add to its wealth and the expenditures made on acquiring wealth. Although the word 'expenditure' is commonly used in capital accounts, we need to be clear that such capital expenditure is a very different type of expenditure from current expenditure such as consumers' expenditure. The difference between current expenditure and capital expenditure is that the latter results in a stream of future income (or benefits), the former does not.

The capital account of the personal sector is shown in Table 3.5. The flow of personal-sector saving (brought down from the income and expenditure account – Table 3.1) is the main source of capital-account receipts (92 per cent). As previously explained, additions

TABLE 3.5 *Personal-sector capital account for 1980*

	£ million	Percentage of total receipts
Receipts		
Gross saving (brought down from income and expenditure account)	24,643	92.2
Additions to tax reserves	775	2.9
Capital transfers	1,324	5.0
Total receipts on capital account	26,742	100.0
Expenditure		
Gross domestic fixed capital formation:		
Dwellings (new, i.e. excluding value of existing dwellings and land)	3,450	12.9
Purchase *less* sales of land and existing buildings	947	3.5
Other fixed capital formation	2,668	10.0
Total fixed capital formation	7,065	26.4
Increase in (book) value of stocks and work in progress	355	1.3
Taxes on capital	957	3.6
Capital transfers to public corporations	65	0.2
Total expenditure on capital account	8,442	31.6
Balance of receipts over expenditure		
Financial surplus (+) or deficit (−), 'net acquisition of financial assets'	18,300	68.4

Source: Central Statistical Office, *National Income and Expenditure 1981 Edition*, table 4.2, p. 29.

to tax reserves have to be added back in at this juncture so that we can strike an accurate balance on the net acquisition of financial assets, even though the acquisition of financial assets to cover these unpaid tax liabilities is only a temporary matter: in the United Kingdom one can even acquire a special financial asset, the Tax Reserve Certificate, bearing interest, which one can surrender to the Inland Revenue when payment of tax is due in settlement of the tax liability. The personal sector also receives capital transfers, almost entirely from the government sector: these are such things as grants to universities to cover capital expenditure (£136 million in 1980); grants to housing associations (£567 million); grants to farmers for farm improvements or field drainage (amount unspecified); or local authority grants to households for the conversion or improvement of houses (£202 million). Although these transfers have to be spent in the 'proper' way (that is, on the capital purposes for which they are given), they are transfers, or gifts, which do not contain any obligation to repay the money; in other words, and importantly, they are not loans.

Total receipts on capital account thus amounted to £26,742 million during 1980. How were these receipts spent?

The main form of capital expenditure undertaken by the personal sector is the acquisition of new dwellings (excluding the cost of land). Improvements to, or conversions of, dwellings are included in consumers' (current) expenditure unless they are being paid for by a local authority grant (capital transfer). The figure includes items of equipment which are an integral part of the dwelling, such as central heating. The purchase of a second-hand house is not counted as capital formation from the point of view of the personal sector as a whole because one household's investment will be another household's disinvestment. However, some land and existing buildings may be purchased from other sectors (as will happen with the sale of council houses) and this does count as capital formation by the personal sector (although not for the economy as a whole). In 1980 the personal sector spent £3,450 million on acquiring new houses, 12.9 per cent of total capital-account receipts, and £947 million on net purchases of land and buildings from other sectors. The cost of land is excluded from the cost of the new dwellings; this is because capital formation relates to the increase in the capital stock and the quantity of land cannot be increased. From a financial point of view, if a household buys a new house, then the cost of the land may either be a payment to another household, in which case the payment cancels out (apart from the transfer costs of stamp duties, legal fees, estate agent's commission), or a payment to another sector of the economy, in which case it appears in 'purchases *less* sales of land', but this will cancel out for the economy as a whole. The net transfer costs of land and buildings are counted as capital expenditure: although they do not result in an addition to the country's stock of fixed capital, they are an indispensable part of the process of capital formation. The personal sector has often been a net seller to other sectors of land and existing buildings, and this may be by reason of farmers' sales of land. In 1980 the sale of council houses from the local authority sector to the personal sector is probably the reason why the net purchases were positive.

The personal sector also engages in a considerable amount of fixed capital formation other than in dwellings, and we have to recall that this sector includes all farmers, all unincorporated enterprises, and charities (including the universities). These will be purchasing various types of capital equipment – tractors, new barns, computers, and so on – which is included here.

The next item of expenditure is the increase in the value of stocks, a mixture of the value of the physical increase in stocks and work in progress – capital formation in stocks – and stock appreciation. However, the increase in the book value of stocks has to be paid for, so this total increase in the value of stocks (including stock appreciation) must be deducted from capital-account receipts. Stock appreciation in the personal sector during 1980 was £854 million, so the value of the physical increase in stocks was −£499 million; in other words, the personal sector reduced the volume of stocks held.

The personal sector has also to pay taxes on capital and, by convention, these non-recurrent capital taxes are recorded as expenditures in the capital account: they are assessed on the basis of capital, not of income, so the capital account is a more appropriate account for them. The bulk of these taxes are taxes levied on the estates of people who die – death duties or estate duties, now called capital transfer tax because it also (since 1974) includes taxes levied on gifts made by the living (to catch people who tried to evade estate duty by giving away their estates before they died). This also includes capital gains tax, a tax at the rate of 30 per cent on any realised capital gain, i.e. if one buys shares in a company and subsequently sells them for more than one paid (due to the market value of the shares having risen), then one may have to pay tax on the capital gain. Capital gains tax is levied on all capital assets but owner-occupied houses are exempt, as are government securities held for more than one year, and this acts as a considerable inducement to invest in these types of assets. Nor is the tax levied on an asset changing hands at the death of the owner because it then becomes subject to capital transfer tax.

The other 'expenditure' on the capital account is a relatively small amount of capital transfers to public corporations. This is a rather strange item and it arises because consumers have generally to pay to have their (new) houses connected to electricity and gas supplies: that is, they have to pay for, say, the cables and for the meters to be installed; this would count as capital formation by households except that the cables and meters remain the property of the electricity or gas boards (they do not become the property of the householder). Therefore, although households pay for this they do not, legally, become the owners of anything in return, and these payments must therefore be treated as a 'transfer payment' and not as an 'expenditure', which implies that the person acquires ownership rights in return.

The total of personal-sector expenditure on capital account in 1980 was £8,442 million, or only 31.6 per cent of total receipts on capital account, so that the balance, which is the greater part, 68.4 per cent, of personal-sector capital account receipts was used to acquire financial assets. The use of over 68 per cent of receipts on capital account, or £18,300 million a year, to acquire financial assets is the reason why I remarked earlier that this was an important structural feature of personal-sector accounts, the obvious point being that £18.3 billion a year is a large flow. So we must now consider the main types of financial assets which the personal sector tends, each year, to acquire.

Financial-asset acquisition

The personal-sector financial account shows how the personal sector used its financial surplus to acquire financial assets. However, the personal sector may also acquire financial liabilities. The *net* acquisition of financial assets is the balance, or difference, between assets acquired and liabilities taken on. There are two important things one needs to be clear about when looking at a financial account.

First, the figures given in a financial account are *flows per period*; that is the figures relate to a change (during a year, say) in an outstanding stock of assets or liabilities. Essentially, financial assets and financial liabilities themselves are stocks existing at a moment of time, whereas the acquisition of assets or liabilities are flows per period. To illustrate simply: at the end of last month I had £20 in my pocket (a stock at a moment of time); at the end of this month I had £25 in my pocket (ditto); during the month I acquired £5 (extra) of money (a financial-asset acquisition, a flow during the month). Financial accounts are concerned with this latter flow. To illustrate with some real figures: Table 3.6 shows both financial stocks and flows. Most people are familiar with bank deposits or building society deposits as a financial asset; and also with loans from banks or from building societies as financial liabilities. (Loans from building societies for house purchases are popularly called 'mort-

TABLE 3.6 *Some financial assets and liabilities of the personal sector, end-1979 and end-1980*

	£ million		
	Amount outstanding at 31 December (i.e. stocks)		Change in stock during 1980 (i.e. annual flow)
Personal sector	1979	1980	
Financial assets			
Deposits with banking sector	30,818	37,404	6,586
Deposits with building societies	42,442	49,460	7,018
Financial liabilities			
Loans from banking sector	14,017	17,617	3,600
Loans from building societies ('mortgages') [a]	36,986	42,708	5,722

[a] Mortgages to all sectors of the economy, but in practice nearly all of this is to the personal sector.

Sources: Central Statistical Office, *Financial Statistics*, August 1981, tables 8.7 and 10.4, pp. 93 and 114.

gages' because, in return for the loan, the house is pledged, or mortgaged, as security, with the proviso that the property shall be reconveyed upon repayment of the loan. If the loan is not repaid as agreed, the creditor (the building society) may take possession of the house and sell it in order to recoup the loan.) Table 3.6 shows these two types of assets and liabilities. At the end of 1979 the personal sector had bank deposits totalling £30,818 million. (These were current-account, or cheque-account, or 'sight', deposits which can be drawn 'on demand' and which do not normally earn interest (£13,192 million); deposit accounts or 'time' deposits, for which notice of withdrawal may be required but which earn interest (£17,142 million); and deposits in foreign currency (but valued in sterling, £484 million).)* At the end of 1980 these bank deposits owned by the personal sector had increased to £37,404 million. So during 1980 the personal sector had acquired £6,586 million of (extra) bank deposits: a flow, during the year, of financial-asset acquisition. Likewise, in increasing its stock of deposits with building societies from £42,442 million at the end of 1979 to £49,460 million at the end of 1980, the personal sector had, during 1980, acquired an extra £7,018 million of financial assets with (claims against) the building societies. On the other hand, the personal sector had outstanding loans from the banking sector of £14,017 million at the end of 1979: that is, the personal sector owed that amount to the banks. At the end of 1980 the personal sector owed the banks £17,617 million, so during 1980 the personal sector had acquired an extra £3,600 million of financial liabilities (amounts owing) to the banks; this is a flow of financial-liability acquisition. Likewise, the value of outstanding mortgages increased from £36,986 million at the end of 1979 to £42,708 million at the end of 1980, so the flow of personal-sector acquisition of (extra) financial liabilities to the building societies during 1980 was £5,722 million. Financial accounts report flows of this sort, and do not (generally) give the corresponding stocks. Thus, for example, when you see in the personal-sector financial account for 1980 (Table 3.7) the figure of £7,175 million reported as 'Deposits with building societies' it means that the personal sector increased its deposits with building societies by that amount during 1980; this figure does *not* refer to the total deposits with building societies standing to the credit of the personal sector. This is the first thing that it is important to be clear about.

* 'Sight deposits' are credit balances on customers' accounts with banks (whether interest-bearing or not) which are transferable or withdrawable on demand without interest penalty; 'time deposits' are all other deposit liabilities of banks.

The second thing that is important about financial accounts is the convention regarding the plus or minus signs. When you look at a financial account you will see minus signs as well as plus signs (it is, of course, conventional simply to omit the plus signs and print only the minus signs, it being understood that a number without a sign is positive). Therefore, it is important to understand what the signs mean. The basic rule is that a plus sign indicates a *use* of finance *by* the sector concerned; a minus sign indicates a *provision* of finance *to* the sector concerned. Now, finance can be used by a sector either to add to its stock of financial assets or to reduce its stock of financial liabilities. To illustrate this latter point, if you owed the bank £100 at the beginning of the month and during the month you had a financial surplus (out of earnings) of £10, then you could use this financial flow to reduce your outstanding liabilities to the bank to £90.

Conversely, finance can be provided to a sector either by an increase in the sector's liabilities, or by a reduction in the sector's stock of outstanding assets. To illustrate, if during the month you had a financial deficit of £10, finance could be provided either by borrowing £10 from the bank (increasing your liabilities to the bank); or if you had £100 in your bank deposit at the bank, then you could meet your financial deficit (your excess of total outgoings over total income) by reducing your bank balance to £90. We may therefore summarise:

+ *indicates* a USE of finance BY the sector	*either*
	(i) to increase a stock of financial assets
	or
	(ii) to reduce a stock of liabilities (amounts owed)
− *indicates* a PROVISION of finance TO the sector	*either*
	(i) through increasing a stock of liabilities (amounts owed)
	or
	(ii) through reducing a stock of financial assets

When the figures of Table 3.6 appear in the personal-sector financial account, the acquisition of financial assets of bank deposits and deposits with building societies will have a plus sign, indicating a use of finance by the personal sector; whereas the acquisition of financial liabilities of loans from banks and loans (mortgages) from building societies will have a minus sign, indicating a provision of finance to the personal sector.

The word 'net' in the term 'net acquisition of financial assets' means, therefore, the acquisition of financial assets net of the acquisition of financial liabilities; or the algebraic sum of all the flows (the sum having regard to signs).

In order to be able to follow financial accounts, it is necessary to practise your understanding of these two important things: that the figures refer to flows; and that signs must be correctly interpreted. Now we can turn to the personal-sector financial account itself.

Table 3.7 gives the personal-sector financial account for 1980. For some types of assets and liabilities there is sufficient information to give the gross flows, but in other cases we have information only on the net flows.

TABLE 3.7   *Personal-sector financial account for 1980*

Financial-asset acquisition or use of finance (+), or financial-liability acquisition or provision of finance (−)	£ million	
	Gross acquisition	Net acquisition
Notes and coin		356
Gross deposits with banking sector	6,630	
Gross loans from banking sector [a]	−3,099	
Net assets with banks [a]		3,531
Gross deposits with building societies	7,175	
Gross loans from building societies	−5,715	
Net assets with building societies		1,460
Other loans for house purchase		−1,570
Hire purchase and other trade credit and loans [b]		−335
British government securities		2,345
National savings		1,378
Local authority debt, public corporations debt, tax instruments		−140
Company and overseas securities and unit trusts		−1,603
Funds of life assurance and superannuation schemes		11,113
Miscellaneous, unidentified, and accruals adjustment [c]		1,765
Total net acquisition of financial assets: financial surplus (+)/deficit (−)		18,300

[a] Excluding banking-sector loans for house purchase.
[b] Comprising credit extended by retailers, identified trade credit, other public-sector lending, other lending by financial institutions.
[c] Comprising deposits with other financial institutions, miscellaneous domestic instruments, unidentified transactions, accruals adjustment.

Source: Central Statistical Office, *National Income and Expenditure 1981 Edition*, table 13.3, p. 92.

The first-mentioned financial asset acquired by the personal sector is simply its acquisition of notes and coin. Because these do not bear any interest and are held simply for the convenience of being able to pay for transactions, the personal sector tends to keep its holdings of notes and coin to a minimum and so the amount held does not increase very much year to year. Obviously, with inflation the average value of transactions undertaken by households goes up and so it is convenient if more notes and coin are held. But relatively speaking, this increase is very small. The personal sector increased its holdings of notes and coin during 1980 by £356 million. The personal sector's stock of notes and coin was estimated to be £7,784 million at the end of 1979 (Central Statistical Office, *Financial Statistics*, February 1982, supplementary table S12, p. 158). Thus the addition during 1980 to the personal sector's stock of money, the flow of £356 million, represented about a 4½ per cent increase in its stock of notes and coin held at end-1979. The total stock of notes and coin in circulation with all sectors of the economy increased by £724 million during 1980; from £9,701 million at the end of 1979 to £10,425 million at end of 1980 (*Financial Statistics*, February 1982, table 7.1, p. 74), so the personal sector took up half of the total increase.

As we have seen in Tables 3.6 and 3.7, the personal sector used part of its financial surplus to increase its gross deposits with banks by £6,630 million; but it also took loans from (increased its liabilities to) the banking sector amounting to £3,099 million. This provision of finance to the personal sector from the banking sector is entered in Table 3.7 with the appropriate negative sign to denote a provision of finance in the form of an increase in liabilities, so that the increase in the personal sector's deposits with the banks net of the increase in the personal sector's liabilities to the banks was £3,531 million shown in the net acquisition column (the figures in Tables 3.6 and 3.7 are not exactly identical, and the reason appears not to be explained in either of the two sources).

As we saw in Tables 3.6 and 3.7, relatively large amounts of money were also deposited by the personal sector with the building societies: the personal sector increased its deposits by £7,175 million during 1980; but it also obtained a large amount of loans for house purchase (mortgages) during 1980: this provision of finance was £5,715 million, entered with the appropriate negative sign; so the personal sector's net acquisition of assets with building societies was only £1,460 million.

The personal sector generally acquires, year by year, a small increase in its financial liabilities in the form of hire-purchase debt and other trade credit, and this net item normally appears with a negative sign denoting a provision of finance of −£335 million. There are some exceptional years when the personal sector reduces the amount of outstanding hire-purchase liabilities, and as a reduction in liabilities represents a use of funds such a reduction in the stock of outstanding liabilities then appears with a positive sign.

Saving with the government

During 1980, as during most other years, the personal sector acquired, net, a substantial amount of financial assets in the form of British government bonds and in various instruments of national savings. The central government (and also local authorities) meet part of their annual expenditure by borrowing. This they do by issuing 'bonds' repayable at a stated date and bearing interest. There are several attractive features of government bonds:

(a) They are a very secure form of asset – no risk of the government going bankrupt – and are therefore sometimes known as 'gilt-edged securities'.
(b) If held for over a year, any capital gain is free of capital gains tax.
(c) They are readily marketable so that if you need your money back before the stated date for repayment (or 'redemption date', as it is known) you will be able to sell the bond to someone else.

In 1980 the personal sector directly acquired (net) £2,345 million worth of British government securities. That is, £2,345 million was the annual increase in the stock of securities held: it was the difference between the gross acquisition of government securities and the gross sale or redemption of government securities. Such government securities are often called 'bonds'.

The personal sector also acquired £1,378 million in the form of national savings during 1980. National savings are basically government-guaranteed schemes intended to make available to lower income-earners facilities for saving and the original purpose, to enable small amounts of money to be put by with a minimum of trouble, continues as the hallmark of national savings. Often (but not always) the interest is free of tax and usually the interest is not paid out but is simply added on to the amount deposited; the accrued interest thus needs to be distinguished from the principal, as the deposits are known.

There is also a tendency to encourage savers to hold their savings rather than to spend them (or, conversely, to penalise the early withdrawal of savings). The stocks and flows relating to national savings are shown in Table 3.8. There is a National Savings Bank,

TABLE 3.8   *National savings: amounts outstanding and transactions by type of asset*

	£ million		
	Amount outstanding at 31 December (i.e. stocks)		Change in stock during 1980 (i.e.
Personal sector	1979	1980	annual flow)
Deposits with National Savings Bank			
ordinary account	1,833.3	1,739.9	−93.4
Premium savings bonds	1,403.5	1,448.0	44.5
British savings bonds	705.3	474.5	−230.8
National savings certificates (not indexed)			
Principal	3,864.5	4,091.8	227.3
Accrued interest	996.9	1,162.8	165.9
National savings certificates (indexed linked)			
Principal	1,150.5	2,110.0	959.5
Accrued index linking/bonus	310.7	524.2	213.5
Save as you earn			
Principal	401.1	449.2	48.1
Accrued interest/bonus/index increase	56.7	100.3	43.6
National savings stamps and gift			
tokens	10.7	9.7	−1.0
Total	10,733.2	12,110.4	1,377.2

Source: Central Statistical Office, *Financial Statistics*, August 1981, table 3.13, pp. 44–5.

formerly (and still commonly) known as the Post Office Savings Bank. There are two forms of account: the ordinary account, which can be opened with a 25p deposit, and from which withdrawals up to £50 can be made on demand at any post office, and the investment account, which can be opened with a £1 deposit, and which pays a higher rate of interest than the ordinary account, but withdrawals require one month's notice. In the statistics the ordinary account is treated as part of national savings but the investment account is reported separately as part of deposits with (other) savings banks. The National Savings Bank is often used by children and other 'small savers', and the average size of deposits is quite small. At the end of 1979 the personal sector held £1,833.3 million on deposit with the National Savings Bank ordinary account, and at the end of 1980 £1,739.9 million; so during the year the personal sector reduced these deposits by £93.4 million. (The trustee savings banks were the forerunners of the Post Office Savings Bank, and many of them suffered from the competition of the Post Office Savings Bank: but in 1929 they were reorganised as part of the national savings and deposits in the ordinary account of trustee savings banks were guaranteed by the government. Accordingly, such deposits were included with national savings; however, as a result of recent legislative changes giving the trustee savings banks more independence, these deposits are not, after the third quarter 1979, regarded as part of national savings.)

Premium bonds are another and popular method of saving: there is no interest on the bonds (which are repayable at face-value at any time) but there are periodic draws and prizes awarded to the holders of bonds with winning numbers: the maximum prize of £250,000 is awarded each month and there are many smaller prizes. In 1980 the personal

Government bonds (or 'gilt-edged securities')

A government bond is basically a promise (a) to pay the bearer a stated percentage rate of interest a year, and (b) to repay the money at a stated date. Suppose you buy a £100 bond at 7 per cent redeemable in 1999. For such a bond you may initially pay £100, or perhaps £98 if the bond is issued at a 2 per cent discount, and, for each £100 bond purchased, you become entitled to receive £7 a year. In 1999 the government will redeem the bond for £100 cash. Now suppose that the following year the rate of interest rises to 14 per cent: that is to say, the government starts issuing bonds bearing interest at 14 per cent. A new investor who puts up £100 becomes entitled to an annual income stream of £14, so that if the holder of the 7 per cent bond had to sell his bond on the stock market, he would receive only £50 for it: that is, any new investor is indifferent to putting his £100 into the (new) 14 per cent bond or to buying two lots of 7 per cent bonds at £50 each. The new investor's annual income stream (in return for his £100) will be the same in both cases. If you tried to sell your 7 per cent £100 bond for more than £50, you would not find any buyers because they could do better by acquiring new 14 per cent bonds. Conversely, if you have a 14 per cent bond and the rate of interest falls to 7 per cent, the market value of the 14 per cent bond will double. Of course, as one nears the redemption date for a bond, its market value will get closer to its redemption value. The moral is that one should only buy bonds if one intends to hold them till 'maturity' (the date of redemption). In times when interest rates fluctuate, purchasing bonds can be a risky business if you do not intend to hold them until maturity. Nevertheless, if you do intend to do this, government bonds do provide an absolutely secure stream of income: hence it is sometimes said that 'widows and orphans buy bonds'. With the high interest rates prevailing in 1980, the personal sector certainly added considerably to its holdings of government bonds.

sector put £44.5 million (net) into premium bonds and increased its holdings of premium bonds from £1,403.5 million at the end of 1979 to £1,448.0 million at the end of 1980.

British savings bonds and national savings certificates are popular methods of saving: on the bonds (taxable) interest is payable half-yearly, but if the bonds are held for a full five years a 4 per cent tax-free bonus is payable. The bonds may be encashed at a month's notice. During 1980 the personal sector *decreased* its holdings of savings bonds from £705.3 million at the end of 1979 to £474.5 million at the end of 1980. Accordingly, this decrease in assets, which represents a *provision* of finance (not a use of finance) is reported with a negative sign.

With savings certificates, the interest is tax-free and the certificates may be encashed at eight days' notice. Interest is payable at maturity and simply added on to the encashable value of the certificate, and the longer you hold the certificates the greater the annual yield becomes. The personal sector holds a large amount of savings certificates: £3,864.5 million at the end of 1979 and £4,091.8 million at the end of 1980, so the personal sector put £227.3 million into these certificates during 1980. The personal sector also obtained £165.9 million of accrued interest to be added on to the principal; this accrued interest is, of course, included in the personal sector's receipt of income in the income and expenditure account. Although this accrued interest has not actually been paid as income, the convention in national accounting is to report flows on an accruals basis rather than on a cash-flow basis; so the interest is given as accruing in the income and expenditure account, even though there is no actual cash inflow.

One snag with all these forms of savings is that they lose their value with inflation. What is ultimately of concern to savers is not the financial assets themselves but the ability to purchase things with the proceeds, so that if prices rise (and go on rising) the real purchasing power of one's stock of financial assets will decline. If you have a stock of

The origin of national savings

The national savings movement has a long history, and it is useful to pause for a moment to consider the origin of national savings. In the 1850s Mr Charles Sikes, a banker with the Huddersfield Banking Company, made a study of the facilities for 'saving' (i.e. for acquiring financial assets) which were available to ordinary wage-earners. He concluded that such facilities were most inadequate: the hours of opening of the banks were too short and so inconvenient to working men (and they tended not to be open every week day); and there were not enough banks, so the distances from working men's homes were too great. In 1856 Sikes pointed out these deficiencies to the government and subsequently gave evidence to a Select Committee of the House of Commons in which he proposed that the post offices (open for longer hours and more widely distributed) should act as a receiver of deposits and payer of withdrawals. Sir Rowland Hill, then Permanent Secretary of the Post Office, welcomed the idea, and the idea of encouraging working men to be thrifty and prudent appealed greatly to Mr Gladstone, then Chancellor of the Exchequer. So the necessary legislation (The Post Office Savings Bank Act) was passed in 1861 to enable the post office to take in deposits and to meet withdrawals, with a rate of interest of $2\frac{1}{2}$ per cent per annum payable on deposits.

financial assets of £30,000, you might have expected to purchase a three-bedroomed detached house with it; but if house prices rise you might be able to buy only a two-bedroomed semi-detached house. That is an example of what is meant by the term 'decline in purchasing power'. In June 1975 the government introduced a scheme, then limited to retired people, to protect the value of savings against inflation. These are the index-linked National Savings Certificates Retirement Issue (popularly nicknamed 'Granny bonds'), and their encashable value (after being held for a full year) is increased in line with the rise in the Retail Price Index: for example, if you buy a £10 certificate and hold it for a year during which prices rise by 10 per cent, then at the end of the year you can cash the certificate for £11. Additionally, if the certificates are held for five years, a 4 per cent bonus (on the initial value) is payable. Initially, this form of savings was meant to protect the assets of retirement pensioners against inflation, but since 7 September 1981 these index-linked certificates have been available to everybody without regard to age, though the maximum amount that any one person can hold in the bonds is £5,000 (excluding bonds inherited on the death of the previous bondholder).*

The net acquisition by the personal sector of index-linked savings certificates during 1980 was £959.5 million, which increased the holding from £1,150.5 million at the end of 1979 to £2,110.0 million at the end of 1980. Additionally the personal sector gained an extra £213.5 million from the index-linking. Granny bonds are a good form of investment (financial-asset acquisition) in times of inflation and are conveniently available for purchase at post offices and trustee savings banks.

There is one other type of inflation-proofed national savings scheme available to people; this is the Save As You Earn scheme. Save As You Earn is open to any individual aged 16 or over: the individual must enter into a savings contract to pay sixty monthly contributions of an amount to be decided by the individual (not less than £4 per month nor more than £50 per month). At the date for repayment, each month's contribution is revalued by the extent of price inflation between the repayment date and the date on which the contribution was paid in; these revaluations are free of income tax. The repayment may be either after five years or after seven years, in which latter case a bonus of two months'

*This upper limit may be revised from time to time; index-linked National Savings certificates became available to everyone regardless of age on 7 September 1981.

contributions is also payable. Save As You Earn has not, however, attracted a large flow of funds: holdings at the end of 1980 were only £449.2 million.

In total, as shown in Tables 3.7 and 3.8, the personal sector used part of its financial surplus during 1980 to increase its holdings of national savings by £1,377.2 million during 1980, from £10,733.2 million at the end of 1979 to £12,110.4 million at the end of 1980.

The personal sector also has some financial-asset transactions with local authorities. On the one hand, it acquires some local authority debt (a financial asset); and on the other hand, it borrows from local authorities for house purchase (takes on a financial liability). The personal sector acquired net liabilities of £124 million from the local authorities during 1980 and another £16 million (net) of liabilities (or reduction of financial assets) in the form of other public-sector financial instruments.

Company securities

An important type of financial asset in a modern industrial economy is company shares. There are two main institutional methods whereby people may join together to provide the finance necessary to start and run an enterprise and to enlarge it if and when the occasion arises.

One is the legal form of *partnership* wherein two or more people, but not more than twenty, may join as partners, each supplying part of the required finance and then sharing in the profits in agreed proportions. The important economic aspect of partnerships is that all partners are jointly liable for the partnership's debts, up to the full extent of their own (private) assets. The liability of partners is therefore unlimited and partnerships mostly comprise active partners who take a day-to-day hand in running the business so they are closely in touch with the debts which the partnership may incur. Certain professions, such as solicitors, accountants and stockbrockers, are always conducted as partnerships.

However, the amounts of finance one can get hold of through partnerships will be restricted, and manufacturing and trading enterprises often require larger amounts of finance. So the second method of acquiring finance is to form a *joint-stock company with limited liability*. this means that one invites any number of people each to contribute a share of the finance. Their liability for the enterprise's debts will be limited to the extent of their contribution: that is, if the enterprise goes into liquidation with debts greater than its assets, all that the individual shareholder loses is his or her contribution; unlike a partnership, his or her other private assets cannot be seized to settle the debts. In return for subscribing to the enterprise's finance, a shareholder becomes entitled to a share in the profits, such payments being called *dividends*; dividends are usually payable half-yearly, an interim dividend and a final dividend. Such enterprises are called 'public limited companies' – their names end with the abbreviation 'Plc' – and we should in future reserve the word 'company' to refer to such legal entities.* If one wishes to establish a limited liability company, or if a limited company wishes to expand, an invitation to subscribe to the issue of shares may be published and the new issue of shares will then (it is hoped) be acquired as a financial asset by the investing public. There is also a considerable market in 'second-hand' shares – the 'stock market', where shares are traded – but in Table 3.7 we are concerned only with the net acquisition of shares by the personal sector; either its purchases of new issues, or its purchases from or sales to other sectors of the economy. One advantage of investing in company securities – as the Blue Book calls shares – is that, if the

---

* Public limited companies may offer securities in the company for sale to the public; private limited liability companies – whose name must end with the word 'Limited' or 'Ltd' – are forbidden by law from doing this (see below, p. 184). Public limited companies and private companies, all registered with the Registrar of Companies, make up the company sector.

company does well the value of the shares will rise; though if the company does badly its share value will fall.

It follows that, when investing in shares, one has to be careful to choose a company which will do well and so provide a good dividend and whose shares may consequently rise in value, rather than a company which may make losses, not be able to pay dividends, and whose shares may fall in value. Part of the solution to this problem is to study each company's performance and prospects before one buys its shares; another part is to 'spread the risk' by investing in a number of companies. However, most individuals have neither the time nor the expertise to do the former; and most households do not have enough to invest to make the latter feasible. To overcome this there arose in the United Kingdom the institution of the *unit trust*. A unit trust is a fund which accepts sums of money from individuals (often in small amounts), pools those sums, and buys shares. In return the individual obtains a certain number of 'units' in the trust fund, and the fund is under a legal

TABLE 3.9 *Personal sector net acquisition of company (and overseas) securities and of funds of life assurance and superannuation schemes, 1953 to 1980*

	Net acquisition of financial assets, £ million			
Year	UK company securities	Overseas securities	Life assurance and superannuation schemes	All financial assets: financial surplus (+), or deficit (−)
1953	n.a.		393	−65
1954	n.a.		437	−233
1955	n.a.		478	−179
1956	n.a.		515	114
1957	n.a.		579	76
1958	−165		649	−44
1959	−377		717	14
1960	−373		816	346
1961	−301		869	628
1962	−392		934	485
1963	−561		1,074	497
1964	−634		1,157	592
1965	−684		1,163	970
1966	−465		1,230	1,138
1967	−581		1,359	866
1968	−704		1,502	526
1969	−481		1,500	755
1970	−734	−96	1,719	1,481
1971	−1,257	25	2,115	490
1972	−1,199	−23	2,955	1,458
1973	−1,678	−391	3,412	2,978
1974	−669	−305	3,695	4,234
1975	−540	−505	4,333	5,394
1976	−1,358	−203	5,576	5,588
1977	−1,493	−408	6,423	5,221
1978	−1,503	273	7,798	9,223
1979	−1,971	176	10,008	13,026
1980	−1,630	35	11,113	18,300

Sources: Central Statistical Office, *National Income and Expenditure*: *1964*, table 51, p. 61; *1965*, table 69, p. 81; *1966*, table 75, p. 88; *1967*, table 74, p. 88; *1968*, table 74, p. 90; *1969*, table 71, p. 84; *1970*, table 70, p. 82; *1971*, table 73, p. 86; *1972*, table 72, p. 84; *1973*, table 72, p. 84; *1963–73*, table 74, p. 86; *1964–74*, table 82, p. 90; *1965–75*, table 14.3, p. 93; *1966–76*, table 13.3, p. 95; *1967–77*, table 13.3, p. 99; *1979 Edition*, table 13.3, p. 97; *1980 Edition*, table 13.3, p. 92; *1981 Edition*, table 13.3, p. 92.

obligation to buy those units back from the individual should he or she wish to sell. The value of each 'unit' is determined by the market value of the shares held divided by the units: if the value of shares held by a unit trust is, say, £10 million, and there are 5 million units in the trust, then each unit will have a value of £2; if the value of shares rises to £15 million, the value of each unit will increase to £3. The advantage of a unit trust is that it can afford to employ full-time experts to assess the prospects and performance of each company it invests in, and, because of the large amount of money at its disposal, the unit trust can invest in a diversified portfolio of shares, so spreading the risk. The unit trust will also receive the dividends on the shares and, normally twice a year, will distribute the dividend income to the unit holders.

Taking unit trusts and the direct acquisition of company securities together, we see in Table 3.7 that during 1980 the personal sector reduced its holdings of shares by £1,603 million. In fact, in all years since 1958 (when the figures first became available) the personal sector has reduced its holdings of company securities (see Table 3.9). Such net disposals of shares by the personal sector appears not to be typical of industrial countries. The reasons for the peculiar pattern of behaviour in the United Kingdom are complex, but one significant factor appears to be the sale of shares on the death of the shareholder. The personal sector in the United Kingdom had, over a long period, built up a very large total holding of shares: the market value of personal-sector holdings of company securities at the end of 1979 was estimated to be nearly £35 billion. In 1980 the personal sector reduced its holdings of all shares by £1.6 billion, so the relative reduction then was not large in relation to the market value of holdings (about 5 per cent). It may be that people inheriting shares need to sell the shares to pay estate duty, or they may prefer to receive a cash inheritance. It may also be that, if the estate is to be divided among several persons, it is simpler to sell the shares and divide the proceeds rather than to divide the share holding itself.

Life assurance and pension funds

Towards the end of Table 3.7 we see where the bulk of the personal sector's net acquisition of financial assets goes: to the acquisition of funds of life assurance and superannuation schemes, amounting to £11,113 million in 1980. At the end of 1979 the personal sector's 'equity' in life assurance and pension funds was estimated to be £76 billion, so the addition during 1980 amounted to a 15 per cent increase. Table 3.9 shows that in each year since 1953 (when figures first became available), the personal sector has acquired relatively large amounts of these particular financial assets. Why?

Because of their obvious importance in personal-sector financial-asset acquisition we need to consider life assurance and superannuation in some detail. Moreover, it is necessary that an economist should understand the basic principles of these savings schemes.

Death is an important fact of life. It is a no less important fact that in old age we all get to a stage of greater or lesser physical infirmity, and this fact is institutionalised in the UK economy by retirement from employment, for men at the age of 65, for women at the age of 60. (These are the ages at which men and women become eligible to draw the National Insurance retirement pension.)

These two facts mean that every family dependent for its living on the earnings of labour must try to provide both against the contingency of the death of the chief wage-earner and also against the certainty of retirement of the chief wage-earner, either of which leads to no income from work. This means that it is prudent, while working, for the chief wage-earner to make such provision. We have in the United Kingdom a system of compulsory provision for retirement known as National Insurance (which also covers other contingencies such as

Annuity

An annuity is an annual payment for the duration of the life of the individual receiving the annuity. Such an annuity can be purchased because for an individual of any age we can estimate the life expectancy, on average, of individuals of that age.

Table 3.10 shows an extract from the *English Life Table No. 13, 1970–2*. This shows, for various ages, the probability that a person of that age will die within one year. These probabilities differ by sex. These probabilities are calculated as the ratio of the annual flow of deaths between age X and age $X+1$ (taken as an average of the three years 1970 to 1972 inclusive) and the number of people who survive to age X. For example, out of 100,000 English males aged 20, 106 will, at the mortality rates prevailing in 1970–2, die within one year. Using these probabilities of death, it is possible to estimate how long, on average, an individual of any age will live, given that the individual is subjected to those mortality risks. This 'expectation of life' represents the average number of complete years lived after attaining age X. The expectation of life must be specific to a starting age. For example, suppose we have four men who die at ages 55, 59, 66 and 88. Their expectation of life at birth was 67 years:

$$\tfrac{1}{4}(55 + 59 + 66 + 88).$$

However, at age 65 the expectation of life is *not* 2 years, because by this age the weaker individuals have died and those surviving to age 65 have better prospects; at age 65 the two survivors (who eventually die) live for 1 year and 23 years, an average of 12 years beyond 65, which is then the expectation of life (in this example) for those who survive to age 65.

The actual statistics show that in 1970–2 in England and Wales the life expectancy of males aged 65 was 12.2 years. Therefore, if by age 65 an English male had accumulated a stock of savings totalling £24,000, then a financial institution specialising in this sort of transaction could afford, in return for the £24,000, to guarantee this man an annual payment for the rest of his life – an annuity – of:

$$\frac{£24,000}{12.2} = £1,967$$

The institution can afford to give this guarantee because it will be selling a large number of such annuities, and although some men will live for more than 12.2 years (and so receive more than they paid), others will live for less than 12.2 years (and so receive less than they paid in). On average over a large number of men the total of the 'underpayments' ought to counterbalance the total of the 'overpayments': what the financial institution loses on the swings of longevity it can expect to gain on the roundabouts of premature death. The important thing is to be right 'on average'; and the financial institution can be right (a) because of the information in the life

TABLE 3.10   *Extract from* English Life Table No. 13, 1970–2 [a]

Age X in years	Probability that a person aged X would die within one year		The expectation of life: the average future lifetime in years which would be lived by a person aged X [b]	
	Male	Female	Male	Female
0	0.01980	0.01523	69.0	75.2
10	0.00034	0.00023	60.7	66.7
20	0.00106	0.00045	51.1	56.9
40	0.00226	0.00160	32.0	37.5
60	0.02075	0.01025	15.4	20.0
65	0.03453	0.01641	12.2	16.1

[a] Applicable to England and Wales; based on the 1971 population census and the average number of deaths registered in the years 1970, 1971 and 1972.

[b] Given that the person is subject to the death probabilities given.

Source: Central Statistical Office, *Annual Abstract of Statistics 1982 Edition*, table 2.33, p. 53.

tables, and (b) because it sells a large number of annuities.

The calculation of the annuity is a little more complicated than we have just indicated because there will be interest earned on the (remaining) balance of the £24,000 (this serves to increase the annuity) and there will be administration costs (these serve to reduce the annuity). If the rate of interest earned were, say, 5 per cent per annum, then the annuitant could expect at the end of the first year approximately:

$$£1,967 + 5\% \text{ of } £24,000$$
$$- \text{Administration costs } (A)$$
$$= £3,167 - A$$

and, at the end of the second year:

$$£1,967 + 5\% (£24,000 - £1,967) - A$$
$$= £3,069 - A$$

In fact, financial institutions selling annuities adjust their payments so as to give a constant annual payment, paying less than is due under this formula in the early years and more in the later years.

We can appreciate how annuities work if we imagine a man holding £24,000 at age 65 trying to escape the administration costs: he could invest the £24,000 at 5 per cent and spend each year £1,967 plus the interest on the remaining balance and not have administration costs deducted. However, for the lone individual this may bring a serious predicament if he lives beyond the age of 77 when his capital will have been exhausted; any individual wishing to take this course of action has either to commit suicide at 77 or fall back on charity. As this is a most unattractive proposition, it is preferable at 65 to hand over one's stock of saving in return for an annuity.

---

unemployment or sickness). But we are not here concerned with this basic compulsory system of social security, partly because the benefits are minimal, but mostly because the benefits are paid for on a pay-as-you-go basis by contributions, with extra funding from general taxation when necessary. In 1980 the contributions to National Insurance were £12,726 million, and payment of benefits totalled £14,526 million and most of the deficit had to be met by a grant from the central government out of general taxation (there was also some earnings of interest which accrued to the National Insurance Fund). Moreover, the National Insurance Fund cannot be deemed to 'belong' to its members in the same way that the funds of a private pension scheme may be said to belong to its members.

So we are concerned with those 'funded' schemes for saving by individuals whereby they can provide for their retirement or possible death. We shall first consider schemes of saving for retirement. The purpose of such schemes is to enable the individual to save an amount of money sufficient to purchase, at the time he or she retires, an adequate 'annuity'.

Superannuation schemes (occupational pension schemes)

A superannuation scheme is basically a scheme for saving regularly throughout one's working life in order to provide, at the age of retirement, a capital sum which enables one to purchase an adequate annuity on which to live during retirement. The word 'superannuation' comes from the verb 'to superannuate', which means to pension off or to cause to retire from service on a pension. In superannuation schemes it is usual for both employer and employee to pay regular contributions to the scheme. For example in the Universities Superannuation Scheme, the employee-member contributes 6 per cent of his/her gross salary and the university (the employer) contributes 9 per cent. The employee's contribution is deductible from income assessable to tax, and the employer's contribution is not counted as part of income assessable to tax. Because of this tax-deductible element, such schemes have to be approved by the Inland Revenue, which sets upper limits to contributions (15 per cent in this case). The Universities Superannuation Scheme is one which only university staff are entitled to join by virtue of their occupation, and so it is known as an 'occupational pension scheme'. These annual contributions of 15 per cent of gross salary are credited to each member and the capital sum so accumulated is used to provide an annuity at retirement. The value of the annuity may be calculated on a different basis than that just described; often the annuity is calculated as 1/60th of final salary for each year of service; so someone who has contributed for forty years receives 40/60ths, or two-thirds, of final salary. Although this calculation is different from the strict annuity calculation, it cannot in practice be too far from the result of the latter calculation without eventually causing the occupational pension scheme either to run into deficit (if the 1/60th basis were too generous) or to accumulate a surplus (if the 1/60th rule were too niggardly).*

There are in the United Kingdom a large number of such occupational pension schemes where the annuities (pensions) are supposed to be fully funded by contributions from both employees and employers. These are known as 'funded schemes'. There are also some occupational pension schemes to which no, or only voluntary, contributions are made by employees, and where the pensions are paid almost entirely on a pay-as-you-go basis by employers' contributions. Such schemes are known as 'unfunded schemes' and they apply mainly to the civil service. In an unfunded scheme, the employer has to be prepared to pay whatever total of contributions is necessary to meet the pensions currently being paid.

The basic working of a funded scheme is shown in Diagram 3.2. When the employee starts work there is an annual flow of saving into the scheme comprising the employee's contribution and the employer's contribution (this flow is not shown on the diagram).

DIAGRAM 3.2   *A funded superannuation sheme*

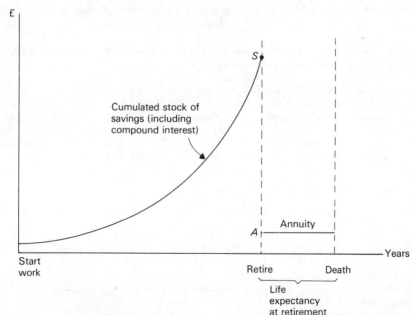

These contributions are left to accumulate, but as each year's contribution will be invested and will earn (compound) interest throughout the employee's working life, the cumulated stock of savings will grow in the manner shown. Eventually, at retirement, the annual contributions plus compound interest will amount to £S, and this capital sum of accumu-

---

*Some pension schemes, instead of giving a pension of n/60ths of final salary (where n = years of pensionable service), give a smaller fraction together with a lump sum (usually related to final earnings at retirement).

lated saving can then be used to purchase an annuity of £A per annum, where the basic formula for computing A is:

$$A = \frac{S}{\text{Life expectancy at retirement}}$$

Although, as explained, this calculation will in practice be modified by the addition of interest on the remaining balance, by the deduction of administration costs and by 'smoothing' to give a constant, instead of a diminishing, annual payment.

Although the state now pays a National Insurance retirement pension to all employees and self-employed, the annual National Insurance retirement pension permits only the barest standard of living, so it is most attractive for an employee to have an additional occupational pension, especially as the employer bears part of the cost of the contributions. Accordingly, as shown in Table 3.11, membership of occupational pension schemes has grown rapidly from 2.6 million employees in 1936 to 11.8 million in 1979, and the coverage of such schemes has increased from 13 per cent of employees to 51 per cent. The public sector has always tended to be ahead of the private sector in the provision of occupational pension schemes and, as shown in Table 3.12, in 1979 nearly three-quarters of public-sector employees were members of occupational pension schemes, whereas only about 40 per cent of private-sector employees were so. (Because public-sector employment has tended to grow faster than private sector employment, this has also boosted the relative coverage of occupational pension schemes.)

Most of the schemes are confined to salaried 'white-collar' workers: that is, to higher-paid employees, though there are also some schemes for lower-paid 'blue-collar' workers. Higher-paid workers can afford to save a larger proportion of their pay, and so these

TABLE 3.11   *Employees in superannuation schemes in the United Kingdom, 1936 to 1979*

	Millions					
	Employees in superannuation schemes			Number of pensions being paid [b]	Employees in employment [c]	Percentage of employees in superannuation schemes
Year	Private sector	Public sector [a]	Total			
1936	1.6	1.0	2.6	0.2	20.7 [d]	13
1953	3.1	3.1	6.2	0.9	21.9	28
1956	4.3	3.7	8.0	1.1	22.7	35
1963	7.2	3.9	11.1	1.8	22.9	48
1967	8.1	4.1	12.2	2.3	23.2	53
1971	6.8	4.3	11.1	2.9	22.4	50
1975	6.0	5.4	11.4	3.4	23.0	50
1979	6.2	5.6	11.8	3.8	23.2	51

[a] Including HM Forces.
[b] Payments to former employees and to their widows and dependants.
[c] Excluding self-employed and unemployed; including HM Forces.
[d] Figure for 1936 includes self-employed.

Sources: Government Actuary, *Occupational Pension Schemes 1975*, fifth survey by the Government Actuary (HMSO, 1978) tables 3.2 and 4.1, pp. 9 and 19; C. H. Feinstein, *National Income, Expenditure and Output of the United Kingdom 1855–1965* (Cambridge University Press, 1972) table 57, p. T126; Department of Employment, *British Labour Statistics Historical Abstract 1886–1968* (HMSO, 1971) table 118, p. 220; Department of Employment, *British Labour Statistics Year Book 1976* (HMSO, 1978) table 55, p. 122; Department of Employment, *Employment Gazette*, December 1980, 'Pension scheme members in 1979', tables 1, 2 and 3, pp. 1209–10.

schemes, with fewer contributors paying relatively large contributions, are administrative-ly more convenient. There are now many hundreds of occupational pension schemes in the United Kingdom, and Table 3.13 gives a few examples from the big to the small. It is the growth in number and size of schemes such as these which partly explains why the annual net acquisition by the personal sector of financial assets with superannuation schemes and life assurance (shown together in Table 3.7) is now so large. The other part is explained by the increase in life assurance, to which we now turn.

TABLE 3.12 *Membership of occupational pension schemes in 1979*

Sector	Millions		
	Members of occupational pension schemes	Total UK employment	Members of schemes as percentage of UK employment
Private sector			
Establishments with less than 100 employees	0.74	5.80	13
Establishments with 100 or more employees	5.46	9.90	55
All establishments	6.20	15.70	39
Public corporations	1.90	2.06	92
Central government (civilians)	1.54	2.00	77
Local authorities	1.85	3.07	60
Sub-total: public sector	5.29	7.13	74
Sub-total: civil employment	11.49	22.83	50
HM Forces	0.31	0.32	97
Grand total	11.80	23.15	51

Source: Department of Employment, *Employment Gazette*, December 1980, 'Pension scheme members in 1979', table 3, p. 1210.

TABLE 3.13 *Some examples of superannuation schemes, 1978*

	Number in United Kingdom		£ million	
	Current members	Pensioners	Annual contributions	Capital value of fund
Universities Superannuation Scheme	47,000	1,500	39.6	365
ICI Staff Pension Fund	35,500	20,500	36.9	384
ICI Workers' Pension Fund	52,000	29,000	25.0	188
British Rail Superannuation Fund (staff) and BR Pension Fund (operatives)	210,000	54,000	113.0	800
Daily Telegraph Pension Fund	3,000	500	0.7	4
ATV (Central TV) Pension Scheme	2,850	300	1.7	15

Source: National Association of Pension Funds, *Year Book 1979*.

Life insurance and life assurance

The economic analysis of life assurance is a little complex because there are two different but related issues. The first is insurance proper against the risk of death within a certain short time period such as a year. In this, life insurance is just like any other insurance, say against one's house burning down. The second is to plan against the inevitability of eventual death. Because there is no inevitability that one's house must burn down, there is no need to plan against that contingency (as opposed to insuring against the risk); but because death is inevitable it is sensible to plan for it. It is the inevitability of death which gives life assurance its second aspect: namely, the provision of a sum of money at a future date. In principle, this sum of money should provide a benefit to one's heirs and dependants, but in practice the sum may also be obtained and used by the insured before he or she dies. This second aspect of life assurance can perhaps be understood if we imagine a mysterious law of nature whereby all houses inevitably burned down eighty years after being built. If this were the case, then all house-owners would seek not only to insure against the short-term risk of fire but also to assure themselves, by saving over a long period of time, of a sum of money sufficient to replace the house when it suffered its inevitable fate. It is sometimes said that the purpose of life assurance is 'to spread the risk of death over a period of time' but this statement confuses the two issues:

(1)   *insuring* against the risk of death during any one year;
(2)   *assuring* a sum of money against the certainty (not the risk) of death.

It is, of course, this second aspect that makes life assurance schemes closely akin to superannuation schemes.

Let us consider the first aspect first. If you look at Table 3.10, you will see that for a man aged 20, there is a probability of 0.00106, or 106 in a 100,000, of his dying within one year. So that, if a life insurance company were to insure for one year 100,000 English males aged 20 against the risk of death for £1,000 each, it could expect that 106 would die within the year, and it would therefore have to pay out £106,000. Thus, if the life insurance company charges each of the 100,000 men a life insurance premium of £1.06 per £1,000 insured, it should break even on the operation. This we shall call 'the breakeven' premium.*

In fact, it should more than break even, because it will have the use through part of the year of £106,000 on which it can earn interest. If the deaths occur at an even rate throughout the year – one every three-and-a-half days – then the insurance company should have an average bank balance of £53,000, and if that were earning 5 per cent per annum interest, the company would earn £2,650 interest. But against this there would be administration expenses, so even allowing for interest, the premium might have to be a little higher than £1.06 per £1,000.

However, at the breakeven premium of £1.06 per £1,000, life insurance looks very attractive to the young man who may want to see that his wife and young baby were not left destitute in the event of his death. For £31.80 a year, or 61p a week, he can insure his life for £30,000, which would provide something for his widow and child.

One can see from Table 3.10 that as one gets older, the annual breakeven life insurance premiums must rise. For males aged 40 the breakeven premium is £2.26 per £1,000, and at 65 the breakeven premium is £34.53 per £1,000. Now, most people want life insurance each year but as one gets beyond 65 the annual premiums become too high. So consider the following scheme for a man aged 20. His prospective working life is forty-five years and suppose he would like (a) to have his life insured each year until then, but (b) if he were still alive at 65, to receive £1,000. If we divide £1,000 by 45, we have an annual contribution of £22.22; suppose that the insurance company then offers the twofold scheme: in return for the breakeven life insurance premium *plus* an annual contribution of £22.22, the insurance company will (1) provide the man's estate with £1,000 in the event of his death, or (2) pay the man himself £1,000 should he still be alive at 65.

This twofold scheme is shown on Diagram 3.3. Along the horizontal axis we mark the man's age in years; up the vertical axis we measure the annual premium per £1,000 of

---

*Please note that we are using this concept simply for the purpose of providing an elementary exposition, in terms of basic vital statistics and economics, of life insurance.

DIAGRAM 3.3   *A life assurance scheme*

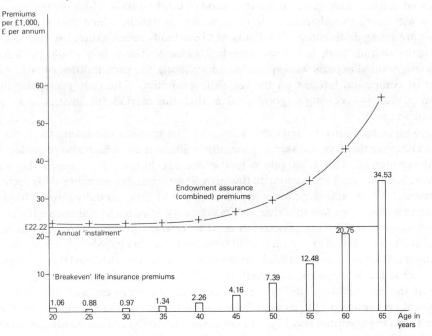

insurance. The first thing to do is to draw in the 'breakeven' life insurance premiums taken from the *English Life Table No. 13, 1970–2*. These show the annual premium per £1,000 of life insurance; for example, it costs a man of age 20 £1.06 to insure his life for £1,000 for one year; a man of age 45 £4.16, and so on. The next thing to do is to calculate the annual 'instalment' necessary to accumulate savings of £1,000 by the age of 64 (that is, £1,000/45 = £22.22). Finally, if we add the 'breakeven' life insurance premium to the annual 'instalment', we get, as shown by the linked crosses, the total annual premium necessary at any age to pay for a life insurance policy which (1) pays £1,000 in the event of the man's death before the age of 65, and (2) pays the man £1,000 at the age of 65 if he is then alive. Such a twofold scheme is known as 'endowment life assurance' because it provides, in addition to life insurance, an 'endowment' of £1,000 at the age of 65 if the man is still alive. It is, of course, possible to obtain an endowment assurance scheme for any multiple of £1,000; for an endowment assurance of £10,000 one would simply multiply all the figures on the vertical axis by 10.

It should be noted that Diagram 3.3 represents only the basic principles of an endowment assurance scheme. In actual practice, the schemes are complicated by the fact that life assurance companies will usually not quote a rising annual premium, as shown by the linked crosses, but will quote a constant annual premium which collects the same total over the forty-five years; this is done by charging more in the early years and less in the later years. Furthermore, and most importantly, we have calculated the annual instalment simply by dividing £1,000 by 45, the number of years over which the 'instalments' are to be paid, but in practice the annual 'instalment' element would be much less than this because each (lower) instalment will be invested at compound interest to provide the total savings of £1,000 in forty-five years' time. Finally, we have made no allowance for administration charges. However, endowment assurance is much more 'expensive' than pure life insurance: for example, for a man aged 30, to insure his life for fifteen years would cost about £1.70 per annum per £1,000 of insurance, but endowment *assurance*, with a return of a capital sum of £1,000 at age 45, would cost about £50 per annum per £1,000. (The marked effect of compound interest can be seen in this premium: because our simple calculation gives £1,000/15 = £66.67 and the actual annual premium quoted by life assurance companies is 25 per cent lower. Clearly, working out the 'right' premiums, premiums which lead neither to too great an accumulation of surplus funds, which means that insured persons are being overcharged, nor to a mounting deficit, which means that insured persons are being undercharged and may not eventually receive their benefits due to the bankruptcy of the fund, is a very complex business. There is a whole profession of 'actuaries', trained experts who specialise in assessing the probabilities of risks and the impact of compound interest on the requisite premiums. The only guarantee that the insured person is receiving a good deal is that the market for insurance is quite a competitive one.)

Endowment assurance policies are a form of savings-with-life-insurance scheme. As such, you can see that they are akin to superannuation schemes which also provide a capital sum at retirement. This is largely why the two are lumped together in the national accounts. Such endowment assurance has proved an attractive form of savings scheme to the personal sector, and large amounts of money now flow annually into such schemes. This is partly due to the fact that there is a tax concession on such premiums which reduces their effective cost. The tax concession used to operate by permitting the taxpayer to deduct $16\frac{1}{2}$ per cent of the premiums paid from his or her tax payable; for example, if one were paying £100 per annum in life assurance premiums one calculated the tax payable on gross income less allowances, and then, from the tax payable, one deducted £16.50, to arrive at the over-all tax liability. From April 1979 the system was changed and the taxpayer then deducted $17\frac{1}{2}$ per cent from the premium due (as calculated per Diagram 3.3) and paid the premium less $17\frac{1}{2}$ per cent deduction to the life assurance company. The life assurance company then claimed the deducted $17\frac{1}{2}$ per cent direct from the Inland Revenue. The taxpayer, of course, is not now able to make any deduction from his tax bill on account of life assurance premiums. So far as everybody is concerned, the net result is the same, except for the fact that the rate of 'relief' was increased from $16\frac{1}{2}$ per cent of premiums to $17\frac{1}{2}$ per cent and then reduced to 15 per cent in 1981–2.

We have mentioned only the two basic types of life assurance policy: pure insurance for one year against risk of death, and endowment assurance, which, for an increased premium, not only insures against death but also provides an endowment or capital sum at a stated age, usually 65. However, it is possible to take out pure life insurance for a term of years, such as five or ten years, paying the requisite annual premium, and this is known as 'term assurance': it is simply the annual insurance extended for the stated period. A 'whole life policy' is an endowment assurance scheme with the stipulation that the capital sum is payable only at the holder's death (not, say, at retirement). With whole life policies, it is usual to cease paying premiums at age 65. Many endowment assurance schemes are 'with-profits', which means that some of the capital gains profits made from investing your premiums are added on to the endowment; 'with-profits' premiums may be a bit more expensive but as a way of obtaining some protection against inflation the extra expense tends to be worth while.

The nature of the connection between pension schemes and life assurance schemes can now be seen. Not only are both based on the *Life Table*, but also an annuity is the converse of a whole life policy. To get an annuity, one pays a lump sum now in return for an annual payment until one's death; to get a whole life policy one pays annual premiums (for a certain period) in return for a lump sum on one's death. An endowment assurance policy is equivalent to a superannuation scheme *plus* the provision of life insurance up to the 'maturity' date when the lump sum becomes due (if one is still alive). For this reason, many superannuation schemes also contain life insurance provisions ('death in service' benefits). Such provisions might provide, for example, an annuity to one's widow; in effect, the life insurance cover would be used to purchase that annuity.

Such provision of financial security for one's retirement and/or for one's dependants is an attractive proposition for most households. It is a wise parent who takes out some term assurance on the birth of each child (say for fifteen or twenty years to cover the period until the child becomes financially independent).* A final attraction about endowment assurance needs to be noted. If one borrows money from a building society to buy a house, only the payment of interest on the loan is tax deductible; the annual instalments repaying the loan are not tax deductible. However, it is possible to take out an endowment assurance policy (maturing, say, at 65) to cover the amount of the loan, and then to assign the policy to the building society (that is, the building society will collect the lump sum on retirement or death). One then pays only interest (tax deductible) to the building society, and makes repayment via the endowment assurance (also attracting a tax concession). Endowment assurance can also be used to pay for a child's (private) education: the parent pays premiums in advance, claiming the tax-deductible concession, and then, after the requisite period or at the parent's death, the assurance company will pay an agreed sum towards school fees. If the parent simply paid the school fees himself, he would not be able to obtain the benefit of the tax concession.

So, as we have seen in Tables 3.9 and 3.11, there has been a considerable growth in the flow of funds into life assurance and superannuation schemes and in membership of superannuation schemes. Membership of superannuation schemes was, in 1979, 11.8 million, or about half of the total number of employees in employment. Given that superannuation schemes are so obviously attractive, perhaps we ought to ask why the other 11.4 million employees are *not* members of pension schemes. From the 1975 survey by the Government Actuary, we know that 3.5 million employees were then employed with an employer who had no occupational pension scheme, and 3.7 million employees were employed by an employer who had a scheme but they were not members because their job was ineligible for membership of the scheme (1.7 million) or because they were excluded by reason of being only part-time or temporary employees (2 million). A further 2.6 million employees were not members of schemes because they were too young or too old or their service was too short. One million employees had refused to join schemes (joining means that the employee's contribution will be deducted from wages). While there appears to be scope for further expansion of pension schemes among those employers who have no schemes, we know that these tend to be concentrated among the smaller companies (small in terms of employment) who may be more cautious about committing themselves to paying employers' contributions to pensions, and it may be that the lack of relative expansion since 1967 will continue.

One important feature in the expansion of pension schemes is that, initially, contributions (from employers and employees) rise much more quickly than do payments to pensioners: between 1953 and 1963, membership of occupational pension schemes rose by 4.9 million, while the number of pensions being paid rose by only 0.9 million (see Table 3.11). This meant that superannuation schemes built up large accumulations of financial assets. Between 1963 and 1979, membership did not expand much but the number of pensioners grew by a further 2 million. However, superannuation schemes and life assurance schemes still have a substantial surplus for investment each year.

Table 3.14 shows the incomings, outgoings and surpluses during 1980 of the life assurance and superannuation schemes in the United Kingdom. The funded schemes, including life assurance, received a total income of £19.9 billion: £6.2 billion from employers' contributions; £2 billion from employees' contributions; £4.7 billion for life insurance premiums; and £6.9 billion from interest and dividends on their financial assets and from rent on property (the pension funds tend to own considerable amounts of

*'Term assurance' is the (somewhat confusing) phrase used by insurance companies for life insurance coverage during a specified term of years, say ten or twenty years, during which term your annual premiums simply cover your heirs (dependants) against your death during the term; there is no end-term endowment capital sum should you survive.

TABLE 3.14   *Incomings, outgoings and surpluses of life assurance and superannuation schemes in 1980*

	£ million
Funded schemes (including life assurance)	
Contributions of employers	6,204
Contributions of employees	1,950
Individual premiums for life policies [a]	4,744
Rent, dividends and interest receipts	6,936
Transfers from notionally funded schemes	33
Total receipts	19,867
Pensions and other benefits paid	7,146
Administrative costs, and taxes	1,920
Total outgoings	9,066
Surplus available for investment	10,801
Notionally funded schemes[b]	
Contributions of employers	728
Contributions of employees	645
Pensions and other benefits paid[c]	1,061
Surplus available for investment	312
Unfunded schemes	
Contributions of employers and employees	2,328
Pensions and other benefits paid	2,328
Total net acquisition of assets by life assurance and superannuation schemes	11,113

[a] Including premium (tax) relief from central government to life assurance funds of £524 million in 1980.

[b] Involving some contributions from employees but where the employer pays the future pension out of future income without setting up a fund.

[c] Including transfer of liabilities to funded schemes.

Source: Central Statistical Office, *National Income and Expenditure 1981 Edition*, table 4.5, p. 31.

commercial property). The schemes paid out only £7.1 billion by way of pensions (annuities) and life assurance payments (for deaths or endowments), and incurred £1.9 billion of administrative costs (including tax on their investment income). This left a net surplus for funded schemes and life assurance of nearly £10.8 billion with which to acquire financial assets and real assets against their future liabilities. The notionally funded and unfunded schemes which receive nearly all their income from employers' contributions operate basically on a pay-as-you-go basis and so had only a relatively small surplus of £312 million. The total surplus of the funded and unfunded schemes during 1980 was £11,113 million and this surplus is deemed to belong to the personal sector because households are the beneficiaries (present or eventual) of these assets.

An over-all view

The net acquisition of financial assets by the personal sector then 'closes the books' on the personal-sector accounts for 1980. Looking at these accounts has been a lengthy process (although the reader must by now realise that our scrutiny has been but an introductory glance at a complex reality).

Diagram 3.4 provides a summary picture of the flows leading up to the personal sector's

DIAGRAM 3.4   *Personal-sector accounts*

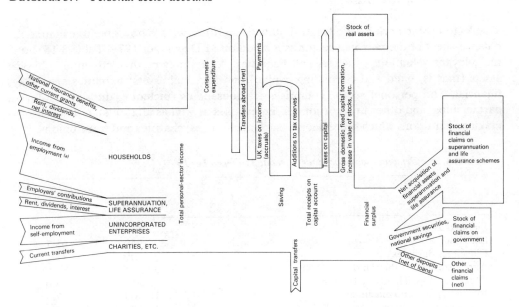

(a) Excluding employers' contributions.

financial surplus. We begin with all the inflows on the income and expenditure account, marking the distinctions among the sub-sectors of the personal sector. (Diagram 3.4 is not drawn exactly to scale.) All these flows add up to a total personal-sector income of £200,985 million in 1980. From this income are disbursed the various current expenditures: consumers' expenditure; net transfers abroad; and taxes on income (accruals of liabilities). The remaining balance on income and expenditure is saving, the flow which is transferred or 'carried down' to the capital account as a receipt. There it is joined by the flow of capital transfers and also by the additions to tax reserves; accruals of tax liabilities are divided into two streams – a stream of payments, and a stream of (temporarily) retained additions to tax reserves which will (temporarily) supplement the personal sector's holdings of financial assets. Together these make up the total receipts on capital account. From these receipts are paid taxes on capital and expenditure on capital formation (including the increase in the book value of inventories). This latter flow of expenditure, unlike all the other flows, does not leave the personal sector, but flows into the 'pool', or balance-sheet, of real assets owned by the personal sector. The remaining balance on capital account is the personal sector's net acquisition of financial assets. As this flow has for many years been positive, we may call it a financial surplus. As we have seen, there are very many types of financial assets which the personal sector acquires each year, as well as several sorts of liabilities (such as loans from building societies). But we may divide the flow of financial-asset acquisition net of liabilities taken on into three main categories: the largest is the net flow of funds into the superannuation and life assurance schemes; there is also the inflow into government securities and national savings, including here the acquisition of notes and coin, and all financial transactions with local authorities; and a third residual category comprises all other net financial transactions (acquisition of assets with net acquisition of liabilities to). This comprises financial transactions with banks (deposits net of loans), with building societies, and with all other financial institutions and companies. These three flows of financial transactions again do not leave the personal sector but flow into the balance-sheets of financial assets and liabilities belonging to the personal sector.

Personal-sector balance-sheet

Thanks to recent work by the Central Statistical Office, we are now able to examine the balance-sheet of the personal sector as it stood on 31 December 1979. Table 3.15 shows the relevant valuations of assets and liabilities. Assets may be divided among physical assets (that is, fixed and circulating capital) and financial assets; liabilities are always financial. The personal sector comprises all households (including the self-employed, partnerships, and other unincorporated enterprises as well as all farms) and non-profit-making institutions which serve people, such as churches, charities and trade unions.

TABLE 3.15   *Personal-sector balance-sheet at 31 December 1979*

	£ million	Percentage of sub-totals
Physical assets		
Dwellings	270,949	65.7
Consumer durables	71,100	17.2
Agricultural and other land	32,791	8.0
Other developed land and buildings	16,618	4.0
Vehicles, plant and machinery	10,400	2.5
Stocks and work in progress	10,372	2.5
Sub-total: physical assets	412,230	100
Financial assets		
Equity in life assurance and pension funds	76,000	32.0
Building society shares and deposits	42,207	17.8
Company and overseas securities, unit trusts	35,060	14.8
Sight and other bank deposits (inc. savings banks)	37,714	15.9
National savings (inc. SAYE)	10,725	4.5
British government securities	9,900	4.2
Notes and coin	7,784	3.3
Local authority and other public-sector securities [a]	3,724	1.6
Trade and other debtors in United Kingdom (accounts receivable)	8,000	3.4
Property overseas	380	0.2
Other [b]	5,985	2.5
Sub-total: financial assets	237,479	100
Liabilities		
Loans for house purchase [d]	44,964	64.2
Bank loans and advances (exc. house purchase)	11,647	16.6
Creditors and accounts payable	5,900	8.4
Hire purchase and other instalment debt	4,315	6.2
Other liabilities [c]	3,230	4.6
Sub-total: financial liabilities	70,056	100
Net wealth (including property overseas)	579,653	—

[a] Comprising temporary deposits with local authorities, certificates of tax deposit, Ulster savings certificates and bonds, Northern Ireland government securities, local authority listed securities and bonds, other public corporation securities, long-term loans to local authorities.

[b] Comprising deposits with finance houses, short-term loans not elsewhere included, other long-term loans, and accrued interest, tax, etc.

[c] Comprising commercial bills, short-term loans not elsewhere included, other public-sector loans, other long-term loans, and accrued interest, tax, etc.

[d] Of which (in £ million): building societies 36,981; banks, 2,370; public sector 3,744; insurance societies 1,847; trustee savings banks, 22.

Source: Central Statistical Office, *Financial Statistics*, February 1982, supplementary table S12, p. 158; see also Central Statistical Office, *Personal sector balance sheets and current developments in Inland Revenue estimates of personal wealth*, Studies in Official Statistics No. 35 (HMSO, 1978).

This balance-sheet differs slightly from the flows and stocks reported in the national accounts: in the first place the value of consumer durables and private vehicles is included (in the national accounts flows of expenditure on acquiring these assets are counted as part of current expenditure in the income and expenditure account); in the second place the value of land owned is included, but the national accounts figures on the stock of physical capital owned by the personal sector excludes this (as well as consumer durables and private vehicles). Nevertheless, despite the national accounting conventions, consumer durables do form a subjectively important part of households' holdings of fixed capital, and so should be included in a reckoning of household balance-sheets; from Table 3.15 we can see that consumer durables also form an objectively (i.e. quantitatively) important part of the personal sector's ownership of physical assets.

However, as one might expect, most of the sector's ownership of physical assets is in dwellings: the value of dwellings is nearly two-thirds of the total value of physical assets owned by the personal sector.

Because of the inclusion in the personal sector of farms, partnerships and the self-employed, etc., the personal sector is also reported as owning considerable amounts of stocks and work in progress (agricultural circulating capital), of agricultural and other land, and of other developed land and buildings (e.g. the offices and shops belonging to the partnerships, the self-employed). Non-profit-making bodies in the personal sector (such as charities, trade unions, universities, churches), also own most of their physical assets in the form of other developed land and buildings. All in all, the personal sector owned £412 billion worth of physical assets at the end of 1979.

A great deal of the personal sector's wealth is held in the form of financial assets. The total value of financial assets belonging to the household sector at end-1979 was £237 billion. This is the gross value of assets held: that is, it takes no account of counterbalancing financial liabilities. The personal sector was estimated to have held £8 billion of notes and coin at the end of 1979; about £140 per person of the population. But it is difficult to know quite what to make of this figure. In the first place, the date is just after Christmas when, one assumes, people's holdings of cash might have been depleted (due to buying Christmas presents); or, perhaps, holdings of cash might have been boosted by people anticipating the New Year sales! Furthermore, the *per capita* figure must be increased by the presence of unincorporated enterprises such as farms and the self-employed.

Two big items of personal-sector financial assets are deposits with banks (both at current-account or 'sight' deposits and interest-bearing deposits) and with building societies. But these financial assets are before we take account of the corresponding financial liabilities of outstanding loans from banks and building societies.

Another large item of financial assets is personal-sector holdings of company and overseas securities, broadly known as 'shares' or 'equities'. As we have seen, the personal sector has tended each year to reduce its holdings of these securities – a reduction which has been ascribed to sales of shares from the estates of the deceased.

The largest single item of households' financial assets is their stake in the funds of life assurance and occupational pension schemes, amounting to £76 billion at the end of 1979. Looking back at Table 3.9, we can see that personal-sector net acquisition of such funds during 1980 amounted to £11.1 billion, so we can see that this stake tends to be growing at a rapid rate: around 15 per cent per annum.

All in all, the personal sector owned nearly £237 billion worth of financial assets at the end of 1979.

The personal sector also has a number of financial liabilities: not only to banks and to building societies, but also to the finance companies who make available hire-purchase credit and other 'instalment debt', i.e. liabilities incurred mainly for the purchase of consumer durables and repayable in regular instalments. Households also have a large amount, £5.9 billion, of debt outstanding in the form of accounts payable and to other creditors; this will comprise things like electricity, gas and telephone bills due for payment, as well as accounts to be settled with shopkeepers, other suppliers, and so on. The average amount appears to be about £295 per household (assuming about 20 million households in the United Kingdom); but, again, we do not know whether this figure is temporarily boosted by Christmas, nor to what extent the figure is affected by farmers' and the self-employed's accounts payable.

All in all, the personal sector 'owned' about £70 billion of financial liabilities at the end of 1979; that is to say, the sector owed this amount to other sectors.

The net wealth of any person, household or other organisation may be defined as:

$$\text{Net wealth} = \begin{array}{c}\text{Value of}\\ \text{physical}\\ \text{assets owned}\end{array} + \begin{array}{c}\text{Value of}\\ \text{financial}\\ \text{assets owned}\end{array} - \begin{array}{c}\text{Value of}\\ \text{financial}\\ \text{liabilities owed}\end{array}$$

So the net wealth of the personal sector at the end of 1979 was £580 billion.

If we divide the personal sector's net wealth by the 1979 mid-year population of 55,881 million, we can see that wealth holdings were £10,373 per person. The average size of household in the United Kingdom was about 2.8 persons, so that there were then about 20 million households, and this would give an average net wealth per household of £28,983 at the end of 1979.

'Saving' is different from 'financial-asset acquisition'

In common parlance the word 'saving' is often used to refer to the (net) acquisition of financial assets, but in economics it is important to maintain (and to understand) the distinction between the two: saving is the balance of flows on current account (the excess of current income over current expenditure) and is used either to acquire capital (real assets) or financial assets. The net acquisition of financial assets (what people often mean by 'saving') is the balance of capital-account receipts over capital-account expenditure (on real assets) and so is a flow quite distinct from the flow of saving (in the economist's use of the term).

There has been a lot of discussion about what determines the pattern of personal-sector spending, and we shall return to this question subsequently. At this point I just wish to remark that the arrangement of the accounts may tempt us into regarding the net acquisition of financial assets by the personal sector as a *residual*: that is, financial assets are what you acquire out of whatever happens to be left over from your income after your current-account and capital-account expenditures have been paid for. Now, although the net acquisition of financial assets appears, like a residual, at the end of the accounts, this should not be taken to imply that financial-asset acquisition is simply the leftovers. It might well be the case that households operate with a budget the first item of which is the acquisition of financial assets (to provide security for the family), the second item being capital expenditure to purchase a house (to provide shelter), the third item (no choice here) being payment of taxes, leaving expenditure on consumption as the difference between income and planned financial and real asset acquisition (after allowing for taxes, etc.). In the economic or behavioural sense, consumers' expenditure could merely be the 'residual' flow. In fact, it is likely that households try to reach an over-all balance by considering all their needs – for consumption, for real-asset purchase, and for financial-asset acquisition – simultaneously, so that it is probably not sensible to regard any of the flows as 'residuals'. This is just a warning not to be led astray by accounting conventions.

The consumption function

If it is reasonable to suppose that, in regard to their use of income, households try to achieve some sort of 'balance' in their expenditures, saving and financial-asset acquisition, then can we discern any regular pattern in the relationship between income and expenditure? That is to say, if we suppose that households try to allocate their income in accordance with some preferences, so making definite decisions and not just acting haphazardly and randomly, then it ought to be the case that patterns of expenditure conform to some regularity. Following on from this, because consumers' expenditure takes up proportionately the largest share of total personal-sector income, is it therefore the case that the relationship between consumers' expenditure and income is over time or among households a reasonably stable one exhibiting the supposed regularity of behaviour?

Appendix 3.1 provides the figures on consumers' expenditure and total personal-sector income in the United Kingdom for the years 1946 to 1980 inclusive. If we take consumers' expenditure as a proportion of total personal-sector income and plot these proportions for each of the years in Diagram 3.5, then we can see that there is a regularity in the 'average propensity to consume' (as we shall call the ratio between total consumers' expenditure and total personal-sector income). Although the average propensity to consume does not change much from year to year, it does tend to decline slowly over the period as a whole, from something over 0.8 in the early years (1946 to 1959) to between 0.8 and 0.75 in the period 1960 to 1969 and to something below 0.75 in the 1970s. What could explain both the year-to-year regularity and the slow downward trend of the average propensity to consume?

DIAGRAM 3.5   *The relationship between consumers' expenditure and personal-sector income*

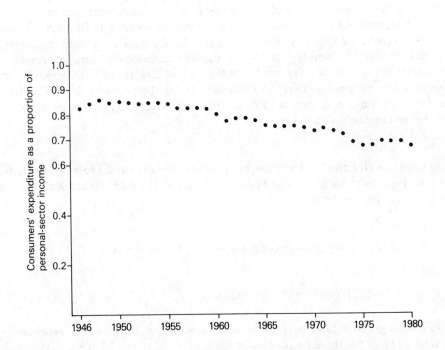

Our basic supposition is that there is some definite relationship between consumers' expenditure and income. This assumed relationship says, moreover, that the amount of customers' expenditure is related to, or depends upon, personal-sector income. To put exactly the same idea a little more technically, we may say that consumers' expenditure is a function of personal-sector income. The point of doing this is to write this technical statement as follows:

$$\text{Consumers' expenditure} = f \,(\text{Personal-sector income})$$

where the symbol '*f*' followed by brackets and preceded by an equals sign means that the 'dependent' variable on the left-hand side of the equals sign is dependent on, or being 'caused' by, the independent variable (or variables if there are more than one) mentioned in the brackets. The implication of writing the statement in this technical form is that the independent variable 'causes', or explains the amount of, the dependent variable. (In analysing economic data, we shall be much concerned, first with general statements which assert that one variable is a function of another variable, and second with ascertaining more specifically the precise form of that function.)

Now, if the functional relationship between consumers' expenditure and personal-sector income were of the specific straight-line, or linear, form then we have:

$$\frac{\text{Consumers'}}{\text{expenditure}} = a + b \,(\text{Personal-sector income})$$

where the symbols '*a*' and '*b*' are constants, or parameters, of the relationship which relate the independent variable to the dependent variable. Note that *a* and *b* are called *constants* or *parameters* in order to contrast them to consumers' expenditure and income, which are both called *variables* because they can vary (from year to year in the time series of Appendix 3.1, or among households, as the case may be). Such a general relationship between consumers' expenditure and personal-sector income is known as a 'consumption function'. The consumption function need not be of the simple linear form just given; and it might include other independent, explanatory variables. But, for the present analysis, we shall use this particular specification of the general consumption function. Now if the parameter *a* in the specific consumption function is positive (is greater than zero) and if the parameter *b* is positive but less than one (is a fraction between 0 and 1), then, providing income is rising over time, we have a relationship which is capable of explaining the pattern charted in Diagram 3.5, namely year-to-year stability and a slow downward trend.

This assertion needs to be explained with the help of Diagram 3.6. Diagram 3.6 shows the specific consumption function just described. Using the symbols '*C*' and '*Y*' to stand for the variables consumers' expenditure and personal-sector income respectively, we can write the consumption function as:

$$C = a + bY$$

This is a linear, or straight-line, relationship because this form of the relationship between *C* and *Y* will appear as a straight line. For example, if *a* = 10 and *b* = 0.5, then if we have *Y* values (in, say, £ per week) of:

40   60   80

we have the corresponding amounts of consumers' expenditure (*C*):

30   40   50

(that is, 10 + 0.5(40), 10 + 0.5(60), 10 + 0.5(80)).

If you draw a graph with income on the horizontal axis and consumers' expenditure on the vertical and plot the three pairs of co-ordinates (40, 30), (60, 40), (80, 50) you will see that a straight line joins the three points. This will be true whatever initial values are chosen for the constants *a* and *b*.

It follows from the equation that when *Y* = 0, *C* = *a*, so the parameter *a* is sometimes called the 'intercept' on the vertical axis. The parameter *a* represents what consumers' expenditure would be in the (hypothetical) case of zero income; but it is reasonable to suppose that, if income fell to zero, people would not stop consuming altogether but would borrow in order to pay for a positive amount of consumers' expenditure. Hence the positive intercept.

DIAGRAM 3.6 *A consumption function*

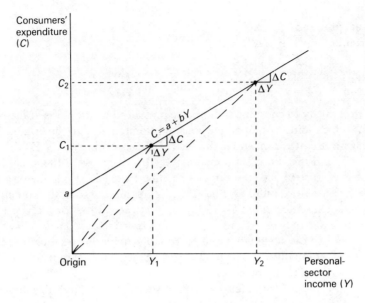

The parameter *b* has a different, and slightly more complicated interpretation, and it is important that this interpretation be fully understood. The slope of a straight line is measured by rise over run. If we say that the slope of a hill-road is 1 in 2, we mean that if we are walking uphill, we rise one yard vertically for every two yards we move horizontally:

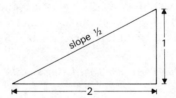

So, the road has a slope of $\frac{1}{2}$, or one-half. A slope of $\frac{1}{4}$, or one-quarter is less steep than a slope of one-half; and a slope of 2 in 1, or 2, is much steeper. In the case of the linear consumption function, the slope of the consumption function is measured by *b*, and it shows the extent to which consumption increases (the extent of the vertical rise) with respect to an increase in income (the extent of the horizontal movement). The Greek symbol capital delta, denoted by 'Δ', is conventionally used to mean 'change in', so 'ΔC' means a change (an increase) in *C*. As shown in Diagram 3.6, the slope, or rise over run, of the consumption function, *b*, is thus equivalent to:

$$b = \frac{\text{Increase in consumption}}{\text{Increase in income}} = \frac{\Delta C}{\Delta Y}$$

Because *b* measures the extent to which an increase in consumption will result from an increase in income, we call *b* 'the marginal propensity to consume'; that is, the extent to which an incremental or marginal change in income will cause a corresponding incremental or marginal change in consumption. The marginal propensity to consume relates only to (relatively small) changes of income and consumption; it is different from the average propensity to consume, which is the relationship between total consumption and total income:

$$\text{Marginal propensity to consume} = \frac{\Delta C}{\Delta Y}$$

$$\text{Average propensity to consume} = \frac{C}{Y}$$

The average propensity to consume is therefore measured by the slope of the broken line in Diagram 3.6 which joins a point on the consumption function to the origin: the slope of such a line is again rise over run, and in the case of the co-ordinate (C_1, Y_1) the rise is total consumption, C_1, and the run is total income, Y_1. If income were to increase to Y_2, the average propensity to consume (the slope of the line from (C_2, Y_2) to the origin) is lower than at the (C_1, Y_1) co-ordinate. So that if the aggregate consumption function for the whole of the personal sector in the United Kingdom were of the form $C = a + bY$ with a greater than zero and b between 0 and 1, then, as income increased from year to year, the average propensity to consume would be reasonably stable in the short run, but in the longer run would gradually decline in the way shown in Diagram 3.5. Is the actual consumption function of this form?

Diagram 3.7 plots the co-ordinates of personal-sector income and consumers' expenditure for each of the years from 1946 to 1980 inclusive (see also Appendix 3.1). The points all fall pretty much along a straight line, and the parameters of this straight line (which fits most closely to all the points) are (in terms of £ million):

$$C = 2,634 + 0.666\ Y$$

The coefficient of correlation between C and Y (see Chapter 1) is 0.9998, so the relationship between the two variables is very close indeed. The intercept, £2,634 million, represents the (very) hypothetical total of consumers' expenditure were total personal-sector income to fall to zero. The slope, 0.666, indicates that for every increase in personal sector income of £1, consumers' expenditure increases by 66.6p; or, the same thing, for

DIAGRAM 3.7   *The consumption function in the United Kingdom, 1946 to 1980*

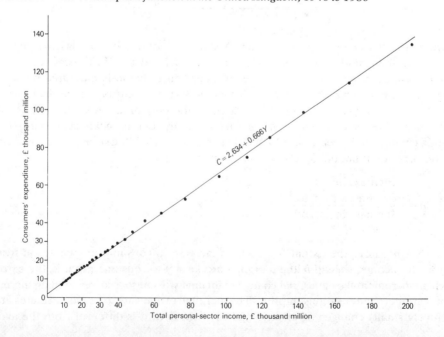

every increase in total personal-sector income of £100 million, consumers' expenditure would increase by £66.6 million. The marginal propensity to consume in the United Kingdom appears to be 0.666 or two-thirds. (I say 'appears to be' because we have to be a little cautious about this result: in the first place this is the simplest possible form of the consumption function and takes no account of, for example, the effect of taxation or stock appreciation; in the second place all the data are at current prices and we have as yet to take the impact of inflation into account. But these are matters which will be dealt with subsequently; the present purpose is simply to become acquainted with the concept of a consumption function, and see that the actual UK data appear to conform to such a regular pattern.)

Thus we have estimated a linear aggregate consumption function for the United Kingdom: 'linear' because the relationship between consumers' expenditure and income appears to be a straight-line one; 'aggregate' because this is a relationship between total, or aggregate, consumers' expenditure and total, or aggregate, personal-sector income. We could use such an aggregate consumption function to forecast the total of consumers' expenditure if we were given an estimate of what personal-sector income would be. For example, if in 1979 we had been told that personal-sector income in 1980 would be £200,985 million (as it actually was), then we could have forecast consumers' expenditure in 1980 (in £ million) as:

$$2,634 + 0.666\,(200,985)$$
$$= 136,490$$

In fact, consumers' expenditure in 1980 turned out to be £135,403 million, so our forecast would have been only 0.8 per cent too large, which is a negligible error.

Cross-section consumption function

When we analyse consumers' expenditure by relating it to total personal-sector income, we find that, taken over a period of time, there appears to be a reasonably stable aggregate consumption function. The presumption is that this is the result of a decision by households to spend or save their income. We regard the household as the basic decision-making unit, and therefore infer that its decisions create the regular pattern of expenditure in relation to income. It is therefore useful to enquire more closely into the pattern of expenditure among different groups of households during the same period. In contrast to the previous *time-series* analysis of aggregate consumers' expenditure, this analysis uses a *cross-section* among households themselves: it is therefore called a cross-section analysis.

The Family Expenditure Survey

Since 1957 the United Kingdom has run an annual survey of household expenditure called the *Family Expenditure Survey*. This is an important source of information on expenditure and income: for instance, Table 3.3 is based on it. It also enables us to analyse the pattern of expenditure and income among households, and so it is worth while becoming acquainted with the survey before we look at the figures themselves.

First of all, the *Family Expenditure Survey* is a sample survey: that is, information is obtained from only a sample of households, not from all households in the United Kingdom. The size of the sample is about 7,000 households: about 11,000 addresses are visited each year by the interviewers of the Office of Population Censuses and Surveys, and about 70 per cent of the households visited agree to co-operate in the survey. Given that there are about 20 million households in the United Kingdom, the sample is only a very small percentage of the total; this is because the emphasis is on obtaining reliable and very detailed data and this requires quite careful supervision by the interviewer of each sampled household.

The interviewer obtains from each member of the household aged 16 and over information on his or her income from all sources, and the interviewer also makes a record of major items of regular expenditure (such as electricity bills, mortgage payments, insurance premiums). The interviewer also records the details of household composition: by age, sex, occupation. Each member of the household aged 16 and over is then given a diary containing fourteen pages, two pages a day for the ensuing week: in these pages the spenders record each and every item of expenditure. At the end of the week, the interviewer calls back, checks that each diary for the first week has been kept satisfactorily, and supplies another diary for the second week. Household expenditure is recorded only for two weeks, so that households are being brought into, and then dropping out of, the survey regularly and continuously throughout the year. This means that the final figures, averaged over all households, are not affected by seasonal factors.

Although great care is taken in collecting and checking information, some care may be required when considering the finer details from the survey. For instance, it is known that spenders tend to underreport the amount spent on alcoholic drink: the estimated average expenditure of all households on alcohol is about 40 per cent below the estimate derived from the statistics produced by HM Customs and Excise! Also there is some difficulty in estimating expenditure on sweets and toys, because the (adult) spenders record only the amount given as pocket-money to children; what the children spend their pocket-money on is not recorded. However, these are problems which affect only a few of the fine details of the survey. The important thing is that, over all and despite its relatively small size, the survey produces reasonably reliable and accurate figures on expenditure. The figures on income may be slightly less reliable; it is suspected that income may be underrecorded, and that higher-income families may be underrepresented in the co-operating households.

Table 3.16 gives the summary details of the 1979 *Family Expenditure Survey*. The households are banded into income groups ranging from households with incomes of under £30 per week to households with incomes of £250 per week or over. The number of sampled households in each income group is given; this shows the small sample size in each group even though a total of 6,777 households provided information to the survey. Next we need to consider the average age of the head of household, because it is quite clear that the households with lowest income are headed by elderly and mostly retired persons (other data indicate a predominance of single-person households in the lower-income brackets and that most of their income is derived from social security benefits, i.e. National Insurance retirement pensions). This bears out what we said previously about the problem of providing an income for one's retirement. In these low-income groups, weekly consumption expenditure tends to exceed weekly income, because the definition of income excludes withdrawals from savings and many elderly persons will be living on their accumulated savings. As income increases, so the average propensity to consume declines: households with incomes from £70 to under £80 per week spent 94 per cent of their income; households with incomes from £200 to under £250 per week spent only 69 per cent of their income. The decline in the average propensity to consume is quite consistent through the income groups.

Diagram 3.8 shows the cross-section consumption function for this sample of UK households in 1979. The correlation coefficient for the straight-line consumption function which best fits the points is 0.995, so the relationship between household average income and household average consumption expenditure is quite a close one. The cross-section data on household income and expenditure confirm the hypothesis that consumers' expenditure tends to be a function of income: it seems that household expenditure is functionally related to household income in a regular and systematic way. This cross-section function gives a different and lower value for the (1979) cross-section marginal

TABLE 3.16　*Weekly income and expenditure per household in the United Kingdom, 1979*

Income bracket, gross normal weekly income per household, £ per week [a]	Number of households in 1979 FES sample	Average age of head of household, in years	Average gross normal weekly income per household £	Average weekly consumption expenditure per household [b] £
Under 30	524	68	25.02	27.51
30 and under　40	507	66	34.51	34.97
40 and under　50	438	64	44.86	46.73
50 and under　60	331	60	54.71	51.68
60 and under　70	294	52	65.03	66.75
70 and under　80	279	48	75.27	70.93
80 and under　90	326	47	84.88	74.07
90 and under 100	354	46	95.01	81.44
100 and under 110	360	45	104.73	86.06
110 and under 120	317	43	114.99	100.13
120 and under 140	696	42	129.85	103.81
140 and under 160	623	43	149.76	113.15
160 and under 180	428	43	169.50	127.99
180 and under 200	339	42	189.42	135.83
200 and under 250	525	45	221.99	153.78
250 or more	436	47	312.01	204.67
All households	6,777	50	120.45	94.17

[a] Income includes all cash receipts from earnings, from interest, etc., on investments, from annuities and pensions, and from social security benefits; it also includes an imputed income from owner-occupancy of dwellings; but it excludes withdrawals from savings and windfall receipts such as legacies or proceeds from the sale of a house.

[b] Comprising all expenditure on current consumption, including purchase of consumer durables; excludes income tax, National Insurance contributions, purchase of dwellings, life assurance premiums, contributions to pension funds, and other financial-asset acquisition.

Source: Department of Employment, *Family Expenditure Survey 1979*, appendix 8, table A, p. 169.

DIAGRAM 3.8　*The cross-section household consumption function in the United Kingdom, 1979*

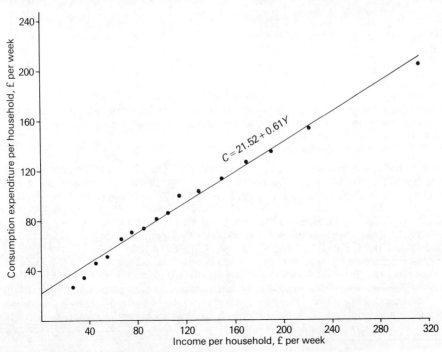

$C = 21.52 + 0.61Y$

propensity to consume of 0.61 as compared with the (1946 to 1980) time-series marginal propensity to consume of 0.67. It may be that in the cross-section data the high-income families are taking time to adjust their consumption upwards, while the low-income families are taking time to adjust their consumption downwards: such a situation would appear as a lower cross-section marginal propensity to consume. There is also a downward 'bias' introduced into the cross-section marginal propensity to consume by the fact that the lower-income households are almost certainly making withdrawals from savings, which withdrawals are not included in income as conventionally defined.

However, these questions of bias and the lower cross-section marginal propensity to consume take us into relatively advanced economic analysis, and we have two other more important issues to hand. The first of these concerns the estimation of the straight-line or linear consumption functions which we have just looked at in Diagrams 3.7 and 3.8. The second is the effect of price inflation on the analysis of income and consumption.

First, by comparing Diagram 3.8, and especially the equation of the straight line, with the last two columns of Table 3.16 (or by comparing Diagram 3.7 with Appendix 3.1), it ought to be obvious that the device of graphing the pairs of observations on the two

TABLE 3.17   *Cross-section household consumption functions in the United Kingdom, 1963 to 1979*

Year of Family Expenditure Survey	Regression constant, or intercept, £ per week	Regression coefficient, or marginal propensity to consume	Correlation coefficient	Number of observations [b]	£ per week Average household income [c]	£ per week Average household expenditure [c]	Average propensity to consume
1963 [a]	4.21	0.660	0.993	9	22.03	19.14	0.869
1964 [a]	4.45	0.634	0.994	9	21.35	19.50	0.913
1965 [a]	5.91	0.604	0.976	9	24.64	21.25	0.863
1966 [a]	4.79	0.628	0.996	9	27.27	22.28	0.817
1967 [a]	4.96	0.635	0.997	12	28.25	23.32	0.826
1968 [a]	5.75	0.625	0.995	12	29.98	24.93	0.832
1969 [a]	5.09	0.624	0.985	12	32.47	26.37	0.812
1970	8.94	0.551	0.992	12	35.40	28.57	0.807
1971	8.76	0.576	0.994	12	38.48	30.99	0.805
1972	7.98	0.629	0.995	12	42.85	35.06	0.818
1973	9.84	0.595	0.993	14	49.41	39.43	0.798
1974	11.73	0.579	0.991	15	58.33	46.13	0.791
1975	13.55	0.561	0.992	16	72.87	54.58	0.749
1976	16.16	0.543	0.995	16	82.30	61.70	0.750
1977	18.57	0.566	0.993	16	92.98	71.84	0.773
1978	19.12	0.578	0.994	16	106.13	80.26	0.756
1979	21.52	0.607	0.995	16	120.45	94.17	0.782

[a] Regression calculated on original data as reported in shillings; regression constant divided by 20 to convert to £s. Average propensity to consume also based on original data.
[b] Number of household income brackets.
[c] Weighted average for all households.

Sources: Calculated from data on average household income and consumption expenditure by income bracket in Department of Employment (formerly Ministry of Labour, etc.): *Family Expenditure Survey 1963*, tables 0 and 2, pp. 12 and 32–3; *Family Expenditure Survey 1964*, tables T and 2, pp. 18–19 and 44–5; *Family Expenditure Survey 1965*, table 2, pp. 28–9 and 36–7; *Family Expenditure Survey 1966*, table 2, pp. 24–5 and 32–3; *Family Expenditure Survey 1967*, table 2, pp. 10–11 and 18–19; *Family Expenditure Survey 1968*, table 3, pp. 16–17 and 24–5; *Family Expenditure Survey 1969*, table 1, pp. 6–7 and 14–15; *Family Expenditure Survey 1970*, appendix 6A, p. 138; *Family Expenditure Survey 1971*, appendix 6A, p. 144; *Family Expenditure Survey 1972*, appendix 6, table A, p. 146; *Family Expenditure Survey 1973*, appendix 6, table A, p. 148; *Family Expenditure Survey 1974*, appendix 6, table A, p. 148; *Family Expenditure Survey 1975*, appendix 6, table A, p. 150; *Family Expenditure Survey 1976*, appendix 7, table A, p. 152; *Family Expenditure Survey 1977*, appendix 7, table A, p. 158; *Family Expenditure Survey 1978*, appendix 8, table A, p. 159; *Family Expenditure Survey 1979*, appendix 8, table A, p. 169.

variables in the space created by the two axes is a 'powerful' way of presenting the lengthy array of information contained in Table 3.16. It is powerful not only because it shows the relationship which exists between the two variables but also because the resulting equation summarises, in one short formula, the whole of the two columns (no matter how long those columns may be). The parameters of the equation also have, as we shall see, important economic implications, and this is generally true of such estimated relationships. For this reason, a considerable amount of economic analysis is based on this sort of equation which summarises a complex set of statistical data. To exemplify this, Table 3.17 shows the estimated cross-section household consumption functions for each year between 1963 (when average income of each of the income brackets was first tabulated) and 1979 inclusive.

Behind each of the rows in Table 3.17 lies the complex sort of information on average household income and expenditure by income bracket which is shown for 1979 in Table 3.16. We can immediately see that the intercept of the cross-section consumption function increases over the period, and this must be largely due to inflation, whereas the marginal propensity to consume tends to decrease slightly; we can also see that the range of variation in the cross-section marginal propensity to consume is not very large: between about 0.66 (1963) and 0.54 (1976). The correlation coefficient tells us that the relationship between the two variables is pretty close in each year. Thus the cross-section consumption function is, by all this evidence, very well supported. Households appear to relate their consumption expenditure to their income in a quite definite and regular way which, allowing for the impact of inflation, does not alter much over time. The average propensity to consume drifts slowly downwards, but this is quite explicable in terms of the regular form of the consumption function with rising average incomes.

The sort of analysis presented in Table 3.17 is therefore much used by economists and accordingly it is necessary to understand how such relationships are estimated.

The method of least squares

If you look at Diagram 3.8 (or Diagram 3.7), you will see that the straight line falls in between the scatter of points representing the paired observations, but naturally it cannot join all the points. The problem is therefore to find that straight line which, in some sense, 'best' or 'most closely' fits the points. A solution to this problem had been invented in 1794 by Karl Friedrich Gauss, then aged 17 (Gauss was one of the world's greatest mathematicians and made important discoveries in many fields including those of astronomy and magnetism). Gauss's solution is known as the *method of least-squares*.

The method of least squares can be explained with the aid of Diagram 3.9. The first part of Diagram 3.9 simply shows three points representing the co-ordinates $(X_1, Y_1), (X_2, Y_2)$ and (X_3, Y_3); we have also drawn in the average or mean of the Y-values, denoted $\bar{Y}$ ('Y-bar'), where:

$$\bar{Y} = \frac{1}{3}(Y_1 + Y_2 + Y_3)$$

or more generally:

$$\bar{Y} = \frac{1}{n} \sum_{i=1}^{n} Y_i$$

The Y-values vary about this mean, as shown by the vertical distances drawn in Diagram 3.9, and the total sum of these distances squared (to avoid negative and positive differences cancelling) is:

$$\Sigma(Y_i - \bar{Y})^2$$

the average of this sum of squares being known as the *variance* of Y. As is shown in the second part of the diagram, which reproduces these three points, it is clear that no straight line can join all these three points; therefore, we have to find that straight line which 'best' fits the points. What is meant by 'best' in this context?

DIAGRAM 3.9   *The method of least squares: 'explaining' why Y varies about its mean*

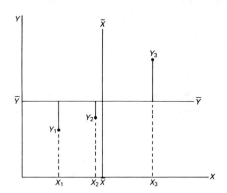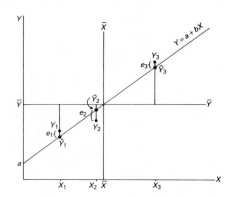

It is clear that the variation of the Y_i about the mean depends in some way upon the corresponding X_i: Y_1 is furthest below $\bar{Y}$, and so X_1 (the corresponding X_i) will be furthest below its mean, $\bar{X}$; at the other end, Y_3 is well above $\bar{Y}$ and so X_3 is also well above $\bar{X}$. This means that the variation of Y_i about the mean $\bar{Y}$ may be 'explained' by the variation of the corresponding X_i about the mean $\bar{X}$. Therefore, if we draw *between* the points some sloping straight line of the form:

$$Y = a + bX$$

we may be able to 'explain' the position of any point Y_i by the equation and the corresponding value of X_i. We can see that the co-ordinates (X_1, Y_1) and (X_3, Y_3) are 'above' the sloping straight line and that the co-ordinate (X_2, Y_2) is 'below' the line; here 'above' and 'below' refer to the vertical distance, the distance along the vertical Y-axis. The value for Y on the sloping straight line corresponding to any value X_i for X we denote by $\hat{Y}_i$, where the symbol '^', commonly referred to as 'hat', denotes an estimated value of Y. So that:

$$\hat{Y}_i = a + bX_i$$

In the next part of Diagram 3.9, the $\hat{Y}_i$ are indicated as exactly on the line. As can be seen, $\hat{Y}_i$ ('Y hat i' or 'estimated Y_i') differs from the actual Y_i by a vertical distance e_i, that is:

$$Y_i - \hat{Y}_i = e_i$$

or:

$$Y_i - (a + bX_i) = e_i$$

where e_i may be positive or negative. These distances, e_i, are known as the residuals.

Now, we can see that the vertical distance of any Y_i from $\bar{Y}$ can be divided into two distinct parts: first, the distance from the (actual) Y_i to the (estimated) $\hat{Y}_i$ (this distance we have called the residual); second, the distance from the (estimated) $\hat{Y}_i$ to $\bar{Y}$. This second distance from the estimated point on the sloping straight line to the average is the distance which is 'explained', or accounted for, by the equation for the sloping straight line in conjunction with the corresponding value of X_i.

To illustrate all this, take the (X_3, Y_3) co-ordinate:

$$Y_3 - \bar{Y} \qquad = Y_3 - \hat{Y}_3 \; + \; \hat{Y}_3 - \bar{Y}$$

(the vertical	(the	(the
distance from	residual	'explained'
Y_3 to $\bar{Y}$)	distance)	distance)

In general:

$$Y_i - \bar{Y} = Y_i - \hat{Y}_i + \hat{Y}_i - \bar{Y}$$
$$= e_i + \hat{Y}_i - \bar{Y}$$

We call the $\hat{Y}_i - \bar{Y}$ part of this distance the 'explained' distance because it is explained by the equation and the corresponding value of X_i. That is, substituting for $\hat{Y}_i$ in the 'explained' distance:

$$\hat{Y}_i - \bar{Y} = a + bX_i - \bar{Y}$$

so we have an 'explanation' in terms of the equation and X_i for this part of the distance of Y from its average. The other part is then the 'unexplained' part of the distance because we have no 'explanation' why the actual Y_i differs from its 'estimated' value.

Of course, we need to consider not only the distances for all the co-ordinates, but also the squared distances, in order that we may relate what we have said above to the total sum of squares of the distances of Y_i about its average: that is, we wish to see how much of the total variance in Y:

$$\frac{1}{n} \Sigma (Y_i - \bar{Y})^2$$

may be 'explained' by the use of the straight-line equation and the corresponding values of X_i. Accordingly:

$$(Y_i - \bar{Y})^2 = (e_i + \hat{Y}_i - \bar{Y})^2$$
$$= e_i^2 + (\hat{Y}_i - \bar{Y})^2 + 2e_i(\hat{Y}_i - \bar{Y})$$

Thus the total sum of squares of deviation of Y_i about the mean is:

$$\Sigma (Y_i - \bar{Y})^2 = \Sigma e_i^2 + \Sigma (\hat{Y}_i - \bar{Y})^2 + 2\Sigma e_i(\hat{Y}_i - \bar{Y})$$

Now, in a large number of observations, the cross-products of e_i and $(\hat{Y}_i - \bar{Y})$ will result in a mixture of positive and negative numbers, so the sum of these is likely to be very small: that is, for practical purposes we can disregard this last, sum of cross-products, term, and concentrate on the sum of squared residuals and the 'explained' sum of squares. If the total sum of squares of Y_i about the average value of Y can be partitioned into two separate component sum of squares (neglecting the sum of cross-products), one of which is 'explained' by the straight-line equation, namely $\Sigma(\hat{Y}_i - \bar{Y})^2$, and the other of which is the residual 'unexplained' sum of squares, namely $\Sigma(Y_i - \hat{Y}_i)^2$, then it makes sense to try and see that the 'unexplained' sum of squares is as small as possible; in this way we shall ensure that the 'explained' sum of squares is, conversely, as large as possible.

The method of least squares is therefore designed to ensure that the sum of all the e_i squared, the 'unexplained' sum of squares, is the minimum attainable. How may this be achieved? We have:

$$e_i = Y_i - \hat{Y}_i$$
$$= Y_i - (a + bX_i)$$
$$= Y_i - a - bX_i$$

Therefore:

$$\Sigma e_i^2 = \Sigma(Y_i - a - bX_i)^2$$

so that Σe_i^2 is a function of the parameters a and b: that is, the values of Y_i and X_i are given to us by the observations, but we can choose various values of a and b. The method of least squares involves ascertaining those values of a and b which will make Σe_i^2 as small as can be obtained.

The value of b which will provide this result is given by the formula:

$$b = \frac{\frac{1}{n}\Sigma(X_i - \bar{X})(Y_i - \bar{Y})}{\frac{1}{n}\Sigma(X_i - \bar{X})^2}$$

$$= \frac{\text{Covariance between } X \text{ and } Y}{\text{Variance of } X}$$

and the corresponding value of a is given by:

$$a = \bar{Y} - b\bar{X}$$

where b is the value from the previous equation (note that in this previous equation we may, if we wish, divide out or cancel the $1/n$). The proof of these assertions involves some calculus and algebra, and I have relegated it to Appendix 3.3. For those who cannot follow Appendix 3.3, this is no matter; the important thing is to appreciate from Diagram 3.9 that the formulae just given are those which will make the sum of squared residuals, Σe_i^2, as small as possible, so, conversely, making the 'explained' sum of squares, $\Sigma(\hat{Y}_i - \bar{Y})^2$, or $\Sigma(a + bX_i - \bar{Y})^2$, as large as possible. This is what is meant by finding the straight line, $a + bX$, which 'best' fits the points (X_1, Y_1), (X_2, Y_2) and (X_3, Y_3).

There is one remaining point that we need to understand and this concerns the relationship between the method of least squares and the coefficient of correlation, which we considered towards the end of Chapter 1. There the correlation coefficient was explained as a measure of the covariance between X and Y, taken relatively to the product of the standard deviation of X and the standard deviation of Y: that is, we said that the covariance was the basic measure of association between two variables, but as it was expressed in rather awkward absolute terms it was useful to put it into a standardised relative form of the correlation coefficient, R, that is:

$$R = \frac{\text{Covariance between } X \text{ and } Y}{\text{Standard deviation of } X \times \text{Standard deviation of } Y}$$

$$= \frac{\frac{1}{n}\Sigma(X_i - \bar{X})(Y_i - \bar{Y})}{\sqrt{\frac{1}{n}\Sigma(X_i - \bar{X})^2}\sqrt{\frac{1}{n}\Sigma(Y_i - \bar{Y})^2}}$$

whence the square of the correlation coefficient, R^2, is:

$$R^2 = \frac{\left[\frac{1}{n}\Sigma(X_i - \bar{X})(Y_i - \bar{Y})\right]^2}{\frac{1}{n}\Sigma(X_i - \bar{X})^2\,\frac{1}{n}\Sigma(Y_i - \bar{Y})^2}$$

$$= \frac{[\Sigma(X_i - \bar{X})(Y_i - \bar{Y})]^2}{\Sigma(X_i - \bar{X})^2\Sigma(Y_i - \bar{Y})^2}$$

(obtained by cancelling out the expression $(1/n)^2$). The remaining point which we need to understand is that the square of the correlation coefficient is identically equal to the ratio of the 'explained' sum of squares to the total sum of squares, that is:

$$R^2 = \frac{\Sigma(\hat{Y}_i - \bar{Y})^2}{\Sigma(Y_i - \bar{Y})^2}$$

so that in maximising the 'explained' sum of squares by ascertaining the appropriate values of a and b we obtain at the same time the (squared) correlation coefficient between X and Y. Or, to put the matter in a more usual way, the square of the correlation coefficient gives the proportion of total variance in Y_i about the mean $\bar{Y}$ which is 'explained' by the straight-line equation $\hat{Y} = a + bX$, where a and b are calculated according to the least-squares formula just given.

To demonstrate the equivalence between the square of the correlation coefficient and the proportion of the explained sum of squares, note first that:

$$a = \bar{Y} - b\bar{X}$$

and as:

$$\hat{Y}_i - \bar{Y} = a + bX_i - \bar{Y}$$

substituting for a we get:

$$\hat{Y}_i - \bar{Y} = \bar{Y} - b\bar{X} + bX_i - \bar{Y}$$
$$= b(X_i - \bar{X})$$

Therefore:

$$\Sigma(\hat{Y}_i - \bar{Y})^2 = \Sigma[b(X_i - \bar{X})]^2$$
$$= b^2\Sigma(X_i - \bar{X})^2$$

But, second, recall that the value of b which minimised the sum of squared residuals was (with $1/n$ cancelled out):

$$b = \frac{\Sigma(X_i - \bar{X})(Y_i - \bar{Y})}{\Sigma(X_i - \bar{X})^2}$$

whence:

$$b^2 = \frac{[\Sigma(X_i - \bar{X})(Y_i - \bar{Y})]^2}{[\Sigma(X_i - \bar{X})^2]^2}$$

Substituting this value for b^2 into the equation for the 'explained' sum of squares gives:

$$\Sigma(\hat{Y}_i - \bar{Y})^2 = \frac{[\Sigma(X_i - \bar{X})(Y_i - \bar{Y})]^2}{[\Sigma(X_i - \bar{X})^2]^2} \times \Sigma(X_i - \bar{X})^2$$
$$= \frac{[\Sigma(X_i - \bar{X})(Y_i - \bar{Y})]^2}{\Sigma(X_i - \bar{X})^2}$$

The ratio of the 'explained' sum of squares to the total sum of squares is, using this result:

$$\frac{\Sigma(\hat{Y}_i - \bar{Y})^2}{\Sigma(Y_i - \bar{Y})^2} = \frac{[\Sigma(X_i - \bar{X})(Y_i - \bar{Y})]^2}{\Sigma(X_i - \bar{X})^2\Sigma(Y_i - \bar{Y})^2}$$
$$= R^2$$

(using the result for R^2 previously obtained). Thus fitting a straight line by least squares and obtaining the correlation coefficient are equivalent ways of looking at the relationship between X and Y: that is to say, they are both ways of finding out whether or not a relationship does exist between the two variables such that above- (or below-) average values of Y tend to be associated with above- (or below-) average values of X (or vice versa).

We have just gone through a considerable amount of theoretical statistics. There is no escaping this, even in elementary economic analysis, because economists are much concerned with analysing relationships among economic variables. Even so, it is appropriate to note that we have covered only the bare technical essentials; beyond this there is still a considerable amount of statistical theory dealing, for example, with questions such as why it is appropriate to minimise the sum of squared residuals measured in vertical distance. Consideration of these matters would lead us to understand why the straight-line equation we have been using is usually called a 'regression line' and why the method of least squares is also called 'linear regression'. But this is not a textbook on statistical theory, and we have simply covered enough ground to provide a basic understanding of these techniques of analysis. Having gone through all this we may return to Table 3.17, which we should now be in a position to understand.

In the first place, using the data from Table 3.16, we now know how the first three numbers in the last row of Table 3.17 were calculated (to give the result illustrated in Diagram 3.8). Table 3.18 shows the basic working data required.

Columns (1) and (2) are taken from Table 3.16. We then need to calculate the average of each of these columns as given at the bottom of each (note that these are simply unweighted averages; the averages for all households in Table 3.16 are weighted according to the number of households in each income bracket). Columns (3) and (4) of Table 3.18 give the squared differences of the X_i and Y_i about their respective means. Column (5) gives the cross-products. From the formula previously given for the correlation coefficient, we have:

$$R = \frac{\text{Covariance between } X \text{ and } Y}{\text{Standard deviation of } X \times \text{Standard deviation of } Y}$$

$$= \frac{\frac{1}{n}\Sigma(X_i - \bar{X})(Y_i - \bar{Y})}{\sqrt{\frac{1}{n}\Sigma(X_i - \bar{X})^2}\sqrt{\frac{1}{n}\Sigma(Y_i - \bar{Y})^2}}$$

$$= \frac{3{,}364.76}{74.478 \times 45.424}$$

$$= 0.99458$$

which result we can see, rounded to three decimal places, in Table 3.17 (last row, under 'correlation coefficient'). We know that, if we compute a least-squares straight-line equation for these observations, then we may explain the following proportion of variance in the observations on Y_i:

$$R^2 = (0.99458)^2 = 0.9892$$

So the straight-line cross-section consumption function:

$$\text{Average expenditure per household} = a + b \ \text{Average income per household}$$

in 1979 'explains' 98.92 per cent of the variation in average expenditure per household by income bracket. In other words, household income plus the least-squares consumption function provide a 'good' explanation of household consumption expenditure.

TABLE 3.18 The method of least squares: data required for computing a and b, and the correlation coefficient

Income bracket, £ per week, i	Average weekly income per household, X_i (1)	Average weekly expenditure per household, Y_i (2)	$(X_i - \bar{X})^2$ (3)	$(Y_i - \bar{Y})^2$ (4)	$(X_i - \bar{X})(Y_i - \bar{Y})$ (5)	$\hat{Y}_i$ [a] (6)	$e_i = Y_i - \hat{Y}_i$ (7)	$(\hat{Y}_i - \bar{Y})^2$ (8)	e_i^2 (9)
Under 30	25.02	27.51	8,455.03	4,219.64	5,973.04	36.692	−9.182	3,111.046	84.309
30 and under 40	34.51	34.97	6,799.86	3,306.11	4,741.42	42.449	−7.479	2,501.975	55.935
40 and under 50	44.86	46.73	5,200.03	2,092.03	3,298.28	48.727	−1.997	1,913.341	3.988
50 and under 60	54.71	51.68	3,876.46	1,663.72	2,539.56	54.702	−3.022	1,426.327	9.132
60 and under 70	65.03	66.75	2,697.89	661.45	1,335.86	60.962	5.788	992.675	33.501
70 and under 80	75.27	70.93	1,738.99	463.92	898.19	67.173	3.757	639.875	14.115
80 and under 90	84.88	74.07	1,029.85	338.51	590.44	73.003	1.067	378.915	1.138
90 and under 100	95.01	81.44	482.30	121.63	242.21	79.147	2.293	177.469	5.258
100 and under 110	104.73	86.06	149.85	41.07	78.45	85.043	1.017	55.142	1.034
110 and under 120	114.99	100.13	3.93	58.69	−15.18	91.267	8.863	1.444	78.553
120 and under 140	129.85	103.81	165.86	128.62	146.06	100.281	3.529	61.031	12.454
140 and under 160	149.76	113.15	1,075.10	427.71	678.11	112.358	0.792	395.582	0.627
160 and under 180	169.50	127.99	2,759.27	1,261.76	1,865.89	124.332	3.658	1,015.267	13.381
180 and under 200	189.42	135.83	5,248.82	1,880.20	3,141.47	136.415	−0.585	1,931.273	0.342
200 and under 250	221.99	153.78	11,028.94	3,759.07	6,438.83	156.172	−2.392	4,058.104	5.722
250 or more	312.01	204.67	38,040.11	12,589.12	21,883.59	210.777	−6.107	13,996.842	37.295
Total: Σ	1,871.54	1,479.50	88,752.29	33,013.25	53,836.22	1,479.50	0	32,656.308	356.784
Average: $\frac{1}{n}\Sigma$	116.97125	92.46875	5,547.02	2,063.33	3,364.76	92.46875	0	2,041.019	22.299
Standard deviation: $\sqrt{\frac{1}{n}\Sigma(\ )^2}$	—	—	74.478	45.424	—	—	—	45.1776	4.722

[a] Computed to eight decimal places from full formula:

$$\hat{Y}_i = 21.51521061 + 0.606589562\, X_i$$

Source: Table 3.16.

From the formula given for the least-squares value of b, we have:

$$b = \frac{\frac{1}{n}\Sigma(X_i - \bar{X})(Y_i - \bar{Y})}{\frac{1}{n}\Sigma(X_i - \bar{X})^2}$$

$$= \frac{3,364.76}{5,547.02}$$

$$= 0.60659$$

which result we can see, rounded to three decimal places, in Table 3.17 (last row, under 'regression coefficient').

Finally, from the least-squares formula for a, we have:

$$a = \bar{Y} - b\bar{X}$$
$$= 92.46875 - 0.60659 \times 116.97125$$
$$= 21.5152$$

which result we can also see rounded to two decimal places, in Table 3.17 (last row, under 'regression constant').

Column (6) in Table 3.18 gives the $\hat{Y}_i$ computed from the full formula (using a and b as estimated to eight decimal places and the corresponding value of X_i). You will observe that the average of the $\hat{Y}_i$ is the same as the average of the Y_i. Column (7) gives the values of the residuals, e_i, computed as $Y_i - \hat{Y}_i$; you will observe that the average of these residuals is zero, as it must be from the computational formula. Column (8) gives the 'explained' squared distance, $(\hat{Y}_i - \bar{Y})^2$: that is, where $\hat{Y}_i$ is 'explained' by the a and b parameters of the straight-line equation in conjunction with the corresponding value of X_i, a and b having been calculated by the least-squares method. The sum of these 'explained' squares is then the maximum we can obtain with a straight-line equation. We have already seen that $R^2 = 0.9892$ and we have observed that this is equal to the ratio of the 'explained' sum of squares to the total sum of squares. This is shown in the following arithmetic:

$$\frac{\text{Explained sum of squares}}{\text{Total sum of squares}} = \frac{\Sigma(\hat{Y}_i - \bar{Y})^2}{\Sigma(Y_i - \bar{Y})^2}$$

$$= \frac{32,656.308}{33,013.25}$$

$$= 0.9892$$

The final column gives the squared residuals, and the sum of squared residuals, computed as:

$$\Sigma e_i^2 = \Sigma(Y_i - \hat{Y}_i)^2$$
$$= \Sigma[Y_i - (a + bX_i)]^2$$

is, when a and b are obtained by the method of least squares, the smallest possible sum of squares. Note that we have partitioned the total sum of squares, $\Sigma(Y_i - \bar{Y})^2$, into the 'explained' sum of squares, $\Sigma(\hat{Y}_i - \bar{Y})^2$, and the 'unexplained' residual sum of squares, Σe_i^2, as follows (apart from a small error due to rounding):

$$\Sigma(Y_i - \bar{Y})^2 = \Sigma(\hat{Y}_i - \bar{Y})^2 + \Sigma e_i^2$$

or:

$$33,013.25 = 32,656.308 + 356.784$$

Table 3.18 gives the full details needed to calculate the least-squares values of *a* and *b* and the correlation coefficient. It is possible to take a number of short cuts in the computing process, and these short-cut formulae are attached to Appendix 3.3. The best short cut is, of course, to get an electronic calculator which will produce all the results for you simply by entering the first two columns of data!

Constructing and using a price index: 'real' income and expenditure

From Table 3.17 we can see that average income per household rose from £22.03 per week in 1963 to £120.45 per week in 1979, while consumption expenditure per household rose from £19.14 per week in 1963 to £94.17 per week in 1979. Or, from Appendix 3.1, we can see that total personal-sector income rose from £8.8 billion per annum in 1946 to £170.3 billion per annum in 1979, while total consumers' expenditure rose from £7.3 billion per annum to £116.7 billion per annum in 1979.

Obviously, increases of this order of magnitude, which imply that household average weekly income increased by 11.2 per cent per annum between 1963 and 1979, are partly due to the impact of 'inflation'; nobody expects that households in 1979 were nearly $5\frac{1}{2}$ times 'better off' than in 1963. So what is inflation and how do we take it into account when examining changes over time in income and expenditure?

The word 'inflation' covers a multitude of sins, but its basic meaning is a *continuing* rise in prices *in general*; a once-for-all price rise would not usually be called 'inflation', and in any case such once-for-all changes hardly ever occur. Second, the rise must be a rise of prices in general: a continuing rise in the price of one commodity, say oil, while all other prices remained stable (also an unlikely event) would not be called 'inflation'. The sustained, continuing and intractable nature of rises in prices is not presently our concern; we must first understand what we mean by, or how we measure, a rise in prices in general. This means we need to understand what a price index is.

Price indices can cover the prices of various sorts of goods: the most commonly referred to price index is that for the prices of consumer goods, the so-called general index of retail prices, calculated monthly. As its name implies, this covers prices in the (retail) shops of goods that households purchase. But there are also other price indices dealing with wholesale prices, such as the price index of materials and fuels purchased by manufacturing industry, or the price index of housebuilding materials, or the wholesale price of manufactured products sold in the United Kingdom, or price indices for stock (inventories) held by industries, or many others. So what is a price index?

A price index can be understood in two ways, each of which is equivalent to the other. In the first, we can consider the percentage change in a price index as measuring exactly the percentage change in the amount of money we would have to spend in order to purchase an identical bundle or basket of goods if the prices of some or all of those goods were to increase (or, indeed, decrease). In the second, we can consider the percentage change in the price index as a 'weighted' average of the percentage changes in prices of each of the goods making up a certain bundle or basket of goods. The word 'weighted', and the reason for using 'weights', will be explained in due course.

First, let us consider a very simple example of a family which lives on bread and butter with a once-a-week treat of a chocolate bar for the children. Suppose that during one particular week, which we shall denote by the subscript 0 (which is conventionally used to refer to the 'base', or starting period), the household budget can be shown as in Table 3.19.

The three items in the household budget are each given a subscript, *i*, where $i = 1$, or $i = 2$, or $i = 3$, as the case may be, to identify them. Bread is measured in units of a loaf, butter in units of a lb, and chocolate in units of a bar. The price, during the base week of a

TABLE 3.19   *Household budget (hypothetical) I*

i	Item (i), and unit	Price per unit		Units purchased per week		Total expenditure per week	
		Pence	Symbol	Number	Symbol	Pence	Symbol
1	Bread, loaf	30	$p_{0,1}$	5	$q_{0,1}$	150	$p_{0,1}q_{0,1}$
2	Butter, lb	80	$p_{0,2}$	1	$q_{0,2}$	80	$p_{0,2}q_{0,2}$
3	Chocolate, bar	2	$p_{0,3}$	1	$q_{0,3}$	2	$p_{0,3}q_{0,3}$
$\sum_{i=1}^{i=3}$	All items	—	—	—	—	232	$\sum_{i=1}^{i=3} p_{0,i}q_{0,i}$

loaf of bread, is 30p; this is referred to by the symbol $p_{0,1}$; 'p' standing for price, the subscript 0 denotes the base period, and the subscript 1 denotes the first item. The quantity (number of units or loaves) of bread which the household purchases is 5 per week; this is referred to by the symbol $q_{0,1}$, where 'q' stands for quantity and the subscripts are as before. Total money expenditure on bread is therefore $5 \times 30 = 150$ pence per week; in symbols this is (omitting the multiplication sign) $p_{0,1}q_{0,1}$. And the same goes for butter and chocolate. Total household weekly expenditure on all items is:

$$150 + 80 + 2 = 232 \text{ pence per week}$$

or in symbols:

$$p_{0,1}q_{0,1} + p_{0,2}q_{0,2} + p_{0,3}q_{0,3} = 232$$

But as the left-hand side of this formula becomes tedious when the list is a long one, we adopt the convention of using the Greek symbol sigma, Σ, to denote summation and write the total of expenditure as:

$$\sum_{i=1}^{i=3} p_{0,i}q_{0,i}$$

which means exactly the same as the formula just given: that is, it says 'let $i = 1$; take the product $p_{0,1}q_{0,1}$; and then let $i = 2$, take the product $p_{0,2}q_{0,2}$ and add it to the preceding product; and then let $i = 3$, take the product $p_{0,3}q_{0,3}$ and add it to the preceding sum'. We stop at $i = 3$ because the range of summation is given as $i = 1$ (written below the Σ) to $i = 3$ (written above the Σ). If we have a long list of items, say n items, where $n = 350$, then we can simply substitute 350 for 3 in the formula above: 350 is, in fact, about the number of items listed for the general index of retail prices.

Now suppose that in some week following week 0, which week we shall denote by the subscript 1, prices have risen: suppose the price of bread has risen by 10 per cent to 33p per loaf ($p_{1,1}$), the price of butter by 20 per cent to 96p per lb ($p_{1,2}$), and the price of a bar of chocolate by 100 per cent to 4p per bar ($p_{1,3}$). The question is: by how much have prices *in general* risen? One simple answer to this question is to say that prices in general have risen by the simple average of the straightforward percentage increases. Thus:

$$\frac{1}{3}(10\% + 20\% + 100\%) = 43.3\%$$

or:

$$\frac{1}{3}10\% + \frac{1}{3}20\% + \frac{1}{3}100\% = 43.3\%$$

But this simple answer is not really meaningful because it gives equal weight (1/3) to the large rise in the price of chocolate as to the smaller rise in the price of bread, despite the fact that expenditure on bread is much more 'important' in the total household weekly expenditure than is expenditure on chocolate. If we work out the amount of money the household would have to spend per week in order to buy exactly the same quantities of exactly the same items at the new prices, we have the budget shown in Table 3.20.*

TABLE 3.20 *Household budget (hypothetical) II*

i	Item (i), and unit	Price per unit		Units purchased per week		Total expenditure per week	
		Pence	Symbol	Number	Symbol	Pence	Symbol
1	Bread, loaf	33	$p_{1,1}$	5	$q_{0,1}$	165	$p_{1,1}q_{0,1}$
2	Butter, lb	96	$p_{1,2}$	1	$q_{0,2}$	96	$p_{1,2}q_{0,2}$
3	Chocolate, bar	4	$p_{1,3}$	1	$q_{0,3}$	4	$p_{1,3}q_{0,3}$
$\sum_{i=1}^{i=3}$	All items	—	—	—	—	265	$\sum_{i=1}^{i=3} p_{1,i}q_{0,i}$

Thus the household has to spend 265 pence per week, or 33 pence more per week than it did in the base period. This represents an increase in expenditure of 14.22 per cent $(33/232 = 0.1422)$. We may express this change not in the form of a straightforward percentage as $(265 - 232)/232 = 0.1422$, but in the form of an index as $265/232 = 1.1422$, because the index tells us by what factor, 1.1422, base-period weekly expenditure must be increased if the same quantities of the same items are to be purchased at the higher prices. This I shall call the *index in proportionate form*, because it has a value of 1 in the base period. However, it is more usual to give the price index with a value of 100 in the base period, and this gives a value of 114.22 in period 1 for the index above; and I shall refer to this as the *index in percentage form*. The difference between the proportionate form and the percentage form is merely a matter of convenience of presentation.

In proportionate form, the price index is calculated as follows:

$$\frac{\sum_{i=1}^{i=3} p_{1,i}q_{0,i}}{\sum_{i=1}^{i=3} p_{0,i}q_{0,i}} = \frac{265}{232} = 1.1422$$

The index (proportionate form) is calculated as the ratio of the same base-period quantities, $q_{0,i}$, multiplied by the new prices, $p_{1,i}$, and summed to give $\sum p_{1,i}q_{0,i}$, to the base-period quantities multiplied by the base-period prices and summed to give $\sum p_{0,i}q_{0,i}$. This index tells us the proportionate increase in money expenditure required to purchase the same basket of goods at the new (higher) prices. It is therefore a measure of (the effect of) price rises *in general*. Note that, in order to answer the question 'by how much have prices in general risen?' we must hold the quantities and items of goods constant and let only prices vary. Doing this, we can isolate the impact of price rises in general. If we allowed the q_i to vary as well as the p_i, then we would have a mixture of price and quantity changes and we would not be able to isolate the impact of price rises.

*The essential part of calculating a price index is to have the quantity of each of the items purchased each week (period) remaining unchanged: that is, our family consumes the same quantities of the same items each week (period). Hence $q_{1,i} = q_{0,i}$ $(i = 1, 2, 3)$, and similarly in all ensuing weeks (periods): $q_{2,i} = q_{0,i}$; $q_{t,i} = q_{0,i}$.

The general form of a price index for n items for any period t, with reference to a base period 0, is therefore (in percentage form):

$$\frac{\sum\limits_{i=1}^{i=n} p_{t,i} q_{0,i}}{\sum\limits_{i=1}^{i=n} p_{0,i} q_{0,i}} \times 100$$

And in this (percentage rather than proportionate) form, it tells us the percentage by which money expenditure, during period t, has to change in order to purchase exactly the same basket or bundle of goods (per period) as in the base period 0. The formula just given is usually simplified by omitting all reference to the *i*s, it being taken for granted that the range of summation is understood, and the formula can then be written simply as:

$$\frac{\sum p_t q_0}{\sum p_0 q_0} \times 100$$

We can now appreciate why the simple answer to the question as to the extent of the rise in prices in general is not meaningful. In fact the simple answer, if it is taken to imply that a household would need to spend 43.3 per cent more money to keep up with price rises in general, is now seen to be downright misleading. Suppose, then, that we took an average of the price increases, but 'weighted' each item's price increase by the 'importance' of expenditure on that item in total household expenditure. In this context, 'importance' can be measured by the proportion of total household expenditure on the item in question: for example, expenditure on bread in the base period is $150/232 = 0.6466$ or 64.66 per cent of total expenditure; so 0.6466 is a measure of the 'importance' of bread. We can then multiply each percentage price rise by its corresponding proportionate share in base period expenditure, and sum the results; this is what is meant by taking a 'weighted' average price rise, the weights being the proportionate shares in base period expenditure. For bread, butter and chocolate, the weights are respectively:

In numbers	*In symbols*
$\dfrac{150}{232} = 0.6466$	$p_{0,1} q_{0,1} / \sum p_{0,i} q_{0,i}$
$\dfrac{80}{232} = 0.3448$	$p_{0,2} q_{0,2} / \sum p_{0,i} q_{0,i}$
$\dfrac{2}{232} = 0.0086$	$p_{0,3} q_{0,3} / \sum p_{0,i} q_{0,i}$

And the weighted average price rise is:

$$0.6466 \times 10\% + 0.3448 \times 20\% + 0.0086 \times 100\% = 14.22\%$$

This weighted average is to be contrasted to the previous simple average where each price increase was given the same 'weight' of 1/3, such simple averages usually being called 'unweighted' averages. You will observe that the weighted average price rise is exactly the same as the answer we obtained (in index form, p. 157) when we compared the cost of the (base-period) basket of goods at the new prices with the (base-period) basket of goods at the base period prices. This equivalence is not accidental because the two formulae are algebraically identical. We can prove this by calculating the weighted average price rise using, not the straightforward percentages, $(3/30)100$, and so on, but the index (proportionate) form of 33/30 and so on:

Price of bread per loaf rises from	Price increase as straightforward percentage	Price increase as index (proportionate) form: 'price relative'
30p to 33p	$\left(\dfrac{33-30}{30}\right) \times 100$	$\dfrac{33}{30}$
	$= \left(\dfrac{3}{30}\right) \times 100$	$= 1.10$
	$= 0.10 \times 100$	
	$= 10\%$	

so that we can calculate the weighted average price increase alternatively as:

$$0.6466 \times 1.10 + 0.3448 \times 1.20 + 0.0086 \times 2.00 = 1.1422$$

If this be expressed in symbols, we have the (weighted) average of the 'price relative':

$$\frac{p_{0,1}q_{0,1}}{\Sigma p_{0,i}q_{0,i}} \times \frac{p_{1,1}}{p_{0,1}} + \frac{p_{0,2}q_{0,2}}{\Sigma p_{0,i}q_{0,i}} \times \frac{p_{1,2}}{p_{0,2}} + \frac{p_{0,3}q_{0,3}}{\Sigma p_{0,i}q_{0,i}} \times \frac{p_{1,3}}{p_{0,3}}$$

or, using summation, the weighted average of the 'price relative' is:

$$\Sigma \left(\frac{p_{0,i}q_{0,i}}{\Sigma p_{0,i}q_{0,i}} \times \frac{p_{1,i}}{p_{0,i}} \right)$$

But, inside the bracket of this formula for the weighted average, the $p_{0,i}$ in the numerator and in the denominator cancel each other, leaving:

$$\Sigma \left(\frac{q_{0,i}}{\Sigma p_{0,i}q_{0,i}} \times p_{1,i} \right) = \frac{\Sigma p_{1,i}q_{0,i}}{\Sigma p_{0,i}q_{0,i}}$$

which is exactly the same formula as that for comparing the money expenditure on the same (base-period) quantities at the new prices with the money expenditure on the base-period quantities at base-period prices.

To measure the impact of price rises in general between the base period 0 and any other period t we have the following equivalent formula:

$$\frac{\Sigma p_t q_0}{\Sigma p_0 q_0} = \Sigma \left(\frac{p_0 q_0}{\Sigma p_0 q_0} \times \frac{p_t}{p_0} \right)$$

This way of measuring the impact of price inflation is known as a *base-weighted index*, because the weights used are the proportionate shares in base-period expenditure. This is also called the Laspeyres price index after Etienne Laspeyres, the statistician who, in 1864, first used this formula. It is possible to use other systems of weights, and the actual weights used in the UK general index of retail prices do vary slightly from year to year to allow for changing patterns of consumption (obviously base-period shares will become out of date), but these are matters which we do not pursue here.

Having seen how we can construct a price index we must now consider how to use it. One common use of a price index is to 'deflate' money incomes in order to determine the rise in 'real' incomes. The operation of deflating is done by dividing money income by the price index (proportionate form). The simplest example is to suppose that the money income of the household is equivalent to its expenditure:

Period	Money income, £ per week	Price index, period 0 = 1	'Real' income per week in £ of period-0 purchasing power
0	2.32	1.0000	2.32
1	2.65	1.1422	2.32

Then we can see that in 'real' terms, in terms of the basket of goods which can be purchased with the weekly money income, nothing has changed. Now let us take an example where money income remains unaltered:

Period	Money income, £ per week	Price index, period 0 = 1	'Real' income per week in £ of period-0 purchasing power
0	2.32	1.0000	2.32
1	2.32	1.1422	2.03

Then we can see that in 'real' terms the household's income has fallen to a proportion 0.8755 of its former level, where 0.8755 = 1/1.1422. This means that at the new prices and with the same money income the household must reduce the quantities of the goods it buys in the same proportion if expenditure is to match income (imagining for the sake of the example that it is possible to buy 0.8755 of a chocolate bar, etc.):

	Units purchased per week	Price per unit, pence	Total expenditure per week, pence
Bread, loaf	$5 \times 0.8755 = 4.3775$	33	144.4575
Butter, lb	$1 \times 0.8755 = 0.8755$	96	84.0480
Chocolate, bar	$1 \times 0.8755 = 0.8755$	4	3.5020
All items	—	—	232.0075

and we may ignore the third and fourth decimal places as errors due to rounding. So the fall in 'real' income in period 1 to proportion 0.8755 of its period-0 value, a fall of 12.45 per cent (100 − 87.55), means that the quantity of each of the items in the basket of goods must be reduced by 12.45 per cent to 0.8755 of the quantity purchased in the base period.

Now let us consider an example where 'real' income rises. Suppose that money income rises from £2.32 per week to £2.90 per week, an increase of 25 per cent (2.90/2.32 = 1.25). But prices rise by only 14.22 per cent. Then, using the price index to deflate money income gives 'real' income as follows:

Period	Money income, £ per week	Price index, period 0 = 1	'Real' income per week in £ of period-0 purchasing power
0	2.32	1.0000	2.32
1	2.90	1.1422	2.539

In 'real' terms income has risen by 9.44 per cent (2.539/2.32 = 1.0944). This means that at the new prices and with the higher money income, the household can increase the quantities of each of the items it buys by 9.44 per cent and expenditure will still remain level with income:

	Units purchased per week	Price per unit, pence	Total expenditure per week, pence
Bread, loaf	$5 \times 1.0944 = 5.4720$	33	180.576
Butter, lb	$1 \times 1.0944 = 1.0944$	96	105.062
Chocolate, bar	$1 \times 1.0944 = 1.0944$	4	4.378
All items	—	—	290.016

So an increase in 'real' income indicates the extent to which a household could increase the quantities of each of the items purchased in the base period and still keep expenditure within income, even though prices have increased. If a household saves a certain proportion of its income, as do most households, then the increase in 'real' income indicates the extent to which a household can increase the quantities of each of the items it purchases and still save the same proportion of its money income. For example, suppose the money income of our household in the base period were £3 per week, so that the household was saving 68p a week (£3–£2.32), or 22.7 per cent of its income. If money income in period 1 were to rise to £3.75 per week, an increase of 25 per cent, then 'real' income would have risen to £3.75/1.1422 = £3.28 per week, an increase of 9.44 per cent; if the household increased, in this proportion, the quantities of each of the goods purchased, it would be spending £2.90 per week and saving 85p per week; and this is, as before, 22.7 per cent of its money income.

So, using a base-weighted price index to deflate money incomes indicates the extent to which households can increase each of the quantities of the base-period items they purchase, at the new prices, and still save the same proportion of their money incomes.

We have considered the meaning of an increase in 'real' income. But if one deflates money income by a base-weighted price index to obtain 'real' income, then it is also necessary to deflate consumers' expenditure to obtain a comparable measure of 'real' expenditure. Such a measure of 'real' expenditure is, in effect, a form of a quantity index of goods consumed, or a weighted average of proportionate changes in quantities purchased.

Having gone through price indices and their use, we now need to see the course of price inflation in the UK economy.

The retail price index (for consumers' expenditure) and price inflation in the United Kingdom

Retail prices covering 'all items' in household budgets have been officially collected monthly in the United Kingdom since July 1914, though there are official partial indices covering food, coal and clothing (separately) back to 1892, with various wholesale price indices back to 1871, and some estimates by statisticians back to 1661 (these are all given in B. R. Mitchell and Phyllis Deane, *Abstract of British Historical Statistics*, Cambridge University Press, 1962, pp. 468–78).

The cost of living index, which started in July 1914, used as weights the results of surveys of food expenditure in family budgets in 1904, of expenditure on rents in 1912, and of expenditure on other items in 1914. The index covered only the prices of 'basic' goods such as bread, potatoes, clothing materials. Naturally this pattern of weights was much criticised, but the index can be used to indicate trends in retail prices during the interwar period.

In 1947 this cost of living index was replaced by an interim index of retail prices which used the weights from a survey in 1937–8 into the family budgets of manual workers in general and non-manual workers earning less than £250 a year. This index continued until January 1956, though the weights were slightly revised in 1952. During 1953–4 a comprehensive survey of household expenditure was carried out, and this provided a reasonably up-to-date and comprehensive set of weights for the general index of retail prices which replaced the interim index in January 1956. This base-weighted index continued until 1962, when the index began to use a changing set of weights based on the *Family Expenditure Survey* (conducted annually since 1957). In January 1974 the base was changed from 16 January 1962 = 100 to 15 January 1974 = 100.

The general index of retail prices covers the prices of 350 items, and many price quotations are obtained for each item from a representative variety of shops throughout the United Kingdom; items such as the price of national newspapers or letter postage which are nationally uniform require only one price quotation, but, for example, about 800 price quotations are obtained for sugar (these are the prices actually charged for cash transactions and the price may vary according to whether the sugar is bought from a 'corner shop' or from a supermarket which may be using sugar as a 'loss leader' – a specially priced item designed to attract shoppers). The price quotations are collected by the staff of Department of Employment local offices on a predetermined Tuesday near the middle of each month (except for December when, for obvious reasons, the earlier Tuesday may be taken – e.g. in 1979, Tuesday the 11th rather than Tuesday the 18th). An average UK price is then obtained for each of the 350 items and each of these prices is then taken relative to the price in January of that year. For convenience the 350 price relatives are combined into eleven sections. Although some information on the sub-groups and items within each section is published, the weights used to make up the weighted average section price relative are not published: for example, the price relative for section VII 'Clothing and footwear' is a weighted average of price relatives for men's outer clothing; men's underclothing; women's outer clothing; women's underclothing; children's clothing; other clothing including hose, haberdashery, hats and materials; and footwear. The weights are the proportions of the expenditure by an average household on clothing and footwear which are used on each of these sub-sections; but these weights are not published. The price relative, for, say, men's outer clothing will, in turn, be an average of the price relatives for representative items.

Because the weights are changed each year, the procedure is to take a weighted average of the section price relatives for each month in relation to January for that year and then to link this to the January 1974 base. Table 3.21 shows how the calculation is done for the index for 14 October 1980. In column (1) we have the section price relatives (in percentage form) for 15 January 1980 with the 'all items' index then standing at 245.3 (15 January 1974 = 100). So we know that the weighted average of all the percentage increases in the prices of each of the items in a typical UK household budget was 145.3 per cent between January 1974 and January 1980. Column (2) gives the section price relatives for 14 October 1980 (15 January 1974 = 100). Column (3) gives the percentage increase, in index form, of the section prices between 15 January 1980 and 14 October 1980. Column (4) gives the proportionate weights used in 1980; these weights are derived from the latest available *Family Expenditure Survey* according to the proportionate allocation of total weekly expenditure on each of the sections. The percentage change in the 'all items' index is calculated in two stages. First, a weighted average is derived for the percentage change between January and October 1980. This percentage change in index form is 110.83, indicating that the price level rose by 10.83 per cent between January and October. Second, the index for January 1980 (15 January 1974 = 100) is then increased by this proportion, namely 1.1083, to give the value of the 'all items' index for October 1980 (15 January 1974 = 100) of 271.87, which is rounded to one decimal place and published as 271.9. The average of all the monthly values so derived is then taken as the index for the year 1980, that is:

$$\tfrac{1}{12} (245.3 + 248.8 + 252.2 + 260.8 + 263.2 + 265.7 + 267.9 + 268.5 +$$
$$270.2 + 271.9 + 274.1 + 275.6)$$
$$= 263.7$$

The calculation of the January 1980 value follows a similar procedure but uses January 1979 as the base and 1979 weights – the working is shown in Appendix 3.2.

Column (5) of Table 3.21 shows the calculation of the straightforward percentage change in the 'all items' index: to illustrate with the food section, instead of taking the percentage increase in the index form of 105.92, we take the straightforward percentage increase as 5.92 per cent and multiply it by the proportionate 1980 weight for the food section, 0.214: this gives, in the fifth column, food's weighted contribution, namely 1.27 percentage points, to the 'all items' percentage increase of 10.83 per cent. The final column shows the percentage points contribution as a percentage of the 'all items' percentage increase. A section can make a big relative contribution to price inflation because it has a large weight, or because it has a substantial price increase, or both. In

TABLE 3.21 Calculation of the 'all items' general index of retail prices for 14 October 1980

Section	15 January 1974 = 100		15 January 1980 = 100	Proportionate weight, 1980 (4)	Contribution to percentage price rise in	
	Index on 15 January 1980 (1)	Index on 14 October 1980 (2)	Index on 14 October 1980 (a) (3)		Percentage points (5)	Per cent
I Food	244.8	259.3	105.92	0.214	1.27	11.7
II Alcoholic drink	241.4	274.6	113.75	0.082	1.13	10.4
III Tobacco	269.7	297.9	110.46	0.040	0.42	3.9
IV Housing	237.4	283.7	119.50	0.124	2.42	22.4
V Fuel and light	277.1	337.4	121.76	0.059	1.28	11.8
VI Durable household goods	216.1	230.8	106.80	0.069	0.47	4.3
VII Clothing and footwear	197.1	208.4	105.73	0.084	0.48	4.4
VIII Transport and vehicles	268.4	295.1	109.95	0.151	1.50	13.9
IX Miscellaneous goods	258.8	287.9	111.24	0.074	0.83	7.7
X Services	246.9	267.4	108.30	0.062	0.51	4.7
XI Meals out	267.8	301.5	112.58	0.041	0.52	4.8
All items	245.3(d)	271.9(c)	110.83(b)	1.000	10.83	100

(a) Index 14 October 1980 *divided by* index 15 January 1980 (percentage form).

(b) Weighted average, obtained by using weights given in column (4).

(c) Calculated as 245.3 × 1.1083 = 271.9.

(d) See Appendix 3.2 for derivation of this value.

Source: Department of Employment, *Employment Gazette*, November 1980, table 6.4, pp. S58–S59.

TABLE 3.22   *Price indices and price inflation in the United Kingdom, 1915 to 1980*

Year (average for twelve months) (a)	Cost of living index, all items, July 1914 = 100	Percentage change over previous year	Year (average for twelve months) (a)	Interim index of retail prices, all items, 17 June 1947 = 100	General index of retail prices, all items, 17 Jan 1956 = 100	General index of retail prices, all items, 16 Jan 1962 = 100	General index of retail prices, all items, 15 Jan 1974 = 100	Chained index, base 1946 = 100 (b)	Percentage change over previous year
1915	123	—	1946	100.246 (c)				100	—
1916	146	18.7	1947 (17 June)	100				—	—
1917	176	20.5	1947	100.9 (d)				100.65	0.7
1918	203	15.3	1948	107.7				107.44	6.7
1919	215	5.9	1949	110.7				110.43	2.8
1920	249	15.8	1950	114.1				113.82	3.1
1921	226	-9.2	1951	124.5				124.19	9.1
1922	183	-19.0	1952	135.9				135.57	9.2
1923	174	-4.9	1953	140.1				139.76	3.1
1924	175	0.6	1954	142.7				142.35	1.9
1925	176	0.6	1955	149.1				148.73	4.5
1926	172	-2.3	1956 (17 Jan)	153.4	100.0			—	—
1927	167.5	-2.6	1956	156.5 (e)	102.0			156.12	5.0
1928	166	-0.9	1957		105.8			161.94	3.7
1929	164	-1.2	1958		109.0			166.83	3.0
1930	158	-3.7	1959		109.6			167.75	0.6
1931	147.5	-6.6	1960		110.7			169.44	1.0
1932	144	-2.4	1961		114.5			175.25	3.4
1933	140	-2.8	1962 (16 Jan)		117.5	100.0		—	—
1934	141	0.7	1962		119.4 (f)	101.6		182.75	4.3
1935	143	1.4	1963			103.6		186.35	2.0
1936	147	2.8	1964			107.0		192.46	3.3

Year								
1937	154	4.8		1965	112.1		201.64	4.8
1938	156	1.3		1966	116.5		209.55	3.9
1939	158	1.3		1967	119.4		214.77	2.5
1940	184	16.5		1968	125.0		224.84	4.7
1941	199	8.2		1969	131.8		237.07	5.4
1942	200	0.5		1970	140.2		252.18	6.4
1943	199	−0.5		1971	153.4		275.92	9.4
1944	201	1.0		1972	164.3		295.53	7.1
1945	203	1.0		1973	179.4		322.69	9.2
1946	203.5	0.2		1974 (15 Jan)	191.8	100.0	—	—
1947 (17 June)	203	—		1974	208.2 (g)	108.5	374.49	16.1
				1975		134.8	465.26	24.2
				1976		157.1	542.23	16.5
				1977		182.0	628.18	15.9
				1978		197.1	680.29	8.3
				1979		223.5	771.41	13.4
				1980		263.7	910.16	18.0

(a) Unless otherwise stated.
(b) Calculated so as to give the same year-to-year percentage changes as in the given indices.
(c) Calculated with reference to June 1947 = 100 index, i.e. (203.5/203) × 100.
(d) Calculated by using separate monthly indices for 1947 and averaged; working not shown.
(e) Calculated with reference to 17 Jan 1956 = 100 index, i.e. (102/100) × 153.4.
(f) Calculated with reference to 16 Jan 1962 = 100 index, i.e. (101.6/100) × 117.5.
(g) Figure given in *Department of Employment Gazette*, October 1975, table 132, p. 1100.

Sources: Department of Employment, *British Labour Statistics Historical Abstract 1886–1968*, tables 89, 90, 91, 93 and 94, pp. 166, 171, 172, 173, 176 and 177; *Department of Employment Gazette*, October 1975, table 132, p. 1100; Department of Employment, *Employment Gazette*, November 1980, table 6.4, p. S58; Department of Employment, *Employment Gazette*, February 1981, table 6.4, p. S58.

January to October 1980 the substantial 19.5 per cent rise in housing costs (including rates and mortgage interest) made a relatively large contribution to over-all inflation because housing also had a large proportionate share (weight) in total household expenditure of 12.4 per cent in 1980.

Table 3.22 gives the retail price indices in the United Kingdom since 1915, with a continuous index based at 1946 = 100 calculated by linking the various indices which have been used over the postwar period. The purpose of this linking is quite simply to preserve the percentage changes in the index. For example, the 17 June 1947 = 100 index comes to an end on 17 January 1956 with a value of 153.4; the value of the 17 January 1956 = 100 index for the whole of 1956 (averaged over twelve monthly values) is 102.0 – that is, the year average is a 2 per cent increase on the January figure; so 153.4 must be increased by 2 per cent, i.e. multiplied by 1.020, to give a value for the year average of 1956 (with 17 June 1947 = 100), namely 156.5; this can then be compared with the value of 149.1 for 1955 to obtain the percentage change in prices between 1955 and 1956. Making an index for the whole period involves dividing the interim index of retail prices by 1.00246, the estimated value for 1946. This carries us to a value for 1956 of 156.12 (156.5/1.00246). For the next year, 1957, we must increase 156.12 by the percentage increase in the 17 January 1956 = 100 index, namely 105.8/102.0; so the 1957 value is 156.12 × (105.8/102.0) = 161.94. The 1958 value is then calculated as the percentage increase between 1956 and 1958 times 156.12; that is, 156.12 × (109.0/102.0) = 166.83. And so on. The value of the chained index, 1946 = 100 in 1980 is 910.6, showing that prices have risen ninefold since 1946.

Much of this rise has occurred in recent years. Diagram 3.10 charts the year-to-year percentage changes in price inflation since 1915–16. During the First World War inflation was quite rapid (the wholesale price index increased by 23 per cent in 1915 over 1914) and after the war there was a brief boom followed by a slump in 1921 and 1922 when prices fell

DIAGRAM 3.10   *Annual percentage price inflation in the United Kingdom, 1915–16 to 1979–80*

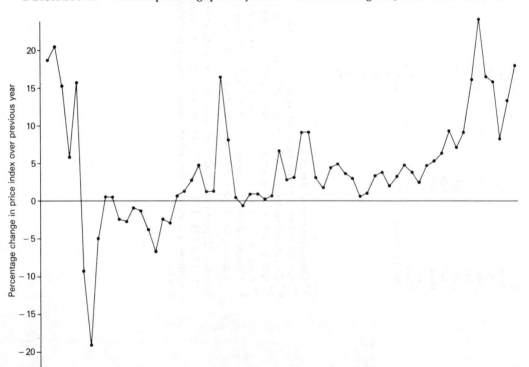

steeply. For much of the interwar period, prices tended to fall, and, although there was a spurt of inflation in 1940, for most of the Second World War price inflation was controlled, largely through rationing. After the end of the Second World War there was a brief period of inflation in 1951 and 1952, mostly due to the effect of the Korean war on world commodity prices. (The Korean war started in June 1950 when North Korea invaded South Korea which was then given military support by the USA; the Chinese became actively involved in the war, supporting North Korea, in November 1950, and by the beginning of 1951 it seemed as if a long and large-scale war threatened; these fears rapidly increased the prices of raw materials, throughout the world, before truce talks began in July 1951 and American military operations largely ceased in November 1951; the armistice was finally signed in July 1953.) After 1952 price inflation fluctuated between about 1 per cent and 5 per cent a year until 1969, when the rate increased to 5.4 per cent and continued to rise until it reached a peak of 24.2 per cent in 1974–5. We shall subsequently be considering the causes of inflation, but we must now consider how the price index may be used to determine the amount of 'real' income and consumers' expenditure in the United Kingdom.

Trend growth rates (using the method of least squares)

If we divide ('deflate') the figures in Appendix 3.1 on total personal income and consumers' expenditure by the price index in Table 3.22 (1946 = 100 but used in proportionate, not percentage, form), we get the series on 'real' income and 'real' consumers' expenditure given in Table 3.23. I have referred to these flows as '£ million at 1946 prices' because this is the usual form of reference, mentioning the base date of the price deflator. But this terminology is not literally accurate – for example, one cannot 'value' income in 1947 at 1946 prices; the meaning is that the proportionate increase in 'real' income in 1947 over 1946 indicates the extent to which households could in 1947 have increased the 'real' quantities of goods purchased and still saved the same proportion of their income.

How rapidly did 'real' income and expenditure increase during these postwar years? There are three different ways of answering this apparently simple question. We can calculate the year-to-year percentage changes, as shown in Table 3.23, and then take the average of these. Or we can calculate the compound annual proportionate change, r, using 'real' income in the first and last years, together with the formula explained in Chapter 1:

$$r = \sqrt[34]{\frac{\text{Income}_{1980}}{\text{Income}_{1946}}} - 1$$

Or we can compute a trend growth rate. Such growth rates were presented for the UK labour force in Table 1.3, but as their computation uses the method of least squares the explanation of this method has had to wait until now. We need therefore to consider how, and why, we may compute a trend growth rate to answer the question: How fast did real income (or any other variable) grow over any particular period?

The compound growth rate formula just cited was explained by the formula for compounding:

$$Y_n = Y_0(1 + r)^n$$

where Y stands for any variable (in Chapter 1, population), and 0 and n were the initial-and end-years respectively, except that n stands for the number of years elapsing between the initial-year and the end-year (in Chapter 1, between population censuses). Suppose we have a time series of observations, Y_t, where Y_t stands for the flow of real income during

TABLE 3.23   *Personal-sector 'real' income and consumers' expenditure in the United Kingdom, 1946 to 1980*

		£ million at 1946 prices			Percentage change over previous year	
Year 't'		Total personal sector income, Y_t	Trend value of real income, [a] $\hat{Y}_t$	Consumers' expenditure, C_t	Trend value of expenditure, [b] $\hat{C}_t$	Y_t	C_t
1946	0	8,830.0	8,359.3	7,273.0	7,370.3	—	—
1947	1	9,414.8	8,609.4	7,976.2	7,532.9	6.6	9.7
1948	2	9,318.7	8,867.0	8,012.8	7,699.2	−1.0	0.5
1949	3	9,571.7	9,132.3	8,121.9	7,869.1	2.7	1.4
1950	4	9,699.5	9,405.5	8,312.2	8,042.8	1.3	2.3
1951	5	9,655.4	9,686.9	8,225.3	8,220.3	−0.5	−1.0
1952	6	9,436.5	9,976.7	7,941.3	8,401.7	−2.3	−3.5
1953	7	9,708.1	10,275.1	8,210.5	8,587.2	2.9	3.4
1954	8	10,073.1	10,582.5	8,544.4	8,776.7	3.8	4.1
1955	9	10,464.6	10,899.1	8,814.6	8,970.4	3.9	3.2
1956	10	10,714.2	11,225.2	8,852.8	9,168.4	2.4	0.4
1957	11	10,885.5	11,561.0	9,004.6	9,370.7	1.6	1.7
1958	12	11,103.5	11,906.9	9,168.6	9,577.6	2.0	1.8
1959	13	11,704.9	12,263.1	9,607.7	9,788.9	5.4	4.8
1960	14	12,485.8	12,629.9	9,993.5	10,005.0	6.7	4.0
1961	15	13,060.8	13,007.8	10,176.9	10,225.8	4.6	1.8
1962	16	13,172.6	13,396.9	10,354.6	10,451.5	0.9	1.7
1963	17	13,710.8	13,797.7	10,795.8	10,682.2	4.1	4.3
1964	18	14,322.5	14,210.5	11,159.2	10,918.0	4.5	3.4
1965	19	14,919.2	14,635.6	11,329.6	11,158.9	4.2	1.5
1966	20	15,370.6	15,073.5	11,577.2	11,405.2	3.0	2.2
1967	21	15,761.5	15,524.4	11,869.0	11,656.9	2.5	2.5
1968	22	16,234.2	15,988.9	12,222.5	11,914.2	3.0	3.0
1969	23	16,552.9	16,467.2	12,331.0	12,177.2	2.0	0.9
1970	24	17,225.0	16,959.9	12,601.3	12,445.9	4.1	2.2
1971	25	17,347.8	17,467.2	12,901.9	12,720.6	0.7	2.4
1972	26	18,500.0	17,989.8	13,596.9	13,001.4	6.6	5.4
1973	27	19,725.4	18,528.0	14,180.5	13,288.3	6.6	4.3
1974	28	20,178.6	19,082.3	14,063.9	13,581.6	2.3	−0.8
1975	29	20,607.8	19,653.2	13,916.7	13,881.4	2.1	−1.0
1976	30	20,406.8	20,241.1	13,822.9	14,187.8	−1.0	−0.7
1977	31	19,744.7	20,846.7	13,690.5	14,500.9	−3.2	−1.0
1978	32	21,089.5	21,470.3	14,544.8	14,820.9	6.8	6.2
1979	33	22,071.4	22,112.7	15,130.3	15,148.1	4.7	4.0
1980	34	22,082.4	22,774.2	14,876.8	15,482.4	0.1	−1.7

[a] Computed from the formula estimated by least squares (the derivation of this formula is explained in the text):
$$\hat{Y}_t = 8,359.346672 e^{0.02947789t}$$
where $R = 0.991045$.

[b] Computed from the formula estimated by least squares:
$$\hat{C}_t = 7,370.250924 e^{0.0218309191t}$$
where $R = 0.99003$.

Source: basic data obtained by dividing money values in Appendix 3.1 by price index in Table 3.22.

year t, starting with $t = 0$ (i.e. 1946 in Table 3.23), going on to $t = 1$ (i.e. 1947 in Table 3.23), and so on, ending with $t = n$ ($= 34$, i.e. 1980 in Table 3.23), and note that by starting with $t = 0$ when we get to n we have also the number of years elapsing between the initial year and the base year. Then, each year throughout the period, the value of any observation Y_t will, if Y grows steadily at rate r per annum, be given by:

$$Y_t = Y_0(1 + r)^t$$

Of course, as we have seen, real income has not grown at the same rate each year. However, suppose real income had grown at a constant trend rate, r, throughout the period but that, in any year, the trend growth rate value may have been modified upwards or downwards by a 'disturbance' in that year which we can represent by the term D_t. If the disturbance takes the value of Y_t 5 per cent above trend, then $D_t = 1.05$; if 5 per cent below trend, then $D_t = 0.95$. We now have a model in terms of a trend growth rate and a disturbance term to represent the actual growth path of Y_t, namely:

$$Y_t = Y_0(1 + r)^t D_t$$

If we take the logarithm to base 10 of this equation, we get:

$$\log_{10}(Y_t) = \log_{10}(Y_0) + t \times \log_{10}(1 + r) + \log_{10}(D_t)$$

(For the reader who has not grappled with the intricacies of logarithms, the above transformation has to be taken on trust; but it may help to ponder the following: $2 \times 2 \times 2 = 2^3 = 8$; $\log_{10}(2^3) = 3 \times \log_{10}(2) = 3 \times 0.30103 = 0.90309$; antilog $0.90309 = 8$.) In this logarithmic transformation, $\log_{10}(Y_0)$ is a constant, or parameter, and so may be represented by the letter a; $\log_{10}(1 + r)$ is also a constant, or parameter, and may be represented by the letter b; $\log_{10}(D_t)$ is a variable 'disturbance' so let us call it d_t. We can then write the equation in a familiar straight-line form:

$$\log_{10}(Y_t) = a + bt + d_t$$

where, using the previous ^ (hat) notation:

$$\log_{10}(\hat{Y}_t) = a + bt$$

and the parameters a and b may be estimated by the method of least squares treating the time series t, shown in Table 3.23, exactly as any other variable; d_t plays the same role as the error term, that is:

$$d_t = \log_{10}(Y_t) - \log_{10}(\hat{Y}_t)$$

If we apply the method of least squares to real income and 't' in Table 3.23 we get the following results:

$$a = 3.922172337$$
$$b = 0.012802085$$
$$R = 0.9910452$$
$$R^2 = 0.9821706$$

Because $a = \log_{10}(Y_0)$ and $b = \log_{10}(1 + r)$, we must take antilogs (using the base 10):

$$Y_0 = \text{antilog}(a) = 8{,}359.3466$$
$$(1 + r) = \text{antilog}(b) = 1.02991667$$

Because antilog $b = (1 + r)$ we may deduce from this last value that the trend growth rate in our model is $r = 0.02991667$, or 2.991667 per cent per annum (t being measured in years). Thus we can write the model for the growth rate of real income either in logarithmic form as:

$$\log_{10}(\hat{Y}_t) = 3.922172337 + 0.012802085t$$

and:

$$\log_{10}(Y_t) = 3.922172337 + 0.012802085t + d_t$$

or in its straightforward, 'multiplicative', form as:

$$\hat{Y}_t = 8{,}359.3466(1 + 0.02991667)^t$$

and

$$Y_t = 8{,}359.3466(1 + 0.02991667)^t D_t$$

We know from the value of the correlation coefficient squared that this model gives quite a good fit to the actual data in Table 3.23 on real income, and so one answer to the question 'How rapidly did real income increase in the period 1946 to 1980?' is this estimate of the trend growth rate: namely, 2.992 per cent per annum.

Having explained the basic model for a trend growth rate, using the compound growth rate formula of Chapter 1, we need to note that this model has a slightly inappropriate form and so produces estimates of the trend growth rate which are slightly biased upwards, though the bias is likely to be only relatively very small. Strictly speaking, the basic model for compound growth:

$$Y_t = Y_0(1 + r)^t$$

assumes that, during the course of each year t, Y_{t-1} remains constant, and that the growth then occurs on the last day of the year to result in Y_t. This is, strictly speaking, the compound interest model where the 'principal', Y_{t-1}, which is a stock, remains constant during the course of the year and where the annual flow of 'interest', or amount by which it grows, is added on at the end of the year. This model is therefore appropriate only for those situations, common in banking and finance, where the interest flow is added at the end of the period to the stock of principal, and where growth therefore occurs in discrete steps like this:

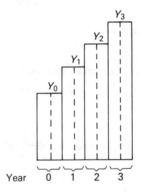

In this process Y is generally a stock variable, so that Y_t refers to the average value of that stock during the period (year) t.

Accordingly, we may call the model we have just used the 'discrete' model of a trend growth rate. But the discrete model is not appropriate for a flow variable like real income, which, it seems reasonable to assume, grows continuously throughout the year, and not in discrete jumps at the end of the year. For a model of continuous growth, where there are no discrete jumps, and where the annual flow is the sum of monthly (or even weekly) flows, each of which shows some growth over its predecessor, we should imagine the growth process as looking like this:

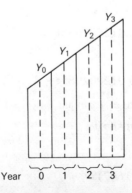

If Y is a stock, then Y_t is the mid-year value of the stock; but if Y is a flow variable, then, of course, Y_t is the value of the flow during the year t.

For this type of growth we require a slightly different formula which can be explained as follows.

In the compound growth model of discrete growth, if interest were added, at proportionate rate r per annum, to the 'principal', Y, twice a year (i.e. regularly at the end of each half-year), then the principal at the end of the first half-year would be:

$$Y_{\frac{1}{2} \text{ year}} = Y_0 \left(1 + \frac{r}{2}\right)$$

and the principal at the end of the first year would be:

$$Y_1 = Y_0 \left(1 + \frac{r}{2}\right)^2$$

and the principal at the end of t years would be:

$$Y_t = Y_0 \left(1 + \frac{r}{2}\right)^{2t}$$

If the interest were added at m regular intervals during the year, then at the end of t years the principal would be:

$$Y_t = Y_0 \left(1 + \frac{r}{m}\right)^{mt}$$

Clearly, if interest is added on monthly, weekly or daily (that is, $m = 12$, or $m = 52$ or $m = 365$ regular intervals) then this formula begins to approximate to a process of 'continuous' growth. Unfortunately, the formula just given is an awkward one, in that it involves m, an indeterminate number. We can, however, both simplify the formula by eliminating m and also at the same time approximate exactly to a process of continuous growth (where m becomes indefinitely large) if we manipulate the formula as follows.

Let $r/m = 1/N$; then m is equal to Nr; as N becomes very large, so too does m, the number of regular intervals a year when interest is added on. Substituting these values for r/m and m, we can then write the formula as:

$$Y_t = Y_0 \left(1 + \frac{1}{N}\right)^{Nrt}$$

or:

$$Y_t = Y_0 \left[\left(1 + \frac{1}{N}\right)^N\right]^{rt}$$

Now consider the behaviour of the expression $(1 + 1/N)^N$ as N becomes very large:

N	1	10	100	100,000	1,000,000	1,000,000,000
$\left(1 + \dfrac{1}{N}\right)^N$	2	2.5937	2.7048	2.71827	2.71828047	2.71828183

It is clear from the arithmetic that the expression $(1 + 1/N)^N$ approaches a limit of 2.71828 as N gets very large, or, technically, as N tends to infinity. Therefore, if we have a continuous process of growth which is going on all the time, so that the number of times interest is added during the year becomes very large, then we may substitute the number 2.71828 for $(1 + 1/N)^N$ in the formula, and derive the following:

$$Y_t = Y_0(2.71828)^{rt}$$

Now consider the following simple analogy: $10^1 = 10$; thus $\log_{10}(10) = 1$; because we can take logs to any base we like, then $\log_{2.71828} 2.71828 = 1$; so that, if in the above equation we take logs to base 2.71828, we have:

$$\log_{2.71828} Y_t = \log_{2.71828} Y_0 + rt \times \log_{2.71828} 2.71828$$

or (because $\log_{2.71828} 2.71828 = 1$):

$$\log_{2.71828} Y_t = \log_{2.71828} Y_0 + rt$$

In this equation Y_t stands for any variable which is growing continuously, so that if we take logarithms to the base of 2.71828 of real income and compute the least-squares straight-line equation between the log (to the base 2.71828) of real income and t, we would have an equation where the intercept was $a = \log_{2.71828} Y_0$ and where the slope, b, was directly equal to r, where (and this is the important part) r is the trend proportionate growth rate per annum when growth is continuous throughout the year (in other words, where 'interest' is added on at exceedingly (infinitely) frequent regular intervals throughout the year).

In more general terms, the conventional mathematical symbol for the number 2.71828183..., or, more strictly, for the number obtained from the formula $(1 + 1/N)^N$ when N tends to infinity, is the letter e, and logs to the base e are conventionally written as ln (instead of $\log_{2.71828}$). So we can write the general formula for continuous growth as:

$$Y_t = Y_0 e^{rt}$$

and using 'natural logarithms', i.e. logs to base 2.71828:

$$\ln(Y_t) = \ln(Y_0) + rt$$

The formula $Y_t = Y_0 e^{rt}$ is called an *exponential function* and the value of r which is derived from such a function is called the *exponential growth rate*: that is, the growth rate where growth is continuous throughout the year, and *not* growth which occurs at discrete intervals. We have gone through a considerable amount of mathematics in order to get here, but this exponential function is very important in economics where we encounter variables which are growing continuously. The analysis of almost any process of growth requires the use of this exponential function.

If we apply the exponential function in natural logarithms to the time series on real income in Table 3.23, we get the following results:

$$a = 9.031135555$$
$$b = 0.02947789$$
$$R = 0.9910452$$
$$R^2 = 0.9821706$$

Because $a = \ln(Y_0)$ we need to take the antilog (using the base $e = 2.71828...$):

$$\text{anti-ln}(a) = 8,359.3466$$

but, in this case, b is a direct estimate of r, so that we can see that the growth rate per annum, where growth is continuous, is 0.02948, or 2.948 per cent. We can observe that this estimate is slightly lower than the estimate from the discrete model, which was 2.992 per cent per annum. This is because continuous growth is always building up the base and growing from the new and higher base, so to get from Y_0 to Y_1 requires a slightly lower growth rate than if the jump from Y_0 to Y_1 were done at one discrete step.

We can also see that the antilog of the constant and the correlation coefficient are exactly the same in both models, and it is furthermore the case that the series of $\hat{Y}_t$ are identical for both models. That is to say, both the discrete growth model and the continuous growth model chart an identical path with exactly the same goodness of fit; the only difference is that the continuous proportionate growth rate is slightly lower, for the reason just explained. Because most variables we encounter are growing in a continuous rather than a discrete manner, the exponential function:

$$Y_t = Y_0 e^{rt}$$

should be the preferred method for estimating trend growth rates. (The trend growth rates of Table 1.3 were, accordingly, estimated in this way.) Table 3.23 gives the trend values of real income and real consumption, computed from their respective exponential functions. It is possible to see that these trend values, $\hat{Y}_t$ and $\hat{C}_t$, do not differ too greatly from their corresponding actual values, Y_t and C_t; in other words, the goodness of fit is satisfactory (see the correlation coefficients).

We are now in a position to choose an answer to the question 'How rapidly did real income and real consumers' expenditure grow during the period 1946 to 1980?' Table 3.24 shows the various answers obtainable. Which answers should we choose or not choose?

TABLE 3.24 *Annual growth rates of real income and real consumers' expenditure over the period 1946 to 1980*

	Per cent change per annum over period 1946 to 1980			
	Average annual change	Compound growth rate	Trend growth rate	
			Discrete	Continuous
Real income	2.768	2.733	2.992	2.948
Real consumers' expenditure	2.159	2.127	2.207	2.183

Source: calculated from Table 3.23, as explained in text.

The compound growth rate, estimated by taking the 34th root of the quotient of the end-year and the initial-year, is not preferred on two counts. First, it does not use all the data we have available: out of the thirty-five observations only two are used, and this represents a waste of information. Second, this estimate will obviously be influenced by the position of the initial- and end-year observation: if the initial-year is the bottom of a cyclical trough and the end-year is the top of a cyclical peak, then this method, in some sense, 'overestimates' the growth rate, and vice versa. Only if the initial- and end-years are 'comparable' years with regard to the general state of economic activity, and so provide trend values of the variables, i.e. where trend Y is close to actual Y, does this estimate correspond to the trend growth rate. This being said, it is sometimes the case that we have only two observations, one at the beginning of the period and another at the end. In this case, the compound growth rate formula is the only one applicable, and it can be seen in Table 3.24 that it does not differ 'excessively' from the other estimates. Furthermore, the compound growth rate may be calculated very speedily (especially if one has a calculator with an exponent key, x^y or $x^{1/y}$, which can automatically extract the yth root of a number). Provided one is aware of its limitations, the compound growth rate formula is handy in its speed of calculation, and for this reason its use may be excusable.

The average of the annual percentage changes answers the question what the average experience was, in any year, of percentage growth and it does use all the information available. But this average may be affected by one or two years in which growth was very rapid (or the converse). Furthermore, it is generally the case that such averages have relatively large standard deviations so that the 'representativeness' of the average is, in any case, questionable (the averages of 2%, 2% and 2% on the one hand, and −4%, 2% and

8% on the other, are both 2%, but how 'representative' is 2% of the latter series?). To illustrate, the standard deviations of the annual percentage growth rates of real income and real consumers' expenditure in Table 3.23 are 2.55 per cent and 2.53 per cent respectively, so that the standard deviations are large relative to their respective averages. For this reason, the average of the annual percentage changes should probably not be used as a measure of growth over any period, though its calculation does have the advantage of being easily understood.

We have already argued that the model of the discrete growth rate is inappropriate in the context where the variable is a flow variable and so is likely to be the subject of a continuous process of growth. If one has all the data and is able to use the method of least squares to compute a trend growth rate, then one should use the exponential function $Y_t = Y_0 e^{rt}$. The trend growth rate, in a continuous process, is an estimate of the growth rate which uses all the information available, and, because of the least-squares method, is less affected by those few years in which growth or decline were abnormally rapid. This trend growth rate answers a quite specific question in giving the general trend over a period in which the cyclical ups and downs more or less cancel out, and it is sensible, from an economic point of view, to interpret the question 'How rapidly did real income grow over the period 1946 to 1980?' as meaning 'What was the trend rate of growth over this period?'

Therefore, unless one has specific reasons for doing otherwise, it is preferable to use the trend growth rate, estimated from the continuous model, as a measure of annual growth over any period of years. And so we shall say that, over the years 1946 to 1980, real personal-sector income in the United Kingdom grew by 2.948 per cent per annum, and real consumers' expenditure grew by 2.183 per cent per annum. This implies that personal-sector real income was doubling every twenty-four years or so; and the fact that real consumers' expenditure was growing more slowly than real income implies that real saving was probably growing more rapidly than real income. Using the compound growth rate formula we can make a quick check on this assertion: 'real' saving before deduction of taxes and National Insurance contributions (note this qualification well) was £8,830m.−£7,273m. = £1,557m. in 1946, and £22,082.4m.−£14,876.8m. = £7,205.6m. in 1980, so the compound annual growth rate of real saving before taxes was:

$$\sqrt[34]{\frac{7,205.6}{1,557}} - 1 = 0.0461$$

or 4.61 per cent per annum. (This illustrates what I meant by the compound growth rate formula being a handy one to apply.)

Having explained the process of deflation by a price index to obtain a series on 'real' values, and also the computation of trend growth rates, we may now use the data of Table 3.23 to see what the time-series consumption function looks like when we take away the impact of price inflation. You may recall that one objection to estimating a time-series consumption function using variables expressed in money terms is that, in years of rapid price inflation, both money incomes and consumers' expenditure are likely to rise rapidly because of the effects of inflation rather than because of the underlying consumption-function relation between the two. In this way, inflation may disguise or bias the estimate of the time-series consumption-function relationship, and so it is preferable, when trying to estimate this relationship, to use price-deflated data on 'real' incomes and consumers' expenditure.

If we estimate a time-series consumption function for the period 1946 to 1980 using the 'real', price-deflated, data of Table 3.23 we obtain the following result:

$$\hat{C}_t = 2,916 + 0.557 Y_t$$

with a correlation coefficient of $R = 0.9957$, so that the equation and the variation in Y_t explain 99.1 per cent of the variance in C_t. The value of the marginal propensity to consume is considerably smaller than the value of 0.666 obtained by using money, or current-price, data (see Diagram 3.7). However, the goodness of fit is not greatly affected by price inflation (the correlation coefficient for the current-price time-series consumption function being $R = 0.9998$: $R^2 = 0.9996$). Thus the consumption function measured by using real income and real consumers' expenditure still provides a good explanation of consumers' expenditure.

Conclusion

This chapter has looked at the main aspects of the personal-sector accounts, as these descriptive items are basic ingredients in understanding the economic behaviour of households. In addition, we have considered several statistical matters (the method of least squares, price indices, exponential growth), an understanding of which is essential to economic analysis. Using the statistical techniques and the descriptive data relating to personal-sector (household) accounts, we can begin to analyse, precisely and in economic and quantitative terms, what households do: for example, through the consumption function, which applies a statistical method to descriptive data to provide an analytic understanding of the (main) influences on consumers' expenditure, an important aggregate in the national accounts.

Exercises

3.1 *(To practise finding data.)*

(i)   Update Table 3.1.
(ii)   Update Table 3.2.
(iii)   Update Table 3.3.
(iv)   Update Table 3.5.

3.2 *(To practise your understanding of accounts.)* The personal sector does not have an operating account as such, but it does have the middle block of accounts in Diagram 2.7; using the results of Exercise 3.1 and the middle part of Diagram 2.7, explain with updated figures the difference between personal-sector saving and the personal-sector financial surplus.

(*Hint:* aggregate the figures of the tables into the requisite totals for Diagram 2.7; i.e. do not try to put in all the details; to cope with receipts on capital account other than saving, put in an extra arrow from the side.)

3.3 *(A puzzle.)* Appendix 1.2 gives an average figure for the stock of unemployed in the United Kingdom in 1980; Table 3.2 gives the total National Insurance unemployment benefit paid in the United Kingdom during 1980. What was the average payment per unemployed person per annum (per week)?

(As the rates of unemployment benefit were £18.50 per week from January to 27 November

1980 and £20.65 per week thereafter (with £11.45 per week for a dependent adult (rising to £12.75) and £1.70 per week for each child (altered to £1.25 per week; data on rates of unemployment benefit may be obtained in DHSS, *Social Security Statistics 1980*, s.1), the results of this exercise would take some explaining, probably in terms of the number of unemployed who do not claim, or are not eligible for, unemployment benefit (payable for 52 weeks only). In other words, this exercise might be better done via an alternative route: dividing the total annual amount paid by (the weekly rate of benefit *multiplied by* fifty-two) to see how many unemployed could have been paid for a full year.)

3.4 *(To practise using data – and to stir your conscience to indignation.)* In 1979 the number of persons in the United Kingdom receiving retirement pensions (including persons residing overseas) was 8.937 million (CSO, *Social Trends 1981 Edition*, no. 11, table 6.8, p. 89). Matching this figure with the total amount of retirement pensions paid in the United Kingdom in 1980 (not a very correct procedure – can you update the figure on the number of retirement pensioners?), what was the average payment per pensioner per annum (per week)?

(The standard rate of National Insurance retirement pension for most of 1980 was £23.30 per week (DHSS, *Social Security Statistics 1980*, table 13.01, p. 70), so the result of this exercise, at least, is not puzzling.)

3.5   *(To practise income tax sums. I promise that this will become a relevant exercise!)* Using the 1980–1 tax rates and the following data, work out the income tax bill for Mr Jones: Mr Jones's income from employment, £25,000 per annum: Mr Jones's own contribution to a superannuation scheme, £1,250 per annum; Mr Jones's interest payable on the mortgage on his own residence, £3,000 per annum (all interest eligible for tax relief); Mr Jones is married. Now do the exercise again but using 1982–3 tax bands. What happens to Mr Jones's tax bill and mortgage interest payment after April 1983?

3.6   *(To practise 'looking at' tables and seeing the difference between stocks and flows.)* What was the personal sector's net asset position with the banking sector at 31 December 1979? What proportionate change in that net asset position occurred during 1980?

3.7   *(A puzzle.)*

(i)   Show on a graph the probabilities that an English male will die within one year at ages 10, 15, 20 and 25 (using 1970–2 mortality rates). What is the pattern? Can you suggest an explanation? (You will need the original source to do this exercise.)

(ii)   What would be the annual breakeven premium to insure the life of an English male aged 25 for £10,000 for one year?

3.8   *(To practise compound growth again.)* Calculate and tabulate the compound annual growth rates of private-sector employees in superannuation schemes between each of the successive pairs of years in Table 3.11.

3.9   *(To estimate your family's net wealth.)* Make up, as completely as you can, a balance-sheet for your household following Table 3.15. (Put approximate guesses for some of the figures if you do not have, or cannot get, exact figures.)

3.10   *(To practise finding data and to practise looking at an important source of data.)*

(i)   Update Table 3.16.
(ii)   Into what category of household and what income group does your household fit?
(iii)   How does your family's weekly expenditure on food compare with the average for UK families of your category and income group.

(To do this exercise you need a library which takes the Department of Employment *Family Expenditure Survey*.)

3.11   *(To practise finding out things.)* The *Family Expenditure Survey* for 1979 sampled 6,777 households, which contained 18,314 persons. The total population of the United Kingdom in mid-1979 was 55,881,000 (CSO, *Monthly Digest of Statistics*, January 1982, table 2.1, p. 16). How many households were there in the United Kingdom in 1979? Upon what assumption is your estimate based?

3.12   *(To practise your understanding of a price index.)* The average household in the United Kingdom in 1979 incurred the following expenditure on fuel, light and power (DoE, *Family Expenditure Survey 1979*, table 6, p. 35):

	£ per week
Gas (inc. hire of gas appliances)	1.52
Electricity (inc. hire of electricity appliances)	2.51
Coal	0.66
Coke	0.13
Fuel oil and other fuel and light	0.43
Total: fuel, light and power	5.25

Between June 1980 and June 1981 price rises were as follows: gas 25 per cent; electricity 22 per cent; coal 9 per cent; coke (smokeless fuels) 10 per cent; oil and other fuel and light 14 per cent (DoE, *Employment Gazette*, August 1981, table 6.2, p. S56). Construct a price index in June 1981 for fuel, light and power with June 1980 = 100.

3.13   *(To practise finding data.)*

(i)   Update Table 3.22.
(ii)   Update Diagram 3.10.

3.14   *(To use price indices.)* What was consumers' expenditure in the United Kingdom in 1979 and 1980? What was the increase in the general index of retail prices between 1979 and 1980? What happened to 'real' consumers' expenditure between 1979 and 1980? (Show all your figures and calculations and explain carefully what your answer means.)

3.15   *(To practise presenting a scatter diagram.)* Draw the consumption function for personal-sector income and consumers' expenditure both at constant 1946 prices and draw in the least-squares line estimated at the end of this chapter.

APPENDIX 3.1 *Personal-sector income and consumers' expenditure in the United Kingdom, 1946 to 1980*

	£ million			£ million Change over previous year		
Year	Total personal income	Consumers' expenditure	Average propensity to consume	Total personal income	Consumers' expenditure	Marginal propensity to consume
1946	8,830	7,273	0.824	—	—	—
1947	9,476	8,028	0.847	646	755	1.169
1948	10,012	8,609	0.860	536	581	1.084
1949	10,570	8,969	0.849	558	360	0.645
1950	11,040	9,461	0.857	470	492	1.047
1951	11,991	10,215	0.852	951	754	0.793
1952	12,793	10,766	0.842	802	551	0.687
1953	13,568	11,475	0.846	775	709	0.915
1954	14,339	12,163	0.848	771	688	0.892
1955	15,564	13,110	0.842	1,225	947	0.773
1956	16,727	13,821	0.826	1,163	711	0.611
1957	17,628	14,582	0.827	901	761	0.845
1958	18,524	15,296	0.826	896	714	0.797
1959	19,635	16,117	0.821	1,111	821	0.739
1960	21,156	16,933	0.800	1,521	816	0.536
1961	22,889	17,835	0.779	1,733	902	0.520
1962	24,073	18,923	0.786	1,184	1,088	0.919
1963	25,550	20,118	0.787	1,477	1,195	0.809
1964	27,565	21,477	0.779	2,015	1,359	0.674
1965	30,083	22,845	0.759	2,518	1,368	0.543
1966	32,209	24,260	0.753	2,126	1,415	0.666
1967	33,851	25,491	0.753	1,642	1,231	0.750
1968	36,501	27,481	0.753	2,650	1,990	0.751
1969	39,242	29,233	0.745	2,741	1,752	0.639
1970	43,438	31,778	0.732	4,196	2,545	0.607
1971	47,866	35,599	0.744	4,428	3,821	0.863
1972	54,673	40,183	0.735	6,807	4,584	0.673
1973	63,652	45,759	0.719	8,979	5,576	0.621
1974	75,567	52,668	0.697	11,915	6,909	0.580
1975	95,880	64,749	0.675	20,313	12,081	0.595
1976	110,652	74,952	0.677	14,772	10,203	0.691
1977	124,032	86,001	0.693	13,380	11,049	0.826
1978	143,470	98,947	0.690	19,438	12,946	0.666
1979	170,261	116,717	0.686	26,791	17,770	0.663
1980	200,985	135,403	0.674	30,724	18,686	0.608

Sources: *National Income and Expenditure 1968*, table 22, p. 30; *National Income and Expenditure 1969*, table 19, p. 24; *National Income and Expenditure 1970*, table 19, p. 24; *National Income and Expenditure 1971*, table 20, p. 26; *National Income and Expenditure 1972*, table 19, p. 24; *National Income and Expenditure 1973*, table 19, p. 24; *National Income and Expenditure 1963–73*, table 21, p. 26; *National Income and Expenditure 1964–74*, table 21, p. 26; *National Income and Expenditure 1965–75*, table 4.1, p. 26; *National Income and Expenditure 1966–76*, table 4.1, p. 28; *National Income and Expenditure 1967–77*, table 4.1, p. 32; *National Income and Expenditure 1979 Edition*, table 4.1, p. 32; *National Income and Expenditure 1980 Edition*, table 4.1, p. 28; *National Income and Expenditure 1981 Edition*, table 4.1, p. 28.

APPENDIX 3.2   *Calculation of the retail price index*

		15 January 1974 = 100		16 January 1979 = 100	Proportionate weight
	Section	Index on 16 Jan 1979	Index on 15 Jan 1980	Index on 15 Jan 1980 [a]	1979
I	Food	217.5	244.8	112.55	0.232
II	Alcoholic drink	198.9	241.4	121.37	0.077
III	Tobacco	231.5	269.7	116.50	0.044
IV	Housing	190.3	237.4	124.75	0.120
V	Fuel and light	233.1	277.1	118.88	0.059
VI	Durable household goods	187.3	216.1	115.38	0.064
VII	Clothing and footwear	176.1	197.1	111.93	0.082
VIII	Transport and vehicles	218.5	268.4	122.84	0.143
IX	Miscellaneous goods	216.4	258.8	119.59	0.069
X	Services	202.0	246.9	122.23	0.059
XI	Meals out	218.7	267.8	122.45	0.051
	All items	207.2	245.3 [c]	118.40 [b]	1.000

[a] Index 15 January 1980 *divided by* index 16 January 1979 (percentage form).
[b] Weighted average, obtained by using weights given in last column.
[c] Calculated as $207.2 \times 1.1840 = 245.3$.

Source: Department of Employment, *Employment Gazette*, November 1980, table 6.4, pp. S58–S59.

APPENDIX 3.3   *The method of least squares*

The sum to be minimised is:

$$\sum_{i=1}^{n} e_i^2 = \sum_{i=1}^{n} (Y_i - a - bX_i)^2 \qquad (1)$$

Because this sum of squares is a function of the parameters a and b (which we are free to choose, the Y_i and X_i being given by the observations), we may minimise the sum of squares by using calculus and finding those values where the first-order differentials of (1) with respect to a and to b are zero, that is, where:

$$\frac{\partial}{\partial a}(\sum e_i^2) = 0$$

and:

$$\frac{\partial}{\partial b}(\sum e_i^2) = 0$$

Applying the rules of calculus:

$$\frac{\partial}{\partial a}(\sum e_i^2) = \frac{\partial}{\partial a}(\sum (Y_i - a - bX_i)^2)$$
$$= -2\sum(Y_i - a - bX_i) \qquad (2)$$

and:

$$\frac{\partial}{\partial b}(\sum e_i^2) = \frac{\partial}{\partial b}(\sum (Y_i - a - bX_i)^2)$$
$$= -2\sum X_i(Y_i - a - bX_i) \qquad (3)$$

Equating these to zero to ascertain the values of a and b which give the minimum value for $\sum e_i^2$ we have:

$$-2\sum(Y_i - a - bX_i) = 0 \qquad (4)$$

and:

$$-2\sum X_i(Y_i - a - bX_i) = 0 \qquad (5)$$

Dividing out the -2s, multiplying out the brackets and rearranging gives:

$$\sum Y_i = na + b\sum X_i \qquad (6)$$

where n is the range of summation (that is, $i = 1, \ldots, n$), and:

$$\sum X_i Y_i = a\sum X_i + b\sum X_i^2 \qquad (7)$$

Equations (6) and (7) are two simultaneous equations in two unknowns, a and b. Let us eliminate the a term by multiplying equation (6) by $\sum X_i$ to give:

$$\sum X_i \sum Y_i = na\sum X_i + b\sum X_i \sum X_i \qquad (8)$$

and by multiplying equation (7) by n to give:

$$n\sum X_i Y_i = na\sum X_i + nb\sum X_i^2 \qquad (9)$$

and by then subtracting equation (8) from equation (9), so eliminating the common term $na\sum X_i$, to give:

$$n\sum X_i Y_i - \sum X_i \sum Y_i = nb\sum X_i^2 - b\sum X_i \sum X_i \qquad (10)$$

In order to proceed further, we need to digress to note the following equivalences:

$$\bar{X} = \frac{1}{n}\Sigma X_i \quad \text{or} \quad \Sigma X_i = n\bar{X} \tag{11}$$

Likewise:

$$\bar{Y} = \frac{1}{n}\Sigma Y_i \quad \text{or} \quad \Sigma Y_i = n\bar{Y} \tag{12}$$

The covariance between X and Y is:

$$\frac{1}{n}\Sigma(X_i - \bar{X})(Y_i - \bar{Y})$$

$$= \frac{1}{n}\Sigma(X_iY_i - \bar{Y}X_i - \bar{X}Y_i + \bar{X}\bar{Y})$$

$$= \frac{1}{n}(\Sigma X_iY_i - \bar{Y}\Sigma X_i - \bar{X}\Sigma Y_i + n\bar{X}\bar{Y})$$

$$= \frac{1}{n}(\Sigma X_iY_i - \bar{Y}n\bar{X} - \bar{X}n\bar{Y} + n\bar{X}\bar{Y})$$

$$= \frac{1}{n}\Sigma X_iY_i - \bar{X}\bar{Y} \tag{13}$$

The variance of X is:

$$\frac{1}{n}\Sigma(X_i - \bar{X})^2$$

$$= \frac{1}{n}\Sigma(X_i^2 - \bar{X}X_i - \bar{X}X_i + \bar{X}^2)$$

$$= \frac{1}{n}(\Sigma X_i^2 - \bar{X}\Sigma X_i - \bar{X}\Sigma X_i + n\bar{X}^2)$$

$$= \frac{1}{n}(\Sigma X_i^2 - \bar{X}n\bar{X} - \bar{X}n\bar{X} + n\bar{X}^2)$$

$$= \frac{1}{n}\Sigma X_i^2 - \bar{X}^2 \tag{14}$$

That is, using (13) and (14):

$$\frac{\text{Covariance between } X \text{ and } Y}{\text{Variance of } X} = \frac{\frac{1}{n}\Sigma X_iY_i - \bar{X}\bar{Y}}{\frac{1}{n}\Sigma X_i^2 - \bar{X}^2} \tag{15}$$

Returning now to equation (10) we may factor out the b on the right-hand side:

$$n\Sigma X_iY_i - \Sigma X_i\Sigma Y_i = b(n\Sigma X_i^2 - \Sigma X_i\Sigma X_i) \tag{16}$$

whence:

$$b = \frac{n\Sigma X_iY_i - \Sigma X_i\Sigma Y_i}{n\Sigma X_i^2 - \Sigma X_i\Sigma X_i}$$

Using (11) and (12):

$$b = \frac{n\Sigma X_iY_i - n\bar{X}n\bar{Y}}{n\Sigma X_i^2 - n^2\bar{X}^2}$$

Factoring out n^2:

$$b = \frac{n^2(\frac{1}{n}\Sigma X_iY_i - \bar{X}\bar{Y})}{n^2(\frac{1}{n}\Sigma X_i^2 - \bar{X}^2)}$$

Dividing out n^2:

$$b = \frac{\frac{1}{n}\Sigma X_iY_i - \bar{X}\bar{Y}}{\frac{1}{n}\Sigma X_i^2 - \bar{X}^2}$$

Using (13) and (14), or (15):

$$b = \frac{\text{Covariance between } X \text{ and } Y}{\text{Variance of } X} \tag{17}$$

Having ascertained that value of b which will satisfy the simultaneous equations for giving the minimum sum of squared residuals, we can return to equation (6) and divide through by n to give:

$$\bar{Y} = a + b\bar{X} \tag{18}$$

whence:

$$a = \bar{Y} - b\bar{X} \tag{19}$$

where b is that value ascertained by equation (17).

Chapter 4

The Company Sector

___

Contents

___

Chapter guide

Chapter 4 continues our grass-roots scrutiny of the economy, looking at the sector of *industrial and commercial companies*, which are important because they produce nearly half of the United Kingdom's value added and undertake nearly four-tenths of the United Kingdom's gross fixed capital formation. We consider some economic-legal features of companies (which economists should know about) and, following the exposition of types of accounts in Chapter 2, we examine the workings of industrial and commercial companies (taken as a sector) through the appropriation account, the capital account, and the financial account.

We look at their sources of *income* – or, more properly, their receipts on appropriation account – and how they 'appropriated', or spent, these receipts. One of the important appropriations is *Corporation Tax*, which is explained in full with particular reference to the *(tax credit) imputation system* known as *Advance Corporation Tax* and we illustrate what this means to the (personal-sector) taxpayer who receives dividends on company shares. We look briefly at the system of *capital allowances* as a tax-deductible item. We look at long-run data on the appropriation of trading profits and especially at the (large) positive balance on appropriation account, or *company saving*, because it is an important feature of company behaviour that companies retain a large proportion of their total receipts on appropriation account.

Looking at the capital account explains why companies save so much: they pay for their fixed capital formation mainly out of their *retentions* (or saving). We also consider some relevant details of the capital account; such as why companies in the United Kingdom get *regional development grants* and what the composition of their investment is.

The balance on the capital account is the financial surplus or deficit; unlike the personal sector, which always runs a financial surplus, the company sector, quite frequently nowadays, runs a *financial deficit*, and we see how this financial deficit is covered, first through the *National Income and Expenditure's* financial account, which gives mostly *net* flows of finance on an *accruals basis*, and second through the *Financial Statistics' flow-of-funds analysis*, the purpose of which is to give more details on the *gross* flows of finance on an actual *cash-flow* basis. (There is a technical section which explains the difference between an accruals basis and a cash-flow basis, with reference to profits and investment to and from abroad.)

Having described what the sector of industrial and commercial companies does, we analyse the most important feature of company behaviour: namely, their use of retentions to finance investment, which implies also that 'profits' (appropriation–account receipts) will affect investment. (In order to do this analysis properly, we must allow for the impact of price inflation, so there is a section explaining how we may obtain and use an *implied price index* (or *'implied price deflator'*) for investment and profits.) We can then use the technique of correlation (Chapter 1) and the method of least squares (Chapter 3) to see whether and how profits relate to investment. This is an important piece of economic analysis because it shows the key role of profits in financing investment and so in helping the economy to grow and prosper.

The company sector: industrial and commercial companies

The personal sector is the major 'consuming' sector of the economy; the company sector is the major 'producing' sector of the economy and, in order to be able to produce, it must hold stocks of fixed capital, so the company sector is also a major 'investing' sector.

Most of the factories, shops and other commercial enterprises with which you are familiar are part of the company sector, so first let us take a quick look in Table 4.1 at the position industrial and commercial companies occupy in the UK economy. In 1980 they produced 49.7 per cent of the United Kingdom's value added; they were responsible for 39.1 per cent of the United Kingdom's gross investment in fixed capital during that year; and they owned 30.6 per cent of the net capital stock (net of cumulated depreciation). Industrial and commercial companies therefore occupy an important position in the economy. Before considering their economic operations, we require some understanding of what sort of entities make up this sector. We need to know a little bit about the legal status of these enterprises as a first step (this is obviously a big subject but we shall consider only the briefest details).

What, legally, is a 'company'? Most companies are *registered companies*, having been formed in acccordance with and registered under one of the Companies Acts. Some

TABLE 4.1   *Industrial and commercial companies in the UK economy in 1980*

	£ million		Industrial and commercial companies as percentage of UK
	Industrial and commercial companies	United Kingdom	
Gross domestic product (value added)	96,252	193,488	49.7
Gross fixed capital formation	15,640	40,050	39.1
Net capital stock (end-year)	227,200	743,000	30.6

Source: Central Statistical Office, *National Income and Expenditure 1981 Edition*, tables 1.10, 10.3, 11.11, pp. 13, 71, 83.

companies may have been established by Royal Charter – such as the Charter granted by King Charles II in 1670 to the 'Governor and Company of Adventurers of England tradeing into Hudson's Bay'. Registered companies are divided between the 'private companies', who may not offer to the public securities in the company and consequently whose shares are not 'quoted' – or traded – on The Stock Exchange, and the larger 'public companies', who may offer securities in the company for sale to the public and some of these securities may be 'quoted' and traded on The Stock Exchange. All public and nearly all private companies are 'limited liability' companies, in the important sense that each shareholder's legal liability for the debts of the company is limited to the extent of his or her shareholding. That is, if the company becomes unable to pay its debts, all that the shareholder loses is the value of his or her shares. The creditors of the company do not have the right to make the shareholder sell, say, his or her house in order to meet (part of) the debts owing. (This is in contrast to the situation which would arise for a partnership which became insolvent – partners have *unlimited* liability for the debts of the partnership and the partners' personal property is at risk.) Because of this limitation on shareholders' liability companies are subjected to considerable legal requirements concerning their formation and their operation.

A company has three important economic-legal features.

First it has corporate status: that is, it is a legal entity in its own right distinct from the persons who own shares in it, and as such the company owns the fixed assets and can be sued for damages, etc. For example, a shareholder cannot wander into an ICI factory and take away an electric drill saying he owns shares in ICI and therefore the drill is 'his'. Or if an ICI factory blows up damaging nearby houses, the householders sue the company, not its shareholders.

Second a company is privately controlled: it is managed by a Board of Directors elected by the shareholders: the most important rights which a shareholder has are to receive an annual dividend on each share held (if a dividend is paid) and to vote on such issues at meetings of shareholders.

Third, the company is supposed to operate with a view to making profits. Profits are important not only because they enable shareholders to receive a return on their funds (and so induce them to supply finance to industry) but also because, as we shall see, the profits retained by companies pay for a large proportion of company investment.

The UK national accounts do not make a distinction between private and public companies. A distinction is made between industrial and commercial companies on the one hand and financial companies on the other. The sector of financial companies comprises banks, building societies, insurance companies, superannuation funds and many other institutions which specialise in accepting liabilities (deposits of money) in return for which they issue assets. In other words, the purpose of financial companies is fundamentally to borrow money at one rate of interest and lend or invest it at a higher rate of interest, thereby making their living on the 'turn' – or margin – between the two. Industrial and commercial companies are all the others which make their living by providing goods and/or services and by charging for what they supply. This sector includes property companies – companies which obtain finance in order to build offices, shops, etc. and to earn a living from the rents. We should note, however, that farming companies (registered limited liability companies) are excluded from the company sector and included in the personal sector; this is because most farms are run by self-employed persons or by partners (and so are in the personal sector) and it would be statistically inconvenient to separate the accounts of those farms run as companies.

Because of the different way in which each of these sub-sectors make its living, it is preferable to consider their accounts separately. First let us consider the industrial and commercial companies.

The appropriation account

Table 4.2 shows the appropriation account of industrial and commercial companies for 1980. These figures include stock appreciation, the amount companies are reported to

TABLE 4.2   *Industrial and commercial companies' appropriation account (income and expenditure account) for 1980*

	£ million	Percentage of total income
Income		
Total gross trading profit (arising in UK) [a]	28,129	78.5
Rent and non-trading income (arising in UK) [b]	2,909	8.1
Income from abroad (net of taxes paid abroad)	4,803	13.4
Total income	35,841	100.0
Expenditure		
Interest on loans	7,049	19.7
UK taxes on income (accruals) [c]	5,623	15.7
Profits due abroad	4,077	11.4
Dividends, etc., to shareholders [d]	4,970	13.9
Current transfers to charities	40	0.1
Total expenditure	21,759	60.7
Balance on appropriation account: 'undistributed income' or gross saving [e]	14,082	39.3

[a]   Accounting profits including stock appreciation of £5,049 million; but this is not an inflow into the sector like other inflows and has to be allocated to maintaining the volume of inventories.
[b]   Including interest received from financial institutions and other sectors.
[c]   Accrued liabilities during year; includes amounts set aside to pay taxes as well as actual payments during the year.
[d]   Including payment of interest on debenture shares, etc.
[e]   Including stock appreciation.

Source: Central Statistical Office, *National Income and Expenditure 1981 Edition*, table 5.4, p. 40.

Starting a company and 'going public'

Under the Companies Act 1980,* there are two basic legal classifications of registered companies: *public limited companies*; and all other companies, namely private companies (apart from some transitional arrangements). The important economic difference between the two classes is that only a public limited company may offer securities (shares or debentures) for sale to the public; any other type of company will be guilty of an offence (punishable by fine) if it offers to the public (whether for cash or otherwise) securities in the company.

In order to ensure that public limited companies are of some 'financial substance', a public limited company must have a nominal (proposed) share capital of at least £50,000, of which at least one-quarter (£12,500) has been 'paid up'. The name of a public limited company must end with the words 'public limited company' (which may be abbreviated to 'plc' – public limited companies with registered offices in Wales may use the Welsh equivalents '*cwmni* [company] *cyfyngedig* [limited] *cyhoeddus* [public]' or 'ccc'). Private limited liability companies must, in most cases, have a name ending with 'limited' ('ltd' – '*cyfyngedig*' or '*cyf*').

In order to start a company, the promoters must submit to the Registrar of Companies the following documents so that they can obtain from the Registrar a 'certificate of incorporation' which confers a legal personality upon the company.

(1) A *Memorandum of Association*, about the 'external relations' of the company, containing clauses setting out, among other things: the name of the company (there are certain restrictions on names, such as not being the same or too like the name of another registered company, or not implying a connection with the Crown); the situation of the registered office (which establishes residence for purposes of Corporation Tax); a statement that the liability of the shareholders or members is limited; and a state-

ment of the objectives of the company (this 'objects clause' will usually be quite widely drawn and will contain some such loophole clause as 'and the doing of all other such things as are incidental or conducive to the attainment' of the company's stated object or objects).

(2) The *Articles of Association*, about the 'internal affairs' of the company, containing the rules by which the company is to be managed: for example, the appointment and powers of directors; the holding of general meetings; the requirement to present audited accounts; the powers to borrow; and, most important, the rights of shareholders.

(3) A *Statutory Declaration*, made by a solicitor or a person named as a director or secretary of the company to the effect that all the requirements of the Companies Acts have been complied with.

(4) The address of the registered office and a statement of the directors and (administrative) secretaries of the company. The registered office is the place where legal notices may be served on the company and where relevant documents may be inspected (companies must notify the Registrar of any subsequent change in the address of the registered office).

(5) A statement of the nominal capital of the company (a small tax is levied upon this at incorporation).

If the Registrar is satisfied that all the requirements of the Companies Acts have been complied with, then he must, on payment of the requisite fee, issue a *certificate of incorporation*. The certificate of incorporation establishes the company as a legal person – a 'body corporate' – which may own property, enter into contracts, sue (and be sued), etc.: in short, which may undertake business with limited liability for its members or shareholders (the *company's* liability for its debts is, of course, unlimited in the sense that it must discharge its liabilities so long

have 'gained' from the rise in the value of their inventories due to price inflation. It would be preferable to deduct stock appreciation from the start, and not to report it as income at all, but (a) it is useful to keep an eye on stock appreciation, and (b) it gets deducted in the capital account where companies have to 'pay' for the increase in the value of their inventories.

Gross trading profits as reported here are what remains out of sales receipts (which are

as it has assets to do so; limited liability means only that the shareholders' or members' liability for the company's debts is limited to the extent of the capital they have subscribed).

A private company may commence business operations immediately after receiving its certificate of incorporation, but a company registered *originally* as a public company requires, additionally, a second certificate of compliance with the minimum share capital requirements (£50,000; £12,500 paid up) known formerly as a 'trading certificate' and now as a '*section 4 certificate*' (after section 4 of the Companies Act 1980). This section 4 (trading) certificate is issued when the Registrar is satisfied that the legal requirements regarding the company's minimum share capital have actually been complied with. The reason for this two-stage procedure is so that a public limited company can first obtain incorporation and, with its legal personality so established, can then set about obtaining its share capital, and when the capital has been successfully raised, it can obtain its section 4 certificate to commence business operations. (A company originally registered as a private company does not require a section 4 certificate because it can obtain a certificate of incorporation as a public limited company only if the Registrar is satisfied that the minimum capital requirements have already been met.)

A public limited company which wishes to offer securities to the public may publish a prospectus inviting the public to subscribe to the securities offered. For the protection of the investing public against fraudulent flotations a copy of the prospectus must be delivered to the Registrar of Companies before publication, and the prospectus must reveal the information about the company as required by the Companies Acts and must include a report by the company's auditors on the financial position of the company (and on its subsidiaries if it has any).

If, as is usually the case, the securities are to be traded – 'listed' – on The Stock Exchange (such marketability making the securities much more attractive to the buyer), then The Stock Exchange's own disclosure requirements for the prospectus (to be published in two leading newspapers) necessitates further description of the company's activities and accounts for at least the preceding five years so that 'no matter relevant to the making of an informed investment decision and to arriving at a judgment on management's ability is omitted' (Committee to Review the Functioning of Financial Institutions (Chairman: Sir Harold Wilson), *Evidence on the Financing of Industry and Trade, Volume 3: Export Credits Guarantee Department, Insurance Company Associations, National Association of Pension Funds, The Stock Exchange*, HMSO, 1978, 'Written evidence by The Stock Exchange', p. 240). A history of the business must be given; the names and ages of the directors; details about the labour force; information on the company's fixed and working capital; a detailed accountant's report; and a statement about any special factors which could affect the company's profits. The Stock Exchange has a lengthy codification of the rules to be observed when preparing prospectuses known as the *Admission of Securities to Listing* (or the 'Yellow Book' after its cover) and draft prospectuses are vetted before publication by The Stock Exchange's Quotations Department.

The Stock Exchange also imposes some quantitative restrictions on new issues because the minimum size of the issue must be £200,000 and companies must have a minimum market valuation of £$\frac{1}{2}$ million – i.e. The Stock Exchange is not for 'small' companies.

*This Act (together with the Companies Act 1981) gives effect to the various provisions of the Second [EEC] Council Directive (13 December 1976) on the co-ordination among EEC Member States of safeguards 'in respect of the formation of public limited liability companies and the maintenance and alteration of their capital, with a view to making such safeguards equivalent' (*Official Journal of the European Communities Legislation*, vol. 20, no. L26, 31 January 1977, pp. L26/1–13).

---

the result of trading activities) after the cost of bought-in-materials *and* the cost of labour have been paid for: it is value added (including stock appreciation) *minus* employee compensation. These trading profits are, in fact, the surpluses carried forward from production accounts – the accounts which would give receipts from sales, cost of materials and cost of labour (see Table 2.2, and Diagrams 2.5 and 2.7) but we do not have a production account for companies, largely because companies are required to report only their profits and not how they arrived at their profits – although some companies now publish a value-added statement (see Table 2.3), and when a complete census on production and distribution is carried out it is possible to derive an aggregate production account for the economy as a whole (Table 2.6).

The gross trading profits made by industrial and commercial companies in 1980 was £28,129 million, including the accounting 'income' of £5,049 million of stock appreciation. As explained in Chapter 2, this stock appreciation does not flow into the company sector; it is a 'book value' of an income flow which would materialise in company bank accounts only if companies reduced the volume of stocks to zero (in effect, went into liquidation or ceased trading). Because we assume that the company sector is going to continue operating, and so must maintain stocks, this stock appreciation is not properly income and must be used to maintain the volume of stocks. Subsequently in the accounts this fact is recognised by deducting the whole of the increase in the book value of stocks. Gross trading profits comprised nearly 80 per cent of the total income accruing to companies because companies have sources of income other than their profits arising from trading activities in the United Kingdom.

Companies receive income arising in the United Kingdom but not from trading activities. First, they receive interest payments on financial assets which they own (such as government bonds). Second, some (property) companies receive rents on property owned by them and let to persons or institutions in other sectors (as a consolidated account for the company sector, rent paid by companies to companies is not included). Such income amounted in total to 8.1 per cent of total company income in 1980.

The other form of income is derived from activities not taking place in the United Kingdom. Many companies own subsidiaries, branches, factories which operate abroad or they may own shares in companies operating abroad. The income which they derive from such ownership (net of taxes abroad to foreign governments and net of depreciation) is separately reported. This figure includes estimates of unremitted income: that is, it is the net income derived (whether actually sent back to the United Kingdom or not). It amounted to 13.4 per cent of total company income in 1980, so that it is a quite significant part of the total. Over all, then, companies received £35,841 million of income in 1980. How did they 'spend' it, or rather, since 'spend' is not quite the right word, how did they 'appropriate', or allocate to current uses, this income?

In the first place, £7,049 million, or 19.7 per cent, went on paying interest on loans from banks. Companies may take on loans or overdrafts from banks, and for this finance they must pay interest. The series of figures in the national accounts show us why businessmen were at this time complaining about the high interest rates they had to pay because in 1969 or 1970 their payment of interest amounted to only 7½ per cent of total income.

Skipping over taxes for the moment, we come to profits due abroad. Some of the companies operating in the United Kingdom are owned by foreign companies, and their profits, whether sent abroad or not, are counted as profits due abroad; that is, the whole amount of such profits needs to be 'appropriated' and therefore not counted as part of the saving of UK companies. If, as they do, foreign-owned companies operating in the United Kingdom leave some of their profits here to pay for capital formation, then this is subsequently treated as investment from abroad: that is, to get a consistent treatment of these flows, the national income statisticians adopt the convention (or 'pretence') that all foreign-company profits are duly sent abroad and that some of those profits may then 'return' to the United Kingdom to pay for investment (this convention is discussed in more detail subsequently).

After payment of interest, taxes, and profits due abroad, companies distributed dividend income to their shareholders. In 1980 this amounted to £4,970 million (as will be explained, this is net of tax at the basic rate). This payment was 13.9 per cent of total income, and, as the accounts of Delta Metal say, this was 'to pay providers of capital' (Table 2.3); but it is clear that shareholders do not receive all that large a share of gross profits. Finally, before we consider company taxation, we should note that companies paid a small amount of money to charities: £40 million in 1980.

Corporation Tax – the imputation system

A fairly substantial amount of tax liabilities accrued in 1980 and companies paid or made provision for £5,623 million of taxes. How and why are companies taxed on their profits? After all, company profits (after interest and depreciation) notionally 'belong' to shareholders who will presumably be paying income tax on the dividends they receive. So are company profits being taxed twice, once as profits accrue to companies, and again when dividends are distributed to shareholders?

This provision for taxation on profits was made under *Corporation Tax*, which is a tax on company profits net of depreciation and after interest charges. In the case of unincorporated enterprises, such as partnerships and sole traders, the whole of the profit made by the undertaking is distributed among the owners and then taxed as their income. But an incorporated enterprise may not distribute all its net profits. In principle, it would be possible simply to tax the distributed profits as the (dividend) income of the recipients and to leave the rest untaxed, but during the First World War the need for extra public finance, combined with the apprehension that firms were making 'excessive' profits out of wartime scarcities, led in 1915 to the Excess Profits Duty levied on wartime profits in excess of the average of profits in the best two of the three prewar trading years (or on the extent to which its return on capital exceeded a statutory minimum return on capital, but most firms preferred to opt for the peacetime profits basis, as 1912 and 1913 had been good years for trading). The Excess Profits Duty provided one quarter of total revenue in the period 1915–21 and it was the first time that company profits had been taxed additionally to income. In 1921 the Excess Profits Duty was repealed, but in 1920 a Corporation Profits Tax of 5 per cent had been imposed on total profits. When Britain began to re-arm in 1937 the need to raise substantial amounts of additional tax revenue again emerged and companies were required to pay a tax – called the National Defence Contribution – on 'excess' profits; additionally in the spring budget of 1939 an Armaments Profits Duty was imposed on the 'excess' profits of munitions firms. The two concerns which led to such a tax – the need to raise revenue and to prevent firms 'profiteering' out of the war – are clearly seen in both these new taxes. In the first wartime budget, an Excess Profits Tax was introduced to tax profits in excess of peacetime 'normal' profits.

From 1946 to 1973 taxation of profits continued by means of a profits tax levied on the profits of a company, the shareholder then paying additional income tax on any distributed dividends. This meant that profits were being taxed twice, as illustrated in Table 4.3.

Suppose we have a rate of profits tax of 52 per cent (the current rate of corporation tax) and a basic rate of income tax at 30 per cent. Under the so-called 'classical system', taxes would be levied twice: first on net profits and then on any dividends. Total net profits would, first, attract tax of £52 (in actual fact, the rate at which profits tax was levied under this system was much lower than this). Suppose the company then distributed the remaining post-tax profits of £48 as dividends (retaining nothing). The basic-rate taxpayer then had to pay, additionally, £14.40 of income tax on the receipt of dividends, so that in all, £66.40 of tax will have been levied. The first snag with this 'classical' system of double taxation is that it discourages distributions and encourages retentions: if the company reduced its dividend to £20, the basic-rate taxpayer would pay only £6 in income tax, and total tax levied on the £100 of net profit would be reduced from £66.40 to £58. The

TABLE 4.3   *Taxing profits*

Item	Annual flow in £	Pro-portionate rate of taxation	Tax paid in £		Notes on imputation system
			'Classical' system: profits taxed twice	'Imputation' system: profits taxed once	
Company net profits (after interest)	100	0.52	52	52	If distributed income is £D this £52 in-cludes an imputed tax credit to the per-son(s) receiving the dividend of 30/70 £D.
Distributed profits (dividend income)	48	0.30	14.40 *less* *equals*	20.57 20.57 0	Calculated as: 0.30 of (£D + 30/70 £D) Imputed tax credit of 30/70 £D Tax payable by basic-rate taxpayer.
Total tax paid	—	—	66.40	52	Total amount of tax does not vary under imputation system (for basic-rate taxpayer), but does vary under classical system according to amount distributed.

company would have more money to invest and presumably the shareholder would benefit from seeing the value of his or her shareholding rise to reflect the increased real assets 'behind' the shares (even though capital gains tax would be levied on this share apprecia-tion when the shares were sold). The second snag is that shareholders claim, with justification, that they are being 'taxed twice': given that the net profits of £100 'belong' to the shareholder, he or she can claim that, with a distribution of all the post-tax profits, the effective rate of tax is 66.4 per cent. Furthermore, the effective tax rate varies according to the extent of the distribution: from 52 per cent with no distributed profits to 66.4 per cent with all post-tax profits distributed.

In order to relieve the shareholder from this 'double' burden of taxation, in the United Kingdom in 1973 the method of taxing profits was changed to the 'imputation' system whereby the shareholder is deemed to receive an imputed tax credit so that

(a)   the basic-rate income taxpayer has no further tax to pay, and
(b)   the total rate of tax levied on profits (when distributions are made to basic-rate income taxpayers) will not exceed 52 per cent (unlike the classical system, where the total tax rate varied with the amount distributed).

Statements (a) and (b) are simply different ways of expressing the same result. In effect, the tax on profits is split into two parts, one of which covers the shareholder's liability to income tax (at the basic rate) on income distributed out of profits (i.e. on dividends), the other of which is a tax on profits proper. The figures for the imputation system are shown in the last column of Table 4.3 but they require a little explanation, which also covers the rather confusing terminology now surrounding UK Corporation Tax. (Because many readers of this book may one day own or inherit company shares, it is of some personal importance to understand the system and its terminology.)*

In the first place, under the imputation system, Corporation Tax of £52 will be levied on every £100 of net profits after interest. If the company then distributes the remaining £48 as dividend income to shareholders, then this £48 is deemed to be a dividend to the shareholders *net* of income tax at the basic rate. Suppose there is only one shareholder who receives the £48, then the shareholder's liability to income tax (at the basic rate) on the dividend is deemed to have been already paid as part of the £52 of Corporation Tax. Or, to

* Corporation Tax was introduced in 1965 but operated under the 'classical system' until 1973, when the present 'imputation system' was introduced.

put it another way, notionally but not actually the shareholder 'receives' along with the £48 dividend an imputed 'tax credit', which is deemed to be part of the £52 of Corporation Tax. Thus the shareholder, as an income taxpayer has no further income tax to pay arising out of the dividend income of £48 – but only if he or she is paying the income tax at the basic rate of 30 per cent. How, then, is the amount of the imputed tax credit calculated?

We can best understand the right answer as to how to calculate the tax credit if we consider a wrong answer. The wrong answer arises if we try to give the following 'straightforward' solution by saying that if £48 is distributed as dividends and the basic-rate taxpayer is paying income tax at the rate of 30 per cent, then the tax credit should be calculated, quite straightforwardly, as £48 × 0.30 = £14.40; so that, it may seem, £14.40 should be the amount of the imputed tax credit.

Unfortunately, this is the wrong answer because under the imputation system the distributed dividend income is income *after* tax, and the straightforward answer fails to take account of this complication. We can see this because the straightforward, and wrong, answer gives the wrong rate of taxation. The rate of taxation is always calculated as:

$$\frac{\text{Tax paid}}{\text{Income } before \text{ tax}} = \frac{\text{Tax paid}}{\text{Income } after \text{ tax} + \text{Tax paid}}$$

So the straightforward, and wrong, answer results in the shareholder apparently paying tax at the following rate:

$$\frac{£14.40}{£48 + £14.40} = \frac{14.40}{62.40} = 0.23$$

but the basic rate of income tax is 30 per cent, not 23 per cent. So the straightforward approach to calculating the imputed tax credit does not give the right answer. In order to get the right answer, the amount of the imputed tax credit (for the basic-rate taxpayer) has to be calculated by starting from the formula just given which defines the basic rate of tax, namely:

$$\text{Basic rate of tax} = 0.30 = \frac{\text{Tax paid}}{\text{Income } after \text{ tax} + \text{Tax paid}}$$

because tax paid divided by *gross* income (income *before* tax) must, for the basic-rate taxpayer, be 30 per cent. In the imputation system the tax 'paid' is, of course, the imputed tax credit. In the equation just given, we know the basic rate of tax, 0.30, and we know the amount of income *after* tax, namely distributed dividends of £48. What we do not know is the amount of income tax which has been deemed to be paid as part of the Corporation Tax. But it is possible to work out correctly the appropriate imputed tax credit as follows:

$$0.30 = \frac{\text{Tax credit}}{£48 + \text{Tax credit}}$$

therefore:

$$0.30 \, (£48 + \text{Tax credit}) = \text{Tax credit}$$

whence:

$$0.30 \times £48 + 0.30 \times \text{Tax credit} = \text{Tax credit}$$

whence:

$$0.30 \times £48 = \text{Tax credit} - 0.30 \times \text{Tax credit}$$

whence:

$$0.30 \times £48 = (1 - 0.30) \text{ Tax credit}$$

whence:

$$\frac{0.30}{1 - 0.30} \times £48 = \text{Tax credit}$$

whence:

$$£20.57 = \text{Tax credit}$$

So the imputed tax credit of the corporation tax is £20.57 or thirty-seventieths (0.30/0.70) of £48. More generally, the imputed tax credit will be 30/70 of whatever amount of profit is distributed as dividends. And more generally still, in case the basic rate of income tax should alter, the imputed tax credit will be:

$$\frac{\text{Basic rate of income tax}}{1 - \text{Basic rate of income tax}} \textit{ multiplied by } \text{Distributed profits}$$

The company is required to pay this imputed tax credit to the Inland Revenue on the same date on which it distributes the dividends to shareholders. (This is to ensure that, should the Inland Revenue have to make refunds to shareholders exempt from income tax, the tax has already been paid.) Accordingly, the imputed tax credit is known as *Advance Corporation Tax* (ACT), a somewhat misleading name since it is really the (basic rate of) income tax on dividends which is being paid directly by the company, on behalf of the shareholders, to the Inland Revenue. Subsequently, when the full corporation tax of £52 falls due (and companies generally pay taxes in arrears), the company pays £52 *minus* £20.57 (the already paid advance corporation tax) *equals* £31.43. This latter residual amount is known as *mainstream corporation tax*, possibly because it is the tax on company profits proper. The amount of mainstream corporation tax (per £100 of net profits after interest) will, of course, vary according to how much net profit has been distributed as dividends. But this does not matter, because the total amount paid in taxes will remain at £52 (per £100 of net profit). The whole purpose of the imputation system of profits tax is to ensure that the total tax paid on net profits of £100 will be exactly and only £52 (or according to whatever the rate of Corporation Tax happens to be). The amount of tax will not vary if the amount of distributed profits varies.

If all this should seem rather complex, the reader who may well become a shareholder must bear in mind that when he or she receives a dividend payment of, say, £48 the cheque will be accompanied by a 'voucher' certifying that a 'tax credit' of £20.57 has also been paid to the Collector of Taxes. The shareholder must then on his or her income tax return enter the (notional) gross of tax dividend of £68.57 to be added to his or her other income in order to compute his or her tax liability. But, at the end, the taxpayer can note that tax of £20.57 has already been paid on this pre-tax dividend income of £68.57; so that if the taxpayer is paying tax at the basic rate, the tax credit exactly offsets the tax liability. However, if the taxpayer is paying a higher marginal rate of tax, then he or she will have to pay an extra amount to the Inland Revenue of:

$$\left\{ \begin{array}{c} \text{Marginal rate applicable to taxpayer} \end{array} - \begin{array}{c} \text{Basic rate} \end{array} \right\} \times \begin{array}{c} \text{Gross of tax dividend} \end{array}$$

$$= \begin{array}{c} \text{Marginal rate applicable to taxpayer} \end{array} \times \begin{array}{c} \text{Gross of tax dividend} \end{array} - \begin{array}{c} \text{Tax credit} \end{array}$$

Two examples to illustrate the imputation system of Corporation Tax

In order to understand this let us consider two contrasting pairs of cases as shown in Table 4.4. In the first pair, we have taxpayer A, who, not being a shareholder, receives no dividends, while taxpayer B receives a dividend payment of £48. Both A and B earn the same income from employment, £10,000 a year, and both can claim the higher (married man's) personal allowance of £2,145 (at 1980–1 rates). A's taxable income is £7,855, all of which is taxed at the basic rate of 30 per cent, so the tax due is £2,356.5. B, by contrast, has to enter the receipt of dividends *before* tax, namely £68.57, comprising the after-tax payment of £48 *plus* the imputed tax credit of £20.57. So B's taxable income is £7,923.57, all of which is taxed at the basic rate, so total tax due is £2,377.07; but tax of £20.57 has already been paid by the company in its payment of Advance Corporation Tax, so this tax credit can be deducted from the total due, and the amount B has to send to the Collector of Taxes is £2,356.5, exactly the same as A.

In the second pair, we have two higher-rate taxpayers, C and D, both of whom receive £20,000 a year from employment: D receives, additionally, a dividend of £48; both claim the same personal allowance. C's taxable income is £17,855; tax at the basic rate of 30 per cent is levied on the first £11,250 of this (£3,375 of tax); at the higher rates of 40 per cent on the next £2,000 (£800), 45 per cent on the next £3,500 (£1,575), and 50 per cent on the remaining £1,105 (£552.5). Total tax due is £6,302.5 and this is the amount C has to pay. D's taxable income is £17,923.57 because he has to add on the £68.57 of dividends before tax (£48 as received *plus* £20.57 of tax credit at the basic rate). Tax at the basic rate is levied on the first £11,250 (£3,375), at 40 per cent on the next £2,000 (£800), at 45 per cent on the next £3,500 (£1,575), and at 50 per cent on the remaining £1,173.57 (£586.79). Total tax due is £6,336.79, but a tax credit of £20.57 has already been paid, so D must pay to the Collector of Taxes £6,316.22; this is £13.72 more than C has to pay because the tax credit at the basic rate does not entirely match D's liability to tax at the higher marginal rate of taxation, which is 50 per cent in this case. Because of the receipt of dividends, D has to pay an additional amount of tax computed, by applying the formula given on p. 190, as:

$$(0.50 \times £68.57) - £20.57 = £13.72$$

TABLE 4.4   *Tax credit under the imputation system of Corporation Tax (1980–1 rates)*

	£ a year			
	A	B	C	D
Income from employment	10,000	10,000	20,000	20,000
Plus Dividend (before tax)	0	68.57	0	68.57
less Personal allowance	2,145	2,145	2,145	2,145
equals Taxable income	7,855	7,923.57	17,855	17,923.57
Tax due:				
Basic rate: 30% on first £11,250	2,356.5	2,377.07	3,375	3,375
Higher rates: 40% on next £2,000	—	—	800	800
45% on next £3,500	—	—	1,575	1,575
50% on next £5,500	—	—	552.5	586.79
Total due	2,356.5	2,377.07	6,302.5	6,336.79
Less Tax credit	—	20.57	—	20.57
Total to be paid	2,356.5	2,356.5	6,302.5	6,316.22

So far, we have considered the mechanics of levying a tax on company profits. Although this is a complex issue, it is not really as important as the problem of defining what constitutes taxable profits in the first place. What, then, are the profits on which tax is levied – what calculations must we do in order to arrive at the £100 of Table 4.3?

The gross profits of a company may be defined as value added *minus* employee compensation. But this flow is not an appropriate measure of the benefits which the company (or its shareholders) derive from its activities because this flow is gross of both depreciation and also of interest payable on loan finance made available to the company.

In the first place, because interest received by the company is taxable, interest paid by companies has always been a tax-deductible expense (which, of course, makes loan finance an attractive method of getting hold of money, up to the point where the risk of not being able to meet, out of gross profits, the interest payments or debt repayment comes into play).

In the second place, the fixed capital which was initially purchased with the shareholders' funds will be depreciating in value as it is 'used up' in the process of production (this was explained in Chapter 2 by the example of the lady with the sewing-machine).

Therefore, it is justifiable to permit the deduction of depreciation as a tax-deductible expense, because it is the net profits, after deducting interest and depreciation, which most appropriately measure the benefit derived by the shareholders from the company's trading activities. Companies have therefore been allowed to deduct depreciation from profits before arriving at taxable (net) profits. However, because the government wished to encourage investment, there developed a policy of allowing more of the depreciation to be deducted in the year in which the investment was made; this reduced taxable profits and taxes in the year in which the company's cash flow came under strain because of paying for the investment and so relieved that strain. The converse of permitting such 'accelerated' depreciation is, of course, that taxable profits and taxes were higher in subsequent years because correspondingly less depreciation could be deducted in those years. What is now the case in the United Kingdom is that annual depreciation cost, as calculated by the accountants, say on a straight-line basis, is *not* allowable as a tax-deductible expense; instead, under the 1972 Finance Act, companies (and partnerships and sole traders) are permitted to deduct the entire capital expenditure in the first year. This applies to plant, machinery, ships and aircraft, and is intended to act as an incentive to investment because it relieves the firm's cash-flow problems in the investment year.

In Chapter 2 we saw how stock appreciation – the rise in the book value of the same volume of inventories, or, what comes to the same thing, the rise in the book value of inventories *less* the value of the physical increase in inventories – would enhance accounting profits. We also saw in Table 2.9 how stock appreciation had, in the 1970s, become very large relative to company profits: in 1974 stock appreciation amounted to 41 per cent of company gross profits (including stock appreciation).

Clearly, if firms were to be taxed on these 'book-value' accounting profits, then a good part of the taxation would fall upon that part of profits (stock appreciation) which was required to be put straight back into simply maintaining the volume of inventories. If it is unreasonable to tax profits gross of depreciation, because depreciation is that part of (gross) profits which must be put back into maintaining the stock of (fixed) capital intact, then it is likewise unreasonable to tax that part of profits which must be reserved for maintaining the physical volume of inventories.

During the 1950s and 1960s the unreasonableness of taxing accounting profits including stock appreciation had neither been apparent nor had it mattered, because stock appreciation was relatively small. (The analogy would be if house-owners were taxed annually on the annual rise in the capital value of their dwellings: as long as this rise were small in relation to house-owners' incomes, such taxation would not, in practice, matter: but if the annual rise became relatively large, then the annual taxation of the annual capital gain would seriously affect the other expenditures which could be made by households.) After 1969, as stock appreciation grew relatively large, it became clear that taxation of these

An example to illustrate the system of capital allowances

Suppose we have a firm earning gross profits of £125 a year derived from investing in a machine costing £100 with a life of four years and so requiring depreciation provisions of £25 a year. In the economist's view, the firm should be permitted to deduct, each year, £25 from gross profits to arrive at taxable profits of £100 on which (at 52 per cent) tax of £52 could be levied each year. Over the four years as a whole, the firm would earn £500 of profits, be allowed £100 for depreciation, and so pay tax of £208 as shown in Table 4.5.

But this is *not* what happens under the United Kingdom's current tax laws. Instead, the firm is permitted to deduct the £100 cost of the machine in the first year of profits. So taxable profits in the first year are assessed as £25 and the Corporation Tax payable (at 52 per cent) is only £13. In the second and subsequent years there is no allowance against gross profits and tax of £65 has to be paid in those years. Over the period as a whole the result is exactly the same: it is only the timing that is different. The advantage to the firm is that under the depreciation system it had to find, in the first year, cash amounts of £100 for the machine and £52 for tax, putting a strain on its cash flow from gross profits of £125 (i.e. forcing the company to borrow and so, perhaps, discouraging investment). By contrast, under the capital allowance system it has to find in the first year cash amounts of £100 for invest-

ment and only £13 for Corporation Tax, so the lower tax payment relieves its cash-flow difficulty. Industrial buildings qualify for a first-year capital allowance of 79 per cent of their cost (comprising a capital allowance of 75 per cent and annual depreciation of 4 per cent); for motor-cars a 25 per cent (normal) depreciation allowance is all that is permitted; for agricultural buildings and works, one-tenth of the cost of construction may be deducted from gross profits each year for ten years; and expenditure on scientific research related to the company's trade activities may be entirely deducted in the year in which it is incurred. Capital expenditure on most 'commercial' buildings is not eligible (an economically nonsensical discrimination).

If the capital allowances exceed profits for any year, then the excess may be carried forward and deducted from future profits, or in the case of plant and machinery may be offset against profits in the three immediately preceding years. To illustrate, suppose the firm (unexpectedly) made gross profits of only £60 in the first year; then £60 of the £100 capital expenditure could be deducted from gross profits, giving zero taxable profits so that no tax at all would be payable; in the second year (gross profits having returned to their expected £125) the remaining £40 of the capital expenditure could be carried forward and offset against gross profits to give taxable profits of £85 and a tax payment of £44.20.

TABLE 4.5 *Depreciation and capital allowances*

| Item | Flows in £ per annum | | | | Total over four years |
	First year	Second year	Third year	Fourth year	
Previous system					
Gross profits after interest	125	125	125	125	500
Straight-line depreciation [a]	25	25	25	25	100
Taxable net profits	100	100	100	100	400
Tax	52	52	52	52	208
Present system					
Gross profits after interest	125	125	125	125	500
Capital allowance [b]	100	0	0	0	100
Taxable profits	25	125	125	125	400
Tax	13	65	65	65	208

[a] On machine costing £100 with a life of four years.

[b] Cost of machine in year of purchase – sometimes called an 'initial allowance' or 'free depreciation' if entire cost deductible in year of purchase ('accelerated depreciation' if depreciation may all be put into, say, first three years).

accounting profits was adversely affecting companies' ability to invest in fixed capital and to maintain the volume of inventories required for production. Therefore, in November 1974 the Chancellor of the Exchequer introduced 'stock relief' to remove the burden of taxation (the relief was retrospective to 1973: the forces which compelled this relief are clearly obvious in Table 2.9). In effect, companies were permitted to deduct stock appreciation from their accounting profits (net of depreciation) in order to calculate taxable profits. However, there remained the problem of calculating stock appreciation in each company so that the proper relief could be obtained. The simple rise in the book value of stocks (one possible method of calculating the permitted deduction) might include also the value of the physical increase in stocks, and so permitting the whole of the rise in the book value of stocks to be deducted could be over-generous to companies (that is, the worry was it might be 'under-generous' to the Inland Revenue). This problem was solved, in a rough-and-ready way, by requiring companies to adjust the increase in the book value of stocks downwards by 10 per cent of profits after capital allowances. This 10 per cent of profits was meant to do duty as a uniform estimate of the value of the physical increase in stocks, the remainder being an estimate of stock appreciation. The increase in the book value of stocks, adjusted downwards by this 10 per cent of net profits, could then, as a measure of stock appreciation, or 'stock relief', approved and accepted by the Inland revenue, be deducted from profits to strike the balance of taxable profits on which Corporation Tax would be levied (the downward adjustment was raised to 15 per cent in 1975–6 to 1978–9, then put back to 10 per cent in 1979–80). From November 1980 stock relief is to be (more sensibly) calculated by applying the percentage change in an all stocks price index* to the opening value of an enterprise's stocks *less* £2,000.

This concludes our consideration of Corporation Tax, but it is an interesting question as to how much tax companies actually paid in the years when all these changes were taking place. We can also take this opportunity to look at trends in the other main appropriations of profits. Table 4.6 shows the main items in the appropriation account of industrial and commercial companies (unlike Table 2.9, this table excludes financial companies). We can start the series in 1964 because this is the first year for which information on profits excluding stock appreciation is available. Before 1973 payment of dividends was reported gross of (income) tax; after 1973 payment is net of Advance Corporation Tax, and Advance Corporation Tax itself is included in the UK taxes on income. It is therefore necessary to make the series consistent by adding Advance Corporation Tax on to dividends and deducting it from UK taxes on profits. The item 'other interest' is mainly interest payments to banks. Table 4.6 relates these payments to UK gross trading profits after deduction of stock appreciation: that is, we ignore income from other sources.

The trends revealed by this comparison are interesting. We see that dividends gross of tax have fallen considerably as a proportion of UK gross trading profits after stock appreciation: from about 40 per cent in the 1960s to about 25 per cent in the late 1970s. This may be due partly to the effect of restrictions on the payment of dividends which formed part of some of the incomes policies which were imposed in the late 1960s and 1970s, but there may also be other reasons which we shall explore subsequently. However, it is clearly not the case that the greater proportion of profits is distributed as dividend income. An even more striking feature in the appropriation accounts of industrial and commercial companies is the rise in other interest payments, mainly to banks. From being well under 10 per cent of gross trading profits in the 1960s, interest payments rose to near or over 20 per cent in the later 1970s and to 30.5 per cent in 1980; on the one hand, as we shall see, this was due to increased borrowing from the banks, and on the other, to higher interest rates charged by banks.

UK taxes on profits have fluctuated as a proportion of UK gross profits after stock appreciation. Over the whole period, 1964 to 1980, taxes have averaged 17 per cent of profits; but there have been years when the proportion has been higher, and years when it

*For which see Department of Industry, *Price index numbers for Current Cost Accounting*, no. 14, 1981, table 7, p. 118.

TABLE 4.6   *Industrial and commercial companies: appropriation of trading profits, 1964 to 1980*

	£ million				Percentage of gross trading profits after stock appreciation		
Year	Gross trading profits after stock appreciation [a]	Dividends gross of tax [b]	Other interest [c]	UK taxes on profits (accruals) [d]	Dividends gross of tax	Other interest	UK taxes on profits (accruals)
1964	4,602	1,709	242	823	37.1	5.3	17.9
1965	4,799	1,980	344	461	41.3	7.2	9.6
1966	4,654	2,022	383	964	43.4	8.2	20.7
1967	4,815	1,999	376	1,028	41.5	7.8	21.3
1968	5,167	1,996	476	1,341	38.6	9.2	26.0
1969	5,579	2,179	566	1,527	39.1	10.1	27.4
1970	5,688	2,041	611	1,314	35.9	10.7	23.1
1971	6,555	2,241	585	1,142	34.2	8.9	17.4
1972	7,692	2,284	733	1,399	29.7	9.5	18.2
1973	8,850	2,661	1,560	2,119	30.1	17.6	23.9
1974	8,300	3,155	2,489	456	38.0	30.0	5.5
1975	9,452	3,163	2,429	542	33.5	25.7	5.7
1976	12,248	3,508	2,892	1,519	28.6	23.6	12.4
1977	17,424	4,181	2,765	1,967	24.0	15.9	11.3
1978	20,588	4,663	3,112	2,704	22.6	15.1	13.1
1979	22,459	6,411	5,036	3,278	28.5	22.4	14.6
1980	23,080	6,715	7,049	3,878	29.1	30.5	16.8

[a]   Income arising in the United Kingdom.
[b]   Dividends on ordinary shares plus other dividends and debenture and loan interest; *plus* (in 1973 and after) Advance Corporation Tax as given in note (3) to table 5.4 in the 1981 Blue Book; before this date dividends were reported gross of tax: see the note to table 5.1 on p. 116 of *National Income and Expenditure 1981 Edition.*
[c]   According to CSO, *Financial Statistics Explanatory Handbook 1980 Edition*, p. 90, these payments 'consist largely of payments [of interest] on bank advances . . . [estimated] by applying appropriate interest rates to levels of liabilities'.
[d]   Reported figures on accruals *less*, in 1973 and after, Advance Corporation Tax.

Sources: Central Statistical Office, *National Income and Expenditure 1964–74*, table 35, p. 39 (the first to give estimates of stock appreciation in industrial and commercial companies); Central Statistical Office, *National Income and Expenditure 1965–75*, table 5.4, p. 39; Central Statistical Office, *National Income and Expenditure 1966–76*, table 5.4, p. 42; Central Statistical Office, *National Income and Expenditure 1967–77*, table 5.4, p. 46; Central Statistical Office, *National Income and Expenditure 1979 Edition*, table 5.4, p. 46; Central Statistical Office, *National Income and Expenditure 1980 Edition*, table 5.4, p. 40; Central Statistical Office, *National Income and Expenditure 1981 Edition*, table 5.4, p. 40.

has been much lower. The retrospective stock relief introduced in November 1974 had a considerable impact in reducing the tax burden in that year and in 1975; but since then taxes have again risen: first, as a result of the lessening of stock relief (due to the increase in the downward adjustment from 10 to 15 per cent of net profits), and, after the third quarter of 1978, by the increasing revenues from Petroleum Revenue Tax on companies' production of North Sea oil.

Saving by industrial and commercial companies

The total amount of income 'spent', or appropriated, on the appropriation account in 1980, was £21,759 million; against this, industrial and commercial companies received £35,841 million of income from all sources (including stock appreciation). This left a

The origins of regional policy

Before the Second World War, the government, through the Industrial Transference Board, spent money on a 'regional policy' aimed at retraining unemployed industrial workers and transferring them (and their families) to areas where there was work (mainly the Midlands and the South-East, where the 'new' industries such as motor-cars and consumer electrical goods were established). Between 1929 and 1938 an average of about 20,000 adults and 7,000 juveniles were assisted to move each year (Gavin McCrone, *Regional Policy in Britain* (Allen & Unwin, 1969) p. 98; A. J. Brown, *The Framework of Regional Economics in the United Kingdom* (Cambridge University Press, 1972) ch. 11). This was basically a policy of taking workers to work-places. In 1934, under the Special Areas (Development and Improvement) Act, the government began a policy of taking work to the workers. This was attempted by giving firms assistance of various sorts if they located or expanded their factories in designated 'special' [development] areas'. By 1938 firms starting up in these areas were being given loans, provided with subsidised industrial premises (the origin of trading estates), and granted various tax concessions (such as exemption from the profits tax – the National Defence Contribution).

The Second World War greatly alleviated the regional problem, largely by the very great increase in the demand for labour and partly by stimulating a revival of the shipbuilding indus-

try. After the war, regional policy continued, partly through grants and loans to firms in 'development areas' under the Distribution of Industry Act 1945, and partly by the direct control of industrial building through the granting or withholding of industrial development certificates under the Town and Country Planning Act of 1947. During this immediate postwar phase many firms moved into wartime factories which had been built in the 'development areas', so providing substantial extra employment, and in the 1950s there was not much concern for further measures of regional policy.

However, by 1960, the problems of the development areas were once more claiming attention, and the Local Employment Act 1960 (and subsequent amending Acts) expanded the various measures of financial assistance available to firms in the scheduled development areas. Under the Industry Act 1972 regional development grants are available in the various categories of assisted areas to help meet the cost of building and works in manufacturing and in certain areas towards the cost of plant and machinery as well. Thus in the last few years quite substantial amounts have been paid directly as regional development grants to firms to finance capital expenditure (the difference between a grant and a loan is that a grant does not have to be repaid but it has to be spent on an agreed project – that is why these grants appear as receipts on the capital account).

---

positive balance of income over appropriations of £14,082 million, or 39 per cent of total income. This positive balance of unappropriated income, or 'undistributed income' as it is known in the national accounts, is the amount properly called 'saving'. (Remember that the flow of saving is the balance on appropriation account – or on income and expenditure account, in the case of the personal sector, or on current account, in the case of the government.) It seems that companies saved a substantial proportion of their gross income in 1980. Even if we deduct stock appreciation from both saving and income (on the grounds that stock appreciation simply represents unrealised 'book' profits which do not flow into the company and which are 'used up' in financing the increase in the book value of stocks), then it still transpires that, in 1980, industrial and commercial companies saved 29 per cent of their income. Diagram 4.1, based on the figures in Appendix 4.1, shows that such a relatively high savings ratio is typical of all years for which we have records. Indeed, the savings ratio has often been above 40 per cent. These high savings ratios are an important feature in the behaviour of industrial and commercial companies; we may recall from Table 2.3 that the Delta Metal Company in 1974 saved, or 'retained', 29 per cent of its gross profits.

DIAGRAM 4.1 *Saving by industrial and commercial companies as a percentage of total income, 1953 to 1980.*

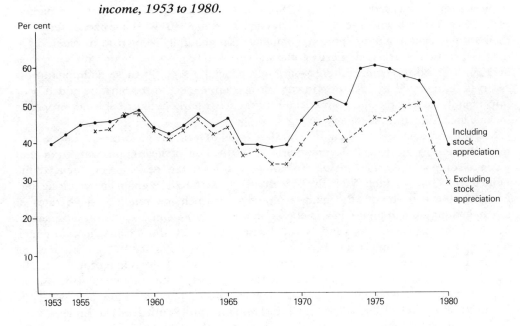

In order to understand why companies retain such a high proportion of their income we need to consider the uses to which they put their saving; this means we must look at their capital account.

Capital account and investment financing

Table 4.7 shows the capital account for industrial and commercial companies in the United Kingdom in 1980. Saving made up 96 per cent of total receipts on capital account, and there were two other small inflows.

TABLE 4.7 *Industrial and commercial companies' capital account for 1980*

	£ million	Percentage of total receipts
Receipts		
Saving [(a)]	14,082	96.0
Addition to tax reserves	86	0.6
Capital transfers	496	3.4
Total receipts	14,664	100.0
Expenditure		
Gross domestic fixed capital formation	15,640	106.7
Increase in (book) value of stocks and work in progress	1,853	12.6
Taxes on capital	44	0.3
Capital transfers to public corporations	69	0.5
Total expenditure	17,606	120.1
Balance of receipts over expenditure, i.e. financial balance: financial surplus (+) or financial deficit (−) (including net investment abroad)	−2,942	−20.1

[(a)] Excluding balance of unremitted profits.

Source: Central Statistical Office, *National Income and Expenditure 1981 Edition*, table 5.4, p. 40.

First, there are additions to tax reserves. The reported flow of UK taxes on income (seen in the appropriation account – Table 4.2) referred to tax liabilities accruing to companies: part of these accruals will have been paid by companies, but part will have been reserved by them for payment in a future period (company taxes generally being paid considerably in arrears). Until they are paid, these earmarked reserved funds will remain with companies and can be used to acquire interest-earning financial assets. So these additions to tax reserves (earmarked by inclusion in current-account expenditure) must be added back into capital-account receipts; but because of their earmarked nature, it is not proper to include them directly in company saving.

Second, companies receive capital transfers (grants) from the government, intended to help them pay for fixed capital formation. In 1980 the bulk of these grants was the amount given to companies establishing or expanding factories in the 'development areas' of the United Kingdom (see table 5.2 in the Blue Book). The United Kingdom has for a long time had a 'regional problem', the main symptoms of which are relatively high rates of unemployment in certain areas and consequent lower *per capita* incomes in those areas. Much of this problem was (and is still being) caused by the decline in 'traditional' nineteenth-century 'Industrial Revolution' industries such as textiles or shipbuilding which tended to be regionally concentrated. The existence of a regional problem can be seen in Table 4.8, which shows the difference among rates of unemployment in the various regions of the United Kingdom: in 1967 ranging from 7.3 per cent of the regional labour force (Northern Ireland) to 1.6 per cent (East Midlands and South-East) and in 1980 from 13.7 per cent (Northern Ireland again) to 4.8 per cent (South-East).

TABLE 4.8   *Regional rates of unemployment in the United Kingdom, 1967 and 1980*

Region	Percentage of region's labour force unemployed	
	1967	1980
Northern Ireland	7.3	13.7
Wales	4.0	10.3
Scotland	3.7	10.0
North [a]	3.9	10.9
North-West [b]	2.3	9.3
South-West [c]	2.5	6.7
East Anglia [d]	2.0	5.7
Yorkshire and Humberside [e]	1.9	7.8
West Midlands [f]	1.8	7.8
East Midlands [g]	1.6	6.4
South-East (including Greater London) [h]	1.6	4.8
United Kingdom	2.3	7.4

[a] Northumberland, Durham, Cleveland, Cumbria and metropolitan county of Tyne and Wear.
[b] Lancashire, Cheshire and metropolitan counties of Greater Manchester and Merseyside.
[c] Gloucestershire, Wiltshire, Avon, Dorset, Somerset, Devon, Cornwall.
[d] Cambridgeshire, Norfolk, Suffolk.
[e] North Yorkshire, Humberside and metropolitan counties of West Yorkshire and South Yorkshire.
[f] Warwickshire, Hereford and Worcester, Shropshire, Staffordshire and metropolitan county of the West Midlands.
[g] Northamptonshire, Leicestershire, Derbyshire, Nottinghamshire, Lincolnshire.
[h] Hampshire, Berkshire, Oxfordshire, Buckinghamshire, Bedfordshire, Hertfordshire, Essex, Kent, Surrey, West and East Sussex, Isle of Wight and Greater London.

Source: Central Statistical Office, *Regional Trends 1982 Edition*, table 7.4, p. 109, and p. 7 (for maps of standard regions).

Total receipts on the capital account of industrial and commercial companies in 1980 thus came to £14,664 million. All and more of this was used to pay for fixed capital formation; the detailed analysis of this capital formation, amounting to £15,640 million, is shown in Table 4.9. Much of it, 56.8 per cent, was spent on plant and machinery, and another substantial proportion, 25.1 per cent, was spent on other new buildings and works. Most of the remainder went on vehicles, ships and aircraft. Given the structure of their stock of fixed capital formation (Diagram 1.7), such a division of the investment flow is to be expected.

TABLE 4.9   *Gross domestic fixed capital formation by industrial and commercial companies in 1980*

Type of asset	£ million	Percentage of total
Vehicles, ships and aircraft	2,848	18.2
Plant and machinery	8,888	56.8
Dwellings	32	0.2
Other new buildings and works	3,927	25.1
Purchases *less* sales of land and existing buildings	−55	−0.4
Total fixed capital formation	15,640	100.0

Source: Central Statistical Office, *National Income and Expenditure 1981 Edition*, table 10.3, pp. 70–1.

Another part of companies' expenditure on capital account was taken up in 'paying for' the increase in the (book) value of stocks and work in progress. Part of this is investment in increasing the volume of inventories – in the Blue Book this is called the value of the physical increase in stocks and work in progress; but most of it was stock appreciation: in 1980 stock appreciation for industrial and commercial companies was £5,049 million, so we can deduce that their investment in stocks was £1,853 million *less* £5,049 million *equals* −£3,196 million; in other words, companies reduced their inventories during 1980. Just above I put the words 'paying for' in inverted commas, because meeting the cost of stock appreciation as such does not entail signing cheques. To go back to the example shown in Table 2.5, the firm had to pay £15 to suppliers for the physical increase in its stocks from 100 to 110 tonnes, but it did not have to pay suppliers for the £105 of stock appreciation due to the doubling of price. However, it is also the case that although £105 of stock appreciation may be reported in accounting profits on the appropriation account, no actual money was received by the firm. So the deduction, at this stage in the capital account, of the increase in the value of stocks deducts a hypothetical outflow from a hypothetical inflow and so leaves the accounts square.

In 1980 companies paid a small amount of taxes on capital, some of which may be the Development Land Tax chargeable on the difference between the disposal proceeds of land and its 'base value', which is generally the cost of acquisition adjusted to take account of any improvements, and also made capital transfers to public corporations (for connections to electricity, gas and water supplies).

Total expenditure by industrial and commercial companies on capital account in 1980 was therefore £17,606 million, which exceeded total receipts on capital account by 20.1 per cent, or £2,942 million. This meant that industrial and commercial companies had a financial deficit of this amount: in other words, they had to borrow money and/or issue new shares to make up the deficit and they had therefore a negative net acquisition of financial assets, or a financial deficit. How, then, did companies obtain the finance necessary to cover their financial deficit? In order to answer this question we must turn to the financial accounts.

The financial account

Table 4.10 shows the presentation of industrial and commercial companies' financial account as given in the national income and expenditure accounts (with some minor consolidation to reduce the length of the table). It is clear that companies are engaged in a wide variety of financial transactions (unfortunately for the student of economics this tends to be true of any sector in a financially developed economy). However, it is possible to pick out three main features before ploughing through the fine details.

TABLE 4.10   *Industrial and commercial companies' financial account for 1980*

Financial asset acquisition or use of finance (+), or financial liability acquisition or provision of finance (−)	£ million	
	Gross acquisition	Net acquisition
Notes and coin		354
Deposits with banking sector	2,929	
Loans from banking sector	−6,640	
Net finance from banking sector		−3,711
Other liquid assets [a]		281
British government securities		133
Credited extended by retailers and identified trade credit		1,044
Overseas securities		1,274
Direct and other investment abroad	2,021	
Overseas direct and other investment in UK	−3,087	
Net overseas		−1,066
UK company securities [b]		−937
All other transactions [c]		−20
Accruals adjustment [d]		−294
Total net acquisition of financial assets: financial surplus (+) or deficit (−)		−2,942

[a] Comprising (in £ million): market Treasury bills (20); tax instruments (332); local authority debt (−48); deposits with building societies (−22); deposits with other financial institutions (−1).

[b] Comprising UK capital issues (new money raised by share issues); capital issues by UK companies overseas; other transactions including cash expenditures or takeovers.

[c] Comprising (in £ million): Bank of England's transactions in (discounting of) commercial bills (−403); loans for house purchase (−7); other public-sector lending (75); other lending by financial institutions (−194); miscellaneous domestic instruments (−59); miscellaneous overseas instruments (794); unidentified items (−226).

[d] Comprising among others: tax, National Insurance contributions, VAT, etc., collected by companies and not yet paid to collecting revenue departments.

Source: Central Statistical Office, *National Income and Expenditure 1981 Edition*, table 13.4, p. 93.

First, it seems that companies obtained a considerable amount of finance from loans made available by the banking sector: in 1980 the banks made £6,640 million-worth of loans to industrial and commercial companies. This flow of loans, of course, is an acquisition of liabilities from the point of view of industrial and commercial companies, so it appears in Table 4.10 with a minus sign. However, industrial and commercial companies also increased their deposits with the banking sector by £2,929 million: this increase in deposits is an acquisition of assets, so it appears with a positive sign. The 'net' acquisition of finance from (liabilities to) the banking sector is, accordingly, −£3,711 million: you will not see this net balance in the Blue Book; it is put in just to show the principle involved in assessing the net acquisition of financial assets.

Second, it seems that companies are involved in a considerable two-way investment to and from abroad. During 1980 overseas companies invested £3,087 million in the United Kingdom: this represents the acquisition of a liability (from the UK viewpoint) and so has a minus sign. But at the same time as overseas companies were supplying £3,087 million-worth of finance to the UK sector of industrial and commercial companies, UK companies were also investing abroad: in 1980, they invested £2,021 million abroad; this represents the acquisition of a financial asset (from the UK viewpoint) and so has a positive sign. We should note that, in the national accounts, the acquisition of *any* asset overseas is regarded as an acquisition of a *financial* asset, as a claim on an overseas enterprise. Even if the asset abroad comprises, say, a factory, this is not treated as fixed capital formation – because the fixed capital is not located in the United Kingdom – but is treated as acquiring a financial claim. The gross flows in Table 4.10 make it clear that international investment by (multinational) companies is, for the United Kingdom, both sizeable and two-way; the net flow indicates that in 1980 UK companies invested less abroad than was invested in the United Kingdom.

Third, companies obtained some finance by issuing, during 1980, ordinary and other shares and securities, thereby obtaining £937 million. This appears as an increase in liabilities but, as explained, shares are a peculiar form of liability: shares are only a promise to pay the shareholder a dividend out of profits, if any; shares also carry the right to vote at the annual general meeting. But a purchaser of, or 'subscriber' to, new shares cannot subsequently demand repayment from the company. Nor can he claim redress if a dividend is not declared (apart from complaining at the annual general meeting – where, of course, a majority of shareholders can dismiss the Board of Directors). If the shareholder wishes to get his money back, he must sell the shares, for whatever they will fetch, on the market for second-hand securities – The Stock Exchange. This is in complete contrast to a loan liability, say, to a bank: in the case of a loan, a bank can legally insist on the payment of interest and repayment of the loan, according to the time-table agreed when the loan was made. If a company fails to meet either its loan interest or repayment obligations, the creditors can appoint a 'receiver' who may put the company 'into liquidation' and sell the assets in order to get their interest and repayments. Because of the 'non-repayability' of shares and the non-obligatory nature of dividends, share issues have been an important and useful method of financing the (risky) fixed capital formation undertaken by industrial and commercial companies.

These are the three main features of Table 4.10. But there are still several details which need to be considered if we are to get an over-all understanding of company finance. In order to operate, companies must hold stocks of means of ready payment; not only do companies need bank accounts, but they must also hold notes and coin (for petty cash, payment of wages, etc.). With inflation, companies may need to increase their stocks of ready payment, and in 1980 they increased their holdings of notes and coin by £354 million. This is roughly the same as the increase in notes and coin held by the personal sector, and this may be considered surprising, especially when one imagines the flows of transactions in which companies are engaged. The reason for this is, of course, that notes and coin are not interest-bearing assets, so any profit-conscious well-run company will keep its holdings of cash to the minimum essential. Companies also acquired £281 million of other 'liquid' assets during 1980: these comprise interest-bearing assets, but assets which can be turned quickly and without risk of loss into means of payment. For the same reason, companies acquired £133 million-worth of government securities.

Companies, and especially retailers, get involved in extending credit to other sectors (although, if they can, they prefer this to be done by the specialist financial institutions). In 1980 they extended trade credit worth £1,044 million to other sectors (including the overseas sector) and so acquired this amount of financial assets (claims on others).

Companies may raise capital by issuing instruments other than ordinary shares. Debentures are loans secured on the (freehold) assets of the company: that is, if the company goes into liquidation, the debenture-holders have a prior claim to repayment out of the proceeds of selling the assets against which the debenture loan was secured. Preference shares carry the right to a specified dividend which must be paid before dividends on ordinary shares. In 1980 companies issued £897 million of ordinary shares (*Financial Statistics*, October 1981, table 9.2, p. 106).

From time to time a big take-over battle for one company by another will hit the headlines. A take over bid often entails the bidding company buying shares from the other sectors (the personal sector, or the financial sector). In 1980 companies spent £903 million on this form of asset acquisition (*Financial Statistics,* October 1981). Not all these purchases, however, will have been the result of contested take-over bids; some may have been the result of amicably agreed mergers, and some may have been the result of 'dawn raids' when the share-buying company buys quietly through agents in the Stock Exchange (although new rules relating to 'substantial' acquisitions – between 15 and 30 per cent – of a company's shares may now make dawn raids more difficult to accomplish).

There is some provision of finance from various miscellaneous sources: mostly loans and mortgages from financial institutions other than banks.

Finally, we come to a fiddly item called 'accruals adjustment', which comprises two components (the details are not given in the Blue Book). The adjustment mainly concerns items of tax (not profits tax). In the companies' operating account (which we have not seen) the deduction from sales receipts of, say, income from employment must include the PAYE income tax deducted at source. For example, if a company pays its workers £100 each as their gross pay, the company is obliged to withhold, say, £30 for eventual payment under PAYE to the Inland Revenue: the amount an employee is actually paid by the company is £70. Clearly, in order to calculate profits, the £100 of accrued gross pay (and not the cash outflow of £70) must be deducted. The problem of accruals adjustment arises because there may be a slight delay in paying the £30 over to Inland Revenue, and during this delay the £30 will go, say, temporarily to increase the company's bank deposit. Therefore, it is necessary to deduct £30 as an 'accruals adjustment' from any such increase in bank deposits (financial asset acquisition). (It is called an 'accruals adjustment' because the flows in the national accounts are reported on an accruals basis, and not on an actual cash-flow basis. To illustrate from the previous example: £100 of wages accrues as an outgoing, but the actual cash outflow is only £70.)

At any one moment of time, companies will have a stock of liabilities due for payment to the Inland Revenue on account of withheld PAYE income tax, etc. If from one year-end to the next, this stock of liabilities increases, then it will give rise to a flow of financial liability acquisition.

Although most of the financial transactions are tracked down and recorded by the national income statisticians, there inevitably remains a residual amount of unidentified items. Some of the residual is simply ascribable to delays in data collection, and the residual for any year is often revised downwards in subsequent publications. The unidentified residual in 1980 was only − £226 million (Table 4.10).

Flow-of-funds analysis

This completes the description of the national accounts' financial account for industrial and commercial companies. This particular financial account is basically designed to show how the 'books were closed' on the 1980 accounting period: that is, how the financial deficit was financed. From this point of view, the national accounts are really only interested in the *net* flows, such as the net flow of finance from the banking sector, though we were able to insert some gross flows (e.g. to and from the banking sector) for illustrative purposes. However, it is clear that all the various gross flows are of interest in their own right, because only such gross flows can fully demonstrate all the financial links between companies and other sectors of the economy. The reporting of gross flows has therefore been much extended in recent years in what is commonly called a 'flow-of-funds analysis'; here the word 'funds' basically means finance but with the implication of a broader perspective – flow-of-funds analyses generally include the acquisition of real assets as well as of financial assets. Flow-of-funds analysis therefore combines capital and financial accounts. For example, *Financial Statistics* (Central Statistical Office), the *Bank of England Quarterly Bulletin,* and *United Kingdom Flow of Funds Accounts: 1963–1976* (Bank of England) are concerned with gross flows of finance (to and from) which fully indicate both the financial articulation of the economy and also all uses to which funds were put. Any economist who is going to be professionally concerned with finance needs therefore to develop and practise his or her understanding of flow-of-funds analysis, so we shall start with the presentation of the gross flows of finance involving industrial and commercial companies; this is fundamentally an elaboration of the net flows of Tables 4.7 and 4.10 (both the capital and the financial accounts) so it follows those accounts quite closely.

Table 4.11 shows the flow-of-funds analysis for industrial and commercial companies from *Financial Statistics.* First, look at the arrangement of items. The (gross) sources of funds are given, with the distinction being made between internal funds (finance which the company sector itself generates – that is, but speaking loosely, finance which does not generate a financial liability to outsiders) and external funds (finance which is provided from other sectors to companies and which does result in the creation of additional financial liabilities). Credit for imports and other trade credit is here given a distinct category on its own. All these add up to total (gross) sources of funds. The next part of the table then shows all the (gross) uses of finance, including uses both for (real) capital formation and also for financial asset acquisition (gross).

So there is nothing mysterious about flow-of-funds analysis; it is simply an extension of the financial accounts to include more of the gross flows. However, there is one wrinkle we have to sort out before we can look at the figures themselves; this is because the national accounts are concerned with reporting figures on an accruals basis, while the flow of funds tends to be more concerned with reporting actual cash flows. You can appreciate that in the example of £100 of wages comprising a £70 cash outflow to workers and retention of £30 for (subsequent) payment of PAYE income tax to the Inland Revenue, the accruals deduction of £100 is the only appropriate deduction from value added when calculating profits; however, you can also appreciate that the cash-flow retention (however temporarily) of £30 complicates matters in the flow-of-funds accounts, where it necessitates an accruals adjustment to report the acquisition of financial assets on a cash-flow basis. In the example just given, £30 would have to be added back to convert retentions on an accruals basis to retentions on a cash-flow basis.

Table 4.11 shows the flow-of-funds account on a cash-flow basis for industrial and commercial companies during 1980. Because unremitted profits retained in the United Kingdom by overseas-owned companies exceeded unremitted profits retained abroad by UK-owned companies, the effect of the net balance of unremitted profits was to augment cash flows in the United Kingdom, so the undistributed income in the flow-of-funds analysis is larger than undistributed income on an accruals basis. Flow-of-funds analysis then reports capital transfers-in net of capital taxes and transfers-out (instead of putting them separately under income and expenditure on capital account) before showing, separately, the increase in tax balances (the change in the stock of PAYE income taxes, National Insurance contributions, VAT, etc., collected by companies but not yet paid over to the revenue-collecting departments) because such temporarily retained funds augment companies' cash flows (albeit only temporarily). In the national accounts Blue Book this flow is not given as a positive item in the inflows, but as a negative adjustment on the financial account (the 'accruals adjustment' of Table 4.10).

TABLE 4.11   *Industrial and commercial companies' sources and uses of capital funds in 1980 (flow-of-funds analysis)*

Industrial and commercial companies	£ million
SOURCES OF FUNDS	
Internal funds:	
Undistributed income [a]	15,781
Capital transfers net of capital taxes and transfers out [b]	383
Increase in tax balances [c]	478
Total internal funds	16,642
Import and other credit received	−226
Other external funds:	
Bank borrowing	6,640
Other loans and mortgages	691
UK capital issues	
Ordinary shares	897
Debentures and preference shares	423
Capital issues overseas	4
Overseas direct investment in securities	516
Overseas direct and other investment [d]	378
Total other external funds	9,549
Total sources of funds	25,965
USES OF FUNDS:	
Gross domestic fixed capital formation	15,640
Increase in book value of stocks	1,853
Investment in UK company securities	903
Investment in overseas securities	1,274
Direct and other investment abroad [e]	925
Export and other credit given	818
Bank deposits	2,929
Notes and coin	354
British government securities	133
Other liquid assets [f]	281
Other identified assets [g]	897
Other accruals adjustments [h]	184
Total identified uses of funds (inc. adjustments)	26,191
Unidentified transactions (residual)	−226
Total uses of funds	25,965

[a]   Including balance of unremitted profits to and from abroad (see Tables 4.12 and 4.13).

[b]   Comprising (in £ million) the balance of: capital transfers (investment and other grants) (496); taxes on capital (−44); capital transfers to public corporations (−69).

[c]   Increase in amount collected on behalf of, but not yet paid to, government revenue departments, mainly income tax, National Insurance contributions, VAT.

[d]   Excluding unremitted profits due to abroad.

[e]   Excluding unremitted profits due from abroad.

[f]   Comprising: Treasury bills, tax instruments, local authority debt, deposits with building societies and other financial institutions.

[g]   Comprising: various loans to public sector, other identified lending to financial institutions, and other identified overseas assets.

[h]   Adjustment for accrued but yet unpaid local authority rates, North Sea oil royalties and other miscellaneous items: that is, the difference between accruals of these liabilities (as reported in national accounts) and the corresponding cash payments.

Source: Central Statistical Office, *Financial Statistics,* October 1981, table 9.2, p.106; Central Statistical Office, *National Income and Expenditure 1981 Edition,* tables 5.4 and 13.4, pp. 40 and 93; the figures from October 1981 edition of *Financial Statistics* are those which are comparable with the *National Income and Expenditure* statistics (some of the figures cited may be subject to slight revision).

Cash flow vs accruals – profits and investment to and from abroad

On one set of figures especially, the flow-of-funds statisticians need to use actual cash flows. This set of figures concerns profits and investment arising from or due to companies abroad. The national accounts statisticians work on the convention that profits arising in the United Kingdom in foreign-owned companies are *all* remitted abroad to the parent companies – that is, they are regarded as accruing to the foreign-owned companies; conversely, profits arising abroad in UK-owned companies are treated as all being remitted to the United Kingdom – as accruing. This is the meaning of the accruals convention. However, UK-owned companies operating abroad may not actually remit all their profits from abroad; they may leave some profits abroad to be directly invested in expanding their foreign operations. In this case the national accounts statisticians adopt the convention of then treating these unremitted profits from abroad as part of the outflow of UK direct company investment abroad: having pretended that the unremitted profits have flowed into the United Kingdom, they then pretend that the unremitted profits flow out again as 'direct investment'.* The 'pretence', or convention, is perfectly reasonable if one wishes to strike a proper estimate of income *accruing* to UK companies; the fact that they may choose to use their income in a particular way (invest it abroad without first remitting it) should not be allowed to affect (diminish) their measured income. And likewise and conversely with profits arising in the United Kingdom but due to foreign-owned companies.

Therefore, having, in the appropriation account, added on all profits made abroad and accruing to UK-owned companies (whether actually remitted to the United Kingdom or not) and likewise deducting total profits accruing in the United Kingdom to foreign-owned companies, in the financial accounts the Blue Book treats profits kept abroad by UK-owned companies as a direct investment outflow from the United Kingdom, and profits kept in the United Kingdom by foreign-owned companies as a direct investment inflow into the United Kingdom. This also produces a consistent and appropriate treatment of UK direct investment abroad and foreign-company direct investment in the United Kingdom; the accruals treatment is appropriate because one would not want one's measurement of UK company direct investment abroad to be affected by the way that investment was financed: to illustrate, measured on an actual cash outflow basis, UK company direct investment abroad would appear to diminish if more of it were financed by unremitted profits abroad; this does not happen on an accruals basis.

Unfortunately, from the point of view of flow-of-funds analysis, unremitted profits arising abroad do affect (adversely) companies' ability to acquire financial assets in the United Kingdom: that is, the pretend inflows on an accruals basis do not enable them to acquire financial assets in the United Kingdom; whereas foreign-company profits arising in the United Kingdom and not remitted abroad (the pretend outflows on an accruals basis) do increase the company sector's ability to acquire (gross) financial assets in the United Kingdom. So the flow-of-funds analysis adopts a cash-flow treatment of unremitted profits, and, correspondingly, a cash-flow treatment of direct company investment to and from abroad. Naturally this produces different gross figures in the flow-of-funds table.

In the national accounts appropriation account – see Tables 4.12 and 4.7 – the balance of industrial and commercial companies' undistributed income (after allowing for profits from abroad and profits due abroad on an accruals basis – i.e. whether or not remitted) was £14,082 million in 1980; when we include additions to tax reserves of £86 million, total retentions on an accruals basis were £14,168 million (Table 4.12). The flow-of-funds analysis in *Financial Statistics* gives a figure for undistributed income of £15,781 million, including additions to tax reserves *and* adjusted for unremitted profits – see Tables 4.12 and 4.13. Because the latter (cash-flow) figure exceeds the former (accruals-based) figure, it is clear that foreign-owned companies in the United Kingdom must have retained (not remitted) more of their profits (aris-

---

*A 'direct investment' means that the investor has a 'significant influence on the operations of the company [invested in]'; as opposed, say, to simply acquiring shares in an (independent) company which would be listed as investment in overseas (company) securities, i.e. as 'indirect' investment (see Central Statistical Office, *United Kingdom Balance of Payments 1981 Edition*, p. 80).

TABLE 4.12   *Reconciliation of company undistributed income for 1980 in national accounts (accruals basis) and in* Financial Statistics *(cash-flow basis)*

Industrial and commercial companies	£ million
National accounts	
Undistributed income (excluding balance of unremitted profits)	14,082
Additions to tax reserves	86
Undistributed income plus additions to tax reserves	14,168
Financial Statistics	
Undistributed income (including balance of unremitted profits) plus additions to tax reserves	15,781
Balance of unremitted profits	−1,613 [a]

[a] Minus sign indicates provision of finance from abroad through balance of unremitted profits.

Sources: Central Statistical Office, *National Income and Expenditure 1981 Edition*, table 5.4, p. 40; Central Statistical Office, *Financial Statistics*, October 1981, table 9.2, p. 106.

ing in the United Kingdom) than UK-owned companies retained (not remitted) profits from abroad. In other words, there was a net supply of finance from abroad due to the balance of unremitted profits.

By comparing the two sets of figures for intracompany investment overseas, we can see exactly how this balance of unremitted profits arose. Table 4.13 shows the relevant figures. During 1980 UK-owned companies invested £2,021 million overseas (direct investment, that is), including that part of direct investment financed by unremitted profits arising abroad; the actual cash outflow part of this was, according to *Fi-nancial Statistics*, only £925 million, so that £1,096 million of the direct investment abroad must have been financed by unremitted profits arising abroad. From the point of view of the United Kingdom, this represents a use of funds, and so has a notional plus sign. On the other side, during 1980, overseas companies invested £3,087 million (direct investment) in the United Kingdom, although on a cash-flow basis the actual cash inflow was only £378 million; they must, therefore, have used £2,709 million of their profits arising in the United Kingdom to complete their payment for this direct investment.

The total cash flows (funds) accruing to companies from internal sources in 1980 was thus £16,642 million. Companies also receive finance from other sources. The sign convention in flow-of-funds accounts is to give such inflows of funds straightforwardly with a positive sign, as representing an increase in liabilities, unless it represents a reduction of liabilities, in which case the sign will be negative. Flow-of-funds accounts can afford to do this because one of their main purposes is to sort all the (minus-sign) provisions of finance into one group (gross) and then to give all the (positive-sign) uses of funds in another group (also gross). (When dealing with flows of finance it is necessary to look sharp about the sign conventions being used in any table, and always, when you examine the figures, deliberately and consciously to sort out the sign conventions.) For example, bank borrowing is a large external contribution to finance: £6,640 million in 1980. We saw this gross flow in Table 4.10, where it had a negative sign to indicate that finance was being provided to industrial and commercial companies by banks. In that table it had to have a negative sign because it was going to be set against the increase in bank

TABLE 4.13 *The balance of unremitted profits from and to abroad in 1980*

	£ million		
Industrial and commercial companies	By UK companies overseas (+) [a]	By overseas companies in UK (−) [b]	Balance for UK
National accounts (including unremitted profits)	2,021	3,087	−1,066
Financial Statistics (excluding unremitted profits)	925	378	547
Unremitted profits [c]	1,096	2,709	−1,613 [b]

[a] Use of finance by UK industrial and commercial companies.
[b] Provision of finance to UK industrial and commercial companies.
[c] National accounts *minus Financial Statistics*.

Sources: Central Statistical Office, *National Income and Expenditure 1981 Edition,* table 13.4, p. 93; Central Statistical Office, *Financial Statistics,* October 1981, table 9.2, p. 106.

The balances for 1980 in Table 4.13 then work out as follows (all references are to direct investment only). Going across the first row, UK companies invested less abroad than did overseas companies in the United Kingdom, so the net balance for the UK economy of −£1,066 million represents a net source of finance to the UK economy and so has a negative sign. Going across the second row, UK companies sent abroad a cash outflow to pay for investment abroad that was greater than the cash inflow to the UK economy from overseas companies and this excess too represents a (positive) net use of funds by the UK economy. Going across the third and last row, UK companies kept an amount of unremitted profits abroad which was smaller than the amount of unremitted profits kept in the United Kingdom by overseas companies; the excess of overseas companies' unremitted UK profits over UK companies' unremitted overseas profits thus represents a net provision of finance to the UK economy, and so has a negative sign to denote that finance was being provided (net) to the company sector. This negative balance of unremitted profits is the reconciling figure which brings *Financial Statistics'* cash-flow figure for undistributed income into conformity with the national accounts' accruals-based figure (Table 4.12). This is rather a technical matter, but it is necessary to grasp it because otherwise one cannot understand why the national accounts and *Financial Statistics* give two widely different figures for the undistributed income of industrial and commercial companies.

deposits of £2,929 million, a use of finance, which has a positive sign, in order to strike the net balance. In the flow-of-funds account the two are clearly separated, so the minus sign is here not explicitly attached to bank borrowing by companies. The figure for bank borrowing in the flow-of-funds account means that companies increased the gross amount of bank loans outstanding by £6,640 million in 1980.

We can see, but only very approximately, what the outstanding liabilities were. Table 4.14 shows the outstanding liabilities to banks of manufacturing and other production industries and various service industries all combined. This grouping is *not* equivalent to industrial and commercial companies because some nationalised industries are included with production, as is agriculture, forestry and fishing, some of which will be in the personal sector, as may be some of the services; excluded is transport and communication, which may contain companies in addition to the nationalised industries. Furthermore, the 'year' runs from 21 November to 19 November, the two dates on which the banks reported the make-up of the stock of outstanding loans. However, we can see that the outstanding

TABLE 4.14   *Advances (loans) to UK residents by banks in the United Kingdom*

	£ million		
	Amount outstanding		Change (flow) during period
	21 November 1979	19 November 1980	
Advances by all banks to UK residents engaged in manufacturing, other production, retail and other distribution, and professional, etc., services	29,031	36,137	7,106

Source: Central Statistical Office, *Financial Statistics*, February 1981, table 6.17, pp. 74–6.

loans increased from £29,031 million on 21 November 1979 to £36,137 million on 19 November 1980: a change, or flow, over this period of £7,106 million. This part of the economy increased its indebtedness to the banks by 25 per cent in '1980', and with indebtedness running at nearly £36 billion one can appreciate why producers were complaining in 1981 about the burden of high interest rates. It would, of course, have been possible in principle for companies to have reduced the amount of bank loans outstanding: in such a case the figure reported for bank 'borrowing' would have been given a negative sign in the flow-of-funds account, to indicate a reduction in liabilities.

The other external funds of Table 4.11 have already been discussed, and we can see that total external sources of funds came to £9,549 million in 1980; so total funds available amounted to £25,965 million (gross). The flow-of-funds account then goes on to show how these funds were used both to acquire capital assets and to acquire financial assets.

Gross domestic fixed capital formation used up £15,640 million of the flow of funds (we have already examined this flow in Tables 4.7 and 4.9); a further £1,853 million went on financing the increase in the book value of stocks (remember that profits included stock appreciation, which is only a nominal, or pretend, cash inflow; here there is a corresponding deduction of the same nominal or pretend cash outflow and this squares the accounts for this particular item). We then go to the use of funds to acquire financial assets. A considerable amount of money was used in acquiring (from other sectors, chiefly the personal sector) UK company securities (remember that in 1980 the personal sector disposed of £1,630 million-worth of company securities – Table 3.9). Companies also acquired overseas securities and sent cash out of the United Kingdom to invest (directly) in their susidiaries overseas: this cash outflow of £925 million was to supplement the £1,096 million of unremitted profits retained by those subsidiaries. Together these two flows made up the total of £2,021 million of company direct investment overseas by UK companies which is the total reported in the national accounts Blue Book's table 13.4 and in Table 4.13 above.

Companies also acquired some British government securities and other 'liquid' assets (financial assets which can readily and without risk of loss be turned into cash – to meet unforeseen contingencies or to pay tax bills when these fall due). A small adjustment has to be made for accruals other than those on account of tax balances (income tax, etc.); this adjustment is mainly for local authority rates, North Sea oil royalties and unpaid interest on bank loans (interest payment on bank loans – in the appropriation account – is reported on as it accrues, not on an actual payment, cash-outflow, basis).

Finally, not all transactions are identified, and total identified uses of funds including accruals adjustment is less than total sources of funds, so there is a relatively small amount of unidentified transactions (amounting to about 0.9 per cent of total uses – given the magnitude and diversity of the flows it is perhaps surprising that the residual is so small;

and this is a tribute to the UK system of statistics). In subsequent publications, the residual may even decline, as late information flows in. It may also be the case that the unidentified residual includes some accruals adjustments which cannot be made because of inadequate information about the precise timing of payments.

Importance of internal finance

This examination of the capital and financial accounts of industrial and commercial companies has been quite lengthy and complex, because this is what the real world is like. But, putting aside all the details, the single most important feature of these accounts is that most, and often all, of companies' fixed capital formation is paid for out of their own (internally generated) undistributed income or saving: that is, the balance on appropriation account is usually sufficient to pay for investment expenditure on the capital account.

We can show this diagrammatically for 1980. Diagram 4.2 gives all the relevant flows of funds and is also drawn roughly to scale so the relative sizes of each of the flows of funds can be seen. Diagram 4.2 combines the national accounts accruals-based flows and the *Financial Statistics* cash flows. The basic principle in any such flow-of-funds analysis is that uses of funds must equal sources of funds; in other words, the analysis must account for what happens to all sources of finance – hence at the top of the diagram we write 'Sources *equals* Uses'.

DIAGRAM 4.2   *Sources of finance to and uses of finance by industrial and commercial companies in 1980 (figures in £ million)*

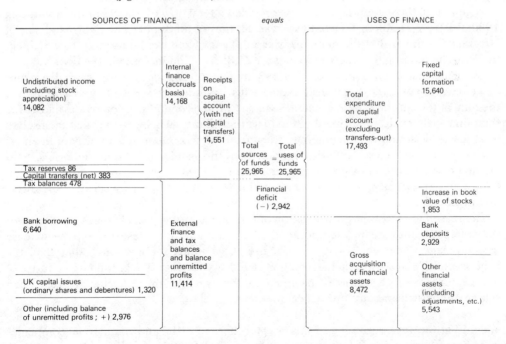

The left-hand side of Diagram 4.2 gives all the inflows or sources of finance; one may think of the two outer lines as being the banks of a river with streams flowing in from various sources. The right-hand side then gives the uses of finance like a river flowing into various channels or uses. We must remember that we are dealing with the aggregate of industrial and commercial companies; because some companies will be borrowing money (acquiring financial liabilities) and others will be acquiring financial assets, the aggregate of companies taken as a whole – the company sector – will be both acquiring financial liabilities (left-hand side, or sources of funds) and also acquiring financial assets (right-hand side, or uses of funds).

One important flow is the flow of 'internal finance' or funds retained from the appropriation account; this is known as the flow of company saving gross of depreciation provision and of stock appreciation; the flow is also sometimes referred to as 'retentions'. You can see this flow in Table 4.2 as the balance on the appropriation account or 'undistributed income' or 'gross saving'. But we should note that:

Gross saving before stock appreciation		£14,082m.
less	Stock appreciation	£5,049m.
equals	Gross saving after stock appreciation	£9,033m.

(Here the word 'gross' means gross of depreciation provisions.) This was supplemented by relatively small flows of capital transfers-in (here calculated net of transfers-out) and additions to tax reserves to give total receipts on capital account, or 'internal finance plus net capital transfers' of £14,551 million.

Companies then obtained a relatively large flow of 'external finance'. A large part of this comprised borrowing from banks of £6,640 million. Capital issues in the United Kingdom, i.e. issues of new shares, provided another source of external finance. This source consisted of issuing a total of £1,320 million-worth of ordinary shares and debenture and preference shares – see Tables 4.10 and 4.11 above. Loans from sources other than banks and other miscellaneous finance including the balance of unremitted profits and adjustments then made up the 1980 total of £11,414 million-worth of finance provided from external sources to the sector of industrial and commercial companies.

Together all these sources of finance provided a total flow of sources of finance during 1980 of £25,965 million. To what uses was this flow of funds put? The right-hand part of Diagram 4.2 shows that the main use was to pay for fixed capital formation of £15,640 million. The other major use was to pay for £1,853 million increase in the book value of stocks. This made up a total of £17,493 million of expenditure on capital account (excluding, as noted, capital transfers-out). This expenditure exceeded by £2,942 million the total of receipts on capital account, so industrial and commercial companies had this as their financial deficit, requiring them to issue (net) financial liabilities against themselves to at least this amount. In actual fact, they acquired more than this by way of financial liabilities, but the 'excess' liabilities were offset by the acquisition of financial assets.

The gross acquisition of financial assets during 1980 comprised mainly deposits with banks, export and other trade credit given, investment in overseas securities, and direct investment abroad.

The reason for such a large acquisition of UK financial assets is, of course, that some of the sources of funds are only temporary, such as additions to tax reserves and the increase in tax balances and enterprises cannot use these funds for anything other than the acquisition of 'liquid' financial assets: that is, assets which can quickly and without risk of loss be turned into a means of payment to, for example, the collector of taxes when settlement of such amounts owing becomes due.

We said at the very beginning of this chapter that industrial and commercial companies were a major producing, and therefore investing, sector of the economy: at the end of 1980 they owned 31 per cent of the net stock of fixed assets in the United Kingdom and during 1980 they undertook 39 per cent of gross domestic fixed capital formation in the United Kingdom. We have noted that the most important feature of the capital account of industrial and commercial companies, seen also in the flow-of-funds analysis, is that most, and often all, of their fixed capital formation is paid for out of their own, internally generated, undistributed gross income, or gross saving. Diagram 4.2 shows the truth of this assertion for 1980: saving during 1980 (undistributed income) of £14,082 million paid for about 81 per cent of capital-account expenditure of £17,493 million (both flows here including stock appreciation). If we were to exclude stock appreciation, we would have for industrial and commercial companies in 1980:

Saving (excl. stock appreciation)	£9,033 million
Capital expenditure (ditto)	£12,444 million
Saving as percentage of capital expenditure	72.6 per cent

It is clear that in 1980 industrial and commercial companies relied heavily on their own saving to pay for their capital expenditure. But is the same true for years other than 1980?

Figures on fixed capital formation go back only to 1959, because the information required to construct a separate capital account for industrial and commercial companies was not available before 1959. Stock appreciation in industrial and commercial companies (separate from financial companies and institutions) is available from 1964 onwards, but it is possible to obtain figures on stock appreciation in all companies, including financial companies and institutions, for the years 1956 to 1963 inclusive. Because financial companies and institutions have very little stock appreciation – they are not in business to hold inventories of goods – we can reasonably apply company-sector stock appreciation to industrial and commercial companies for these years to get an estimate of saving after providing for stock appreciation in industrial and commercial companies.

Table 4.15 gives the relevant figures, comparing the flow of saving (after stock appreciation) each year with the flow of fixed capital formation for that year, and Diagram 4.3 charts, for each year between 1959 and 1980 inclusive, the proportionate extent to which such saving was more or less than sufficient to pay for fixed capital formation. The line drawn at 100 per cent shows where saving would be exactly sufficient to pay for all gross investment. In eleven out of the twenty-two years the flow of saving has been larger than the flow of investment in fixed assets; and on average over the twenty-two years the flow of saving (after stock appreciation) has been almost exactly equal to the flow of gross fixed capital formation. Over the period as a whole there have only been two years in which saving has been 20 per cent below the flow of fixed capital formation.

DIAGRAM 4.3 *Industrial and commercial companies: saving as a percentage of gross fixed capital formation, 1959 to 1980*

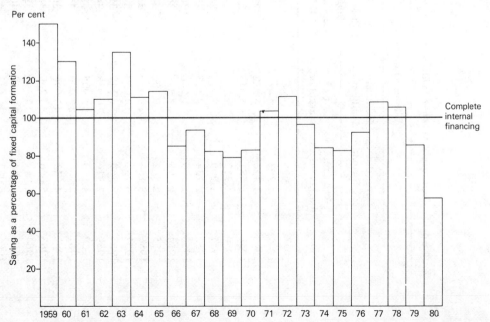

TABLE 4.15   Industrial and commercial companies: income, saving and investment at current and constant prices, 1956 to 1980

| | Whole economy | | | Industrial and commercial companies | | | | | |
| | Gross domestic fixed capital formation, £ million | | Implied price index for capital goods, 1975 = 100 | Current prices, £ million | | | Constant prices, £ million | | |
Year	At current market prices	At 1975 market prices		Total gross income (a)	Undistributed income, or saving (a)	Fixed capital formation	Total gross income (a)	Undistributed income, or saving (a)	Fixed capital formation
1946	929	—	—	—	—	—	—	—	—
1947	1,203	—	—	—	—	—	—	—	—
1948	1,426	6,082	23.45	—	—	—	—	—	—
1949	1,581	6,645	23.79	—	—	—	—	—	—
1950	1,712	7,025	24.37	—	—	—	—	—	—
1951	1,909	7,074	26.99	—	—	—	—	—	—
1952	2,134	7,123	29.96	—	—	—	—	—	—
1953	2,395	7,908	30.29	—	—	—	—	—	—
1954	2,595	8,597	30.18	—	—	—	—	—	—
1955	2,882	9,106	31.65	—	—	—	—	—	—
1956	3,164	9,536	33.18	3,883	1,672	—	11,702.8	5,039.2	—
1957	3,451	10,058	34.31	4,110	1,800	—	11,979.0	5,246.3	—
1958	3,569	10,142	35.19	4,278	2,021	—	12,156.9	5,743.1	—
1959	3,816	10,918	34.95	4,566	2,181	1,453	13,064.4	6,240.3	4,157.4
1960	4,190	11,905	35.20	4,986	2,151	1,649	14,164.8	6,110.8	4,684.7
1961	4,704	13,070	35.99	4,841	1,980	1,888	13,451.0	5,501.5	5,245.9
1962	4,833	13,096	36.90	4,872	2,106	1,917	13,203.3	5,707.3	5,195.1
1963	5,066	13,269	38.18	5,454	2,521	1,866	14,285.0	6,602.9	4,887.4
1964	6,041	15,494	38.99	6,021	2,546	2,288	15,442.4	6,529.9	5,868.2
1965	6,504	16,240	40.05	6,336	2,791	2,447	15,820.2	6,968.8	6,109.9
1966	6,923	16,643	41.60	5,658	2,063	2,423	13,601.0	4,959.1	5,824.5

TABLE 4.15 *continued*

	Whole economy			Industrial and commercial companies					
	Gross domestic fixed capital formation, £ million		Implied price index for capital goods, 1975 = 100	Current prices, £ million			Constant prices, £ million		
Year	At current market prices	At 1975 market prices		Total gross income [a]	Undistributed income, or saving [a]	Fixed capital formation	Total gross income [a]	Undistributed income, or saving [a]	Fixed capital formation
1967	7,524	18,052	41.68	5,854	2,216	2,362	14,045.1	5,316.7	5,667.0
1968	8,200	18,878	43.44	6,308	2,153	2,615	14,521.2	4,956.3	6,019.8
1969	8,591	18,954	45.33	6,927	2,364	2,987	15,281.3	5,215.1	6,589.5
1970	9,470	19,460	48.66	7,111	2,790	3,359	14,613.6	5,733.7	6,903.0
1971	10,517	19,743	53.27	7,989	3,590	3,462	14,997.2	6,739.3	6,499.0
1972	11,606	19,823	58.55	9,324	4,323	3,888	15,924.9	7,383.4	6,640.5
1973	14,238	21,195	67.18	11,764	4,741	4,907	17,511.2	7,057.2	7,304.3
1974	16,833	20,567	81.84	11,701	5,058	6,023	14,297.4	6,180.4	7,359.5
1975	20,416	20,416	100.00	12,321	5,728	6,910	12,321.0	5,728.0	6,910.0
1976	23,567	20,649	114.13	16,147	7,467	8,107	14,147.9	6,542.5	7,103.3
1977	25,753	20,161	127.74	21,185	10,505	9,690	16,584.5	8,223.7	7,585.7
1978	29,741	20,836	142.74	25,076	12,578	11,872	17,567.6	8,811.8	8,317.2
1979	34,251	20,898	163.90	30,357	11,784	13,713	18,521.7	7,189.7	8,366.7
1980	40,050	20,761	192.91	30,792	9,033	15,640	15,961.8	4,682.5	8,107.4

[a] Excluding stock appreciation.

Sources: Central Statistical Office. *Economic Trends Annual Supplement 1981 Edition*, pp. 9 and 14; Central Statistical Office, *National Income and Expenditure 1981 Edition*, tables 1.1, 2.1 and 5.4, pp. 3, 17 and 40; Appendix 4.1 in this book and sources there cited.

Profits affect investment

Is it the case, then, that investment in fixed capital and internal finance are related to each other? We may investigate this matter by enquiring whether the changes, from year to year, in the supply of internal finance are related to the year-to-year changes in fixed capital formation. Of course, it is clear from the current price data that the later years are affected by price inflation, so it would be preferable to investigate this relationship without the effect of price inflation. To do this we need a series on price deflated 'real' gross income, 'real' saving and 'real' capital formation. Now, when we were considering personal-sector income and consumers' expenditure, it made sense to deflate the current price series by the general index of retail prices, because that price index related to what consumers were buying. 'Real' income could therefore be computed with reference to the prices of the goods which that income was mainly being spent on. But here we are dealing with expenditure on an entirely different category of goods, namely capital goods, so the retail price index for consumers' goods is clearly not an appropriate price index. Clearly we need a price index for capital goods, and then we could determine changes in the volume of capital expenditure and likewise changes in 'real' company gross income and saving with reference to capital goods' prices because this income and saving is mainly being spent on capital goods (see p. 216 and Table 4.15 for the appropriate price index).

It can be seen that while there has been considerable growth in real fixed capital formation by industrial and commercial companies over the period 1959 to 1980, there has over this same period been less growth in real gross income or in real gross saving. Even if we omit the years 1974 to 1980 inclusive, because of the world recession following successive oil price rises, this conclusion still holds. To see this we may apply the least squares method of estimating continuous trend growth rates and thereby compute the growth rates given in Table 4.16. While fixed capital formation has grown at about 3 per cent per annum, the trend rate of growth of real income and real saving has been at under one-third of this rate. As we shall see, these contrasting trends have caused increasing difficulties in financing fixed capital formation by industrial and commercial companies. We can see in Diagram 4.3 that there has been a tendency towards less self-sufficiency in financing fixed capital formation.

TABLE 4.16   *Industrial and commercial companies: growth of real income, saving and investment*

Period	Trend growth rates, per cent per annum		
	Real total gross income	Real gross saving	Real fixed capital formation
1959 to 1980	0.91	0.74	2.80
1959 to 1973	1.31	0.54	3.26

Source: calculated by fitting an exponential function to data in Table 4.15.

We can now return to our original problem: is there any relation between the year-to-year changes in company gross income ('profits' for short), saving and fixed capital formation ('investment' for short)? For this purpose, it seems preferable to use percentage changes rather than absolute changes (whether in current price £s or constant price £s). So Table 4.17 shows these percentage changes both in the current price series and in the constant price series.

It is apparent from the percentage changes in the 'real', constant price series that the volume of investment formation and the profits and saving of industrial and commercial

TABLE 4.17 *Industrial and commercial companies: annual percentage changes in income, saving and investment*

	Percentage change from year to year					
	Current prices			Constant 1975 prices		
Year to year	Total gross income [a]	Undistributed income [a]	Fixed capital formation	Total gross income [a]	Undistributed income [a]	Fixed capital formation
t	$\dot{\Pi}$	$\dot{S}$	$\dot{I}$	$\dot{\Pi}^*$	$\dot{S}^*$	$\dot{I}^*$
1956–7	5.8	7.7	—	2.4	4.1	—
1957–8	4.1	12.3	—	1.5	9.5	—
1958–9	6.7	7.9	—	7.5	8.7	—
1959–60	9.2	−1.4	13.5	8.4	−2.1	12.7
1960–1	−2.9	−7.9	14.5	−5.0	−10.0	12.0
1961–2	0.6	6.4	1.5	−1.8	3.7	−1.0
1962–3	11.9	19.7	−2.7	8.2	15.7	−5.9
1963–4	10.4	1.0	22.6	8.1	−1.1	20.1
1964–5	5.2	9.6	6.9	2.4	6.7	4.1
1965–6	−10.7	−26.1	−1.0	−14.0	−28.8	−4.7
1966–7	3.5	7.4	−2.5	3.3	7.2	−2.7
1967–8	7.8	−2.8	10.7	3.4	−6.8	6.2
1968–9	9.8	9.8	14.2	5.2	5.2	9.5
1969–70	2.7	18.0	12.5	−4.4	9.9	4.8
1970–1	12.3	28.7	3.1	2.6	17.5	−5.9
1971–2	16.7	20.4	12.3	6.2	9.6	2.2
1972–3	26.2	9.7	26.2	10.0	−4.4	10.0
1973–4	−0.5	6.7	22.7	−18.4	−12.4	0.8
1974–5	5.3	13.2	14.7	−13.8	−7.3	−6.1
1975–6	31.1	30.4	17.3	14.8	14.2	2.8
1976–7	31.2	40.7	19.5	17.2	25.7	6.8
1977–8	18.4	19.7	22.5	5.9	7.2	9.6
1978–9	21.1	−6.3	15.5	5.4	−18.4	0.6
1979–80	1.4	−23.3	14.1	−13.8	−34.9	−3.1

[a] Excluding stock appreciation.

Source: calculated from data in Table 4.15.

companies can fluctuate quite markedly from year to year. These fluctuations in the year-to-year changes in real profits and real investment are shown in Diagram 4.4. Because, we shall show, it appears that changes in profits appear to determine changes in investment, rather than vice versa, Diagram 4.4 shows the percentage change in profits lagged one year: that is, and using the function notation introduced previously in connection with the consumption function, the sequence of events seems to be:

$$\begin{pmatrix}\text{Changes in}\\\text{investment}\\\text{in year } t\end{pmatrix} = f\begin{pmatrix}\text{Changes in}\\\text{profits in}\\\text{year } t-1\end{pmatrix}$$

and we may postulate a straight-line form of functional relationship for the percentage changes:

$$\begin{pmatrix}\text{Percentage change}\\\text{in investment}\\\text{in year } t\end{pmatrix} = a + b\begin{pmatrix}\text{Percentage change}\\\text{in profits}\\\text{in year } t-1\end{pmatrix}$$

A price index for capital goods

We can obtain a price index for capital goods in the following way. The national income statisticians have published data on annual fixed capital formation at current prices since 1946; here the phrase 'at current prices' means 'at the prices currently ruling during the year to which the figure refers'. If we let $p_{t,i}$ stand for the price of the ith capital good during year t, and $q_{t,i}$ for the quantity of the ith capital good purchased during the year t, then (summing over i but omitting the i subscript) the total purchase of capital goods during year t at current prices is

$$\Sigma p_t q_t$$

And this is the algebraic expression for the current price series given in the first column of Table 4.15. As you can see in Table 4.15, the national income statisticians have also published data on annual fixed capital formation at constant 1975 prices for all years since 1948. Their calculations for this are necessarily complex, but basically this series is derived by repricing each of the $q_{t,i}$ at 1975 prices and summing to get the amount that would have been spent on year t quantities had 1975 prices then applied. That is, the algebraic formula for each of the annual flows in Table 4.15's second column is, for each year t:

$$\Sigma p_{1975} q_t$$

You will observe that, for 1975 itself, this total is the same as the current price total.

Now, if we divide the current price total by the constant price total we obtain for each year t:

$$\frac{\Sigma p_t q_t}{\Sigma p_{1975} q_t} = \sum \frac{p_t}{p_{1975}} \frac{p_{1975} q_t}{\Sigma p_{1975} q_t}$$

which is a weighted average of the price relatives, p_t/p_{1975}, where the weights are the proportionate share of expenditure on the ith item in year t valued at 1975 prices in total expenditure on capital goods in year t valued at 1975 prices.

The weights thus change from year to year as they depend on q_t. This form of price index is therefore known as a current-weighted index; it is also called a Paasche price index after the statistician Hermann Paasche, who, in 1874, first used this formula. So by dividing the current price series on fixed capital formation by the constant 1975 price series on fixed capital formation we can obtain the price index which is implied by the ratio of the two series. For this reason such a price index is called an 'implied price index'. We are thus able to compute (see Table 4.15) the implied price index for capital goods, using capital expenditure in the economy as a whole.

If we assume that changes in this price index are likely to be very similar to the weighted average changes in the prices of capital goods purchased by industrial and commercial companies, then we may use the index to deflate the series on company income, saving and fixed capital formation. It is obviously possible to raise objections to this assumption, because fixed capital formation in the whole economy includes roads, bridges, new dwellings and other items not much purchased by industrial and commercial companies, and if the prices of these items moved in a markedly different way from the items purchased by companies, then the use of the implied price deflator for all capital goods to deflate company-sector fixed capital formation would be inappropriate. However, it seems unlikely that any such divergence, if it existed at all, would be sufficiently large; furthermore, the only alternatives to using this price index are to use other price indices (which are likely to be even less satisfactory) or not to use a price index at all (which fails to solve the initial problem of getting away from the impact of price inflation). Therefore, we use this implied price index to deflate the current price series on company income, saving and fixed capital formation to obtain the constant price series shown in the last three columns of Table 4.15.

Because changes in profits are 'lagged' one year behind the changes in investment, this is technically known as a 'lagged time-series function'; such lagged functions are commonly used in economic analysis and it is clearly implied by the relationship of changes in investment following in time the changes in profits that the latter 'causes' the former – the general principle being that a cause precedes its consequence. If we lag changes in profits, then we can see that there appears, in Diagram 4.4, to be a reasonably close coincidence both of levels, and of directions in movement, of the points which give the percentage

DIAGRAM 4.4   *Industrial and commercial companies: year-to-year changes in real investment and in real profits (lagged one year)*

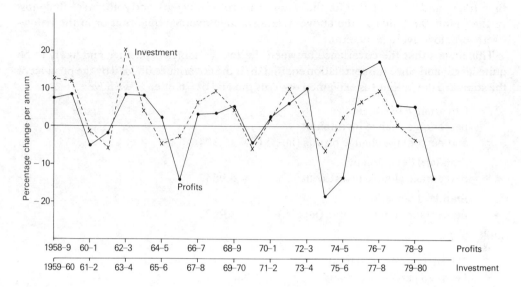

changes. If profits are up (or down) in one year, then in the following year investment tends to be up (or down) by an approximately similar percentage.

This visual presentation of Diagram 4.4 is easy to comprehend; but for precise analysis we require a systematic statistical method of determining the degree of 'closeness' in the relationship; after all there are several places in Diagram 4.4 where the points diverge. We can get such a systematic statistical presentation by correlating the percentage change in real investment (year to year) with the percentage change in real profits (lagged by one year). This is given in Diagram 4.5, which shows a 'scattergram' of the pairs of co-ordinates

DIAGRAM 4.5   *Industrial and commercial companies: alternative presentation in 'scattergram' of relationship between year-to-year changes in investment and in profits (lagged one year)*

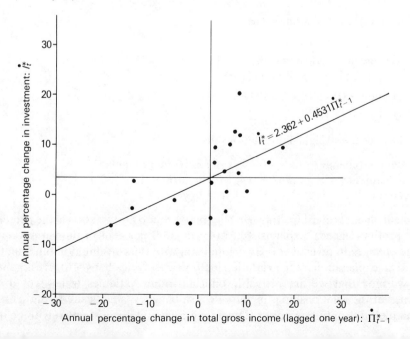

in Table 4.17: $(12.7, 7.5)$, $(12.0, 8.4)$, $(-1.0, -5.0)$, $(-5.9, -1.8)$, and so on. Diagram 4.5 also draws in the averages, namely 3.47 per cent for the changes in investment and 2.44 per cent for the changes in profits (lagged), and you can see that most of the points fall either in the above-average/above-average quadrant or in the below-average/below-average quadrant.

This means that the covariance between the two variables is positive and likely to be quite large; and since the correlation coefficient is the covariance divided by the product of the standard deviations (as explained towards the end of Chapter 1) we have:

Covariance between
percentage change investment
and percentage change profits (lagged) $= 36.3946$

Standard deviation of
percentage change investment $\quad = 6.9842$

Standard deviation of
percentage change profits (lagged) $\quad = 8.9622$

Whence, for Diagram 4.5:

Coefficient of correlation
between percentage change $\quad = \dfrac{36.3946}{6.9842 \times 8.9622}$
investment and percentage
change profits (lagged)

$$= 0.5814$$

From the method of least squares we know that the coefficient b for the straight-line relationship may be estimated as:

$$b = \frac{\text{Covariance}}{\begin{array}{c}\text{Variance percentage}\\ \text{change in profits (lagged)}\end{array}}$$

$$= \frac{36.3946}{(8.9622)^2}$$

$$= 0.4531$$

and the constant a may be estimated as:

$$a = \begin{array}{c}\text{Average}\\ \text{change in}\\ \text{investment}\end{array} - b\left(\begin{array}{c}\text{Average}\\ \text{change in}\\ \text{profits (lagged)}\end{array}\right)$$

$$= 3.4667 - (0.4531 \times 2.4381)$$

$$= 2.362$$

so that we have as the straight-line relationship:

$$\begin{array}{c}\text{Percentage change}\\ \text{in investment}\\ \text{in year } t\end{array} = 2.362 + 0.4531 \left(\begin{array}{c}\text{Percentage change}\\ \text{in profits}\\ \text{in year } t-1\end{array}\right)$$

So the straight-line relationship, drawn in Diagram 4.5, and the variation in the percentage change in profits (lagged) 'explains' $(0.5814)^2$ or 33.8 per cent of the variation in the percentage changes in investment. By comparison with the consumption function this is not as good an explanation for the variation in the year-to-year changes in investment, and this is a warning that we are probably omitting other variables which would affect investment, but the relationship is nevertheless statistically 'significant' in the sense that such a 'sample' of twenty-one points (Diagram 4.5) would be most unlikely to be drawn from a 'population' of points where the correlation for the population were zero. Specifically, we can tell from special statistical tables that there is less than one chance in 100 (1 per cent) that we would obtain a correlation coefficient of (plus or minus) 0.549 or greater from a sample of twenty-one paired observations when the 'true', or population, correlation coefficient were zero (in these tests we make no judgement beforehand as to the sign of the correlation coefficient, though we might feel entitled to predict that the covariance will be positive rather than negative). The correlation coefficient for the twenty-one observations is in fact 0.5814, so we can reject the alternative hypothesis that there is no relationship between the two variables quite confidently. (This is what is meant by saying that 'the correlation coefficient is significant at the 1 per cent level', which is the statistician's short-hand expression. Making no judgement beforehand about the sign of the correlation coefficient results in what is known technically as a 'two-tail test'. The special table for the significant correlation coefficients are generally given in the appendices to statistical textbooks.)

So there is a relationship of some sort between the percentage change in real investment and the percentage change in real profits lagged one year. We need now to justify the choice of lagging profits by one year. One way of doing this is to look at the correlation coefficient and the straight-line relationship without the lag. We may use the notation given in the column headings of Table 4.17. Here the Greek symbol 'Π' (pi) stands for profits (to avoid confusion with *p*, which is generally used to denote prices); '*S*' stands for savings and '*I*' for investment. To distinguish between the current price and the constant price series, an asterisk '*' is added to denote the latter. A dot '·' placed over each of the symbols is the conventional way of denoting a percentage change. Finally, we use the subscript '*t*' to refer to a particular percentage change, such as 1959–60, and the subscript '*t* − 1' denotes a lag of one year. These short-hand symbols are used here not only because they are convenient, but also because this sort of notation is quite commonly seen in economic analysis and it is therefore necessary for students of economics to become accustomed to their use and not to shy away from them as being some sort of unintelligible gobbledygook. Table 4.18 provides the analysis we require. In the first row we have the

TABLE 4.18   *Relationships between changes in investment, profits and saving of industrial and commercial companies*

Straight-line relationship estimated by method of least squares	Correlation coefficient	Number of observations
$\dot{I}_t^* = 2.36 + 0.453 \ \dot{\Pi}_{t-1}^*$	0.581 [a]	21
$\dot{I}_t^* = 3.01 + 0.317 \ \dot{\Pi}_t^*$	0.433 [b]	21
$\dot{I}_t^* = 4.04 - 0.228 \ \dot{\Pi}_{t+1}^*$	−0.313 [b]	20
$\dot{I}_t = 6.33 + 0.579 \ \dot{\Pi}_{t-1}$	0.732 [c]	21
$\dot{S}_t^* = -1.06 + 1.069 \ \dot{\Pi}_t^*$	0.684 [c]	24
$\dot{S}_t = -0.80 + 0.971 \ \dot{\Pi}_t$	0.655 [c]	24
$\dot{I}_t^* = 2.99 + 0.248 \ \dot{S}_{t-1}^*$	0.448 [d]	21
$\dot{I}_t = 9.11 + 0.326 \ \dot{S}_{t-1}$	0.562 [a]	21

[a] Statistically significant at the 1 per cent level.
[b] Not statistically significant.
[c] Statistically significant at the 0.1 per cent level.
[d] Statistically significant at the 5 per cent level.

Source: computed from data in Table 4.17; significance table from E. S. Pearson and H. O. Hartley, *Biometrika Tables for Statisticians* (3rd edn) Cambridge University Press, 1970, vol. I, table 13, p. 146.

relationship between percentage changes in real investment and real profits lagged one year, which we have already studied in Diagram 4.5. In the second row we have the relationship without the lag; the correlation coefficient drops to 0.4327, which is not statistically significant. In the third row we advance, or 'lead', the percentage change in real profits by one year and the correlation coefficient becomes negative at -0.313; but it is not statistically significant. It is only when thnage change in real profits is lagged by one year that we get a statistically significant relationship between the two series on percentage changes. Therefore, we may conclude that we are justified in saying that changes in the profits of industrial and commercial companies tend to determine changes in investment by industrial and commercial companies.

If we take the percentage changes in the current price variables (fourth row of Table 4.18), there is a strong positive correlation of 0.732 between the percentage change in investment and in profits lagged one year.

The next thing we need to look at is the relationship between the year-to-year percentage changes in retained income (saving) and the year-to-year percentage changes in profits. We saw in Diagram 4.1 that between 1956 and 1980, saving tended to vary between about 35 to 45 per cent of total income, excluding stock appreciation. We can see in Table 4.18 that there is a positive correlation between changes in profits (total income) and changes in saving whether we take constant price data ($R = 0.684$) or current price data ($R = 0.655$). This is exactly what one would expect if the proportion of total income saved were reasonably constant over time. Finally, we can see that there is a positive relationship between year-to-year percentage changes in investment and year-to-year percentage changes in savings lagged one year.

It does seem therefore that a 'good' year for profits (that is, a year when the increase in profits is above average) tends to be associated with an above-average increase in investment in the year following, and this relationship may partly work through the mechanism of an increase in profits leading to an increase in saving, which latter increase in retained funds then permits the financing of more investment.

On this evidence it appears, therefore, that one important function of profits, or company income, through being retained by companies, is to finance fixed capital formation (Diagram 4.3). Profits play a twofold role in the economy.

In the first instance, profits provide the return to, and inducement to undertake, investment. If money is borrowed or acquired through an issue of shares, in order to pay for investment, then the profits from that investment will be required to pay the interest on the borrowed money or the dividends on the shares.

In the second instance profits also provide much, if not all, the finance for investment in fixed capital. In the case of borrowed money, the repayment of principal would also be found from the profits flow. Ordinary shares are not, of course, repaid; but part of the flow of profits may be retained for further investment, and this will lead to an appreciation in the value of the initial shares so permitting those who (a) assumed the initial risk, and (b) accepted non-repayability to participate in the benefits resulting from a (successful) business venture.

We have seen objectively the importance of profits and retentions (saving) in the financing of fixed capital formation by industrial and commercial companies, and this is a theme to which we shall return because it is a central pivot of the economic behaviour of companies. It is therefore fitting to conclude with some evidence on the subjective importance attached by companies to profits and retentions. Table 4.19 gives the results of an enquiry among two samples of senior company directors, one in the United Kingdom and the other in West Germany, as to why their companies were 'interested in pursuing a high level of profitability'. The intriguing feature about the preferences given is twofold: first, 'to provide finance for expansion' is the reason given top priority in *both* samples; second, in the United Kingdom and West Germany, this reason appears in the scoring of priorities to stand well clear of the other reasons. It seems that senior management in the United Kingdom and in West Germany concur in the great importance they attach to profits as a source of internal finance for expansion. Sociological data on the subjective views of management are scarce, but it is most striking that such a survey should conform so well to the objective statistics of the appropriation and capital accounts of industrial and commercial companies in the United Kingdom as shown in Diagram 4.3.

TABLE 4.19   *Why the company is interested in pursuing a high level of profitability (rate of return on capital employed; asked only of directors of parent company)*

Ranking in importance [a]	Stated reason for interest in profitability	Mean score (lower value indicates greater importance attached to reason)	
		United Kingdom [b]	West Germany [c]
1	To provide finance for expansion	1.90	2.10
2	Because it is a yardstick of efficiency	2.43	3.21
3	To reduce the cost or difficulty of raising finance	2.61	3.03
4	To provide a larger cake for everybody	2.48	3.24
5	To maintain/increase the price of the company's shares	2.83	2.94
6	To pay dividends to the shareholders	3.02	3.03
7	To maintain high morale among the work-force	2.82	3.48
8	To attract good managers to the company	2.56	4.51
9	To minimise the threat of takeover	4.10	4.36

[a] Ranking according to unweighted average of UK and West German scores.
[b] Average number of directors stating reasons: 61.
[c] Average number of directors stating reasons: 37.

Source: Andreas Budde, John Child, Arthur Francis and Alfred Kieser, *Corporate Goals, Managerial Objectives and Organizational Structures in British and West German Companies*, University of Aston Management Centre Working Paper Series, No. 206, June 1981; published in *Organization Studies*, vol. 3, issue 1, 1982; table 4.

Exercises

4.1 *(To practise finding data and making trend comparisons.)*

(i)   Update Table 4.1.
(ii) Find comparable relevant data for 1969 and compare these with your updated figures. Does anything in your comparison surprise you?

(*Hint:* what has happened to the proportion of value added invested? Have you checked that your value-added figures for 1969 relate to *industrial and commercial* companies?)

4.2 *(To practise finding data and interpreting the appropriation account.)*

(i)   Update Table 4.2.

(ii)   Briefly explain each of the items listed under 'allocation of income' in the *National Income and Expenditure* accounts.

(iii) In your updated table, calculate the balance on appropriation account excluding stock appreciation and explain why this balance would be a more helpful figure to a manager thinking of buying a piece of machinery (imagining that these accounts refer to a single company).

(iv)   Draw a pie-chart to show the allocation of income (including stock appreciation) in your updated appropriation account, and in the pie-chart show stock appreciation separately.

(v)   Following the pattern of Diagram 2.5 (adapted as necessary), draw a diagram to illustrate the flows on your updated appropriation account.

4.3   *(To practise your understanding of the imputation system of corporation tax.)* A married man receives in the 1980–1 tax year a dividend payment of £800; his income from employment during this tax year is £22,000; and he has no outgoings allowable against tax (such as mortgage interest).

(i)   What is the tax credit on the dividend payment?

(ii)   What is the implied gross of tax dividend that he is deemed to be receiving? (*Check:* what answer do you get when you divide the tax credit by the implied gross of tax dividend?)

(iii) What is his taxable income?

(iv)   How much income tax is due to be paid?

(v)   How much tax does he himself actually have to hand over to the Inland Revenue?

4.4   *(To practise finding data and interpreting the capital account.)*

(i)   Update Table 4.7 and make one small change in your updated table: namely, give the 'increase in (book) value of stocks and work in progress' as the sum of its two components. (*Hint:* you will find the required information in chapter 12 (1981 numbering) of the *National Income and Expenditure* accounts.)

(ii)   Following the pattern of Diagram 2.6, but showing taxes on capital and capital transfers separately and distinguishing in the capital expenditure flow between the increase in the value of stocks and gross domestic fixed capital formation, illustrate your updated capital account.

4.5   *(It is always useful to know something about the 'standard regions' of the United Kingdom.)*

(i)   Update Table 4.8 to the latest available date. (Apart from the source cited, this information may be found in the Department of Employment *Employment Gazette* or in the Central Statistical Office *Monthly Digest of Statistics.*)

(ii)   Draw a map of the standard regions of England and Wales and on this map draw bars (or cylinders or blocks if your draughtsmanship extends that far) to represent the updated percentage rates of unemployment in each standard region of England and Wales.

4.6   *(To practise presenting data.)*

(i)   Update Table 4.9.

(ii)   Draw a pie-chart to illustrate your updated table. (What are you going to do about puchases *less* sales of land and existing buildings, if negative?)

(iii) To make your pie-chart more lively, list and draw beside it a (or some) typical example(s) of each of the major types of asset. (If you were a journalist presenting this in an article to readers not entirely familiar with the terminology, isn't this the sort of thing you would do?)

4.7   *(To practise using a most important table.)*

(i)   Present from table 9.2 of the Central Statistical Office's *Financial Statistics* (1982 numbering) the sources and uses of funds (flow-of-funds analysis) of industrial and commercial companies for the latest available *quarter.*

(ii)   What proportion of the quarter's fixed capital formation was financed by the quarter's saving?

4.8   *(Further to practise flow-of-funds analysis.)*

(i)   Using the Central Statistical Office *Financial Statistics'* table 9.2 'continued', explain how the 'net borrowing requirement of industrial and commercial companies' arose in 1980, illustrating your answer with reference to the data for 1980.

(ii)   What is the consequence of gross borrowing in excess of the net borrowing requirement by industrial and commercial companies?

4.9   *(Further to practise flow-of-funds analysis.)*

(i)   Present from table 10.2 of the Central

Statistical Office's *Financial Statistics* (1982 numbering) the sources and uses of funds of the personal sector in 1980. (Advice: you will need a copy of *Financial Statistics* of or after October 1981 and before mid-1982 in order to get figures matching those in the *National Income and Expenditure 1981 Edition*.)

(ii) Reconcile 'saving' in the flow-of-funds analysis with 'saving' in Table 3.5 above.

(iii) Using Table 3.5 above, show how the flow-of-funds figure for 'investment in fixed assets and stocks' was arrived at.

(iv) Using your flow-of-funds analysis table, show how the financial accounts' figure in Table 3.7 for 'other loans for house purchase' was arrived at.

(v) What other figures in table 10.2 of *Financial Statistics* exactly match the figures in Table 3.7 above?

4.10 *(To practise calculating implied price indices.)* Using the appropriate data from chapter 10 of the latest *National Income and Expenditure* accounts, derive implied price indices for the period given for the following types of asset: (i) buses and coaches; (ii) plant and machinery; (iii) dwellings.

4.11 *(To practise using implied price indices.)*

(i) In the *National Income and Expenditure* accounts find and tabulate the expenditure by industrial and commercial companies on plant and machinery at current prices over the given period. Using your implied price index for plant and machinery from Exercise 4.10(ii), calculate industrial and commercial companies' investment in plant and machinery at constant 1975 prices.

(ii) Calculate the year-to-year percentage changes in 'real' investment in plant and machinery by industrial and commercial companies.

(iii) The Central Statistical Office's *Economic Trends* contains a time series on 'Average price of new dwellings: mortgage approved' in index form with 1975 = 100 (this index includes the cost of land). How does this series compare with your implied price index for fixed capital formation in dwellings (which does not include the cost of land)?

4.12 *(To practise your understanding of how a company works.)* The principal activities of the Esso Chemical Company Ltd comprise the manufacturing and the marketing of a range of industrial chemicals and other speciality chemical products together with the research to develop these products. With reference to the following extracts from the *Report and Accounts 1980* (to which I have added three notes):

ESSO CHEMICAL LIMITED

Value-added statement 1980 [a]	£ million
Total sales including excise duties and VAT	245.2
Less excise duties and VAT collected for government	(13.5)
Less payments to suppliers for goods and services	(206.8)
VALUE ADDED	24.9
Allocated as follows:	
TO EMPLOYEES AND ANNUITANTS	
As salaries, wages, pensions and benefits [b]	12.7
TO CENTRAL AND LOCAL GOVERNMENT	
Provisions for taxation on profits	0.3
Rates and other taxes	1.5
TO PROVIDERS OF CAPITAL	
Dividends [c]	—
RETAINED IN THE BUSINESS	10.4
Other items	
Interest receivable net of interest payable	2.2
Capital expenditure	11.0

[a] Year ended 31 December.

[b] Of which, £10.7 million as remuneration to 970 employees.

[c] The 'Statutory report of the directors' recommended that 'no dividend should be paid for the year'; the 'Chairman's statement' commented: 'The year 1980 was a very difficult one and was marked by low sales, low margins and a very much reduced trading profit.'

Source: Esso Chemical Limited, *Report and Accounts 1980*, pp. 3, 7, 9, 10, 12 and 14.

(i)   What was Esso Chemical's flow of 'saving' in 1980?

(ii) What was Esso Chemical's 'financial balance' in 1980?

(iii) What would you say about Esso Chemical's 'internal financing' of capital expenditure?

(iv) How does average remuneration per employee compare with average 'output' per employee in 1980?

4.13   *(To practise your understanding of legal niceties.)* Write an explanation of the term 'limited liability'. (This assignment can be tackled as ambitiously as you wish: it is helpful to start with a basic reference work such as the *Penguin Dictionary of Commerce* or the *Penguin Dictionary of Economics*; one can progress through the article on 'Company' in the *Encyclopaedia Britannica*; and (for the ambitious) one can end up with any textbook on company law such as L. C. B. Gower, *Gower's Principles of Modern Company Law*, 4th edn, Stevens, 1979, ch. 5 'The consequences of incorporation'.)

4.14   *(To practise your understanding of an important financial instrument.)*

(i)   Write a brief explanation of the term 'ordinary share'.

(ii) Tabulate and draw a chart of the annual issue of ordinary shares by UK industrial and commercial companies on the UK capital market over the past five years.

4.15   Write an essay entitled 'The connection between the profits of and investment by industrial and commercial companies in the United Kingdom and the implications of that connection.' (Further reading: W. A. Thomas, *The Finance of British Industry 1918–1976*, Methuen, 1978, especially chs 8 and 11; Committee to Review the Functioning of Financial Institutions (the Wilson Committee), *Report*, Cmnd 7937, HMSO, June 1980, ch. 10; G. Meeks, 'Cash flow and investment', and G. J. Anderson, 'Investment and profits in the industrial and commercial sector', chs 4 and 5 of *The Economics of the Profits Crisis*, ed. W. E. Martin, HMSO, 1981.)

APPENDIX 4.1   *Industrial and commercial companies' total income and saving, 1953 to 1980*

£ million

Year	Before deduction of stock appreciation		Stock appreci- ation	After deduction of stock appreciation		Saving as a percentage of total income	
	Total gross income on appropriation account	Undistri- buted income, or saving		Total gross income on appropriation account	Undistri- buted income, or saving	Before stock appreci- ation	After stock appreci- ation
1953	3,114	1,236	—	—	—	39.7	—
1954	3,418	1,444	—	—	—	42.2	—
1955	3,810	1,712	—	—	—	44.9	—
1956	4,042	1,831	159 [a]	3,883	1,672	45.3	43.1
1957	4,251	1,941	141 [a]	4,110	1,800	45.7	43.8
1958	4,260	2,003	−18 [a]	4,278	2,021	47.0	47.2
1959	4,643	2,258	77 [a]	4,566	2,181	48.6	47.8
1960	5,063	2,228	77 [a]	4,986	2,151	44.0	43.1
1961	4,962	2,101	121 [a]	4,841	1,980	42.3	40.9
1962	4,982	2,216	110 [a]	4,872	2,106	44.5	43.2
1963	5,565	2,632	111 [a]	5,454	2,521	47.3	46.2
1964	6,259	2,784	238	6,021	2,546	44.5	42.3
1965	6,588	3,043	252	6,336	2,791	46.2	44.0
1966	5,955	2,360	297	5,658	2,063	39.6	36.5
1967	6,003	2,365	149	5,854	2,216	39.4	37.9
1968	6,783	2,628	475	6,308	2,153	38.7	34.1
1969	7,503	2,940	576	6,927	2,364	39.2	34.1
1970	7,974	3,653	863	7,111	2,790	45.8	39.2
1971	8,831	4,432	842	7,989	3,590	50.2	44.9
1972	10,399	5,398	1,075	9,324	4,323	51.9	46.4
1973	14,054	7,031	2,290	11,764	4,741	50.0	40.3
1974	16,415	9,772	4,714	11,701	5,058	59.5	43.2
1975	16,604	10,011	4,283	12,321	5,728	60.3	46.5
1976	21,413	12,733	5,266	16,147	7,467	59.5	46.2
1977	25,018	14,338	3,833	21,185	10,505	57.3	49.6
1978	28,450	15,952	3,374	25,076	12,578	56.1	50.2
1979	37,354	18,781	6,997	30,357	11,784	50.3	38.8
1980	35,841	14,082	5,049	30,792	9,033	39.3	29.3

[a] Stock appreciation for all companies, including financial companies and institutions.

Sources: Central Statistical Office, *National Income and Expenditure 1964*, table 28, p. 33; Central Statistical Office, *National Income and Expenditure 1965*, table 28, p. 36; Central Statistical Office, *National Income and Expenditure 1966*, table 33, p. 41; Central Statistical Office, *National Income and Expenditure 1967*, table 32, p. 40; Central Statistical Office, *National Income and Expenditure 1968*, table 32, p. 42; Central Statistical Office, *National Income and Expenditure 1969*, table 29, p. 36; Central Statistical Office, *National Income and Expenditure 1970*, table 28, p. 34; Central Statistical Office, *National Income and Expenditure 1971*, table 29, p. 36; Central Statistical Office, *National Income and Expenditure 1972*, table 28, p. 34; Central Statistical Office, *National Income and Expenditure 1973*, table 28, p. 34; Central Statistical Office, *National Income and Expenditure 1963–73*, table 30, p. 36; Central Statistical Office, *National Income and Expenditure 1964–74*, table 35, p. 39; Central Statistical Office, *National Income and Expenditure 1965–75*, table 5.4, p. 39; Central Statistical Office, *National Income and Expenditure 1966–76*, table 5.4, p. 42; Central Statistical Office, *National Income and Expenditure 1967–77*, tables 1.2 and 5.4, pp. 4 and 46; Central Statistical Office, *National Income and Expenditure 1979 Edition*, tables 1.2 and 5.4, pp. 4 and 46; Central Statistical Office, *National Income and Expenditure 1980 Edition*, tables 1.2 and 5.4, pp. 4 and 40; Central Statistical Office, *National Income and Expenditure 1981 Edition*, table 5.4, p. 40.

Chapter 5

The Individual Enterprise

Contents

Chapter guide

The pivot on which Chapters 5, 6, 7, and 8 all turn is the relation between prices and costs as a determinant of profits. We begin in Chapter 5 by considering the enterprise as an entity which tries in its *corporate strategy* to look ahead, especially with regard to financing its (planned) investment. We consider briefly the use of *external finance* to pay for investment, but concentrate upon *internal finance*, which is quantitatively more important when it comes to financing investment. The amount of internal finance (or *retentions*) which an enterprise can generate depends, given its *dividend policy*, upon the difference between *price* and *unit cost* – that is, on the *mark-up* which the enterprise can charge on cost – and upon the quantity it can sell.

We examine the classification of costs so that we may better understand the terms *unit production cost* and *unit gross margin*, and then we see how all these elements fit together in the framework of a *business economic plan* which gives the enterprise's projected *cash flow* as the 'bottom line'.

Introduction

In the preceding chapter we considered the important role that undistributed income appeared to play in financing fixed capital formation. We did this by looking at the aggregate statistics for the sector of industrial and commercial companies and we also looked at some subjective opinions on the subject. But such an aggregate result can emerge only as the consequence of deliberate decisions taken by a large majority of the individual companies which make up the company sector. Therefore, this and the following three chapters turn our attention to the behaviour of an individual company. Because company decisions, particularly about pricing, cannot be taken in isolation from market forces, we shall also have to look at the behaviour of buyers whose purchasing decisions provide the market for companies' products. This furthers our understanding of consumers' expenditure out of personal-sector income, which was also a matter examined in Chapter 3.

When delving into the complexities of company behaviour, we cannot hope to follow reality in all its diverse circumstances. We need therefore to simplify by using a model which will schematically represent the important elements so that we can see (a) how these elements run through all the economic processes, and (b) how these elements relate to one another. It follows that different models of company behaviour can be devised depending on which elements of reality are selected. There are indeed a variety of such models presented as 'theories of the firm' rather as though the models were necessarily competing rather than possibly complementary. A deficiency of teaching in this field is that the interlocking nature of such models is not made explicit to the student, whose understanding of company behaviour remains correspondingly incomplete. Accordingly, these next few chapters are concerned to show how the various models of company behaviour are linked together.

The enterprise as a forward-looking economic entity

Diagram 5.1 shows the over-all model of enterprise behaviour which we shall be examining as a first approximation. Having explained this model, we shall also examine, in detail, the two circles labelled 'consumer behaviour' and 'production economics' in the chapters following.

DIAGRAM 5.1   *A model of enterprise behaviour*

Capital expenditure plan: 'corporate strategy'

Total finance required

| New share issues | Borrowing | Depreciation | Net retentions |

External finance | Internal finance

Financial markets

| Internal finance | Dividends | Interest | Tax |

Gross profits

| Gross profits | Wages | Materials |

Sales receipts

Production economics

Consumer behaviour

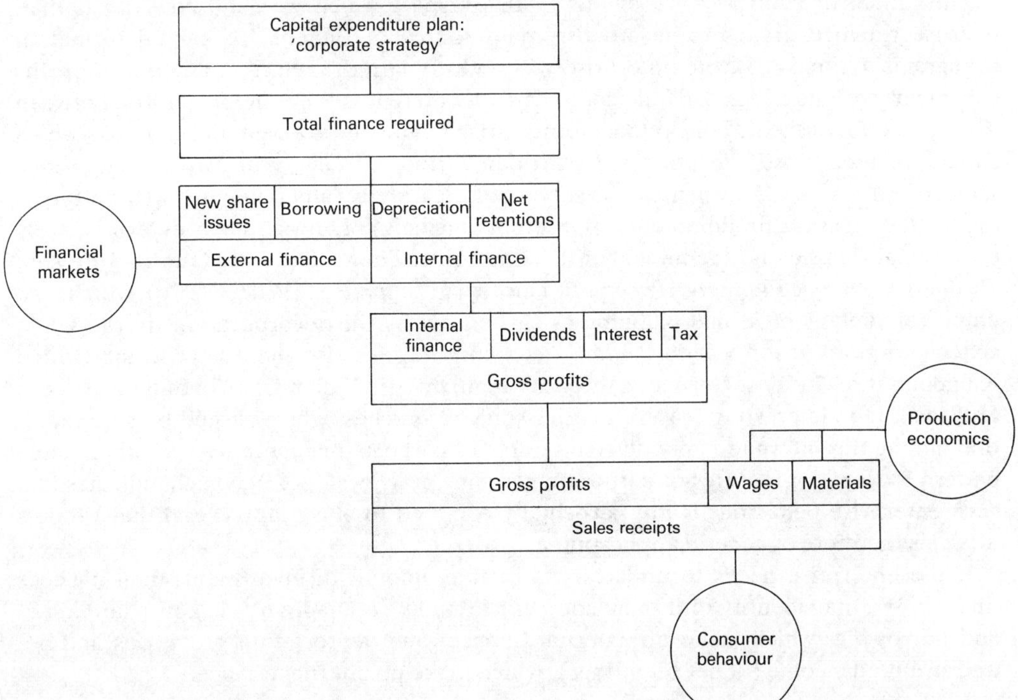

At the outset, we need to note that we are concerned with the behaviour of economic undertakings generally, not solely with limited companies, though most large undertakings are companies. Accordingly, we shall in the present chapter use the word 'enterprise' rather than 'firm', because the model of enterprise behaviour is also applicable to much of the behaviour of the nationalised industries, and while one thinks of, say, British Rail or the National Coal Board as enterprises, the word 'firm' is not usually applied to them. However, when I use the word 'company' – e.g. in relation to dividend policy – this signals that we are discussing a particular class of enterprise.

An important set of decisions made by the enterprise concerns its medium- to long-range plans for development. Although we shall subsequently examine production economics, or the manner in which the enterprise should do whatever it is currently engaged in, the crucial decisions are often those which determine the future activities of an enterprise, or what it will be doing in, say, five years' time. That is to say, we must make a distinction between 'operating decisions', concerned with current production, and 'strategic decisions', concerned with the enterprise's objectives and goals. This is despite the fact that strategic and current operating decisions are very closely linked, as we shall see. In a changing world the importance for an enterprise of seeing whether its product (slide rules, say) may become obsolete (replaced by cheaper and more effective electronic calculators), and then planning accordingly, is obvious.

We need therefore to consider the corporate strategy of enterprises if we are to understand the economic aspects of their behaviour. 'Corporate strategy' has been well defined as 'the determination of the basic long-term goals and objectives of an enterprise, and the adoption of courses of action and the allocation of resources necessary for carrying out those goals' (Alfred Chandler, *Strategy and Structure*, MIT Press, 1962, p. 13). From the economist's point of view, the important consequence of corporate strategy is that it results in a 'plan' – or set of intentions – for capital formation. Subsequently we shall consider how the capital expenditure plan arises from enterprise forecasts, or plans, of sales, but if the enterprise has a corporate strategy, then the immediate implication is a need for total financing of investment. The economic question which then arises is how this finance is to be obtained.

The model of enterprise behaviour in this respect which we shall consider is that, because retained gross profits are the main source of finance for capital formation (Diagrams 4.2 and 4.3), the enterprise will seek to earn the requisite amount of profits consonant with its needs for finance. In this way there arises an important link between pricing and investment. This model of enterprise behaviour is based on two books which should be mentioned. The first is by Adrian Wood, *A Theory of Profits* (Cambridge University Press, 1975), which is a largely theoretical study (albeit keeping a sharp eye on the facts, such as the predominance of internal financing) of how and why enterprises rely on internal finance and the impact of this on profits. The second is by Gunnar Eliasson, *Business Economic Planning: Theory, Practice and Comparison* (Wiley, 1976), which is an empirical analysis of formal planning as carried out by thirty corporations in the USA, sixteen corporations in Sweden, and sixteen corporations elsewhere (five in the United Kingdom, three in West Germany, three in Japan, three in Finland, one in Italy, and one in Holland). One interesting feature of Eliasson's researches, which should be stressed, is that among this internationally diverse sample of corporations there was 'a rather stable pattern as to major features of corporate planning practices' (p. 29), which indicates that such enterprise behaviour is not parochially confined to one country, and that Wood's model is therefore of general applicability.

If the enterprise needs to undertake a certain amount of investment, then it needs finance. We may identify four main sources of finance in Diagram 5.1: new share issues and borrowing, which make up external finance; and depreciation provisions and net undistributed income (or net retentions), which make up internal finance.

Costs of a new issue

Together with other (legal, etc.) costs, all costs may amount to a considerable proportion of the proceeds ('the average costs for an issue of around £250,000 have been 10% of issue size or over since 1959, and about 12% in 1971'; issues of over £1 million incur costs of about 4% to 5%: E. W. Davis and K. A. Yeomans, *Company Finance and the Capital Market*, Cambridge University Press, 1974, p. 18). If there is a shortfall in the public's subscription, then the underwriters take up their portion of shares at the issue price.

If the price is set 'too low', then the issue is likely to be oversubscribed, in that total demand from the general public will exceed supply, and in this case the company will have 'wasted' money, in the sense that it could have charged a higher price and still have sold the whole issue.

Perhaps more important than these considerations of the costs of a new issue and the difficulty in setting the 'right' issue price is the fact that, so far as existing shareholders are concerned, a new issue amounts to inviting others to share in the ownership of the company, so 'diluting' their ownership interest. Even worse, by increasing the number of shares, a new issue of shares tends to reduce the price per share, so inflicting a capital loss on existing shareholders. This happens because the new issue must, in order to be successful, offer new shares at a discount in order to induce the public to subscribe. To take the example used in F. W. Paish and R. J. Briston, *Business Finance* (Pitman, 1978, p. 107), if a company has one million ordinary shares valued on the stock market at £2 each, and the company issues a further quarter of a million shares at a discount of 50p per share, i.e. at £1.50, to ensure that the new issue will be fully subscribed, the new valuation of the 1¼ million shares will be:

	£
Old shares (1 million at £2 each)	2,000,000
New shares (¼ million at £1.50 each)	375,000
Enlarged issue (1¼ million at £1.90 each)	2,375,000

Existing shareholders therefore suffer a capital loss of 10p per share. Because of this, when companies make new issues in the United Kingdom, they must now give existing shareholders the 'right' to subscribe to the new issue in proportion to the number of shares they already hold.* Such issues are known as 'rights issues' and if, in the example just quoted, shareholders are given the right to buy one new share for every four old shares they own then they can buy for £1.50 a share which will be worth £1.90, a gain of 40p: and this gain will exactly counterbalance the $4 \times 10p = 40p$ capital loss they will suffer on their holding of four old shares when the market valuation of those shares falls from £2 to £1.90 each.

*This requirement, to give 'pre-emption' rights to existing shareholders in any new issue, has been imposed by the Companies Act 1980.

The economic problems in raising finance are that there are constraints on the amount of external finance which can be raised, and that the flow of depreciation provisions is predetermined by the enterprise's past investments and by the tax laws. This tends to leave net retentions as the key flow which the enterprise may have to maximise if it is to make up the total finance required. In practice, enterprises appear to estimate what their maximum flow of internal finance is likely to be, to match this against estimated uses of capital and then to treat external finance as a residual source of funds to make up the difference.

The constraints on external finance are reasonably obvious: it is at this juncture, as shown by the circle in Diagram 5.1, that the enterprise confronts the outside world, in the form of financial markets (broadly defined).

If an enterprise sees good prospects in its corporate strategy, it may well try to finance some, or indeed all, of the required investment in fixed capital by an *issue of new shares*. But this depends on being able to convince the outside world that the prospects are as good as the enterprise thinks they are. To issue new shares means that the company invites the public to buy, or 'subscribe to', new shares in the company; the proceeds from issuing new shares then provide finance for the company's investment. One problem is that making a new share issue tends to be a quite costly affair in terms of publishing a prospectus and paying the fees and commissions of the financial institutions which undertake the process of issuing shares. The company will be intending to sell to the public a very large number of shares in a single day, so it must advertise its issue adequately, and it must attract the public by setting an 'appropriate' price per share.

Here there arises the difficulty that if the price per share is set 'too high', the issue may not be fully subscribed to by the public, in which case it will be taken up by prearrangement with the 'underwriters' – institutions which, in return for an appropriate commission, undertake to buy any shares left unsold if the response from the general public falls short of the total issue. The commission is payable to the underwriters whether or not the issue is fully subscribed.

For all these reasons, new issues tend to play a relatively minor role in the over-all financing of fixed capital formation by companies.

Different constraints apply to borrowing. When an enterprise borrows it commits itself (a) to a definite amount of interest payments, and (b) to a schedule of repayment of principal. Interest is payable whether or not profits are made, and if not paid the lender has the right to put the company into liquidation and to receive payment of interest due and repayment of principal out of the proceeds of selling the company's assets. Because profits may fluctuate and interest payments may not be passed over, as may dividends on shares, such borrowing has obvious risks for the borrower. Furthermore, a large burden of interest payments increases the possibility that, if profits decline, dividends may not be paid, and this possibility may reduce the market valuation of shares, so inflicting a capital loss on shareholders. The stock market, or rather the professionals who operate therein, keep an eye on the ratio of fixed-interest debt to the value of total assets, or a company's 'gearing' as it is known, so that share values will almost certainly be adversely affected by too much borrowing. If a company's gearing becomes 'too high', then further loans will become more costly and difficult to obtain, so that if the enterprise runs into adverse economic conditions it may not be able to obtain finance to tide it over the crisis, in the way that an enterprise with lower gearing would. The advantage of gearing is that if the company can earn more than the interest payments by using the borrowed funds, then the excess accrues as extra income to shareholders without their having to provide the additional capital. Therefore, a certain amount of loan capital will be used by companies, but only within the limits deemed prudent. There is evidence that companies do not like to utilise fully all their borrowing possibilities, but prefer to hold a reserve of borrowing powers in case they need these to surmount unexpected and temporary cash-flow problems.

For all the reasons we have discussed (and more besides), the amount of external finance which may be obtained by an enterprise and committed to capital formation is likely to be limited and subject to constraints. If the enterprise's corporate strategy requires more finance than can be made up by internal finance supplemented by external finance, then it generally happens that the expenditure plan of the corporate strategy is itself revised downwards.

Any enterprise is likely to have a fairly large flow of *depreciation provisions* which it can set aside from the current flow of profits; the enterprise must, of course, be making profits through on-going operations for depreciation provisions to be a source of finance. The flow of provisions for depreciation depend on the tax laws – the amount that is permitted to be deducted by the Inland Revenue applying the provisions of the Finance Acts – and on the past investments of the enterprise. Depreciation provisions cannot therefore be altered by the enterprise: they are what they are.

So this leaves *net retentions* – undistributed income after depreciation (and stock appreciation) – as the key flow in the make-up of total finance required. The precise distinction between retentions gross and net of depreciation is, in any case, not very important. What matters is that the (gross) flow of internal finance is adequate to the financing needs of the enterprise, given its total requirement for finance and the constraints on external financing.

What, then, determines the size of the flow of internal finance? If you look at Diagram 5.1, you will see that internal finance is what remains from the flow of gross profits after interest, tax, and dividends have been paid (see also Diagram 2.2 and Table 4.2). The flow of interest is determined by the past borrowing of the enterprise and by the level of interest rates (over which the enterprise naturally has no influence); tax payments are likewise determined by the flow of taxable profits and the rate of taxation on profits. The flow of tax payments is not something which can be greatly varied by the enterprise (of course, it can and should minimise its tax payments by taking full advantage of all the concessions on free depreciation – Table 4.5).

A company can vary its dividend payments – specifically, a company with a given flow of gross profits can increase its flow of internal finance by reducing its payout of dividends. However, there are limits to which this can be done. Most dramatically, if a majority of shareholders object to a reduced dividend they – the majority – have the power to vote the board of directors out of office and to elect new directors who will, presumably, restore the dividend. Such explicit revolts by shareholders are rare events. Much more likely is that shareholders, failing to receive an adequate dividend, may 'vote with their feet' and sell their shares, thus depressing the market price of those shares.

Now, while it may be the case that the low share price should be only temporary – because the increased flow of retentions resulting from the reduced dividend is being put into (presumably) profitable assets – nevertheless the fall in the share price leaves the company vulnerable to a takeover bid by anyone who spots that the share price is 'artificially' low and so creating stock market valuation of the company below the 'proper' valuation of its assets. A takeover bid is an offer made to the shareholders of a company by any person or organisation intending to gain control of the company. If a majority of shareholders accept the offer, then the existing board of directors and management lose control of the company and, very likely, their posts. The term 'takeover' implies that the offer is made against the wishes of the existing management, in contrast to a 'merger' undertaken with the agreement and consent of both parties.

The statistical evidence on company dividend policy suggests that managements prefer to choose some initially appropriate ratio of dividends to net profits – the 'payout ratio' – and then to try to maintain that ratio as far as possible. The evidence is that the option of reducing dividends does not enter into corporate planning; the dividend payment is predicated on the basis of a traditionally established policy. However, we have seen in Table 4.6 that dividends (gross of tax) have tended to decline as a proportion of gross profits (after stock appreciation) from about 40 per cent in the mid-1960s to under 30 per cent in the later 1970s (although part of this may have been imposed upon companies by legislative restrictions on dividends under the various incomes policies).

All this implies that if the enterprise wishes to generate a sufficient flow of internal finance in order to prevent it from having to look for 'too much' external finance or having to revise its capital expenditure plans, then it has to look to its flow of profits and to ensure that this flow is sufficiently large. The flow of profits is what remains from sales receipts after wages and materials costs have been paid, so the question should be asked as to how the enterprise may set about ensuring that the difference between sales receipts, on the one hand, and wages and materials costs, on the other, may be increased to the largest possible extent. By and large, the whole of this and the following three chapters are concerned, one way or another, with the answers to this question; nearly everything that we shall discuss has a bearing on this question.

Classifying costs

Cost accountants are basically concerned to provide, as fully as possible, details of all the enterprise's costs, so that these may be monitored and thereby controlled. For this cost accountants need a detailed classification of costs. Diagram 5.2 shows how costs may be classified.

In the first instance, costs will be classified by function: that is, whether the cost is incurred during the process of production, or in selling the product (advertising, salesmen, etc.), or in distributing the product from factory to purchaser, or in undertaking research and development for improvement of a product or creation of a new one (occasionally selling and distribution costs may be put together), or in administration such as payrolls, invoicing, industrial relations, etc. These are the main functions, but there could be others of a special nature: running computers or

DIAGRAM 5.2   *Classification of costs*

Function: →	Production				Selling/ distribution	Research and development	Administration
Cost centre: →	Department *A*		Department *B*				
Cost unit: →	Product *A₁*	Product *A₂*	*B₁*	*B₂*			
Cost element: ↓							
Directly allocable costs Materials	*Plastics*						
Labour	*Operatives*						
Other expenses	*Fuel*						
Total direct costs, or 'prime costs'	Variable costs						
Indirectly apportionable costs Materials	*Spare parts*						
Labour	*Maintenance*						
Other expenses	*Rent*						
Total indirect costs, or 'overheads'							

Source: adapted from John Sizer, *An Insight into Management Accounting*, Penguin, 1969, ch. 3.

Pricing and costs: the mark-up

We know from the system of accounting that:

$$
\text{Sales receipts} = \left.\begin{array}{l}\text{Materials costs} \\ + \text{Wages costs}\end{array}\right\} \textbf{Production costs}
$$

$$
\left.\begin{array}{l}+ \text{Interest} \\ + \text{Tax} \\ + \text{Dividends} \\ + \text{Depreciation} \\ + \text{Net retentions}\end{array}\right\} \textbf{Gross margin}
$$

This is so because net retentions is the residual (in an accounting framework) remaining from sales receipts after all the other flows have been deducted. We shall simplify the

obtaining economic intelligence, for instance.

Under each function there may be one or more cost centres, perhaps called 'departments', which may be a place, or a group of persons, or items of equipment, for which costs may be separately ascertained for purposes of cost control (and hence cost responsibility). Within each department, there may be one or more cost units, which could be specific batches of products. Within each cost centre and cost unit, there are classified distinct cost elements, or individual items of costs. Cost elements may be distinguished as follows:

(a)   those which may be directly allocated to a specific cost unit and which are called 'direct costs'; and

(b)   those which cannot be directly associated with any particular product batch but which may be indirectly apportioned to that cost unit and which are called 'indirect costs'.

Within each of direct and indirect costs, there may be distinguished the costs of materials (commodities supplied to the enterprise), the costs of labour (wages and salaries, employers' contributions, etc.), and other expenses such as electricity, rent and depreciation. The total of direct costs is sometimes called 'prime costs', and the term 'prime costs' is usually confined to those costs incurred under the function of production. The total of indirect costs of production together with the total of all costs under other functions is called, by cost accountants, the 'overheads'.

Because all prime costs can be directly associated with a cost unit (a batch of products), it follows that prime costs vary according as the volume of production per period varies: if the quantity of product A_1 being produced per month increases, then the cost per month of materials used will rise, as will the costs per month of operatives (e.g. more overtime payments). Accordingly all prime costs are 'variable costs', meaning that they vary with the volume of production. Generally, variable costs are only those which are associated with the function of production.

By contrast, most (but not all) overhead costs tend to be largely unaffected by changes in the volume of production. Most overhead costs accrue simply as a function of time; for example, the rent per month or fire insurance accrues regardless of the volume of production. The costs of research and development, of administration, or depreciation on fixed capital also accrue without being much affected by the volume of production. Costs which are thus functions of simply the passage of time are known as 'fixed costs', implying that they are 'fixed', or invariant, with respect to the volume of production (the term does not imply that these costs are unalterable; for example, the enterprise may rent cheaper premises or reduce research and development expenditure, or, if it puts in more expensive machinery, increase its depreciation charges). Note that Diagram 5.2 does not include such 'costs' as interest charges or taxes on profits.

---

analysis by referring to the costs of materials and all labour as 'production costs' and to the total of all the other flows as the 'gross margin'. The terminology of costs is complex and it is necessary even for the beginner student in economics to have at least a glance at the complexity of the costing situation so as properly to appreciate the degree of simplification involved in the preceding equation.

The costing situation relates to another 'confrontation' with the outside world, of the enterprise's suppliers and also its labour force, as shown by the circle in Diagram 5.1.

In the analysis that follows, the accountant's classification of costs will be drastically simplified. We shall lump together direct costs and indirect costs (except depreciation) under *all* functions as 'production costs' – using the word 'production' in a sense much broader than the operation of manufacture – and all other flows, such as depreciation, *and including* tax, interest, dividends and net retentions, will be lumped together as the 'gross margin' – the margin of sales receipts over all production costs – gross of depreciation.

This simplification enables us to write the following equation:

$$\frac{\text{Sales}}{\text{receipts}} = \frac{\text{Production}}{\text{costs}} + \frac{\text{Gross}}{\text{margin}}$$

What we are calling production costs tends to be a relatively large flow. For example, if we apply this equation to the accounts of the Delta Metal Company for 1974 (Table 2.3) we have:

	£ million	Percentage
Sales receipts	399.81	100
Production costs	358.82	90
Gross margin	40.99	10

Now, if we imagine an enterprise producing a single product, then:

$$\frac{\text{Sales}}{\text{receipts}} = \text{Price} \times \text{Quantity}$$

The flow of sales receipts per period is the product of the price per item *multiplied by* the quantity of items produced (and sold) per period. (In what follows we assume that the quantity produced per period and the quantity sold per period are equal: that is to say, the enterprise is neither increasing nor decreasing its inventory of finished products.) We may therefore write:

$$\text{Price} \times \text{Quantity} = \frac{\text{Production}}{\text{costs}} + \frac{\text{Gross}}{\text{margin}}$$

and, dividing through by quantity we may express price as:

$$\text{Price} = \frac{\dfrac{\text{Production}}{\text{costs}}}{\text{Quantity}} + \frac{\dfrac{\text{Gross}}{\text{margin}}}{\text{Quantity}}$$

The term we shall use for production cost per item produced is 'unit production cost': that is, the cost of production per unit of output by quantity. The term we shall use for the gross margin per item produced is likewise 'unit gross margin'.

Unit production cost and unit gross margin are simply the accounting flows per item produced. For example, if the price is £1 per item, and 100 items are produced per period, say per week, then total sales receipts will be £100 per week; if total production costs are £90 per week, then the gross margin will be £10 per week; unit production cost will be 90p (per item) and unit gross margin will be 10p (per item).

So far we have dealt simply with accounting flows as they might emerge after the close of the production period. The next step in building a model of the enterprise's pricing behaviour is to step back in time and to contemplate the situation as it might look to an enterprise embarking on the production of a new product and for which no price has yet been established. We need to suppose that the enterprise can estimate its production costs for any given volume of production with a reasonable degree of accuracy. The cost accountants, with their cost classifications, and the engineers, with information on what is required by way of materials, labour time, etc., should be able to get together to produce an estimate of total production costs and from this an estimate of unit production cost. If the enterprise can now determine its unit gross margin, it will have established the price to be charged as the sum of unit production cost *plus* unit gross margin. It is possible, and is often done, for the enterprise to determine its unit gross margin as some proportion, m, of its unit production cost:

Unit gross margin = $m \times$ Unit production cost

The proportion m may take on any value: it is, of course, certain to be larger than zero; it may be a fraction between 0 and 1; but there is nothing which necessarily stops it from being greater than 1.

If the enterprise proceeds in this way, with some conventional value of *m*, perhaps based on past experience, then we may write the price to be charged as determined by the estimated unit production cost and the proportion *m*:

Price = Unit production cost + *m* × Unit production cost

or, simplifying:

Price = (1 + *m*) Unit production cost

The expression *m* may then be called the 'mark-up' on unit production cost which determines the price to be charged; this means either that *m* × Unit production cost is added to unit production cost to determine price, or (what comes to the same thing) that unit production cost is multiplied by 1 + *m* to determine price. This is known as the *mark-up theory of pricing*, or sometimes, for obvious reasons, as the *cost-plus* theory of pricing or *full-cost* pricing.

Whatever may be the enterprise's desired or target mark-up, the mark-up actually achieved is quite simply the ratio of the gross margin to production costs. To show this:

$$1 + m = \frac{\text{Price}}{\text{Unit production cost}}$$

$$= \frac{\text{Price} \times \text{Quantity}}{\text{Unit production cost} \times \text{Quantity}}$$

$$= \frac{\text{Production costs} + \text{Gross margin}}{\text{Production costs}}$$

$$= 1 + \frac{\text{Gross margin}}{\text{Production costs}}$$

whence:

$$m = \frac{\text{Gross margin}}{\text{Production costs}}$$

For example, we can see that the average mark-up achieved by Delta Metal in 1974 was:

$$m = \frac{£40.99\text{m.}}{£358.82\text{m.}}$$

$$= 0.114$$

or 11.4 per cent.

The mark-up method of pricing appears, from various surveys, to be a fairly widely applicable description of what enterprises often do, but it cannot be a fully fledged theory of pricing until we can describe the factors which determine the mark-up, the ratio of gross margin to production costs, that the enterprise tries to achieve. The gross margin comprises the following flows:

Interest, Tax — *Predetermined variables*
Dividends — *Constrained policy variable*
Depreciation — *Determined*
Net retentions — *Target variable*

Of these, interest, tax and depreciation are more or less predetermined for the enterprise, and are not freely variable. Dividends (or distributions out of net income) may be altered by the enterprise, but we have seen that there are likely to be limits to the extent to which dividends may be reduced and that companies generally keep to a set policy with regard to dividends. If, therefore, the enterprise has forecasts of its future interest, tax and depreciation flows, and has made some decision on the flow of dividends to be paid, then that leaves net retentions as the remaining undetermined variable. However, in view of the importance of internal financing, we have argued that enterprises may wish to achieve a certain flow of net (or gross) retentions, in order to be able to obtain, without excessive recourse to external funds, the financing required to pay for the fixed capital formation which the enterprise intends, as a result of its corporate strategy, to try to undertake. If this is the case, then, looking forward in time, the flow of net retentions is no longer simply an accounting residual, passively to be accepted, but is part of the enterprise's forward planning. At this juncture, the flow of net retentions becomes a target variable which the enterprise must try to achieve if it is to be able to carry out its long-range plans. If this is so, then the mark-up is determined, because the denominator, production cost, is known, and all the flows in the numerator, the gross margin, are also the subject of determinate estimates (whether predetermined or targets) made in advance.

That is to say, the way in which the enterprise may seek to achieve the requisite flow of internal finance is by establishing, in the price charged, an appropriate mark-up on unit production cost. The mark-up, and hence the price, is the critical variable which the enterprise may seek to vary in order to achieve its long-range goals with regard to the financing of fixed capital formation.

Having said this, we must immediately stress that many factors may intervene to prevent the enterprise achieving its desired mark-up, and we shall subsequently examine the impact of the market environment in which the enterprise must sell its product.

Another critical area in which the enterprise confronts the outside world is in the reactions of its *customers*; these may be studied under the heading of 'consumer behaviour', as shown by the circle in Diagram 5.1. It may well be that, because of consumer behaviour, at the end of the day, the enterprise is unable to achieve through pricing the flow of internal finance it requires, and this may force modifications to the corporate strategy.

In this way, the pricing/mark-up decisions of the enterprise are the key links between its current and its future operations. From a behavioural point of view, 'profits' should not be thought of as simply a balancing accounting residual, but as the subject of targets established in advance, and targets to be achieved through appropriate mark-ups and pricing. Products which fail, because of market price conditions and/or cost overruns, to achieve a 'satisfactory' mark-up are likely to be dropped from production, while products which provide 'good' margins will be expanded. Many enterprises nowadays establish, for each product line, fairly detailed budgeting and planning systems with forecasts of sales quantities, prices and gross margins to be generated. Lack of fulfilment of these plans may then lead to early remedial action such as an increased sales drive by the selling staff or a drive to reduce production costs. We must not be misled by the residual accounting nature of profits into thinking that enterprises do not actively pursue a target flow of profits. Enterprises do try to determine their profits in advance; one of the more important methods of doing this is through pricing policy: that is, through setting prices with mark-ups on unit production costs which will generate the required profits; and the main reason they do this is not simply for the sake of profits themselves but because the enterprise needs the gross retentions out of profits – the internal finance – to pay for its planned investment.

Business economic planning

So far we have spoken of corporate strategy in a rather loose way because all we required was to trace the links in Diagram 5.1. It is now necessary to consider how enterprises set about strategic planning, because this not only elucidates the concept of corporate strategy but also shows more clearly how the enterprise encounters external constraints. Most business economic planning starts from plans for prices and quantities (volume) of production; this is shown in the flow chart of Diagram 5.3 as the originating basis of an enterprise's plan.

DIAGRAM 5.3   *Business economic planning: flow chart*

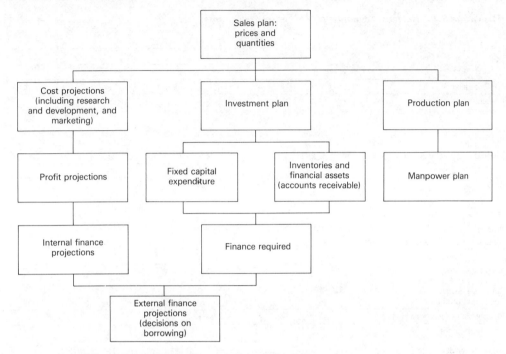

Source: adapted from Gunnar Eliasson, *Business Economic Planning: Theory, Practice and Comparison*, Wiley/Swedish Industrial Publications, 1976, diagram I-1B, p. 25.

From these plans for sales there will be:

(a)   a corresponding production plan (which may also imply a manpower plan – recruitment and/or training of various skills);

(b)   an investment plan (to be discussed); and

(c)   a set of cost projections, which will probably include not only the variable costs associated with the volumes of each product but also all the 'overheads' (it appears to be common business practice to classify research and development costs with 'overhead costs').

Together, the sales plan and the cost projections result in a set of projections of gross operating profit. When the profit projections are matched against payments of taxes, interest, and dividends, projections of internal finance may be obtained.

To return to the investment plan: the enterprise will have to assess not only all the expenditure required to be undertaken on fixed capital for purposes of maintaining production of existing products (and possibly reducing costs) and of producing new products, but also the expenditure which will have to go into 'working capital' such as inventories or financial assets like accounts receivable. Despite the apparent lesser importance of the latter in the aggregate flows reported in the national accounts, it appears that businesses have to plan quite systematically for annual increases in working capital and that these flows may frequently be larger than expenditure on fixed capital. Together, the plans for expenditure on fixed capital and on working capital determine the total finance required. When matched against the projections of internal finance, the amount of external finance may be projected, and decisions can be taken on borrowing and/or new issues. Unacceptable, or unattainable, projections for external finance may then result in revisions to various parts of the plan; common among these are reductions in fixed capital formation plans and attempts to reduce costs (but seldom, apparently, research and development).

DIAGRAM 5.4   *Business economic planning: set of accounts*

			Year		
			1	2 ...	h
(1) Sales plan	Price, p	Quantity, q	pq		pq
Product 1	$p_{1,1}$	$q_{1,1}$			
Product 2	$p_{2,1}$	$q_{2,1}$			
.					
Product n	$p_{n,1}$	$q_{n,1}$			
All products: total value of sales, £		$\Sigma p_1 q_1$	$\Sigma p_2 q_2$	...	$\Sigma p_h q_h$
(2) Cost projections		£	£		£
Product 1		$C_{1,1}$			
Product 2		$C_{2,1}$			
.					
Product n		$C_{n,1}$			
All products: total 'costs of production'		ΣC_1	ΣC_2	...	ΣC_h
(3) Profit projections		£	£		£
Total value of sales		$\Sigma p_1 q_1$			
Total 'costs of production'		ΣC_1			
Total 'overheads'		O_1			
Total gross profits		$\Pi_1 = \Sigma p_1 q_1 - \Sigma C_1 - O_1$	Π_2	...	Π_h
(4) Internal finance projections		£	£		£
Total gross profit		Π_1			
plus Other income		Y_1			
minus Taxes		T_1			
minus Interest		I_1			
minus Dividends		D_1			
equals Internal finance (gross retentions) (F)		$F_1 = \Pi_1 + Y_1 - T_1 - I_1 - D_1$	F_2	...	F_h
(5) Investment plan		£	£		£
Expenditures necessary to:					
Maintain volume of production (existing products)		$K_{a,1}$			
Equipment for new products		$K_{b,1}$			
Cost-reducing investments		$K_{c,1}$			
Contingencies		$K_{d,1}$			
Total investment in fixed capital		ΣK_1	ΣK_2	...	ΣK_h
(6) External finance and cash flow projections		£	£		£
Sources of funds					
Internal finance		F_1			
plus New issues (proceeds)		N_1			
plus Borrowing (long-term and short-term)		B_1			
plus Increase in accounts payable		A_1			
equals Total sources (excluding cash)		$S_1 = F_1 + N_1 + B_1 + A_1$	S_2	...	S_h
Uses of funds					
Investment in fixed capital		ΣK_1			
plus Increase in inventories		V_1			
plus Repayment of borrowing		R_1			
plus Increase in accounts receivable		A_1'			
equals Total uses (excluding cash)		$U_1 = \Sigma K_1 + V_1 + R_1 + A_1'$	U_2	...	U_h
Balancing item					
Change in cash (liquid assets)		$L_1 = S_1 - U_1$	L_2	...	L_h

Note: all variables, except prices, are flows per annum.

Source: adapted from Gunnar Eliasson, *Business Economic Planning: Theory, Practice and Comparison*, Wiley/Swedish Industrial Publications, 1976, supplement 2 'A set of standard forms', pp. 267–74.

We may give a greater concreteness to this flow chart by looking at a standard (and simplified) set of tables which enterprises use in their business planning (see Diagram 5.4). Planning is usually done annually (but shorter periods can be used) over a time horizon of about five years ($h = 5$). The basic ingredient of the plan are forecasts, by product, of prices and quantities, and hence forecasts for each year from year 1 to year h of total receipts from sales. Some of these products may, of course, be new products to be introduced within the planning horizon.

The next stage is a set of cost projections, also by product and generally confined to 'variable costs'. A considerable amount of detailed specification goes into each of the cost projections, and subsequently attempts may be made to reduce the initial cost estimates.

The third stage is to prepare, from the sales and cost projections, with added projections for overhead costs, a projection of gross profits.

In the fourth stage these projections of gross profits can be matched with projections of appropriations – that is, taxes, interest, and dividends – to produce a projection of internal finance, or gross retentions.

The fifth stage in the process of planning is to request, from operating divisions, details of required capital expenditures over the time horizon. These estimates are, apparently, the subject of much discussion and negotiation between 'headquarters' and the divisions, especially as they will eventually form the basis of final authorisation for capital expenditure (Eliasson makes the point strongly that the plan itself never implies actual authorisation; that has to wait until nearer the time). Normally, this fifth stage relates to fixed capital only – equipment and structures – classified in a variety of ways, of which one way is shown in Diagram 5.4: maintenance; new product equipment; cost-reducing investment; and 'contingencies'. The total will make up the annual flow of expenditure on fixed capital over the time horizon.

The sixth and final stage in the planning process is to bring together the sources and uses of funds in a statement which will leave the enterprise's 'cash', or liquidity, position to be determined as the 'bottom line'. That is, the enterprise will add together its internal finance, the amounts of external finance it plans on trying to obtain, excluding 'cash' borrowing such as overdrafts, but including possible increases in accounts payable, to give a total of sources of funds (excluding 'cash'). Then it totals the various uses of funds: fixed capital formation; increase in inventories (usually calculated on the basis of the increase in sales); repayments of borrowing; and increase in accounts receivable.

Finally, on the bottom line, the enterprise will determine the implications of the balance between total sources of funds and total uses of funds for its liquidity, or 'cash', position, to see whether it is likely either to be accumulating 'cash' (liquid assets) or requiring to draw down its reserves of 'cash' or use up short-term financing such as a bank overdraft. In the medium term the enterprise must be in balance on its 'bottom line'; it should neither be accumulating excessive liquidity, nor requiring continuous increases in its liquid liabilities. This means that, all the preceding items must somehow be brought into over-all conformity with one another over the planning period taken as a whole.

An 'unacceptable' result at the bottom line, i.e. a continuous negative net acquisition of liquid financial assets, can then lead to various courses of action. The furthest-reaching of these, and the one of greatest interest to economists, goes all the way back to an upward revision of prices, or, as we previously described it, an increase in the mark-up. But there are other possibilities. A downward revision of costs is often instigated at this juncture, and Eliasson describes the constant pressure which his sixty-two enterprises brought to bear to 'maintain and improve performance', which usually meant that profits as a percentage of sales had to be increased, or at least maintained. This is tantamount to requiring (a) a cost reduction per unit of output, or (b) a price increase, or (c) both. The gross profit margin, which we shall denote by r, is (and using the notation of Diagram 5.4):

$$r = \frac{\Pi}{\Sigma pq}$$

$$= \frac{\Sigma pq - \Sigma C - O}{\Sigma pq}$$

$$= 1 - \frac{\Sigma C}{\Sigma pq} - \frac{O}{\Sigma pq}$$

If the flow of variable costs, ΣC, or the flow of overhead costs, O, can be reduced in relation to the flow of sales receipts, Σpq, then the profit margin on sales receipts, r, will rise; alternatively, a rise in prices, p, if it does not affect the quantities sold, q (a most important qualification), will also increase r. However, it appears that enterprises usually fear the adverse impact of price rises on the volume of sales (with good reason, as we shall subsequently see), so that cost reductions tend to be the first line of attack.

If the results of these courses of action, vigorously pursued, still leave an unacceptable bottom line, and if the enterprise cannot or will not increase its external financing, then the projects for new investment will probably be trimmed, in the light of estimated rates of return on capital employed in each product.

It may be, of course, that the result on the bottom line is an embarrassing accumulation of liquid assets continuing over a number of years. One response to this is simply to reduce all external finance to zero, and possibly even to adopt the absence of external financing as company policy. If the accumulation of cash (liquid assets) still continues, then the enterprise may seek either to expand its investment programme, but it may here encounter shortages of skilled manpower, including a shortage of good managerial talent. Another possibility, not mentioned in Diagram 5.4, is to embark on acquiring other companies: that is, on using funds to purchase shares and/or make takeover bids (this adds a new line to the uses of funds mentioned in Diagram 5.4). We have seen (in Tables 4.10 and 4.11) that companies purchase the shares of other companies as part of their uses of funds. Such a use of funds appears quite frequently in enterprise business planning and may be the subject of much discussion and concern within the enterprise.

Of course, there are more aspects to detailed business planning than are shown in Diagram 5.3. We have shown one offshoot: the detailed production plan, and an associated manpower plan. But there may be other aspects of planning, such as a detailed inventory management plan, or plans, for improving marketing and distribution. But mostly these are offshoots from the basic sales plan and they are of specialist, rather than general economic, interest.

We considered previously in some detail one of the important areas where the enterprise confronts the outside world: namely, the financial markets from which external finance might be sought (full discussion of financial markets awaits subsequent consideration of financial institutions in the United Kingdom). We also pointed to two other critical areas in which the enterprise confronts the outside world: production economics, concerned with costs; and consumer behaviour, concerned with pricing. We have seen that cost reductions often appear to have priority in enterprise planning. This is largely because consumer behaviour sets fairly stringent limits to the extent to which enterprises can raise prices. After all, if prices could be raised to any extent imaginable without adverse consequences for quantities sold, then enterprises could simply achieve all desired objectives in Diagram 5.4 merely by determining the requisite mark-up on unit production costs and not worrying unduly about what those costs happened to be. Unfortunately (or fortunately), consumer behaviour (customer reaction) prevents this from happening, and we must now see why this is so, before going on to a consideration of production economics and how enterprises seek to minimise unit production costs.

Exercises

5.1 *(To practise your understanding of the mark-up.)* In 1977 total sales receipts, etc., for UK manufacturing industry, were £132,030.1 million, total cost of bought-in materials, etc. (used) was £88,038.1 million, and total labour costs were £27,413 million (Exercise 2.2). What was the average percentage mark-up on all costs achieved by UK manufacturing industry in 1977?

(*Hint*: in an exercise like this what is important is not so much to get the arithmetically right answer (14.36 per cent), as to set forth fully the economics and algebra behind your answer; for example, start by defining the total gross margin and go on from there to identify all the relevant variables *before* putting the above numbers to them, *before* doing the arithmetic.)

5.2 *(Further to practise your understanding of the mark-up and the gross margin.)* With reference to the data given in Exercise 4.12:

(i) what was Esso Chemical's total gross margin in 1980?
(ii) What was Esso Chemical's average proportionate mark-up on production costs?
(iii) With reference to your answer to (ii), do you think the Chairman's statement quoted in note (*c*) to the table in Exercise 4.12 was reasonable? (Delta Metals in 1974 provides one possible standard of comparison.)

5.3 *(To practise your understanding of Diagram 5.1.)*
(i) To what extent have statutory depreciation allowances contributed to the 'internal finance' of UK companies over the past decade? (Depreciation allowances are given for *all* companies in an un-numbered table in section 15 'Notes' of the *National Income and Expenditure* accounts.)

(ii) In the light of table 5.4 in the *National Income and Expenditure* accounts you will see that the 'gross profits' bar in Diagram 5.1 (the second from bottom) is somewhat simplified; draw an unsimplified bar, showing all the components and with relevant figures inserted for the latest year for industrial and commercial companies; but, first, decide what you will do about stock appreciation.

5.4 *(To practise your understanding of business economic planning.)* Because you are good at and like (a) carpentry or (b) sewing – you should choose between (a) or (b) according to inclination* – but cannot find paid employment, you are going into business for yourself as (a) a manufacturer of solid-wood garden furniture made from elm, or (b) a producer of soft toys. You plan to produce the following product lines: (a) a chair, a bench, a table, and a large tea-tray; or (b) a teddy bear, a rag doll, a rabbit, and a glove puppet. To start up in business you need: some (powered) equipment; an inventory of (a) seasoned timber or (b) cloth, kapok, and cotton, etc.; and premises. Establish, with all the relevant figures, a business economic plan to present to your bank manager to show him how, and convince him that, you can service the loan which you are going to request from the bank in order to get started.

5.5 *(To practise your understanding of cost classification.)* Using the data assembled for Exercise 5.4, classify your costs as per Diagram 5.2 (adapted if necessary).

*If you wish, you can choose any other activity you know about, but you must produce more than one product and you must require fixed capital, circulating capital, and premises.

Chapter 6

Consumer Behaviour and Market Constraints on the Enterprise

Contents

Chapter guide

At the end of Chapter 5 we left enterprises confronting the problem that they cannot charge any mark-up they wish to without this affecting the quantity which they can sell: *price* and *quantity sold* are interdependent, so this chapter is about the market constraints which consumer (or customer) behaviour imposes on enterprises. This constraint can be expressed in a (downward-sloping) *demand curve*, which effectively limits the mark-up by forcing on the enterprise a choice between price charged (mark-up) and quantity sold: the higher the one, the lower the other.

Fully understanding this (rather obvious) constraint involves analysing consumer behaviour through the interaction of *indifference curves* (which depict a consumer's preferences, or what he or she would like to do) and the *budget constraint* (which depicts what the consumer is able, given his or her income, to do). This interaction produces, for the individual, a *ceteris paribus* downward-sloping demand curve and this can be generalised for the totality of consumers to give a *market demand curve*.

The practical impact on *total sales receipts* of the inverse interdependence between price and quantity sold along the market demand curve is governed by *own-price elasticity of demand*. This important relationship of price elasticity to total sales receipts is fully explained and demonstrated with reference to a case study of an actual demand curve.

But choosing the 'right' price/quantity combination on the market demand curve requires also that costs be brought into the reckoning, and *profit maximisation* with reference to *marginal costs* and *marginal sales receipts* is explained and examined with reference to the same case study.

We consider also how competitors' likely reactions to price changes by an enterprise may 'trap' the enterprise between two adverse price elasticities.

Demand curves

We have considered a simplified model of enterprise pricing, for any particular product, as:

$$\text{Price} = (1 + m) \times \text{Unit production cost}$$

where *m* is the mark-up which the enterprise may seek to establish with reference to its need for profits, gross retentions out of profits being required to make up the total finance needed for the enterprise's capital formation. Gross retentions are determined as the residual remaining from sales receipts after production costs have been paid and appropriations such as interest, tax and dividends have been met. Sales receipts are, of course, price *multiplied by* quantity of goods sold. Thus:

$$\frac{\text{Gross}}{\text{retentions}} = \text{Price} \times \text{Quantity} - \frac{\text{Production}}{\text{costs}} - (\text{Interest} + \text{Tax} + \text{Dividends})$$

Clearly, from this equation, if an enterprise could increase the price per item without suffering any reduction in the quantity of items sold, then it could generate almost any flow of gross retentions it wished. Unfortunately, price and quantity are interdependent variables such that a price increase is certain to result in a quantity decrease, and we must now investigate the nature of this interdependency which establishes the conditions under which the enterprise confronts its customers in the outside world.

The key analytic device in understanding the interaction between an enterprise and its customers is the concept of a 'demand curve', or a schedule which relates the quantity of items that may be sold to the various prices which may be charged for that item. Intuitively, we can all appreciate that the higher the price of a good the less is likely to be sold during any period. For example, if all ice-cream cones were £100 each, even the hottest summer would not be likely to promote any sales. But this intuition is too vague and impressionistic to be the basis of an adequate understanding of consumer behaviour, so we need to be more specific in our analysis, even though we are only 'spelling out' a quite familiar, everyday experience of price–quantity interdependency.

A *demand curve*, or *demand schedule* (I would prefer the latter term but for the former being standard textbook terminology), relates the total flow of sales, measured in number of items sold, during a period to the price per item. Note that the word 'demand' is being used in a precise sense of being measured by quantity of items sold. Let us illustrate this with an example of an actual demand curve taken from one of the case studies by D. C. Hague, *Pricing in Business* (Allen & Unwin, 1971). Hague studied the pricing practices of thirteen enterprises in the United Kingdom between 1964 and 1968, and subsequently published a book based on these researches, including in the book nine cases which he was given permission to publish by the participating enterprises. All the cases were disguised with regard to identity. One of the case studies, that for 'Fourways Manufacturing Ltd' (not its real name, but some comments point to it being an engineering company), was concerned with the introduction of a new product, Product *F*. Fourways tended to follow a practice of mark-up pricing:

> there was the operational objective that, for every group of similar products within each product line, there should be a standard percentage rate of recovery, or margin (expressed as gross invoice value [i.e. sales receipts] *less* commission, labour costs and material cost [i.e., and loosely, 'production cost']) (p. 69).

Fourways' cost estimator had estimated the unit cost of the new product at about £196 (per unit), and 'multiplying the cost figure by the traditional Fourways' percentage [mark-up] suggested a price of £260 per unit' (p. 147). We can infer from this that the 'traditional' mark-up at Fourways was 0.33 or 33 per cent. However, Fourways had incurred quite heavy 'indirect' costs of research and development, design, market development, and sales promotion, and they were anxious to try to 'recover' some of these 'overheads' also from the gross margin (p. 148), and this led them, in the later stages, to conclude that if the desired gross margin over unit costs, including all development costs, were to be achieved the price should be £450 to £500 per unit (pp. 290–1). Unfortunately, however, prices then being charged in the United Kingdom for comparable products were around £350 to £400 per unit; eventually Fourways charged £390 per unit (p. 291).

While the arguments about 'recovering' the development costs were going on within the company, Fourways' sales manager asked his area managers and the company's agents overseas to estimate how many units of the product could be sold if it were priced at £250, £300, £350, £400, or £450 respectively. The results obtained by totalling all the answers are given in Table 6.1 (as noted, the results were initially in the form of ranges from low to high; for example, at £250 the estimate was that quantity of sales per annum would be between 1,286 to 1,456, but in Table 6.1 I have simplified by taking the mid-points of these ranges). At the lowest price of £250 per unit, about 1,371 units of Product *F* would probably have been sold per annum, while at the highest price of £450 per unit only 166 would probably have been sold each year. If we plot these points as in Diagram 6.1, we obtain the scatter of points shown, and we can fit by least squares a straight-line relationship of the form:

$$\text{Price per unit} = 451 - 0.1587 \begin{pmatrix} \text{Number of} \\ \text{units sold} \\ \text{per annum} \end{pmatrix}$$

with a correlation coefficient of −0.967. This is the relationship known as a 'demand curve' – here given in the form of a straight line.

TABLE 6.1   *Fourways Manufacturing Ltd: demand curve for Product F*

Possible price in £ per unit:	*p*	250	300	350	400	450
Estimates made by area managers and overseas agents of number of units per annum which could be sold at that price: [a]	*Q*	1,371	840	509	307	166

[a] The estimates were originally provided in the form of ranges, as follows: 1,286 to 1,456, 763 to 916; 476 to 541; 294 to 319; and 161 to 171 respectively; the figures given in the table are the mid-points of these ranges.

Source: D. C. Hague, *Pricing in Business* (Allen & Unwin, 1971) p. 292.

Logarithmic form for demand curves

Although this straight line gives quite a good fit, it should be apparent from Diagram 6.1 that a straight-line relationship is not altogether satisfactory, as the points fall more along a curve. A curvilinear, or logarithmic relationship gives a better fit, with a correlation coefficient of -0.992; but for purposes of exposition, such a form of the relationship becomes mathematical-ly complex. The important thing is, at this stage, to understand the basic principles, and this compels the use of the mathematically simpler, if less appropriate, demand curve. It is worth noting that a curvilinear relationship is a form much more likely to occur in the real world, and this confirms the basic accuracy of the replies which the sales manager received.

DIAGRAM 6.1   *Demand curve for Product F*

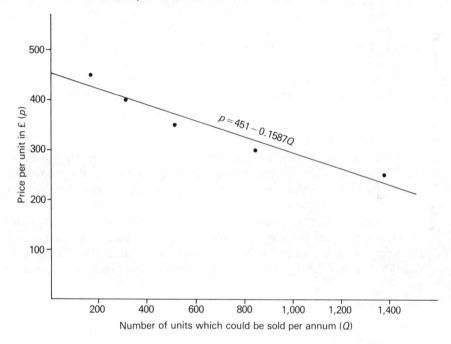

In drawing demand curves, it is usual to put price on the upright vertical axis and quantity on the horizontal axis; this is also a convenient arrangement for economic analysis, as we shall see. And so the general expression for the demand curve (in a straight-line form) is:

$$p = a + bQ$$

and, as we shall show, the sign of the coefficient b is, almost entirely without exception, negative.

Why can we be so sure that the sign of b will be negative? In other words, why can we be certain that the interdependence between price and quantity results in an inverse relationship: the higher the one, the lower the other? In order to answer this question – and we know from our equation for gross retentions that the inverse interdependence of price and quantity has important consequences (that is, if we increase price in order to increase gross retentions, we may not achieve our aims because quantity will decline) – we need to consider the theoretical economics of consumer behaviour.

The economic analysis of consumer behaviour – indifference curves

The total quantity of sales during a year (or during any other period) comprises the totality of sales to many consumers, and in order fully to understand the demand curve drawn in Diagram 6.1, we need first of all to investigate theoretically the factors which influence the *individual* consumer in his or her purchases of a good. What are the things which affect the individual consumer in his or her decision-making process when deciding how much of a good to buy?

The three things which determine each consumer's purchases of a good are:

(a)   his or her 'tastes', or pattern of preferences;
(b)   his or her income, in other words what he or she is able to do; and
(c)   the other things on which the consumer might alternatively spend income.

It is important to appreciate that the price of a good measures not only how much one has to pay for the good itself; it also indicates, when taken in conjunction with the price of another good, the amount of the other good which must be forgone as a result of purchasing the first good. That is, the analysis of consumer behaviour is an analysis of the process of choosing between competing uses of (limited) income so as best to satisfy our preferences. To put it technically, each purchase has an 'opportunity cost' in terms of the alternatives which are thereby forgone (as anyone living on a limited income knows full well). So it is necessary to analyse the decision-making process in terms of this opportunity cost; we cannot, that is, simply look at the decision to buy good X in isolation from the opportunity cost (the corresponding 'decision' not to buy good Y).

The first problem is to represent the consumer's 'tastes' or pattern of preferences. We may do this diagrammatically in two-dimensional form by limiting the analysis to two goods, X and Y. Suppose, then, that we establish in Diagram 6.2 a two-dimensional space in which can be represented the purchases of combinations of the two goods. Along the horizontal axis, we measure, in number of items, the quantity of good X which the individual may purchase (and consume) during any period (such as a year). Along the vertical axis, we measure, in number of items, the quantity of good Y which the consumer may purchase during that same period. The 'items' may be any convenient and conven-

DIAGRAM 6.2   *An indifference curve*

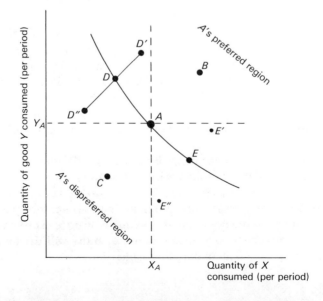

tional units of measurement, such as kg of apples, number of shirts, litres of petrol, and so on. Prices must then be expressed in £ or pence per 'item' as thus measured. In this analysis we make no distinction between purchases and consumption; to purchase is to consume.

The consumer gets 'satisfaction' from consuming quantities of goods X and Y. So that the combination of any initial combination such as that represented by co-ordinate A, representing X_A of good X and Y_A of good Y, on Diagram 6.2, affords the consumer an initial 'level' of satisfaction. The problem in determining the consumer's pattern of preferences is to compare other points in the X–Y space with this initial combination. Clearly, any point such as B in the quadrant above and to the right of Y_A and X_A, which represents more of *both* Y and X, will afford an unambiguously higher level of satisfaction than does A, because B offers everything that A offers and more besides. Conversely, any point such as C, in the quadrant below and to the left of Y_A and X_A, representing less of both Y and X, offers an unambiguously lower level of satisfaction than does A. So any point in the upper-right quadrant is preferred to A and any point in the lower-left quadrant is not preferred to A, but is 'dispreferred' – if we may coin the word.

So far, so good. But what may we conclude about points such as D or E? Are they preferred or dispreferred to A? The problem for the consumer is that a point such as D represents more of Y (it is above Y_A) but less of X (below X_A). The question is whether the increase in the consumption of Y more than 'compensates' for the diminution in the consumption of X, or whether it less than compensates, or perhaps whether it exactly compensates. We can imagine a point such as D' (D prime) where the relatively large increase in the consumption of Y is more than sufficient to compensate for the relatively small reduction in the consumption of X, so that D' would be preferred to A (or, as we shall say, is in A's preferred region). Alternatively, we may take a point such as D'' (D double prime), where the relatively small increase in the consumption of Y is not sufficient to compensate for the relatively large reduction in the consumption of X, so that D'' would be dispreferred to A – or is in A's dispreferred region.

If we move along the straight line joining D' (in A's preferred region) and D'' (in A's dispreferred region), we must somewhere come to the boundary between A's preferred region and A's dispreferred region. For the sake of exposition let us suppose that D is exactly on this boundary line. What can we then say about D compared with A? We know that on one side of the boundary line it would be preferred to A, and on the other dispreferred. But if it is exactly on the boundary line, then the consumer can neither prefer nor disprefer it to A; in other words, it is a matter of indifference to the consumer whether he or she has combination A or combination D.

We could repeat the analysis with points such as E, E' and E'', again imagining that E is exactly on the boundary line between A's preferred region and A's dispreferred region. If the consumer is indifferent between A and D and between A and E, then it follows that the consumer must be indifferent as to the choice between D and E.

If we repeated this analysis over and over, we could eventually trace out most of the boundary line between A's preferred region and A's dispreferred region on which points such as D and E lay. Because this boundary line marks out the points, or combinations of X and Y, between or among which the consumer is indifferent, such a line (drawn in Diagram 6.2) is known as an 'indifference curve'. The indifference curve, as explained, divides the X–Y space into two regions: one to the upper right of the curve which contains all the points (combinations of X and Y) preferred to A, the other to the lower left which contains all the points dispreferred to A.

It is obvious that the indifference curve must slope downwards to the right: if the consumer is to suffer a reduction in the consumption of one good, then he or she must be compensated for this by an increase in consumption of the other good. But there is more to the indifference curve than simply a downward slope. In Diagram 6.2 the indifference curve has been drawn with a definite shape, known as convex to the origin; if one stands at the origin, the curve appears as convex, thus: →(. We could have had a downward-sloping straight line as the boundary; or even a concave (towards the origin) downward-sloping curve, thus: →). Let us demonstrate the peculiarity that would be implied by a straight-line boundary or indifference curve.

The peculiar implication is that, with a straight line, moving down it would imply that an equal amount of increase in *X* would always exactly counterbalance a given reduction in *Y*, *regardless of how much Y was being consumed to start with*. Thus, if consumption of *Y* were initially high, a given reduction in consumption would be compensated for by a certain increase in *X* (according to the slope of the straight line); and if the consumption of *Y* were very low, a further given reduction in its consumption would be compensated by the same increase in *X* as previously. This is peculiar, because we know that as consumption of a good falls, our resistance to further declines in consumption grows; in operational terms, we require greater increases in consumption of the other good in offsetting compensation. In other words, the shape of the indifference curve is likely to be convex rather than a straight line.

Diagram 6.3 illustrates the point. If we are initially at point *A*, consuming a lot of *Y* and a little of *X*, then we are likely to be 'keen' to consume more of *X*, while conversely it does not matter greatly if we consume less of *Y*; so at point *A* an extra unit of *X*, Δ*X*, would adequately compensate for a reduction of, say, 1 unit in *Y* so the consumer is indifferent between *A* and *A'*. However, at point *B* consumption of *Y* is significantly lower and consumption of *X* is now approaching satiation. Thus a further reduction in the consumption of *Y* by 1 unit now requires, as matching compensation, an increase in the consumption of *X* by, say, 3 units: this is a measure of 'increased resistance' to further reductions in the consumption of *Y*. The rate at which extra units of *X* substitute for a unit reduction in *Y*, which we may express as the ratio of the value of the change in *Y* disregarding sign (or the 'modulus' of Δ*Y*, where 'Δ' means 'change in' and 'modulus' means disregarding sign and is expressed by two parallel lines, thus $|\Delta Y|$: the modulus of $+1$ being 1, and the modulus of -1 being 1) to the change in *X* disregarding sign, goes from:

$$\frac{|\Delta Y|}{|\Delta X|} = \frac{|-1|}{|1|} = \frac{1}{1}$$

to:

$$\frac{|\Delta Y|}{|\Delta X|} = \frac{|-1|}{|3|} = \frac{1}{3}$$

and the ratio will continue to decrease as we move downwards to the right.

Because we are dealing all the time with small changes such as those from *A* to *A'* or *B* to *B'* (and not with 'wholesale' changes such as the change from *A* to *B*), the terminology which has become conventional in economics is to refer to the change from *A* to *A'*, which combines $|\Delta Y|$ with $|\Delta X|$, as 'marginal' changes (or 'incremental' changes) and to refer to the rate at which *X* substitutes for *Y* over such small changes as the 'marginal rate of substitution'.

(The best translation of the word 'marginal', while it is unfamiliar, is 'over a small change' – so the term 'marginal rate of substitution' reads 'rate of substitution when taken over a small change'. Likewise, 'marginal rate of taxation' means 'the change in taxation taken over a small change in income'; or 'marginal propensity to consume' means 'the change in consumption when taken over a small change in income'. The word 'incremental' is also synonymous with 'marginal'.)

The principle that the marginal rate of substitution of *X* for *Y* should change from 1/1 to 1/3 and so on as the consumption of *X* increases and the consumption of *Y* falls is known as the *principle of diminishing marginal rate (or ratio) of substitution*. The effect of a diminishing marginal rate of substitution (illustrated in Diagram 6.3) is simply to make it

DIAGRAM 6.3   *Diminishing marginal rate of substitution*

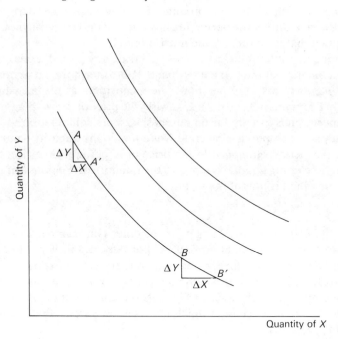

harder and harder, in terms of extra (or marginal) compensating increases of one good, to induce the consumer to forgo marginal units of another good the lower becomes the over-all level of consumption of the latter good. Clearly, if we are to draw an indifference curve, or boundary line, between a preferred and a dispreferred region which shows such a diminishing marginal rate of substitution, then it must be a curve which changes its slope in the way shown in Diagram 6.3. The slope, always measured by rise over run, represents the rate at which a small marginal change in the consumption of one good is compensated for by a small marginal change in the consumption of another good.

Having derived an indifference curve with reference to point *A*, we could repeat the process starting at any other point (combination of *X* and *Y*) and derive the indifference curve with respect to that point. We can thus derive a family of indifference curves, as shown in Diagram 6.3, to represent, diagrammatically, the 'tastes', or pattern of preferences, of the given individual consumer. It follows from their construction that indifference curves (for the same individual and the two goods *X* and *Y* during the same time period) cannot, logically, intersect and cross. If that happened, it would produce an area which would be simultaneously both preferred and dispreferred with regard to the point of intersection. This is a logical contradiction; therefore, indifference curves cannot intersect.

As one moves upwards to the right, away from the origin, in Diagram 6.3, each of the successive indifference curves represents a higher 'level' of satisfaction (is in the preferred region with respect to the preceding indifference curve). We may assume that each consumer tries to reach the highest level of satisfaction possible; in operational terms, each consumer tries to reach that indifference curve which is furthest away from the origin.

The budget constraint

So far we have been concerned simply with a consumer's preferences: that is, with what the consumer would *like* to do. But we are generally constrained from freely doing exactly what we would like to do, and so we need to introduce these constraints in order to analyse what the consumer is *able* to do. The most common constraint on consumer expenditure is the amount of money he or she has to spend. This is commonly known as the *budget constraint* because it refers to the total amount of money a consumer budgets to spend on the two goods X and Y during the period in question; but ultimately all budget constraints derive from the fact that a consumer's income is limited.

Suppose that the consumer budgets to spend, during any period, exactly £C (no more, no less) on a combination of the two goods X and Y. Furthermore, let us note that X has a price, denoted p_X, in terms of £ per unit (the same units as are measured along the horizontal axis in Diagrams 6.2 and 6.3). Likewise, the price of Y is p_Y per unit. We assume that the consumer spends exactly £C on purchasing some combination of X and Y. The amount of money spent on purchasing good X is equal to the quantity – number of units – of X purchased per period *multiplied by* the price of X per unit; likewise, the amount of money spent on purchasing good Y is equal to the quantity of Y *multiplied* by the price of Y. The budget constraint is thus of the form:

$$p_X \times X + p_Y \times Y = C$$

More generally, of course, the budget, or income, constraint is that the combined expenditures on X and Y must not exceed £C per period; but it would complicate the analysis to work in terms of an inexact inequality rather than an exact equality, and so we shall assume that the equality expresses the budget constraint. This budget constraint can also be expressed in another way, which says that the amount of money spent on good Y must be equal to the amount of money that is not spent on good X: that is, to the difference between £C and $p_X X$. Thus:

$$p_Y \times Y = C - p_X \times X$$

From this form of the budget constraint we may derive an expression relating the quantity of Y purchased during the period (rather than the amount of money spent on Y, as above) to the quantity of X purchased during the period. We may do this by dividing the preceding equation through by the price of Y, p_Y, as follows:

$$Y = \frac{C}{p_Y} - \frac{p_X}{p_Y} \times X$$

(This form of the budget constraint will be used in conjunction with indifference curves: it expresses an inverse relationship between quantities of X and quantities of Y in the form of a straight line with a downward slope of $-p_X/p_Y$ and an intercept (on the Y-axis) of C/p_Y.)

Let us see how this equation works out. If no X is purchased ($X = 0$), then, conversely, all of £C is spent on Y, and the number of units of Y purchased is equal to C divided by the price of Y per unit. Second, purchases of X and Y 'compete', in that the more of X is purchased the less of Y must be purchased. In money terms, for every one extra unit of X that is purchased, p_X less *money* must be spent on Y; if we divide this money amount by the price of Y, p_Y, we get, in quantity terms (number of units), the amount by which purchases of Y must be reduced. For example, if the price of X is £2 per unit and the price of Y is £1 per unit, then purchasing one extra unit of X means that £2 (the price of X per unit) less money must be spent on Y; if we divide this by the price of Y, £1 per unit, we see that purchases of Y (by quantity) must be reduced by 2 units.

So the inverse, or 'competing', relationship between Y and X, in quantity terms, is measured by the ratio of the price of X to the price of Y. The higher the price of X per unit relative to the price of Y per unit, the 'stronger' is this competing relationship. The ratio of the prices, p_X/p_Y, indicates the rate at which quantities of X and Y may be substituted for each other along the budget constraint without changing total expenditure on both.

The budget constraint, expressed thus in terms of quantities, can be represented graphically as a straight line, with a (downward) slope of $-(p_X/p_Y)$, and an intercept on the Y-axis of C/p_Y. In this form the budget constraint indicates what the consumer is able to do (given the constraint of the budget, £C). If we now put the consumer's preferences, as represented by the indifference curves, together with the possibilities as represented by this form of the budget constraint, we have a match between what the consumer would like to do and what the consumer is able to do, and so we can predict what the consumer will in fact do, and how he or she will react to price changes (this latter being the fundamental purpose of the whole analysis).

Diagram 6.4 shows the combination of a budget constraint of a consumer with that consumer's indifference curves. We assume that the budget constraint has a slope of -2 (that is, $p_X/p_Y = 2/1$). If the consumer tries to reach the highest possible indifference curve, then he or she will be at point E (for 'equilibrium') consuming Y_E of Y and X_E of X. Point E is the point of tangency between the (highest) indifference curve and the budget constraint. It is a unique point, in that there is, under these conditions, only one such point of tangency in the X–Y space. Why is E a point of 'equilibrium' at which the consumer will remain, period in period out, so long as these same conditions apply? We need to answer this question slightly less directly than simply saying it is on the highest indifference curve (and therefore in the preferred region of every other point which can be reached with the budget constraint).

Suppose the consumer were, by some accident, initially at a point such as A. Is this a combination at which the consumer would rest content? Point A lies at the intersection of the budget constraint and an indifference curve; at this point the modulus of the slope of the budget constraint, 2, is greater than the modulus of the slope of the indifference curve, which is at A 1/1 or 1. This means that by moving upwards along the budget constraint to A', the consumer is able to substitute 1 (marginal) unit of X by 2 (marginal) units of Y; but we know that along the indifference curve at point A all that the consumer requires in exact compensation for reducing consumption of X by 1 unit is a 1-unit increase in the consumption of Y. Therefore, in moving upwards along the budget constraint by reducing consumption of X by 1 (marginal) unit, the consumer gains more (along the budget constraint) in terms of a marginal increase in Y than he requires as an exactly compensating marginal increase in Y (along the indifference curve). So the consumer makes a net gain and can increase his or her 'satisfaction' by doing this; A' is in A's preferred region. Therefore, perceiving this, the consumer will make the transition from A to A'. The analysis can now be repeated, so long as the difference in slopes persists. It is only when a point is reached such that the ratio of prices (the slope of the budget constraint) equals the marginal rate of substitution along an indifference curve that no further net gain is possible by any movement.

DIAGRAM 6.4   *Indifference curves and the budget constraint*

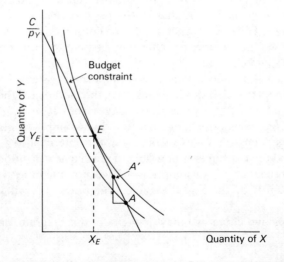

Formally stated, the condition that the consumer should be in a position of equilibrium (a position towards which he or she will move, and away from which he or she will not move so long as conditions remain) is that:

$$\frac{p_X}{p_Y} = \frac{|\Delta Y|}{|\Delta X|}$$

This condition must apply to *any* pair of goods, so if we introduce good Z then equilibrium comprises that combination of the three goods where:

$$\frac{p_X}{p_Y} = \frac{|\Delta Y|}{|\Delta X|}$$

$$\frac{p_Z}{p_Y} = \frac{|\Delta Y|}{|\Delta Z|}$$

$$\frac{p_X}{p_Z} = \frac{|\Delta Z|}{|\Delta X|}$$

Such theorising about consumer preferences in the presence of constraints is important because it can be used to analyse the choices a consumer makes and to predict reactions to changes such as an alteration in the price of one good or an increase in income. As the student progresses to more advanced economics, this sort of theoretical analysis will be found in analysing such topics as the choice between work and leisure (theoretical labour economics) or between consumption today and consumption tomorrow (theories about interest rates). Here and now, we simply use the analysis to predict the consumer's reaction to a change in the price of X, all other things being held constant. This is a key step in the theoretical derivation of a demand curve.

Deriving a demand curve – the substitution effect and the income effect

Diagram 6.5 shows the theoretical derivation of a demand curve (for an individual consumer) from a set of indifference curves and the budget constraints. The budget constraint is initially:

$$Y = \frac{C}{p_Y} - \frac{p_X}{p_Y} \times X$$

with equilibrium at E and consumption pattern Y_E and X_E, just as in Diagram 6.4.

Now suppose that the price of X falls from £2 per unit to £1.50 per unit *while all other things remain exactly as they were*: that is, the price of Y does not alter; the amount budgeted to be spent, £C, does not alter; and the consumer's tastes, represented by the pattern of indifference curves, does not alter. This assumption, that nothing other than the price of X alters, is sometimes called by a Latin tag *ceteris paribus*, meaning all other things ('*ceteris*') being equal ('*paribus*'). It is a most important assumption in the theoretical derivation of a demand curve. If this happens, then the modulus of the slope of the budget constraint falls from 2 to 1.5 (the price ratio changes from 2/1 to 1.5/1). The intercept on the vertical axis, C/p_Y, does not change because, by assumption, neither C nor p_Y have changed. The budget constraint now pivots about this intercept to a new position with a less steep slope, and the consumer is now able to reach a new position of equilibrium, E', on a higher indifference curve. Consumption of X will now increase to $X_{E'}$, and (as we shall show) it will necessarily be the case that the consumption of X will increase: $X_{E'}$ will be larger than X_E.

To derive the demand curve, we may draw under this diagram, and vertically aligned

DIAGRAM 6.5   *The theoretical derivation of a demand curve*

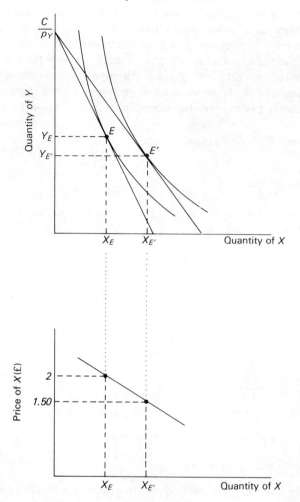

with it, another diagram with the same horizontal axis measuring quantity of X consumed per period but where the vertical axis measures the price of X (as in Diagram 6.1). On this diagram we may plot the co-ordinates which relate the equilibrium levels of consumption of X, X_E and $X_{E'}$, to their respective prices of £2 and £1.50. If we were then to repeat the process for other prices of X (but still keeping to the *ceteris paribus* assumption), and to join up all the co-ordinates so derived, we would then have the individual's demand curve for good X. The demand curve so drawn need not necessarily be a straight line; it could be curved in a number of different ways, but it must have a downward slope indicating that the lower the price the more will be sold (to that consumer with that budget and that pattern of preferences). In this derivation of the demand curve, other things must be held constant. If C and/or the price of Y is allowed to vary at the same time, then whatever one gets in the lower part of the diagram (plotting the price of X against the consumption of X) is not properly called a demand curve. A demand curve is concerned to analyse the changes in quantity consumed occurring in response solely to changes in that good's own price.

We cannot say in advance what is likely to happen to the consumption of Y when the price of X falls. In Diagram 6.5 the consumption of Y (at the equilibrium position) falls; but it could have risen. How then can we be certain, on the other hand, that the (equilibrium) consumption of X will rise in response to a fall in the price of X? The answer to this lies in appreciating that a fall in the price of a good affects the demand for that good in two different ways. The effect of the fall in the price of *X* was to enable the consumer to reach position *E'* on the higher indifference curve in Diagram 6.5. Because the consumer is at a higher level of satisfaction we can say that the 'real' value of the money income *C* has risen as a result of the fall in price (or, going the other way from *E'* to *E*, 'real' income has fallen as a result of the rise in price; which theoretically supports the use in Chapter 3 of a price index to deflate money income). Suppose, then, that prices had not altered but that, as illustrated in Diagram 6.6, the consumer had been given an increase income (that is, in *C*) which enabled him or her to reach the same higher indifference curve on which *E'* lay.

DIAGRAM 6.6   *Income effect and substitution effect*

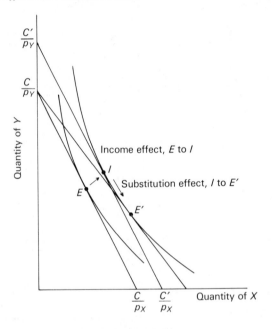

The maintenance of the slope of the budget constraint with an alteration in its intercept means that the budget constraint moves upwards to the right parallel to the original budget constraint. The value of the rise in money income to *C'* necessary to achieve the 'same' result (at unchanged prices) as the fall in the price of *X* (with unchanged *C*) is a measure of the extent to which the fall in the price of *X* increases the consumer's 'real' income. (In the preceding sentence, the word 'same' means to reach the same indifference curve.) Because of this increase in the amount budgeted to be spent on *X* and *Y* (more generally, increase in income), the consumption of both *X* and *Y* will rise to the equilibrium point *I*. This movement is known as the *income effect*, and it is nearly always the case that the income effect on the consumption of both goods is positive. (There are a few exceptions to this rule which define a peculiar class of goods, known as *inferior goods*, whose consumption may fall with increases in income; paraffin or margarine might be examples of this class.)

So in any price reduction there is a 'real' income effect which is likely to increase consumption of both goods. However, the consumer, enjoying a price reduction in p_X (but with an unaltered *C*) ends up not at *I* but at *E'*. And we may get the consumer from *I* to *E'* by reducing the budgeted amount spent and also reducing p_X but all the time keeping the consumer on the same indifference curve. This sliding down the indifference curve from *I* to *E'*, substituting *X* and *Y* as the price of *X* is reduced, is known as the *substitution effect*, and the substitution effect ensures that the equilibrium consumption of *X* will rise in a response to a fall in the price of *X*. We may also now describe more adequately the problem of the change in the consumption of *Y* in response to a fall in the price of *X*. The income effect will very likely raise the consumption of Y; but the substitution effect will certainly diminish it. If the substitution effect on Y outweighs the income effect, then, as in Diagram 6.5, the consumption of Y will fall; but there is no necessary reason why this should be so, and if the income effect on Y is larger, then the consumption of Y may nevertheless rise. However, it is certain that the equilibrium consumption of X will rise in response to a fall in the price of X because both income and substitution effects work in the same, positive, direction.

This means that the *ceteris paribus* demand curve for an individual consumer must slope downwards to the right, as shown in Diagram 6.5. We have spent quite some time on demonstrating something that appears intuitively obvious; and we have done so because thereby we have learnt about several useful concepts, especially indifference curves, which are frequently used in economic analysis. We have also seen more clearly the theoretical nature of a change in 'real' income consequent upon changing prices, so our use of price indices in Chapter 3 now has a sounder theoretical footing.

We need finally to go from the demand curve for an individual to the sort of market demand curve such as that which appeared to confront Fourways Manufacturing Ltd for their Product F. This is an easy step. The 'market' for a good comprises the totality of all individuals purchasing that good. Therefore, in order to get the market demand for a good at any particular price, all we need to do is aggregate the quantities each individual would buy at that price; we can then do this again for another price; and so on. The path traced out by this process will be a market demand curve. Because all the individuals who comprise the market have downward-sloping *ceteris paribus* demand curves, so too must the *ceteris paribus* market demand curve slope downwards. As we have seen, this inverse price–quantity interdependence has important economic consequences for enterprises.

If the enterprise is small in relation to the market, i.e. if its output is only a small fraction of total sales in the market, then the enterprise may be able to sell any quantity of output it can produce without affecting the market price. In this case the market demand curve is not a factor for consideration by the enterprise, which simply takes price as given and concerns itself with the decision as to what quantity to produce. Farm enterprises are usually in this position, but among enterprises in manufacturing industry it is generally the case that the enterprise will have some choice as to price–quantity combinations: that is, the enterprise will be facing a downward-sloping market demand curve, and this forces the enterprise to choose a price–quantity combination constrained by this demand curve.

Sales receipts and the demand curve

The enterprise must perforce be greatly concerned with the demand curve because the demand curve effectively determines the enterprise's total sales receipts, that is:

$$\text{Sales receipts} = \text{Price} \times \text{Quantity}$$

In choosing a price–quantity combination on the (externally given) demand curve, the enterprise is also choosing a certain level of sales receipts. Because the enterprise can choose different price–quantity combinations *along the demand curve*, so too it chooses the corresponding flow of sales receipts.

The enterprise cannot, of course, determine *both* price and quantity. It can establish one or the other but then it has, more or less, to accept the market determination of the other variable. To illustrate, in Diagram 6.7 the enterprise faces a demand curve of the form $p = a - bQ$. If it sets price at £8, then it will be able to sell only 4 units per period. If it wishes to produce and sell 5.6 units per period, then it will be forced to charge price £7.20. The enterprise cannot determine both price and quantity such as the £8–5.6 units combination; given the demand curve, this latter combination is not feasible. If the enterprise started by establishing a price of £8 and planning to produce 5.6 units, then it would find that its sales were running at a rate of only 4 per period and the remainder of its production would remain unsold. Obviously, no enterprise can afford to produce for stockpiling indefinitely, because this causes cash-flow problems (the enterprise is incurring production costs – cash outflow – without generating sales receipts – cash inflows). Thus the enterprise will eventually be forced either to cut its production to 4 units per period, if it wishes to retain the price of £8, or to lower its price to £7.20 if it wishes to maintain its production at 5.6 units. The price–quantity combination the enterprise chooses must lie on the demand curve.

DIAGRAM 6.7   *Price elasticity of demand and total sales receipts*

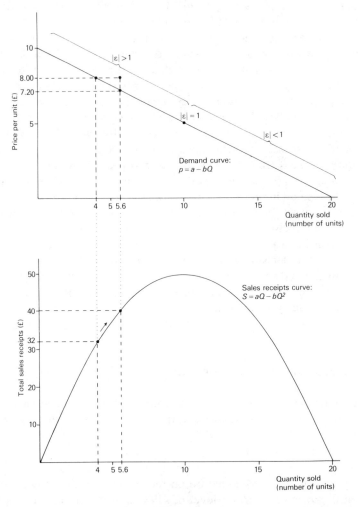

The question remains as to the implications for sales receipts of the different price–quantity combinations along the demand curve. In the demand curve diagram, sales receipts are represented by the area of the rectangle under any point on the demand curve (the formula for the area of a rectangle is height *multiplied by* base; in this case price is the height and quantity is the base). It is obvious that under the demand curve some rectangles will be larger than others. To illustrate, if we start at the top left-hand portion of the demand curve and charge a price so high that quantity sold is zero, then we have zero sales receipts; if we charge a slightly lower price, we have a positive value of Q and sales receipts will be represented by the area of the tall narrow rectangle; as we reduce price and increase quantity, so too does the area of the rectangle increase. However, this does not happen continuously, because as we approach the bottom right-hand portion of the demand curve the rectangle diminishes in size and eventually becomes zero when a zero price is charged.

We can represent this pattern of change by drawing a second diagram below the demand curve, vertically aligned with it and again putting Q on the horizontal axis. On the vertical axis we measure total sales receipts, so this lower diagram maps out a quantity–sales receipts space in which we can plot sales receipts as a function of Q. In terms of algebra this latter function is quite simply derived. Let p stand for price in £ per unit, Q for quantity (number of units) sold per period, and S for total sales receipts in £ per period. Then we have the demand curve:

$$p = a - bQ$$

and sales receipts as:

$$S = pQ$$

and substituting for p we get:

$$S = (a - bQ)Q$$

or:

$$S = aQ - bQ^2$$

Now the latter function traces out what is known as a *parabola*, and given the values of the parameters a and b encountered in a straight-line demand curve this parabola will rise at first as Q increases (because the positive effect of aQ is at first dominant) and then falls (as the negative effect of $-bQ^2$ becomes dominant). So we may construct this sales receipts function, derived from the demand curve, in the lower part of the diagram. This set of relationships, from price to quantity to sales receipts, is obviously a matter of considerable importance to the enterprise, and we need to spend a little time analysing Diagram 6.7 further.

Own-price elasticity of demand

What in effect happens in a left-to-right downward movement along the demand curve is that, at first, any given proportionate reduction in price (say, by 10 per cent) leads to a greater than equiproportionate increase in quantity sold (say, by 40 per cent), so that the loss to total sales receipts resulting from the reduction in price is more than offset by the gain to total sales receipts resulting from the increase in quantity sold. Consequently, total sales receipts rise if price is reduced.

To illustrate arithmetically on Diagram 6.7: if price is £8 per unit and quantity sold is 4 units per period, then total sales receipts are £32 per period; if a 10 per cent reduction in price to £7.20 per unit 'causes' (along the demand curve) a 40 per cent increase in quantity sold to 5.6 units per period, then total sales receipts *rise* to £7.20 × 5.6 = £40.32 per period. Eventually a point is reached where any given proportionate reduction in price leads to only an equiproportionate increase in quantity sold, so that the loss to sales receipts from the price reduction is only just counterbalanced by the gain from the increased quantity sold. Consequently, total sales receipts remain unchanged. After this point on the demand curve, we reach points where any given reduction in price leads to a less than equiproportionate increase in quantity sold, so the loss to sales receipts is less than counterbalanced by the rise in quantity sold. Consequently, total sales receipts fall if price is reduced.

This relationship between the proportionate change in price and the proportionate change in quantity sold (the two proportionate changes, because of the downward-sloping demand curve, always being of opposite signs) is known as the 'own-price elasticity of demand': 'own-price' because we are concerned with the effect of changes in the good's own price: the word 'elasticity' is used to refer generally to any relationship between a *proportionate* change in one variable and a corresponding *proportionate* change in any other functionally related variable. (To contrast: 'income elasticity of demand' refers to the relationship between the proportionate change in quantity sold and a proportionate change in income.) The own-price elasticity of demand is thus measured by the proportionate change in the quantity sold divided by the corresponding proportionate change in the good's own price. The formal definition of own price elasticity of demand is as follows:

$$\text{Own-price elasticity of demand} = \frac{\text{Proportionate change in quantity sold}}{\text{Proportionate change in own-price}} = \frac{\dfrac{\Delta Q}{Q}}{\dfrac{\Delta p}{p}} = \varepsilon$$

Where the Greek symbol 'Δ', delta, means change in, and the Greek symbol 'ε', epsilon, is used to denote the own-price elasticity of demand. Thus defined, ε will always be negative because the numerator and denominator will always have opposite signs. In economics it has become conventional to ignore the negative sign of ε: that is, to take the modulus of ε, $|\varepsilon|$, as the elasticity. For example, if a price reduction of 10 per cent led to a quantity increase in sales of 40 per cent, then we say that the own-price elasticity of demand is 4, not -4:

$$|\varepsilon| = \left|\frac{+0.40}{-0.10}\right| = |-4| = 4$$

Thus when economists loosely use the abbreviated term 'elasticity of demand', we mean precisely 'the modulus of the own-price elasticity of demand'.

Elasticity of demand is an important concept because it tells you what will happen to total sales receipts if price is altered. We may use the following mnemonic table:

	Elasticity of demand greater than 1	*Elasticity of demand less than 1*
If price is reduced	Sales receipts rise	Sales receipts fall
If price is increased	Sales receipts fall	Sales receipts rise

We can see this on Diagram 6.7. On the upper left-hand portion of the demand curve, $|\varepsilon|$ is greater than 1, so reduced prices lead to rises in sales receipts in a rightward movement *up* the total sales receipts curve; but if price is increased, then moving backwards and upwards along the demand curve leads to a leftward movement *down* the total sales receipts curve. Conversely, on the lower right-hand portion of the demand curve, $|\varepsilon|$ is less than 1, so reduced prices lead to falls in sales receipts in a rightward movement *down* the total sales receipts curve; but if price is here increased, then moving backwards and upwards along the demand curve leads to a leftward movement *up* the total sales receipts curve. Finally, at that point on the demand curve where $|\varepsilon|$ is neither greater nor less than 1, i.e., is exactly equal to 1, total sales receipts will be stationary with respect to a change in price, and at this point total sales receipts will be at a maximum. It is possible to work out the table above with reference to Diagram 6.7 (simply memorising the table is not the way to understand these important relationships). It is also possible to demonstrate these propositions algebraically, and that proof is in Appendix 6.1.

Note that price elasticity of demand is a property of a *point on the curve*; it is not a property of the entire curve. In other words, price elasticity of demand will vary depending on the point on the demand curve (the price–quantity combination) from which one starts. If the exact form of the demand curve is:

$$p = a - bQ$$

then:

$$Q = \frac{a}{b} - \frac{1}{b} \times p$$

and:

$$\frac{\Delta Q}{\Delta p} = -\frac{1}{b}$$

Thus:

$$\frac{\dfrac{\Delta Q}{Q}}{\dfrac{\Delta p}{p}} = \frac{\Delta Q}{\Delta p} \times \frac{p}{Q} = -\frac{1}{b} \times \frac{p}{Q} = \varepsilon$$

so the value of ε depends not only on the value of the constant $1/b$ but also on the initial ratio of p to Q, which, of course, varies along the demand curve; specifically, this ratio falls as one moves downwards to the right along the demand curve and so, therefore, the modulus of ε, $|\varepsilon|$, falls likewise.

Although the demand curve analysis is based on strict *ceteris paribus* assumptions which may not hold (for example, incomes may be rising), it is nevertheless important to understand and appreciate such basic propositions as, for example, if the price elasticity of demand is greater than 1, then raising prices is likely to cause a fall in total sales receipts. In the United Kingdom this phenomenon is frequently seen; we may take the example of British Rail, which tries to recoup increased costs by raising rail fares; generally the effect of this is to reduce the volume of rail travel sharply and so British Rail's total sales receipts fall, leaving BR in a worse position than before. If British Rail wishes to increase its sales receipts, it can do this only by *reducing* fares, because the price elasticity of demand for rail

TABLE 6.2 *Fourways' sales receipts for Product F, estimated from the linear demand curve, and elasticities of demand*

Price, £ per unit, p	Number of units sold according to demand curve, [a] units per annum, $\hat{Q}$	Estimated total sales receipts, £ per annum, $p\hat{Q} = a\hat{Q} - b\hat{Q}^2$	Elasticity of demand at that price–quantity combination, [c] $|\varepsilon|$
400	323.59	129,436	7.788
350	638.60	223,510	3.453
300	953.61	286,083	1.982
250	1,268.62	317,155	1.242
225.68 [b]	**1,421.84** [b]	**320,881**	**1.000**
200	1,583.63	316,726	0.796
150	1,898.64	284,796	0.498

[a] Demand curve $p = a - b\hat{Q}$ estimated by least squares from Table 6.1 as $p = 451.3615587 - 0.15872464\hat{Q}$; correlation coefficient $R = -0.9666$.
[b] Price–quantity combination which maximises sales receipts.
[c] Estimated from formula:

$$\varepsilon = -\frac{1}{b} \times \frac{p}{\hat{Q}} = -\frac{1}{0.15872464} \times \frac{p}{\hat{Q}}$$

travel is apparently quite high. A converse case is that of Sir Freddie Laker, whose Skytrain providing reduced airfares between the United Kingdom and the USA considerably expanded the volume of sales and thereby total sales receipts on the North Atlantic route.*

We can apply this analysis to the demand curve for Fourways Product F. Table 6.2 shows the possible prices, p, and the quantities, Q, which might be sold at those prices, not as directly estimated by the area sales managers, but according to the demand curve estimated from those data (we need to do this because we are working to an exact mathematical and straight-line model of the demand curve). The quantities of units sold which are exactly related to prices and the demand curve are designated $\hat{Q}$ and these points are shown on the demand curve in Diagram 6.8 (the demand curve having been estimated by least squares in Diagram 6.1).

DIAGRAM 6.8   *Fourways' Product F: demand curve, sales receipts curve, cost curve, and total gross margin*

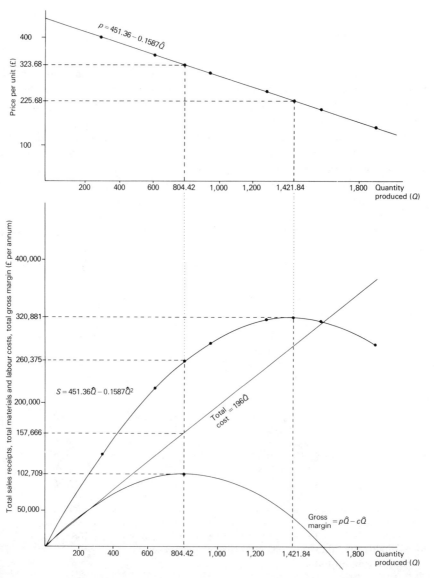

*Unfortunately, Sir Freddie Laker then borrowed most of the money to finance the expansion of Laker Airways – rather than relying on, and largely limiting himself to, company retentions! – and, becoming unable to service the debt, had to go into receivership on 5 February 1982.

From this set of prices and quantities, we may calculate estimated total sales receipts, according to the demand curve, in £ per annum, $p\hat{Q}$; because we are assuming that an exact model applies, we also have that $p\hat{Q} = a\hat{Q} - b\hat{Q}^2$, where a and b are the parameters of the demand curve $p = a - bQ$, the values of these parameters being given in note *(a)* to Table 6.2*. The prices are listed in descending order from highest to lowest; conversely, quantity of sales occurs in ascending order. It can be seen in the lower part of Diagram 6.8 that, as prices are reduced, estimated total sales receipts rise at first. Total estimated sales receipts reach a maximum of £320,881 per annum at the price–quantity combination of £225.68 and 1,421.84. (These latter values can be ascertained by differentiating the sales receipts function $aQ - bQ^2$, equating to zero and solving for that value of Q at which the rate of change (the slope) of the function is zero; the corresponding price can then be ascertained by inserting this value of Q in the demand curve.) After this point, estimated total sales receipts fall as prices go below £225.68.

We can calculate, in the last column of Table 6.2, the elasticity of demand at these various price–quantity combinations according to the formula just given for ε. We can see that at the higher prices the elasticity of demand is greater than 1, indicating that if price is reduced total sales receipts rise. At the lower prices, the elasticity of demand is less than 1, indicating that if price is reduced total sales receipts fall. At the price–quantity combination which maximises total estimated sales receipts, price elasticity of demand is equal to 1 (these are two different ways of getting at the same thing).

The important thing about Table 6.2 and Diagram 6.8 is that it presents a paradigm picture of the situation confronting nearly all enterprises which face a downward-sloping demand curve for their products: namely, that sales receipts will at first rise, reach a maximum, and then fall. It is mathematically possible for the demand curve to take a form which will not do this, but such a form is, as a matter of economics, not very likely to occur, and so the mathematical possibility may be ignored.

The demand curve and the cost curve

The question facing Fourways concerned the most advantageous price–quantity combination to choose for Product F. It might be thought that the combination which maximised sales receipts would be the best, but this is mistaken: seeking to maximise sales receipts is not necessarily the most advantageous thing to do because it takes no account of the behaviour of costs. The cost accountants at Fourways estimated that the material and labour costs were about £196 per unit of output. Specifically, they provided the management with the following figures (Hague, *Pricing in Business*, p. 292):

Quantity produced	1,286	763	475	294	161
Total material and labour cost (£000)	252.1	149.5	93.1	58.6	31.6
Materials and labour cost per unit of output (£)	196	196	196	199	196

If we plot, in the lower part of Diagram 6.8, these total material and labour costs against the quantity produced, we obtain that part of the cost curve relating to the variable 'material and labour costs'. Specifically, we have a cost curve of the form:

$$\text{Total material and labour costs} = 196 \times \text{Quantity produced}$$

which is a form of a linear cost curve:

$$\text{Total variable cost} = c \times \text{Quantity produced}$$

*As explained in Chapter 3 (p. 148), we use the 'hat' symbol of '^' to denote an *estimated* value.

where the parameter *c* is the constant average variable cost per unit of output.

Because the total gross margin is the difference between total sales receipts and total material and labour costs, we can calculate in Table 6.3 the gross margin at the various price–quantity combinations, and we can plot, on Diagram 6.8, the total gross margin as a function of the quantity sold. It is immediately apparent that the total gross margin is not at a maximum where sales receipts are at a maximum. This is what we meant by saying that maximum sales receipts is not the most advantageous position. The most advantageous position for the enterprise is where the total gross margin is maximised, because that leaves the enterprise with the maximum amount of money, after materials and labour costs have been paid, to meet its 'overheads', or fixed costs, to pay interest, taxes and dividends, and so leave it with maximum retentions. In Table 6.3 the price–quantity combination, along the straight-line demand curve, which maximises the total gross margin (the difference between sales receipts and materials and labour costs) is £323.68 and 804.42. At this combination, and with the given linear cost curve, the total gross margin would be £102,709 per annum. At a higher price, such as £350, the total gross margin is lower, £98,344; and at a lower price, such as £300, the gross margin is also lower, £99,175.

Maximising profits

In what way may the price–quantity combination which maximises the total gross margin be determined? We could proceed arithmetically by trial and error, but that is not a systematic method and it fails to impart an understanding of what is going on. To proceed systematically we need first to note that:

Total   Total   Total
gross   = sales   – production
margin   receipts   costs

Second, on Diagram 6.8 to the left of the quantity of sales at which the maximum gross margin occurs, the gross margin rises as quantity increases because total sales receipts are rising faster than total production costs. That is to say, the increase in total sales receipts, ΔS, with respect to a given increase in quantity sold, ΔQ, is greater than the increase in total production costs with respect to the same given increase in quantity sold. Writing *C*

TABLE 6.3   *Fourways' gross margin for Product F, and marginal sales receipts*

Price per unit, £, p	Estimated units sold per annum number, $\hat{Q}$	Estimated totals, £ per annum			Marginal sales receipts, £ $(\Delta p\hat{Q})/\Delta\hat{Q}$ $= a - 2b\hat{Q}$
		Sales receipts $p\hat{Q} = a\hat{Q} - b\hat{Q}^2$	Materials and labour costs [a], $c\hat{Q}$	Gross margin, $p\hat{Q} - c\hat{Q}$	
400	323.59	129,436	63,424	66,012	348.6
350	638.60	223,510	125,166	98,344	248.6
323.68 [b]	**804.42** [b]	**260,375**	**157,666**	**102,709**	**196.0**
300	953.61	286,083	186,908	99,175	148.6
250	1,268.62	317,155	248,650	68,505	48.6
225.68	1,421.84	320,881	278,681	42,200	0
200	1,583.63	316,726	310,391	6,335	−51.4
150	1,898.64	284,796	372,133	−87,337	−151.4

[a] Calculated from the cost formula:
    Total material and labour cost = 196 × *Quantity sold.*
[b] Price–quantity combination which maximises the gross margin.

Source: Table 6.2.

for total production costs and ΔC for the increase in production costs, we have in this region:

$$\frac{\Delta S}{\Delta Q} > \frac{\Delta C}{\Delta Q}$$

Because sales receipts are rising faster (as Q increases) than are costs, it follows that the gross margin must rise as Q increases. Conversely, to the right of the position which maximises the gross margin, the increase in total sales receipts with respect to a given increase in quantity sold is less than the increase in total production costs with respect to the same given increase in quantity sold. That is:

$$\frac{\Delta S}{\Delta Q} < \frac{\Delta C}{\Delta Q}$$

From this it follows that the total gross margin reaches a maximum when it is momentarily stationary with respect to changes in Q; this happens when the increase in total sales receipts with respect to a given increase in quantity sold is equal to the increase in production costs with respect to the same given increase in quantity sold – that is, when:

$$\frac{\Delta S}{\Delta Q} = \frac{\Delta C}{\Delta Q}$$

Now the formula for total production costs is quite simply:

$$C = 196 \times Q$$

because each unit of Q has the same, constant, production cost of £196. This means that if we increase production by 1 unit, $\Delta Q = 1$, then the increase in total production cost, ΔC, is £196. That is:

$$\frac{\Delta C}{\Delta Q} = \frac{196}{1} = 196$$

and this is the case for any volume of production. The increase in production costs with respect to the increase in quantity is, of course, the slope (rise over run) of the total production cost curve in Diagram 6.8; because this cost curve is a straight line, its slope does not vary as Q varies: the slope is always 196/1. There is a technical name for the increase in costs with respect to a given (small or marginal) increase in quantity produced, and that term is 'marginal cost'. In the case of Fourways Product F, the marginal cost is £196 taking the smallest practicable increase in $\hat{Q}$ as being 1 unit.

However, the slope of the sales receipts curve does vary as quantity sold varies. It has a positive slope in the left-hand region; but the steepness of the slope declines as Q increases. Eventually, at maximum sales receipts, the slope is zero; and thereafter the slope is negative (the slope is then measured by *fall* over run). Differential calculus tells us what this slope will be at any point. We have:

Sales receipts = Price × Quantity

or:

$$S = p \times \hat{Q}$$

because the demand curve is:

$$p = a - b\hat{Q}$$

we have by substitution:

$$S = (a - b\hat{Q})\hat{Q}$$

whence:

$$S = a\hat{Q} - b\hat{Q}^2$$

Two ways of measuring slopes

Strictly speaking, in mathematical terms we measure the slope at a given point (given value of Q) by the slope of the straight-line tangent to the curve at that point. Thus:

Tangential slope   *Marginal sales receipts*

But in economic terms, we are concerned with what happens to sales receipts if we increase Q by a *small* (marginal) amount, say $\Delta Q = 1$. At any point on the sales receipts curve above a value of $\hat{Q}$ in Diagram 6.7, the tangential slope of the sales receipts curve is equal to $a - 2b\hat{Q}$, where a and b are the parameters of the demand curve and $\hat{Q}$ is the value of Q at which the

tangential slope is being ascertained (this result is derived from the rules of differential calculus, not further explained here: the student may consult P. Abbott, *Teach Yourself Calculus*, English Universities Press, 1959, ch. 4; or J. Parry Lewis, *An Introduction to Mathematics for Students of Economics*, Macmillan, 1965, chs 9 and 10). We can work out the tangential slope according to this formula simply by inserting the value of $\hat{Q}$ (in the second column of Table 6.3) and using the values of a and b from Table 6.2. The resulting values for marginal sales receipts are given in the last column of Table 6.3. To verify the first of these results, if we increased $\hat{Q}$ by 1 unit from 323.59 to 324.59, the price would have to fall from £400 to £399.841 (because to get $\Delta \hat{Q} = 1$ we have to move downwards along the demand curve), and sales receipts would increase from £129,436 ($= 400 \times 323.59$) to £129,784.4 ($= 399.841 \times 324.59$), an increase of £348.4; so the tangential slope is a very close approximation to what would happen to total sales receipts were we to increase $\hat{Q}$ by 1 unit.

From this sales receipts curve (expressing S as a function of $\hat{Q}$) we have by calculus:

$$\frac{\Delta S}{\Delta \hat{Q}} = a - 2b\hat{Q}$$

So the slope depends both upon the values of the constants a and b, and also upon the value of the variable $\hat{Q}$; furthermore, because of the negative sign, the larger the value of $\hat{Q}$, the smaller the slope, and clearly at some point as $\hat{Q}$ increases the slope will become negative. We have a technical name for the change in total sales receipts with respect to an increase in quantity sold when the increase in quantity sold is relatively small (for example, $\Delta \hat{Q} = 1$): the technical term is 'marginal sales receipts' (sometimes, in other textbooks, it is called 'marginal revenue', but the word 'revenue' is rather a vague term in most contexts and so will not be used here). Marginal sales receipts is thus measured by the slope of the total sales receipts curve.

The maximum gross margin occurs at that value of $\hat{Q}$ where marginal sales receipts equals marginal cost:

$$\frac{\Delta S}{\Delta \hat{Q}} = \frac{\Delta C}{\Delta Q}$$

which condition we can now write as:

$$a - 2b\hat{Q} = 196$$

or solving for $\hat{Q}$:

$$\hat{Q}^* = \frac{a - 196}{2b}$$

where the asterisk denotes the particular value of $\hat{Q}$ which maximises the total gross margin. Specifically, for Fourways Product F and the estimated demand curve:

$$\hat{Q}^* = \frac{451.3615587 - 196}{2 \times 0.15872464}$$

$$= 804.42$$

with a corresponding price, p^*, of:

$$p^* = 451.3615587 - 0.15872464 \times 804.42$$

$$= 323.68$$

At this price–quantity combination, total sales receipts are £260,375 per annum and total materials and labour costs are £157,666 per annum, giving a total gross margin of £102,709 per annum. Assuming that quantity sold is determined exactly according to the least-squares straight-line demand curve, and that the cost curve is of the form given, then this is the maximum gross margin per annum that Fourways could obtain by producing and selling Product F. We can see in the final column of Table 6.3 that at this value of $\hat{Q}$, $\hat{Q}^* = 804.42$, marginal sales receipts (according to the tangential slope) are exactly equal to marginal costs.

We know from the case study that Fourways first put Product F in their price list at £390 per unit, and left it unchanged (Hague, *Pricing in Business*, p. 291). We can calculate that under the assumption of a linear demand curve the volume of sales at this price would have been 386.59 units per annum (in fact, actual sales in the first two years were far lower than this, indicating either that a non-linear demand curve would be a more appropriate model, or that the sales manager's estimates related more to what would happen when the product became 'established'). This would have produced sales receipts of £150,770 per annum ($= 390 \times 386.59$) with materials and labour costs of £75,771.64 ($= 196 \times 386.59$), so giving a total gross margin of £74,998.36 per annum ($= 150,770 - 75,771.64$), about 27 per cent less than the maximum theoretically achievable according to the linear demand curve. This fact was clearly appreciated by Fourways' sales manager, who recommended a selling price of £330 to £340 which 'would provide the largest margin to cover fixed costs and overheads' (Hague, *Pricing in Business*, p. 293, quoting from the report written by the sales manager).

We began this consideration of pricing by seeing how enterprises may try to set their prices with reference to some mark-up on unit production costs. We can now see that the market forces of consumers' behaviour will constrain the mark-up that can be established: if the mark-up is set too high, then the adverse effect of a high price on volume of sales will reduce the total gross margin; while if the mark-up is set too low, then the margin between price and unit cost will be too small, despite the volume of sales, to generate a large total gross margin flow. So the enterprise must have a regard for this constraint. But the constraint imposed by the *ceteris paribus* demand curve, by consumers' behaviour, is not the only one which enterprises encounter.

So far we have considered the pricing problem – the question of the most advantageous price–quantity combination for the enterprise – in isolation from external factors other than the *ceteris paribus* demand curve. We have concentrated simply on spelling out the constraints on the enterprise implied by the downward-sloping demand curve which embodies the reactions of consumers to changes in the price of a good. But it is obvious that *ceteris paribus* is a very restrictive assumption: recall that the downward-sloping demand curve was derived from indifference curves and a budget constraint which moved as a consequence of a change in the good's own price only. Specifically, under the *ceteris paribus* assumption the price of the other competing good was not permitted to change. But enterprises operate in a world where their competitors are very likely to respond to a price change. What happens in this case?

Competitors' reactions

In Diagram 6.5 we derived a *ceteris paribus* demand curve from a set of indifference curves by allowing the price of X only to fall from p_X to p_X' and so pivot the budget constraint to a new position where a greater quantity of X could be bought with the same amount of money. In Diagram 6.9 (which reproduces Diagram 6.5 in its derivation of the *ceteris paribus* demand curve) the consumer's equilibrium purchases of X, given that the consumer continues to spend £C on the X–Y combination, would rise from X_1 (at p_X) to X_2 (at p_X' with unchanged price of Y, p_Y). This change causes the equilibrium quantity of Y, whose price had been held unaltered, to fall. Suppose that the manufacturers of Y, an enterprise competing with the manufacturers of X, in response to such a reduction in the price of X, reduced their price also from p_Y to p_Y'. Let us suppose that they reduce the price of Y by the same proportion, thus restoring the original price ratio.

The sequence of events is thus: price of X reduced; adjustment in consumer behaviour takes place; manufacturers of Y react and reduce price of Y so as to restore original relationship between the price of X and the price of Y; adjustment in consumer behaviour to equilibrium position takes place.

Diagram 6.9 shows what is then likely to happen. There is now a third budget constraint representing the combined impact of the reduction in the price of X and in the price of Y; because the reduction in the price of Y restores the original price ratio, this budget constraint is parallel to the first (but this is not essential to the argument). Restoring the price ratio leads to substitution and income effects, the combined impact of which is to

DIAGRAM 6.9   *A ceteris paribus demand curve and a competitive demand curve*

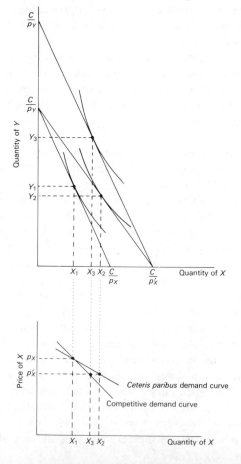

raise the consumption of Y to Y_3 and to reduce the consumption of X from what it had become after the price of X had been reduced (but before the price of Y had been correspondingly reduced also); accordingly, the equilibrium consumption of X alters again, from X_2 to X_3.

(Diagram 6.9 also further explains the impact of an increase in 'real' income, in this case due to a reduction in the prices of both goods. The consumer, without any increase in the amount budgeted to be spent on X and Y, moves to a higher indifference curve and to a higher level of consumption of quantities of both goods.)

In the lower part of Diagram 6.9 we may plot a line tracing out what is likely to happen to consumption of X, at equilibrium points, if the prices of both X and Y were altered equiproportionately but no other prices or the budgeted amount to be spent on X and Y changed. This would give a curve with a steeper slope than the *ceteris paribus* demand curve. There is no recognised name for this latter curve, so we shall call it 'a competitive demand curve' to indicate that the prices of competitive goods are changed also in line with the price of X.

One of the things which induce businessmen to adhere to the practice of using a 'conventional' or standard mark-up on unit production costs as a method of pricing is that they believe that charging less than this would cause competitors to follow the cuts, while there is a corresponding fear that competitors would *not* follow an increase in price, and so the price-raising enterprise would lose sales to competitors. (Empirical evidence for this assertion was first adduced by R. L. Hall and C. J. Hitch in a famous article 'Price theory and business behaviour', *Oxford Economic Papers*, 1939, reprinted as chapter 3 in T. Wilson and P. W. S. Andrews (eds), *Oxford Studies in the Price Mechanism*, Oxford University Press, 1951: see tables 3 and 4, p. 115, of this reprint.)

In terms which we have been using, businessmen seem to believe that at any established price–quantity combination they are exposed to two demand curves: if they increase price, their competitors will *not* react and the price–quantity combination of X will move along the *ceteris paribus* demand curve; however, if they reduce price, their competitors *will* react and the price–quantity combination of X will move along the steeper competitive demand curve. To practise our understanding of elasticity of demand, we may say exactly the same thing as follows. Businessmen believe that if they raise the price of a product they will be exposed to a 'high' price elasticity of demand; if they lower the price of a product they will be exposed to a 'low' price elasticity of demand. Let us translate 'high' and 'low' into specific terms of 'greater than 1' and 'less than 1'. To reproduce part of our mnemonic table:

	$|\varepsilon| > 1$	$|\varepsilon| < 1$
If price is reduced		Sales receipts fall
If price is increased	Sales receipts fall	

Businessmen seem to believe that they are 'trapped' by the adverse elasticities between the two quadrants of falling sales. Their belief may not be as specific as this because the column headings may indicate only the appropriate (adverse) difference in price elasticities, in which case the entry in the upper-right quadrant may be 'Sales receipts may fall and certainly won't rise much', while the lower-left quadrant may be 'Sales receipts are quite likely to fall'. Whatever the case, businessmen's pessimism about the adverse price elasticities confronting them in the event of a change in price seems theoretically quite reasonable (Diagram 6.9) and there is some empirical evidence that they are thus pessimistic.

If businessmen are right to think of their pricing situation in this way, what are the economic consequences? Diagram 6.10 shows a product with an established price–quantity combination: increasing the price takes the price–quantity combination up

DIAGRAM 6.10   *An enterprise 'trapped' by adverse price elasticities due to competitors' reactions*

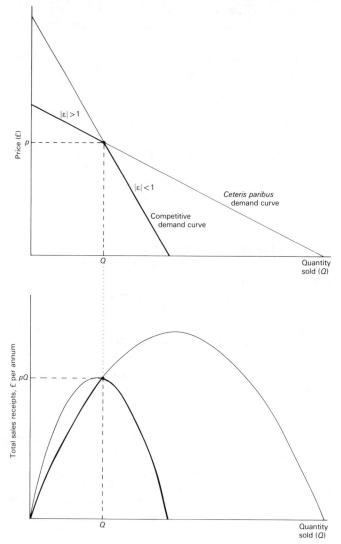

the *ceteris paribus* demand curve (no reaction from competitors) where the elasticity of demand is greater than 1; reducing the price, however, takes the price–quantity combination down the competitive demand curve (reaction from competitors) where the elasticity of demand is less than 1. These operative portions of the demand curves are drawn in heavy lines. The lower part of Diagram 6.10 draws the respective sales receipts curves for these two demand curves; again, the operative portions, corresponding to the two parts of the demand curves which come into play, are drawn in heavy lines.

It can be seen that with regard to total sales receipts the enterprise is more or less stuck at the pinnacle created by the intersection of the two operative portions of the two sales receipts curves. There is now a wide range over which marginal costs may vary and this position will still remain the one which achieves the maximum difference between total sales receipts and total production costs (i.e. the maximum total gross margin). In other words, the enterprise cannot increase its total gross margin by altering its price–quantity combination. Paradoxically this leads to the conclusion that, for an enterprise 'trapped' between two adverse elasticities, the demand curves are not all that important a consideration. The *fact* of the demand curves is important in constraining the enterprise to a particular pinnacle; but the precise *shapes* of the demand curves, and the slopes of the operative parts of the sales receipts curves each side of the pinnacle, are not matters of operational significance for the enterprise.

What, then, becomes of operational significance to the enterprise is the level of unit production costs. If the enterprise is 'stuck' at a given pinnacle of total sales receipts (at a given price–quantity combination), then the way to increase the total gross margin is to ensure that unit production costs are as low as possible. We must therefore turn to the theoretical analysis of production costs.

Exercises

6.1 *(To practise your understanding of a demand curve.)* In his autobiography *My Life and Work*, Henry Ford gives the following data for his touring car (p. 145):

Accounting year	Price in $	Production in cars
1909–10	950	18,664
1910–11	780	34,528
1911–12	690	78,440
1912–13	600	168,220
1913–14	550	248,307
1914–15	490	308,213
1915–16	440	533,921
1916–17	360	785,432

(i) Draw a scatter diagram of price (vertical axis) against production (horizontal axis) on ordinary graph paper.

(ii) Draw a scatter diagram of price (vertical axis) against production (horizontal axis) on double-logarithmic paper (you need a log 1 Cycle × 2 Cycles; Chartwell C5912 has the requisite scale).

(iii) Describe the difference between the two graphs.

(iv) Explain why the curves fitting these points cannot strictly be considered as demand curves.

(v) *(To practise a stand-by method.)* If you cannot get double-logarithmic paper (and even if you can), take the logarithms of price and production and plot the *logarithms* on *ordinary* (arithmetic) graph paper. How does this compare with (ii) above?

6.2 *(To practise your understanding of price elasticity of demand.)*

(i) Draw, as accurately as you can, a straight line to fit the points on the double-logarithmic scatter diagram of Exercise 6.1(ii) – or 6.1(v). Notwithstanding your answer to 6.1(iv), does the shape of this line suggest that the demand for cars was responsive to price reductions? (This question is, deliberately, vaguely worded: answer it precisely and technically.)

(ii) Tabulate what happened to Ford's sales receipts as the price was reduced, and plot, on ordinary graph paper, total sales receipts (vertical scale) against volume of production (horizontal scale).

(iii) Comment on the economics of Ford's business philosophy:

'Our policy is to reduce the price, extend the operations, and improve the article. You will notice that the reduction of price comes first. We have never considered any costs as fixed [i.e. unalterable]. Therefore we first reduce the price to a point where we believe more sales will result. Then we go ahead and try to make the price. We do not bother about the costs. The new price forces the costs down. The more usual way is to take the costs and then determine the price, and although that method may be scientific in the narrow sense, it is not scientific in the broad sense, because what earthly use is it to know the cost if it tells you you cannot manufacture at a price at which the article can be sold? But more to the point is the fact that, although one may calculate what a cost is, and of course all of our costs are carefully calculated, no one knows what a cost ought to be. One of the ways of discovering what a cost ought to be is to name a price so low as to force everybody in the place to the highest point of efficiency. The low price makes everybody dig for profits. We make more discoveries concerning manufacturing and selling under this forced method than by any method of leisurely investigation.' (*My*

Life and Work, Heinemann, 1926, pp. 146–7.)

6.3 *(To practise your understanding of indifference curves and budget constraints.)*

(i)   Explain how indifference curves represent, or 'map', a consumer's tastes or pattern of preferences.

(ii) Explain to your mother why she buys fewer tomatoes when the price of tomatoes goes up.

(iii) Your spending money is £20 a month and you devote all of it to two leisure-time activities: going to discos and going to the ice-skating rink.* Establish prices for a disco session and for an ice-skating session and graph your 'budget constraint' (make sure you label your axes properly).

6.4 *(Further to practise your understanding of price elasticity of demand.)* With reference to Exercise 5.4, having successfully persuaded the bank manager to give you a loan you have started up in business but things are not going as well as you hoped and the volume of your sales is insufficient to cover your costs and monthly interest on the bank loan. Your bank manager wants to see you and is likely to suggest that you 'put up your prices in order to bring in more money'. But you suspect that the (modulus of the) price elasticity of demand for your product lines is greater than unity. Prepare your explanation to the bank manager as to why, in the circumstances, you are going to *reduce* prices.

6.5 *(To practise your understanding of Diagram 6.10.)* Consider the following questionnaire results (questionnaire asked of thirty-eight businessmen):

*If you wish, you can substitute any other two leisure-time activities, but each must involve a determinate cost per 'session'.

Reasons for adhering to full-cost principle [a]	*Number of responses*
Reasons for not charging more than full-cost:	
Fear of competitors or potential competitors (including belief that others would not follow an increase)	17
They do not go in for a high profit	2
They prefer a large turnover	2
Buyers technically informed regarding costs	3
Reasons for not charging less than full cost:	
Demand unresponsive to price	9
Competitors would follow cuts	11
Difficult to raise prices once lowered	2
Trade Association minimum prices	3
Convention with competitors	1
Quasi-moral objections to selling below cost	8
Price cuts not passed on by retailers	1

[a] The principle that a price should be 'based on full average cost [of production] including a conventional allowance for profit' (source,* p. 113); note that some of the reasons cited for not charging less than full cost would not now be legally permissible.

(i)   Explain fully whether you think the figures support or confute Diagram 6.10 and its argument.

(ii) Are the first two reasons for not charging less than full cost really different?

*Source: R. L. Hall and C. J. Hitch, 'Price Theory and Business Behaviour', reprinted in T. Wilson and P. W. S. Andrews (eds), *Oxford Studies in the Price Mechanism* (Oxford University Press, 1951) p. 115; the article originally appeared in *Oxford Economic Papers*, May 1939.

APPENDIX 6.1 *Own-price elasticity of demand and sales receipts*

	Elasticity of demand, $|\varepsilon|$, greater than 1	Elasticity of demand, $|\varepsilon|$, less than 1
If price is reduced	Sales receipts rise	Sales receipts fall
If price is increased	Sales receipts fall	Sales receipts rise

Proof

p = initial price p' = changed price
Q = initial quantity Q' = changed quantity
S = initial sales receipts S' = changed sales receipts
$S = pQ$ $S' = p'Q'$

$>$ means: left-hand expression is greater than right-hand expression

$<$ means: left-hand expression is less than right-hand expression

$$p' = p\left(1 + \frac{p' - p}{p}\right)$$

$$Q' = Q\left(1 + \frac{Q' - Q}{Q}\right)$$

Therefore:

$$S' = p'Q' = p\left(1 + \frac{p' - p}{p}\right)Q\left(1 + \frac{Q' - Q}{Q}\right)$$

$$= pQ\left\{1 + \frac{p' - p}{p} + \frac{Q' - Q}{Q} + \left[\frac{p' - p}{p} \times \frac{Q' - Q}{Q}\right]\right\}$$

$$\simeq S\left\{1 + \frac{p' - p}{p} + \frac{Q' - Q}{Q}\right\}$$

because the term

$$\frac{p' - p}{p} \times \frac{Q' - Q}{Q}$$

the product of two small proportions (e.g. $0.10 \times 0.20 = 0.02$) may be ignored as being of the second order of smallness. (We shall there-fore treat this approximate equality as an exact equality in what follows, because the inaccuracy resulting from this is very small.)

From:

$$S' = S\left\{1 + \frac{p' - p}{p} + \frac{Q' - Q}{Q}\right\}$$

we have that S' is greater than, equal to, or less than S, $S' \gtreqless S$, depending on whether:

$$1 + \frac{p' - p}{p} + \frac{Q' - Q}{Q} \gtreqless 1$$

Subtracting 1 from both sides (a permissible operation) gives this condition as:

$$\frac{p' - p}{p} + \frac{Q' - Q}{Q} \gtreqless 0$$

If price is reduced, $(p' - p)/p$ is negative and $(Q' - Q)/Q$ is positive, so adding the modulus of $(p' - p)/p$ to both sides gives:

$$\frac{Q' - Q}{Q} \gtreqless \left|\frac{p' - p}{p}\right|$$

as the condition for $S' \gtreqless S$. Or dividing through the inequality by $|(p' - p)/p|$ (a permissible operation) gives:

$$\frac{(Q' - Q)/Q}{|(p' - p)/p|} \gtreqless 1$$

as the condition for $S' \gtreqless S$, which proves the first row of the table.

If price is increased, $(p' - p)/p$ is positive and $(Q' - Q)/Q$ is negative, so adding the modulus of $(Q' - Q)/Q$ to both sides gives:

$$\frac{p' - p}{p} \gtreqless \left|\frac{Q' - Q}{Q}\right|$$

as the condition for $S' \gtreqless S$. Or dividing through the inequality by $(p' - p)/p$ gives:

$$1 \gtreqless \frac{|(Q' - Q)/Q|}{(p' - p)/p}$$

as the condition for $S' \gtreqless S$, which proves the second row of the table.

Chapter 7

Efficient Production: Capital–Labour Substitution and Economies of Scale

Contents

Chapter guide

In Chapters 5 and 6 we assumed that the enterprise's costs are the minimum achievable. But how is this to be? Chapters 7 and 8 are largely concerned with the enterprise's problem of attaining and maintaining minimum unit costs of production: Chapter 7 explains how unit costs are affected by capital–labour substitution and by economies of scale; Chapter 8 explains how unit costs are affected by technological change and by the learning curve. Together with the preceding Chapters 5 and 6, these two chapters on cost-effective production complete the economic analysis of the price/unit cost/profits nexus which is so important to enterprises because of the relationship, explained at the beginning of this chapter, between cost-effective production and profitability.

The key concept in analysing all these issues of minimising unit costs is that of the *production function* – the systematic relation between output and inputs. From the production function, we may derive the analytically important concept of an *isoquant* (which is really a production function in another form). These two concepts are first explained through relatively straightforward arithmetic models (which anyone having a calculator with an x^y key should be able to follow). Subsequently, we look at the relevant time-series and cross-section data relating to the UK economy.

Attaining the *least-cost position* on a production function (or on an isoquant) depends also on the relative prices of labour and capital inputs, and we examine how this is so before proceeding to look at some actual data from the United States economy on *capital–labour substitution* – the first important ingredient in achieving cost-effective production.

The second important ingredient in cost-effective production is *increasing returns to scale* (or '*economies of scale*'). This important concept is fully explained via a simple arithmetic production function model which introduces the concept of a *unit isoquant* so that we can more readily perceive what happens when the scale of production expands under conditions of increasing returns. We then look at some data on economies of scale in sixteen industries and we examine, with the illustrative help of this real-world data, the powerful implications of economies of scale for the enterprise's prospects of commercial success (or failure!)

Economic efficiency and unit cost

The economics of production is basically concerned with the problem of keeping costs to the minimum when producing any given flow of output. In other words, it is concerned with the problem of *economic efficiency*. Economic efficiency is different from technical efficiency: for example, it may be the case that the circuitry of electronic equipment made with gold would be technically the most efficient because of gold's superior ductility, but if other, and cheaper, metals or alloys would perform almost as well, then these would be economically more efficient or 'cost effective'. There are occasions when considerations of technical efficiency are overriding, as shown by the use of gold in the circuitry of computers controlling the voyages to the moon; nor, for different reasons, would one think much of a brass wedding ring; but in everyday life where an occasional breakdown or malfunction can be tolerated, the principle of cost effectiveness is more important because in reducing the cost, and therefore the price, of the product it brings the product within the reach of more people: that is, cost effectiveness raises standards of living.

Economic efficiency, or cost effectiveness to use another term for the same thing, is quite complicated because it depends not only upon the quantities of inputs and output but also upon the prices of inputs and outputs. Diagram 7.1 shows this twin dependence. In the first instance, economic efficiency depends upon the ratio of the quantity of output to the quantity of inputs; this ratio is generally referred to as 'productivity'. A familiar example of productivity is the ratio of number of items produced per period (e.g. cars per annum, Q) to the number of units of input required (e.g. man-years, N_i). This would be called 'labour productivity', to signify that it referred to the labour input. But there are as many types of productivity as there are distinguishable inputs: one might measure tonnes of wheat per

DIAGRAM 7.1   *Economic efficiency is measured (inversely) by unit cost*

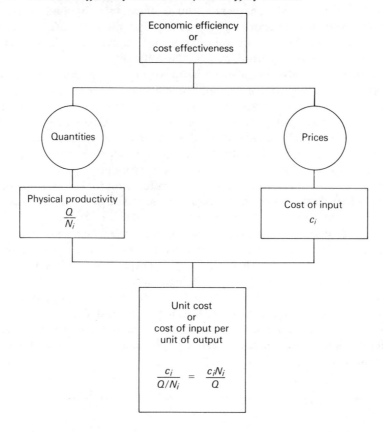

hectare, or litres of milk per cow, or tonne-km per litre of fuel (for jet planes or heavy-goods vehicles): so you would have, respectively, land productivity, cow productivity, or fuel productivity. Labour productivity is only one type of productivity, albeit the most important. Note also that the word 'productivity' should almost always be prefixed with the word 'physical' to denote a relationship between physical quantities (number of cars and man-years, tonnes and hectares, litres and cows, tonne-km and litres). Occasionally we may deviate from this, and use a monetary measure of output, especially value added, but always a physical measure of input is denoted when we use the word 'productivity'.

In the second instance, economic efficiency depends upon the prices of inputs. For example, because of its ductility one might be able to make more electronic circuits per *kilogramme* of gold, but the high price of gold nevertheless makes its use uneconomic or not 'cost effective' when there are other much cheaper metals available to be used. So we must also take the prices of the inputs, the c_i, into account.

When we put physical productivity and the price of inputs together we get a measure of the cost of input per unit of output, or 'unit cost' as we shall call it for short. If we are referring only to one input such as labour or litres of fuel, then we have the cost of labour input per unit of physical output, 'unit labour cost' for short, or the cost of fuel input per unit of output, 'unit fuel cost' for short. Unit cost is a very important concept which needs to be studied and thought about carefully until one is thoroughly familiar with it. We have the following definitions:

$$\frac{\text{Unit}}{\text{cost}} = \frac{\text{Price of input}}{\text{Productivity of input}}$$

or, equivalently:

$$\text{Unit cost} = \frac{\text{Total cost of input}}{\text{Quantity of output produced}}$$

To demonstrate this, for any ith input, let N_i be the physical quantity (number) of the ith input used (total man-years, total litres of fuel), c_i the price per unit of input (annual wage, price per litre), and Q the physical quantity of total output produced (number of cars, tonne-km travelled). Then:

$$\text{Unit cost} = \frac{c_i}{Q/N_i}$$

$$= \frac{c_i N_i}{Q}$$

To put some illustrative arithmetic flesh on these algebraic bones, suppose a factory produces 1,000 desks per annum ($Q = 1,000$) the price of labour is £5,000 per annum (i.e. the annual wage is $c_i = £5,000$), and the factory uses 10 man-years (it employs ten workers throughout the year, so $N_i = 10$). Then we have:*

$$\text{Unit labour cost} = \frac{5,000}{1,000/10} = \frac{5,000}{100} = 50$$

or:

$$\text{Unit labour cost} = \frac{5,000 \times 10}{1,000} = \frac{50,000}{1,000} = 50$$

We can similarly calculate the unit cost for any other input, and having done so we can add them all up to get the unit total cost (for all inputs):

$$\text{Unit total cost} = \frac{\Sigma c_i N_i}{Q}$$

Economic efficiency, or cost effectiveness, is then assessed by unit total cost: the lower is unit total cost, the greater is economic efficiency, and the aim of efficient production is to keep all unit input costs, $c_i/(Q/N_i)$, to the minimum possible. We can now see why gold electronic circuitry is not cost effective: although Q/N_i (where $N_i = $ kg of gold) may be higher than for other metals, c_i (the price of gold per kg) is extremely high and so causes unit gold cost to be very high, and therefore its use is not economic.

Efficiency and profits

Next, we need to see how over-all economic efficiency is related to net profit, profit net of depreciation charges. First we must have a picture of the whole enterprise as a cycle of production. Diagram 7.2 shows the enterprise as a producing entity. The enterprise, using its organisation and know-how, combines the factors of production, labour, land and capital, into a combined factor input; by working on and with the bought-in materials and

---

*Again, note very carefully and remember that 'unit labour cost' means the labour cost incurred in producing a unit of *output*; it does NOT mean the cost of a unit of labour (and likewise with 'unit capital cost' or 'unit total cost').

services, the enterprise produces annually a quantity of production measured in physical units; by selling these products or services the enterprise gets its cash flow of sales receipts; from this it pays its suppliers leaving the enterprise with value added; from this value added, the enterprise has to meet the costs incurred by its use of factors of production (these costs are also, from the factor's point of view, income). These payments to the factors of production are those which permit the enterprise to obtain and use the services of these factors, so closing the cycle of production.

DIAGRAM 7.2   *The cycle of production*

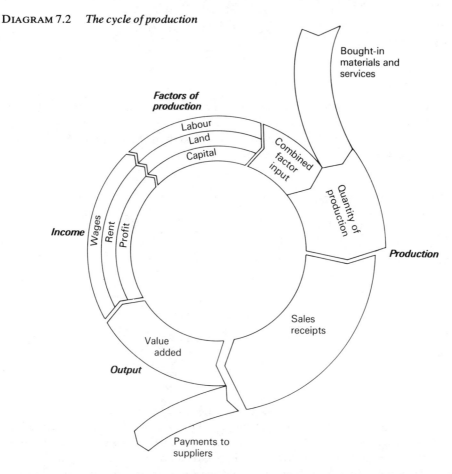

We saw in Diagram 5.2 that enterprises classify the costs incurred during the process of producing, selling and distributing their products in quite complex ways because one cannot hope to control and minimise costs unless one knows exactly where and for what purposes the costs are being incurred. But for the purposes of economic analysis we require only a rudimentary classification into four basic categories, as in Diagram 7.2:

1. Cost of bought-in materials and services (payments to suppliers).
2. Cost of labour.
3. Cost of rented or hired capital or land (assets which the enterprise does *not* own).
4. Cost of capital (including land) which the enterprise *does* own.

The first three categories comprise flows of payments which are actually made, and so measuring these costs presents no problem (except for the slight difficulty which arises when the 'outside' supplier is another department within the same company, in which case an appropriate 'transfer price' has to be agreed, generally on the basis of 'outside' market prices). Measuring the cost of labour presents no difficulty: this is the annual wage bill plus whatever the employer has to pay by way of contributions to National Insurance and to superannuation schemes as well as such costs as subsidised canteens or sports facilities. Ascertaining the cost of assets which are not owned but which are rented or hired is also straightforward: this is simply the annual rental or hire charge. Because land (and premises) is very often a non-owned, rented factor of production, Diagram 7.2 gives 'rent' and 'land' in the cycle of production followed by 'profit' and 'capital'; but we should be clear that the distinction is really between non-owned assets (of any type) and owned assets, and that when I use the word 'profits' I mean the return, or income, accruing to owned assets. I shall also use the word 'capital' to refer to owned assets.

Because no money changes hands to pay for the cost of owned assets we have in principle a problem of assessing the cost of its use so that we may impute a cost. If we do not impute a cost to capital, then we shall be unable to assess the unit capital cost, and so an important part of unit total cost will be missing. On what basis, then, may we derive the imputed cost incurred by using the services of owned capital?

In answering this question it is necessary to appreciate that we must work to a uniform solution. In other words, if two enterprises use identical capital equipment, the imputed cost of the capital equipment must be the same for each. Now one uniform answer is simply to take the annual flow of depreciation – the sum of money which has to be set aside each year in order to enable the enterprise to continue in business. This is a low estimate of the cost of capital, and for most purposes it will suffice as a measure of the imputed cost of capital. However, we need to note that an enterprise which has borrowed the funds necessary to acquire its capital equipment will annually incur a cost greater than the depreciation (or amortisation) necessary to repay the loan, because it will have to pay an annual interest charge. If we add on an annual interest charge to the depreciation flow, then we may derive a higher estimate of the cost incurred in the use of capital equipment. But this may give a non-uniform solution. The difficulty which arises from including interest charges may be seen if we imagine two enterprises using identical capital equipment but where one enterprise has used no borrowed funds while the other has financed all its capital equipment by borrowing: if we include interest charges, then the latter enterprise will record a higher imputed cost of capital than the former, and, from the point of view of analysing cost efficiency, it is a mistake to let the method of financing capital equipment affect the measurement of the efficiency of use of that capital equipment. If we are to include interest charges in our measure of the imputed cost of capital, then not only must we count the actual interest charges but we must also impute an interest charge to all capital not financed by borrowed money.

In general, it seems preferable in the context of analysing efficiency simply to use the lower cost measure of depreciation. Using depreciation as our measure of the cost of capital does, however, create a problem in the case of owned land, because land does not depreciate. In any such case we simply have to price the use of the asset at what it would cost to rent it. So depreciation provisions on owned assets must be taken to include an imputed rental in those cases where depreciation is not applicable. This still maintains uniformity in costing: for example, if we imagine two identical farms, one of which owns its land, the other renting all its land, both incur the same cost for the use of land.

We may now consider how over-all economic efficiency is related to net profit, pausing to note that this is not an issue of purely academic interest: Table 4.19 showed that among company directors in both the United Kingdom and West Germany, the second most important reason given for interest in profitability was 'Because it is a yardstick of efficiency'. And when Eliasson's sample of companies stressed the need to maintain or improve past performance, they, too, meant performance or efficiency as indicated by net profitability.

From the system for accounts we may derive the annual flow of profits (before interest and tax) net of depreciation provisions (including imputed rentals where appropriate) as:

$$\frac{\text{Net}}{\text{profits}} = \text{Sales receipts} - \text{Cost of bought-in materials}$$
$$- \text{Cost of labour} - \text{Rental costs (non-owned assets)}$$
$$- \text{Depreciation provisions (owned assets)}$$

In order to make progress with the analysis we need to transpose this to algebraic symbols. Let:

p = price per unit of output
Q = total quantity (number of units) of output produced per annum
c_i = cost per unit of ith bought-in material
N_i = total quantity (number of units) of ith bought-in material per annum
w = cost per unit (man-year) of labour, annual wage
L = total quantity (number of man-years) of labour used
R = total annual rental on non-owned assets
D = total annual flow of depreciation provisions
      (including imputed rental) on owned assets
Π = net profits (before interest and tax but after depreciation) per annum

The equation, with appropriate summation, thus becomes:

$$\Pi = pQ - \Sigma c_i N_i - wL - R - D$$

If we divide through by Q, the quantity of output, we get net profits per unit of output as follows:

$$\frac{\Pi}{Q} = p - \frac{\Sigma c_i N_i}{Q} - \frac{wL}{Q} - \frac{R}{Q} - \frac{D}{Q}$$

$$= p - \left\{ \frac{\Sigma c_i N_i}{Q} + \frac{wL}{Q} + \frac{R}{Q} + \frac{D}{Q} \right\}$$

Now, the expression on the right-hand side in brackets is, of course, total costs incurred per unit of output produced. So, for an enterprise with a given price and quantity of output produced, the lower its unit cost of production – that is, the greater its economic efficiency or cost effectiveness – the higher its net profit per unit of output produced. Given that net profits are a residual remaining from sales receipts after all other costs of production have been met, then inefficiency (high unit costs) in the use of any inputs ultimately impinges on (reduces) the flow of net profits per unit of output. Thus net profit per unit of output provides the 'ultimate' measure of an enterprise's over-all efficiency.

This assertion depends somewhat on the enterprise's inability to fix the price (and still sell a similar or only slightly reduced flow of output). For instance, a monopoly supplier of some essential commodity such as salt might increase net profits per unit of output by raising the price of salt (we assume this has little effect on the volume of salt sold; in other words, the price elasticity of demand for salt is low) and such an increase in net profits has nothing to do with efficiency and everything to do with 'exploiting' the consumer. This explains why most governments keep some sort of a watch on monopolies or cartels (which are formal agreements among firms to charge mutually acceptable prices), if indeed monopolies or cartels are permitted at all.

Using these equations, we can see the importance of balancing marginal sales receipts against marginal costs, if over-all economic efficiency in production is to be achieved. The balancing of the marginal impact on production of a marginal increase in inputs applies to any and every input.

An example to illustrate marginal cost

For example, it is a common problem in arable farming as to how much fertiliser should be applied. The application of fertiliser tends to be accompanied by diminishing marginal returns: that is to say, on unfertilised land, the first 'dose' of fertiliser will have a dramatic impact on increasing yields; but the impact of the second 'dose' will not raise the yield by so much again, and finally one reaches a point where extra fertiliser has no effect at all. Accordingly, the cost of the first dose of fertiliser may be exceeded by its impact on the volume of output *multiplied by* price so that (first equation) total net profits increase as a result of applying more fertiliser, or (second equation) unit costs incurred in fertiliser application fall. But as the farmer increases his application of fertiliser, a point is eventually reached where the cost of extra fertiliser is not outweighed by its impact on output (and sales receipts) and after this point any further application of fertiliser would cause net profits to fall, or unit fertiliser costs to rise. So at this point the total application of fertiliser will be the most *economically* efficient with the lowest unit cost of fertiliser. The basic argument is really quite straightforward and obvious, but the student must practise 'seeing' or interpreting this argument in the appropriate analytic framework of the above equations. Note also the importance of the price of a unit of fertiliser: clearly, if fertiliser prices were to rise excessively, then we could reach a point where the quantity/sales receipts impact of even the first 'dose' of fertiliser would not outweigh its cost, and if this were the case it would be economically efficient (though certainly not technically efficient) to apply no fertiliser at all. A less extreme case is that rises in the price of fertiliser are likely to lead to a reduction in its application (and to reductions in total output) so that unit fertiliser costs are minimised. Of course, reductions in total output could lead to rises in product prices and so partially restore the application of the more costly fertiliser. The whole process of adjustment is complex, but it needs to be seen in the context of enterprises striving for economically most efficient production, for minimum unit costs.

(It is worth noting that the fertiliser example is not simply of academic interest: in the twenty years between 1952 and 1972 the application of fertilisers in the world – especially in the developing countries – rose very steeply because fertiliser prices actually fell during this period. Consequently, world food production rose, even a little more rapidly than did population. However, in 1973 and 1974 fertiliser prices rose very steeply (by about fourfold) and its use subsequently seems to have declined, thus putting downward pressure on the volume of production and upward pressure on food prices.)

If an enterprise is not economically efficient in its use of an input (such as fertiliser), then it will have a smaller net profit per unit of output. The same is true of any other input or factor of production. If an enterprise uses more labour than that which gives minimum unit labour costs, then its economic efficiency, its net profits per unit of output, will be lower than it could otherwise be. We do know that the cost of labour, the annual wage rate, tends usually to be rising; this naturally leads the enterprise, in its search for economically efficient production, to try to reduce its use of labour. One way of doing this is to mechanise: if the cost of dairymaids becomes 'excessive', the farm switches to milking-machines; if the cost of lorry-drivers increases, can we not use bigger lorries so as to offset this with more tonne-km per driver-hour (bigger lorries, of course, represent more fixed capital)? Of course, such mechanisation may raise the flow of depreciation per unit of output, and we must never forget that the only thing which counts in the long run is over-all unit cost.

Long-run changes in the efficiency of production

The conditions under which mechanisation takes place, and the appropriate extent of mechanisation, are traditionally important subjects in the economic analysis of production, and very rightly so, because this seemingly abstract subject is a key *historical* determinant of your standard of living and was a most important aspect of the Industrial Revolution:

> The result [of the Industrial Revolution] has been an enormous increase in the output and variety of goods and services, and this alone has changed man's way of life more than anything since the discovery of fire: *the Englishman of 1750 was closer in material things to Caesar's legionnaires than to his own great-grandchildren* (David Landes, *The Unbound Prometheus: Technological Change and Industrial Development in Western Europe from 1750 to the Present*, Cambridge University Press, 1969, p. 5, italics added).

We saw in Chapter 1, especially Diagram 1.10, how capital per worker and output (value added) per worker have increased in the UK economy between 1871 and 1980: over this period of a little more than a century capital stock per worker in work (at 1975 prices) rose from £5,488 to £22,144, while value added per worker (at 1975 prices) rose from £1,148 per annum to £4,144 per annum (Appendix 1.3). It is clear from David Landes's work (and that of others) that in the century prior to 1871 capital per worker and output per worker had also risen rapidly, far more so than in any preceding century. Now, the impact of increases in capital per worker on output per worker tend to be a complex synthesis or fusion of three ingredients which lead to higher labour productivity. For analytic purposes, we need to consider the three separately:

1. Capital–labour substitution (or 'mechanisation'), within a given technology.
2. Economies of large-scale production, within a given technology.
3. Technical progress, or changes in technology.

In practice, these three things are often inextricably fused into one single change embodying all three, but theoretically they are distinct and we need therefore to examine them one by one. The basic analytic device for describing and analysing these three ingredients is the concept of a *production function*, from which we may derive another key analytic concept, that of an *isoquant*. Before we can systematically examine these three ingredients we need to understand these two concepts and the way in which least-cost production is determined.

Production function and least-cost production (capital–labour substitution)

A production function is basically like a recipe which tells you that if you put in this particular combination of inputs you will get such-and-such output, while if you put in another combination of inputs you will get another level of output (see Table 7.1).

TABLE 7.1   *Production function (schedule)*

Quantity of labour	*together with this*	Quantity of capital	*results in this*	Quantity of output
L_1		K_1		Q_1
L_2		K_2		Q_2
⋮		⋮		⋮

The two inputs, or factors of production, with which we are most concerned are labour and capital. Most production functions are only partial recipes in that they give the relationship between, say, labour and capital inputs on the one hand and output on the other. It is simply taken for granted that the other inputs will be adjusted as necessary; a production function for wheat output in relation to fertiliser and land input would simply assume that the required amount of labour would be used as well. In the production functions we shall be analysing it is assumed that the input of materials is adjusted to the volume of output. A production function should be considered a 'partial' relationship between physical quantities: quantities of some inputs and quantities of output. Furthermore, a production function relates to a given technology or state of knowledge; changes in technology have to be represented by a bodily shift in the whole production function itself.

Now, how are the quantities of inputs and outputs to be measured?

Labour as a factor of production can be measured by counting the number of workers – a stock – engaged in the process of production. Alternatively, and preferably, one can count the flow of labour-time, such as man-hours per annum. This counting may appear to be a simple matter but it is not: for example, should one count a labour-hour supplied by a skilled craftsman as equivalent to a labour-hour supplied by an unskilled worker? But this is not a question we shall attempt to answer here and we shall simplify by treating all labour as alike.

It is difficult also to measure capital as a factor of production. In practice we have to use the gross capital stock at constant prices (see Tables 1.9 and 1.11 and Chapter 1, *passim*), assuming that an unchanging proportion of this is utilised in the process of production.

Output will be measured in whatever are the appropriate units: numbers of cars; tonnes of wheat; tonne-km of freight carried. So a production function is of the general, abstract form:

$$\frac{\text{Quantity}}{\text{of output}} = \textit{Function of} \left(\frac{\text{Quantity}}{\text{of labour}} \quad \textit{and} \quad \frac{\text{Quantity}}{\text{of capital}}\right)$$

Or, in algebraic terms, with Q for quantity of output, L for quantity of labour, and K for quantity of capital, and using our functional notation f (see Chapter 3, pp. 139–40), we may write:

$$Q = f(L, K)$$

We now need to give this indeterminate production function a determinate mathematical form. To do this we have to get over the barrier that while most students are familiar with additive functions – functions which depend on addition (or subtraction) – many students find it difficult to adjust to the less familiar multiplicative functions – functions which use only multiplication (or division). Because production functions are concerned generally with the *proportionate* impact on output of *proportionate* changes in inputs, a multiplicative function is the appropriate one.

Understanding a production function

A production function can best be understood as coming from a weighted average of the growth rates of the inputs. It is therefore helpful to approach a multiplicative production function via an additive growth function: in this way we shall step from the familiar to the unfamiliar. If output and inputs are functionally related, then it is reasonable to assert that the growth rate of output is a function of the growth rates of the inputs. Specifically we suppose that the growth rate of output is likely to be a weighted sum of the growth rates of inputs:

$$\frac{\Delta Q}{Q} = a\frac{\Delta L}{L} + b\frac{\Delta K}{K}$$

(We may find it convenient here to fix our minds

on a time-series production function, so that the proportionate changes are the year-to-year proportionate changes for the same producing entity; however, we could also be dealing with a cross-section production function, in which case the proportionate changes would be those between, say, one enterprise and another.)

This additive growth rate function has, as variables, the three growth rates, and, as parameters, the weights a and b. These weights can be interpreted quite simply. If we let $\Delta K/K = 0$, then we have:

$$a = \frac{\Delta Q/Q}{\Delta L/L}$$

so that a is the elasticity of output with respect to the labour input (when capital input is held constant). Likewise, b is the elasticity of output with respect to capital input when labour input is held constant. Now, because changes in the logarithm of a variable measure proportionate, not absolute, changes (see the discussion of logarithmic, or ratio, scales in Chapter 1), they can be written equivalently as:

$$a = \frac{\Delta \log Q}{\Delta \log L}$$

and:

$$b = \frac{\Delta \log Q}{\Delta \log K}$$

so that the additive growth rate function can be equivalently written in logarithmic form as:*

$$\log Q = a \log L + b \log K$$

But adding logarithms of variables is equivalent to multiplying those variables themselves, so from this logarithmic form of the additive growth rate function we may derive:

$$Q = L^a K^b$$

which, but for one thing, is the required multiplicative production function. The one thing required is an adjustment factor: if Q is measured in, say, number of cars, L in number of man-years, and K in £ at constant prices, how can we multiply man-years (raised to an exponent) by £ at constant prices (raised to an exponent) and get numbers of cars? The answer is we cannot unless we put in an adjustment factor which 'scales' man-years (exponentiated) *multiplied by* £ at constant prices (exponentiated) to conformity with numbers of cars. Let us denote this adjustment factor by the letter Z. Then we may write the multiplicative production function as:

$$Q = ZL^a K^b$$

Another way of dealing with the adjustment problem is to measure Q, L and K not in their original units but as indices, each with a base (index) value of unity, and in this case the adjustment factor Z will also be equal to 1, because in the base index values the production function will be:

$$1.00 = 1 \times 1.00^a \times 1.00^b$$

because 1 raised to any power is still 1. This form of the production function is known as the Cobb–Douglas production function after the mathematician Charles Cobb and the American economist Paul Douglas who in 1928 derived the function to explain the output and capital and labour inputs of manufacturing industry in the USA between 1899 and 1922 (see Paul Douglas, *The Theory of Wages*, 1934; republished Augustus Kelley, 1964). (The basic work on production functions goes back to Philip Wicksteed's *An Essay on the Co-ordination of the Laws of Distribution*, Macmillan 1894; reproduced by University Microfilms International, 1980.)

---

*For the sake of mathematical completeness, it should be noted that this equation derives from the weighted average growth rate equation by integration, and so there should be a constant of integration; this constant of integration is subsequently brought into the analysis when we introduce the adjustment factor Z; that is, the full equation here is: $\log Q = a \log L + b \log K + \log Z$, where $\log Z$ is the constant of integration.

Labour productivity and capital per worker

Now there are two important things about a production function. First, we can show that (physical) labour productivity is a function of the capital–labour ratio. Let us suppose that we have the following values for the parameters a and b:

$$a = 0.75, \quad b = 0.25$$

The reason for choosing these values (which sum to 1), apart from arithmetic convenience, will become clear when we consider the economies of large-scale production. Let us also measure Q, L and K in index terms, with base values of 100 (in this case, too, the adjustment factor Z will be equal to 1). The production function is therefore:

$$Q = L^{0.75} K^{0.25}$$

If we divide through by L we get a production function for output per worker as related to capital per worker:

$$\frac{Q}{L} = L^{0.75} L^{-1} K^{0.25}$$

$$= L^{-0.25} K^{0.25}$$

$$= \left\{ \frac{K}{L} \right\}^{0.25}$$

(using the rule for indices, or exponents, that $1/L = L^{-1}$). We shall see in a moment what this looks like in a diagram.

Isoquants

The second thing about a production function is that the same quantity of output can be produced with different combinations of labour and capital inputs. Suppose we hold Q constant, say, at 100, denoting this constant value as $\bar{Q}$. Then we have:*

$$\bar{Q} = L^{0.75} K^{0.25}$$

whence:

$$K^{0.25} = \bar{Q} \times \frac{1}{L^{0.75}}$$

so that:

$$K = \bar{Q}^{\frac{1}{0.25}} \times \frac{1}{L^{\frac{0.75}{0.25}}}$$

$$= \bar{Q}^4 \times \frac{1}{L^3}$$

If we put into this function any chosen values of L, we may calculate the requisite quantities of K needed, in conjunction with that value of L, to produce 100 units of output. These combinations of L and K trace out what is known as an *isoquant*, from 'iso' meaning equal with an abbreviation for quantity of output. Let us see how this works out arithmetically.

Table 7.2 shows in its first row that if we have 100 (index) units of labour and 100 (index) units of capital, then the production function gives us 100 (index) units of output: $31.6228 \times 3.1623 = 100$. Suppose we want to construct an isoquant for $\bar{Q} = 100$ (index) units; let us choose values of L at 60, 70, 80, 120, 140 and 200, and then let us ascertain, using the formula just derived, the corresponding values of K which would be required, in combination with those values of L, to produce 100 (index) units of output. These values of K are given in the second column of Table 7.2, and if we insert these values of L and K into the production function we find that, throughout, the quantity of production remains constant at 100 (index) units. Plotting the combinations of L and K in the first two columns in a two-dimensional $L-K$ space, or diagram, gives us the isoquant for $\bar{Q} = 100$.

*This $\bar{Q}$ notation is different from, and should not be confused with, the bar notation used in previous chapters to denote an average.

TABLE 7.2   *Schedule for hypothetical production function and isoquant* [a]

L	K	$L^{0.75}$	$\times$ $K^{0.25}$	= $\bar{Q}$	$\dfrac{K}{L}$	$\left\{\dfrac{K}{L}\right\}^{0.25}$	$\dfrac{\bar{Q}}{L}$
100	100	31.6228	3.1623	100	1.00	1.00	1.00
60	462.9630	21.5582	4.6386	100	7.72	1.67	1.67
70	291.5452	24.2005	4.1322	100	4.16	1.43	1.43
80	195.3125	26.7496	3.7384	100	2.44	1.25	1.25
120	57.8704	36.2565	2.7581	100	0.48	0.83	0.83
140	36.4431	40.7002	2.4570	100	0.26	0.71	0.71
200	12.5000	53.1830	1.8803	100	0.06	0.50	0.50

[a] The production function is $Q = ZL^{a}K^{b}$. Taking Q, L, and K as measured by indices with base values of 100 means the adjustment factor, Z, is 1. The isoquant for $\bar{Q} = 100$ has the derived formula for K (with $a = 0.75$ and $b = 0.25$):

$$K = \bar{Q}^{\frac{1}{b}} \times \frac{1}{L^{\frac{a}{b}}} = 100^{4} \times \frac{1}{L^{3}}$$

We may also derive, in the sixth column of Table 7.2, the ratio of capital to labour (measured in index units with a base value of 1.00). If we raise this capital–labour ratio to the power 0.25 (that is, take its fourth root), we should, according to the previously derived production function for output per worker, get the corresponding values for output per worker (also measured in index values with a base of 1.00). We can verify this production function by directly calculating, in the final column, the value of $\bar{Q} = 100$ divided by the labour input (in index value); the two columns are identical.

DIAGRAM 7.3   *Production function for output per worker*

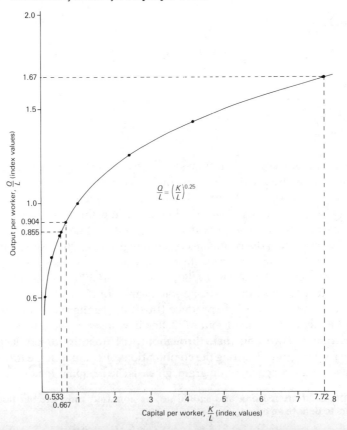

Diagram 7.3 shows this production function for output per worker (by having output per worker and capital per worker we can reduce the production function to two dimensions). On the horizontal axis we measure the capital–labour ratio (in index values, base = 1.00) and on the vertical axis output per worker (ditto). In this space we can then plot the co-ordinates of the sixth and eighth columns of Table 7.2 and, because the production function is continuous, we may join these by a smooth curve to represent the whole production function. The production function is at first quite steep, showing that (for a given technology) when capital per worker is low there are considerable (absolute) gains to be made in terms of output per worker by increasing capital per worker (or by 'mechanising'). But as we move along the capital–labour axis the extra gains become smaller and smaller. Within the confines of a given technology this result seems quite in accord with common sense. We shall not, in this introductory textbook, be making much use of Diagram 7.3, which is meant simply to give a visual impression of a production function and so take the sting out of the algebra and the arithmetic. But the student should note that this production function is used quite extensively in advanced economic analysis, so that it is useful to have an understanding of Diagram 7.3 (for example, for its use see F. H. Hahn and R. C. O. Matthews, 'The theory of economic growth: a survey', *The Economic Journal*, December 1964).

Least-cost production

Diagram 7.4 shows the isoquant for $\bar{Q} = 100$ as derived in Table 7.3. This isoquant is, of course, simply another way of representing a production function. Along the horizontal axis we measure the quantity of labour input (in index values, base = 100); up the vertical

DIAGRAM 7.4 *Isoquant for $\bar{Q} = 100$, isocost line, and least-cost combination of L and K*

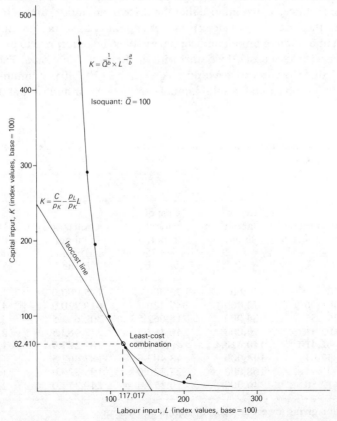

$$K = \bar{Q}^{\frac{1}{b}} \times L^{-\frac{a}{b}}$$

Isoquant: $\bar{Q} = 100$

$$K = \frac{C}{p_K} - \frac{p_L}{p_K} L$$

Isocost line

Least-cost combination

Capital input, K (index values, base = 100)

Labour input, L (index values, base = 100)

axis we measure the quantity of capital inputs (ditto). In the diagram's L–K space we may plot the co-ordinates representing the different combinations of labour and capital required to produce 100 (index) units of output, as given in the first two columns of Table 7.3. Again, because the function is continuous, we may connect these points by a continuous curve; any point on this curve represents a combination of labour and capital which will enable us to produce 100 units of output. There will, of course, be other, differently positioned isoquants for other levels of output.

Both Diagram 7.3 and Diagram 7.4 tell us something important about production within the confines of a given technology: namely, that it is possible to substitute capital for labour in the process of production. Diagram 7.3 tells us very clearly that if we increase the capital–labour ratio we shall raise output per worker; and Diagram 7.4 illustrates the possibility of substituting capital for labour and still producing the same quantity of output. The possibility and process of substituting one input for another input (and still producing the same quantity of output) is very important to economically efficient production and is empirically well attested; although the present analysis is in terms of capital and labour, it can be applied to any other substitutable inputs (plastic and wood, synthetic and natural fibres).

Clearly, in producing 100 (index) units of output we must have a combination of capital and labour somewhere on the isoquant: to produce $\bar{Q} = 100$ with any combination above and to the right of the isoquant is simply wasteful; and it is not technically possible, given the state of technology as represented by this isoquant, to produce $\bar{Q} = 100$ with any combination below and to the left of the isoquant. But the question as to which of the combinations along the isoquant to choose can only be answered if we bring in the prices (costs) of labour and capital: economically efficient production depends on prices as well as on quantities (Diagram 7.1). The most important step in the economic analysis of production is to appreciate that, for any given set of prices, there is one unique combination of capital and labour inputs which gives the lowest combined unit costs of production.

To see this in practice, let us suppose that the price of an (index) unit of labour is £1,200 per annum and the price of an (index) unit of capital is £750 per annum. Given these prices, what combination of labour and capital enables the enterprise to produce $\bar{Q} = 100$ units per annum with least cost? If we start with the first combination in Table 7.2, we can see in Table 7.3 that the enterprise would be spending £120,000 per annum on labour and £75,000 per annum on capital, a total annual cost for labour and capital of £195,000 to

TABLE 7.3   *Hypothetical isoquant with labour and capital costs and unit labour and capital costs combined*

			£		
Quantities required to produce $\bar{Q} = 100$		Cost of labour input, $p_L = £1,200$, $p_L \times L$	Cost of capital input, $p_K = £750$, $p_K \times K$	Total cost of labour and capital input	Unit cost of labour and capital input
L	K				
100	100	120,000	75,000	195,000.0	1,950.00
60	462.96	72,000	347,220	419,220.0	4,192.20
70	291.55	84,000	218,662.5	302,662.5	3,026.63
80	195.31	96,000	146,482.5	242,482.5	2,424.83
117.017 [a]	62.410 [a]	140,420.4	46,807.5	187,227.9	1,872.28
120	57.87	144,000	43,402.5	187,402.5	1,874.03
140	36.44	168,000	27,330.0	195,330.0	1,953.30
200	12.50	240,000	9,375.0	249,375.0	2,493.75

[a] Combination giving lowest unit cost of capital and labour.

produce 100 (index) units of output, or combined labour and capital costs of £1,950 per unit of output. This is clearly a lower cost than if we were to use 60 (index) units of labour and 462.96 (index) units of capital (second row of Table 7.3) because with this combination the total annual costs are £419,220 and the unit labour and capital costs are £4,192.2. But the first combination is not as economical as the combination of 120 units of labour and 57.87 units of capital, because this combination gives total annual costs of £187,402.5 and unit labour and capital costs of £1,874.03. However, if we go on to the combination of 140 units of labour and 36.44 units of capital, the total cost and the unit cost rise.

Now, we could go on by trial and error for all the various combinations along the $\bar{Q} = 100$ isoquant, but from an analytical point of view this is not a satisfactory method of ascertaining the least-cost combination of labour and capital to use. So how can we proceed in systematic way?

The amount of money, £C per annum, which the enterprise is going to spend on labour and capital is given by:

$$C = p_L \times L + p_K \times K$$

where p_L and p_K are the prices per unit of labour and capital respectively. We can turn this cost equation into a functional relationship between K and L as follows:

$$K = \frac{C}{p_K} - \frac{p_L}{p_K} \times L$$

This is a straight-line relationship between K and L with a (downward) slope of $-p_L/p_K$. If we hold C constant, this equation shows the combinations of L and K which can be bought for that constant total cost. This equation is sometimes called an *isocost line* because of this.

What we need on Diagram 7.4 is the lowest isocost line which still permits us to produce $\bar{Q} = 100$. Obviously such an isocost line must only just touch, or be tangential to, the isoquant. The formal condition for tangency is that the slope of the isoquant, at the point of tangency, is equal to the slope of the isocost line. The slope of the isocost line is:

$$\frac{\Delta K}{\Delta L} = - \frac{p_L}{p_K}$$

and, because the prices of L and K are given, this slope is a constant (the line is a straight line). For the prices given:

$$\frac{\Delta K}{\Delta L} = - \frac{1,200}{750} = -1.6$$

The general formula for the isoquant (omitting the adjustment factor Z, which, by fiddling with index units, we have contrived to make equal to 1) is:

$$K = \bar{Q}^{\frac{1}{b}} \times L^{-\frac{a}{b}}$$

So the slope of the isoquant is:

$$\frac{\Delta K}{\Delta L} = - \frac{a}{b} \times \bar{Q}^{\frac{1}{b}} \times L^{-\frac{a}{b} - 1}$$

In the case of the production function and isoquant being used, $\bar{Q} = 100$, $a = 0.75$ and $b = 0.25$, so:

$$\frac{\Delta K}{\Delta L} = -3 \times 100^4 \times L^{-4}$$

The slope of the isoquant is variable, because it depends (inversely) on L, which is a variable: the bigger is L, the smaller (less steep) the negative slope (rise over run).

For the point of tangency we need that position on the isoquant where the slope of the isoquant equals the slope of the isocost line. That is, where:

$$-3 \times 100^4 \times L^{-4} = -1.6$$

which may be solved for L to give:

$$L^* = 117.017$$

The corresponding value of K, estimated from the isoquant equation, is:

$$K^* = 62.410$$

where the asterisks denote the least-cost combination, at the prices given, of L and K required to produce $\bar{Q} = 100$. Any combination other than this will, at these prices, result in higher total and unit labour and capital costs of production.

For those students whose algebra and calculus are not sufficiently advanced, it should be noted that the really important point is that, along the isoquant and with a given set of labour and capital prices, there is one determinate combination, and only one, of labour and capital inputs which gives the lowest labour and capital costs combined per unit of output. It is essential to grasp this firmly (whether the argument is understood via calculus, or via Diagram 7.4, or via trial and error by arithmetic in Table 7.3, matters far less).

The existence of one least-cost combination of labour and capital inputs is obviously important to every enterprise engaged in production. Given that labour and capital costs are a significant part of an enterprise's costs, any enterprise which operates at a combination other than the least-cost combination is likely to lose business to enterprises which operate at or nearer the least-cost combination because the economically efficient enterprises can charge lower prices and still be profitable. In the long run the economically inefficient enterprise is likely to go bankrupt.

At this least-cost combination of labour and capital, capital per worker (in index units) is $62.410/117.017 = 0.533$ and output per worker (in index units) is $100/117.017 = 0.855$. This position may be plotted on Diagram 7.3, in order to show that the least-cost position is *not* that of maximum labour productivity. Sometimes, people talk as if maximising labour productivity were all that mattered when increasing efficiency. This is not the case, because simply raising labour productivity to the greatest possible extent takes no account of the capital costs incurred in raising labour productivity. It would be technically possible (Table 7.2) to produce $\bar{Q} = 100$ with 60 units of labour, giving labour productivity of $100/60 = 1.67$ and capital per worker of $462.96/60 = 7.72$ and so be much further up the production function in Diagram 7.3. But this does *not* lead to the lowest unit cost of production, to the most economically efficient production, because it requires an 'excessive' and uneconomic use of capital in order to raise physical labour productivity to that level. The argument is elementary, but it is forgotten or overlooked surprisingly often, and woe betide the enterprise which does so because it ends up with higher-than-minimum unit total costs.

The economist's analytic prescription for least-cost production – operate at the point of tangency between the isoquant and the isocost line – is not likely to make sense to the businessman who is not normally accustomed to thinking in these abstract theoretical terms. But this does not matter, because we can easily translate the least-cost conditions into a statement which is readily comprehensible in business terms, and it will advance our practical understanding of the least-cost combination to do so, because it shows how the least-cost combination arises naturally from the attempt to cut costs.

In theoretical terms, the least-cost combination occurs where the modulus of the slope of the isoquant is equal to the ratio between the prices or the modulus of the slope of the isocost line:

$$\left|\frac{\Delta K}{\Delta L}\right| = \frac{\dot{p}_L}{p_K}$$

Along the isoquant, ΔK and ΔL are linked: if there is a certain decrease in labour input, $(-)\Delta L$, then there must, along the isoquant, be a certain compensating increase in capital input, $(+)\Delta K$, in order that the enterprise can continue to produce the same quantity of output. This relationship is measured in terms of physical units; for this reason $|\Delta K/\Delta L|$ is known as the *marginal physical rate of substitution* between K and L. If we multiply these marginal changes, $-\Delta L$ and ΔK, by their respective prices, p_L and p_K, we can 'translate' the marginal physical rate of substitution into a marginal money-cost rate of substitution. Thus, using the equation just given, we can see that the least-cost combination occurs where:

$$|p_K \Delta K| = |p_L \Delta L|$$

We can see what this condition of equality means if we consider the situation at some other point, say A in Diagram 7.4, where:

$$\left|\frac{\Delta K}{\Delta L}\right| < \frac{p_L}{p_K}$$

so that:

$$|p_K \Delta K| < |p_L \Delta L|$$

This inequality means that, at point A, if the enterprise reduces its input of labour by ΔL, it saves $|p_L \Delta L|$ in costs; in order to compensate for the marginal reduction in labour input it has to increase its capital input by ΔK (according to the slope of the isoquant at A), and this compensating marginal increase in capital input costs the enterprise $p_K \Delta K$. The inequality tells us that this marginal compensating increase in capital costs *less* than the marginal reduction in labour costs, so that there is a net reduction in costs to be made by moving up the isoquant away from A: the enterprise saves more by reducing labour input than it has to pay out in extra capital costs. Only where the marginal money-cost rate of substitution is equal:

$$|p_K \Delta K| = |p_L \Delta L|$$

is it not possible to make a net saving on costs by substituting between inputs.

The terminology in which we have described this process may be unfamiliar to a practising businessman, but the process of seeing whether or not the enterprise can effect a net saving in costs by substituting one input for another is certainly not. Businessmen are continually considering such questions as whether or not the introduction of a machine will save more on annual labour costs than the annual cost of the machine, or whether a different material may be substituted, or partly substituted, for another material with a net saving in costs. In this way, the enterprise's search for lower costs, or net cost savings, is likely to lead it to the least-cost combination of all inputs. Again, we should remind ourselves of the broader significance and desirability of this process, because economically efficient production brings the product into the reach of more people: that is, raises standards of living.

Having seen that there is a least-cost combination of inputs which depends upon the ratio of prices – upon relative prices – of the inputs and upon the isoquant itself, we can now examine the process of capital–labour substitution, or 'mechanisation' as it is loosely called. This is the first of our list of three ingredients in rising labour productivity (see p. 280). Historically, the tendency in most economies has been towards a rising cost of labour *relative* to the cost of capital; put the other way round, capital has tended to become relatively cheaper than labour. In a way we shall examine, this change in relative factor prices has been important in inducing mechanisation.

The historical record

We cannot here pause to demonstrate these assertions through an examination of economic history and the story of changes in technology, but the student in search of some muscles to articulate the economic-analytic skeleton of capital–labour substitution could read from among the following: David Landes, *The Unbound Prometheus: Technological Change and Industrial Development in Western Europe from 1750 to the Present* (Cambridge University Press, 1969); T. K. Derry and T. I. Williams, *A Short History of Technology* (Oxford University Press, 1960); H. J. Habakkuk, *American and British Technology in the Nineteenth Century: The*

Search for Labour-saving Inventions (Cambridge University Press, 1962); G. C. Allen, *The Industrial Development of Birmingham and the Black Country 1860–1927* (Frank Cass, 1966; 1st edn 1929); Barry Supple (ed.), *Essays in British Business History* (Oxford University Press, 1977); William Alexander and Arthur Street, *Metals in the Service of Man* (Penguin, 1979; 1st edn 1944). I mention these books because it is important for students of economics to have in mind the flesh-and-blood historical processes in the real world as a background to the rather abstract, theoretical paragraphs which follow.

Capital–labour substitution

Suppose that the price of labour per (index) unit rises from $p_L = £1,200$ per annum to $p_L' = £1,500$ per annum, while the price of capital remains constant at £750 per unit per annum (it would make no difference if the price of capital also rose slightly so long as it rose proportionately less than the rise in the price of labour; what matters is that the price of labour rises *relatively* to the price of capital). Diagram 7.5 reproduces the isoquant of Diagram 7.4, but we now have a different isocost line of:

$$K = \frac{C'}{750} - \frac{1,500}{750} \times L$$

Because the cost of labour has risen, we will now have to spend more on producing $\bar{Q} = 100$, and the question is: what is now the least-cost combination? Using calculus, we know that we have to be at that point on the isoquant where the marginal physical rate of substitution between capital and labour (the slope of the isoquant) is equal to the new price ratio (with a minus sign). That is:

$$\frac{\Delta K}{\Delta L} = - \frac{1,500}{750}$$

or:

$$-3 \times 100^4 \times L^{-4} = -2$$

Solving gives the least-cost labour input, L^*, for producing $\bar{Q} = 100$ as:

$$L^* = 110.668$$

and from the isoquant the corresponding capital input, K^*, is:

$$K^* = 73.779$$

The total cost of producing $\bar{Q} = 100$ is now $(£1,500 \times 110.668) + (£750 \times 73.779) = £221,336.25$, with a unit labour and capital combined cost of £2,213.36. (The student without calculus needs to demonstrate this either by arithmetic trial and error, or by drawing a graph.) This unit cost is the lowest which can be achieved

DIAGRAM 7.5   *Capital–labour substitution in response to changing relative factor prices*

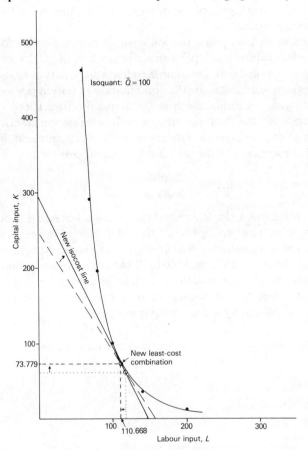

with the new set of prices; the new least-cost unit cost is, of course, higher than the previous least-cost unit cost; this is inescapable because the cost of the labour input has risen and it is not possible entirely to offset this (that is, the enterprise cannot cut back proportionately on its labour input *and at the same time not* expand its capital input while maintaining production at $\bar{Q} = 100$). Instead, because, at the old least-cost capital–labour combination (62.410 and 117.017), we now have a situation with the new price ratio, where:

$$\left|\frac{\Delta K}{\Delta L}\right| < \frac{p'_L}{p_K}$$

or:

$$|p_K \, \Delta K| < |p'_L \, \Delta L|$$

it pays the enterprise to substitute some (marginal) amount of the relatively cheaper capital for some (marginal) amount of the relatively more expensive labour, and so seek out a new capital–labour combination of 73.779 and 110.668 where no net cost savings can be made by further capital–labour substitution. So, the rise in the price of labour relative to the price of capital leads, via the search for the least-cost combination, to a substitution of capital for labour, or to 'mechanisation'. Note that at the new least-cost combination labour productivity is higher (Diagram 7.3), having increased from $100/117.017 = 0.855$ to $100/110.668 = 0.904$: this movement can be traced out along the production function in Diagram 7.3, so that the rise in labour productivity, at the least-cost combination, is due to the rise in the capital–labour ratio from 0.533 to 0.667. So mechanisation in response to changing relative factor prices increases labour productivity. This process is an important part of the skeleton of the Industrial Revolution and of subsequent economic progress.

To demonstrate this, we may pause to look again at the time-series data on output per worker in work and on capital stock per worker in work in the UK economy since 1871 (Appendix 1.3 and Diagram 1.10). Diagram 7.6 charts these data not as two separate time series but plotting the co-ordinates for the combination of output per worker and capital per worker in each year (omitting the first 1920 and the first 1960). There is a good correlation coefficient for the data: the square of the correlation coefficient is 0.962, so that 96.2 per cent of the variance in output per worker is 'explained' by the associated variance in capital per worker and the least-squares linear equation:

$$\frac{\text{Output per}}{\text{worker}} = 328.28 + 0.189 \times \frac{\text{Capital per}}{\text{worker}}$$

The points do not trace out a single production function because a production function represents (or should be taken to represent) the relationship between output per worker and capital per worker *in a given state of technology*, and it is clear that there has been much technological change between 1871 and 1980. These are therefore rather to be thought of as points on different production functions, which were probably shifting upwards over time. But it is quite clear that, however we may explain it, there is a close positive association between productivity and capital per worker.

DIAGRAM 7.6   *Labour productivity and capital per worker in the UK economy, 1871 to 1980*

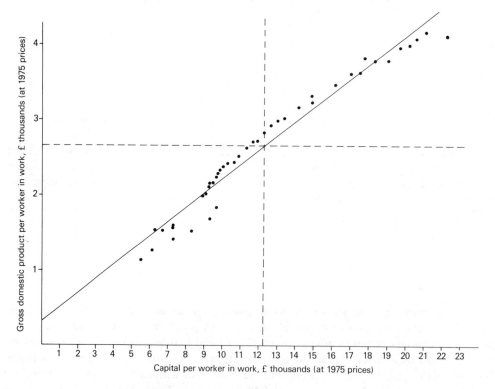

We may also reconsider the cross-section data on output per worker and capital per worker in the branches of the UK economy in 1971 (Table 1.14 and Diagram 1.11). Diagram 7.7 reproduces Diagram 1.11, but instead of fitting a straight line to the data, we can fit a form of the production function to give:

$$\text{Output per worker} = 237.19 \times \left(\text{Capital per worker}\right)^{0.254}$$

with a correlation coefficient squared of 0.675. It would, however, not be very sensible to treat this as a single production function because we are probably dealing with very different technologies in each of the branches of the economy: that is to say, the observation for each branch of the economy represents a point on a production function specific to that branch. But despite this, the diagram and the fitted function make it clear that, for cross-section data, there is a strong positive association between output per worker and capital per worker of a form which can be represented by a multiplicative production function.

DIAGRAM 7.7 *Output per worker and capital per worker in branches of the UK economy, 1971*

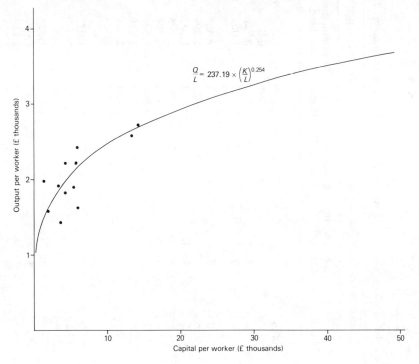

The purpose of capital–labour substitution is to economise on unit labour costs by increasing unit capital costs; unit labour costs are reduced because capital–labour substitution raises labour productivity. In the hypothetical example we considered, labour productivity, at the least-cost position, increased from $100/117.017 = 0.855$ to $100/110.668 = 0.904$, or by 5.7 per cent. The bigger the increase in labour productivity, the bigger the saving in unit labour cost. In the real world, increases in labour productivity resulting from capital–labour substitution have often been very much bigger than this. There is, unfortunately, very little hard data to demonstrate this, but we do have some detailed data on labour productivity and unit labour costs (but not, alas, on unit capital costs) in the US glass-making industry around 1925. These data are of more than mere historical interest because, although the earlier part of this century saw a great amount of capital–labour substitution, or 'mechanisation', it may well be that the advent of the micro-processor and 'robotics' will now bring similar productivity gains to many branches of industry.

Table 7.4 shows how the substitution from hand processes of manufacture through semi-automatic processes to automatic mechanised processes raised labour productivity

TABLE 7.4   *Impact on labour productivity and unit labour cost of capital–labour substitution in the US glass industry, 1925: twenty-nine products*

Item	Number produced per man-hour [a]			Labour cost per 'unit' $ [b]			Automatic machine unit labour cost as percentage of hand unit labour cost
	Hand [c]	Semi-automatic machine [d]	Automatic machine [e]	Hand	Semi-automatic machine	Automatic machine	
Bottles (unit cost per gross)							
¼ oz prescription ovals	102.8	—	3,617.3	0.940	—	0.028	3.0
2 oz prescription ovals	92.6	122.4	3,617.0	1.006	0.874	0.028	2.8
4 oz prescription ovals	77.2	114.8	3,172.0	1.177	0.720	0.032	2.7
8 oz prescription ovals	64.2	92.7	1,744.8	1.472	1.052	0.057	3.9
6 dram extract panels	82.2	—	2,365.9	1.170	—	0.046	3.9
2 oz extract panels	72.0	102.4	1,808.4	1.377	1.027	0.061	4.4
¼ pint sodas	56.6	72.7	929.2	1.622	1.299	0.108	6.7
¼ pint whisky dandies	64.2	94.8	495.9	1.382	1.042	0.142	10.3
1 pint whisky dandies	51.4	73.2	381.5	1.790	1.295	0.185	10.3
1 pint milk bottles	51.4	133.1	758.2	2.390	0.796	0.120	5.0
1 quart milk bottles	41.2	111.6	596.9	2.980	1.096	0.152	5.1
¼ gallon packer jugs	25.8	37.9	212.7	3.710	2.018	0.340	9.2
1 gallon packer jugs	20.6	29.1	167.8	5.150	2.784	0.431	8.4
5 gallon water carboys	3.7	—	37.9	25.308	—	1.880	7.4
Glasses and dishes (unit cost per 100)							
8–9 oz common tumblers	31.00	64.93	380.71	1.951	1.073	0.130	6.7
10 oz common tumblers	28.86	—	357.86	2.075	—	0.138	6.7
9–10 oz punch tumblers	25.69	—	364.57	1.900	—	0.133	7.0
4¼–5 inch dishes ('nappies')	39.61	58.71	300.87	1.718	1.053	0.148	8.6
6–7 inch dishes ('nappies')	27.37	45.69	134.39	2.549	1.418	0.338	13.3
3¼ oz dessert dishes ('sherbets')	33.55	58.21	274.10	1.806	1.147	0.162	9.0
4¼–5 oz dessert dishes ('sherbets')	30.45	41.66	192.00	1.917	1.721	0.246	12.8
Light bulbs (unit cost per 1,000)							
25 watt	56.19	116.06	1,699.22	13.044	4.197	0.471	3.6
40 watt	55.78	116.55	1,703.59	13.048	4.180	0.470	3.6

Lamp chimneys (unit cost per 100)							
Chimneys (No. 2 sun-crimped)	27.434	37.387	—	2.740	1.712	—	—
Pounds of glass tubing (unit cost per 100 lb)							
Sizes 19–21 (1,100 to 890 inches per lb)	9.957	—	58.932	6.905	—	1.281	18.6
Sizes 32–34 (270 to 216 inches per lb)	10.067	—	75.169	6.830	—	1.004	14.7
Boxes of window glass each containing 50 square feet (unit cost per box)							
Single-strength glass	0.709	1.654	1.851	0.955	0.407	0.299	31.3
Double-strength glass	0.561	0.972	1.280	1.320	0.699	0.433	32.8
Square feet of plate glass (unit cost per 100 square feet) (f)							
Rough plate glass	43.887	—	63.630	1.812	—	1.357	74.9
Polished plate glass (from rough plate)	7.664	—	12.300	10.397	—	6.939	66.7

(a) The units of output measurement for productivity refer to the first words of the italicised headings: for example, number of bottles; pounds of tubing; boxes of window glass. Output and labour hours data refer mostly to 1925, but some data refer to other years, especially for semi-automatic machinery, where data may be the totals (weighted averages) for earlier years. Labour input (hours and costs) refers only to the 'shop' workers directly engaged in production: for example, blowers, mould boys, etc., or machine foremen, machine operators, etc. All other workers are excluded.

(b) The 'units' of measurement are given in brackets in the italicised headings: e.g. labour costs per gross (12 dozen) of bottles; labour costs per 100 dishes; labour costs per *box* (50 square feet) of window glass. Labour costs are based on 1925 wage rates, regardless of year of output data; unit labour costs include piece-rate costs and time-rate costs. Again, costs refer only to 'shop' workers directly engaged in production; the term 'shop' refers to a group of workers such as two blowers, a finisher and assistants, or machine foreman, machine operator and assistants.

(c) Where hand methods were no longer used continuously, the figures given are the 'ideal' figures representing the concerted opinions of experienced bottle blowers, foreman and employers: the figures 'really show what a "shop" of three experienced blowers and four helpers could produce when working on any one kind of bottles for a complete eight-hour day without changing molds' and under favourable conditions (*Productivity of Labor in the Glass Industry* (see below), p. 45).

(d) Where data on more than one semi-automatic machine are given, priority is given to the process with *lowest* productivity (as representing the intermediate stage of capital–labour substitution).

(e) There were usually several varieties of automatic machine; the one with highest labour productivity is given in this column (as best representing the then most advanced stage of capital–labour substitution).

(f) 'Hand' methods here indicate the discontinuous process, and 'automatic' the continuous process; nor are the products distinct: rough plate glass is an intermediate input into polished plate glass.

Source: United States Department of Labor Bureau of Labor Statistics, *Productivity of Labor in the Glass Industry*, Bulletin No. 441, July 1927, prepared by B. Stern (US Government Printing Office, 1927) tables A, B, C, D, E, F, 8, 9; pp. 59–87, 101–9, 116, 128–31, 136, 144, 13, 14.

throughout the US glass industry. The increases in the volume of output per man-hour almost defy percentages: the man-hour productivity for small medicine-bottles ($\frac{1}{4}$ oz prescription ovals) rose from 102.8 bottles to 3,617.3 bottles, or by 3,419 per cent and for 4 oz prescription ovals productivity rose by 4,009 per cent!

Even a casual inspection of this table amply demonstrates that productivity increases were not only enormous but that they affected every single product. Using a consistent set of labour costs, we can see that these increases in productivity slashed unit labour costs in the automatic mechanised processes to very small fractions of the unit labour costs under hand processes. For example, the labour costs per 144 small prescription bottles was reduced from 94 cents to 2.8 cents and for 4 oz bottles unit labour costs (per gross) fell from 117.7 cents to 3.2 cents. Unfortunately, no data were collected on the cost of the capital equipment installed, so we do not know how great was the increase in unit capital costs required to obtain these reductions in unit labour costs. Accordingly, we do not know what happened to unit total costs, but it is obvious that such remarkable savings in unit labour costs were obtained only at the price of substantial increases in capital costs. The hand processes in producing bottles involved a skilled blower taking from the furnace an exact blob of molten glass on a tube and then blowing it while at the same time rolling and smoothing it before putting it into a mould held by a 'mould boy' to obtain its completed shape. The automatic machine – known as the Owens, after its inventor in 1904, M. J. Owens – was a system of ten rotating arms each carrying a number of moulds (usually six): as the arms rotated, each arm paused momentarily over the molten glass and by vacuum the moulds were filled with the exact quantity of glass; the moulds were then sealed and the bottles blown by compressed air:

> One of these machines blows 6 bottles at one time and thus throws out 60 bottles with each revolution. At the rate of four revolutions per minute, this machine throws out 240 bottles per minute, or almost as many bottles as a hand shop of 7 workmen could make in 20 minutes ... The average Owens machine requires one operator ... [and] a machinist or foreman is needed to adjust the speed of the machine ... he usually takes care of at least two machines. This is the total direct labour needed in attending an Owens machine (*Productivity of Labor in the Glass Industry*, p. 38).

Thus the saving in labour due to the introduction of machinery was considerable. There were also incidental welfare gains: prior to mechanisation in 1899, 14 per cent of the workers in the glass industry were children under 16 years of age, employed as assistants – e.g. 'mould boys' – to the skilled workers; the conditions of work – squatting close to the ground in temperatures over 100°F, and hand workers had to work next to the furnace – were appalling and injuries (mostly burns) were common. The need for such labour was all but eliminated by mechanisation, and by 1919 only 2 per cent of the glass industry's labour force were minors under 16 (*Productivity of Labor in the Glass Industry*, p. 24). The rising standard of living brought about by the search for profitability has dimensions other than simple increases in productivity and real wages.

It can be seen from Table 7.4 that the manufacture of plate glass was least affected by mechanisation, and indeed, radical advance here had to await the development of the Pilkington Float process in the 1950s (for which, see B. Supple (ed.), *Essays in British Business History*, Oxford University Press, 1977, ch. 10).

We shall subsequently return to capital–labour substitution, because it is clear that advances in technology usually require to be introduced through new capital equipment, but we must now go on to a consideration of economies of scale.

Economies of scale

The second of our ingredients which cause higher labour productivity is economies of large-scale production, or, alternatively, 'increasing returns to scale'. The term 'returns to scale' refers to what happens to output, according to a production function, when both (all) inputs are increased by the *same* proportion. Suppose we increase labour and capital inputs (and all other necessary inputs) by, say, 10 per cent. There are then three possibilities for the resulting change in output:

1. Output increases by more than 10 per cent: *'increasing returns'*.
2. Output increases by exactly 10 per cent: *'constant returns'*.
3. Output increases by less than 10 per cent: *'decreasing returns'*.

The terminology is reasonably self-evident; let us examine it formally using a production function.

We were working with a production function of the form:

$$Q = ZL^aK^b$$

Suppose we increase both labour and capital inputs by 10 per cent, i.e. multiply them by 1.10, to get the new levels of labour and capital inputs:

$$L' = 1.10L$$
$$K' = 1.10K$$

What then happens to the new level of output Q' compared with Q defines the situation regarding economies of scale:

$$Q' = ZL'^aK'^b$$
$$= Z(1.10L)^a(1.10K)^b$$
$$= 1.10^{a+b}ZL^aK^b$$
$$= 1.10^{a+b}Q$$

whence:

$$\frac{Q'}{Q} = 1.10^{a+b}$$

Now, for any number greater than 1, we have: if it is raised to the power 1, then it remains the same; if to a power greater than 1, then it increases; if to a power less than 1, then it decreases. So that:

1. If $a + b > 1$, output increases by more than 10 per cent.
2. If $a + b = 1$, output increases by exactly 10 per cent.
3. If $a + b < 1$, output increases by less than 10 per cent.

So, in the Cobb–Douglas production function, the sum of the exponents indicates the situation regarding returns to scale. We have been working so far with a constant returns to scale production function ($a = 0.75$, $b = 0.25$, $a + b = 1$).

Having defined 'returns to scale' we now need to examine its implications for the economic analysis of production. Because increasing returns to scale tends to be an important economic force (historically and contemporary), we shall examine this case in detail.

The important economic consequence of increasing returns to scale is that *both* the labour requirement per unit of output and the capital requirement per unit of output decrease if the scale of output increases; in other words (and given that input prices remain unchanged), the (least-cost) unit labour and capital cost combined decreases as the quantity of output increases. In order to analyse this, we need one more theoretical concept, that of the *unit isoquant*.

The unit isoquant

The unit isoquant gives, not the total requirements for labour and capital to produce a given level of output, but the requirements for labour per unit of output and for capital per unit of output to produce (of course) one unit of output. Table 7.5 shows the isoquants for $\bar{Q} = 100$ (reproduced from Table 7.3) and for $\bar{Q} = 200$; from these we may derive the unit isoquants by dividing each total labour input and total capital input by 100 or by 200. It will be seen that, under the production function used, which is one of constant returns to scale (i.e. $0.75 + 0.25 = 1.00$), the two unit isoquants are identical; in other words, unit labour requirements, $L/\bar{Q}$, and unit capital requirements, $K/\bar{Q}$, are *not* affected by the scale of output, and this is true whatever the scale of output.

TABLE 7.5   *The derivation of a unit isoquant under constant returns to scale* [a]

Isoquant to produce $\bar{Q} = 100$		Unit isoquant when $\bar{Q} = 100$ [b]		Isoquant to produce $\bar{Q} = 200$		Unit isoquant when $\bar{Q} = 200$ [b]	
L	K	$\dfrac{L}{\bar{Q}}$	$\dfrac{K}{\bar{Q}}$	L	K	$\dfrac{L}{\bar{Q}}$	$\dfrac{K}{\bar{Q}}$
100	100	1.00	1.0000	200	200	1.00	1.0000
60	462.96	0.60	4.6296	120	925.92	0.60	4.6296
70	291.55	0.70	2.9155	140	583.09	0.70	2.9155
80	195.31	0.80	1.9531	160	390.63	0.80	1.9531
117.017	**62.410**	**1.17**	**0.6241**	**234.034**	**124.82**	**1.17**	**0.6241**
120	57.87	1.20	0.5787	240	115.74	1.20	0.5787
140	36.44	1.40	0.3644	280	72.89	1.40	0.3644
200	12.50	2.00	0.1250	400	25.00	2.00	0.1250

[a] From the production function $Q = L^{0.75} K^{0.25}$; whence, for $\bar{Q} = $ constant, the isoquant is:

$$K = \bar{Q}^{\frac{1}{0.25}} L^{-\frac{0.75}{0.25}} = \bar{Q}^4 L^{-3}$$

[b] The unit isoquant is derived by dividing the points on the 'total isoquant' by the relevant output, $\bar{Q}$.

This unchanging unit isoquant is drawn in Diagram 7.8. It is instructive to see that the least-cost combination of labour and capital input can be determined according to the isocost line for a unit of output. The combined labour and capital cost per unit of output is:

$$\frac{C}{\bar{Q}} = p_L \left(\frac{L}{\bar{Q}}\right) + p_K \left(\frac{K}{\bar{Q}}\right)$$

whence the unit isocost line is:

$$\frac{K}{\bar{Q}} = \frac{C/\bar{Q}}{p_K} - \frac{p_L}{p_K} \times \frac{L}{\bar{Q}}$$

so that the slope of the isocost line is, as before, the negative of the ratio of the price of labour to the price of capital, $-p_L/p_K$. The condition for minimum unit cost production is to be at that point on the unit isoquant which is tangential to (just touches) the (lowest) unit isocost line. The formula for the unit isoquant may be simply derived from the production function for $\bar{Q}$:

$$\bar{Q} = L^a K^b$$

$$K = \bar{Q}^{\frac{1}{b}} L^{-\frac{a}{b}}$$

(using $X^{-y} = 1/X^y$). From this the unit isoquant may be derived by (a) dividing through by $\bar{Q}$, and (b) obtaining an appropriate term in $L/\bar{Q}$:

$$\frac{K}{\bar{Q}} = \bar{Q}^{\frac{1}{b}} \bar{Q}^{-1} L^{-\frac{a}{b}}$$

$$= \bar{Q}^{\frac{1}{b}} \bar{Q}^{-1} L^{-\frac{a}{b}} \bar{Q}^{\frac{a}{b}} \bar{Q}^{-\frac{a}{b}}$$

$$= \bar{Q}^{\frac{1}{b}} \bar{Q}^{-1} \bar{Q}^{-\frac{a}{b}} \left(\frac{L}{\bar{Q}}\right)^{-\frac{a}{b}}$$

$$= \bar{Q}^{\frac{1}{b}-1-\frac{a}{b}} \left(\frac{L}{\bar{Q}}\right)^{-\frac{a}{b}}$$

DIAGRAM 7.8   *Unit isoquant (invariant under constant returns to scale)*

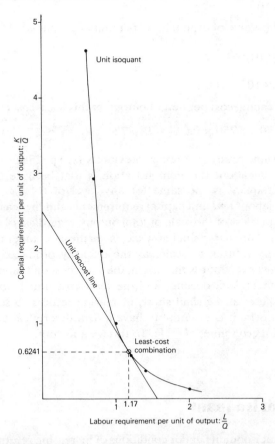

In the case of the production function where $a = 0.75$ and $b = 0.25$, $(1/b) - 1 - (a/b) = 0$, and anything raised to the power zero is equal to 1, so in this case the unit isoquant is (conveniently):

$$\frac{K}{\bar{Q}} = \left(\frac{L}{\bar{Q}}\right)^{-\frac{0.75}{0.25}} = \left(\frac{L}{\bar{Q}}\right)^{-3}$$

and the slope of the unit isoquant is:

$$\frac{\Delta(K/\bar{Q})}{\Delta(L/\bar{Q})} = -3\left(\frac{L}{\bar{Q}}\right)^{-3-1}$$

$$= -3\left(\frac{L}{\bar{Q}}\right)^{-4}$$

The larger the value of $L/\bar{Q}$, the smaller the slope of (the less steep is) the unit isoquant (as can be seen in Diagram 7.8).

If the ratio of prices is £1,200/£750 = 1.6, we need that point on the unit isoquant where:

$$-3\left(\frac{L}{\bar{Q}}\right)^{-4} = -1.6$$

whence the required value of $L/\bar{Q}$ which minimises unit costs, $(L/\bar{Q})^*$, is:

$$\left(\frac{L}{\bar{Q}}\right)^* = \left(\frac{-3}{-1.6}\right)^{\frac{1}{4}}$$

$$= 1.17017$$

and the corresponding value of capital input per unit of output is:

$$\left(\frac{K}{\bar{Q}}\right)^* = (1.17017)^{-3}$$

$$= 0.62410$$

And the labour and capital cost per unit of output, at this least-cost combination, is:

$$£1,200 \times 1.170 + £750 \times 0.624 = £1,872$$

which is exactly the same result as obtained previously (see p. 288).

The important point about this demonstration is that because, for this production function, the unit isoquant is the same for any level of total output, the least-cost combination of unit labour and unit capital requirements and the least-cost total unit cost remain the same, regardless of the scale of total output, regardless of whether $\bar{Q} = 100$ or $\bar{Q} = 200$ or whatever. This, as we shall now see, is *not* the case under increasing returns to scale. With increasing returns to scale, as the quantity produced increases, the unit isoquant shifts downwards towards the origin, the least-cost unit labour requirement and unit capital requirement *both* decline, and the least-cost unit labour and capital cost combined falls. Because, as we shall show, increasing returns to scale is an important feature of the real world, it is essential to have a firm theoretical understanding of the impact on unit costs of economies of scale. To this we now turn.

Shifts in the unit isoquant

In order to derive unit isoquants under conditions of increasing returns to scale, we need a production function which shows increasing returns to scale. I shall use the following production function:

$$Q = ZL^{0.9}K^{0.3}$$

Because $a + b = 0.9 + 0.3 = 1.2$ this function is characterised by increasing returns, as we have defined the term. Specifically, if labour and capital were both to be increased by 10 per cent, output would increase by a factor of:

$$(1.10)^{1.2} = 1.121$$

that is to say, output would increase by 12.1 per cent. Because the exponents of this functiion do not add to 1, if we are to measure outputs and inputs in index values with a base of 100, then we cannot dispense with an adjustment factor, Z, which makes the following relation hold (for the base values):

$$100 = Z \times 100^{0.9} \times 100^{0.3}$$

The value of Z which does this is 0.398107, so the production function now is:

$$Q = 0.398107 L^{0.9} K^{0.3}$$

Table 7.6 shows in the first two columns the isoquant derived from this production function for $\bar{Q} = 100$. This isoquant is the same as the isoquant for $\bar{Q} = 100$ under the constant returns to scale production function and consequently, for $\bar{Q} = 100$, the unit isoquant is also the same. (The fact that the starting positions are the same has been artificially contrived, for the purpose of facilitating comparison, by increasing each exponent of the production function in the same proportion.)

TABLE 7.6   *Unit isoquants under increasing returns to scale* [a]

Isoquant to produce $\bar{Q} = 100$		Unit isoquant when $\bar{Q} = 100$		Isoquant to produce $\bar{Q} = 200$		Unit isoquant when $\bar{Q} = 200$	
L	K	$\dfrac{L}{\bar{Q}}$	$\dfrac{K}{\bar{Q}}$	L	K	$\dfrac{L}{\bar{Q}}$	$\dfrac{K}{\bar{Q}}$
100	100	1.00	1.0000	200	125.99	1.00	0.6300
60	462.96	0.60	4.6296	120	583.30	0.60	2.9165
70	291.55	0.70	2.9155	140	367.32	0.70	1.8366
80	195.31	0.80	1.9531	160	246.08	0.80	1.2304
117.017	**62.410**	**1.17**	**0.6241**	**234.034**	**78.632**	**1.17**	**0.3932**
120	57.87	1.20	0.5787	240	72.91	1.20	0.3646
140	36.44	1.40	0.3644	280	45.92	1.40	0.2296
200	12.50	2.00	0.1250	400	15.75	2.00	0.0787

[a] From the production function $Q = 0.398107 L^{0.9} K^{0.3}$; whence, for $\bar{Q}$ = constant:

$$K = 0.398107^{-\frac{1}{0.3}} \, \bar{Q}^{\frac{1}{0.3}} \, L^{-\frac{0.9}{0.3}}$$

$$= \left(\frac{\bar{Q}}{0.398107}\right)^{\frac{1}{0.3}} L^{-3}$$

If we now derive the unit isoquant for $\bar{Q} = 200$, we get the figures shown in the seventh and eighth columns of Table 7.6: we use the same L figures as in Table 7.5, but the $K/\bar{Q}$ figures are now different *and lower*. (If we had used in Table 7.6 the same K figures for $\bar{Q} = 200$ as in Table 7.5, the $L/\bar{Q}$ figures would have been different *and lower*.) Consequently the unit isoquant for $\bar{Q} = 200$ is different under increasing returns from the unit isoquant for $\bar{Q} = 200$ under constant returns. (The algebra and the arithmetic formula for the unit isoquants under increasing returns are given in Appendix 7.1.)

Diagram 7.9, using the figures of Table 7.6, shows what happens to the unit isoquant under increasing returns to scale: it shifts inwards (downwards) towards the origin; if we were to construct the unit isoquant for $\bar{Q} = 300$, that would again be further in towards the origin. The position of the whole unit isoquant now depends upon the scale of production.

DIAGRAM 7.9   *Unit isoquants (shifting under increasing returns to scale)*

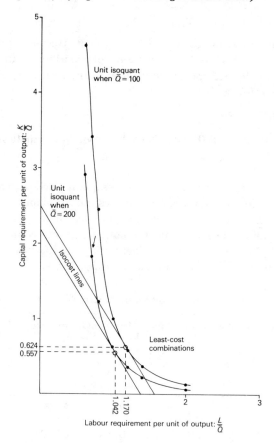

From this it follows that the least-cost combination of labour and capital inputs per unit of output changes with the scale of production: specifically, unit labour requirement and unit capital requirement (at the least-cost combination and given an unchanged price ratio) *both* fall. If $\bar{Q} = 100$, the least-cost combination is the same as it was under constant returns (with a price ratio of £1,200/£750 = 1.6). In Table 7.6 unit labour requirement is 1.170 and unit capital requirement is 0.624, so the least-cost unit cost is (at this scale of output):

$$£1,200 \times 1.170 + £750 \times 0.624 = £1,872$$

But, and this is the important point, if the scale of output rises to $\bar{Q} = 200$, the least-cost combination of labour and capital input per unit of output becomes:

$$\left(\frac{L}{\bar{Q}}\right)^* = 1.042; \quad \left(\frac{K}{\bar{Q}}\right)^* = 0.557$$

(The algebra for this is given in Appendix 7.1.) The least-cost unit cost for the scale of output $\bar{Q} = 200$ is accordingly:

$$(£1,200 \times 1.042) + (£750 \times 0.557) = £1,668.15$$

So, as a result of doubling the scale of output under these conditions of increasing returns to scale, the least-cost unit cost has fallen by:

$$\frac{1,668.15}{1,872.00} = 0.891$$

or by 10.9 per cent. So we can represent the economic impact of increasing returns to scale in Table 7.7. Because of the awkwardness of comparing absolute money values of the least-cost unit cost, we may put the least-cost unit cost into index form, as in the last row of Table 7.7. From this last row we can see that the enterprise which produces at a scale of output of $\bar{Q} = 200$ will have a 10.9 per cent labour and capital cost advantage over an enterprise which produces at a scale of output of $\bar{Q} = 100$. Obviously, this has considerable economic implications, in that the enterprise producing on a larger scale will be able to charge lower prices (and still be as profitable); so the larger enterprise should be able to take business away from its smaller competitor; and in the long run the prospects for the economic survival of the smaller enterprise look bleak.

TABLE 7.7   *Theoretical representation of increasing returns to scale*

	Scale of output	
	100	200
Least-cost unit labour requirement: $\left(\dfrac{L}{\bar{Q}}\right)^*$	1.170	1.042
Least-cost unit capital requirement: $\left(\dfrac{K}{\bar{Q}}\right)^*$	0.624	0.557
Least-cost unit labour and capital cost, £	1,872.00	1,668.15
Index of least-cost unit labour and capital cost	100	89.1

Empirical data on economies of scale

There is empirical evidence that increasing returns to scale are quite prevalent in manufacturing industry. Table 7.8 shows some of the data published by C. F. Pratten in his valuable book *Economies of Scale in Manufacturing Industry* (Cambridge University Press, 1971). This table gives the real-world counterparts to the scale of output and to the last row of Table 7.7.

In most cases the decline in unit costs between the smallest and largest capacity is quite substantial. In the theoretical example through which we have just worked a doubling in the scale of output led to a 10.9 per cent decline in labour and capital costs per unit of output; in Pratten's data doubling the scale of initial output causes declines in unit costs ranging from 28 per cent (bakeries) and 25 per cent (oil refining) to about 4 per cent (sulphuric acid) and 2 per cent (diesel engines). So the theoretical example of Table 7.7 is quite realistic, and we can, on the basis of the sixteen examples in Table 7.8, which cover quite a wide range of industries, accept Pratten's conclusion that 'there are important economies of scale in many industries' (*Economies of Scale*, p. 313). The implications of this conclusion are manifold and far-reaching: enterprises producing on a larger scale should be able to produce at lower cost; expansion of markets (such as joining the EEC) should assist enterprises to reduce costs; 'aggressive' pricing policies of keeping prices as low as possible and thereby producing and selling at maximum output may be indicated by economies of scale; increasing returns to scale may well be an important part of economic growth, and may help to economise on scarce factors of production. However, we have not the space fully to explore all these economic consequences of increasing returns.

TABLE 7.8   *Sixteen examples of increasing returns to scale*

Oil refining

Refinery capacity, million tons crude oil p.a.	1	2	5	10	20
Index of refinery costs per ton (excl. crude oil) [a]	100	75	56	44	40

Cement works

Works capacity, thousand tons cement p.a.	100	200	500	1,000	2,000
Index of unit labour and capital costs [b]	100	80	69	58	49

Crude steel

Plant output, thousand tons of iron p.a.	250	1,000	2,000	5,000	10,000
Index of total costs per ton (incl. materials)	100	80	75	73	72

Cylinder block foundry

Foundry output, thousand tons p.a.	10	25	50	100	200
Index of combined labour and capital costs per unit of output [c]	100	86	74	69	65

Motor-vehicles (three basic bodies with variants)

Factory output, thousands of cars p.a.	100	250	500	1,000	2,000
Index of labour and all capital costs per vehicle [d]	100	73	61	54	49

Footwear

Plant capacity, pairs of shoes per day	300	600	1,200	2,400	4,800
Index of unit labour and overhead costs	100	94	90	87	85

Beer brewing

Brewery capacity, thousand barrels p.a.	100	200	500	1,000
Index of unit labour and capital costs [b]	100	77	43	28

Diesel engines (25–100 brake horse power)

Plant capacity, number of engines p.a.	1,000	2,000	5,000	100,000
Index of labour and capital costs per engine	100	98	96	58

Machine-tool (standard model)

Factory output, number of machines tools p.a.	10	50	100	800
Index of ex-factory cost per machine-tool [e]	100	55	49	39

Domestic electrical appliances

Factory output, thousands of units p.a.	10	50	150	500
Index of unit labour and capital costs [b] [f]	100	90	85	75

Polymerisation plants (nylon, polyester)

Plant capacity, thousand tons p.a.	4	20	40	80
Index of costs per ton (excl. materials)	100	81	57	41

Sulphuric acid

Plant capacity, thousand tons p.a.	100	250	500	1,000
Index of total costs per ton (incl. materials)	100	96	94	93

Synthetic fibre

Plant capacity, thousand tons of yarn p.a.	4	15	40
Index of unit costs (excl. materials)	100	91	78

Ethylene plants

Plant output, thousand tons p.a.	100	200	300
Index of labour and depreciation costs per ton	100	80	64

Bakeries

Oven capacity in sacks of flour per hour	9.5	19.0	28.5
Index of capital and labour costs per unit of output [g]	100	72	54

Bricks (tunnel kilns)

Capacity, million bricks p.a.	10	25
Index of labour and capital costs per thousand bricks	100	66

[a] Refinery costs include works fuel.
[b] Index of value added per unit of output.
[c] Using the weighting of 15/55 for the unit capital cost index and 40/55 for the unit labour cost index.
[d] Including initial costs per vehicle; initial costs comprise initial tooling costs (particularly for body pressings), costs of design, building of prototypes, and other costs associated with the introduction of a new model.
[e] Including initial costs per machine-tool.
[f] Excluding the costs of tooling: based on plants of different vintages: 'if economies of scale for factories equipped with new machinery were calculated, they could well show appreciably larger economies of scale' (Pratten, *Economies of Scale*, p. 212).
[g] Using the cost structure on p. 78 to weight the indices of unit capital and labour costs: 18/33 and 15/33 respectively; oven capacity and index values taken at mid-point of range given.

Sources: C. F. Pratten, *Economies of Scale in Manufacturing Industry*, Cambridge University Press, 1971 (sources in sequence, except for footwear): table 4.2, p. 35; table 10.5, p. 92; table 12.2, p. 105; table 13.3, p. 129; table 14.4, p. 142; table 7.3, p. 75; p. 183; table 17.5, p. 173; table 21.5, p. 212; table 6.4, p. 65; p. 50; table 6.5, p. 66; table 5.2, p. 47; table 8.3, p. 79 and cost structure p. 78; table 11.3, p. 99; footwear from C. Pratten, R. M. Dean and A. Silberston, *The Economies of Large-scale Production in British Industry: An Introductory Study*, Cambridge University Press, 1965, table 3.9, p. 53.

Some reasons for economies of scale

What causes increasing returns to scale? Many things, apparently. One simple reason is that if one is incurring the capital costs of constructing a container, the materials required do not expand in proportion to the volume of the container: for example, a box of 1 cubic foot (1 foot by 1 foot by 1 foot) requires 6 square feet of metal; a box 2 feet by 2 feet by 2 feet provides 8 cubic feet for 24 square feet of metal: increasing cubic capacity eightfold has increased material (capital) costs only fourfold. Much fixed capital is in the general form of containers: distillation towers in oil refineries; furnaces in steel production; ovens in bakeries; kilns in brick-making. Annual production in these cases is related to cubic capacity, so that capital costs either in the form of initial investment per unit of output or in the form of depreciation charges per unit output will be lower the greater the scale of output. A practical example occurs in the production of iron from iron ore: commenting on Japan's development of very large blast furnaces, William Alexander and Arthur Street say, in *Metals in the Service of Man*:

An important economic factor in running a blast-furnace, and indeed any process, is to achieve maximum output with minimum breakdown time. The really costly breakdown in a blast furnace involves re-lining, which is made necessary by the attack of the molten cascade of iron and slag descending the furnace and the red-hot air blast hurricaning up it. This is related to the surface area of the furnace lining; but quadrupling the volume of any container involves only doubling the inner surface area, so the bigger blast furnace will be expected to give less breakdown cost per tonne of iron produced than the smaller furnace (p. 52).

Another reason for economies of scale in capital costs is that certain pieces of equipment may not need to be (greatly) altered if capacity is increased: the carrying capacity of a lorry can be increased without increasing the cost of the gearbox, the drive-shaft, or the number of wheels and axles. This sort of situation occurs quite frequently. Another cause of reduced costs per unit is that the enterprise may have to incur considerable development and start-up costs, and if these indivisible lump-sum costs are spread over a greater volume of production the unit costs are thereby reduced.

Economies of scale are not confined to capital costs; they also affect labour costs. In many process plants it is possible to handle a greater volume of production with a less than proportionate increase in labour input: 'In the process industries we have shown that the labour required to man plants increases very slowly as the scale of plants is increased' (Pratten, *Economies of Scale*, p. 282). Obviously one would not need to double the number of workers at an oil refinery if one doubled the scale of output; nor does one double the number of lorry-drivers if the capacity of the lorry doubles. Also, the labour cost in 'set up' time or in design work is not proportionately increased with the scale of output.

Most of the figures in Table 7.8 exclude materials costs per unit of output: 'economies for these costs are generally small compared to those for other costs' (Pratten, *Economies of Scale*, p. 282). Clearly, one cannot increase output from an oil refinery without increasing in equal proportion the input of crude oil. There may be some scope for such things as savings in fuel costs or, if the producers of the enterprise's bought-in materials themselves enjoy economies of scale, for obtaining some reductions in the price of bought-in components.

Practical consequences of economies of scale

Some of the figures gathered by Pratten show these influences clearly. Let us consider three examples to strengthen our understanding of the real-world forces leading to economies of scale.

First, Table 7.9 shows the details of costs for ethylene production at three different scales of output. (Ethylene is a gas which by undergoing 'polymerisation' becomes polyethylene, which you will encounter as sheets for wrapping or packets (frozen foods) or 'plastic' containers (the 'plastic' is polyethylene). Polymerisation is the process whereby many molecules are united (often by heat and pressure but also by other processes) to give a molecule (polymer) with different physical properties. In reaction with chemicals, ethylene is used in the manufacture of detergents, paints, antifreeze, synthetic rubber, and plastics proper.) It cost (in terms of the prices prevailing in the early 1960s, to which these data refer) £8.4 million to set up an ethylene plant with a capacity for producing 100,000 tons of ethylene a year; if the plant capacity were increased by 100 per cent to be twice as big, the cost of the fixed capital does not double (to £16.8 million) but increases by only 61 per cent to £13.5 million – this is probably the consequence of the sort of factors we have mentioned, and it results in quite considerable reductions in the fixed capital costs per ton of annual capacity (third row of Table 7.9).

TABLE 7.9   *The structure of increasing returns to scale in ethylene production*

Scale of ethylene plant, thousand tons p.a.	100	200	300
Investment costs			
Plant and off-site facilities, £ million	8.4	13.5	16.6
Fixed capital investment per ton capacity, £	84.0	67.5	55.3
Operating costs per ton of ethylene			
Feedstock costs and chemicals and utilities, £	41.2	41.2	41.2
Operating labour, supervision and maintenance labour, £	3.5	2.7	2.1
Depreciation on fixed capital, £	8.4	6.8	5.5
Interest at 10 per cent on finance for fixed and working capital, £	6.7	5.5	4.6
Total operating costs, £	59.8	56.2	53.4
less Value of all by-products, £	28.6	27.4	26.3
equals Average cost per ton of ethylene, £	31.2	28.8	27.1
Index of unit labour cost	100	77	60
Index of unit capital costs (depreciation but not interest)	100	81	65
Index of unit labour and capital costs (excluding interest)	100	80	64
Index of average cost per ton (allowing for by-products)	100	92	87

Source: C. F. Pratten, *Economies of Scale in Manufacturing Industry*, Cambridge University Press, 1971, table 5.2, p. 47.

There appears to be no scope for economies of scale in the use of feedstock materials; unit materials costs are constant at £41.2 per ton over all scales of output. But there are economies of scale in the use of labour: although the total labour costs increase with increasing scale, they increase less than the proportionate increase in output, and so unit labour costs decline from £3.5 per ton when $\bar{Q} = 100,000$ tons to £2.1 per ton when $\bar{Q} = 300,000$ tons. Following the reduced initial investment costs per ton, the annual depreciation charges per ton (the flow of capital costs, excluding interest) also decline with increasing scale of output: from £8.4 per ton at $\bar{Q} = 100,000$ tons to £5.5 per ton at $\bar{Q} = 300,000$ tons. Although combined unit labour and capital costs decline by 36 per cent if the scale of output is trebled (from an index value of 100 to 64), the decline in effective production costs per unit (allowing for the value of by-products) is only 13 per cent (from 100 to 87). This is because there are no economies of scale in materials costs, which form the largest proportion of costs, and, of course, increasing returns over all is a weighted average of the increasing returns to each of the inputs. (The value of by-products must be deducted; effectively, the value of by-products amounts to a recovery of (reduction in) the cost of materials input to ethylene production considered alone.)

Using the figures of Table 7.9 we can explore the sort of economic impact that increasing returns to scale are likely to have on enterprises. Suppose plants were to (try to) price their products on the basis of a 25 per cent mark-up on unit production costs. Because unit production costs vary with the scale of plant, this would (theoretically) give rise to three different prices for ethylene, as shown in the third row of Table 7.10.

TABLE 7.10 *Possible economic consequences of increasing returns to scale in ethylene production: impact on profitability*

Scale of ethylene plant, thousand tons p.a.	100	200	300
Unit production cost per ton, £ [a]	31.2	28.8	27.1
Price per ton at 25 per cent mark-up, £	39.0	36.0	33.88
'Competitive' price (established by cheapest producer), £	33.88	33.88	33.88
Total gross margin at 'competitive' price, £ thousands p.a. [b]	268	1,016	2,034
Total gross margin p.a. as percentage of initial investment costs: 'profitability', per cent [c]	3.2	7.5	12.3

[a] Including interest charges at 10 per cent, and allowing for (deducting) the value of by-products.

[b] Calculated as:

$$\left(\begin{array}{l}\text{'Competitive'} \\ \text{price}\end{array} - \begin{array}{l}\text{Unit production} \\ \text{cost}\end{array}\right) \times \begin{array}{l}\text{Scale of} \\ \text{output}\end{array}$$

[c] Initial investment cost in second row of Table 7.9.

Source: Table 7.9.

In practice, the small-scale plant is unlikely to be able to sell its output if larger-scale plants are offering *the same* product at a cheaper price. Let us suppose, therefore, that the largest-scale enterprise establishes a 'competitive' price of £33.88 per ton which is charged by all enterprises. The consequence of this is that the gross margins of the smaller-scale plants are 'squeezed' by the effects of price competition from the larger-scale plant; and, taking total gross margins in relation to initial capital stock invested, the smaller-scale plants show a very much reduced rate of profit (last row of Table 7.10). Because of this, one may expect small-scale plants eventually to disappear. In some industries, smaller-scale plants may be able to produce a 'better' product, say in terms of quality; in this case, the smaller-scale plants can charge a premium for quality (or whatever) and so can get away with a pricing structure as per the second row of Table 7.10; but, then, the plants are not (strictly speaking) producing 'the same' product. It is reasonably common to find small-scale 'specialist' producers (either or both a special product or special production process) in industries where one would expect economies of scale to operate. So we cannot conclude from Table 7.10 that small-scale producers inevitably disappear, only that special conditions must intervene to enable them to survive. Such special conditions do exist: the Campaign for Real Ale enables small-scale breweries with a 'better' product to sell their beer despite its higher cost; Pratten shows that transport costs (a factor we have not discussed, but whose impact is reasonably self-evident) intervene to protect smaller brickworks, which may also survive on the basis of producing special or 'local-style' bricks. And Rolls-Royce have managed to be profitable in motor-vehicles production despite their relatively small scale of output.

The second example concerns the production of cars. Table 7.11 shows Pratten's figures for the production costs of motor-cars (a range of similar models, i.e. variations on a 'standard' model), assuming a production run of four years. The important feature of this example is the effect of scale of output on 'initial costs'. The main initial costs are the costs of establishing the requisite fixed capital equipment, or 'tooling up', the cost of design, and the cost of building and testing prototypes. The scale of production has but little effect on total initial costs: if annual output capacity increases tenfold from 100,000 cars to 1 million cars, initial costs increase only twofold from £40 million to £80 million (at the prices then prevailing). If we assume that the production run is for four years, then these initial costs are spread over four times the annual production (i.e. the total number of vehicles produced), and there is, as shown in the third row of Table 7.11, a marked impact of

TABLE 7.11   *The structure of increasing returns to scale in motor-car production: economies of scale in initial costs*

	100	250	500	1,000	2,000
Output of cars, thousand cars p.a. (for 4 years)	100	250	500	1,000	2,000
Initial costs for model, £ million	40	50	60	80	110
Costs per car produced over 4-year run					
Initial costs, £	100	50	30	20	14
Materials and bought-in components, £	290	270	255	247	240
Labour (direct and indirect), £	120	100	92	87	84
Capital charges for fixed and working capital, £	75	65	58	53	48
Total ex-works cost, £	585	485	435	407	386
Index of unit initial costs	100	50	30	20	14
Index of unit materials, etc., costs	100	93	88	85	83
Index of unit labour costs	100	83	77	73	70
Index of unit capital costs	100	87	77	71	64
Index of unit ex-works cost	100	83	74	70	66

Source: C. F. Pratten, *Economies of Scale in Manufacturing Industry*, Cambridge University Press, 1971, table 14.4, p. 142.

increasing returns to scale on initial costs per vehicle produced (which is the cost which has to form part of the price if the initial costs are to be 'recovered'): at an output of 100,000 cars per annum (for four years) initial costs per vehicle are £100; at an output of 2 million cars per annum they are only £14 per vehicle. This alone helps the larger-scale producer to a substantial price advantage.

This sort of situation, where large initial or development costs have to be recovered, is reasonably common (jet engines and Rolls-Royce's problems with the RB211 engine come to mind), and so it is important to appreciate its role in economies of scale. In Table 7.11 note also that there are economies of scale in unit materials costs, as was not the case for ethylene production. This is probably due to the fact that suppliers of bought-in components themselves enjoy economies of scale and so they can pass on some or all of this to the car manufacturer. Economies of scale in the use of capital are due to various technical factors, including the ability to utilise capital more fully when the throughput of vehicles is higher. It is interesting to note that, even in this production industry (as opposed to the process industry exemplified by ethylene production or oil refining), there is scope for substantial economies of scale in the use of labour, part of which seems to arise from the fact that the greater the volume of production the more it 'pays' to substitute capital for labour: for example (but not at the date of Pratten's survey), to use computers to control the production line. Over all, then, the largest-scale producer of motor-vehicles could, on the basis of Pratten's figures, offer a price advantage of 34 per cent (386/585 = 0.66) over the smallest-scale producer in a market which is very sensitive to price differences. This fact is not unconnected on the one hand with the success of Japanese car manufacturers and on the other hand with the lack of success of some European car manufacturers.

The third and final example of economies of scale concerns possible increasing returns to the use of fuel. Obviously, as energy prices rise relatively to all other prices, this becomes correspondingly more important. Furthermore, economies of scale in the use of fuel were historically, and are still, important in the generation of electricity. Table 7.12 shows Pratten's figures, 'from a very reliable source' (*Economies of Scale*, p. 99), for the costs of brick production at two different scales of output: 10 million and 25 million bricks per annum. Note the fact that the cost of the kilns – basically a 'container' costed by square feet in which the bricks are fired – increases much less than in proportion to the increase in output (bascially dependent on cubic capacity): so investment cost in kilns alone per unit of 1,000 bricks declines from £12.5 to £8 with the increase in scale. Note also that the 'associated works' (mainly for clay preparation, moulding and handling) benefit from

TABLE 7.12   *The structure of increasing returns to scale in brick production: economies of scale in fuel*

	10	25
Capacity of (tunnel) kilns, million bricks p.a.	10	25
Investment costs		
Kiln alone, £ thousands	125	200
Associated works, £ thousands	59	96
Total investment, £ thousands	184	296
Kiln cost per thousand bricks, £	12.5	8.0
Associated works cost per thousand bricks, £	5.9	3.84
Operating costs per thousand bricks		
Fuel and power, £	1.78	1.50
Labour, £	1.27	0.86
Capital charges at 15 per cent of initial fixed capital cost, £	2.76	1.78
Total operating cost (excl. materials), £	5.81	4.14
Index of unit fuel and power cost	100	84
Index of unit labour cost	100	68
Index of unit capital cost	100	64
Index of unit total cost (excl. materials)	100	71
Total number of employees required (estimate of 1947)	33	66
Labour productivity, thousand bricks p.a. per employee (1947)	303	379

Source: C. F. Pratten, *Economies of Scale in Manufacturing Industry*, Cambridge University Press, 1971, table 11.3, pp. 98, 99.

increasing returns to scale, and that labour costs do likewise: 'it is possible for operatives to control a number of extrusion lines, pressing machines, etc., simultaneously. Similarly it would not be necessary to duplicate the management if extra kilns were added to a works' (Pratten, *Economies of Scale*, p. 98). There are some (admittedly out-of-date) figures on labour requirements from which we can see that (in 1947) an increase of 2½-fold in output required only a doubling in labour input from thirty-three to sixty-six man-years; consequently, labour productivity, the inverse of labour requirement per unit of output, rises from 303,000 bricks per man-year to 379,000 bricks per man-year, simply as a consequence of economies of scale in the use of labour.

Most important, however, note that there appears to be quite significant economies in the use of fuel and power: the costs of these fall from £1.78 per thousand bricks at a scale of annual output of 10 million to £1.50 per thousand bricks at a scale of annual output of 25 million: a decline of 16 per cent. If it is generally the case that the use of energy may be subject to increasing returns to scale, then, in an era of rising energy costs, this may give an extra competitive edge to large-scale plants, and small-scale, 'energy-inefficient' plants may be driven out of business by their inability to cope with higher fuel prices.

This nearly completes our discussion of economies of scale. We have dealt at some length with this second ingredient in rising labour productivity because it is an important feature of the real world, and it is much used in economic analysis. The concept is often rather loosely defined, and so it is essential to have a soundly based understanding, via production functions and unit isoquants, of the impact of increasing returns to scale on unit costs. Only in this way can data such as Pratten's be adequately understood. But there is one question remaining. If economies of scale are so ubiquitous and significant, why is not each industry dominated by one single enterprise reaping maximum benefits from economies of scale? We may observe that increasing concentration of production has indeed been a feature of most economies this century – and this may be partly due to economies of scale (although other factors, associated with financing fixed capital formation, may also be important), but nevertheless we have not reached a situation of one industry–one enterprise which seems the logical consequence of economies of scale. Apart from government hostility to monopolies, it may sometimes be the case that *diseconomies* of scale set in at a certain point and so prevent enterprises from expanding to dominate the industry.

Such diseconomies of scale have often been interpreted in managerial terms – very big plants may become less manageable; quality control may become more difficult – but there may also be technical diseconomies of scale. For example, in distillation towers, the distillation process is less efficient outside the area of a square bounded by the circumference of the tower; it appears that as long as the diameter of the tower is less than about 8 feet this area of inefficiency does not too greatly affect the distillation process; but as the diameter goes beyond 8 feet the inefficient area impinges adversely on production. So it is possible to reap economies of scale in distillation towers up to 8 feet in diameter, but diseconomies set in thereafter, for technical reasons. In other words, 'real-world' production functions may produce rather oddly shaped curves, quite different from the smooth shape of Diagram 7.3. It may be that, even if there are no diseconomies of scale, enterprises simply cannot expand sufficiently rapidly to reach a dominant position: in order to put economies of scale into operation an enterprise has to grow, and if there are (as there appear to be) limits on the rate of expansion, then such constraints could suffice to explain why no single enterprise suddenly comes to dominate an industry. If enterprises depend largely on internal finance to pay for fixed capital formation, then we can see why any single enterprise may never be able to take full advantage of all the economies of scale available to it: limitations of finance simply preclude the possibility of a rapid twentyfold or hundredfold increase in capacity (and there are quite a few such ranges in Pratten's data shown in Table 7.8).

Exercises

7.1 *(To practise your understanding of unit costs and its relation to price and profitability.)* The following data relate to the operating costs of a cement plant in Peru with an annual production capacity of 80,000 metric tonnes (source: J. A. King, *Economic Development Projects and their Appraisal: Cases and Principles from the Experience of the World Bank* (Johns Hopkins University Press, 1967, case 27):

Item	Costs of producing 80,000 metric tonnes of cement per annum, Soles
Limestone	2,310,400
Shale	272,800
Gypsum	263,200
Fuel	3,316,800
Power	1,068,000
Sacks (5-ply)	3,199,200
Direct labour	321,600
Indirect labour (admin., sales, maintenance, etc.)	3,549,600
Social benefits, payroll taxes, etc.	610,400
Depreciation on plant	3,254,400
Interest payments on loans	1,872,800

(i)   What is the unit materials and fuels costs? (Answer in Soles please, the national currency of Peru; at that time the Sole was about 5 cents US or $1 = S20.) What is the unit labour cost? What is unit total production cost?

(ii) How would you define unit capital cost in this case? What is the unit capital cost on your definition?

(iii) The proposed selling price was 360 Soles per metric tonne (excluding freight, which would be charged separately; this price was considered 'conservative' by the World Bank). What flow of net profits would have resulted from production at full capacity?

(iv) What mark-up was being proposed on unit production cost to achieve this price?

(v)   By the year ending 1958, the cement company was operating with capital of 115.6 million Soles. Assuming production at full capacity, to what extent was this a profitable operation?

7.2 *(To practise your understanding of a production function and an isoquant.)*

(i) In Table 7.3 what level of capital input would have been required to produce $\bar{Q} = 100$ were the labour input to be 50? (To do this exercise you need a calculator with an x^y key, otherwise you will have to resort to four-figure logarithm tables – a practical example of capital–labour substitution!)

(ii) At this point on the isoquant, what is output per worker and capital per worker (see Diagram 7.3)? Do your answers fit the production function for output per worker?

7.3 *(To practise your understanding of unit costs and isoquants.)*

(i) With reference to Exercise 7.2 and Table 7.3, if the price of a unit of labour is £1,200 and the price of a unit of capital is £750 (annual flows), what is the unit labour cost, the unit capital cost, and the unit cost of labour and capital combined, when producing $\bar{Q} = 100$ with $L = 50$ and with the requisite quantity of capital? Explain why this is not the least-cost unit cost position at which to operate.

(ii) Explain the difference between 'unit labour cost' and 'the cost of a unit of labour'!

7.4 *(To practise seeing what can happen to unit labour cost under capital–labour substitution.)* With reference to Table 7.4:

(i) What was the labour cost (in cents) of *one* 5-gallon water carboy when made by hand? When made by automatic machine?

(ii) What was the labour cost (in cents) of *one* 2-oz prescription oval when made by hand? When made by semi-automatic machine? When made by automatic machine?

(iii) What was the labour cost (in cents) of *one* 40-watt bulb when made by hand? When made by semi-automatic machine? When made by automatic machine?

(This question provides useful practise in handling decimal places; you should work to about four decimal places.)

7.5 *(To practise your understanding of the relationship between productivity and unit labour costs and to demonstrate the usefulness of algebra.)* In 1925 average hourly earnings of produc-

tion workers in all manufacturing industries in the USA were $0.54 (US Department of Commerce Bureau of the Census, *Historical Statistics of the United States: Colonial Times to 1970*, Bicentennial Edition, part I, series D 802, p. 170). How do the hourly earnings implied by Table 7.4 compare, with the all-manufacturing average, for workers engaged in producing: (i) $\frac{1}{2}$-oz prescription ovals by hand; (ii) $\frac{1}{2}$-oz prescription ovals by automatic machine; (iii) 8–9 oz common tumblers by hand; 8–9 oz common tumblers by semi-automatic machine; (iv) 8–9 oz common tumblers by automatic machine; (v) 25-watt light bulbs by hand; (vi) 25-watt light bulbs by semi-automatic machine?

(*Hint:* it is difficult for anyone to see the method for answering this question unless one uses algebra, so proceed as follows: let w = average hourly earnings; L = number of man-hours used; Q = flow of output (number of items) produced during these man-hours; n = number of items making up a 'unit'. Using these symbols, define 'number (of items) produced per man-hour' and 'labour cost per "unit"'; using these two algebraic definitions work out the calculation required to derive w. This question is important more for its demonstration of the 'power' or usefulness of algebra than for the numerical answers; it is often the case in complex arithmetic problems that one can only be sure of doing the right thing if one first reduces the problem to algebra.)

7.6 *(To practise your understanding of economies of scale.)*

(i) With reference to Table 7.6 but at points $L = 200$, 240, 280, 400 and 520, derive the isoquant and unit isoquant when $\bar{Q} = 400$.

(ii) Redraw Diagram 7.9 with the unit isoquants for $\bar{Q} = 100$, $\bar{Q} = 200$ and $\bar{Q} = 400$.

(iii) What, for $\bar{Q} = 400$, is the least-cost unit labour requirement and unit capital requirement when $p_L = £1,200$ and $p_K = £750$? (See Appendix 7.1.)

(iv) What, for $\bar{Q} = 400$, is the least-cost unit capital and labour cost combined at these prices? What reduction does this represent on the least-cost unit labour and capital cost when $\bar{Q} = 200$?

7.7 *(To practise seeing what economies of scale can do to production costs.)*

(i) The labour and capital costs in 1965 for a new brewery with a capacity of 0.5 million barrels per annum were £1.76 per barrel;

the cost of brewery materials and other costs, at £4.26 per barrel, may be assumed to be relatively unaffected by economies of scale (at least for the purpose of this exercise). Work out the actual cost of producing a barrel of beer in breweries with the capacities given in Table 7.8 and with the economies of scale there given (data on brewery costs from C. F. Pratten, *Economies of Scale in Manufacturing Industry*, table 7.2, p. 74).

(ii)   Comment on the implications of all this for the Campaign for Real Ale!

7.8   *(To practise the interpretation of data relating to economies of scale.)*

(i)   Explain how the third row of Table 7.9 is derived and what it means.

(ii)   With reference to Table 7.9, tabulate for the different capacity plants (taking care to specify the units of measurement): total annual feedstock costs and chemicals and utilities; total annual operating labour, supervision and maintenance labour costs; total annual depreciation on fixed capital; total annual interest on finance for fixed and working capital; total annual total operating costs; total annual value of all by-products; total annual total costs.

(iii)   Express all the items in (ii) in index form with the absolute values for the scale of plant of 100 tons per annum as = 100. By comparison with the figures of 300 for the scale of the largest ethylene plant (being regarded as an index value), what do you observe in general about your indices?

(iv)   Include with your indices for (iii) the index for total plant and offsite facilities. Which item among all the indices shows the greatest impact of economies of scale?

(v)   This chapter gave a general definition of 'increasing returns to scale' in terms of proportionate output changes resulting from a proportionate change in all inputs (the same proportionate change for all inputs); using your answers to (iii) and (iv) suggest another definition for 'economies of scale' that might be applied to specific items of inputs (or input costs).

(vi)   On graph paper, plot against scale of output (horizontal axis): operating labour, supervision and maintenance labour costs per ton of ethylene; depreciation on fixed capital per ton of ethylene; interest at 10 per cent on finance for fixed and working capital per ton of ethylene; and average cost per ton of ethylene (after taking account of the value of all by-products per ton of ethylene). What, in general, can you say about the curves joining each set of points?

7.9   *(How to put your understanding of economies of scale to good use.)* Write a memo to your mother demonstrating, *exactly, where* and *how* economies of scale would affect her baking of chocolate cakes, making it imperative that she reduce the unit cost of chocolate cakes by baking two each time she bakes instead of just one.

7.10   *(Further to practise understanding economies of scale – and its practical implications.)*

(i)   'There is widespread agreement that individual [car] models should be produced at levels exceeding 200,000 per year and that, ideally, a firm should have an overall output of not less than 1 million cars per year' (Krish Bhaskar, *The Future of the UK Motor Industry* (Kogan Page, 1979) p. 25). With reference to the data in Table 7.11, explain why there is this widespread agreement.

(ii)   With reference to the table below, consider the implications for BL (now BL and Honda) of your answer to (i).

Manufacturing group	Total (world) production in 1978, millions of cars
General Motors (incl. Isuzu)	9.9
Ford (incl. Toyo Kogyo)	7.2
Toyota (incl. Daihatsu and Hino)	3.5
Chrysler (incl. Mitsubishi but excl. Chrysler Europe)	3.2
Nissan/Datsun (incl. Nissan Diesel and Fuji)	2.9
PSA Peugeot-Citroen (incl. Chrysler Europe)	2.7
Volkswagen Group	2.4
Renault (incl. American Motors and Volvo)	2.4
Fiat (incl. Seat)	1.9
BL and Honda	1.6

Source: Krish Bhaskar, *The Future of the World Motor Industry* (Kogan Page/Nichols Publishing Company, 1980), table 4.1, p. 46.

APPENDIX 7.1 *Increasing returns to scale*
The production function for the base index value is:

$$100 = Z100^{0.9}100^{0.3}$$

Whence:

$$Z = \frac{100}{100^{0.9}100^{0.3}} = 0.39810717$$

The isoquant is derived as follows:

$$\bar{Q} = ZL^{a}K^{b}$$

$$K = \left(\frac{\bar{Q}}{Z}\right)^{\frac{1}{b}} L^{-\frac{a}{b}}$$

Or, inserting the numerical values, for $\bar{Q} = 100$ the isoquant is:

$$K = \left(\frac{100}{0.398107}\right)^{\frac{1}{0.3}} L^{-\frac{0.9}{0.3}}$$

$$= (251.1886)^{\frac{1}{0.3}} L^{-3}$$

For $\bar{Q} = 200$ the isoquant is:

$$K = \left(\frac{200}{0.398107}\right)^{\frac{1}{0.3}} L^{-3}$$

$$= (502.3773)^{\frac{1}{0.3}} L^{-3}$$

The unit isoquant is derived as follows:

$$K = Z^{-\frac{1}{b}} \bar{Q}^{\frac{1}{b}} L^{-\frac{a}{b}}$$

$$\frac{K}{\bar{Q}} = Z^{-\frac{1}{b}} \bar{Q}^{\frac{1}{b}} \bar{Q}^{-1} L^{-\frac{a}{b}}$$

$$= Z^{-\frac{1}{b}} \bar{Q}^{\frac{1}{b}} \bar{Q}^{-1} L^{-\frac{a}{b}} \bar{Q}^{\frac{a}{b}} \bar{Q}^{-\frac{a}{b}}$$

$$= Z^{-\frac{1}{b}} \bar{Q}^{\frac{1}{b}-1-\frac{a}{b}} \left(\frac{L}{\bar{Q}}\right)^{-\frac{a}{b}}$$

Or, inserting the numerical values, for $\bar{Q} = 100$ and $\bar{Q} = 200$ the unit isoquants are respectively:

$$\frac{K}{\bar{Q}} = 0.398107^{-\frac{1}{0.3}} 100^{-0.6667} \left(\frac{L}{\bar{Q}}\right)^{-3}$$

$$\frac{K}{\bar{Q}} = 0.398107^{-\frac{1}{0.3}} 200^{-0.6667} \left(\frac{L}{\bar{Q}}\right)^{-3}$$

The slope of the unit isoquant is:

$$\frac{\Delta(K/\bar{Q})}{\Delta(L/\bar{Q})} = -\frac{a}{b} Z^{-\frac{1}{b}} \bar{Q}^{\frac{1}{b}-1-\frac{a}{b}} \left(\frac{L}{\bar{Q}}\right)^{-\frac{a}{b}-1}$$

Or, inserting the numerical values, for $\bar{Q} = 100$:

$$\frac{\Delta(K/\bar{Q})}{\Delta(L/\bar{Q})} =$$

$$-3 \times 0.398107^{-\frac{1}{0.3}}100^{-0.6667}\left(\frac{L}{\bar{Q}}\right)^{-4}$$

So that, at $\bar{Q} = 100$, the least-cost unit labour input, $(L/\bar{Q})^*$, is at that point on the isoquant where its slope is equal to the slope of the isocost line, $-1,200/750 = -1.6$ (given $p_L = 1,200$ and $p_K = 750$):

$$-3 \times 0.398107^{-\frac{1}{0.3}} 100^{-0.6667} \left(\frac{L}{\bar{Q}}\right)^{-4} = -1.6$$

whence the value of $L/\bar{Q}$ which satisfies this equation may be calculated as:

$$\left(\frac{L}{\bar{Q}}\right)^* = \left[\frac{-3}{-1.6} 0.398107^{-\frac{1}{0.3}} 100^{-0.6667}\right]^{\frac{1}{4}}$$

$$= 1.17017$$

And from the unit isoquant for $\bar{Q} = 100$, the corresponding value of the unit capital requirement is:

$$\left(\frac{K}{\bar{Q}}\right)^* = 0.398107^{-\frac{1}{0.3}} 100^{-0.6667} 1.17017^{-3}$$

$$= 0.62410$$

So that the least-cost unit cost, when the scale of output is $\bar{Q} = 100$, is:

$$(£1,200 \times 1.170) + (£750 \times 0.624) = £1,872$$

This is the same as the least-cost unit cost for $\bar{Q} = 100$ under constant returns to scale, and so establishes a common basis for comparison. Under constant returns to scale, the unit isoquant does not alter if the scale of output changes (Table 7.5) so the least-cost unit cost remains the same whatever the scale of output. But the same is not the case for increasing returns to scale: under increasing returns to scale, the slope of the unit isoquant, when the scale of output is $\bar{Q} = 200$, is:

$$-3 \times 0.398107^{-\frac{1}{0.3}} 200^{-0.6667} \left(\frac{L}{\bar{Q}}\right)^{-4}$$

And, solving for the appropriate value of $L/\bar{Q}$, with the slope of the isocost line at -1.6, we have:

$$\left(\frac{L}{\bar{Q}}\right)^* = \left[\frac{-3}{-1.6} \quad 0.398107^{-\frac{1}{0.3}} \quad 200^{-0.6667}\right]^{\frac{1}{4}}$$

$$= 1.042$$

whence:

$$\left(\frac{K}{\bar{Q}}\right)^* = 0.39811^{-\frac{1}{0.3}} \quad 200^{-0.6667} \quad 1.042^{-3}$$

$$= 0.557$$

So that the least-cost unit cost, when the scale of output is $\bar{Q} = 200$, is, under the increasing returns to scale production function:

$£1{,}200 \times 1.042 + £750 \times 0.557 = £1{,}668.15$

To summarise:

	Increasing returns to scale [a]	
	Scale of output: $\bar{Q} = 100$	*Scale of output:* $\bar{Q} = 200$
Least-cost		
$\left(\dfrac{L}{\bar{Q}}\right)^*$	1.170	1.042
$\left(\dfrac{K}{\bar{Q}}\right)^*$	0.624	0.557
Least-cost unit cost, £ [b]	1,872.00	1,668.15

[a] Production function $Q = 0.398107 L^{0.9} K^{0.3}$.
[b] Prices as $p_L = £1{,}200$, $p_K = £750$.

Chapter 8

Technical Progress: Technological Change, the Learning Curve, and Economic Growth

Contents

Chapter guide

Technical progress is the single most important factor shaping the economy in which we live. The term 'technical progress' encompasses all those forces which raise simultaneously the productivity of all factors of production combined (but is distinguished from economies of scale by not necessarily requiring an increase in the scale of production to achieve this improvement in total factor productivity). Technical progress has two aspects which may in the real world be difficult to distinguish but which analytic clarity requires us to consider separately.

The first and most important aspect of technical progress is *technological change*. This concept is defined and its impact on (total) factor productivity and unit total cost is fully explained, again via a simple arithmetic production function model, before we look at some relevant empirical data. These data are also used to illustrate the practical consequences of technological change for enterprises and their corporate strategy.

The second aspect of technical progress is the *learning curve* effect. The learning curve is concerned with the improvement in the efficiency of a given plant using a given technology as the cumulative experience of production enables (total) factor productivity to rise (or factor requirement per unit of output – the inverse of productivity – to fall). The learning curve refers especially to (rising) labour productivity or (falling) unit labour requirement. We examine the behaviour of unit labour requirement, and therefore also of *unit labour cost*, along a learning curve, again using a simple arithmetic production function model. We then look at some data, drawn from the careful records of US wartime production, on the learning curve. We consider the practical consequences for enterprises and for corporate strategy of the learning curve and its associated, but more broadly based, *experience curve*.

Finally, we look at the quantitative impact which all these ingredients – capital–labour substitution, economies of scale, and technical progress – have been assessed to have had on the growth of nine industrial market economies in the postwar period.

Technological change

The third of our ingredients in rising labour productivity is technical progress. At its most dramatic, technical progress leads to an increase in output combined with a reduction in (all) inputs: that is, the productivity of all inputs ('total factor productivity') increases. Less dramatically, technical progress leads to a maintenance of output while inputs are reduced; or to an increase in output without a corresponding increase in inputs (but, unlike economies of scale, technical progress at plant level requires no alteration in the scale of production).

Technical progress can be divided between two broad categories of progress: first, increases in total factor productivity due to technological change; second, increases in total factor productivity due to 'learning' or 'experience'. These two categories form the subject of this chapter, and we shall discuss them in turn.

Technology consists of society's stock of knowledge relating to the production of goods and services: *what* can be produced and *how* to produce it. Technological change is a change in such 'production technology'. Technological change is thus a complex phenomenon because it concerns either the products/services produced or the methods of producing those products/services or (very often) both product and method. Therefore, we need a three-by-three matrix (at least) to describe what we mean by technological change:

	Methods of production		
Products/services	Existing methods	'Improved' methods	'New' methods
Existing products/services	1	4	7
Changed ('improved') products/services	2	5	8
'New' products/services	3	6	9

Position 1 in the matrix describes the present state of production technology; but the present state is rarely static: movement is continually being made from position 1 to the other eight positions, and any such movement may be described as 'technological change'. Obviously, it is not always easy to draw the line between 'improved' and 'new', but it is generally possible to put a change into one or other of the eight boxes. Of course, the most dramatic and far-reaching changes occur during a change from 1 to 9, but any of the other changes may be just as important.

Another way of describing the 'size' of the technology change involved in any innovation is with reference to 'the amount of any change required in a textbook of the sort that would be used for a university course' dealing with the body of knowledge or industrial practice concerned (see Table 8.1).

TABLE 8.1   *Five-point scale of size of change in technology*

5	Innovation leads to a new technology: new textbook with new title required
4	Innovation makes several chapters of the standard textbook out of date
3	Innovation requires major change in one or two chapters of the standard textbook or additions of new chapters
2	Innovation requires alterations or additions of a few paragraphs in standard textbook
1	Innovation makes no or only very slight difference to standard textbook

Source: J. Langrish, M. Gibbons, W. G. Evans and F. R. Jevons, *Wealth From Knowledge: Studies of Innovation in Industry*, Macmillan, 1972, pp. 65, 66.

The authors who devised this scale investigated in their book, *Wealth From Knowledge*, eighty-four innovations in the United Kingdom which had won the Queen's Award for innovation in 1966 and 1967 (there were sixty-six Awards involving innovation in these years but some contained more than one innovation). Most of the innovations were at points 3 and 2 on their scale (*Wealth From Knowledge*, p. 67):

Size of change in technology	5	4	3	2	1
Percentage of innovations ($n = 84$)	1.2	11.9	42.9	39.3	4.8

There is likely to be a correspondence between the *Wealth From Knowledge* scale and the numbers in the 3×3 technological change matrix, but it is in any case clear that technical progress is a complex issue when examined in detail.

Now, as one way of studying technological change it would be possible to run through a long catalogue of specific technological changes from economic history and from the present day (for example, the thirty-six detailed case studies in *Wealth From Knowledge*). Such a catalogue would certainly illustrate the very great impact which technological change has on the economy and on society. From the point of view of economic analysis, however, the problem with such a catalogue, fascinating and relevant though it may be, is that at the end of it all we cannot systematically assess what it all 'adds up to'. Having read and digested such books as David Landes's *The Unbound Prometheus*, Derry and Williams's *A Short History of Technology*, the collection of papers edited by Barry Supple, *Essays in British Business History*, or the case studies in *Wealth From Knowledge*, we may feel a satisfying sense of the broad panorama of technological change and an awareness (which in any case is with us at every moment of our daily lives and which may, from time to time, be an uneasy rather than a comfortable awareness) of how technology affects our standards of living. What we do not know is how the over-all impact of technological change may be assessed in a systematic way from a purely economic point of view, in terms of its impact on outputs and inputs.

Economic theory has devised a method of doing this. There is, naturally, considerable argument about the method, which argument is also complicated by the fact that theory has run considerably in advance of empirical data. Nevertheless it is necessary for an economist to have a theoretical understanding of how technological change affects the productivity of factors of production, and we shall then return to some of these questions about the feasibility of applying theory to data.

Neutral technological change

We shall deal first of all with 'neutral' technological change, where the word 'neutral' means that the exponents in the production function to the labour and capital inputs remain unchanged (or, more generally, that the ratio of the exponents remains constant). The force of this proviso will subsequently become apparent when we consider non-neutral technical change. The definition of 'neutral technological change', *in economic terms* and supposedly or assumedly encompassing all the complexity of the eight possible different changes referred to earlier, is that it is an increase in actual output (as measured), in excess of the increase in output which can be ascribed, via a production function, to the increase in labour and capital inputs (as measured). Of course, with the parenthetical 'as measured' we are sliding over a number of awkward questions, especially when 'new' products and 'new' methods are involved. This issue will be briefly taken up later, but at this juncture it would seriously delay us. This is rather a complicated definition, so let us explain it as follows (following conventional terminology, we shall refer to 'technological change' under the broader category of 'technical progress'). Because technical progress is something that happens through time, we need to introduce a time subscript, t, into the production function, and in order to be able to represent technical progress, we must now let Z, the previously introduced adjustment factor, vary through time rather than remaining constant; so, like Q, L and K, Z will have a time subscript indicating that its value may vary with time. Thus for period t (with the subscript for flows and stocks being appropriately interpreted) we have, for the consecutive time periods t and $t+1$, the production functions:

$$Q_t = Z_t L_t^a K_t^b$$

and:

$$Q_{t+1} = Z_{t+1} L_{t+1}^a K_{t+1}^b$$

The increase in output between t and $t+1$ which can be ascribed *solely* to the increase in labour and capital inputs can be measured with reference to Q', the hypothetical output determined by the old value Z_t in conjunction with the new values of L_{t+1} and K_{t+1}, as follows:

$$Q' = Z_t L_{t+1}^a K_{t+1}^b$$

So, the change from Q_t to Q' is due to the change in L and K, and the change from Q' to Q_{t+1} is due to 'technical progress'. We may therefore measure the proportionate impact, or rate, of technical progress as:

$$\frac{Q_{t+1} - Q'}{Q'} = \frac{Q_{t+1}}{Q'} - 1$$

$$= \frac{Z_{t+1} L_{t+1}^a K_{t+1}^b}{Z_t L_{t+1}^a K_{t+1}^b} - 1$$

$$= \frac{Z_{t+1}}{Z_t} - 1$$

So the proportionate change in the adjustment factor, Z, measures the rate of technical progress. If we can measure Q, L and K accurately, and if we can establish values for the production function parameters a and b, then we can estimate the Z values quite simply as:

$$\frac{Q_t}{L_t^a K_t^b} = Z_t$$

and

$$\frac{Q_{t+1}}{L_{t+1}^a K_{t+1}^b} = Z_{t+1}$$

Using these two expressions, the proportionate change in Z may be ascertained from:

$$\frac{Z_{t+1}}{Z_t} = \frac{Q_{t+1}/Q_t}{(L_{t+1}^a K_{t+1}^b)/(L_t^a K_t^b)}$$

The right-hand side of this equation is the proportionate change in actual output (the numerator) divided by the proportionate change in 'combined factor input' (the denominator), where the term 'combined factor input' refers to the product $L^a K^b$. The product $L^a K^b$, taken as a whole, thus serves as an index of the 'total' factor input combined, and is analogous, say, to a weighted price index which serves to measure the 'total' price change for a basket of goods combined.

As a matter of algebra, although this last expression does not overtly contain Q', it is formally equivalent to an expression containing Q'. This can be seen if we multiply the denominator on the right-hand side by $Z_t/Z_t = 1$:

$$\frac{Z_{t+1}}{Z_t} = \frac{Q_{t+1}/Q_t}{(Z_t L_{t+1}^a K_{t+1}^b)/(Z_t L_t^a K_t^b)}$$

$$= \frac{Q_{t+1}/Q_t}{Q'/Q_t}$$

$$= \frac{Q_{t+1}}{Q'}$$

So much for the basic algebra of the definition of 'technical progress'. Let us now see what neutral technical progress means in terms of an arithmetic example and the behaviour of the unit isoquant. For this, we shall use the constant returns to scale production function so as to avoid any possibility of confusing technical progress with the impact of increasing returns to scale. Assuming that the price ratio is still £1,200/£750 = 1.6, the enterprise should be operating with the least-cost combination of L and K, and during period t its inputs and output are (Table 7.3):

$$Q_t = 1.00 \times 117.017^{0.75} 62.410^{0.25}$$

$$= 100$$

where we have added $Z_t = 1.00$ to the production function. Suppose now that in period $t+1$ both labour and capital inputs are doubled and that the value of $Z_{t+1} = 1.5$. (We double the inputs so as to get a standard of comparison with Table 7.5, where the unit isoquant did not change when output and inputs doubled. We also have a proportionately big increase in Z so as to make the example obvious and to keep the arithmetic simple. In practice, of course, we would be dealing with much smaller changes than this.) For actual output in $t+1$ we now have (at the least-cost position: see Table 7.5):

$$Q_{t+1} = 1.5 \times 234.034^{0.75} 124.820^{0.25}$$

$$= 300$$

But the output which would be produced, were the labour and capital inputs alone to change, is given with an unchanged value of $Z - L$ and K only changing:

$$Q' = 1.00 \times 234.034^{0.75} 124.820^{0.25}$$

$$= 200$$

So that the impact of technical progress is measured by:

$$\frac{Q_{t+1} - Q'}{Q'} = \frac{300 - 200}{200}$$

$$= 0.50 = 50 \text{ per cent}$$

which is exactly the proportionate change in Z from $Z_t = 1.00$ to $Z_{t+1} = 1.50$. This change can also be measured as the ratio between the proportionate change in actual output and the proportionate change in total (combined) factor input, both proportionate changes being expressed in index form:

$$\frac{300/100}{(234.034^{0.75}124.820^{0.25}/117.017^{0.75}62.410^{0.25})} = \frac{3.00}{2.00} = 1.50$$

This we shall call the practical way of measuring the impact of technical progress; it uses actual outputs and inputs and so dispenses with the need to calculate the hypothetical value of Q' (although, as we showed above, it is formally equivalent to the ratio Q_{t+1}/Q').

We now need to see what neutral technical progress does to the unit isoquant and to unit cost itself. Table 8.2 shows in its first four columns the isoquant and unit isoquant for $\bar{Q} = 100$; these columns are identical to those in Table 7.5 so as to establish a basis for comparison. In Table 7.5, which had a production function without technical progress, we then showed the isoquant for double the level of output with double the level of inputs and a correspondingly unchanged unit isoquant (this was to establish a basis for comparison with the situation under an increasing returns to scale production function). In Table 8.2 the second group of four columns shows what happens when inputs are doubled *and* when there is neutral technical progress; the flow of output is, in this case, trebled (not doubled); the isoquant for $\bar{Q} = 300$ (with technical progress) is the same as the isoquant for $\bar{Q} = 200$ (without technical progress); and, accordingly, the unit isoquant after neutral technical progress is considerably lower than the unit isoquant before neutral technical progress.

The important effect of neutral technical progress is on the unit cost of production at the least-cost combination. Assuming factor prices of $p_L = £1,200$ and $p_K = £750$, the least-cost combination for $\bar{Q} = 100$ is $L = 117.017$ and $K = 62.410$, determined as previously; and the least-cost combination for $\bar{Q} = 300$ is $L = 234.034$ and $K = 124.82$. The least-cost *unit* cost for $\bar{Q} = 100$, i.e. before neutral technical progress, is £1,872, as shown in the second-last column of Table 8.2. The least-cost unit cost *after* neutral technical progress is £1,248 (last column, Table 8.2). Thus neutral technical progress has effected a one-third reduction in unit labour and capital costs at the least-cost combination. *This* is the important aspect of neutral technical progress from an economic point of view: namely, that it raises the productivity of both labour and capital (equivalently, shifts the unit isoquant downwards) and so reduces production costs per unit of output. Such increased factor productivity/reduced unit production costs (two sides of the same coin) is, and has always been, a powerful factor in raising standards of living.

We considered the case of neutral technical progress occurring in conjunction with an increase in labour and capital inputs because we needed to make clear the difference between that part of the increase in actual output which could be ascribed, via the production function, to the increase in inputs and that part of the increase in actual output which was in excess of the former. It is helpful now to consider neutral technical progress in two other, but formally equivalent, ways. The first is neutral technical progress as that increase in output which occurs without any increase in labour and capital inputs as measured; the second is neutral technical progress as a reduction in measured labour and capital inputs for the same (constant) level of output. Both ways are illustrated in Table 8.3.

TABLE 8.2 *Unit isoquants under constant returns to scale and with neutral technical progress*

Labour and capital								£ [(e)]	
Before neutral technical progress				After neutral technical progress				Before	After
Isoquant to produce $\bar{Q} = 100$ [(a)]		Unit isoquant when $\bar{Q} = 100$ [(b)]		Isoquant to produce $\bar{Q} = 300$ [(c)]		Unit isoquant when $\bar{Q} = 300$ [(d)]		Unit cost from unit isoquant for $\bar{Q} = 100$	Unit cost from unit isoquant for $\bar{Q} = 300$
L	K	$\dfrac{L}{\bar{Q}}$	$\dfrac{K}{\bar{Q}}$	L	K	$\dfrac{L}{\bar{Q}}$	$\dfrac{K}{\bar{Q}}$		
100	100	1.00	1.00	200	200	0.6667	0.6667	1,950	1,300
60	462.96	0.60	4.6296	120	925.92	0.4000	3.0864	4,192	2,795
70	291.55	0.70	2.9155	140	583.09	0.4667	1.9436	3,027	2,018
80	195.31	0.80	1.9531	160	390.63	0.5333	1.3021	2,425	1,616
117.017	62.410	1.17	0.6241	234.034	124.82	0.7801	0.4161	1,872	1,248
120	57.87	1.20	0.5787	240	115.74	0.8000	0.3858	1,874	1,249
140	36.44	1.40	0.3644	280	72.89	0.9333	0.2430	1,953	1,302
200	12.50	2.00	0.1250	400	25.00	1.3333	0.0833	2,494	1,662

[(a)] From production function $Q = 1.00 L^{0.75} K^{0.25}$. Whence:

$$K = 1.00^{-\frac{1}{0.25}} \bar{Q}^{\frac{1}{0.25}} L^{-\frac{0.75}{0.25}}$$

[(b)] From the production function in (a):

$$\frac{K}{\bar{Q}} = 1.00^{-\frac{1}{0.25}} \bar{Q}^{\left(\frac{1}{0.25}\right) - 1 - \frac{0.75}{0.25}} \left(\frac{L}{\bar{Q}}\right)^{-\frac{0.75}{0.25}}$$

The middle term becomes 1 because $(1/0.25 - 1 - 0.75/0.25) = 0$; and 1 raised to any power remains 1, so $K/\bar{Q} = (L/\bar{Q})^{-3}$; minor discrepancies due to rounding.

[(c)] From the production function (with technical progress) $Q = 1.50 L^{0.75} K^{0.25}$. Whence:

$$K = 1.50^{-\frac{1}{0.25}} \bar{Q}^{\frac{1}{0.25}} L^{-\frac{0.75}{0.25}}$$

[(d)] From the production function (with technical progress) in (c):

$$\frac{K}{\bar{Q}} = 1.50^{-\frac{1}{0.25}} \bar{Q}^{\frac{1}{0.25} - 1 - \frac{0.75}{0.25}} \left(\frac{L}{\bar{Q}}\right)^{-\frac{0.75}{0.25}}$$

$$= 1.50^{-4} \left(\frac{L}{\bar{Q}}\right)^{-3}$$

(minor discrepancies due to rounding).

[(e)] Assuming unchanging factor prices of $p_L = £1,200$ and $p_K = £750$, this is computed, for the respective unit isoquants as:

$$\left(p_L \times \frac{L}{\bar{Q}}\right) + \left(p_K \times \frac{K}{\bar{Q}}\right)$$

In the first instance, we may imagine neutral technical progress occurring in an enterprise which does not alter its factor inputs. Assuming that the enterprise was producing at the least-cost combination of $L = 117.017$ and $K = 62.410$, the enterprise finds that, after neutral technical progress (that is, after Z in its production function has increased from 1.00 to 1.50), its output has increased to 150, its unit isoquant has shifted downward correspondingly, and its labour and capital costs per unit of output are now $(£1,200 \times 0.7801) + (£750 \times 0.4161) = £1,248$, instead of £1,872 before neutral technical progress.

TABLE 8.3   *Alternative (but equivalent) ways in which neutral technical progress may affect factor productivity*

After neutral technical progress: increase in output with no increase in factor inputs				After neutral technical progress: same output produced with reduction in factor inputs			
Isoquant to produce $\bar{Q} = 150$		Unit isoquant when $\bar{Q} = 150$		Isoquant to produce $\bar{Q} = 100$		Unit isoquant when $\bar{Q} = 100$	
L	K	$\dfrac{L}{\bar{Q}}$	$\dfrac{K}{\bar{Q}}$	L	K	$\dfrac{L}{\bar{Q}}$	$\dfrac{K}{\bar{Q}}$
100	100	0.6667	0.6667	66.667	66.667	0.6667	0.6667
60	462.96	0.4000	3.0864	40.000	308.640	0.4000	3.0864
70	291.55	0.4667	1.9436	46.667	194.366	0.4667	1.9436
80	195.31	0.5333	1.3021	53.333	130.207	0.5333	1.3021
117.017	62.410	0.7801	0.4161	78.011	41.607	0.7801	0.4161
120	57.87	0.8000	0.3858	80.000	38.580	0.8000	0.3858
140	36.44	0.9333	0.2429	93.333	24.293	0.9333	0.2429
200	12.50	1.3333	0.0833	133.333	8.333	1.3333	0.0833

In the second instance, we may imagine an enterprise which continues to produce output of 100, but which finds that, at the least-cost combination of labour and capital inputs, it needs only 78.011 of labour input (instead of the previous 117.017) and 41.607 of capital input (instead of the previous 62.410). The enterprise's unit isoquant has shifted downward correspondingly and its least-cost unit cost becomes £1,248. Note that in both these instances, and in the case of Table 8.2, where inputs increased, the unit isoquant after technical progress is exactly the same. Regardless of what is happening to factor inputs and outputs, neutral technical progress can be represented by exactly the same downward shift of the unit isoquant.

The commonly accepted view of technical progress (especially among employees threatened with redundancy) is probably the pessimistic one of a reduction in factor inputs with no increase in output. Theoretically, and under certain conditions which we shall consider, this should be unlikely: for the simple reason that the reduction in least-cost unit labour and capital cost (given unchanged factor prices) should permit a reduction in the price of the product and so lead to an expansion in the volume of output. Precisely what happens when price is reduced depends on the price elasticity of demand: we could see that technical progress in, say, the production of salt could lead to redundancies in the salt mines; but technical progress in the production of, say, computers is much more likely to lead to an expansion of employment and capital used in the electronics industry. This 'optimistic' view of technical progress depends on the condition that the reduction in unit labour and capital cost is passed on in the form of a price reduction to customers; in this way the benefit of technological progress is spread amongst the widest group attainable.

However, if the effect of technical progress accrues in the form of increased income to the factors of production in the enterprise (or industry) so that instead of unit labour and capital cost falling from £1,872 to:

$$£1,200 \times 0.7801 + £750 \times 0.4161 = £1,248$$

what happens is that both factor prices rise so that unit labour and capital cost (at the least-cost combination) remains at £1,872:

$$£1,800 \times 0.7801 + £1,125 \times 0.4161 = £1,872$$

Price remains constant, so there is no possibility of increased demand from this source; the rise in incomes of the factors of production may or may not increase demand for this particular product, but there is obviously no necessary connection as is the case with a price reduction.

Non-neutral technological change

So far we have explained technical progress with reference to a 'neutral' shift in the production function: that is, from a shift which does not alter the exponents in the production function; or, more generally, which does not alter the ratio of the exponents. The defining characteristic of 'neutral' technical progress is that it does not alter the *ratio* of capital to labour inputs (although it alters the amounts of those inputs) at the least-cost combination (given that factor prices remain unchanged). This is because, if the production function is:

$$Q = ZL^aK^b$$

then, as shown in Appendix 8.1, the capital–labour ratio, at the least-cost combination of capital and labour, is given by:

$$\frac{K^*}{L^*} = \frac{p_L/p_K}{a/b}$$

Thus, if the ratio a/b is not changed by technical progress (and the price ratio is also constant), the capital–labour ratio is unaffected by technical progress. However, it is obviously possible that technical progress could not only shift the production function (that is, increase the value of Z) but that technical progress could also alter the ratio of the exponents. If this happens, the technical progress is called 'non-neutral' or 'biased', technical progress. If the ratio a/b falls, the capital–labour ratio at the least-cost combination will rise, so this is called capital-using/labour-saving (non-neutral or biased) technical progress; conversely, if the ratio a/b rises, the capital–labour ratio at the least-cost combination will fall, so this is called capital-saving/labour-using (non-neutral or biased) technical progress. Thus non-neutral technological change is defined as any change which causes an alteration in the ratio a/b, where a and b are, respectively, the exponents on the labour and capital inputs to the production function; and there are two types of non-neutrality which we shall refer to, respectively, as labour-saving or capital-saving technical progress. Labour-saving technical progress tends to raise the rate of increase of labour productivity, so such a bias has obvious implications for standards of living.

Measuring the impact of non-neutral technical progress is only slightly different from measuring the impact of neutral technical progress. Let a and b be the exponents before non-neutral technological change, and a' and b' be the exponents after non-neutral technological change. Then:

$$Q_t = Z_t L_t^a K_t^b$$

and:

$$Q_{t+1} = Z_{t+1} L_{t+1}^{a'} K_{t+1}^{b'}$$

As before, we must derive a hypothetical value of output, Q', which would result solely from the increase in factor inputs (that is, no change in Z and no change in the exponents):

$$Q' = Z_t L_{t+1}^a K_{t+1}^b$$

The impact of non-neutral technological change can then be measured as:

$$\frac{Q_{t+1}}{Q'} = \frac{Z_{t+1} L_{t+1}^{a'} K_{t+1}^{b'}}{Z_t L_{t+1}^a K_{t+1}^b}$$

$$= \frac{Z_{t+1}}{Z_t} \times L_{t+1}^{a'-a} \times K_{t+1}^{b'-b}$$

The impact of non-neutral technical progress will accordingly be greater or less than Z_{t+1}/Z_t depending on whether $L_{t+1}^{a'-a} K_{t+1}^{b'-b}$ is greater or less than 1. To illustrate this, suppose that we have initially a production function of the form $Q = ZL^{0.75}K^{0.25}$; that Z rises from 1.00 to 1.5; that the factor price ratio remains unchanged at $p_L/p_K = 1{,}200/750 = 1.6$; and that constant returns to scale are maintained under all changes. We may then illustrate the impact of neutral, and the two types of non-neutral, technical progress as follows:

	$\dfrac{a'}{b'}$	$\dfrac{p_L/p_K}{a'/b'} =$	$\dfrac{K^*}{L^*}$
Neutral technical progress	$\dfrac{0.75}{0.25}$	$\dfrac{1.6}{3}$	$= 0.5333$
Labour-saving/capital-using technical progress	$\dfrac{0.70}{0.30}$	$\dfrac{1.6}{2.3333}$	$= 0.6857$
Capital-saving/labour-using technical progress	$\dfrac{0.80}{0.20}$	$\dfrac{1.6}{4}$	$= 0.4000$

The least-cost capital–labour ratio is higher under labour-saving technical progress than under neutral technical progress: that is, a labour-saving bias in technical progress leads to capital–labour substitution (at an unchanging factor price ratio).

Table 8.4 shows the unit isoquants for each of the three possibilities just given, together with the unit isoquant before technical progress. For each of these isoquants we can establish the least-cost combination of labour and capital along the unit isoquant.

TABLE 8.4   *Non-neutral technical progress and the unit isoquant*

Before technical progress [a]		After neutral technical progress [b]		After labour-saving technical progress [c]		After capital-saving technical progress [d]	
$\dfrac{L}{\bar{Q}}$	$\dfrac{K}{\bar{Q}}$	$\dfrac{L}{\bar{Q}}$	$\dfrac{K}{\bar{Q}}$	$\dfrac{L}{\bar{Q}}$	$\dfrac{K}{\bar{Q}}$	$\dfrac{L}{\bar{Q}}$	$\dfrac{K}{\bar{Q}}$
1.000	1.0000	0.6667	0.6667	0.6667	0.6667	0.6667	0.6667
0.600	4.6296	0.4000	3.0864	0.4000	2.1956	0.4000	5.1440
0.700	2.9155	0.4667	1.9436	0.4667	1.5323	0.4667	2.7766
0.800	1.9531	0.5333	1.3021	0.5333	1.1221	0.5333	1.6276
				0.74656 [e] **0.5119** [e]		0.74656	0.4239
1.17017 [e] **0.6241** [e]		**0.7801** [e] **0.4161** [e]		0.7801	0.4620	0.7801	0.3556
				0.80075	0.4347	**0.80075** [e] **0.3203** [e]	
1.40	0.3644	0.9333	0.2430	0.9333	0.3041	0.9333	0.1735
2.00	0.1250	1.3333	0.0833	1.3333	0.1323	1.3333	0.0417

[a]   From the production function $Q = 1.00L^{0.75}K^{0.25}$.
[b]   From the production function $Q = 1.50L^{0.75}K^{0.25}$.
[c]   From the production function $Q = 1.50L^{0.70}K^{0.30}$.
[d]   From the production function $Q = 1.50L^{0.80}K^{0.20}$.
[e]   Least-cost combination for $p_L = £1{,}200$ and $p_K = £750$.

It can also be seen that non-neutrality in technical progress 'twists' the unit isoquant in a way which is illustrated in Diagram 8.1. The least-cost position with neutral technical progress is on the same capital–labour ratio; but a labour-saving/capital-using bias in technical progress twists the isoquant so that the least-cost combination of labour and capital is at a higher capital–labour ratio and a higher level of labour productivity than is the case under neutral technical progress. If the non-neutrality, or bias, in technical

DIAGRAM 8.1   *Unit isoquants with neutral and non-neutral technical progress*

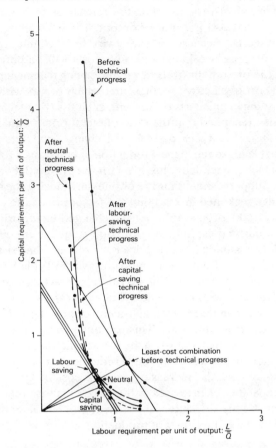

progress were consistently of a labour-saving/capital-using type, then, independently of any change in the factor price ratio towards relatively more expensive labour, this would be a factor causing the capital–labour ratio to rise, thus enhancing the growth of labour productivity.

Table 8.5 shows the sort of difference non-neutrality makes to the impact of technical progress: with neutral technical progress both output and labour productivity rise by 50 per cent. If there is in the technical progress a labour-saving bias, then labour productivity rises by 57 per cent. It is this aspect of an 'enhanced' increase in labour productivity which is important in labour-saving technical progress.

TABLE 8.5   *The impact of non-neutral technical progress on labour productivity and on unit costs (assuming no change in the factor price ratio)*

	Least-cost capital–labour ratio	Labour productivity	Percentage change in labour productivity	Unit labour and capital cost, £	Percentage reduction in unit cost
Before technical progress	0.5333	0.855	—	1,872	—
Neutral technical progress	0.5333	1.282	50	1,248	−33.3
Labour-saving technical progress	0.6857	1.339	57	1,280	−31.6
Capital-saving technical progress	0.4000	1.249	46	1,201	−35.8

Source: Table 8.4, assuming p_L = £1,200, p_K = £750 throughout.

However, what the businessman is really interested in is not the neutrality or non-neutrality aspects of technical progress, but the impact of technical progress on the combined labour and capital cost per unit of output. Table 8.5 shows in its last column what happens to unit costs. Because of the 'twist' in the unit isoquant caused by non-neutral technical progress we know that unit costs will be different according to whatever happens. In the present illustration, labour-saving technical progress will result in a reduction in unit cost of slightly less than that which occurs with neutral technical progress; the biggest saving in unit costs occurs with capital-saving technical progress. So, supposing a businessman reckoned that the ratio of factor prices would not alter and had the choice between the three types of technical change, the one chosen would be capital-saving because it leads to the biggest reduction in unit costs. However, as a matter of empirical, historical fact, the tendency has been for the price of labour to rise relatively to the price of capital. Suppose, then, that the businessman facing the choice of the three types of technical change reckoned instead that the factor price ratio would change from £1,200/£750 = 1.6 to £1,600/£400 = 4.00. At the changed factor price ratio, the least-cost combination of labour and capital along the unit isoquant are different from those given in Table 8.4 (which assumed a factor price ratio of 1.6); the least-cost positions on the unit isoquants at the changed factor price ratio are given in Table 8.6, together with the least-cost combination before technical progress (at the old factor price ratio) to provide a basis for comparison. The unit costs (at the new factor prices) are given in the second-last column, and it can now be seen that the labour-saving technical progress gives by a slight margin the largest reduction in unit costs. This is a quite common-sense result: labour-saving technical progress economises most on the factor which has become relatively more costly, and so may provide for the largest possible reduction in unit costs as capital–labour substitution is necessitated by the increasing relative cost of labour. A belief in the inevitability and inescapability of increases in the price of labour relative to the price of capital could thus stimulate the search for labour-saving technical innovation as the most promising way towards reduced unit costs of production.

The historical record

The preceding paragraphs may seem to the student rather abstract and theoretical, but the contrasting positions in Tables 8.5 and 8.6 probably contain a large part of the explanation for the fact that, as early as 1850, technology in manufacturing industry in the USA had gone ahead of manufacturing technology in Britain: it has been plausibly argued that one of the main reasons for this was the rising relative cost of scarce labour in a country where there were many economic opportunities more attractive than those of industrial employment. The early technological superiority of American industry quickly became obvious, and was clearly one important cause of high and rising standards of living in the USA. We have not the space here to go over all the evidence, but the student who might be tempted to dismiss the previous paragraphs as being only of (minor) theoretical importance should read H. J. Habakkuk's penetrating study *American and British Technology in the Nineteenth Century: The Search for Labour-saving Inventions* (Cambridge University Press, 1962). And from the viewpoint of the businessman today, whose most important long-run decisions may lie in this area of technological innovation, it is vital to have a well-founded understanding of non-neutral technical progress and its impact on unit costs under conditions of changing factor price ratios.

TABLE 8.6   *The impact of non-neutral technical progress on unit costs when the price of labour rises relatively to the price of capital*

	Least-cost combination [a]		Labour and capital cost per unit of output, £ [a]	Percentage reduction in unit cost
	$\dfrac{L^*}{Q}$	$\dfrac{K^*}{Q}$		
Before technical progress	1.17017	0.6241	1,872	—
After neutral technical progress	0.62040	0.8272	1,324	−29.3
After labour-saving technical progress	0.56713	0.9722	1,296	−30.8
After capital-saving technical progress	0.66667	0.6667	1,333	−28.8

[a] Before technical progress the factor price ratio is $p_L/p_K = 1,200/750 = 1.6$; for all cases after technical progress, the factor price ratio is changed to $p_L/p_K = 1,600/400 = 4$; thus labour is relatively more expensive.

Empirical data on technological change

So far we have treated technological change in an abstract, theoretical way as an increase in output which (somehow) arises to an extent greater than that which could be explained by an increase in labour and capital inputs (and, if necessary, allowing also for the effects of economies of scale). In a formal, algebraic way we have incorporated technical progress into the analysis via a change in Z, the adjustment factor, perhaps accompanied by a change in the production function's exponents. But algebra is not economics, so what sorts of influences explain why Z rises? There appear to be two main categories of influences: the first is *technological change* proper; the second is the effect of what is called the *learning curve*. We shall now discuss these in turn.

Since, as we described earlier, technological change itself is a complex phenomenon affecting both products and production methods, it is difficult to give any general account of the process; there is simply a myriad of changes, some small, some large, which make production more efficient – what matters is the economic effects of these changes. So, what are the implications, for economic analysis, of technological change proper?

We have seen in Table 8.5 that technical progress raises labour productivity. We saw in Table 7.4 how capital–labour substitution had raised productivity in the US glass industry. Table 8.7 shows in some detail the successive steps whereby output per man-hour of 25-watt electric light-bulbs was raised from 53 in 1916 to 1,699 in 1925 and thence to 4,539 in 1932, and this was not the end of the story! The technology and speed of the production process changed considerably during this period, and the result, shown clearly in Table 8.7, was a substantial decline in unit labour costs: from $14.75 per 1,000 bulbs (25-watt) when produced by hand to 5.3 cents when produced by the most advanced machinery. The purpose of Table 8.7 is to demonstrate just how great are the savings in unit labour costs which may be achieved, though, of course, this is at the expense of higher capital costs. As new processes came into operation, they rapidly displaced the older plants, and enterprises had to adopt the advanced processes or go out of business; even after allowing for capital costs (on which we have, unfortunately, no information), the automatic processes produced much cheaper light-bulbs.

Labour productivity grew rapidly also in the motor-car tyre industry. Manufacturing tyres is basically a process of mixing, assembling and moulding ingredients for 'curing' tyres by heat under pressure. The 'output' of these various processes can therefore be measured by weight of materials processed, and Table 8.8 shows that there was, in the

TABLE 8.7   Changes in the productivity and unit cost of labour directly engaged in producing electric light-bulbs, USA, 1916 to 1932

'Technology', or method of production; type of machine (and model)	'Vintage': year of operation	25-watt bulbs Number produced Per 'unit' hour[a]	Number produced Per man-hour	Labour cost (1925) per 1,000 bulbs, $ [b]	40-watt bulbs Number produced Per unit hour[a]	Number produced Per man-hour	Labour cost (1925) per 1,000 bulbs $ [b]
Hand production: Plant A	1916	118.17	52.52	14.750	118.44	52.64	14.716
Hand production: Plant B	1923	126.43	56.19	13.044	125.51	55.78	13.048
Semi-automatic machine (Empire E)	1925	406.24	116.06	4.197	407.91	116.55	4.180
Automatic machine (Empire F with feeder)	1925	1,870.91	801.82	0.570	1,837.50	787.50	0.580
Automatic (24-spindle Westlake, old type)	1925	2,139.38	1,283.63	0.584	2,198.59	1,319.15	0.568
Automatic (24-spindle Westlake, new type)	1925	2,336.43	1,699.22	0.471	2,342.44	1,703.59	0.470
Automatic (24-spindle Westlake, improved)[c]	1931	3,537.70	2,573.70	0.311	3,341.80	2,430.20	0.329
Automatic (48-spindle Ohio)[c]	1932	6,242.20	4,538.90	0.176	5,186.10	3,772.10	0.212
Ribbon bulb machine (Corning)[c]	1932	20,762.00	—	0.053	19,633.00		0.056

[a] Total output divided by total number of hours for which 'unit' operated; a 'unit' comprises the handful of workers (blowers and assistants, or machine operators and assistants) directly engaged in production: output per unit-hour divided by output per man-hour gives number of workers per unit (fractions indicate that some workers (e.g. assistants or foremen) may work for more than one unit).

[b] Labour costs are calculated on the basis of 1925 wage rates, regardless of year of output; this figure is calculated as:

Total labour cost per unit hour × 1,000 ÷ Output per unit hour

[c] Labour cost per unit hour calculated on the assumption that labour cost per unit-hour is the same as that for the 24-spindle new type unit ($1.100, comprising ⅓ machine foreman at $1 per hour; ½ mechanic at 90 cents per hour; and 1 machine operator at 75 cents per hour); the number of workers per unit for the 24-spindle improved unit and the 48-spindle unit is the same (1½), so in these first two cases the assumption is partly supported by the data; there are no data on the labour requirements of, and pay rates for, the Corning ribbon bulb machine, but some remarks indicate that its labour requirement must have been minimal, so that, even with higher rates of pay, this estimate must indicate approximately the extent of the reduction on the previous unit labour cost.

Sources: United States Department of Labor Bureau of Labor Statistics, *Productivity of Labor in the Glass Industry*, Bulletin No. 441, July 1927 (prepared by B. Stern), table D, pp. 128–131 (and table 28, p. 127); United States Department of Labor Bureau of Labor Statistics, *Technological Changes and Employment in the Electric Lamp Industry*, Bulletin No. 593, 1933 (prepared by W. Bowden), table 8, p. 45.

TABLE 8.8   *Changes in the productivity of labour directly engaged in producing motor-car tyres and inner tubes, USA, 1922 to 1931*

Materials handling by department	Per man-hour										Trend rate of increase, 1922–31, per cent per annum
	1922	1923	1924	1925	1926	1927	1928	1929	1930	1931	
All six surveyed plants, weighted average											
Washing, milling, compounding, and calendering of rubber, lb	68.47	72.08	77.95	86.30	98.01	102.76	108.10	116.70	129.89	152.57	8.5
Stock preparation and tyre (carcass) building, lb [a]	21.15	23.13	22.99	24.34	28.97	33.89	38.98	42.54	50.53	57.09	11.5
Curing, finishing and inspecting tyres, lb [a]	44.14	45.88	48.98	56.12	65.94	74.16	80.56	88.48	97.66	118.75	11.1
Manufacturing inner tubes, lb [b]	11.56	12.55	12.46	13.27	15.07	16.19	17.04	18.99	18.30	21.15	6.7
Whole plant, tyres by weight, lb	11.28	12.28	12.71	13.77	16.48	18.82	20.97	22.80	26.17	30.67	11.3
Tyres, number	0.70	0.78	0.82	0.80	0.92	0.98	1.05	1.07	1.14	1.37	6.6
Tubes, number	5.15	5.69	5.59	5.67	6.21	6.48	6.43	6.91	6.79	8.03	4.1

[a] Data for 1922 to 1924 inclusive is for five plants only.
[b] Data for five plants only.

Source: United States Department of Labor Bureau of Labor Statistics, *Labor Productivity in the Automobile Tire Industry*, Bulletin No. 585, July 1933 (prepared by B. Stern), tables 5, 19, 22, 27, 30, pp. 7, 44, 55, 63, 72.

period 1922 to 1931, a rapid growth in output (by weight) per man-hour of between 9 and 12 per cent per annum in the three main processes of tyre manufacture: preparing the materials; building the 'green' tyre; and curing the tyre. The average tyre became somewhat heavier during this period, so output of the whole plant by number of tyres per man-hour did not rise quite so rapidly: 6.6 per cent per annum. Similar productivity growth affected the manufacture of inner tubes. Closer inspection of Table 8.8 reveals that progress was especially rapid in the years 1928 to 1931, and this was a period when many new methods of materials handling were introduced in all departments; Appendix 8.2 provides a long and detailed catalogue of improvements in one plant between 1928 and 1931, each with its consequent reduction in man-hours per day. If one is not familiar with the processes of tyre manufacture and the attendant terminology, this list conveys only a rough impression of the changes which were going on. But it matters not if our comprehension of most of the items in Appendix 8.2 is hazy: what is important is (a) the length of the list, which indicates how technical change (in various forms) could affect every part of the manufacturing process, and (b) the fact that all these changes had a recorded impact on man-hours required per day and that this obviously increased labour productivity very considerably. The purpose of Table 8.8 and Appendix 8.2 is to demonstrate how the cumulative impact of technical progress raises labour productivity (or, equivalently, reduces unit labour requirements).

We have had occasion to observe that technological change may have to be 'embodied' in new capital equipment: word-processors may greatly increase the productivity of clerical staff, but in order to benefit from the new technology an enterprise has to invest in new sorts of fixed capital, perhaps scrapping its 'old' typewriters, even though these may still be very serviceable. This apparently rather obvious fact about technical progress has considerable economic implications, which were analysed by W. E. G. Salter in his important study *Productivity and Technical Change* (Cambridge University Press, 1960). Because capital equipment is durable, the process of adjustment, *within an industry*, to technical change is likely to be subject to delay: plants constructed on the basis of last year's technology (and still very serviceable) will not immediately be scrapped and replaced with plant embodying this year's technology.

Salter demonstrates what he means with reference to some data on the US blast-furnace industry: blast-furnaces produce (crude) pig-iron from iron-ore by heating ore, coke and limestone together and then casting the pig-iron into ingots. Although these data refer to the USA many years ago, this itself does not matter because the sort of situation depicted – considerable variation in labour productivity among the plants which make up the industry – is typical of most industries in all countries today. The figures in Table 8.9 show that productivity in the plants of highest productivity, or 'best-practice' plants as Salter calls them, rose by 83 per cent in the fifteen years 1911 to 1926, from 0.313 tons per man-hour to 0.573 tons per man-hour, or by about 4 per cent per annum. For the whole sample of plants, productivity rose even faster: by 111 per cent in fifteen years, or 5.1 per cent per annum. As the sample was a fairly large one, we may take these results as representative of the entire industry: the average number of plants in the sample during 1911 to 1926, excluding 1915 and 1916, was forty-two and the average number of 'stacks' (actual furnaces) was sixty-four (some plants comprise more than one stack); for the entire US blast-furnace industry the average number of plants during these years was 161, with 365 stacks (data from *Productivity of Labor in Merchant Blast Furnaces*, appendix 5, p. 138), so the coverage of the sample was about one-quarter of the industry.

But, between 1911 and 1918, there was little if any increase in productivity, and it was only in the period 1919 to 1926 that productivity advance occurred. For the sample as a whole, one important cause of the increase in productivity during the postwar period was the cessation of production by the inefficient, low-productivity plants: the recession in 1921 and 1922 forced out many of the high-cost, low-productivity plants, and although

TABLE 8.9 *Productivity and technical progress in the US blast-furnace industry, 1911 to 1927*

Year	Productivity: tons (2,240 lb) of pig-iron per man-hour [c]			Scale of output: tons per stack-day [e]			Highest productivity plant	
	Highest product-ivity plant	Sample average	Lowest product-ivity plant [d]	Highest product-ivity plant	Sample average [f]	Lowest product-ivity plant [d]	Plant serial number in survey	Vintage [g]
1911	0.313	0.140	0.068	385.0	260.5	136.1	16	1911
1912	0.299	0.150	0.075	385.3	261.4	140.2	16	1911
1913	0.308	0.151	0.082	389.0	258.3	81.9	16	1911
1914	0.274	0.160	0.078	382.4	262.3	72.0	16	1911
1915 [a]	0.313	0.159	0.088	450.9	252.5	190.2	16	1911
1916 [a]	0.294	0.147	0.095	445.9	231.9	182.4	16	1911
1917	0.326	0.150	0.059	376.8	249.8	109.1	4	1912, rebuilt 1914 and 1916
1918	0.310	0.131	0.067	337.6	225.6	120.7	32	1917
1919	0.328	0.144	0.060	308.0	246.6	109.1	9	1918
1920	0.446	0.157	0.063	464.7	247.5	115.2	1	1914, re-lined 1919
1921	0.428	0.178	0.064	574.4	287.1	218.1	1	1914
1922	0.442	0.232	0.077	557.3	329.8	86.9	1	1914
1923	0.462	0.213	0.069	508.3	294.9	77.7	1	1914
1924	0.466	0.244	0.096	320.7	327.2	132.6	23	1923
1925	0.512	0.285	0.105	596.7	353.5	229.1	3	1911, new furnace 1919 and 1925
1926	0.573	0.296	0.115	648.7	369.1	124.2	3	1911
1927 [b]	0.630	0.300	0.122	657.9	397.5	124.0	3	1911

[a] Sample considerably reduced in number.

[b] First six months only.

[c] Gross tons per man-hour of all labour concerned with production (furnace crew labour and other labour); general office clerks and accountants, sales and delivery workers are excluded.

[d] For which figures are given on both labour productivity and output per stack-day.

[e] Stacks (furnaces) are not operated every day of the year, so tons of output per each calendar day of actual operation best indicates plant capacity; tonnage is usable product (not total metal cast; excludes 'runner and ladle scrap').

[f] Some years exclude a very few plants for which days operated were not reported.

[g] Apparent date of construction and/or rebuilding as listed in table A, last column.

Source: United States Department of Labor Bureau of Labor Statistics, *Productivity of Labor in Merchant Blast Furnaces*, Bulletin No. 474, December 1928 (US Government Printing Office, 1929), table 2, p. 5; table 6, p. 27; appendix 1, table A, pp. 71–103, table B, pp. 104–15.

some of these plants came back into production in the boom of 1923, the same reasons – high unit costs – subsequently forced many out of business:

> Less than three-fourths of the merchant plants operating in 1923 remained active until 1926, and the high-productivity average of the later year is due in no small degree to the closing down of inefficient plants (*Productivity of Labor in Merchant Blast Furnaces*, p. 1).

However, for individual plants, especially perhaps the best-practice plants:

> another important factor causing the increase in productivity has been the improvement of blast furnaces and the technical improvements in [methods of] operation, both of which are reflected in greater daily production per furnace… The most important labor-saving devices have been *(a)* mechanical charging and *(b)* machine casting, which have eliminated large numbers of hand laborers engaged in charging materials into the stack and in handling the pig-iron after it has been cast (*Productivity of Labor in Merchant Blast Furnaces*, p. 2).

Table 8.9 shows that the best-practice plant from 1911 to 1916 was Plant No. 16, which had been newly built in 1911. The furnace of this plant was mechanically charged and the pig-iron was cast by machine. This means it had a mechanised system whereby rail-cars could directly unload their ore into bins and thence into smaller skips for delivery by hoist to the top of the stack (installation of a skip-hoist could double labour productivity) and that its metal was cast into steel moulds running on an endless chain dipping through a trough of water to cool the iron before dumping the 'pigs' (ingots) straight into rail-cars for shipping out (rather than cast into sand-beds, left to cool, and then manually picked up and loaded).

Between 1917 and 1920 the best-practice plants at the top of the table changed each year, but always to a plant recently built or refurbished, and all of these plants had for long used mechanical charging and machine casting.

Between 1920 and 1923 Plant No. 1 held the leadership: not only was this plant mechanised and refurbished but it operated on a much larger scale of output, so it benefited also from economies of scale.

In its turn, Plant No. 1 was displaced by a smaller-scale but more up-to-date plant in 1924, and from 1925 onwards, Plant No. 3, obviously benefiting from economies of large-scale production, held the leadership.

The interesting feature of this 'league table' is that the plants at the top of the league were always those which had incorporated the most advanced methods and which operated on a large scale; thus they gained their position because they simultaneously took advantage of technical progress and economies of scale.

We may assume, as seems reasonable, that these best-practice plants represented the least-cost position at each date according to the prevailing factor price ratios and technology (isoquant). If so, and providing there were no economies of scale and no capital–labour substitution induced by changing factor price ratios, we could then ascribe the entire 83 per cent change in labour productivity in best-practice plants to technological progress (whether neutral or non-neutral). The first condition is, however, not applicable: it is known that there are economies of scale in pig-iron production; and Table 8.9 demonstrates that the scale of operation of best-practice plants did increase substantially over this period, so that the 83 per cent increase in labour productivity was partly due to economies of scale.

(Economies of scale would also be likely to explain some part of the difference in productivity between best-practice plants, as a comparison of Table 8.9 shows that the high-productivity plants were operating at a considerably greater scale of output: the best-practice plant in 1911 – Plant No. 16 – had a scale of output per stack day of 385 tons compared with the sample average of 261 tons and 136 tons for the worst-practice plant.)

The condition of a constant factor price ratio also did not apply: between 1911 and 1926 average hourly earnings of mainly union labour in manufacturing industries in the USA rose from 26.3 cents per hour to 64.7 cents per hour, an increase of 146 per cent; over approximately the same period the implied price of producers' durables capital formation rose by 83 per cent (data from US Department of Commerce Bureau of the Census, *Historical Statistics of the United States: Colonial Times to 1970*, part I, series D 766, p. 168, and series F 85 and F 112, pp. 231–2). The price of labour relative to the price of capital thus rose by about one-third during this period, and we must reckon that this also induced capital–labour substitution along the isoquants (which were at the same time shifting because of technical progress and economies of scale).

Therefore, we must conclude that the 83 per cent rise in labour productivity was partly due to capital–labour substitution, partly due to economies of scale, and partly due to technical progress. In practice, it is difficult (in the absence of complete data, especially on capital inputs) to distinguish which caused what. But the combined effect of all these influences is clearly apparent in Table 8.9. Whatever the combination of technical progress, economies of scale, and capital–labour substitution, their combined impact on labour productivity, or conversely on unit labour requirements, was substantial.

Practical consequences of technological change

Table 8.9 also shows the weighted average performance of the sample of blast-furnace plants taken as a whole: total tons of pig-iron produced annually by the sample divided by total man-hours used per annum. It is a significant fact that, at any date, the average productivity of the whole sample is only about half that in the best-practice plants. One important reason for this continuing difference seems to be the 'delay' in the adoption, by other plants in the sample, of mechanical charging and casting, techniques which were first introduced in 1905; more than twenty years after this date only 70 per cent of the plants had fully adopted these techniques. Salter argues that such situations are typical; he gives other instances for other industries at other times and in other countries and his argument is in any case very plausible on *a priori* grounds (serviceable plant is not immediately scrapped and replaced when it becomes technically obsolete).

But this fact is of considerable significance for a proper understanding of the process of competition among plants, and we need to explore its implications fully. If we examine the dispersion among blast-furnace plants of unit labour requirements (measured by man-hours per ton of pig-iron), we can see that there is a wide range of unit labour requirements. Appendix 8.3 gives the details for sixty plants in 1923; this was a boom year and a number of low-productivity (high unit labour requirement) plants were brought into (temporary) production, so we can see just how widely unit labour requirements may vary given favourable circumstances. Plant No. 1 had the lowest unit labour requirement of 2.166 man-hours per ton of pig-iron and Plant No. 71 had the highest unit labour requirement of 14.405 man-hours per ton followed by Plant No. 65 at 11.713 man-hours per ton. In Appendix 8.3 the plants are listed in ascending order of unit labour requirement, and we can see that, by and large, the plants with the lowest unit labour requirement were operating at bigger scales of output and vice versa (the coefficient of correlation between unit labour requirement and scale of output is -0.783 and the minus sign shows that the covariance is negative: that is, below-average unit labour requirement (man-hours per ton) tends to be associated with above-average scale of output (tons per stack-day).

Now, it would be cumbersome to analyse the working of the blast-furnace industry with reference to all sixty plants, so Table 8.10 reproduces the details for seven plants spaced

TABLE 8.10 *Variation in unit labour requirements among plants and competition in the US blast-furnace industry, 1923 and 1925*

Plant No.	Unit labour requirement, man-hours per ton		Scale of output, tons per stack-day	
	1923	1925	1923	1925
3 [a]	—	1.954	—	596.7
1	2.166	2.271	508.3	578.7
5	3.141	3.390	444.6	457.7
45	4.459	3.471	287.5	276.8
46	5.447	4.865	298.1	291.9
43	6.571	5.614	192.4	220.8
40	8.139	9.560	269.1	229.1
65 [b]	11.713	—	136.2	—

[a] Recorded as 'new furnace built' in 1925.
[b] Recorded as 'idle since 1923'.

Source: Appendix 8.3 and United States Department of Labor Bureau of Labor Statistics, *Productivity of Labor in Merchant Blast Furnaces*, Bulletin No. 474, December 1928, appendix I, table B, pp. 105–8.

throughout the sample, and arranged in ascending order of unit labour requirement, the most efficient plant first. Table 8.10 also gives the same information on unit labour requirement and output per stack-day for the same plants in 1925, except that a new plant, No. 3, is top of the list in 1925, having had a new furnace built, and the bottom plant in 1923, No. 65, had ceased production by 1925 (I have taken, from Appendix 8.3, the second-last plant to represent the worst-practice plant, because Plant No. 71 is really too exaggeratedly bad).

If this sample of plants can be taken as representative of the whole industry, and if all plants operated more or less the same number of days per annum, then we can represent the entire industry in 1923, according to unit labour requirements and output, in the top part of Diagram 8.2. Along the horizontal axis we measure tons of pig-iron, and starting with the most efficient plant, Plant No. 1, next to the origin mark off the output per stack-day of that plant as this corresponds (on a reduced scale) to its annual output; on to the position so reached we then add the output per stack-day of the next-most efficient plant, and so on *cumulatively* (each time measuring not from the origin but from the position previously reached). At the end, therefore, we have marked off a representation of the annual output of the whole industry. We can see, in line with the negative correlation for the whole sample, that the scale of output per plant tends to be greater in the more efficient plants and that these produce more per annum than do the less efficient plants. The width of the column, representing annual plant output, therefore becomes narrower as we move on to the less efficient plants. Up the vertical axis of Diagram 8.2 we may then measure the unit labour requirement of each plant. The range of plants in 1923 shows the effect not only of economies of scale but also the effect of new technology installed; we may argue that the most efficient (lowest unit labour requirement) plants embody the newest techniques, and that the less efficient plants embody techniques of less recent 'vintage' (we shall use the word 'vintage' to refer to the date at which the plant was constructed). As Salter puts it:

> Given a continuous stream of improvements in techniques of production, the plants in existence at any one time, are, in effect, a fossilised history of technology over the period spanned by their construction dates – the capital stock represents a petrified chronicle of the recent past (Salter, *Productivity and Technical Change*, p. 52).

Thus, the situation depicted in Diagram 8.2 is probably typical of most industries in most countries at all times (unless there are peculiar circumstances to the contrary such as may occur when the industry comprises either a single plant or plants all of very nearly the same vintage).

Unit costs of production – labour *plus* capital charges *plus* bought-in materials and services per ton of pig-iron – may plausibly be argued to be lower in the newer, more efficient plants than in the older, less efficient plants. In the first place, we may argue that either through the operation of a competitive labour market or through the influence of an industry-wide trade union, wages per man-hour will be approximately the same in each plant regardless of vintage: the same hourly rate of pay together with declining unit labour requirements would produce lower unit labour costs in the plants of newer vintage. A situation in which markedly lower average wages were paid in plants of older vintage could exist, but would be peculiar.

A parallel argument may be made, but with less certainty, for unit capital costs; if there were cases where the bias in technical progress had actually led to higher unit capital requirements in plants of newer vintage, then, correspondingly, we could expect the reduction in unit labour requirements to have been enhanced by such a labour-saving/capital-using bias. However, this argument abstracts entirely from the method of financing the capital formation: for example, if the newer plant were financed by borrowing and the older plant not, then the newer plant could be incurring heavier interest

DIAGRAM 8.2   *Unit costs, prices and competition among plants*

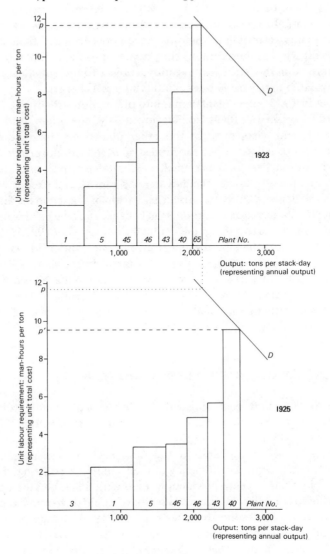

and debt repayment charges (per unit of surplus) than the older plant. In what follows we ignore this important (financial) possibility in order to concentrate on the purely economic aspects of production.

Unit material costs may or may not be affected by technical progress and economies of scale; if not, then the addition of the same unit materials cost to declining unit labour and capital costs to give the unit total cost of production (for each vintage) will reduce the proportionate difference between the plants of newest and oldest vintage, but there will still remain a difference. To save drawing another diagram (for which we have in any case no hard data) we may simply pretend that the height of the columns in Diagram 8.2 also represents unit total costs of production. The impression of cost differences may be a little exaggerated but it will serve to emphasise an important economic aspect of production by plants in an industry: namely, that plants of newest vintage (and largest scale of production) should be operating at the lowest unit cost of production in the industry (and so should be the most profitable). If by this pretence we transpose the vertical axis into unit total cost per ton of pig-iron, we may also record price per ton of pig-iron on it and draw in an assumed demand curve for pig-iron such as *D* (remembering that we are also pretending that the horizontal axis represents annual output). The total supply of pig-iron being what it is, the price of pig-iron in 1923 will be p; this price is just sufficient to keep the least efficient plant, No. 65, in operation; and this price provides 'extra' profits for the more efficient plants according to the difference between p and their unit total costs of production. Plant No. 1 is therefore making greatest profits, before interest charges, and should therefore be in the 'strongest' position, subject to the qualification that its profits may be appropriated to pay for greater capital (interest) charges.

Suppose that in 1925 a new plant comes into production – Plant No. 3, as shown in the bottom part of Diagram 8.2: Plant No. 3 is now next to the origin. It has a large capacity (see Table 8.10), and, also, most of the other plants may increase their production somewhat. In order to sell its output, the newest plant reduces the price of pig-iron to p', as shown in the bottom part of Diagram 8.2. This lower price must now become the 'competitive' price for all plants in the industry. As a result of the reduced price two things happen: along the demand curve there is an expansion of sales; and the least efficient plant in 1923, Plant No. 65, has to cease production because the new price is below its unit total costs of production. These two things mean that the new plant of 1925 vintage is able to sell all its output. Note also that the disappearance of the (low-productivity) plant and its 'replacement' by the (high-productivity) 1925 plant means that, in 1925, the *average* productivity of the industry as a whole will have risen; so we have here an explanation for the rise in industry average labour productivity shown in Table 8.9 (assuming, of course, that this process of pushing out plants of oldest vintage and replacing them with newest vintage plant is something that goes on all the time).

Technological change and corporate strategy

If this sort of situation – unit costs rising with the vintage of plant and inversely with scale of operation – is widespread, then the situation depicted in Diagram 8.2, i.e. perpetual displacement of outdated, small-scale plants, may typify the process of change and growth in all industries. If so, it explains, in the first place, why managers are always so preoccupied with increasing the efficiency of their plants: by so doing, they postpone the day when that plant has to cease production. In Diagram 8.2, had the managers of Plant No. 65 been able to cut unit costs, then Plant No. 65 could have remained in business (for the time being at least) despite the advent of the 1925-vintage plant. Previously, in Chapters 5 and 7, we noted from Eliasson's survey of sixty-two large corporations (*Business Economic Planning: Theory, Practice and Comparison*) the importance which he found that managers attached to maintaining and improving plant performance. Given the pervasiveness of technological change allied with economies of scale, this finding is not surprising: the length of time for which a plant survives is probably determined by the ability of its managers to do just this.

We have from time to time discussed the significance of internal financing of fixed capital formation. The analysis of Diagram 8.2 was carried through entirely in terms of plants, not of firms (or companies). Obviously, there are two very different possibilities in Diagram 8.2: the 1925 vintage Plant No. 3 belongs to the same company that owns Plant No. 65; or Plant No. 3 belongs to some other company. In the former case, the company owning Plant No. 65 continues in business. In the latter case, it goes into liquidation (assuming the company has no interests other than its pig-iron plant). It seems reasonable to argue that companies desire to continue in business and wish to avoid bankruptcy. In that case, Plant No. 65 must, over the period of its economic lifetime, accumulate sufficient retained earnings which (together, possibly, with an additional injection of external funds) will enable the company to construct the new Plant No. 3 in 1925. From the day it begins production, the managers of any plant must be looking ahead to the economic demise of that plant and its replacement by an up-to-date, cost-competitive plant. The more rapid the pace of technological change, the shorter is likely to be the economic lifespan of a plant, and the more keenly must the managers of a company be aware of this need to accumulate replacement funds. It is not simply a coincidence that senior managers in both the United Kingdom and West Germany stated that the most important reason for their interest in profitability was 'to provide finance for expansion' (Table 4.19). If managers do not obtain this finance to invest in new plant, embodying technological progress and economies of scale, and facilitating capital–labour substitution (if the price of labour is rising relatively to the price of capital), then they must eventually encounter the liquidation of the company, probably through the mechanism displayed in Diagram 8.2.

Given that technological change is an ongoing, willy-nilly process, companies have no alternative but to try to accumulate funds for investment in new plant; the alternative to company growth is not simply stagnation, it is death (in the form of liquidation). As Ricardo remarked in another context (and with reference to an entirely different principle): 'The clearly understanding this principle is, I am persuaded, of the utmost importance to the science of political economy.'

We may use Diagram 8.2, broadening it out from its purely pig-iron application, to analyse issues other than the displacement of old plants by new best-practice plants. The source of additional output for sale may come not from a new domestic plant but from imports, thus displacing domestic production and employment.

A leftward shift of the demand curve (because of the arrival of a new product substitute, or because of a change in 'fashion' (people's tastes), or because of a reduction in government (or other) expenditure on the product or on products into which it is an input, or because of a general recession), will hasten the liquidation of plants of older vintage, leaving only the more modern, lower-cost plants to survive.

Conversely, a rightward shift of the demand curve may, if it does not lead to an increase in imports, cause (temporary) upward pressure on prices (the total volume of production being approximately fixed in the short term), and this will lead to an increase in profits which (if the extra profits are not expropriated by increased wages) will provide both the incentive and the wherewithal (internal financing) to invest in new capacity; and the company who is quickest off the mark (or even anticipates the change) may gain the most. A rise in wages (or other costs), unaccompanied by a corresponding shift in the demand curve, may also lead to the demise of plants of older vintage, because their unit costs then rise above the prevailing price; the consequent disappearance of output (if not replaced by imports – which replacement is a most likely possibility), may then lead to higher prices via an upward movement along the demand curve; this then relieves the cost pressure on the surviving plants, but leaves the employees of the liquidated plants with no prospect of re-employment within the industry. One 'solution' to such a situation is to subsidise (e.g. from tax revenues) the plant(s) of older vintage and so enable them to continue production.

Thus the implications, for economic analysis, of technological change (allied with economies of scale and capital–labour substitution) are far-reaching, especially with regard to understanding the operations of, and the pressures on, the enterprise sector of the economy.

The learning curve

We have seen why and how the pressure is always on management continually to improve the performance of plants. In this task management may be assisted by the 'learning curve', which is the second category of influences causing 'technical progress', in the form of a rise in Z: increases in output not accompanied by corresponding increases in labour and capital inputs. The learning curve represents a specific, and important, type of technical progress and it deserves to be studied with some care. The learning curve refers only to a (steady) movement from position 1 straight to position 4 in our three-by-three matrix of technological change (p. 316): it concerns only the production of an existing product but with a movement towards 'improved' methods of production.

Let us start by summarising how we see technical progress as affecting the production function, now that we have looked at some data on technical progress and productivity change. Such a summary usefully paves the way for a proper consideration of the learning curve.

Suppose, in Table 8.9, that at each date we had a different, most-recent vintage plant as the best-practice plant. This is not in fact the case, because we know that Plants 16, 1 and 3 each held their lead for several years (and the learning curve may help explain why), but for purposes of exposition we may envisage a succession of plants each year: the basic principle is that best-practice plants will, sooner or later, be displaced by newcomers as the most efficient plant, so all our supposition does is to speed up and make more regular the process of displacement. So we now have Table 8.9 with a different serial number each year in the second-last column – a new best-practice plant each year. If we could fit a production function to the data on output, labour and capital inputs of this regular sequence of best-practice plants, we would most likely find that, as we progressed from plant to plant, the output from each succeeding best-practice plant rose by more than could be accounted for by the increase (if any) in the measured labour and capital inputs (after allowing also for the effect of any economies of scale). This 'extra' increase in output we would ascribe to technical progress.

To take a simple example (but an entirely possible one). The 'output' of the best-practice plant of a given vintage will be 'gross' output of all items (whether defective or not) *minus* the wastage of sub-standard, defective items. Let us suppose that the wastage rate is 10 per cent of 'gross' output: that is, only 90 items (or tons) out of every 100 are up to quality standards (anyone familiar with the sale of 'seconds' will appreciate that such a situation is entirely realistic and there is in fact some wastage of unusable 'runner and ladle scrap' in the blast-furnace industry). Suppose that a quality-control device is invented and installed in a plant of new vintage and that this device reduces the wastage rate to 6 per cent; 94 items (or tons, etc.) out of every 100 are now up to standard. Compared with the older-vintage plant, the new best-practice plant adopting such a quality-control device now has 4.4 per cent more net output (94/90) for no extra cost other than that of installing and operating the quality-control device. If we assume that this extra cost is relatively small, then the newer best-practice plant shows a 4.4 per cent increase in output with hardly any increase in measured labour and capital inputs, and so this 4.4 per cent increase shows up as an increase in Z_t, the adjustment factor; and thus we measure technical progress. If we know the values of the exponents a and b, then we may estimate Z_t as:

$$Z_t = \frac{Q_t}{L_t^a K_t^b}$$

If we do not know the values of a and b, but want to estimate them by fitting a least-squares (multiple) regression line to data on Q, L and K, then we cannot estimate Z_t in this way. One method of getting round this problem is to assume that, over the whole period, Z_t will increase at a constant proportionate rate, r, each year: for example, to assume that there will be a 4.4 per cent increase in Z each year. Obviously such an assumption is only an approximation, but it will nevertheless serve. If we are prepared to proceed on the basis of such an assumption, then we can relate the adjustment factor in year t simply to the passage of time as follows (see Chapter 3 for an explanation of e):

$$\hat{Z}_t = Z_0 e^{rt}$$

where Z_0 is the initial value, t is the date (measured as 0 in the base year, 1911, and so on: $1 = 1912$, etc.), and r is the proportionate rate of technical progress per annum. Note that in this expression there is a hat on Z to denote that it is an *estimate* of Z_t based on the assumption of a steady rate of technical progress (in other words, we are assuming that any inaccuracy caused by this assumption is relatively small). We may now write the production function for successive best-practice plants as:

$$Q_t = \hat{Z}_t L_t^a K_t^b$$
$$= Z_0 e^{rt} L_t^a K_t^b$$

or taking logarithms to the base e (ln):

$$\ln Q_t = \ln Z_0 + rt + a \ln L_t + b \ln K_t$$

and this linear equation in logarithms may be estimated by statistical methods, using observations on Q_t, t, L_t and K_t; $\ln Z_0$ is the constant term in the equation, and r, a and b will be estimated by least squares as the parameters (or coefficients) of the equation. In this procedure, we have envisaged Z_t as increasing simply because, steadily through time, innovations become available and are adopted and incorporated into the best-practice process of production.

The way in which technical progress, represented thus, would affect output can be shown very simply if we imagine a situation in which the labour and capital inputs do not change but are constant throughout at their least-cost combination (as given in Table 7.3, assuming a price ratio of £1,200/£750 = 1.6). Let us assume that technical progress occurs at a constant and continuous rate of 0.04 = 4 per cent per annum. (Recall that labour productivity in the best-practice plants in Table 8.9 increased by about 4 per cent per annum.) In this case, with constant labour and capital inputs, output will change in the way shown in Table 8.11; requirements for labour and capital per unit of output will decline, and labour and capital cost per unit of output will fall steadily, as shown in the last column. Within four years, unit costs will have declined by 15 per cent, and if these were a series of best-practice plants (all with the same labour and capital input and no economies of scale), the best-practice plant built in year 4 would have a considerable cost advantage over the best-practice plant in year 0.

However, there are many cases where, if one considered the data on outputs and labour and capital inputs for the *same* plant over a number of years, one would find that the annual flow of output increases each year without any change in the labour and capital inputs used. It is not quite so easy to imagine that the same plant can adopt, each and every year, innovations like, say, quality control which continuously improve its performance: such a process is quite understandable in the case of a series of new, best-practice plants, but it is difficult to envisage the process occurring continually in a plant of a given vintage.

Nevertheless, as we shall see, the phenomenon of continually improving performance in the same plant does exist. One possible explanation is that even a plant of a given vintage is simply a composite of lots of pieces of equipment, and piecemeal improvements to various parts of the plant could account for such technical progress. But there is another explanation of more general applicability. This is the explanation that, as the work-force becomes accustomed to, and experienced in, the production process, the workers steadily learn how to do tasks more efficiently and quickly. Consequently, either the output for the same input of labour-time goes up; or (what amounts to the same thing) the amount of labour-time required to produce a unit of output goes down. The experience gained by the labour force is related to the *cumulated* amount of output produced.

Such a process of 'learning by doing' is well known to occur in such assembly industries as aircraft production, and it is quite understandable that the labour-time taken to assemble the first aircraft of a given model should be much greater than the labour-time

TABLE 8.11 *Impact of a constant rate of technical progress, r = 4 per cent per annum, on best-practice plants*

Vintage of best-practice plant, year t	Production function			Index of annual output, Q_t	Unit requirements		Unit labour and capital cost, £
	Technical progress effect, $Z_0 e^{rt}$ $1.00 \times 2.71828^{0.04t}$	Labour input, L^a $117.017^{0.75}$	Capital input, K^b $62.410^{0.25}$		Labour input, L/Q_t $117.017/Q_t$	Capital input, K/Q_t $62.410/Q_t$	$p_L\left(\dfrac{L}{Q_t}\right) + p_K'\left(\dfrac{K}{Q_t}\right)$ $1{,}200\left(\dfrac{117.017}{Q_t}\right) + 750\left(\dfrac{62.410}{Q_t}\right)$
0	1.0000	35.578	2.811	100.0	1.17017	0.62410	1,872
1	1.0408	35.578	2.811	104.1	1.12408	0.59952	1,799
2	1.0833	35.578	2.811	108.3	1.08049	0.57627	1,729
3	1.1275	35.578	2.811	112.8	1.03738	0.55328	1,660
4	1.1735	35.578	2.811	117.4	0.99674	0.53160	1,595
⋯	⋯	⋯	⋯	⋯	⋯	⋯	⋯

taken to assemble the nth aircraft. The reasons for this are fairly obvious (and will be understood by any reader with experience, say, of building a first and subsequent model aircraft, or of cooking a first and subsequent cake, of the same model or recipe, or of knitting a first and subsequent jersey): at the beginning (the first item), nothing is routine, everything is unfamiliar, and it takes times to learn how to cope with snags; by the nth item, everything is routine and familiar, and the quickest and best way of dealing with snags and awkward parts is well known to the now experienced work-force. Additional to this 'informal' process of learning by doing, the plant may institute 'formal' work study – time-and-motion study – to decrease the labour-time required per unit of output; theoretically speaking, improvements in labour productivity achieved by such formal methods are independent of the cumulated volume of production, but in practice there is likely to be a close relation: the importance attached by most plants to work study emphasises the significance of the whole process of economising on labour inputs.* As a result of all these influences, the labour-time required per unit of output (aircraft, real or model, or per cake or per knitted garment) falls as the cumulated output rises because producing this output provides the work-force with experience – the greater the (cumulated) output, the greater the experience gained.

We may, for the purposes of economic analysis, represent the effect on productivity of learning from experience by relating Z not to the passage of time as previously, but to the *cumulated* amount of output: in other words, to the serial number of the item produced when the items are numbered in sequence – first item = 1, second item = 2, ..., ith item = i, and so on. Here we need to have in our mind's eye a picture of the production of relatively 'big' but nevertheless standardised items, such as aircraft (of a specific type and model), or ships (such as a standard size oil tanker), or a large piece of machinery (turbine generator). Suppose we go back to the production function of Table 7.3, where at the least-cost position we had 117.017 units of labour and 62.410 units of capital producing 100 units of output per annum. From this production function labour productivity is $100/117.017 = 0.855$, and conversely the unit labour requirement is $117.017/100 = 1.17017$. When dealing with 'big' items it is preferable to work in terms of the labour requirement per unit (item) of output. Let us see how this expression for unit labour requirement was derived, using (general) symbols instead of specific numbers. The production function is:

$$Q_t = Z_t L_t^a K_t^b$$

Therefore, labour requirement per unit of output is:

$$\frac{L_t}{Q_t} = Z_t^{-1} L_t^{1-a} K_t^{-b}$$

If there were no change in Z, L and K, then the unit labour requirement, averaged in this way over the year's production, Q_t (assuming t represents one year), would at the same time be the unit labour requirement for each item produced: that is, each item, no matter what its sequence in the year's production, would require L_t/Q_t (e.g. 1.17017) units of labour input. Thus for any ith item (where i is the serial number in sequence) we could write the unit labour requirement for that item, u_i, as:

$$u_i = Z^{-1} L^{1-a} K^{-b}$$

where the t subscripts on Z, L and K have been removed to indicate that they are being held constant. In the absence of learning from experience, u_i is simply a constant (e.g. 1.17017) for all i. Now, the important characteristic of learning from experience is that unit labour requirement decreases as cumulated output – experience, measured by the serial number i

*A close inspection of Appendix 8.2 will show at least eight such 'work-study' items in the motor-car tyre and inner-tube production processes.

– increases. Therefore, if we make Z a variable which increases with i, then u_i will *decrease* with i (because u_i is related to Z^{-1}, or to $1/Z$). Thus, if we want to incorporate learning from experience into the production function, we must make Z vary with cumulated output, as measured by the serial number of each item:

$$u_i = Z_i^{-1}L^{1-a}K^{-b}$$

(we still hold L and K constant because, for instance, we do not wish the effect of an increase in capital per worker on output per worker, or unit labour requirement, to affect the analysis). This now leaves us with the problem of devising an expression for Z_i.

Let us suppose (and we shall subsequently see the evidence for this supposition) that the effect of cumulated output on unit labour requirement is a *proportionate* effect: that is, that each 1 per cent increase in cumulated output produces, or 'causes', an increase of $d \times 100$ per cent in Z. Thus, with Z_0 still as the initial value of the adjustment factor, we have:

$$Z_i = Z_0 i^d$$

Thus d is the 'elasticity' of the adjustment factor with respect to cumulated output as measured by the serial number i: in other words, d is the proportionate (or percentage) change in Z with respect to a proportionate (or percentage) change in i. The expression for unit labour requirement on the ith item to be produced is now:

$$u_i = [Z_0 i^d]^{-1}L^{1-a}K^{-b}$$
$$= Z_0^{-1}i^{-d}L^{1-a}K^{-b}$$

So that as i increases u_i will decrease, because u_i is related to i^{-d}, or to $1/i^d$. Using the constant returns to scale production function and the least-cost combination of labour and capital inputs given in Table 7.3, we can see what happens to unit labour requirements per item if the value of d is 0.20 or 20 per cent (this is near to the value for d which we shall subsequently find in the empirical data). For the following values $Z_0 = 1.0000$, $L = 117.017$, $K = 62.410$, $a = 0.75$, $b = 0.25$ and $d = 0.20$, we may calculate:

$$Z_i = Z_0 i^d$$

and:

$$u_i = \frac{L^{1-a}K^{-b}}{Z_i} = Z_0^{-1}i^{-d}L^{1-a}K^{-b}$$

for $i = 1$ to 16, the first sixteen items to be produced, as shown in Table 8.12. The relationship between u_i, as the dependent variable and i, as the independent variable, is known as the learning curve. Given that Z_0, L and K are constant (as are the parameters a and b in the production function), then $Z_0^{-1}L^{1-a}K^{-b} = F$, a constant (in the case under consideration, $F = 1.17017$) and we may write the learning curve in a simple form as:

$$u_i = Fi^{-d}$$

The graph of this learning curve is shown in Diagram 8.3, where i is measured along the horizontal axis, and unit labour requirement, for the ith item, up the vertical axis. You can see that the resulting set of points, when joined together, give a curve which is steep at first and then flattens out. This represents the situation that 'learning' is fastest at the beginning when everything is new and unfamiliar but that later on it slows down. Formally, we gave this shape to the learning curve when we supposed that the effect of cumulated output on unit labour requirement was a *proportionate* effect; the increase from item 1 to item 2 is a 100 per cent increase in cumulated output but the increase from item 2 to item 3 is only a 50 per cent increase in cumulated output; therefore, the effect on unit labour requirement of the move from item 1 to item 2 is almost twice as great as the effect of the move from 2 to 3.

TABLE 8.12   *The impact of learning from experience on unit labour requirement and hence on unit labour cost*

Item (serial number in production process), [a] i	Adjustment factor in production function, [b] Z_i	Unit labour requirement for ith item, [c] u_i	Unit labour cost for ith item, £ $p_L = £1,200$ $p_L \times u_i$	Cumulative total labour cost, [d] £	Cumulative average unit labour cost, [e] £ $\frac{1}{i} \Sigma p_L \times u_i$
1	1.000000	1.170170	1,404.2040	1,404.2040	1,404.2040
2	1.148698	1.018692	1,222.4306	2,626.6346	1,313.3173
3	1.245731	0.939344	1,127.2129	3,753.8475	1,251.2825
4	1.319508	0.886823	1,064.1876	4,818.0351	1,204.5088
5	1.379730	0.848115	1,017.7385	5,835.7736	1,167.1547
6	1.430969	0.817747	981.2958	6,817.0695	1,136.1782
7	1.475773	0.792920	951.5040	7,768.5734	1,109.7962
8	1.515717	0.772024	926.4291	8,695.0026	1,086.8753
9	1.551846	0.754051	904.8606	9,599.8632	1,066.6515
10	1.584893	0.738327	885.9928	10,485.8560	1,048.5856
11	1.615394	0.724387	869.2639	11,355.1200	1,032.2836
12	1.643752	0.711890	854.2676	12,209.3876	1,017.4490
13	1.670278	0.700584	840.7009	13,050.0886	1,003.8530
14	1.695218	0.690277	828.3323	13,878.4209	991.3158
15	1.718772	0.680817	816.9810	14,695.4019	979.6935
16	1.741101	0.672086	806.5034	15,501.9053	968.8691

[a] First item produced has serial number 1, second number 2, and so on.
[b] Calculated as $Z_i = Z_0 i^d = 1.000 i^{0.2}$.
[c] Calculated as $(L^{1-a}K^{-b})/Z_i = (117.017^{1-0.75}62.41^{-0.25})/Z_i$.
[d] Cumulative sum of unit labour costs.
[e] Preceding column divided by i.

DIAGRAM 8.3   *The learning curve*

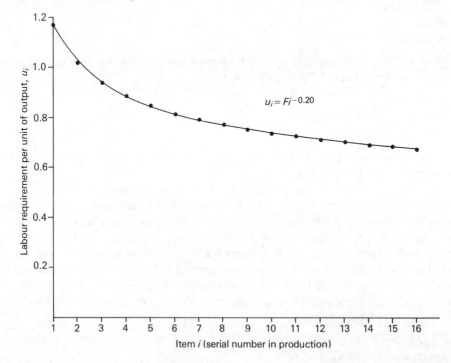

In fact the learning curve is often used (e.g. by cost accountants) in terms of its proportionate effect on unit labour requirement (or unit labour cost) as cumulated output successively doubles:

Cumulated output	1	2	4	8	16
Unit labour requirement	1.17017	1.018692	0.886823	0.772024	0.672086
Ratio to preceding unit labour requirement	—	0.871	0.871	0.871	0.871

At each doubled level of output, the unit labour requirement is 0.871, or 87.1 per cent, of its preceding value. The proportion 0.871 arises because, if the learning curve is:

$$u_i = Fi^{-0.2}$$

then for u_j, where $j = 2 \times i$, i.e. where j represents a doubling of cumulated output:

$$u_j = Fj^{-0.2} = F(2 \times i)^{-0.2}$$
$$= 2^{-0.2}Fi^{-0.2}$$
$$= 0.871u_i$$

A learning curve that is derived from the unit labour requirement (or unit labour cost) and cumulated output, with an elasticity of d, can therefore also be referred to as an X per cent learning curve, where X is computed as:

$$(2^{-d}) \times 100$$

In this way, we might refer to the learning curve in Table 8.12 as 'an 87.1 per cent learning curve', thereby indicating that each time cumulated output doubled, unit labour requirement (or cost) was reduced to 87.1 per cent of its preceding value.

The relation of unit labour cost to the ith item is simply the relation for unit labour requirement multiplied by the price per unit of labour. If a unit of labour is priced at $p_L = £1,200$ (Table 7.3), and this is unchanging, then:

$$\text{Unit labour cost for } i\text{th item} = p_L \times F \times i^{-d}$$

This can be verified if we actually estimate, by least squares, the learning curve for unit labour cost as given in Table 8.12:

$$\text{Unit labour cost for } i\text{th item} = 1,404.204 i^{-0.2}$$

So the learning curve in terms of unit labour cost for the ith item has the same slope as the learning curve in terms of unit labour requirements.

Another variant of the learning curve used by cost accountants is to relate the *cumulative* average unit labour cost, i.e. the sum of all the unit labour costs incurred divided by the number of items produced, to the cumulated output produced. The reason for doing this is that if the cost accountant has an estimate of the learning curve with cumulative average unit labour cost as the dependent variable, then, when this function is multiplied by i, the cost accountant has an estimate of the total labour cost incurred in producing those i units – which total cost is important to the process of cost accounting.

The learning curve for cumulative average unit labour cost, as given in Table 8.12, is (when estimated by least-squares):

$$\text{Cumulative average unit labour cost} = 1,442 \times i^{-0.1391}$$

Note that the rate at which cumulative average labour cost declines with i is less than the rate at which unit labour cost for the ith item declines, because, of course, cumulative

The learning curve on double-logarithmic scales

We noted in Chapter 1 in connection with Diagram 1.3, which showed the working population of the United Kingdom from 1851 to 1980 on semi-logarithmic paper, that there was also 'double-logarithmic' paper with log scales in both directions. We now have an opportunity to see the use of double-log paper, because learning curves are usually drawn on such scales; the reason for this is that the curved line of Diagram 8.3, drawn on arithmetic scales both ways, becomes a straight line when drawn on paper with logarithmic scales both ways.

Diagram 8.4 shows the data of Table 8.12 plotted on double-log paper. The horizontal axis is again i, starting from 1, but on this logarithmic, or ratio, scale the ruler distance from 1 to 2 (a doubling) is the same as the ruler distance from 2 to 4, or 4 to 8 or 5 to 10 (all of which representing a doubling, or the same proportionate increase). The vertical axis represents the unit labour requirement, starting at 0.1 and going to 1.0 and then on to 1.1 (the next line above 1.0, which is, however, not marked). You will observe that logarithmic scales start at 1 or 0.1 (or 10 or 100, as you choose) but never at 0; this is because we are dealing with proportionate changes and the proportionate change from 0 to anything is infinite; in other words, it is nonsensical to speak about a proportionate change starting from 0 (the reader may recall Alice's offended reply to the March Hare's invitation to 'take some more tea': 'I've had nothing yet, so I can't take more.'). Plotting the co-ordinates from Table 8.12 on the double-log paper in Diagram 8.4 produces a straight line. Because the data of Table 8.12 were derived from the learning curve:

$$u_i = Fi^{-d}$$

if we take logarithms we get:

$$\log u_i = \log F - d \log i$$

which is the form of an equation for a straight line (in the logarithms of the variables). Because many functional relationships result in proportionate effects, and because straight lines are more convenient than curves, economists often use such logarithmic relationships as shown in Diagram 8.4.

DIAGRAM 8.4   *The learning curve of Diagram 8.3 drawn on double-logarithmic paper*

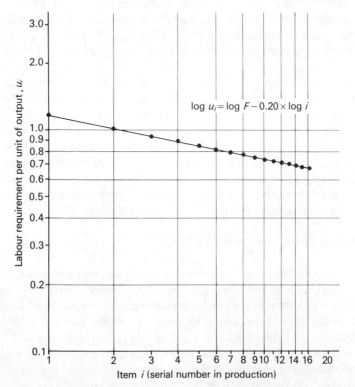

$\log u_i = \log F - 0.20 \times \log i$

Labour requirement per unit of output, u_i

Item i (serial number in production)

average unit labour cost is 'held back' by the tail of higher unit costs on all preceding items. (Note also that, because of the least-squares fit ($R = -0.995$), the function has become a little approximate, rather than mathematically exact, and the constant is 1,442 instead of 1,404. The constant, or intercept, term in this equation ought to be exactly the unit labour cost for producing the first item.) From the learning curve in terms of cumulative average unit labour cost we may estimate the total labour cost for producing the first i items as:

$$\text{Total labour cost in producing } i \text{ items} = 1{,}442 \times i^{-0.1391} \times i$$

$$= 1{,}442 \times i^{-0.1391+1}$$

$$= 1{,}442 \times i^{0.8609}$$

And this total labour cost function is exactly the equation which may be derived by applying the method of least squares to the relevant data in Table 8.12. So that, if the cost accountant can make an estimate of the elasticity of cumulative average unit labour cost with respect to cumulated output, then, together with an estimate of the unit labour cost for the first item, he can estimate the total labour cost for producing the first i items. And it is clearly important to be able to do this, particularly if the cost accountant is then going to make a recommendation about the price to be charged which will cover costs, but which at the same time will be as low as possible – i.e. taking into account falling unit labour costs – so as to enable a maximum penetration into the market.

In Table 8.12 we made a sneaky transition from the preceding production functions, which were all in terms of the passage of time, to a production function in terms of the passage of units of output. Fully to explore the exact relationship between the two would take us rather too far afield, but two remarks are called for.

First, falling unit labour requirements per unit of output mean rising labour productivity; therefore, if through successive periods of time one applies equal amounts of labour to production, but with rising productivity, then output per period of time per worker (or per total man-hours) will rise. To illustrate (approximately) from Table 8.12, in the first period of time, one might produce the first four items, in the second (equal) period of time, one might produce the next *five* items, and in the third period, the next *six*; and (more or less) so on.

Second, if the idea of for ever declining unit labour requirements (and therefore unit labour costs, given constant prices) seems disturbing, then one must recall that the basis of the decline is *cumulated* output, and so the amount of time required to effect, say, an 87.1 per cent reduction in unit labour requirements will rise enormously; the flattening out of the curve, seen in Diagram 8.3, shows that, sooner rather than later, the reduction in unit costs per period of time becomes almost imperceptible and unit labour requirements will, for all practical purposes, appear constant. The gains from the learning curve mostly accrue during the first few periods of production, as can be seen in the unit labour cost for the ith item column in Table 8.12.

Empirical data on learning curves

Having considered learning curves from a theoretical aspect, with hints as to their practical importance to production and costing, we need to consider some of the actual statistics which demonstrate, quite conclusively, that learning from experience does affect industrial production, especially the production, by assembly, of 'big' items. The first set of data we shall be considering in Tables 8.13 and 8.14, and Appendices 8.4 and 8.5, comes from the production of military ships and aircraft in the USA during the Second World War. Apart from the fact that this appears to be the only detailed, systematic data published on this matter, there are several good reasons for using these data.

First, the production of military equipment was a very widespread operation: shipyards and aircraft plants were established or expanded quickly into full-capacity operation which then ran fairly uninterruptedly for several years; at the peak, over 1.7 million workers were employed in private and navy shipyards, and over 1.5 million in aircraft production. Although there may have been some capital–labour substitution, some economies of scale, and some other sorts of technical progress, given the short time scale involved, these effects may be assumed to have been relatively small (e.g. 'outdated' plants were not being superseded by 'best-practice' plants), so that most of what we see in the figures is the effect of learning from experience.

Second, the fact of virtually uninterrupted production, whether by trade cycles or strikes, and the fact that the work-force was probably reasonably co-operative throughout, also makes the data more readily applicable to an analysis of production economics, pure and simple, because we do not have to be worried about any such 'extraneous' effects.

Third, because of the contractual nature of the work, the US government agencies kept (or ensured the keeping of) records relating to production, so one can have at least reasonable confidence in the accuracy of the figures which, let us emphasise again, relate to a very sizeable economic operation.

Fourth, and most important, many of today's large industries, especially the mechanical and electrical engineering industries, to say nothing of the motor-vehicles or electrical-appliance industries, take the general form of repetitive assembly of pieces of machinery or equipment, often quite 'big' pieces. To the extent that this is so, then the phenomenon of learning by experience, demonstrated in the US wartime statistics, is likely to be quite widespread throughout contemporary industry.

In 1941 the US Maritime Commission, the government agency in charge of merchant shipbuilding, authorised the construction of over 300 'Liberty Ships', the EC–2 cargo vessels, designed to meet an emergency demand for cargo-carrying capacity for the USA and its allies. The Liberty Ships were 10,800 deadweight tons, of a standardised design and equipment. The first Liberty Ships were delivered in December 1941 and by the end of October 1944, when the construction programme was winding down, 2,404 Liberty Ships had been built in sixteen shipyards. The US Maritime Commission made estimates of the total contractual man-hours per vessel including direct labour specifically chargeable to ship construction – machinery, hull and superstructure – and outfitting, and indirect man-hours including the allocated time of supervisory, technical, clerical, office, mainte-nance and other employees (the time of corporation officers, auditors, general managers, superintendents was excluded from the figures, as was subcontracted work, which was, however, considered a negligible percentage). Although there were obvious problems with keeping such records on a consistent basis, the Bureau of Labor Statistics believed that 'the figures are sufficiently reliable to indicate the trend' (US Department of Labor Bureau of Labor Statistics, 'Increased Productivity in the Construction of Liberty Vessels', *Monthly Labor Review*, November 1943, p. 862; see also 'Productivity Changes in Selected Wartime Shipbuilding Programs', *Monthly Labor Review*, December 1945).

The resulting figures of man-hours per vessel, averaged over successive groups of ten vessels (by sequential serial number in order of delivery dates), are given for sixteen shipyards separately and for all yards combined in Table 8.13. The outstanding feature of this table is that, in all cases, there are substantial declines between the higher unit labour requirements for the early groups of vessels delivered and the lower unit labour require-ments for the later groups. Taking Yard *A*, the first ten vessels to be produced required an average of 1.024 million man-hours per vessel, but the last completed group of ten vessels (nos 371 to 380) required an average of 0.442 million man-hours per vessel: a reduction of 57 per cent (!) over the production run.

Diagram 8.5 illustrates the shape of the learning curve for two shipyards, *K* and *L* (chosen because they can be conveniently fitted on to a diagram, but similar curves could,

TABLE 8.13 Average man-hours required to build EC-2 cargo vessels ('Liberty Ships') delivered through 31 October 1944 in sixteen US shipyards [a]

Average for vessels nos (in order of delivery dates) [b]	Average man-hours per vessel, thousands																
	Yard A	Yard B	Yard C	Yard D	Yard E	Yard F	Yard G	Yard H	Yard I	Yard J	Yard K	Yard L	Yard M	Yard N	Yard O	Yard P	All yards
1 to 10	1,024	1,009	899	1,241	1,395	1,217	915	740	1,164	1,342	1,837	1,667	1,571	1,057	1,528	2,347	1,310
11 to 20	818	809	749	1,209	1,022	973	644	566	898	1,026	1,135	1,055	1,106	889	1,095	1,404	931
21 to 30	732	687	656	915	935	924	564	601	727	895	928	781	746				776
31 to 40	692	635	613	749	847	949	558	517	658	743	745	666	620				692
41 to 50	673	590	661	820	772	750	592	473	640	692	670	651	607				661
51 to 60	655	598	606	694	772	718	558	452	577	707	645	594	570				628
61 to 70	642	573	553	552	777	700	536	422	660	700	601	553					610
71 to 80	625	571	502	550	720	661	450	418	648	697							574
81 to 90	622	569	479	571	665	710	430	403	680								569
91 to 100	616	544	437	515	599	690	409	392	661								540
101 to 110	608	493	418	510	613	652	390	395	633								524
111 to 120	593	456	401	494	528	620	414	398									488
121 to 130	581	379	377	498	552	593	470	401									485
131 to 140	567	331	392	487	526	577	562										490
141 to 150	559	321	402	501	519	550											475
151 to 160	549	319	385	492	550	545											473
161 to 170	537	314	368	458	519	530											454
171 to 180	527	311	361	420	454	525											421
181 to 190	517	313	348	413	427												402
191 to 200	515	301	348	421													396
201 to 210	510	293	354	425													396
211 to 220	525	288	357	417													397
221 to 230	536	284	363	417													400
231 to 240	535	287	361	430													403
241 to 250	511	292	343	438													396

	1	2	3	4	5	6	7	8	9	10	11	12	13	14	15	16	Total
251 to 260	502	298	323	441													391
261 to 270	499	282	313	440													384
271 to 280	495	270	301	433													375
281 to 290	494	266	300	447													377
291 to 300	485	275	327	448													384
301 to 310	494	300	337	456													390
311 to 320	496	296	365														386
321 to 330	493	285	464														414
331 to 340	466	286															376
341 to 350	466	328															397
351 to 360	474	364															464
361 to 370	479																
371 to 380	442																
381 to 390	450																
Per vessel																	
Maximum man-hours	1,199	1,164	1,095	1,532	1,596	1,529	1,200	1,073	1,424	1,701	2,279	2,488	1,878	1,148	1,714	3,159	3,159
Minimum man-hours	409	247	219	406	406	525	367	368	527	660	581	551	529	798	950	1,404	219
Average, all vessels delivered	566	413	438	559	700	723	535	478	722	867	963	897	891	973	1,384	2,261	604
Number of vessels delivered	384	351	330	306	186	173	138	126	110	72	65	61	56	20	15	11	2,404

(a) The programme was started in June 1941 when the US Maritime Commission authorised the construction of the first 300 standard 'Liberty Ships': 'The vessel was specifically designed to enable the utilization of mass-production shipyard methods. Standardization of structural members, elimination of all but essential equipment, the use of prefabricated parts, and the utilization of new materials not only made large-scale production possible but materially reduced the time necessary for the completion of each ship' (*Wartime Employment, Production, and Conditions of Work in Shipyards* (see below), p. 37). The 'Liberty Ship' had a length of 441 feet; a deadweight tonnage of 10,800 tons; a 9,000 horsepower steam reciprocating engine.

(b) Groups of ten vessels or part thereof (at the end of the production run – see very last row for number of vessels averaged; for example, for Yard A the last average figure is the average for the last four vessels built, i.e. for vessels 381 to 384; for Yard B the figure is for the 351st vessel only).

Source: United States Department of Labor Bureau of Labor Statistics, *Wartime Employment, Production, and Conditions of Work in Shipyards*, Bulletin No. 824, 1945, table 23, pp. 40–1.

DIAGRAM 8.5   *The learning curve in two US shipyards building 'Liberty Ships'*

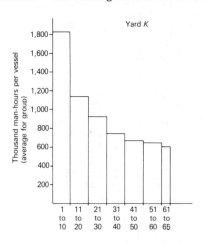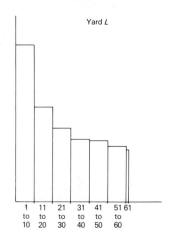

as we shall show, be drawn for any of the yards). The profile of the hypothetical learning curve of Diagram 8.3 is clearly seen in these group-average data for shipbuilding: the decline in unit labour requirement is steep at first, but then slows down. The data for Yard L shows that while the first ten ships took an average of 1,667,000 man-hours per vessel, the 61st vessel required only 553,000 man-hours (this is one of the few 'point' estimates of unit labour requirements provided by these data). In other words, over the cumulated output produced by Yard L, unit labour requirement fell by two-thirds to one-third of the initial value. Such a decline is substantial; furthermore, declines of this order of magnitude seem to have been quite common.

It is also clear that there was considerable variation among shipyards in efficiency: at any given stage of the production process (i.e. going across Table 8.13) some shipyards would have a substantially lower unit labour requirement than others. Part of this may have been due to the fact that some yards used all-welding techniques, which took less labour time than the combination of riveting and welding used by other yards, and part of it was due to some yards having more space than others in which to lay out a systematic sequence of work.

Appendices 8.4 and 8.5 show that learning curves also applied to the building of 'Victory Ships', a faster and slightly larger cargo or troop transport ship (troop transports required more fitting out than cargo vessels, and so had a higher unit labour requirement) and to the building of destroyer–escort vessels carrying torpedo tubes, depth charges and heavy machine-guns. Throughout all these data, the decline in unit labour requirement as cumulated output increases is clearly evident.

The Bureau of Labor Statistics considered that these figures showed 'without a doubt that among the most important factors affecting man-hour requirements to build Liberty Ships has been experience' (*Wartime Employment*..., p. 43). The Bureau noted also that the policy of awarding prizes to employees who made suggestions for promoting efficiency and curtailing waste resulted in 3,000 such suggestions between August 1942 and December 1944 and that these suggestions 'resulted in a saving of over 31 million man-hours and 44 million dollars' with $143,000 in prizes being paid (*Wartime Employment*..., pp. 46–7). From this we may conclude that the practical experience gained by workers was put to good use.

Nor was the situation of falling labour requirement confined to the shipbuilding industry. Table 8.14 shows some time-series data on the production of military aircraft. The scale of this operation was clearly very large: in the peak month of March 1944 no less than 9,117 aircraft were delivered to the military during the month, and total employment in the prime contracting airframe, engine and propeller plants rose to over $1\frac{1}{2}$ million. But the interesting feature of this enormous programme is again the decline in unit labour requirement from 61.44 employees (per thousand lb of aircraft delivered) in January 1941 to 14.31 employees per thousand lb in August 1944, by which time the cumulated output amounted to 221,047 aircraft. (Weight is the most appropriate measure of physical output for a diverse assortment of aircraft.)

If we plot, on double-log paper, the points of unit labour requirement against cumulated output measured, not to the end of the month as in Table 8.14, but to the middle of the month, in Diagram 8.6, we can see that though the over-all trend in unit labour requirement is downward, there are several irregularities, particularly round about the beginning of 1943. The problem with these data is that they contain all types of aircraft under production (separate figures for each model were not published), so differences in the product-mix, or the introduction of new (and therefore unfamiliar) models, could affect over-all unit labour requirement. The explanation for increases in unit labour requirements in 1943 appears to be that prior to 1943 production was concentrated on lighter aeroplanes, such as fighters and trainers. But, beginning in 1943, heavy bombers and cargo planes became a more significant part of production; so it is likely that the switch to different types of aircraft temporarily disturbed the learning-curve progress – and this is exactly what we would expect to find. However, once the production of heavy planes was under way, the learning effect manifested itself in a further sharp fall in unit labour requirements.

Tables 8.13 and 8.14 and Appendices 8.4 and 8.5 present again the problem of a large amount of data which need somehow to be summarised if we are to obtain more than an over-all impression that the learning curve exists in reality. Again, the solution lies in using least-squares regression to fit the proportionate form of the learning curve (as given in Table 8.12) to the data. This enables us to 'reduce' each column of data to an estimate of the coefficient d, the elasticity of unit labour requirement with respect to cumulated output, and to a correlation coefficient which shows how accurately that particular form of the learning curve represents the real-world data.

DIAGRAM 8.6   *The learning curve for aircraft production (all models) in the USA*

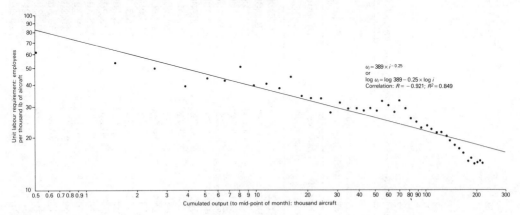

Table 8.15 shows the learning curves which can be estimated for all these US shipyards. There are two important main facts to be gathered from this table.

First, where applicable, the correlation coefficients are high, indicating that the theoretical learning curve of Table 8.12 and Diagrams 8.3 and 8.4 is well fitted to representing these data. That is, the form, or 'shape', of the learning curve we have been discussing is strongly supported by this empirical evidence.

TABLE 8.14   US production of military aircraft, monthly, January 1941 to August 1944

Year and month	Acceptances by military of aircraft during month		Total employment number (c)		Cumulative number of aircraft produced by end of month	Unit labour requirement: number of employees per thousand lb of aircraft produced	
	Number of aircraft (a)	Total weight of aircraft, lb ths (b)	Airframe plants	Airframe, engine and propeller plants		Airframe employees only	Employees in all plants
1941 Jan	1,012	3,420.3	162,200	210,138	1,012	47.42	61.44
Feb	963	4,120.1	170,600	222,008	1,975	41.41	53.88
Mar	1,136	4,699.5	179,200	234,125	3,111	38.13	49.82
Apr	1,391	6,386.9	191,200	250,062	4,502	29.94	39.15
May	1,329	6,056.2	203,100	265,972	5,831	33.54	43.92
Jun	1,478	6,908.0	222,300	291,099	7,309	32.18	42.14
Jul	1,462	6,263.6	242,900	317,636	8,771	38.78	50.71
Aug	1,854	8,713.5	265,500	346,076	10,625	30.47	39.72
Sep	1,946	9,077.1	283,800	369,454	12,571	31.27	40.70
Oct	2,284	10,588.2	310,800	405,237	14,855	29.35	38.27
Nov	2,138	9,658.1	327,600	427,479	16,993	33.92	44.26
Dec	2,462	13,497.1	356,300	466,030	19,455	26.40	34.53
1942 Jan	2,977	15,021.7	388,600	507,353	22,432	25.87	33.77
Feb	3,047	16,660.5	423,700	556,784	25,479	25.43	33.42
Mar	3,483	21,318.0	448,300	596,082	28,962	21.03	27.96
Apr	3,506	20,057.4	479,900	639,589	32,468	23.93	31.89
May	3,984	23,237.0	510,200	682,284	36,452	21.96	29.36
Jun	3,738	24,846.3	553,800	736,068	40,190	22.29	29.62
Jul	4,106	27,402.7	594,300	784,385	44,296	21.69	28.62
Aug	4,281	29,025.0	658,200	858,385	48,577	22.68	29.57
Sep	4,307	32,148.8	710,500	917,951	52,884	22.10	28.55

Oct	4,063	30,848.4	774,100	991,906	56,947	25.09	32.15
Nov	4,812	35,064.7	840,500	1,070,897	61,759	23.97	30.54
Dec	5,501	41,178.6	913,000	1,153,364	67,260	22.17	28.01
1943 Jan	5,014	37,532.1	975,500	1,232,943	72,274	25.99	32.85
Feb	5,423	43,961.6	1,013,100	1,285,618	77,697	23.05	29.24
Mar	6,265	51,038.9	1,037,800	1,324,616	83,962	20.33	25.95
Apr	6,472	55,252.1	1,062,300	1,361,969	90,434	19.23	24.65
May	7,087	60,692.7	1,084,200	1,394,511	97,521	17.86	22.98
Jun	7,097	61,535.6	1,115,100	1,437,440	104,618	18.12	23.36
Jul	7,376	65,458.5	1,139,600	1,472,401	111,994	17.41	22.49
Aug	7,613	69,296.7	1,148,100	1,498,429	119,607	16.57	21.62
Sep	7,598	71,103.9	1,170,900	1,536,209	127,205	16.47	21.61
Oct	8,363	76,256.5	1,179,100	1,559,756	135,568	15.46	20.45
Nov	8,791	82,444.6	1,185,500	1,575,379	144,359	14.38	19.11
Dec	8,802	86,353.4	1,167,900	1,555,840	153,161	13.52	18.02
1944 Jan	8,789	89,989.0	1,156,100	1,550,962	161,950	12.85	17.24
Feb	8,761	93,500.0	1,137,900	1,534,826	170,711	12.17	16.42
Mar	9,117	101,400.0	1,108,400	1,500,634	179,828	10.93	14.80
Apr	8,331	96,400.0	1,084,300	1,475,157	188,159	11.25	15.30
May	8,902	102,400.0	1,063,400	1,450,773	197,061	10.38	14.17
Jun	8,049	97,800.0	1,027,600	1,413,951	205,110	10.51	14.46
Jul	8,000	93,900.0	1,009,000	1,392,890	213,110	10.75	14.83
Aug	7,937	93,900.0	973,300	1,343,937	221,047	10.37	14.31

(a) Excludes spares.
(b) Including spares.
(c) Including estimate of subcontracting labour for airframe plants.

Source: United States Department of Labor Bureau of Labor Statistics, *Wartime Development of the Aircraft Industry*, Bulletin No. 800, 1944 (prepared by H. B. Byer) tables 2 and 10, pp. 5 and 22.

TABLE 8.15 Learning curves for shipyards in the USA during the Second World War

Yard, and type of ship	Number of observations	Regression equation [a] Intercept: thousand man-hours required to build first ship	Coefficient: elasticity of unit labour requirement w.r.t. cumulated output	Correlation R	Proportion of variance in unit labour requirement explained, R^2	Fitted point on learning curve Unit labour requirement (thousand man-hours) for ships with: Serial No. 25	Serial No. 50	Serial No. 100	Learning gradient [b]
Liberty Ships: EC–2									
Yard A	39	1,355	−0.179	−0.991	0.981	762	673	594	0.883
Yard B	36	2,239	−0.360	−0.938	0.879	702	547	426	0.779
Yard C	33	1,599	−0.277	−0.939	0.882	655	540	446	0.825
Yard D	31	2,269	−0.306	−0.958	0.919	848	686	555	0.809
Yard E	19	2,576	−0.317	−0.974	0.948	927	744	597	0.803
Yard F	18	1,997	−0.250	−0.972	0.944	894	752	633	0.841
Yard G	14	1,225	−0.214	−0.864	0.747	615	530	457	0.862
Yard H	13	1,077	−0.214	−0.975	0.952	540	466	402	0.862
Yard I	11	1,481	−0.197	−0.890	0.793	786	686	599	0.873
Yard J	8	2,123	−0.274	−0.980	0.960	879	727	601	0.827
Yard K	7	4,040	−0.463	−0.998	0.996	910	660	479	0.725
Yard L	7	3,587	−0.456	−0.995	0.991	827	603	440	0.729
Yard M	6	3,625	−0.473	−0.986	0.972	791	570	411	0.721
Yard N	2	1,405	−0.167	(e)	(e)	821	731	651	0.891
Yard O	2	2,957	−0.387	(e)	(e)	850	650	497	0.765
Yard P	2	8,305	−0.741	(e)	(e)	764	457	273	0.598
All yards [c]	32	2,176	−0.310	−0.994	0.988	802	647	522	0.807
Victory Ships						*3*	*6*	*12*	
AP–3: general cargo									
Yard A	7	1,405	−0.193	−0.995	0.990	1,137	994	870	0.875
Yard B	7	1,224	−0.160	−0.938	0.879	1,027	919	823	0.895
Yard C	2	1,931	−0.480	(e)	(e)	1,140	817	586	0.717
All yards [d]	7	1,290	−0.173	−0.970	0.942	1,066	946	839	0.887

						5	10	20	
AP–5: troop transport									
Yard D	4	2,483	−0.270	−0.983	0.966	1,845	1,530	1,269	0.829
Yard E	2	2,490	−0.258	(e)	(e)	1,876	1,569	1,312	0.836
Yard A	2	2,288	−0.276	(e)	(e)	1,689	1,395	1,151	0.826
AP–2: general cargo									
Yard C	2	704	−0.153	(e)	(e)	595	535	481	0.899
Yard F	2	1,108	−0.242	(e)	(e)	849	718	607	0.845
Destroyer–escorts									
Yard A	31	1,064	−0.100	−0.773	0.598	906	845	789	0.993
Yard B	25	1,946	−0.327	−0.979	0.959	1,150	917	731	0.797
Yard C	21	2,740	−0.290	−0.936	0.877	1,718	1,405	1,149	0.818
Yard D	15	1,370	−0.084	−0.612	0.375	1,198	1,130	1,067	0.944
Yard E	6	784	−0.225	−0.880	0.774	546	467	400	0.856
Yard F	5	2,839	−0.488	−0.958	0.918	1,294	922	658	0.713
Yard G	4	578	−0.043	−0.724	0.524	540	524	509	0.971
Yard H	4	607	0.155	0.948	0.899	779	867	965	—
Yard I	4	1,703	−0.149	−0.997	0.993	1,340	1,208	1,090	0.902
Yard J	3	1,402	−0.287	−0.999	0.999	884	725	594	0.820
All yards [d]	25	1,523	−0.196	−0.888	0.788	1,110	969	846	0.873

(a) Where u_i is thousand man-hours per vessel (averaged for a group of vessels) and i is the mid-point of the group's serial numbers (cumulated output), the equation is: $u_i = F i^{-d}$, fitted in logarithmic form; the intercept is F and the coefficient is d. Using the mid-point effectively fits the curve to the unit labour requirements for each vessel in sequential serial number.

(b) Ratio of unit labour requirement at successive doubling of cumulated output: can be computed from the fitted points given (but to one decimal place) or as 2^{-d}.

(c) At least three yards in the average.

(d) At least two yards in the average.

(e) Correlation not applicable to a line fitted to two points.

Source: computed from Table 8.13 and Appendices 8.4 and 8.5.

Second, in every case but one, the elasticities of unit labour requirement with respect to cumulated output are not only negative but are also quite large: the unweighted average of the thirty-three shipyards' elasticities (excluding those for 'all yards' and the one positive coefficient) is −0.282. On first encountering the learning curve, one might have been tempted to regard the hypothetical elasticity of −0.20 used in Table 8.12 as exaggeratedly excessive; but we can now see that, if anything, this hypothetical value erred on the side of understatement and that elasticities of −0.25 or more can occur.

There are also two other points to be gathered from Table 8.15.

First, the intercept, which gives according to the fitted curve the man-hours required to build the first vessel, may be thought of as indicating each shipyard's initial efficiency. It is apparent from considering the variation in these intercepts, for each type of ship, that shipyards differed considerably in their efficiency. Unfortunately, there are no data on capital input which would permit us to explore the reasons for this inter-yard variation in efficiency, but as the significance of inter-plant differences in productivity was previously discussed it is worth noting the extent to which such differences existed among the shipyards.

Second, the way in which the curve has been fitted (to the mid-points of the grouping by serial numbers) means that we can, from the fitted curve, provide point-estimates of the man-hours required to build a ship of any given serial number (in order of delivery date, which must be pretty well the order of construction). Because of the high correlation coefficients throughout, we can be reasonably confident that these 'predicted' point estimates are not too far from the (unknown) real values. The table gives sets of three such point-estimates, representing two successive doublings of cumulated output. The purpose of this is to enable the reader to study the 'learning gradient', defined as the proportion of its former value to which unit labour requirement is reduced when output *doubles*. The reader can verify that the learning gradient is the ratio:

$$\frac{u_{2 \times i}}{u_i} = 2^{-d}$$

by working out, separately, each side of the equation. (The reader should also verify the fitted points by using the intercept and the coefficient: for instance, that $762 = 1{,}355 \times 25^{-0.179}$ or that $594 = 1{,}355 \times 100^{-0.179}$, and so on. Take nothing on trust!)

Diagram 8.6 gives the learning curve as fitted to the aircraft production data of Table 8.14. We are on less firm ground here, because these data cover all types of aircraft and so refer to the composite learning experience on different types of aircraft, and not to a complete run of one model (as does the shipyard data). Nevertheless, the learning elasticity, taken over all models, was −0.25, and the correlation coefficient of −0.92 shows that the fit is reasonable. Again, the size of the elasticity and the shape of the learning curve are supported by empirical data.

Practical consequences of the learning curve

The main practical consequences of the learning curve may be divided between two different but related areas: cost accounting, and strategic management.

Cost accounting is concerned with collecting data on all costs incurred in production and selling, analysing those data (so that, for example, costs may be more precisely allocated to the point at, or function in, which they are incurred), and then, using the data as analysed, making projections of costs so as (a) to enable the enterprise to control its costs, and (b) to permit the enterprise to plan prices and hence (it is to be hoped) profits per unit of output (via the mark-up – but always subject to market constraints).

The learning curve is obviously relevant to the issue of projecting costs, because, if the curve is applicable to a product, it means that a straightforward 'linear' projection of, say, unit labour cost and therefore of total labour cost in producing i units of output will not give accurate results. To illustrate, if we simply assume constant unit labour cost, then the linear projection of total labour costs incurred in producing i items is:

$$\text{Total labour cost in producing } i \text{ items} = \frac{p_L \times L}{Q} \times i$$

where p_L is the (constant) price of a unit of labour. But if the unit labour requirement, L/Q, varies with i, i.e. declines as i increases, then this approach leads to erroneous cost projections. Accordingly, as explained previously (pp. 343–6), the cost accountant may have to use a non-linear function for total labour cost of the form:

$$\text{Total labour cost in producing } i \text{ items} = A \times i^g$$

where A is some constant and g is some positive fraction: in other words, total labour cost increases less than in proportion to the proportionate increase in the number of items produced. Accordingly, the cumulative average unit labour cost will decline as the number of items increases:

$$\text{Cumulative average unit labour cost} = \frac{\text{Total labour cost in producing } i \text{ items}}{i} = A \times i^g \times i^{-1}$$

$$= A \times i^{g-1}$$

and the exponent on i will be negative (because g is less than 1); in other words, cumulative average unit labour cost decreases as i increases.

We may take the step from cost accounting to the implications of the learning curve for strategic management by noting that up to now we have discussed the learning curve simply in terms of unit labour requirements and unit labour cost. Because unit labour cost tends to be a significant part of unit production cost we could argue that, providing unit materials cost did not rise with cumulated output (which seems, *a priori*, an unlikely eventuality), unit production cost would tend to follow a similar, if less marked, decline with increasing cumulated output. Such a curve for unit production cost we may call the 'experience curve' (following the usage which has become conventional in referring to the broader all-costs curve as an 'experience curve' so as to distinguish it from the narrower labour cost only 'learning curve'). The argument that the experience curve depends on the learning curve is rather a minimum argument: it has further been argued that something akin to the learning effect will benefit inputs other than labour, but (a) the empirical evidence for this is a little sketchy, and (b) this seems to introduce technological progress into the experience curve – but a technological progress which can only be garnered by the cumulative experience of producing output (i.e. it is not technological progress accessible to those without the necessary cumulative production experience). While this further argument may be a realistic one (especially when considerations of quality are taken into account), we shall here rely on the minimum argument only.

In our discussion of the learning curve we have tended to imply that the decrease in unit labour requirement and in unit labour cost would simply occur, though the remarks on work study and on prizes for suggestions from workers (pp. 341 and 350) indicated that full advantage of the learning curve effect might need to be deliberately 'managed': in other words, careful management might be required to 'force' the production unit down the learning curve. We should also note that the reduction in unit labour costs will not be commensurate with the reduction in unit labour requirement if employees are being paid according to piece-rates or according to productivity bonuses; in such cases, the advantage of reduced unit labour requirement (increased labour productivity) accrues to the employees. So that, if the enterprise is to reap (at least some of) the cost savings from the learning curve, it must allow for learning-curve effects in its incentive pay schemes.* However, in what follows we shall assume that the enterprise itself (that is, its operating account) reaps the full benefit of learning-curve effects.

The implications for business strategy of falling unit cost as the number of items produced increases are powerful ones. The first enterprise to go into a product market is likely, *ceteris paribus*, to have an advantage over late-entrant competitors because, at any moment in time, its cumulated output *i* will be greater than its rivals' and its unit costs correspondingly lower. However, the *ceteris paribus* clause is most important, because the late-entrant competitors may overcome their 'experience-curve disadvantage' either by taking advantage of technological change, since the first entrant began production (a very real possibility), or by producing on a larger scale (if economies of scale operate), or both. Having taken due note of these important qualifications, most of the following remarks concerning the practical consequences of the learning curve will assume *ceteris paribus* (continually to repeat these obvious qualifications simply becomes tedious).

DIAGRAM 8.7   *Experience curves and the first entrant's unit cost advantage*

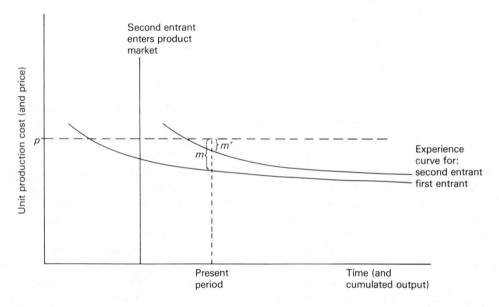

Diagram 8.7 illustrates these important possibilities, showing clearly the cost advantage which the first entrant is likely, *ceteris paribus*, to have over a subsequent entrant. Up the vertical axis we measure unit production costs (all costs, not labour costs only); we can also show price on this axis, with the vertical distance between price and unit production cost being the unit gross margin. The horizontal axis has now to have several scales: first, starting at the origin, we measure time, say in years. Assuming a steady flow of production through time, we can also measure, on a matching horizontal scale, the cumulative output during each year of the first entrant. (To illustrate: if the items are produced at the rate of one per month (e.g. aeroplanes), then the end of the first year will be marked 12 on the cumulative-output scale of the first entrant; if the first entrant's annual production is growing at, say, 10 per cent per annum, then the second year's cumulative-output scale has

---

*Such problems seem to have occurred in the UK motor industry where piece-work payment systems caused the earnings of production workers to rise rapidly due (partly) to the learning-curve effect: see H. A. Turner, Garfield Clack and Geoffrey Roberts, *Labour Relations in the Motor Industry* (Allen & Unwin, 1967) ch. V 'Wages in the motor industry'.

to be adjusted to incorporate 10 per cent more units, so that the scale at the end of the second year reads 25.2, at the end of the third year, 39.72, and so on.)

At the point of time at which the second entrant enters the product market we may start the second entrant's experience curve, which we shall assume, *ceteris paribus*, to be a replica of the first entrant's experience curve.* The second entrant's experience curve has its own cumulated production axis (e.g. if the second entrant enters at the beginning of the third year and produces at the same annual rate, then by the end of the third year the second entrant's cumulative production scale reads 12, as against the first entrant's 39.72, and so on).

The first entrant can set a price, p, at which its unit gross margin, m, is greater than the unit gross margin for the second entrant, m'; it is clear that the first entrant is likely to have the economic ability to set prices in this particular product market. We may note that the first entrant's relative experience-curve advantage will decline with the passage of time, because it is on the less steeply sloping part of the curve, while the second entrant is still on the steeply sloping part. But during the 'present period' the first entrant clearly has a greater flow of profits, and so the first entrant can more readily finance from retentions an expansion in production facilities and, in quantitative terms, the first entrant will probably dominate the market in terms of annual sales volume. Dominance in the market and greater profitability thus stem from the same underlying cause – the cost advantage created by being further along the experience curve.

If it is the case that market 'dominance' and profitability are positively related, then we may devise an interesting method of considering the strategy of an enterprise which produces several different products (or different sets of related products). This method has obviously appealed to practising businessmen, to judge by the success of the Boston Consulting Group – the commercial business consultancy firm which initially devised the method and which uses the method (or variations of it) in its consultancy practice.†

The method is known as the business portfolio matrix, sometimes also referred to as the growth-share matrix. The matrix is illustrated in Diagram 8.8. Each product (or set of products) produced by the enterprise is first classified according to whether the annual growth rate of the market (and, consequently, of the product's sales) is 'high' or 'low'. An arbitrary dividing-line between 'high' and 'low' used to be 10 per cent per annum in volume terms, but clearly this dividing-line is going to depend on the general performance of the economy, and so we shall here refrain from naming any currently applicable dividing-line.

The second classification of products is according to their 'competitive position' in the market and, by implication from the learning curve, etc. (see Diagram 8.7), the profitability of (the proportionate mark-up on) the product. We need to pause to clear up a confusion in the conventional presentation of the business portfolio matrix. It is obvious that market share by itself is an uninformative measure of competitive position. If an enterprise has a 20 per cent share of the market (by volume or value), then we know but little about its

---

*The importance of *ceteris paribus* can now be clearly seen: taking advantage of technological progress and/or economies of scale means a lower experience curve for the second entrant. For a practical example of the deliberate use by an enterprise of the learning curve to achieve and maintain market dominance (*à la* Diagram 8.7), see D. F. Channon, 'Texas Instruments Inc.', in John M. Stopford, Derek F. Channon and John Constable (eds), *Cases in Strategic Management*, Wiley, 1980.
†The most accessible statement of the Boston Consulting Group's views is in two articles by Barry Hedley: 'A fundamental approach to strategy development' and 'Strategy and the "business portfolio"' in *Long Range Planning*, vol. 9, no. 6, December 1976, pp. 2–11; and vol. 10, no. 1, February 1977, pp. 9–15, respectively. See also the 'Management Page' articles in the *Financial Times*: 1 December 1978, p. 15; 17 October 1980, p. 17; 11 November 1981, p. 14; 13 November 1981, p. 16; 16 November 1981, p. 16; 20 November 1981, p. 10; and 27 November 1981, p. 16 (the *Financial Times*' interest in this topic presumably mirrors that of (many of) its readers).

DIAGRAM 8.8   *The business portfolio (growth-share) matrix: Boston Consulting Group*

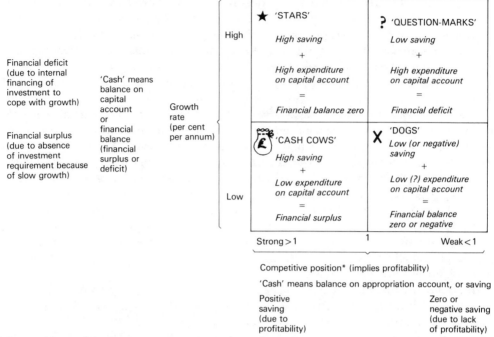

Financial deficit (due to internal financing of investment to cope with growth)

Financial surplus (due to absence of investment requirement because of slow growth)

'Cash' means balance on capital account or financial balance (financial surplus or deficit)

*Competitive position is measured by:

$$\frac{\text{Proportionate market share by volume or value}}{1/\text{Number of competitors}}$$

relative 'competitive position' in the market: if there are fifty competitors in the market (i.e. the firm plus forty-nine competitors), then the firm with a 20 per cent share dominates the market; but if there are two competitors in the market (i.e. itself plus one other), then clearly it does not.

The conventional presentation of the business portfolio matrix seeks to get round this problem by measuring the competitive position of any product through the ratio of its share to the share of the competitor with the largest share, save that the competitive position of the largest competitor is measured by taking its share relative to that of the next largest competitor. This is logically sloppy and confusing. The logically correct, and informative, measure of competitive position that is required is the ratio of the product's *actual* share of the market (whether by volume or by value) to the *hypothetical* share it would have had were all competitors to be equal in size. This hypothetical share can be measured very simply by:

$$\frac{1}{\text{Number of competitors}}$$

that is, if there were fifty competitors, equal shares for all would be 0.02. The firm having a 20 per cent share of the market with fifty competitors thus scores a competitive position of $0.20/0.02 = 10$, indicating its relatively dominant position; while a firm having a 20 per cent share of the market with only one other competitor scores a competitive position of $0.20/0.5 = 0.4$, indicating its lack of dominance. We shall (arbitrarily) take the dividing-line between a 'strong' and a 'weak' competitive position as 1.

Having clarified the matter of competitive position, we may now establish a two-by-two matrix which gives the appropriate cross-classification of products, as shown in

Diagram 8.8. The conventional presentation of the business portfolio matrix then proceeds to analyse the four cells of the matrix in terms of their 'cash flows'. Here, too, the use of words tends to be imprecise and the term 'cash flow' is used without distinction to refer to both the balance on the appropriation account, or saving, and also the balance on the capital account – the financial balance or financial surplus or deficit (see Diagrams 2.5 and 2.6). It is important carefully to maintain the distinction between the two, because the competitive position essentially relates to the balance on the appropriation account – the (cash) flow of saving; while the growth-rate classification essentially involves the balance on the capital account – the (cash) flow of the financial surplus or deficit.

The analysis proceeds as follows: a product with a strong competitive position will (following Diagram 8.7) be generating a large flow of profits and hence a large positive balance on appropriation account: its contribution to the flow of saving will be positive and large. Conversely, a product with a weak competitive position will *not* be generating a large flow of profits (it may even be making a loss), so its contribution to the flow of saving will be zero or negative. Turning to the growth-rate classification (rapidly growing) product sales in a rapidly growing market will require considerable expenditure on capital account (fixed and circulating capital formation) in order to provide the extra production capacity to meet the growth rate. Conversely (slowly growing) product sales in a slowly growing market will require little if any expenditure on capital account (possibly some replacement of fixed capital but no extra circulating capital).

The product's saving flow and its capital expenditure flow can then be put together to see the product's contribution to the financial balance.

We may start in the upper-right quadrant of Diagram 8.8 and move anti-clockwise. The symbolic names of the quadrants are those that have been popularised by the Boston Consulting Group and which have accordingly become familiar (they are graphic and useful mnemonics).

In the upper-right quadrant we have those 'question-mark' products whose competitive position is weak but which are in rapidly growing markets. Their profitability is low but their requirements for capital expenditure are large, so these products generate a large financial deficit (the modulus of the financial deficit is large). These 'question-mark' products therefore pose both a threat and a challenge to the enterprise: the threat is that they will continue to run financial deficits and the challenge is to move some (as many as possible) of these products into the upper-left quadrant with a strong competitive position and improved profitability; those products which cannot be moved leftwards by careful management may be candidates for divestment by the enterprise.

In the upper-left quadrant the enterprise has its 'star' products. These are the profitable products (in a strong competitive position) whose sales are growing rapidly. Although their rapid growth necessitates capital expenditure, they are contributing considerably to the profit flow and so to the saving flow, and 'stars' may, on balance, be self-financing on capital account, so that their financial balance is zero.

If the growth rate of a 'star' drops away, then the product descends into the 'cash-cow' quadrant. This quadrant contains those (lucrative) products which are profitable in their strong competitive position and which contribute heavily to the flow of saving. However, because the growth rate is low, little if any expenditure is incurred on their behalf in the capital account, and so they generate a large financial surplus. The financial surplus of the 'cash cows' can then be 'milked' to cover the financial deficit incurred by the 'question-marks' in the hope that some of the 'question-marks' will, in due course, become 'stars'.

In the lower-right quadrant we have the unfortunate 'dogs'. The chief characteristic of 'dogs' is that they have little realistic prospect of moving sideways into the 'cash-cow' quadrant or up into the 'question-mark' quadrant: their weak competitive position and lack of profitability is likely to be permanent, and the growth rate of the market and of sales is unlikely to pick up. As such, 'dog' products trundle along, not making any profits and possibly making a loss, but probably not incurring much expenditure on capital account, and generating a financial deficit (or, at best, a zero financial balance). They may occupy managerial time and attention (which could be better devoted to 'question-marks'), and it is potentially dangerous to incur expenditure on capital account on their behalf as this may not benefit the enterprise. The Boston Consulting Group tends to advocate that 'dogs' be sold to other enterprises to whom the dogs may be worth more by reason of bringing in economies of scale, reducing (for the buyer) a major source of competition, or adding to its customers in a way beneficial to the buyer.

The over-all aim of the enterprise, according to the Boston Consulting Group, should be to have a 'balanced' portfolio of products, and here the term 'balanced' means with respect to its over-all financial balance. Apart from deliberate decisions to issue new equity (share) capital (together perhaps with a little judicious borrowing), the unspoken implication of business portfolio analysis is that enterprises should rely largely on internal financing for capital expenditure and new product development: 'stars' provide the enterprise's growth; 'cash cows' provide the financial surplus to cover the new product development in the 'question-mark' quadrant, so ensuring a supply of 'stars' for the future.

The interest among businessmen in the product portfolio analysis (or business portfolio analysis, if there are sets of products) is another piece of evidence supporting our general argument about the importance of internal financing to pay for investment. It also supports the system of cost classification and business economic planning which we considered in Chapter 5 because such a framework of information is designed to supply the detailed cost, investment and cash-flow data necessary to plan and monitor the performance of a 'balanced' product (or business) portfolio. And we have seen in this and the preceding two chapters the economic forces which make such planning and investment an urgent necessity to ensure the enterprise's survival in a competitive world.

This concludes our discussion of capital–labour substitution, economies of scale, and technical progress (in both its forms) all as seen from the point of view of producing enterprises. We have seen, both theoretically and empirically, that these are powerful forces in the shaping of our material existence and in the provision of our creature comforts. But, the reader may well ask, if all these forces are continuously at work in modern industry, can we not measure their over-all, aggregate, impact on the growth of the whole economy? This is a very proper question to ask, and it is one which economists *have* attempted to answer.

Impact on economic growth

The most consistent attempt to analyse the impact of technical progress, economies of scale and the growth of factor inputs on the growth of the economy is to be found in the work of Edward Denison, *Why Growth Rates Differ: Postwar Experience in Nine Western Countries* (Brookings Institution, 1967). When considering the growth of the aggregate economy there are some complicating factors, not so far mentioned, which have to be taken into account.

First, the economy's output may increase simply because of an improved allocation of resources, such as may occur when labour (and capital) transfer from a sector of low productivity, such as agriculture, to a sector of high productivity, such as industry (although productivity in agriculture is no longer so low – Table 1.14). This has nothing to do with an increase in total factor input, nor with economies of scale, nor with technical progress: increased output results simply from an improved allocation of resources and it has been an important factor in postwar growth in some European economies (notably

Italy, West Germany and France). There are other causes of improved resource allocation, and most of these are taken into account by Denison, but it would take too long to explain them all here.

Second, the measurement of the stock of labour and capital inputs needs to be adjusted for changes which may affect the flow of services from those inputs: the simplest case is where a change (reduction) in hours of work may change (reduce) the input of labour-time from a given stock of workers; less obviously, an improvement in the educational qualifications of the labour force may increase the effective flow of labour services from a given stock (number) of (more highly educated) workers. Such changes were also taken into consideration by Denison in his measurement of factor inputs. Denison's procedure was:

1.   To measure the growth of net national income (at constant prices).
2.   To ascertain what part of that growth could be ascribed to: (i) the growth of (quality, etc., adjusted) factor inputs under the assumption of constant returns to scale; (ii) the improved allocation of resources; (iii) a separately estimated effect of economies of scale.

The remaining 'residual', or otherwise 'unascribable' part of growth, may then be put down to the impact of 'technical progress': that is, Denison's method was to measure (and define) the impact of technical progress as that part of the growth in output which is left over after we have accounted, as far as possible, for the impact of all other sources of growth.

This method has caused considerable controversy; some economists have simply dismissed such a measure of technical progress as 'the coefficient of ignorance' because it indicates that part of output growth about whose sources we know nothing; other economists have argued that the residual arises because of inadequate (or otherwise imperfect) measurement of factor inputs. These arguments cannot be dismissed, but we are all aware of the impact of technological change as a source of improved living standards so that if one can remove most other causes of growth it is probably not unreasonable to suppose that the remaining part could be due to technological change. A relevant analogy may be that it was possible to produce an outline map indicating the size of Africa by sailing round its shores, though the early map-makers knew nothing about the interior of the Dark Continent until much later; but because of that ignorance one could not dismiss the early maps of Africa as entirely useless. The objection about the proper measurement of inputs is partly one of practice, and it may be possible in future to do better on this score. For the time being we have to make do with what data we have.

Table 8.16 shows the results of Denison's researches. To illustrate what the figures mean, let us take the United Kingdom. During the period 1950 to 1962, the United Kingdom's net national income at constant prices increased by 2.29 per cent per annum. The growth of (quality-adjusted) factor inputs, according to a constant returns to scale production function, contributed 1.11 percentage *points* to this annual growth rate: that is, 48.5 per cent (1.11/2.29) of the United Kingdom's growth during this period may be ascribed to the growth of the factor inputs. The remaining part of growth was thus due to increased output per unit of input. Such increased total factor productivity may be ascribed to three sources: improved allocation of resources; economies of scale; and a residual called 'technical progress'.

Improved allocation of resources contributed only 0.03 percentage points to the growth rate of output: the United Kingdom, with only a small proportion of its labour force in agriculture in 1950 (see Diagram 1.2), had very little scope (unlike other economies) for benefiting from a transfer of labour from (low-productivity) agriculture to (high-productivity) industry. Economies of scale is estimated by Denison to have contributed

TABLE 8.16 *Contribution to growth in output of: growth in input, economies of scale, technical progress and improved resource allocation in nine Western economies, 1950 to 1962*

Country [a]	Growth rate of net national income (at constant prices) 1950 to 1962, per cent per annum [b]	Contribution, in percentage points, to growth rate of national income from:					Contribution, in percentages, to growth rate of national income from:				
		Growth of total factor input: $L^a K^{b}$ [c]	Growth of total factor productivity:				Growth of total factor input: $L^a K^{b}$ [c]	Growth of total factor productivity:			
			Due to improved allocation of resources [d]	Due to economies of scale	Residual due to 'technical progress'	Total		Due to improved allocation of resources [d]	Due to economies of scale	Residual due to 'technical progress'	Total
West Germany	7.26	2.78	1.31	1.61	1.56	4.48	38.3	18.0	22.2	21.5	61.7
Italy	5.96	1.66	1.43	1.22	1.65	4.30	27.9	24.0	20.5	27.7	72.1
France	4.92	1.24	1.17	1.00	1.51	3.68	25.2	23.8	20.3	30.7	74.8
Netherlands	4.73	1.91	0.84	0.78	1.20	2.82	40.4	17.8	16.5	25.4	59.6
Denmark	3.51	1.55	0.87	0.65	0.44	1.96	44.2	24.8	18.5	12.5	55.8
Norway	3.45	1.04	0.94	0.57	0.90	2.41	30.1	27.2	16.5	26.1	69.9
USA	3.32	1.95	0.25	0.36	0.76	1.37	58.7	7.5	10.8	22.9	41.3
Belgium	3.20	1.17	0.68	0.51	0.84	2.03	36.6	21.3	15.9	26.3	63.4
United Kingdom	2.29	1.11	0.03	0.36	0.79	1.18	48.5	1.3	15.7	34.5	51.5

[a] Listed in descending order of growth in output.

[b] Measured at factor cost.

[c] Growth of labour input, L, incorporates changes in hours of work, changes in age–sex composition of employed persons, and changes in educational qualifications. A constant returns to scale production function was assumed by Denison, separate estimates then being made of the impact of economies of scale.

[d] Improved allocation of resources comprises: (i) changes in allocation of inputs to agriculture; (ii) changes in allocation of inputs to non-agricultural self-employment; (iii) reduction in international trade barriers; (iv) effect of irregularities in capacity utilisation; (v) effect of irregularities in agricultural output; (vi) balancing of capital stock; (vii) reduction in age of capital stock; (viii) miscellaneous effects due to adjustment to deflation procedures. These categories are separately given in Denison's tables.

Source: Edward F. Denison, *Why Growth Rates Differ: Postwar Experience in Nine Western Countries* (Brookings Institution, 1967) tables 20.1, 21.1, 21.5, 21.7, 21.9, 21.11, 21.13, 21.15, 21.17 and 21.19; pp. 281, 298, 302, 304, 306, 308, 310, 312, 314 and 316.

0.36 percentage points to the annual UK growth rate of output. The sum now goes as follows:

				Contribution of				Residual
Growth in output	minus	Growth in inputs	minus	Improved allocation	minus	Economies of scale	equals	'technical progress'
2.29	−	1.11	−	0.03	−	0.36	=	0.79

So that the impact of technical progress contributed 0.79 percentage points, or just over one-third, to the United Kingdom's annual growth during this period. The right-hand part of the table gives the proportionate contributions to the annual growth rate of each country, so we can make comparisons among countries.

For present purposes, the most important point to emerge from Table 8.16 is that the impact of 'technical progress', in all these Western economies, made a quite substantial contribution to their annual growth rate: ranging from one-eighth in Denmark to just over one-third in the United Kingdom. It is therefore clear that there is a substantial portion of the growth in output which cannot be accounted for by the impact of things which we can measure, such as increased factor inputs, improved allocation of resources, and economies of scale. This analysis at an aggregate level therefore demonstrates that technical progress contributes in a quantitatively significant way to over-all economic growth in most economies.

Another interesting feature of Table 8.16 is that, in all countries except the USA, the growth of total factor productivity contributed more to annual growth than did the simple growth of total factor inputs. Improvements in resource allocation cannot be a lasting source of economic growth, as the case of the United Kingdom seems to demonstrate. Economies of scale also seem to make an impact on the growth of output, so here too the macroeconomic figures give empirical support to the microeconomic data on economies of scale considered earlier.

Conclusion

The fulcrum of Chapters 5–8 has been the price/unit cost/profit nexus, vital to all enterprises operating in the market. Accordingly, we have considered: the economic analysis of price (with special reference to consumer behaviour, using the analytic device of the demand curve); the economic analysis of influences on unit cost (especially capital–labour substitution, economies of scale, and technical progress); and we have seen in Chapter 5 (Diagrams 5.1 and 5.4) and in Chapter 7 (Diagram 7.2) how all these things relate to the results achieved by an enterprise.

Exercises

8.1 *(To practise seeing the impact of technical progress.)*

(i)   In Table 8.2, what is the isoquant value for K in the isoquant and in the unit isoquant, before and after technical progress, when

L in the isoquant is 150?

(ii)   With reference to Table 8.2, draw on one graph the unit isoquants before and after technical progress.

8.2 *(To practise deriving isoquants from pro-*

duction functions.) With reference to Table 8.4, derive the formulae for K and $K/\bar{Q}$ after capital-saving technical progress, and verify your formulae with reference to the figures given (take $\bar{Q} = 1$ for simplicity).

8.3 *(To see the impact of technical progress in the real world.)*

(i)   With reference to Table 8.7, draw a graph to show the impact over time of technical progress (as embodied in capital equipment) on the unit labour cost of producing 40-watt electric light-bulbs.

(ii)   With reference to Table 8.8, draw a graph to show the impact over time of technical progress on the number of tyres produced per man-hour and on tyres by weight per man-hour.

(iii) Calculate and tabulate the changing average weight of tyres over this period.

(iv)   With reference to Appendix 8.2, in your opinion how many purely technological innovations are listed for the period given.

8.4 *(Further to practise seeing the impact of technical progress.)* With reference to Table 8.9:

(i)   Draw a graph to show the impact over time of technical progress (among other things) on labour productivity in the 'best-practice' plant.

(ii)   Draw a graph to show how the scale of output in the best-practice plant changed over the period.

8.5 *(To articulate your knowledge.)*

'The variation between industries in the extent of increases in labour productivity can be explained primarily by the uneven impact of three influences: (i) improvements in technical knowledge, (ii) potential economies of scale and the extent of their realisation, and (iii) factor substitution. Although analytically distinct, these three influences are highly interrelated: realisation of economies of scale depends upon increases in output which are in part induced by technical advances; while factor substitution is prompted by changes in relative factor prices which to some extent originate in technical change itself' (W. E. G. Salter, *Productivity and Technical Change*, Cambridge University Press, 1960, p. 143).

(i)   Explain fully what this statement means.

(ii)   By what mechanism or mechanisms would increases in output be 'in part induced by technical advances'?

(iii) How could technical change affect relative factor prices?

(iv)   To what extent do the data in Tables 8.7, 8.9 and in Appendix 8.2 support Salter's argument?

8.6 *(To consider the implications of technical progress, etc.)*

(i)   With reference to Table 8.10 and Diagram 8.2, describe the competitive process whereby 'inefficient' plants are eliminated from an industry.

(ii)   Argue the case that such elimination is desirable on economic grounds.

(iii) Consider the implications for social policy of your argument in (ii).

8.7 *(To practise your understanding of how technical progress works.)* With reference to Table 8.11:

(i)   Calculate the rows for years 5 and 6.

(ii)   Plot on a unit isoquant diagram the successive unit labour requirement and unit capital requirement for years 0 to 6 inclusive.

(iii) Draw a graph to show the behaviour of unit labour and capital costs in the years 0 to 6 inclusive.

8.8 *(To show that the hallmark of most technical progress is that it simultaneously saves on all costs.)* You are a works manager of a steel-making plant with an open-hearth furnace. Using the following data, write a memo to your Managing Director to convince him (and the Board of Directors) that technical progress requires you to scrap the open-hearth furnace and to invest in the oxygen steel process (source: G. F. Ray, 'The diffusion of new technology: a study of ten processes in nine industries', *National Institute Economic Review*, May 1969, table 6, p. 45):

	Percentages of total conversion costs for open-hearth process	
	Open-hearth process	*Oxygen process*
Wages and salaries	10.4	6.7
Fuel and power	23.4	10.4
Materials (excl. pig-iron), furnace relining, maintenance, etc.	42.5	23.3
Total processing costs	76.3	40.4
Depreciation and interest	23.7	16.0
Total conversion costs	100.0	56.4

8.9 *(To illustrate the gigantic effect of technical progress and economies of scale combined – a drama in three acts entitled 'So you think petrol is expensive?')* Using the following data calculate the total cost of producing petrol (gasoline) in cents (at 1939 prices) per gallon at the three dates given. Draw a graph to illustrate your results. What has been the percentage reduction in unit costs (at constant 1939 prices) between 1913 and 1960? What has been the percentage reduction per annum in unit costs (at constant 1939 prices) between 1913 and 1960? (You will find a quick read of 'Petroleum' in the *Encyclopaedia Britannica* very helpful as to how all this happened.)*

A	Burton process, 1913	Fluid process, 1942	Improved fluid process 1960
Plant capacity, barrels per day	88.5	12,750	36,000
Inputs per 100 gallons of petrol (gasoline) produced			
Crude oil, gallons	396	238	170
Energy, millions of BTUs	8.4	3.2	1.1
Process labour, man-hours	1.61	0.09	0.02
Capital costs, $ at 1939 prices	3.60	0.82	0.52

B	Prices in 1939
Crude oil, cents per gallon	2.43
Energy (gas), cents per million BTUs	18.82
Labour, skilled and semi-skilled males, cents per hour	80.80

*Source for A is C. Freeman, 'Chemical process plant: innovation and the world market', *National Institute Economic Review*, August 1968, table 7, p. 40; source for B is United States Department of Commerce Bureau of the Census, *Historical Statistics of the United States from Colonial Times to 1970 (Bicentennial Edition)* series M139, S203 ÷ S198, and D842, pp. I 593, II 832, I 172.

8.10 *(To practise your understanding of the learning curve in theory.)*

(i)   Calculate the rows for item 17 and item 32 in Table 8.12 (for the 32nd item, do not do the cumulative total labour cost and the cumulative average unit labour cost).

(ii)   Compare the unit labour requirement for item 32 with the unit labour requirement for item 16. Compare the unit labour cost for item 32 with the unit labour cost for item 16 (how can you test whether or not your answer to this question is right?).

(iii)   Draw a diagram to illustrate the behaviour of unit labour requirement from items 1 to 17 and item 32.

(iv)   Draw a diagram to illustrate the behaviour of unit labour cost from items 1 to 17 and item 32.

8.11 *(To practise seeing what learning curves may mean in reality.)*

(i)   Draw a diagram to illustrate the learning curve for Yard *H* in Table 8.13. Compare this diagram with 8.10(iii).

(ii)   Average hourly earnings in shipyards in the USA during the relevant period were $1.22 (US Department of Labor, *Wartime Employment, Production, and Conditions of Work in Shipyards*, table 12, p. 18). Calculate and tabulate unit labour cost per vessel (averaged over successive groups of ten vessels) for Yard *H*. Draw a graph to illustrate the behaviour of unit labour costs. Compare this diagram with 8.10(iv).

8.12 *(To articulate your knowledge.)*

'The realisation of cost reductions through experience is not automatic but depends crucially on a competent management that seeks ways to force costs down as volume expands. Effective competition has an important role to play in the process' *(A Review of Monopolies and Mergers Policy: A Consultative Document*, Cmnd 7198, HMSO, May 1978, p. 85).

(i)   Explain what this statement means.
(ii)   What are the implications for anti-monopoly policy?

8.13 *(To see the implications for an enterprise of the learning curve.)*

'The learning curve has many ramifications for business strategies. For example, competitive bidding in defense contracting would be affected by the predicted learning effects. The expected volume could have a dramatic influence on the unit price. The cost per airplane is much less if 500 are manufactured than if 50 are manufactured' (Charles T. Horngren, *Cost Accounting: A Managerial Emphasis* (4th edn), Prentice Hall, 1977, p. 208).

Explain this statement and illustrate your answer with reference to the data in Table 8.14.

8.14 *(To practise familiarity with learning curves.)*

(i)   Using the fitted regression equation in Table 8.15, calculate the unit labour requirement (thousand man-hours) for the EC–2 Liberty ships produced by Yard *A* with serial numbers 75, 150 and 1,000 (had production extended so far). Check your result by comparing the first of these with the actual average for the relevant group.

(ii) What is the ratio of the estimated unit labour requirement for ship no. 75 to the estimated unit labour requirement for ship no. 150?

(iii) Using the hourly labour cost of $1.22, calculate the estimated labour cost for EC–2 Liberty ships built in Yard *A* of serial nos. 75, 150 and 1,000.

(iv) What is the percentage reduction in unit labour cost between Liberty ship no. 75 and Liberty ship no. 150? How does this relate to the 'learning gradient'?

8.15 *(To practise presentation of data and seeing the impact of technical progress.)* With reference to Table 8.16, draw a bar chart to illustrate the differences in growth rates among countries and the differences in contributions to those growth rates.

(*Hint:* the height of the bar should represent the growth rate and each bar should then be divided appropriately among the contributing elements.)

APPENDIX 8.1   *Least-cost inputs, the factor price ratio, and the production function's exponents*

The production function is:

$$Q = ZL^aK^b$$

The isoquant for $\bar{Q}$ is:

$$K = \left(\frac{\bar{Q}}{Z}\right)^{\frac{1}{b}} L^{-\frac{a}{b}}$$

The least-cost labour input, L^*, is found where the slope of the isoquant is equal to the slope of the isocost line:

$$\frac{dK}{dL} = -\frac{p_L}{p_K}$$

or:

$$\frac{d[(\bar{Q}/Z)^{\frac{1}{b}} L^{-\frac{a}{b}}]}{dL} = -\frac{p_L}{p_K}$$

Whence, by differentiation:

$$-\frac{a}{b}\left(\frac{\bar{Q}}{Z}\right)^{\frac{1}{b}} L^{-\frac{a}{b}-1} = -\frac{p_L}{p_K}$$

And solving this for L^* gives:

$$L^* = \left(\frac{a/b}{p_L/p_K}\right)^{\frac{1}{(a/b)+1}} \left(\frac{\bar{Q}}{Z}\right)^{\frac{1}{a+b}}$$

Using the isoquant equation gives the corresponding least-cost capital input, K^*:

$$K^* = \left(\frac{\bar{Q}}{Z}\right)^{\frac{1}{b}} L^{*-\frac{a}{b}}$$

$$= \left(\frac{\bar{Q}}{Z}\right)^{\frac{1}{b}} \left[\left(\frac{a/b}{p_L/p_K}\right)^{\frac{1}{(a/b)+1}} \left(\frac{\bar{Q}}{Z}\right)^{\frac{1}{a+b}}\right]^{-\frac{a}{b}}$$

$$= \left(\frac{\bar{Q}}{Z}\right)^{\frac{1}{b}} \left(\frac{a/b}{p_L/p_K}\right)^{\frac{-a/b}{(a/b)+1}} \left(\frac{\bar{Q}}{Z}\right)^{\frac{-a/b}{a+b}}$$

$$= \left(\frac{\bar{Q}}{Z}\right)^{\frac{1}{b}-\frac{a/b}{a+b}} \left(\frac{a/b}{p_L/p_K}\right)^{\frac{-a/b}{(a/b)+1}}$$

Whence the capital–labour ratio at the least-cost combination is:

$$\frac{K^*}{L^*} = \left(\frac{\bar{Q}}{Z}\right)^{\frac{1}{b}-\frac{a/b}{a+b}} \left(\frac{a/b}{p_L/p_K}\right)^{\frac{-a/b}{(a/b)+1}}$$

$$\left(\frac{a/b}{p_L/p_K}\right)^{\frac{-1}{(a/b)+1}} \left(\frac{\bar{Q}}{Z}\right)^{\frac{-1}{a+b}}$$

$$= \left(\frac{a/b}{p_L/p_K}\right)^{\frac{-(a/b)-1}{(a/b)+1}} \left(\frac{\bar{Q}}{Z}\right)^{\frac{1}{b}-\frac{a/b}{a+b}-\frac{1}{a+b}}$$

$$= \left(\frac{a/b}{p_L/p_K}\right)^{-1}$$

Now, the exponent of $\bar{Q}/Z$ is zero, as follows:

$$\frac{1}{b} - \frac{a/b}{a+b} - \frac{1}{a+b} = \frac{1}{b} - \frac{(a/b)+1}{a+b}$$

$$= \frac{1}{b} - \frac{(a+b)/b}{a+b}$$

$$= \frac{1}{b} - \frac{1}{b}$$

$$= 0$$

So the exponential $\bar{Q}/Z$ term becomes equal to 1, and simplifying the other exponent, which is equal to -1, gives:

$$\frac{K^*}{L^*} = \left(\frac{a/b}{p_L/p_K}\right)^{-1}$$

$$= \frac{p_L/p_K}{a/b}$$

So that, if the factor price ratio is unaltered and if the ratio of the production function exponents, a/b, stays the same, the capital–labour ratio at the least-cost combination will not alter.

APPENDIX 8.2 *Details of reasons for labour productivity increases in 'plant 1'[a] in the US automobile tyre industry, 1928 to 1931*

Brief details of innovation by production department	Reduction in man-hours per day [b]	Percentage increase in output (by weight) per man-hour
Crude rubber milling, compounding and calendering, 1928–31		
New cutter for crude-rubber bales installed	16	
Two Banbury mixers installed with necessary conveyors and other equipment	960	
Additional spray-cooled Banbury mixer and three spray sheeting mills installed, together with all accessory equipment	480	
Two tread calenders equipped with automatic feed devices	48	
Tandem calenders equipped with push-button controls	32	
Total reduction in man-hours per day, 1928 to 1931	1,536	
Percentage increase in department's productivity, 1927 to 1931		**99.1**
Stock-preparation and tyre carcass-building, 1928–31		
Machine process replacing hand operations in flippering wire beads	84	
Hand process of cushioning bands replaced by machine process	20	
Speeding up of operations on bead-covering machines	84	
New conveyor installed to supply stock to builders	100	
New device for covering and flippering beads in one operation	50	
Applying filling gum to bands directly on band-building machine	100	
Cementing treads on one end instead of both	48	
New method of rolling stock in liners	118	
New bead-building machine	48	
Automatic stops installed on four stock-cutting machines	56	
Combination knife and brush installed on tread conveyor	32	
Festoon racks installed at several tyre-building machines	60	
Electric controls installed on three stock-cutting machines	36	
New method for building tread bands on machines	80	
Automatic device eliminates need for changing rolls on cutting machines	200	

APPENDIX 8.2 (continued)

Brief details of innovation by production department	Reduction in man-hours per day [b]	Percentage increase in output (by weight) per man-hour
Eight core-building machines replaced by the shoulder drum process of tyre-building	200	
Filling gum devices on band-building units eliminate the need for rolling filling gum in liners	240	
Banner machine replaces hand unit for forming and covering beads	50	
Bead flippering machine replaces hand process	240	
New process of cutting, splicing and making finishing strips	240	
Automatic knife eliminates hand-cutting on water-cooled tread unit	24	
Automatic device eliminates feeders on water-cooled tread unit	72	
New method of 'booking' treads	60	
New bias-cutting unit for flipper stock	60	
New method of building tread bands	336	
Change in the application of cushion stock on large tyre bands	60	
Bias cutting machines are equipped to gum and flipper stock as well as to apply gum on finishing strip	120	
New method of applying gum tip to flipper stock	120	
New method of servicing plies to tyre builders on drum machines	36	
New method of cutting cord fabric for tyres	120	
Rerolling gum stock on slitting machines eliminated	72	
Total reduction in man-hours per day, 1928 to 1931	3,166	
Percentage increase in department's labour productivity, 1927 to 1931		**88.0**
Curing, finishing and inspecting, 1928–31		
Machine for inserting water tubes into core-built tyres before curing	24	
New device eliminating need for soap-stoning tyre carcass	48	
Elimination of ringing tyres and removing rings from cured tyres by using moulds with rings permanently attached	160	
Automatic device for spraying lids of curing moulds replacing hand process on three units	72	
Improved method of removing tyres from curing conveyor	84	
Automatic spray for bottom mould on two curing units	80	
New method of shaping drum-built bands for one unit	118	
Automatic tyre extractor to remove tyre from hot mould after curing	72	
Additional new moulds with rings attached, eliminating necessity of ringing tyres and removing rings	330	
Automatic mould opener on one curing unit	21	
New system of balancing tyres on belt while inspecting	24	
Special process eliminating trimming tyres by hand	36	
Revamping and consolidating all white sidewall-handling operations, such as inspection, buffing, balancing, washing	180	
Air machine extracting water bags from cured tyres	50	
New system of balancing tyres	60	
Total reduction in man-hours per day, 1928 to 1931	1,359	

Brief details of innovation by production department	Reduction in man-hours per day [b]	Percentage increase in output (by weight) per man-hour
Percentage increase in department's labour productivity, 1927 to 1931		**106.4**
Manufacturing inner tubes, 1928–31		
Complete unit of moulded-built inner tubes displacing the mandrel process	380	
Rearranging mandrel process of inner tubes for building, wrapping and stripping operations	240	
Automatic valve pad punching machine installed on tube calender	24	
Automatic trimmer installed for inner tubes	24	
Automatic device for measuring inner tubes	36	
Splice presses added to rubber flap conveyor	144	
Cutting flaps on utility cutting machine	30	
Hand stamping of flaps replaced by electric branding	20	
Machine process for application of gum to flaps for rerolling liners for flaps	50	
Tube calender equipped with electric knife	18	
Changes in system of curing, classifying and inspecting mandrel-built tubes	252	
Classifying and water-testing operations of inner tubes combined	16	
Calender and rolling device method replaces drum process of building moulded inner tubes	230	
Machine replaces hand process of skiving inner tubes	120	
Automatic strip feeder installed on tubing machine	36	
Conveyor installed between the two test-water tanks on inner tubes	16	
Final inspection of inner tubes consolidated	16	
Change in method of curing moulded inner tubes	60	
Inspection and boxing of inner tubes combined	30	
Total reduction in man-hours per day, 1928 to 1931	1,742	
Percentage increase in department's labour productivity, 1927 to 1931		**135.1**

[a] The study is written by chapters, each concerned with the distinct processes (departments); the author (to preserve plants' anonymity) warns that identical numbers throughout the study do not denote identical plants; however, it would seem unlikely that, *within chapters*, the author would vary the identity of plants, and so we may thus relate the percentage increase in departmental productivity (given in one table in a chapter) to the list of innovations (given in another table in the same chapter).

[b] The author fails to say what is meant by 'day': a period of twenty-four hours; or a single shift of eight hours (and the plants worked multiple shifts)? The former would seem the obvious interpretation, but where the reduction in number of employees is also given, the hours saved tends to be eight times the reduction in employees. The number of employees by plant for plant 1 is not known (because of the changed identity of plants), so it is not possible to ascertain exactly the proportionate impact of the reduction in man-hours; however, the average total employment in three plants in 1927 was 2,922 employees; the aggregate saving in man-hours (1928 to 1931) over all departments was 7,803, which divided by 8 gives a saving of 975 employees, or one-third of the 1927 'total'. In other words, we can reasonably surmise that the impact was relatively substantial.

Source: United States Department of Labor Bureau of Labor Statistics, *Labor Productivity in the Automobile Tire Industry*, Bulletin No. 585 (prepared by B. Stern), July 1933, tables 18, 20, 21, 23, 26, 28, 29, 31; pp. 43, 46, 53, 56, 62, 65, 71, 74.

APPENDIX 8.3 *Unit labour requirement, output per stack-day and methods of charging and casting in sixty merchant blast-furnace plants in the USA in 1923*

Plant No.	Unit labour requirement: man-hours per ton of pig-iron	Scale of output: average output per stack-day, tons	Method of [a] Charging	Casting	Plant No.	Unit labour requirement: man-hours per ton of pig-iron	Scale of output: average output per stack-day, tons	Method of [a] Charging	Casting
1	2.166	508.3	M	M	53	5.092	212.1	M	S
25	2.179	356.0	M	M	46	5.447	298.1	M	M
3	2.194	477.5	M	M	59	6.198	182.1	M	M
4	2.434	517.7	M	M	41	6.282	290.9	H	S
13	2.510	462.6	M	M	52	6.316	224.8	M	S
32	2.816	336.1	M	M	66	6.338	120.8	M	S
12	2.917	330.7	M	M	17	6.474	265.0	H	M
23	3.037	253.4	M	M	38	6.509	223.1	M	S
22	3.055	431.0	M	M	57	6.531	199.7	H	S
5	3.141	444.6	M	M	49	6.566	207.6	M	S
36	3.240	260.5	M	M	43	6.571	192.4	M	S
8	3.407	382.0	M	M	48	6.841	250.0	H	S
16	3.566	493.4	M	M	44	6.904	281.6	[b]	M
24	3.729	[b]	M	M	54	6.986	159.0	M	M
33	3.760	308.0	M	S	73	7.199	104.1	H	S
6	4.033	325.4	M	M	30	7.204	319.1	M	S
2	4.102	330.8	M	SM	55	7.421	183.9	H	M
28	4.150	402.4	H	S	15	7.494	237.3	H	S
7	4.322	346.8	M	M	31	7.542	181.0	M	S
45	4.459	287.5	H	M	40	8.139	269.1	M	S
21	4.466	448.0	M	M	47	8.218	155.8	HM	S
50	4.559	212.5	M	S	68	8.536	198.7	H	S
14	4.588	341.0	H	M	51	8.575	209.0	M	S
39	4.688	255.1	M	M	42	8.827	230.8	H	M
20	4.708	377.0	H	M	60	9.257	130.7	H	S
18	4.919	226.5	M	S	76	9.471	114.0	H	S
19	4.924	344.8	H	M	11	9.509	171.1	HM	SM
27	4.942	360.7	M	M	78	11.574	119.2	H	S
34	5.000	197.1	HM	M	65	11.713	136.2	H	S
35	5.041	370.0	[b]	M	71	14.405	77.7	H	S

[a] Charging: M = Mechanical; H = Hand; HM = Hand and Mechanical; Casting: M = Machine; S = Sand; SM = Sand and Machine.
[b] Not reported.

Source: United States Department of Labor Bureau of Labor Statistics, *Productivity of Labor in Merchant Blast Furnaces*, Bulletin No. 474, December 1928, appendix I, table B, pp. 107–8.

APPENDIX 8.4 *Average man-hours required to build VC–2 vessels ('Victory Ships') delivered through 31 October 1944 in six US shipyards*

	Average man-hours per vessel, thousands										
Average for vessels nos (in order of delivery dates)	General cargo: VC–2–S–AP3				Troop transport: VC–2–S–AP5				General cargo: VC–2–S–AP2		
	Yard A	Yard B	Yard C	All yards	Yard D	Yard E	Yard A	All yards	Yard C	Yard F	All yards
1 to 5	1,118	1,042	1,140	1,100	1,811	1,876	1,689	1,792	595	849	772
6 to 10	949	878	712	846	1,456	1,457	1,364	1,426	517	704	611
11 to 15	880	802		841	1,288						
16 to 20	808	770		788	1,094						
21 to 25	771	699		735							
26 to 30	732	691		711							
31 to 35	708	776		741							
Per vessel											
Maximum man-hours	1,273	1,285	1,630	1,630	2,029	2,627	1,887	2,627	635	988	988
Minimum man-hours	694	673	642	642	1,011	1,395	1,339	1,011	497	574	497
Average, all vessels delivered	866	811	926	850	1,429	1,662	1,596	1,526	560	807	668
Number of vessels delivered	32	32	10	74	19	10	7	36	9	7	16

Source: United States Department of Labor Bureau of Labor Statistics, *Wartime Employment, Production, and Conditions of Work in Shipyards*, Bulletin No. 824, table 25, p. 45.

APPENDIX 8.5 *Average man-hours required to build destroyer-escort vessels delivered through 31 October 1944 in ten US shipyards*

Average for vessels nos (in order of delivery dates)	Average man-hours per vessel, thousands										
	Yard A	Yard B	Yard C	Yard D	Yard E	Yard F	Yard G	Yard H	Yard I	Yard J	All yards
1 to 3	1,129	1,519	2,141	1,346	727	1,852	563	687	1,539	1,149	1,265
4 to 6	995	1,174	1,798	1,213	511	1,434	546	740	1,327	886	1,062
7 to 9	848	1,025	1,413	1,149	447	1,175	507	871	1,264	786	954
10 to 12	817	930	1,455	1,145	414	852	537	876	1,186		912
13 to 15	799	786	1,408	1,099	476	698					878
16 to 18	763	758	1,227	1,067	453						882
19 to 21	762	733	1,086	1,050							908
22 to 24	749	689	1,050	1,014							876
25 to 27	730	655	988	921							824
28 to 30	732	677	943	921							818
31 to 33	627	654	921	905							777
34 to 36	780	636	947	949							828
37 to 39	753	603	1,137	1,254							937
40 to 42	726	553	1,240	1,144							916
43 to 45	697	498	1,007	1,087							822
46 to 48	649	465	906								673
49 to 51	677	555	835								689
52 to 54	668	547	789								668
55 to 57	670	557	804								677
58 to 60	684	526	795								668
61 to 63	703	497	800								629
64 to 66	714	486									600
67 to 69	699	478									589
70 to 72	692	476									584
73 to 75	683	552									618
76 to 78	712										
79 to 81	728										
82 to 84	722										
85 to 87	731										
88 to 90	795										
91 to 93	814										
Per vessel											
Maximum man-hours	1,187	1,621	2,224	1,390	963	2,180	595	951	1,714	1,266	2,224
Minimum man-hours	630	457	782	888	396	666	487	654	1,166	786	396
Average, all vessels delivered	749	681	1,139	1,084	508	1,202	538	794	1,329	960	873
Number of vessels delivered	*91*	*75*	*61*	*45*	*17*	*15*	*12*	*12*	*12*	*8*	*348*

Source: United States Department of Labor Bureau of Labor Statistics, *Wartime Employment, Production, and Conditions of Work in Shipyards*, Bulletin No. 824, 1945, table 26, p. 48.

Chapter 9

General Government Expenditure and Income

Contents

Chapter guide

The public sector – loosely, the government and the nationalised industries – is an important part of the economy and Chapters 9 and 10 provide the basic account of the public sector, thus completing the essential groundwork for the analysis in Chapters 11 to 14 of macroeconomics and economic policy.

Chapter 9 is concerned with the sector of *general government,* which (in the United Kingdom) is divided between *central government* and *local authorities.* First, there are a number of descriptive facts which need to be known, such as the names and functions of the central government's bank accounts with the Bank of England: the *Consolidated Fund*; the *National Loans Fund*; and the *National Insurance Fund.* We look also at data on the historical growth of general government expenditure.

We turn next to the task of understanding how items of general government expenditure may be classified, with special attention to the distinction between *resource-using expenditures* and *transfer payments.* We then look at the data on actual expenditures so as to obtain a clear picture of what the general government spends the taxpayers' money on. We examine the division of expenditures between central government and local authorities and the historical trends in total government outgoings (including transfer payments).

After expenditure comes revenue. We look at the ways in (and the extent to) which the central government levies taxes and at how taxes and benefits together affect households. We explain, fairly fully, the most important central government taxes: *Petroleum Revenue Tax*; *excise duties*; *Value Added Tax*; *National Insurance contributions* (including here an explanation of *contracting out*); *Capital Transfer Tax* (which has replaced the former 'death duties'); *Capital Gains Tax*; and *Development Land Tax* (income tax and Corporation Tax were explained in Chapters 3 and 4 respectively). We also look at local authority *rates* and *rents.*

Given that we now know about the items, and totals, of general government expenditure and revenue, we are in a position to understand two very important concepts: the *general government financial deficit* and the *general government borrowing requirement.* These two concepts are fully explained with reference to actual data (including an explanation of the *accruals adjustment*).

The relationship of the *public sector borrowing requirement* (PSBR) to the general government borrowing requirement is then explained. Because the PSBR plays a key role in our subsequent analysis of economic policy, it is most important to understand exactly how it arises and so we bring together in one table all the items which gave rise to the PSBR in 1980. We look at the data on trends in the public sector borrowing requirement over the period 1952 to 1980 to see why the size of the PSBR has become an issue of such note in recent years, and we consider some employment trends which help to explain the increasing relative importance of the public sector in the UK economy.

Introduction

The main difference between the private sector and the public sector is that while organisations or entities in the private sector have (by and large) to determine their expenditure according to their income, the general government sector tends to be in the enviable position of being able to determine its income according to its expenditure. The power of the government to levy taxes means that it can, by and large, first decide its expenditure and then raise the revenue necessary to pay for those expenditures. It is thus logical, when considering the operations of general government, to start with expenditures, then to consider revenues, and finally to examine the general government financial deficit. Thus, while we shall progress according to the regular sequence of accounts, the emphasis – expenditure first, income second – is different from that to which we have become accustomed in dealing with the private sector.

Sectors of the economy

It may be helpful at this stage to consider again the sectors of the economy in general and the public sector in particular. Diagram 9.1 shows the four major sectors of the UK economy, including the overseas or rest of world sector, which is not a sector *in* the economy but which is *of* the economy, in the sense that entities in the UK economy have transactions with entities in the overseas sector. We have already considered the personal sector and the company sector in some detail and have also discussed the subdivisions within those sectors.

The public sector in the UK economy divides into two main categories of general government and public corporations. The term 'general government' is used to describe the combined sectors of central government and local authorities.

The public corporations are public trading bodies, dominated by the nationalised industries, which have a substantial degree of financial independence from the public authority (central or local government) which created them; this financial independence is reflected in their powers to borrow funds and to maintain their own financial reserves – that is, if public corporations make profits, then their financial surpluses (if any) are retained by them. It is now the practice to present the accounts for the general government and the public corporations separately, except for a consolidation in the public-sector financial accounts which show the combined financial deficits of general government and public corporations. The reason for consolidating the financial accounts and showing the com-

DIAGRAM 9.1   *Sectors of the UK economy*

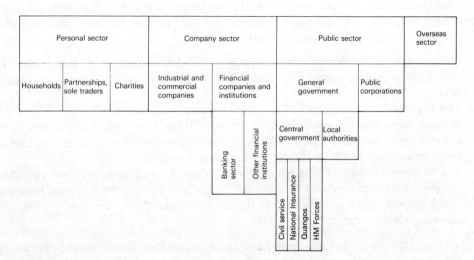

bined public-sector financial deficit (there is only very rarely a public-sector financial surplus) is that financing the deficit is the over-all responsibility of the central government and the issuing of debt (acceptance of liabilities) by the central government may well be used to finance public corporations' deficit in addition to the general government's deficit.

Apart from this, general government and public corporations comprise very different entities.

Most of the public corporations are similar in their operations to industrial and commercial companies – they produce goods or services for sale to customers – and some are similar to financial companies – they provide finance and make their living on the 'turn' between interest rates charged and interest rates paid. Therefore, we shall postpone consideration of the public corporations to the next chapter, and here concentrate on the general government.

The sector of general government in the United Kingdom comprises the twin pillars of central government and local authorities. A division between a central government concerned with 'national' affairs and local governments concerned with 'local' affairs is commonly found in most countries and, where there are written constitutions, the powers of each tend to be carefully defined (which does not prevent complex legal wrangling over the issue). The 'localities' may have several tiers of 'government' with varying responsibilities and powers. The picture can rapidly become very complex. However, we can cling on to one broad generalisation: in all countries, national defence and trading relations with other countries (tariffs, customs duties) are the responsibility of central government, and the main revenue-raising authority is also central government (for reasons usually connected with its sole responsibility for military expenditure).

Although the description we shall give of general government is that pertaining to the United Kingdom and to the accounts of central government and local authorities, the description should be adaptable, with suitable changes, to most other countries. However, it is not possible always to pretend in this chapter to broad generalisations: in previous chapters it effectively mattered little whether the household or business enterprise were British, American, French or German: the restriction was only to industrialised, market economies (the description of the operations of a peasant household in a subsistence-agriculture economy or a producing entity in a centrally planned communist economy would be different in important ways). But where governments are concerned it is difficult to strike quite such a general note all the time.

In the United Kingdom the term 'central government' embraces all entities for whose activities a Minister of the Crown, or other responsible person, is accountable to Parliament. Four main types of entities may be distinguished:

1. Government departments – the 'civil service' – which are the main instruments for giving effect to government policy when Parliament has passed the necessary legislation.
2. HM Forces.
3. Bodies administering public policy, separate from government departments but without financial independence (such as the University Grants Committee, which receives and then hands on the money for the universities).
4. The National Insurance Fund, whose operations we have studied previously (although the system of social security is operated by the government, the National Insurance Fund is held apart as a fund 'belonging' to its members, and, on occasion, its transactions are separately reported).

In the United Kingdom the term 'local authorities' covers local government comprising in England and Wales the county authorities, the district authorities, and the Greater

The central government's bank accounts

Like any other entity, the central government must have a bank account for receiving money and for making payments, though unlike other entities in the economy such a bank account must be established by, and operated according to, Act of Parliament. The central government's bank accounts therefore have special names, indicated by the use of capital letters. There are three main accounts, all with the government's bank, the Bank of England:

1. The Consolidated Fund, which receives all revenues other than receipts from borrowing and from which all payments (except for loans given by government interest on borrowings and National Insurance benefits) are made.
2. The National Loans Fund, which receives all money raised by the issuing of debt and which also pays interest on debt and from which loans by the government are disbursed.
3. The National Insurance Fund, which receives an appropriate transfer from the Consolidated Fund and which disburses National Insurance benefits.

The Consolidated Fund (the government's cash account) is not allowed as a matter of bookkeeping to go into deficit (to become 'overdrawn'); each day's deficit is made up by a transfer from the National Loans Fund, and it is this Fund (debt account) which has then to borrow the necessary from somewhere. The Comptroller and Auditor General is the person charged with the statutory duty to verify that all moneys payable to the Consolidated Fund and the National Loans Fund are duly paid over and that all payments from these Funds are as authorised by Act of Parliament; he audits and reports on these accounts annually. We shall return to these accounts subsequently when we consider the operations of the Bank of England; for the moment all that is necessary is to know that these impressive-sounding names are merely the names given by Act of Parliament to the government's bank accounts, and that there is a 'cash account' (called the Consolidated Fund) and a 'borrowing or debt account' (called the National Loans Fund).

London Council; and in Scotland and Northern Ireland the district councils. Before 1 April 1974 the term 'local authorities' included bodies with special functions such as regional water boards, river and drainage authorities and harbour boards, but from 1 April 1974 these were included with the public corporations. Local authorities have a power to levy property taxes, called 'rates', on all land and buildings in their area; they also have, as we shall see, some other income mainly from rents on houses owned by them, but a large proportion (about half) their income is derived from central government.

One hundred years or so ago it would not have been necessary to devote much space in a book such as this to general government because government expenditures were then only a small part of the economy; but since then things have changed considerably, and it is salutary to begin by putting general government expenditure into historical perspective.

Why the government is (nowadays) economically important

Diagram 9.2 shows total expenditure by general government on goods and services and on fixed capital formation and also its 'current' expenditure on goods and services only, both taken not in their 'raw' or *absolute* form in £ million but as a percentage of gross domestic product: in other words, this diagram shows a *relative* measure of general government spending – namely, the proportion of total expenditure in the economy which was made by general government. Note carefully that these figures refer only to the government's 'real' expenditure and do *not* include transfer payments, such as pensions, unemployment or

DIAGRAM 9.2   *UK general government expenditure in relation to gross domestic product, 1870 to 1980*

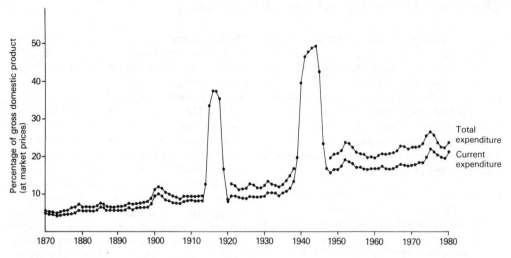

sickness benefits, or capital transfers (the distinction between 'real' expenditure and transfer payments is a matter to which we shall return).

The lower line in Diagram 9.2 shows (in relation to gross domestic product) the general government's current expenditure on goods and services: that is, its 'consumption' expenditure on such things as wages for those employed in the general government sector or heating and lighting for offices or schools, and so on. The upper line shows (relatively to GDP) the general government's total expenditure: that is, its current expenditure *plus* its capital expenditure (expenditure on fixed capital formation – such as new schools, hospitals, offices, roads, council houses, and so on). The vertical distance between the two lines shows the proportion of GDP going to general government fixed capital formation, while, of course, the vertical distance from the horizontal axis to the lower line shows the proportion of GDP going to general government current expenditure. Note, however, that expenditure on fixed capital for the armed forces counts as current expenditure. There are no figures on general government capital expenditure for the years 1939 to 1947 inclusive; figures for the years up to 1920 include Southern Ireland but the Republic of Eire is excluded for the years thereafter.

In the years between 1870 and 1898, total general government expenditure annually averaged 6.5 per cent of the UK gross domestic product. In October 1899 the South African war, having been in the offing for most of the year, officially began; at first the rather small British army suffered defeats and volunteer forces were raised in Britain. The need to pay soldiers and to arm and provision them raised government total expenditure rapidly to 12.0 per cent of GDP in 1901 (nearly double its previous long-run average). The South African war formally ended in May 1902, and government expenditure declined, but not to its former peacetime level: total expenditure averaged 9.4 per cent of GDP between 1903 and 1913 inclusive. Part of this increase in expenditure was due to increased expenditure on the navy: developments in explosives, guns and marine engineering meant that, if Britain were to retain her superiority over the expanding German navy, there had to be considerable expenditure on the construction of *Dreadnought*-type battleships capable of firing eight or ten 12-inch guns in a single broadside (compared with the previous maximum of four) and four such battleships were laid down in 1906 and thirteen more were constructed in the years following and before the First World War. The First World War began between the United Kingdom and Germany on 4 August 1914. In preparation for the war and in the months following the formal declaration, government expenditure rose to 13.9 per cent of GDP in 1914 and then to 33.8 per cent in 1915 and 37.4 per cent in 1916. The peace treaty – the Armistice – ending the war was signed by the Germans on 11 November 1918, and in 1919 government expenditure declined to 17.3 per cent of GDP and then declined still further to 9.9 per cent in 1920. Again, however, expenditure did not fall back to its former peacetime level: between 1921 and 1938 inclusive, government total expenditure averaged 12.6 per cent of GDP, the proportion of GDP spent on fixed capital formation by the government increased considerably: in the years 1870 to 1913 such capital expenditure had averaged 1.1 per cent of GDP; but in the period 1921 to 1937 it averaged 2.7 per cent of GDP.

Much of this expansion in government capital expenditure was due to the building of dwellings by local authorities for renting. There had been very little construction of houses during the First World War, and after the war there was a considerable demand for housing of all types, and the construction by local authorities of dwellings for letting to working-class tenants was encouraged by various Acts of Parliament which provided central government subsidies towards the capital cost of local authority, or 'council', housing. In the general election of 1918 Lloyd George had campaigned on a promise of making Britain 'a fit country for heroes to live in' and the first subsidies were provided in 1919 in (partial) fulfilment of this pledge (the government also subsidised house-building by private constructors for sale to owner-occupiers). Although local authority house-building fluctuated according to the availability of subsidies, between 1920 and 1938 local authorities constructed an average of 70,000 houses a year at a total cost averaging £38 million a year – in relation to total fixed capital expenditure by general government as a whole averaging £123 million a year. So local authority expenditure on dwellings in the interwar period accounted for nearly one-third of government capital expenditure; such local authority house building continued after the Second World War, with the result, as we saw in Chapter 1 (Diagram 1.7) that local authorities now own a considerable proportion – about 35 per cent by value – of the stock of dwellings in the United Kingdom.

During the Second World War, general government expenditure rose to a peak of 49.2 per cent of GDP in 1944, and although expenditure declined after the end of the war in 1945 it remained at a much higher level than had previously been the case: in the years 1948 to 1980 total general government expenditure averaged 22 per cent of GDP, and its capital expenditure averaged 4.1 per cent of GDP.

What analytical conclusions may be drawn from this brief historical survey? Most obvious is the rise in the proportion of gross domestic product being used up in general government expenditure: from an annual average of 6¼ per cent in the last quarter of the nineteenth century to 22 per cent in the third quarter of the twentieth century. This means that expenditure by the general government, and the need to finance that expenditure, now has a major impact on the economy. In turn, this means that a substantial part of any modern textbook on economics must be devoted to the public sector, which is now an essential rather than a merely peripheral part of the economy.

Second, it is also obvious that wars have had a major effect on public expenditure: the three 'large' wars in which the United Kingdom has been engaged this century have each raised public expenditure to relative levels not previously seen. Furthermore, each successive war tended to be relatively more expensive. This is due partly to the increasing 'scale' of the wars, but also to the increasing 'capital' cost of equipping the armed forces – a trend which is clearly discernible from the first decade of this century when increasing amounts had to be spent on bigger and better battleships. The cost for a nation to equip its defence forces 'adequately' is nowadays very large indeed.

Third, it seems that each peak of wartime public expenditure has been followed by a level of peacetime expenditure higher than the previous peacetime average. If we look at the successive peacetime averages of total expenditure, we see the sequence of percentages: 6.5, 9.4, 12.6, and 22. While the first upward step in this sequence was partly due to naval armaments, there was also (as we have seen) an increased awareness of the 'social responsibilities' of the state which led to the introduction of the first old-age pension in 1908. After the First World War the social responsibility of the state was extended with the growth of local authority housing – 'houses for heroes' – and with the gradual widening of unemployment benefit (although note that neither pensions nor unemployment benefit are included in the figures we have been considering, which relate only to the government's 'direct' expenditure). Again, after the Second World War the social responsibilities of the state were greatly extended into the provision of health and education and into more housing, with a concomitant expansion of government capital expenditure. Over the past century, then, this 'ratchet' effect has increased the relative level of government expenditure by more than threefold; taxes have therefore also had to rise concomitantly, and so we need now to examine the government's present-day expenditures and revenues in more detail.

Classifying general government expenditure

Before we get into the details of the government's expenditure we need a system of classifying public expenditures (excluding loans) into a few manageable basic categories. Such a classification can best be based on the different reasons for which the government incurs expenditures. There are, in my opinion, five distinct sorts of reasons.

First, the government undertakes to provide a category of services known as 'public goods'. Public goods are those goods, or benefits, which must be enjoyed, or 'consumed', by the public at large in the sense that it is not really possible to supply different amounts to different individuals *and* where the benefit accruing to one individual does not diminish, or impinge on, the benefit accruing to another. Obvious examples of public goods are defence and law and order. Although one might be a pacifist and object to military expenditure, it is inescapable that you must, along with everybody else, 'consume' or enjoy your share of collective security against external aggression. Furthermore, the fact that you are 'consuming' external security in no way impinges on my 'consumption' of external security. Another example of a public good is the maintenance of public health, an area in which public expenditure expanded considerably during the nineteenth century.

The economic problem with providing public goods, and one of the reasons why they are provided by the government, is that because it is impossible to deny an individual access to, or enjoyment of, such goods, it is in each individual's interests *not* to pay for such goods if he or she can manage this: it is possible to have the benefit without contributing to its cost. Therefore, such goods tend to be paid for on a compulsory basis: everybody is taxed to pay for them, and only the government has the power to do this; or rather, the authority that has this power is the government. 'For the impositions, that are laid on the people by the sovereign power, are nothing else but the wages, due to them that hold the public sword, to defend private men in the exercise of their several trades, and callings' (Thomas Hobbes, *Leviathan*, 1651, ch. XXX). The class of public goods was, historically, one of the first categories of expenditure to be incurred by the state, and there were early controversies over taxes to pay for it. You may recall that one of the difficulties preceding the English Civil War was the dispute over the King's right to levy 'ship money' as a general tax to pay for an increased naval fleet to protect Britain against a Franco–Dutch alliance.

The second category of goods provided by the government is the class of goods, almost entirely falling into the category of services from fixed capital whose initial provision costs a considerable amount, but whose use thereafter (up to the limits of congestion) has no, or only a very low, cost. A good example of this is a bridge: to provide a bridge over a river costs a lot, but once the bridge is there its use by individuals costs nothing, in the sense that if an extra individual crosses the bridge the cost imposed by that crossing is (to all intents and purposes) zero. Suppose a private company borrowed money to put up a bridge and then charged a toll to cross the bridge – the toll money then being used to pay the interest on the loan. Those people who can afford to do so will use the bridge, but we may with certainty assume both that there will be people who would wish to use the bridge but who will refrain from doing so because of the toll and also that there will be excess capacity on the bridge in the sense that the bridge could carry a greater flow of crossings without congestion. Obviously, the conjunction of unsatisfied desires to use the bridge and unutilised river-crossing capacity is undesirable and wasteful: one must take account not only of the money raised by the toll, but also of the 'loss' sustained by people who do not pay the toll because they cannot afford to. Suppose, then, that one adopts a different method of financing the bridge's construction: a compulsory levy on all who are likely to use the bridge, with no charge thereafter for crossing. This spreads the cost of the bridge across a large number of people; more people will then use the bridge so the facility will not be under-used. Clearly, this method of financing the bridge is preferable because more benefits (crossings) will be obtained without any extra cost being incurred. There is therefore a compelling reason for the public provision of certain facilities in this way: these are facilities with heavy initial costs but virtually no, or only low, costs thereafter.

Many 'public works' fall into this category: not only bridges, but roads, canals, harbours, public parks, museums, and so on. They all have the feature in common that, once their heavy initial costs are met, their benefit to the community should be maximised by encouraging maximum use of them, and this entails levying no direct charge (at least up till the limits of congestion).

A third class of goods and services on which public expenditures are incurred are those goods and services whose provision costs something, often quite a lot, but whose consumption the state wishes to encourage because of the general benefits provided by such consumption. This encouragement takes the form of providing the good or service at a subsidised, or zero, price to whomever is consuming the good or service. Education is one of the most conspicuous examples of this sort of good. If there were a direct, commercial charge for education, then many children might be 'under-educated' in the sense of having fewer years of education than if the education were free of direct charge. But, it can be argued, the *general* economy, and also society, will benefit from the presence of better-educated (more highly skilled) workers. Therefore, from a social point of view it is worth encouraging the consumption of education by charging less than it costs to provide (even by charging zero) and then paying for education by a compulsory levy on taxpayers generally. Similar arguments may be applied to the provision of employment services (job centres) or health services.

The fourth category of public expenditures is undertaken in order to redistribute consumption, mostly via a redistribution of income, to disadvantaged individuals who for various reasons are unable to provide for themselves by participating in economic activity. These individuals fall into many different groups: the elderly, the unemployed, the sick, orphans, and so on. There is a long history of state provisions for such, especially where the scale of the problem is large and not easily managed by private charity. The main forms of such redistributive expenditures in the United Kingdom are the various social security payments, expenditures on welfare services, and the provision of housing to lower-income families. Sometimes, instead of making payments in the form of income to households (pensions, unemployment benefit, sickness benefit, etc.), the government gives subsidies to certain enterprises so that they may charge less to certain groups of consumers (for example, to British Rail); such subsidies are also redistributive expenditures. The United Kingdom also makes grants of money available to other countries, mostly to the world's poorer countries, known as 'aid'; such aid expenditures could be counted as redistributive expenditure in a broader international context.

The fifth category is the payment of interest on the National Debt: the annual charges which the government incurs because of its past borrowing.

Consumption *vs* capital expenditure*

Cutting across these five types of public expenditure there are two other sets of distinctions which need to be made. The first distinction is the familiar one between current (or income and expenditure account) 'consumption' expenditures and capital account 'investment' expenditures. Obviously, from Diagram 9.2, the greater part of general government expenditures is current, consumption expenditure, but increasingly since 1920 there has been relatively more expenditure on capital goods.

Resource-using expenditures *vs* transfer payments

The second distinction is that between 'actual' expenditures, which directly involve using up real resources, and 'transfer payments', which merely involve a redistribution of value added. This is a conceptually complex distinction which may not be fully understood until we subsequently discuss the concept of final expenditure; for the moment a partial understanding of the distinction will suffice. If the government pays out money to employ a teacher or a civil servant or to build a school or a road, then that expenditure is a resource-using expenditure which directly involves the production *and* using up of value added; so that, if there is unemployment or excess capacity in the construction industry, and the government employs an extra teacher or civil servant or builds an extra school or ten miles of road, then the gross domestic product is thereby increased to the extent of the additional employment income and profits (if the construction is contracted out to private companies). If there is no unemployment or no excess capacity in the construction industry, then the additional government (resource-using) expenditure, whether on teachers, etc., or on construction, has an 'opportunity cost' in that, say, a scientist employed in industry becomes a teacher or a bank clerk joins the civil service, while, say, private house-building is postponed to enable the construction company to get on with building the school or the road. Such resource-using expenditures therefore involve a real-resource 'burden' on the economy (although obviously there are important differences in the nature of this 'burden' depending on whether the resources used were, or were not, previously unemployed or idle).

On the other hand, transfer payments have no direct implication for the production of value added; they do not involve the use of resources; they merely alter the distribution of an existing flow of value added. Such redistribution is mostly among consumers (households). To illustrate, suppose, as was the case at the beginning of this century, that there were no state retirement pensions, and the elderly just existed as best they could supported by their own savings (if any), charity or family. Suppose that the government then decides to institute a non-contributory retirement pension to all elderly persons (as did Lloyd George's Old Age Pensions Act 1908: the pension was five shillings a week payable from post offices to those over 70 with incomes of less than £21 a year; the cost had been estimated at £6 million a year, but in its first year the cost was £8 million (about 4½ per cent of general government current expenditure); and this rose to £12 million in 1913 (nearly 6 per cent); the number who were eligible was much greater than expected and it became, accordingly, a programme of quite substantial expenditure).

Now, such expenditure would have no direct impact on the production of value added; no productive resources are used up by this expenditure (apart from the small administrative expenses involved); the gross domestic product (of 1909 and onwards) was not

*This distinction, or rather, the decline in the relative proportion of general government capital expenditure has been the subject of recent debate; it is an important issue and the reader might care to consult the paper by HM Treasury ' "Capital" and "current" public expenditure' in *Economic Progress Report*, No. 135, July 1981.

thereby increased: these government expenditures themselves employed no idle resources, nor did they have any opportunity cost; these transfer-payment expenditures on pensions for the elderly poor simply redistributed an existing flow of consumption from those who were being taxed to those who were receiving the pension. Nowadays, such transfer payments to the personal sector are very large; this is how it comes about that total personal income can be larger than the gross domestic product (at factor cost) because total personal income includes (non-resource-using) transfer payments which are not part of the gross domestic product.

Subsidies and transfers abroad (aid) also count as transfer payments. For example, the production of value added by British Rail is not affected by whether BR's income is derived wholly from fares or partly from (lower) fares and partly from subsidies; the economic activity of British Rail is the same in both cases. It is obviously not possible for the government to raise the UK domestic product by giving more foreign aid (apart, of course, from the entirely indirect effects if aid recipients should spend money here – which indirect effects *may* be important).

The interest on the National Debt is also regarded as a transfer payment because otherwise the size of the national income would not be independent of the means of financing government expenditure; it would be nonsensical to assert that if the government borrows more this year, so raising its debt interest payments in future years, the size of the national product will in future years be larger by the amount of that debt interest. Accordingly, this possibility is ruled out by treating interest on the National Debt as a transfer payment.

Finally, in addition to these resource-using and transfer-payment expenditures, the general government also makes loans to other sectors, chiefly to the public corporations (nationalised industries). In the national accounts the word expenditure sometimes also includes loans made *by* the government (net of repayments to the government of past loans). It is clear that the word 'expenditure' is being hopelessly overworked: our vocabulary is just not extensive enough. We ought to have something like the following schema:

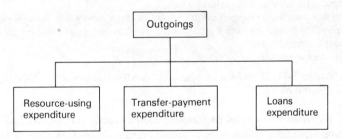

Instead, the word 'expenditure' is used, usually without qualifying adjectives, to cover all types of outgoings. As with the word 'income', we need to look sharp when we see the word 'expenditure'.

General government expenditure

The distinction between real resource-using expenditure and transfer payments is often the basis of the following sort of examination question: 'To what extent is government expenditure a "burden" on the economy?' Answering such a question involves relating the government's resource-using expenditure to gross domestic product, but the snag, as we shall see, is that revenues have also to be raised to finance transfer-payments expenditure, so these latter are not themselves without considerable economic implications.

As a preliminary introduction to the general government's expenditure, let us see what the answer to the examination question is. Table 9.1 shows, in the first place, all the general government's expenditure during 1980, in the second place its resource-using expenditure only, and finally its transfer-payment expenditure, all under the national accounts' rather broad headings whose detail will be subsequently scrutinised.

TABLE 9.1   *UK general government expenditure in relation to gross domestic product, 1980*

General government	1980 £ million	Percentage of GDP
All expenditure		
Expenditure [a] on current account	92,145	40.9
Expenditure [b] on capital account	8,082	3.6
less Stock appreciation	(−)181	−0.1
Total general government expenditure	100,046	44.4
Resource-using expenditure only		
Final consumption expenditure [c]	48,337	21.4
Gross domestic fixed capital formation [d]	5,500	2.4
Value of physical increase in stock and work in progress [d]	119	0.1
Total resource-using expenditure	53,956	23.9
Remainder: transfer-payment expenditure	46,090	20.4
Comprising:		
Current grants to personal sector [c]	25,476	11.3
Subsidies [c]	5,215	2.3
Current grants paid abroad [c]	1,832	0.8
Debt interest [c]	11,285	5.0
Capital grants and transfers [d]	2,282	1.0
Gross domestic product at market prices	225,560	100.0

[a] Including transfer payments, but excluding loans.
[b] Including transfer payments (for capital purposes), and the increase in the value of stocks (i.e. the value of the physical increase in stock *plus* stock appreciation), but excluding loans.
[c] Current-account expenditure.
[d] Capital-account expenditure.

Source: Central Statistical Office, *National Income and Expenditure 1981 Edition*, tables 1.1, 9.1, 10.1, 12.4; pp. 3, 59, 69, 89.

The general government's total expenditure on current account in 1980 was £92,145 million, and its reported expenditure on capital account (in table 9.1 of the Blue Book) was £8,082 million. At this juncture we must iron out a minor wrinkle: reported capital expenditure includes stock appreciation of £181 million on (central government) inventories; these are inventories held both by central government trading bodies (for example, stocks of growing timber held by the Forestry Commission) and by central government emergency and strategic stocks of food and raw materials. Such book-value stock appreciation is not part of the gross domestic product, and so we ought properly to deduct it before making the comparison with GDP. As you can see, the adjustment is not quantitatively of much significance. Over all, then, general government expenditure was £100,046 million, or 44 per cent of GDP, in 1980. This is far greater than the proportion we saw in Diagram 9.2, and this is because the figures just cited include transfer-payment (non-resource-using) expenditures. Therefore, we need to separate the resource-using expenditures from the transfer-payment expenditures. General government expenditures which used up real resources amounted in 1980 to £48,337 million of consumption expenditures on current account (mostly the pay-bill for those employed by central government and local authorities plus the cost of HM Forces), or 21.4 per cent of GDP (as we saw in Diagram 9.2; see also Appendix 9.1); £5,500 million of fixed capital formation, or 2.4 per cent of GDP (again in Diagram 9.2; see also Appendix 9.1); and a relatively negligible £119 million of circulating capital formation ('value of the physical increase in stocks and work in progress' – not included in Diagram 9.2). Total resource-using expenditure in 1980 was thus £53,956 million, or 23.9 per cent of the gross domestic product. A century ago this figure (but excluding the negligible circulating capital formation) was only 5½ to 7 per cent.

The remaining part of general government expenditure is transfer-payment expenditure comprising the items listed in the table, the biggest being transfer payments ('current grants') to the personal sector. The term 'current' means that these were for purposes of current expenditure: retirement pensions, unemployment benefit, student grants, money for universities to pay salaries, and so on. They are distinct from 'capital grants', which are for purposes of capital expenditure only: for example, if the government, through the University Grants Committee, gives money to a university to build a new building, then that money may not be spent on 'current' items such as salaries or stationery; or if the local authority gives a householder a grant to damp-proof a house (fixed capital formation), the householder must spend the money on just that. The word 'grant' means that the money is a 'gift', without obligation to repay: the distinction has to be drawn between grants and loans, the latter carrying an obligation to repay. Table 9.1 does not include loans made by the general government; if the local authority made a loan to a householder to damp-proof a house, then this would not appear in Table 9.1. In order to get a complete picture of the general government's outgoings we need to go to Table 9.2 (where stock appreciation has been added back in to make the figures tally with those reported in the Blue Book and elsewhere: e.g. *Economic Trends Annual Supplement 1982 Edition*, p. 151). In 1980 the general government lent £3,493 million to other sectors of the economy (net of repayments from those sectors of past loans) and this pushed up total government outgoings to £103,720 million, all of which had to be financed by taxation and borrowing, as we shall see.

TABLE 9.2   *Total outgoings of the UK general government, 1980*

	£ million
Total general government expenditure [(a)]	100,046
plus Stock appreciation	181
Lending to other sectors (net of repayment to government of past loans)	3,493
Total general government outgoings [(b)]	103,720

[(a)] Resource-using and transfer-payment expenditure; excludes net lending expenditure.
[(b)] Including stock appreciation; reported in the Blue Book (table 9.1 last line) as 'Total government expenditure'.

Source: Table 9.1 and Central Statistical Office, *National Income and Expenditure 1981 Edition*, table 9.1, p. 59.

Having seen in broad outline what total general government expenditure amounted to in 1980, we now need to consider in detail what this expenditure comprised. This list of general government expenditure is necessarily lengthy, but it is important for the student to build up an adequate descriptive picture of general government expenditures. Only in this way can we obtain a proper understanding, in economic terms, of the term 'general government expenditure'. The list deals with *general* government expenditure: that is, without distinguishing between central government and local authorities, because it is necessary, in the first instance, to see government expenditure as a whole. Subsequently,

TABLE 9.3   *UK general government expenditure (total outgoings) by category of expenditure, 1980*

Category [a]	1980 £ million	1980 Percentage of total
Public goods		
Military defence	11,388	11.0
Civil defence	31	0.03
Fire service	459	0.4
Police	2,100	2.0
Prisons	471	0.5
Parliament and law courts	709	0.7
External relations	2,072	2.0
Finance and tax collection	1,426	1.4
Records, registration and surveys	71	0.07
Public health services	302	0.3
Miscellaneous local government services	1,387	1.3
Other general government services	431	0.4
Sub-total: all goods	20,847	20.1
Public works		
Roads and public lighting	2,302	2.2
Water, sewerage and refuse disposal	1,185	1.1
Land drainage and coastal protection	211	0.2
Parks, pleasure grounds	743	0.7
Libraries, museums and arts	592	0.6
Sub-total: all goods	5,033	4.9
General-benefit goods and services		
Education	11,886	11.5
National Health Service	11,494	11.1
Research	797	0.8
Employment services	1,692	1.6
Agriculture, forestry, fishing, food	1,589	1.5
Other industry and trade	4,075	3.9
Transport and communications	1,243	1.2
Sub-total: general benefit goods and services	32,776	31.6
Redistributive expenditure		
Social security benefits	22,211	21.4
Housing	7,156	6.9
Personal social services	2,127	2.1
School meals, milk and welfare foods	510	0.5
Sub-total: redistributive expenditure	32,004	30.9
Interest on the National Debt	11,285	10.9
Non-trading capital consumption [b]	1,775	1.7
Total expenditure including net lending	103,720	100.0

[a] Each category may include resource-using expenditure, transfer-payment expenditure, and net lending expenditure.

[b] National income accounting item; comprises mainly imputed rents on owner-occupied buildings (as an item of 'income' in the national income) and is reported, in general government accounts, twice: once as imputed income; and once, as here, as imputed expenditure.

Source: Central Statistical Office, *National Income and Expenditure 1981 Edition*, table 9.4, pp. 61–4.

we shall consider the division of expenditure between central government and local authorities. Although thirty distinct items are recorded in the national accounts' analysis of total general government expenditure, the 'big four' – social security benefits, education, military defence, and the National Health Service – account for over one-half of general government total outgoings.* Nevertheless, it is important to have at least some knowledge of the other twenty-six items as well.

Table 9.3 gives the figures on these thirty items categorised (by me) under the five types of general government expenditure (by reason for the expenditure) with sub-totals for each type. This categorisation of items into five sets is not found in the national accounts, which simply gives a straightforward list of thirty items (each subdivided by current/capital, expenditure/grants, and net lending; these sub-divisions are not given here). Furthermore, the composition of some items is not wholly consonant with the categorisation: for example, 'roads and public lighting' contains a great deal of expenditure on the current maintenance of roads and on payment for electricity, which is not quite what one has in mind under the category of 'public works' – the latter implying the initial provision, rather than the subsequent maintenance and running, of fixed capital. The national accounts' analysis includes all outgoings, whether as expenditure on goods and services, expenditure on transfer payments and subsidies, or net lending. Rather than alter the items given in the Blue Book, I have simply taken them as they are given so that the reader can more easily examine the trends over time when consulting the Blue Book (as with all tables involving Blue Book data, Table 9.3 is intended as an introduction to the national income and expenditure accounts – the reader will derive much less benefit if tables like this one are read without additionally studying the Blue Book). The Blue Book's figures are from accounts derived for the purpose of ensuring parliamentary and departmental control over, and accountability for, expenditure, so we cannot expect them always to fall in with theoretical classification.

General government expenditure on public goods

The central government is responsible for all military expenditure, amounting to 11 per cent of total outgoings in 1980. This comprises wages and salaries (about 43 per cent of all expenditure on defence), purchases of supplies and equipment (the other 55 per cent) and a small amount of current grants abroad (military aid, etc.). Some expenditure by the United Kingdom Atomic Energy Authority is included here. About three-quarters of civil defence expenditure is incurred by the central government on acquiring inventories of, and on storage and distribution facilities for, food, petroleum and other strategic materials. The remaining one-quarter of civil defence expenditure is incurred by local authorities for civil defence establishments or for the capital costs of emergency water supplies, sewage facilities, fire-fighting appliances, and so on. Expenditure on the regular fire brigades service is nearly all under local authorities, who have a statutory duty (i.e. a duty laid on them by Act of Parliament) to provide adequate fire-fighting facilities. Nearly all expenditure on the police also comes under local authorities and mostly comprises police pay and pensions and equipment; however, the costs of police training are met directly by the central government.

The cost of prisons is entirely met by central government. Expenditure on Parliament and the law courts is incurred partly by central government for the House of Lords, the

---

*There are actually thirty-one items, but one item, 'War damage compensation: capital grants to private sector' – to rebuild or replace houses bombed or ships sunk during the Second World War – has for many years had no entries, though it did record a negative figure (a repayment?) of £1 million in 1980.

Local control of the police – or the importance of history

There are important historical (and constitutional) reasons for keeping 'local' control of police services: in the first part of the nineteenth century, when police forces were gradually being organised to combat the increase in (mainly urban) crime, there were very strong objections to any central government control of the police which, it was feared, would 'reduce England to the level of the continental "police-states"' (E. L. Woodward, *The Age of Reform 1815–1870*, The Oxford History of England, vol. 13, Oxford University Press, 1938, p. 448), and so the system of local police forces gradually evolved in the attempt to 'reconcile an effective system of police with that perfect freedom of action and exemption from interference which are the great privileges and blessings of society in this country' – to quote the words of the Report of the 1822 Select Committee on the Police of the Metropolis. Consequently there are now forty-three police forces in England and Wales, eight in Scotland and one in Northern Ireland, each responsible for law enforcement in its own area and each operating under a local police authority committee of local authority councillors and magistrates. Although under local control, more than half of the local authorities' expenditure on the police is met from a grant given by central government for this purpose. This practice, too, is a product of history: resistance to an 1856 Act of Parliament giving the Home Office power to inspect local police forces had been overcome by the provision of central government grants to local bodies to enable them to pay for an efficient police force. The reason for explaining the complicated arrangements the United Kingdom has for financing its police forces is to demonstrate the influence of history on matters such as this. Indeed, most of the items in Table 9.3 are the product of history, and can only be fully understood in the context of that history; however, we shall not, for lack of space, be able to pursue these historical explanations in any detail.

House of Commons, the High Courts, and the Crown Courts (for serious cases) and partly by local authorities who bear the cost of the local magistrates' courts (for less serious cases). Current grants to the personal sector for legal aid are included under this item.

The cost of external relations includes overseas aid, expenditures on the diplomatic service and on the administration of overseas aid by the Foreign and Commonwealth Office, expenditure on the Secret Service, payments to the BBC for its external services, and subscriptions to certain international organisations. Under this heading come also the contribution to the European Economic Community (these contributions are counted net of UK receipts from the budgets of the EEC): such net contributions amounted to £825 million in 1980 – Blue Book, table 7.2).

Expenditure on finance and tax collection consists of the expenses of the Treasury, of the Board of Inland Revenue, of Customs and Excise, of the National Savings Committee, and of the Exchequer and Audit Department (whose function it is to see that all money payable to the Consolidated Fund and to the National Loans Fund are duly paid over and that all issues of money from these Funds are as authorised by statute). This also includes the cost of administering the National Debt and the cost of producing coins and notes. Local authorities incur under this item the administrative cost of rate collection and of valuations for rating. Records, registrations and surveys comprise current expenditures by local authorities on the registration of births, marriages and deaths, and on the compilation of the electoral register. Central government expenditure under this item includes the costs of making Ordnance Survey maps, and of maintaining various central registries and public records. The cost of undertaking the population census is also included here, which is why this item shows a large increase each census year. Expenditure on public health services (not to be confused with the National Health Service) comprises local authority expenditure on public lavatories, on sanitary inspection, on the inspection of food and drugs, and on port health services.

Miscellaneous local government services are mainly administrative expenses on such items as town and country planning, local elections, and general administration. Other general government services include various costs of government not covered elsewhere, such as the Meteorological Office, the Civil Service Commission (responsible for the recruitment of all permanent civil servants), the Ombudsman (whose proper title is the Parliamentary Commissioner for Administration), the *ad hoc* Royal Commissions, and (most important of all) the Civil List for the cost of the monarch's public expenditure on carrying out official duties as head of state.

Together these twelve items constitute the provision of public goods which are collectively 'consumed' by the public at large. This category makes up about one-fifth of total general government outgoings. As you can see, a large part of what we would think of in connection with the word 'government' is included among these twelve items, and the list would not have unduly surprised any Briton visiting us from preceding centuries.

General government expenditure on public works

The next category is that of public works: those items characterised by high initial fixed costs but thereafter with relatively low operating costs. This is the reason why their provision is undertaken by the state; the actual flows of expenditure in Table 9.3 relate more to the costs of maintenance and operation, as most of these facilities have been built up gradually over the years. In this category we have: expenditure on roads and public lighting (including the capital costs of new roads); water supply, sewerage, and refuse disposal; land drainage and coastal protection (including, for example,the cost of the Thames barrage); public parks and pleasure grounds, including the preservation of historic buildings and ancient monuments, and, for local authorities, the cost of maintaining and running all recreational facilities (net of charges for admission to those facilities); and expenditure on libraries, museums and arts, such as the British Museum, the Victoria & Albert Museum, the National Gallery, the Tate Gallery, and grants to, for example, the Royal Opera House, Covent Garden. This category makes up only about one-twentieth of total outgoings, and the greater proportion is on roads and public lighting.

General government expenditure on general-benefit goods and services

The third category is that of general-benefit goods and services: the provision of these, in terms of current costs, is expensive, and it is feasible to provide the services privately with direct charges to users, but the state tries to encourage the consumption of these services by providing them at a low or zero price to users and obtaining the necessary finance through general taxation. This is done because of some general benefit that is supposed to be derived from an increased consumption or provision of the good or service concerned. Education is foremost among these general-benefit goods and services (or 'merit goods', as they are sometimes called). Education expenditure comprises all current and capital expenditure on schools (excluding school meals), institutions of further education, and universities, as well as maintenance of grants to students. Education is one of the single biggest items in the list, taking up 11.5 per cent of total outgoings in 1980.

The National Health Service has been classified under this heading even though there is a redistributive element in NHS expenditure, i.e. making medical and surgical treatment more readily available to the lower-income groups, but, of course, the NHS is not specifically aimed at lower-income groups. Central government expenditures cover the hospital service (current and capital expenditures), payments to general practitioners, and the costs of dental, ophthalmic and pharmaceutical services, net of charges levied (such as prescription charges). Local authorities provide services such as health centres, health visiting and home nursing, ambulance services, and most vaccination and immunisation services. The central government's annual subscription to the World Health Organisation is included here. The National Health Service is another of the big items in the list and accounted for 11.1 per cent of total outgoings in 1980.

Research expenditures constitute the most obvious example of expenditures undertaken in the hope of providing a general benefit to society. This covers expenditure by the various research councils (the Medical Research Council, the Science Research Council, the Social Science Research Council, etc.) including the payment of postgraduate research scholarships.

Employment services are mainly the services of the Department of Employment's Job Centres and training centres. Expenditure on special employment schemes for young people or for the disabled are included. The administrative costs of the Redundancy Fund and the rebates of redundancy payments to employers are included (employers are required initially to meet the whole cost of redundancy payments and may then claim a rebate of about one-half the payment from the Redundancy Fund, which is financed by a general payroll levy on all employers). The central government's subscription to the International Labour Organisation is included here.

Expenditures on agriculture, forestry, fishing and food are mainly the services and subsidies provided by the Ministry of Agriculture, Fisheries and Food, the Forestry Commission and other related bodies (such as the White Fish Authority). Occasionally the government has to pay compensation to farmers for animals slaughtered to prevent outbreaks of infectious disease, such as foot and mouth disease, from spreading and such compensation payments would be included here.

Expenditure on other industry (i.e. industries other than agriculture) and trade comprises most of the services provided by the Department of Trade and Industry; this includes assistance to the aerospace industry (such as for building *Concorde*), to the shipbuilding industry, the provision of factories for leasing in development areas, and the expenses of the Export Credits Guarantee Department. This latter offers two main facilities to Britsh exporters: insurance against the risk of not being paid for goods and services exported; and access to special fixed interest rates for export finance. The ECGD also provides support for 'buyer credits', which are loans made directly to overseas buyers of capital goods manufactured in the United Kingdom; such financial backing for their exporters is indulged in by most governments of industrialised countries, and as it can materially affect the terms on which bids by tender may be made for export orders it is important in the over-all drive to maintain and increase UK exports that the UK government does likewise. One might ask why the banks do not undertake such financing: the answer is that they do, but they will insure only against normal, assessable commercial risk and not against abnormal, unassessable political risk, which may be significant as many of the contracts are with foreign governments. By filling this gap in the financial market, the government hopes to ensure more jobs and profits in British industry as well as more foreign exchange earnings, so generally benefiting the economy. Grants and loans to private industry and to the public corporations concerned with fuel and power and iron and steel are included, and it is in fact the net lending to these nationalised industries which was largely responsible for this item being so big in 1980, such net lending amounting to £2,417 million (table 9.4, p. 62 of the Blue Book).

Expenditure on transport and communications covers fixed capital formation (other than that on roads and public lighting, which is separately reported) paid for by capital transfers or net lending to the various transport and communications public corporations (e.g. British Rail, British Airways, the Post Office, etc.) and subsidies to these corporations to cover loss-making operations which it is thought desirable to keep running (e.g. rural train or bus services).

All these general-benefit goods and services comprise nearly one-third (31.6 per cent) of total general government outgoings. It is a category whose relative size has expanded considerably this century, and the list (apart from primary education) would not really be familiar to a visitor from the nineteenth century, to whom government involvement here would doubtless take much explaining.

General government redistributive expenditure

Fourth, we have the category of redistributive expenditure to disadvantaged persons – although we must interpret the word 'disadvantaged' broadly to include, for example, those who have retired from economic activity. The largest single item comprises all the various social security benefits, such as all the National Insurance benefits (retirement pension, unemployment and sickness benefits – as discussed in Chapter 3), family allowances, supplementary benefits, and war pensions. The administrative costs of social security are also included here. I have classified the cost of public provision of housing under redistributive expenditure because this is specifically intended to benefit the lower-income group. Much of this is either for building new houses by local authorities or on subsidies to rents – that is, the excess of local authority expenditure, including loan charges, repairs and other housing expenses, over the amounts received in rents from tenants. Capital grants to the personal sector to enable individuals to improve houses are included, as is net lending to the personal sector by local authorities to enable people to buy houses.

Personal social services is mainly local authority expenditure on care of the aged, handicapped and homeless and on child care. This expenditure goes on social workers' salaries and on running various homes for disadvantaged groups. The cost of school meals, milk and welfare foods (net of receipts from those receiving meals) and the administrative expenses thereof are classified as redistributive expenditures because it seems that these are often used in a redistributive way with some children from lower-income families not having to pay for the meals.

The sub-total of these redistributive expenditures is nearly one-third of general government outgoings. This category has also increased in relative size this century. To the visitor from the nineteenth century, many of the items would be familiar, but as private charity rather than as government expenditure.

Interest on the National Debt and imputed capital consumption

Fifth, we come to the interest on the National Debt, which is *sui generis* (Latin for 'a kind [*generis*] of its own [*sui*]'). This is about 11 per cent of general government outgoings.

Finally, there is an item not so far mentioned which is to do with national income accounting conventions rather than with (actual) general government outgoings. The gross domestic product must include the value added derived from owner-occupied buildings. If, say, all hospitals and government offices belonged to some property company which, having financed their construction, rented them to the government, then those rents would quite naturally and properly appear as value added produced by the property company sector. The fact that the government owns most of the buildings it occupies, and that no rents are therefore paid, cannot be allowed to 'diminish' the national product, because a real benefit is being derived from the use of those buildings. Therefore, the national accounts statisticians impute a rental on such owner-occupied buildings which they call 'non-trading capital consumption', and this appears as an item of expenditure (just as would happen if the government were paying rent). Because the government owns the buildings, it must, correspondingly, be deemed to be receiving these imputed rentals as income (as would the hypothetical property company); so the same imputed non-trading capital consumption also appears as a general government receipt on current account. This balances out so far as general government accounts are concerned, but the expenditure, or the corresponding income, then appears as part of the gross domestic product, or national income.

The reader should appreciate that we have the space to give only the most superficial treatment of these thirty items of general government expenditure, most of which could readily be discussed each in a whole chapter. Elsewhere in this book we have considered some of them – such as the more important social security benefits which appear as a significant part of personal-sector income. The purpose of this brief glance at government expenditure is simply to provide a bird's-eye view of the main areas of government expenditure, and the reader should appreciate, even after the fag of toiling over Table 9.3, that he or she still has a lot more to learn to obtain a full knowledge of government activities. The book most useful for starting such a fuller study is *Britain 1981: An Official Handbook*, published each year by HMSO. After that, the reader will have to delve into the more specialist literature concerned with specific topics. But at least we should now have a more concrete understanding of the term 'general government expenditure'.

Central government and local authorities

Table 9.3 dealt with general government expenditure making no distinction between central government and local authorities, though we sometimes mentioned in our description of the items the responsibilities of each. It is necessary to look briefly at the division of expenditures between central government and local authorities, because a substantial part of local authority expenditure is financed by the central government and, correspondingly, central government efforts to control local authority spending have become an important issue in British politics (and such conflict between central and local government is not unknown in other countries).

Table 9.4 shows the division of general government expenditure between central government and local authorities. Table 9.4 focuses on the general government total outgoings in 1980 of £103,720 million, but because of financing provided by central government to local authorities, with one item (interest payments) from local authorities to central government, the table also has some extra items at the bottom. Such intersectoral transactions between central government and local authorities do not, of course, affect general government as a whole, just as the income and expenditure of a family as a whole is not affected by transfers from one member of a family to another. For example, if a father gives his son pocket-money, that transaction affects the father's expenditure and the son's income, but it does not alter the total expenditure and the total income of the family. Although Table 9.4 is quite lengthy, its main features are relatively few: resource-using expenditure accounted for 52.2 per cent of total general government expenditure with 30.2 per cent of total general government expenditure being undertaken by central government and 22 per cent by local authorities. In other words, resource-using expenditure was divided very approximately half and half between central government and local authorities. However, note that local authorities were responsible for about seven-tenths of general government fixed capital formation. Transfer-payment expenditures took up 44.4 per cent of total general government outgoings, and nine-tenths of this was the responsibility of the central government.

TABLE 9.4 *Division of UK general government expenditures (total outgoings) between central government and local authorities, 1980*

	1980					
	£ million			Percentage of total general government outgoings		
	Central govern-ment	Local auth-orities	General govern-ment	Central govern-ment	Local auth-orities	General govern-ment
Current consumption expenditure on goods and services	28,679	17,883	46,562	27.7	17.2	44.9
Non-trading capital consumption	675	1,100	1,775	0.7	1.1	1.7
Gross domestic fixed capital formation	1,679	3,821	5,500	1.6	3.7	5.3
Increase in value of stocks	300	—	300	0.3	—	0.3
Sub-total resource-using expenditure (including stock appreciation)	31,333	22,804	54,137	30.2	22.0	52.2
Subsidies	4,231	984	5,215	4.1	0.9	5.0
Current grants to personal sector	24,383	1,093	25,476	23.5	1.1	24.6
Current grants abroad	1,832	—	1,832	1.8	—	1.8
Capital transfers to private sector	1,617	202	1,819	1.6	0.2	1.8
Capital transfers to public corporations	323	140	463	0.3	0.1	0.4
Capital transfers abroad	0	—	0	0	—	0
Debt interest to non-government sectors [b]	8,662	2,623	11,285	8.4	2.5	10.9
Sub-total: transfer payment expenditure	41,048	5,042	46,090	39.6	4.9	44.4
Net lending to private sector	55	463	518	0.1	0.4	0.5
Net lending to public corporations (including 'public dividend capital' [c])	3,358	—	3,358	3.2	—	3.2
Net lending to overseas sector	−439	—	−439	−0.4	—	−0.4
Cash expenditure on company securities	56	—	56	0.1	—	0.1
Sub-total: financial expenditure	3,030	463	3,493	2.9	0.4	3.4
Total expenditure (excluding inter-sectoral transactions)	75,411	28,309	103,720	72.7	27.3	100.0
Intersectoral transactions						
Current grants to local authorities allocated to specific services	2,733	—	[a]			
Current grants to local authorities not allocated to specific services	10,542	—	[a]			
Capital transfers to local authorities	337	—	[a]			
Net lending to local authorities	1,229	—	[a]			
Debt interest to local authorities/central government [b]	−1	1,606	[a]			
Sub-total: inter-sectoral transactions	14,840	1,606	[a]			
Grand total (including, for sectors, intersectoral transactions)	90,251	29,915	[a]			

[a] Intersectoral transactions between central government and local authorities cannot meaningfully be aggregated into general government expenditure as this results in doublecounting.

[b] Debt interest payments to local authorities by central government is not directly reported, but may be calculated with figures in £ million as: Central government total debt interest (8,661) *minus* {General government total debt interest (11,285) *minus* Local authority debt interest payment to sectors other than central government (2,623)}.

[c] The chief feature of which is that no dividends are payable until the industry becomes profitable: such 'equity-type' capital has been used for British Shipbuilders and the British Steel Corporation.

Source: Central Statistical Office, *National Income and Expenditure 1981 Edition*, tables 7.2, 7.3, 7.4, 8.2, 8.3, 8.4, and 9.4; pp. 49, 50, 52, 55, 56, 57, and 65.

Net lending to other sectors took up 3.4 per cent of general government total outgoings, and most of this was net lending by central government to public corporations (national-ised industries). However, note that most general government net lending to the private sector is undertaken by local authorities. Over the three types of expenditure taken together – resource-using, transfer payments, and net lending – the central government was in 1980 responsible for about three-quarters (72.7 per cent) and local authorities for about one-quarter (27.3 per cent). Local authorities may be the junior partner in general government, but they are a significant junior partner, as shown by their 27.3 per cent share.

We have mentioned from time to time that local authorities have certain duties laid upon them by Act of Parliament, for example to provide a fire-fighting service or a police force. Because of this, and because local authorities' own sources of income were insufficient to these purposes, the central government provides local authorities with additional income, partly as specific grants for specific purposes, for example for the police or for education or for capital expenditure, and partly as a general 'rate support grant' to supplement local authorities' income in a general way: that is, each local authority is (more or less) free to allocate the rate support grant among individual services as it sees fit.

For each local authority, the amount it receives in rate support grant from the central government is worked out with reference to:

(a)   its 'needs', so that authorities which most need to undertake expenditure (for example, on slum clearance) receive more;
(b)   its 'resources', so that authorities with less rateable income per head of population receive more; and
(c)   its 'domestic' requirement to give rate reductions to certain householders.

The whole formula was an attempt, with reasonable success, to equalise matters among authorities so that, for example, a local authority with much poor-quality housing – giving rise to both low rate income *(per capita)* and high spending needs *(per capita)* – received more rate support grant *(per capita)* than did an affluent suburban local authority with high *per capita* rate income and a low *per capita* spending need. With the inflation of the 1970s the rate support grant rose rapidly as the central government struggled with the following options involved in trying to contain the grant's rise:

1.   Curb local authorities' expenditure.
2.   If expenditure rose but the rate support grant were not increased, accepting that the rates levied by local authorities would rise.

In Table 9.4, we can see that in 1980 the central government provided a gross total of £14,840 million worth of finance to local authorities (the net amount being somewhat reduced by the fact that local authorities had to pay to the central government £1,606 million of interest on borrowings from the central government). Of this, £2,733 million comprised current grants for specific purposes, and £10,542 million comprised the general rate support grant. It can be seen that the rate support grant is a significant part (11.7 per cent) of total central government outgoings of £90,251 million.

We can see in Table 9.4 that grants and lending from central government (net of interest paid by local authorities to central government) financed about one-half of local authority spending. This means that the central government must be closely concerned with local authorities' spending, because such spending inevitably affects the central government's accounts, in no small measure, and this concern has become an issue of some political controversy.

Trends in general government total outgoings

Having examined these aspects of government expenditure, we need to return to the historical trends in total outgoings. Diagram 9.2 showed the ratchet-like growth in relative resource-using expenditure only – in the extent to which the general government was using real resources. Diagram 9.2 left transfer payments and net lending out of the reckoning. But transfer payments and lending need nevertheless to be financed; they are tax-using expenditures just as much as are resource-using expenditures. If we want to see the extent to which the government has had to raise taxes to finance its outgoings, we need to examine total outgoings relative to the total tax base. The best measure of the total tax base is gross *national* product (at factor cost); that includes net property income from abroad.

Diagram 9.3 shows total general government outgoings as a percentage of gross national product from 1900 to 1980, with the basic data shown in Appendix 9.2. Because of the rise in transfer payments – grants to the personal sector and interest on the national debt – there has during this century been a very great change in the relative size of tax-using expenditures, as the following summary from Appendix 9.2 shows:

	1903 to 1913	1920 to 1938	1948 to 1980
General government total outgoings as percentage GNP: annual average for period	11.8	26.9	44.0

DIAGRAM 9.3   *UK general government total outgoings in relation to the gross national product, 1900 to 1980*

Excluding wartime years (and their immediate aftermath, when expenditure may have been winding down from their wartime levels), we can see that total general government outgoings rose from an average of 11.8 per cent of GNP before the First World War to 26.9 per cent in the interwar years, and then to 44.4 per cent after the Second World War. This is, of course, a rather different picture from that given in Diagram 9.2. We can also see that, during the period after the Second World War, general government total outgoings, and hence the need for finance, rose quite steeply in two phases: first in the years 1965 to 1968, and then in 1974 and 1975, when the percentage rose to 54.1 per cent. It is interesting to note that ever since 1967 the government's need for finance has consistently been much greater than it was when the United Kingdom was fighting the First World War.

One of the main reasons for this relative expansion in general government total outgoings is the growth of transfer payments, such as retirement pensions, unemployment benefit, student grants, and subsidies, these transfer payments being associated with the development in the United Kingdom of the welfare state. Diagram 9.4 shows the historical growth of such transfer payments as a percentage of general government expenditure on current account (consumption of goods and services, grants and subsidies, and debt interest). We leave out the abnormal wartime years and their immediate aftermath.

DIAGRAM 9.4   *Grants (transfer payments on current account) and subsidies paid by general government as a percentage of general government current expenditure, 1900 to 1980*

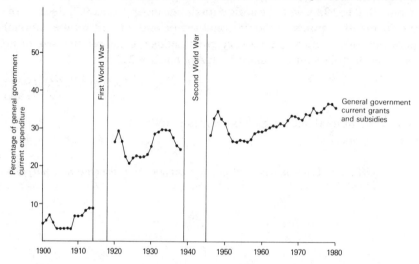

Sources: C. H. Feinstein, *National Income, Expenditure and Output of the United Kingdom 1855–1965*, table 14, pp. T35–T36; *Economic Trends Annual Supplement 1981 Edition*, p. 151; *National Income and Expenditure 1981 Edition*, table 9.1, p. 59.

The impact of Lloyd George's retirement pensions, first paid in 1909, is clearly to be seen. In 1911 Lloyd George's National Insurance Act provided sickness insurance for all employees and unemployment benefit for employees in certain industries prone to industrial fluctuations, and the effect of this too can be seen in the further rise in transfer payments (as a proportion of current expenditure) in 1912. In 1920 unemployment insurance was extended to all employees, and this, together with war pensions and retirement pensions, meant that transfer payments in the interwar years were relatively much greater than previously, and they tended to rise as the rate of unemployment rose after 1929 (see Diagram 1.5). Since 1955 there has been a steady rise in the relative importance of transfer payments, partly due to the inevitable rise in pension payments as the proportion of elderly in the population increases – for Great Britain we may calculate the following figures from Table 1.6:

	1951	1961	1971	1981	1991 (projected)
Percentage of population over retirement age	13.6	14.7	16.3	17.7	17.4

It is, however, clear that the causes of the relative increase in general government total outgoings may be many and varied, and may be quite apart from 'political' decisions to increase the size of general government expenditure. Such matters are not really the concern of an introductory textbook on economics (readers who wish to follow up these topics could consult F. T. Blackaby (ed.), *British Economic Policy 1960–74*, Cambridge University Press, 1978, especially ch. 3).

Having now examined general government expenditure in its constituent components, with some historical perspective, we must now consider the general government revenues which, in 1980, paid for this expenditure of £103,720 million.

General government revenue

Much learned work is devoted to the economics of taxation, and it would indeed be pleasing if the process of raising revenue were subordinate to rational, economic criteria. Unfortunately this is not, and can never be, the case. Given the rise in general government outgoings to over one-half the gross national product, there is only one operative law of taxation: this is to raise as much tax revenue as it is politically feasible to do. Successive governments have been able to raise these sorts of relative levels of tax revenues because they have been able to tax the gross national product twice: once as income, and then again as expenditure. Were it not for the general acceptance by the population of this 'double taxation', financing for general government expenditure would long ago have been in serious difficulty. The pressure to raise revenue means also that a large variety of taxes is used. It is therefore not surprising that the tax 'system' in the United Kingdom today, to use the words of a committee of experts, 'contains a number of anomalous complications and inconsistencies' (*The Structure and Reform of Direct Taxation*, Report of a Committee chaired by Professor J. E. Meade (Allen & Unwin, 1978, p. 3). Other experts have observed that anyone seeing it for the first time

> would regard the present [tax] system with some incredulity ... No one would design such a system on purpose and nobody did. Only a historical explanation of how it came about can be offered as a justification. That is not a justification, but a demonstration of how seemingly individually rational decisions can have absurd effects in aggregate (J. A. Kay and M. A. King, *The British Tax System*, 2nd edn, Oxford University Press, 1980, p. 239).

From the point of view of the need to finance public expenditure, none of these anomalies or absurdities really matters, and we shall not therefore discuss the system of taxation as we would like it to be. In the first place, we have already considered some of the taxes elsewhere (e.g. income tax in Chapter 3); in the second place, there are already excellent books on this subject – especially the work of Kay and King just cited – and we have not here the space to go over this well-trodden ground; in the third place, it is important simply to establish the descriptive (rather than the analytic) background to taxation and public finance in the United Kingdom, and this latter task is what we shall try to accomplish. The reader must appreciate that in order properly to criticise the tax system, it is necessary first of all to know what that system comprises: we must have description before analysis.

The government may raise money to finance total outgoings from three sources: first, it may raise compulsory levies ('taxes' of various sorts); second, it may borrow from voluntary lenders (compulsory borrowing has also been known, for example, as once in Ghana where salary-earners were required to subscribe to 'development bonds', but is not very common); third, the government may receive revenue from other sources – for example, if the government owns shares in a company or has lent money to a household, it may receive dividends or interest, and if a government trading enterprise, e.g. Export Credits Guarantee Department, makes a profit, that profit will be a source of revenue to the government. Here again we need to be careful in our use of words, and we shall try to stick to the terminology given in Diagram 9.5 on the classification of general government receipts.

Because of the different ways in which central government and local authorities raise taxes it is necessary from the outset to consider the two separately. We shall deal first with

DIAGRAM 9.5   *Classification of general government receipts*

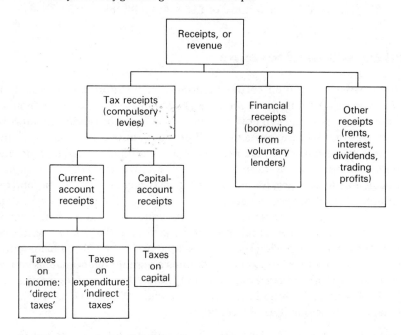

the tax and other receipts of both sectors, before going on to consider financial receipts.

Central government tax receipts are paid into the Consolidated Fund (month-by-month receipts into and disbursements from the Consolidated Fund – the central government's cash account with the Bank of England – are given in *Financial Statistics*, table 3.1). Table 9.5 gives the figures for central government receipts for the calendar year 1980. These figures are reported on an 'accruals basis' – that is, these are the taxes payable, falling due, in the calendar year 1980, whether or not actually paid over in 1980. We saw in our analysis of company accounts that, in order to strike a meaningful figure for profits after taxes, the taxes deducted had to be tax liabilities payable – falling due – not the taxes which were actually paid. If some part of those tax liabilities were not in fact paid, but temporarily held in the company's bank account, we might subsequently in the accounts have to add back these temporarily held tax liabilities before striking the company's cash-flow balance. But it would not have been meaningful to strike a figure for after-tax profits which included these temporarily held tax liabilities, which figure would result from deducting taxes actually paid rather than tax liabilities accruing. Now, if we adopt for the other sectors an accruals convention for deducting taxes, then, to be consistent, we must adopt for the government sector an accruals basis for tax receipts. In practice, the central government tends to receive less actual cash payment of taxes during the year than tax liabilities accruing (because other sectors temporarily postpone payment of tax liabilities), so when we strike the government's cash balance we have to allow for this in what is called an 'accruals adjustment'. In the meantime it is simply necessary to realise that the figures in Table 9.5 relate to receipts on an accruals basis – a falling-due or payable basis – and not on an actual cash-payment basis.

Table 9.5 contains a lengthy list of some thirty-two items of central government receipts, given in much the order and classification as appears in the Blue Book. This bears out what we said about a multiplicity of taxes. There is a theoretical typology of taxes, the terminology of which is still used and which to some extent lies behind the sub-headings of Table 9.5. This theoretical classification divides taxes into two kinds: direct taxes and indirect taxes.

TABLE 9.5   *UK central government receipts, 1980*

	£ million	Percentage of total
Current account		
Taxes on income		
Income tax	24,326	30.2
Surtax	6	—
Petroleum Revenue Tax	1,798	2.2
Corporation Tax (*less* overspill relief)	4,758	5.9
Sub-total: taxes on income	30,888	38.3
Taxes on expenditure: administered by Customs and Excise		
Beer, wines, etc., spirits, and tobacco	5,216	6.5
Hydrocarbon oils (*less* bus fuel rebates)	3,347	4.2
Customs and protective duties	869	1.1
EEC agricultural levies	252	0.3
Value-added tax (*less* export rebates)	11,379	14.1
Car tax	456	0.6
Betting and gaming duties, and other duties	469	0.6
Sub-total: Customs and Excise administered taxes	21,988	27.3
Taxes on expenditure: others		
Motor-vehicle duties	1,322	1.6
National Insurance surcharge	3,500	4.3
Royalties and taxes from seaward activities	1,156	1.4
Stamp duties	630	0.8
Television contractors' additional payments	51	0.1
Northern Ireland rates	88	0.1
Fines and penalties	111	0.1
Passport fees and miscellaneous	141	0.2
Sub-total: other taxes on expenditure	6,999	8.7
National Insurance contributions		
National Insurance	12,726	15.8
National Health	1,040	1.3
Redundancy Fund, etc.	211	0.3
Sub-total: National Insurance	13,977	17.3
Rent, dividends and interest		
Rent	33	—
Dividends and interest from local authorities	1,606	2.0
Dividends and interest from public corporations	1,908	2.4
Dividends and interest from other sectors	1,244	1.5
Sub-total: rent, dividends and interest	4,791	5.9
Gross trading surplus of central government enterprises (including stock appreciation)	39	—
Imputed charge for consumption of non-trading capital	675	0.8
Sub-total: receipts on current account	79,357	98.5
Capital account		
Taxes on capital		
Death duties	433	0.5
Tax on other capital transfers	14	—
Taxes on capital gains	718	0.9
Development Land Tax	42	0.1
Sub-total: tax receipts on capital account	1,207	1.5
Grand total: all receipts by central government	80,564	100.0

Source: Central Statistical Office, *National Income and Expenditure 1981 Edition*, tables 7.2 and 9.7, pp. 48 and 68.

Direct and indirect taxes

Because these terms are still used – for example, see the title of the Meade Committee's Report: *The Structure and Reform of Direct Taxation* – it is necessary to pause briefly to explain them. The basis for the classification was most clearly stated by John Stuart Mill in the nineteenth century. Mill said:

> 'A direct tax is one which is demanded from the very persons who, it is intended or desired, should pay it. Indirect taxes are those which are demanded from one person in the expectation and intention that he shall indemnify himself at the expense of another' (*Principles of Political Economy*, book V 'On the influence of government', ch. III 'Of direct taxes').

To illustrate, income tax is a direct tax in that it is meant to be levied on and paid by the income-earner himself or herself; it is neither intended nor expected that the income-earner will ask for higher pay to 'indemnify' himself or herself against the tax. Value-added tax or the duty on beer is an indirect tax in that it is intended and expected that the person (the shopkeeper or the brewer) paying over the tax shall pass the tax on in the price charged to the customer and so 'indemnify' himself – i.e. recover the tax.

Because income tax and the well-known expenditure taxes are examples of direct and indirect taxes respectively, the term 'direct tax' is sometimes used synonymously with 'income tax' and 'indirect tax' with 'expenditure tax'. Strictly speaking this is not the case. To quote Mill again:

> 'Direct taxes are either on income, or on expenditure. Most taxes on expenditure are indirect, but some are direct, being imposed not on the producer or seller of an article, but immediately on the consumer. A house-tax, for example, is a direct tax on expenditure, if levied, as it usually is, on the occupier of the house. If levied on the builder or owner, it would be an indirect tax' (ibid.).

So that, local authority rates or motor-vehicle licence duties are direct taxes on expenditure. It is also arguable that employees may ask for higher wages to counteract the impact on take-home pay of higher taxes. Furthermore, some taxes on capital cannot readily be allocated into one or other of these two theoretical categories. For these reasons, we shall not make much use of the terms 'direct taxes' and 'indirect taxes'; but because of their widespread common use it is necessary to understand the terms properly.

Despite the length of Table 9.5, its three main features are obvious. First, taxes on income account for nearly 40 per cent of total central government receipts. Second, Customs and Excise taxes on expenditure account for over one-quarter of total receipts. And third, National Insurance and related social security contributions make up 17.3 per cent of receipts and so these are quantitatively also important. Together these three sub-groups make up over 80 per cent of central government's total receipts.

We need now to run through the items in Table 9.5, because it never does to be ignorant of how and where the government is taking its 'tax bite', even though some of the bites, such as stamp duties or death duties, are only little nips.

Taxes on income – at what rate is income taxed?

In 1980 the sub-total of taxes on income was £30,888 million. These taxes are administered and collected by the Board of Inland Revenue and they comprise the taxes on the various forms of income accruing to the personal sector, to the company sector, and to non-residents. Table 9.6 provides a breakdown of these taxes by sector paying tax. The personal sector pays over 80 per cent of total taxes on income, most of this in the form of taxes on pay (which provide two-thirds of total taxes on income); companies pay 9.9 per

TABLE 9.6   *Who paid taxes on income in 1980*

Sector paying taxes on income (payments, not accruals)	Amount of tax, £ million	Percentage of total taxes on income
Personal sector		
Taxes on wages and salaries [a]	20,738	67.1
Taxes on current grants from general government to personal sector	570	1.8
Surtax	6	—
Taxes on other income (inc. Advance Corporation Tax)	4,583	14.8
Sub-total: taxes on personal-sector income	25,897	83.8
Companies (excluding Advance Corporation Tax)	3,066	9.9
Public corporations	52	0.2
Non-residents	1,873	6.1
Total taxes on income	30,888	100.0

[a] Including taxes on pay of HM Forces.

Source: Central Statistical Office, *National Income and Expenditure 1981 Edition*, table 9.7, p. 68.

cent of total taxes on income; and non-residents pay 6.1 per cent. The personal sector pays tax on some, but not all, of the current grants from general government to the personal sector; the more important of these taxable grants are the retirement pension, widows' benefits and guardians' allowance, but excluding that part of these benefits payable in respect of children (all payable as part of National Insurance), and war pensions and war-service grants. Some National Insurance benefits, such as unemployment benefit, used not to be taxed but it was decided in 1980 to tax from 1982 the social security benefits paid to the unemployed and to those on strike whose families received supplementary benefits. The taxation of some other social security benefits, such as sickness benefits, maternity allowance, injury and invalidity benefit, is also under discussion – all of which goes to illustrate the general principle that the search for extra taxes knows no rational bounds. Surtax was a tax levied at higher rates on income over a certain amount, but in 1972–3 the tax system was unified, with surtax being integrated into the rates of tax on bands of taxable income; the amount reported for 1980 (which is negligible) must therefore consist of residual tax relating to previous years' income as assessments can be made up to six years after the end of the year of assessment.

The total amount of tax accruing on personal-sector incomes in 1980 was £26,672 million (see Table 3.1). Excluding the £775 million of taxes accruing but not paid and the £6 million of surtax on previous years' income, the personal sector paid in 1980 income taxes of £25,891 million on taxable income, estimated in Table 9.7 to be £158,681 million. This gives an over-all average tax rate on personal-sector income of 16.3 per cent. We can allocate the taxes among the various categories of personal-sector incomes to answer the juicy question of how much tax, proportionately, the personal sector actually pays on its income.

Table 9.7 gives some of the relevant figures. As we remarked in Chapter 3, employers' contributions (on behalf of employees) to National Insurance and to occupational pension schemes are not assessable to tax; strictly speaking, we should therefore take only taxable pay for comparison with the income tax paid. If we do this, it turns out that the average rate of taxation on pay is 17.3 per cent. If we were to disregard the convention and take total income from employment (i.e. including employers' contributions) as the economically relevant tax base, we would have:

TABLE 9.7   *Average rates of taxation on various categories of personal-sector income in 1980*

	£ million		Percentage average rate of taxation
	Amount of income	Tax paid on amount [a]	
Taxable income			
Wages and salaries	117,145	20,322	17.3
Pay of HM Forces	2,435	416	17.1
Current grants from central government	11,164 [b]	570	5.1
Self-employment incomes, rents, dividends, interest [c]	27,937	4,583 [d]	16.4
Total of above	158,681	25,891	16.3
Surtax in respect of previous years' income		6	
Additions to tax reserves		775	
Total taxes accruing		26,672	

[a] Except for the last two rows, this refers to actual payments (not to accruals).

[b] Comprising (in £ million) the main taxable social security benefits for which separate data are available (the Blue Book does not distinguish carefully between taxable and non-taxable social security benefits): retirement pensions (10,177); widows' benefit and guardians' allowance (637); industrial death benefit (41); one-half of war widows' pensions ($\frac{1}{2} \times 386$ rough estimate of amount taxable); old persons' pension (36; 1979–80); mobility allowance (80; 1979–80); for the list of taxable and non-taxable social security benefits see Kenneth Tingley (ed.), *Daily Mail Income Tax Guide 1981–82*, pp. 9–10.

[c] Self-employment income is after stock appreciation and depreciation; dividends, etc., includes receipts by life assurance and superannuation schemes but excludes (non-taxable) imputed rent.

[d] Including Advance Corporation Tax (ACT) tax credits of £1,512 million; calculated as a residual.

Sources: Central Statistical Office, *National Income and Expenditure 1981 Edition*, tables 4.1, 4.3, 7.2, 7.6, and 9.7; pp. 28, 29, 49, 53, and 68; Central Statistical Office, *Social Trends No. 11 1981 Edition*, table 6.9, p. 90; and Table 9.6 of this book.

Total income from employment (including HM Forces)	£137,083 million
Tax on pay	£20,738 million
Average rate of taxation	15.1 per cent

However, this calculation ignores the fact that many employees regard their own National Insurance contributions as simply another form of taxation, and quite a substantial tax at that: National Insurance contributions from insured employees (including HM Forces) amounted to £4,703 million in 1980 (Blue Book, table 7.6). Incorporating this into the analysis gives:

Total income from employment (including HM Forces)	£137,083 million
Tax and employees' National Insurance contributions	£25,441 million
Average rate of taxation	18.6 per cent

We might go even further, and say that because the typical employee tends to disregard the 'benefit' he or she derives from the (largely invisible) employers' contributions, the way in which the typical employee *feels* he or she is being taxed is as follows:

Pay (including HM Forces; excluding employers' contributions)	£119,580 million
Tax and employees' National Insurance contributions	£25,441 million
Average rate of taxation	21.3 per cent

The point of all this is to demonstrate how tricky it is to answer such an apparently simple question as: How much 'tax' do employees pay as a proportion of their 'income'? Depending on how one chooses to define the words 'tax' and 'income' in the question, one has (at least) four possible answers:

	Average rate of taxation, per cent	
	Definition of 'tax'	
Definition of 'income'	*Excludes employees' NI contributions*	*Includes employees' NI contributions*
Excludes employers' contributions	17.3	21.3
Includes employers' contributions	15.1	18.6

There is no single 'right' answer to the question. It is arguable that any one answer is more appropriate than others. For instance, it may be that most employees would regard 21.3 per cent as the rate of deductions from pay which they feel as being most relevant. On the other hand, an economist might assert that National Insurance contributions are different from tax (one does not, after all, regard (compulsory) motor insurance as a tax) and that employers' contributions ought not to be disregarded as part of the total benefits derived from employment, and so conclude that 15.1 per cent was an 'economically realistic' measure of the rate of taxation. However, choosing an answer is not half so important as appreciating how tricky it is to answer such questions.

A relatively small amount of income tax is levied on certain social security benefits, mostly retirement pensions; and the list of taxable benefits is likely to be extended. The average rate of taxation on these incomes in 1980 was low, 5.1 per cent, because the total income of most recipients would not greatly have exceeded the personal (tax) allowance; to illustrate: the retirement pension payable to a single man or woman on own insurance and under the age of 80 would have been, during the tax year 1979–80, £1,093.80 (thirty-one weeks at £19.50 per week and twenty-one weeks at £23.30 per week: Department of Health and Social Security, *Social Security Statistics 1980*, table 13.01, p. 70); the 'age allowance' for taxpayers aged 65 or over (the 'age allowance' being the substitute for the 'personal allowance' which is applicable only to persons under the age of 65) was, in the tax year 1979–80, £1,540 for single persons.* Therefore, no tax would have been payable by a retirement pensioner dependent solely on the state retirement pension; he or she would have had also to be in receipt of other income (excluding non-taxable social security benefits) to come above the tax threshold.

The average rate of tax levied on rental, dividend, interest, and trading (self-employed) income appears to be 16.4 per cent over all. Due to insufficient data, we cannot make a further distinction between taxes on rents, dividends and interest on the one hand, and trading income on the other. This average rate of taxation may seem 'low', but the tax on trading incomes net of depreciation and stock appreciation may be subject to deductions in respect of capital expenditure, and some interest and dividend income, especially that accruing to life assurance and superannuation schemes, is subject to effectively low tax rates: for example, the first £70 (in 1980–1) of interest on deposits with the National Savings Bank is disregarded for tax purposes.

Taking all taxable incomes and all income taxes the average percentage rate of taxation on the personal sector appears to have been 16.3 per cent in 1980. If we were, additionally, to take employers' contributions (£17,503 million) and non-taxed current grants from

* Since altered as follows: 1980–1 and 1981–2, £1,820; 1982–3, £2,070.

general government (£14,312 million) into reckoning on the income side, and employees' National Insurance contributions on the taxation side, then we would have:

Personal-sector income (including employers' contributions and non-taxed social security benefits)	£190,496 million
Tax and employees' National Insurance contributions	£30,594 million
Average rate of taxation	16.1 per cent

So that the average percentage rate of taxation on personal-sector incomes, taking the broad view, is much the same as on the narrower definitions: 16.1 per cent. However, this is obviously a very incomplete picture of taxation because we have taken no account of how indirect taxes on expenditure affect households, nor of the benefits in kind provided by the state more or less free of charge (such as education and health services) which households enjoy. Mention of households should provoke another question about such an over-all average rate of taxation: namely, how meaningful/sensible/useful is a global average when the rate of taxation varies considerably among groups of households?

The average rate of taxation (as measured by total taxes *divided by* total incomes) should not be confused with the rate of taxation on the 'average' or representative household because the progressivity of the tax system makes the latter a higher rate (the former measure – at which we have just been looking – is also affected by the distribution of incomes). Table 9.8, calculated from data in Appendix 9.3, shows the proportions of average (male) earnings which are taken in taxation – not only in income tax but also in taxes on expenditure, the incidence of which we have not so far considered. These figures are worked out for a married man whose wife is not working and who has two dependent children. This is not exactly an 'average' household, but it is at least reasonably representative. In 1981–2 income tax together with National Insurance contributions took 29.45 per cent of gross weekly earnings. The weekly amount of VAT which the family incurred on its expenditure was 4.9 per cent of gross weekly earnings (if this seems low, note that, as we shall see, food – a large item in family budgets – is zero-rated). What is more surprising is that other taxes on expenditure (including, for example, motor-vehicle licence duties) took 11.1 per cent of gross weekly income. These other expenditure taxes are therefore relatively quite substantial. Rates took 3.9 per cent of weekly earnings. Over all, taking all taxes into account, a (reasonably) representative household in the United Kingdom paid 49.35 per cent (nearly one-half) of gross earnings in taxation. Table 9.8 also shows that taxation has risen considerably between 1978–9 and 1981–2 by 5.55 percentage points or by 12.7 per cent.

TABLE 9.8   *The incidence of income tax and of expenditure tax on a 'representative'* [a] *household, 1978–9 and 1981–2*

	Percentage of average earnings	
	1978–9	1981–2
Income tax	20.1	21.7
National Insurance contributions	6.5	7.75
Value Added Tax	2.9	4.9
Other central government indirect taxes	11.0	11.1
Rates	3.3	3.9
Total	43.8	49.35

[a] A 'representative' household is here taken to comprise a married man on average earnings with two children whose wife is not working (this definition is forced on us by the availability of data, but it is not too inappropriate for present purposes).

Source: computed from Appendix 9.3.

It is often said that income tax is a 'progressive tax', meaning thereby that the proportionate 'take' increases as income rises, whereas expenditure tax is a 'regressive tax', meaning thereby that the proportionate 'take' falls as income rises. We can show this with the data from Appendix 9.3 for 1981–2:

	Percentage of earnings taken by:		
	---	---	---
Man's earnings	Income tax and National Insurance contributions	All expenditure taxes	All taxes
Three-quarters of average earnings	26.7	22.2	48.9
One-and-one-half times average earnings	31.4	17.7	49.1

While the man on higher earnings pays proportionately more in income tax than does the man on lower earnings, the reverse is the case so far as taxes on expenditure are concerned, and so over all both households pay pretty much the same proportion of earnings in taxation. However, these figures take no account of state benefits as they vary among households, and it is to these that we now turn.

Taxes and benefits among poor, average, and rich households

The Central Statistical Office does, in fact, make detailed calculations, from a representative sample, of how taxes and benefits vary among households. Table 9.9 gives an extract from these figures for the poorest tenth of households, for a middle tenth, and for the richest, or top, tenth. There were 6,944 households in the whole sample investigated. The poorest one-tenth of households had, on average, hardly any income from work or investments – only £8 per annum per household on average. These households were therefore entirely dependent on the state for their cash income, most of which came from retirement pensions topped up by supplementary benefit; over three-quarters (522 in number) of these 694 households comprised one or two retired adults only; another forty-six households consisted of single-parent families (*Economic Trends*, January 1982, tables 5 and 7, pp. 124 and 126). Because of their low original incomes, these households paid almost no direct tax: on average, £2 a year per household. On average these poorest households received £1,036 a year as the value of benefits in kind, mainly from the consumption of health services provided free of charge, but partly also in the form of subsidised housing. The grand total of their cash incomes and value of benefits in kind was £3,081 per annum per household, or £59 per week. Although these poorest households paid almost no direct taxes, they did, of course, incur indirect taxes on their consumption expenditures, and these indirect taxes averaged £510 per annum per household. So although their rate of direct taxation was negligible, they paid taxes of about 16½ per cent on their total incomes and benefits in kind.

For the sample of middle-ranking households, direct taxes were on average 16.8 per cent of cash incomes; and for the richest households direct taxes were 22.8 per cent of cash incomes. The over-all rate of taxation (including indirect taxes in the numerator and the value of benefits in kind in the denominator) was, for the middle-ranking households, 33.2 per cent and, for the top-ranking households, 36.0 per cent. It can be seen, therefore, that indirect taxes on expenditure have a substantial impact on rates of taxation. It is also clear that rates of taxation vary substantially among households, so that an over-all rate, such as that calculated in Table 9.7, may conceal more than it reveals.

TABLE 9.9   *Incomes, taxes, and benefits by household group, 1980*

	Average per household		
	Poorest [a] 694 (10%) households	Middle [a] 694 (10%) households	Richest [a] 694 (10%) households
£ per annum			
Original income from work and investments [b]	8	5,255	17,578
Direct state benefits in cash			
Age-related benefits [c]	1,134	260	87
Income-related benefits [d]	622	91	66
Child-related benefits [e]	77	225	193
Other cash benefits [f]	204	101	36
Sub-total: direct cash benefits	2,037	677	382
Total gross cash income	2,045	5,932	17,960
Allocable state benefits in kind			
Education [g]	232	481	656
National Health Service [h]	557	479	469
Housing subsidy [i]	206	134	71
Other allocated benefits [j]	41	68	150
Sub-total: state benefits in kind	1,036	1,162	1,346
Total cash income and benefits in kind	3,081	7,094	19,306
Direct taxes (including NI contributions)	2	999	4,088
Indirect taxes on expenditure [k]	510	1,353	2,855
Total taxes	512	2,352	6,943
Percentage rates			
Direct taxes as percentage of total cash income	0.1	16.8	22.8
Total taxes as percentage of total cash income and benefits in kind	16.6	33.2	36.0

[a] 'Poorest', etc., in terms of original income from work and investments; there were 6,944 households in the whole sample, so the poorest 694 households represent the bottom one-tenth (or first 'decile') of households; the middle one-tenth is the fifth decile, and the richest one-tenth is the tenth decile.

[b] Original income is pre-tax income from employment, from self-employment and from investments of all members of the household; it excludes imputed income from owner-occupied dwellings; occupational pensions are included (but not the state retirement pension).

[c] Retirement and old persons' pension, widows' benefit, and Christmas bonus for pensioners.

[d] Unemployment benefit, Family Income Supplement, Supplementary Benefit, electricity discounts, rent rebates, student maintenance awards.

[e] Child benefit, maternity benefits and grants.

[f] War and invalidity pensions, sickness benefit, invalid care and attendance allowances, industrial injury disablement benefit, death grant, other benefits.

[g] Cost per pupil or student of providing education service *multiplied by* number of pupils/students in household.

[h] Cost per person of providing health services (excluding maternity services) by age–sex group allocated according to household composition; average cost of maternity services assigned separately to households in receipt of maternity benefit.

[i] To local authority tenants; cost of housing *minus* rents payable.

[j] Rail travel subsidies, life assurance premium relief, option mortgage schemes (household borrower charged low rate of interest by building societies, which receive additional payment from central government).

[k] Local authority rates (including water rates), excise duties, VAT and car tax, motor-vehicle duties and driving licences, television licences and stamp duties, customs duties, *plus* indirect taxes on producers, which taxes are assumed to be shifted to consumers.

Source: Central Statistical Office, *Economic Trends*, January 1982, table 3, p. 117, and related article 'The effects of taxes and benefits on household income, 1980', pp. 97–126.

Petroleum Revenue Tax (PRT)

Returning to Table 9.5, £1,798 million worth of Petroleum Revenue Tax was levied in 1980. Under the Oil Taxation Act 1975, Petroleum Revenue Tax (PRT) is charged on the profits from the 'winning' (as opposed to refining) of hydrocarbons in the United Kingdom including the UK continental shelf and territorial waters; in 1980 PRT was charged at 70 per cent on the net income from each field, where net income is defined as gross revenue from the field *minus* operating costs (but excluding interest payments) and royalties and *minus* an allowance for capital expenditure. Gross revenues are assessed at the value of sales on the open market to an independent purchaser, whether or not such sales actually occur (much North Sea oil, of course, goes straight into the extractor's own refinery). Royalties are charged at 12.5 per cent of gross revenues and are regarded as a separate tax because in the United Kingdom oil and natural gas reserves are owned by the Crown and the pseudo-rationale for royalties would be that they are a compensation from the licensee to the Crown for the right to exploit these mineral resources. In fact, of course, royalties are simply a means of obtaining more tax revenue from the oil producers. Royalties may be refunded to a licensee as an incentive to develop, or to continue production from, a field which would not otherwise satisfy normal commercial criteria. Because the capital expenditure involved in North Sea exploration and development is massive (think of the cost of the oil rigs), a concession was granted to the levying of Petroleum Revenue Tax: companies could, for capital expenditures incurred or contracted for before 1 January 1979, deduct 1.75 times the capital expenditure from gross revenue before calculating net revenue assessable to PRT (this is described as an 'uplift' of 75 per cent). For contracts signed on or after 1 January 1979 the uplift was reduced to 35 per cent (i.e. 1.35 times the capital expenditure could be deducted). Abortive exploration costs elsewhere in the North Sea or losses on an abandoned field elsewhere can also be included in these deductible capital expenditures. The purpose of these tax concessions on capital expenditure was to ease the companies' cash-flow problems in the early periods of exploration and development.

It is forecast that government revenues from North Sea activities will rise very sharply in the 1980s, partly because the effect of capital expenditure deductions will be ending and partly because of the rise in the price of oil (which increases gross revenue). By the mid-1980s it is estimated by the Treasury that government receipts from the North Sea could be about £8 billion (other forecasts are higher, but compare this with total general government outgoings in 1980 of £104 billion). An important topic for public debate, already emerging, is what best to do with the oil revenues, but this is not a topic we can pursue here (the reader might care to start by reading my article 'A world without oil', *New Society*, 17 August 1978).

Finally, Corporation Tax of £4,758 million, or 5.9 per cent of total receipts, was levied in 1980 (including ACT tax credits on distributed profits). The overspill relief is a temporary transitional concession to companies with overseas income who suffered under corporation tax a loss of the reliefs previously given where the overseas rate of taxation exceeded the UK rate (the excess being the 'overspill').

Taxes on expenditure

As we can see in Table 9.5, taxes on expenditure are rather numerous, partly for historical reasons. Diagram 9.6 sets out the main divisions of general government expenditure taxes; we shall postpone consideration of local authority rates and concentrate on central government taxes. The main authority concerned with collecting expenditure taxes is the Board of Customs and Excise, which is also responsible (more excitingly!) for the

DIAGRAM 9.6   *Classification of taxes on expenditure*

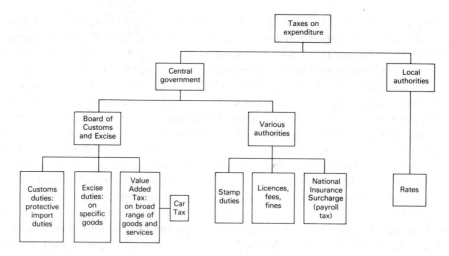

enforcement of prohibitions on the import and export of certain classes of goods, and for the compilation of overseas trade statistics. But there are also other authorities which collect various items classified as taxes on expenditure: for example, the Passport Office collects passport fees.

The Customs and Excise Board collects three main types of taxes: first, protective customs duties; second, excise duties imposed on specific goods; third, VAT imposed on a broad, general rate of goods and services. We shall now deal with each of these in turn.

Protective customs duties (or 'tariffs') nowadays provide relatively little revenue for the UK government: including the EEC agricultural levies, these protective duties contributed only 1.4 per cent of total central government revenue. This is because of a long-run trend towards 'free trade', dating back to Sir Robert Peel's tax reforms of 1842 which reduced import duties and which – so far as Peel was concerned – culminated in the repeal of the duties on imported corn in 1846. Free trade has for long been an important issue in British politics. The relatively small amount of revenue from import duties, fairly typical of industrial market economies, is also in contrast to the situation in Third World economies, many of which rely heavily on import duties and on export duties (a tax almost unknown in Britain). The present UK protective customs duties are chargeable in accordance with the common customs tariff of the EEC (no such duties are chargeable on goods which qualify as Community goods). There is also an EEC agreement with the developing countries of Africa, the Caribbean, and the Pacific, known as the Lomé Convention (after Lomé, the capital city of Togo in West Africa where it was negotiated – there were two Lomé conventions, the first in 1975, the second in 1980), whereby there is free entry into the EEC of all industrial and almost all agricultural products exported by these developing countries.

Excise duties

The various excise duties (with corresponding customs duties) are levied, as can be seen from the list in Table 9.5, on specific items, such as beer, wine, etc., tobacco. The noun 'excise duties' came, after 1643, to mean a tax charged on home-produced, as opposed to foreign-produced, goods before sale to the consumer (1643 was the year in which Parliament, then engaged in fighting the Civil War, imposed excise duties on a number of articles of consumption, including beer and cider, the list being soon greatly extended to such things as salt, iron, soap and glass: excise was and remained a very unpopular tax both in its imposition and the manner of its collection, an army of commissioners being required to collect it).

These duties are levies at specific rates: £ per gallon, etc., except that since 1 January 1980 the duties have become metric; some examples of rates of duty are shown in Table 9.10. Duty is charged on spirits in accordance with their alcoholic strength: spirit of standard strength, containing 57.1 per cent of alcohol by volume, is known as 'proof spirit'; most spirits sold in the United Kingdom are at a strength of 70 per cent proof, equivalent to alcohol content of $0.7 \times 57.1 = 40$ per cent of alcohol by volume. From 1 January 1980

TABLE 9.10 *Some excise rates of duty, 1963 to 1982*

Date in force	Mature spirits: home-produced, £ per proof gallon	Beer: £ per bulk barrel	Hydrocarbon fuel: full rate; £ per gallon	Tobacco, cigars: full rate; £ per lb
1963 4 Apr	11.60	6.15	0.1375	4.04
1964 15 Apr	12.87½	7.35	0.1375	4.31
1964 11 Nov	12.87½	7.35	0.1625	4.31
1965 7 Apr	14.60	8.55	0.1625	4.81
1967 12 Apr	16.06	9.43	0.1792	4.81
1968 20 Mar	17.14	9.43	0.1958	5.03
1969 16 Apr	18.85	10.37½	0.2250	5.485
1971 15 Feb	18.85	10.37½	0.225	5.485
1973 1 Apr	15.45	6.90	0.225	4.749
1973 1 Jul	15.45	6.90	0.225	4.749
1974 1 Jan	15.45	6.90	0.225	4.690
1974 27 Mar	17.01	9.36	0.225	6.090
1975 1 Jan	17.01	9.36	0.225	6.061
1975 15 Apr	22.09	13.68	0.225	8.111
1976 1 Jan	22.09	13.68	0.225	8.081
1976 7 Apr [a]	24.63	15.84	0.30	8.991 [b]
1977 30 Mar	27.09	17.42	0.35	9.853 [c]
1978 1 Jan	27.09	17.42	0.300	9.500 [d]
1979 12 Jun	27.09	17.42	0.368	9.500
1980 1 Jan	27.09	17.43	0.368	9.498

	Metric rates (from 1 January 1980)			
	£ per litre [e]	£ per hectolitre	£ per litre	£ per kilogram
1980 1 Jan	10.44	10.65	0.081	20.94
1980 26 Mar	11.87	13.05	0.10	25.60
1981 11 Mar	13.60	18.00	0.1382	34.29
1982 10 Mar	14.47	20.40	0.1554	39.00

[a] From 1 January 1977 to 29 March 1977 all items (except hydrocarbon fuel) were subject to 10 per cent Regulator surcharge; surcharge for tobacco started on 16 December 1976.

[b] Comprising customs duty of £6.226 per lb and new tobacco products (excise) duty of £2.765 per lb.

[c] Comprising excise duty of £6.811 per lb and tobacco products duty of £3.0415 per lb.

[d] Tobacco products duty only; customs duty was abolished on 1 January 1978; henceforth all figures refer to tobacco products duty.

[e] Per litre of alcohol in the spirit.

Sources: Central Statistical Office, *Annual Abstract of Statistics 1975*, table 371, pp. 359–60; Central Statistical Office, *Annual Abstract of Statistics 1982 Edition*, table 16.21, pp. 397–401; the *Financial Times*, 11 March 1981, p. 18; the *Financial Times*, 10 March 1982, p. 17.

this 'proof' system was replaced by a standard European system of charging for alcoholic strength in which duty is levied on the alcohol in the spirits; a proof gallon is equivalent to 2.595 litres of alcohol. On 26 March 1980 the excise duty on mature spirits was £30.80 per proof gallon, or, equivalently, £11.87 per litre of alcohol, and on 11 March 1981 the duty was raised to £13.60 per litre of alcohol in the spirits. This is equivalent to nearly £4.60 on a bottle of blended whisky. The duty on beer is levied also with regard to the technicalities of its production, but the duty in 1981 was equivalent to over 16p per pint. Duty on hydrocarbon fuels in 1981 was 13.82 pence per litre, equivalent to about 63 pence per gallon. Enough has been said to show why these excise duties are such large revenue-raisers: in 1980 the beer, etc., and hydrocarbon oil duties contributed 10.7 per cent of total central government revenue.

Value Added Tax (VAT)

The single biggest tax on expenditure is Value Added Tax (VAT), which in 1980 raised £11.4 billion, or 14.1 per cent of total central government receipts. VAT is therefore an important tax and it is accordingly necessary to know how it works. In order to do this, let us go back to Table 2.1, which gave a model showing the production of value added by productive industry. Table 9.11 reproduces the figures from this model, but now we imagine that VAT is being levied at the rate of 10 per cent (the actual rate of VAT in the United Kingdom in 1981 was 15 per cent, but 10 per cent – the rate at which VAT was first levied on its introduction in April 1973 – keeps the arithmetic simpler).* Tables 2.1 and 9.11 happen to be in terms of physical goods, but services are also included in VAT (e.g. the woodcutter could have been a maintenance mechanic or a lawyer). We have to make a change to the first heading of Table 2.1 and talk in terms of enterprises, for it is enterprises (strictly speaking 'taxable persons' as defined by the Finance Act 1972) which act as the agents for collecting VAT. It is important to appreciate that enterprises (taxable persons) themselves do not bear the cost of VAT (apart from the incidental but nevertheless troublesome, administrative burden involved): that is to say, the total wage and profit incomes of the enterprise are not altered by VAT (as they would be by income tax or profits tax). (The purchasing power of those incomes is affected by VAT, but this is a different issue.)

The administrative arrangements for getting enterprises to collect VAT on behalf of the Board of Customs and Excise (the body responsible for VAT) are in three steps as follows.

The first step is that each enterprise charges its customer(s) an extra 10 per cent on its sales (sales excluding VAT). This is known as the 'output tax'. Thus, before VAT, the farmer who supplied his customer the miller with £20-worth of wheat would send the miller a bill (an 'invoice') saying simply:

To supplying wheat	£20
Total due (within 30 days, please)	£20

(we suppose that the farmer's normal credit terms are thirty days). After the imposition of VAT, the farmer has to send the miller the following invoice:

To supplying wheat	£20
VAT @ 10% ('output tax')	£ 2
Total due (within 30 days, please)	£22

*We use this example solely to follow on from the previous table; in terms of VAT in the United Kingdom, this is a misleading example because (see later) food is 'zero-rated': that is, food is not subject to VAT.

TABLE 9.11 A model showing how Value Added Tax is levied

£ a year (flow)

Enterprise	Sales receipts excluding VAT	VAT at 10% charged to customer: 'output tax'	Total charged to customer	Cost of bought-in materials to purchaser		VAT invoiced to enterprise by supplier 'input tax'	VAT payable by enterprise to Customs and Excise [a]	Value added		Factor incomes	
				Excluding VAT	Including VAT			Excluding VAT	Including VAT	Wages	Profits
Farmer	20	2	22	0	0	0	2	20	22	8	12
Miller	30	3	33	20	22	2	1	10	11	6	4
Woodcutter	5	0.5	5.5	0	0	0	0.5	5	5.5	0	5
Baker	45	4.5	49.5	35	38.5	3.5	1	10	11	6	4
Total	—	—	—	—	—	—	4.5	45	49.5	20	25

[a] Calculated at VAT charged to purchaser *minus* VAT paid by enterprise to supplier: that is, 'output tax' *minus* 'input tax'.

Source: adapted from Table 2.1.

So the miller now has £2 of VAT invoiced to him as an 'output tax' by his supplier. Likewise, the miller's invoice to the baker now reads:

To supplying flour	£30
VAT @ 10% ('output tax')	£ 3
Total due (within 14 days, please)	£33

(the terms on which the miller extends credit are not so generous as the farmer's). The baker will also have 50p VAT invoiced to him by the woodcutter.

The second step in the administrative arrangements is for the enterprise to calculate the total amount of VAT for which it has been invoiced by its suppliers. This is known as the 'input tax'. For example, the miller, buying only wheat knows that VAT invoiced to him by suppliers is £2. The baker, buying flour and wood, works out that VAT invoiced to him by suppliers is:

VAT invoiced by miller	£3
VAT invoiced by wood-cutter	£0.50
Total VAT invoiced by suppliers	£3.50
('input tax')	

The third, and final, step in the administrative arrangements for VAT is for the enterprise to calculate the difference between the total amount of VAT it has charged to (and received from) its customers and the total amount of VAT for which it has itself been invoiced by its suppliers: that is, 'output tax' *minus* 'input tax'. This difference is then the amount payable to Customs and Excise (nicknamed, for this purpose, the VAT-man). Strictly speaking, it is this net amount which is the Value Added Tax, but this strict nomenclature is usually disregarded. For example, the miller has charged £3 VAT ('output tax') to his customer the baker, and has been invoiced (and paid to) the farmer £2 VAT ('input tax'); the difference, £3 − £2 = £1, must be sent off (within one month) to the VAT-man. The amount due to the VAT-man from the baker is, following the rule:

VAT charged to customers, *minus* 'output tax'	VAT invoiced by suppliers, *equals* ('input tax')	Sum due to VAT-man
£4.50 −	(£3 + £0.50) =	£1

Note that although the baker has paid £3.50 VAT as input tax to suppliers and £1 VAT to the VAT-man, the baker is not himself bearing the cost of VAT, because he is 'indemnifying' himself by charging his customers £4.50. To put the equation the other way round:

VAT invoiced by suppliers, *plus* input tax	Sum Due to VAT-man, VAT (proper)	VAT charged to (i.e. recovered from) customers, *equals* output tax

The term 'Value Added Tax' is, accordingly, rather complicated; in the preceding paragraphs we have been using it a little loosely (the discussion is complicated enough without burdening ourselves at the outset with legal niceties). The Finance Act 1972 defines only the terms 'output tax' and 'input tax'; the Act contains no explicit, formal definition of the term 'Value Added Tax'; but of course the whole of Part I of the Act comprises, in effect, the regulations for levying VAT, and to that extent the provisions of part I of the Act (and the Schedules thereto) in their entirety comprise the definition. We can, accordingly, derive from the Act the following implicit definition of the term 'Value Added Tax' (adapted from Finance Act 1972, Sections 2 and 3):

Implicit legal *definition of 'Value Added Tax'*

'Output tax'	*minus* 'Input tax'
Tax on the supply of chargeable goods and services by a taxable person in the course of a business carried on by him, payable by the person supplying the goods or services (but subject to the deduction of input tax)	Tax on the supply to a taxable person of any goods or services for the purpose of a business carried on by him, which may be deducted from the tax chargeable on supplies by him

Who, then, bears the cost of VAT? The answer is that it is the final consumer – the household which is not a 'taxable person' acquiring goods for 'business purposes'. In the model of Table 9.10 it is the household purchasers of bread who find that bread now costs them £4.50 more than before the imposition of VAT at 10 per cent and who cannot 'indemnify' themselves against the extra cost. Households will be invoiced as follows:

To supplying bread	£45
VAT @ 10%	£ 4.50
Total due	£49.50

The tax is 'payable' by the baker to the VAT-man (the baker is the person legally responsible for charging £4.50 and for handing over the tax *minus* permitted deductions) but the tax is 'paid' by the households because, unlike the baker, they cannot recover the amount paid.

The household consumes the bread, so the VAT of £4.50 is an expenditure tax on consumption. The VAT-man will have received a total of £4.50, collected in stages from the various enterprises engaged in contributing to the production of bread, these enterprises simply acting as the agents for the VAT-man.

It may help our understanding of VAT if we ask the obvious question: Why not simply levy a tax of 10 per cent on sales of bread? That is, instead of imposing all this administrative work on the farmer, the miller, the woodcutter and the baker, why not make just the baker the tax-collecting agent: the baker charges his customers £4.50 and sends the cheque straight off to the Customs and Excise. Such a system used to operate in the United Kingdom before 1973 for some goods and was known as *purchase tax*. The problem, which prevents this solution, is that many goods are used both as inputs into the production process and as final consumption goods: the bread might be bought by a hotel instead of a household. Under the VAT system the hotel can recover the VAT charged on bread and it makes no difference whether the hotel buys its bread from a bakery or bakes the bread itself. Under the purchase tax system, hotel charges for meals will reflect the tax on bread (as they will under VAT), but if a hotel bakes its own bread and thereby avoids the purchase tax on bread, it can still charge higher prices for meals (in line with other hotels who are purchasing bread from bakers) and thereby make extra profits (to the extent of the avoided purchase tax). Thus the purchase tax system, if widely applied, encourages vertical integration and mergers and all sorts of economic distortions. For this reason, purchase tax used to be levied only on a specific sort of consumer goods, such as refrigerators or washing-machines or cars.

Having seen how Value Added Tax is administered and collected, we can return to Table 9.11 to see how the accounts of enterprises and of the economy are amended to incorporate VAT. Because value added is defined as sales receipts *less* cost of bought-in materials (ignoring inventory changes as, in this context, inessential), and because national income is the sum of values added in all the enterprises in the economy, we now have two ways of measuring value added and the national income: first, excluding VAT; second, including VAT. That is:

Sales		Bought-in		Value
receipts	*minus*	materials	*equals*	added
exc. VAT		exc. VAT		exc. VAT

Sales		Bought-in		Value
receipts	*minus*	materials	*equals*	added
inc. VAT		inc. VAT		inc. VAT

From time to time we have spoken of gross domestic product at factor cost and gross domestic product at market prices. We have also used such terms as 'consumers' expenditure' or 'government consumption expenditure'. In Chapter 11 we shall explain all these terms fully in the context of explaining the important concept of *final expenditure*; properly to understand these concepts and their place in the scheme of economic analysis is a little difficult, but not insuperably so providing we go one step at a time; the two rather obvious equations we have just set forth are the first steps.

Thus Table 9.11 has two columns for value added, one excluding VAT, the other including VAT. In what follows VAT represents all taxes on expenditure: that is, if you wish, you can substitute for the term 'VAT' the term 'all taxes on expenditure', but we shall stick to the VAT example and terminology having told you that the analysis is of generally applicable validity and not narrowly confined to VAT alone. In the column totals we have therefore total value added (that is, gross domestic product if we assume Table 9.11 models an entire economy) excluding VAT and including VAT. It is important to note also that:

Value					
added	*equals*	Wages	*plus*	Profits	
exc. VAT					

but that:

Value					
added	*equals*	Wages	*plus*	Profits	*plus* VAT
inc. VAT					

So that total value added excluding VAT, or, more generally, gross domestic product excluding taxes on expenditure, equals the sum of total wages and total profits, or the sum of total incomes of the factors of production. Accordingly, gross domestic product excluding taxes on expenditure is known as gross domestic product at the cost of factors of production, or gross domestic product at factor cost for short. In Table 9.11 gross domestic product at factor cost is £45.

On the other hand, total value added including VAT, or, more generally, gross domestic product including taxes on expenditure, equals the sum of total wages, total profits, and the taxes on expenditure. Accordingly, gross domestic product including taxes on expenditure is known as gross domestic product at market prices, because it is valued at the across-the-counter prices which people pay. In Table 9.11 gross domestic product at market prices is £49.5. Note, therefore, as you can see in the bottom row of Table 9.11:

Total		Total		
value added	*equals*	value added	*plus*	VAT
inc. VAT		exc. VAT		

or, more generally:

Gross domestic		Gross domestic		Taxes
product at	*equals*	product at	*plus*	on
market prices		factor cost		expenditure

And to show you that the rigmarole of Table 9.11 is relevant to the real world, we may apply the equation just given to the UK economy in 1980:

£225,560m. = £193,488m. + £32,072m.

(from Central Statistical Office, *National Income and Expenditure 1981 Edition*, table 1.1, p. 3, where total taxes on expenditure are net of subsidies which are simply negative expenditure taxes: £193,488 million is a figure we have seen before in Tables 2.7 and 2.8; we have indirectly encountered £225,560 million in Appendix 9.1 – but we shall not be discussing this fully until Chapter 11 on final expenditure). Taxes on expenditure comprise the sub-totals in Table 9.5 of £21,988 million (Customs and Excise) and £6,999 million (other taxes on expenditure) *plus* £8,300 million of local authority rates (which figure we shall come to shortly) *minus* the £5,215 million of subsidies from the general government which we saw in Table 9.4.

We need to take one more preliminary step which will not at this juncture seem to be important, but which is nevertheless significant (although its full significance will not be apparent until Chapter 11). The whole economy in Table 9.11 produces only one good: a good for consumption, namely bread. We may therefore think of the expenditure on bread, which expenditure includes VAT, as standing for consumers' expenditure, a category of 'final' expenditure. Remember that in Table 3.3 we analysed UK consumers' expenditure in 1980 in some detail. The real economy produces categories of goods ('final expenditures') other than consumers' goods, but to return to our simplified model economy which produces only consumers' goods (bread) we can note that in Table 9.11:

Expenditure		Total
on bread	*equals*	value added
by households		inc. VAT

Or, for this simple economy:

Expenditure		Gross domestic
on bread	*equals*	product at
by households		market prices

This equation becomes a little more intriguing if we substitute it for gross domestic product at market prices and at factor cost as follows:

Expenditure		Gross domestic		Taxes
on bread	*equals*	product at	*plus*	on
by households		factor cost		expenditure

or

Expenditure				Taxes
on bread	*equals*	Wages *plus* Profits	*plus*	on
by households				expenditure

Subsequently, we shall see that this equation between (all forms of 'final') expenditure on the one hand and factor incomes plus expenditure tax on the other is a most important equation in the analytic scheme of modern macroeconomics ('Keynesian economics'), but at this point we shall for the moment leave these first steps towards understanding how categories of final expenditure and taxes on expenditure fit into the system of national accounts, and why this system owes so much to J. M. Keynes.

Three more important points relating to VAT follow. First, in Table 9.11 note that in each enterprise, and therefore for the economy as a whole, value-added tax payable by the enterprise to Customs and Excise is 10 per cent of value added excluding VAT. This is an arithmetic result, but it explains why Value Added Tax is called 'Value Added' Tax. The arithmetic is straightforward:

$$\begin{array}{l} \text{VAT payable} \\ \text{by enterprise} \\ \text{to Customs} \\ \text{and Excise} \end{array} \; equals \; 10\% \; of \begin{bmatrix} \text{Sales} \\ \text{receipts} \\ \text{exc. VAT} \end{bmatrix} \; minus \; 10\% \; of \begin{bmatrix} \text{Bought-in} \\ \text{materials} \\ \text{exc. VAT} \end{bmatrix}$$

$$equals \; 10\% \; of \begin{bmatrix} \text{Sales} \\ \text{receipts} \\ \text{exc. VAT} \end{bmatrix} \; minus \begin{bmatrix} \text{Bought-in} \\ \text{materials} \\ \text{exc. VAT} \end{bmatrix}$$

$$equals \; 10\% \; of \begin{bmatrix} \text{Value} \\ \text{added} \\ \text{exc. VAT} \end{bmatrix}$$

(where 10 per cent is the rate of VAT). It would therefore be feasible (subject to the qualification to be made in the following paragraph) for an enterprise to calculate VAT payable by it to the VAT-man on the basis of its accounts for value added excluding VAT as in the last line of the equation; this would be an accounts basis for levying VAT. The system which is actually used is the system based on invoices, as previously described and as here represented by the first line of the equation. The invoice-based system is required by law, which lays down general requirements as to the information to be given on invoices and as to the records to be kept by taxable persons.

Second, and this is a most important qualification to the equation just given and to the whole preceding discussion of VAT, so far as enterprises are concerned no distinction is made between goods purchased as current inputs into the process of production – the cost of bought-in materials and services – and goods purchased as fixed capital. This means that the equation just given must be modified to read:

$$\begin{array}{l} \text{VAT payable} \\ \text{by enterprise} \\ \text{to Customs} \\ \text{and Excise} \end{array} \; equals \; 10\% \; of \begin{bmatrix} \text{Sales} \\ \text{receipts} \\ \text{exc. VAT} \end{bmatrix} \; minus \; 10\% \; of \begin{bmatrix} \text{Bought-in} \\ \text{materials} \\ \text{exc. VAT} \end{bmatrix}$$

$$minus \; 10\% \; of \begin{bmatrix} \text{Expenditure} \\ \text{on fixed} \\ \text{capital exc. VAT} \end{bmatrix}$$

$$equals \; 10\% \; of \begin{bmatrix} \text{Value} & & \text{Expenditure} \\ \text{added} & minus & \text{on fixed} \\ \text{exc. VAT} & & \text{capital exc. VAT} \end{bmatrix}$$

Because VAT paid on capital goods acquired by enterprises in the course of (fixed) capital formation is deductible from the output tax, VAT as administered in the United Kingdom becomes a tax on consumption expenditure only. This is an important modification to the principle that VAT is a tax on value added. If the amount in brackets in the equation's last line is negative, which is possible if the enterprise has either been saving up previously for, say, a new piece of equipment, or has borrowed or issued new shares to pay for the investment, then the Customs and Excise have to refund the (negative) amount to the enterprise, reversing the normal process of the enterprise paying to Customs and Excise. That is the meaning of a negative sign in the equation, should it occur.

Third, certain enterprises may be either exempt from VAT or be zero-rated for VAT. Exemption means that the enterprise does not have to charge VAT on its sales; there is no output tax and the equation given simply does not apply to the enterprise, which of course will still be paying VAT on goods supplied to it and, of course, that amount of VAT will be reflected in the enterprise's prices. But the exempt trader may not recover any of the input tax. Zero-rating means that the equation just given applies to the enterprise but the rate at which VAT is charged to its customers by the enterprise is zero. For a zero-rated enterprise, its transactions with Customs and Excise are determined by the following equation:

$$\begin{array}{l}\text{VAT payable}\\\text{by enterprise}\\\text{to Customs}\\\text{and Excise}\end{array} \text{ equals } 0\% \text{ of } \begin{bmatrix}\text{Sales}\\\text{receipts}\\\text{exc. VAT}\end{bmatrix} \text{ minus } 10\% \text{ of } \begin{bmatrix}\text{Bought-in}\\\text{materials}\\\text{exc. VAT}\end{bmatrix}$$

$$\text{minus } 10\% \text{ of } \begin{bmatrix}\text{Expenditure}\\\text{on fixed}\\\text{capital exc. VAT}\end{bmatrix}$$

A zero-rated enterprise can therefore claim refunds of input tax, and a zero-rated enterprise *receives* a continual stream of payments from Customs and Excise as a refund of VAT it has paid on its supplies (of materials and fixed capital). The point of this is that, because of refunds, no VAT at all is incorporated into the end-price of the zero-rated good. This is why, for example, food is zero-rated. Strictly speaking it is not enterprises as such which are exempt or zero-rated, but categories of goods: an enterprise is only exempt or zero-rated to the extent that it supplies exempt or zero-rated goods. In the United Kingdom the following are the main categories of goods which are zero-rated (full details to be found in Schedule 4 to the Finance Act 1972):

(a)   food (except a supply in the course of catering, and except ice-cream, soft drinks, excisable drinks, confectionery);
(b)   water supply;
(c)   books, newspapers, periodicals;
(d)   young children's clothing and footwear;
(e)   passenger transport, including ship (15 tons and over) and aircraft (18,000 lb and over) building and repair and maintenance;
(f)   drugs and medicines supplied on prescription;
(g)   construction of all buildings;
(h)   exports.

The second-last category (g) explains why an alteration of a house which amounts to an improvement counts as 'construction' and so is zero-rated, whereas house maintenance attracts VAT. As you might imagine, this has attracted much litigation by householders as to what constitutes an 'improvement' and what is merely 'maintenance'; for example, the case of a householder who replaces a leaking flat roof with a new pitched roof would probably have the work zero-rated because that would constitute an 'improvement' rather than maintenance, but replacement with a new flat roof would be 'maintenance' attracting VAT.*

The main categories of goods which are exempt are (full details available in Schedule 5 of the Finance Act 1972):

(a)   insurance;
(b)   finance;
(c)   letter and parcel post;

*Almost every other week, it seems, the Finance and the Family 'agony column' in the Saturday *Financial Times* contains some correspondence from worried (and irate) householders as to whether or not they should be paying VAT on 'improvements'.

(d)   education;

(e)   health services.

Enterprises dealing entirely in exempt goods do not have to register for VAT. 'Small' traders (with a turnover, gross sales receipts, of less than £17,000 a year – the threshold announced in the 1982 budget) are also exempt from registering for VAT. Such a trader does not have to invoice his customers for VAT, but he is not eligible to reclaim VAT paid on his own purchases. A 'small' trader may register if he so wishes (and it can be to his advantage to do so because he can then reclaim the tax invoiced to him providing he has invoiced his customers for VAT).

Other taxes on expenditure

To return to Table 9.5. Car tax is a special tax levied on the sale of new motor-cars in addition to VAT. At the time of the introduction of VAT, cars bore purchase tax at a high rate of 30 per cent (reduced in 1972 to 25 per cent). The 10 per cent rate at which VAT was levied when first introduced would, because VAT replaced purchase tax, have led to a substantial fall in the retail price of cars and to a considerable loss of tax revenue. Accordingly, the special extra car tax was imposed to prevent this happening. Car tax brought in £456 million in 1980, or 0.6 per cent of total central government receipts. Cars on which car tax has been paid and which are exported may have the tax rebated; this is one of the reasons for export rebates in Table 9.5, which rebates, however, I have deducted from the VAT total.

Finally, the Customs and Excise are responsible for collecting duties on betting and gaming (including bingo), mostly as a percentage of the stake money, or in the case of casinos as a half-yearly licence fee related to the rateable value of the premises and the number of tables provided for gaming; the licence fee is basically a fee per table, but the rate per table depends on the rateable value of the premises.

All in all, the Customs and Excise Board were responsible for administering and collecting just over one-quarter of the central government's revenue in 1980.

In addition to these taxes on expenditure administered by the Customs and Excise, there are other taxes on expenditure administered by various different authorities.

In the United Kingdom all motor-vehicles in use have to be registered once and licensed annually, and all drivers of motor-vehicles must have a valid driving licence. This task, and collecting the fees, is undertaken by the Driver and Vehicle Licensing Centre at Swansea (but it is also possible to renew a vehicle's licence at certain post offices which act as agents for the DVLC). These motor-vehicle duties brought in 1.6 per cent of central government receipts in 1980; nearly all of this comes from the licences for vehicles known as the 'motor vehicle excise duty', but a small amount comes from the administration fee charged for driving licences.

Skipping over the National Insurance surcharge for the moment and royalties and taxes from seaward activities (discussed in the section on Petroleum Revenue Tax), we come to stamp duties. Many kinds of commercial and legal documents, especially relating to the transfer of property, have to have stamps affixed. Stamps may be purchased from Inland Revenue offices, and the main sanction is that documents which are not duly stamped cannot (except in criminal proceedings) be given in evidence in court, though failure to stamp documents is subject to other penalties. Such inadmissibility can of course be very damaging, so stamp duties are virtually self-enforcing. Northern Ireland rates are constitutionally (since the imposition of 'direct rule' in 1974) collected as part of central government taxes on expenditure.

Fines, such as for traffic offences, constitute a small proportion of central government receipts, as do passport fees (administered by the Passport Office) and other miscellaneous receipts such as gun licences.

One of the more controversial taxes on expenditure is the National Insurance surcharge, which in 1980 provided 4.3 per cent of central government revenue. The National Insurance surcharge was introduced at the start of the 1977–8 fiscal year. It has, despite its name, little to do with National Insurance; it is effectively a payroll tax on employers administered via the National Insurance system (which is how it got its name). It is a levy paid by employers, along with their 'proper' or 'regular' National Insurance contributions in respect of their employees, at a rate of 3.5 per cent of employees' earnings up to £200 per week, the maximum current in 1981 (i.e. there is a maximum payable of $0.035 \times £200 = £7$ per week per employee). It is assumed that employers pass this tax on to the prices they charge so the National Insurance surcharge (but not employers' 'regular' National Insurance contributions) counts as a tax on expenditure. The tax is controversial: it was originally intended as a temporary measure but has become permanent because abolishing it now would 'cost' too much in lost revenue ($4\frac{1}{2}$ per cent of central government receipts is not insignificant – although some of this money is being paid by central government and local authorities); it is criticised as a tax which falls on exports but not on imports (with adverse consequences for the competitiveness of British industry); as a tax on jobs, it is alleged to reduce employment (for example, by encouraging employers to use overtime for existing employees rather than take on additional workers); and finally, it is said that by reducing profits it reduces investment. However, in view of its revenue-raising power, its abolition would be surprising unless another form of revenue (Petroleum Revenue Tax, perhaps) can take its place. (The NI surcharge was reduced to $2\frac{1}{2}$ per cent in the 1982 Budget with effect from 2 August 1982 – with a further temporary reduction of $\frac{1}{2}$ percentage point between 2 August 1982 and 5 April 1983 to compensate for the 'unavoidable delay' in bringing the reduction into effect after the Budget.)

The total of all these other taxes on expenditure contributed 8.7 per cent of central government revenue in 1980.

National Insurance contributions

Next in Table 9.5 we come to the 'proper' or 'regular' National Insurance contributions. The National Insurance scheme was discussed in Chapter 3: this is the system of social security funded by joint contributions from insured persons (employees and the self-employed) and from employers, with supplementation from the central government when necessary. These National Insurance contributions by insured persons and by employers (excluding the National Insurance surcharge levied on employers) raised 17.3 per cent of total central government receipts in 1980. This is a substantial contribution, and the reason for its being so large is readily appreciated once we look at the rates of contribution. These rates are given (for the year 1981–2) in Table 9.12. For employees, the rate of contribution depends on whether the employee is or is not a member of a 'contracted-out' occupational pension scheme run by the employer.

In Table 9.12 we can see that for employees the total rate of combined contribution was (in 1981) 17.95 per cent of pay (up to the Upper Earnings Limit) for not-contracted-out employees and 10.95 per cent for contracted-out employees between the Lower Earnings Limit and the Upper Earnings Limit, as explained in note *(e)*. The contribution rates for the self-employed are a mixture of a percentage rate of 5.75 per cent of income and a 'flat-rate' contribution of £3.40 per week. All these rates are quite substantial – employees' contribution rates having been increased by 1 percentage point, the Class 4 contribution rate by $\frac{3}{4}$ of a percentage point, and the Class 2 contribution by 90p per week as from April 1981. Being levied on large annual flows, they raise a considerable amount

TABLE 9.12   *Standard rates of National Insurance contributions from April 1981* [a]

Contributions [d]	Rate of contributions as a percentage of earnings, [b] subject to Lower Earnings Limit of £27 per week and Upper Earnings Limit of £200 per week [c]			
	National Insurance Fund	National Health Service	Redundancy Fund and Maternity Pay Fund	Total
Class 1 contributions for persons in employment: 'normal rate' [e]				
Employee's contribution	7.10	0.65	—	7.75
Employer's contribution [f]	9.40	0.60	0.20	10.20
Combined contribution	16.50	1.25	0.20	17.95
Class 1 contributions for persons in employment: 'contracted-out rate' [e]				
Employee's contribution	4.60	0.65	—	5.25
Employer's contribution [f]	4.90	0.60	0.20	5.70
Combined contribution	9.50	1.25	0.20	10.95
Class 4 contributions for self-employed persons: earnings-related percentage [g]	4.90	0.85	—	5.75
Class 2 contributions for self-employed persons: *flat-rate £ per week* [h]	*3.01*	*0.39*	—	*3.40*

[a] Excludes reduced rate for employees who are married women or widows and who have opted for reduced rates, which right is being phased out but retained for those so eligible at 5 April 1978.

[b] Except for Class 2 self-employed flat-rate contributions which are in *£ per week and italicised.*

[c] Lower and Upper Earnings Limits applicable to employed persons only; for self-employed persons see *(h)* below.

[d] Following (except for the new Class 4) the Beveridge classification of contributors described in Chapter 3 above (see Diagram 3.1).

[e] The arrangements for levying NI contributions are now rather complicated. First, there is no liability to pay contributions by or on behalf of an employee whose weekly earnings are below the Lower Earnings Limit (whether or not contracted out). Second, for employees who are not contracted out and whose earnings are equal to or above the Lower Earnings Limit, contributions must be paid at the 'normal rate' *times* weekly earnings, but only up to the Upper Earnings Limit (that is, the maximum contribution payable is $r \times$ Upper Earnings Limit, where r is the relevant proportionate rate of contribution). Third, for employees who are contracted out and whose earnings are equal to or above the Lower Earnings Limit, contributions are calculated in two stages: (a) the 'normal rate' is applied to earnings up to the Lower Earnings Limit; (b) the 'contracted-out rate' is applied to earnings between the Lower Earnings Limit and the Upper Earnings Limit – the contracted-out contribution then being the combined sum of these two.

[f] Excluding the 3.5 per cent National Insurance surcharge on earnings up to the Upper Earnings Limit (but not payable for employees with earnings below the Lower Earnings Limit).

[g] Levied on annual profits (income) starting at £3,150 per annum but subject to an upper limit of £10,000 p.a.

[h] Payable by self-employed persons with incomes above the £1,475 per annum threshold.

Sources: the *Financial Times*, 25 November 1980, p. 12; the *Financial Times*, 26 November 1980, p. 13 (corrected for misprint); the *Financial Times*, 6 April 1981, p. 4.

Contracting-out

A brief word on contracting-out. The state retirement pension scheme is now divided into a basic pension plus an earnings-related additional pension, but employers may 'contract out' their employees from the additional pension providing that their occupational pension scheme is at least as good as the state additional pension; in return lower National Insurance contributions are payable by and on behalf of contracted-out employees (who are not then eligible for the state additional pension).

Contracting-out is optional, and some employers with good occupational pension schemes have decided to 'ride on top' of the additional state retirement pension; this means that they and their employees pay higher rates of contribution. The arguments for or against contracting-out are complex and basically depend on whether one thinks that by paying lower contracted-out contributions one can invest the money so saved to provide a better return than the state additional retirement pension.

of revenue. The wage and salary bill (excluding employers' contributions) on which these contributions are being levied (in this complicated way and subject to the Upper Earnings Limit) is about 60 per cent of gross domestic product, while income from self-employment (after deducting depreciation and stock appreciation) is about 8 per cent of GDP, with about 1.9 million self-employed most of whom were paying Class 2 flat-rate contributions. So it is not surprising that National Insurance contributions contribute so heavily to central government revenue.

Central government non-tax receipts

We now come, in Table 9.5, to the non-tax receipts on current account. Because the central government owns some property which it lets to other sectors, it receives a small amount of rental income. (This is different from and excludes the imputed rental income which the central government is deemed to 'receive' by virtue of owner-occupation of its own offices, hospitals, etc. – but this treatment began only in *National Income and Expenditure 1966–76*.) The central government makes loans to local authorities for capital purposes – such as house-building or civil engineering works – mostly through the Public Works Loan Board of the central government's National Investment and Loans Office, which manages the National Debt. On these loans, the local authorities have to pay interest, and because the amounts outstanding are relatively large and rates of interest quite high – on 31 March 1980 the total local authority indebtedness to the Public Works Loan Board was £14 billion at rates of interest varying between 13 and 15 per cent (CSO, *Financial Statistics*, September 1981, tables 4.4, and 13.14, pp. 52 and 141) – the total interest paid per annum is relatively large; but, as we saw in Table 9.4 this intersectoral transaction does not count as *general* government revenue. The central government also lends money to the public corporations, mainly to the nationalised industries, and also provides public dividend capital to the nationalised industries: interest and dividends are payable on these financial assets of the central government. The central government also makes loans to other sectors of the economy including overseas governments (including loans at low rates of interest to Third World countries) and receives interest on these loans as well. The total of rents, dividends and interests made up 5.9 per cent of total central government receipts in 1980.

Finally, there is the 'income', imputed for purposes of national accounting, from imputed rents on owner-occupied buildings called 'consumption of non-trading capital' –

these capital assets are called 'non-trading' to distinguish them from fixed assets which are held for the purposes of industrial and commercial trading. We have already encountered this exact flow as an 'expenditure' in Table 9.4; from the point of view of the government account, these imputed flows of income and expenditure simply cancel out, but of course, as with owner-occupied houses, it is necessary to include in the national 'output' a measure of the benefits derived from owner-occupied (non-trading) buildings such as government offices, hospitals, etc.

All the foregoing items in Table 9.5 comprise what is known as total receipts on current account and they provided 98.5 per cent of total central government revenue in 1980. These receipts are the income part of the government's 'income and expenditure' account: the balance of receipts over expenditure on this account being known as 'saving'. The taxes received on current account are all taxes on *flows*, such as taxes on the flow of income or on a flow of expenditure. But in order to see the totality of government receipts, Table 9.5 goes on to give the tax receipts on capital account, which consist of the various taxes on capital.

Taxes on capital

Taxes on capital are taxes on or pertaining to a *stock* of 'capital', and here the word 'capital' embraces land and financial assets as well as physical assets. As shown in Diagram 9.7, taxes on capital are basically of two sorts: those that are levied at a change of ownership; and those that are levied without there being any change of ownership. The United Kingdom has, so far, no examples of the latter category, though a wealth tax, were such to be introduced, would fall into this category. All UK taxes on capital are taxes levied at change of ownership; these taxes fall into two main categories: taxes levied on (in

DIAGRAM 9.7   *Classification of taxes on capital*

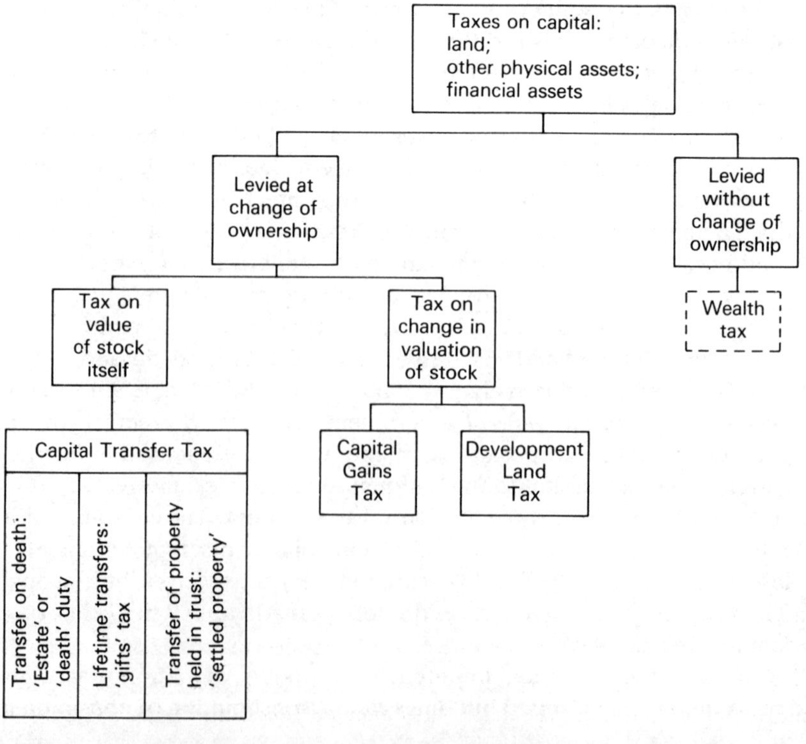

proportion to) the entire value of stock itself; and taxes levied on the change in the value of the stock. The UK tax on the entire value of the stock is known as Capital Transfer Tax; and the United Kingdom has two taxes on the change in the value of stock (assessable when the asset is disposed of), one known as Capital Gains Tax, the other as Development Land Tax.

Capital Transfer Tax (CTT)

Capital Transfer Tax was introduced in the Finance Act 1975. This Act abolished 'estate duty', which was the tax on property changing hands on the death of the owner, and replaced these 'death duties' by Capital Transfer Tax levied in three main areas: lifetime transfers or 'gifts'; transfers at death; and transfers relating to 'settled property', i.e. to property held in trust for, but not owned outright by, the beneficiaries of the trust. Capital Transfer Tax was intended to close the loophole whereby a person could evade estate duty by giving away his or her property before his or her death; this loophole was closed by making gifts during the person's lifetime taxable (with certain exemptions from tax, such as gifts made by a person up to a value of £3,000 in one tax year, or gifts in consideration of marriage, and transfers between husband and wife in life or on death). Estate duty had also been avoided by another loophole: namely, by the establishment of a discretionary trust which could distribute income from the trust to named beneficiaries, such a trust not attracting estate duty. Capital Transfer Tax is intended to close this particular loophole as well.

The rates at which Capital Transfer Tax is levied are given in Table 9.13. The important

TABLE 9.13 *Rates of Capital Transfer Tax, 1981*

Slice of chargeable transfer, £[d]		Rates of Capital Transfer Tax [a] per cent of transfer	
		On lifetime [b] transfers, 'gifts'	On transfers at death [c]
0 to	50,000	0	0
50,001 to	60,000	15	30
60,001 to	70,000	17.5	35
70,001 to	90,000	20	40
90,001 to	110,000	22.5	45
110,001 to	130,000	25	50
130,001 to	160,000	30	55
160,001 to	510,000	35	60
510,001 to	1,010,000	40	65
1,010,001 to	2,010,000	45	70
2,010,001 and over		50	75

[a] Applicable to lifetime transfers on or after 10 March 1981 and to deaths on or after 26 March 1980 and before the 1982 Budget revised slices come into effect.

[b] Other than within three years before death.

[c] Including transfers within three years of death.

[d] The slices of chargeable transfers were altered in the 1982 Budget as follows (figures in £ thousands – the rates of taxation remained unchanged; however, it was announced that in future the slices would be revised annually in the light of changes in the retail prices index): 0 to 55; over 55 to 75; over 75 to 100; over 100 to 130; over 130 to 165; over 165 to 200; over 200 to 250; over 250 to 650; over 650 to 1,250; over 1,250 to 2,500; and over 2,500.

Sources: Kenneth Tingley (ed.), *Daily Mail Income Tax Guide 1981–82*, p. 128; and the *Financial Times*, 11 March 1981, p. 21; the *Financial Times*, 10 March 1982, p. 17.

Three examples to illustrate Capital Transfer Tax

In order to see what this means, and how the rates of CTT are applied, let us consider three cases:

1. Mr *A* makes a gift during his lifetime of £115,000 and then, more than three years after making the gift, dies with an estate value at nothing (if he died within three years, the death transfer rates of tax would become applicable to the gift).
2. Mr *B* makes three separate gifts during his lifetime: one of £58,000, one of £28,500 and another one of £28,500 (totalling £115,000, the same as Mr *A*) and then, more than three years after making the last gift, dies with an estate valued at £105,000 (the periods between gifts 1 and 2, 2 and 3, and 3 and death not being, in any case, more than ten years).
3. Mr *C* makes no gifts and dies with an estate valued at £220,000 (equal to the total value of Mr *B*'s lifetime gifts plus Mr *B*'s estate).

All these events take place on or after 10 March 1981 (Budget day) and before the 1982 Budget revisions come into force. Table 9.14 gives the resulting calculations of capital transfer tax payable (using pre-1982 chargeable slices).

Mr *A*'s Capital Transfer Tax is quite straightforward. The first £50,000 is subject to a zero rate of tax, so no tax is payable on this portion; the next £10,000 falls into the £50,001 to £60,000 chargeable slice and is subject to tax at 15 per cent, so £1,500 of CTT ($0.15 \times £10,000$) is payable on this portion; the next £10,000 falls into the £60,001 to £70,000 slice and is subject to tax at 17.5 per cent; the next £20,000 to tax at 20 per cent (following the rates in Table 9.13); the next £20,000 to tax at 22.5 per cent; and the remaining £5,000, which falls into the £110,000 to £130,000 slice, is taxed at 25 per cent and so tax of £1,250 ($0.25 \times £5,000$) is payable on this last portion. In all, £13,000 of CTT is payable on this gift of £115,000 or 11.3 per cent of the value of the gift. Mr *A* (the 'transferor' or person making the transfer – the 'transferee' is the person receiving the transfer) is responsible for informing the Capital Taxes Office of the transfer and for paying the CTT which is due.

Having seen how the rates of CTT are applied to successive slices of chargeable transfers, let us now see how the principle of cumulation works. Mr *B* makes the same total of lifetime gifts as does Mr *A*, but Mr *B* makes three separate gifts (it does not matter whether these gifts are to the same or different persons). The first gift is £58,000, so the first £50,000 of this is taxed at a zero rate, and the remaining £8,000 is taxed, in the £50,001 to £60,000 slice, at 15 per cent, and so £1,200 of tax ($0.15 \times £8,000$) is payable on this gift. The second gift is £28,500; of this the first £2,000 falls, cumulatively, into the £50,001 to £60,000 slice to be taxed at 15 per cent: that is, as shown by the linking, the last £8,000 from the first gift fell into this slice, and as the second gift starts, for Capital Transfer Tax purposes, where the first gift left off – in accordance with the principle of cumulation – the first £2,000 from the second gift falls into the £50,001 to £60,000 slice, so 'completing' this slice. The next £10,000 of the second gift falls into the £60,001 to £70,000 slice and is taxed at 17.5 per cent, and the remaining £16,500 of the second gift falls into the £70,001 to £90,000 slice and is taxed at 20 per cent. In all, £5,350 of CTT is payable on this second gift, or 18.8 per cent. Continuing on with the principle of cumulation, the third gift of £28,500 starts where the second gift left off, so the first £3,500 (which then exhausts the £70,001 to £90,000 slice) is taxed at 20 per cent; the next £20,000 is taxed at 22.5 per cent; and the remaining £5,000, in the £110,001 to £130,000 slice, is taxed at 25 per cent. In all, £6,450 of CTT is payable on the third gift, or 22.6 per cent. We can now see why the principle of cumulation is adopted: Mr *A* with one gift of £115,000 and Mr *B* with three separate gifts totalling £115,000, both pay exactly the same CTT on their lifetime transfers. Note that Mr *B*'s second and third gifts, equal in value, attract different amounts of Capital Transfer Tax.

Let us now see how the principle of cumulation applies also to transfers on death. More than three years but less than ten years after making his third gift, Mr *B* dies leaving an estate valued at £105,000. The principle of cumulation means that, for CTT purposes, the tax rates on the £105,000 estate start from where the cumulated lifetime transfers left off, but the rates to be applied are now those applicable to transfers on death (see the second column of Table 9.13). So in Table 9.14 we had the last £5,000 of Gift 3 going into the £110,001 to £130,000 slice; now, the first £15,000 of the estate is chargeable in this slice, but taxable at the death transfer tax rate for this slice of 50 per cent; the next £30,000

TABLE 9.14   *Three examples of Capital Transfer Tax to illustrate the principle of cumulation*

	Portion of transfer, £		Capital Transfer Tax [a]		
			Slice of chargeable transfer, £ thousands	Rate of CTT, per cent	Tax payable, £
Mr A					
Gift of £115,000	First	50,000	0 to 50	0	0
	Next	10,000	50 to 60	15	1,500
	Next	10,000	60 to 70	17.5	1,750
	Next	20,000	70 to 90	20	4,000
	Next	20,000	90 to 110	22.5	4,500
	Remaining	5,000	110 to 130	25	1,250
Total tax payable					13,000
Mr B					
Gift 1 of £58,000	First	50,000	0 to 50	0	0
	Next	8,000	50 to 60	15	1,200
Tax payable on Gift 1		(b)			1,200
Gift 2 of £28,500	First	2,000	50 to 60	15	300
	Next	10,000	60 to 70	17.5	1,750
	Remaining	16,500	70 to 90	20	3,300
Tax payable on Gift 2		(b)			5,350
Gift 3 of £28,500	First	3,500	70 to 90	20	700
	Next	20,000	90 to 110	22.5	4,500
	Remaining	5,000	110 to 130	25	1,250
Tax payable on Gift 3					6,450
Tax payable on Gifts 1, 2, and 3		(b)			13,000
Transfer of remaining estate on death, £105,000	First	15,000	110 to 130	50	7,500
	Next	30,000	130 to 160	55	16,500
	Remaining	60,000	160 to 510	60	36,000
Tax payable on death transfer					60,000
Total Capital Transfer Tax payable					73,000
Mr C					
Transfer of £220,000 on death	First	50,000	0 to 50	0	0
	Next	10,000	50 to 60	30	3,000
	Next	10,000	60 to 70	35	3,500
	Next	20,000	70 to 90	40	8,000
	Next	20,000	90 to 110	45	9,000
	Next	20,000	110 to 130	50	10,000
	Next	30,000	130 to 160	55	16,500
	Remaining	60,000	160 to 510	60	36,000
Total Capital Transfer Tax payable					86,000

[a] For transfers or deaths occurring on or after 10 March 1981 (different rates applicable before then); more than three years elapse between Mr *B*'s Gift 3 and his death; Gifts 1, 2, 3, and death, have not more than ten years between each. This uses the pre-1982 slices.

[b] Portions linked in slice of chargeable transfer by principle of cumulation; the two linked portions sum to the chargeable slice.

Source: calculated using rates given in Table 9.13.

of the estate falls into the £130,001 to £160,000 slice (cumulated on from the lifetime transfers) to be taxed at 55 per cent; and the remaining £60,000 falls into the broad slice for death trans- fers of £160,001 to £510,000 to be taxed at 60 per cent. So £60,000 of CTT is payable on Mr *B*'s estate of £105,000, or 57.1 per cent of the estate. In all Mr *B* (and his estate) will have paid

£73,000 of CTT, or 33.2 per cent of lifetime transfers plus estate.

Because the rates of taxes on lifetime transfers, 'gifts', are lower than the rates on transfers at death (see Table 9.13), it is still advantageous to make gifts at least three years before death. We can see this if we consider Mr C, who dies leaving an estate of £220,000, equivalent to Mr

B's lifetime transfers and estate. The CTT levied on Mr C's estate is £86,000 or 39.1 per cent (to be contrasted to Mr B's 33.2 per cent on lifetime transfers and estate of the same total value: in other words, Mr B saves £13,000 by transferring some of his estate more than three years before his death).

feature about CTT is that it is cumulative. The cumulation used to be without time limit, but the 1981 budget introduced a new rule restricting cumulation to transfers made within a period of ten years before the transfer in question. For the moment we shall disregard the ten-year rule and consider only transfers made within ten years of each other. CTT is cumulative in two ways: first, the value of gifts (lifetime transfers) is cumulated for tax purposes; second, on death the value of the estate is added to the cumulated value of lifetime transfers in order to determine the rates of taxation on the estate.

As we have mentioned, Capital Transfer Tax has a number of exemptions, mostly in relation to lifetime transfers. Transfers between husband and wife in life or on death are exempt; transfers made *by* a person in any one tax year up to a value of £3,000 plus the amount by which transfers in the previous year fall short of £3,000 – that is, in any two consecutive tax years, a total of £6,000 can be transferred, howsoever apportioned as between the two years; gifts *to* any one person of £250 or less; gifts forming part of 'normal expenditure'; gifts made in consideration of marriage; gifts to charity, political parties, or for national purposes. It is important, if CTT is to be avoided, for parents to utilise to the full the occasion of children's marriage for making tax-exempt gifts; and the £3,000 a year exemption has led to a lively trade in people creating 'shares' in the house that they own and transferring an exempt value of such 'shares' each year to a beneficiary.

Capital Gains Tax (CGT)

Capital Gains Tax is a tax on gains accruing from the disposal of assets by persons resident, or normally resident, in the United Kingdom. The word 'assets' includes all forms of capital, financial assets and real assets including jewellery and antiques. There are certain exemptions such as an individual's principal private residence, private motor-vehicles, and sums from the sale of most chattels with a life of less than fifty years. For business, capital gains tax may be deferred if the sale proceeds are used to replace the assets sold – so-called 'rollover relief' – but any such deferred tax will become due when and if the asset is sold without being replaced.

Capital Gains Tax is levied at 30 per cent of the 'chargeable gain' and applies to disposals taking place on or after 7 April 1965, the date on which CGT came into force. If an asset were acquired on or after 7 April 1965, the chargeable gain is calculated as the difference between the disposal proceeds and the cost of acquisition; losses may be offset against chargeable (positive) gains. If assets are disposed of as a gift or for an 'inadequate' sum, an imputed market value of the transaction will be substituted for disposal proceeds. If an asset were acquired before 7 April 1965, only that portion of the gain occurring after 7 April 1965 is chargeable to tax. If an asset can be given a valuation for 6 April 1965, this valuation can be used in the calculation; if not, the total gain can be multiplied by the proportion of total time for which the asset was owned elapsing after 7 April 1965.

To illustrate, suppose an asset were acquired on 7 April 1960 and sold on 7 April 1975;

then the asset will have been owned for fifteen years, ten of which fell after 7 April 1965, so ten-fifteenths of the total gain will be chargeable to CGT. The taxpayer can choose which method to use – market valuation on 6 April 1965 or proportion of time (which is usually worked out in months for greater accuracy). Starting in 1980–1, if the net gains from all disposals do not exceed £3,000 (the 'basic exemption'), then no tax is payable; thereafter, net gains in excess of the basic exemption of £3,000 are chargeable. So that in calculating CGT one first works out chargeable gains as disposal proceeds *minus* cost of acquisition (using the provisions just described for assets acquired before 7 April 1965); then one deducts allowable capital losses if any; then one deducts the basic exemption of £3,000; and on the remaining sum tax is payable at a rate of 30 per cent of this remaining sum.

In the 1982 Budget, the basic exemption for Capital Gains Tax was increased to £5,000 and it was announced that this basic exemption would in future be revised annually in the light of changes in the Retail Price Index. Furthermore, it was proposed in the 1982 Finance Bill that, for disposals on or after 6 April 1982, there would be an additional 'indexation allowance', also to be deducted from the capital gain before assessing the taxable gain. The indexation allowance is to be calculated by applying to the *original* cost of the asset either (1) for assets purchased before March 1981, the proportionate change in the retail price Index from March 1982 to the date of disposal of the asset; or (2) for assets purchased after March 1981, the proportionate change in the Retail Price Index from the acquisition date *plus* twelve months to the date of disposal of the asset (see the *Financial Times*, 27 March 1982, p. 5). Let us illustrate for case (2). Suppose you purchased an asset for £100,000 in June 1981 which you sold in May 1983 for £110,000, and suppose that the Retail Price Index increased by 5 per cent between June 1982 and May 1983; the indexation allowance is then calculated as $0.05 \times £10,000 = £500$; the chargeable gain for CGT is: Actual gain *minus* Basic exemption *minus* Indexation allowance, which in this case is $£10,000 - £5,000 - £500 = £4,500$, and the CGT payable will be 30 per cent of this chargeable gain, i.e. $0.30 \times £4,500 = £1,350$. But the indexation allowance is not allowed to create a loss: that is, the equation 'ceases' at zero and negative taxes will not be paid out to the taxpayer! The indexation allowance is a major change and will almost certainly reduce quite substantially the amount of CGT collected.

Development Land Tax (DLT)

Development Land Tax, introduced in 1976 is, in effect, a special category of capital gains tax applied to land used for property development. It is charged at 60 per cent of the realised 'development value' and, unlike CGT, it applies also to non-residents. Calculating 'development value' is a complex process but fundamentally it represents the difference between the proceeds from sale and what is called the 'base value'. Base value is fundamentally the value the land would have without planning permission for property development (in the United Kingdom, the Town and Country Planning Act 1947 requires that permission be obtained from the local authority for any change in land use, including property development). Base value may be calculated as the (estimated) 'use value' (without planning permission) current at the time of disposal *plus* 15 per cent *plus* cost of any improvements.

For all their complexity and administrative costliness, these taxes on capital contribute only a small fraction of central government receipts: 1.5 per cent in 1980. Given the various costs of raising these taxes, including the cost of the effort put into avoiding them, one might conclude that we could just as well do without them; but the overriding need to raise taxes by all means possible means that such rational cost–benefit considerations will continue to be disregarded.

An example to illustrate Development Land Tax

Suppose someone, having obtained planning permission for houses to be built on a piece of farmland he had bought, sells the piece of land; the development value is the difference between the proceeds of the sale and the value of that land as farmland. For disposals on or after 1 April 1980, a basic exemption of £50,000 is deductible from development values arising in any one tax year. No DLT is payable when development value is realised by an owner-occupier on the sale or development of his sole or main residence (with land up to one acre). DLT is not charged on land or buildings held by building firms as 'stock-in-trade' because the (capital) gains realised on the sale of stock-in-trade are assessable to income (profits) tax. If a

portion of a gain bears Development Land Tax, then that portion is not assessable to Capital Gains Tax.

To illustrate, Diagram 9.8 shows the case of someone who bought a piece of farmland for £60,000 and who sells it, with planning permission to 'develop' the land, for £180,000; at the time of its sale, the land, if sold as farmland, would, it is estimated, realise only £100,000, so this latter may be taken as its 'base value'. The development value is thus £180,000 *minus* £100,000 *equals* £80,000. Subject to the DLT basic exemption of £50,000, this is subject to Development Land Tax at 60 per cent: that is, £18,000 of DLT is payable. Capital Gains Tax is levied, not on the whole gain (£180,000 *minus*

DIAGRAM 9.8   *Development Land Tax and Capital Gains Tax on the sale of a piece of land (with planning permission)*

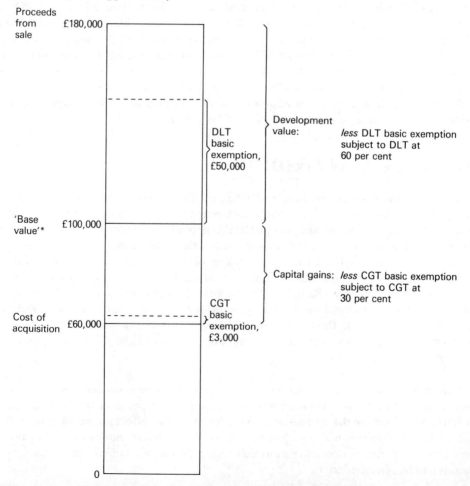

£60,000) but only on that portion not bearing Development Land Tax: that is, on the base value *minus* the cost of acquisition.

The rationale for Development Land Tax was a feeling that the state, rather than the individual, should benefit from planning permission to develop land.

*Value without permission for property development; calculated as current 'use value' or as cost of acquisition *plus* 15 per cent *plus* cost of improvements (whichever is highest). (Note that the CGT basic exemption was raised to £5,000 in the 1982 Budget.)

This concludes our consideration of central government receipts, amounting to £80,564 million in 1980. Examining Table 9.5 has been quite a lengthy process, but it is not possible to understand government finances unless one has at least some descriptive knowledge of the various taxes levied by the central government. We proceed now to consider local authority receipts, a somewhat shorter process since local authorities have only two main sources of revenue apart from what the central government gives them: namely, rates and rents.

Local authority receipts

Table 9.15 shows the structure of local authority receipts in 1980. Rates are local taxes paid by occupiers of land and property. Each occupier's annual payment is calculated by multiplying the 'rateable value' of the property by the 'rate poundage'. Rateable value is supposed to represent the property's annual rental value on the open market (with the tenant responsible for repairs, maintenance and insurance); rateable values in England and Wales are assessed periodically by the Board of Inland Revenue (this is done by independent assessors in Scotland). Because there is not much in the way of a market for rented dwellings, the annual market rental value is something of a fiction, but this does not matter: what matters is that the valuation is consistent among all types of property. Because of this fiction, rates are classified as a tax on expenditure: that is, on the implied benefit derived from having a building.

Table 9.15 shows that local authorities derived 30.8 per cent of their total receipts from rates in 1980. Rates paid by the personal sector provided approximately 13 per cent of total receipts, and rates paid by all other sectors provided approximately 17.8 per cent of total receipts.* A further 11.4 per cent came from rents on local authority housing net of repairs and supervision expenses. Some income is derived from interest, mainly on local authority mortgages – if more people buy council houses using local authority mortgages, then rental income should alter and interest payments should increase. A small amount of income is derived as the gross trading surplus of local authority enterprises, chiefly bus services. Finally, there is the imputed income derived from owner-occupied buildings of £1,100 million, or 4.1 per cent of the total. All in all, local authorities' 'own' income provided 49.3 per cent of their total receipts.

The rest came mainly from current and capital grants given by the central government. The central government gives grants to local authorities for four main reasons:

(a)   to meet the cost of specific services;

---

*These are only approximate figures because water charges should be excluded from personal-sector rates, but there appears to be no separate figure, and because other sector rates are calculated as a residual from total rates.

TABLE 9.15   *Local authority receipts, 1980*

	£ million	Percentage of total
Receipts on current account		
Rates [a] paid by personal sector (including water charges)	3,506	13.0
Approximate rates [a] paid by other sectors (understated by water charges)	4,794	17.8
Net rent (gross rents and subsidies *minus* repairs, etc.) [b]	3,059	11.4
Interest (of which −£1m. from central government)	683	2.5
Gross trading surplus [c]	131	0.5
Imputed charge for consumption of non-trading capital	1,100	4.1
Sub-total: 'own income' (including interest from central government)	13,273	49.3
Current grants from central government		
Grants not allocated to specific services	10,542	39.2
Grants allocated to specific services [d]	2,733	10.2
Sub-total: current grants from central government	13,275	49.3
Sub-total: receipts on current account	26,548	98.6
Receipts on capital account [e]		
Capital grants from central government [f]	337	1.3
Miscellaneous capital receipts	41	0.1
Total receipts on current and capital account	26,926	100.0

[a] Excluding Northern Ireland rates, recorded as central government receipts since 1974.

[b] Comprising (in £ million): rent paid by tenants (1,808) *plus* rent rebates (520) *plus* subsidies (2,153) *plus* rent on other properties (83) *plus* other income (exc. interest) (183) *minus* repairs (976) *minus* supervision and management (632) *minus* other current expenditure (exc. interest) (80); full details in Blue Book's table 8.5 'Housing: operating account'. This 'net rent' is net of expenses only; it is still gross of depreciation.

[c] From, for example, passenger transport services; includes stock appreciation.

[d] Comprising (in £ million): transport (374); housing (320); police (1,052); administration of justice (144); education (inc. grants for school meals) (697); other specific services (146).

[e] Excluding surplus on current account (saving).

[f] These are given for specific purposes and comprise (in £ million): roads and public lighting (34); water, sewerage and refuse disposal (14); land drainage and coast protection (6); education (32); other (251).

Source: Central Statistical Office, *National Income and Expenditure 1981 Edition*, tables 4.8, 8.2 and 8.3, pp. 36, 55 and 56.

(b)   to help authorities with high spending needs;

(c)   to supplement the income of authorities where rate income *per capita* is low; and

(d)   to compensate authorities for any reductions in rate poundage which the authorities were required to give to householders.

Items (b) and (c) comprise the 'rate support grant' or block grant which each local authority is more or less free to spend as it sees fit.

The central government provides a large proportion of local authorities' receipts, and so it is that recent attempts by the central government to control public expenditure have also affected the amount of money given to local authorities, and the way in which those amounts are determined. The financial relationship between central government and local authorities is a complex matter: we can here provide only the basic descriptive categories, and the reader who wishes to take this subject further can begin with chapter 10 'Local taxation' of *The British Tax System* by J. A. Kay and M. A. King.

Current and capital grants from central government to local authorities do not, of

An example to illustrate rates

The 'rate poundage' is the amount of rate per £ of rateable value and is fixed by the local authority according to its projected financial needs. For example, the author's house in Birmingham has a rateable value of £555, and the City of Birmingham District Council's annual rate poundage in 1981–2 is 123.50 pence in the £ (i.e. per £ of rateable value), so the author's annual rates for 1981–2 are 1.2350 × £555 = £685.425. The rate poundage is calculated by dividing the yield of a 'penny rate' (i.e. the yield of one pence per £ of total rateable values in the local authority area) into the sum which the local authority needs to raise. For example, the rateable value of the City of Birmingham was estimated to be £163.5 million at 1 April 1981, so the product of a penny rate was £1.6 million: in 1981–2 the City of Birmingham needed to raise £168.8 million, so its rate poundage was approximately 168.8/1.6 = 105.52 pence in the £, but this rate poundage had to be increased by about one-fifth to meet the West Midlands County Council's rate precept for police and fire services (for which the County Council, not the City Council, is responsible).

course, form part of general government receipts, because such grants come out of central government tax (etc.) receipts and we cannot count them twice. But the 'own' income of local authorities and their miscellaneous capital receipts (mainly from public corporations – see Table 10.5) are an additional extra source of income from other sectors to general government.

Having now examined the items of expenditure and income of general government – and it is necessary that an economist should have some descriptive knowledge of these items – we can now begin to consider the general government borrowing requirement. The general government borrowing requirement, when supplemented by the borrowing requirement of the public corporations (nationalised industries) from the non-government sector, becomes the public sector borrowing requirement. The PSBR is a key concept in understanding how the financial sector of the economy works and so it is not possible to understand how an economy works unless one understands it. The public corporations' contribution to the PSBR will be considered in the next chapter. But the greater part of the PSBR arises in the general government borrowing requirement, as we shall see.

The general government borrowing requirement

The general government borrowing requirement – an annual flow – is the amount of money the general government needs to borrow each year in order to cover both:

1. Its (annual) financial deficit.
2. Its (annual) net lending to other sectors.*

Let us first explain these terms using a simple example. Suppose your income were £100 per week, and you spent £110 during the week and lent £5 to a friend (against your friend's IOU); suppose also you started off the week with no financial assets. Your financial deficit is the difference between your income and your expenditure and you need to borrow £10

---

*The borrowing requirement is always in terms of *net* finance required: that is, gross borrowing *less* redemption of maturing debt. Subsequently we shall consider also the gross borrowing (but zero net borrowing) to finance debt redemption. However, from the point of view of the outstanding stock of debt, borrowing to finance redemption merely substitutes new debt for old.

to cover your financial deficit (i.e. if you do not borrow, you will not be able to spend in excess of your income). In addition, you need to borrow £5 (against your own IOU) so you can lend on the money to your friend. You will thus have borrowed during the week £15 – this is your total (weekly) borrowing requirement – and so will have acquired financial liabilities of £15; but against this you have also acquired a £5 financial asset (your friend's IOU), so your *net* acquisition of financial liabilities is £10; exactly the excess of expenditure over income.

In order to understand how the general government borrowing requirement arises, we thus need to understand, first, how the general government runs a financial deficit, and, second, the extent to which the general government lends money to other sectors. The total of the general government financial deficit and its net lending to other sectors would be the general government borrowing requirement, but there is the further matter of the accruals adjustment. This comes about as follows. We have been taking general government receipts on an accruals basis – the annual flows (mainly of taxes) falling due, or 'accruing' – but in the real world there may be differences (of timing) between taxes falling due (accruing) and tax payments actually flowing in as cash to the Consolidated Fund. This happens because the private sector pays some of its taxes in arrears – this being simply part of the administrative arrangements for tax payments. Now the government's borrowing requirement relates to actual cash flows, rather than to accruals, so if cash flows are less than accruals, then the borrowing requirement, calculated on the basis of accruals, has to be adjusted upwards: this is known as the 'accruals adjustment' and in the United Kingdom, because the private sector tends to pay taxes with a time lag, the accruals adjustment to the borrowing requirement is nearly always upwards.

The accruals adjustment can, moreover, be relatively large, so it is necessary to understand it fully. Suppose we had reported your income accruing during the week as £100, but your employer had for some reason paid you actual cash of only £96, deferring, for some legitimate reason, £4 of your income for payment in a subsequent week. Then, although your borrowing requirement for that week on an accruals basis is £15 – and this represents your long-term position regarding gross acquisition of liabilities – you will also have to borrow (temporarily, until your employer hands over the other £4) an extra £4, so this 'accruals adjustment' will increase your actual borrowing requirement, on a weekly cash-flow basis, to £19: namely, £10 to cover your financial deficit (accruals basis accounting), £5 to cover lending to a friend, and £4 to cover the actual cash-flow deficiency (i.e. to go from accounting on an accruals basis to accounting on a cash flow basis – because actual borrowing always relates to cash flows rather than to accruals). The reason for going through this rigmarole of a separate accruals adjustment is that it is economically more meaningful to say that your income for the week is £100 (the amount falling due) rather than to say that your income for the week is £96 (the amount of cash actually handed over).

Having dealt with these preliminary definitions via a simplified example (and the reader whose recollection of Diagrams 2.6 and 2.7 and the relevant pages of Chapter 2 is a little hazy should at this juncture revise those pages), we may see how these definitions applied to the general government in the United Kingdom in 1980 (to save repeating the word 'general', hereafter 'government' should be taken to mean general government). Table 9.16 gives the relevant figures, all of which (apart from the accruals adjustment) have been seen before.

The accounts preserve the distinction between current and capital accounts (Diagrams 2.5 and 2.7) so the sequence in Table 9.16 is:

Receipts on *minus* Expenditure *equals* Current surplus,
current a/c   on current a/c   or 'saving'

The current-account surplus is then 'transferred' as a receipt to the capital account, and the sequence then is:

TABLE 9.16   *The UK general government borrowing requirement: balance of receipts and expenditures, 1980*

	£ million
Receipts on current account	
Taxes on income	30,088
Taxes on expenditure (including rates)	37,287
National Insurance contributions	13,977
Gross trading surplus (including stock appreciation)	170
Rent	3,092
Interest and dividends	3,836
Imputed charge for consumption non-trading capital	1,775
Total receipts on current account	91,025
Expenditure on current account	
Current expenditure on goods and services	46,562
Non-trading capital consumption	1,775
Subsidies	5,215
Current grants to personal sector	25,476
Current grants paid abroad	1,832
Debt interest	11,285
Total expenditure on current account	92,145
Balance on current account: current surplus or 'saving'	−1,120
Receipts on capital account	
Current surplus	−1,120
Taxes on capital and miscellaneous local authority receipts	1,248
Total receipts on capital account	128
Expenditure on capital account	
Gross domestic fixed capital formation	5,500
Increase in value of stocks	300
Capital grants and other capital transfers	2,282
Total expenditure on capital account	8,082
Balance on capital account: net acquisition of financial assets or financial balance; financial surplus (+) or financial deficit (−)	−7,954
Therefore: borrowing requirement to finance deficit	+7,954
Financial expenditure (net lending to other sectors) [a]	3,493
Total borrowing requirement (accruals basis) to finance deficit and financial expenditure, before accruals adjustment	11,447
Accruals adjustment (including miscellaneous financial transactions): actual cash-flow receipts *minus* accounting receipts	−927
Miscellaneous financial transactions	−561
Therefore: extra borrowing requirement caused by accruals after allowing for miscellaneous financial transactions	+1,488
Total borrowing requirement (cash-flow basis), after accruals adjustment	12,935
Memorandum items (to be dealt with in following chapters)	
Borrowing requirement of public corporations not financed by general government	−691
Total public sector borrowing requirement (PSBR)	12,244

[a] Mostly to public corporations.

Source: Central Statistical Office, *National Income and Expenditure 1981 Edition*, tables 9.1 and 13.12, pp. 58−9 and 101.

Receipts on capital a/c (i.e. saving *plus* other receipts)	*minus*	Expenditure on capital a/c	*equals*	Financial balance: financial deficit (if negative); financial surplus (if positive); or net acquisition of financial assets

The algebraic signs now become a little tricky and cannot be treated mechanically; when dealing with financial balances, there is no substitute for keeping a sharp look-out as to what we are doing. The government's annual net acquisition of financial assets is nearly always negative: that is, the government tends each year to run a financial deficit (negative sign). This financial deficit creates a matching need to borrow money, so we shall report this borrowing requirement with a positive sign. The accounts thus continue:

Borrowing requirement to cover financial deficit	*plus*	Borrowing requirement to cover net lending	*equals*	Total borrowing requirement before accruals adjustment

Total borrowing requirement before accruals adjustment	*plus*	Accruals adjustment	*equals*	Total borrowing requirement on cash-flow basis

The items in the foregoing four equations are the building blocks for the general government borrowing requirement; Diagram 9.9 shows what these equations look like in pictorial form (but excludes the accruals adjustment). The excess of receipts over expenditure on current account (if positive) is saving; this is transferred to the capital account, there to be joined by other capital-account receipts; the excess of expenditure over receipts on capital account is the financial balance; if the financial balance is negative, it creates a need for borrowing, and so we may transfer it as a (positive) use of funds to the financial account, there to be joined by other financial uses of funds (lending), and the two combined create a total borrowing requirement. The financial deficit, or the negative net acquisition of financial assets, is always the same, because borrowing to finance lending always cancels out so far as the *net* financial liabilities/assets situation is concerned.

Now let us look at the 1980 figures. Total receipts on current account during 1980 were

DIAGRAM 9.9 *The sequence of accounts which give the general government total borrowing requirement*

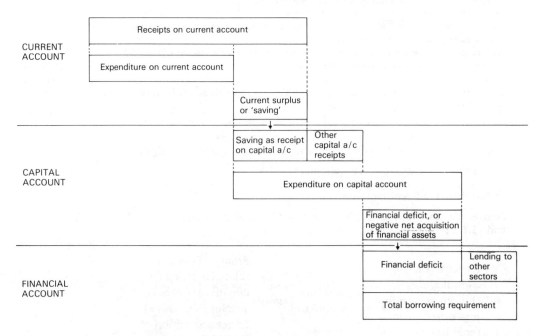

£91,025 million. This comprises £77,751 million of central government receipts on current account *excluding* interest from local authorities (see Table 9.5 above and do the calculation), and £13,274 million of local authorities' 'own' income *excluding* interest from central government (see Table 9.15 above and do the calculation).

In order that this total of £91,025 million be not an anonymous aggregate, Table 9.16 also gives some details of its composition. The figures in Table 9.16 are taken straight from the Blue Book's table 9.1 'General government: summary account', but we have already encountered most of them in previous tables in this chapter. Taxes on income were analysed in Tables 9.5 and 9.6; taxes on expenditure of £37,287 million comprise, from Table 9.5, £21,988 million of Customs and Excise taxes, £6,999 million of other central government taxes on expenditure, and from Table 9.15, £3,506 million of rates paid by the personal sector and £4,794 million of rates paid by other sectors. National Insurance contributions are as in Table 9.5. The gross trading surplus (including stock appreciation) of £170 million comprises £39 million from central government enterprises (Table 9.5) and £131 million from local authority enterprises (Table 9.15). Rent of £3,092 million comprises £3,059 million of local authority rent receipts (Table 9.15 – which is why council house rents are an important part of government revenues) and £33 million of rents received by central government (Table 9.5). Interest and dividends, received from sectors outside the general government totalled £3,836 million, and this sum may be worked out from Tables 9.5 and 9.15, as may the combined imputed charge for consumption of non-trading capital.

Total general government expenditure on current account in 1980 was £92,145 million. The items making up this expenditure on current account have also been seen previously in Table 9.4. But note that the figures in Table 9.3 each tend to be a mixture of current- and capital-account expenditures as we did not there distinguish (as does the original source for that table) between the two accounts. Note also that, for the government accounts, the inclusion under current expenditure of the imputed charge for non-trading capital consumption means that this item cancels out, though it still goes into the national income.

The total income and expenditure on current account thus give us the figures for the first equation towards the general government borrowing requirement. This is the equation which gives government saving:

$$£91,025m. - £92,145m. = -£1,120m.$$

Thus we see that, in 1980, government saving was negative. This has not often been the case, but was so in 1976, 1978 and 1979. Government saving is 'transferred' as a receipt to capital account (see Diagrams 2.5 and 2.7). To these (negative) receipts are added the central government taxes on capital (see Diagram 9.7 and Table 9.5) of £1,207 million and the miscellaneous capital receipts of local authorities of £41 million (Table 9.15): a total of £1,248 million of tax and other receipts, so the total receipts on capital account is the algebraic sum of this and the negative current-account surplus, which is £128 million.

Expenditure on capital account in 1980 amounted to £8,082 million, comprising fixed capital formation, increase in the value of stocks, and capital grants and transfers (including capital transfers to public corporations), all of which can also be seen in Table 9.4. So we now have the figures for the second equation towards the general government borrowing requirement. This is the equation which gives us the government's net acquisition of financial assets (its financial balance):

$$£128m. - £8,082m. = -£7,954m.$$

Thus we can see that in 1980 the government had a sizeable financial deficit (see Diagram 2.6 and pp. 434–6): it was spending on current and capital account more than it had coming in. This negative financial balance, or negative 'net acquisition of financial assets', means that the government had to borrow to cover the deficit. The wording of the previous sentence is not quite accurate enough: the reality is that, in order to be able to make expenditures in excess of income, the government had first to arrange this amount of borrowing.

To illustrate, if you had no financial assets to start with, and your income for the week were £100, then in order to make expenditures during the week of £110, you would have had to borrow £10 somehow, perhaps just by running up an unpaid bill at the butcher's, perhaps by letting your bank account go into an overdraft. Mentioning a bank account indicates why we tend to use the rather clumsy, but more generally applicable, term 'negative net acquisition of financial assets' to denote a financial deficit: if you had £10 standing to your credit in the bank at the start of the week, then you could have covered your financial deficit, your excess of expenditure over income, simply by running down your stock of financial assets (your credit at the bank) to zero – this is a negative acquisition of financial assets. A financial deficit gives rise to a borrowing requirement (of equal size) only if there are no financial assets to start with. Or to put it another way round: a financial deficit must be financed by a negative net acquisition of financial assets, and this negative net acquisition of financial assets may take the form either of a reduction in an initial stock of financial assets or of an increase in a stock of financial liabilities (or, of course, a mixture of the two). Because the government is basically in the position of having no (at least, very few) financial assets (which in any case it would be reluctant to reduce), it is the case that the government's financial deficit requires it to borrow in order to cover its excess of expenditure over income. So the government's financial deficit creates a matching borrowing requirement.

(Note that we are also ruling out of consideration the possibility that the government might sell physical assets to cover its financial deficit; such sales would be one way of financing the financial deficit without recourse to borrowing – just as you might sell your watch for £10 to cover a financial deficit of that amount rather than borrow from the bank or run up a butcher's bill. As a matter of accounting, however, such sales of fixed capital by the government would be reported either as positive income on capital account if the original expenditure had been a financial transaction (for instance, this was the treatment adopted whenever plants belonging to the nationalised iron and steel industry was sold back into private ownership in the period 1953 to 1964) or as negative expenditure on capital account (i.e. a deduction from gross fixed capital formation) if the original expenditure had been treated as part of fixed capital formation resulting in the creation of new assets for the nation – this would be the treatment for the sale of council houses, i.e. sales of council houses count as reductions in government investment.)

With these remarks in mind, we may proceed in Table 9.16 to write, after the line containing the financial deficit, that therefore (i.e. arising from the financial deficit – negative sign) the government has an exactly equivalent borrowing requirement to finance the deficit – but we now report the borrowing requirement with a positive sign as +£7,954 million (at this point the presentation of Table 9.16 departs from the rather complicated, and hard-to-follow, presentation of the Blue Book's table 9.1).*

In addition to incurring this excess of expenditure over income, the government also lends money to other sectors: £3,493 million in 1980. As can be seen in Table 9.4, this financial expenditure is rather complex, but most of it is central government lending to the public corporations, with some local authority lending to the private sector (mostly in the form of local authority mortgages), but there are some negative financial expenditures: that is, net financial receipts from disposals of company securities owned by the govern-

---

*Please note that this departs from the usual sign convention, that a source of funds should be reported with a *minus* sign.

ment or net repayments of loans previously made by the central government to the overseas sector (mostly to other governments). So we now have the figures for the third equation towards the general government borrowing requirement. This is the equation which gives us the total borrowing requirement before the accruals adjustment:

$$£7,954m. + £3,493m. = £11,447m.$$

This borrowing requirement represents the government's 'long-term' position. However, because the government tends to receive in less money by way of actual cash flows than is accruing (falling due) we need finally to switch from the accruals-based accounting to cash-flow accounting, because actual borrowing depends on cash flows rather than on amounts falling due. The accruals adjustment as reported on the *receipts* side of the summary account in the Blue Book was −£927 million. This figure of −£927 million means that the tax actually paid to the government during (the calendar year) 1980 was less than the amount falling due to the government during (the calendar year) 1980; that is, cash-flow actual receipts were less than accruals-based receipts (much of this 'shortfall' appears to occur in VAT and income tax). Rather than reduce the accruals-based tax receipts reported in Table 9.16, we keep them on that basis, and at this last stage in the accounts we note that the borrowing requirement (on an accruals basis) has to be increased to cover the accruals adjustment or shortfall. There was, however, also a negative amount of miscellaneous financial receipts of −£561 million to be added to the negative accruals adjustment, so the net increase in the borrowing requirement is £1,488 million, and so we have the figures for the fourth and final equation giving the general government borrowing requirement on a cash-flow basis:

$$£11,447m. + £1,488m. = £12,935m.$$

The economic significance of the general government borrowing requirement and of the general government financial deficit will not be fully understood until we have, in the chapters to follow, considered the workings of the financial institutions and the macroeconomic 'Keynesian' system relating to the determination of flows of final expenditure. The purpose of the present chapter is simply to explain, as a matter of description, how the general government financial deficit and the general government borrowing requirement arises. In order to understand *what* the government's financial deficit and borrowing requirement are requires that we have some (descriptive) knowledge of all the items in Table 9.16. Acquiring this descriptive knowledge has been a necessarily lengthy process (and it is a process most unfortunately shirked in nearly all textbooks on economics). *How* the deficit and the borrowing requirement fit into the analysis of the modern economy will be dealt with later but the reader may be assured that they are very important concepts so the current effort of descriptive understanding will eventually pay off.

Meanwhile we may conclude our description with two memorandum items in Table 9.16. The public corporations (nationalised industries − to be discussed in the next chapter) run each year a fairly large financial deficit, as we shall see. Much of this is covered by loans from the central government to the public corporations (see Table 9.4) and so enters into the general government borrowing requirement. But the public corporations also borrow some money from other sectors of the economy, which borrowing is guaranteed by the central government; this 'extra' borrowing by public corporations is, from a financial point of view, little different from general government borrowing and so what matters at the end of the day for monetary economics is the borrowing requirement of the whole of the public sector combined: central government, local authorities, and public corporations. The memorandum items in Table 9.16 show that the extra borrowing of the public corporations was −£691 million in 1980, and so the borrowing requirement of the whole of the public sector was £12,244 million in 1980.

The trend of the public sector borrowing requirement

The PSBR has, in the last few years, become the focal point of much of government policy and of economic debate. To instance this we may quote from the 1981 budget speech of the Chancellor of the Exchequer:

> Some people, I know, are tempted to regard the PSBR as an entirely mystical concept, of interest only to economists. How I wish they were right! But, alas, the size of public borrowing is, as it must be, a critically important constraint. There should be no surprise in that. For Governments are not so different from individuals. The PSBR, in plain language, is broadly the difference between what Government spends, or lends to others, and what it collects in revenue, mainly through taxation. It necessarily includes what the nationalised industries borrow; most of this comes from the Government, and where they borrow from other sources, the Government stands behind them. So the PSBR is the amount central and local Government and the public corporations have to borrow. It is the experience of Governments around the world that if they try to borrow too much, then either interest rates or inflation or both begin to soar. Britain's experience tells the same story. If we are to stay on course for lower inflation and for lower interest rates, then we must borrow less. Public borrowing as a proportion of the national income must be brought down (the *Financial Times*, 11 March 1981, p. 15).

In order to begin to see why the Chancellor of the Exchequer said that public borrowing as a proportion of national income must be brought down, it is helpful to look at the trend of the PSBR in relation to the gross national product.

Table 9.17 and Diagram 9.10 show the United Kingdom's public sector borrowing requirement in relation to gross national product (at factor cost). In 1952 the PSBR was 5.6 per cent of GNP (this was due to the increase in public expenditure during the Korean war, unaccompanied by comparable rises in taxes), but it fell as a proportion in the next two years, and thereafter, for twelve years to 1966, remained between 2 and 4 per cent of GNP. In 1967 it rose to 5.3 per cent, but was during the following two years brought down to a negative level (and in 1969 the public sector was receiving more by way of taxes (etc.) than it was spending). After 1970 the PSBR as a percentage of GNP rose rapidly to a peak of 11 per cent in 1975, before being reduced, though it rose again in 1978 and 1979. Clearly, it is this recent history that the Chancellor of the Exchequer had in mind when he spoke of the need to reduce public borrowing as a proportion of the national income. The

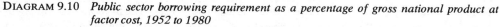

DIAGRAM 9.10   *Public sector borrowing requirement as a percentage of gross national product at factor cost, 1952 to 1980*

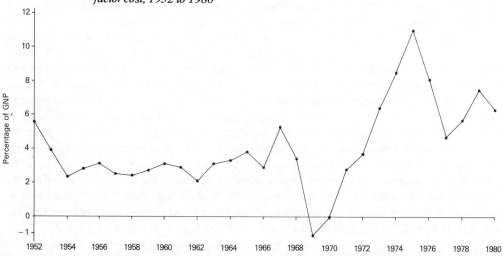

TABLE 9.17   *The UK public sector borrowing requirement (PSBR) in relation to gross national product, 1952 to 1980*

| | £ million | | |
Year	Public sector borrowing requirement	Gross national product at factor cost	PSBR as percentage of GNP at factor cost
1952	794	14,088	5.6
1953	593	15,147	3.9
1954	371	16,011	2.3
1955	470	17,079	2.8
1956	573	18,530	3.1
1957	487	19,653	2.5
1958	491	20,520	2.4
1959	571	21,520	2.7
1960	710	22,870	3.1
1961	704	24,482	2.9
1962	546	25,618	2.1
1963	844	27,311	3.1
1964	990	29,604	3.3
1965	1,208	31,654	3.8
1966	964	33,518	2.9
1967	1,860	35,313	5.3
1968	1,295	37,910	3.4
1969	−445	40,131	−1.1
1970	4	44,128	—
1971	1,382	49,992	2.8
1972	2,054	55,885	3.7
1973	4,209	65,604	6.4
1974	6,437	76,076	8.5
1975	10,480	95,248	11.0
1976	9,128	112,950	8.1
1977	5,993	127,047	4.7
1978	8,356	145,896	5.7
1979	12,611	167,310	7.5
1980	12,244	193,450	6.3

Sources: PSBR 1952 to 1962, Bank of England, *Statistical Abstract*, no. 1, 1970, table 12(2), p. 79; PSBR 1963 to 1969 and GNP, Central Statistical Office, *Economic Trends Annual Supplement 1981 Edition*, pp. 38 and 154; PSBR and GNP 1970 to 1980, Central Statistical Office, *National Income and Expenditure 1981 Edition*, tables 1.1 and 13.12, pp. 3 and 101.

movements of the PSBR in the 1970s, compared with the 1950s and 1960s, are unusual and partly explain why the PSBR is at the centre of the debate about economic policy.

Part of the reason for the rise in the relative size of the PSBR during the 1970s is seen in Diagram 1.5 and Appendix 1.2 which show that the numbers unemployed in the United Kingdom rose quite steadily in the 1970s; this caused part of the rise in the relative size of total general govenment outgoings (Diagram 9.3) because transfer payments to the unemployed rose. At the same time as outgoings were rising rapidly, tax receipts were not rising so fast because there were fewer people in work paying income taxes and National Insurance contributions. So an economic recession tends to cause an increase in the PSBR both by holding back the rise in receipts and by forcing up expenditure quite rapidly. This is an important point, and it can be quite clearly demonstrated by figures which contrast actual borrowing with what borrowing would have been had constant employment, or a constant unemployment rate, been maintained: that is, if rising unemployment had not caused transfer payments (unemployment benefits) to go up and had not held back tax receipts.

Table 9.18 presents the figures for the period since 1964. The definitions used by Ward and Neild differ slightly from those we have been using: capital taxes have been excluded, as these do not vary cyclically; net lending to the private sector is also excluded, so we are considering only the borrowing required to cover the public-sector financial deficit rather than the total public sector borrowing required to cover the financial deficit and net lending; but the financial deficit has been calculated on a cash-flow basis and not on an accruals basis (i.e. accruals-based receipts include – are reduced by – the accruals adjustment). Against these actual cash-flow receipts and expenditures and actual borrowing to cover the financial deficit, the authors match a hypothetical computation of what (cash-flow) receipts and expenditures would have been (at prevailing, changing, tax rates and expenditure plans) had a constant rate of unemployment been maintained. From this they compute the hypothetical borrowing required to finance the resulting hypothetical 'constant employment budget deficit' (where 'budget deficit' is simply the excess of expenditure over income). If the actual borrowing requirement (as a percentage of GNP) is greater than the hypothetical borrowing requirement (as a percentage of hypothetical constant employment GNP), then this indicates that unemployment has increased the need to borrow either by forcing up expenditure and/or by holding back receipts, the former – expenditure – effect having been, in practice, the most important. Comparison of the last two columns of Table 9.18 shows that in the 1970s actual public-sector borrowing tended increasingly to exceed hypothetical constant employment borrowing, thus demonstrating the quite marked impact that the rising levels of unemployment had on the government's financial situation.

The borrowing required to finance the constant employment budget deficit also indicates the government's 'fiscal policy': that is, what the effects of changes in tax rates and/or changes in public expenditure plans were. Table 9.18 shows clearly in the last three

TABLE 9.18　*Public-sector borrowing to cover financial deficit (cash-flow basis): actual and hypothetical at constant employment, 1964 to 1977*

| Year | Percentage of gross national product at factor cost | | | |
	Actual cash receipts [a]	Actual cash expenditure [b]	Actual borrowing to finance deficit (cash-flow basis) [c]	Borrowing had constant employment been maintained [d]
1964	38.0	41.9	3.9	5.9
1965	40.0	43.1	3.1	4.4
1966	41.2	44.6	3.3	4.5
1967	43.7	48.8	5.1	5.5
1968	45.9	49.6	3.7	4.2
1969	48.3	48.5	0.3	−0.1
1970	49.1	48.5	−0.6	−1.4
1971	46.6	48.3	1.7	0.0
1972	43.9	48.1	4.3	2.2
1973	42.8	47.6	4.8	4.0
1974	46.0	52.7	6.7	5.1
1975	47.0	55.6	8.6	5.7
1976	47.7	56.7	9.0	3.8
1977	49.0	54.1	5.1	−1.1

[a] Excluding receipts from capital taxes.
[b] Excluding government lending to the private sector and public-sector net purchases of existing assets and company securities.
[c] Excess of cash expenditure over cash receipts (as defined).
[d] Based on a constant rate of unemployment of $2\frac{1}{2}$ per cent.

Source: T. S. Ward and R. R. Neild, *The Measurement and Reform of Budgetary Policy*, Institute for Fiscal Studies/Heinemann, 1978, table 4.2, p. 42.

figures of the last column that between 1975 and 1977 the government's fiscal policy 'tightened' considerably and this appears to have been caused both by increased taxation and by reductions in public expenditure.

The role of fiscal policy in the economy will be considered further in the following chapters; the main purpose here is simply to establish the basic categories of government expenditures, receipts, financial balance, and borrowing requirement.

However, we should note that increasing unemployment and its associated increase in transfer payments has not been the only cause of the rising relative level of public expenditure: we saw in Diagram 9.2 that general government current resource-using expenditure (i.e. excluding transfer payments) had risen relatively in the period since 1960. The main reason for this is the rise in employment in general government, especially in local authorities. In 1980 about one-half of central government current expenditure on goods and services went on wages and about three-quarters of local authority current

TABLE 9.19 *Total UK working population in employment by sector, 1956 to 1980*

	Central government		Local authorities	Public corporations [b]	Private sector [c]	Total working population in employment
At mid-year [a]	HM Forces	Civilians [b]				
1956	761	1,309	1,588	2,419	18,432	24,509
1957	702	1,287	1,628	2,409	18,511	24,537
1958	614	1,281	1,656	2,375	18,344	24,270
1959	565	1,287	1,703	2,299	18,487	24,341
1960	518	1,303	1,737	2,200	19,016	24,774
1961	474	1,302	1,782	2,196	19,303	25,057
1962	442	1,329	1,848	2,192	19,404	25,215
1963	427	1,346	1,913	2,132	19,405	25,223
1964	424	1,350	2,085	2,081	19,012	24,952
1965	423	1,370	2,154	2,028	19,217	25,192
1966	417	1,402	2,259	1,962	19,311	25,351
1967	417	1,455	2,364	1,937	18,814	24,987
1968	400	1,485	2,444	2,069	18,443	24,841
1969	380	1,484	2,505	2,041	18,447	24,857
1970	372	1,533	2,559	2,025	18,264	24,753
1971	368	1,572	2,651	2,009	17,799	24,399
1972	371	1,608	2,771	1,929	17,712	24,391
1973	361	1,637	2,890	1,890	18,194	24,972
1974	345	1,751	2,834	1,985	18,144	25,059
1975	336	1,915	2,974	2,035	17,672	24,932
1976	336	1,978	3,016	1,980	17,455	24,765
1977	327	1,978	2,984	2,089	17,454	24,832
1978	318	1,989	2,997	2,061	17,595	24,960
1979	314	2,005	3,060	2,065	17,676	25,120
1980	323	2,004	3,027	2,036	17,330	24,720

[a] 1956 is the earliest year for which a sectoral analysis of employment is available (see CSO, *National Income and Expenditure 1967*, p. 101).

[b] Between 1956 and 1960 inclusive the Post Office was treated, in the Blue Book's figures, as part of central government civilian employment; in 1961 and after Post Office employment is given, in the Blue Book's figures, as part of public corporations. An adjustment has therefore been made, in this table, to exclude Post Office employees from central government employment and include them in public corporations for the years 1956 to 1960 inclusive. Post Office employment (industrial and non-industrial) in thousands was: 1956, 335.3; 1957, 336.6; 1958, 336.8; 1959, 337.7; 1960, 338.8. These figures relate to 1 April of each year (source: *Annual Abstract of Statistics No. 100, 1963*).

[c] Including self-employed.

Sources: Central Statistical Office, *National Income and Expenditure: 1967*, table 13, p. 15; *1968*, table 13, p. 15; *1969*, table 13, p. 15; *1970*, table 13, p. 15; *1971*, table 13, p. 15; *1972*, table 13, p. 15; *1973*, table 13, p. 15; *1963–73*, table 13, p. 15; *1964–74*, table 13, p. 15; *1965–75*, table 1.10, p. 13; *1966–76*, table 1.10, p. 15; *1967–77*, table 1.11, p. 17; *1979 Edition*, table 1.11, p. 17; *1980 Edition*, table 1.12, p. 15; *1981 Edition*, table 1.12, p. 15; Central Statistical Office, *Annual Abstract of Statistics No. 100, 1963*, tables 135 and 137, pp. 111 and 112.

expenditure on goods and services went on wages; so employment costs are a significant part of general government total current resource-using expenditure. Table 9.19 shows that local authority employment rose from 1.6 million in 1956 to 3 million in 1980. Local authority employment thus increased from 6¼ per cent of the working population in 1956 to 12¼ per cent in 1980. Central government employment as a whole has not risen quite so rapidly over this period because a fall of nearly 60 per cent in HM Forces partly offset a rise of over 50 per cent in the number of central government civilian employees: total central government employment rose from 8.4 per cent of the working population in 1956 to 9.4 per cent of the working population in 1980. General government employment thus rose from 14.9 per cent of the working population in 1956 to 21.7 per cent in 1980.

The figures of Table 9.19 show quite startling changes in the sectoral composition of employment in the United Kingdom; we may summarise the changes as follows:

Sector of employment	*Change 1956 to 1980 in millions*
Local authorities	1.4
Central government civilian employment	0.7
HM Forces	−0.4
Public corporations	−0.4
Private sector (including self-employed)	−1.1
Total UK working population in employment	0.2

These figures clearly indicate why 'the size of the public sector' (or of general government) is an important issue of economic policy, and especially why the operations of local authorities are coming under increasing scrutiny. We cannot pause here to analyse the vast economic consequences of these changes, but such an analysis is available in the book by Robert Bacon and Walter Eltis, *Britain's Economic Problem: Too Few Producers* (Macmillan, 1976; 2nd edn 1978).

Meanwhile, we need to complete our examination of the public sector by considering the public corporations.

Exercises

9.1   *(To provide basic knowledge.)* Read, and make notes on, the chapter entitled 'Government' in *Britain 1981; An Official Handbook* (HMSO, 1981) – or a later edition if available – with special attention to the sections on government departments and on local government.

9.2   *(To practise your understanding of some basic terms.)* Write brief explanations of the following:

(i)   central government
(ii)   Consolidated Fund
(iii)   public goods (with examples and amounts spent)
(iv)   transfer payments (with examples and amounts spent).

9.3   *(To practise your understanding of resource-using expenditure vs transfer payments, and so that you can begin to find out for yourself about government expenditure.)*

(i)   Update Table 9.1.
(ii)   Using your updated table, write an essay to answer the question: 'To what extent is general government expenditure a "burden" on the UK economy?'

9.4   *(To become familiar with general government expenditure: this may seem a rather useless exercise, but its purpose is to get you to look at all the items of general government expenditure, big and small, so that when you discuss public expenditure you will have the relevant background knowledge.)* Update Table 9.3.

9.5 *(This exercise provides some background information to the subsequent chapters on money and monetary policy.)* For the period in the latest *National Income and Expenditure* accounts, calculate, tabulate and graph general government debt interest as a proportion of total general government outgoings including net lending. Comment on your findings.

9.6 *(To look at the division of expenditure in the United Kingdom between central government and local authorities.)* Update Table 9.4.

9.7 *(To look at the income of, and problems for, local authorities.)* For the period covered by the latest *National Income and Expenditure* accounts, calculate and tabulate the percentages of local authority total receipts on current account coming from: (i) current grants from central government; and (ii) rates. (iii) What changes do you observe? (iv) Explain and discuss the following statement:

> Because of the [central] government's preoccupations they [the local authorities] found that they were being compelled either to leave needs unmet or to push up their own sources of revenue (chiefly rates and council house rents), imposing an unacceptable rising burden on local residents (University of Cambridge Department of Applied Economics, Economic Policy Group, *Cambridge Economic Policy Review: Urban and Regional Policy with Provisional Regional Accounts, 1966–78*, vol. 6, no. 2, July 1980, ch. 4 'The conflict over local government spending', p. 43).*

9.8 *(To examine a serious and important long-run problem and to demonstrate that you need an adequate background knowledge before you can properly discuss such issues.)* Explain, with all relevant data, why a rising proportion of elderly in the population causes 'financial problems' for the government and what the problems are which face the elderly. (Further reading: J. Walley, *Social Security: Another British Failure?*, Charles Knight, 1972, ch. XI 'Old age'; P. Townsend, *Poverty in the United Kingdom: A Survey of Household Resources and Standards of Living*, Penguin, 1979, ch. 23 'Old people'; G. C. Fiegehen, P. S. Lansley and A. D. Smith, *Poverty and Progress in Britain 1953–73*, Cambridge University Press, 1977, ch. 5 'The life-cycle and causes of poverty'; Royal Commission on the Distribution of Income and Wealth (Chairman: Lord Diamond), *Lower Incomes*, Report No. 6, Cmnd 7175, May 1978.)

9.9 *(To practise your knowledge of central government receipts.)* Update Table 9.5.

9.10 *(Income tax is quantitatively the government's most important tax: to practise your knowledge about how the total is raised.)* With reference to Table 9.20 (p. 446), calculate:

(i)   the average annual income in each income range (including that for all ranges);

(ii) the average annual tax paid in each income range (ditto);

(iii) the average percentage rate of taxation in each income range (ditto).

(iv) What was the over-all average rate of taxation in 1977–8? Draw a graph to show how this over-all average rate of taxation resulted from different average rates of taxation on the different income ranges.

(v)   Using the changes in average annual income and average annual taxation between successive income ranges, calculate the percentage 'marginal rate of taxation' consequent upon moving from one average income to the next average up.

9.11 *(To examine Petroleum Revenue Tax and to look at the Consolidated Fund.)* With reference to tables 3.1 and 3.2 of the CSO's *Financial Statistics* (latest available edition), describe the contribution of Petroleum Revenue Tax to Consolidated Fund total revenue during the past few financial years.

9.12 *(To study the way in which the tax-benefit system works to redistribute income.)*

(i)   With reference to Table 9.9, describe how the system of income taxation and social security and other state benefits affects the distribution of 'income' in the United Kingdom. (The (updated) *Economic Trends* article – published annually – is basic reading; also J. L. Nicholson, 'The distribution and redistribution of income in the United Kingdom', in Dorothy Wedderburn (ed.), *Poverty, Inequality and Class Structure*, Cambridge University Press, 1974.)

*Further reading: A. Midwinter and E. Page, 'Cutting local spending – the Scottish experience, 1976–80', and R. Greenwood, 'Fiscal pressure and local government in England and Wales', chs 3 and 4 respectively of C. Hood and M. Wright (eds), *Big Government in Hard Times*, Martin Robertson, 1981.

TABLE 9.20　*Distribution of total personal incomes before and after tax, 1977–8*

Range of income, £ per annum	Number of incomes in that range, thousands	£ million, tax year	
		Total income before tax	Total income tax paid
810 to under　1,000	573	523	2
1,000 to under　1,500	1,840	2,300	111
1,500 to under　2,000	2,150	3,770	383
2,000 to under　2,500	2,410	5,410	747
2,500 to under　3,000	2,270	6,230	1,000
3,000 to under　3,500	2,100	6,800	1,160
3,500 to under　4,000	1,900	7,120	1,270
4,000 to under　4,500	1,720	7,300	1,330
4,500 to under　5,000	1,560	7,400	1,360
5,000 to under　6,000	2,380	13,000	2,500
6,000 to under　7,000	1,480	9,530	1,950
7,000 to under　8,000	813	6,070	1,330
8,000 to under　10,000	720	6,360	1,520
10,000 to under　12,000	268	2,910	798
12,000 to under　15,000	163	2,160	677
15,000 to under　20,000	105	1,790	664
20,000 to under　50,000	81	2,170	1,100
50,000 to under 100,000	4	249	175
100,000 and over	0.6	106	78
All ranges	22,500	91,200	18,200

Source: Board of Inland Revenue, *Inland Revenue Statistics 1980*, table 2.3, p. 38 (using table 1.4, p. 10, to correct a misprint in table 2.3's figure for total tax paid in the income range £6,000 to under £7,000).

(ii)　With reference to the data in Appendix 9.3, calculate for 1981–2 the 'marginal' rate of income tax as one goes from three-quarters of average earnings to average earnings, and from average earnings to one-and-one-half of average earnings (exclude National Insurance contributions in these calculations). Explain why you get these answers – see Table 3.4 note (c)! 'The average rate rises if the marginal rate is above the average rate.' Is this true?

(iii)　With reference to Appendix 9.3, how has the relative incidence of over-all taxation on the three household types (i.e. ¾ of average earnings, average earnings, and 1½ times average earnings) changed proportionately over the period 1978–9 to 1981–2? Are you surprised by your answer?

(iv)　With reference to Appendix 9.3 and your answer to (iii), to what extent have these three households incurred proportionate increases in the relative incidence of (a) income taxes including National Insurance contributions, and (b) all other (expenditure) taxes? Comment on your answers.

9.13　*(To develop your understanding of VAT in particular and the problems of taxation in general.)*

(i)　Explain, with illustrative data, the following statement:

VAT is the only major tax in the UK for which inflation poses no problems (J. A. Kay and M. A. King, *The British Tax System*, 2nd edn, Oxford University Press, 1980, p. 135).

(ii)　What problems does inflation pose for income taxation and capital taxation in a system of progressive taxation? (Reading: J. E. Meade, *The Structure and Reform of Direct Taxation*, Allen & Unwin, 1978, ch. 6 'Indexation for inflation'; *Inflation Accounting*, Report of the Inflation Accounting Committee, Cmnd 6225, Chairman F. E. P. Sandilands, HMSO, September 1975, ch. 15 'Implications for taxation'.)

9.14　*(To provide background knowledge of the National Insurance system.)*

(i)　Calculate, and graph, the percentage contribution made by National Insurance (etc.) contributions to central government total receipts on current account over the period covered by the latest available *National Income and Expenditure* accounts. Comment on your findings.

(ii) To what extent has the central government had, through grants, to supplement the receipts of the National Insurance Fund from employers and insured persons? Comment on the trend.

9.15 *(To provide background knowledge of capital taxes.)* In some of the (relevant) boxes of Diagram 9.7 insert the figures for the latest available year (treat 'death duties' and 'taxes on other capital transfers' as Capital Transfer Tax).

9.16 *(Further to see the working of local authorities.)*

(i) Describe the structure of current grants from central government to local authorities which are allocated to specific services (use data for the latest available year).
(ii) Describe the structure of local authority expenditure on current account (ditto).
(iii) Describe the structure of local authority expenditure on capital account (ditto).

9.17 *(Further workings of local authorities.)* 'Rent' is an important item of local authority receipts on current account. With reference to the 'Housing: operating account' in the *National Income and Expenditure* accounts, explain what 'rent' comprises.

9.18 *(This is a most important exercise if you are to understand the public sector borrowing requirement properly.)*

(i) Update Table 9.16.
(ii) Using your updated table, express the general government financial balance as:

Total of receipts on current and on capital account *minus* Total of expenditure on current and on capital account

9.19 *(To see something interesting.)*

(i) Tabulate, and graph, the general government 'saving' over the period given in the latest *National Income and Expenditure* accounts.

(ii) Comment, but not too acidly, on your findings.

9.20 *(To practise your understanding of the general government borrowing requirement, and to put the United Kingdom into an international perspective.)*

(i) Explain, with data, how one gets from the general government financial balance to the general government borrowing requirement.
(ii) Calculate the United Kingdom's general government borrowing requirement as a percentage of total expenditure plus net lending (including the accruals adjustment and miscellaneous financial transactions) for the latest available year.
(iii) What does Table 9.21 show about the UK central government's borrowing requirement in relation to other countries with regard to the period 1973 to 1978?

TABLE 9.21   *Central government borrowing requirement as a percentage of central government total expenditure plus net lending, seventeen countries, 1973 and 1978*

Country (listed in order of 1973 borrowing)	Per cent [a]	
	1973	1978
Italy	25.6	32.5
Ireland	17.9	24.9
United Kingdom	9.8	12.8
Belgium	8.7	14.9
New Zealand	7.9	21.0
Australia	7.1	12.2
USA	6.3	12.8
Canada	5.9 [b]	22.3
Austria	5.6	10.8
Sweden	4.3	11.3
Norway	2.3	14.9
Spain	1.2	9.0
Netherlands	0.1	6.0
France	−1.3	3.1
Switzerland	−2.8	0.4
West Germany	−5.4	7.0
Luxembourg	−8.4	−7.2

[a] Borrowing requirement (financial deficit) given with a + sign; minus sign indicates a lending requirement (financial surplus); this reverses the sign conventions used in the source.

[b] 1974 (data not available for 1973).

Source: International Monetary Fund, *Government Finance Statistics Yearbook*, vol. V, 1981, p. 24.

APPENDIX 9.1   *UK general government expenditure in relation to the gross domestic product, 1870 to 1980*

	£ million, current prices				Percentage of GDP		
	General government				General government		
Year	Current expenditure on goods and services	Gross domestic fixed capital formation	Total expenditure	Gross domestic product at market prices	Current expenditure on goods and services	Gross domestic fixed capital formation	Total expenditure
1870	55	6.5	61.5	1,120	4.9	0.6	5.5
1871	56	6.5	62.5	1,220	4.6	0.5	5.1
1872	57	7.5	64.5	1,278	4.5	0.6	5.1
1873	55	9.5	64.5	1,313	4.2	0.7	4.9
1874	58	12.5	70.5	1,348	4.3	0.9	5.2
1875	60	11.5	71.5	1,313	4.6	0.9	5.4
1876	61	13.5	74.5	1,300	4.7	1.0	5.7
1877	62	16.5	78.5	1,280	4.8	1.3	6.1
1878	64	17.5	81.5	1,268	5.0	1.4	6.4
1879	69	15.5	84.5	1,187	5.8	1.3	7.1
1880	70	15.5	85.5	1,330	5.3	1.2	6.4
1881	71	13.5	84.5	1,303	5.4	1.0	6.5
1882	74	11.5	85.5	1,342	5.5	0.9	6.4
1883	76	11.5	87.5	1,386	5.5	0.8	6.3
1884	76	13.5	89.5	1,336	5.7	1.0	6.7
1885	83	12.5	95.5	1,294	6.4	1.0	7.4
1886	80	11.5	91.5	1,285	6.2	0.9	7.1
1887	78	12.5	90.5	1,349	5.8	0.9	6.7
1888	78	9.5	87.5	1,367	5.7	0.7	6.4
1889	80	9.5	89.5	1,412	5.7	0.7	6.3
1890	85	10.0	95.0	1,456	5.8	0.7	6.5
1891	87	14.0	101.0	1,500	5.8	0.9	6.7
1892	87	14.0	101.0	1,472	5.9	1.0	6.9
1893	89	18.0	107.0	1,455	6.1	1.2	7.4
1894	91	17.0	108.0	1,513	6.0	1.1	7.1
1895	97	17.0	114.0	1,543	6.3	1.1	7.4
1896	102	18.5	120.5	1,611	6.3	1.1	7.5
1897	106	21.0	127.0	1,633	6.5	1.3	7.8
1898	112	26.0	138.0	1,734	6.5	1.5	8.0
1899	136	30.0	166.0	1,860	7.3	1.6	8.9
1900	182	34.5	216.5	1,950	9.3	1.8	11.1
1901	202	41.0	243.0	2,019	10.0	2.0	12.0
1902	190	43.0	233.0	2,001	9.5	2.1	11.6
1903	169	38.0	207.0	1,997	8.5	1.9	10.4
1904	163	38.0	201.0	2,015	8.1	1.9	10.0
1905	163	33.0	196.0	2,059	7.9	1.6	9.5
1906	163	29.0	192.0	2,114	7.7	1.4	9.1
1907	163	26.5	189.5	2,156	7.6	1.2	8.8
1908	167	24.5	191.5	2,079	8.0	1.2	9.2
1909	173	24.0	197.0	2,143	8.1	1.1	9.2
1910	182	24.0	206.0	2,233	8.2	1.1	9.2
1911	188	23.0	211.0	2,316	8.1	1.0	9.1
1912	196	24.5	220.5	2,378	8.2	1.0	9.3
1913	203	30.0	233.0	2,517	8.1	1.2	9.3
1914	324	30.0	354.0	2,553	12.7	1.2	13.9
1915	1,045	17.0	1,062.0	3,139	33.3	0.5	33.8
1916	1,332	9.0	1,341.0	3,588	37.1	0.3	37.4
1917	1,685	6.0	1,691.0	4,537	37.1	0.1	37.3
1918	1,842	8.0	1,850.0	5,243	35.1	0.2	35.3
1919	935	33.0	968.0	5,586	16.7	0.6	17.3
1920 [a]	520	—	—	6,230	8.3	—	—
1920	488	103	591	5,982	8.2	1.7	9.9
1921	489	159	648	5,134	9.5	3.1	12.6
1922	435	120	555	4,579	9.5	2.6	12.1
1923	395	88	483	4,385	9.0	2.0	11.0
1924	398	97	495	4,419	9.0	2.2	11.2
1925	412	122	534	4,644	8.9	2.6	11.5
1926	420	137	557	4,396	9.6	3.1	12.7
1927	423	143	566	4,613	9.2	3.1	12.3

APPENDIX 9.1 *continued*

| | £ million, current prices | | | | Percentage of GDP | | |
| | General government | | | | General government | | |
Year	Current expenditure on goods and services	Gross domestic fixed capital formation	Total expenditure	Gross domestic product at market prices	Current expenditure on goods and services	Gross domestic fixed capital formation	Total expenditure
1928	425	125	550	4,659	9.1	2.7	11.8
1929	435	121	556	4,727	9.2	2.6	11.8
1930	443	126	569	4,685	9.5	2.7	12.1
1931	443	132	575	4,359	10.2	3.0	13.2
1932	431	107	538	4,276	10.1	2.5	12.6
1933	430	84	514	4,259	10.1	2.0	12.1
1934	446	89	535	4,513	9.9	2.0	11.9
1935	483	108	591	4,721	10.2	2.3	12.5
1936	536	132	668	4,905	10.9	2.7	13.6
1937	617	165	782	5,289	11.7	3.1	14.8
1938	749	188	937	5,572	13.4	3.4	16.8
1939	1,179	—	—	5,958	19.8	—	—
1940	2,952	—	—	7,521	39.3	—	—
1941	4,097	—	—	8,831	46.4	—	—
1942	4,581	—	—	9,591	47.8	—	—
1943	4,983	—	—	10,208	48.8	—	—
1944	5,056	—	—	10,272	49.2	—	—
1945	4,190	—	—	9,831	42.6	—	—
1946	2,348	—	—	10,009	23.5	—	—
1947	1,810	—	—	10,704	16.9	—	—
1948	1,836	485	2,321	11,751	15.6	4.1	19.8
1949	2,061	497	2,558	12,412	16.6	4.0	20.6
1950	2,149	532	2,681	12,970	16.6	4.1	20.7
1951	2,522	630	3,152	14,473	17.4	4.4	21.8
1952	2,999	754	3,753	15,701	19.1	4.8	23.9
1953	3,136	825	3,961	16,910	18.5	4.9	23.4
1954	3,213	759	3,972	17,831	18.0	4.3	22.3
1955	3,273	755	4,028	19,196	17.1	3.9	21.0
1956	3,531	788	4,319	20,754	17.0	3.8	20.8
1957	3,681	814	4,495	21,947	16.8	3.7	20.5
1958	3,751	789	4,540	22,864	16.4	3.5	19.9
1959	3,988	834	4,822	24,071	16.6	3.4	20.0
1960	4,224	860	5,084	25,522	16.6	3.4	19.9
1961	4,557	921	5,478	27,262	16.7	3.4	20.1
1962	4,882	1,030	5,912	28,555	17.1	3.6	20.7
1963	5,138	1,110	6,248	30,371	16.9	3.7	20.6
1964	5,466	1,396	6,862	33,131	16.5	4.2	20.7
1965	5,994	1,486	7,480	35,607	16.8	4.2	21.0
1966	6,520	1,680	8,200	37,992	17.2	4.4	21.6
1967	7,213	1,964	9,177	40,131	18.0	4.9	22.9
1968	7,662	2,169	9,831	43,490	17.6	5.0	22.6
1969	7,997	2,244	10,241	46,573	17.2	4.8	22.0
1970	8,991	2,431	11,422	51,107	17.6	4.8	22.3
1971	10,250	2,562	12,812	57,339	17.9	4.5	22.3
1972	11,675	2,732	14,407	63,461	18.4	4.3	22.7
1973	13,380	3,661	17,041	73,025	18.3	5.0	23.3
1974	16,618	4,376	20,994	83,114	20.0	5.3	25.3
1975	23,039	4,984	28,023	104,907	22.0	4.8	26.7
1976	26,776	5,410	32,186	124,656	21.5	4.3	25.8
1977	29,237	4,815	34,052	143,911	20.3	3.3	23.7
1978	32,969	4,622	37,591	164,901	20.0	2.8	22.8
1979	38,241	5,004	43,245	192,329	19.9	2.6	22.5
1980	48,337	5,500	53,837	225,560	21.4	2.4	23.9

[a] From 1870 to the first 1920 Southern Ireland (Eire) is included; thereafter it is excluded.

Sources: 1870 to 1945, C. H. Feinstein, *National Income, Expenditure and Output of the United Kingdom 1855–1965*, tables 2, 3, and 39, pp. T8–11, T85–86; 1946 to 1969, Central Statistical Office, *Economic Trends Annual Supplement 1981 Edition*, pp. 9 and 48; 1970 to 1980, Central Statistical Office, *National Income and Expenditure 1981 Edition*, tables 1.1 and 10.1, pp. 3 and 69.

APPENDIX 9.2   *UK general government total outgoings* [a] *in relation to the gross national product, 1900 to 1980*

Year	£ million Total general government outgoings	Gross national product at factor cost	General government outgoings as percentage of GNP at factor cost	Year	£ million Total general government outgoings	Gross national product at factor cost	General government outgoings as percentage of GNP at factor cost
1900	259.5	1,926	13.5	1941	5,223	7,921	65.9
1901	290.0	1,989	14.6	1942	5,765	8,540	67.5
1902	286.0	1,964	14.6	1943	6,246	9,080	68.8
1903	257.0	1,963	13.1	1944	6,334	9,140	69.3
1904	247.0	1,977	12.5	1945	5,735	8,754	65.5
1905	243.0	2,030	12.0	1946	4,531	8,855	51.2
1906	239.0	2,095	11.4	1946 [c]	4,584	8,908	51.5
1907	235.5	2,145	11.0	1947	4,330	9,511	45.5
1908	237.5	2,080	11.4	1948	4,381	10,549	41.5
1909	252.0	2,150	11.7	1949	4,459	11,168	39.9
1910	262.0	2,239	11.7	1950	4,522	11,782	38.4
1911	269.0	2,326	11.6	1951	5,371	13,021	41.2
1912	282.5	2,393	11.8	1952	5,962	14,088	42.3
1913	300.0	2,542	11.8	1953	6,172	15,147	40.7
1914	434.0	2,572	16.9	1954	6,145	16,011	38.4
1915	1,173.0	3,096	37.9	1955	6,466	17,079	37.9
1916	1,515.0	3,566	42.5	1956	7,041	18,530	38.0
1917	1,962.0	4,533	43.3	1957	7,633	19,653	38.8
1918	2,287.0	5,237	43.7	1958	7,971	20,520	38.8
1919	1,591.0	5,468	29.1	1959	8,449	21,520	39.3
1920	—	6,098	—	1960	8,832	22,870	38.6
1920 [b]	1,209	5,858	20.6	1961	9,743	24,482	39.8
1921	1,312	4,910	26.7	1962	10,387	25,618	40.5
1922	1,162	4,317	26.9	1963	10,970	27,311	40.2
1923	1,047	4,107	25.5	1964	12,004	29,604	40.5
1924	1,046	4,185	25.0	1965	13,326	31,654	42.1
1925	1,106	4,447	24.9	1966	14,467	33,518	43.2
1926	1,170	4,184	28.0	1967	16,691	35,313	47.3
1927	1,141	4,373	26.1	1968	18,311	37,910	48.3
1928	1,136	4,406	25.8	1969	19,008	40,131	47.4
1929	1,158	4,494	25.8	1970	20,896	44,128	47.4
1930	1,190	4,443	26.8	1971	23,483	49,992	47.0
1931	1,217	4,063	30.0	1972	26,357	55,885	47.2
1932	1,180	3,913	30.2	1973	30,544	65,604	46.6
1933	1,117	3,927	28.4	1974	39,167	76,076	51.5
1934	1,117	4,173	26.8	1975	51,561	95,248	54.1
1935	1,184	4,380	27.0	1976	58,438	112,950	51.7
1936	1,247	4,543	27.4	1977	61,816	127,047	48.7
1937	1,360	4,912	27.7	1978	71,848	145,896	49.2
1938	1,593	5,177	30.8	1979	84,818	167,310	50.7
1939	2,006	5,478	36.6	1980	103,539	193,450	53.5
1940	3,808	6,878	55.4				

[a] Expenditure and transfers on current and capital account and (from the second 1920 onwards) net lending to other sectors; figures for 1940 to 1946 include payments in respect of war-damage claims (transfers to private capital accounts). Figures for 1970 to 1980 (inclusive) exclude central government stock appreciation (previously negligible or not calculated).
[b] This and all following figures exclude the Republic of Ireland (Southern Ireland); previously included.
[c] Start of CSO (consistent) series: but matches closely with other series for 1946.

Sources: 1900 to 1946: C. H. Feinstein, *National Income, Expenditure and Output of the United Kingdom 1855–1965*, tables 2, 14, 34, 36, and 39, pp. T8–T9, T35–T36, T79, T81, and T85–T86; HM Treasury, *National Income and Expenditure of the United Kingdom 1938 to 1946*, Cmd 7099, April 1947, tables 19, 20 and 23, pp. 33, 35 and 37; 1946 [c] to 1969, Central Statistical Office, *Economic Trends Annual Supplement 1981 Edition*, pp. 38 and 151; 1970 to 1980, Central Statistical Office, *National Income and Expenditure 1981 Edition*, tables 1.1, 9.1 and 12.4, pp. 3, 59 and 89.

APPENDIX 9.3   *Income taxes, National Insurance contributions, and expenditure taxes for a household of a man (employed), wife (not working) and two (dependent) children, 1978–9 to 1981–2*

	£ per week			
	1978–9	1979–80	1980–1	1981–2
Earnings ($\frac{3}{4}$ × *average*)	70.82	83.39	100.24	111.56
Income tax	11.20	13.82	17.69	21.09
National Insurance contributions	4.60	5.42	6.78	8.65
Value Added Tax	2.02	3.85	4.65	5.31
Other central government indirect taxes	9.01	10.13	11.65	13.99
Rates	2.91	3.33	4.35	5.51
Total taxes	29.74	36.55	45.12	54.55
Earnings (*average earnings*)	94.42	111.18	133.65	148.75
Income tax	18.99	22.16	27.72	32.25
National Insurance contributions	6.14	7.23	9.02	11.53
Value Added Tax	2.75	5.26	6.39	7.33
Other central government indirect taxes	10.41	11.84	13.68	16.44
Rates	3.07	3.52	4.60	5.82
Total taxes	41.36	50.01	61.41	73.37
Earnings ($1\frac{1}{2}$ × *average*)	141.63	166.77	200.48	223.13
Income tax	34.57	38.84	47.76	54.56
National Insurance contributions	7.80	8.78	11.14	15.50
Value Added Tax	4.28	8.24	10.06	11.55
Other central government indirect taxes	13.36	15.46	17.97	21.51
Rates	3.40	3.92	5.14	6.48
Total taxes	63.41	75.24	92.07	109.60

Source: House of Commons Parliamentary Debates, *Weekly Hansard*, issue no. 1224, 27 November to 3 December 1981, 'Written answers to questions', Thursday, 3 December 1981, cols 188–92.

Chapter 10

Public Corporations

Contents

Chapter guide

Chapter 10 describes the *public corporations* in the UK economy and analyses the basic problems of economic policy towards the *nationalised industries* (which form the greater part of the sector of public corporations).

Following some data on the size of the public corporations relative to the whole economy and a brief account of their historical origins, we look at a classification of all the public corporations so as to get a full and accurate picture of the entities which make up this sector.

In the *National Income and Expenditure* accounts, the sector of public corporations is uniquely distinguished by having an *operating account*, which shows how this sector's value added is produced, so we seize the opportunity to show the whole sequence of accounts from beginning to end, to look at the details of an operating account, and to explain some technicalities relating to the calculation of value added such as *sales to own capital account*.

We then look, in turn, at data from the public corporations' *appropriation account*, *capital account*, and *financial account*, and we can then see how all the accounts connect, especially with regard to the final outcome: namely, the public corporations' *financial deficit* (which contributes to the public sector borrowing requirement).

This raises the question of the *economic performance* of the public corporations, and we look at some measures of, and data on, *indicators of performance*: namely, the share of trading surplus in value added; the rate of profitability; trends in 'real' (inflation-adjusted) labour productivity as measured by value added per employee; and unit labour costs. The adjustment for inflation requires us to explain the *implied GDP price deflator* – how it is calculated and how it may be used.

We then analyse the main problems of *economic policy* towards the public corporations as expressed in various *White Papers* on the nationalised industries, and we show the relationship between prices charged by nationalised industries and their ability (or inability) to finance investment out of retentions.

Introduction

The state-owned public corporations are an important part of the UK economy. Table 10.1 shows that in 1980 they produced 10.9 per cent of UK gross domestic product, undertook 17.1 per cent of the investment in fixed capital, owned 17.2 per cent of the net capital stock (valued at current replacement cost), and employed 8.2 per cent of the working population – employing just over 2 million people: one in twelve of the employed labour force works for a public corporation. What, then, are the public corporations?

TABLE 10.1   *Public corporations in the UK economy, 1980*

	£ million [a]		Public corporations as percentage of United Kingdom
	Public corporations	United Kingdom	
Gross domestic product (value added)	21,174	193,488	10.9
Gross fixed capital formation	6,846	40,050	17.1
Net capital stock (end-year)	127,900	743,000	17.2
Employed labour force [b] *thousands*	*2,036*	*24,720*	*8.2*

[a] Except for employment (italicised).
[b] Including, for the United Kingdom, self-employed and HM Forces.

Source: Central Statistical Office, *National Income and Expenditure 1981 Edition*, tables 1.10, 1.12, 10.3 and 11.11, pp. 13, 15, 71 and 83.

The nationalised industries are all public corporations, but the sector of public corporations includes bodies other than the nationalised industries. 'Nationalised industries' is, in fact, rather a vague term and 'public corporations' is the precise, and therefore preferable, term; but we shall use the term 'the major nationalised industries' to refer to the fifteen major organisations in this sector.

A public corporation – and note the difference between a ('state-owned') public *corporation* and a ('privately owned') public *company* – is basically a financially independent but publicly controlled trading body. A public corporation is thus distinguished from other types of trading body by two main characteristics:

1. It is publicly controlled to the extent that a Minister of the Crown appoints (and may dismiss) the whole or the majority of the board of management.
2. It is a corporate body free to manage its affairs without *detailed* control by Parliament or the government; in particular its financial independence includes the power to borrow, within limits laid down by Parliament, and to maintain its own financial reserves.

Nevertheless, the government does impose certain requirements of general policy upon the public corporations, as we shall see. Statutorily, the responsible Minister may issue general directions as to how a public corporation should be run.

It is a fairly complex matter to classify and list all of them, but Diagram 10.1 presents a classification based on the distinction among public corporations between 'nationalised

DIAGRAM 10.1   *Public corporations in the United Kingdom, 31 December 1980*

Public corporations: financially independent but publicly controlled trading bodies				
'Nationalised industries'			Other public corporations	
Public utilities: 'essential service monopolies'	Transport and communications: 'near monopolies'	Manufacturing or extractive industries: 'basic supply or technology'	Quasi-financial and development institutions	Cultural activities
*British Gas Corporation and Area Gas Boards *Central Electricity Generating Board and all Area Electricity Boards, etc. Electricity Council National Water Council, Regional Water Authorities	*British Rail *National Bus Company *National Freight Corporation Passenger Transport Executives Northern Ireland Transport Holding Co. *Scottish Transport Group National Ports Council *British Transport Docks Board National Dock Labour Board Trust Ports *British Waterways Board *British Airways Board British Airports Authority Civil Aviation Authority *Post Office[b] Cable & Wireless Ltd	*National Coal Board *British Steel Corporation *British Shipbuilders *British Aerospace *British National Oil Corporation Royal Ordnance Factories[d] Royal Mint[d] Property Services Agency (Supplies)[d] HM Stationery Office	Bank of England[a][b] National Enterprise Board[c] Commonwealth Development Corporation Scottish Development Agency Northern Ireland Development Agency Welsh Development Agency Development Board for Rural Wales Land Authority for Wales New Town Development Corporations Housing Corporation Northern Ireland Housing Executive Scottish Special Housing Association Covent Garden Market Authority National Film Finance Corporation National Research Development Corpn Crown Agents Highlands and Islands Development Board	British Broadcasting Corporation Independent Broadcasting Authority

*Officially designated 'nationalised industry'.

[a] Excluding the Issue Department included in the central government sector.

[b] In the financial accounts the Banking Department of the Bank of England and the Post Office Giro (the National Girobank) are treated as part of the banking sector; but in the appropriation and capital accounts they are included in public corporations.

[c] Subsidiary companies of the NEB (e.g. British Leyland) treated as part of the company sector.

[d] Central government trading funds treated for statistical purposes as if they were public corporations.

Sources: Central Statistical Office, *Financial Statistics Explanatory Handbook 1981 Edition*, p. 54; HM Treasury/Central Statistical Office, *Guide to Public Sector Financial Information*, No. 1, 1979, pp. 107–8; Central Statistical Office, *National Income and Expenditure 1981 Edition*, p. 119.

Origins of the independent public corporation

From an economic point of view, the public corporation is an important twentieth-century innovation, permitting government 'intervention' in some or other sphere of economic activity while still trying to maintain a 'normal' commercial pattern of operations, including especially the making of profits; however, as the word 'profit' is normally reserved for privately owned companies, it is officially taken to be an inappropriate word to apply to a public corporation and the term 'trading surplus' is officially used instead.

The need to ensure commercial independence and flexibility for the public corporations was recognised as early as 1931 by Clement Attlee, who had been Postmaster General in the second Labour government in 1931 (the Post Office then being part of the Civil Service) and who expressed the opinion that control by the Treasury hampered the efficient running of the Post Office. The political problem of government control was, of course, critical in relation to radio broadcasting when it developed in the 1920s and so one of the first public corporations to be established was the British Broadcasting Corpo-ration, created by Royal Charter in 1927. The claim to being the first public corporation should probably go to the Port of London Authority, established in 1908 by the Port of London Act 1908; and in 1919 the Electricity Supply Commission and the Forestry Commission were established, also by Act of Parliament – however, the Forestry Commission's activities are now treated as part of central government trading activities.

Most of the United Kingdom's public corporations were established by the postwar Labour government when the 'major' nationalised industry public corporations were created: coalmining in 1947; electricity in 1948 (although the Central Electricity Generating Board had been established in 1926 to construct and operate a nation-wide system of interconnected generating stations known as the 'national grid'); gas in 1949; and iron and steel in 1951 (subsequently denationalised in 1953 and renationalised in 1967). In addition to these major nationalised industry public corporations, a large number of other corporations have been established at one time or another.

industries' and other public corporations. Within the nationalised industries, we may distinguish the main sorts of undertakings based on the service provided and the approximate (economic) reason for having a degree of public control over such undertakings.

First, we may distinguish the public utilities, which provide the 'essential services' of gas, electricity and water, and in the provision of which there is a strong case for having one (monopoly) supplier, to avoid 'wasteful' duplication of fixed capital – such as two gas or water mains running along the same street. In the nineteenth century, gas and water were supplied either by municipally owned undertakings or by municipally regulated but privately financed and owned companies, and where the latter competed for customers the waste in double or treble sets of mains and the inconvenience of having roads and pavements dug up separately for repairs and maintenance soon became apparent and led to the emergence of 'natural monopolies' often through outright amalgamations or more discreet agreements between companies. In the case of water supplies, there was always the additional argument that the provision of an ample supply of pure drinking and washing water was too important to be dictated by the need of a private company to make profits. So, today in the United Kingdom, gas, electricity and most water (there are still some private water companies) are supplied by public corporations, and this tends to be the case in most other countries.

Second, there are the 'near monopolies' in transport and communications. Here there is also a case for monopoly: to duplicate railway lines and its equipment or canals or telephone lines or a postal distribution service would be wasteful; but there are areas, such as road or air transport, where competition is possible and is therefore permitted. So the

United Kingdom has the major nationalised industries of British Rail, British Airways and the Post Office (which became a public corporation in April 1961 having previously been a department of central government). In the United Kingdom nearly all the major seaports and airports are in public ownership, and it is obviously essential to have one organisation, vested with considerable powers, to control the movement of civil aircraft – this is the Civil Aviation Authority.

It is reasonable to say that there is no great political controversy over the existence of these two types of public corporations, but the third type of nationalised industry public corporation does generate more disagreement. These are the public corporations concerned either with the extraction of natural resources or with manufacturing. The economic arguments for having public corporations operate in these areas are at least more arguable, but these industries are in many ways 'basic' to the economy or, in the case of aerospace, are concerned with advanced (and expensive) technology which is closely connected with defence; there are five of the fifteen major nationalised industries in this category, all with large numbers of employees and a considerable annual turnover.

Next we come to those other public corporations not normally considered as falling under the heading of 'nationalised industry'. Most of these are quasi-financial or development organisations: that is, much of their activity is concerned with the provision of finance or being directly responsible for some other type of development. The Bank of England was nationalised in 1946, but before that it had acted in very much the same way as the government's banker, and we shall subsequently consider its role more fully.

Finally, we come to two different types of public corporation: the BBC, which obtains its main income from licence fees and broadcasts on radio and television, pretty well independent of the government; and the regulatory commission, the Independent Broadcasting Authority, whose task it is to supervise and license the independent television companies and the commercial radio companies and to own and provide the broadcasting transmitters for the television companies to use under hiring arrangements.

We have now considered, rather briefly, the composition of the sector of public corporations and we can now look at the accounts for this sector with at least a background knowledge of the organisations concerned.

Further reading

A full historical survey of public corporations may be obtained from William Robson, *Nationalized Industry and Public Ownership*, rev edn (Allen & Unwin, 1962); an analysis of the recent performance of the main public corporations is given by Richard Pryke, *The Nationalised Industries: Policies and Performance since 1968* (Martin Robertson, 1981); with a comprehensive survey of the period up to 1968 in Richard Pryke, *Public Enterprise in Practice: The British Experience of Nationalization over Two Decades* (MacGibbon & Kee, 1971); and there is a useful collection of various important documents in Leonard Tivey (ed.), *The Nationalized Industries Since 1960: A Book of Readings* (Allen & Unwin, 1973).

The accounts of the public corporations

The accounts of the public corporations are especially interesting because the Blue Book presents their operating account in addition to their appropriation and capital accounts, so this is one sector for which we can trace the complete cycle of accounts as shown in Diagram 2.5. The sequence of accounts through which we shall go is shown in Diagram 10.2 (note that Diagram 10.2 is is not drawn to scale, nor is it in proportion).

DIAGRAM 10.2 *The sequence of accounts which give the public corporations' financial deficit and borrowing requirement*

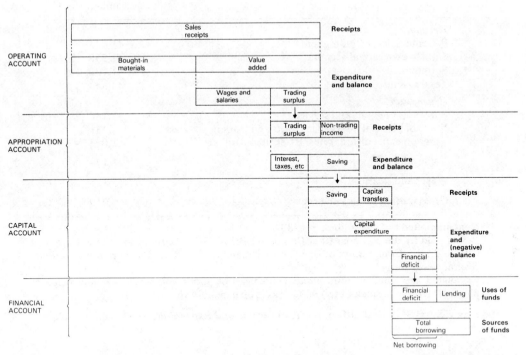

We start with the operating account, which shows how the public corporations derived their gross trading surplus – the balance on the operating account. The trading surplus is transferred to the appropriation account, there to be joined by (a small amount of) non-trading income; part of this combined income is appropriated for interest payment on loans and for taxes on income, and the balance, saving, is transferred to the capital account as a receipt. There it is joined by capital transfers. However, capital expenditure – mostly on fixed capital formation – tends each year to be considerably greater than total receipts on capital account (this is shown in Diagram 10.2 by the greater length of the bar representing capital-account expenditure), so the difference between income and expenditure, the financial balance (which in this case is a financial deficit), creates a requirement to borrow money. We can transfer the financial deficit to the financial account as a 'use of funds' or requirement for finance; and there it is joined by the (relatively small amount of) lending (financial asset acquisition) which the public corporations do (mainly in the form of trade credit to their customers). Together the financial deficit and the lending make up a total uses of funds, and all of this has to be financed by borrowing, mostly, as we shall see, from the central government. Diagram 10.2 is thus a guide to the set of accounts which follow.

The operating account

First, let us look at the operating, or production, account (Table 10.2), which shows how the sector derived its 'profits' – called the 'surplus' in the case of public corporations. As we have noted, the public corporations derive their income by producing and selling goods and services to customers (including other public corporations). In the case of the BBC 'sales revenue' derives from the 'sale' or issuing of broadcast receiving licences and the IBA's income comes from 'rentals' or charges for the use of its transmitting stations. These sales to customers are known as revenue sales, but because the accounts include, on the

TABLE 10.2   *Operating account of public corporations, 1980*

	£ million
Revenue	
Revenue sales, including rent [a]	41,047
Sales to own capital account	1,558
Subsidies	1,739
Total revenue	44,344
Expenditure	
Purchases of goods and services	22,168
Value of physical increase in stocks and work in progress	31
Taxes on expenditure: rates, ECSC levies, others [b]	1,033
Value added [c]	21,174
Wages and salaries	15,155
Gross trading surplus and rent	6,019

[a] Rent amounted to £397 million in 1980.

[b] Levies paid by the National Coal Board and British Steel Corporation to the European Coal and Steel Community; other taxes on expenditure includes the employers' National Insurance surcharge.

[c] Calculated as: Total revenue *minus* (Purchases of goods and services *minus* Value of physical increase in stocks, etc.) *minus* Taxes on expenditure.

Source: Central Statistical Office, *National Income and Expenditure 1981 Edition*, table 6.1, p. 45.

expenditure side, the costs of repairs and maintenance on property owned and let by the public corporations (which it is not possible to separate from other costs) the rents obtained from such property-letting are included with revenue sales; in any event, the New Town Corporations (to whom rents mostly relate) are largely in business to provide property (new towns) for rent.

The public corporations also make and 'sell' to themselves considerable amounts of capital equipment. For example, much of British Rail's rolling stock is built by British Rail's wholly owned subsidiary, British Rail Engineering Ltd, which also produces railway wagons for export to other countries. These 'internal' sales are valued at their cost price (cost of materials and wages) and, of course, they must be included in the calculation of value added.

In the public corporations' operating account, total revenue in 1980 included £1,558 million of 'sales' to own capital account (which amount, of course, is also subsequently included as 'expenditure' in the capital account).

During 1980 the public corporations also received subsidies (mostly from central government but local authorities also grant subsidies to their passenger transport executives) in the main given to help the public corporations keep their prices down (that is, subsidies came to be extensively used as an 'anti-inflationary' measure). Now, the revenue from subsidies should be included in 'sales' revenue, because, or so the public corporations would argue, if they were not receiving this subvention from the taxpayer they would have raised their prices in order to obtain the same amount from their customers. In this argument it is presumed that the volume of goods and services provided would have remained the same, only the method of paying for it would have altered. Now, while a part of this argument is suspect (at higher prices a lower volume would probably have been purchased), in general terms the argument is sound and the value-added figure needs to be calculated with subsidies included – the taxpayer must be regarded as 'obtaining' (indirectly) a good or a service in return for the subsidy and the value-added measure of output would be misleadingly low were subsidies to be excluded from 'sales receipts'.

Sales to own capital account

It is worth digressing on own sales for a paragraph, because many enterprises do make their own capital equipment using bought-in materials and their own employees' working time. In this case the cost of the equipment so acquired must, if the capital account is to have any meaning, be shown on the expenditure side of the capital account (and, of course, the value of the equipment must go into the balance-sheet). However, this entails that the cost price of the equipment must be entered into 'sales receipts' so that the operating, appropriation and financial accounts come out as they should. For example, suppose we have an enterprise (see Table 10.3) which sells £100-worth of metal-working lathes to outside customers, buys in £60 of materials and pays its employees £30; at the end of the year this enterprise will have a financial surplus of £10 (assuming no taxes, interest or dividends). But suppose that this enterprise uses part of its £60-worth of materials and £30 of employees' time to produce one lathe for its own use, valued (at the cost of materials and labour-time) at £10; and suppose that, as in the first column of Table 10.3, it does not enter this £10 lathe as a 'sale to own capital account'. Then, if its financial surplus figure is to be correct (and there will be this rise in its bank deposit), the enterprise must report a zero under capital expenditure, and, indeed, it will not have signed a cheque to any outside supplier for this lathe.

However, the zero under capital expenditure is misleading because the enterprise has acquired during the year not only financial assets of £10 but also a fixed capital asset – the lathe – worth £10, and both need to be shown in the balance-sheet if this is to present 'a true and fair view' of the enterprise's position (and an auditor will be required to certify that the balance-sheet presents such a view). Suppose that when this misleading omission under capital expenditure is pointed out, the enterprise amends the accounts by putting the £10 capital expenditure into the accounts as shown in the second column. The immediate consequence of this is that the financial surplus appears to be zero; and this is quite wrong because the enterprise will have the extra money in the bank. The way to put this problem right is to report, in total sales receipts (third column), a figure of £10 for sales to own capital account (even though no money is actually received for the 'sale' of this lathe). The enterprise's total sales of lathes are now reported as £110, its value added becomes £50, its profits are £20, against which capital expenditure of £10 is charged (even though no money is paid outside the enterprise) and its reported financial surplus is right.

Furthermore, we may note that these last value-added and profits figures are more economically meaningful than those in the preceding columns. Suppose that the enterprise

TABLE 10.3 *An example to show why own capital formation must be included in total sales*

	£		
	Wrong		**Right**
	Financial surplus right; capital expenditure misleading	Capital expenditure right; financial surplus wrong	Capital expenditure right; financial surplus right
Sales to outside customers	100	100	100
Sales to own capital a/c	0	0	10
Total sales	100	100	110
Materials used	60	60	60
Value added	40	40	50
Wages	30	30	30
Profits	10	10	20
Capital expenditure	0	10	10
Financial surplus	10	0	10

had, at the last minute, changed its mind and sold the lathe to an outside customer. Then its sales receipts, value added and profits for the year would have been £110, £50 and £20 respectively; the lesson is that we must not allow an inessential feature (such as retaining one of its own lathes) to 'distort' the measurement of value added (as is done in the first two columns).

Total revenue of the public corporations in 1980 was thus £44,344 million; their purchases of goods (materials) and services (both from outside the sector and from other public corporations) amounted to £22,168 million. From this cost of bought-in materials and services must be subtracted any increase in the volume of inventories, because such increases do not represent a use (in the current production period) of materials and services. We must also deduct, from sales receipts, taxes on expenditure, these being treated as a kind of input. Total revenue *minus* total use of materials *minus* taxes on expenditure then gives the value added produced by the public corporations (this figure is not reported in the Blue Book's operating account but is given in table 1.10 of the Blue Book).

The other item of expenditure charged on operating account is wages and salaries. This leaves the balance on operating account known as the *gross trading surplus and rent*. This balance is then transferred to the appropriation account, so that if you look back at the first row of Table 4.2, the appropriation account of industrial and commercial companies, you can now better appreciate where the gross trading profits came from – in other words, how those profits arose – because behind that figure there will have been just such an operating account for companies as we have been considering for the public corporations.

TABLE 10.4   *Appropriation account of public corporations, 1980*

	£ million	Percentage of total income
Income		
Gross trading surplus (net of stock appreciation)	5,622	80.2
Rent	397	5.7
Gross trading surplus and rent [a]	6,019	85.8
Stock appreciation	393	5.6
Non-trading income	518	7.4
Income from abroad (net of taxes paid abroad)	82	1.2
Total income (including stock appreciation)	7,012	100.0
Allocation of income		
Interest payment to central government	1,908	27.2
Other interest payments, including additions to reserves (£40m.)	994	14.2
UK taxes on income, [b] including additions to reserves (£30m.)	82	1.2
Total allocation	2,984	42.6
Balance of income over allocations (saving): undistributed gross income including stock appreciation	4,028	57.4

[a] Balance transferred from operating account.
[b] From 1965–6 public corporations became subject to corporation tax.

Source: Central Statistical Office, *National Income and Expenditure 1981 Edition*, table 6.2, p. 45.

The appropriation account

To turn then to the public corporations' appropriation account in Table 10.4, the first items recorded are the gross trading surplus and rents – the balance from the operating account – but the Blue Book gives, at this stage, separate figures for trading profits and for rent. Added to the accounts at this stage is a figure for stock appreciation (because subsequently in the capital account expenditure is reported on the increase in the value of stocks). The public corporations have also a small amount of non-trading income, mostly from financial investments, and some income from abroad (net of taxes paid abroad), presumably mostly profits on the operations of the Commonwealth Development Corporation (formerly the Colonial Development Corporation established under the Overseas Resources Development Act 1948 to invest in projects for developing the resources of the colonial territories, particularly foodstuffs and raw materials, though nowadays the Commonwealth Development Corporation invests also in manufacturing industry and does not confine its investments to the Commonwealth).

Public corporations' total income on appropriation account in 1980 (including stock appreciation) was £7,012 million; they spent £1,908 million paying interest to central government, which provides them with most of their loan finance (see Table 9.5); a further £994 million on paying interest to other suppliers of finance; £82 million on corporation tax (to which public corporations, like public companies, are subject); making a total allocation of income of £2,984 million. This left public corporations with a flow of saving of £4,028 million to be transferred to their capital account.

The capital account and the financial account

Table 10.5 gives the figures for the capital account in 1980. To the transfer of the surplus from the appropriation account must be added some other receipts: grants for capital expenditure from central government (see Table 9.4); capital transfers from local authorities and from private consumers paying to be connected to public utility supplies (because ownership of the connections remains vested in the public corporations the consumers obtain no ownership of anything in return for their payment, which has therefore to be treated as a transfer; and the transfer is regarded as a capital-account receipt for the public corporations because it helps them pay for fixed capital formation – see Tables 3.5 and 4.7 and associated discussion there of this item).

In total, then, the public corporations received £4,695 million on capital account in 1980; and they spent £6,846 million, or 45.8 per cent more than they received, on fixed capital formation in the United Kingdom. They had also to 'pay' for a £424 million increase in the value of their stocks (remember that saving, and therefore capital-account receipts, include stock appreciation for which no money is actually received, so that here stock appreciation has to be deducted, as well as paying for any physical increase in stocks). Looking back at the figures in the appropriation and operating accounts, we can see that this increase in the value of stocks comprises £393 million of stock appreciation *plus* a £31 million increase in the volume of stocks. Public corporations also transferred £46 million to other sectors; this item comprises payment by the Scottish and Welsh Development Authorities to local authorities for capital works (see Table 9.15) and by the Highlands and Islands Development Board to the private sector. The total of expenditure on capital account was therefore £7,316 million; and as this exceeded capital-account receipts by 55.8 per cent, the public corporations had a corresponding financial deficit; or, as we should say, they had a negative net acquisition of financial assets of −£2,621 million in 1980. As we shall now see, public corporations had to borrow to cover not only this financial deficit, but also to cover further lending of £181 million (gross acquisition of

TABLE 10.5   *Capital account of public corporations, 1980*

	£ million	Percentage of total receipts
Receipts		
Undistributed gross income	4,028	85.8
Additions to interest, dividend and tax reserves [a]	70	1.5
Capital transfers from central government [b]	323	6.9
Capital transfers from local authorities	140	3.0
Capital transfers from private sector [c]	134	2.9
Total receipts	4,695	100.0
Expenditure		
Gross domestic fixed capital formation	6,846	145.8
Increase in value of stocks and work in progress	424	9.0
Capital transfers to other sectors	46	1.0
Total expenditure	7,316	155.8
Balance of receipts over expenditure: financial deficit (−) (net acquisition of financial assets)	−2,621	55.8

[a] These additions to reserves were included in interest, etc., payments on appropriation account, and so were deducted there to give 'true' saving; but as they are (temporarily) retained by the corporations they must be added back in the capital account as a (temporary) source of finance.
[b] Government grants to finance capital expenditure; excluding loans written off (see Table 9.4).
[c] Contributions by private consumers towards the cost of connecting consumers' premises to public utilities' supplies.

Source: Central Statistical Office, *National Income and Expenditure 1981 Edition*, table 6.3, p. 46.

financial assets) which they undertook. Most of this lending was done by the quasi-financial public corporations such as the National Film Finance Corporation, which lends money for the production of feature films, or the National Research Development Corporation, which provides finance for innovation by industrial companies. The Scottish, Welsh, and Northern Ireland Development Agencies also lend money to companies.

As Table 10.6 shows, the public corporations' main source of borrowing to finance all this is the central government; in 1980 they borrowed £3,358 million directly from the central government; this was in fact more than they needed, so some of the 'excess' borrowing was used to redeem outstanding debt (reduce financial liabilities), which is the meaning of the minus signs in the 'sources of funds' section. There was a quite large source of funds in the £648 million of trade credit extended to public corporations by other sectors of the economy. Usually this flow is more than counterbalanced by the flow of extra trade credit extended by the public corporations, but in the financially stringent year in 1980 public corporations actually reduced their lending to trade debtors by £51 million. In the 'uses of funds' section we can see that some public corporations, probably the National Enterprise Board, acquired some company securities as well as a small amount of other sorts of financial assets. There was also an accruals adjustment (negative) for subsidies receivable (but not yet paid). All in all, public corporations acquired (gross) £181 million of financial assets during 1980; so they had to borrow £2,802 million: comprising £2,621 million to cover their financial deficit (93.5 per cent of their borrowing requirement), and £181 million to cover their acquisition of financial assets – their 'lending' to other sectors (the remaining 6.5 per cent).

From where did they borrow this money? Table 10.6 shows that an excess, £3,358 million or 119.8 per cent, was borrowed from the central government, either in the form of

TABLE 10.6   *Financial account of public corporations, 1980*

	£ million	Percentage of total borrowing required
Borrowing required to cover financial deficit	2,621	93.5
Financial uses of funds (transactions in financial assets)		
Net lending to private sector	106	3.8
Net lending and investment abroad	118	4.2
Cash expenditure on company securities	150	5.4
Lending to trade debtors	−51	−1.8
Increase in bank deposits	28	1.0
Acquisition of other financial assets	−70	−2.5
Accruals adjustment: subsidies receivable	−100	−3.6
Total transactions in financial assets	181	6.5
Total borrowing required to cover financial deficit and transactions in financial assets	2,802	100.0
Sources of funds (transactions in financial liabilities)		
Direct borrowing from central government:		
loans and public dividend capital	3,358	119.8
Accruals adjustment: taxes (etc.) payable [a]	119	4.2
Trade credit	648	23.1
Unidentified items	−632	−22.6
'Extra' contribution to PSBR		
Government guaranteed stock ('−' indicates redemptions)	−30	−1.1
Other sterling stock, borrowing under exchange cover scheme, foreign currency borrowing, other identified sterling, other unidentified items	−586	−20.9
Transactions in central government and local authority debt	−75	−2.7
Sub-total: 'extra' contributions to PSBR [b]	−691	−24.7
Total sources of funds	2,802	100.0

[a] Algebraic sum of *Financial Statistics'* (sources of funds) accruals adjustment (total) and Blue Book's (uses of funds) accruals adjustment (subsidies receivable).

[b] See *National Income and Expenditure 1981 Edition*, table 13.12, p. 101.

Sources: Central Statistical Office, *National Income and Expenditure 1981 Edition*, tables 6.4 and 13.12, pp. 46 and 101; further identification of flows of funds from Central Statistical Office, *Financial Statistics*, October 1981, table 5.2, p. 56.

loans (£1,942 million) on which interest is payable, or as public dividend capital on which no dividends are payable until the corporation becomes profitable (£1,416 million). Public dividend capital was introduced in 1966 to finance the (then) British Overseas Airways Corporation; it was non-redeemable capital on which BOAC was required to pay an annual (variable) dividend instead of (fixed) interest. The dividend could be varied, by agreement with the Treasury, according to circumstances. In other words, public dividend capital is, for a public corporation, the equivalent of equity capital (shares) for a private-sector company. In 1969 the device of public dividend capital was again used for financing the British Steel Corporation, and since then it has been used more frequently (see the discussion in Leonard Tivey (ed.), *The Nationalized Industries Since 1960: A Book of Readings*, pp. 116–21). In addition to borrowing this £3,358 million from the central government – which is thus subsumed into the central government borrowing requirement (see Tables 9.4 and 9.16) – a further −£691 million, the sub-total of the last three distinct items of Table 10.6 is counted by the Treasury as an extra contribution to the 'public sector' borrowing requirement (see the memorandum items in Table 9.16).

Although the financial accounts of the public corporations appear complicated, the main structure in 1980 is quite clear – and this structure applies also to most other years:

1. Public corporations have a relatively large financial deficit (their flow of saving is insufficient to cover their expenditure on fixed capital).
2. Most of the money borrowed to cover their financial deficit and their net lending has to come from the central government (and so has been subsumed into the central government borrowing requirement).

For these reasons it is clear why the central government is so concerned that the public corporations, especially the nationalised industries, should operate 'profitably' – a concern which we shall soon consider at length.

How the accounts connect

Having looked at each of the accounts of public corporations in some detail, it may be helpful to take an overview of the public corporations' activities in 1980. This we can do quite simply by applying the model of Diagram 2.5 (as modified by Diagram 2.6) to the figures in the national income and expenditure accounts. Diagram 10.3 shows how the public corporations made and spent their income in 1980. It also shows why (as in Diagram 10.2) the balance from one account is 'transferred' to the succeeding account, because the flows follow on in a logical progression.

In the operating account we have total sales revenue, subsidies and rent; deducting from this the purchases of materials (less any additions to inventories – i.e. the use of materials) and the taxes on expenditure gives the flow of value added; deducting wages and salaries and taxes on expenditure then gives the gross trading surplus and rent (where 'gross' means that provisions for depreciation are included); this balance on the operating account then becomes a receipt on the appropriation account, to which must be added the

DIAGRAM 10.3   *The accounts of the public corporations, 1980*

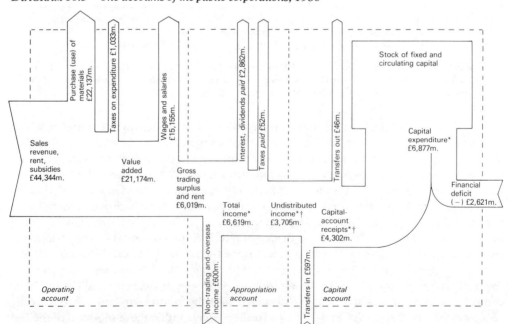

*Excluding stock appreciation.
†Including additions to reserves.

inflow of non-trading income and income from abroad to give total income on appropriation account (we do not add in stock appreciation because it is not 'really' a receipt;
conversely, under capital expenditure, we count only the cost of the *physical* increase in
inventories). From this total income on appropriation account, we must deduct the flows of
interest, dividends and taxes actually paid out (i.e. excluding earmarked flows which are
put into public corporations' 'reserves' for interest (etc.) payments in the future), to give
the flow of undistributed income (including additions to reserves). This balance on the
appropriation account is then transferred as a receipt to the capital account and we must
add the capital transfers received to get total capital-account receipts. Against these
receipts, we must charge the capital transfers paid out and expenditure on both fixed
capital formation and the physical increase in inventories. As capital-account expenditure
in 1980 was greater than capital-account receipts (this has always been the case with the
sector of public corporations), we are left with a financial deficit to make up the excess of
expenditure over receipts. This financial deficit – the negative net acquisition of financial
assets – must comprise either a running up of financial liabilities or a running down of an
existing stock of financial assets. Because the public sector does not own a large stock of
financial assets, the financial deficit generally has to be met by borrowing.

We now have the framework within which we can analyse the economic performance of
the public corporations.

Economic performance of the public corporations

Assessing, in economic terms, the performance of any undertaking is a complicated
matter, because it requires consideration of both 'real' and 'financial' indicators of
performance. Financial indicators are those which relate to the balancing, or residual,
flows on the various accounts:

1. Gross profits (trading surplus)   The balance on operating account
2. Gross saving (undistributed income)   The balance on appropriation account
3. Financial balance, surplus or deficit The balance on capital account

Real indicators are those which relate to output and inputs – materials, labour, capital, etc.
– and include not only the physical quantities but also the costs of inputs and the price of
output. Accordingly, while there is uniformity among enterprises in financial indicators,
there are many different indicators of real performance, and differences may be suited to
enterprises. One task of a manager is to know which of the real indicators are of most
importance to – have the greatest impact on – the financial indicators of his or her
particular enterprise. There are not only many real indicators, but there also tend to be
specialised variants of each. A necessarily incomplete list of real indicators of performance
is the following:

(a) materials and fuels conversion rates (ratios between materials, etc., inputs and
     outputs);
(b) labour productivity and associated variables (such as unit labour costs);
(c) capacity utilisation, or use of fixed capital;
(d) use of circulating capital (e.g. stock turnover rates);
(e) prices of inputs;
(f) prices of output(s).

The list makes it clear that real indicators may often be of a delicate and confidential nature
and will not be readily bandied about in public; for this reason we have few examples of
real indicators, but this should not hide from us their importance. While Diagram 7.2

above shows how all the real indicators will fit together to determine the enterprise's financial performance, it is often the case that financial performance may depend on only one or two critical indicators. For example, in copper mining (or other similar types of mining such as diamonds or bauxite) what matters most is the 'ore grade' as measured by the copper produced per tonne of ore (rock) mined and processed. Because the bulk of costs incurred relate to the mining and processing of ore, and because revenue is earned only from selling the refined copper, the conversion rate from ore to copper is the key factor in determining a mine's profitability. This rate, of course, is partly a matter of nature, but the decisions of the mining engineers on where to mine are also important in determining ore grades.

Stock turnover as an indicator of real performance

If we turn from mines to shops (retail or wholesale), we find that one important real indicator is the annual rate of stock turnover, measured by annual sales divided by the average value of stock held during the course of the year, and retailers will often be heard talking about 'slow-moving lines' (bad) and 'fast-moving lines' (good). To illustrate: if there are two goods A and B, each retailing at £1 and each earning 20p on each occasion of sale (i.e. each is bought at a wholesale price of 80p) and suppose good A 'turns over' fifty-two times during the year (has to be replaced once a week) while good B 'turns over' only twelve times during the year (has to be replaced once a month); then £1 invested in good A (and replaced out of sale proceeds as frequently as necessary) earns:

$$52 \times 20p = £10.40 \text{ per annum}$$

while £1 invested in good B earns only

$$12 \times 20p = £2.40 \text{ per annum.}$$

The same amount of money is tied up as circulating capital in an item of A and an item of B, but A is a much more 'profitable' item because of its higher rate of stock turnover.

Sometimes performance is measured inversely with reference to failure rates. For example, in the manufacture of silicon chips a certain proportion will be found to be defective and will have to be rejected (this arises because of technical difficulties with the manufacturing process). A key determinant of profits is therefore the rejection, or failure, rate, and attention is naturally concentrated on reducing this.

These examples should indicate why the list of real indicators of performance is necessarily incomplete: each enterprise may well have its own special indicator(s) that management regards as being of critical importance. The fact that labour productivity and the percentage utilisation of fixed capital capacity are in widespread use in manufacturing industry as real indicators of performance should not prevent us from appreciating the multitude of other relevant indicators.

Thus, when assessing the performance of the public corporations, we need to have regard to both real and financial indicators. The performance of public corporations in the United Kingdom tends to be a controversial subject, and in any case a proper appraisal can only be done corporation by corporation (as is done by Richard Pryke in *The Nationalised Industries: Policies and Performance Since 1968*). The purpose of the following paragraphs is merely to show how the data in the accounts we have been considering may be used to analyse performance, how these data need to be supplemented, and how all of this fits together in a framework to explain the main problem for economic policy concerning the public corporations.

Appendix 10.1 gives the operating account of the public corporations for each (calendar) year between 1950 and 1980 inclusive (1950 is the earliest year for which complete information on the public corporations is available – some data are available for earlier years, but information on stock appreciation starts only in 1950). The operating account gives the sequence:

$$\text{Sales receipts} \quad minus \quad \text{Use of goods and services} \quad equals \quad \text{Value added}$$

followed by:

$$\text{Value added} \quad minus \quad \text{Wages and salaries} \quad equals \quad \text{Gross trading surplus}$$

The balance on the operating account – the gross trading surplus – is the most important financial indicator because it largely determines the other financial indicators.

The most common use of this financial indicator is to relate it to the stock of capital employed in the form of a rate of profit. Data on the net fixed capital stock of the public corporations are available from 1955, and so we may calculate the public corporations' profitability as their gross trading surplus divided by their net fixed capital stock, expressed as a percentage. These figures are given in Appendix 10.1 and charted in Diagram 10.4. We can see that, with some fluctuations, the profitability of the public corporations increased between 1955 and 1963 and thereafter declined. If we look at the share of the gross trading surplus in value added, we can see that this share, with fluctuations, increased up to 1968 and thereafter declined.

DIAGRAM 10.4   *Public corporations: share of trading surplus in value added and rate of profitability, 1950 to 1980*

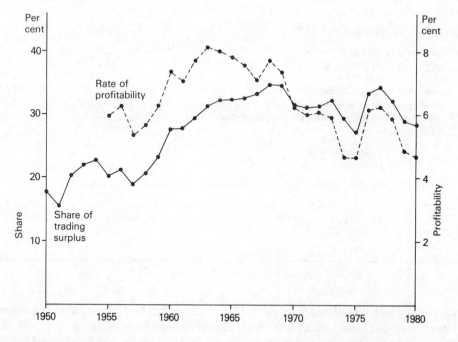

One reason for this change appears to be the rapid increase in unit labour costs after 1968. Unit labour costs – the cost of labour used per unit of output produced – may be measured by average earnings divided by output per worker. If w represents annual average earnings per employee, L the number of employees, and Q the volume of output produced, then:

$$\text{Unit labour cost} = \frac{wL}{Q} = \frac{w}{Q/L}$$

Calculating the implied GDP price deflator

The implied GDP price deflator is calculated by dividing the gross domestic product measured at current prices by the gross domestic product measured at constant prices. Table 10.7 gives, for the three years 1975 to 1977 inclusive, data on GDP at current and constant (1975) prices.

GDP at current prices is simply the total of values added, at the prices currently (then) ruling and excluding taxes on expenditure, in all the industries in the economy. The second row gives GDP measured at constant (1975) prices. There are two ways in which the national income statisticians may obtain this figure.

The first is to calculate the value added of each industry at constant prices; this is usually done by deflating each industry's current-price value added by a price index for the output of that industry. The resulting, deflated or constant-price values added are then totalled for all industries to give constant-price GDP (based on output data).

The second way in which the statisticians may obtain GDP at constant prices is to deflate each of the items of final expenditure by a price index appropriate to that item and then to total the resulting constant-price estimates of final expenditures. This gives constant-price GDP based on expenditure data. (The rationale for this procedure will not be understood until we have considered, in the next chapter (on final

TABLE 10.7   *The implied GDP price deflator, 1975 = 100*

	1975	1976	1977
GDP at current prices, £ million [a]	94,475	111,585	126,943
GDP at constant 1975 prices, £ million [a]	94,475	97,948	99,240
Implied GDP price deflator, 1975 = 100 [b]	100	113.923	127.915
Percentage changes over previous year:			
GDP at current prices	—	18.111	13.763
GDP at constant prices	—	3.676	1.319
Implied GDP price deflator	—	13.923	12.282

[a] Based on expenditure data; and at factor cost.

[b] Calculated as

$$\frac{\text{GDP at current prices}}{\text{GDP at constant prices}} \times 100$$

Officially called 'the implied index of total home costs (per unit of output)'.

Source: Central Statistical Office, *National Income and Expenditure 1981 Edition*, tables 1.1 (GDP at current prices), 2.1 (GDP at constant 1975 prices), and 2.6 (implied GDP price deflator), pp. 3, 17, and 23.

Thus we may measure changes in unit labour costs with reference to changes in average (money) earnings, w, and changes in (real) output per employee, Q/L.

However, in the operating account of Appendix 10.1, we do not have information on employment, L; nor do we have information on the volume of output, Q. Therefore, we need to supplement the conventional operating-account data. Note that, given supplementary information on employment, we may derive average annual earnings, w, by dividing the total annual wage and salary bill (Appendix 10.1) by the number of employees.

The implied GDP price deflator is a form of a price index (see Chapters 3 and 4) applicable to the entire gross domestic product. Using the implied GDP price deflator,

expenditure), why GDP can also be measured as the sum of final expenditures.)

The complex technicalities of measuring GDP at constant prices are not as important as grasping the (quite straightforward) fact that constant-price GDP measures what GDP would be had prices not changed, in this case from their 1975 level. That is to say, it is a way of measuring for 1976 (or for 1950 or any other year) what GDP would have been if 1975 prices had applied in that year.

The implied GDP price deflator, as it is usually known, or the implied index of total home costs (per unit of output), as it is officially called, can then be calculated by dividing current-price GDP by constant-price GDP. To illustrate for 1976:

$$\frac{\text{£111,585m.}}{\text{£97,948m.}} \times 100 = 1.13923 \times 100$$
$$= 113.923$$

We multiply by 100 to put the ratio into index form with 1975 = 100. The index is called an 'implied' price index because it is implied by the ratio between current- and constant-price GDP (rather than being 'explicitly' calculated as the weighted average of a set of price relatives). The index is called a 'deflator' because it is usually used to deflate (or adjust for price changes) some or other current-price data.

The way in which the implied GDP price deflator works is as follows. What we are doing is to partition the proportionate change in GDP measured at current prices between (a) the proportionate change in GDP measured at constant prices, and (b) the proportionate change in the 'over-all' price level. The excess of the proportionate change in GDP at current prices over the proportionate change in GDP at constant prices is ascribed to the proportionate change in

over-all prices. To illustrate: in 1976, by comparison with 1975, GDP at current prices increased by 18.111 per cent, or by a factor of 1.18111 (Table 10.7 – calculated as £111,585m./ £94,475m.; the reader must practise these alternative ways of looking at percentage changes). We know that GDP at constant prices (expenditure data, not output data) increased by 3.676 per cent, or by a factor of 1.03676. The proportionate excess of the former factor over the latter factor must be ascribed to price changes; the proportionate excess is properly measured as the ratio between the two (not the arithmetic difference):

$$\frac{1.18111}{1.03676} = 1.13923$$

(The arithmetic difference:
$$18.111 - 3.676 = 14.435$$
gives an approximate, but strictly speaking incorrect, answer; when working with price indices, one must always stick to division (or multiplication) and never use subtraction (or addition).) So the GDP price deflator works by partitioning the 18.111 per cent change in current-price GDP into a 3.676 per cent change in 'volume' and a 13.923 per cent change in 'prices'.

It follows that the implied GDP price deflator is the most comprehensive, all-embracing price index in the economy. The problem we started with – not having a long-run price index for the output of all the public corporations – may therefore be solved by using the implied GDP price deflator. This is not a completely satisfactory solution, but the only alternative, the nationalised industries' price index for goods and services sold to consumers, does not go back far enough, and moreover covers only a part of the output of the public corporations.

given in Appendix 10.2, we may then estimate the public corporations' value added at constant prices by 'deflating' (dividing) current-price value added by the implied price deflator. To illustrate: public corporations' value added in 1976 at current (i.e. 1976) prices was £13,005 million; the implied GDP price deflator for 1976 was 113.9 (1975 = 100); so value added in 1976 at constant (1975) prices can be calculated as:

$$\frac{\text{£13,005m.}}{1.139} = \text{£11,418m.}$$

(Note that instead of dividing by 113.9 and multiplying the result by 100, we have taken a short cut by dividing by 113.9/100 = 1.139.) We thus use the implied GDP price deflator to deflate (or revalue) the current-price value added. Likewise the public corporations' current-price value added in 1950 (at the, lower, 1950 prices) is revalued ('deflated' being not quite the applicable word) to 1975 prices as follows:

$$\frac{£983m.}{0.232} = £4,237m.$$

We may thus derive estimates of public corporations' value added at constant (1975) prices. This series then serves as the measure of the volume of output, Q, and by dividing by the mid-year figures on employment, L, we may obtain estimates of real labour productivity, Q/L, measured (as is usually done) by value added at constant prices per employee. Fitting an exponential function (see Chapter 3) to these data gives a trend growth rate for productivity of 3.67 per cent per annum over the whole period 1956 to 1980. Using our rule 'divide the annual percentage growth into 70' to ascertain the time taken by the variable to double, we may see that productivity in the public corporations should, at this growth rate, double every nineteen years, and, in the nineteen years between 1956 and 1975, productivity *did* double.

What happened to unit labour costs? We can measure unit labour costs by dividing average (money) earnings by average (real) labour productivity (or, what comes to the same thing, by dividing the total, money, wage and salary bill by total, real constant-price, value added). The result may be expressed as the cost, per £ of value added measured at 1975 prices, of labour used. To illustrate: in 1956 average annual earnings were £628 per employee and average (real) productivity was £2,534 of value added (at 1975 prices) per employee per annum; unit labour costs in 1956 were accordingly:

$$\frac{£628}{£2,534} = 0.248$$

or 24.8 pence per £ of value added (at 1975 prices). We may, however, express unit labour costs in index form with, say, 1956 = 100; this is because we are here concerned not with comparing absolute levels of unit labour costs across enterprises during any one year but with comparing relative changes of unit labour costs in the same sector (set of enterprises) over several years. If we use this index form of unit labour costs, we can see that between 1956 and 1968 unit costs, with some fluctuations, rose quite slowly at 1.2 per cent per annum (exponential trend rate); but between 1968 and 1980 (inclusive) unit labour costs rose much more rapidly at a trend rate of 13 per cent per annum. It was this rapid growth of unit labour costs, probably combined with political pressure on the nationalised industries to keep the rate of increase of their prices down, which led to their deteriorating financial performance (share of profits in value added and rate of profitability) in these later years.

The public corporations' financial performance has always been affected by two other things: a considerable amount of interest charges, and the need to invest in quite substantial amounts of fixed capital each year – this latter need is clearly shown by the amounts of capital consumption attributed to the public corporations. The interest charges have the effect of reducing the public corporations' saving – the balance on appropriation account – while gross fixed capital formation (when matched against this 'small' flow of saving) then led, each and every year, to a substantial financial deficit – negative balance on capital account.

Appendix 10.3 gives the appropriation account of public corporations for the years 1950 to 1980; Appendix 10.3 also gives, as a memorandum item, the capital consumption attributed by the national accounts statisticians to the public corporations. From this we can see that the public corporations have never had a flow of saving sufficient to match, let alone exceed, their capital consumption. Indeed, in most years capital consumption has exceeded gross saving by a substantial margin.

Appendix 10.4 gives the capital account of the public corporations for the years 1950 to 1980. Total receipts on capital account have always been considerably less than total expenditure on capital account, and so each year the public corporations have run a substantial financial deficit. In turn, this has created each year a substantial borrowing requirement, supplemented by their lending to other sectors (such lending stemming, in the main, from those public corporations – such as the Welsh or Scottish Development Agencies or the Commonwealth Development Corporation – established for the purpose of lending).

This continual need by the public corporations for relatively large annual borrowing has created an uneasy relationship between the public corporations and the central government, the 'uneasiness' of this relationship seeming to vary directly with the size of the borrowing required, as the central government is responsible for meeting most of the public corporations' financing requirements. Accordingly, the government's policies concerning the running of the public corporations – especially the nationalised industries – has evolved against this financial background, and has often been directed towards reducing the financial deficit. Accordingly, it is not possible to appreciate policy concerning the nationalised industries until one sees their performance as measured by the financial indicators in Appendices 10.1, 10.3 and 10.4.

Economic policy towards the public corporations

The basic economic problem with which policy has had to cope centres on the interrelated matters of pricing, investment and finance. The essence of the problem (which the student must see in the context of the sequence of accounts in Diagrams 10.2 or 10.3) is that prices which are 'too low' will increase (the modulus of) the financial deficit, while investment that is 'too high' will do likewise.* We may illustrate, in a schematic way for any specific public corporation, the basic analytics of this interrelationship in Diagram 10.5.

We start off, in the upper-right quadrant, with a modified version of a demand curve, to be called a 'demand growth function', which relates price not to the flow of annual sales volume, but to the annual percentage growth in sales volume. The argument here is that while demand will be growing 'naturally' as incomes and the economy grow, a 'low' price will additionally boost the naturally occurring growth, while a 'high' price will retard growth; so this demand growth function slopes downwards.

In the lower-right quadrant we may relate the need for annual (gross) investment to the annual growth in sales volume: the higher the rate of growth of sales volume, the greater is the annual flow of investment required to increase production capacity. Even if growth in demand were zero there would have to be some investment simply to cover depreciation,† so the gross investment function starts at the amount of depreciation, D, and is then an increasing function of the growth in sales volume. 'Investment' here includes circulating capital formation, but, of course, is dominated by fixed capital formation.

Ignoring the 'minor' elements on capital account (transfers in, transfers out), the annual investment creates a need for financing, either by saving (internally generated finance) or by borrowing (external finance). We may therefore use a 45° line, in the lower-left quadrant, to switch the annual flow of investment to the horizontal axis of the upper-left quadrant, which axis indicates the total annual flow of financing required.

Now we know (Chapter 6) that the downward-sloping demand curve (charting price

---

*The words 'modulus of' are used to avoid misunderstanding; an increase is properly a change in a positive direction, e.g. the change from -4 to -3 is an increase (of $+1$); what is meant here is, for example, an 'increase' from -4 to -5, hence the need for the words 'modulus of', which tells us to disregard the sign.
†Or, strictly speaking, retirements.

DIAGRAM 10.5   *The pricing–investment–financing problem of public corporations*

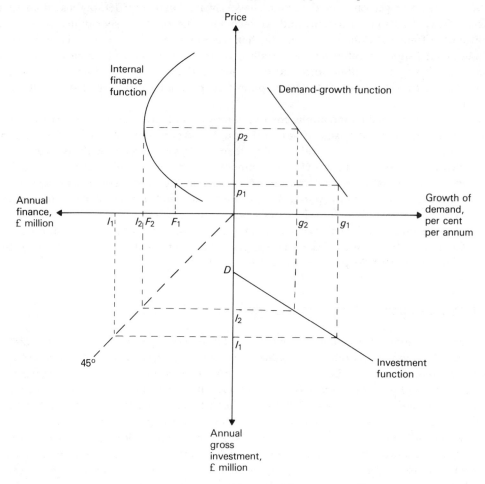

against annual quantity sold) generates a parabolic sales receipts curve: that is, a sales receipts curve which first rises then falls as sales volume increases (see Diagram 6.7). Given some regular behaviour of costs the parabolic sales receipts curve will result in a parabolic total profits – or total gross margin – curve (see Diagram 6.8). Given some regular deductions from profits on appropriation account, this implies that undistributed income, or gross saving, will also be parabolic. Specifically: the flow of annual saving will be low if the price is high (and hence sales volume low); the flow of saving will at first rise with decreasing price/increasing sales volume. Saving will reach a maximum at some point; and thereafter saving will decline with decreasing price/increasing sales volume. We may therefore draw a schematic 'internal finance function' in the upper-left quadrant, showing, for any price charged, the annual flow of saving which should be generated via the production account (which starts with sales receipts *equals* price *multiplied by* quantity sold) and the appropriation account.

We can now use Diagram 10.5 to analyse the basic problem of economic policy concerning the nationalised industries. Initially the industries were enjoined, in the Acts of Parliament which established them, first to raise such revenues that, taking one year with another, would be not less than sufficient to meet all items properly chargeable to revenue including interest, depreciation, the redemption of capital, and a contribution to the provision of services (i.e. to the expansion of fixed capital capacity). Second, they were enjoined to be run 'in the public interest'. Now, the nationalised industries were mostly monopolies, so there was public concern to see that they did not 'take advantage' of their monopoly position by charging 'excessive' prices. Consequently, what happened was that prices tended to be kept 'low' – serving the 'public interest'. This led to a rapid growth in demand, which in turn caused a corresponding need for considerable investment. In the illustrative scheme of Diagram 10.5: prices were set at p_1; annual growth of sales volume was 'rapid' at g_1; and the need for annual investment, and correspondingly for total finance, was 'high' at I_1. For example, between 1948 and 1956 the price of electricity to household consumers rose by only 20 per cent (over the whole period), compared with a rise of 45 per cent in the retail price index and compared with a 32 per cent rise (no less) in the prices for fuel used in manufacturing electricity (Ministry of Power: *Statistical Digest 1956*, tables 95 and 106, pp. 128 and 138–9; *Statistical Digest 1963*, tables 77 and 84, pp. 104 and 110–11 – the 'price' figures refer to net selling value per kilowatt hour to domestic (private residential premises) consumers and average fuel costs per kilowatt hour sent out; and Table 3.22 above). So electricity became relatively much cheaper and consumption of electricity by households rose rapidly, thus pushing up annual investment in electricity-generating capacity.

But the consequence of this strategy of setting 'low' prices for the public corporations meant that the annual flow of saving was also 'low' (Appendix 10.3); to the price of p_1 in Diagram 10.5 there was a corresponding flow of internal finance (saving) of only F_1, while the need for financing was I_1. The difference between F_1 and I_1 is (ignoring minor elements) the financial deficit, or need for external finance – borrowing. So in these early years the financial deficits of the public corporations were relatively large (Appendix 10.4).

There were then two government 'White Papers' which set forth policies intended to deal with this problem (among others): the 1961 White Paper, *Financial and Economic Obligations of the Nationalised Industries* (Cmnd 1337) and the 1967 White Paper, *Nationalised Industries: a Review of Economic and Financial Objectives* (Cmnd 3437).

White Papers

A 'White Paper' is a means whereby the government – i.e. a Departmental Minister, but with the agreement of the Cabinet – presents statements of policy to Parliament: 'A White Paper indicates the broad lines of the legislation the Government intend to introduce and, very often, of executive action that will be taken' (the Prime Minister, Harold Wilson, 13 May 1969, quoted in J. E. Pemberton, *British Official Publications*, 2nd rev edn, Pergamon Press, 1973, p. 58).

White Papers are one of a class of Parliamentary Papers which state on their title page that they were 'Presented to Parliament by Command of Her Majesty' and these are accordingly known as Command papers. Each is identified by a Command number: a number preceded by an abbreviation of the word 'Command'. The series Cmd 1 to Cmd 9889 appeared in 1919 to 1956; after 1956 the numbering started again at Cmnd 1.

The 1961 White Paper said that there should be increased internal financing of investment by the nationalised industries:

> there are powerful grounds in the national interest for requiring these undertakings to make a substantial contribution towards the cost of their capital development out of their own earnings, and so reduce their claims upon the nation's savings and the burden on the Exchequer: this is particularly so for those undertakings which are expanding fast and which have relatively large capital needs (1961 White Paper, Cmnd 1337, para. 22;

reproduced in L. Tivey (ed.), *The Nationalized Industries Since 1960: A Book of Readings*, p. 70).

The government expressed the hope that reductions in unit costs and increases in prices (but preferably the former) would permit a greater degree of self-financing:

> The aim of the industries generally will naturally be to secure the necessary additions to their net revenue [i.e. to their saving] as far as possible by reduction in costs. The government recognize, however, that the industries must have freedom to make upward price adjustment especially where their prices are artificially low (1961 White Paper, Cmnd 1337, para. 30; Tivey, pp. 72–3).

The 1967 White Paper said that nationalised industries should assess their investment projects more thoroughly and systematically and that such assessments should be done within the framework of a pricing policy aimed at making the consumer 'pay the true costs of providing the goods and services he consumes' (1967 White Paper, Cmnd 3437, para. 18; Tivey, p. 80).

Ignoring the (nevertheless important) requirement of reducing unit operating costs which would serve to shift the internal finance function outwards to the left, these White Papers indicated the need for nationalised industries to raise their prices and thereby reduce their financial deficits; in terms of Diagram 10.5, raising prices should, in the first instance, reduce the annual need for investment and so reduce the requirement for financing, and in the second instance, should increase the flow of internal finance (saving) becoming available. We can, rather artificially, draw a neat 'solution' to the whole problem in Diagram 10.5 by setting a configuration where the price charged results in maximum saving and also, with purely artificial coincidence, results in an annual flow of investment (and consequent need for financing) exactly equal to the flow of saving, so causing there to be a zero financial deficit: in Diagram 10.5, I_2 and F_2 then coincide. Such an artificially neat coincidence would be unlikely to occur in practice, but the aim of policy – to raise prices and so, it is hoped, to maximise savings and also to reduce the need for investment and thereby reduce (the modulus of) the financial deficit to a minimum (pulling F_1 and I_1 towards each other) – is quite clear.

In the years immediately following 1961 this policy pushed up the profitability of the public corporations (Diagram 10.4) and helped to contain their financial deficit (Appendix 10.4), but in 1970 and the years following the public corporations' financial performance was affected by the government's requirement that they keep their prices down as their contribution to anti-inflation policies. In the face of rising unit labour costs (Appendix 10.2), this was bound adversely to affect profitability and financial performance. The government even paid out subsidies to compensate the public corporations for the revenue forgone by restraining their price rises. This was subsequently admitted by the government in the 1978 White Paper *The Nationalised Industries* (Cmnd 7131), from which we may quote at length to illustrate the official recognition of the policy problems analysed in this chapter, particularly in Diagram 10.5:

> the main single factor which undermined the principles in the 1967 White Paper was the price restraint policies of the early 1970's . . . It is essential that the mistakes of the early 1970s should not be repeated. The Government intends that the nationalised industries will not be forced into deficits by restraints on their prices . . . Now that the industries are generally in better shape, public attention – and sometimes criticism – is focussing on the size of their profits which result from the progressive return to economic pricing. However, although these reported profits may appear big when looked at in isolation they are by no means large when related to the net assets of the industries which are generating them . . . An adequate level of nationalised industry profits is essential to the continuing well being of the industries and their customers and of the economy as a

whole. They provide some of the funds for the very large investment programmes necessary to maintain supplies and services to the public ... It is sometimes suggested that financial targets should be in the form of self-financing ratios. However, although forecasts of these ratios are very important in estimating the industries' requirements for Government finance, they are not a suitable basis for financial targets. Performance in relation to a target is a measure of how well an industry is using its total assets, and it is therefore necessary to relate profits earned to the total capital employed in the business rather than to the amount of its investment in a particular year. Moreover, a number of the industries have a record of shortfall on their estimates of annual investment and so a self-financing ratio target could be met or beaten for reasons in no sense attributable to efficient management (*The Nationalised Industries*, March 1978, Cmnd 7131, paras 5, 54, 55 and 71; pp. 6, 22, 23 and 26).

The 1978 White Paper went on to acknowledge that the profitability (financial) indicator might, if taken alone, be an insufficient guide to performance 'since to the extent that there is a monopoly situation the targets could be achieved by price rises or changes in the level of service' (Cmnd 7131, para. 76). Accordingly, the nationalised industries were to be asked to select and publish appropriate and relevant real indicators of performance:

> The indicators will vary from industry to industry and the Government recognises that some of the industries in a competitive position have to take account of requirements of commercial confidentiality. However, there will probably be some indicators common to most including, for example, labour productivity, and standards of service, where these are readily measurable (Cmnd 7131, para. 78).

What I have tried to show in this chapter on the public corporations is that it is not possible to discuss the problems of the nationalised industries, and government policy towards them, without first having a clear understanding of their basic accounts and of how their financial deficit (or borrowing requirement) is meshed in with the general government borrowing requirement to give the over-all PSBR. Using this framework, we can begin to appreciate why the government must inevitably take a close interest in the operations of the public corporations, and we can begin to understand the sorts of economic requirements which governments place upon the nationalised industries.

Exercises

10.1 *(An important exercise* (a) *to practise working with an operating account, and* (b) *to see a real-life example of the calculation of value added and its distribution as income.)* Insert the relevant figures of Table 10.2 to the operating account part of Diagram 10.2. (Work more or less* to scale, and note the meaning in Diagram 10.2 of 'bought-in materials' so that the appropriate figure for insertion can be calculated from Table 10.2; the first bar of Diagram 10.2 has to be appropriately divided to bring the real-life complications into the picture.)

10.2 *(Another important exercise* (a) *to practise working with an appropriation account, and* (b) *to*

see a real-life calculation of saving.) The appropriation account part of Diagram 10.2 is a simplification to basic essentials; redraw this part of the diagram to include, with figures, all the details of Table 10.4. (Work more or less* to scale; but not to the same scale as for Exercise 10.1, otherwise it gets too difficult to draw properly – unless you start by using a huge sheet of paper!)

10.3 *(Yet another important exercise* (a) *to practise working with a capital account, and* (b) *to*

*'More or less' means that you are permitted somewhat to enlarge the representations of the very small amounts so as to make it practicable to show them on the diagram.

see a real-life calculation of a financial deficit.)
The capital-account part of Diagram 10.2 is a
simplification to basic essentials; redraw this
part of the diagram to include, with figures, all
the details of Table 10.5. (Work more or less* to
scale but not to the same scale as for
Exercise 10.2.)

10.4 *(To practise seeing how all the accounts fit
together.)* Update, to the latest available year,
Diagram 10.3. (For this exercise you will have to
go to the latest *National Income and Expenditure*
tables, as given in the sources to Tables 10.2,
10.4 and 10.5.)

10.5 *(Further to practise working with an
operating account.)*

(i)   For the most recent eleven-year period,
      tabulate public corporations' total sales re-
      venue and gross trading surplus after de-
      ducting stock appreciation. Calculate,
      tabulate and graph the gross trading surp-
      lus as a percentage of total sales revenue,
      which percentage we shall call the 'rate of
      profit on sales'.

(ii) If we call the gross trading surplus after
      deducting stock appreciation the public
      corporations' 'gross margin', what propor-
      tionate mark-up on 'production costs' did
      the public corporations achieve in each of
      these eleven years? (Your recollection of
      the mark-up may need to be refreshed by
      re-reading   Chapter 5,   especially
      pp. 232–5.)

10.6 *(To demonstrate the relationship between
the proportionate mark-up and the rate of profit on
sales.)*

(i)   Using the results of Exercise 10.5, show by
      arithmetic that the following relationship
      holds:

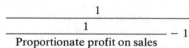

Proportionate mark-up =

$$\frac{1}{\dfrac{1}{\text{Proportionate profit on sales}} - 1}$$

(ii) Prove by algebra that this equation neces-
      sarily holds.

10.7 *(To practise calculating and using the implied GDP price deflator.)*

(i)   Tabulate GDP (at factor cost) at current
      and constant 1975† prices for the period
      1974 to the latest available year (inclu-

sive) and calculate from your data the
implied   GDP   price   deflator   with
1975† = 100. Check your answers in the
relevant table of the *National Income and
Expenditure* accounts.

(ii) Taking the data on personal-sector money
      income from Appendix 3.1 (updated by
      you as per Exercise 3.1(i)) for the period
      1974 to the latest available year, use the
      implied GDP price deflator from (i) to
      deflate personal-sector income to con-
      stant 1975† (GDP) prices.

(iii) Following the discussion on pp. 159–61
      of the meaning of an increase in 'real
      income' (where 'real income' meant
      money income deflated by an index of
      retail prices to the consumer), write a
      short explanation of the meaning of an
      increase in 'real income', where 'real in-
      come' means money income deflated by
      the implied GDP price deflator.

10.8 *(To practise your understanding of how
producing enterprises work – albeit using sector
accounts.)* Using Diagram 7.2, explain why the
trend decrease in public corporations' profitability, as measured in Appendix 10.1 and as shown
in Diagram 10.4, could be due: (i) to a decrease
in economic efficiency; or (ii) to enforced 're-
straint' on prices charged for output; or (iii) to
'aggressive' employee action to raise average
earnings.

10.9 *(To see one of the things which results in
changed productivity.)*

(i)   On the same sheet of semi-logarithmic
      paper (log 2 cycles: Chartwell C5521 (A4
      size) or C5221 (A3 size)), chart public
      corporations' value added per employee
      at 1975 prices from 1956 to 1980 inclusive
      (taking the vertical scale as £ thousands)
      and public corporations' total value added
      at 1975 prices for the same years (taking
      the vertical scale now as £ thousand
      million).

(ii) Describe the relationship between the two
      lines joining the relevant set of time-series
      points. (Comment on the importance of
      footnote *(a)* to Appendix 10.2.)

*'More or less' means that you are permitted
somewhat to enlarge the representations of the
very small amounts so as to make it practicable
to show them on the diagram.
†If the base has been changed from 1975 to
some later year, then use this later year.

(iii) Looking at the series on employment in public corporations, can you suggest an explanation for this relationship?

10.10 *(To practise analysing the economic problems of public corporations through their accounts, and to practise your ability to interpret those accounts.)*

(i) In a critique of the public corporations, the Oxford economist Walter Eltis alleges that the official presentation of the public corporations' accounts is misleading:

> The national income accounts do not show the full scale of loss making and indebtedness that occurred [in the public corporations], and the manner in which they are presented obscures this totally ... For private sector companies, the CSO shows the effect on the trading surplus of deducting capital consumption, but strangely it omits to show the effect of deducting capital consumption from the so-called 'trading profits' of the public corporations, perhaps precisely because the effect is to remove the entire surplus or more in most years (Walter Eltis, 'The true deficits of the public corporations', *Lloyds Bank Review*, no. 131, January 1979, pp. 4–6).

With reference to Appendices 10.1 and 10.3, explain, verify and discuss this statement.

(ii) Eltis also argues that 'overinvestment' by public corporations has contributed to their 'deficits':

> In the aggregate the nationalized industries clearly have produced financial problems for the remainder of the economy for the two main reasons outlined: pricing in many cases to cover not even wage costs plus capital consumption, and very loose government authorizations for investment programmes, which no commercially minded concern could tolerate (ibid, p. 10).

With reference to the data in Appendices 10.1, 10.3 and 10.4, and to Diagram 10.5, explain and discuss this argument.

APPENDIX 10.1   *Operating account of public corporations and profitability, 1950 to 1980*

Year	Sales receipts [a]	Use of goods and services [b]	Value added [c]	Wages and salaries	Gross trading surplus and rent [d]	Net fixed capital stock at current replacement cost, £ thousand million [e]	Gross trading surplus etc as a percentage of value added	Profitability: gross trading surplus as percentage of net fixed capital stock
1950	1,831	848	983	808	175	n.a.	17.8	n.a.
1951	2,512	1,301	1,211	1,023	188	n.a.	15.5	n.a.
1952	2,831	1,399	1,432	1,141	291	n.a.	20.3	n.a.
1953	3,000	1,470	1,530	1,193	337	n.a.	22.0	n.a.
1954	2,966	1,397	1,569	1,210	359	n.a.	22.9	n.a.
1955	2,933	1,395	1,538	1,227	311	5.2	20.2	5.98
1956	3,014	1,356	1,658	1,308	350	5.6	21.1	6.25
1957	3,152	1,440	1,712	1,386	326	6.1	19.0	5.34
1958	3,150	1,400	1,750	1,387	363	6.4	20.7	5.67
1959	3,211	1,412	1,799	1,384	415	6.6	23.1	6.29
1960	3,465	1,479	1,986	1,435	551	7.5	27.7	7.35
1961 [f]	4,040	1,668	2,372	1,711	661	9.4	27.9	7.03
1962	4,440	1,794	2,646	1,868	778	10.1	29.4	7.70
1963	4,670	1,863	2,807	1,930	877	10.8	31.2	8.12
1964	4,957	1,974	2,983	2,023	960	12.0	32.2	8.00
1965	5,224	2,064	3,160	2,138	1,022	13.1	32.3	7.80
1966	5,465	2,172	3,293	2,215	1,078	14.2	32.7	7.59
1967	6,111	2,531	3,580	2,393	1,187	16.7	33.2	7.11
1968	7,085	3,043	4,042	2,630	1,412	18.3	34.9	7.72
1969	7,651	3,423	4,228	2,759	1,469	20.0	34.7	7.35
1970	8,355	3,868	4,487	3,067	1,420	22.6	31.6	6.28
1971	9,018	4,095	4,923	3,394	1,529	25.5	31.1	6.00
1972	9,931	4,319	5,612	3,863	1,749	28.8	31.2	6.07
1973	11,274	4,899	6,375	4,328	2,047	34.5	32.1	5.93
1974	14,635	6,662	7,973	5,615	2,358	50.4	29.6	4.68
1975	18,758	8,203	10,555	7,691	2,864	61.4	27.1	4.66
1976	23,052	10,047	13,005	8,655	4,350	70.5	33.4	6.17
1977	27,008	12,484	14,524	9,534	4,990	79.8	34.4	6.25
1978	31,410	15,009	16,401	11,098	5,303	90.4	32.3	5.87
1979	38,190	20,116	18,074	12,835	5,239	107.8	29.0	4.86
1980	44,344	23,170	21,174	15,155	6,019	127.9	28.4	4.71

[a] Including rents received, and subsidies.

[b] Defined as follows: Purchases of goods and services *less* Value of physical increase in stocks and work in progress *plus* Rents paid out *plus* Taxes on expenditure; where Value of physical increase in stocks (etc.) *equals* Increase in value of stocks (etc.) *less* Stock appreciation (having regard to the sign conventions adopted in the Blue Book). For value of physical increase in stocks and work in progress (inventories) see column 5, Appendix 10.4.

[c] Including rent received; excluding stock appreciation.

[d] Before providing for depreciation but after deducting stock appreciation.

[e] At end-year.

[f] From 1 April 1961 the Post Office is treated as a public corporation.

Sources: Central Statistical Office, *National Income and Expenditure: 1961*, tables 12 and 31, pp. 8 and 29; *1962*, tables 12 and 31, pp. 13 and 33; *1963*, tables 12 and 31, pp. 13 and 33; *1964*, tables 12 and 31, pp. 11 and 35; *1965*, tables 12 and 31, pp. 17 and 39; *1966*, tables 13, 36 and 66, pp. 15, 44 and 79; *1967*, tables 13, 36 and 65, pp. 15, 44 and 79; *1968*, tables 13, 36 and 65, pp. 15, 46 and 81; *1969*, tables 13 and 33, pp. 15 and 40; *1970*, tables 13, 32 and 61, pp. 15, 38 and 73; *1971*, tables 13, 33 and 64, pp. 15, 40 and 77; *1972*, tables 13, 32 and 63, pp. 15, 38 and 75; *1973*, tables 13, 32 and 63, pp. 15, 38 and 75; *1963–1973*, tables 13, 34 and 65, pp. 15, 40 and 77; *1964–74*, tables 13, 41 and 72, pp. 15, 44 and 81; *1965–75*, tables 1.10, 6.1 and 12.11, pp. 13, 44 and 84; *1966–76*, tables 1.10, 6.1 and 11.11, pp. 15, 46 and 86; *1967–77*, tables 1.11, 6.1 and 11.11, pp. 17, 50 and 90; *1979 Edition*, tables 1.11, 6.1 and 11.11, pp. 17, 50 and 88; *1980 Edition*, tables 1.10, 6.1 and 11.11, pp. 13, 45 and 83; *1981 Edition*, tables 1.10, 6.1 and 11.11, pp. 13, 45 and 83.

APPENDIX 10.2   *Public corporations: average earnings, p'oductivity, and unit labour costs, 1950 to 1980*

Year	Mid-year employment, thousands	Average earnings per employee, £ per annum	Price deflator: implied index of total home costs, 1975 = 100	Value added revalued to 1975 prices, £ million	Value added per employee at 1975 prices, £ per annum	Unit labour cost	
						Average earnings per £ of value added[b] at 1975 prices, pence	Index, 1956 = 100
1950	n.a.	n.a.	23.2	4,237	n.a.	n.a.	n.a.
1951	n.a.	n.a.	24.9	4,863	n.a.	n.a.	n.a.
1952	n.a.	n.a.	27.2	5,265	n.a.	n.a.	n.a.
1953	n.a.	n.a.	28.0	5,464	n.a.	n.a.	n.a.
1954	n.a.	n.a.	28.6	5,486	n.a.	n.a.	n.a.
1955	n.a.	n.a.	29.6	5,196	n.a.	n.a.	n.a.
1956	2,084	628	31.4	5,280	2,534	24.8	100.0
1957	2,072	669	32.7	5,235	2,527	26.5	106.9
1958	2,038	681	34.2	5,117	2,511	27.1	109.4
1959	1,961	706	34.8	5,170	2,636	26.8	108.1
1960	1,861	771	35.4	5,610	3,015	25.6	103.3
1961 [a]	2,196	779	36.6	6,481	2,951	26.4	106.6
1962	2,192	852	37.8	7,000	3,193	26.7	107.7
1963	2,132	905	38.7	7,253	3,402	26.6	107.4
1964	2,081	972	39.9	7,476	3,593	27.1	109.2
1965	2,028	1,054	41.5	7,614	3,754	28.1	113.3
1966	1,962	1,129	43.1	7,640	3,894	29.0	117.0
1967	1,937	1,235	44.3	8,081	4,172	29.6	119.5
1968	2,069	1,271	45.6	8,864	4,284	29.7	119.8
1969	2,041	1,352	47.3	8,939	4,380	30.9	124.6
1970	2,025	1,515	51.0	8,798	4,345	34.9	140.7
1971	2,009	1,689	56.5	8,713	4,337	39.0	157.2
1972	1,929	2,003	62.3	9,008	4,670	42.9	173.1
1973	1,890	2,290	67.3	9,473	5,012	45.7	184.4
1974	1,985	2,829	78.7	10,131	5,104	55.4	223.7
1975	2,035	3,779	100.0	10,555	5,187	72.9	294.1
1976	1,980	4,371	113.9	11,418	5,767	75.8	306.0
1977	2,089	4,564	127.9	11,356	5,436	84.0	338.9
1978	2,061	5,385	142.6	11,501	5,580	96.5	389.5
1979	2,065	6,215	161.7	11,177	5,413	114.8	463.6
1980	2,036	7,444	190.9	11,092	5,448	136.6	551.5

[a] From April 1961 the Post Office is treated as a public corporation.
[b] Per employee.

Sources: Appendix 10.1; Central Statistical Office, *Economic Trends Annual Supplement 1981 Edition*, p. 5 (implied index of total home costs); and Central Statistical Office, *National Income and Expenditure: 1967*, table 13, p. 15; *1968*, table 13, p. 15; *1969*, table 13, p. 15; *1970*, table 13, p. 15; *1971*, table 13, p. 15; *1972*, table 13, p. 15; *1973*, table 13, p. 15; *1963–1973*, table 13, p. 15; *1964–74*, table 13, p. 15; *1965–75*, table 1.10, p. 13; *1966–76*, table 1.10, p. 15; *1967–77*, table 1.11, p. 17; *1979 Edition*, table 1.11, p. 17; *1980 Edition*, table 1.12, p. 15; *1981 Edition*, tables 1.12 and 2.6, pp. 15 and 23.

APPENDIX 10.3   *Appropriation account of public corporations, 1950 to 1980*

£ million

Year	Gross trading surplus and rents (a)	Non-trading income (b)	Income from abroad (c)	Total receipts	Interest and dividends paid (d)	UK taxes paid (d)	Balance: undistributed income and additions to reserves	Additions to tax and interest reserves	Balance: undistributed income, gross 'saving' (e)	CSO capital consumption	Percentage by which capital consumption exceeded gross saving
1950	175	16	1	192	91	3	98	9	89	191	114.6
1951	188	13	0	201	106	4	91	29	62	229	269.4
1952	291	18	1	310	118	3	189	38	151	273	80.8
1953	337	19	2	358	134	24	200	17	183	290	58.5
1954	359	21	2	382	148	37	197	-8	205	291	42.0
1955	311	28	3	342	162	32	148	-15	163	304	86.5
1956	350	28	4	382	157	30	195	7	188	327	73.9
1957	326	34	4	364	190	22	152	-3	155	350	125.8
1958	363	30	5	398	225	21	152	-15	167	376	125.1
1959	415	30	6	451	254	11	186	6	180	392	117.8
1960	551	38	6	595	288	12	295	7	288	413	43.4
1961	661	40	8	709	345	12	352	7	345	505	46.4
1962	778	41	8	827	420	8	399	-28	427	561	31.4
1963	877	28	7	912	333	6	573	37	536	600	11.9
1964	960	31	8	999	394	6	599	10	589	640	8.7
1965	1,022	40	8	1,070	421	3	646	17	629	696	10.7
1966	1,078	46	9	1,133	473	31	629	-8	637	745	17.0

1967	1,187	47	10	1,244	552	9	683	17	666	817	22.7
1968	1,412	66	13	1,491	636	17	838	27	811	937	15.5
1969	1,469	80	15	1,564	722	8	834	-4	838	1,024	22.2
1970	1,420	90	14	1,524	779	10	735	5	730	1,202	64.7
1971	1,529	88	14	1,631	864	8	759	24	735	1,393	89.5
1972	1,749	90	17	1,856	926	7	923	50	873	1,561	78.8
1973	2,047	202	20	2,269	1,133	8	1,128	71	1,057	1,778	68.2
1974	2,358	268	30	2,656	1,586	11	1,059	45	1,014	2,282	125.0
1975	2,864	284	40	3,188	1,905	12	1,271	59	1,212	2,972	145.2
1976	4,350	466	56	4,872	2,395	2	2,475	74	2,401	3,567	48.6
1977	4,990	470	52	5,512	2,537	21	2,954	70	2,884	4,135	43.4
1978	5,303	523	66	5,892	2,507	28	3,357	227	3,130	4,699	50.1
1979	5,239	542	71	5,852	2,808	68	2,976	131	2,845	5,408	90.1
1980	6,019	518	82	6,619	2,862	52	3,705	70	3,635	6,497	78.7

(a) Excluding stock appreciation.
(b) Excluding rent received (included in first column).
(c) Net of taxes paid abroad.
(d) Actual payments (not accruals: i.e. excluding additions to reserves).
(e) After deduction of additions to reserves; also excludes stock appreciation.

Sources: Central Statistical Office, *National Income and Expenditure: 1961*, tables 12, 32 and 61, pp. 8, 29 and 61; *1962*, tables 12, 32 and 62, pp. 13, 33 and 65; *1963*, tables 12, 32 and 63, pp. 13, 33 and 72; *1964*, tables 12, 32 and 65, pp. 11, 35 and 74; *1965*, tables 32 and 58, pp. 39 and 71; *1966*, tables 37 and 63, pp. 44 and 77; *1967*, tables 37 and 62, pp. 44 and 77; *1968*, tables 37 and 62, pp. 46 and 79; *1969*, tables 34 and 59, pp. 40 and 73; *1970*, tables 33 and 58, pp. 38 and 71; *1971*, tables 34 and 58, pp. 40 and 73; *1972*, tables 33 and 57, pp. 38 and 71; *1973*, tables 33 and 57, pp. 38 and 71; *1963–1973*, tables 35 and 59, pp. 40 and 73; *1964–74*, tables 42 and 66, pp. 44 and 66, pp. 44 and 77; *1965–75*, tables 6.2 and 12.9, pp. 44 and 82; *1966–76*, tables 6.2 and 11.9, pp. 46 and 84; *1967–77*, tables 6.2 and 11.9, pp. 50 and 88; *1979 Edition*, tables 6.2 and 11.9, pp. 50 and 86; *1980 Edition*, tables 6.2 and 11.9, pp. 45 and 82; *1981 Edition*, tables 6.2 and 11.9, pp. 45 and 82; and Appendix 10.1.

APPENDIX 10.4 *Capital account of public corporations, 1950 to 1980*

£ million

Year	Undistributed income and additions to reserves (a)	Capital transfers in (b)	Total receipts (b)	Gross domestic fixed capital formation	Value of physical increase in inventories	Capital transfers out	Total expenditure (a)	Financial balance: net acquisition of financial assets	Transactions in financial assets, or lending (c)	Total borrowing requirement
1950	98	3	101	288	−15	—	273	−172	20	192
1951	91	5	96	358	4	—	362	−266	−70	196
1952	189	6	195	414	51	—	465	−270	30	300
1953	200	7	207	488	−25	—	463	−256	1	257
1954	197	7	204	538	−69	—	469	−265	39	304
1955	148	12	160	571	22	—	593	−433	76	509
1956	195	16	211	589	16	—	605	−394	−106	288
1957	152	9	161	660	54	—	714	−553	51	604
1958	152	7	159	694	36	—	730	−571	3	574
1959	186	7	193	758	11	—	769	−576	8	584
1960	295	7	302	788	−25	—	763	−461	8	469
1961	352	8	360	905	−3	—	902	−542	25	567
1962	399	8	407	933	−1	—	932	−525	7	532
1963	573	9	582	1,024	−35	—	989	−407	11	418
1964	599	10	609	1,187	3	—	1,190	−581	−1	580
1965	646	11	657	1,294	−14	—	1,280	−623	30	653
1966	629	11	640	1,458	30	—	1,488	−848	45	893
1967	683	16	699	1,669	76	—	1,745	−1,046	49	1,095

Year									
1968	838	69	907	1,624	8	—	1,632	−725	113	838
1969	834	70	904	1,487	−73	—	1,414	−510	107	617
1970	735	76	811	1,679	−38	—	1,641	−830	122	952
1971	759	84	843	1,862	66	1	1,929	−1,086	121	1,207
1972	923	122	1,045	1,774	13	1	1,788	−743	396	1,139
1973	1,128	152	1,280	2,073	−28	2	2,047	−767	610	1,377
1974	1,059	215	1,274	2,859	−52	2	2,809	−1,535	507	2,042
1975	1,271	285	1,556	3,920	433	2	4,355	−2,799	6	2,805
1976	2,475	381	2,856	4,695	293	4	4,992	−2,136	1,191	3,327
1977	2,954	442	3,396	4,774	−157	15	4,632	−1,236	789	2,025
1978	3,357	529	3,886	4,944	−6	31	4,969	−1,083	1,266	2,349
1979	2,976	519	3,495	5,635	−45	41	5,631	−2,136	2,421	4,557
1980	3,705	597	4,302	6,846	31	46	6,923	−2,621	181	2,802

(a) Excluding stock appreciation.

(b) Excluding: loans from central government written off; transfer of liability for stock to central government; transfer of capital redemption funds to central government. Up to 1970, capital transfers are reported net.

(c) Comprising: net lending to private sector; net lending and investment abroad; cash expenditure on company securities; accruals adjustment; and other transactions in financial assets.

Sources: Central Statistical Office, *National Income and Expenditure: 1961*, tables 12 and 33, pp. 8 and 29; *1962*, tables 12 and 33, pp. 13 and 33; *1963*, tables 12 and 33, pp. 13 and 33; *1964*, tables 12 and 33, pp. 11 and 35; *1965*, tables 12 and 33, pp. 17 and 39; *1966*, tables 13 and 38, pp. 15 and 45; *1967*, tables 13 and 38, pp. 15 and 45; *1968*, tables 13 and 38, pp. 15 and 47; *1969*, tables 13 and 35, pp. 15 and 41; *1970*, tables 13 and 34, pp. 15 and 39; *1971*, tables 13 and 35, pp. 15 and 41; *1972*, tables 13 and 34, pp. 15 and 39; *1973*, tables 13 and 36, pp. 15 and 41; *1964–74*, tables 13 and 43, pp. 15 and 45; *1965–75*, tables 1.10 and 6.3, pp. 13 and 45; *1966–76*, tables 1.10 and 6.3, pp. 15 and 47; *1967–77*, tables 6.2 and 6.3, pp. 50 and 51; *1979 Edition*, tables 6.2 and 6.3, pp. 50 and 51; *1980 Edition*, tables 6.2, 6.3 and 6.4, pp. 45 and 46; *1981 Edition*, tables 6.2, 6.3 and 6.4, pp. 45 and 46; and Appendix 10.3.

Chapter 11

Final Expenditure
and Aggregate Demand

Contents

Chapter guide

Having now looked at all the sectors of the economy (with the exception of the sector of financial companies and institutions – which sector is considered subsequently when we can more readily appreciate its role), Chapters 11 and 12 explain how the aggregate economy 'works'. In Chapter 11 we consider the problem of *aggregate demand*; in Chapter 12 we consider the *financial balances (surpluses or deficits)* of sectors of the economy as part of the macroeconomic system.

In order to understand how the aggregate 'macro economy' works, we need first to understand the concept, and categories, of *final expenditure*, and this is fully explained in Chapter 11 first via a sequential development of the simple 'model' economy of Chapter 2, and then with reference to data from the UK economy (which data are explicitly related to the figures from the 'model' economies). We explain why total value added in the economy (i.e. gross domestic product) can also be measured as the sum of final expenditures and how imports and exports must be taken into the reckoning. The role of *taxes on expenditure* (less *subsidies*) is explained, so that the difference between gross domestic product at *market prices* and gross domestic product at *factor cost* can be fully understood. We show how final sales and *intermediate sales* relate to the production of value added by industries of the UK economy, thus completing Chapter 2's explanation of the gross domestic product. We see how transactions with the overseas sector fit into the framework of national accounts, especially with regard to the *overseas sector's financial balance*.

All the foregoing is a necessary preliminary to understanding how *aggregate demand* (total final expenditure) is determined. The explanation of this is known as 'Keynesian macroeconomics' because of its exposition by John Maynard Keynes in his book *The General Theory of Employment, Interest and Money* (1936). We first explain the problem which *Say's 'law'* created for economic theory; how the Polish economist Michał Kalecki propounded in 1935 (an incomplete) explanation of the problem of aggregate demand; and how Keynes gave the complete and systematic account in 1936 of how the *aggregate consumption function* and the *multiplier* worked, in conjunction with investment and final expenditure, to determine the total size of the flows of final expenditure in the economy. The multiplier process and its effect on incomes is fully explained, using a simple model economy, and we examine also the impact on the multiplier of 'leakages' into *imports*. We explain the important (and, at the time, revolutionary) assertion that total output (i.e. gross domestic product) and hence the volume of employment (and, consequently, the amount of unemployment) was determined by aggregate demand (and not by the capacity to produce). In other words, we consider Keynes's demonstration that mass unemployment could be a situation of *stable equilibrium*, with no automatic self-righting tendency. We see why and how Keynes argued, against the Treasury, that public-sector expenditure could be effectively expanded to reduce unemployment, and why, as part of his argument, Keynes insisted upon the *equality of saving and investment*.

Finally we look at the *Keynesian macroeconomic system* as a whole, with the aid of a diagram (Diagram 11.7) which puts together in one framework all the main elements of Keynes's explanation of how 'investment' determines total final expenditure.

Introduction

In an economy all transactions concerning goods and services (where the word 'transactions' covers sales of goods or services, or – the other side of the coin – expenditure on goods or services) can be divided into two mutually exclusive and jointly exhaustive classes of transactions: the class of final expenditures (or sales) and the class of intermediate expenditures (or sales). In this chapter we shall use the words 'expenditure' and 'sale' almost interchangeably because it does not really matter whose view of the transaction we take (the buyer's – expenditure; or the seller's – sale); so sometimes we shall use the term 'final expenditure', sometimes 'final sale' and sometimes 'final sale/expenditure'. Note that in this context 'expenditure' does not include expenditure on acquiring financial assets, nor does it include expenditure on transfer payments; we are concerned solely with transactions relating to goods and services. The reason for making the distinction between final and intermediate expenditures is so that we can analyse how the economy works.

The purpose of this chapter is twofold. First, to explain the concepts of final and intermediate expenditures and to show why gross domestic product (hitherto explained as the sum of values added) can also be measured as the sum of the various categories of final expenditures. Second, to explain how the total, or aggregate, flow of final expenditures is determined – in other words, to explain what determines the size of the gross domestic product in any one year. And, because the flow of GDP is, at any given technology, a determinant of total employment available in the economy, while unemployment is approximately determined by the difference between the demographically determined total labour force available for work and the economically determined total employment available, we are at the same time explaining some of the factors which determine unemployment.

This theory of what determines aggregate final expenditure (called *aggregate demand*) and hence aggregate employment/unemployment is variously called '*macro*economics' (the prefix 'macro' meaning large – in this context, large aggregates – and contrasted with the prefix 'micro' meaning small in size or extent; so we would talk about the *micro*economic analysis of a (single) household's expenditures but the *macro*economic analysis of all (aggregated) households' expenditure), or 'Keynesian economics' after the economist John Maynard Keynes, who, in 1936, published his book *The General Theory of Employment, Interest and Money* in which the theory was first systematically expounded.

Final expenditure

Because the concept of final expenditure is the key concept in understanding macroeconomics, we shall take its explanation in three separate steps aimed at explaining not only the concept itself but also the different categories of final expenditure.

In the first step we shall concentrate on distinguishing final expenditure from intermediate expenditure and we shall consider only two categories of final expenditure: namely, consumers' expenditure (or consumption), and investors' expenditure (or investment).

In the second step we shall concentrate more on explaining all the various categories of final expenditure (consumers' expenditure, investors' expenditure, government expenditure, and exports) and on explaining the role of expenditure on imports.

In both these steps we shall explain why the sum total of final expenditures by category is necessarily equal to the gross domestic product – it might be better to say 'is another way of looking at, or measuring, the gross domestic product'. These two steps will be taken with aid of a simple model elaborating the schematic economy of the farmer, miller, woodcutter and baker which we first used in Chapter 2 (see Table 2.1) to explain the concept of value added.

The third step is to go from the expanded model economy (Table 11.2) to the real figures on 'gross national product by category of [final] expenditure' which appears as table 1.1 of the *National Income and Expenditure* Blue Book – and we may note the symbolic importance of final expenditures being the very first table in the Blue Book.

In this third step we can complete the transition from the model of Table 2.1 to the real-world economy in Table 2.6 by dividing the sales receipts column of Table 2.6 into intermediate and final sales and distinguishing among the various categories of final expenditure – this is done in Table 11.10 below. We may also take the opportunity to look more closely at the international transactions of the UK economy – this is done in Table 11.11. All this should demonstrate the links between total value added (gross domestic product and gross national product) and total final expenditure. These three steps should fulfil the first purpose of this chapter, and we can then proceed to the second purpose – namely, to explain what determines aggregate final expenditure.

The model economy of Table 2.1 ended up by producing only bread for sale to consumers. Because we need also to consider the production of fixed capital goods for sale to investors, we shall now introduce the following three additional industries: a quarry, which produces cut or 'dressed' stone for sale to a millstone-maker and to an oven-maker;

a millstone-maker who produces mill-stones for sale to the miller (for grinding the wheat into flour); and an oven-maker who produces stone ovens for sale to the baker (for baking the bread). The sale of millstones and ovens, which are both fixed capital, introduces the requisite sale to investors. Table 11.1 gives the figures for the production of value added by this economy, and the table is annotated for the purpose of understanding the categorisation of sales receipts. Diagram 11.1 accompanies Table 11.1 for the purpose of making explicit the distinction between final sales/expenditures and intermediate sales/expenditures.

As noted, in this chapter we may use the words 'expenditure' and 'sale' interchangeably because they refer to the same transaction seen from different standpoints. Intermediate sales are sales of (or expenditure on) those goods and services which are used up in the same period's production of value added: they are sales from one producing industry to another producing industry for direct use in the immediate production of value added. Final sales (or expenditures) are sales of (or expenditure on) those goods and services which are not used up in the same period's production of value added: they are sales from a producing industry either to a 'final' consumer or to a 'final' investor. To put it crudely: final sales of (final expenditure on) goods and services are sales of goods and services which are wanted for their own sake (consumer goods) or for the sake of their contribution, to be made in future periods, to production (capital goods), while intermediate sales are sales of goods and services which are wanted for direct use in current production.

The classification of expenditures on (sales of) goods and services into these two mutually exclusive and jointly exhaustive classes is a classification of *transactions* by purpose of transaction. It is *not* a classification of products: the same product can be sold in either transaction; for example, if the miller sells flour to the baker for use by the baker in baking bread, that counts as an intermediate sale from one producer to another producer, but if the miller sells flour to a housewife for use by her in cooking for the family, that counts as a final sale to a consumer, and if the miller sells flour to the baker and the baker does not use that flour up in the production of value added but puts it aside (for future use) as inventory investment, that counts as a final sale to an investor. It is therefore misleading to talk of 'final products' and 'intermediate products' – the transactions, not the products, are what is being classified. Thus, in Chapter 9, where I implied that bread (a product) was in the class of final expenditures, I was talking loosely: it is the expenditure on bread (the transaction) which is being classified.

The distinction may be put more exactly, if a little less comprehensibly, by saying that intermediate sales are distinguished by appearing, in Table 11.1, *both* in the sales receipts column *and* in the bought-in materials column, while final sales are distinguished by appearing only in the sales receipts column. Let us see how these definitions work in Table 11.1. The farmer produces £20 worth of wheat a year and sells this to the miller; because the miller uses up all of this wheat during the year in producing value added, £20 appears again in the bought-in materials column for the milling industry. So the £20 for wheat appears twice in Table 11.1 – once in the sales receipts column and once in the bought-in materials column – and this transaction counts as an intermediate sale (by the farmer) or expenditure (by the miller). (We shall not, at this juncture, be considering taxes on expenditure, so Table 11.1 is devoid of these – see Table 9.11.)

The miller sells £30 of flour, all of it to the baker for use in the production of bread, so this, too, appears again in the cost of bought-in materials column and is classified as an intermediate sale/expenditure. The self-employed woodcutter sells £5 of wood to the baker, and this is likewise classified as an intermediate sale/expenditure.

The baker sells £45 of bread to consumers: this then 'disappears' from the process of production and plays no further role in producing value added (apart from its indirect effect of feeding the workers). Specifically, the £45 does not appear again in the cost of bought-in materials column, so, appearing once only, it is classified as a final

TABLE 11.1   *A model showing the production of value added and the distinction between final sales/expenditure and intermediate sales/expenditure*

£ a year (flow)

Productive industry (and product)	Production of value added						Distribution as income			
	Sales receipts	(Classification)	minus	Cost of bought-in materials	equals	Value added	equals	Employees' wages	plus	Gross profits
Farming (wheat)	20	(Intermediate sale to producers)		0		20		8		12
Milling (flour)	30	(Intermediate sale to producers)		20		10		6		4
Woodcutting (fuel)	5	(Intermediate sale to producers)		0		5		0		5
Baking (bread)	45	(Final sale to consumers)		35		10		6		4
Quarrying (cut stone)	10	(Intermediate sale to producers)		0		10		6		4
Millstone-making (millstones)	12	(Final sale to investors)		4		8		5		3
Oven-making (ovens)	18	(Final sale to investors)		6		12		9		3
Whole economy	140			65		75		40		35

Total final sales/expenditures   75
Of which:
  Final sales to consumers or consumers' (final) expenditure   45
  Final sales to investors or investment (final) expenditure   30

sale/expenditure. Within the class of final sales we shall be distinguishing several categories of final expenditure, according to the end-purpose of the expenditure; the end-purpose of expenditure on bread is consumption, so this falls into the category of final sales to consumers or consumers' expenditure.

Continuing with Table 11.1, the quarry produces and sells £10 worth of dressed (cut) stone a year: £4 to the millstone-maker and £6 to the oven-maker. Because this £10 appears again in the bought-in materials column, it counts as an intermediate sale to producers. The millstone-maker sells £12 worth of millstones to the miller. Millstones for grinding wheat are fixed capital (Chapter 1). Although fixed capital is used in the production of (future periods') value added, it is not used up (directly) in the production of the current period's value added. Accordingly, this £12 does not appear again in the cost of bought-in materials column and it is classified as a final sale to an investor. If the millstones are sold to the miller, we classify this as a (final) sale to the miller-as-investor (in contrast to the (intermediate) sale of wheat to the miller-as-producer). Because the end-purpose of this final expenditure is gross fixed capital formation (investment), the expenditure falls into the category of final sales to investors or investment expenditure. The miller may either be replacing a worn-out millstone (making good his depreciation or capital consumption) or expanding his milling capacity (net investment), or, of course, both.

The oven-maker sells £18 of stone ovens during the year to the baker. As with the millstones, this is classified as a final sale to investors. (We could imagine an awkward complication here: some of the ovens could be sold to households as 'consumer durables'

DIAGRAM 11.1 *The production boundary and intermediate and final sales*

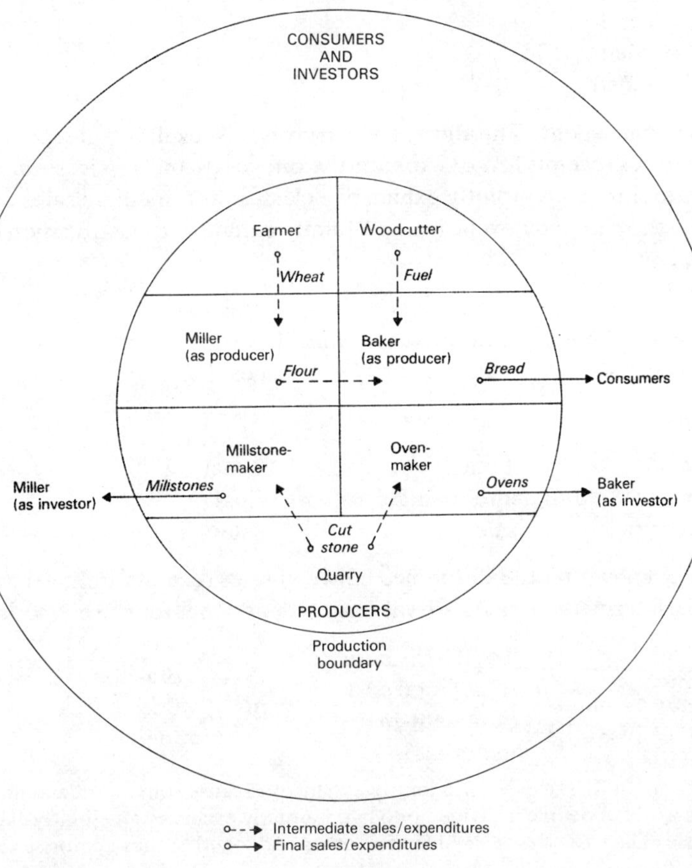

o-- -▶ Intermediate sales/expenditures
o——▶ Final sales/expenditures

where, although they would provide services to their owners, the ovens would not be used in the production of (future periods') value added. Such sales to households would not therefore count as fixed capital formation, and would be classified as consumers' expenditure on 'consumer durables'.)

We may look at Table 11.1 graphically if we depict the economy as comprising an inner circle of producers surrounded by an outer ring of consumers and investors (Diagram 11.1). The producers are separated from the consumers and investors by the 'production boundary'. All transactions within the production boundary are intermediate transactions; all transactions across the production boundary are final sales/expenditures. But in drawing such a diagram it is very important to keep in mind the distinction between the miller-as-investor buying millstones (a transaction which crosses the production boundary) and the miller-as-producer buying wheat (a transaction within the production boundary). The miller (and also the baker) does business under two hats, as investor and as producer, and we must be aware of which hat he is wearing (and therefore where he is standing in the diagram) when we consider his transactions.

The total of all sales receipts in the economy is £140 (Table 11.1), but this is simply an unuseful aggregate of the two classes of sales: final sales of £75 and intermediate sales of £65. The total of intermediate sales is simply the total of the figures appearing in the cost of bought-in materials column. The total of final sales has to be derived from selecting, in the sales receipts column, those transactions which we have classified as final sales. We may distinguish, in this class, the category of consumers' expenditure (final sales to consumers) and the category of investment expenditure (final sales to investors or gross fixed capital formation).

We can see arithmetically in Table 11.1 a most important equivalence, namely:

$$\begin{array}{lll} \text{Total} & \text{Total} & \\ \text{final} & = \text{value} & = £75 \\ \text{sales} & \text{added} & \end{array}$$

How does this come about? The algebra which gives this result is quite straightforward. All transactions – sales receipts for, or expenditure on, goods and services – are classified into two mutually exclusive and jointly exhaustive classes: intermediate sales and final sales.* Algebraically, this mutually exclusive and jointly exhaustive classification can be expressed as follows:

$$\begin{array}{llll} \text{Whole} & & \text{Total} & \text{Total} \\ \text{economy's} & \textit{equals} & \text{intermediate } \textit{plus} & \text{final} \\ \text{sales receipts} & & \text{sales} & \text{sales} \end{array}$$

and therefore:

$$\begin{array}{llll} \text{Whole} & & \text{Total} & \text{Total} \\ \text{economy's} & \textit{minus} & \text{intermediate } \textit{equals} & \text{final} \\ \text{sales receipts} & & \text{sales} & \text{sales} \end{array}$$

But we already know that the difference between sales receipts and the cost of bought-in materials – i.e. intermediate sales – is value added, and that for the economy as a whole:

$$\begin{array}{llll} \text{Whole} & & \text{Total intermediate} & \\ \text{economy's} & \textit{minus} & \text{sales (total cost} & \text{Total} \\ \text{sales receipts} & & \text{of bought-in} & \textit{equals} & \text{value} \\ & & \text{materials)} & \text{added} \end{array}$$

*Lest the term 'mutually exclusive and jointly exhaustive' cause some puzzlement, the reader may reflect that the world of people is divided into two mutually exclusive and jointly exhaustive classes: male and female. The two classes exclude each other and together they comprise the entire class of people.

From these last two equations we have:

Total   Total
final *equals* value
sales   added

And because gross domestic product is the total value added, we may thus measure GDP in this economy as the total of final expenditures (subject to subsequent remarks about dealing with imports).

The discussion of Table 11.1 and Diagram 11.1 should have clarified the concepts of final sales/expenditures and intermediate sales/expenditures. Before continuing to the second step, it may be helpful to consider further the difference between intermediate sales and final sales to investment. We made a distinction between transactions on goods and services where the goods and services were required for using up in the current period's production of value added (calling these intermediate sales/expenditures) and transactions on goods and services where the goods and services were required for their own sake (consumption final expenditures) or for the sake of their future contribution to the production of (subsequent periods') value added (investment final expenditure). Thus sales of millstones count as (gross) fixed capital formation (investment final sales); or the sale of a bag of flour for storage as circulating capital (not for use in the *current* period's production of value added) counts as circulating capital formation (investment final sales – in the national accounts' terminology this would be called the 'value of physical increase in stocks and work in progress'). Now, while we can see clearly that consumption expenditures are on goods (such as bread) which are 'wanted for their own sake', we can also see that investment final expenditures are on goods which are wanted only for the sake of the contribution they make to the production of value added (albeit in future periods), just as intermediate goods are wanted for their contribution to value added (albeit in the current production period). Furthermore, fixed capital goods are gradually, if indirectly, 'used up' in the production of value added. So, one might ask, should not investment final sales be excluded from the national product, like intermediate sales? Furthermore, we might ask, suppose millstones wear out very rapidly, lasting say only three months; then, is not the miller's investment in a millstone 'used up' in the current period's production of value added? So how is the distinction between intermediate sales and investment final sales maintained?

The answer to these questions is twofold. First, the distinction is maintained by a set of accounting rules or conventions; but, second, the accounting conventions do permit subsequent adjustment to take account of the questions raised. First, on the question of accounting conventions we maintain a strict division between fixed and circulating capital (Chapter 1), and any expenditure on an item of fixed capital (no matter how short the item's economic life) counts as a final expenditure. Regarding circulating capital, we maintain a strict division between sales/expenditures which appear twice – once in the sales receipts column and once in the cost of bought-in materials column – and so count as intermediate sales, and sales/expenditures which do not appear again in the cost of bought-in materials column, as would happen if the baker bought a sack of flour for storage, count as a final sale/expenditure. (It must be understood that the cost of bought-in materials column must, in an accounting sense, contain figures relating only to the *use* in that production period of materials – see the adjustments we had to make in Chapter 10 to distinguish between 'purchases' of materials and 'use' of materials by public corporations before we could properly calculate their value added. Spelled out, 'cost of bought-in materials' means cost of bought-in materials actually used during this period.)

Second, the accounting conventions do take account of the questions raised. Any using-up of a circulating capital stock in subsequent periods will be taken into the reckoning when calculating value added (see the discussion in Chapter 2 of the need to calculate value added with reference to both opening and closing stocks – inventories of circulating capital). The depreciation of fixed capital (or capital consumption) will be taken into the reckoning if we choose to use the distinction between gross and net profits; we normally take value added as gross of depreciation and then derive gross profits, from which we may reckon the net profits, but it is possible to take value added net of capital consumption, and indeed this is done when we reckon *the* national income as being the net national product (see Table 2.6 and the discussion in Chapter 2).

These accounting conventions are adopted because they lead to 'sensible' or 'meaning-ful' results. For example, if fixed (or circulating) capital formation increases the economy's *capacity* to produce output (value added), then it seems sensible to treat such expenditure differently from intermediate sales. The distinction is meaningful also because there is a sense in which intermediate sales are very closely tied to ongoing final sales – the flow of intermediate sales (Diagram 11.1) depends almost immediately upon the final sales: one can see that the baker's expenditure on flour (an intermediate expenditure) depends almost one-for-one on how much bread he is selling; if consumers alter their bread-buying habits, then this will rapidly lead to a corresponding and matching change in expenditure by the baker on flour. It is the final sales of/expenditure on bread which directly 'drives' the intermediate sales of/expenditure on flour. Conversely, there is a sense in which invest-ment final sales/expenditures are not quite so closely or directly related to the currently ongoing sales of bread; to be sure, investment will be influenced by the 'state of the market', but the baker might, as a young and aggressive salesman with a keen eye on the increasing participation of women in the labour market and the consequent decline of home-baking, take an optimistic view of the future and so set out to expand his baking capacity by ordering more ovens, at the same time beginning to increase his inventories to cope with the anticipated greater throughput of materials. Here there is no direct, one-for-one tie between ongoing final sales of bread and final investment expenditure, as there is between final sales of bread and intermediate expenditure on bought-in materials. This is an important economic difference between intermediate sales and final investment sales, and so is a reason for maintaining the accounting conventions as illustrated in Diagram 11.1 – there is an economic-behavioural difference between the baker-as-producer and the baker-as-investor.

Categories of final expenditure

We have given the distinction between final and intermediate sales/expenditures a fairly good airing and we must move on to the second step of explaining the various categories within the class of final expenditures and the role of imports. For this we need an expanded model economy which includes, besides the household (personal) sector and the enter-prise sector of Table 11.1, a government sector and an overseas sector. The introduction of the overseas sector and sales to and purchases from that sector (exports and imports respectively) makes the model a little more complex, because we now have to record separately sales at home (to residents) and sales abroad (to non-residents), and likewise we have to distinguish in cost of bought-in materials between materials produced at home and materials produced abroad. Among the sales at home, we record in separate columns intermediate sales and final sales. Table 11.2 gives this expanded model economy.

Table 11.2 has the same values added in the productive industries which appeared in Table 11.1, but we have now inserted two other industries or branches of activity: an industry which refines and distributes imported petroleum, the product here being petrol (gasoline); and a government sector (branch of activity) which provides (a) a refuse-collection service for the public, and (b) military defence. Let us run through this model economy to see how it works and how its national accounts are arranged.

Table 11.2   An expanded model showing the main categories of final expenditure

Industry and type of expenditure	Sales receipts 'Sales' at home Intermediate sales	Final sales	Sales abroad: exports	Total sales	Bought-in materials Produced at home	Produced abroad: imports	Total	Value added	Employees' wages	Gross profits
Farming	15	—	5	20	0	0	0	20	8	12
Milling	24	—	1	25	15	0	15	10	6	4
Woodcutting	5	—	0	5	0	0	0	5	0	5
Baking	—	40	5	45	30 (a)	5	35	10	6	4
Quarrying	10	—	0	10	0	0	0	10	6	4
Millstone-making	—	8	4	12	4	0	4	8	5	3
Oven-making	—	10	8	18	6	0	6	12	9	3
Petroleum refining										
Sales to households	—	4 ⎫								
Sales to enterprise	1	2 ⎬	0	7	0	2	2	5	4	1
Sales to government	—	2 ⎭								
Government: refuse collection	—	8	—	8	(b)	(b)	(b)	8	8	(b)
Government: military defence	—	12	—	12	(b)	(b)	(b)	12	12	(b)
Whole economy	55	84	23	162	55	7	62	100	64	36

Final expenditure:
Consumers' expenditure	44	—	—
Fixed capital formation	18	—	—
Government final consumption	22		
Total domestic expenditure	84		
Exports	—	23	23
Total final expenditure	84	23	107
less Imports	—	—	7
Total gross domestic product	—	—	100

(a) Comprising: £24 flour; £5 wood fuel; £1 petrol.
(b) Inapplicable because purchases of materials by government are, by accounting convention, treated as a final sale to government consumption and not as an intermediate expenditure.

The farmer produces and sells £20 of wheat as before, but £5 worth of wheat is now sold abroad as an 'export' and only £15 of wheat is sold 'at home' to the miller as an intermediate sale (i.e. within the economy to a resident producer for use in the production of value added); the farmer has no bought-in materials, so his value added is £20, that is:

$$\text{Total sales} \quad minus \quad \text{Total bought-in materials}$$

and this is distributed as £8 of wages and £12 of gross profits (and rent if he pays any). The miller buys in and uses £15 of wheat from the farmer and sells flour worth £25 a year: £24 to the baker (an intermediate sale) and an export (final) sale of £1 a year. The self-employed woodcutter sells £5 of wood a year to the baker as an intermediate sale. The baker buys in the following materials for use: £24 of flour from the miller; £5 of wood fuel from the woodcutter; £1 of petrol from the petroleum-refiners and distributors (we suppose that the baker delivers the bread to households, and for this he needs petrol to drive his van); and £5 of imported yeast purchased directly from abroad. The baker's total intermediate expenditure on bought-in materials is £35 and the baker sells £45 worth a year: £40 to resident consumers (a final sale) and £5 as an export to non-residents in the overseas sector (also a final sale). So the baker's value added is £10, distributed as £6 of wages and £4 of gross profits. The quarry produces £10 of cut stone a year, selling £4 to the millstone-maker and £6 to the oven-maker (both of these are intermediate sales); the quarry has no purchases of bought-in materials, so its value added is £10. The millstone-maker sells £12 worth of millstones a year: £8 to a resident customer for investment (a final sale) and £4 as an export to an overseas, non-resident customer (also a final sale); value added in millstone-making is £8 a year. The oven-maker sells £18 worth of ovens a year: £10 to a resident customer (final investment sale) and £8 as an export to an overseas, non-resident customer (also a final sale); value added in oven-making is £12 a year.

The petroleum-refining and distributing sector buys in as imports £2 a year of crude petroleum (it has no other purchases) and refines and sells £7 worth of petrol a year. Although the refinery's accounts show only the total of £7 of sales, we know from other sources (the annual household expenditure survey, the annual census of industrial production, and the government's accounts) that households spent £4 a year on petrol (a final expenditure); enterprises spent £1 a year on petrol (an intermediate expenditure); and the government spent £2 a year on petrol, so we can enter these in the way shown. Note that any sale of goods to the government counts as a final sale to government consumption (this accounting convention will be discussed in the following paragraphs). Value added in petroleum-refining and distribution is £5 a year, distributed as £4 of wages and £1 of gross profits.

We come now to government activities. The government in this model economy employs people to provide two services to the public: refuse collection and military defence. As with nearly all government services, these services are provided free of direct charge to the user – the refuse collectors just turn up at homes and empty dustbins and no money changes hands then and there (as happens, say, with the milk delivery). Nor is there any direct charge for military protection – it would in any case be a puzzle to know how such charges could be made. Instead the government finances, or partly finances, the provision of these services from taxation on incomes (there are no taxes on expenditure in this economy) but these income taxes are not seen in Table 11.2. Because the government does not 'sell' its services but provides them free of direct charge, it is difficult to see how we can arrive at a figure in the sales at home column; indeed, you will see that the heading to the column contains the word 'sales' in inverted commas to indicate that for the government's activities sales are an accounting fiction. In the case of commercial enterprises we have always worked from sales receipts to value added to wages and profits. In the case of government activities, this starting-point – sales receipts – is absent; what is obvious, however, is that wages are being earned by employees engaged in refuse collection and by members of the armed forces. Therefore, we can start from this datum, and fill in the accounts by working backward as follows. Suppose income from employment is £8 a year for refuse collectors and £12 a year is paid as wages to the armed forces; government (non-trading) activities are deemed by definition to be non-profit-making – that is, in the nature of things there are no trading profits; so that, if value added is the sum of wages and profits, and as profits are non-existent, then 'value added' by these government activities must be equal to the wages paid. This is a 'pretend', or imputed, valuation for value added. (Note that we are not here concerned with those relatively small government trading activities such as the Forestry Commission, where there are sales receipts – from selling timber – and where a profit can be made.)

The reason for putting a figure in the value-added column (derived by working backward from wages) is that we – the public – presumably benefit from the services provided by the use of these workers: if the government did not provide a 'free' refuse-collection service, householders and enterprises would simply turn to private contractors to take away their rubbish and things would be much as before, except that refuse collection would then be a private-sector activity with value added calculated in the usual way. Therefore, we should not allow the peculiar method of financing government refuse collection (from taxes on income) to interfere with the economic reality that people are deriving a 'real' benefit from these workers' services. Put the other way, suppose refuse collection had been done by private contractors with their value added entering the gross domestic product, but that the private service had not proved satisfactory and the government therefore took over the services and provided a comprehensive service free of direct charge, paying for the service out of taxes on income. In this event it would not be sensible to have the size of the GDP diminished by the disappearance of the private contractors' value added; therefore, we need to insert a figure in the value-added column; and the only way we can now do this is to work backward from the wage bill (the value added will have been somewhat diminished by the disappearance of contractors' profits but the wage element will still be there).

So we have now entered an imputed value-added figure for government activities in the value-added column, which column gives GDP by industrial origin. In the real world this figure will also include both the benefit which the government derives from its owner-occupation of buildings and also any profit which it may make on its trading activities. But this is how the value-added figure for government activities is constructed – by working backward from factor incomes.

This way of arriving at the value added in government activities means that the cost of bought-in materials is inapplicable to government activities: instead any materials which the government buys – and in our model economy the government buys £2 of petrol to run the refuse-collection trucks – is classified separately as a final sale to government consumption; the fact that such sales are treated as final sales by accounting convention means, of course, that they cannot be entered in the bought-in materials column of intermediate sales. So these columns are inapplicable in so far as government non-trading, tax-financed activities are concerned.

We can now complete the accounts by entering for the government activities an imputed or 'pretend' sales figure in the sales receipts column. The fiction, or accounting convention, is that the government not only produces these refuse-collection and military-defence services but that the government then sells these services to itself, at cost valuation – buying the services up on behalf of the public. That is, the government itself is the final consumer of the services it produces, just as households are final consumers of bread. The valuation of these pretend purchases is simply the value added, which in turn has been derived from the wage bill. So in the 'sales' receipts column we enter imputed sales receipts based on this cost valuation, and these imputed sales receipts are treated as final sales; in this way we preserve the relationship that total final sales in the economy equal total value added in the economy (allowing for imports, with which we shall deal shortly). In other words, the purpose of entering a figure for 'sales' receipts on these government activities is to preserve this basic national accounting relationship between total final sales and total value added. Although these contortions, or fictions, relating to government non-trading activities may seem at first sight peculiar, they are necessary in order to preserve a coherent and sensible system for national accounts.

Having explained the treatment of government activities, we may now turn to consider how the relationship between total final sales and total value added works out and how we must allow for imports.

In the national accounts, five categories of final sales/expenditure are distinguished as follows:

1. Consumers' expenditure
2. General government final consumption
3. Gross domestic fixed capital formation
4. Value of physical increase in stocks and work in progress
5. Exports

The first four add up to what is known as 'total domestic expenditure', and total domestic expenditure *plus* exports *equals* total final expenditure. Let us consider these categories of final expenditure using the model economy of Table 11.2. Consumers' final expenditure is £44 a year, comprising £40 of bread and £4 of petrol (you should tick these figures in Table 11.2). General government final consumption is £22 a year, comprising £2 of petrol, £8 of refuse collection (under the convention that the government buys from itself, on behalf of the public, the services it is producing), and £12 of military defence (ditto). The £2 of petrol counts as final consumption expenditure, as does the 'expenditure' on refuse collection and military defence. In this economy, the government does not engage in any fixed capital formation; but if it had, this would have been classified as final expenditure on capital formation. Gross domestic fixed capital formation is £18 a year, comprising £8 of millstones (bought by the miller) and £10 of ovens (bought by the baker). This model economy has no inventory investment (value of physical increase in stocks and work in progress). Total domestic (final) expenditure – that is, final expenditure by residents – is therefore £84.

Export final sales/expenditure – that is, final expenditure by non-residents – is £23 a year, comprising £5 of wheat sold abroad by the farmer, £1 of flour sold abroad by the miller, £5 of bread sold abroad by the baker, £4 of millstones sold abroad by the millstone-maker, and £8 of ovens sold abroad by the oven-maker.

Therefore, total final expenditure is £107, comprising £84 of total domestic (final) expenditure and £23 of export final expenditure.

All figures in the sales receipts columns which have not been ticked are the intermediate sales which ought to appear in the figures in the bought-in materials produced at home column. Thus the farmer's £15 of wheat sold to the miller appears as the miller's bought-in materials produced at home. The £24 of flour, the £5 of wood, and the £1 of (refined) petrol appear as £30 in the baker's bought-in materials produced at home. The quarry's £10 of dressed stone appears as £4 bought by the millstone-maker and £6 bought by the oven-maker. All sales abroad are, by definition, final sales, so we have now classified all sales receipts (in the first three columns of Table 11.2) into two mutually exclusive and jointly exhaustive classes (i.e. nothing has been left out).

The problem which now arises is that, 'embodied' in total final expenditure of £107 is some expenditure on imports, and imports do not constitute domestic value added: by definition, expenditure on imports is expenditure on overseas, non-residents' value added and generates incomes only for non-residents. The total of imports into our model economy is £7 a year, comprising £5 of yeast imported by the baker, and £2 of crude petroleum imported by the oil refinery. This £7 of total expenditure on imports represents income (value added) which accrues to non-residents; it is *not* part of domestic value added and incomes, though it is (its cost is) 'embodied' in the final sales of petrol and bread. Note that the value of yeast imports is also (partly) embodied in the value of bread exports. In an economy nearly all goods produced and sold in final sales/expenditure will be an inextricable mixture of home-produced value added and imported value added: for example, a British Leyland car will contain copper (probably from Zambia), rubber (probably from Malaysia), synthetic fibres (probably made from petroleum from Saudi Arabia), and so on. The only way we can extricate the imported value added from final sales is to make an over-all adjustment to the total final expenditure and deduct aggregate imports from total final expenditure. Thus we have:

Total final expenditure (embodying some foreign value added) *minus* Total imports (foreign value added) *equals* Total domestic value added

Total domestic value added in the model economy of Table 11.2 can be quite straightforwardly calculated as the total of the figures in the value-added column (using the conventions for calculating value added by government activities), and is £100. Total final expenditure is £107 and imports total £7, so the above equation works out as:

£107 − £7 = £100

There is nothing 'magical' about this equality; it is simply an algebraic rearrangement of the way in which we have, for each industry and therefore in aggregate, calculated value added. Thus, for each industry, the value-added equation is:

Sales at home *plus* Sales abroad (exports) *minus* Intermediate purchases (home-produced) *minus* Imports *equals* Value added

Therefore, in aggregate we have:

Total sales at home *plus* Total sales abroad (exports) *minus* Total intermediate purchases (home-produced) *minus* Total imports *equals* Total value added (GDP)

equals
Total final expenditure

As indicated, the first three terms on the left-hand side of the equation constitute total final expenditure and this gets us back to the previous equation.

As we shall see, this equation is important in the analysis of the working of the economy. Inserting the categories of final expenditure we have:

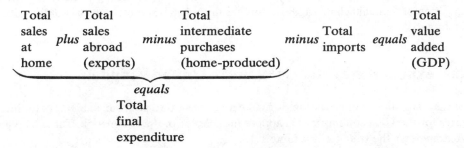

Consumers' expenditure *plus* Gross domestic fixed capital formation *plus* Value of physical increase in stocks, etc.

(*Continued over*)

plus General government final consumption   *plus* Exports *minus* Imports

equals Gross domestic product   *equals* Income from employment   *plus* Gross profits and rents

where incomes (wages, etc., profits, and rents) are all measured before deduction of taxes on income. This equation ignores taxes on expenditure, but we had in Chapter 9 a preliminary look at the way these fit into the picture and we shall subsequently see how expenditure taxes come into the UK national accounts.

Another way of looking at this equation, used by Wilfred Beckerman in his book *An Introduction to National Income Analysis* (Weidenfeld & Nicolson, 3rd edn, 1980), is to say that the benefit which residents derive from economic activity is of two sorts: consumption benefits and investment benefits. Consumption benefits may be enjoyed privately (consumers' expenditure) or publicly (government consumption). Investment benefits may take three forms: the accumulation of fixed capital; the change in inventories (circulating capital formation); and the accumulation of (financial) claims on non-residents, which claims may be earned by selling to non-residents more than is purchased from them, i.e. by an excess of exports over imports. This is how Beckerman puts it (p. 86):

Private consumption [consumers' expenditure]
Public consumption [government final consumption] } Total consumption

Gross domestic fixed capital formation
Change in stocks [value of physical increase in
    inventories]
Exports *less* Imports } Total investment

Note that although we exclude from capital formation (or investment) the acquisition of financial claims by a resident against a resident (because the financial claim and matching financial liability cancel each other), the acquisition of a financial claim by a resident against a non-resident does not, for the nation, have a cancelling liability; so the net acquisition of financial claims against non-residents can be counted as part of the nation's investment.

Final expenditures and GDP in the United Kingdom

The third step in our explanation of final expenditure is to go from Table 11.2 to the real figures for the UK economy which appear in table 1.1 of the Blue Book. Table 11.3 gives an extract from the Blue Book's table 1.1.

Table 11.3 starts by giving the real-world counterparts of the whole economy's employees' wages (income from employment) and gross profits (gross profits, self-employment income and rents) to be found for the model economy at the bottom of the last two columns of Table 11.2: we have already encountered these two real-world figures for the UK economy in 1980 in Table 2.7, to which reference should be made. The whole economy's value added is then given; this is the real-world counterpart to the figure at the end of the third-last column in Table 11.2. These three figures are familiar and accordingly provide a known starting-point from which to explore the real-world figures on final expenditures by category.

Consumers' expenditure, excluding taxes on expenditure, was £113,446 million in

TABLE 11.3   *Final expenditures and gross domestic product in the United Kingdom, 1980*

	£ million	Percentage of GDP
Income from employment [a]	137,083	70.8
Gross profits, self-employment income and rents [a][b]	56,405	29.2
Gross domestic product at factor cost	193,488	100.0
Consumers' expenditure [c]	113,446	58.6
Gross domestic capital formation (fixed and circulating) [c]	33,031	17.1
General government final consumption [c]	44,636	23.1
Total domestic expenditure [c]	191,113	98.8
Exports of goods and services	60,207	31.1
Total final expenditure [c]	251,320	129.9
less Imports of goods and services [d]	57,832	29.9
Gross domestic product at factor cost	193,488	100.0

[a] See Table 2.7 in Chapter 2 above.
[b] Including imputed output from dwellings; adjusted for doublecounting of financial services and residual error. Excludes stock appreciation.
[c] At factor cost, i.e. excluding taxes on expenditure (see Diagram 2.3).
[d] Excluding taxes on expenditure levied on imports.

Source: Central Statistical Office, *National Income and Expenditure 1981 Edition*, tables 1.1 and 1.2, pp. 3 and 5 (see also Table 2.7 above).

1980. The figure which we encountered previously in Tables 3.1 and 3.3 for consumers' expenditure, including taxes on expenditure, was £135,403 million in 1980. From this we can infer that expenditure taxes paid by consumers on their expenditure were £135,403 million *minus* £113,446 million *equals* £21,957 million, or 16.2 per cent of tax-inclusive expenditure. The figure comprises those Customs and Excise taxes on expenditure paid by the personal sector (see Table 9.5 for total Customs and Excise taxes, not all of which are paid by the personal sector), motor-vehicle duties paid by the personal sector (Table 9.5), and rates paid by the personal sector (Table 9.15), *less* subsidies on expenditure made available to the personal sector (see Table 9.4 for total subsidies – not all of which go to the personal sector). Taxes on expenditure paid by the personal sector are allocated by the national income statisticians, and Table 11.4 gives their allocation; this table is important for understanding the distinction between final expenditure at market prices and final expenditure at factor cost (and hence value added – gross domestic product – at market prices and at factor cost: see Diagram 2.3 and Table 9.11 and related discussion in the text).

Total taxes on consumers' expenditure in 1980 were £26,422 million, of which the most important were taxes on alcoholic drink, taxes on tobacco, rates, and taxes on the running costs of motor-vehicles. However, VAT (see Tables 9.5 and 9.11) ensures that nearly all items of consumers' expenditure are taxed. Total subsidies on consumers' expenditure in 1980 were £4,465 million, of which the most important were subsidies on rents and rates (rebates to poor families) and on travel (e.g. payments to British Rail and to bus services to run 'uneconomic' routes at 'low' fares). Subsidies are a negative tax, so the total of taxes and subsidies, i.e. taxes *less* subsidies, was £21,957 million. Consumers' expenditure excluding these expenditure taxes (*less* subsidies) was £113,446 million in 1980; this is known as 'consumers' expenditure at factor cost' and the reason for this slightly peculiar terminology can be seen if you look at the illustrative model of VAT (a tax on expenditure) in Table 9.11. In that model we have two figures for consumers' final expenditure on bread: £45 excluding VAT; and £49.5 including VAT. But when we look at the factor incomes (labour's income and profits) generated in the production of this final expenditure

TABLE 11.4   *Taxes on expenditure and subsidies allocated to consumers' expenditure, 1980*

	£ million	Percentage of total taxes (*less* subsidies)
Taxes on expenditure		
Food (household expenditure, excluding meals out)	877	4.0
Alcoholic drink	3,707	16.9
Tobacco	3,331	15.2
Housing (rates, water charges, VAT on maintenance, etc.)	3,840	17.5
Fuel and light	66	0.3
Clothing	1,243	5.7
Consumer durables (cars, furniture, electrical goods, etc.)	1,621	7.4
Running costs of motor-vehicles (petrol duties, licences, etc.)	3,324	15.1
All other household goods [a]	1,642	7.5
All services (including catering)	2,607	11.9
Not allocated to categories	4,164	19.0
Total taxes on expenditure	26,422	120.3
Subsidies on expenditure		
Food	493	2.2
Rent, rates, water charges	2,481	11.3
Travel	733	3.3
Others	201	0.9
Not allocated to categories	557	2.5
Total subsidies on expenditure	4,465	20.3
Taxes on expenditure *less* subsidies	21,957	100.0
Consumers' expenditure, excluding taxes (*less* subsidies), i.e. 'at factor cost'	113,446	—
Consumers' expenditure, including taxes (*less* subsidies), i.e. 'at market prices'	135,403	—

[a] Comprising (in £ million) taxes on: other household goods (519); chemists' goods (254); miscellaneous recreational goods (517); other miscellaneous goods (352).

Source: Central Statistical Office, *National Income and Expenditure 1981 Edition*, table 4.8, p. 36.

we see that the factor incomes, the factor cost of production of value added, sum to £45: namely, £20 wages and £25 profits. This is therefore known as 'value added at factor cost', and therefore final expenditure on bread excluding taxes on expenditure is known as 'final expenditure at factor cost'.

Final expenditure at factor cost measures the factor incomes generated in the course of producing the good or service which is the object of the final sale/expenditure, all the way through the chain of intermediate sales/expenditure (wheat, flour, etc.) to the last producer (the baker). Final expenditure at market prices measures factor incomes generated *plus* the taxes on expenditure received as 'income' by the government (Table 9.11). So if we were comparing the real-life figures in Table 11.4 with their model counterparts in Table 9.11 we would have:

	Model economy, Table 9.11 £	UK economy 1980, Table 11.4, £ million
Consumers' final expenditure at factor cost	45	113,446
Taxes on expenditure (*less* subsidies)	4.5	21,957
Consumers' final expenditure at market prices	49.5	135,403

Returning to Table 11.3, final expenditure on gross domestic capital formation (fixed capital formation and the value of the physical change in inventories) was £33,031 million (excluding such taxes on expenditure as fall on capital formation, but not VAT, which does not apply to capital expenditure). The total of capital formation including taxes on expenditure was £36,454 million in 1980, so we may infer that final expenditure on capital formation carried expenditure taxes of £3,423 million, or 9.4 per cent of the tax-inclusive total. The Blue Book gives no analysis of these expenditure taxes on capital formation (they must *not* be confused with taxes on capital, such as capital gains tax or capital transfer tax).

An analysis of capital formation at market prices by sector making the expenditure is given in Table 11.5. In order to relate the figures in Table 11.5 to the capital accounts of the various sectors (Tables 3.5, 4.7, 9.1, 9.4 and 10.5) the increase in the book value of stocks is given, but the stock appreciation part of this does not count as capital formation (see Table 2.5), so we must deduct from the increase in the book value of stocks and work in progress the amount of stock appreciation to get the value of the physical increase in stocks and work in progress; it is this latter which counts as income-generating final capital expenditure. The economy was in a recession in 1980, so there was in fact disinvestment in inventories, i.e. a running down of stocks or 'de-stocking' of £3,596 million in 1980. The second-last column of Table 11.5 gives the amount of gross fixed capital formation undertaken by each sector (gross, that is, of capital consumption or depreciation). We know (Table 3.5) that a large proportion (49 per cent in 1980) of personal-sector fixed capital formation is on new dwellings (Table 4.9 had a breakdown, by type of asset, of industrial and commercial companies' gross domestic fixed capital formation).

TABLE 11.5   *Final expenditure on gross domestic capital formation, 1980*

	£ million at market prices				
	Increase in book value of stocks and work in progress	Stock appreci- ation	Value of physical increase in stocks, etc.	Gross domestic fixed capital formation	Domestic capital formation
Personal sector [a]	355	854	−499	7,065	6,566
Industrial and commercial companies [b]	1,853	5,049	−3,196	15,640	12,444
Financial companies and institutions	−51	—	−51	4,999	4,948
Public corporations [c]	424	393	31	6,846	6,877
Central government [d]	300	181	119	1,679	1,798
Local authorities [d]	—	—	—	3,821	3,821
All sectors	2,881	6,477	−3,596	40,050	36,454

[a] See Table 3.5.
[b] See Tables 2.9 and 4.7.
[c] See Table 10.5.
[d] See Tables 9.1 and 9.4.

Source: Central Statistical Office, *National Income and Expenditure 1981 Edition*, tables 10.3 and 12.4, pp. 71 and 89.

The figure for gross fixed capital formation in Table 11.3 includes gross fixed capital formation undertaken by central government and local authorities, this government expenditure being separated from government final consumption expenditure. We did not pause in Chapter 9 to consider the government's capital expenditure in any detail save to note (Table 9.4) that a large proportion (69 per cent) was undertaken by local authorities, so Table 11.6 gives a breakdown of government fixed capital formation by type of asset (see also, for comparison, Diagram 1.7 on the disposition of the net capital stock). We can

TABLE 11.6   *Final expenditure on fixed capital formation by central government and local authorities, 1980*

	£ million at market prices		
	Central government	Local authorities	General government
Vehicles, ships, and aircraft [a]	32	161	193
Plant and machinery	348	236	584
Dwellings	37	2,213	2,250
Other new buildings and works	1,316	1,886	3,202
Purchases *less* sales of land and existing buildings	−54	−675	−729
Total	1,679	3,821	5,500

[a] Not including military vehicles, ships and aircraft, purchases of which are classified as government final consumption expenditure.

Source: Central Statistical Office, *National Income and Expenditure 1981 Edition*, table 10.3, pp. 70–1.

quickly see that the three big items were expenditure on new dwellings by local authorities, and expenditure on other new buildings and works by both central government and local authorities. Note that capital expenditure by a sector includes purchases *less* sales of existing land and buildings; as one sector's net purchases tend to be another sector's net sales, this tends to cancel for the economy as a whole except for the (mainly legal) costs of transferring land and buildings (which by accounting convention is classed as final capital expenditure). The local authorities have a large negative figure of purchases *less* sales of existing land and buildings because of the sale of council houses to the personal sector.

General government final consumption expenditure in Table 11.3 was £44,636 million (at factor cost) in 1980. This is the real-world counterpart to the final expenditure of £22 in Table 11.2 comprising £20 of wages and £2 of petrol. Table 11.7 shows that a large proportion (59.7 per cent) goes on wages and salaries. Other government final consumption expenditure, excluding taxes on expenditure, amounted to £13,996 million; including taxes on expenditure, other final consumption expenditure came to £16,929 million, of which £6,416 million, or 37.9 per cent, was for military defence supplies (including vehicles, ships, aircraft, etc.); £4,526 million or 26.7 per cent was for the National Health Service supplies; and £1,847 million or 10.9 per cent was for education supplies. Finally, the National Insurance surcharge (which the government, like all other employers, pays is

TABLE 11.7   *General government final consumption expenditure, 1980*

	£ million	Percentage of total at market prices
Current expenditure on goods and services		
Wages and salaries	28,865	59.7
Other payments (excluding taxes on expenditure)	13,996	29.0
Imputed consumption of non-trading capital	1,775	3.7
Total expenditure (excluding taxes on expenditure)	44,636	92.3
National Insurance surcharge	768	1.6
Other taxes on expenditure	2,933	6.1
Total expenditure (including taxes on expenditure)	48,337	100.0

Source: Central Statistical Office, *National Income and Expenditure 1981 Edition*, tables 1.1, 9.1, 9.5 and 9.6, pp. 3, 59, 65 and 67.

classified as a tax on expenditure, and so total general government final consumption expenditure at market prices (including imputed capital consumption) was £48,337 million in 1980.

Together, all these categories of final expenditure totalled £191,113 million of domestic expenditure by residents in 1980; to this must be added £60,207 million of exports of goods and services (final expenditure by non-residents). This gives £251,320 million of total final expenditure in 1980 (this is the real-world counterpart of the £107 of total final expenditure in Table 11.2). But part of this total final expenditure consisted of expenditure on imports amounting to £57,832 million in 1980. This expenditure on imports does not generate income for residents, and so we must deduct it to give the total final expenditure which does generate income for residents: as we have previously demonstrated, and as the figures in Table 11.3 show, this last total is equivalent to (is another way of looking at) the gross domestic product at factor cost.

It is important that one should understand thoroughly this (rather complex) way of looking at gross domestic product (total value added) as the sum of all final expenditures adjusted for (i.e. *minus*) imports. Table 11.8 shows in full the parallel figures for the model economy of Table 11.2 and the UK economy final expenditures in 1980 and the student should practise by inserting the UK figures for final expenditure into Table 11.2, though we do not have all the other information (on intermediate and total sales) for the economy. However, there are data on these for 1963, and we shall subsequently return to a form of Table 11.2 for the UK economy in 1963.

TABLE 11.8   *Final expenditure: comparison of model economy and UK economy, 1980*

	Model economy Table 11.2 £	UK economy, 1980, Table 11.3 £ million
Consumers' expenditure	44	113,446
Government final consumption	22	44,636
Gross domestic capital formation	18	33,031
Total domestic expenditure	84	191,113
Exports of goods and services	23	60,207
Total final expenditure	107	251,320
less Imports	7	57,832
Gross domestic product at factor cost	100	193,488
Of which:		
Income from employment	64	137,083
Gross profits, self-employment income, and rents	36	56,405

Before this we need to make the transition from expenditures at factor cost, which exclude expenditure taxes, to expenditures at market prices, which include taxes on expenditure. Table 11.9 shows in its first column the factor cost final expenditure (i.e. excluding taxes on expenditure) which we have so far been considering. The last three rows also give total taxes on expenditure and total subsidies. The second column gives the taxes on expenditure *less* subsidies which are levied on each category of final expenditure, and the third column gives the resulting final expenditures at market prices. The row of gross domestic product gives GDP, calculated from final expenditures *less* imports first at factor cost (the sum of income from employment and profits, self-employment income and rents – see Table 2.7 above), and then at market prices (see Diagram 2.3 above). The fourth column of Table 11.9 gives, for the sake of comparison, the figures for final expenditure at market prices in 1963, and we can best make this comparison by looking not at the absolute money figures but at the relative percentages. The obvious features are that over

TABLE 11.9 Final expenditure at factor cost and at market prices, 1980, and final expenditure at market prices, 1963

	£ million				Percentage structure of GDP at market prices	
	1980			1963	1980	1963
	Expenditure at factor cost	Taxes on expenditure *less* subsidies	Expenditure at market prices	Expenditure at market prices	1980	1963
Consumers' expenditure	113,446	21,957 [c]	135,403 [e]	20,195	60.0	66.7
General government final consumption	44,636	3,701 [d]	48,337 [f]	5,080	21.4	16.8
Gross domestic fixed capital formation	33,031	3,423	40,050	4,906	17.8	16.2
Value of physical increase in stocks and work in progress			−3,596	212	−1.6	0.7
Total domestic expenditure	191,113	29,081	220,194	30,393	97.6	100.5
Exports of goods and services	60,207	2,991	63,198	5,814	28.0	19.2
Total final expenditure	251,320	32,072	283,392	36,207	125.6	119.7
less Imports of goods and services	57,832	0	57,832	5,950	25.6	19.7
Gross domestic product	193,488	32,072	225,560	30,257	100.0	100.0
Taxes on expenditure	37,287 [a]	—	—	4,048		
less Subsidies	5,215 [b]	—	—	560		
Taxes *less* subsidies	32,072	—	—	3,488		

[a] See Tables 9.5 and 9.15 above: this comprises (in £ million): Customs and Excise administered (22,081); other taxes on expenditure (6,906); rates (8,300). The first two of these figures, as given in Table 9.5, were different by virtue of the inclusion of export rebates and bus fuel rebates (−£16 million and −£77 million respectively) in Customs and Excise administered taxes.

[b] See Table 9.4 above.

[c] See Table 11.4 above.

[d] See Table 11.7 above.

[e] See Table 3.1 above.

[f] See Table 9.4 above (third column, first two rows).

Sources: Central Statistical Office, *National Income and Expenditure 1968* (unrevised data) tables 1 and 7, pp. 3 and 11; Central Statistical Office, *National Income and Expenditure 1981 Edition*, table 1.1, p. 3.

the period consumers' expenditure has fallen as a percentage of GDP at market prices, while government consumption expenditure has risen. There has also been a large rise in both exports and imports as a percentage of GDP at market prices: the UK economy has become a more 'open' economy with not only a greater degree of import 'penetration' into final expenditure but also with a greater degree of exporting of production.

Another reason for looking at the categories of final expenditure in 1963 is that the input–output table for that year, as published in *National Income and Expenditure 1968* (table 19), enables us to complete the sequence of 'model' and real-life tables which started with Table 2.1 and continued to Tables 2.6, 11.1 and 11.2. Using the 1963 input–output table we can derive the real-life equivalent for the UK economy in 1963 of Table 11.2 (in a slightly expanded form). This table is given in Table 11.10. (In case it should give rise to puzzlement, the 1963 figures we shall be using are the unrevised figures; slightly revised figures appeared subsequently for the input–output table in Central Statistical Office, *Input–Output tables for the United Kingdom 1963*, and for final expenditures in subsequent Blue Books. However, no subsequent Blue Book brought together the revised industry-by-industry input–output table and the revised final expenditures, and as our purpose here is to enable the student to see how the production of value added and sales by final expenditure fit together in the framework of national income accounting, we shall stick to the more handy version of the unrevised figures. The revisions were, in any case, relatively minor in most cases: GDP at market prices was revised upwards by 0.4 per cent, consumer's expenditure was revised downwards by 0.3 per cent. The only problem is that, however small the differences, the figures in Tables 11.9 and 11.10, taken from the 1968 Blue Book, are not identical with those appearing in subsequent Blue Books.)

Table 11.10 is simply an expanded version of Table 2.6 and, if the student is not to lose his or her way in the ensuing thicket of figures, Table 11.10 must continually be viewed as such (in turn Table 2.6 is only a real-life elaboration of Table 2.1). The expansion consists first of dividing the sales receipts column of Table 2.6 into intermediate sales and final sales and also distinguishing the categories of final sales (as we did in a simple way in Table 11.2). Second, the single 'cost of bought-in materials' column in Table 2.6 is divided between home-produced sales and imports. Third, the rows at the bottom of the table are slightly differently arranged so as to give the totals of the various sales and bought-in materials. The last row of Table 11.10 contains the same figures as are given in the fourth column of Table 11.9. Fourth, and finally, Table 11.10 has to include a row for sales by imports; in this context 'imports' can be regarded as a foreign industry (we can imagine it simply as one foreign factory) selling to the UK economy: such sales/expenditure must, of course, appear in the total expenditure figures – total consumers' expenditure is total consumers' expenditure regardless of whether it is on British-produced or foreign-produced goods – but of course 'imports' is not an industry which produces domestic value added (and incomes for residents), so there is no value-added figure for imports, and, consequently, total imports must be deducted from total final expenditure to give the total final expenditure generating total domestic value added.

As I have said, Table 11.10 may look elaborate and complicated, but it is no more than an expanded version of Table 2.6 – the student will note that all of the figures in the first three columns of Table 2.6 are to be found in the eighth, eleventh and twelfth (respectively matching) columns of Table 11.10. And, once again, value added is the anchor-point: the student studying Table 11.10 should start from its last column and work backwards from there, also bearing in mind that part of Table 2.6 which does not appear (for reasons of space) in Table 11.10: namely, the distribution of value added as income either in the form of wages or in the form of profits, etc.

Let us now see how Table 11.10 works. The first column gives all the intermediate sales; for example, the figure in the first row tells us that the industry (branch of economic

TABLE 11.10   *The UK gross domestic product in 1963 by value added and by final expenditure, also showing intermediate sales*

£ million

Industry (sales by which to column headings, and likewise for bought-in materials and value added)	Inter-mediate sales	Sales receipts — Final sales/expenditure — Consumption expenditure — Personal sector	General government	Capital formation — Fixed capital	Stocks and work in progress	Exports	Total final sales	Total sales	Bought-in materials, etc. — Produced at home (from intermediate sales column) (a)	Produced abroad: imports	Total	Value added at factor cost
Agriculture, forestry and fishing	503	1,083	14	9	24	43	1,173	1,676	572	151	723	953
Mining and quarrying	812	208	26	21	−23	51	283	1,095	354	8	362	733
Manufacturing industry	7,646	4,995	1,274	1,832	174	3,902	12,177	19,823	8,356	2,593	10,949	8,874
Construction	260	386	303	2,170	21	10	2,890	3,150	1,232	146	1,378	1,772
Electricity, gas, and water	716	653	81	158	—	4	896	1,612	765	19	784	828
Transport and communication	1,705	868	156	51	1	785	1,861	3,566	670	604	1,274	2,292
Distributive trades	488	3,679	101	197	—	311	4,288	4,776	1,569	35	1,604	3,172
Other services	2,018	2,362	506	181	1	371	3,421	5,439	1,466	38	1,504	3,935
Public administration, etc. (b)	—	343	2,732	—	—	—	3,075	3,075	—	—	—	3,075
Ownership of dwellings (c)	—	1,135	—	—	—	—	1,135	1,135	—	—	—	1,135

Sales by final buyers to one another (d)	199	194	-393	-75	—	75	-199	0	—	—	—	(f) —
Imports (e)	3,594	1,641	189	250	14	262	2,356	5,950	—	—	—	—
Total expenditure at factor cost	17,941	17,547	4,989	4,794	212	5,814	33,356	51,297	14,984	3,594	18,578	26,769
Taxes on expenditure *less* subsidies	637	2,648	91	112	—	—	2,851	3,488	—	—	—	3,488
Total expenditure at market prices	18,578	20,195	5,080	4,906	212	5,814	36,207	54,785	—	—	—	30,257 (g)

(a) Including taxes on expenditure levied on industries' intermediate purchases and totalling £637 million.

(b) Public administration and defence, public health and educational services, domestic services to households, and services to private non-profit-making bodies serving persons.

(c) In the input–output table this figure is included with public administration, etc.; it is separately reported to table 11 of the 1968 Blue Book and is given separately here.

(d) Sales of second-hand equipment from one sector to another or for export, and payments by persons to central government for services provided under the National Health Service or to local authorities for various services; note that the total of this row is zero as such sales/purchases cancel out in aggregate (this is why this row did not appear in Table 2.6).

(e) A row has to be included for imports (unlike Table 2.6) so we can get the expenditure totals correctly (from the point of view of, say, total consumers' expenditure, expenditure on a Japanese car is the same as expenditure on a British Leyland car; from the point of view of total *domestic* value added, of course, imports have to be deducted from total expenditure).

(f) Inapplicable; see note (e).

(g) At market prices.

Source: Central Statistical Office, *National Income and Expenditure 1968*, table 19, pp. 24–5 (data on ownership of dwellings from table 11, p. 13).

Allocating consumers' expenditure by industry

We need to pause for a moment to clear up a slight technical point, because every reader knows that he or she rarely, if ever, buys food directly from the farmer or fish directly from the fisherman: we buy our food from shops, so why is all consumers' expenditure not concentrated on distributive trades (shops)? It would of course be possible to proceed in this way; nearly all sales by agriculture would then appear as intermediate sales to shops. But this would lose sight of how much agricultural produce was being sold to consumers (via shops) and this is in itself an interesting piece of economic information. So the national income statisticians adopt a different convention: they pretend that shops act only as agents who sell, not the produce itself, but merely their services in bringing the producer-seller and consumer-buyer together. This accounting fiction has two useful results:

(a)   it preserves valuable detail, in that we can see what industries are supplying consumers' needs;
(b)   it means that what is presented as sales by distributive trades is basically the sales of shops' *services* in distributing goods, and is not the less economically useful figure of total (checkout till) sales receipts by shops, which confuses in one total the cost of the goods sold and the cost of distributive services – providing the buildings (etc.) and sales persons (etc.).

For economic analysis, this latter figure of the cost of distributive trades' services is of greater relevance. So, if the farmer were to sell, via a health-food shop, natural wheat for home-grinding to a housewife, this would count, in Table 11.10, as a sale by the farmer to the personal sector at cost price (farmgate price) and if the health-food shop incurred £X expense in selling that wheat (the consumer paying the farmgate price *plus* £X), then this £X would be reported as a final sale of £X worth of (agent's) services by the shop to the consumer. The statistical fiction is a bit tortuous, but it produces a much more useful arrangement of the figures. Of course, only the distributive trades are treated in this way (as agents); if the farmer sells wheat to the miller, then this sale for processing (not simply for distribution) is treated as an intermediate sale to a producer. So now you can look at your next checkout till-receipt total in a different light: as comprising so much for the producer (at farmgate or factory-door price) and so much for the distributive trades (wholesale and retail) who have acted as agents in bringing you and the factory together – unfortunately, of course, the checkout total will not give you these figures, but they are nevertheless the economic reality behind the total. (The checkout bill will also contain VAT – see Chapter 9 – but the sales receipts figures in Table 11.10 contain no taxes on expenditure; these are introduced only in the second-last row. Again, this is because we are interested mainly in what the farmer (etc.) receives for his produce.)

activity) of agriculture, forestry and fishing in 1963 sold £503 million worth of produce to other industries for their use in producing value added. So this figure is identical in principle to the farmer's sale of wheat to the miller (Table 11.2). The next figure in the first row tells us that agriculture, forestry and fishing sold £1,083 million worth of their produce to the personal sector for consumption.

Agriculture, forestry and fishing sold in 1963 £14 million worth of products to general government (this would probably have been food for HM Forces, etc.). Agriculture (etc.) is also recorded as selling £9 million worth of products to fixed capital formation. This is at first sight a little odd, because agriculture (etc.) does not produce the sort of things we would think of as fixed capital – tractors, barns, etc. However, farmers may well engage in producing drainage ditches, building fences and even barns, etc., and such production for 'sale' to their own capital account must be counted – see the discussion in Chapter 10 of public corporations' sales to own capital account (Table 10.3). We note that, in any case, the amount involved is relatively small, and that, as we should expect, most of the sales to fixed capital formation by all sectors comes from manufacturing industry (plant and equipment) and from construction (buildings and works). More understandably, agriculture (etc.) made considerable sales to investment in stocks and work in progress: to illustrate, if the farmer sold wheat to the miller not for immediate use in the production of flour, but for the miller to add physically to his stock of wheat, then this would count as inventory investment and would appear in this column. Finally, UK farmers (etc.) exported £43 million of produce in 1963. The United Kingdom is not, of course, a country noted for the volume of its agricultural exports but I have been on farms in foreign countries where the proudest possession has been livestock of British-bred dairy cows or beef cattle or horses, so it is clear that British agriculture has a small but important export trade. Total final sales by agriculture (etc.) in 1963 was £1,173 million, and together with their intermediate sales, total sales receipts were £1,676 million (see Table 2.6).

Agriculture (etc.) bought in £572 million of materials for use in producing their output, fertiliser from the chemical industry, electricity to run the farms, etc., and also bought in £151 million worth of imports (some fertiliser could of course be foreign-produced). The total of bought-in materials from all sources was £723 million in 1963, so value added in agriculture (etc.) was £953 million in 1963 (see Table 2.6).

The story is much the same for all the other rows dealing with the enterprise sector of the economy. Mining and quarrying sells most of its output to intermediate sales (coal to the power-stations, gravel and sand to the builders) and not too much to final consumers. Conversely, construction sells only a little to intermediate sales (probably mostly in building maintenance and repair services to factories), more to consumers (maintenance and repair services for households), but most of their sales are, of course, to fixed capital formation (new buildings, including new dwellings and works).

For public administration the story is different. This sector is rather complex in that it includes domestic services and private non-profit-making bodies which sell a small amount of services to the personal sector. The major item here is the services of central and local government, including public health and educational services; these, of course, are not 'sold' in any direct way – the accounting convention is adopted that the government, which is also the producing sector, itself 'buys' these services on behalf of the public.

The row of sales by final buyers to one another is basically meant to cover the problem that some expenditures may be on already existing capital goods (such as second-hand equipment). Such expenditures will, of course, figure in any one sector's expenditure; but there must be a corresponding negative 'expenditure' elsewhere and so, for the economy as a whole, such transactions cancel out.

Finally, for the purposes of getting the correct totals of expenditure, we must include 'imports' as a foreign industry selling to intermediate and final sales. We can see that 60 per cent of the sales by 'imports' (£3,594m./£5,950m.) were intermediate sales for further processing by UK producers, and this figure of £3,594 million is the real-world counterpart to the £7 of yeast and crude petroleum imports in Table 11.2. Note that Table 11.2 contained no direct sales by 'imports' to consumers, investors or the government; this was deliberately to keep Table 11.2 uncomplicated, but of course in real life consumers and investors buy goods directly from 'imports', and 27.6 per cent of total imports were sold to consumers. 'Imports' also sold £262 million as export final sales: this happens because of what is known as 're-exports': goods which are imported and then exported without further processing. This happens typically, for example, with metals which are imported and sold on the London metal market, some of it to overseas residents, and these latter sales count as re-exports.

The figures reported under sales receipts in Table 11.10 are all at sellers' value (the amount received by the seller), as distinct from purchasers' value (the amount paid by the purchaser). They thus exclude taxes on expenditure, and so the first total given is the total of sales at factor cost (excluding taxes on expenditure). The second-last row then gives taxes on expenditure (net of subsidies) allocated to the expenditures, and the final row then gives total expenditure at purchasers' values, or 'at market prices', i.e. including taxes on expenditure. The second to the sixth figures in the last row then match the figures in Table 11.9, which are at market prices.

We may now see how Table 11.10 fits together in the system of national accounts. The best point to start from is total value added, or gross domestic product, at factor cost, which is £26,769 million – a familiar figure from Table 2.6 – and to keep referring back to this figure.

First, let us go from gross domestic product at factor cost to gross domestic product at market prices. Total taxes on expenditure *less* subsidies was £3,488 million in 1963, so (Diagram 2.3) this step is simply made:

	Gross domestic product at factor cost	£26,769m.
plus	Total taxes on expenditure *less* subsidies	£ 3,488m.
equals	Gross domestic product at market prices	£30,257m.

Second, we had previously said that all sales in the economy were divided into two mutually exclusive and jointly exhaustive classes: intermediate sales and final sales. Taking the market price totals in the last row we can see that total sales were £54,785 million, divided between £18,578 million of intermediate sales and £36,207 million of final sales. In the simple model (without imports) we could then write:

$$\text{Total sales} \quad minus \quad \text{Total intermediate sales} \quad equals \quad \text{Total value added}$$

to show why the total of final sales was necessarily just another way of looking at the gross domestic product (total value added). However, in the real world of Table 11.10 we must reckon with imports which are not value added produced by, or accruing as income to, residents, so we have for 1963:

	Total final sales/expenditure (including expenditure on imports) at market prices	£36,207m.
less	Total imports	£ 5,950m.
equals	Gross domestic product at market prices	£30,257m.

So that total final sales/expenditure is another way of looking at GDP if we allow for expenditure on foreign value added (imports).

If we take the view that the gross domestic product constitutes the benefits which residents derive both from consumption (private and public) and also from investment, including any net increase in residents' stock of financial claims on foreigners, we have for 1963:

Private consumption at market prices	£20,195m.
Public consumption at market prices	£ 5,080m.
Fixed capital formation at market prices	£ 4,906m.
Inventory investment	£ 212m.
Increase in financial claims on foreigners (Exports *minus* Imports)	−£ 136m.
Total gross domestic product at market prices	£30,257m.

As you will see, in 1963 UK residents did not increase their stock of claims on foreigners; the minus sign indicates that the reverse happened and foreigners increased their net stock of claims against UK residents. Note, by the way, that the surplus of exports over imports, called the balance of trade surplus (or deficit if negative, as in 1963) represents the extent to which the United Kingdom has a financial balance (surplus or deficit) with the overseas sector on account of trading transactions. At its simplest, such a surplus (or deficit) will result in an increase (or reduction) in the nation's stock of foreign currency. And we may put the converse relationship: namely, that a surplus of imports over exports represents the extent to which the overseas sector has, due to trading, a positive net acquisition of assets – these assets being a claim against the United Kingdom. So, in 1963:

> Overseas sector's financial balance (due to trading) or financial surplus
> (+) or deficit (−) is given by:

Imports (into UK), a credit for overseas sector	£5,950m.
less Exports (from UK), a debit against overseas sector	£5,814m.
Overseas sector financial balance (due to trading)	+£ 136m.

Note also that at this stage, because we are dealing with gross *domestic* product, we have so far been concerned only with exports and imports of goods and services. This means that property income (interest, profits, dividends) received from and paid to abroad have been left out of the reckoning, so although the trade surplus/deficit is one part of the overseas sector's financial balance, it is not the only part. We need to complete our consideration of the international transactions of the United Kingdom, so Table 11.11 gives the figures which lead up to the complete financial balance of the overseas sector.

Transactions with the overseas sector

There are three sorts of international transactions which occur in the United Kingdom's current account with the overseas sector: transactions due to trade and commerce; transactions on account of 'property' ownership; and transfers.

First, transactions due to trade and commerce arise from exports and imports of goods ('visibles') and services ('invisibles'). It is the balance of trade which is the relevant balance when going from total domestic (final) expenditure to gross domestic product (the student must study the figures in Table 11.11 and see how they fit with the figures in Table 11.9).

Second, the United Kingdom also receives income from abroad (net of foreign taxes on that income) because of UK residents' ownership of property abroad, where 'property' includes financial assets as well as real assets: UK residents may own bonds issued by foreign governments on which they receive interest, they may own shares in foreign companies on which they receive dividends, and they may directly own property – subsidiary companies, branches, etc., and other real estate – from which they receive profits. Because non-residents can also own 'property' in the United Kingdom, this transaction goes both ways (also taking the property income paid to abroad net of UK taxes on that income). The balance of property income received from abroad over property income paid to abroad is known as *net property income from abroad* ('net' simply means the balance of receipts over payments, and has nothing to do with depreciation or with the netting off of taxes). It is the addition of this net balance which converts gross domestic product to gross national product (see Tables 2.6 and 2.7 for this use of the figures in Table 11.11).

Third, the United Kingdom has various international transfers: if immigrants here remit money to relatives abroad such a transfer counts as a UK debit (anything on current account which represents a using up of foreign currency is a UK debit; conversely, anything which represents a gain of foreign currency is a UK credit). One of the big transfer debits in recent years has been the UK government's payments to the European Economic Community.

The total of all the credits *minus* the total of all the debits (alternatively, and identically, the algebraic sum of the balance of trade, net property income from abroad, and the balance on transfers) is known in the *Balance of Payments* Pink Book as the 'current

TABLE 11.11   *International transactions of the United Kingdom leading to the overseas sector's net acquisition of financial assets, 1963 and 1980*

	£ million	
	1963	1980
Trade [a]		
UK credits		
Exports and re-exports of goods ('visibles')	4,282	47,389
Exports of services ('invisibles') [b]	1,532	15,809
Total exports [c]	5,814	63,198
UK debits		
Imports of goods ('visibles')	4,362	46,211
Imports of services ('invisibles')	1,588	11,621
Total imports [c]	5,950	57,832
Balance of trade		
Visible balance	−80	1,178
Invisible balance (trade only)	−56	4,188
Balance of trade [d]	−136	5,366
Transactions on account of 'property' ownership [e]		
UK credits		
Property income received from abroad (net of foreign taxes)	838	8,204
UK debits		
Property income paid to abroad (net of UK taxes on such income)	444	8,242
Balance of (i.e. net) property income from abroad [f]	394	−38
Other transactions [g]		
UK credits		
Current transfers received from abroad	113	1,751
UK debits		
Current transfers paid to abroad	260	3,873
Balance on transfers	−147	−2,122
Total credits	6,765	73,153
Total debits	6,654	69,947
Over-all balance on current transactions: current balance or net UK 'investment' abroad	111	3,206
Conversely: overseas sector's net acquisition of financial assets (financial deficit) *vis-à-vis* the UK [h]	−111	−3,206

[a] Trade is recorded at a 'free on board' (f.o.b.) valuation; this means at the cost loaded on board the point of departure, leaving the 'cost of insurance and freight' (c.i.f.) to be entered separately as a credit or debit according to the nationality of the carrier. This must be done in order that the appropriate balance of payments may be struck.

[b] 'Invisibles' consists of services such as passenger and freight (international) transport, financial services including insurance, banking and commodity trading fees, tourism (expenditure by UK residents in overseas countries – see Table 3.3 above, second last line – and expenditure by overseas residents in the United Kingdom), royalties, construction work overseas (fees and profits of architects, engineers, etc.), and government diplomatic expenditure. This list is not complete: see, CSO, *United Kingdom Balance of Payments 1981 Edition*, pp. 18–22, for a full list. In the official statistics the invisibles balance includes the balance of net property income from abroad and the balance of current transfers. 'Visibles' are, of course, simply goods which one can see being loaded.

[c] See, for 1963, Tables 11.9 and 11.10, and for 1980 Table 11.9 above.

[d] It is this balance which has to be added to total domestic (final) expenditure to give gross domestic product: see Table 11.9 and apply these figures.

[e] 'Property' covers real assets and financial assets, so the income here comprises interest, profits and dividends (usually abbreviated as IPD).

[f] See, for 1963, Table 2.6, and for 1980, Table 2.7; this gives the transition from gross *domestic* product to gross *national* product.

(Continued opposite)

balance' or in the *National Income and Expenditure* Blue Book as 'net investment abroad', where 'net' means investment abroad by UK residents net of investment in the United Kingdom by non-residents, and where 'investment' must be taken to include the acquisition of financial assets as well as the acquisition of real assets. In the financial accounts section of the Blue Book, the table which deals with the overseas sector reports mainly the overseas sector's net acquisition of financial assets; here the word 'financial' is misleading because it must be taken to include real assets. Because there are two sides to any 'financial' transaction, the overseas sector's net acquisition of financial assets is equal to the United Kingdom's current balance on the balance of (foreign) payments, with the sign of that balance changed (this is subject to a small qualification, not often occurring in practice, that the overseas sector's net acquisition of financial assets may benefit additionally from any capital transfers abroad which the United Kingdom may make).

To illustrate with the simplest possible example. Suppose the United Kingdom exports £100 worth of goods to the USA, which is the only overseas country, and imports £70 worth of goods from the USA. There are no other international transactions, so the balance of trade is also the current balance on the balance of (foreign) payments. The exchange rate is $2 = £1. We may set forth these transactions in Table 11.12. The United Kingdom has earned $200 = £100 from its exports to the USA and has spent $140 = £70 on its imports from the USA. Conversely, the USA has spent $200 = £100 on exports from the United Kingdom and has earned £140 = £70 from supplying imports to the United Kingdom. The UK balance of trade surplus (exports, credits, valued in £ *minus* imports, debits, valued in £) represents a converse trade deficit for the USA (which represents the overseas sector). In practice, we in the United Kingdom must calculate the USA's (the overseas sector's) deficit in £ sterling because this is the only way of reducing the (various) foreign currency transactions to a common base (in reality, the $ column in Table 11.12 represents a large number of foreign countries and currencies according to the destination and origin of UK exports and imports).

The USA must, of course, finance its deficit with the United Kingdom, so, looked at from the standpoint of the overseas sector, the UK balance of trade surplus is the USA's (the overseas sector's) financial deficit; accordingly, simply by changing the sign of the UK current balance on the balance of payments we obtain the overseas sector's financial balance *vis-à-vis* the United Kingdom. In the model of Table 11.12 the United Kingdom has (see Table 11.11) a balance-of-payments surplus (+), so the overseas sector has a corresponding but negative net acquisition of financial assets; were the UK balance of payments to be in deficit (as happened in 1974 and 1979), then the overseas sector would have a positive net acquisition of financial assets.

All sequences of accounts must be 'closed' with a statement of how a financial surplus was used or how a financial deficit was financed and this sequence is no exception. So we must show, in the financial account for the overseas sector, how this overseas sector deficit was financed.

In Table 11.12 we first note in the overseas sector's financial account that there is a deficit to be financed (the deficit is transferred down from the balance-of-payments account – and as we are using the UK balance-of-payments account we must change the

---

(g) Transfers include such things as remittances abroad (e.g. by the personal sector – see Table 3.1), pensions paid abroad, government military receipts and payments, and also government transfers paid to and received from the EEC.

(h) See *National Income and Expenditure 1981 Edition*, table 13.11 'Financial transactions: overseas sector'.

Sources: Central Statistical Office, *National Income and Expenditure 1968*, table 7, p. 11 (note that the unrevised figures are being used for 1963); Central Statistical Office, *National Income and Expenditure 1981 Edition*, table 1.6, p. 9; see also Central Statistical Office, *United Kingdom Balance of Payments 1981 Edition*.

TABLE 11.12   *A model showing the sign conventions on the balance of (foreign) payments and on the overseas sector's financial account*

	+ denotes credit to (earnings by) sector;[a] − denotes debit to (spending by) sector[a]		
	United Kingdom	USA	
	£	$	£[b]
Balance-of-payments account (for international transactions):			
Exports from UK to USA	+100	−200	−100
Imports into UK from USA	−70	+140	+70
Balance	+30	−60	−30
		(change sign en route)	
Overseas sector financial account:			
Financial surplus (+) or deficit (−)		[b]	−30
Financed by:			
UK bank lending to the USA			−20
Increase in UK official holding of $ reserves			−10

[a] The word 'sector' here means either the whole UK economy or the whole US economy, as the case may be; the USA is simply representing what is called, from the UK standpoint, 'the overseas sector' in the UK national accounts.

[b] In practice, we must work the overseas sector's account in £ sterling, because in reality there will be not one foreign currency but many, and the overseas sector transactions need therefore to be reduced to a common base which in this case is the £.

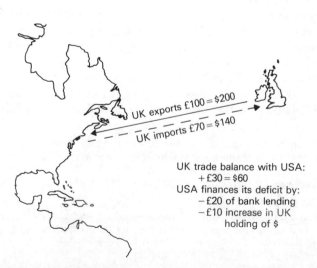

UK exports £100 = $200
UK imports £70 = $140

UK trade balance with USA:
+£30 = $60
USA finances its deficit by:
−£20 of bank lending
−£10 increase in UK
  holding of $

sign of the UK balance en route to the overseas sector's financial account). There are many ways in which the USA could finance the deficit, and two are illustrated in the model. We may suppose that one of the US importers borrows £20 from a UK bank to settle its debt for some of the exports supplied by the United Kingdom to the USA. Accordingly, the US importer's liabilities to the UK bank rise by £20, and this increase in the overseas sector's liabilities is denoted by a minus sign (exactly as would be the case if you borrowed from the bank to finance an excess of spending over income). Another way in which the overseas sector's deficit may be financed is through an increase in UK official reserves of dollars (foreign exchange). This happens if another US importer hands over $20 in return for £10 to settle his debt and so UK holdings of dollars rise by £10 worth of foreign currency (usually called 'foreign exchange'). Again, we must work in terms of valuations in £ sterling to reduce all the foreign currencies to a common base. So far as UK exporters are concerned, they have up to this stage been paid £30 (via a bank loan and via an increase in UK foreign currency reserves), and this leaves £70 owing to them from US importers; but as UK importers owe £70 to US exporters, the $140 = £70 handed over by the remaining American importers is 'cancelled' (so far as UK foreign exchange reserves are concerned) by the £70 = $140 which must be handed over by UK importers.

The important point about this simple model is to see that some part of the overseas sector's financial deficit may be financed by an increase in UK reserves of foreign currency: just as the UK bank's loan to the US importer represents an increased UK claim on the USA – an increased liability by the USA to the United Kingdom and so given a minus sign in the USA's (the overseas sector's) financial account – so does a rise in UK holding of dollar (foreign currency) reserves represent an increased UK claim on the USA – an increased liability by the USA to the United Kingdom and so has a minus sign in the overseas sector's financial account. This explains the accounting convention that a *rise* in UK foreign currency reserves appears with a *negative* sign: changes in official reserves of foreign exchange are always viewed from the standpoint of the overseas sector's financial account. This sign convention sometimes seems paradoxical, but in the context of Table 11.12 (with the analogous bank loan example as well) it should be quite understandable.

From the UK standpoint, an increase in financial claims on the overseas sector represents investment abroad, so the current balance on the balance of foreign payments is referred to in the Blue Book as 'net investment abroad'.

Of course, in the real world the overseas sector may finance a financial deficit (or use a financial surplus) in many other ways. Indeed, the change in UK official reserves of foreign currency tends to be merely the end-result of a considerable number of other financial transactions: the overseas sector not only takes loans from the UK banking sector but it also makes deposits with the UK banking sector, and the scale of these loans and deposits is nowadays very large, thanks to London's position as a centre for international finance. Table 11.13 shows the overseas sector's financial account for 1963 and 1980, and the very large flow of financial transactions by the overseas sector with the UK banking sector is apparent – especially in 1980. There is also a considerable two-way annual flow of intra-company investment overseas: overseas companies investing in the UK company sector and UK companies investing abroad. The overseas sector may acquire (+) or sell (−) company securities, or they may likewise acquire (+) British government securities. At the end of the day, all these transactions will affect the official UK reserves of foreign currency.

In these last few sections we have set out to explain, in three steps, the concept of final expenditure, including its relation to gross domestic product (total value added). This explanation was the first of two purposes to be accomplished in this chapter. The student should by now feel familiar with the concept of final expenditure, with its various

TABLE 11.13 *The overseas sector's financial account, 1963 and 1980*

Acquisition of assets by, or reduction of liabilities of, overseas sector is positive (+); sale of assets or increase in liabilities is negative (−)	£ million	
	1963	1979˙
Deposits with banking sector	378	33,631
Bank lending to overseas sector	−321	−33,097
Overseas direct and other investment in the United Kingdom [a]	208	3,179
Direct and other investment abroad [a]	−253	−2,444
Company and overseas securities	−41	−3,473
British government securities and local authority debt	89	1,273
Other and unidentified [b]	−224	−1,984
Total above	−164	−2,915
Official reserves of UK (drawings on +/additions to −)	+53	−291
Overseas net acquisition of financial assets	−111	−3,206

[a] New classification introduced in *National Income and Expenditure 1981 Edition*; comparison with 1963 classification may not be exact.
[b] Including HM government borrowing and transactions with International Monetary Fund (IMF) and other overseas monetary authorities.

Sources: Central Statistical Office, *National Income and Expenditure 1968*, table 79, p. 95; Central Statistical Office, *National Income and Expenditure 1963–1973*, table 79, p. 91 (for intra-company investment overseas); Central Statistical Office, *National Income and Expenditure 1981 Edition*, table 13.11, p. 100.

categories, and also with the way in which exports and imports fit into the picture. The second purpose of this chapter is to explain how the size of the total flow of aggregate final expenditure is determined.

Aggregate demand

We are now going to consider what is known as macroeconomics, or Keynesian economics, named after J. M. Keynes, the Cambridge economist (1883–1946) who published his major work, *The General Theory of Employment, Interest and Money*, in 1936. The essence of the 'Keynesian revolution' in macroeconomics was to focus attention on the aggregate of final sales and on its constituent components in Keynes's (successful) attempt to explain how a situation could arise *and* could persist where:

Total final sales (actual GDP)	*was less than*	Economy's *capacity* to produce value added (at full employment)

The economy's capacity to produce value added is determined, for any given level of technology, by its stock of fixed capital and its stock of workers. If total final sales (actual GDP) were less than the economy's capacity to produce value added, then there would be idle fixed capital and unemployed workers. This may seem trite to the reader, but it only seems so because our very description of the situation is due to Keynes's theory that total output (and hence total employment) would depend upon the total of final expenditure – upon aggregate demand, or 'effective demand' as Keynes called it. Before Keynes this description of the situation, emphasising total expenditure, would not have been understood, let alone its subsequent analysis.

Although Keynes provided the first full explanation of mass unemployment, another economist, Michał Kalecki, had published in 1935 an article (in Polish) which partly analysed the problem. It is instructive to consider Kalecki's discussion because by seeing where Kalecki stopped short of a complete explanation we can better appreciate the completeness of Keynes's treatment.*

In his 1935 article 'The mechanism of the business upswing' Kalecki begins by considering the mass unemployment existing at the time; he observed that unemployment existed alongside unused capital equipment and that therefore the cause of unemployment was not due to inadequate supplies of fixed capital: 'the idle capital equipment is the counterpart of the unemployed force' (M. Kalecki, 'The mechanism of the business upswing', in *Selected Essays on the Dynamics of the Capitalist Economy*, Cambridge University Press, 1971, p. 26). Kalecki asked whether this situation could be remedied by a general reduction in wages, it then being a popular argument that if labour were to become cheaper more of it would be employed (just as if apples were to become cheaper more apples would be purchased). Kalecki argued that a general reduction in wages, despite its attractiveness for a single entrepreneur, would not solve the problem: 'If one entrepreneur reduces wages he is able *ceteris paribus* to expand production; but once all entrepreneurs do the same thing – the result will be entirely different' (ibid, p. 26). And the reason for this is that there still remains the problem of selling all the goods produced. A general reduction in wages would cause a general reduction in workers' (i.e. consumers') expenditure, so only if entrepreneurs expanded their investment out of their (hoped-for) higher profits (consequent on the wage reductions) would production (in aggregate) continue to be sold (with, of course, a shift from consumption to investment). Unfortunately, this is most unlikely to happen because entrepreneurs will not invest (expand production capacity) if they are faced with falling consumer demand. Consequently a general reduction of wages does not constitute a way out of the depression.

We may restate this part of Kalecki's argument very straightforwardly if we use our concept of final expenditure together with the relation that the sum of final expenditures equals gross domestic product (allowing for imports). This concept and this relationship had not then been systematically expounded, and so Kalecki did not, as we do, have these analytic tools available (you will recall that at the beginning of this chapter we made the distinction between final and intermediate expenditures so that we could see how the economy works). Let us keep the argument simple to start with, and imagine an economy with no government final expenditure and no foreign trade; to expound the basic principle we need only consumers' expenditure and investment:

Restatement of Kalecki's argument

Components of final expenditure	After wages are reduced	After investment rises
Consumers' expenditure *plus*	Falls	Rises
Investment	Falls (or at best, remains the same)	Rises
equals Gross domestic product	∴ Falls	∴ Rises

*A warning footnote: the following exposition is intended only to enable the student to understand the basic mechanics of aggregate demand; it is emphatically not intended as an exposition in the history of economic thought of exactly what Kalecki or Keynes said or meant to say; nor is it intended to demonstrate who got where first. Readers requiring accurate historical exegesis should consult Phyllis Deane, *The Evolution of Economic Ideas* (Cambridge University Press, 1978) ch. 12, or G. L. S. Shackle, *The Years of High Theory: Invention and Tradition in Economic Thought 1926–1936* (Cambridge University Press, 1967) chs 9–14, as well as the writings of Kalecki and Keynes referred to here. Keynes had outlined some of his ideas much earlier: see *The Means to Prosperity* (Macmillan, 1933), a pamphlet reprinting an enlarged version of four articles published in *The Times* in March 1933.

Say's law and saving

Prior to Keynes, it had never been understood how, or even that, such a paradoxical conjunction of idle machinery (with its owners wanting profits) and unemployed workers (desperately wanting work and wage incomes) could exist in a permanent, long-run situation. Economists had accepted an old-established 'law' of economics that 'supply creates its own demand' – a law going back to the French economist Jean-Baptiste Say, who first expounded it in his *Treatise of Political Economy* published in 1803. According to Say's law, permanent unemployment is just not possible because any goods or services the unemployed workers and idle capital produced would find a purchaser somewhere in the market – that is, there could not be an over-all deficiency of purchasers.

In a non-barter economy, with which we are familiar, we can make Say's law work by imagining a situation where every recipient of income (wage-earner, dividend-receiver, or residual profit-taker) is paid, say, on the last Thursday of each month for services provided in producing that month's value added. We have further to imagine a peculiar rule that income-recipients are paid with money which must be used for a purchase by mid-day on the Saturday immediately following the Thursday, or else the money loses its validity and cannot be used at all for anything. But if the money has changed hands in return for goods or services, then it retains its validity and may continue in use. We can now imagine quite well what happens to total income each Thursday: all income recipients will go to market on Friday and themselves purchase goods or services, and if they have not spent all their money then they will on Saturday morning lend the remaining money (their financial surplus) to someone in return for an IOU and that someone will, before mid-day, purchase something he needs (like a piece of machinery) with the money. Thus no one gets stuck with invalid money at mid-day on Saturday. The purpose of our peculiar rule is to ensure that all the month's income (wages, dividends and profits) is spent by the end of the month. If this happens, then all the goods and services – value added – produced during the month, which value added gives rise to an equivalent amount of income, must be sold at the end of the month, because there is a total demand guaranteed (by the operation of our peculiar rule) to be equal to total value added. In such an economy there can be no permanent unemployment and idle machinery because any extra production/ income is guaranteed to find a buyer because all the incomes received will be spent: (extra) supply creates (extra) demand. There can be no over-all deficiency of purchasers in the market.

Now, although we made Say's law 'work' by virtue of a peculiar rule about money and the immediate spending of all incomes, if one imagines a poor but growing and dynamic economy then it is quite reasonable to suppose that all wage incomes are spent on the necessities of life, while all profits are invested (spent) by entrepreneurs anxious to expand their businesses. That expenditure would always press against the limits of income is a quite natural assumption to make if one has no evidence on this matter, and

---

In terms of these two categories of final demand, Kalecki's argument is obvious. Total consumers' expenditure falls because wages have been reduced; investment probably falls also; and the result is that gross domestic product falls and, consequently, unemployment rises.

Kalecki then went on to argue a converse case: that a rise in investment not accompanied by a reduction in wages would cause a rise in output, and so reduce unemployment and idle capital capacity. He imagined the case of a general increase in investment associated with some important invention – that is, Kalecki imagined a situation in which investment was increased because of factors outside the normal economic process (he might have had in mind the increased availability of cheap electricity due to technical progress in electricity supply which had a marked impact on production technology in the interwar period). Suppose, Kalecki argued, the extra investment were financed by borrowing from the banks – the capitalists not yet having the profits with which to pay for the investment. In the first

indeed the assumption was probably quite close to the truth back in 1803. The basic assumption – that everybody works only to have an income to *spend* – is so 'obvious' that one can appreciate why it was never questioned. However, with our access to national income and expenditure accounts by sector, we know very well that the personal sector, especially, tends to work not only to have an income to spend but also to have an income from which to save; and not only to save but also to accumulate financial assets. We must bear in mind that information on income and expenditure by sector within the UK economy has been available only within the last forty years. The early estimates of national income contained no data on total expenditure, let alone expenditure by sector (A. L. Bowley and Sir Josiah Stamp, *The National Income 1924: A Comparative Study of the Income of the United Kingdom in 1911 and 1924*, Oxford University Press, 1927; *Inland Revenue Report on National Income 1929*, reprinted with an Introduction by Richard Stone, Department of Applied Economics, Cambridge, 1977). The *Inland Revenue Report* of 1929 (which was not published until 1977) tried to make an over-all estimate of the annual flow of saving, but it was not until the Treasury White Paper of 1941, *An Analysis of the Sources of War Finance and an Estimate of the National Income and Expenditure in 1938 and 1940* (Cmd 6261, April 1941) that the United Kingdom had its first estimates of personal-sector saving showing that personal saving in 1938 (£151 million) was 3.4 per cent of the national income (£4,415 million). So we must not be too quick to deride those economists who, in the absence of any relevant statistical information, took Say's law as applying to the British economy.

However, we know from Chapter 3 that the personal sector saves an appreciable proportion of its income (Table 3.1), and although some of this saving is spent on capital formation the personal sector has, annually, a relatively large financial surplus (Table 3.5) which they are not themselves spending. So that, if this financial surplus is not borrowed from the personal sector and spent on their behalf, it is possible – to revert to our illustrative economy but now suspending the rule about the Saturday mid-day invalidation of unspent money – for producers to go to market at the end of the month there to encounter an over-all deficiency of purchasers in the market: in aggregate, there will be unsold goods when the market ends. Aggregate demand will be less than supply. The consequence is likely to be that in the next month's production, producers who are carrying inventories of unsold goods will reduce the monthly volume of production and, as total employment is related to total production, total employment will consequently fall. Say's law that total supply will always meet a matching demand no longer works.

If we look back at the statistics on unemployment in interwar Britain (Diagram 1.5 and Appendix 1.2) it is clear in any case that the facts were greatly at variance with Say's law: mass unemployment and idle capital could exist and persist. The question for economics in the 1920s and 1930s was how such permanent unemployment could come about. The explanation for this was provided by Keynes, and with the explanation came the possibility of eliminating such mass unemployment.

---

instance, there is a setting to work of idle equipment and unemployed labour to provide the investment goods. Following this, 'the increased employment is a source of additional demand for consumer goods and thus results in turn in higher employment in the respective [consumer goods] industries' (ibid, p. 29). All this additional spending causes total profits (not necessarily the rate of profit) to rise and so, indirectly, finances the initial extra investment by enabling capitalists to repay their bank loans.

Again, using the categories of final expenditure, the restatement of this argument is very straightforward. Initially investment rises, propelled by 'outside' forces (and financed by borrowing); this extra investment expenditure leads to additional incomes being earned; Kalecki explicitly makes the assumption that workers do not save, so the newly employed workers spend their income or consumer goods, and consumption (final) expenditure rises. The end-result is that gross domestic product rises and unemployment falls. Kalecki then concludes his argument by demonstrating that a similar chain of events could occur if the government were to expand public spending financed initially by borrowing (not by taxation, which reduces people's spending ability).

One of the most important points in Kalecki's argument is that there will be an induced increase in consumption expenditure resulting from the initial increase in investment (or in public spending). There is a twofold impact on the gross domestic product: first from the initial increase in (final) expenditure (however caused), and second from the *induced* increase in consumers' expenditure. Kalecki did not elaborate on the connection between the two, but Keynes did, and that is why *The General Theory of Employment, Interest and Money* constitutes the first complete explanation of this matter.

The consumption function and the multiplier

One of the most important contributions to economics in *The General Theory* was Keynes's systematic explanation of the way in which, *and* of the extent to which, an increase in investment (and so in incomes) would induce an increase in consumers' expenditure. This part of Keynes's argument was based explicitly on the concept of a *consumption function* and on the derived *multiplier* effects of an increase in any component of final expenditure.

In Chapter 3 we spent some time examining the relationship which existed between personal-sector consumption expenditure and personal-sector income, which relationship we called the 'consumption function'. We saw in Diagram 3.7 that, over the period 1946 to 1980, there existed in the United Kingdom a time-series function which could be estimated, using data at current prices for the whole of the personal sector, as:

$$\text{Consumers' expenditure,} = 2{,}634 + 0.66 \times \text{Personal sector income,}$$
$$\text{£ million p.a.} \qquad\qquad \text{£ million p.a.}$$

We also saw in Diagram 3.8 and Table 3.17 that among households there tended to be a quite close cross-section relationship in any given period between household income and household consumption expenditure, where we took the averages for households grouped according to a bracket for household income. An example of this cross-section relationship for households surveyed in 1979 was given in Table 3.16 and Diagram 3.8:

$$\text{Consumption expenditure per household,} = 21.52 + 0.61 \times \text{Income per household,}$$
$$\text{£ per week} \qquad\qquad \text{£ per week}$$

So we know from the statistics that there tends to be a quite close relationship between consumption and income.

In Chapter 8 of *The General Theory* Keynes postulated that consumption would be determined as a function of income but that not all income would be spent – the often-cited passage is:

> The fundamental psychological law ... is that men are disposed, as a rule and on the average, to increase their consumption as their income increases, but not by as much as the increase in their income. That is to say, if C is the amount of consumption and Y is income ... ΔC has the same sign as ΔY but is smaller in amount, i.e. dC/dY is positive but less than unity (*The General Theory of Employment, Interest and Money*, book III 'The propensity to consume', ch. 8 'The propensity to consume: I The objective factors', p. 96 (of 1st edn)).

We have already seen that this is so in Chapter 3, where we ascertained for the United

Kingdom the following values for the marginal propensity to consume (Keynes's dC/dY):

Time series: aggregate data, current price	+ 0.666
Time series: aggregate data, constant price	+ 0.56
Cross section: household, average of 17 estimates	+ 0.60

Suppose we take as our estimate of the marginal propensity to consume the arithmetically simple value of 0.6. What then follows?

Remember that Kalecki said that if investment increased, the extra employment due to such an increase 'is a source of additional demand for consumer goods'. Using the consumption function we can analyse precisely both *how* this additional demand for consumer goods comes about and also the *extent* to which it will come about. To keep the mathematics straightforward let us assume that the extra investment final expenditure – the extra value added in the investment-goods industry and all the (intermediate) industries – is all distributed as income to households (either as wages or as dividends). If the extra investment were, say, 10 (e.g. £10 million), then what happens is that households (the personal sector) receive additional income of 10 (i.e. more heads of households are in work – remember that throughout we are assuming that there are unemployed resources to hand). By the consumption function we know that 0.6, or 60 per cent, of this extra income will be spent on consumption, so:

Extra
consumers' $= 0.6 \times 10 = 6$
expenditure

So now, through the consumption function's marginal propensity to consume, we have analysed precisely and quantitatively the link which Kalecki referred to in rather general, verbal, terms.

However, having expressed the link in this way, we must immediately see that this cannot be the end of the matter because the extra 6 of consumers' final expenditure represents extra value added in the consumer-goods industry and their (intermediate) suppliers; in turn, this means that extra incomes are being earned in those industries. Sticking to our simplifying assumption that all value added is distributed as income to the household sector, we can see that, via the consumption function, which operates for *all* additional incomes, there must be 'second-round' induced increases in consumers' expenditure out of these additional incomes:

Extra
consumers'
expenditure $= 0.6 \times 6 = 3.6$
(second round)

And, of course, the chain cannot end at 3.6 but must continue as follows in the full sequence:

Initial increase in investment
    final expenditure   10

First-round induced increase in
    consumers' final expenditure $0.6 \times 10 = 6$

Second-round induced increase in
    consumers' final expenditure $0.6 \times 6 = 0.6 \times 0.6 \times 10$
        $= 0.6^2 \times 10 = 0.36 \times 10 = 3.6$

Third-round induced increase in
    consumers' final expenditure $0.6 \times 3.6 = 0.6 \times 0.6^2 \times 10$
        $= 0.6^3 \times 10 = 0.216 \times 10 = 2.16$

And so on ... the sum of the series is:

$$10 + 0.6 \times 10 + 0.6^2 \times 10 + 0.6^3 \times 10 + \cdots$$

This is known as a 'geometric series': a geometric series is one where the *ratio* between successive terms is always the same (a constant), in this case 0.6 (i.e. divide the first term into the second, or the second into the third). (An 'arithmetic series' is one where the difference – subtraction – between the successive terms is constant.)

We need to find what this series sums to, and this is quite straightforward. We want to ascertain the value of Z where:

$$Z = 10 + 0.6 \times 10 + 0.6^2 \times 10 + 0.6^3 \times 10 + \cdots$$

and where the three dots means that the series theoretically continues to infinity – but going on to infinity is not of any practical consequence in this sequence because, for example, $0.6^{10} = 0.00647$, so by the tenth round we are down to relatively small numbers. We may ascertain the value in two steps. First, multiply the above equation by the constant ratio between successive terms, namely 0.6, to give:

$$0.6 \times Z = 0.6(10 + 0.6 \times 10 + 0.6^2 \times 10 + \cdots$$
$$= 0.6 \times 10 + 0.6^2 \times 10 + 0.6^3 \times 10 + \cdots$$

Second, if we subtract this second equation from the first equation for Z above we eliminate all but the first term in the awkward sequence to infinity:

$$Z - 0.6 \times Z = 10$$

whence:

$$Z(1 - 0.6) = 10$$

whence:

$$Z = \frac{1}{1 - 0.6} \times 10 = \frac{1}{0.4} \times 10$$
$$= 2.5 \times 10 = 25$$

This can be demonstrated arithmetically by using a calculator. For example, taking the first six terms gives:

10		10
$0.6 \times 10 = 0.60$	$\times 10 =$	6
$0.6^2 \times 10 = 0.36$	$\times 10 =$	3.6
$0.6^3 \times 10 = 0.216$	$\times 10 =$	2.16
$0.6^4 \times 10 = 0.1296$	$\times 10 =$	1.296
$0.6^5 \times 10 = 0.07776$	$\times 10 =$	0.7776

Total for first 6 terms   23.8336

The value:

$$\frac{1}{1 - 0.6} = \frac{1}{0.4} = 2.5$$

indicates in a precise quantitative way the total multiple (chain) effects on income and expenditure of any given increase in final expenditure. So we can now go back to Kalecki's comment that the extra employment (income) is 'a source of additional demand for consumer goods' and say that not only will this be the case but that if 10 were the increase in investment and 0.6 were the value of the marginal propensity to consume, then the additional income produced by the whole process (including the initial increase in investment) would be:

$$\frac{1}{1-0.6} \times 10 = 25$$

comprising the increase in investment *plus* all the induced increases in consumers' expenditure. So by using Keynes's consumption function we know, not only *how* it comes about that there is an extra induced demand for consumer goods, but also the *extent* of this extra induced demand. In general, the formula of the total impact is:

$$\frac{1}{1-b} \times \Delta I$$

where *b* is the marginal propensity to consume and ΔI is the initial increase in final expenditure.

One simple diagrammatic way of looking at this sequence of events (of the geometric series) is shown in Diagram 11.2. Let us represent the initial increase of 10 in investment final expenditure by a horizontal bar. As we shall see in a moment, this 10 represents value added in the investment-goods industry and in its supplying (intermediate) industries (e.g.

DIAGRAM 11.2 *How an increase in investment final expenditure leads to a chain of induced increases in consumers' final expenditure*

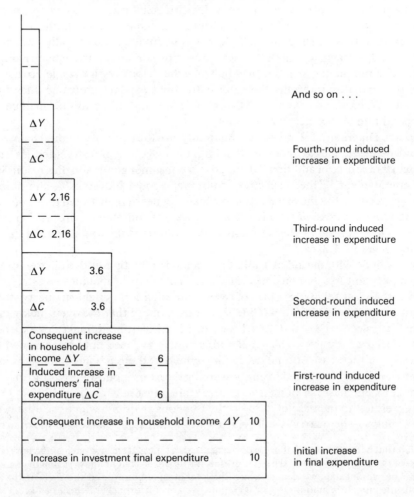

And so on . . .

Fourth-round induced
increase in expenditure

Third-round induced
increase in expenditure

Second-round induced
increase in expenditure

First-round induced
increase in expenditure

Initial increase
in final expenditure

if the 10 final sale of investment goods contains 3 of bought-in materials, then there will be 7 of value added/incomes in the investment-goods industry and 3 of value added/incomes in the industries supplying the bought-in materials). Because this final sale of investment goods creates a corresponding total of value added/incomes we may draw, as part of the investment final expenditure bar, an exactly corresponding bar of 10 (still maintaining our assumption, which merely serves to simplify the diagram without affecting the basic principle, that all value added is distributed to households as income through wages or dividends). The income is the other side of the coin of investment final expenditure – that is, there is in the first step of Diagram 11.2 only one number – '10' – which we may look at as comprising investment final expenditure (bottom of the bar) or incomes received from producing those investment goods (top of the bar). Out of this extra income, denoted by ΔY, there is induced, via the consumption function, extra consumption final expenditure, or ΔC, and, given the value of the marginal propensity to consume which we have taken (namely, 0.6), this first-round induced increase in consumption final expenditure will total 6.

But this extra consumption final expenditure creates value added/incomes in the consumer-goods industry and in the supplying (intermediate) industries of 6, so the bar representing the induced increase in consumption final expenditure must also contain an exactly corresponding income part of 6. Out of this extra income there is induced, via the consumption function, a second-round of induced increase in consumption final expenditure of $0.6 \times 6 (= 0.6 \times 0.6 \times 10 = 0.6^2 \times 10) = 3.6$.

The chain of events continues, theoretically with an infinite series of steps, but the sum of all the bars (counting either final expenditure or income – but not both!) is 25.

Although the bars in Diagram 11.2 do not constitute a geometrically perfect triangle (Diagram 11.2 is drawn to scale), they do make approximately a triangular shape, and for purposes of subsequent exposition, we shall take the shape to be a triangle, so that the total *area* of the triangle represents the total extra final expenditure/value added/incomes generated.* When we take the area of the triangle, we must take only one set of bars: either final expenditure or incomes, but not both.

Although Diagram 11.2 gives an apparently obvious picture of the chain of events whereby increased employment in the investment-goods industry (and its supplying industries) 'is a source of additional demands for consumer goods and thus results in turn in higher employment in the respective [consumer-goods] industries' – the point which Kalecki appreciated but the mechanism of which Keynes demonstrated fully and systematically – the 'obviousness' of the picture covers a quite complicated process in reality, and we need to look a little further into this reality in order fully to understand the chain of events in Diagram 11.2.

This we can do with the aid of Table 11.2, changing the figures therein to represent the increased expenditures and incomes. In Table 11.2 the oven-making (investment-goods) industry is shown as selling 18 worth of ovens and using 6 of bought-in quarry stone (note the input–output ratio of $6/18 = 0.3333$). Let us suppose that the oven-making industry finds that its sales rise by 10 to 28 (this extra 10 of investment final sales expenditure is equivalent to the increase we have been discussing – we need not be concerned with the reasons why this increase occurs; we can imagine that there is some important invention leading to a new and improved oven). Assuming the same input–output ratio of 0.333, the oven-maker's purchases of bought-in quarry stone must now rise to $0.3333 \times 28 = 9.33$, which represents an increase of 3.33 on the previous sales of 6 which the quarry made to the oven-maker. The quarry is still selling 4 to the millstone-maker, so the quarry's total

---

*Note well that in Diagram 11.2 there is no vertical axis as such. If we give each of the bars (i.e. either the bar representing final sales or the bar representing incomes – but not both) a height of 1 unit, then along the horizontal axis we can measure the monetary amount, and the *area* of the bar then represents the monetary amount; so, in aggregate, we are concerned with the area of the 'triangle'.

sales are 13.33. So for the two rows relating to quarrying and oven-making in Table 11.2, we now have the figures:

	Total sales	Bought-in materials	Value added	Wages	Profits
Quarrying	13.33	0	13.33	8	5.33
Oven-making	28	9.33	18.67	14	4.67
Both combined	—	—	32	22	10

By comparison with Table 11.2, where both industries combined were producing 22 worth of value added, value added has now risen by 10 to 32; so the 10 of extra investment final sales has created 10 of extra value added: 3.33 extra in the quarrying (intermediate) industry, and 6.67 extra in the oven-making industry. The extra value added has led to a rise in both the wage bill and in gross profits; and assuming that gross profits are all distributed as household income to the owners of the quarry and the oven-making factory, household incomes will have risen likewise by 10.

The consumers' expenditure of these households is governed by the consumption function: households 'are disposed, as a rule and on the average, to increase their consumption as their income increases, but not by as much as their income increases'. If there were unemployment, we may imagine that unemployed heads of households with zero income obtained employment and extra wage income, and that households receiving profits simply have an increase in their distributed-profit income. All households are assumed to have the same marginal propensity to consume of 0.6 – for the economy as a whole it may be permissible thus to average all the reactions.

Applying this consumption function (this marginal propensity to consume of 0.6) means that the consequence of this rise of 10 in household income is to produce a first-round induced increase in the consumption of bread by 6 from 45 to 51 (bread being the only consumer good in this economy). In turn, this will raise incomes in the baking industry and in its supplying industries (including the overseas industries supplying imports). Out of the extra domestic incomes so created there will be a second-round induced increase in consumers' expenditure.

However, the presence of imports causes a problem, as we shall see. In Table 11.2 the baker sold £45 worth of bread using £35 worth of bought-in materials (flour £24; wood fuel £5; petrol £1; imported yeast £5), so the ratio of input to output was 35/45 = 0.7778; the baker's final sales rise to £51 due to the additional £6 spent on bread (consumer goods) out of the extra £10 of income in the investment-goods industry and its suppliers. So, assuming that there are no price changes (and no technical progress which affects the efficiency of materials conversion), the baker's total purchases of bought-in materials must rise to £51 × 0.7778 = £39.67. Another way of looking at it is that the baker's sales have risen by 13.33 per cent (51/45), so his total purchases of bought-in materials rise also by 13.33 per cent (£35 × 1.1333 = £39.67). Each of the items purchased must rise in a like proportion, so the baker's purchases of bought-in materials become: flour £27.20; wood fuel £5.67; petrol £1.13; imported yeast £5.67).

The miller's total sales of flour (including his unaltered £1 of exports) rise from £25 to £28.20 or by 12.8 per cent, so the miller's purchases of wheat rise from £15 to £16.92; consequently, the farmer's total sales of wheat (including his unaltered £5 of exports) rise from £20 to £21.92. Finally, petroleum-refining, which used to sell £7 of petrol in total (with £1 of sales going to the miller) using £2 of imported crude oil, finds that its sales now rise to £7.13 because sales of petrol to the miller go up by £0.13 to £1.13), so imports of crude oil must rise to £2.04 (= £2 × 7.13/7). We may bring all these figures together as they would be at the end of the first round (but, as in Table 11.10, we must insert a row for imports to take account of foreign value added):

	Total sales	Bought-in materials	Value added	Value added in Table 11.2
Farming	21.92	0	21.92	20
Milling	28.20	16.92	11.28	10
Woodcutting	5.67	0	5.67	5
Petroleum-refining	7.13	2.04	5.09	5
Baking	51	39.67	11.33	10
Total domestic industries	—	—	55.29	50
Imports (yeast, crude oil)	—	—	7.71	7
Grand total (domestic and overseas value added)	—	—	63	57

Value added in domestic industries has risen by £5.29 from £50 to £55.29 as a result of the increase in consumers' final expenditure, and value added in overseas industries (yeast-making and crude oil extraction) has risen by £0.71 from £7 to £7.71. So total 'world' value added (and incomes) in this group of industries has risen by £6 (£5.29 + £0.71) as a result of the increase in consumers' final expenditure, but domestic income has risen by only £5.29. At this stage, let us note that of the extra consumers' final expenditure on bread of £6 generating additional 'world' value added and incomes of £6 proportion:

$$0.118 = \frac{0.71}{6}$$

has accrued as income to overseas residents (because of the extra imports resulting), while conversely proportion:

$$1 - 0.118 = \frac{5.29}{6}$$

has accrued as domestic income to residents.

The problem for the multiplier analysis (as depicted in Diagram 11.2) is that, while we can assume that the rise in domestic income will cause the demand for British bread (UK consumers' expenditure) to rise, we can make no such assumption about the impact of the income which accrues to overseas residents. In fact, the only sensible assumption is that the extra overseas income will not affect (or will affect only very slightly) the demand for British goods. So we must assume that the second-round induced increase in consumers' expenditure will be only out of the £5.29 of extra *domestic* income, as depicted in Diagram 11.3.

So, taking the extra domestic income as $(1 - 0.118) \times 6 = 5.29$, the second-round induced increase in consumers' final expenditure will be (bearing in mind the initial origin of the extra £6 of consumers' expenditure was 0.6×10, where £10 was the increase in investment in ovens):

$$0.6 \times 5.29 = 0.6 \times (1 - 0.118) \times 6$$
$$= 0.6 \times (1 - 0.118) \times 0.6 \times 10$$
$$= 0.6^2 \times (1 - 0.118) \times 10 = 3.17$$

In turn this second-round induced increase in consumers' expenditure on bread will give rise to an extra £3.17 of 'world' value added and incomes. And again, only proportion $(1 - 0.118)$ of this will accrue as domestic income to residents. (The proportions 0.118 and $(1 - 0.118)$ will be maintained – assuming no price changes nor any changes in the input–output coefficients – as can be ascertained by working through the whole sequence of input–output relations for baking, petroleum-refining, woodcutting, milling and farming, using the extra £3.17 expenditure on bread, with £54.17 instead of £51 as the total final sales by baking; such a calculation would again give the same porportions.) If

DIAGRAM 11.3   *The impact upon induced increases in consumers' final expenditure of 'leakages' into overseas income because consumer goods contain an import component*

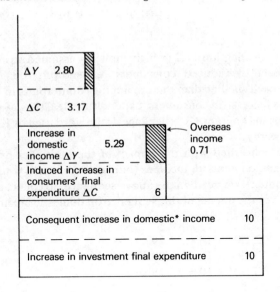

proportion $(1 - 0.118)$ of this additional 'world' income of £3.17 accrues as domestic income, we then have for the extra domestic income at this second round the expression:

$$(1 - 0.118) \times 3.17$$

and substituting in the expression above for 3.17 gives:

$$(1 - 0.118) \times 0.6^2 \times (1 - 0.118) \times 10$$
$$= 0.6^2 \times (1 - 0.118)^2 \times 10 = 2.80$$

And, in turn, the induced consumers' expenditure out of this extra domestic income is:

$$0.6 \times 0.6^2 \times (1 - 0.118)^2 \times 10$$
$$= 0.6^3 \times (1 - 0.118)^2 \times 10 = 1.68$$

We thus have the sequence (illustrated in Diagram 11.3):

1. Initial increase in investment
   final expenditure   10

2. First-round induced increase in
   consumers' final expenditure 0.6×10 $= 6$

3. Consequent increase in
   domestic incomes $(1 - 0.118) \times 0.6 \times 10$ **= 5.29**

4. Second-round induced increase in
   consumers' final expenditure $0.6 \times (1 - 0.118) \times 0.6 \times 10$
         $= 0.6^2 \times (1 - 0.118) \times 10$ $= 3.17$

5. Consequent increase in
   domestic incomes $(1 - 0.118) \times 0.6^2 \times (1 - 0.118) \times 10$
         $= 0.6^2 \times (1 - 0.118)^2 \times 10$ **= 2.80**

6. Third-round induced increase in
   consumers' final expenditure $0.6 \times 0.6^2 \times (1 - 0.118)^2 \times 10$
         $= 0.6^3 \times (1 - 0.118)^2 \times 10$ $= 1.68$

*Here it is assumed that investment goods contain no imported components; otherwise the same rule about leakage into overseas income would apply.

7. Consequent increase in
    domestic incomes

$$(1 - 0.118) \times 0.6^3 \times (1 - 0.118)^2 \times 10$$
$$= 0.6^3 \times (1 - 0.118)^3 \times 10 \qquad\qquad = \mathbf{1.48}$$

And so on ...

By comparison with Diagram 11.2 (which implicitly assumed no imports) the successive steps of the impact of induced consumers' expenditure on *domestic* incomes in Diagram 11.3 are each smaller than their matching counterparts in Diagram 11.2. This is because part of the increase in consumers' expenditure 'leaks' away overseas, as shown by the shaded portions in Diagram 11.3 ('leakage' is the word used by Keynes in his pamphlet *The Means to Prosperity*).

Because we are concerned with the impact of the multiplier process, resulting from increased investment, on *domestic* incomes (our basic concern is with the determination of gross domestic product), we need, in the above sequence, to collect all the *odd*-numbered terms. This then gives the impact of this sequence on domestic incomes, i.e. the series:

$$10 \qquad\qquad\qquad\qquad 10$$
$$0.6 \times (1 - 0.118) \times 10 = 5.29$$
$$0.6^2 \times (1 - 0.118)^2 \times 10 = 2.80$$
$$0.6^3 \times (1 - 0.118)^3 \times 10 = 1.48$$
$$\ldots$$

The sum of this series gives the total effect of the multiplier process on domestic incomes of the extra investment final expenditure of 10. Let us denote the sum by Z. Then:

$$
\begin{aligned}
Z = \ & 10 \\
& + 0.6 \times (1 - 0.118) \times 10 \\
& + 0.6^2 \times (1 - 0.118)^2 \times 10 \\
& + 0.6^3 \times (1 - 0.118)^3 \times 10 \\
& + \cdots
\end{aligned}
$$

And multiplying Z by the constant ratio between successive terms gives:

$$
\begin{aligned}
0.6 \times (1 - 0.118) \times Z = \ & 0.6 \times (1 - 0.118) \times 10 \\
& + 0.6^2 \times (1 - 0.118)^2 \times 10 \\
& + 0.6^3 \times (1 - 0.118)^3 \times 10 \\
& + \cdots
\end{aligned}
$$

so that:

$$Z - 0.6 \times (1 - 0.118) \times Z = 10$$

or:

$$Z[1 - 0.6 \times (1 - 0.118)] = 10$$

whence:

$$
\begin{aligned}
Z & = \frac{1}{[1 - 0.6(1 - 0.118)]} \times 10 \\[2mm]
& = \frac{1}{1 - 0.6 \times 0.882} \times 10 \\[2mm]
& = \frac{1}{1 - 0.5292} \times 10 \\[2mm]
& = 2.124 \times 10 \\
& = 21.24
\end{aligned}
$$

In the multiplier process shown in Diagram 11.2 there was no 'leakage' into imports, so the multiplier was larger at $1/(1 - 0.6) = 2.5$, and the impact of an extra 10 of investment final expenditure would have been to raise total domestic incomes by 25. But if there is a 'leakage' into imports of, say, 0.118 of consumers' final expenditure (that is, each extra £1 spent on bread involves an extra £0.118 of imports), then the multiplier is reduced to:

$$1/[1 - 0.6(1 - 0.118)] = 1/(1 - 0.6 + 0.118 \times 0.6) = 2.124$$

and the impact of an extra 10 of investment final expenditure will be to raise domestic incomes by 21.24.

We could arrive at this multiplier by a different short-cut route which is sometimes used in textbooks. Let us use the following symbols:*

Y = Gross domestic product
C = Consumers' final expenditure
I = Investment final expenditure
X = Exports
M = Imports

(we are leaving out government consumption expenditure).

We have a consumption function:

$$C = bY$$

(we have been working with a value for b, the marginal propensity to consume, of 0.6). We now add an import function which makes imports a function of consumers' final expenditure (effectively continuing our simplifying assumption that neither investment final expenditure nor exports contain any imported components). This we can write:

$$M = mC$$

In the example above we had a value for m of 0.118; this is the marginal propensity to import in terms of consumers' final expenditure. We may substitute the consumption function into this expression to give:

$$M = mbY$$

We have the gross domestic product defined in terms of final expenditure as:

$$Y = C + I + X - M$$

Substituting in the consumption function and the import function (expressed as a function of Y) gives:

$$Y = bY + I + X - mbY$$

whence:

$$Y - bY + mbY = I + X$$

and:

$$Y(1 - b + mb) = I + X$$

so that:

$$Y = \frac{1}{(1 - b + mb)} \times (I + X)$$

$$= \frac{1}{[1 - b(1 - m)]} \times (I + X)$$

*These symbols will be used with the same meaning throughout this chapter and the next. This notation is fairly standard in economics; if it is unfamiliar to you, please learn it by heart.

So that the increase in income will be a function of the increase in investment and exports (the example above did not have any exports):

$$\Delta Y = \frac{1}{[1 - b(1 - m)]} \times \Delta(I + X)$$

This is exactly the multiplier we derived earlier. This short-cut to the multiplier is convenient, but it unfortunately tends to lose sight of the macroeconomic processes involved.*

Diagram 11.4 illustrates the multiplier process with and without imports; the diagram is in effect a schematic (triangular) representation of Diagrams 11.2 and 11.3. The effect of the leakage of expenditure into imports is seen in the smaller area of the triangle, which represents the total effect on domestic value added of the initial increase in final expenditure (represented by the length of the base of the triangle). The total increase in incomes will clearly depend on the initial increase in expenditure (the length of the base) and the values of the marginal propensity to consume, b, and the marginal propensity to import, m: the larger is b, the larger will be the ratio $1/(1 - b)$ and so the triangle will be 'taller' with a bigger area. The larger is m, the smaller will be the ratio $1/(1 - b + mb)$ and the triangle will have a smaller area.

DIAGRAM 11.4   *The over-all impact of leakages into imports*

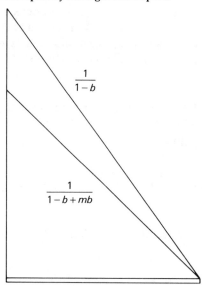

Output is determined by aggregate demand

So far we have discussed the process simply in terms of the *increase* in total income (value added) consequent upon an *increase* in investment: that is what the triangle in Diagram 11.4 schematically represents. It is now necessary to convert this analysis from one of the relationship between increased investment and consequent increased income to one of the relationship between *total* investment and *total* income (value added). Here we are following Keynes in chapter 10 of *The General Theory*, the opening words of which are:

---

*However, note that Keynes used the term 'multiplier' to refer to the relationship between the flow of *total* investment (and exports) and *total* output; and did not use it to refer to the ratio between *increases*; this is discussed further in the section following.

We established in Chapter 8 that employment can only increase *pari passu* with investment. We can now carry this line of thought a stage further. For in given circumstances a definite ratio, to be called the *Multiplier*, can be established between [total] income and [total] investment . . . This further step is an integral part of our theory of employment, since it establishes a precise relationship, given the propensity to consume, between aggregate employment and income and the rate [i.e. total flow] of investment (*The General Theory of Employment, Interest and Money*, book III, ch. 10 'The marginal propensity to consume and the multiplier', p. 113 (1st edn); '*pari passu*' is Latin for 'in step with' – literally (but not in this context) 'with equal step').

The determinate relationship between total income/final expenditure/output on the one hand and total investment on the other hand comes about as follows (and as illustrated in Diagram 11.5). Suppose that total annual investment in the economy is planned to be *OC*, the base of the triangle in Diagram 11.5 (let us assume that there are no government expenditures or exports, and no imports). We know that if the marginal propensity to consume is *b*, induced consumption final expenditure should then build up in successive steps to give a total flow of final expenditure/income of the area of triangle *OCA*, where this area will be:*

$$\frac{1}{1-b} \times OC$$

Strictly speaking, the area of the triangle *OCA* represents the plans, or intentions, of final spenders (investors and consumers) as to the extent of their total final expenditure over the course of the year.

DIAGRAM 11.5   *How expenditure causes production to vary so making gross domestic product a variable*

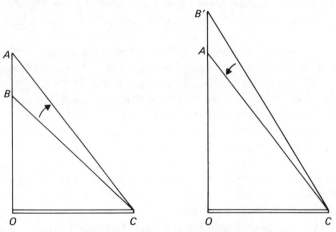

OCA = 'Planned' total final expenditure, depending on *OC* and the multiplier
OCB and *OCB'* = Initially 'planned' total production

However, because expenditure plans and production plans are made by two different sets of people (households and investors in the former case and enterprises in the latter case), it is quite feasible that manufacturers, initially unaware of what is happening, plan to produce at a lower annual rate as represented by the area of the triangle *OCB* on the left-hand side of Diagram 11.5. (Note that the only significance of *OCB* is in its area representing the volume of planned production; unlike *OCA*, which represents the

---

*Bear in mind that this 'area' representation is only approximated by the triangle.

sequence of diminishing steps, the triangular shape of *OCB* has no special significance: we could have represented *OCB* as a circle or square but always with a lesser *area* than that of triangle *OCA*. However, a circle or a square would not fit the diagram so neatly!)

We may assume that the manufacturers of investment goods (and their intermediate suppliers) are directly in touch via their order books with investment plans so that there is a ready adjustment of the production of investment goods to the total demand for investment goods as represented by *OC*. But what about the manufacturers of consumer goods (and their intermediate suppliers)? They might be intending to produce, for the year, at rate represented by the area of *OCB*, because they are not directly in touch with planned consumers' expenditure for the whole year. As time goes by, these producers of consumer goods will find that, month by month, the monthly flow of (induced) consumers' final expenditure outruns the monthly flow of (planned) production of consumer goods and that stocks of already produced consumer goods are reduced – running down inventories being the only way in which ongoing expenditure can outrun ongoing production (remember that imports are not here entering into consideration). Manufacturers of consumer goods are then likely to be stimulated by falling inventories into increasing production; as retailers and wholesalers find themselves short of stocks, they will increase their orders to manufacturers and (always assuming that there is some spare capital capacity and some unemployed labour) the manufacturers of consumer goods will respond to these orders by increasing production so that their initially planned volume of production, *OCB*, will gradually be modified and the actual rate of production will approximate to *OCA*.

Conversely, on the right-hand side of Diagram 11.5, given an initial total planned investment of *OC*, manufacturers of consumer goods might have been planning to produce at *OCB'*, so the planned rate of annual production is larger than the rate of consumers' (induced) expenditure, *OCA*. In this case, month by month, production outruns expenditure and inventories of (unsold) goods must rise. Sooner rather than later, this will force a downward revision of production plans (no manufacturer can withstand the strain on cash flows caused by paying for production without receiving the sales revenue from selling that production). In this case, production will fall from the initially planned annual rate of *OCB'* to the annual rate determined by aggregate final expenditure, *OCA*.

Actual total output, and hence total employment, will be determined, *not* by the capacity to produce at full employment, but by the aggregate of final expenditure, in turn determined by the initial flow of investment, *OC*, and the marginal propensity to consume which governs the multiplier impact of the initial flow of investment. This is a far cry from Say's law; the assessment of Professor Shackle regarding this part of *The General Theory* is that 'the great revolution of Book III was the mere recognition that, even in its shortest period, a theory of employment must treat aggregate income as a variable' (G. L. S. Shackle, *The Years of High Theory*, p. 147). That is to say, output (income) will adjust to whatever aggregate is determined by the initial final expenditure and the multiplier: output is determined by aggregate demand.

We can now return to the problem stated earlier: how could a situation arise and persist where total output was less than the economy's capacity to produce at full employment? The right-hand side of Diagram 11.5 illustrates the answer. We may postulate that, were all the labour and capital in the economy to be fully employed, total annual output would be represented by area *OCB'*. But if *OC* remains, year in and year out, the total flow of initial annual investment final expenditure, and the multiplier $1/(1 - b)$ stays the same, so that total annual aggregate demand is represented by *OCA*, then total annual actual production will also be *OCA*, because it is only at this volume of annual production that manufacturers can sell all they produce. The other side of the coin is that the 'wedge' *ACB'* represents *permanently* unused production capacity in the form of idle capital and unemployed labour. For as long as *OC* and the multiplier both persist, so too will the unemployed 'wedge' persist, with no tendency for the situation to alter. As economists might say, such a configuration with mass unemployment is a situation of stable equilibrium.

Saving and investment

Having dealt with the basic mechanics of aggregate demand as the determinant of output, we can turn now to the implications for economic policy of Keynes's analysis. Our understanding of Keynes's economics at this point will be helped by some knowledge of the history of the times (the full story is told by Donald Winch, *Economics and Policy: A Historical Study*, Hodder & Stoughton, 1969, chs 6–9, and by A. J. P. Taylor, *English History 1914–1945*, Oxford History of England, Vol. 15, Oxford University Press, 1965, ch. 8).

In the campaign leading up to the general election of May 1929, Lloyd George's election manifesto *We Can Conquer Unemployment* pledged a programme of public works – roads, houses, electricity, telephones, railways – all to be financed by borrowing: each year for three years £100 million would be spent by the government (if Lloyd George were elected) on capital expenditure. Public-sector expenditure on fixed capital formation in 1928 was £125 million, so Lloyd George's campaign pledge represented a substantial increase. Although this was before the Wall Street crash of October 1929, unemployment in the United Kingdom in 1928 was $1\frac{1}{4}$ million, or about $7\frac{1}{2}$ per cent of the labour force. In the event, the Labour party under Ramsay MacDonald won the election, but in any case the senior civil servants at the Treasury did not accept the view that increased public-sector investment could reduce unemployment because, they believed, any addition to public-sector investment would simply reduce private-sector investment so that there could be no net gain. The Treasury argued that resources available to provide investment were limited so that increased public-sector investment could only be at the expense of private-sector investment: in their words, 'the supply of capital in this country being limited, it was undesirable to divert any appreciable proportion of this supply from normal trade channels' (quoted in Winch, *Economics and Policy*, p. 106). With rapidly worsening unemployment after 1929 (see Diagram 1.5) these arguments and counter-arguments became more important (the Treasury view tending to prevail, notwithstanding the rows and splits this occasioned in the Labour government). This forced Keynes to concentrate his attention on demonstrating the fallacy of the official Treasury argument, which argument had been largely (if reluctantly) accepted by the Labour party. This is the historical background to much of chapter 10 of *The General Theory*, especially the following passage:

> An increment of investment [in real terms] ... cannot occur unless the public are prepared to increase their savings [in real terms]. [So far Keynes conceded that there was some truth in the Treasury view, but] Ordinarily speaking, the public will not do this unless their aggregate income [in real terms] is increasing. Thus their effort to consume a part of their increased incomes will stimulate output until the new level (and distribution) of incomes provides a margin of saving sufficient to correspond to the increased investment. The multiplier tells us by how much their employment has to be increased to yield an increase in real income sufficient to induce them to do the necessary extra saving ... If saving is the pill and consumption is the jam, the extra jam has to be proportioned to size of the additional pill (*The General Theory of Employment, Interest and Money*, ch. 10, pp. 117–18).

Keynes's argument, important for economic policy, is that extra public investment would, through the multiplier effect, produce extra resources for investment so that the Treasury view that public investment would simply displace an equivalent amount of private investment was, in economic analysis, wrong. The argument can be illustrated in Diagram 11.6. Extra public investment of, say, 10 creates an equivalent amount of domestic income (assuming no leakage into imports). Of this extra income, proportion 0.6 goes on consumers' expenditure, and proportion $(1 - 0.6)$ is saved. So there is extra consumption expenditure, denoted by ΔC, of $0.6 \times 10 = 6$, *and* extra saving, denoted by ΔS, of $(1 - 0.6) \times 10 = 4$. The extra consumers' expenditure creates matching additional incomes, of which proportion 0.6 is spent and proportion $(1 - 0.6)$ is saved. So at the second round $\Delta C = 0.6^2 \times 10 = 3.6$ and $\Delta S = (1 - 0.6) \times 0.6 \times 10 = 2.4$.

DIAGRAM 11.6   *How an increase in final expenditure leads also to an equivalent total increase in saving*

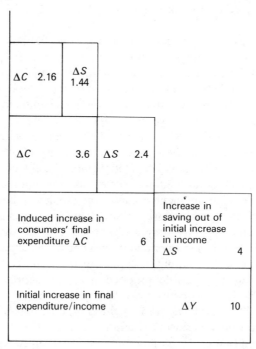

For extra saving we thus have the sequence:

1. Increase in saving out of
    initial increase in income $\qquad\qquad (1 - 0.6) \times 10 = 4$

2. Increase in saving out of
    increase in income consequent
    upon first-round induced increase
    in consumers' expenditure $\qquad (1 - 0.6) \times 0.6 \times 10 = 2.4$

3. Increase in saving out of
    increase in income consequent
    upon second-round induced increase
    in consumers' expenditure $\qquad (1 - 0.6) \times 0.6^2 \times 10 = 1.44$

4. Increase in saving out of
    increase in income consequent
    upon third-round induced increase
    in consumers' expenditure $\qquad (1 - 0.6) \times 0.6^3 \times 10 = 0.864$

    And so on . . .

The sum of this geometric series is:

$$Z = (1 - 0.6) \times 10$$
$$+ (1 - 0.6) \times 0.6 \times 10$$
$$+ (1 - 0.6) \times 0.6^2 \times 10$$
$$+ (1 - 0.6) \times 0.6^3 \times 10$$
$$+ \cdots$$

Again, to solve the sum we multiply by the constant ratio between successive terms, 0.6, to get:

$$0.6 \times Z = (1 - 0.6) \times 0.6 \times 10$$
$$+ (1 - 0.6) \times 0.6^2 \times 10$$
$$+ (1 - 0.6) \times 0.6^3 \times 10$$
$$+ \cdots$$

So that:

$$Z - 0.6 \times Z = (1 - 0.6) \times 10$$

and:

$$Z(1 - 0.6) = (1 - 0.6) \times 10$$

whence:

$$Z = 10$$

because $(1 - 0.6)$ on both sides divides out. So that the total of extra savings, Z, resulting from this process is exactly equal to the initial increase in expenditure – 'the new level of incomes ... provides a margin of saving sufficient to correspond to the increased investment' (Keynes, *The General Theory*, p. 117). The multiplier process determining the increase in aggregate income determines at the same time a flow of additional saving equal to the initial increase in expenditure. So the official Treasury view that extra public expenditure would simply displace private investment expenditure was wrong; knowledge of the multiplier process demonstrated that additional output (incomes) would be produced some of which would *not be consumed*, i.e. there would be extra saving, and this additional unconsumed output – exactly matching the initial extra expenditure – could then be available for investment.

So far we have discussed Keynes's argument about a flow of saving to match the initial flow of expenditure in terms of increases in saving and increases in expenditure (as would have followed had Lloyd George's £100 million plan been put into effect). But the same analysis applies to the total flow of investment and the division of total income between consumption expenditure and saving, and so enables us to see the coherence of the whole of Keynes's system of macroeconomic relationships.

The Keynesian macroeconomic system

We can best see the whole system with the aid of Diagram 11.7 (which effectively translates the 'impressionistic' Diagram 11.5 into its functional equivalent). To keep the diagram uncomplicated (we are expounding the basic principle, not the details), we assume, first, that all income is distributed as income to households (we shall subsequently move to a more realistic assumption), and second that the economy has no government consumption expenditure and no foreign trade. We have a simple consumption function relating total consumers' expenditure, C, to total household income, Y (which by virtue of our first assumption is also total value added, or gross domestic product):

$$C = 0.6 \times Y$$

whence the marginal propensity to consume is:

$$\frac{\Delta C}{\Delta Y} = 0.6$$

and so the multiplier is:

$$\frac{1}{1 - 0.6} = 2.5$$

If the total of investment expenditure, I, remains as a constant annual flow and is the only 'non-induced' final expenditure (by virtue of our second assumption ruling out government consumption expenditure, determined by politics, and exports, determined by overseas), then the multiplier process gives the value for total income (output), Y, as depending on the total of investment final expenditure, I (which creates income in the investment-goods, and supplying, industries) and on the total of induced consumers' expenditure (which creates income in consumer-goods, and supplying, industries). Thus for a marginal propensity to consume of 0.6 we have:

$$Y = \frac{1}{1 - 0.6} \times I$$

as the multiplier relationship between total income (as the dependent variable) and investment.

This multiplier relationship is drawn in the upper-right quadrant of Diagram 11.7. Along the horizontal axis we measure the annual flow of investment, I (were the model more complicated, this axis would measure the combined total of investment, government consumption expenditure and exports). Up the vertical axis we measure total income, Y. We may then draw in the multiplier relationship with a slope (rise over run) of $1/(1 - 0.6) = 2.5$; this shows the total final expenditure/output/income generated for any level of investment.

For any income flow so arising, total consumers' expenditure is given by the consumption function, $C = 0.6 \times Y$. We may draw the consumption function in the upper-left quadrant, where the horizontal axis, measuring leftwards from the origin, is simply marked off in money units to measure such things as total consumers' expenditure, total saving, and total final expenditure. This is not, of course, a separate process from what is going on in the upper-right quadrant, but is another representation of it because the multiplier relationship depends on the consumption function.

The consumption function then shows us what will be the total of consumers' expenditure for any income flow (where income is measured from the origin up the vertical axis). We also have a saving function, which is, so to speak, the converse of the consumption function. Total saving by households, S, is the difference between total household income, Y, and total consumers' expenditure, C, as follows:*

$$S \equiv Y - C$$

Substituting the consumption function for C gives the saving function expressing total household saving as a function of total household income:

$$S = Y - 0.6 \times Y$$
$$= (1 - 0.6) Y$$

*Three lines ($\equiv$) denotes a definitional identity, and is to be read as: '[the left-hand side] is defined as [the right-hand side]'.

DIAGRAM 11.7 *The Keynesian system of macroeconomics: the multiplier relationship with total saving equal to total investment*

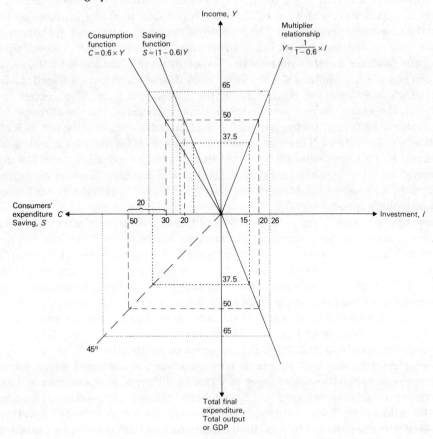

We can draw the saving function also in the upper-left quadrant of Diagram 11.7. You can see that this saving function is a 'mirror image' of the multiplier relationship in the upper-right quadrant and because of this mirror image the matching S and I co-ordinates will always be equidistant from the origin: total saving will always equal total investment.

Down the vertical axis from the origin we can measure total final demand, putting a 45° line in the lower-left quadrant so that we can switch from the leftward horizontal axis to the downward vertical axis.

As in Diagram 11.5, everything depends, given the multiplier, on the flow of investment, I (in Diagram 11.5, OC). Suppose that the flow of annual investment final expenditure is 20 (e.g. £20,000 million). This expenditure will give rise to an annual flow of output – and incomes – in the investment-goods and consumer goods (and intermediate supplying) industries. The total of all these expenditures/incomes will be:

$$Y = \frac{1}{1 - 0.6} \times 20 = 2.5 \times 20 = 50$$

Given that total income is 50, total consumers' expenditure is:

$$C = 0.6 \times 50 = 30$$

and total saving is:

$$S = (1 - 0.6)50 = 20$$

thus demonstrating that total saving equals total investment. We may now determine total final expenditure leftward along the horizontal axis by adding total investment to total consumers' expenditure and we may then switch this total final expenditure, via the 45° line, to the downward vertical axis. The relation, in the lower-right quadrant between total final expenditure and investment, is a 'mirror image' of the multiplier relationship in the upper-right quadrant, but showing total final expenditure as a function of total investment.

We can now see the whole of Keynes's system. A flow of investment will lead to a flow of saving which is exactly the equivalent of the investment flow. The greater is total investment, the greater is income (via the multiplier process), and the correspondingly greater will be the flow of saving (via the saving function) – this was the nub of Keynes's refutation of the official Treasury argument about the futility of expanding public investment. Keynes here demonstrates that there would be extra resources (saving) for investment, so greater public investment need not necessarily displace an equivalent amount of private-sector investment: the 'supply of capital' (saving) was *not* limited but could and would expand.

A flow of investment results also in a flow of induced consumers' expenditure via the multiplier process and this is shown in the consumption function. When the two flows of final expenditure (investment and consumers') are added together, we get the total flow of final expenditure, or aggregate demand, in the economy, which can (using the 45° line) be switched to the vertical downward axis in Diagram 11.7 (this linear measurement is then the same as the *area* of the triangle *OCA* in Diagram 11.5).

We might suppose that total output (value added) at full employment was 65, and that all producers had been intending to produce at full capacity. However, the investment-goods industries soon ascertain through their order books that they will be able to sell only 20 of investment goods. And, sooner or later, producers of consumer goods will realise that consumers' expenditure is running at a rate of 30 per annum and they will have to adjust their production downward (not being able to withstand the strain on business cash flows of unsold goods). Eventually total production (gross domestic product) will settle at the level of 50 as determined by total final expenditure. At this total output, producers in aggregate will be selling all they produce and the system will be in an 'equilibrium' from which it will not move so long as investment runs at 20 per annum and the multiplier continues to be 2.5. The unemployment of labour and idle capital capacity will simply continue for as long as this 20–30–50 configuration exists. If there is likely to be any change, the probability is that it will be a change for the worse because manufacturers suffering excess capacity (and hence a reduced rate of profit on total capital) are likely to reduce investment to, say, 15 per annum. This then has multiplier repercussions on total annual incomes, which fall to $2.5 \times 15 = 37.5$. Consequently, total annual saving declines to $(1 - 0.6) \times 37.5 = 15$ and consumers' expenditure to $0.6 \times 37.5 = 22.5$ per annum. The volume of production will again be forced downwards to conform to the new total of final expenditure of 37.5, and unemployment will rise. The multiplier effect of such a contraction in investment can be readily seen: a reduction of 5 in annual investment has brought about a fall in annual production of 12.5.

One way to get to full employment would be to raise investment to 26 per annum. Investment by the public sector (an act of Lloyd George politics) could do this because the extra income would produce extra saving to match the increased investment: at an income level of 65 total saving would be 26, and so public-sector investment would not merely displace an equivalent amount of private-sector investment. The consumer-goods industries (and their intermediate suppliers) would come under the pressure of falling inventories and increased orders and would therefore expand production to meet the new rate of annual consumers' expenditure running at 39 per annum.

Having seen how the Keynesian system of macroeconomics works in a simplified model we now need to consider models which involve more elements of the real world.

Exercises

11.1 *(To practise your understanding of final expenditure.)*

(i) For the latest available year, calculate and tabulate the percentage structure of GDP at factor cost by category of final expenditure at factor cost.

(ii) Compare this structure with that for ten years previously and comment on any changes which seem to you significant.

(iii) Explain, with illustrative data from the *National Income and Expenditure* accounts, the difference between final expenditure at factor cost and final expenditure at market prices.

11.2 *(To practise your understanding of the relationship between GDP, incomes and aggregate final expenditure.)*

(i) With illustrative data for the latest available year from the *National Income and Expenditure* accounts, show the equivalence between the following:

    (a) Sum of values added (at factor cost) in industries of the economy after adjusting for financial services and the residual error.

    (b) Sum of factor incomes after providing for stock appreciation and including the residual error.

    (c) Total of final expenditures at market prices after deducting imports, *minus* taxes on expenditure less subsidies.

    (d) Total of final expenditures at factor cost after deducting imports.

    (e) Gross domestic product at factor cost.

(ii) Explain why the second item is equal to the first item.

(iii) Explain why the second-last item is equal to the first item.

11.3 *(To practise your knowledge of the categories of final expenditure.)*

(i) Update Table 11.5.
(ii) Update Table 11.6.
(iii) Update Table 11.7.
(iv) Update Table 11.9.
(v) Update Table 11.11.
(vi) Update Table 11.8 and briefly explain each of the items in the table.

11.4 *(To practise your understanding of the multiplier.)* Suppose that there is an economy wherein the personal sector has a marginal propensity to consume of three-quarters (0.75), that this economy has no transactions with the overseas sector and that there is no government sector (and hence there are no 'leakages' into imports or taxes), and that all profits are distributed as dividend income to the personal sector.

(i) Explain what is meant by 'marginal propensity to consume of three-quarters'.

(ii) In this economy there is an increase in (annual) investment final expenditure of 10. Explain fully the manner and extent of the consequent increase in (annual) aggregate demand.

(iii) The increase in investment of 10 in this economy has brought the total annual flow of investment to 100, which annual rate of investment now continues. What is the total aggregate demand annually in the economy? Explain why aggregate 'output' will be adjusted to this aggregate demand (you may assume that there is sufficient 'excess capacity' in the economy).

11.5 *(To practise your understanding of leakages into imports.)* Suppose that the economy of Exercise 11.4 engages in foreign trade and that imports form one-fifth of consumers' expenditure according to the import function:

$$\text{Imports} = 0.20 \times \text{Consumers' expenditure}$$

(but neither investment nor exports contain any imported components).

(i) If (annual) investment expenditure and exports together increase by a total of 10, i.e. $\Delta(I + X) = 10$, explain fully the manner and extent of the consequent increase in (annual) domestic incomes.

(ii) In this economy the total flow of (annual) investment and exports after the increase is 160, comprising 100 of investment and 60 of exports. What is the total of (annual) domestic incomes in this economy? What is the total of (annual) consumers' expenditure? What is the total of (annual) imports? What is the economy's balance of trade?

Chapter 12

The Macroeconomic System and Sector Financial Balances

Contents

Chapter guide

The previous chapter explained the basic Keynesian macroeconomic system, but we cannot fully understand the working of a modern economy until we see how the consumption function/multiplier/final expenditure mechanism affects the income and expenditure of each sector to create that sector's *financial surplus or deficit*. Chapter 12 is therefore concerned to explain how the *financial balance equations* for each sector relate to the working of the macroeconomic system as a whole and why, in principle, the sum of sectors' financial balances (including the *residual error* in the national accounts) must be zero. All this is a complex issue, so we proceed through a staged series of simple 'model' economies: first, a two-sector household/enterprise economy; then a three-sector household/enterprise/government economy (which introduces the impact on the multiplier of 'leakages' into taxes); and finally a four-sector household/enterprise/government/overseas sector model economy.

Having seen how these model economies work as a macroeconomic (multiplier) system to generate the sector financial balances, we then look at an exactly parallel arrangement of the actual national accounts data on final expenditures and sector financial balances for the UK economy in 1980. Understanding this table of data (Table 12.8) in terms of the multiplier process and sector financial balances (Diagram 12.3) ties all the preceding chapters into an analytically unified view of the UK economy as a whole and how it 'works'.

The financial balance equations

In other chapters we have looked at the financial balances (net acquisition of financial assets) of the sectors of the UK economy. We need now to examine the main macroeconomic processes which result in the financial balance for each sector, and we shall do this within the framework provided by (a) the financial balance equations for each sector, and (b) the equation for the sum of all the sectors' financial balances. In conjunction with the multiplier process, this framework is the key to understanding how the economy works and provides the basis from which to examine the working of financial institutions in the following chapter.

A financial balance equation for a sector simply comprises, for the variables relating to that sector:

Income on current account	*minus*	Expenditure on current account	*equals*	Saving
Receipts on capital account (saving)	*minus*	Expenditure on capital account (investment)	*equals*	Financial balance (net acquisition of financial assets; financial surplus +, financial deficit −)

It is most important to note, and always to bear in mind, that in this context the word 'balance' refers to a *flow* (it does not, most emphatically, refer to a stock). This is so important that it would be preferable to refer to the financial balance as the net acquisition of financial assets – which term clearly indicates a flow – were it not for the length of this latter term. The reader should note also that 'net acquisition of financial assets' was the official term used in the national income and expenditure accounts.* Additionally, it should be noted that because only *domestic* capital formation is recorded as expenditure on capital account, the net acquisition of financial assets includes any investment in fixed capital abroad.

We are using the term 'current account' to cover what is called the income and expenditure account for the personal sector or the appropriation account for the company sector. In the expository models we shall simplify slightly by running saving (the balance on current account) and receipts on capital account together and so writing the financial balance equation for each sector as:†

---

* The 1981 Blue Book introduced a change in terminology from 'Net acquisition of financial assets' to 'Financial surplus or deficit'.
† This simplification assumes away the small amounts of additions to reserves and capital transfers; these flows are not, in principle, important, and they will subsequently (Table 12.8) be brought back into the picture.

$$\begin{array}{c} \text{Current} \\ \text{income} \end{array} - \begin{array}{c} \text{Current} \\ \text{expenditure} \end{array} - \begin{array}{c} \text{Capital} \\ \text{expenditure} \end{array} = \begin{array}{c} \text{Financial} \\ \text{balance} \end{array}$$

The sum of sectors' financial balances is then the adding together of the left-hand sides of the equation for each sector.

The simple two-sector model we have been considering (no government sector, no overseas sector – no foreign trade) has only a household (personal) sector and an enterprise sector. We also made the simplifying assumption that all profits received by enterprises (enterprise-sector current income) were distributed as (dividend) income to households, such distributions comprising the current expenditure of enterprises, so that enterprises had no retained profits (saving). We also simplified further by assuming that the personal sector made no capital expenditure. Under these assumptions the sum of sectors' financial balances may be written in abbreviated form as:

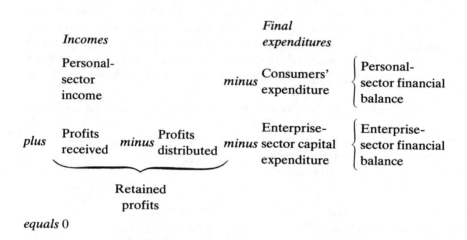

There are several points to note carefully (and understand) about this equation because these points apply to all such equations for the sum of sectors' financial balances. The sum of sectors' financial balances, taking *all* the sectors of the economy including the overseas sector, is always zero; or at least it would be zero if all the flows in the equations were recorded exactly. In practice there may be some inaccuracies in the recorded flows which give rise to a residual error: in this case the sum of sectors' financial balances *plus* the residual error in the national accounts will be zero.

Why do the sectors' financial balances sum, in principle, to zero? There are three answers (really three different ways of looking at the same thing).

In the first place and taking retained profits so as to avoid counting distributed profits twice (once in enterprise profits and again in personal-sector income), the terms with a plus sign in the equation will generally be the incomes accruing to each sector, while the terms with minus signs will generally be the final expenditures made by each sector (the slight qualification is due to the fact that government tax receipts appears, as we shall subsequently see, with both plus and minus signs, so cancelling out). Thus the equation for the sum of financial balances is simply a way of rearranging the equation in which total incomes equal total final expenditure (both being equal to total value added):

$$\begin{array}{c} \text{Personal-} \\ \text{sector} \\ \text{income} \end{array} \textit{plus} \begin{array}{c} \text{Retained} \\ \text{profits} \end{array} \textit{equals} \begin{array}{c} \text{Consumers'} \\ \text{expenditure} \end{array} \textit{plus} \begin{array}{c} \text{Enterprise-} \\ \text{sector capital} \\ \text{expenditure} \end{array}$$

The sum of financial balances equation for all sectors involves subtracting the right-hand side from the left-hand side and so must result in the total sum being equal to zero.

In the second place, the equation for the sum of the financial balances is a restatement of the Keynesian argument that saving equals investment. Rearranging the equation gives:

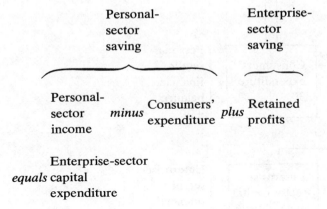

Personal-
sector
saving

Enterprise-
sector
saving

Personal-
sector   *minus*   Consumers'   *plus*   Retained
income   expenditure   profits

equals Enterprise-sector
capital
expenditure

(We shall subsequently relax the assumption that enterprises retain no profits, i.e. have no saving, because they distribute as dividends to households all their income on appropriation account: you can see that if enterprises kept retained profits, then this would be by reducing distributions to the personal sector, so *ceteris paribus* personal-sector saving would decline by the rise in enterprise saving.)

Thus any system of financial balance equations can be rearranged to show the equivalence of the total flow of saving to the total flow of investment. To subtract total investment from total saving, as does the equation for the sum of financial balances, must therefore give a total of zero. It should be noted that in this first simple model the personal sector is assumed not to engage in any capital expenditure (so in this case the personal-sector financial balance and personal-sector saving are the same) but it would be a simple matter to insert personal-sector capital expenditure (with a minus sign) into the financial balance equation and then rearrange to the equation where personal-sector capital expenditure would appear on the right-hand side with a plus sign, again demonstrating the equality between total saving and total investment.

In the third place, it appears to make common sense that the sum of *all* the sectors' financial balances must in principle sum to zero because a financial asset (a claim on someone) cannot be acquired without a corresponding acceptance of a financial liability by someone else: for the system as a whole the total of – new – financial assets acquired (plus) and total – new – financial liabilities accepted (minus) must in principle match each other exactly, so that their algebraic total is zero.

Another point to bear in mind about the equation for the sum of sectors' financial balances is that the expenditure items are connected to the income items and vice versa. This we shall try to demonstrate with linking arrows, which point to the sort of connections we explored in Chapter 11 when we explained what would happen to the output and income figures in Table 11.2 were, say, investment to rise by 10.

Taking the simple economy depicted in Diagram 11.7 (p. 537), how does the sum of financial balances equation work for that economy? With investment of 20 and a multiplier of 2.5 total income is 50, and with the given consumption function total consumers' expenditure is 30. Assuming still that all profits are distributed as income to households so that total retained profits (enterprise saving) is zero, we have for the sum of sectors' financial balances:

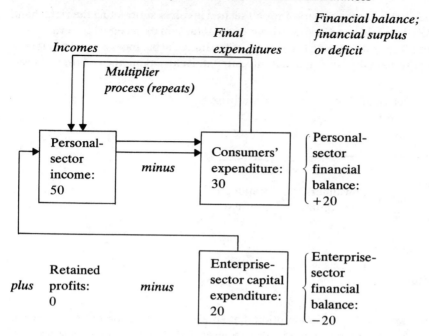

equals 0

In this case the enterprise sector has no retained profits (saving) with which to pay for its capital expenditure of 20. It has therefore to finance its capital expenditure by issuing financial liabilities (shares) to the personal sector, while the personal sector uses its financial surplus to acquire such shares. Clearly this is not the only method by which the enterprise sector could acquire the requisite finance (but it would be running ahead to the next chapter here to discuss the possibility that the personal sector could increase its deposits with the banks by 20 while the enterprise sector could borrow 20 from the banks). What is clear is that, somehow, the enterprise sector must finance its financial deficit.

Financial balances in the macroeconomic process

We need to tie in the financial balance equations with the production accounts to show the over-all pattern: so far, total wages and total profits have been missing and this omission must now be put right. Table 12.1 shows the full set of national income and expenditure accounts for this two-sector economy.

We can aggregate the consumer-goods industries and their intermediate suppliers into one set because we are concerned with value added; and the same goes for investment goods.* This compression is further convenient because it means that we can also see the final expenditures in the production account, and so do not have to produce a separate set of final expenditure accounts. We make throughout this chapter the assumption that wages

---

*This simplification is retained throughout this chapter with value added being measured by final expenditure: that is, where you see in these tables 'consumer goods' you must understand that it means 'consumer goods including related value added in (intermediate) supplying industries'. For example, in Table 11.1, 'consumer goods' value added' would, in the present context, mean the 45 of value added (as measured by final sales of bread) in all of farming, milling, and woodcutting as well as in baking: that is, it means total value added in the economy due to the final sale of bread. Likewise for 'Investment goods', etc.

TABLE 12.1 *National accounts for a two-sector economy with investment of 20, with all profits distributed as dividend income, and with a multiplier of $1/(1 - 0.6) = 2.5$*

Production account	£ p.a.			Sector (financial balance) accounts	£ p.a.	
	Value added [a]	Wages	Profits		Personal sector	Enterprise sector
Consumer				Current account		
goods	30	21	9	Income	50 [b]	15
Investment				Expenditure	30	15 [c]
goods	20	14	6	Saving	20	0
Total	50	35	15	Capital account		
				Expenditure	0	20
				Financial balance	+20	−20

[a] Value added is distributed 70 per cent as wages and 30 per cent as profits.
[b] Comprising 35 of wages and 15 of distributed profits.
[c] All profits are distributed as (dividend) income to the personal sector.

take up 70 per cent of value added and profits receive the remaining 30 per cent (in 1980 wages and salaries took $72\frac{1}{2}$ per cent of value added in UK manufacturing industry, so 70 per cent is a convenient and realistic round number). Total wages are thus 35 and total profits are 15. On current account (another name for the income and expenditure or appropriation account), the personal (household) sector receives 35 of wage income plus 15 of distributed profits by reason of our assumption that all profits are distributed. From this total income of 50 the personal sector spends 30 on consumers' goods. Note that this follows the consumption function from which the multiplier derived. Personal-sector saving is thus 20. In order to keep the model simple, the personal sector has no expenditure on capital account (for the sake of saving space in Table 12.1 we take saving – the balance on current account – to be the receipts on capital account; this saves repeating a line). So the personal sector's financial balance (its net acquisition of financial assets) is +20. The enterprise sector receives 15 of profits on current account, and distributes all of this as (dividend) income to households. The enterprise sector therefore has zero saving (retained profits) and, with capital-account expenditure of 20, the enterprise sector incurs a financial deficit of −20 (it has a negative net acquisition of financial assets). The sum of sectors' financial balances is zero, as it must be in this economy where all the flows are accurately recorded.

We know, of course, that enterprises do not distribute all their profits (as dividends, etc.) income to the personal sector but that they retain a fairly substantial proportion of their profits as their own saving from which most of their capital expenditure is financed (see Diagrams 4.2 and 4.3 and Table 4.15). So we can readily imagine that the enterprises in Table 12.1, rather than distributing all their profits (a policy of zero retentions) year in and year out, decide to try to solve at least some of their financing problems by, say, adopting a policy of paying 70 per cent value added as wages to employees, paying a further 10 per cent of value added (or 33 per cent of profits: $10/(100 - 70)$) as dividend income to households, and retaining the remaining 20 per cent of value added (67 per cent of profits) as their own saving with which to pay for some part of their capital expenditure.

If they do this, it is most important to understand that we cannot simply shuffle the figures around in Table 12.1 with an unaltered total of value added: the macroeconomic processes which created the figures in Table 12.1 will be altered by the new retentions policy of enterprises and it is vital to understand this alteration fully. That is, what follows is important not so much for the sake of incorporating a more realistic assumption about retained profits into the model, but much more for the sake of demonstrating how a changed policy on retentions will alter the macroeconomic multiplier process.

The residual error

We may digress briefly on the residual error. Suppose that, in this economy, personal-sector income were underrecorded by 2 (say by reason of some income not being fully reported), and so the national accounts had entered personal-sector income as 48, whereas the statisticians know from surveys of final expenditure that total final expenditure is 50. This discrepancy gives rise to what is called the 'residual error', defined (for an economy with no foreign trade) as:

$$\text{Total final expenditure} \quad minus \quad \text{Total (recorded) income}$$

$$equals \quad \text{Residual error}$$

In this case, the residual error is $50 - 48 = +2$, so the residual error is treated as an item of (unrecorded) income which may be positive (as here) or negative. To illustrate, in 1980 in the United Kingdom total final expenditure (*less* imports) at factor cost was £193,488 million (Table 11.9 above) but the total of income from employment (£137,083 million) and profits and output from dwellings (adjusted for financial services but *not* adjusted for the residual error) and amounting to £58,450 million (Table 2.7 above) was £195,533 million, so the residual error for 1980 in the 1981 Blue Book was:

$$£193,488\text{m.} - £195,533\text{m.}$$
$$= -£2,045\text{m.}$$

(these figures will be found in the last three lines of the upper half of table 1.2 in the Blue Book). So far as the sum of financial balances is concerned, if personal-sector income in Table 12.1 were to be reported as 48, then personal-sector saving would appear as 18, and the personal-sector financial balance would appear as $+18$; accordingly, the sum of recorded sector balances is $+18 - 20 = -2$, and only the addition of the residual error of $+2$ brings the over-all total to zero. In this hypothetical example you can see that the residual error is in effect an item of unattributable saving, and it is accordingly treated as such in the Blue Book's summary capital account (table 1.7 of the 1981 Blue Book).

We have so far worked out the multiplier on the assumption that the personal sector received 100 per cent, or proportion 1, of all value added (this is the conveniently simplifying effect of the assumption that all profits are distributed as income to households; because households also receive wages, the effect of distributing all profits is to give households all the value added). If enterprises alter their policy from distributing all profits to distributing only one-third of profits (equivalent to 10 per cent of value added – given that wages are always 70 per cent of value added), then the personal sector will receive only 80 per cent, or proportion 0.8, of value added as income (0.7 as wages *plus* 0.1 as dividend income).

The consumption function is:

$$\text{Consumers' expenditure} = 0.6 \times \text{Personal-sector income}$$

But now:

$$\text{Personal-sector income} = 0.8 \times \text{Total value added}$$

from which we have the relationship:

$$\text{Consumers' expenditure} = 0.6 \times 0.8 \times \text{Total value added}$$

Accordingly, the multiplier must now be derived as:

$$\frac{1}{1 - 0.6 \times 0.8} = 1.923$$

The multiplier is now lower because at each step, instead of all value added accruing as household income, proportion 0.8 only accrues. It is important to understand how this new multiplier arises. The multiplier must now be worked out from the following sequence:

1. Investment final expenditure
    (and hence *value added*)   20

2. Consequent increase in
    household income 0.8×20 $= 16$

3. First-round induced consumers'
    final expenditure (and hence
    in *value added*) $0.6 \times 0.8 \times 20$ $= 9.6$

4. Consequent increase in
    household income $0.8 \times 0.6 \times 0.8 \times 20$
                                        $= 0.6 \times 0.8^2 \times 20$ $= 7.68$

5. Second-round induced consumers'
    final expenditure (and
    hence in *value added*) $0.6 \times 0.6 \times 0.8^2 \times 20$
                                        $= 0.6^2 \times 0.8^2 \times 20$ $= 4.6$

    And so on ...

At step 1 investment final expenditure of 20 creates value added of 20, but, because of the new enterprise policy on retentions, at step 2 only 16 is paid as income to households (comprising 14 of wages, 0.7 of value added, and 2 of distributed profits, 0.1 of value added or 0.33 of profits of 6; enterprises keep 4 as retained profits, 0.2 of value added or 0.67 of profits of 6). So, at step 3 induced consumers' expenditure is induced out of only 16 ($= 0.8 \times 20$) of household incomes; the marginal propensity to consume being 0.6, the first-round induced consumers' final expenditure is $0.6 \times 16 = 0.6 \times 0.8 \times 20 = 9.6$. This creates a value added of 9.6; but only 0.8 of this (i.e. 7.68) ends up as household income (step 4). So the next round of induced consumers' expenditure is only $0.6 \times 7.68 = 4.6$ (note that in order to get the series, we always express the numbers in their full form).

Because we are concerned with calculating the creation of total *value added* via the multiplier process (and not simply with the total of household income comprising wages and whatever amount of profit is distributed), we need to take the sequence of *odd-numbered* terms and ascertain the sum of that sequence. This we may do following the usual method:

$$Z = 20$$
$$+ 0.6 \times 0.8 \times 20$$
$$+ 0.6^2 \times 0.8^2 \times 20$$
$$+ \cdots$$

Multiplying Z by the constant ratio between successive terms gives:

$$0.6 \times 0.8 \times Z = 0.6 \times 0.8 \times 20$$
$$+ 0.6^2 \times 0.8^2 \times 20$$
$$+ \cdots$$

and then subtracting gives:

$$Z - 0.6 \times 0.8 \times Z = 20$$

whence:

$$Z(1 - 0.6 \times 0.8) = 20$$

and:

$$Z = \frac{1}{1 - 0.6 \times 0.8} \times 20$$
$$= 1.923 \times 20 = 38.5$$

Assuming that enterprises continue to invest 20 per annum, then total value added resulting from the 20 of investment expenditure and all the induced consumers' expenditure will be $1.923 \times 20 = 38.5$, and total consumers' expenditure, resulting from the equation previously derived, will be:

$$\text{Consumers' expenditure} = 0.6 \times 0.8 \times 38.5$$
$$= 18.5$$

Total consumers' expenditure is now smaller because the 'leakage' of value added into retained profits dampens down the multiplier process by reducing household incomes (the even-numbered terms) below what they would have been had all value added been distributed as incomes (had zero profits been retained).

Thus if enterprises were to increase their saving by retaining profits, we must expect the whole macroeconomic multiplier process to change and so to create a new set of sector financial balances through an entirely altered pattern of economic activity. Table 12.2 shows what the national accounts are under the new retentions policy, and it can be seen that the main aggregates differ considerably from those in Table 12.1; in particular, value added is considerably smaller. Total output in the consumer-goods industry has fallen, output in the investment-goods industry is maintained by virtue of the (somewhat unrealistic) assumption that enterprises continue to spend 20 on capital expenditure. Total wages and total profits are reduced, and total personal-sector income is reduced on two counts: lower total wage receipts and lower distributed profits. Bearing in mind the equality between saving and investment, total saving is the same (because investment is

TABLE 12.2   *National accounts for a two-sector economy with investment of 20, with only one-third of profits distributed as dividend income, and with a multiplier of $1/(1 - 0.6 \times 0.8) = 1.923$*

Production account	Value added [a]	Wages	Profits	Sector accounts	Personal sector	Enterprise sector
	£ p.a.				**£ p.a.**	
Consumer goods	18.5	13	5.5	Current account		
				Income	30.8 [b]	11.5
Investment goods	20	14	6	Expenditure	18.5	3.8 [c]
Total	38.5	27	11.5	Saving	12.3	7.7
				Capital account		
				Expenditure	0	20
				Financial balance	+12.3	−12.3

[a] Value added is distributed 70 per cent as wages and 30 per cent as profits.
[b] Comprising 27 of wages and 3.8 of distributed profits.
[c] One-third of total profits, $0.33 \times 11.5 = 3.8$, is distributed as dividend income to the personal sector; this amounts to 10 per cent of total value added, so the personal sector, taking into account the 70 per cent of value added received as wages, effectively gets 80 per cent of value added as total income.

unaltered) but is now divided between the enterprise sector (7.7) and the household sector (12.3). The sector financial balances are different: the personal sector has a reduced financial surplus of +12.3 while the enterprise sector financial deficit has improved from −20 to −12.3. So the enterprise sector has solved part of its financing problems, but at the cost of imposing a reduction in economic activity, and with it a reduction in the total flow of profits (and, given an almost unaltered capital stock, the rate of profit will also have declined).

The total saving ratio in the economy has risen from $20/50 = 0.4$ (Table 12.1) to $20/38.5 = 0.52$ (Table 12.2): not because of a rise in total saving, but because of a fall in economic activity. In general, any rise in the saving ratio (whatever its cause) will tend to have a 'deflationary' impact: that is, it will reduce total value added because it dampens down the multiplier process. In this example there has been an increase in the enterprise sector's propensity to save (their saving has risen from 0 to 7.7).

The government sector and taxes on income

Having shown how retained profits can be incorporated into the model without any change in the basic principle of the multiplier process, we need to consider the impact of introducing a government sector which not only spends money but which also taxes incomes. In order that we may follow these changes through, let us revert to the economy of Diagram 11.7 and Table 12.1, where the enterprise sector spends 20 on capital formation and distributes all its profits. When discussing Diagram 11.7 we remarked that if total output at full employment were 65, one way to get to full employment would be to raise investment to 26 per annum and that this could be achieved through public-sector investment, as had been argued by Lloyd George in 1929. Suppose, then, that the government, *without* levying *any taxes*, orders 6 of investment goods (say from construction enterprises). Total investment is now 26, as in Diagram 11.7, and, with the multiplier being 2.5 (all profits being distributed as income to the personal sector), total output is 65, with consumers' expenditure at $0.6 \times 65 = 39$. Table 12.3 shows the figures for the production account, again assuming 70 per cent of value added is paid in wages.

TABLE 12.3   *National accounts for a three-sector economy with investment of 26, with all profits distributed as dividend income, with no taxation, and with a multiplier of $1/(1 − 0.6) = 2.5$*

Production account	£ p.a.			Sector accounts	£ p.a.		
	Value added [a]	Wages	Profits		Personal sector	Enterprise sector	Government sector
Consumer				Current account			
goods	39	27.3	11.7	Income	65 [b]	19.5	0
Investment				Expenditure	39	19.5	0
goods	26	18.2	7.8	Saving	26	0	0
Total	65	45.5	19.5	Capital account			
				Expenditure	0	20	6
				Financial balance	+26	−20	−6

[a] Value added is distributed 70 per cent as wages and 30 per cent as profits.
[b] Comprising 45.5 of wages and 19.5 of distributed profits.

For the sector accounts, we must now add, on the right-hand side of the table, the government sector. The personal sector's income is 65, comprising 45.5 wages and 19.5 distributed profits; consumers' expenditure is 39, so personal-sector saving is 26, equal to the higher level of investment. Thus the new level of incomes, to use the words previously quoted from Keynes, 'provides a margin of saving sufficient to correspond to the increased investment'. And we can see that although the personal sector has swallowed the 'additional pill' of extra saving, the pill has been coated with the 'jam' of a substantial increase in consumers' expenditure.

The personal sector has no capital expenditure, so its financial balance is now +26. The enterprise sector's financial balance (given that all profits are distributed) is −20. The government has (at this stage) no tax receipts and no current-account consumption expenditure and so has no saving; but expenditure on capital account of 6 means that the government sector has a financial balance of −6. So the sum of the sectors' financial balances is zero, as it must be. By incurring a financial deficit the government sector has created full employment, just as Kalecki and Keynes argued would be the case.

What happens if the government gets worried about the amount of money it has to borrow to finance its deficit and decides to reduce this by levying a tax on incomes. Looking at the national accounts in Table 12.3, the government might reckon that a tax on personal-sector incomes of 10 per cent would adequately cover its financial deficit, so the government announces that incomes received by the personal sector will be taxed at a rate of 10 per cent or 0.1.

We take what may appear to be a low rate of taxation because we are concerned with taxes paid to the government net of transfer payments (National Insurance benefits, etc.) received from the government (that is, we simply regard transfers received as negative income taxes). For 1980 we have the following figures (Table 3.1 above):

Taxes on income and NI contributions	£40,649m.
less NI benefits, etc.	£25,476m.
Total 'tax reduction' in personal-sector income	£15,173m.
Personal-sector income (excluding stock appreciation of £854 million and miscellaneous); requited income only	£174,246m.
'Effective' rate of taxation, per cent	8.7

So 10 per cent is a convenient (and reasonably realistic) round number.

We need now to distinguish between personal-sector income (gross of tax) and personal-sector incomes after deduction of tax, which we shall call 'disposable income' (the term 'personal-sector income' must now be understood as referring to pre-tax income comprising wages and distributions from profits (dividends and interest)). So we have:

$$\text{Disposable income} = \text{Personal-sector income} - \text{Taxes on income}$$

where taxes on income are total tax payments *less* transfer payments received from government. Because the rate of taxation of income is 10 per cent, we have for total tax payments:

$$\text{Taxes on income} = 0.1 \times \text{Personal-sector income}$$

We may substitute this equation into the previous equation to get:

$$\text{Disposable income} = \text{Personal-sector income} - 0.1 \times \text{Personal-sector income}$$

$$= (1 - 0.1) \text{Personal-sector income}$$

We must now amend the consumption function so as to make consumers' expenditure a function of disposable income:

$$\frac{\text{Consumers'}}{\text{expenditure}} = 0.6 \times \frac{\text{Disposable}}{\text{income}}$$

$$= 0.6(1 - 0.1) \frac{\text{Personal-}}{\text{sector}}_{\text{income}}$$

With proportion $(1 - 0.1)$ of their pre-tax income accruing as disposable income and proportion 0.1 'leaking' away as income-tax payments, the parallel with imports (Diagram 11.3) is quite clear. As illustrated in Diagram 12.1, the investment expenditure of 26 creates 26 of pre-tax income, of which $2.6 (= 0.1 \times 26)$ is taxed away, leaving 23.4 $(= (1 - 0.1) \times 26)$ as disposable income, of which proportion 0.6 will be spent on consumption, so that the first-round induced consumers' expenditure will be $0.6 \times (1 - 0.1) \times 26 = 14$. This 14 of induced consumers' expenditure will create value added and incomes of 14, of which 1.4 will be taxed away leaving $(1 - 0.1) \times 14 = 12.6$ as disposable income, of which proportion 0.6 will be spent on consumption; and so on. Accordingly we have the series:

1. Investment final expenditure (and hence pre-tax incomes)   26

2. Consequent increase in *disposable* income $(1 - 0.1) \times 26$ $= 23.4$

3. First-round induced increase in consumers' final expenditure (and hence in pre-tax incomes) $0.6 \times (1 - 0.1) \times 26$ $= 14$

4. Consequent increase in *disposable* income
$$(1 - 0.1) \times 0.6 \times (1 - 0.1) \times 26$$
$$= 0.6 \times (1 - 0.1)^2 \times 26 \qquad = 12.6$$

5. Second-round induced increase in consumers' final expenditure (and hence in pre-tax incomes)
$$0.6 \times 0.6 \times (1 - 0.1)^2 \times 26$$
$$= 0.6^2 \times (1 - 0.1)^2 \times 26 \qquad = 7.6$$

And so on . . .

DIAGRAM 12.1   *The impact of taxation on the multiplier process*

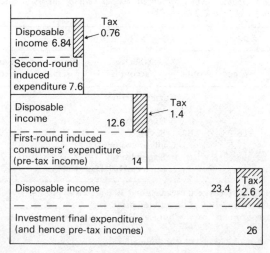

Because we are concerned with the multiplier process as it affects *pre-tax* incomes, we may gather together the odd-numbered terms and calculate the sum of these by the usual method:

$$Z = 26$$
$$+ 0.6 \times (1 - 0.1) \times 26$$
$$+ 0.6^2 \times (1 - 0.1)^2 \times 26$$
$$+ \cdots$$

Multiplying Z by the constant ratio between successive terms gives:

$$0.6 \times (1 - 0.1) \times Z = 0.6 \times (1 - 0.1) \times 26$$
$$+ 0.6^2 \times (1 - 0.1)^2 \times 26$$
$$+ \cdots$$

whence:

$$Z - 0.6 \times (1 - 0.1) \times Z = 26$$
$$Z[1 - 0.6 \times (1 - 0.1)] = 26$$
$$Z = \frac{1}{[1 - 0.6 \times (1 - 0.1)]} \times 26$$
$$= 2.174 \times 26$$
$$= 56.5$$

In general, if b is the marginal propensity to consume out of disposable income and t is the proportionate rate of tax levied on (pre-tax) personal-sector income, then the multiplier is calculated as:

$$\frac{1}{1 - b(1 - t)}$$

Table 12.4 shows the national accounts resulting when the government not only spends 6 on investment, but also levies taxation on incomes at the rate of 10 per cent. Again, by contrast with Table 12.3, there are changes in the macroeconomic processes, so all the main aggregates are altered. In particular, total output is now lower at 56.5, and total wages and profits are smaller. Total saving is still equal to total investment of 26, but the total is divided between 20.3 of personal-sector saving and 5.7 of government saving. The

TABLE 12.4   *National accounts for a three-sector economy with investment of 26, with all profits distributed as dividend income, with taxation at 10 per cent of incomes, and with a multiplier of $1/[1 - 0.6(1 - 0.1)] = 2.174$*

Production account	Value added [a]	Wages	Profits	Sector accounts	Personal sector	Enterprise sector	Government sector
	£ p.a.				£ p.a.		
Consumer				Current account			
goods	30.5	21.4	9.1	Income	56.5 [b]	16.9	5.7 [d]
Investment				Expenditure	36.2 [c]	16.9	0
goods	26	18.2	7.8	Saving	20.3	0	5.7
Total	56.5	39.6	16.9	Capital account			
				Expenditure	0	20	6
				Financial balance	+20.3	−20	−0.3

[a] Value added is distributed 70 per cent as wages and 30 per cent as profits.
[b] Comprising 39.6 of wages and 16.9 of distributed profits.
[c] Comprising 30.5 of consumers' expenditure and 5.7 payment of income taxes to the government sector.
[d] Total taxes on income; levied at 10 per cent of incomes.

personal sector's financial surplus is smaller, and the government sector has all but eliminated its financial deficit. However, the macroeconomic 'cost' of this improvement in the government sector's financial deficit is a lower level of economic activity and hence an increase in unemployment.

We might suppose that the government, perturbed by the adverse impact on economic activity and employment of its (higher) taxation, decides that it will employ some of the unemployed as refuse collectors, that it will spend £4 per annum on providing this service free of charge to the public and that it will not raise the *rate* of taxation but will keep it unaltered at 10 per cent of incomes. Investment continues at 26, comprising 20 of enterprise-sector investment and 6 of government-sector investment.

The total of final expenditures acting as the initial base for the multiplier process is now 30, comprising 26 of investment and 4 of government final consumption expenditure (in this, government consumption expenditure has the same impact as government capital expenditure). The multiplier is still $1/[1 - 0.6(1 - 0.1)]$ because neither the marginal propensity to consume nor the rate of taxation has altered. So, as shown in Table 12.5, total output is 65.2 (just a little bit in excess of full-employment output, so we suppose that more overtime is being worked by the labour force). The important lesson is that the (increased) government final consumption expenditure has resulted in an increase in the level of economic activity; in this, its effect is exactly the same as investment (it is important to note this).

TABLE 12.5 *National accounts for a three-sector economy with investment of 26, with all profits distributed as dividend income, with taxation at 10 per cent of incomes, with government final consumption expenditure of 4, and with a multiplier of $1/[1 - 0.6(1 - 0.1)] = 2.174$*

Production account	£ p.a.			Sector accounts	£ p.a.		
	Value added [a]	Wages	Profits		Personal sector	Enterprise sector	Government sector
Consumer				Current account			
goods	35.2	24.6	10.6	Income	65.2 [b]	18.4	6.5 [d]
Investment				Expenditure	41.7 [c]	18.4	4
goods	26	18.2	7.8	Saving	23.5	0	2.5
Government							
consumption	4	4	—	Capital account			
Total	65.2	46.8	18.4	Expenditure	0	20	6
				Financial balance	+23.5	−20	−3.5

[a] Value added is distributed 70 per cent as wages and 30 per cent as profits except for government final consumption, where all value added accrues as wages.

[b] Comprising 46.8 of wages and 18.4 of distributed profits.

[c] Comprising 35.2 of consumers' expenditure and 6.5 payment of income taxes to the government sector.

[d] Total taxes on income; levied at 10 per cent of incomes.

Total wages and profits have increased, as has total consumers' expenditure. Total saving is still equal to total investment of 26, but is divided between 23.5 of personal-sector saving and 2.5 of government-sector saving. Note that, because of the rise in economic activity, total tax receipts have risen even though the *rate* of taxation is unaltered. Government saving has been reduced and the government financial deficit has worsened to −3.5. But this is inescapable if economic activity is to be stimulated by government expenditure. The sum of sectors' financial balances is zero.

We may illustrate the working of the three-sector economy in Table 12.5 within the framework of the sum of sectors' financial balances:*

---

*We put the important aggregates in boxes so the 'causal' links between one set of aggregates and another can be shown.

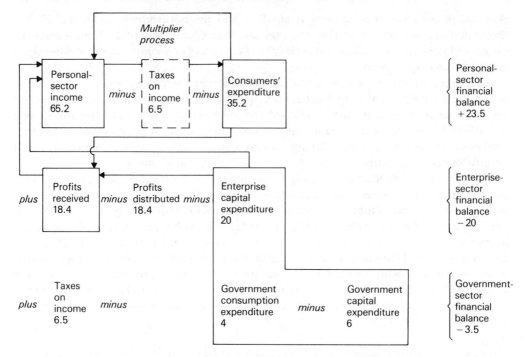

equals 0

What is happening in this economy is that capital expenditure by enterprise (20), capital expenditure by government (6) and consumption expenditure by government (4) provide a basis for the multiplier process (in some textbooks, this total of 30 would be called an 'injection' of 'exogenous' expenditure, where 'exogenous' means that the expenditures are decided by factors outside the economic process itself, as contrasted with the 'induced' nature of consumers' expenditure which is determined within and by the macroeconomic process itself). This initial 'injection' of final expenditure totalling 30 provides a basis for the multiplier process because it creates value added (wages and profits) in the producing industries. By our assumption that all profits are distributed as dividend income, we then have a simplified system, where all the value added so created ends up as household (personal-sector) income. This income, based on the initial final expenditure, then induces consumers' expenditure, though we must note that the multiplier process is affected by incomes being subject to taxation. In turn, the induced consumers' expenditure creates further value added, all distributed as incomes to households also subject to tax, and so the multiplier process works its way through in a series of diminishing steps. This macroeconomic process then results in (a) a flow of saving equal to the total capital expenditure, and (b) a set of financial balances which sum to zero. If the personal sector governs its expenditures so as to create a positive financial balance for itself (and in Chapter 3 we discussed the reasons why the personal sector deliberately acted in this way), then other sectors in the economy must run a financial deficit.

We can see that the households comprising the personal sector can thrust an increased financial deficit on to another sector if they increase their propensity to save. Suppose that the households in Table 12.5 decide that an annual financial surplus of 23.5 is insufficient for their needs (they want more financial assets for retirement – pension entitlement – or better life assurance cover for their families). Faced with this decision, each household does the only thing it can to increase its financial surplus: that is, it reduces its expenditure on consumption. Let us suppose that the effect of this is to alter the consumption function by reducing the (marginal) propensity to consume, and we now have an altered consumption function with a marginal propensity to consume of 0.5 (instead of 0.6 as previously):

$$\frac{\text{Consumers'}}{\text{expenditure}} = 0.5 \times \frac{\text{Disposable}}{\text{income}}$$

The multiplier now becomes (the 10 per cent rate of taxation being unchanged):

$$\frac{1}{1 - 0.5(1 - 0.1)} = 1.818$$

Let us suppose that the government goes on spending 4 on current account and 6 on capital account, as before, but that the enterprise sector, while still carrying out 20 of intended capital-account expenditure, is also determined to maintain the total output of consumer goods come what may (this is not realistic, but it provides a useful illustration). What happens now is depicted in Table 12.6, but the figures require careful attention.

TABLE 12.6   *National accounts for a three-sector economy with investment of 31.9, with all profits distributed as dividend income, with taxation at 10 per cent of incomes, with government final consumption expenditure of 4, and with a multiplier of $1/[1 - 0.5(1 - 0.1)] = 1.818$*

Production account	Value added [a]	Wages	Profits	Sector accounts	Personal sector	Enterprise sector	Government sector
	£ p.a.				£ p.a.		
Consumer				Current account			
goods	29.3	20.5	8.8	Income	65.2	18.4	6.5
Investment				Expenditure	35.8 [b]	18.4	4
goods	31.9	22.3	9.6	Saving	29.4	0	2.5
Government							
consumption	4	4	—	Capital account			
Total	65.2	46.8	18.4	Expenditure	0	25.9 [c]	6
				Financial balance	+29.4	−25.9	−3.5

[a] Value added is distributed 70 per cent as wages and 30 per cent as profits, except for government final consumption, where all value added accrues as wages.
[b] Comprising 29.3 of consumers' expenditure and 6.5 payment of income taxes to the government.
[c] Comprising 20 of intended capital formation and 5.9 of 'unintended' accumulation of inventories.

If total output is maintained at 65.2 (as in Table 12.5), then total consumers' expenditure, given the changed propensity to consume, will be 0.5 × Disposable income; because disposable income is Total income *minus* Taxes on income, i.e. 65.2 − 6.5 = 58.7, consumers' expenditure will be 0.5 × 58.7 = 29.3. This means that if the enterprise sector insists on maintaining the output of consumer goods at 35.2 (as in Table 12.5) despite the fall in aggregate demand, then the enterprise sector must acquiesce in the accumulation of 35.2 − 29.3 = 5.9 worth of inventories of consumer goods. This accumulation of inventories counts as capital expenditure, so enterprise-sector capital expenditure becomes 25.9, which together with government capital expenditure of 6 makes total capital expenditure of 31.9.

Saving by the personal sector is now 29.4 (Table 12.6) instead of 23.5 (Table 12.5) and so the personal sector has increased its saving and hence its financial surplus by 5.9. The government-sector accounts and its financial balance remain the same as in Table 12.5. So the improvement in the personal sector's financial surplus must be mirrored by a deterioration in the enterprise sector's financial deficit; and the enterprise sector's financial deficit has changed from −20 (Table 12.5) to −25.9 (Table 12.6). This has happened because of the 'extra' (and perhaps unintended) inventory investment. It must be appreciated that the improvement in the personal sector's financial surplus and the deterioration in the enterprise sector's financial deficit are *not* two different things but are merely the opposite sides of the same coin: the enterprise sector has persisted in producing the 5.9 of consumer goods which it could not sell to the personal sector because of the households' decision to save more and spend less on consumption. In order to maintain production, the enterprise sector will have been paying wages (and distributing profits) to households; and these wages and distributed profits are not being spent. Thus the personal sector increases its saving and improves its financial balance at the expense of the deterioration in the enterprise sector's financial deficit; the former could not occur without the latter.

Note that saving in Table 12.6 totals 31.9, comprising 29.4 of personal-sector saving and 2.5 of government-sector saving. This is exactly equal to investment of 31.9, comprising government capital expenditure of 6, and enterprise-sector capital formation of 20 of intended investment and 5.9 of inventory investment. When the accounts are reckoned up, taking inventory investment into the calculation, investment will always equal saving.

When discussing Keynes's macroeconomics, we dismissed a scenario such as the change from Table 12.5 to Table 12.6 as rather unlikely, because we doubted whether enterprises could 'withstand the strain on cash flows caused by paying for production without receiving the sales revenue from selling that production'. We have now spelled out exactly what that phrase means, in terms of a concrete example. And it must be recognised that the scenario of Table 12.6 is an unlikely one; it is more probable that enterprises would not acquiesce in such inventory accumulation, and so the result of the change in household behaviour and the reduced propensity to consume, or conversely, increased propensity to save, with its reduced multiplier, would be a decline in the level of economic activity.

So far in this section we have discussed the macroeconomic system and the resulting financial balances without including the overseas sector: that is, none of the models included exports and imports. But we know that 'leakage' into imports has an impact on the multiplier process, and so we must now see how imports and exports come into the picture.

The import function and the multiplier

In order to do this, we must have an import function. While we may plausibly assume that exports are determined by forces outside the domestic economy, we must equally assume that imports are determined by forces within the domestic economy. When illustrating how 'leakage' into imports affected the multiplier process (in Chapter 11, pp. 526–30), we had a simple import function where imports were a function of consumers' expenditure only. This was because the model of Table 11.2 was constructed to have no imports in investment expenditure (to keep things as simple as possible). We also had a marginal propensity to import out of consumers' final expenditure of 0.118 (again a value thrown up by Table 11.2), and we explained and illustrated how imports so determined would affect the multiplier sequence of domestic incomes.

We must now modify (or expand) this previous example on two counts. First, it is not realistic to assume that imports go only into consumers' expenditure; rather, we must assume that all categories of final expenditure will contain imported value added. Second, the import ratio of 0.118 is not realistic with respect to the current situation in the UK economy, where we have the figures for 1980:

Imports of goods and services	£57,832 million
Total final expenditure at factor cost	£251,320 million
Average propensity to import out of final expenditure	0.23

The figure of 0.23 is near to the convenient round number of 0.25, so let us assume that the economy's marginal propensity to import out of final expenditure is 0.25. We now need an import function which makes imports a function of all categories of final expenditure, as follows:

$$\frac{\text{Total}}{\text{imports}} = 0.25 \times \left[\frac{\text{Consumers'}}{\text{expenditure}} + \frac{\text{Capital}}{\text{expenditure}} + \text{Exports} \right]$$

To illustrate the impact of imports only, let us temporarily revert to an economy with no government sector. Using the standard notation given previously, we may write this equation more conveniently as:

$$M = 0.25 \times (C + I + X)$$

The simplifying assumption here is that all categories of final expenditure have the same impact on imports. Keeping to the assumption that all profits are distributed as dividend income, so that the personal sector receives the whole domestic product, Y, as its income, we have the consumption function:

$$C = 0.6 \times Y$$

(reverting to a marginal propensity to consume of 0.6). Gross domestic product may be defined in terms of final expenditures as:

$$Y = C + I + X - M$$

If we use the previously explained (p. 529) short-cut route to the multiplier, we can substitute into this equation both the import function (itself containing the consumption function) and the consumption function, to give:

$$Y = 0.6 \times Y + I + X - 0.25(0.6Y + I + X)$$

whence:

$$Y - 0.6 \times Y + 0.25 \times 0.6Y = I + X - 0.25(I + X)$$

or:

$$Y(1 - 0.6 + 0.25 \times 0.6) = (1 - 0.25)(I + X)$$

or:

$$Y = \frac{1 - 0.25}{1 - 0.6 + 0.25 \times 0.6} \times (I + X)$$

So the multiplier, the increase in Y with respect to an increase in the sum of $I + X$, $\Delta Y / \Delta(I + X)$, is:

$$\frac{1 - 0.25}{1 - 0.6 + 0.25 \times 0.6} = 1.364$$

Clearly, if our assumption of 0.25 as the UK marginal propensity to import out of final expenditure is near the mark (as the figures for 1980 seem to indicate), then the propensity to import has a marked dampening effect on the multiplier process.

Having derived the multiplier by the short-cut textbook route, we really need to see what it means in terms of the macroeconomic process, otherwise the above derivation may remain simply a piece of algebra, rather than becoming a properly understood sequence of economic analysis.

Diagram 12.2 illustrates the sequence. First, we have an initial increase in final expenditure of, say, 10. Out of this expenditure of 10, proportion 0.25 'leaks' away into imports (imports rise by 2.5 and this thus becomes income for overseas, while proportion $(1 - 0.25)$, or 7.5 $(= (1 - 0.25) \times 10)$ accrues as the consequent increase in *domestic* incomes. Out of this increase in domestic incomes, we have a first-round induced increase in consumers' expenditure of $0.6 \times 7.5 = 0.6 \times (1 - 0.25) \times 10 = 4.5$. In turn, out of this induced increase in final expenditure, proportion 0.25, or 1.125, 'leaks' away into imports and income for overseas, while proportion $(1 - 0.25)$, or 3.375, accrues as the consequent increase in *domestic* incomes. Again, it is from this extra domestic incomes that we have the second-round induced increase in consumers' expenditure. And so on.

DIAGRAM 12.2   *The impact of immediate 'leakages' into imports on domestic incomes and on the multiplier process*

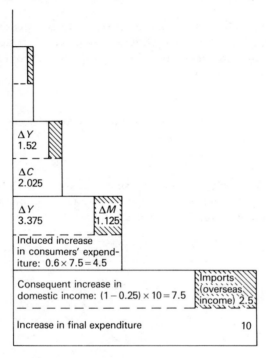

We thus obtain the sequence:

1. Initial increase in final
    expenditure   10

2. Consequent increase in
    domestic incomes $(1 - 0.25) \times 10$ = 7.5

3. First-round induced increase
    in consumers' expenditure $0.6 \times (1 - 0.25) \times 10$ = 4.5

4. Consequent increase in
    domestic incomes $(1 - 0.25) \times 0.6 \times (1 - 0.25) \times 10$
                                 $= 0.6 \times (1 - 0.25)^2 \times 10$ = 3.375

5. Second-round induced increase
    in consumers' expenditure $0.6 \times 0.6 \times (1 - 0.25)^2 \times 10$
                                 $= 0.6^2 \times (1 - 0.25)^2 \times 10$ = 2.025

6. Consequent increase in
    domestic incomes $(1 - 0.25) \times 0.6^2 \times (1 - 0.25)^2 \times 10$
                                 $= 0.6^2 \times (1 - 0.25)^3 \times 10$ = 1.52

    And so on ...

Because we are concerned with the total impact on *domestic* incomes we need to gather the *even*-numbered terms together and sum: as follows:

$$Z = (1 - 0.25) \times 10$$
$$+ 0.6 \times (1 - 0.25)^2 \times 10$$
$$+ 0.6^2 \times (1 - 0.25)^3 \times 10$$
$$+ \cdots$$

The effect of having a 'leakage' immediately from the initial final expenditure means that we can no longer start from 10, as we were accustomed to do, and proceed straight to the sum of a geometric series (because the successive, i.e. first and second, second and third do not bear a constant ratio to each other). However, if we first divide Z by $(1 - 0.25)$, then we can proceed as usual, with the constant ratio between successive terms being $0.6 \times (1 - 0.25)$:

$$\frac{Z}{1 - 0.25} = 10$$
$$+ 0.6 \times (1 - 0.25) \times 10$$
$$+ 0.6^2 \times (1 - 0.25)^2 \times 10$$
$$+ \cdots$$

Proceeding now as per the usual method:

$$0.6 \times (1 - 0.25) \times \frac{Z}{1 - 0.25} = 0.6 \times (1 - 0.25) \times 10$$
$$+ 0.6^2 \times (1 - 0.25)^2 \times 10$$
$$+ \cdots$$

so that:

$$\frac{Z}{1 - 0.25} - 0.6 \times (1 - 0.25) \times \frac{Z}{1 - 0.25} = 10$$

whence:

$$\frac{Z}{1 - 0.25} [1 - 0.6 \times (1 - 0.25)] = 10$$

or:

$$Z = \frac{1 - 0.25}{[1 - 0.6 \times (1 - 0.25)]} \times 10$$
$$= \frac{1 - 0.25}{1 - 0.6 + 0.25 \times 0.6} \times 10$$

This is identical to the multiplier arrived at by the short-cut route, so we shall in future make more use of this route, but the student must always bear in mind that the short-cut route omits the view of diagrams such as Diagram 12.2.

The four-sector economy

We need now to re-introduce the government sector so that we can work out the multiplier and the financial balances for a four-sector economy. We shall use the short-cut route to derive the multiplier; so, with the same symbols as before but with G standing for government (final) consumption expenditure and with 0.1 as the proportionate rate of taxation on incomes, we have the consumption function:

$$C = 0.6 \times \frac{\text{Disposable}}{\text{income}}$$

and as disposable income is pre-tax income minus total taxes on income we have:

$$\frac{\text{Disposable}}{\text{income}} = Y - 0.1 \times Y = (1 - 0.1) \times Y$$

whence:

$$C = 0.6 \times (1 - 0.1) \times Y$$

The import function is (now including government consumption expenditure, G):

$$M = 0.25 \times (C + I + G + X)$$

We have the usual equation for gross domestic product, Y, in terms of final expenditures:

$$Y = C + I + G + X - M$$

So, following the usual algebraic substitution and manipulations:

$$Y = 0.6 \times (1 - 0.1)Y + I + G + X \\ - 0.25 \times [0.6 \times (1 - 0.1)Y + I + G + X]$$

$$Y - 0.6 \times (1 - 0.1)Y + 0.25 \times 0.6 \times (1 - 0.1)Y \\ = I + G + X - 0.25 \times (I + G + X)$$

$$Y[1 - 0.6 \times (1 - 0.1) + 0.25 \times 0.6 \times (1 - 0.1)] \\ = (1 - 0.25)(I + G + X)$$

$$Y = \frac{1 - 0.25}{[1 - 0.6 \times (1 - 0.1) + 0.25 \times 0.6 \times (1 - 0.1)]} \times (I + G + X)$$

$$Y = 1.2605 \times (I + G + X)$$

By comparison with the multiplier without taxes (1.364), we can see that the multiplier incorporating 'leakages' of income into income tax is somewhat smaller. By comparison with the multiplier with taxes but without imports (2.174, Table 12.5) this multiplier is also considerably smaller. However if we have imports with their contractionary multiplier effects, we must also have exports which have an expansionary impact.

Using the last-found multiplier we can set out the national accounts for a four-sector economy as shown in Table 12.7. Because we are now only a few steps away from looking at the real national accounts in this framework, it is necessary to understand Table 12.7 carefully. We assume that, as in Table 12.5, investment is 26, comprising 20 of enterprise-sector capital expenditure and 6 of government-sector capital expenditure, while government consumption expenditure is 4. We have now to add exports, which I have put at 20. All these annual flows are determined by 'outside' forces, so it is permissible to allocate (almost) arbitrary values to them (although we must bear in mind that the output of 65 is still our benchmark for full-employment output, so this constrains our choice somewhat).

Having established these initial final expenditures, we may determine total gross domestic product from the multiplier relationship (we shall work in round numbers as far as is possible):

$$Y = 1.2605 \times (I + G + X) \\ = 1.2605 \times (26 + 4 + 20) \\ = 1.2605 \times 50 \\ = 63$$

TABLE 12.7 *National accounts for a four-sector economy with investment of 26, with government final consumption expenditure of 4, with exports of 20, with all profits distributed as dividend income, with taxation at 10 per cent of incomes, and with a multiplier of $(1 - 0.25)/[1 - 0.6(1 - 0.1) + 0.25 \times 0.6 \times (1 - 0.1)] = 1.2605$*

£ p.a.

Category of final expenditure	Final sales	Imports	Domestic value added	Wages	Profits
Consumers' expenditure	34	8.5	25.5	17.8	7.7
Investment	26	6.5	19.5	13.7	5.8
Government consumption	4	1	3	3	—
Exports	20	5	15	10.5	4.5
Total expenditure	84	21	63		
Imports	21				
Gross domestic product	63		63	45	18

£ p.a.

Account	Personal sector	Enterprise sector	Government sector	Overseas sector
Current account				
Income	63	18	6.3	21
Expenditure	40.3	18	4	20
Saving	22.7	0	2.3	1
Capital account				
Expenditure	0	20	6	—
Financial balance	+22.7	−20	−3.7	+1

This is just within the assumed full-employment output, so the figures chosen for the initial final expenditures are reasonable. We know that consumers' expenditure is determined by the consumption function and that we must also take into account the effect on consumers' expenditure of taxation (at rate 0.1) on incomes. So:

$$C = 0.6 \times (1 - 0.1) \times Y$$
$$= 0.6 \times (1 - 0.1) \times 63$$
$$= 34$$

We must be quite clear that this total of 34 is the result of the macroeconomic, multiplier process of the sort depicted in Diagram 12.1. Using this total of induced consumers' expenditure and the total of 50 of other final expenditures, we can see that total expenditure is 84. The import function informs us that:

$$M = 0.25 \times (C + I + G + X)$$
$$= 0.25 \times 84$$
$$= 21$$

So we can now enter, in the upper half of Table 12.7, the complete column of final expenditures. Because of the presence of imports, Table 12.7 has to be differently arranged: we cannot now assume (as was previously the case when there were no imports) that final sales constitute only domestic value added. Assuming that the import coefficient of 0.25 applies uniformly throughout the economy, we may multiply each of the categories of final expenditure by 0.25 to ascertain the imported component in the final expenditures; this is shown in the second column. If we deduct imports from final sales, we obtain the domestic value added in those final sales; this is shown in the third column. For the sake of completing the accounts, we assume that domestic value added is divided 70/30 between wages and profits, except in the case of government consumption expenditure, all of which accrues as wages (to the refuse collectors).

Thus the upper half of Table 12.7 shows how the macroeconomic multiplier process works out in terms of the economy's production account. The basis of this process is that the initial final expenditures on investment, government consumption and exports generate a multiplier process affecting both consumers' expenditure and imports. To return to Kalecki's initial argument, it is not simply that these initial final expenditures constitute additional demand for consumer goods (and, now, imports), but that, through the multiplier, we can analyse precisely and quantitatively how and to what extent this additional demand occurs.

We must now see how all these flows work out in terms of the sectors' financial balances. These sectoral accounts are shown in the lower half of Table 12.7. Again we have our usual simplifying assumption that all profits are distributed as dividend income to the personal sector (this assumption has already determined the multiplier). So the personal sector receives as income not only 45 of wages but also 18 of distributed profits. This income is taxed by the government at rate 0.1, so the personal sector pays total taxes of 6.3 (see the entry under current-account income for the government sector – note that the tax rate has already been incorporated in the multiplier). The personal sector also spends 34 of consumers' expenditure, so total personal-sector expenditure on current account is 40.3. Personal-sector saving (the balance on current account) is accordingly 22.7, and as the personal sector is assumed to engage in no capital expenditure, its financial balance is +22.7.

The enterprise sector's accounts are as usual straightforward. Their current (appropriation) account is credited with 18 profits, but all of this is by assumption distributed as dividend income to the personal sector, so there is a corresponding debit. Accordingly the enterprise sector's saving is zero, and with capital expenditure of 20, the sector's financial balance is −20.

The government sector receives 6.3 of income taxes (from the personal sector), it has consumption expenditure of 4 on current account, so government-sector saving is 2.3. With capital expenditure of 6, the government sector's financial balance is −3.7.

The overseas sector receives as income on *its* current account the earnings it makes from the 21 of imports into the economy. Conversely, the overseas sector incurs as expenditure on its current account the amount it has to pay for the 20 of exports from the economy. The overseas sector thus has saving of 1 (corresponding, with a change of sign, to the economy's balance of trade deficit – exports *minus* imports. (See illustrative Table 11.12 above as well as Table 11.11.)

The overseas sector cannot, by accounting convention, engage in *domestic* capital expenditure (if it finances investment here, it must do so via agents in the domestic economy to whom the capital expenditure will be attributed, regardless of how financed). So the overseas sector's financial surplus is +1.

So the sum of sectors' financial balances is zero, as it must be if all flows are exactly recorded. We may note that total saving by domestic sectors is 25 (22.7 of personal-sector saving and 2.3 of government-sector saving). But investment expenditure is 26. The equality of saving and investment is fulfilled by bringing in the overseas sector's saving of 1. Whenever saving by domestic sectors is less than domestic capital expenditure, the difference must be made up by overseas sector's saving, or in other words by an excess of imports over exports. If an economy undertakes investment to a greater extent than domestic sectors provide saving, then the balance of trade deficit (the overseas sector's saving) must make up the shortfall in domestic saving.

Using the figures in Table 12.7, we can see how the expenditures generating value added and the sector accounts fit together within the framework of the equation for the sum of financial balances:

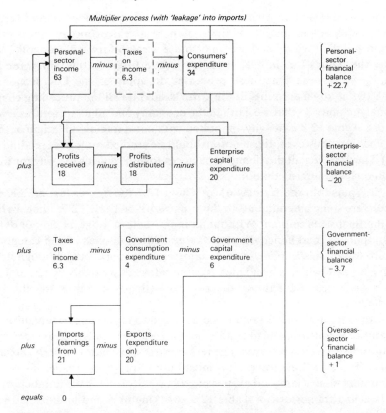

Multiplier process (with 'leakage' into imports)

In the economy, we have capital expenditure by enterprises and by government (20 and 6), consumption expenditure by government (4) and exports (20). This provides an initial 'injection' of final expenditure which is the basis for the multiplier process with its 'leakages' both into taxes on income and also into imports. The initial final expenditures and all the induced final expenditure, allowing for leakages, create domestic value added (gross domestic product). The entire process will result in a flow of saving (including the overseas sector's saving) equal to total capital expenditure, and a set of sector financial balances which sum to zero. This shows the full macroeconomic system which underlies the workings of a modern, industrial and financially developed economy which relies mainly on market forces.

The macroeconomic system and financial balances in the UK economy

Preceding sections have illustrated the macroeconomic multiplier process and financial balances by using a series of schematic, model economies. Such multiplier processes are at work in the UK economy but it is not within the scope of an introductory textbook to develop a value for the multiplier in the UK economy in terms of all its separate parameters (such as the marginal propensity to consume or import, the rate of taxation, of distribution of profits) and to apply it to the categories of final expenditure. The reason for this being out of bounds is not that there are any changes in basic principles but that the real world is a complex place, and sorting out the complexities takes up a great deal of time. For example, different income groups have different marginal propensities to consume, so the distribution of incomes affects the multiplier; it is clearly not the case that all categories of final expenditure have the same impact on imports; and determining the effective rates of taxation of income is also a complex issue.

Nevertheless, the analytic framework which we have developed and illustrated using models is readily applicable to analysis of how a real economy works from a macroeconomic point of view, and we may quite straightforwardly adapt Table 12.7 to encompass the figures for the UK economy in 1980. We do this with three purposes in mind. First, we can see that these processes do apply to the UK economy. Second, presenting the national accounts in this form should tie all the preceding chapters into a greater analytic unity so that we can see the economy and all its sectors 'as a whole'. (For this purpose, Table 12.8 is heavily annotated with notes tracing the origin of the figures in previous chapters; however, these notes should be studied only after reading this section through.) Third, seeing all the financial balances together paves the way for the following chapter on financial intermediation.

Table 12.8 puts into the framework of Table 12.7 the figures for the UK economy in 1980. There are some amendments to the framework of Table 12.7. First, we have figures only for the final sales column. Without an input–output table we cannot determine the import component (and hence domestic value added) in each of the categories of final expenditure (doing this is in any case a major undertaking). But, although it is helpful to have such a breakdown, it is by no means essential; what we really need are the final sales themselves and these we have in the first row (this first row is the third column of Table 11.9 above).

Second, the sector accounts need to be enlarged to report separately different sorts of incomes and expenditures, and to handle small, nuisance details such as stock appreciation and additions to (tax, etc.) reserves. The real world is, most unfortunately, not as neatly cut and dried as Table 12.7. However, it is most important for the reader not to get lost in a thicket of numbers, so it is a good exercise to try brutally forcing the numbers of Table 12.8 into the five-line framework of Table 12.7, working in round billions and ignoring the nuisance details.

Third, we need to represent the UK economy by six sectors, not four. Specifically, the enterprise sector must be divided into three: industrial and commercial companies (discussed in Chapter 4), public corporations (discussed in Chapter 10), and financial companies and institutions (to be discussed in the next chapter).

With these modifications, we can begin to see how things work out in the economy as a whole. In Table 12.8 the 'important' aggregates in the sector accounts have a box drawn round them; these aggregates are the final expenditures made by sectors, and also the saving by sectors.

We start with the 'initial injection' of final expenditures into the economy in 1980, taking these at market prices (i.e. including taxes on expenditure) because it is in this form that these expenditures will occur in the sector accounts. This 'injection' comprised:

General government final consumption	£48,337 million
Gross domestic fixed capital formation	£40,050 million
Value of physical increase in stocks, etc.	−£3,596 million
Exports of goods and services	£63,198 million
Total 'injection'	£147,989 million

Given that gross domestic product in 1980 was £225,560 million, the value of the multiplier implied by these market price figures is:

$$\frac{£225,560m.}{£147,989m.} = 1.524$$

Given this 'injection', total consumers' expenditure of £135,403 million at market prices was induced, though in the real world some of this consumers' expenditure was probably undertaken without the effect of being induced. In other words, the consumption function has a constant term:

$$\frac{\text{Consumers'}}{\text{expenditure}} = a + b \times \frac{\text{Disposable}}{\text{income}}.$$

where the value of *a* indicates that element of consumers' expenditure which is not dependent on income (in the multiplier analysis *a* would simply be incorporated along with investment, etc., as an 'initial injection').

Given this determination of consumers' expenditure, and together with other final expenditure, total imports of £57,832 million were induced, and so the flows of expenditure which lead to the creation of total value added (at market prices) were all determined. These are the flows which lead to the creation of income in the economy's branches of economic activity (and to the flows of expenditure taxes into the government's current account). The wage part of this income (before deduction of income taxes, £137,083 million) flows straight into the personal sector's current account, as does income from self-employment (£18,394 million). The remaining profits (or trading surplus) part of this income flows straight into the current account of the three enterprise sectors; from here some of it was distributed as dividend or interest income to the personal sector (£19,623 million). Some of each enterprise sector's profits may be paid to other sectors (e.g. industrial and commercial companies pay interest to financial institutions; public corporations pay interest to general government). These distributions out of profits (trading surplus) figure as current-account expenditure of these sectors. The reported profits (and self-employment income) figures include stock appreciation, which in this context is merely a nuisance detail to be deducted (note, however, that stock appreciation is not deducted in the general government column, solely for the sake of preserving the identity of that column's figures with those in table 9.1 of the 1981 Blue Book).

Sectors also received other income: in the case of the personal sector most of this is transfer income (National Insurance benefits, etc., £25,476 million *plus* £409 million of miscellaneous transfers – e.g. donations to charity) which is not counted as part of value added. In the case of other domestic sectors most of these receipts were income from abroad on account of property ownership abroad (these income flows have nothing to do with exports).

The overseas sector received income not only from exporting goods and services to the United Kingdom (UK imports of £57,832 million) but also received other income from the United Kingdom: £12,115 million (after deduction of UK taxes due on this income); this comprised property income accruing to the overseas sector in 1980 of £8,242 million (net of taxes), and £3,873 million of transfer payments (e.g. UK government subscription to EEC).

The government sector received as its 'income' on current account: all the (current) taxes on income due to the central government (£30,888 million); all the central government Customs and Excise and other taxes on expenditure (£22,081 million *plus* £6,906 million); all the National Insurance contributions (£13,977 million); other receipts due to central government (£3,899 million – but not counting the payment within the general government sector of £1,606 million interest to central government from local authorities); and all the rent and rates and other income due to local authorities (£13,274 million, excluding −£1 million of interest from central government to local authorities). This 'income' is treated as a transfer payment from taxpayers and consumers to the government.

Thus each sector has its total current income, the components of which are obtained by various means. Out of these current incomes, current expenditures (or appropriations) were made.

The personal sector: spent £135,403 million on consumers' final expenditure (at market prices – i.e. including taxes on expenditure); paid £40,649 million of taxes on income and National Insurance contributions; and made £290 million of transfer payments to abroad. Personal-sector total current-account expenditure was £176,342 million, so personal-

TABLE 12.8 *National accounts and financial balances for the UK economy, 1980*

£ million

	Consumers' expenditure	General government final consumption	Gross domestic fixed capital formation	Value of physical increase in stocks, etc.	Exports of goods and services	Total expenditure	Imports of goods and services	Gross domestic product
Final sales at market prices	135,403	48,337	40,050	−3,596	63,198	283,392	57,832	225,560

Account	Personal sector	Industrial and commercial companies	Financial companies and institutions	Public corporations	General government	Overseas sector
Current account						
Income (inc. stock appreciation)	175,100 (a)	31,038 (i)	18,282	6,412 (p)	—	57,832 (bb)
less Stock appreciation	854	5,049	—	393	—	—
Transfers-in and other receipts	25,885 (b)	4,803 (i)	1,901	600 (q)	91,025 (u)	12,115 (cc)
Total receipts	200,131	30,792	20,183	6,619	91,025 (u)	69,947 (dd)
Expenditure	135,403 (c)	12,019 (j)	13,308	2,902 (q)	48,337 (v)	63,198 (ee)
Taxes accruing (inc. NI contributions)	40,649 (d)	5,623 (k)	964	82 (q)	—	—
Transfers-out payments (abroad)	290	4,117 (k)	343	—	43,808 (w)	9,955 (ff)
Total expenditure	176,342	21,759	14,615	2,984	92,145	73,153
Balance: saving (exc. stock appreciation and additions to reserves)	23,789 (e)	9,033 (l)	5,568	3,635 (r)	−1,120	−3,206 (hh)
Capital account						
Receipts: saving (exc. stock appreciation)	23,789	9,033	5,568	3,635 (s)	−1,120	—
Additions to reserves	775 (f)	86 (m)	50	70 (s)	—	—
Transfers-in	1,324 (f)	496 (m)	4	597 (s)	1,248 (x)	—
Total receipts (exc. stock appreciation)	25,888	9,615	5,622	4,302	128	—
Expenditure on fixed capital formation	7,065 (f)	15,640 (n)	4,999	6,846 (s)	5,500 (y)	—
Value of physical increase in stocks, etc.	−499 (g)	−3,196 (o)	−51	31 (t)	300 (z)	—
Transfers-out, taxes on capital	1,022 (f)	113 (m)	206	46 (s)	2,282 (aa)	—
Total expenditure (exc. stock appreciation)	7,588	12,557	5,154	6,923	8,082	—
Financial balance: net acquisition of financial assets	+18,300 (h)	−2,942	+468	−2,621	−7,954	−3,206 (gg)

(a) See Table 3.1 above, first three items; all references in these notes are to tables in this book.

(b) See Table 3.1, fourth and fifth items.

(c) Consumers' expenditure; see top row this table, first item; also Table 3.3.

(d) See Table 3.1, eighth and ninth items.

(e) See Table 3.1; saving there reported (£24,643 million) includes stock appreciation of £854 million.

(f) See Table 3.5.

(g) See Table 3.5: increase in book value of stock, etc. (£355 million) less stock appreciation (£854 million) equals value of physical increase in stocks, etc. (−£499 million).

(h) See Table 3.7 for uses to which this financial surplus was put.

(i) See Table 4.2: first two items, and third item.

(j) See Table 4.2: comprises interest on loans (£7,049 million) and dividends, etc., to shareholders (£4,970 million).

(k) See Table 4.2: comprises profits due abroad (£4,077 million) and current transfers to charities (£40 million).

(l) See Table 4.2: saving there reported (£14,082 million) includes stock appreciation of £5,049 million.

(m) See Table 4.7.

(n) See Table 4.9.

(o) See Table 4.7: increase in book value of stocks, etc. (£1,853 million) less stock appreciation (£5,049 million) equals value of physical increase in stocks, etc. (−£3,196 million); that is, there was destocking in 1980.

(p) See Table 10.2 for operating account; Table 10.2 reports income net of stock appreciation (that is, £6,019 million less £393 million equals £6,412 million).

(q) See Table 10.4.

(r) See Table 10.4; saving there reported (£4,028 million) includes stock appreciation of £393 million.

(s) See Table 10.5.

(t) See Table 10.5; increase in book value of stocks, etc. (£424 million) less stock appreciation (£393 million) equals value of physical increase in stocks, etc. (£31 million).

(u) See Tables 9.5 and 9.15; this total comprises: total central government receipts on current account (£79,357 million) less dividends and interest from local authorities (£1,606 million, an intra-sectoral transaction) plus local authority 'own' receipts on current account (£13,273 million) less interest from central government (−£1 million) (transactions within the general government sector must be excluded).

(v) See Table 9.1, and Table 9.4, first two rows; also see second item, first row this table.

(w) See Table 9.1, tenth to thirteenth rows inclusive; or Table 9.4 (note that capital transfers are excluded here); includes debt interest.

(x) See Table 9.5 for central government receipts on capital account (£1,207 million) and Table 9.15 for local authority miscellaneous capital-account receipts (£41 million).

(y) See Table 9.1, or Table 9.4 third row.

(z) This is the increase in book value of stocks, etc., of £300 million, comprising £119 million of value of physical increase in stocks and work in progress and £181 million of stock appreciation (this is the only column in which stock appreciation has not been deducted in the second row; this is for the sake of maintaining conformity with the figures in the Blue Book's table 9.1).

(aa) See Table 9.1, and Table 9.4, ninth and tenth rows.

(bb) See this table, first row, second-last item; also Table 11.11, second column, fourth and fifth rows.

(cc) See Table 11.11, second column, eleventh and fourteenth rows.

(dd) See Table 11.11, second column, third-last row.

(ee) See this table, first row, fifth item; also Table 11.11, second column, first and second rows.

(ff) See Table 11.11, second column, tenth and thirteenth rows.

(gg) See Table 11.11, second column, last row.

(hh) Total of this box is £37,699 million; this includes general government stock appreciation of £181 million, excluding which brings the total of saving to £37,518 million.

(ii) Total of this box is £40,050 million; see this table, first row, third item.

(ii) Total of this box is −£3,415 million; this includes general government stock appreciation of £181 million, excluding which brings the total of inventory investment to −£3,596 million; see this table, first row, fourth item.

Sources: see the above notes for details of tables in this book; otherwise: Central Statistical Office, National Income and Expenditure 1981 Edition as follows; first row, table 1.1, p. 3; lower part of table: stock appreciation by sector in table 1.7, p. 11; additions to reserves in table 1.7, p. 10; financial surplus or deficit (net acquisition of financial assets): table 1.7, p. 11 and table 13.1, p. 90; personal sector: tables 4.1 and 4.2, pp. 28 and 29; industrial and commercial companies: table 5.4, p. 40; financial companies and institutions: table 5.5, p. 41; public corporations: tables 6.2 and 6.3, pp. 45 and 46; general government: table 9.1, pp. 58−9; overseas sector: table 1.6, p. 9.

sector saving in 1980 was £23,789 million (the difference between total incomings and total outgoings).

The sector of industrial and commercial companies paid out: dividends, etc., to other sectors (£4,970 million); interest on loans (£7,049 million); taxes on income (£5,623 million); profits due abroad (£4,077 million); and transfers to charity (£40 million). Total expenditure on current account was therefore £21,759 million, so saving by industrial and commercial companies was £9,033 million. Similarly, the other enterprise sectors had a flow of saving during the year.

The government spent £48,337 million on providing services and goods to the community (general government final consumption – part of the initial injection), and a further £43,808 million on transfer payments, so total general government current expenditure exceeded current income and the general government had negative saving.

The overseas sector spent £63,198 million on purchasing exports from the United Kingdom. This is part of the initial injection of expenditure into the economy and is important for that reason. The overseas sector also paid £9,955 million to UK residents, mostly on account of residents' ownership of property abroad, but part of this was transfer payments (such as EEC subsidies). The overseas sector received less income on current account from the United Kingdom than it paid to the United Kingdom, so the overseas sector had negative saving in 1980 of −£3,206 million.

Total recorded saving of all sectors amounted to £37,518 million (excluding government stock appreciation), and so this was the amount of resources available for investment.

The sector capital accounts are complicated by two details (none the less important for financial balances). The balance of a sector's saving is struck after allowing for tax liabilities accruing; after all, if your income were £100, your consumption expenditure of £60, and your tax bill £30 but you delayed paying your taxes, you would not then want to claim that 'your' saving was £40; the 'true' figure for 'your' saving is £10, even though the temporary addition to tax reserves of £30 in your bank account makes your financial balance for the period a flow of +£40. So in the capital account we must add back additions to tax reserves. Furthermore, some sectors have other receipts on capital account; in the case of the government sector this is mostly taxes on capital.

Out of these receipts on capital account, two types of capital expenditure are funded: fixed capital formation, and payments for the value of the physical increase in circulating capital (stocks of materials, finished goods and work in progress). In 1980 the total of final expenditure on fixed capital formation by all sectors was £40,050 million, and the total of final expenditure on circulating capital formation by all sectors was −£3,596 million. Total investment by the economy was therefore £36,454 million, and this total forms part of the initial injection of final expenditures. The totals of the recorded flow of saving and the recorded flow of investment are within 2.8 per cent of each other (a negligible discrepancy given the magnitude of the statistical task), so we can see that the equality of saving and investment in the UK economy is preserved.

Sectors also have some capital transfer/tax expenditures on capital account; for the private sectors this comprises taxes on capital or capital transfers to public corporations, while for the public sector this expenditure comprises capital transfers to the other sectors. For the whole economy, capital transfers-out equal capital transfers-in, so, in aggregate, these cancel out (see the Blue Book's table 1.7 'Summary capital account' for net capital transfers by sector).

Thus we can total each sector's expenditure on capital account and finally strike each sector's financial balance by deducting this total from total receipts on capital account. We can then see that the personal sector and the sector of financial companies and institutions had financial surpluses (a positive financial balance or a positive net acquisition of financial assets), while the sector of industrial and commercial companies, the sector of public corporations, the sector of general government and the overseas sector all had financial deficits (a negative financial balance or a negative net acquisition of financial assets).

Although Table 12.8 looks at first sight complicated (after all, it deals comprehensively with all the transactions taking place in the UK economy), its basic underlying structure is no more complex than the model of the sum of financial balances which we looked at on p. 561). Accordingly, we may apply that structure to showing the over-all macroeconomic system in the UK economy. Diagram 12.3 gives a summary account of the UK economy in terms of the sum of financial balances equation, with the relevant figures for 1980 in round billions (and ignoring the minor details of Table 12.8).

DIAGRAM 12.3   *The sum of financial balances equation for the UK economy, 1980*

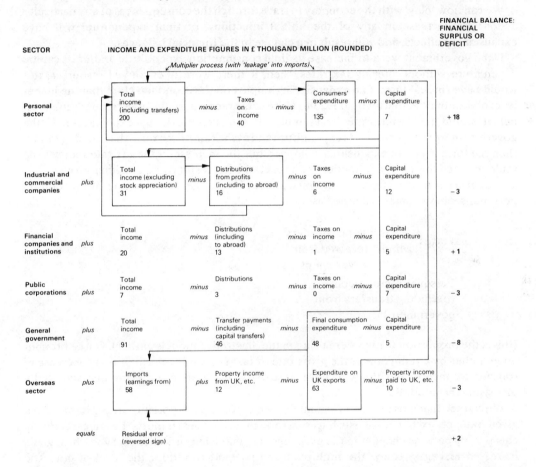

The final expenditures are boxed and lines are drawn to show some (not all) of the main connecting flows. As before, the initial injection of final expenditures (comprising all capital expenditure, government final consumption expenditure, and exports – the box on the right) is (after allowing for 'leakage' into imports) the basis for creating initial domestic value added (wages and profits). Upon the income thus accruing to the personal sector (wages *plus* distributed profits), a multiplier process determining consumers' expenditure is based. This multiplier process is determined not only by the marginal propensity to consume but also by the 'leakage' into imports and the 'leakage' into taxation (which latter leakage is now somewhat offset by return transfer payments from the government to the personal sector). This induced consumers' expenditure is (after allowing for leakage into imports) the basis for further domestic value added (wages and profits). Upon the income thus accruing to the personal sector (wages *plus* distributed profits), there is further induced consumers' expenditure. And so on, in an ever diminishing sequence. Thus all final expenditures, including imports, are determined, and so total domestic value added (gross domestic product) is determined.

In the process the macroeconomic system will lead to a flow of saving equal to total investment (saving includes the overseas' sector's saving, so if domestic sectors invest more than they are prepared to save, the strain of the 'excess' demand will be thrown upon the import–export balance, thus leading to the requisite overseas sector saving to make up the deficiency).

The result of the whole macroeconomic multiplier process will also be a set of sector financial balances which, inaccuracies of recording apart, sum to zero.

We can now 'play' with the economy to trace through the consequences of any particular action. An increase in any of the 'initial injections' of final expenditure will have expansionary effects, and will result in a change in the financial balances.

If the government were to increase its final consumption expenditure and/or its capital expenditure without altering tax rates, then, if there were unemployed resources, this would have (in real terms) an expansionary impact on the economy. Note that the higher level of economic activity would lead to a rise in tax receipts, so the government's financial deficit would not deteriorate by as much as the increase in its expenditure. If the government were to increase its expenditure and at the same time raise the *rate* of taxation, then the former has an expansionary impact, but the increase in the tax rate reduces the multiplier and this has a contractionary impact; the net result could go either way.

A reduction in the effective rate of taxation, where the effective rate of taxation on personal-sector incomes is defined as:

$$\frac{\text{Total taxes paid} \quad minus \quad \begin{array}{c}\text{Total transfers}\\\text{received from}\\\text{government}\end{array}}{\begin{array}{c}\text{Personal-sector income}\\\text{(excluding transfers from}\\\text{government)}\end{array}}$$

(this is the proportion 0.1 we were using in the illustrative models earlier), can be brought about either by a reduction in the gross rate of taxation on incomes, or by an increase in transfer payments, and this will have an expansionary effect on economic activity by increasing the multiplier.

We can see that a rise in the marginal propensity to import (possibly arising because at a given rate of exchange of sterling for foreign currencies imports become relatively cheaper, or because changes in the exchange rate make imports cheaper) will, through its increased leakage, reduce the multiplier and so tend to reduce the level of domestic economic activity. This may be doubly so, because the same forces which increase the propensity to import will probably reduce the volume of exports, thus reducing the initial injection into the economy.

The algebraic sum of the financial balances for the UK economy in 1980, as reported in the 1981 Blue Book, is +£2,045 million. That the sector financial balances do not sum to zero is due to 'errors' of recording in some of the flows. The total of final expenditures at market prices, after deducting imports, is £225,560 million. Taxes on expenditure *less* subsidies were £32,072 million. So the total of recorded final expenditures (*less* imports) at factor cost was £193,488 million, and this is the figure we have been using for gross domestic product at factor cost. But the total of incomes accruing out of value added (income from employment and self-employment, excluding transfers and stock appreciation) was recorded as £195,533 million. The residual error is defined as:

Recorded total   Recorded
final expenditure *minus* total
(*less* imports)   incomes

So, for the 1980 figures in the 1981 Blue Book, we have:

$$\text{Residual error} = £193,488\text{m.} - £195,533\text{m.} = -£2,045\text{m.}$$

So the sum of financial balances and the residual error is zero. The residual error here reported will probably be reduced in subsequent Blue Books, as revisions are made to the data so incorporating late-arriving information.

It is important to note that a financial deficit is not necessarily a 'bad thing'; nor is a financial surplus always a 'good thing'. The financial balance, while having a connection with profitability, is not the same thing *as* profitability. To illustrate, a very profitable enterprise in a growing, dynamic market may be expanding so fast and investing so much that, despite its profits, it runs a large financial deficit. This would be regarded as all to the good. Conversely, an enterprise with a financial surplus may simply be sitting on profits which it has not the entrepreneurial wit to invest dynamically. This would be regarded as rather a poor show.

The pattern of sector financial balances in the postwar UK economy is shown in Diagram 12.4 (and Appendix 12.1). Here we take the financial balances as a percentage of

DIAGRAM 12.4   *Sectors' financial balances as a percentage of gross domestic product at factor cost, 1948 to 1980*

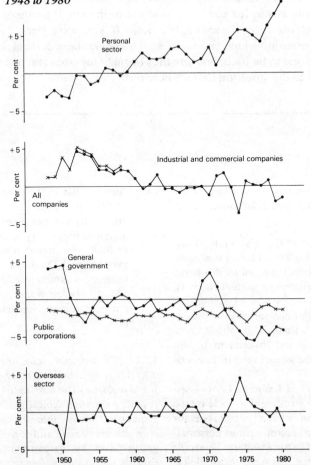

gross domestic product (this abstracts from the effect of inflation to provide a relative picture). In the years after the war the personal sector ran a financial deficit (1948 to 1955 inclusive). This may have been due to the personal sector spending in peacetime those financial assets which had accumulated during wartime when spending was inevitably constrained. We do not have sufficient data to prove whether or not this was the case, but the conjecture seems reasonable, and if so it demonstrates that a financial deficit (a negative net acquisition of financial assets) can be in the form of a reduction in a stock of financial assets owned, and is not always an increase in liabilities owed. But throughout the period there was a generally rising trend in the personal sector's financial surplus.

The sector of all companies ran a financial surplus in the immediate postwar period; but we have insufficient information to tell whether they were acquiring financial assets in the United Kingdom or were acquiring assets abroad. After 1960 the sector of industrial and commercial companies tended to have alternating periods of financial surpluses and deficits, with surpluses tending to occur in economic booms and deficits during recession.

The public corporations have, as already discussed in Chapter 10, consistently run a financial deficit, and the general government has, except for a few short periods, tended also to run a financial deficit. Correspondingly the public sector as a whole has nearly always run a financial deficit. In the 1970s the general government financial deficit deteriorated considerably. The overseas sector has alternated between financial surplus and financial deficit, corresponding (inversely) to the United Kingdom's balance of payments on current account.

What is important about Diagram 12.4 is that the financial balances of the sectors of the UK economy tend usually to be away from the zero line, with (as a generalisation) the personal sector being in surplus and the public sector in deficit. So there is a reasonably consistent 'pattern' of sector financial balances. If you look back at Table 12.8 or Diagram 12.3, the question which must arise is: If there are these deficits requiring finance and surpluses requiring to be used, how are they brought together (as, one way or another, they must be)? It is to this question that we now turn.

Exercises

12.1 *(To practise your understanding of the multiplier process and the financial balance equations.)*

(i)   In the economy of Exercise 11.4(iii), assuming that the personal sector makes no investment expenditure (all of this being made by the enterprise sector), what is: the personal sector's flow of saving; the personal sector's financial balance; the enterprise sector's financial balance? Comment on saving and investment in this economy and the sum of sectors' financial balances.

(ii)   In the economy of Exercise 11.5(ii), assuming that all investment is made by the enterprise sector, what is: personal-sector saving; overseas-sector saving; personal-sector financial balance; enterprise-sector financial balance; overseas-sector financial balance?

(iii)   Assume that in the economy of Exercise 11.5(ii) the personal sector's marginal propensity to import rises to 0.30 while the marginal propensity to consume remains at 0.75, investment remains at 100 and exports at 60. On the same assumptions as before and assuming a 70/30 split of value added between wages and profits, work out each sector's financial balance equation.

12.2 *(To see that your answer to Exercise 12.1(iii) is applicable to a very significant real-world problem.)* The answer to Exercise 12.1(iii) reveals a situation typical in many Third World economies where there is a 'gap' between domestic investment and domestic saving, which gap is 'filled' by the gap between imports and exports (accordingly, this analysis is known in the literature on development economics as the 'two-gap analysis'). In the light of this, explain why your answer to 12.1(iii) might constitute a justification for foreign aid to developing countries. (Further reading: G. M. Meier (ed.), *Leading Issues in Economic Development*, 2nd edn, Oxford University Press, 1970, s. VA1 'Public financial aid – measuring capital requirements'; Tony Killick, *Development Economics in Action: A Study of Economic Policies in Ghana*, Heinemann, 1978, ch. 5 'External performance: the foreign exchange constraint and its causes', esp. pp. 122–5.)

12.3 *(To practise working with the sum of sector financial balances.)*

(i) How would you set about explaining why, in the answer to Exercise 12.1(iii), the sum of sectors' financial balances is zero?

(ii) Demonstrate, for each of the three most recent years available, that the sum of sectors' financial balances in the UK economy (including the overseas sector) equals the residual error with its sign reversed (i.e. the sum of sectors' financial balances and the residual error is zero).

12.4 *(To practise seeing how the four-sector economy works.)* Assume that the economy of Exercise 12.1(iii) has a government sector which levies taxes on incomes at the rate of 10 per cent (but there are no taxes on expenditure); assume that all profits are distributed as income to the personal sector (to be taxed in that sector); and assume that value added is divided 70/30 between wages and profits, except for government consumption expenditure, which is all on wages. For this economy we have the following functional relationships and initial final expenditures:

Consumers' expenditure
  = 0.75 × Disposable income
Imports = 0.30 × Total final expenditure
Enterprise investment = 60
Government consumption expenditure
  = 20
Exports = 120

(i) Show that the multiplier with this rate of taxation and this consumption function

and import function is 1.327 (this may be done via the short-cut method).

(ii) Following the format of Table 12.7, work out and insert all the figures for this economy.

(iii) Unfortunately, the economy of Exercise 12.4(ii) suffers from unemployment; the government therefore decides to expand the level of economic activity by raising government consumption expenditure to 46; enterprise investment and exports remain at 60 and 120 respectively. Following the format of Table 12.7, work out and insert all the figures for this economy.

(iv) Describe, and analyse, the main contrasts between the economy of 12.4(ii) and 12.4(iii).

12.5 *(To practise seeing how the UK economy works.)*

In 1980 the [UK] economy experienced its most drastic fall in economic activity since the early 1930s ... Real GDP fell by 4½ per cent during the year ... As a result unemployment grew by over ¾ million during the year to reach a total of 2.1 million by December, the highest figure since before the war (National Institute of Economic and Social Research, *National Institute Economic Review*, no. 95, February 1981, p. 3).

(i) With reference to Table 12.8, explain why destocking was said to be a deflationary influence in 1980.

(ii) With regard to the sector of industrial and commercial companies in Table 12.8, explain why it was said that destocking 'was the result of powerful financial pressures' (*National Institute Economic Review*, February 1981, p. 41).

(iii) Explain why the government was urged during 1980 to cut taxes or expand expenditure (or both) and explain what this would have meant in principle for sector financial balances. (Further reading: National Institute of Economic and Social Research, *National Institute Economic Review*, February 1981, pp. 3–21 and 32–45.)

APPENDIX 12.1   Sector financial balances in the UK economy, 1948 to 1980 [a]

| | Financial surplus (+) or deficit (−) £ million | | | | | | | Gross domestic product at factor cost [b] | Financial surplus or deficit as percentage of gross domestic product at factor cost | | | | | | |
Year	Personal sector	Industrial and commercial companies	Financial companies and institutions	Public corporations	General government	Overseas sector	Residual error		Personal sector	Industrial and commercial companies	Financial companies and institutions	Public corporations	General government	Overseas sector	Residual error as percentage of GDP
1948	−316	122		−129	410	−145	58	10,314	−3.1	1.2		−1.3	4.0	−1.4	0.6
1949	−257	147		−168	469	−192	1	10,949	−2.3	1.3		−1.5	4.3	−1.8	—
1950	−346	434		−172	510	−475	49	11,386	−3.0	3.8		−1.5	4.5	−4.2	0.4
1951	−412	265		−266	22	322	69	12,679	−3.2	2.1		−2.1	0.2	2.5	0.5
1952	−7	(c) (640) 708		−270	−281	−168	18	13,836	−0.1	(4.6) 5.1		−2.0	−2.0	−1.2	0.1
1953	−65	(646) 685		−256	−445	−151	232	14,918	−0.4	(4.3) 4.6		−1.7	−3.0	−1.0	1.6
1954	−233	(627) 661		−265	−170	−121	128	15,761	−1.5	(4.0) 4.2		−1.7	−1.1	−0.8	0.8
1955	−179	(365) 435		−430	36	155	−17	16,905	−1.1	(2.2) 2.6		−2.5	0.2	0.9	−0.1
1956	114	(399) 479		−394	−150	−208	159	18,301	0.6	(2.2) 2.6		−2.2	−0.8	−1.1	0.9
1957	76	(309) 389		−553	19	−233	302	19,404	0.4	(1.6) 2.0		−2.8	0.1	−1.2	1.6
1958	−44	(450) 522		−571	122	−344	315	20,227	−0.2	(2.2) 2.6		−2.8	0.6	−1.7	1.6
1959	14	421	38	−576	16	−143	230	21,258	0.1	2.0	0.2	−2.7	0.1	−0.7	1.1
1960	346	225	42	−461	−246	255	−161	22,637	1.5	1.0	0.2	−2.0	−1.1	1.1	−0.7
1961	628	−81	79	−542	−205	−6	127	24,228	2.6	−0.3	0.3	−2.2	−0.8	—	0.5
1962	485	49	39	−525	−2	−122	76	25,284	1.9	0.2	0.2	−2.1	—	−0.5	0.3
1963	497	416	9	−407	−426	−124	35	26,913	1.8	1.5	—	−1.5	−1.6	−0.5	0.1
1964	592	−126	−23	−581	−423	355	206	29,210	2.0	−0.4	−0.1	−2.0	−1.4	1.2	0.7

1965	970	−123	−22	−228	26	—	31,219	3.1	−0.4	−0.1	−2.0	−0.7	0.1	—
1966	1,138	−270	−73	−6	−104	163	33,130	3.4	−0.8	−0.2	−2.6	—	−0.3	0.5
1967	866	−30	−93	−411	294	420	34,935	2.5	−0.1	−0.3	3.0	−1.2	0.8	1.2
1968	526	−39	−160	−725	242	375	37,576	1.4	−0.1	−0.4	−1.9	−0.6	0.6	1.0
1969	755	−17	−388	−510	981	−350	39,633	1.9	—	−1.0	−1.3	2.5	−1.2	−0.9
1970	1,481	−541	−301	−830	1,511	−497	43,574	3.4	−1.2	−0.7	−1.9	3.5	−1.9	−1.1
1971	490	711	−209	−1,086	786	432	49,490	1.0	1.4	−0.4	−2.2	1.6	−2.3	0.9
1972	1,458	1,263	−203	−743	−804	−724	55,347	2.6	2.3	−0.4	−1.3	−1.5	−0.4	−1.3
1973	2,978	−67	−108	−767	−2,000	−1,076	64,347	4.6	−0.1	−0.2	−1.2	−3.1	1.6	−1.7
1974	4,234	−2,684	−448	−1,535	−3,178	263	74,661	5.7	−3.6	−0.6	−2.1	−4.3	4.5	0.4
1975	5,394	571	−504	−2,799	−4,903	720	94,475	5.7	0.6	−0.5	−3.0	−5.2	1.6	0.8
1976	5,588	257	−114	−2,136	−6,181	1,705	111,585	5.0	0.2	−0.1	−1.9	−5.5	0.8	1.5
1977	5,221	59	85	−1,236	−4,696	526	126,943	4.1	—	0.1	−1.0	−3.7	0.2	0.4
1978	9,223	1,149	−619	−1,083	−7,070	−661	145,304	6.3	0.8	−0.4	−0.7	−4.9	−0.6	−0.5
1979	13,026	−3,274	−137	−2,136	−6,143	−2,199	166,464	7.8	−2.0	−0.1	−1.3	−3.7	0.5	−1.3
1980	18,300	−2,942	468	−2,621	−7,954	−2,045	193,488	9.5	−1.5	0.2	−1.4	−4.1	−1.7	−1.1

(a) As published according to latest revised estimates to appear in the national income and expenditure accounts; for some later revisions pertaining to 1952 to 1969, see Bank of England, *Statistical Abstract Number 1*, 1970, table 31, pp. 180–91.

(b) Expenditure-based estimates.

(c) Bracketed figures are Bank of England data for industrial and commercial companies only.

Sources: Central Statistical Office, *National Income and Expenditure: 1959*, tables 7 and 46, pp. 4 and 49; *1960*, tables 7 and 47, pp. 4 and 49; *1961*, tables 7 and 48, pp. 4 and 49; *1962*, tables 7 and 48, pp. 8 and 53; *1963*, tables 7 and 48, pp. 8 and 55; *1964*, table 49, p. 59; *1965*, table 67, p. 79; *1966*, table 73, p. 86; *1967*, table 72, p. 86; *1968*, table 72, p. 88; *1969*, table 69, p. 82; *1970*, table 68, p. 80; *1971*, table 71, p. 84; *1972*, table 70, p. 82; *1973*, table 70, p. 82; *1963–73*, table 72, p. 84; *1964–74*, tables 8, 35, 36, 80, 87, pp. 10, 39, 40, 88 and 95; *1965–75*, tables 1.7, 5.4, 5.5, 14.1 and 14.8, pp. 10–11, 39, 40, 91 and 98; *1966–76*, tables 1.7, 13.1 and 13.8, pp. 12–13, 93 and 100; *1967–77*, tables 1.8, 13.1, 13.8, pp. 14–15, 97 and 104; *1979 Edition*, tables 1.8, 13.1, 13.8, pp. 14–15, 95 and 102; *1980 Edition*, tables 1.7, 13.1 and 13.8, pp. 10–11, 90 and 97; *1981 Edition*, tables 1.1, 1.7, 13.1 and 13.11, pp. 3, 11, 90 and 100; Bank of England, *Statistical Abstract Number 1*, 1970, table 31, p. 186; Central Statistical Office, *Economic Trends Annual Supplement 1981 Edition*, p. 5.

Chapter 13

Financial Intermediation, Banking and the Money Supply

Contents

Chapter guide

Having seen in the previous chapter how sector financial surpluses or deficits are generated by the macroeconomic process, Chapter 13 explains the process of *financial intermediation*, which enables sectors (and entities) in financial deficit to borrow from sectors (and entities) running a financial surplus.

The two important problems of *risk assessment* and *liquidity* in the lending/borrowing transaction are explained as providing the basis for financial intermediation, and we look at data on the working of *financial intermediaries* in the UK economy: the *building societies*; *general insurance* and *life assurance* companies; *superannuation (pension) funds*; and a group of smaller financial institutions (*investment trusts, unit trusts, property unit trusts, trustee savings banks*, and *finance houses* (hire-purchase finance companies)). We examine the role of *The Stock Exchange*, particularly with regard to the *issuing* of securities.

The *banks* form the largest group of financial intermediaries, and they are especially important because they are not only financial intermediaries but they also provide the economy's *money transmission service*. We explain how this service works, and examine the *money supply* of the United Kingdom which largely comprises the *deposit liabilities* of the banks.

In order to understand how the money supply changes we need first to explain the function of the *Bank of England*, the nation's *central bank* and, second, to demonstrate how the public sector borrowing requirement (PSBR) can lead to expansion of banks' *reserve assets* with the Bank of England, and so to an expansion of bank lending which then results in the growth of banks' deposit liabilities (i.e. in the growth of the money supply). (The PSBR is the essential starting-point for all monetary economics and as such is the key concept.)

We explain how a change in banks' reserve assets leads to a multiple expansion in deposit liabilities as determined by the reciprocal of the proportionate *reserve asset ratio*. Some related issues, such as the role of finance for the PSBR from the *overseas sector*, the role of *special deposits*, and the concept of *domestic credit expansion*, are explained.

We examine actual data on how the PSBR leads to an expansion of the money supply (*sterling* M_3) and we examine the part which *interest rates* are supposed to play in constraining the growth of the money supply. We see how the system for expansion of the money supply works in theory and we look at various relevant data on the relationship between the PSBR and changes in the money supply, the relationship between the PSBR and short-term interest rates, and at the large amount of 'other currency' business undertaken by the UK banking sector.

The system of monetary regulation in the United Kingdom was considerably altered on 20 August 1981, and so we explain how the old system, known as *'Competition and Credit Control'*, has now been amended to the new system of *'Monetary Control'*.

So far the exposition has been based on the public sector borrowing requirement, which is a *net* requirement for finance by the public sector: that is, the PSBR (as officially defined) does not include the (re-)financing requirement caused by *maturing debt* (existing debt which falls due for redemption – such debt redemption simply replaces 'old' debt by 'new' debt and therefore does not alter the total stock of debt outstanding, unlike the (net) PSBR, which does increase the total of outstanding liabilities). Nevertheless, maturing debt does cause problems for government financing; we explain this through the basic monetary policy equation for *'high-powered money'* and we consider some of the steps taken by the government, through *open-market operations* and other means, to cope with its over-all financing problem.

Financial intermediation: risk assessment and liquidity

We have seen that some sectors in the economy tend to run a financial surplus while others may run a financial deficit. Such financial surpluses and deficits can be taken to be part and parcel of a healthy and growing economy because they result, in general, from an 'affluent' household sector which has more than met its material needs and, conversely, from enterprise and government sectors which are investing (in the future of the economy) more than they have by way of a flow of saving. Within this pattern of sectoral financial balances (which may be seen in the national accounts) there will be, largely hidden from view, some entities inside each sector which are in financial surplus while other entities in the same sector will be in deficit. For example, within the personal sector, some entities in financial surplus deposited £7,175 million with building societies in 1980, while other entities, incurring a financial deficit (by reason of house purchase), borrowed £5,715 million from building societies in 1980 (Table 3.7 above).

Now, it is possible for deficit entities to borrow directly from surplus entities. In this context the word 'borrow' means obtaining the present use of funds in return for:

(a)   a promise (legally binding) to repay the sum lent (called 'the principal') usually at or by a specified date (or by instalments on specified dates) or on request; and

(b)   the promise of an annual (or periodic) payment while the loan is outstanding (this periodic payment is known as 'interest').

It was quite common practice in nineteenth-century England for a factory-owner to borrow directly from families (often perhaps relatives) in the neighbourhood (as had Mr Tulliver in George Eliot's *The Mill on the Floss*). But such a direct transaction has many disadvantages both to lender and borrower. From the borrower's point of view, there is the inconvenience, perhaps even the impossibility, of amassing a sufficiently large sum for his needs; he may have to borrow from many different entities in financial surplus in order to obtain the sum needed. From the lender's point of view, there are two serious inconveniences in making such direct loans.

First, there is the problem that he – the lender – is likely not to have the expertise to assess whether or not the loan will be 'safe'; he will not be able to assess the soundness or otherwise of the borrower's project.

Second, even if the borrower tries to satisfy the lender on this point by offering the lender 'security' – say, in the form of a fall-back claim on the real assets to be obtained with the funds or on some other asset – the lender may still remain worried about being able to retrieve his loan should he wish to do so. That is, the lender might wish to lend for only a short period, and the borrower to borrow for a longer period, quite apart from questions of risk. This second inconvenience is distinct from the first, though not unconnected with it.

The second inconvenience can be mitigated if there is a market in 'second-hand' loans, enabling the initial lender, if he needs to retrieve his money, to 'sell' his loan to someone else, but the inconvenience cannot thereby be entirely eliminated because the initial lender might still have to sell his loan 'at a discount' for less than its face-value of the sum originally lent and promised for repayment (strictly speaking, the lender sells his entitlement to repayment of the loan and to the periodic interest payment). Thus there remains inescapably for the lender the inconvenience that he might suffer a capital loss if he wished to retrieve his money before the due date for repayment. For this reason alone, the borrower has to compensate the lender by paying interest.

This second inconvenience is known as the problem of 'liquidity'. Liquidity is a property of assets. It is generally a property of financial assets, though it can, by extension, be applied also to real assets. Liquidity is the property of an asset being able to be turned *quickly and without the risk of capital loss* into purchasing power or into a means of payment – where the term 'means of payment' means that the tendering of this means of payment constitutes, in law, a settlement of the obligation. In the definition of 'liquidity', the terms 'quickly' and 'without risk of capital loss' are both important terms. I could very quickly turn my house into purchasing power if I were, say, to offer the title deeds to a publican in return for a pint of beer. But I would have sustained a considerable capital loss. Liquidity is a matter of degree: different assets can be less or more liquid. Bank notes and coin of the realm are distinguished as assets by having 100 per cent liquidity: they are *legal* tender and must be accepted in settlement of any debt or in any exchange (subject to minor restrictions on the tendering of coin in settlement of large debts).

Thus the lender of funds faces two problems. First, there is the problem of assessing risk; the lender is unlikely to have the specialist expertise to do this. Second, in parting with his funds, the lender is parting with liquidity; as Keynes argued in *The General Theory of Employment, Interest and Money*, 'the rate of interest is the reward for parting with liquidity for a specified period' (p. 167). Even on an entirely risk-free loan, the lender is likely to want periodic interest payment to compensate for suffering the inconvenience of changing a liquid asset (money) into an illiquid asset (an IOU). All these problems faced by both lenders and borrowers engaged in direct financial transactions can be either entirely overcome or greatly reduced if, instead of dealing one to one, face to face, they deal through a financial intermediary.

A financial intermediary is, in the first instance, a person who (or institution which) specialises in the expert assessment of risk. Financial intermediaries tend, as a rule, to specialise in assessing certain types of risk. This largely explains why there are so many different types of financial intermediary. But if this were all that financial intermediaries did, then they would be no more than specialist advisers, and perhaps agents, assisting in direct financial transactions. So most (but not all) financial intermediaries do more than this: there is usually an equally important second dimension to their activities; this concerns the way in which they affect liquidity.

Most financial intermediaries gather up funds from surplus entities (lenders) and then, using their specialist expertise in risk assessment, they lend funds to deficit entities (borrowers). Usually, financial intermediaries will have more lenders and fewer borrowers: that is, they on-lend agglomerations, or parcels, of funds.

Financial intermediaries can reduce the general riskiness of making loans in two ways: first, by expertly weeding out uncreditworthy projects (requests for loans); second, and only because it is making a large number of loans, the financial intermediary can make provision in its loan charges (the interest payments it receives) to recover the loss of any loan, initially deemed creditworthy, that unexpectedly fails (as happens from time to time). The financial intermediary will also, of course, tend additionally to obtain good security for its loan (which the face-to-face lender can also do; but the face-to-face lender is not usually making so many loans that he can 'insure' himself via the interest charges on a multiplicity of loans). In these two ways, the riskiness of lending is reduced by financial intermediaries.

But there is another very important aspect of financial intermediation. This is that financial intermediaries can, while acting as go-between for (many) lenders and (fewer) borrowers, increase the liquidity available to the lender *without* affecting the loan terms available to borrowers. This is an enormously powerful benefit and conferring it is the main reason for the success (and growth) of financial intermediaries. How does this come about?

If the sources of funds (lenders) are large in number, the financial intermediary who accepts deposits from lenders can safely reckon that, during any given period, only a small proportion of such lenders (or 'depositors', as we shall now call them) will want to retrieve their funds, and such retrievals can readily be accommodated partly by the financial intermediary holding a small 'reserve' of (liquid) assets (such as notes and coin) from which to meet such a contingency, partly from the inflow of new deposits, and partly from the inflow of repayments of past loans (and from the interest thereon). So a financial intermediary operating on a sufficiently large scale is able to assure depositors that, should they so wish, they will readily and speedily be able to retrieve their deposits. In this way, and very importantly, the financial intermediary greatly increases the liquidity available to depositors (lenders). In return for this assurance of liquidity, the financial intermediary will pay depositors of funds (and they will be entirely satisfied with) a lower rate of interest on their deposits (by contrast with a face-to-face loan, lenders depositing funds with – lending to – a financial intermediary who offers such an assurance are not 'parting with liquidity' to as great an extent, and so will accept a lower rate of interest on their loans – deposits).

The other side of the coin (that there will be relatively few depositors retrieving their funds) is that the financial intermediary can afford to 'lend long' to borrowers: that is, there is no need for a financial intermediary to alter the terms on which funds are available to borrowers (in a face-to-face transaction the lender cannot obtain more liquidity except by imposing highly inconvenient restrictions ('repayment on demand') on the borrower – inconveniences against which the borrower is likely to retaliate by offering to pay only a lower rate of interest).

All this means that a financial intermediary can, by offering the assurance of increased liquidity to depositors, pay depositors a lower rate of interest, while conversely, by offering convenient loans for long periods to borrowers, the financial intermediary can charge borrowers a higher rate of interest. Over all, however, rates of interest paid and charged by financial intermediaries are likely to be substantially less than would prevail in the absence of financial intermediaries. To illustrate, if I lent directly to you, I might demand, and you would have to pay, interest of 25 per cent per annum; but if there is a financial intermediary, I might be content with receiving 10 per cent per annum on my (more liquid) deposit, and you would benefit by being charged only, say, 12 per cent per annum (we assume that competition among financial intermediaries to on-lend deposits would act to drive the rate charged down from 25 per cent). The existence and functioning of financial intermediaries therefore lowers rates of interest in the economy, and, if borrowed funds are being used to pay for investment, this means cheaper finance for investment and so an encouragement to investment. So financial intermediation inevitably accompanies economic growth and, indeed, is an integral part of economic development (the reader who wishes to pursue this theme is referred to Raymond Goldsmith, *Financial Structure and Development*, Yale University Press, 1969).

The difference between the interest rate which a financial intermediary pays to depositors (lenders) and the (higher) interest rate which it charges to borrowers is very important. This differential, or 'turn' or 'margin' as it is sometimes called, provides most of the income for financial intermediaries from which they pay for the cost (employees, premises, etc.) of their services. To illustrate, if a financial intermediary has accepted deposits of 100 from lenders on which it pays 10 per cent per annum, and the financial intermediary then lends 90 to borrowers, charging 12 per cent per annum (holding a 'reserve' of 10 in case the depositors want (some of) their deposits back), then the financial intermediary has to pay the depositors $100 \times 0.1 = 10$ per annum, while it receives from the borrowers $90 \times 0.12 = 10.8$ per annum; so the financial intermediary 'makes' 0.8 per annum. Given that the units were, say, in millions (given that the financial intermediary is operating on a sufficiently large scale), this represents an annual income of £800,000, available to a relatively small group of specialist risk assessors. In short, financial intermediation can be a highly profitable business. In actual practice, the interest rate differential, or 'turn', in terms of percentage points may sometimes be less than this example (derived for arithmetic convenience) but the stocks on which the turn arises are very large indeed; for example, the stock of liabilities/assets held by building societies in the United Kingdom at the end of 1979 was £46,126 million and the rate of interest paid to depositors in 1980 was about 8.5 per cent per annum, while the rate of interest charged for mortgages (loans) advanced by the building societies was nearly 11.9 per cent. Although not all building societies' assets were in the form of mortgages, we have theoretically a turn of about 3.4 percentage points on a stock of £46,126 million, or an annual income during 1980 of approximately:

$$0.034 \times £46,126m. = £1,568m. \text{ per annum}$$

(figures from Central Statistical Office, *Financial Statistics*, September 1981, tables 8.7 and 13.13, pp. 93 and 141).

This section has dealt with the general principles of financial intermediation and we now need to examine the actual financial intermediaries operating in the economy.

Financial institutions and financial markets in the United Kingdom

Table 13.1 shows that at the end of 1979 there were about 2,900 financial institutions in the United Kingdom whose total holdings were £362 billion. The banking sector held 55.1 per cent of these assets, and their operations will be discussed subsequently in this chapter. In the sections immediately following we shall consider the financial institutions other than banks, among whom the three biggest are building societies, insurance companies and superannuation funds.

TABLE 13.1   *Financial institutions in the United Kingdom, end-1979*

		Holdings at end of 1979	
	Number of institutions	£ million	Percentage of total
Banking sector [a]	373 (281)	199,590	55.1
Other financial institutions			
Building societies	276	46,126	12.7
Insurance: general	} 870 {	10,486	2.9
Insurance: long-term		42,311	11.7
Superannuation funds	700	42,403	11.7
Investment trusts	202	5,995	1.7
Unit trusts	350	3,487	1.0
Property unit trusts	23	956	0.3
Trustee savings banks	17	5,805	1.6
Special finance agencies, etc.	8	1,332	0.4
Finance houses (inc. other consumer credit agencies)	36	3,467	1.0
Total	2,855	361,958	100.0

[a] Comprising: British banks, overseas banks, consortium banks, listed discount market institutions and five money trading departments of listed banks (see pp. 63–6 of first source). The figure of 281 banks is from the first list of 'recognised banks' issued under the Banking Act 1979 (the *Financial Times*, 6 April 1981). This figure excludes 'licensed deposit-taking institutions'.

Sources: Central Statistical Office, *Financial Statistics Explanatory Handbook 1981 Edition*, pp. 63–6 and 74; data on finance houses' holdings from Central Statistical Office, *Annual Abstract of Statistics 1982 Edition*, table 17.24, p. 435 (adding on net acquisitions to end-1976 holdings); Central Statistical Office: *Financial Statistics*, September 1981, table 6.1, p. 59; *Financial Statistics*, January 1982, table 8.12, p. 100 (giving revised data for holdings of superannuation funds).

In his book *The British Financial System* (Macmillan, 1973) Professor Jack Revell suggests that the way to classify financial institutions is according to the nature of the claims which they issue against themselves, i.e. according to their liabilities. In Revell's scheme of classification we have (p. 74):

1. Deposit institutions – short-term liabilities (e.g. banks, building societies).
2. Insurance and provident institutions – long-term (and contingency) liabilities (e.g. life and other insurance, superannuation funds).
3. Portfolio institutions – liabilities essentially marketable securities, similar to those held as assets (e.g. investment trusts, unit trusts).
4. Special investment agencies – institutions which obtain funds for specialist lending to a branch of industry (e.g. Agricultural Mortgage Corporation, Industrial & Commercial Finance Corporation, Commonwealth Development Corporation).

Clearly this is a more manageable system of classification than one based on specialist risk-assessment expertise, which effectively puts each type of financial institution in its own (specialist) class. The discussion of financial institutions will be confined to the basic components of their balance-sheets and their inflows and outflows.

Further reading

Readers wanting more detail may consult Professor Revell's book, *The British Financial System*, or Christopher Johnson, *The Anatomy of UK Finance 1970–75* (Longman, 1976), Hamish McCrae and Frances Cairncross, *Capital City – London as a Financial Centre* (Methuen, rev. edn, 1983), or the *Report* of the Committee to Review the Functioning of Financial Institutions (the Wilson Report) especially the *Appendices* volume (Cmnd 7937). The best brief guide is *British Banking and other Financial Institutions,* Central Office of Information Reference Pamphlet No. 123 (HMSO, 1974). Readers requiring practical details should consult Margaret Allen, *The Money Book* (Pan, 1978), James Rowlatt, *A Guide to Saving and Investment* (Pan Books, 1981), or Eamonn Fingleton and Tom Tickell, *The Penguin Money Book* (Penguin, 1981). These latter 'practical guides' are most important for students in helping to understand the day-to-day reality of financial intermediation.

Building societies

Most students will have some familiarity with the operation of building societies. Building societies accept deposits (in various forms) from a large number of persons who are 'saving'* (often saving in order to buy a house) and they then 'on-lend' money to a fewer number of persons buying houses (the term officially used is 'dwellings'). In 1980 the building societies had 31.6 million depositors and share investors, and only 5.4 million borrowers on their books: that is, there were nearly 6 times more depositors than borrowers, thus illustrating how the building societies as financial intermediaries make up 'parcels' of finance (figures from Central Statistical Office, *Annual Abstract of Statistics 1982 Edition*, table 17.22, p. 434). This is a 'paradigm' illustration of financial intermediation ('paradigm' literally means pattern or (exact) example). The building society, using its specialist ability to assess property values and the creditworthiness of would-be borrowers,

---

*Strictly speaking, these people are running a financial surplus; in this chapter it is difficult to avoid a rather loose use of the word 'saving' and this qualification must henceforth be taken as read.

makes loans for house purchase, secured by a claim ('mortgage') on the house itself (that is, if the borrower defaults on the payment of interest and/or on repayment of the principal, the building society may 'foreclose' on the mortgage, and sell the house in order to recoup whatever is owed to it – naturally, foreclosure is only a last resort). The funds which building societies lend are nearly all obtained as deposits from the personal sector, mostly short-term deposits (i.e. deposits withdrawable virtually on demand – but building societies will pay depositors slightly higher rates of interest if they will commit their deposits for longer periods). Because building societies provide such (very) liquid assets for savers, Revell asserts roundly that 'building societies are specialised savings banks' (*The British Financial System*, p. 366) and it is this feature which has caused the phenomenal growth in persons saving with building societies from three–quarters of a million in 1920 to two-and-a-quarter million in 1950 to over ten million in 1970 and over thirty million in 1980. Most deposits in building societies are technically in the form of 'shares' (meaning that the depositor is not protected should the building society become insolvent); apart from this, there is nothing in common with (equity) shares in a limited company (furthermore some 'shares' are protected deposits). We shall use the term 'share deposit' to cover both.

So we can see that the building societies provide a very clear example of financial intermediation: they greatly reduce risk to the lender (almost eliminating it) and provide liquidity, while at the same time they reduce inconvenience to the borrower, enabling him or her to obtain a long-term loan.

Table 13.2 shows the balance-sheet for the building societies' stocks of holdings at end-1979 and end-1980, together with the derived changes (flows) in those stocks during 1980. At the end of 1979 the personal sector held share deposits with the building societies of £42,442 million; by the end of 1980 these share deposits had grown to £49,460 million, so this source of funds provided the building societies with an inflow from the personal

TABLE 13.2　*Financial intermediation by the building societies, 1980*

	£ million		
	Holdings at book value		Flow during 1980
	End-1979	End-1980	
Liabilities (sources of funds)			
'Shares' and deposits			
Personal sector [a]	42,442	49,460	7,018
Other sectors	349	490	141
Total shares and deposits	42,791	49,950	7,159
Other liabilities [b]	3,335	4,356	1,021
Total liabilities	46,126	54,306	8,180
Assets (uses of funds)			
Mortgages [c]	36,986	42,708	5,722
Other [d]	9,140	11,598	2,458
Total assets	46,126	54,306	8,180

[a] See Table 3.6, line 2, or Table 3.7, line 5; see also Table 3.15, line 9.

[b] Mainly reserves.

[c] Nearly all of which to personal sector; see Table 3.7, line 6; see also Table 3.15 (for end-1979 data). Liabilities in Table 3.15 include house-purchase loans from other institutions and are latest revised data so may not match exactly (ditto assets).

[d] Mainly short-term (liquid) assets and British government securities, but including real assets.

Source: Central Statistical Office, *Financial Statistics*, October 1981, tables 8.7 and 10.4, pp. 93–4 and 114.

sector of £7,018 million during 1980. The deposits of other sectors (mainly of industrial and commercial companies) also increased during 1980, so the increase in total deposits was £7,159 million. In addition to this source of funds, building societies also had a source of funds from their accumulated surpluses called 'reserves'. Reserves are classified as a liability, even though they may not be a liability specifically owed to any one person (as are deposits). If the building societies were privately owned (which none are, all being officially mutual, non-profit organisations called 'Friendly Societies'), then reserves would be called something like 'owner's equity' – a sort of 'liability' owed by the organisation to the owner. Reserves are, in effect, the amount by which total assets exceed other and specifically owed liabilities. During 1980 building societies increased their reserves by £1,021 million, so the total inflow, their sources of funds, was £8,180 million during the year. How did they use these funds? The greater proportion, 70 per cent, was used in mortgage loans for house purchase; nearly all of these loans were to the personal sector for the purchase of dwellings. During 1980 building societies made, net of repayments of principal, £5,722 million of mortgage advances, and they put the remaining £2,458 million into various assets (such as deposits with banks, government securities, and other assets such as premises).

TABLE 13.3   *Building societies' main flows of funds, 1980*

	£ million
Change in share and deposit liabilities	
Deposits of principal	22,183
less Withdrawals of principal	18,367
Net inflow of shares and deposits	3,816
plus Interest credited to accounts but not paid out	3,343
Net increase in share and deposit liabilities outstanding	7,159
Change in mortgage assets	
Advances of mortgages (to 677,000 borrowers)	9,614
less Repayments of principal	3,892
Net advances of principal	5,722

Source: Central Statistical Office, *Financial Statistics*, October 1981, tables 8.6 and 8.8, pp. 92 and 95.

The net growth in shares and deposits and in mortgage advances disguises the large 'gross' flows involved. Table 13.3 shows the gross flow of funds behind these net changes. During 1980 'savers' (strictly speaking, entities in financial surplus or entities switching funds from other financial assets) deposited £22,183 million with building societies, but 'dissavers' (entities presumably in financial deficit, or switching to other financial assets) withdrew £18,367 million; so the *net* change in shares and deposits was only £3,816 million. Building societies also receive a substantial flow of funds from interest which is credited to share depositors' accounts but which is not actually paid out to share depositors. Adding on this 'left-alone' interest then gives the total increase in deposit liabilities of £7,159 million. So in these gross flows we can see 'liquidity' at work: share depositors can and do withdraw their deposits; but although the building societies maintain reserves of liquid assets from which to meet such withdrawals, we can see that, in reality, most of the withdrawals are 'met' from the gross inflow of new share deposits. This is very often the way with deposit-taking financial institutions (and it partly explains their attempts, via advertising, to persuade the public to make deposits with them: they have ceaselessly to replace withdrawals).

The net change in mortgages of £5,722 million on 1980 is also a little misleading. In gross terms, building societies made £9,614 million worth of mortgage advances to 677,000 borrowers during 1980: an average of about £801 million to 56,000 borrowers a month and £14,200 per borrower. This gives some idea of the scale of the financial intermediation between households that is undertaken by the building societies. A large part of the attractiveness of borrowing from building societies is the tax relief which interest on the loan attracts (see Table 3.4 above): if we take two households in identical circumstances with incomes of £20,000 a year, except that one pays £2,400 a year in mortgage interest, while the other pays £2,400 a year in rent, then the income-tax bill of the first family will be £1,085 lower than that of the second.* Added to this is the fact that the owner-occupier enjoys the benefit of capital gain on the residence, free of Capital Gains Tax. This 'holding gain' is not readily realisable – if one moves house, the capital gain simply has to be put into the next house – but the holding gain can be realised if one 'trades down', as do many households upon the retirement of the head of household. As Fingleton and Tickell emphasise, 'buying a house can be the best investment of your life' (*The Penguin Money Book*, p. 57).

Insurance companies

Insurance companies† do two types of business: general insurance (against various forms of risk); and long-term insurance (which is mainly life insurance). These two classes of insurance are distinguished by the ability to the insurer (and the insured) not to renew an insurance contract in the case of general insurance, and by the long-term commitment of both insurer and insured in the case of long-term (life) insurance (but note that *all* life insurance, most but not all of which is contractually for long periods, is classified as 'long-term' business).

There are six categories of general insurance, as shown in Table 13.4. Motor-vehicle insurance (which is compulsory by law, at least to the minimum standard of claims which

TABLE 13.4 *General insurance business of insurers incorporated in the United Kingdom, '1974'*[a]

Category of business	£ million		Percentage of total	
	Premiums	Claims	Premiums	Claims
Motor-vehicle	938	586	33.8	36.5
Property (e.g. fire and theft)	868	428	31.3	26.7
Marine, aviation and transport	337	249	12.2	15.5
Pecuniary loss	186	98	6.7	6.1
Personal accident	73	36	2.6	2.2
Re-insurance (not included above)	370	208	13.3	13.0
Total	2,772	1,605	100.0	100.0

Holdings of general funds at book value at end-1973   £3,186m.

[a] Aggregate of figures for companies' accounting years ending in the period 1 September 1974 to 31 August 1975 (accounting year varies among companies).

Sources: Central Statistical Office, *Annual Abstract of Statistics 1982 Edition*, table 17.47, pp. 446–47; Central Statistical Office, *Financial Statistics*, March 1976, table 74, p. 86.

* At 1980–1 tax rates.

†Such as: Prudential, Commercial Union, Legal & General, Norwich Union, Guardian Royal Exchange, Sun Alliance & London, Royal, General Accident, and Eagle Star, to name but a few of the largest.

others may have against the driver, though many drivers have comprehensive insurance covering also damage to, or theft of, their own vehicle) is one of the biggest categories of business, quite closely followed by property insurance (fire or other damage and theft). The other four are: (a) marine, aviation and transport (insurance of goods in transit); (b) pecuniary loss; (c) personal accident; and (d) re-insurance.

As you can see in Table 13.4 (which is an incomplete set of accounts), the annual income from premiums was more than sufficient in 1974 to cover the cost of claims. But in addition to the cost of claims, insurers have to meet all their administrative costs (although they have some extra income from the interest on the assets which they own). Table 13.4 also shows (in the last row) the book value of assets held against general insurance liabilities. It is clearly highly undesirable to try to run an insurance business solely on the basis of paying claims out of premium income without having a 'cushion' of financial (and other) assets, so insurers must hold assets, and Table 13.4 shows their substantial assets held against the liabilities which could arise on account of their general business.

Life assurance (as discussed in Chapter 3) is also big business. Table 13.5 shows that in 1973–4 nearly 19 million life policies were held with insurance companies in the United Kingdom, the total sum assured being nearly £64 billion, or an average of £3,361 per policy (bear in mind that many of the policies will have been taken out quite some while ago before inflation took hold). There were also 2½ million annuities paying an average of £919 a year. Against these liabilities, insurance companies held £19.7 billion of assets – a much greater sum than in the case of general insurance. There is, of course, no need for assets held to be equal to liabilities because annual life insurance claims will mostly be paid out of annual premiums received – but in the case of endowment assurance, the assets must be built up to repay the assured at the maturity of the policy.

TABLE 13.5   *Life assurance and annuities in the United Kingdom, 1973–4*

	1973–4 [a]
Life policies: number of policies, [b] thousands	18,980
Total sum assured, £ million	63,793.5
Annuities: [c] number in thousands	2,485
Annuities: [c] per annum, £ million	2,282.8
Average capital sum assured per policy, £	3,361
Average annuity per annuitant, £ per annum	919
Long-term funds, holding at book value at end-1973, £ million	19,732

[a] Aggregate of figures for companies' accounting years ending in the period 1 September 1973 to 31 August 1974 (accounting year varies among companies).
[b] Policies with and without profits.
[c] Both immediate and deferred.

Sources: Central Statistical Office, *Annual Abstract of Statistics 1981 Edition*, table 17.47, p. 448; Central Statistical Office, *Financial Statistics*, March 1976, table 74, p. 86.

Table 13.6 shows a more complete set of business accounts for both general insurance and long-term insurance in 1974 (accounting year). General insurance has a much bigger annual premium income than claims paid, but its expenses of management (with its need for time-consuming inspections and verification of claims) are proportionately heavier and its interest and other income is proportionately lower. The annual surplus of general insurance is not all that large relatively, though there is a surplus part of which can be used to build up a cushion of assets. Long-term insurance has a smaller annual flow of premium income than does general insurance, but it has a much bigger annual flow of interest (etc.) income, mostly the result of its much greater holding of assets (£19.7 billion versus £3.2

TABLE 13.6   *Revenue and expenditure of insurers incorporated in the United Kingdom, 1974* [a]

	£ million		Percentage of total income	
	General insurance	Long-term insurance	General insurance	Long-term insurance
Income				
Premium income	3,161 [b]	2,622	93.5	64.7
Interest, dividends, rent, and other income	218	1,432	6.5	35.3
Total income	3,379	4,054	100.0	100.0
Expenditure				
Claims paid	1,824 [b]	1,654	54.0	40.8
Expenses of management and commission	926	483	27.4	11.9
Taxation and other	156	141 [c]	4.6	3.5
Total expenditure	2,906	2,278	86.0	56.2
Surplus: balance	473	1,776 [d]	14.0	43.8

[a] Aggregate of figures for companies' accounting years ending in the period 1 September 1974 to 31 August 1975 (accounting year varies among companies).

[b] This figure does not match the total premium income or claims paid for general insurance given in Table 13.4; the difference may arise from an exemption in Table 13.4 to mutual insurers from submitting fully detailed accounts, whose detailed income and claims paid are consequently there excluded but whose aggregate income and claims paid are here included.

[c] Excluding transfers to investment reserves.

[d] Including transfers to investment reserves.

Source: Central Statistical Office, *Annual Abstract of Statistics 1982 Edition*, tables 17.41 and 17.42, pp. 441–2.

billion). This is where compound interest will be building up the endowments of the assured (see Diagrams 3.2 and 3.3). The proportion of income going in management expenses is much lower for long-term insurance (the state system of registration of death helps here), and long-term insurance has, of course, a very large annual inflow into investment reserves; it is slightly misleading to call this a surplus because most of it 'belongs' to insured persons who are building up an endowment policy.

All this gives a descriptive picture of the size and importance of the insurance business in the United Kingdom. What of its analysis?

Insurance is a type of financial intermediation, albeit with rather peculiar characteristics. It is, very obviously, based on highly expert and specialist risk assessment. In return for a premium (which is neither a returnable deposit nor the acquisition of a marketable asset), the insured obtains for a specified period a contingent claim against the insurer – a sort of financial asset in potentiality (in the event that the insured-against contingency actually occurs). If a claim materialises, the insured is not a *net* gainer because the claim merely compensates for a loss sustained. By on-lending the premiums, the insurer can earn interest, and so reduce the premium which it is necessary to charge in order to remain solvent. However, all insurance premiums, except for the long-term saving element of endowment life assurance, are charged as expenditure in the personal-sector income and expenditure account (see Table 3.3), and so do not figure as part of the financial surplus of the insured. This makes sense because there is no *net* asset acquisition in the case of insurance claims. So, in respect of this premium income, insurance companies are not acting as financial intermediaries between entities in financial surplus and entities in financial deficit (although they do provide funds to those in deficit). Because the claim which the insured has is only a claim contingent upon certain eventualities, the question of liquidity does not arise for the insured. However, the question of liquidity is very important for the insurer; or, rather, it might be better to say that the insurer needs to have a portfolio of assets which, while earning the highest return possible, is nevertheless sufficiently liquid to permit the insurer to meet all claims arising. It is important for an insurance company to earn a high rate of return on its assets because (providing the administrative costs for any given type of insurance are uniform among companies) a higher rate of return on investments should lead to lower premiums charged (while still remaining profitable), and so to a competitive advantage over other companies in the market for that type of insurance.

This being acknowledged, liquidity is an important consideration in the portfolio of assets held by insurance companies against their contingent liabilities. (Note that considerations of liquidity clash with the desire to earn the highest possible rate of return on financial assets because, generally speaking, rates of interest will be higher the less liquid is the asset – higher rates of interest can be charged on long-term loans than on short-term loans.) Table 13.7 shows the portfolios of assets which insurance companies in the United Kingdom hold against their contingent liabilities both in general insurance and in long-term (life) insurance. The last two columns show the percentage structure of the two portfolios at end-1980, and it is quite clear that a far higher proportion of assets held against general (contingent) liabilities is held in liquid assets than is the case for assets held against long-term (contingent) liabilities of life assurance. To illustrate, in general funds 10.8 per cent of assets were short-term liquid assets (mainly bank deposits), while only 3 per cent of long-term funds were so held; in general funds 9.6 per cent of general funds were in British government securities with five years or less to maturity, while only 1 per cent of long-term funds were so held; conversely, long-term funds held a far higher proportion of long-dated British government securities, and also had a higher proportion of assets in (illiquid but profitable) real estate.

TABLE 13.7   *Insurance companies' investments (assets) held against liabilities, end-1980*

| | Holdings at market values, end-1980 | | | |
| | £ million | | Percentage of total | |
Investment (asset)	General funds [a]	Long-term funds [b]	General funds	Long-term funds
Short-term (liquid) assets [c]	1,248	1,616	10.8	3.0
British government securities				
Up to 5 years' maturity	1,101	513	9.6	1.0
Over 5 and up to 15 years	1,113	3,601	9.7	6.7
Over 15 years and undated	563	10,517	4.9	19.6
Total	2,777	14,632	24.1	27.2
UK company securities	2,743	16,599	23.8	30.9
Unit trust units	13	1,380	0.1	2.6
Overseas securities	937	2,186	8.1	4.1
Land, property and ground rents	1,280	12,362	11.1	23.0
All other investments	2,518	4,971	21.9	9.2
Total investments	11,516	53,746	100.0	100.0

[a] Funds held against general insurance liabilities.
[b] Funds held mostly against life assurance.
[c] Mostly bank balance.

Source: Central Statistical Office, *Financial Statistics*, October 1981, table 8.13, pp. 101–2.

Superannuation funds

Like insurance companies' long-term funds, superannuation (pension) funds have definite long-term liabilities, and against these they need to maintain a portfolio of assets which will earn the highest possible rate of return (many of the superannuation funds are managed by insurance companies; but this business is reported separately). The falling due of superannuation funds' liabilities is known well in advance, so the portfolio need not contain much by way of liquid assets. If we look in Table 13.8 at the proportionate structure of assets held by superannuation funds, we can see that this is indeed the case, with small proportions in short-term assets and large proportions in long-term and relatively illiquid assets.

We saw in Table 3.14 the cash inflows and outflows from the life assurance and superannuation funds. In general, these funds have a large annual surplus of incomings over outgoings and it is this surplus which is invested (on behalf of the personal sector) in the assets shown in Tables 13.7 (second column) and 13.8.

One feature worth noting is the large proportion of long-term funds (life assurance) and superannuation funds held as UK company securities. Consistently, since information first became available in 1964, the personal sector has each year been a net seller of company (and overseas) securities on a quite substantial absolute scale (though personal-sector annual disposals are probably not a large proportion of their total holdings), while equally consistently the life assurance and superannuation funds have annually acquired company (and overseas) securities on a large scale (Appendix 13.1). Consequently, these 'institutional investors' – as they are called – have become important with regard to company dividend and other policy; for example, institutional investors often play a decisive role in (contested) takeover bids.

TABLE 13.8   *Superannuation funds' investments (assets) held against liabilities, end-1980*

	Holdings at market values, end-1980	
Investment (asset)	£ million	Percentage of total
Short-term (liquid) assets [a]	1,934	3.5
British government securities		
Up to 5 years' maturity	277	0.5
Over 5 and up to 15 years	3,306	6.0
Over 15 years and undated	8,140	14.9
Total	11,723	21.4
UK company securities	25,074	45.8
Unit trust units and property unit trusts	1,722	3.1
Overseas securities	4,401	8.0
Land, property and ground rents	8,170	14.9
All other investments	1,688	3.1
Total investments	54,712	100.0

[a] Net of short-term liabilities and long-term borrowing.

Source: Central Statistical Office, *Financial Statistics*, January 1982, table 8.12, p. 100.
These figures are revised figures and may not be fully comparable with the unrevised (and mainly flow) data reported elsewhere.

Other financial intermediaries

We come now to the group of relatively smaller financial institutions: investment trusts, unit trusts, property unit trusts, trustee savings banks, and finance houses. Investment

TABLE 13.9　*Assets of some other financial institutions, end-1979*

	£ million (market values)				
	Investment trusts	Unit trusts	Property unit trusts	Trustee savings banks	Finance houses [a]
Short-term (liquid) assets	243 [b]	248	143	2,262.3 [c]	105
British government securities	260	45	—	1,810.6	—
Listed (Stock Exchange) securities	3,333	2,578	—	222.9 [d]	—
Other UK financial assets	286	17	49	1,508.7 [e]	3,362 [f]
Property	17	—	757	—	—
Overseas securities	1,856	657	—	—	—
Total [g]	5,995	3,545	949	5,804.5	3,467

[a] Including other consumer credit companies.
[b] Includes £38 million overseas net short-term assets.
[c] Comprises: cash, balances with National Debt Office, balances with UK banks and with Central Trustee Savings Bank.
[d] Quoted local authority stock and negotiable bonds only.
[e] Most (£939.9 million) of which is unquoted local authority debt; value of premises included here.
[f] Comprising loans and advances to UK residents, £1,815 million (54 per cent) of which is to individuals (including unincorporated businesses) and £1,307 million (39 per cent) of which is to industrial and commercial companies.
[g] Some of the totals here do not exactly match the holdings as given in Table 13.1 but the differences are very slight.

Sources: Central Statistical Office, *Financial Statistics*, April 1981, tables 8.2, 8.9, 8.11, and 8.12, pp. 87, 96, 98 and 99–100; data on finance houses and other consumer credit agencies from Central Statistical Office, *Annual Abstract of Statistics 1982 Edition*, table 17.24, p. 435, obtained by adding net acquisitions to end-1976 holdings.

trusts and unit trusts (see Chapter 3) fall into Revell's class of portfolio institutions – they obtain funds from investors and with those funds they acquire mostly company securities; this is clearly shown by their asset structure in Table 13.9. By going through this type of financial intermediary, the investor obtains a combination of expert risk assessment and portfolio management. Property unit trusts perform a similar function, but they obtain funds only from pension funds and charities (tax-exempt bodies) and use these funds to invest in commercial property.

While unit trusts, investment trusts and property unit trusts are for investors prepared to take a chance on fluctuations in asset valuation (the hope being, of course, for a rise in valuation, but this must be at the risk of a possible loss), the trustee savings banks are for the 'small' saver who does not wish to risk a capital loss and who wants, accordingly, a guarantee of the nominal value of his or her savings. This means that the trustee savings banks must invest largely in securities having a similar face-value guarantee, and in turn this means largely investing in British government securities. However, the Trustee Savings Banks Act 1976 gave the trustee savings banks power to act more independently and since then they have branched out into making loans to customers.

The finance houses are financial intermediaries who are mainly concerned with financing consumer credit or 'hire purchase', but they also make loans to industrial and commercial companies for the purchase of machinery and plant. Finance houses tend to borrow 'wholesale' from banks, from industrial and commercial companies, and from other financial institutions (i.e. they tend to take only large deposits) on which they can pay a quite high rate of interest because the cost to the user of consumer credit is also quite high.

The Stock Exchange

So far we have described briefly the main financial intermediaries (other than banks), but of course these financial intermediaries and other entities are engaged in a considerable amount of trading in 'second-hand' securities, as well as in subscribing to new issues of securities (of which more shortly). We pointed out earlier how the liquidity, or attractiveness, of a security could be enhanced if there were a second-hand market on which it could be sold. The market in second-hand securities in the United Kingdom is known as The Stock Exchange, and Table 13.10 shows the very large volume of business which it does annually. During 1980 there were over $5\frac{1}{2}$ million transactions (which, on 254 working days, works out at about 22,000 per day) involving the purchase and the sale (duplicated figure) of about £196 billion worth of securities, or if we omit the duplication by halving the figure we could say that sales of second-hand securities during 1980 were £98 billion. We can also see that, during 1980, trading in British government and government-guaranteed securities was far more active relative to the value of stock outstanding than was trading in company securities.

TABLE 13.10 *Securities and transactions on The Stock Exchange,* [a] *1980*

	£ million		Number of transactions 1980, thousands
	Market value of securities quoted, March 1980 [b]	Turnover [c] during 1980	
British government and government guaranteed stocks	57,766	155,517	1,064
Other stocks, inc. overseas governments	11,760	8,219	76
Company securities	210,804	32,551	4,568
Total	280,330	196,287	5,708

[a] 'The Stock Exchange' comprises (since 1973) the union of the stock exchanges of the United Kingdom and the Republic of Ireland.

[b] This is the market value of all securities 'listed' on The Stock Exchange, e.g. the total of shares in company A times the market price per share.

[c] 'Turnover' means the sum of sales *and* purchases; it would seem sensible to halve the figures here given and to avoid duplication, but the table follows the official practice.

Sources: Central Statistical Office, *Annual Abstract of Statistics 1982 Edition*, table 7.14, p. 430; Central Statistical Office, *Financial Statistics*, January 1982, table 12.2, p. 127.

The Stock Exchange is therefore an important market, especially to the government. It operates through 'members' of The Stock Exchange who are divided between 'stockbrokers' who act as agents for the public who want to buy or sell securities and 'stockjobbers' who sell and buy securities to or from brokers (and other jobbers). In order to do this jobbers will carry a 'book' of (temporarily) owned shares – a risky business in a falling market but highly profitable in a rising market.

The Stock Exchange is not only the market for second-hand securities; it is also a market on which new securities can be 'issued' or 'floated'. For company (and other non-government) securities this may be done via a 'public issue' in which a company itself offers directly to the public a fixed number of shares (or securities) at a stated price with a published prospectus including an application form. The application may not be at a stated price but at a price to be tendered by the prospective purchaser, in which case it is an 'issue by tender'. Or the new issue may be done via an 'offer for sale' in which a company sells all its shares to an issuing house or stockbroker who then on-sells the shares in The Stock Exchange. An issuing house is an institution, often a (branch of a) merchant bank, which specialises in this 'wholesale' purchase and 'retail' selling of new securities. Or the issue taken up by the issuing house may be directly placed with clients of the issuing house; this is known as a 'placing' and it may be used only for relatively small issues. Finally, there is the 'rights issue' (see Chapter 4) in which a company already listed on The Stock Exchange offers its shareholders the right to subscribe cash for further shares in proportion to their existing shareholdings.* Shareholders not wishing to exercise their rights may sell them (but it is generally advisable, if ever you are offered a rights issue, to subscribe if you can because the rights issue is generally at a discount and there is likely to be a quick capital gain).

Nearly all new issues are 'underwritten', or insured against not being fully subscribed to, by underwriters (who may be drawn from a wide variety of financial institutions). The underwriters charge a small insurance premium called a 'commission': if the issue is fully subscribed, the underwriters take their commission and depart; if not, they take their commission and buy the (remaining) securities, the disposal of which is then their problem. If an underwriter defaults on the undertaking, the take-up of securities becomes the responsibility of the issuing house.

The government also uses The Stock Exchange in its issuing of securities, but is less dependent on it. Nearly all issues of government stock are made by public offer, often at a tender price. Government issues do not suffer the indignity (or the cost) of being underwritten; any surplus stock left unsold is taken up by the New Issue Department of the Bank of England and is subsequently sold on The Stock Exchange in response to bids from jobbers requiring government securities; this remaining stock is referred to as a 'tap' stock.

Although shares are not redeemable by the company issuing them, most other securities and all government securities (with the exception of a few historical issues) do have a date on (or period in) which they must be 'redeemed' – bought back at face-value from the owner. So that, for example, the government has each year to issue securities not only to finance the government borrowing requirement for that year but also to finance the redemption of stock issued in the past and now falling due.

Table 13.11 shows the flow of issues, the flow of redemptions, and issues *less* redemptions (i.e. the flow of net new money raised) of non-government securities and of British government securities. It is clearly apparent that the activity in government securities is very much larger than that in non-government securities. During 1980 the government sold nearly £15 billion (gross) of securities, say an average of £58½ million each working day.† But one-quarter of this was effectively used in the redemption of stock at or near maturity (the government often buys back stock near to maturity date in order to even out

TABLE 13.11   *Issues and redemptions of securities in the United Kingdom, 1980*

	£ million
Non-government securities *(a)* (wholly Stock Exchange)	
Gross issues	2,083
Redemptions	1,310
Issues *less* redemptions	773
Government securities (partly Stock Exchange)	
Gross issues	14,851
Redemptions	3,606
Issues *less* redemptions	11,245

(a) Excludes international issues.

Source: Central Statistical Office, *Financial Statistics*, October 1981, tables 3.9 and 12.1, pp. 39 and 124.

*For companies whose securities are already listed on The Stock Exchange and who wish to raise further capital, it is now (Companies Act 1980, sections 17 to 19) a statutory requirement that the company shall first offer existing shareholders the right to subscribe, within at least twenty-one days, to the new issue in proportion to their existing holding (similar 'pre-emption rights' are given to shareholders in private companies when further capital is – privately – to be raised).

†The number of Stock Exchange working days is given in *Financial Statistics*, table 12.2: 254 during 1980.

these transactions). Only three-quarters, £11.2 billion, was 'new money' available to finance the government's borrowing requirement.

One-third (34.6 per cent) of this £11.2 billion was taken up by life assurance and superannuation funds (see Table 13.12). One-fifth (20.9 per cent) was taken up directly by the personal sector (but bear in mind it is also the personal sector's financial surplus which is being, indirectly, channelled through the life assurance and superannuation funds). It is important to note that banks, including the discount market, took up 13.6 per cent of the net issue of government securities. Other financial institutions (including the savings banks) took up 11.5 per cent of the £11.2 billion, and 13.3 per cent was taken up by the overseas sector. So the government relies mainly for its finance on the personal-sector financial surplus (indirectly and directly) but also borrows from a variety of other sources. This borrowing via the issuing of securities is, of course, facilitated by the existence of an active market on The Stock Exchange in second-hand securities: that is, the possibility of being able readily to sell the securities enhances their attractiveness.

TABLE 13.12 *Net take-up of British government securities by sector, 1980*

Government securities issued to *less* redemptions from	£ million	Percentage of total
Life assurance and superannuation funds	3,888	34.6
Banks and discount market	1,528	13.6
Other financial institutions (inc. savings banks)	1,294	11.5
Personal sector [a]	2,345	20.9
Industrial and commercial companies [b]	133	1.2
Overseas sector	1,498	13.3
Other [c]	559	5.0
Total	11,245	100.0

[a] See Table 3.7, line 10.
[b] See Table 4.10, line 6.
[c] Including other public-sector transactions *plus* take-up by Bank of England and National Debt Commissioners *plus* sinking funds.

Source: Central Statistical Office, *Financial Statistics*, October 1981, table 3.9, p. 39.

The new issue market for non-government securities is generally dominated by industrial and commercial companies. Table 13.13 shows this pattern for 1980, but it tends to hold in other years as well. Note that in 1980 local authorities and public corporations redeemed more stock than they issued and so have a negative figure. Again, the ability to issue such securities is greatly facilitated by the market which The Stock Exchange provides.

TABLE 13.13 *Net issuing by sector of (non-government) securities, 1980*

Issues *less* redemptions by	£ million
Industrial and commercial companies [a]	939.3
Financial companies	−7.2
Local authorities and public corporations	−164.9
Overseas borrowers	6.0
Total	773.2

[a] See Tables 4.10 (line 12, beware signs) or Table 4.11 (lines 8 and 9); figure there is all-inclusive for industrial and commercial companies, and so is slightly larger than present figure, which refers only to capital issues on The Stock Exchange.

Source: Central Statistical Office, *Financial Statistics*, October 1981, table 12.1, pp. 124–5.

These, in brief, are the financial institutions other than banks. But, as a group, the banking sector holds more assets/liabilities than all the other financial intermediaries put together, and so they warrant consideration at greater length.

The banks and money transmission

Banks are the largest group of financial intermediaries because they not only engage in financial intermediation but also provide a money transmission service which is of very great importance. In order to understand banks, it is not sufficient to describe them as financial intermediaries which accept short-term deposits from lenders and which then on-lend, mostly on a short-term basis, to various borrowers. The banks' prime role is *not* that of financial intermediation (although this role is important); their prime role, the role upon which their size and importance are based, is that of providing a money transmission service. The money transmission service has two aspects:

(a) that of cash distribution – providing notes and coin to those who need cash (and receiving back notes and coin surplus to customers' requirements);
(b) that of providing a means for non-cash payments (exemplified by the use of cheques).

In order to discuss the money transmission service further, we need briefly to dicuss money itself.

Money is what money does. What does money do? Money is used as a means of payment – a means to settle (discharge) obligations. In most countries there are two forms of money: legal tender; and other means of payment. Legal tender comprises coin and bank notes of the country concerned: this means of payment is called 'cash' or legal tender because residents of the country are legally obliged to accept cash in settlement of debts owed to them. While cash is used as a means of payment in most transactions (by number), it is generally used only in transactions of relatively small average size; and non-cash means of payment are used in a larger proportion of transactions by value. The most common means of non-cash payment is by a 'cheque' 'drawn' on a deposit at a bank.

A cheque is an instruction to the banker to transfer the sum stated on the cheque from the deposit of the drawer to the deposit of the 'payee' – the person to whom the cheque is payable. Alternatively, the cheque may instruct the banker to pay cash to the payee.

A cheque must be unconditional (that is, it cannot have conditions attached which must be fulfilled before the banker effects payment); a cheque must be addressed by one 'person' to another 'person' – here 'person' is legally interpreted to cover legal entities; a cheque must be for a sum certain in cash and must be signed by or on behalf of the drawer (cheques generally must have the amount written in words *and* numbers (if there is a discrepancy, the words have priority) and in law the drawer owes a duty to his bank to use reasonable care in drawing cheques so as not to facilitate additions or alterations; finally, cheques must bear a date, the banks having a normal practice of not accepting cheques dated more than six months previously. The bank has a duty to the drawer to pay, or 'honour', the cheque providing that the cheque is presented within reasonable time and that there are sufficient funds on deposit to cover the cheque and providing that the drawer has not 'stopped' the cheque by a countermanding order; notification in any way of the drawer's death also stops all cheques – in this case the cheque will be returned to the payee for settlement by the deceased's personal representative.

There are other circumstances in which a bank may refuse to accept the instructions on a cheque (e.g. notification that the drawer has become of unsound mind, or if the bank receives notice of bankruptcy proceedings against the drawer – in which case the bankrupt's property passes into the control of the Official Receiver). But these legal technicalities apart, a customer who opens an account with a bank on which cheques can be drawn has in law an implied contract that the bank will pay cheques drawn in correct form providing there are funds available. If there are insufficient funds available to cover the cheque, that is another matter: the banker may then return the cheque to the payee marked 'RD' – referred to drawer – in which case the payee must contact the drawer (the bank will not dicuss the drawer's affairs). But this implied contract makes cheques into a very useful instrument; provided that the payee will accept a cheque, payment can be quickly and conveniently made without the inconvenience of carrying large sums in cash.

If a payee banks with one bank and the drawer banks with another, then the value of the cheque is normally credited to the payee's account when paid (the bank can cancel this credit if the cheque is not honoured) and the cheque is then sent to the 'clearing house' – jointly funded premises – where cheques are sorted and 'cleared' for transmission to the drawer's bank. On receipt, the drawer's bank debits the drawer's account. The banks then settle among themselves the net debts incurred in clearing: for example, if Barclays Bank depositors draw in a day £100 million payable to Lloyds Bank depositors, and Lloyds Bank depositors draw in a day £80 million payable to Barclays Bank depositors, then Barclays Bank will, after clearing, pay the £20 million difference to Lloyds Bank. Payment by cheque is known as a 'debit transfer' because after being credited to the payee's account the cheque goes through the clearing system as an instruction to debit the drawer's account.

Payment by cheque is the most common means by which banks effect non-cash payment, but there are others. The *credit transfer* is an instruction given at the bank where the account is held to transfer a stated sum of money to the account of a (named) person at another (named) bank: for example, credit transfers are widely used for payment of wages and salaries – the employee simply has his or her account credited with after-tax pay (and does not receive a cheque from the employer). Many credit transfers are done by computers; it is called a 'credit transfer' because it goes through the clearing system as an instruction to credit the payee's account. The *standing order* – a variation of the credit transfer – is an instruction given by the account holder *regularly* to pay a specified sum to a specified payee; this is widely used by households to pay mortgage interest, life assurance premiums, or local authority rates. The *direct debit* is an instruction given by the account-holder to the bank to permit the payee directly to request an unstated amount for a specific purpose from the account-holder's account (relatively few institutions are granted access to direct-debit facilities). *Credit cards* are another means of effecting payments. In this case the bank or credit-card agency pays the supplier, and subsequently obtains payment from the credit-card user. A *banker's draft* may be used for important large-value payments where the payee will not wait for a cheque to be cleared before the amount is credited to the payee's account. A banker's draft is a cheque drawn by a bank on its own head office; this will be immediately credited to the payee's account – bankers' drafts can be telephoned to the payee's bank, and this method of payment is often used in house purchase.

In all these ways, the banks provide a very important and convenient money – means of payment – transmission service. The banks estimated that they made about 2¼ billion payments by all these means in 1976 in Great Britain, that the money transmission service used about 60 per cent of their staff (i.e. about 120,000 employees), cost about £800 million in 1976 to operate, and required about £1,000 million worth of capital equipment (*The London Clearing Banks*, Evidence by the Committee of London Clearing Bankers to the Committee to Review the Functioning of Financial Institutions, Longman, 1978, p. 35). The total of inter-bank debit and credit clearings in 1976 was £2,232,232 million (this excludes cheques paid by a customer of a bank to another customer of the same bank and so understates the size of the money transmission service – *Annual Abstract of Statistics 1982 Edition*, table 17.3, p. 419).

How many banks?

Counting the number of 'banks' in the United Kingdom is a problematic task, Table 13.1 showed the count from the official list in *Financial Statistics Explanatory Handbook 1981 Edition*, pp. 63–6, which gives a tally of 373; but the Banking Act 1979 provides for official recognition and licensing (by the Bank of England) of deposit-taking institutions, only some of which will be able to use the unqualified word 'bank' in their title, while others will have to attach the term 'licensed deposit-taking institution', and in the first list issued under this Act there were 281 'Recognised Banks' and 297 'Licensed Deposit-taking Institutions', with several pending a decision. The student may be surprised that the numbers are so large, but the list includes many British financial institutions such as merchant banks and finance houses as well as all the multitude of overseas banks operating in London.

In any case, however the classification of the banking sector may change, the only banks which matter significantly in terms of deposits and the UK economy are the six London clearing banks: the 'big four' of Barclays Bank Plc, Lloyds Bank Plc, Midland Bank Plc, and National Westminster Bank Plc, and the two smaller banks, Coutts & Co. (which is a wholly owned subsidiary of the National Westminster) and Williams & Glyn's Bank Plc (16 per cent of the shares in which are owned by Lloyds Bank). They are called 'the London clearing banks' because they fund the operation in London of sorting and 'clearing' cheques between banks. We should mention also the Scottish clearing banks (Bank of Scotland [35 per cent of which is owned by Barclays Bank], Clydesdale Bank Plc [owned by the Midland Bank] and the Royal Bank of Scotland Plc [16 per cent owned by Lloyds]); the Northern Ireland banks (Allied Irish Banks Plc, Bank of Ireland, Northern Bank [owned by the Midland Bank], and Ulster Bank [owned by National Westminster]); and the Co-operative Bank, the National Girobank and the Trustee Savings Bank to complete the list of the institutions that most UK residents would call 'banks' (but the 1979 Banking Act does not apply to the trustee savings banks, which are subject to their own separate Trustee Savings Bank Act).

There are two types of accounts which a person may hold with a bank: *sight deposits* (popularly known as 'current account') which are transferable or withdrawable on demand; and *time deposits*, which are all other deposits (most of these are the deposit-account facility). Cheques, standing orders, etc., may usually be drawn only on sight deposits. Interest is not usually paid on sight deposits, but is paid on time deposits. Theoretically, seven days' notice is required to make a withdrawal from a time deposit, but this can be waived at the cost of a slight penalty of interest forgone. Because time deposits are reasonably readily available, they tend to be counted as 'near-money' from a means of payment point of view: if there are insufficient funds in a customer's sight deposit but sufficient funds in his or her time deposit, a bank will normally honour a cheque drawn in excess of the funds in the current account because it has in law a *lien* on the deposit account (time deposit) to the extent of the 'overdraft' created on the current account (sight deposit). (A *lien* is a right in law to retain possession of property until a debt due in respect of the property is discharged.)

Although the money transmission service is the important facility provided by banks, they are also financial intermediaries, taking in deposits and then on-lending most of what they take in. There are two main ways in which banks in the United Kingdom lend money. The first is a straightforward loan, where a certain agreed sum of money is lent, generally with an agreed date for repayment and an agreed rate of interest to be charged. The loan will be credited to the borrower's current account and a special loan (debit) account will be established in the borrower's name, to be paid off in due course as agreed. The second is the overdraft facility: in this the bank agrees that a customer can go into debit on his or her current account, or can 'overdraw' the account. There will usually be an agreed limit to the extent to which the customer can overdraw. The borrower then draws cheques as required, and interest will be charged each day at $r/365$ on the amount by which the account is overdrawn at close of business (where r is the proportionate rate of interest per annum chargeable to such borrowing). Very often the borrower will use only a part of the agreed overdraft limit. The overdraft form of lending is a convenient and flexible form of lending.*

Because banks' liabilities to their depositors are very short-term liabilities, banks prefer their loans and advances (as used overdrafts are called) also to be fairly short term, often with the aspect of being 'self-liquidating' – such as financing the purchase of inventories where the loan can be repaid out of selling the goods so acquired, or such as a 'bridging loan' where a person has to pay for a house before having sold the old house (the bridging loan can be repaid when the house is sold). However, banks have recently branched out into some more long-term lending, particularly for house purchase, so the old pattern of short-term loans only is changing.

The money supply

The stocks of means of payment in the United Kingdom at end-1980 are shown in Table 13.14. There are three possible measures of the stock of means of payment. The first, known as M_1, comprises only notes and coin in circulation with the public *plus* private-sector sight deposits in sterling (i.e. where the banks' liability is a liability denominated in sterling). The second is known as sterling M_3 (sometimes abbreviated $£M_3$) and this comprises M_1 *plus* private-sector sterling time deposits *plus* all public-sector deposits. The third measure is known simply as M_3 (i.e. without the prefix 'sterling'), and it comprises sterling M_3 *plus* residents' deposits in other currencies (i.e. where the banks'

TABLE 13.14 *Stocks of means of payment – money stock – in the United Kingdom, end-1980*

Amount outstanding (not seasonally adjusted)	£ million	Percentage of M_3
Notes and coin in circulation with the public (legal tender)	10,425	13.7
UK private-sector sterling sight deposits with banks	20,805	27.4
Money stock, M_1 (total of two above)	31,230	41.1
Private-sector sterling time deposits with banks	36,766	48.4
Public-sector sight and time deposits with banks	1,595	2.1
Money stock, sterling M_3 (M_1 *plus* two above)	69,591	91.6
UK residents' deposits in other currencies	6,383	8.4
Money stock, M_3 (sterling M_3 *plus* above)	75,974	100.0

Source: Central Statistical Office, *Financial Statistics*, October 1981, table 7.1, p. 74.

* Banks usually quote a (variable) rate of interest on overdrafts as 'base rate' (see below, p. 619) *plus* one to five percentage points (depending on the status of the borrower – i.e. the borrower is given an interest *rating* rather than an interest rate); for loans, on the other hand, banks must by law give an annual percentage rate (APR) of interest (fixed for the duration of the loan). Note also that interest on overdrafts is charged on what is known as the 'cleared balance', the balance *after* allowing three *working* days for any cheques (debit transfers) paid in to be cleared; for example, if you have an overdraft of £100 and on a Monday you pay in a cheque (not cash) for £100 then (despite the £100 being – provisionally, as it were – credited immediately to your account on Monday) you will pay interest on the £100 overdraft at the close of business on Monday to Wednesday inclusive; on Thursday the cheque will have been 'cleared' and your overdraft will, for purposes of charging interest, have been eliminated. Clearing covering a weekend will take five calendar days, during which interest will be charged; the banks generally 'average' this and tell customers that the cleared balance takes four 'days' (unspecified).

liability to the depositor is denominated in a currency other than sterling; before the abolition of foreign exchange controls with effect from 24 October 1979, these deposits were mainly those of multinational companies – residents could not legally hold foreign currency for more than a certain length of time – but UK residents may now hold foreign currency deposits, and this component may grow as a hedge against depreciation in the external value of sterling). Foreign currency deposits can easily be switched to sterling, so it should be counted as a means of payment.*

Table 13.14 shows that 41.1 per cent of the UK total stock of means of payment was in the form of legal tender and private-sector sight deposits, and a further 48.4 per cent was in the form of private-sector time deposits. To put it another way, private-sector sight and time deposits accounted for three-quarters of the UK means of payment. The division of private-sector deposits between sight and time deposits is determined by the deposit-holders themselves; so what matters for the economic analysis of the stock of means of payment are the forces which determine the size of, and changes in, private-sector sight and time deposits taken together. The amount of legal tender in circulation with the public is determined by the public's need for legal tender to use in transactions (e.g. try paying for your bus fare or a bar of chocolate by cheque) and this need is largely a matter of their convenience (for instance, legal tender in circulation rises by about 4 per cent in mid-December – so before Christmas the banks obtain more notes and coin from the Bank of England to prevent the depletion of their tills as people draw spending-money out, and after Christmas as the traders pay in all the notes and coin the banks send the surplus cash back to the Bank of England).

In order to understand what determines the size of private-sector bank deposits (sight *plus* time), we need to introduce one more actor to the scene: the Bank of England.

The Bank of England

The Bank of England is the United Kingdom's central bank. The essential functions of a central bank are twofold: first it is the government's bank; second, it is the bank for other banks. We have already seen (Chapter 9) that, by law, the central government maintains its accounts with the Bank of England (the Consolidated Fund – the government's current account into which all tax receipts must be paid and from which all outgoings must be disbursed; the National Loans Fund – the government's account for borrowings; and the special National Insurance Fund). Central government may maintain working accounts with other banks, but the balances from these are eventually transferred to the Consolidated Fund. We have mentioned earlier in this chapter that after clearing the daily balance of cheques, Barclays may owe Lloyds £20 million; in this case Barclays will draw a cheque (strictly speaking, a banker's draft) on its account with the Bank of England payable to Lloyds, and settlement is effected by Lloyds paying the cheque into its deposit at the Bank of England, and the Bank of England then 'clears' the cheque internally and debits Barclays' account at the Bank of England.

The Bank of England carries out more tasks than simply these two banking operations.

---

* For the inquisitive, M_2 was a measure used previously when a distinction, abandoned in 1972, was made between 'deposit banks' (comprising the London clearing and Scottish and Northern Ireland banks) and all other banks; and M_2 excluded time deposits with other banks. The definitions then ran: M_1 = notes and coin *plus* private-sector sterling sight deposits with all banks (adjusted for transit items); $M_2 = M_1$ *plus* private-sector sterling time deposits with 'deposit banks' and discount houses (but not with 'other banks'); $M_3 = M_2$ *plus* private-sector sterling time deposits with other banks *plus* private-sector non-sterling deposits with all banks *plus* public-sector deposits (see *Bank of England Quarterly Bulletin*: March 1972, pp. 72, 153; September 1971, table 12, p. 398; September 1970, pp. 320–1). A new M_2 – for transactions balances – is to be introduced; *BEQB*, June 1982, p. 224.

Diagram 13.1 shows the main functions of the Bank of England, including the essential ones of being the government's bank and the banks' bank. As the government's bank, the Bank of England operates the Consolidated Fund just as any ordinary bank operates a customer's current account, and it also operates the National Loans Fund, the account which receives all moneys raised by government borrowing – transfers from the National Loans Fund to the Consolidated Fund cover any deficit which the latter may run (the government is not allowed the privilege of an overdraft – its operations being on too large a scale and so needing to be properly covered by a formal system of borrowing, i.e. by due issuing of securities). As part of operating the National Loans Fund, the Bank of England issues government securities: it regularly announces issues of government securities, such as in 1979 the issue of £1,000 million of 15 per cent stock 1985 (i.e. stock bearing interest at 15 per cent per annum and redeemable in 1985), sometimes inviting the public to subscribe by tender. The money which the Bank of England receives from selling new stock is then credited to the National Loans Fund and transferred as required to the Consolidated Fund to cover any deficit. Parts of an issue which are not subscribed are to be sold 'on tap' during the ensuing months. The Bank of England not only issues securities for the government but it will buy back securities, particularly those nearing maturity, in order to smooth out the flow of repayments (it is, even for the government, inconvenient to find £1,000 million all at one go). Buying back government securities also has another purpose which may be important: it provides cash to the sellers of government securities, and there are times when the sellers may need cash. The Bank of England also keeps the register of current holders of government securities so they can be paid the interest due to them.

DIAGRAM 13.1   *The Bank of England*

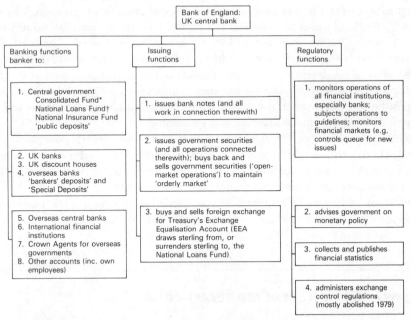

The Bank of England operates the Treasury's Exchange Equalisation Account, which holds the country's official reserves of foreign exchange. If an exporter earns foreign currency, that foreign currency may be changed for sterling (which is the currency in which the exporter must pay his employees, etc.) at the Exchange Equalisation Account (in

*By law, receives all central government receipts (other than those from borrowing) and makes all disbursements for central government expenditure.
†By law, receives all money raised by creation of debt.

practice, the exporter's clearing bank will handle the transaction). If an importer needs foreign currency to settle his debts, then the foreign currency may be obtained in return for sterling at the Exchange Equalisation Account. If the Exchange Equalisation Account requires sterling to pay the exporter, then that money will be drawn from the National Loans Fund. Conversely, sterling received from the importer will be surrendered to the National Loans Fund.

The Bank of England also issues bank notes and undertakes all work in connection with that issue (such as maintaining a register of serial numbers of notes in circulation as a safeguard against forgery). Coin is provided by the Royal Mint, a separate government department.

In addition to all this, the Bank of England acts as banker to certain other institutions (as listed) and is responsible for monitoring and regulating the working of the financial system. It used also to administer the now-abolished regulations concerning the issuing and surrender of foreign currency.

We have not so far mentioned the Bank of England's most important power: this is a power which is seldom used, but its presence and potentiality is an important guarantee of the stability of the banking system. As the bankers' bank, the Bank of England will, if necessary and to any extent, lend (i.e. make cash available) to any bank in need of cash. This is the power to act as 'lender of last resort'. It is easy to appreciate the importance of this power. You have a deposit at bank *X*; you hear rumours that bank *X* is 'in trouble' ('won't be able to meet its deposit liabilities', etc.); you run to be first in the queue to withdraw your deposit and find, to your horror and consternation, that the queue is already three streets long. No problem: the Bank of England stands ready to lend to bank *X* all the cash (legal tender) it needs to satisfy its panicky customers. End of panic. Paradoxically, the very presence of this power means that it has nowadays rarely to be used. This need for the Bank of England to act as lender of last resort was neither understood nor accepted until 1873, when Walter Bagehot published his influential book *Lombard Street: A Description of the Money Market* (especially ch. VII 'A more exact account of the mode in which the Bank of England has discharged its duty to retaining a good bank reserve, and of administering it effectually'). During the nineteenth century financial panics did occur, and Bagehot argued convincingly that the Bank of England had a duty to act as lender of last resort – an argument the Bank eventually accepted.

But because the Bank of England guarantees, in the last resort, your deposit with a clearing bank, this conversely implies that it seeks to impose 'prudent' behaviour on the institutions which it must ultimately support. It seems that nothing in this world is for free: if the banks want the reassurance of ultimate support from the Bank of England, they must follow the Bank of England's requirements as to the conducting of their business. So we must now see what these requirements are and how they work.

Changes to the system of monetary control

Before we can do this we must digress on the change in the system of monetary control which was introduced on 20 August 1981. On this date substantial changes were made to the methods whereby banking operations were controlled: more exactly, a considerable *decontrol* was effected, leaving the banking system freer than had hitherto been the case. This change raises two problems:

1. The system in operation before 20 August 1981 was (relatively) easy to understand: that is, the 'mechanics' of the system could readily be demonstrated (through an exposition of how the reserve asset ratio worked). The new system is less 'mechanical' and is, accordingly, more difficult to grasp.

2. The new system retains some elements of the old system (the special deposits

scheme). Therefore, to try and understand the new system without a thorough grasp of the old system is almost impossible.

The new system gives greater freedom to the banks and, conversely, forces the government to use interest rates more 'vigorously' in its attempt to meet the objectives of monetary policy. It is possible that in the future this feature may prove unacceptable to the government of the day, and that elements of the old 'mechanical' system will be used again (the retention of the special deposits scheme gives the authorities room to do just this). A textbook which expounds (and students who know about) only the new system will then have but half an understanding. Because of these two problems – the need for a groundwork,

and the retention of elements of the old system – we shall proceed first to an exposition of the old system (generally called 'Competition and Credit Control' after the consultative document in which it was initially set forth on 14 May 1971 – see *Bank of England Quarterly Bulletins* for June, September and December 1971), and we shall then describe the modifications made to the old system by the 'Monetary Control' system introduced on 20 August 1981. For convenience a synopsis of the 'Competition and Credit Control' system and the main changes introduced by the new 'Monetary Control' system is given here, but the meaning and purpose of most of the items will not be clear until the basic essentials have been discussed in the following sections.

Competition and Credit Control *(16 September 1971 to 19 August 1981)*		**Monetary Control** *(from 20 August 1981)*

Cash* ratio of $1\frac{1}{2}$ per cent of eligible liabilities, applicable only to London clearing banks		Cash* ratio of $\frac{1}{2}$ per cent of eligible liabilities applicable to the (new) 'monetary sector' comprising:
		    all banks and licensed deposit-takers
		    National Girobank
		    trustee savings banks
		    Banking Department of Bank of England
		    banks in the Channel Islands and Isle of Man opting to join

	plus	for London clearing banks, an unspecified volume of 'operational funds' to be retained voluntarily at the Bank of England for clearing purposes
	plus	for 'eligible banks', an average of 6 per cent of eligible liabilities as secured money with members of the London Discount Market Association and/or as money at call with money brokers and gilt-edged jobbers (the amount held as secured money with the discount market not to fall below 4 per cent of eligible liabilities on any day)
Reserve asset ratio of $12\frac{1}{2}$ per cent of eligible liabilities applicable to all banks in the UK, but for London clearing banks reserve asset ratio includes $1\frac{1}{2}$ per cent cash ratio, and for finance houses reserve asset ratio was 10 per cent of eligible liabilities		Reserve asset ratio abolished but institutions to whom reserve asset ratio formerly applied agree to observe a 'prudent mix' of liquidity
Special deposits: interest-bearing, called as a proportion of eligible liabilities		Special deposits: interest-bearing, applicable to all banks with eligible liabilities of £10 million or more
Supplementary special deposits: non-interest-bearing; called as proportion of interest-bearing eligible liabilities		Supplementary special deposits to be phased out

*Defined as balances with the Bank of England.

Eligible liabilities comprise:
   sterling deposits with original maturity of 2 years or less
   sterling deposits from banks *less* claims on banks
   sterling certificates of deposit issued *less* certificates of deposit held
   net deposit liability in sterling to overseas offices
   net liability in currencies other than sterling *less*
   60 per cent of the net value of transit items in balance-sheet

Eligible liabilities comprise:
   sterling deposits with original maturity of 2 years or less
   sterling deposits from banks *less* claims on banks
   sterling certificates of deposits issued *less* certificates of deposit held
   net deposit liability in sterling to overseas offices
   net liability in currencies other than sterling *less*
   60 per cent of the net value of transit items in balance-sheet
   less
   funds lent by one institution in the 'monetary sector' to another institution in the 'monetary sector'
   less
   money at call placed with money brokers and gilt-edged jobbers in The Stock Exchange and secured on gilt-edged stocks, Treasury bills, local authority bills, and eligible bank bills

Reserve assets comprise
   balances at the Bank of England (exc. special deposits)
   Treasury bills
   money at call with the London money market (i.e. with members of the London Discount Market Association, money brokers and gilt-edged jobbers)
   British government (and government-guaranteed) stock with 1 year or less to final maturity
   local authority bills
   commercial bills eligible for rediscount at the Bank of England (subject to a maximum of 2 per cent of eligible liabilities)

No formally defined reserve assets

Eligible banks (as listed by Bank of England), defined as:
   recognised bank whose bills are eligible for discount at the Bank of England
   criteria for listing:
      has and maintains a broadly based acceptance business in UK (i.e. guarantees or 'accepts' short-dated commercial IOUs or 'bills')
      acceptances command the finest rates
      whether, in the case of foreign-owned banks, British banks enjoy reciprocal rights in foreign owners' domestic market

Interest rates: Bank of England formally announces its short-term interest (discount) rate: known as Bank Rate or, after 13 October 1972, as Minimum Lending Rate

Interest rates: Bank of England ceases formally to announce a Minimum Lending Rate; clearing banks' base rates to be determined to a greater extent by 'market factors'

'Competition and Credit Control': the reserve asset ratio system

The basic requirement, which used to operate before 20 August 1981, was that each bank must maintain, against its deposit liabilities to customers, a 'reserve' of liquid assets amounting to a minimum of $12\frac{1}{2}$ per cent of the value of those liabilities.* Of this, $1\frac{1}{2}$ percentage points (i.e. $1\frac{1}{2}$ per cent of the value of the liabilities) had to be maintained, day by day, as a credit balance of the bank in its account at the Bank of England (these credit balances, like all current accounts or sight deposits, earn no interest). The remaining 11 percentage points could be made up from the following list of four (types of) assets:

1. British government Treasury bills (these are short-term securities redeemable ninety-one days after issue; Treasury bills do not carry interest as such but are sold for less than their redemption value and so they yield a return).
2. Money at call with the London money market ('at call' means that it may be retrieved within twenty-four hours; it must also be placed with certain specified institutions, chiefly the discount houses, which mainly use the money so borrowed to buy Treasury bills; in effect the discount houses here act as agents for the banks in holding Treasury bills, though the discount houses would probably feel demeaned by this description).
3. British government securities (and nationalised industries' securities guaranteed by HM government) with one year or less to final maturity and local authority bills.
4. Eligible commercial bills (i.e. traders', etc., IOUs) backed by a bank guarantee (the total in this category must not amount to more than 2 percentage points).

This $12\frac{1}{2}$ per cent was known as the *reserve asset ratio*. The meaning of the reserve asset ratio cannot be understood until we see what the ratio was intended to accomplish.†

In order to do this the following requirements are absolutely essential:

(a) we need a simplified model to enable us to follow through what happens in the real world; and
(b) we must *start* with the public sector borrowing requirement (which is to say that we must begin at the *beginning*).

In what follows, until explicitly stated otherwise, we shall ignore the problem of government borrowing to refinance maturing debt; in other words, and to keep the initial exposition as simple as possible, we shall pretend that no government debt is maturing. When the basics of the problem have been expounded, we shall then incorporate the supplementary, but important, matter of refinancing. To keep the exposition simple, the exposition following will concentrate upon three elements only: deposit liabilities; credit balances at the Bank of England; and Treasury bills.

How reserve assets arise

Start by supposing that the general government was raising exactly enough annual tax revenue to pay for all its annual expenditure: receipts into and payments out of the Consolidated Fund exactly balanced. Now we must specifically disturb the balance to make the Consolidated Fund run a deficit: let us specifically assume that an extra university student has to be paid a student grant of, say, £1,000 for the year (but that no additional tax revenue is raised). Disregarding the fact that payment is made via a local

---

*The minimum reserve ratio was reduced to 10 per cent on 5 January 1981, and there were other (temporary) reductions during March and April 1981. The following exposition will use the 'normal' $12\frac{1}{2}$ per cent ratio (abolished in August 1981).

†In the practice of monetary control, the important (i.e. operational) part of this ratio was the $1\frac{1}{2}$ per cent credit balance, or 'cash balance', ratio at the Bank of England.

authority, the student receives, in effect, a government cheque drawn on the Consolidated Fund for £1,000. As there are no extra tax receipts, the 'excess' expenditure of £1,000 now becomes the government's financial deficit which, assuming that the government is not lending and that the public corporations are running in exact financial balance, we may equate with the public sector borrowing requirement.

The next thing that happens is that the student pays the cheque into his or her bank account, say with Lloyds Bank (following the percentages in Table 13.14 we disregard the possibility that the student obtains £1,000 cash for the cheque). The deposit liability of Lloyds Bank to the student now increases by £1,000, but Lloyds has the government's cheque for £1,000 and, in its turn, Lloyds will present the cheque to the Bank of England for crediting to Lloyds' account at the Bank of England. The Bank of England duly credits Lloyds deposit with it, and then debits the government's Consolidated Fund with £1,000. The Consolidated Fund now has a deficit of £1,000 and this must be made up by a transfer from the National Loans Fund. Where does the National Loans Fund get the money from?

There are three possibilities. First, the government may borrow from the UK non-bank private sector. Second, it may 'borrow' from the overseas sector. Third, it may borrow from the UK banking sector. If the government cannot borrow from the first two sources, it must end up, willy-nilly, borrowing from the banking sector. Let us see how all this works out.

If the government borrows from the UK non-bank private sector, then what happens is straightforward. Suppose the Bank of England (acting on the government's behalf) sells a security to an individual who banks with Lloyds. In actual practice, as we have seen, the Bank of England is more likely to dispose of the security to a pension fund, but the pension fund will in turn have obtained its funds from a household in financial surplus. (Assuming that the individual banks with Lloyds is simply for convenience – what matters is the position of the whole banking sector's deposits with the Bank of England.) The individual who purchases the government security pays the Bank of England £1,000 with a cheque drawn on his or her account with Lloyds. The Bank of England pays the cheque into the National Loans Fund (the money thence to be transferred to the Consolidated Fund to cover the government's financial deficit). After being credited to the National Loans Fund the cheque is presented to Lloyds account at the Bank of England for payment, and Lloyds' deposit with the Bank of England is reduced by £1,000. This restores Lloyds' Bank of England deposit to the position before it cleared the student's grant cheque. Lloyds now sends the cheque to the security purchaser's account and debits this account with £1,000, so Lloyds' deposit liabilities are reduced by £1,000. This exactly counterbalances the increase in Lloyds' deposit liability to the student and leaves the total of Lloyds' deposit liabilities as it was before the student deposited his or her grant cheque. It is important to note that the effect of the government's borrowing from the non-bank private sector is to leave the total of bank deposits *unaltered*; bank deposits are a large part (about three-quarters) of the money supply, so the money supply is unaffected by government borrowing from the non-bank private sector.

The second possibility is that the government may 'borrow' from the overseas sector. I put the word 'borrow' in inverted commas because this particular form of borrowing is possible only if there is a deficit on the current-account balance of payments. To keep the illustration simple, let us suppose that from a position of exactly balancing earnings from exports and expenditure on imports, an importer buys an extra Japanese motor-cycle costing £1,000 (or its equivalent in yen). The importer asks his bank, Lloyds again, to debit his account with £1,000, to obtain the requisite amount of yen, and to pay the Japanese motor-cycle firm. Accordingly, Lloyds reduces its deposit liability to the importer by £1,000; this matches Lloyds' increased deposit liability to the student, and so restores the total of Lloyds' deposit liabilities to what it was before the student deposited his or her grant cheque. Lloyds now pays out £1,000 from its account with the Bank of England to the Exchange Equalisation Account in return for the requisite amount of yen (we can imagine that yen notes are then posted to the Japanese motor-cycle firm, though in practice the transfer would be effected in a more sophisticated way!). Lloyds' deposit with the Bank of England is thus reduced by £1,000 and this restores Lloyds' Bank of England deposit to what it was before it cleared the student's grant cheque. The Exchange Equalisation Account now holds less yen but has £1,000 in sterling, which is transferred to the National Loans Fund and thence to the Consolidated Fund to cover the government's financial deficit. Again, the important point is that the total of Lloyds' deposit liabilities – the money supply – remains what it was before the student deposited his or her grant cheque. In this way a balance-of-payments deficit (the extra imported motor-cycle) provides sterling finance to cover the government's borrowing requirement (the reduction in foreign exchange reserves being the counterpart to the issuing of a government security).

However, we may suppose that neither the first nor the second possibility come to pass. We can readily imagine that the UK non-bank private sector refuses to buy the £1,000 security, so cutting off that possibility; and we can imagine that the balance of payments remains in balance. In this case the government ends up borrowing from the banks and, significantly, if this happens the total of bank deposits – the money supply – will increase. Let us see how this works out.

How the reserve asset ratio works – the deposit multiplier

Table 13.15 will help us to sort out the sequence of events, which have been separated into numbered stages as shown on the left-hand side. The figures in the table refer to the stocks as they exist at each stage.

First, the student deposits the grant cheque with Lloyds, and so Lloyds incurs a deposit liability to the student (it is against this deposit liability that Lloyds had to end up holding $1\frac{1}{2}$ per cent of the value of the liability as a deposit (credit) at the Bank of England and a further 11 per cent in specified (liquid) reserve assets – this $12\frac{1}{2}$ per cent in all being Lloyd's reserve of liquid assets which can be used (partly) to meet the liability to the student should he or she want to retrieve his or her deposit liability; it gives Lloyds a margin, albeit only a $12\frac{1}{2}$ per cent margin, of 'safety').

At the second stage, which happens quite quickly, Lloyds pays the grant cheque into its account with the Bank of England. At this stage we must get the whole process of government borrowing from the banks off the ground by assuming that the government is *not* borrowing from other sources; in other words, nothing is happening which would reduce, in a counteracting way, Lloyds' (or any other bank's) deposits with the Bank of England. So, at this stage Lloyds is 'stuck' with £1,000 to its credit at the Bank of England.

It is most important for the student to appreciate that at this second stage Lloyds Bank is in an untenable, loss-making situation, and this for the following reasons. Assume the student deposited the grant cheque in a time deposit to earn interest, say at 10 per cent per annum. Lloyds is now contracted during the coming year to pay the student £100. The £1,000 which Lloyds has to its credit at the Bank of England is (by tradition, about which the banks grumble) non-interest-earning (like most sight deposits). So at this second stage Lloyds is in the untenable position of having to pay the student £100 per annum with nothing coming in to pay the interest to the student. (It does not make any difference to the analysis if the student deposits the grant cheque in a non-interest-bearing sight deposit, because the bank is, as we have seen, incurring quite heavy staff and other costs in running such an account.) Thus, if it is to avoid making a loss, Lloyds must look sharp and use its non-interest-earning credit deposit with the Bank of England to acquire some interest-earning assets, the interest from which will cover the interest due to the student or the costs

TABLE 13.15 *The way in which the government borrowing requirement can lead to a multiple expansion of the money supply*

£ (stock)

	Lloyds Bank				Barclays Bank			
		Assets				Assets		
	Deposit liabilities	Bank of England deposits (a)	Other reserve assets (b)	Loans to customers	Deposit liabilities	Bank of England deposits (a)	Other reserve assets (b)	Loans to customers
1. Student deposits grant cheque with Lloyds	1,000							
2. Lloyds clears grant cheque with Bank of England		1,000						
3. Lloyds acquires interest-earning assets		(890)	110	875				
4. Borrower from Lloyds pays first supplier, who deposits with Barclays					875			
5. Barclays clears cheque with Lloyds via Bank of England		15	110	875		875		
6. Barclays acquires interest-bearing assets						(778.75)	96.25	765.625
7. Borrower from Barclays pays second supplier, who deposits with Lloyds	765.625							
8. Lloyds clears cheque with Barclays via Bank of England		765.625				13.125	96.25	765.625
9. Lloyds acquires interest-earning assets		(681.406)	84.219	669.922				
10. Borrower from Lloyds pays third supplier, who deposits with Barclays					669.922			
11. Barclays clears cheque with Lloyds via Bank of England		11.484	84.219	669.922		669.922		
12. Barclays acquires interest-earning assets						(596.231)	73.691	586.182
13. Borrower from Barclays pays fourth supplier, who deposits with Lloyds	586.182							
14. Lloyds clears cheque with Barclays via Bank of England		586.182				10.049	73.691	586.182
And so on ...								

(a) Brackets indicates deposit only temporarily at that level until other bank presents cheque for payment; the deposit figure in this column must end up as 1½ per cent of the bank's deposit liability (e.g. 15 is 1½% of 1,000; 13.125 is 1½% of 875; 11.484 is 1½% of 765.625, and so on).

(b) These other reserve assets must (under the then rules) comprise 11 per cent of the bank's deposit liability (e.g. 110 is 11% of 1,000; 96.25 is 11% of 875; 84.219 is 11% of 765.625, and so on). Together with the (eventual) 1½ per cent deposit at the Bank of England, this makes up the 12½ per cent of reserve assets, the remaining 87½ per cent is lent (at greatest profit) to a borrower from the bank, so the figure in the 'loans to the customer' column is $(1 - 0.125)$ times the deposit liability figure.

of operating his or her current account. It is important to understand and appreciate this powerful pressure on Lloyds to get out of a potential loss-making situation, because it is this pressure which 'drives' the banking system along the subsequent stages of Table 13.15.

So, in stage three, Lloyds looks sharp to get itself out of this potential loss-making situation. First, it buys £110 worth of Treasury bills from a new issue. This provides Lloyds with the 11 per cent of reserve assets (other than deposits with the Bank of England) which it was required to hold against its deposit liability of £1,000 to the student. The Treasury bills are redeemable in ninety-one days, and for its £110 Lloyds will obtain bills redeemable for something like £113 (in round numbers). If Lloyds then resubscribes to Treasury bills four times during the year, it will be a net gainer of something like £12, which can be put towards paying the interest to the student.

For the Treasury bills, Lloyds will have paid £110 to be credited to the National Loans Fund and so its deposit with the Bank of England will be debited with this amount, reducing its deposit to £890. Note that the government has now borrowed £110 towards the total of £1,000 which it needs to borrow to cover the student's grant (the government's financial deficit).

Lloyds is not yet out of a loss-making situation because it has, so far, obtained interest of only about £12 to cover its £100 due during the year to the student. So, next in stage three, Lloyds seeks to lend some money to a borrower to whom it can charge interest. How much money out of the remaining £890 can Lloyds lend? The Bank of England requires Lloyds to maintain $1\frac{1}{2}$ per cent of Lloyds' £1,000 deposit liability to the student as a credit deposit of Lloyds at the Bank of England; $1\frac{1}{2}$ per cent of £1,000 is £15, so Lloyds knows that it can lend only £890 *minus* £15 = £875. So Lloyds lends £875 to a creditworthy borrower, say for one year at $10\frac{3}{4}$ per cent per annum. Lloyds is now home and dry, out of its loss-making situation. The annual interest on its loan to the creditworthy borrower is $0.1075 \times £875 = £94.06$, and Lloyds has another £12 coming in during the year from the profits on its holdings of Treasury bills; in all, Lloyds has secured for itself an annual income of £94.06 + £12 = £106.06 and out of this it can pay the student's interest of £100, and also have something left over for staff (etc.) costs and a bit of profit besides.

Note that it is the creditworthy borrower who has got Lloyds out of its loss-making situation. Most borrowers from banks imagine that the bank is doing them a tremendous favour by lending them money, whereas it is really the other way round: the borrower is doing the bank a great service! Appreciation of this fact should not dispose the reader to a tactless attitude when asking the bank manager for a loan or an overdraft (after all there may be other and more creditworthy would-be borrowers in the queue behind you!) But it is important for a proper economic analysis of banking to stress the essential role of the creditworthy borrower.

The borrower does not, of course, borrow money simply to have it sitting round in his or her bank account with Lloyds. The borrower, perhaps a merchant buying some goods to sell or a householder wanting a new car, uses the borrowed money to pay the supplier; we may suppose that the borrower gives the supplier a cheque drawn on his (the borrower's) Lloyds account (now containing the agreed loan). The supplier, let us assume, banks with Barclays, so at stage four, the supplier pays the cheque into his account at Barclays Bank. Barclays' deposit liabilities to the supplier now increase by £875. Barclays then, stage five, clears the cheque with Lloyds via the Bank of England: that is, Lloyds must pay Barclays £875 out of its £890 held at the Bank of England. This reduces Lloyds deposit at the Bank of England to £15, just sufficient to meet the requirement that Lloyds keeps $1\frac{1}{2}$ per cent of the value of its deposit liabilities as a deposit at the Bank of England.

Barclays Bank is now in an untenable loss-making situation. Assuming the supplier has deposited the money into a time deposit account bearing interest at 10 per cent per annum, Barclays is due to pay the supplier £87.50 p.a. So Barclays must now look sharp and use the

£875 (subject to Bank of England requirements) to acquire interest-earning assets. In stage six, Barclays puts the required 11 per cent of the value of its deposit liability into other reserve assets, such as a new issue of Treasury bills: $0.11 \times £875 = £96.25$. Note that the government has now obtained another £96.25 towards covering its borrowing requirement.

Barclays knows it has (had) to keep $1\frac{1}{2}$ per cent of £875, i.e. £13.125, on deposit at the Bank of England, so, at the next step in stage six, it lends the remaining £765.625 to a creditworthy borrower at $10\frac{3}{4}$ per cent per annum (being in competition with Lloyds it cannot charge more). This interest, together with the return on Treasury bills, enables Barclays to pay interest on the £875 deposit liability and have something left over towards costs and profits.

The borrower from Barclays pays a second supplier who deposits with Lloyds (it should be clear that Lloyds and Barclays are representing the whole UK banking sector, so the names do not particularly matter to the analysis). Lloyds' deposit liabilities rise by £765.625 and the whole process moves on, as before, driven always by the banks' need to keep themselves from making losses and their desire to reap profits.

However, we can see that the process cannot continue indefinitely because each round is successively smaller. For the total of the increases in banks' deposit liabilities (Lloyds and Barclays taken together) we have the series:

Initial deposit from student
(leading to increase in bank's
deposits with the Bank of England)   1,000
First supplier's deposit $0.875 \times 1,000 = (1 - 0.125) \times 1,000$
$= 875$
Second supplier's deposit $0.875 \times 875 = (1 - 0.125) \times 875$
$= (1 - 0.125)^2 \times 1,000 = 765.625$
Third supplier's deposit 0.875×765.625
$= (1 - 0.125)^3 \times 1,000 = 669.922$
And so on ...

We use the term $(1 - 0.125)$ instead of 0.875, because 0.125 or $12\frac{1}{2}$ per cent is the reserve asset ratio (which used to be) required by the Bank of England. As with the multiplier process in Chapter 11, we have a geometric series the sum of all of whose terms is:

$$Z = 1,000$$
$$+ (1 - 0.125) \times 1,000$$
$$+ (1 - 0.125)^2 \times 1,000$$
$$+ \cdots$$

and using the usual method involving the constant ratio between successive terms:

$$Z - (1 - 0.125)Z = 1,000$$

whence:

$$Z(1 - 1 + 0.125) = 1,000$$

or:

$$Z = \frac{1}{0.125} \times 1,000$$
$$= 8 \times 1,000 = 8,000$$

So the total expansion in banks' deposit liabilities is a multiple of:

$$\frac{1}{\text{Proportionate reserve asset ratio}}$$

applied to the initial increase in banks' deposits (but only because, in the absence of government borrowing from other sectors, this initial deposit leads also to a rise in banks' deposits with the Bank of England).

At the end of this process, the government will have borrowed, through the issuing of Treasury bills:

First sale to Lloyds	$0.11 \times 1{,}000$	$= 110$
First sale to Barclays	0.11×875	
	$= 0.11 \times (1 - 0.125) \times 1{,}000$	$= 96.25$
Second sale to Lloyds	0.11×865.625	
	$= 0.11 \times (1 - 0.125)^2 \times 1{,}000$	$= 84.219$
Second sale to Barclays	0.11×669.922	
	$= 0.11 \times (1 - 0.125)^3 \times 1{,}000$	$= 73.691$

And so on . . .

The sum of this series is:

$$Z = 0.11 \times 1{,}000$$
$$+ 0.11 \times (1 - 0.125) \times 1{,}000$$
$$+ 0.11 \times (1 - 0.125)^2 \times 1{,}000$$
$$+ \cdots$$

whence, dividing through by 0.11, gives:

$$\frac{Z}{0.11} = 1{,}000$$
$$+ (1 - 0.125) \times 1{,}000$$
$$+ (1 - 0.125)^2 \times 1{,}000$$
$$+ \cdots$$

The right-hand side is the sum of the increases in bank deposit liabilities previously dealt with, so:

$$\frac{Z}{0.11} = \frac{1}{0.125} \times 1{,}000$$

whence:

$$Z = 0.11 \times 8{,}000 = 880$$

So the government will have borrowed a total of £880 through the take-up of Treasury bills by the banks into their portfolio of reserve assets. This, of course, leaves the government £120 short of its need to borrow £1,000. Here comes the Bank of England to the rescue.

The banks' deposits with the Bank of England will have increased as follows (going straight to the sum of the series):

$$Z = 0.015 \times 1{,}000$$
$$+ 0.015 \times (1 - 0.125) \times 1{,}000$$
$$+ 0.015 \times (1 - 0.125)^2 \times 1{,}000$$
$$+ \cdots$$

whence:

$$\frac{Z}{0.015} = \frac{1}{0.125} \times 1,000$$

so that:

$$Z = 0.015 \times 8,000 = 120$$

The Bank of England is sitting pretty on top of £120 increased balances held by the banks with it; the Bank of England does not pay any interest on these deposit liabilities; and the Bank of England now itself acquires (interest-earning) Treasury bills (or lends to the National Loans Fund in what is called a 'Ways and Means Advance', or acquires other government securities) with this £120. This closes the government's borrowing requirement. Like everybody else, the Bank of England earns interest on its take-up of Treasury bills (or on its Ways and Means Advances), but as it pays no interest to the banks, whose deposits it has used to acquire these assets, the interest received by the Bank of England is all profit – and this is (partly) the way in which the Bank of England earns its living.* (I say 'partly', because it has other sources of income, especially its charges to the government in connection with the issue (etc.) of bank notes – we have not dealt with these sources.)

The schematic model of Table 13.15 shows that expansion in the stock of banks' deposit liabilities depends upon the banks (as a whole) being able to expand both their deposits with the Bank of England and also their holdings of reserve assets. Such an expansion can come about if the government has to borrow from the banks. Broadly speaking, the government has to borrow from the banks if it has a borrowing requirement, based mostly on a financial deficit, *and* if it cannot sell government debt to the UK non-bank private sector *and* if the balance-of-payments account is not in deficit (so providing the government with sterling in return for a reduction in the reserves of foreign exchange).

To illustrate with a metaphor which may help to put the technicalities into a pictorial perspective (it is more important to understand in broad terms the nature of the problem than to follow through all the complex technicalities – for details on which, see Geoffrey Bell and Lawrence Berman, 'Changes in the money supply in the United Kingdom, 1954 to 1964', *Economica*, May 1966). As illustrated in Diagram 13.2, the public sector borrowing requirement is like a river whose flow (represented in one dimension by the

DIAGRAM 13.2   *To illustrate the residual nature of banking-sector lending to the public sector*

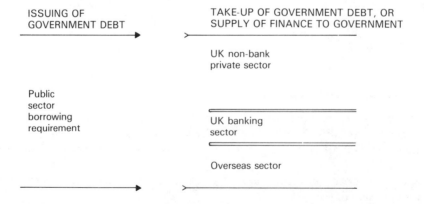

---

*It was estimated that the Bank of England's earnings from the 1½ per cent cash ratio probably amounted to about £35 million in the year 1976–7 (March to February); hence the complaint by the clearing banks that a substantial and discriminatory cost penalty is being applied to them alone (*The London Clearing Banks*, Evidence by the Committee of London Clearing Bankers to the Committee to Review the Functioning of Financial Institutions, paras 7.14–17.18, pp. 183–4).

External finance

We must here add a qualification: importers are not the only residents who come to the Exchange Equalisation Account with sterling to get foreign exchange; residents who are investing abroad (whether acquiring financial assets or real assets overseas) will also come to the Exchange Equalisation Account with sterling in order to get foreign exchange to pay for their overseas asset acquisitions. Because we are concerned with the total (net) inflow of sterling into the Exchange Equalisation Account, from a monetary point of view, although not from other points of view, it does not particularly matter whether the sterling paid into the EEA is used to buy an imported Japanese motor-cycle or, say, shares in an American company. Both these transactions – imports or investment abroad by a resident – will reduce the money supply (provide sterling finance to the government via the EEA). Conversely, exports to or investment from abroad will tend to raise the money supply (require sterling finance from the government via the EEA).

The basic principle is that: *inflows (outflows) of currency from (to) abroad will increase (reduce) the money supply sterling M_3 if sterling is placed in (taken out of) the hands of non-bank UK residents.*

Paying for the Japanese motor-cycle import is a straightforward case of a sterling deposit (with a bank) being taken out of the hands of the importer. Unfortunately, there are many other possibilities involving transactions with the overseas sector, especially since the abolition of foreign exchange control in October 1979. One possibility is that an exporter from the United Kingdom receiving foreign currency in payment for the export simply holds this on a foreign currency deposit with a UK bank (as he is now legally entitled to do). This has then no impact on public-sector finance, nor on the money supply. To illustrate, suppose a motor-cycle were imported for £1,000 and an exporter sold whisky to the USA for £400 = $800, these being the only transactions with the overseas sector. *Prima facie* ('on the face of it – without further investigation'), this would appear to provide the government with £600 of sterling finance towards the PSBR: however, the exporter may, since October 1979, simply hold the $800 in his 'other currency' deposit account with a UK bank, and if this happens, the government would receive £1,000 towards its PSBR, though the balance of trade deficit is only £600. The connection between the balance of payments, the EEA and changes in official reserves, financing to/from the government and the money supply has now become very complex.

In order to calculate the effect on the money supply and on government finance of transactions with the overseas sector we need now to measure the net extent to which private-sector residents buy foreign currency with sterling and sell foreign currency for sterling. It is basically this which is the width of the overseas-sector channel (drawn as positive in Diagram 13.2, but which can be negative, please note). For further discussion of this issue, the best article is C. M. Miles and P. A. Bull, 'External and foreign currency flows and the money supply', *Bank of England Quarterly Bulletin*, December 1978, pp. 523–9; the student should also consult K. K. F. Zawadzki, *Competition and Credit Control*, Blackwell, 1981, ch. 5.

width of the river) must meet a certain take-up of the debt issues to finance the PSBR. The debt so issued must flow into three channels, whose combined width (flow) is equal to the PSBR. The three channels are: the UK non-bank private sector; the overseas sector; and the UK banking sector.

In the over-all channel taking up the debt there are two vanes which can move. The distance from one side to the first vane determines the (width of) the take-up of government debt by the UK non-bank private sector. The government pushes this vane as far out into the middle as it can: by offering a large variety of debt for the personal sector to acquire (personal-sector financial assets) – national savings including index-linked 'granny' bonds, premium bonds, etc. – and, in the last resort, by raising the interest rate paid on new issues in order to attract more purchasers.

The distance from the other side to the second vane measures the flow of sterling finance provided by the overseas sector – we shall refer to this as 'external finance'. Specifically, in this illustration we suppose that there is a balance-of-payments deficit on current account, so importers are bringing more sterling to the Exchange Equalisation Account than exporters are taking sterling proceeds away from the EEA and so providing 'external' finance towards the PSBR (the adjective 'external' is only short-hand for a rather complex reality, and should not be taken too literally).

The distance into the middle of the river of this second vane cannot be greatly influenced in any direct way by the government: the distance depends mostly on the deficit on the current-account balance of payments.* The government can indirectly try to push the overseas sector's vane further into the middle by, for example, relaxing or abolishing controls on investment abroad by the UK private sector, which may lead to residents bringing more sterling to the EEA to get foreign exchange to invest abroad.

Given that the government has pushed the first vane, determining the extent of the UK non-bank private-sector take-up of government debt, out as far as possible towards the middle of the river, and that the position of the second vane is determined by the (somewhat independent) set of forces which acts upon the balance of payments and private-sector capital flows, then the remaining distance in the middle of the river between the two vanes must be the take-up of government sector debt by the banking sector. This happens willy-nilly as previously described by the example of the student's £1,000 grant cheque (which cheque stood for the public sector borrowing requirement). This is the case that the government has not been able to borrow either from the UK non-bank private sector or from the overseas sector (to illustrate, in that example, there could have been not one but three students whose grant cheques, in total, comprised the PSBR, but the government had succeeded in borrowing only £1,000 from the UK non-bank private sector, and there was £1,000 sterling flowing into the EEA on account of a balance-of-payments deficit, leaving £1,000 to be borrowed from the banks, in the manner described in Table 13.15).

If the banking sector uses this opportunity to acquire only the minimum of required deposits at the Bank of England and required other reserve assets and, conversely, to on-lend the maximum amount to the UK private sector (and we have seen that this opportunity is likely to be seized because the banks thereby extricate themselves from a potential loss-making situation and put themselves in a profit-making situation), then the total of bank deposits of the UK private sector will expand in a multiple of the banks' initial lending to the government, where the bank deposit multiplier is the reciprocal of the reserve asset ratio.

If the government wishes (for reasons we shall be considering) to reduce the growth of the money supply (i.e. largely the growth of bank deposit liabilities), then, taking the position of the overseas sector's vane as fixed, the government must:

1. reduce the PSBR; *and/or*
2. increase the acquisition of government debt by the UK non-bank private sector; *and/or*
3. reduce the bank deposit multiplier effect (this may be done either by raising interest rates, which reduces the flow of borrowing from/lending by banks, or by administratively reducing the base upon which the deposit multiplier operates).

The government has resorted to the third measure quite frequently. This it has done not only by raising interest rates (a matter to be discussed shortly), but also by reducing the

Special deposits

The way in which special deposits work is as follows. Special deposits are, in essence, a temporary confiscation from the banks of their (ordinary) deposits with the Bank of England. Although special deposits are held by the Bank of England, banks cannot count them as part of their reserve assets.* To illustrate the impact of a call by the Bank of England for special deposits let us return to the student's £1,000 grant cheque, representing the PSBR, with no government borrowing from the UK non-bank private sector and no balance-of-payments contribution to the PSBR. That is to say, Lloyds Bank ends up with an extra £1,000 in its deposit at the Bank of England (the government not having been able to 'borrow' the money anywhere else) – stage 2 of Table 13.15. In Table 13.15 this increase then became the basis for the whole bank deposit multiplier process, Lloyds keeping back the minimum required reserve assets and on-lending to a creditworthy borrower in the private sector the maximum of all the rest (driven by the need to get out of a loss-making and into a profit-making situation).

Special deposits provide, in effect, a method whereby the Bank of England can put a spanner in the works before Lloyds makes its first loan to the private-sector borrower. Seeing that Lloyds' deposits at the Bank of England have increased by £1,000 (and fearing the inevitable consequences of this for the multiplier expansion of bank deposits), the Bank of England immediately steps in and calls for, say, £300 (of its £1,000) on a 'frozen' special deposit (Lloyds gets some interest on the special deposit, but cannot do anything else with it – in particular, Lloyds cannot count it as part of its reserve assets against deposit liabilities). Therefore, Lloyds now has, on 'ordinary' deposit with the Bank of England, only £700. Out of this £700 Lloyds has as before to keep £15 on 'ordinary' deposit with the Bank of England (to satisfy the requirement that $1\frac{1}{2}$ per cent of deposit liabilities – to the student who deposited the £1,000 grant cheque – be so kept), and it has to keep £110 in the specified other reserve assets (this 11 per cent of the deposit liability together with the $1\frac{1}{2}$ per cent on 'ordinary' deposit at the Bank of England makes up the total $12\frac{1}{2}$ per cent of required reserve assets). So now, after the call for £300 special deposits, Lloyds has only £700 − £15 − £110 = £575 to

lend to the creditworthy borrower. Assuming that the Bank of England does not call for any further special deposits, the whole process then continues as before to give the following series for the total expansion of bank deposit liabilities:

1,000	(student's grant cheque)
+ 575	(first supplier's deposit)
$+ (1 - 0.125) \times 575$	(second supplier's deposit)
$+ (1 - 0.125)^2 \times 575$	(third supplier's deposit)
$+ \cdots$	

The total of this series is:

$$1,000 + \frac{1}{0.125} \times 575$$
$$= £5,600$$

which, from the point of view of limiting the expansion of bank deposits (money supply), is a much better result than an increase of £8,000.

This illustrates how special deposits work in effect. In practice, of course, the Bank of England does not call for special deposits from one single bank (this would be unfair and discriminatory) but simply calls for special deposits from all banks, as a proportion (the same proportion for all banks) of their outstanding deposit liabilities. But the effect of this general call is exactly as described, except that for 'Lloyds' we must substitute 'the UK banking sector'. It should be noted, however, that there is some controversy about the actual impact of special deposits; the arithmetical illustration which we used had a very large proportionate call for special deposits, and in practice calls have been made only on the basis of relatively small proportions, which may have something to do with the alleged ineffectiveness of special deposits. However, banks may have other means whereby they may escape such restrictions (this will be taken up subsequently). Note also that the government can borrow the £300 special deposit from the Bank of England and so still make up its total borrowing requirement.

*Special deposits have been used since 1958, so this was a technique predating 'Competition and Credit Control'; they are to continue in use despite the critical comment they attract; for example see the *Committee on the Working of the Monetary System* (the Radcliffe Report; Cmnd 827, August 1959) para. 508, p. 181.

base upon which the multiplier (the reciprocal of the proportionate reserve asset ratio) works. This reduction has been carried out via the mechanism of 'special deposits' (and the now-abolished 'supplementary special deposits' – humorously called 'the corset' – the main difference between special deposits and supplementary special deposits being that interest was paid to the banks on the former but not on the latter).

We may see how all this works out so far as the expansion of total bank deposits is concerned by using Diagram 13.3. The public sector borrowing requirement leads to a residual take-up of public-sector debt by the banking sector. Subject to calls for special deposits, this provides (as illustrated in Table 13.15) the basis for a flow of bank lending to the private sector, which lending leads to an increase in banks' deposit liabilities. Furthermore, some of the public sector borrowing requirement taken up by the non-bank private sector will be taken up in the form of an increase in the stock of notes and coin in circulation with the public (to be starkly simple, if the government had paid the student not a grant cheque but £1,000 in notes, *and* if the public had continued to hold in its wallets and purses the extra £1,000 of notes, then the government would have met its financial deficit arising from the student's grant by the issue of notes). Because the money stock comprises notes and coin (legal tender) in circulation with the public, and the banks' deposit liabilities, we must add on to the increase in banks' deposit liabilities the increase in notes and coin in circulation with the public to get the total increase in the money stock, or 'money supply' as it is more commonly called. So that if the government wishes to limit the expansion of the money supply, a reduction in the PSBR with the same absolute take-up of government debt by the UK non-bank private sector (and the same provision of finance from the reduction in foreign exchange reserves) will 'squeeze' the take-up of government debt by the UK banking sector, and so, on this smaller base for monetary expansion, the increase in banks' lending and in their deposit liabilities will also be smaller. The same effect can be achieved, at a constant PSBR, by increasing the UK non-bank private-sector take-up of government debt (excluding notes and coin). If neither of these can be achieved, then the Bank of England can directly reduce the base for monetary expansion by calling for special deposits, or it can try to brake the flow of bank lending (and so the expansion in banks' deposits) by raising interest rates.

DIAGRAM 13.3   *The public sector borrowing requirement, the expansion of the money supply, and domestic credit expansion*

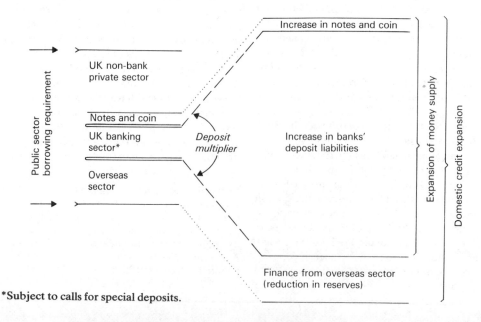

*Subject to calls for special deposits.

Domestic credit expansion

We must now consider the slightly paradoxical situation, so far as increases in the money supply are concerned, of the sterling financing for the PSBR which may be provided by a balance-of-payments deficit on current account (ignoring for the moment the finance provided if UK residents invest overseas).

Generally speaking, a deficit on the balance of payments current account is regarded as a 'bad thing': it means we are spending more on goods and services from abroad (etc.) than we are earning by selling goods and services to abroad (etc.); the country is 'living beyond its means'; and, most obviously, reductions in the country's reserves of foreign exchange cannot continue for ever, and sooner or later the country would have to start borrowing from abroad. However, in Diagram 13.3 it can clearly be seen that were the balance-of-payments deficit to increase and the reduction in foreign exchange reserves to accelerate, the effect, so far as the expansion of the money supply is concerned, is wholly beneficial: the government gets more finance into the National Loans Fund from the Exchange Equalisation Account and thus needs to borrow less from the UK banking sector, which reduces the monetary base for the deposit multiplier process. But a government which concerned itself only with the expansion of the money supply, ignoring the impact of such finance from the overseas sector, and which thought it was doing well because overseas finance (a reduction in foreign exchange reserves) was reducing government borrowing from the banks would clearly be deluding itself.

In order to overcome this delusion, the government needs to consider not only the expansion in the money supply but also the broader situation of 'domestic credit expansion', which is defined as the increase in the money supply *plus* the finance provided by the overseas sector. Domestic credit expansion can be measured, as in Diagram 13.3, as an adjusted or 'corrected' increase in the money supply – adjusted or 'corrected' for the extent to which the balance-of-payments deficit is funding the PSBR. Alternatively (but equivalently), it can be measured (or interpreted) as a flow of lending by the banking sector to the private sector and to the public sector, *plus* the flow of 'lending' by the overseas sector to the public sector (i.e. the reduction in official reserves of foreign exchange) *plus* that special flow of 'lending' by the non-bank private sector to the public sector which comprises the take-up of extra notes and coin in circulation with the public. The concept of domestic credit expansion thus emphasises the role of external finance, and this is why the International Monetary Fund – the international agency which, among other things, lends foreign exchange to governments short of foreign exchange – insists, when it lends, that economic policy should be run with reference to achieving a target (maximum permissible) domestic credit expansion.

Expansion of the money supply

To see how all this works out in the UK statistics on the growth of the money supply, Table 13.16 gives the relevant figures for 1980. So that we may begin at the beginning, the first part of the table shows the origin of the public sector borrowing requirement. We start with general government total receipts (mainly taxes and rates), which are smaller than general government total expenditure, so generating the general government's financial deficit. It is important at this stage for the student to 'see' the general government financial deficit not simply as this algebraic difference, but as the payment, via cheques and giros, by the government to the private sector in excess of what the government is taxing away from the private sector. In other words, the financial deficit must be seen, for monetary analysis, in terms of the first steps which initiated Table 13.15.

TABLE 13.16 *The public sector borrowing requirement, the change in the money stock sterling*
M_3, *and domestic credit expansion, 1980*

			£ million
	(1)	General government tax and other receipts on current and capital account [a]	92,273
less	(2)	General government expenditure on current and capital account [b]	100,227
equals	(3)	General government financial deficit	−7,954
plus	(4)	Public corporation's financial deficit [c]	−2,621
equals	(5)	Public-sector financial deficit	−10,575
change sign	(6)	Borrowing required to finance deficit	10,575
plus	(7)	Public-sector net lending to other sectors, acquisition of company securities, etc. (inc. accruals adjustment) [d]	1,669
equals	(8)	Public sector borrowing requirement	12,244
less	(9)	Net acquisition of public sector debt (exc. notes and coin) by UK non-bank private sector	9,086
less	(10)	Increase in notes and coin in circulation with public	724
less	(11)	Direct external finance	801
less	(12)	Foreign currency borrowing from banks	−730
equals	(13)	Borrowing by public sector in sterling from banks (residual)	2,363
		Banking-sector lending in sterling to:	
	(14)	UK private sector	9,622
	(15)	Overseas sector	2,803
	(16)	UK public sector	2,374
		Increase in banking-sector sterling deposit liabilities to:	
	(17)	UK private sector	9,852
	(18)	UK public sector	338
	(19)	Overseas sector	3,002
	(20)	Change in money stock, sterling M_3: (18) + (17) + (10)	10,914
	(21)	Domestic credit expansion: (15 + (14) + (13) + (12) + (11) + (10)	15,583

Deposit multiplier, via lending

[a] See Table 9.16; comprises £91,025 million on current account and £1,248 million on capital account.
[b] See Table 9.16; comprises £92,145 million on current account and £8,082 million on capital account.
[c] See Table 10.5.
[d] This is a complicated item in its details; it is calculated from the Blue Book's table 13.12 as the sum of items other than the financial deficit on the expenditure side, *plus* the sum of items (other than the PSBR) on the receipts side with their signs reversed.

Sources: Central Statistical Office, *National Income and Expenditure 1981 Edition*, tables 9.1 and 13.12, pp. 58–9 and 101; Central Statistical Office, *Financial Statistics*, October 1981, tables 2.6, 6.2, 7.2, 7.3 and 11.1, pp. 22, 60–1, 76, 78, and 115; the presentation of this table follows that in Central Statistical Office, *Financial Statistics Explanatory Handbook 1982 Edition*, p. 33.

To the general government financial deficit must be added the public corporations' financial deficit to get the public sector financial deficit. Because the government guarantees the debt of the public corporations, borrowing by the public corporations has the same status in the monetary system as does government debt itself.

Reversing the sign of the public-sector financial deficit gives the amount of public sector borrowing required to finance the public-sector financial deficit. In addition, the public sector engages in some net lending to other sectors of the economy, including under the heading 'net lending' the purchase of company securities (a transaction which would not normally be called 'lending'). It is convenient also to put the accruals adjustment in at this juncture (it should really be given separately), and, adding on this 'net lending' together with the accruals adjustment, we get the finance required to meet the public sector borrowing requirement on a cash-flow basis. This public sector borrowing requirement (PSBR) is then the starting-point for the expansion of the money supply in the economy (see Diagram 13.3).

In 1980 the general government received £92,273 million on current and capital account, and paid out £100,227 million on current and capital account (Chapter 9 was largely concerned with these receipts and expenditures). Accordingly, the general government financial deficit was −£7,954 million in 1980. The public corporations' financial deficit in 1980 was −£2,621 million (and we saw in Chapter 10 how this deficit arose). So the combined public-sector financial deficit in 1980 was −£10,575 million. At this juncture it is convenient to reverse the sign on the public-sector financial deficit and to switch to talking about the borrowing needed to cover the financial deficit. So the public sector needed in 1980 to borrow £10,575 million to meet its financial deficit. (The student should appreciate that this last sentence is slightly peculiar in its implied sequence: one is not able to incur a financial deficit unless one simultaneously borrows or reduces a stock of financial assets; the fact that the government is incurring a financial deficit means, by that fact itself, that the government is borrowing.)

In addition to this borrowing to cover the financial deficit, the public sector lent to other sectors £1,669 million in 1980, and this too required borrowing finance. Unlike the financial deficit, however, the liabilities which the government issues to finance this borrowing are 'matched', exactly, by the financial assets which the government acquires.

All in all, therefore, the public sector borrowing requirement in 1980 was £12,244 million. From whom did the public sector borrow the necessary?

The greater part of it, nearly three-quarters, came from the net acquisition of public-sector debt, excluding notes and coin, by the UK non-bank private sector. We have seen, in Chapter 3, that the personal sector runs each year a very substantial financial surplus: £18,300 million in 1980 (Table 3.7), £2,345 million of which was devoted to acquiring British government securities and £1,378 million of which was put into national savings (both of these directly providing finance to the public sector). Furthermore, the personal sector acquired £11,113 million worth of funds with life assurance and superannuation schemes and, in turn, these funds will have acquired public-sector debt with this money, as is indicated by the structure of assets in their balance-sheets in Tables 13.7 and 13.8.*

The public sector gained nearly 6 per cent of its required finance from the increase in notes and coin in circulation with the public. Further amounts of finance were obtained from the external sector, both directly and via borrowing foreign currencies from the banks.

All this left a residual amount of £2,363 million to be borrowed from the UK banking sector in 1980. This is the exact counterpart to the £1,000 in Table 13.15. And, because the public sector is not borrowing this amount from anyone else, this £2,363 million will initiate expansion of the money supply in more or less exactly the manner described in Table 13.15.

This residual borrowing requirement will have initially appeared to the banks as an increase in their deposit liabilities (mostly interest-bearing) as the private sector paid in cheques from the public sector – just as did the student in Table 13.15. So, in the first stage, the banks will have found themselves, as in row 1 of Table 13.15, with £2,363 million in extra (and costly) liabilities; simultaneously, however, they will also have found their deposits with the Bank of England rising by a like amount (as in row 2 of Table 13.15). So, naturally, the banks set about on-lending this money in order to obtain interest-bearing

*Life assurance and superannuation funds took up £3,888 million of British government securities in 1980 (*National Income and Expenditure 1981 Edition*, table 13.2, p. 91).

assets, thus enabling them to meet their obligations to deposit-holders. The banks are driven on by the urgent need to get themselves out of a potential loss-making situation of having to pay out interest on time deposits (or of incurring the administrative costs of running sight deposits) without interest coming in from interest-bearing assets.

The banks thus seek out creditworthy borrowers to whom they can lend money, subject to keeping a minimum in the form of reserve assets and (non-interest-bearing) balances with the Bank of England. Most of these loans will, as per Table 13.15, end up as additional further deposit liabilities in the banking sector as borrowers pay their suppliers and the suppliers deposit the money in their bank accounts. Again, the banks will be driven to on-lend this money to keep themselves out of a loss-making situation. The sequence is not endless, however, because the sequence is diminished at each round by the 'leakage' into reserve assets required under the old 'Competition and Credit Control' system (and the new system will also, but less formally, require a similar leakage into reserves of liquid assets).

So during 1980 the banks lent £9,622 million to the UK private sector and a further £2,803 million (in sterling) to the overseas sector. The magnitude of this last flow of lending is something new in the UK economy because prior to October 1979 borrowing in sterling by non-residents was limited by exchange control regulations. The abolition of exchange control in October 1979 meant, among other things, that non-residents could borrow freely, and this appears to have been happening.

The upshot of this on-lending by the banks was that their deposit liabilities in sterling to the UK private sector increased by £9,852 million in 1980, and this forms the greater part, 90 per cent, of the expansion of the money supply sterling M_3 in 1980.

However, given that the banks had lent the government £2,363 million in 1980, we might with the old reserve asset ratio of 0.125 and a corresponding deposit multiplier of 8, expect that the expansion in bank deposits would have been even larger than £9,852 million. Why was the increase in bank deposits low relative to what might, theoretically, have been expected?

A small part of the answer to this question is that some of the on-lending was to non-residents and, to the extent that this was used to settle accounts with other non-residents, such on-lending does not affect the money stock sterling M_3: as shown by row (19) of Table 13.16, this happened to a considerable extent.

But the important part of the answer to this question is that the flow of bank lending to residents was severely braked during 1980 by very high interest rates (among other things – although this effect may have been partly counteracted by the recession, which forced companies willy-nilly to borrow from the banks, high interest rates notwithstanding).

Interest rates, the PSBR and the growth of the money supply

It was always intended that the system of 'Competition and Credit Control' should be one in which the allocation of credit would be primarily determined by cost – i.e. by interest rates on borrowing – and where the authorities would seek to limit the expansion of credit rather more by causing interest rates to influence the amount of borrowing than by rationing credit through the deposit multiplier (e.g. by calling for special deposits).

From the government's point of view the use of interest rates has a twofold effect: on the one hand, rising interest rates on public-sector debt mean that the authorities are likely to be able to sell more public-sector debt to the non-bank private sector (thus reducing residual borrowing from the banks and so reducing reserve asset creation); on the other hand, higher interest rates for borrowers means that there will be a reduction in the flow of borrowing from/lending by the banks, and this, too, reduces the rate at which the money supply will expand.

The London clearing banks' 'base rate' is the rate of interest (expressed as a per cent per annum) at, or above, which the clearing banks will lend. The base rates may not be exactly the same for all banks, as there is some competition between the banks, but base rates move pretty well in step, for obvious competitive reasons (what would a Lloyds Bank customer do if he could borrow more cheaply from Barclays Bank?) and the rates of interest charged by the banks for loans and overdrafts to customers will depend on who and how creditworthy the customer is – most lending is in a range between 1 and 5 percentage points above base rate. The rate of interest payable by banks on deposits will also be related to base rate and will tend to be a little below base rate.

Diagram 13.4 shows the course of the London clearing banks' base rates between 1972 and 1980. It is clear that rates have changed quite frequently, as it was intended that they should in order to influence borrowing. It is also obvious that the banks' rate of interest in 1980 was relatively high at 17 per cent per annum until July and at 16 per cent per annum for most of the rest of the year. This high rate of interest meant that borrowing from the banks during 1980 was reined back by the high cost of borrowing, and this influenced the extent to which the deposit multiplier worked.

DIAGRAM 13.4   *London clearing banks' base rate of interest, 1972 to 1980*

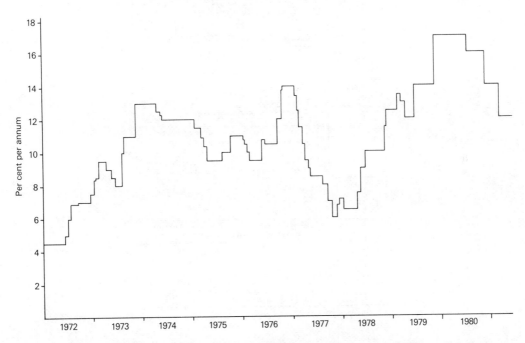

Accordingly, the banks expanded their holdings of British government securities of over one year to maturity by £1,157 million during 1980: from a holding of £2,083 million on 16 January 1980 to £3,240 million on 10 December. These do not count as reserve assets but, effectively, such lending by the banks to the government increases the 'leakage' from the successive rounds of the deposit multiplier process, so making the end-result of that process smaller. High interest rates have a twofold effect: on the one hand, they discourage creditworthy private-sector borrowers (thus disrupting the chain of events described in Table 13.15); on the other hand, they make it more profitable for the banks to acquire non-reserve asset government debt (also disrupting the chain of events described in Table 13.15, which chain depended on banks lending to the government only the *minimum* required).

Because of these high interest rates during 1980, the growth of the money supply sterling M_3 was limited despite the large public sector borrowing requirement. Domestic credit expansion, which takes into account all lending in the economy, including lending to the overseas sector, was larger than the growth of sterling M_3, but this is largely the result of the new situation created by sterling lending to non-residents following the abolition of exchange controls.

While discussing Table 13.16 we have seen that the connection between the public sector borrowing requirement and the expansion of the money supply comprises a long chain of separate links, most of which are subject to various influences. These influences are schematically illustrated in Diagram 13.5, and it is important that the student should appreciate that the sequence from PSBR to the change in sterling M_3 is not a rigid mechanical link, but may be influenced by these influences, some of which comprise the measures of monetary policy.

DIAGRAM 13.5   *The (loose) connection between the public sector borrowing requirement and the expansion of the money supply*

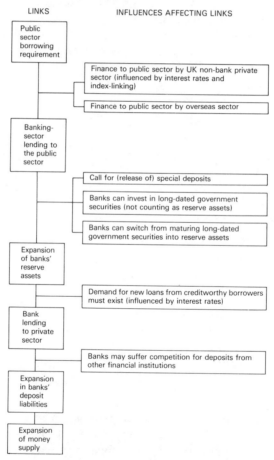

The first link is affected by sources of finance for the PSBR from other sectors of the economy; this flow will thus be conditioned by the rate of interest on government debt, and this is important in checking the growth of reserve assets.

The second link, between banking-sector lending to the public sector and the expansion of banks' reserve assets, is subject not only to calls for (or the release of) special deposits but also to the fact that banks can, and do, invest in long-dated government securities not counting as reserve assets. Conversely, if banks are not doing much lending to the public sector but the demand from the private sector for loans is running strongly, then the banks can switch from maturing long-dated securities into reserve assets (this increases the possible expansion of reserve assets without the banks doing any lending in the current period to the government).

The third link, between the expansion of the banks' reserve assets and bank lending to the private sector, depends crucially on the demand for new loans. If this is braked by high interest rates, then the flow of bank lending (and consequent expansion in banks' deposit liabilities) simply slows down, and, as in 1980, the banks have to make the best of a bad job by investing in long-dated government securities.

Finally, in the fourth link, some of the bank loans may be (permanently) deposited with other financial institutions, and such a leakage also interrupts the expansion of banks' deposit liabilities.

Accordingly, the connection between the public sector borrowing requirement and the change in the money supply, while existing, is not a mechanically rigid connection. Diagram 13.6 (based on data in Appendix 13.2) shows that the annual PSBR and the annual change in the money stock sterling M_3, both taken as a percentage of the year's gross domestic product, tend to move together, though there were occasional divergences. The coefficient of correlation between the two series is $R = +0.361$, indicating a rather loose but nevertheless positive (and just significant) association – which is perhaps exactly what we should expect given that this is a connection so subject to other influences.*

DIAGRAM 13.6 *Public sector borrowing requirement and changes in money stock sterling M_3, both taken as a percentage of GDP, 1952 to 1980*

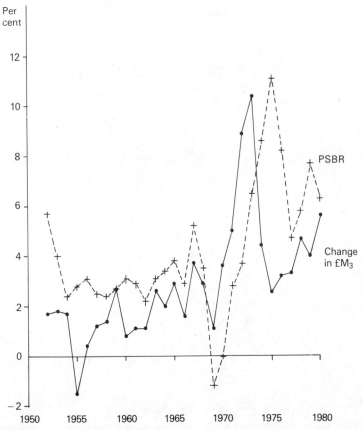

*The relationship is:

$$\left(\frac{\Delta\pounds M_3}{GDP}\right)\% = 1.52 + 0.34\left(\frac{PSBR}{GDP}\right)\%$$

so that expansion in the PSBR/GDP percentage by no means leads to a one-for-one expansion in the expansion in the money supply/GDP percentage.

As we have seen, one of the reasons why the connection between the public sector borrowing requirement and changes in the money supply is rather a loose one is that if, at any given PSBR, the government raises interest rates, then it will sell more debt to the non-bank private sector and reduce its borrowing from the banks, so limiting the expansion of reserve assets upon which the growth of the money supply is based. Conversely, if the government wishes to limit its borrowing from the banking sector, then, as the PSBR increases, it may have to raise interest rates to increase its disposal of debt to the non-bank private sector, so limiting its borrowing from the banks in the face of the rising PSBR.

A rise in interest rates will also have the important impact of slowing down the flow of borrowing from/lending by the banks, and this reduces the effective deposit multiplier (which must be mediated through borrowing).

For both these reasons we should expect there to be a positive relationship between the government's short-term rate of interest and the public sector borrowing requirement. Such a relationship can be seen in the data shown in Diagram 13.7 (taken from Appendices 13.2 and 13.3). The graph covers the period 1952 to 1980, and we take the short-term interest rate (known formerly as Bank Rate and subsequently as Minimum Lending Rate) and express the PSBR as a percentage of GDP (such a relative measure of the PSBR gets round the problem that part of the changes in the PSBR are due simply to inflation). The correlation between the rate of interest and the (relative) size of the public

DIAGRAM 13.7   *The relationship between the public sector borrowing requirement and the short-term interest rate, 1952 to 1980*

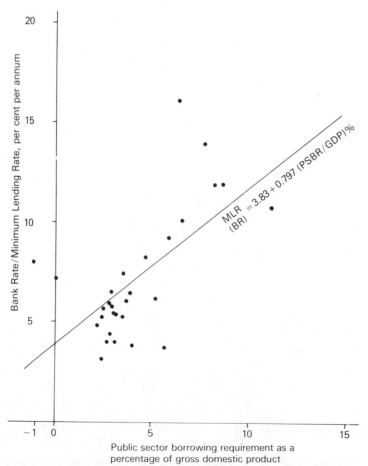

sector borrowing requirement is $R = +0.633$, which is a statistically significant correlation.

The estimated relationship between the two variables is:

Minimum Lending Rate (Bank Rate) $= 3.83 + 0.797$ Public sector borrowing requirement as a percentage of gross domestic product

So that, in general, there has been a tendency for an increase of one percentage point in the PSBR as a percentage of GDP to lead to an increase in the Minimum Lending Rate (Bank Rate) of 0.797 percentage points.

We can see also that there are some 'odd' points on the scatter diagram, such as that for 1969, when there was a negative PSBR in conjunction with a relatively high interest rate. However, these points only serve to 'prove' (in the sense of test) the rule, because in 1969 the increase in the money supply was small (see Appendix 13.2).

Banks' liabilities and assets in sterling and other currencies

Having seen how bank deposit liabilities depend on banks' reserve assets, which assets arise from banks' (residual) lending to the public sector, we can return to the structure of banks' liabilities and assets. When we noted earlier that the size of the banking sector's holdings of assets/liabilities (Table 13.1) depended not only upon their services as financial intermediaries but also (and perhaps mainly) upon the usefulness of the money transmission service they provided, we noted only half of the truth. The 'immediate' reason why the banking sector in the United Kingdom is so big relative to other UK financial institutions is that the UK banking sector is predominantly engaged in international financial transactions with the overseas sector. We may again speculate that this international business rests (at least partly) upon the usefulness of the means of payment service provided by the banks, but it also rests partly upon the usefulness to the overseas sector of being able confidently to place short-term deposits with banks in London, or to borrow in London.

Table 13.17 shows that, at the end of 1980, 62.4 per cent of the UK banking sector's total liabilities were deposit liabilities owed to the overseas sector in currencies other than sterling (but at a sterling valuation so they can all be added together), while 61.3 per cent of the UK banking sector's total assets were loans (etc.) to the overseas sector in currencies other than sterling. Conversely, only about one-quarter of the UK banking sector's business was in sterling with UK residents.

To get this into perspective, Table 13.18 shows the structure of liabilities and assets of the three main groups making up the UK banking sector: the clearing banks; other British banks including the accepting houses (which are merchant banks specialising in accepting – guaranteeing – bills of exchange (short-dated IOUs which are mainly issued to finance transactions in international trade) where the 'acceptance' is important because the guarantee means that the bill can readily be 'discounted', sold for ready cash but at a slight reduction on its face-value); and the overseas banks.

The totals in Table 13.17 do not square with the totals in Table 13.18, because the former table is adjusted to exclude inter-bank deposits (amounting on 10 December 1980 to about £60 billion) and the doublecounting of items in transit (probably about £4 billion). We can see that the clearing banks have most of their business in sterling deposits and lending, while the overseas banks have nearly all their business in other currency deposits and lending. But the clearing banks have also quite substantial other currency

TABLE 13.17   *UK banking sector: liabilities and assets, end-1980*

	£ million			Percentage of over-all total		
	Sterling	Other currencies [a]	Total	Sterling	Other currencies [a]	Total
Liabilities						
UK private-sector deposits	57,571	6,229	63,800	24.7	2.7	27.3
UK public-sector deposits	1,595	154	1,749	0.7	0.1	0.7
Overseas-sector deposits	11,477	145,644	157,121	4.9	62.4	67.3
Total deposits	70,643	152,027	222,670	30.3	65.1	95.4
of which *eligible liabilities* [b]	67,473	–	–	28.9		–
Non-deposit liabilities	10,722	–	10,722	4.6	–	4.6
Total	81,365	152,027	233,392	34.9	65.1	100.0
Assets						
Lending to UK private sector	54,870	8,852	63,722	23.5	3.8	27.3
Lending to UK public sector	17,325	1,485	18,810	7.4	0.6	8.1
Lending to overseas sector	7,879	142,981	150,860	3.4	61.3	64.6
Total	80,074	153,318	233,392	34.3	65.7	100.0
of which *reserve assets* [c]	9,084			(13.5) [d]		

[a] At their value in sterling.

[b] Defined as: sterling deposit liabilities of UK residents (other than banks) (*excluding* deposits having an original maturity over two years) *plus* sterling deposits from banks in UK *less* sterling claims on UK banks *plus* sterling certificates of deposit issued *less* any holdings of sterling certificates of deposit *plus* banks' net deposit liability in sterling to overseas offices *plus* banks' net liability in currencies other than sterling *less* 60 per cent of the net value of transit items (to avoid double counting, e.g. cheques paid into payee's account but not yet debited to drawer's account).

[c] Comprising: balances at the Bank of England (other than special deposits); British government Treasury bills; money at call with the London money market; British government and government-guaranteed stocks with one year or less to final maturity; local authority bills eligible for rediscount at the Bank of England; and commercial bills eligible for rediscount at the Bank of England.

[d] Percentage of reserve assets to eligible liabilities.

Source: Central Statistical Office, *Financial Statistics*, September 1981, tables 6.1 and 6.7, pp. 58–9 and 67.

business and the overseas banks have also some quite substantial sterling business. Thus, while it may be 'unsporting' in Table 13.1 to include the overseas banks with their very large other currency business and then to compare this with the mostly domestic business of the other financial institutions, there is no way of untangling the web of banking finance. Table 13.18 serves to illustrate the size of the international money market so far as the City of London is concerned. The growth of international banking and finance has been very rapid in the last two decades, and Table 13.18 bears witness to the effect of this growth.

The overseas banks are subject to the minimum reserve asset ratio but mostly in respect of their sterling deposits (the same applies to the clearing banks and other British banks); banks are not officially required to hold reserve assets against the gross total of their other currency deposit liabilities (as is the case for sterling deposit liabilities) but they are required to hold reserve assets against the total of other currency deposits *less* other currency assets. That is, to the extent that other currency business is not a straight in-and-out operation – to the extent that it impinges on the availability of finance in the United Kingdom (other currency deposits net of other currency lending being used for sterling business) – it is subject to the reserve asset ratio. As can be seen in the last two rows of Table 13.18 only a small proportion of the overseas banks' business is subject to UK monetary controls; but we should, conversely, note the extent to which the business of the British clearing banks does *not* fall within the scope of the UK monetary controls. British banks are themselves quite heavily engaged in the international banking business.

We have now seen how and why the money stock varies, and how the Bank of England (the government's agent) seeks to control or influence that variation.

TABLE 13.18 *The structure of the UK banking sector: British banks' and overseas banks' liabilities and assets, 10 December 1980*

	£ million			Percentage of respective totals		
	London and Scottish clearing banks and Northern Ireland banks	Accepting houses and other British banks	Overseas banks: American, Japanese, other, and consortium banks	London and Scottish clearing banks and Northern Ireland banks	Accepting houses and other British banks	Overseas banks: American, Japanese, other, and consortium banks
Liabilities						
Sterling deposits	48,911	21,959	20,034	66.9	39.3	11.5
Other currency deposits	13,039	28,199	152,109	17.9	50.5	87.2
Other liabilities	11,082	5,699	2,199	15.2	10.2	1.3
Assets						
Sterling assets	51,770	25,095	22,098	70.9	44.9	12.7
Other currency assets	13,579	28,498	151,521	18.6	51.0	86.9
Other assets [a]	7,687	2,267	728	10.5	4.1	0.4
Total liabilities or assets [b]	73,032	55,858	174,344	100.0	100.0	100.0
of which						
Eligible liabilities	39,550	13,619	14,303	54.2	24.4	8.2
Reserve assets	5,276	1,818	1,992	7.2	3.3	1.1

[a] Comprising sterling and other currency miscellaneous assets.
[b] Total may not equal sum of components due to rounding.

Source: *Bank of England Quarterly Bulletin*, September 1981, tables 3.2 to 3.10 inclusive and table 4.

The new 'Monetary Control' system

So far this exposition has dealt only with the system of monetary control begun in 1971 and called 'Competition and Credit Control.' But on 20 August 1981 a new system came into operation and this we shall now consider. In order to do this we need first to consider some matters of definition. So far we have spoken (rather loosely) of the reserve asset ratio simply as the requirement on the banks to hold a reserve of specified liquid assets (see p. 603) against their 'deposit liabilities to customers'. We did not then complicate the exposition by going into the full details of what those deposit liabilities were defined to comprise, but we must now do so.

The liabilities against which the specified reserve assets had to be held (to the tune of 12½ per cent of the liabilities) were known as 'eligible liabilities'. These eligible liabilities were defined to comprise the following stocks:*

1.   All sterling deposits, of an original maturity of two years or under, from UK residents (other than banks) and from overseas residents.
2.   All sterling deposits – of whatever term – from banks in the United Kingdom, less any sterling claims on such banks.
3.   All sterling certificates of deposit issued – of whatever term – less any holdings of such certificates.
4.   The bank's net deposit liability in sterling to its overseas offices.
5.   The bank's *net* liability in currencies other than sterling.
     less
6.   60 per cent of the net value of transit items in the bank's balance-sheets.

This is rather a lengthy definition; we have so far concerned ourselves simply with the first item: the banks' short-term deposit liabilities in sterling to UK non-bank residents, as these are operationally the most important item.

The provisions of item (2) in the definition can best be explained by imagining in Table 13.15 that Lloyds, after receiving the student's £1,000 deposit, had lent £875 to Barclays (had deposited £875 with Barclays) *and* that Barclays had then on-lent £875 to the Midland Bank *and* that the Midland Bank had then lent £875 to a (creditworthy) non-bank borrower. This may seem a peculiar chain of events, but to cope with temporary cash surpluses or deficits banks do engage in considerable lending and borrowing among themselves. At the beginning of the chain Lloyds has retained £125 of reserve assets against its deposit liability to the student; and it is clearly appropriate that this should be so. At the end of the chain the Midland Bank will have a deposit liability to Barclays Bank, and as the Midland Bank is responsible for lending the money to the non-bank sector it is appropriate that the Midland Bank put aside 0.125 × £875 = £109.375 as reserve assets to cover this deposit liability. The question which arises is whether it is appropriate to make Barclays Bank – the bank in the middle of the chain – also put aside £109.375 to cover its deposit liability to Lloyds. If this were required, one can see immediately that part of the banking sector's deposit liabilities (the deposit liability of £875) would, in effect, be covered by two sets of reserve assets. In order to avoid such double-coverage, Barclays Bank is permitted, by the provisions of item (2) in the definition, to deduct its claim on the Midland Bank from its deposit liability to Lloyds Bank, so leaving Barclays in a zero net position – which requires no reserve assets – and the requirement to hold reserve assets against the £875 deposit liability is thrust on to the Midland Bank, which is responsible for employing the £875 outside the banking sector.

Item (3) has a similar offset to item (2). A certificate of deposit is simply a certificate stating that a deposit of a stated amount has been deposited at a particular bank for a stated

* 'Reserve ratios: further definitions', *Bank of England Quarterly Bulletin*, December 1971.

period at a stated rate of interest; this is called a (negotiable) certificate of deposit, and at the due date the deposit is repayable to the current holder of the certificate (who need not necessarily be the person to whom the certificate was originally issued). This last feature makes the certificate of deposit a marketable financial asset which can be sold and resold as and when necessary; this negotiability is the attractive feature of certificates of deposit, which also pay a slightly higher rate of interest than ordinary time deposits.

We have seen in Table 13.17 the extent to which banks in the United Kingdom are involved in business denominated in currencies other than sterling: that is, accepting deposits of foreign currency and making loans (advances) in foreign currencies. The *net* position regarding these other currency stocks of liabilities and assets, i.e. the excess of foreign currency deposits over foreign currency advances, is also part of a bank's eligible liabilities against which reserve assets must be held.

The deduction of 60 per cent of the net value of 'transit items' is intended to safeguard banks from double-coverage with regard to reserve assets. It can be explained as follows. Suppose, in Table 13.15, that the student had straightaway paid £1,000, by cheque, to the university for fees and lodging; and suppose the university had deposited the student's cheque in its account with Barclays. There would then have been a (very brief) period before the cheque was 'cleared' and the student's account debited (drawn down to zero). During this period both banks would have had deposit liabilities of (essentially the same) £1,000 on their books. The question that arises is: should both banks, during this period, cover the deposit liability with £125 of reserve assets? It seems unnecessary to hold reserve assets against a seeming deposit liability of £2,000 (for the two banks concerned) when in fact there is only one liability of £1,000. The example may seem slightly artificial, but in aggregate the amount of items in transit is substantial, *and* such transit items are occurring all the time (for different transactors of course) so that the transit situation is a large and permanent one. It would therefore seem logical to permit Lloyds to deduct from its deposit liability the value of the cheque in transit; Lloyds would not then have to hold reserve assets against the (very temporary) liability to the student; only Barclays would hold reserve assets, and there would be no double-coverage. With millions of pounds in transit each and every day, failure to disregard transit items would, for the banking system as a whole, lead to a substantial doublecounting of deposit liabilities and so to considerable double-coverage.

This answer explains why all transit items should be deducted from deposit liabilities, and it is an incomplete answer because only 60 per cent of transit items may be so deducted. Why only 60 per cent? The answer to this particular question can be seen if we imagine that the student had not received a grant (say, due to some administrative delay) but had arranged with Lloyds an overdraft to cover his or her £1,000 payment of fees, etc. A cheque for exactly the same amount will then be in transit, but to permit Lloyds to deduct this transit item, when the cheque in question is going to result in an overdraft rather than the reduction of an existing deposit liability, will clearly result in undercounting Lloyds' deposit liabilities. If it were known what cheques in transit were drawn on deposit balances fully in credit and what cheques in transit would result in overdrafts (or the taking up of a loan), then we could deduct the former but not the latter and this would solve the problem of undercounting eligible liabilities were all transit items to be deducted. In practice, such information is not available (it would involve recording the state of every account at the time every cheque was drawn – for example, a cheque for £1,000 on an account £700 in credit where the drawer had agreed a £300 overdraft). The Bank of England has therefore agreed with the clearing banks that, to avoid undercounting, not all transit items would be deducted; and that a uniform 60 per cent of transit items be deducted – it being assumed (on the basis of some evidence) that the other 40 per cent of transit items represents cheques drawn against overdrafts, etc.

It has been necessary to describe the composition of eligible liabilities at some length, not only because the term is relevant to 'Monetary Control', but because the new system has made a concession in the definition of eligible liabilities. In the new system, the definition is amended to *exclude* (or, rather, to permit the deduction of) 'money at call placed with money brokers and gilt-edged jobbers in the Stock Exchange and secured on gilt-edged stocks, Treasury bills, local authority bills and eligible bank bills'.* This gives an added incentive to banks to use the services of the money brokers/gilt-edged jobbers and for the latter group to take up the specified securities.

When we described the old 'Competition and Credit Control' system, we were rather unspecific as to whom, exactly, the $12\frac{1}{2}$ per cent reserve asset ratio and the $1\frac{1}{2}$ per cent deposits at the Bank of England applied. In practice, under the old system, the $12\frac{1}{2}$ per cent ratio applied to all banks operating in the United Kingdom, but the further stipulation that $1\frac{1}{2}$ per cent be deposit balances at the Bank of England applied only to the London clearing banks. In practice, it was the $1\frac{1}{2}$ per cent ratio, supplemented by special deposits, which provided the operational lever whereby the Bank of England influenced (i.e. generally restrained) the growth of the London clearing banks' deposit liabilities. If the monetary authorities could sell more government securities in open-market operations, then the London clearing banks' cash balances with the Bank of England would be depleted (as people paid for the securities, the Bank of England would present their cheques to the clearing banks, so drawing down the clearing banks' deposits at the Bank of England). This depletion would cause the London clearing banks to hold back on making advances (loans and overdrafts) to customers, and this in turn would rein back the expansion of bank deposits. It is important to note that such control applied only to the clearing banks, and would not, in theory, affect other financial institutions (especially other banks to whom the $1\frac{1}{2}$ per cent cash ratio did not apply).

One of the problems that emerged during the 'Competition and Credit Control' period (1971 to 1981) was thus straightforward: if (creditworthy) borrowers could not get advances from the clearing banks, they would go to other banks or even to other financial institutions who were not hampered by having to observe the $1\frac{1}{2}$ per cent cash balance ratio. This process, whereby finance business moved out of the controlled sector, became increasingly obvious during the 1970s and came to be known as 'disintermediation' – although 'credit-control evasion' would have been a better descriptive title. And, following the abolition of exchange control in 1979, borrowers could more easily go abroad for finance.

The new 'Monetary Control' system has abolished the $12\frac{1}{2}$ per cent reserve asset ratio and, for the clearing banks, the $1\frac{1}{2}$ per cent ratio of balances at the Bank of England. In their place have been substituted:

1. A requirement that *all* recognised banks and licensed deposit-takers (under the 1979 Banking Act) maintain $\frac{1}{2}$ per cent of their (redefined) eligible liabilities as (non-interest-bearing) cash balances at the Bank of England.†
2. A requirement that the London clearing banks should 'voluntarily' maintain a further (unspecified) amount of deposits with the Bank of England for the purpose of effecting clearings among themselves and to give the Bank of England some leverage on the clearing banks.

---

*'Monetary Control – provisions', *Bank of England Quarterly Bulletin*, September 1981, pp. 347–9; other relevant documents are the preceding Green Paper *Monetary Control* (Cmnd 7858, March 1980) and five Bank of England papers: 'The gilt-edged market'; 'Monetary base control'; 'Method of monetary control'; 'Monetary control: next steps'; and 'The liquidity of banks', all in *Bank of England Quarterly Bulletins*; June 1979, pp. 137–48; June 1979, pp. 149–59; December 1980, pp. 428–9; March 1981, pp. 38–9; and March 1981, pp. 40–1, respectively. I call the new system the 'Monetary Control' system because of the title of the Green Paper Cmnd 7858.

†The level of these $\frac{1}{2}$ per cent deposits will be set twice a year on the average over the preceding six months of the institution's eligible liabilities; a full list of recognised banks and licensed deposit-takers was published in the *Financial Times*, Monday, 6 April 1981.

3. The stipulation that the special deposits scheme will be retained and will be applicable to all institutions with eligible liabilities of £10 million or more (this widens the scope of calls for special deposits).

Although the reserve asset ratio of 12½ per cent has been formally abolished, the Bank of England has sought and obtained assurances from the banks to which the ratio applied that they will maintain a 'prudential' level of liquidity and will discuss any changes in their management of liquidity with the Bank of England in advance of such changes. The prudential level of liquidity will now include an enlarged area of commercial bills. The previous 12½ per cent reserve asset ratio included, besides British government securities (and government-guaranteed securities), eligible commercial bills issued by the non-bank private sector and guaranteed, or 'accepted', by a few recognised financial institutions specialising in such acceptances. The acceptance implies that the commercial bill would, if necessary, be 'discounted' by the Bank of England – i.e. bought for cash (at a discount) by the Bank. This characteristic made such commercial bills a very safe liquid asset. The list of recognised institutions whose acceptance of a bill means that the bill will be eligible for discount at the Bank of England has been considerably extended under the 'Monetary Control' system with the intention that this will ensure a greater volume of commercial bills.* In return these 'eligible banks' – as the recognised institutions are called – have been required to hold an average of 6 per cent of their deposit liabilities (as previously defined) in the form of money at call with members of the London Discount Market Association and/or with money brokers and gilt-edged jobbers (who use the money so deposited with them to take up government securities and eligible bills). This ensures that at least a minimum of funds will be placed with the specialised discount market institutions which take up short-term government debt (especially Treasury bills). The London clearing banks are among the eligible banks.

Under the 'Competition and Credit Control' system, we could describe a fairly 'mechanical' model wherein any (residual) lending by the banking sector to the public sector could, subject to various conditions, result in a multiple creation of bank deposits according to the deposit multiplier formula of:

$$\frac{1}{\text{Reserve asset ratio}} \times \frac{\text{Bank lending}}{\text{to public sector}}$$

With a reserve asset ratio of 0.125, this gave a deposit multiplier of 8.

Under the 'Monetary Control' system there is no longer a determinate reserve asset ratio, and so there is no determinate deposit multiplier. There now appears to be a set of indeterminate ratios based on 'prudential' considerations and buttressed by the ½ per cent uniform cash balance ratio and the 6 per cent ratio for 'eligible banks', together with an extended ability of the monetary authorities to neutralise the growth of the banks' cash balances at the Bank of England through special deposits. The same basic principles as under 'Competition and Credit Control' will apply to 'Monetary Control', but in a more discretionary and possibly less discriminatory manner.

Part of the new 'Monetary Control' system is that the Bank of England will now regard itself as freer to vary interest rates according to the needs of monetary control: the Bank of England will no longer announce a Minimum Lending Rate (although in certain circumstances it may still do so), but will simply discount bills (i.e. supply cash) within an undisclosed band. In effect, this gives official recognition to the increasing reliance which the authorities placed upon interest rates when attempting to influence the growth of the money supply; the new 'Monetary Control' system formally acknowledges what was happening in any event.

The definition of the new 'monetary sector' – see the synopsis given previously –

*A list of eligible banks was published in *Bank of England Quarterly Bulletin*, September 1981, p. 350.

including all recognised banks, all licensed deposit-takers, the National Girobank, and the trustee savings banks, etc., is larger than the previous banking sector, chiefly due to the inclusion of the trustee savings banks, and because of this there will be a once–for–all increase in the money supply sterling M_3 of about £8,000 million or 13 per cent – about three-quarters coming from the inclusion of deposits with the trustee savings banks.

Maturing debt and the basic monetary policy equation

So far we have assumed that there was no maturing government debt (i.e. debt falling due for redemption), but because of past borrowing there is, in fact, each year a large flow of debt needing to be redeemed and so we must now incorporate maturing debt into the analysis. The term 'public sector borrowing requirement' covers *only* the public sector financial deficit *plus* net lending to other sectors.* This is the official definition of the public sector borrowing requirement, and we shall keep to this definition. However, the government's need to borrow may be greater than this by reason of the need to redeem maturing debt; such borrowing to finance redemption does not, of course, affect the government's total stock of financial liabilities – it simply replaces old (maturing) debt with new debt. The only thing that affects the total of the (net) stock of financial liabilities is the financial deficit. However, from the point of view of the expansion of the money supply, maturing debt can be a problem of significance.

Our explanation of the whole process of monetary expansion started by imagining a situation where the government had initially no financial deficit, but where the payment of a £1,000 grant to a student then created a government financial deficit, and we traced the process of monetary expansion from that source, assuming both that the government was not able to sell counterbalancing debt to the UK non-bank private sector (including notes and coin) and also that the government was not being provided with sterling finance through a balance-of-payments deficit. In this case the government ended up willy-nilly using finance provided by the banking sector; and this banking sector finance *is* the base of extra reserve assets for the banks upon which they can expand their loans and their deposit liabilities. The way this happens should by now be familiar to you.

However, for the purposes of analysing the process of monetary expansion, the imagined payment by the government of a £1,000 student grant (creating a government financial deficit) could just as well have been the repayment of £1,000 of maturing debt (no financial deficit involved at all – the government is just replacing old debt with new debt). It makes no difference in principle to the analysis of monetary changes whether the initial cheque is for a student grant (financial deficit) or to redeem maturing debt (no financial deficit).† If the government cannot finance its maturing debt by the sale of new debt to the UK non-bank private sector, and if there is no sterling finance from a balance-of-payments deficit, then everything in our analysis will proceed as before: the government will have to rely for its (re-)financing on the banking sector, and this provides the banking sector with the extra reserve assets. In other words, whereas Diagram 13.2 and the left-hand side of Diagram 13.3 used only the implied equation:

$$\begin{matrix} \text{Public} \\ \text{sector} \\ \text{borrowing} \\ \text{requirement} \end{matrix} = \begin{matrix} \text{Finance} \\ \text{from UK} \\ \text{non-bank} \\ \text{private} \\ \text{sector‡} \end{matrix} + \begin{matrix} \text{Finance} \\ \text{'from'} \\ \text{overseas} \\ \text{sector} \end{matrix} + \begin{matrix} \text{Finance} \\ \text{from UK} \\ \text{banking} \\ \text{sector} \end{matrix}$$

*It is important to appreciate that the public sector borrowing requirement is strictly a *net* borrowing requirement; there is no recognised term for the gross borrowing requirement which includes the borrowing needed to refinance maturing debt.

†In practice, it may make a difference, because non-bank holders of maturing debt may wish to replace it with new debt.

‡Including, here, the increase in notes and coin in circulation with the public.

(which equation holds because finance from the UK banking sector is the 'residual' which makes the equation always valid). Suppose now that all maturing debt is held by the UK non-bank private sector and that the holders of maturing debt do not wish to renew their holdings (while finance from the overseas sector remains constant) – in this simplified model the UK non-bank private sector switches its maturing government debt into assets (deposits) with the banking sector. Then we must, when maturing debt is taken into the reckoning, write:

$$\begin{matrix} \text{Public} \\ \text{sector} \\ \text{borrowing} \\ \text{requirement} \end{matrix} + \begin{matrix} \text{Maturing} \\ \text{debt} \end{matrix} = \begin{matrix} \text{Finance} \\ \text{from UK} \\ \text{non-bank} \\ \text{private} \\ \text{sector*} \end{matrix} + \begin{matrix} \text{Finance} \\ \text{'from'} \\ \text{overseas} \\ \text{sector} \end{matrix} + \begin{matrix} \text{Finance} \\ \text{from UK} \\ \text{banking} \\ \text{sector} \end{matrix}$$

In pictorial terms, we are simply adding on the left-hand side of Diagrams 13.2 and 13.3 another channel to the public-sector borrowing requirement and so widening the total stream of uses of finance labelled (in Diagram 13.2) 'Issuing of government debt'. We can write this last equation more realistically, for purposes of describing what actually happens in the real world, as follows:

$$\begin{matrix} \text{Finance} \\ \text{from UK} \\ \text{banking} \\ \text{sector} \end{matrix} = \begin{matrix} \text{Public} \\ \text{sector} \\ \text{borrowing} \\ \text{requirement} \end{matrix} + \begin{matrix} \text{Maturing} \\ \text{debt} \end{matrix} - \begin{matrix} \text{Finance} \\ \text{from UK} \\ \text{non-bank} \\ \text{private} \\ \text{sector*} \end{matrix} - \begin{matrix} \text{Finance} \\ \text{'from'} \\ \text{overseas} \\ \text{sector} \end{matrix}$$

This equation (or variants of it) I shall call the 'basic monetary policy equation'. For the purpose of understanding the flows which 'create difficulty' for the government (monetary authorities) when they want to control the growth of the money supply, we need to use the equation which explicitly contains the gross flows. We should now also take into account the fact that one part of the provision of finance to the government by the UK non-bank private sector is itself a direct part of the expansion of the money supply: this, of course, is the *extra* notes and coin which the public may come to hold during the course of the year – the student must ever bear in mind that all the terms in these equations are (annual) flows. To do this we may write:

$$\begin{matrix} \text{Finance} \\ \text{from UK} \\ \text{banking} \\ \text{sector} \end{matrix} + \begin{matrix} \text{Extra} \\ \text{notes} \\ \text{and} \\ \text{coin} \end{matrix} = \begin{matrix} \text{Public} \\ \text{sector} \\ \text{borrowing} \\ \text{requirement} \end{matrix} + \begin{matrix} \text{Maturing} \\ \text{debt} \end{matrix} - \begin{matrix} \text{Finance from} \\ \text{UK non-bank} \\ \text{private sector} \\ \text{(inc. notes,} \\ \text{etc.)} \end{matrix}$$

$$+ \begin{matrix} \text{Extra} \\ \text{notes} \\ \text{and} \\ \text{coin} \end{matrix} - \begin{matrix} \text{Finance} \\ \text{'from'} \\ \text{overseas} \\ \text{sector} \end{matrix}$$

In monetary economics, the sum of the two terms on the left-hand side of this equation is sometimes called the expansion in 'high-powered money'.[†] This is because the first term on the left-hand side provides the ('high-powered') basis upon which the expansion of the money supply proceeds according to the deposit multiplier. If the monetary authorities want to limit the expansion of high-powered money, then, with a given public sector borrowing requirement (determined by taxes and expenditures and including net lending)

---

*Including, here, the increase in notes and coin in circulation with the public.

[†]See Milton Friedman and Anna Schwartz, *A Monetary History of the United States 1867–1960* (Princeton University Press, 1963) p. 50; or C. A. E. Goodhart, *Money, Information and Uncertainty* (Macmillan, 1975) pp. 154–5.

and with a given flow of maturing debt (determined by past borrowing and the terms of that borrowing), and also assuming that little can be done directly and greatly to influence the finance obtained from the overseas sector, the authorities must try to obtain as much finance as possible from the non-bank private sector.

This means that the government must try to entice the public into acquiring as much non-marketable debt as possible. National savings are the main avenue in this effort, and the government has shown considerable ingenuity in devising attractive savings instruments such as the premium bond and the index-linked 'granny' bond (now, be it noted, available to everyone).*

The government will also try, through 'open-market operations', to sell as much marketable debt as possible. The attractiveness of such marketable debt depends upon the interest rates offered on such debt, so, if they wish to limit the expansion of high-powered money, the authorities may have to offer high rates of interest in order to sell debt; and we have seen that there is indeed a positive relationship between the public sector borrowing requirement (taken as a percentage of GDP) and the government's short-term interest rate (Diagram 13.7). The government is also not above rigging the tax system so as to make national savings and government securities more attractive: interest on Save As You Earn, on National Savings Certificates, and the first £70 of interest on ordinary deposits with the National Savings Bank are all exempt from income tax, while government securities (and public corporations' government-guaranteed securities) are exempt from Capital Gains Tax unless the disposal occurs within a period of twelve months following the date of acquisition.

Additionally to this, the operation of calling for special deposits can be seen as an administrative 'back-up' system whereby, if the authorities are failing, through open-market operations and otherwise, to limit the expansion of high-powered money to the rate they wish to see, a discretionary part of the expansion of high-powered money can simply be 'neutralised' by turning part of the expansion into special deposits (over which the deposit multiplier – whether a determinate or an indeterminate ratio – cannot operate).

However, all this may seem like *Hamlet* without the Prince of Denmark – why should the government wish to limit the growth of high-powered money? It is to this question and consequential issues of economic policy that we turn in the next chapter, having established in this chapter the basic descriptive groundwork for an understanding of monetary policy.

Exercises

General reading for all exercises is to be found in the relevant sections of: Central Statistical Office, *Financial Statistics Explanatory Handbook 1981 Edition* (or subsequent editions); Central Statistical Office, *Financial Statistics* (monthly – use the latest available edition); Jack Revell, *The British Financial System* (Macmillan, 1973; 2nd rev. edn forthcoming); Christopher John-

son, *Anatomy of UK Finance 1970–75* (Longman, 1976).

13.1   *(To deepen your appreciation of liquidity.)* Describe, and then analyse, Mr Tulliver's liquidity problems as portrayed by George Eliot in *The Mill on the Floss* (book One, chapter 8 'Mr Tulliver shows his weaker side').

---

*The appeal to the British public's gambling instincts when the *premium bonds* were introduced in Harold Macmillan's 'savings budget' of April 1956 was justified under the slogan 'If we cannot always save sinners, let us at least make sure that sinners save' (Harold Macmillan, *Riding the Storm, 1956–1959*, London, Macmillan, 1971, p. 36).

13.2 *(To practise your understanding of financial intermediation.)*

The largest financial intermediary in our economy is not classified as such because its other functions far outweigh its financial role. This is the central government (Jack Revell, *The British Financial System*, Macmillan, 1973, ch. 4 'Financial institutions', p. 74).

Explain, with illustrative data, the extent to which the central government functions as a financial intermediary.

13.3 *(To develop your knowledge and understanding of financial markets in the United Kingdom.)*

(i)   Your grandmother has just become a widow and has received £20,000 from your grandfather's whole-life assurance policy; your grandmother has turned to you for advice on what to do with the capital sum. Write a letter to her explaining the alternative possibilities, but making your own specific and considered recommendation.

(ii)   Your young brother has won £1,000 on a premium bond; advise him how he could best invest it.

(iii)   Your (patriotic) uncle has promised you £3,000 when you complete your education, on condition that you invest it in the shares of a company operating in the United Kingdom (which company is to be decided by you). Write a letter to him explaining how you have decided on the company of your choice.

(*Further reading:* Margaret Allen, *The Money Book*, Pan Books, 1977; Eamonn Fingleton and Tom Tickell, *The Penguin Money Book*, Penguin, 1981; James Rowlatt, *A Guide to Saving and Investment*, Pan Books, 1981.)

13.4 *(To develop your knowledge about building societies and about financial statistics. This exercise is intended also to give you practice in finding your own data and materials.)*

(i)   Write a project, with illustrative quantitative data and case studies, on the historical development and present position of building societies in the United Kingdom.

(ii)   Describe and explain the recent incursion by the clearing banks into the house-mortgage market (*further material:* Michael Cassell and William Hall, 'Banks and building societies: open war is de-

clared', the *Financial Times*, Saturday, 5 December 1981; also interview your (your father's) bank manager and the manager of the local branch of a building society – it would be polite to write first asking for an interview and explaining why).

13.5 *(To develop your knowledge about insurance.)*

(i)   Describe in detail and from the documents (contracts) themselves the insurance policies held by members of your family's household.

(ii)   Your mother is going to visit some relatives/friends abroad; advise her about 'holiday insurance' (you can get leaflets, application forms, etc., from your local insurance companies or travel agents).

(iii)   Your married sister is expecting her first child; assemble an argument to convince your brother-in-law that he should consider taking out some life insurance and advise him as to the sorts of policies available (*extra reading:* Christopher Gilchrist, *How To Plan Your Life Insurance*, Martin Books, 1979).

(iv)   Describe, with illustrative data, the insurance market in the United Kingdom (*further reading:* Committee to Review the Functioning of Financial Institutions (the Wilson Committee): *Evidence on the Financing of Industry and Trade, Volume 3: Export Credits Guarantee Department, Insurance Company Associations, National Association of Pension Funds, The Stock Exchange*, HMSO, 1978, pp. 55–100).

13.6 *(To develop your knowledge about pensions.)* Describe and explain, with illustrative data, the working of pension funds in the UK economy. (*Further reading:* Michael Pilch and Victor Wood, *Pension Schemes: A Guide to Principles and Practice*, Gower Press, 1979; Committee to Review the Functioning of Financial Institutions (the Wilson Committee), *Report*, Cmnd 7937, HMSO, June 1980, ch. 6 'Pension funds and pension funding'; *Appendices* [to *Report*], Cmnd 7937, HMSO, June 1980, pp. 462–9; *Evidence on the Financing of Industry and Trade, Volume 3: Export Credits Guarantee Department, Insurance Company Associations, National Association of Pension Funds, The Stock Exchange*, HMSO, 1978, pp. 129–85.)

13.7   *(To develop your knowledge of some other financial intermediaries.)* Describe and explain, with illustrative data, the working of investment trusts and the difference between investment trusts and unit trusts. *(Further reading:* Committee to Review the Functioning of Financial Institutions (the Wilson Committee), *Evidence on the Financing of Industry and Trade, Volume 7: Association of Investment Trust Companies, Unit Trust Association, Association of British Chambers of Commerce,* HMSO, April 1978, pp. 1–8 and 27–37; *Appendices* [to *Report*], Cmnd 7937, HMSO, June 1980, pp. 442–53; The Association of Investment Trust Companies, *Investment Trust Year Book,* Association of Investment Trust Companies, 16 Finsbury Circus, London EC2M 7JJ.)

13.8   *(To develop your knowledge of The Stock Exchange.)* Describe and explain, with illustrative data, the working of The Stock Exchange. *(Further reading:* Committee to Review the Functioning of Financial Institutions (the Wilson Committee), *Evidence on the Financing of Industry and Trade, Volume 3: Export Credits Guarantee Department, Insurance Company Associations, National Association of Pension Funds, The Stock Exchange,* HMSO, 1978, pp. 186–267; *Appendices* [to *Report*], Cmnd 7937, HMSO, June 1980, pp. 486–503; *The Stock Exchange Fact Book,* The Council of the Stock Exchange, London EC2B 2PQ.)

13.9   *(To develop your knowledge about banks.)*

(i)   From the leaflets available in your local bank(s), describe the services which banks provide.

(ii)   You are applying for a job with a bank and the selection from among the applicants is to be based on applicants' written appraisals of banking business (in not more than 2,000 words). Write your appraisal.

(Further reading (important source material): *The London Clearing Banks,* Evidence by the Committee of London Clearing Bankers to the Committee to Review the Functioning of Financial Institutions, November 1977, Longman, 1978; Committee to Review the Functioning of Financial Institutions, *Appendices* [to *Report*] Cmnd 7937, HMSO, June 1980, pp. 393–421.)

13.10   *(Further to develop your understanding of banks' business.)*

(i)   For the latest date available, tabulate, and work out the percentage structure of, the stock of outstanding advances made by the London clearing banks to UK residents by branch of industry including the personal sector (Central Statistical Office, *Financial Statistics,* latest edition, table 6.7 'Analysis of advances to UK residents by banks in the United Kingdom').

(ii)   Explain why, by late 1981, the Bank of England was becoming concerned about the growth in banks' advances to the personal sector for house purchase.

13.11   *(To develop your understanding of one of the roles of the Bank of England and also to give you some practice in research using contemporary material.)* Following the failure of Overend, Gurney & Co. Ltd, the financial bill-brokers, on Thursday, 10 May 1866, and the ensuing panic on 'Black Friday', 11 May 1866, with a 'run' on banks by depositors in London and in the provinces, the Governor of the Bank of England, in an address on 13 September 1866, said:

A great strain has within the last few months been put upon the resources of this house [i.e. the Bank of England], and of the whole banking community of London; and I think I am entitled to say that not only this house, but the entire banking body, acquitted themselves most honourably and creditably throughout that very trying period. Banking is a very peculiar business, and it depends so much upon credit that the least blast of suspicion is sufficient to sweep away, as it were, the harvest of a whole year. But the manner in which the banking establishments generally in London met the demands made upon them during the greater portion of the past half-year affords a most satisfactory proof of the soundness of the principles on which their business is conducted. This house exerted itself to the utmost – and exerted itself most successfully – to meet the crisis. We did not flinch from our post. When the storm came upon us, on the morning on which it became known that the house of Overend and Co. had failed, we were in as sound and healthy a position as any banking establishment could hold, and on that day and throughout the succeeding week we made advances [i.e. loans] which would hardly be credited. I do not believe that anyone would have thought of predicting, even at the shortest period beforehand, the greatness of those advances. It was not unnatural that in this state of things a certain degree of alarm should have taken possession of the public mind, and that those who required accommodation from the Bank should have gone to the Chancellor of the Exchequer and requested the Government to empower us to issue notes [bank notes, i.e. currency] beyond the statutory amount, if we should think that such a measure was desirable. But we had to act before we could receive any such power, and before the Chancellor of the Exchequer was perhaps out of his bed we had advanced one-half of our reserves, which were certainly thus reduced to an amount which we could not witness without regret. But we would not flinch from the duty which we conceived was imposed upon us of supporting the banking community, and I am not aware that any legitimate application made for assistance to this house was refused. Every gentleman who came here with adequate security was liberally dealt with, and if accommodation would not be afforded to the full extent which was demanded, no one who offered proper security failed to obtain relief from this house (quoted in Walter Bagehot, *Lombard Street: A Description of the Money Market* (1873), pp. 164–6; see also appendix, note D).

Bagehot's (approving) comment on this speech was: 'It acknowledges a "duty" on the part of the Bank of England to "support the banking community", to make the reserve of the Bank of England do for them as well as for itself.'* In the light of Bagehot's remarks about the Bank of England's 'duty', describe and assess how the Bank of England carried out its 'duty' in the secondary banking crisis of 1973–4.

(*Further reading: Bank of England Quarterly Bulletin*, June 1978, 'The secondary banking crisis and the Bank of England's support operations', paper presented by the Bank to the Research Panel of the Wilson Committee; and the following articles, all in the *Financial Times*: Michael Blanden, 'When flexibility in the banking system can be a weakness', Thursday, 6 December 1973, p. 22; Margaret Reid, 'Institutions in £80m. rescue move for Cedar Holdings', Friday, 21 December 1973, p. 1; Margaret Reid, 'City to the rescue', Friday, 21 December 1973, p. 9; Michael Blanden, 'Bank [of England] in confidence move', Saturday, 22 December 1973, p. 1; Michael Blanden, 'Secondary banks: an end to freewheeling', Monday, 24 December 1973, p. 5; Margaret Reid, 'How the "Bankers Lifeboat" came to the rescue', Tuesday, 29 January 1974, p. 12; Margaret Reid, *The Secondary Banking Crisis 1973–75* (Macmillan, 1982).)

13.12 (*To practise your understanding of the deposit multiplier.*)

(i) Assume, for Table 13.15, that the amount of reserve assets which the clearing banks are required to hold against deposit liabilities is 10.5 per cent of those liabilities, *including* in the 10.5 per cent the (now) $\frac{1}{2}$ per cent (of deposit liabilities) required as bankers' deposits with the Bank of England. Assume that, as per Table 13.15, the government has to borrow £1,500 to pay the (now-increased) student's grant and that the student deposits this with Lloyds Bank. Work out the ensuing sequence of deposit/loans expansion. Using this sequence as illustrative data, derive the deposit multiplier.

(ii) In this sequence, explain, with relevant data, why Lloyds Bank is, at step (2), potentially in a loss-making situation.

13.13 (*To practise your understanding of the financing of the public sector borrowing requirement.*)

(i) In 1980, as compared with 1979, the public sector borrowing requirement fell slightly (by 3 per cent), yet government borrowing in sterling from the banks rose considerably (by 54 per cent). With reference to Diagram 13.3, explain why this is, at first glance, surprising.

(ii) With reference to Central Statistical Office, *Financial Statistics*, latest edition, table 2.6 'Financing the public sector borrowing requirement', explain how it was that the situation described in (i) came about.

13.14 (*To see the practical importance of Special Deposits.*)

The Special Deposits scheme should be retained to guard against the possible effects of excess liquidity in the banking system as a whole (*Monetary Control*, 'Green Paper' presented to Parliament by the Chancellor of the Exchequer (Cmnd 7858, HMSO, March 1980), para. 6.3, p. 15).

With reference to the size in recent years of Special Deposits relative to bankers' deposits with the Bank of England, show that the 'Green

*Bagehot was actually quoting an article in *The Economist* of 22 September 1866, but Bagehot himself was editor and manager of *The Economist* from 1860 until his death in 1877.

Paper' on *Monetary Control* had good reason for coming to this conclusion (Central Statistical Office, *Financial Statistics*, latest edition, table 6.4 'Liabilities of the monetary authorities' – for the purposes of this answer you may ignore the fact that the reported figures on Special Deposits include Supplementary Special Deposits).

13.15   *(To practise your knowledge of the money supply.)*

(i)   Update Table 13.14.
(ii)   Briefly explain what each of the items in your updated table is.
(iii)   Describe the changes in UK residents' deposits in other currencies since the abol-

ition of foreign exchange controls from 24 October 1979.

(iv)   It is said that high interest rates in 1980 and 1981 encouraged the growth of private-sector time deposits (possibly by switching from other assets). Why should this be so? Is the assertion true in the light of the data?

(v)   In the Budget of June 1979 (and subsequently) it was announced that the target for the expansion of the money supply sterling M_3 under the government's 'Medium Term Financial Strategy' would be in the range 7 to 11 per cent per annum. How successful, or unsuccessful, has the government been in meeting its target?

APPENDIX 13.1   *Transactions in company securities by personal sector and by life assurance and superannuation funds, 1964 to 1980*

Year	Transactions in company and overseas securities, £ million	
	Personal sector [a]	Life assurance and superannuation funds [b]
1964	−573	619
1965	−685	601
1966	−574	659
1967	−785	554
1968	−776	674
1969	−616	617
1970	−858	773
1971	−1,165	875
1972	−999	1,358
1973	−1,815	794
1974	−1,324	160
1975	−1,369	1,413
1976	−1,328	1,275
1977	−1,912	1,815
1978	−1,601	2,094
1979	−1,875	2,355
1980[c]	−1,630	2,288

[a] Derived as a residual. Note that the data in Table 3.9 are revised data.

[b] The exact composition of this sector is difficult to determine clearly; from 1964 to 1977 inclusive it is reported as 'insurance companies and superannuation funds' but a note on page 112 of *National Income and Expenditure 1965* states with reference to table 68: 'In this Blue Book the table has been extended to show separately the transactions in financial assets of *life assurance* and superannuation funds' (italics added).

[c] Excludes overseas securities; UK company securities only.

Sources: Central Statistical Office, *National Income and Expenditure: 1965*, table 68, pp. 80 and 112; *1966*, table 74, p. 87; *1967*, table 73, p. 87; *1968*, table 73, p. 89; *1969*, table 70, p. 83; *1970*, table 69, p. 81; *1971*, table 72, p. 85; *1972*, table 71, p. 83; *1973*, table 71, p. 83; *1963–1973*, table 73, p. 85; *1964–74*, table 81, p. 89; *1965–75*, table 14.2, p. 92; *1966–76*, table 13.2, p. 94; *1967–77*, table 13.2, p. 98; *1979 Edition*, table 13.2, p. 96; *1980 Edition*, table 13.2, p. 91; *1981 Edition*, table 13.2, p. 91.

APPENDIX 13.2 *Public sector borrowing requirement, change in money supply, domestic credit expansion, and price inflation in the United Kingdom, 1952 to 1980*

Year	£ million				Percentage of GDP			Percentage increase in implied GDP deflator (a)
	Public sector borrowing requirement	Increase in money stock sterling M3	Domestic credit expansion	Gross domestic product	Public sector borrowing requirement	Increase in money stock M3	Domestic credit expansion	
1952	794	235	51	13,836	5.7	1.7	0.4	9.2
1953	593	267	293	14,918	4.0	1.8	2.0	2.9
1954	371	268	342	15,761	2.4	1.7	2.2	2.1
1955	470	−248	−92	16,905	2.8	−1.5	−0.5	3.5
1956	573	81	75	18,301	3.1	0.4	0.4	6.1
1957	487	228	201	19,404	2.5	1.2	1.0	4.1
1958	491	274	103	20,227	2.4	1.4	0.5	4.6
1959	571	578	746	21,258	2.7	2.7	3.5	1.8
1960	710	182	385	22,637	3.1	0.8	1.7	1.7
1961	704	262	513	24,228	2.9	1.1	2.1	3.4
1962	546	275	275	25,284	2.2	1.1	1.1	3.3
1963	824	697	1,040	26,913	3.1	2.6	3.9	2.4
1964	999	597	1,514	29,210	3.4	2.0	5.2	3.1
1965	1,190	915	1,130	31,219	3.8	2.9	3.6	4.0
1966	965	536	790	33,130	2.9	1.6	2.4	3.9
1967	1,826	1,309	1,766	34,935	5.2	3.7	5.1	2.8
1968	1,318	1,075	1,908	37,576	3.5	2.9	5.1	2.9
1969	−474	454	−181	39,633	−1.2	1.1	−0.5	3.7
1970	4	1,586	1,041	43,574	0.01	3.6	2.4	7.8
1971	1,382	2,459	1,177	49,490	2.8	5.0	2.4	10.8
1972	2,054	4,927	6,691	55,347	3.7	8.9	12.1	10.3
1973	4,209	6,702	8,066	64,347	6.5	10.4	12.5	8.0
1974	6,437	3,255	6,926	74,661	8.6	4.4	9.3	16.9
1975	10,480	2,331	4,530	94,475	11.1	2.5	4.8	27.1
1976	9,128	3,565	7,475	111,585	8.2	3.2	6.7	13.9
1977	5,993	4,130	1,132	126,943	4.7	3.3	0.9	12.3
1978	8,356	6,772	8,065	145,304	5.8	4.7	5.6	11.5
1979	12,611	6,615	10,255	166,464	7.6	4.0	6.2	13.4
1980	12,244	10,898	15,541	193,488	6.3	5.6	8.0	18.1

(a) Over previous year.

Sources: Bank of England, *Statistical Abstract*, No. 1, 1970, tables 12(2) and 12(3), pp. 79−80; Bank of England, *Statistical Abstract*, No. 2, 1975, tables 12(2) and 12(3), pp. 103 and 105; Central Statistical Office, *Economic Trends Annual Supplement 1981 Edition*, pp. 5 and 148; Central Statistical Office, *National Income and Expenditure 1981 Edition*, tables 1.1, 2.6 and 13.12, pp. 3, 23 and 101; Central Statistical Office, *Financial Statistics*, October 1981, table 7.3, p. 79.

APPENDIX 13.3   *Short-term official interest rates, 1945 to 1981*

Year [a]	Per cent per annum Bank Rate	Year [a]	Per cent per annum Minimum Lending Rate [b]
1945	2.00	1970	7.21
1946	2.00	1971	5.92
1947	2.00	1972	6.08
1948	2.00	1973	10.10
1949	2.00	1074	11.90
1950	2.00	1975	10.75
1951	2.08	1976	11.81
1952	3.75	1977	8.25
1953	3.83	1978	9.25
1954	3.17	1979	13.96
1955	4.42	1980	16.17
1956	5.42	1981 [c]	12.57
1957	5.71		
1958	5.25		
1959	4.00		
1960	5.42		
1961	5.79		
1962	4.79		
1963	4.00		
1964	5.25		
1965	6.42		
1966	6.50		
1967	6.21		
1968	7.42		
1969	7.92		

[a] Simple average of rates at end of each month.
[b] Known as Bank Rate before 13 October 1972.
[c] Up to and including July; MLR discontinued in August.

Sources: Bank of England, *Statistical Abstract*, No. 1, 1970, table 29, pp. 169–73; Bank of England, *Statistical Abstract*, No. 2, 1975, table 27, p. 158; Central Statistical Office, *Financial Statistics*, March 1976, table 113, p. 133; *Financial Statistics*, November 1978, table 13.10, p. 146; *Financial Statistics*, October 1981, table 13.9, p. 139.

Economic Policy

Contents

Chapter guide

Chapter 14 is concerned with the basic analytic framework for macroeconomic policy. We explain why, in *monetary policy*, the government might wish to limit the growth of the money supply, and we show how the PSBR, the bank deposit multiplier and interest rates fit together in the framework for monetary policy (Diagram 14.1). We explain the *discounted cash flow* technique of investment appraisal so that the relationship between the rate of interest in the economy at large and the investment decision of individual enterprises can be appreciated (high interest rates are a disincentive to enterprise investment and this provides a powerful reason why the government would prefer to have lower interest rates).

We examine data on the connection between *inflation* and the growth of the money supply, one of the cornerstones of *monetarism*. We explain how the general government's financial deficit may affect the *overseas sector's financial balance* (i.e. the balance of payments, especially the balance of trade) and we also look at empirical data on this important relationship.

The systematic relationships between the PSBR, inflation, the overseas sector's financial balance and *unemployment* are then put together in a unified analytic framework for economic policy (Diagram 14.4). The various options for economic policy are then explained – what they are and how they are supposed to work; we consider, especially, *devaluation, import controls, incomes policy*, and reducing the *full-employment government financial deficit* by expanding private-sector investment and exports.

Monetary policy

Why does the government (the Bank of England) impose the controls on banking described in the previous chapter? Part of the answer is that it is necessary to ensure 'prudent' financial intermediation; financial intermediaries must not become so 'exposed' (with regard to short-term deposit liabilities and long-term assets) that they run the risk of not being able to meet their obligations. For this reason the Bank of England also requires 'reserve asset' or liquidity ratios to be observed by other financial institutions as well.

But another part of the answer is that the government may wish to control the growth of the money supply. In Chapter 12 we could see very clearly the rationale for the government increasing its expenditure and/or decreasing taxation in order to reduce the level of unemployment by stimulating economic activity (e.g. the transition from Table 12.4 to Table 12.5). From this point of view, when there is unemployment, an increased government financial deficit and hence an increased public sector borrowing requirement may be a 'good thing' leading to less unemployment.

However, we can now see (Diagram 13.3) that an increased public sector borrowing requirement leads to either or all of the following:

1. More government borrowing from the UK non-bank private sector – obtained by increasing the rate of interest offered on new issues of government debt.
2. More government borrowing from the UK banking sector – which will increase banks' reserve assets and so possibly lead to an expansion of the money supply (see Diagrams 13.5 and 13.6).
3. A balance-of-payments deficit (a reduction in foreign exchange reserves) which provides sterling finance for the PSBR.

Monetary policy is that part of government policy which is concerned basically with these three items (monetary policy has many other facets, but this definition will serve as an introduction).

We need to understand two basic aspects of monetary policy. The first is that there is an inverse 'trade-off' between the interest rate on new issues of government debt and the expansion of the money supply. The second is that, if the government wishes simultaneously to reduce both the rate of interest and the expansion of the money supply, then it has no alternative but to reduce the public sector borrowing requirement. In other words, with a given public sector borrowing requirement, the government can *either* establish an interest rate and then accept whatever expansion of the money supply ensues, *or* the government can establish a target rate of money supply expansion and then accept the consequences for the interest rate of trying to achieve that target; what the government *cannot* do is to control interest rates and the expansion of the money supply *simultaneously and independently* of each other while at the same time not altering the PSBR.

All this can be explained with the aid of Diagram 14.1 (which spells out, more explicitly with regard to interest rates, the sequence of events illustrated in Diagram 13.3).* We start

*Diagram 14.1 is a 'model', or schematic and simplified representation, of the real world, but it relates to the empirical evidence of the previous chapter as follows. The upper-left quadrant of Diagram 14.1 shows, in schematic form, the relationship between the rate of interest on government debt and government borrowing from the UK non-bank private sector; this schematic relationship relates to the empirical relationship in Diagram 13.7 which showed how the interest rate tended to

DIAGRAM 14.1 *The framework for monetary policy*

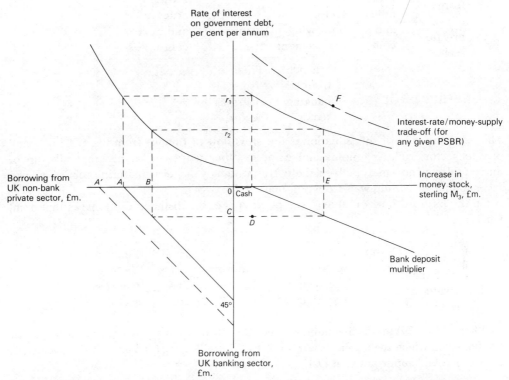

in the upper-left quadrant of Diagram 14.1. Leftwards along the horizontal axis we measure government borrowing from the UK non-bank private sector, but excluding any increase in notes and coin in circulation with the public (which increase we call 'cash' in the diagram).

In terms of the basic monetary policy equation (see p. 631), the distance along this axis would be given by:

$$\begin{array}{l}\text{Finance} \\ \text{from UK} \\ \text{non-bank} \\ \text{private} \\ \text{sector*}\end{array} = \begin{array}{l}\text{Public} \\ \text{sector} \\ \text{borrowing} \\ \text{requirement}\end{array} + \begin{array}{l}\text{Maturing} \\ \text{debt}\end{array} - \begin{array}{l}\text{Finance} \\ \text{from UK} \\ \text{banking} \\ \text{sector}\end{array} - \begin{array}{l}\text{Finance} \\ \text{'from'} \\ \text{overseas} \\ \text{sector}\end{array}$$

but because, for reasons which will become apparent, we want to take 'cash' (the increase in notes and coin in circulation with the public) out of the reckoning – or rather we need to take it into the reckoning elsewhere – what is being measured leftwards along the horizontal axis in Diagram 14.1 is:

be higher, the higher was the extent of total public-sector borrowing (taken as a proportion of GDP). The schematic relationship in the bottom-right quadrant of Diagram 14.1 between the increase in the money supply and public-sector borrowing from the banking sector relates to the empirical evidence of Diagram 13.6 in so far as the two lower quadrants of Diagram 14.1 demonstrate what happens when the PSBR increases, thus shifting the 45° line outwards and downwards: this will produce a positive *ceteris paribus* relationship between the PSBR and the expansion of the money supply, and such a positive relationship is discernible in Diagram 13.6. The schematic relationship in the upper-right quadrant of Diagram 14.1 then follows as a *ceteris paribus* relationship consequent upon all the foregoing.

*Including the increase in notes and coin in circulation with the public.

$$\begin{array}{l}\text{Finance} \\ \text{from UK} \\ \text{non-bank} \\ \text{private} \\ \text{sector*}\end{array} - \begin{array}{l}\text{Extra} \\ \text{notes} \\ \text{and} \\ \text{coin}\end{array} = \begin{array}{l}\text{Public} \\ \text{sector} \\ \text{borrowing} \\ \text{requirement}\end{array} + \begin{array}{l}\text{Maturing} \\ \text{debt}\end{array} - \begin{array}{l}\text{Extra} \\ \text{notes} \\ \text{and} \\ \text{coin}\end{array}$$

$$- \begin{array}{l}\text{Finance} \\ \text{from UK} \\ \text{banking} \\ \text{sector}\end{array} - \begin{array}{l}\text{Finance} \\ \text{'from'} \\ \text{overseas} \\ \text{sector}\end{array}$$

The left-hand side of this equation is the *gross* flow of finance from the UK non-bank private sector excluding notes and coin; in other words, it is the gross take-up of marketable and non-marketable debt (correspondingly the term 'maturing debt' should be taken to include withdrawals from non-marketable debt).

On the leftward horizontal axis, the point *A* (i.e. the distance *OA*) marks that point where:

$$\begin{array}{l}\text{Finance} \\ \text{from UK} \\ \text{non-bank} \\ \text{private} \\ \text{sector*}\end{array} - \begin{array}{l}\text{Extra} \\ \text{notes} \\ \text{and} \\ \text{coin}\end{array} = \begin{array}{l}\text{Public} \\ \text{sector} \\ \text{borrowing} \\ \text{requirement}\end{array} + \begin{array}{l}\text{Maturing} \\ \text{debt}\end{array} - \begin{array}{l}\text{Extra} \\ \text{notes} \\ \text{and} \\ \text{coin}\end{array} - \begin{array}{l}\text{Finance} \\ \text{'from'} \\ \text{overseas} \\ \text{sector}\end{array}$$

In other words, *OA* marks that point at which the UK non-bank private sector provides *all* the financing which the public sector requires (after allowing for finance from overseas); conversely, and importantly, at *OA*:

$$\begin{array}{l}\text{Finance} \\ \text{from UK} \\ \text{banking} \\ \text{sector}\end{array} = 0$$

Up the vertical axis of Diagram 14.1 we measure the rate of interest paid on new issues of government debt. Following the empirical relationship demonstrated in Diagram 13.7, we argue that the greater the amount the government wants to borrow from the UK non-bank private sector, the higher the rate of interest which the government must offer on new issues of debt: that is, the relationship between the amount of borrowing and the interest rate is positive because the greater the amount of debt to be sold during the year to the UK non-bank private sector, the more attractive have to be the terms offered (the rate of interest). Furthermore, we argue that it is likely to get increasingly difficult to persuade the UK non-bank private sector to take up additional government debt, so the curve showing this relationship has an upward-curving twist in it (in what follows we also assume that this curve does not move – i.e. shift 'bodily' – but is stable).† If the government wishes the UK non-bank private sector to take up the entire PSBR plus maturing debt after allowing for increase in notes and coin and after allowing for finance from the overseas sector (to be called 'external finance' for short – in what follows we shall assume that external finance is relatively constant) – that is, if the government wishes to dispose of *OA* to the UK non-bank private sector, then the government will have to offer (a high) rate of interest r_1 on its newly issued debt (including not only marketable debt but also non-marketable debt like National Savings). If the government offers a lower rate of interest,

---

*Including the increase in notes and coin in circulation with the public, which expression we shall shorten to 'extra notes and coin'.

†To some small extent this upward twist can be discerned in Diagram 13.7.

say r_2, then the UK non-bank private sector will take up only *OB* of government debt, leaving the rest, *BA*, to be provided by the UK banking sector.

From *A* we may draw at 45° a line to the downward vertical axis, along which axis is measured government borrowing from the UK banking sector. Using this 45° line we may plot *OC* equal to *BA*. So that, if the given PSBR *plus* maturing debt *minus* cash *minus* external finance without any banking-sector finance determines point *A*, and the government offers rate of interest r_2 on new debt, then we know that the government must borrow *OC* (= *BA*) from the UK banking sector.

In the lower-right quadrant of Diagram 14.1, we may measure, along the horizontal axis rightwards from the origin, the expansion in the money supply. Because increases in the money supply largely comprise increases in bank deposits, this is going to depend mostly upon the extent to which the banking sector is lending to the public sector and so obtaining additional reserve assets (but see Diagram 13.5). However, the increase in notes and coin is directly part of the increase in the money supply (sterling M_3), so we must start along this axis at a distance representing this increase in notes and coin. That is, even if there were zero government borrowing from the banks and consequently no expansion in banks' reserve assets and in their deposit liabilities, there will still be this 'cash' increase in the money supply. After this intercept point, further increases in the money supply depend upon banks acquiring reserve assets by lending to the government (this involves the whole chain of lending (etc.) described in the previous chapter – see Table 13.15).

These further increases in the money supply we may represent as being subject to the bank deposit multiplier; that is, under the previous UK banking system of 'Competition and Credit Control' there was likely to occur an expansion of banks' deposits of 8 for every 1 which the banks lent to the government. Under the new 'Monetary Control' system, we may assume that a similar multiple relationship will continue to hold, though on a less determinate ratio. Note that the line in Diagram 14.1 is not drawn with a slope of 1 in 8 simply because it would be too close to the horizontal axis and would make the diagram difficult to follow.*

So, as can be seen, the bank deposit multiplier relationship is a 'powerful' relationship in multiplying up the money supply increase consequent upon government borrowing from the banking sector. Note that the effect of calls for special deposits is to shift this relationship downwards parallel to itself – if the Bank of England were to call for special deposits of amount *OC*, then *D* indicates the point from which the bank deposit multiplier relationship would start. However, Diagram 14.1 is drawn on the assumption of no calls for special deposits.

If the government borrows *OC* from the UK banking sector, then, given that the bank deposit multiplier is in the position indicated (no calls for special deposits), the expansion in the money supply will be *OE* (subject to the requisite and relevant conditions of Diagram 13.5 being fulfilled). So, with the given PSBR and maturing debt and increase in notes and coin and external finance, the rate of interest r_2 will correspond to *OE* expansion of the money supply sterling M_3, while the rate of interest r_1 corresponds to the 'cash' increase only in the money supply. Clearly, it is possible to plot, in the upper-right quadrant, a continuous downward curve traced out by such points of correspondence, and this curve shows the 'trade-off' between the interest rate on the one hand and the money supply increase on the other (for any given PSBR and maturing debt such as that measured by distance *OA*, after allowing for external finance).

*As drawn, Diagram 14.1 tends to *understate* the impact on the increase in the money supply. However, drawing a straight line to represent the deposit multiplier effect glosses over the important fact that changes in interest rates will, through their impact on the demand for bank loans, affect the deposit multiplier process itself; this should (under certain assumptions) give the deposit multiplier relationship a downward twist, but this intricate complication has not been drawn simply for the sake of keeping Diagram 14.1 to its basic essentials.

Having understood the derivation of this curve in the upper-right quadrant, it is important to appreciate that the only way of simultaneously reducing both the rate of interest offered on new government debt and the increase in the money supply – that is, the only way of shifting the curve downwards – is to reduce the public sector borrowing requirement. To illustrate this (and because it is slightly easier to draw it in the diagram), let us imagine what the situation would be were the PSBR *higher* than initially described in the *OA* configuration.

Suppose that, increase in notes and coin and external finance being constant, the (higher) public sector borrowing requirement (together with the same maturing debt, and minus notes and coin and external finance) were equal to *OA'*. We now have a new 45° line, as shown by the broken line, and correspondingly a new and higher trade-off curve in the upper-right quadrant as shown by the broken curve. If the PSBR *plus* maturing debt *minus* increase in notes and coin and external finance were equal to *OA'*, the interest-rate/money-supply increase trade-off might be at a point such as *F*. In the absence of calls for special deposits, the only way the government can get to the point $r_2 E$ is to reduce the PSBR. Note well that the government has to take action on the PSBR alone; there is nothing it can do about the flow of maturing debt (which is historically determined), and little it can do about the other two variables (cash and external finance) either. But with a reduced PSBR, the government can reduce the rate of interest to r_2 and (with its lower borrowing requirement and consequently a downward shift in the trade-off curve) the money supply will rise by only *OE*.

Reverting to the trade-off curve resulting from the *OA* configuration, if the government wants to have the rate of interest r_2, then, with the given PSBR, it must accept an expansion in the money supply of *OE*. Or, if the government wishes to establish a target for the increase in the money supply, say to that represented by 'cash', then with the given PSBR it will have to accept the necessity for setting rate of interest r_1.

To summarise. Ignoring special deposits and ignoring the matter of external finance (which will be considered subsequently), a government which wishes to reduce the expansion of the money supply (but which does not wish to reduce the PSBR) must increase interest rates. Conversely if it wishes to lower interest rates, it must accept a faster expansion of the money supply. A government which wishes *both* to reduce interest rates *and* to have a reduction in the rate of growth of the money supply must (special deposits apart) reduce the public sector borrowing requirement (i.e. the 45° line in the lower-left quadrant must be shifted upwards towards the origin by reducing its starting-point on the horizontal leftwards axis, so shifting the interest-rate/increase in money supply trade-off curve bodily downwards towards the origin).

Diagram 14.1 thus provides a schematic representation of the problems of monetary policy facing any government. But it leaves us with two immediate and substantive questions relating to economic policy in general and monetary policy in particular. Why should a government want low interest rates? And why should a government want to limit the increase in the money supply?

One relatively unimportant answer to the first question is that high interest rates condemn the government to paying out more (taxpayers') money, over quite long periods, in order to finance its borrowing. Such interest payments are only transfer payments, but they do mean that more tax revenue has to be raised.

A more important answer is that the rate of interest offered on new government debt tends to determine rates of interest in general (because government debt is the 'safest' (least risky) security available to savers, it is difficult for other debt issuers (issuing riskier securities) to offer less than the government rate of return), so high rates of interest on government debt mean that, for example, the rate of interest on mortgages for house purchase will be high, and this is politically unpopular. More importantly, if part of the investment in real assets by industry and commerce is financed by borrowed money (or by new issues), then it is clearly not desirable for industry and commerce to be in stiff competition with the government for the financial surpluses of the personal sector. There is some dispute over the extent to which company investment has been (in actual fact) affected by high interest rates and heavy government borrowing, but the principle is obvious, and in theory at least high interest rates should have an adverse impact on investment (this is especially true if enterprises use the discounted cash flow method of appraising investment). Furthermore, even with internal financing of company invest- ment, there would come a point where companies would find it more profitable to invest in high-interest, risk-free government securities than in productive but risky fixed capital assets.

The answer to the second question – why control the expansion of the money stock? – is much more controversial. The basic answer, not accepted by all economists, is that 'excessive' expansion of the money supply leads to price inflation.

Discounted cash flow

Discounted cash flow is a technique for assessing the 'profitability' of any proposed investment. The purpose of this section is to explain dis- counting (which is an important technique in its own right) and to show that the 'profitability' to the enterprise of an investment will vary *inverse- ly* with the rate of interest in the economy at large, thus making for an important connection between macroeconomic policy and the working of enterprises.

The operation of discounting can be ap- proached initially as the converse of the opera- tion of compounding (but, as we shall explain, it is conceptually more complex than compound- ing). In Chapter 1 we saw that, where P_n is the end-value, P_0 the initial or 'present' value, r the proportionate annual growth rate, and n the number of years elapsing, the formula for com- pound growth was:

$$P_n = P_0(1 + r)^n$$

If P were a sum of money, then this formula tells us what a present sum, P_0, will be worth in the future after waiting n years and if compounded at rate r per annum.

Discounting is the converse operation, which tells us what a future sum, P_n, is worth in the present if we were to have to wait n years to receive it and if we were to *discount* at rate r per annum. The formula for discounting is simply derived from the compounding formula as follows:

$$P_0 = \frac{P_n}{(1 + r)^n}$$

or, writing the same formula in an algebraically

identical way (which we shall henceforth be using):*

$$P_0 = P_n(1 + r)^{-n}$$

In the compound growth formula, r has an easily understood meaning: it is the proportion- ate (annual) rate of growth applicable to a pres- ently existing variable (which is growing) to arrive at the variable's 'future value' (when sub- ject to this compound growth process). As most of us understand the process of growth from our everyday observation, this formula makes ready sense; we can 'grasp' what it means. On the other hand, in the dicounting formula, r has a less familiar significance: we can *say* that it is the proportionate rate of discount applicable to a future variable (i.e. a sum arising in the future) to arrive at its present value, but what does this really mean?

There are two answers to this question, one philosophical and subjective (but nevertheless important), the other businesslike and objective. Let us consider these two answers in turn, so as to elucidate the 'meaning' of discounting.

The philosophical, subjective answer is that the discount rate measures 'impatience', a desire to consume now rather than later, a belief that 'a bird in the hand is worth two in the bush'. To take a simple example, suppose you were of- fered a choice between £100 now ('in the hand') or £102 in two years' time ('in the bush'). You would almost certainly choose the £100 now: that is, your preference would be for the present

*For example: $0.125 = 1/2^3 = 2^{-3}$, as can be demonstrated by a calculator with the requisite x^y key.

sum rather than for the future sum.* Now suppose you were offered a choice between £100 now or £180 in two years' time. You might be strongly tempted to choose the £180 with a two-year wait: that is, your preference would be for the future sum rather than for the present sum. Logically, therefore, at some point, denoted as £X, between £102 and £180 you must switch your preference from the present sum of £100 to the future sum: this switching-point we shall call the 'indifference boundary', because as you approach the boundary you find it increasingly difficult to make up your mind between the present and future sum, and at the boundary you are (by definition) 'indifferent' between £100 now and £X in two years' time. What determines the location of this boundary-point, the £X in two years' time, is the philosophical, subjective question which the discount rate answers.

Suppose, to continue the example, your discount rate were 25 per cent per annum. We could then work out the mathematics of the above two choices by discounting the future sums as follows:

$$102(1 + 0.25)^{-2} = 102 \times 0.64 = 65.28$$
$$180(1 + 0.25)^{-2} = 180 \times 0.64 = 115.20$$

In this mathematics $0.64 \ (= (1 + 0.25)^{-2})$ is the 'discount factor' which is applied to sums of money arising two years hence and discounted at 25 per cent per annum. At your rate of discount, £102 in two years' time has a 'discounted present value' of £65.28, which is a poor show by comparison with the alternative of £100 in the present. But £180 in two years' time has a 'discounted present value' of £115.20, which is attractive by comparison with the alternative of £100 in the present. This, then, is the formal mathematics of discounting which lies behind your choice or your 'decision-making process' when choosing between present and future sums. (And like Molière's *Bourgeois gentilhomme* you may be surprised to learn that you have been discounting future sums/talking prose all your life!)

To illustrate the significance of discounting, you (supposing you to be a bit impatient) might imagine yourself saying: '*I* would jolly well prefer £100 now to £180 in two years' time'; then, in discounting terms, what you are in effect saying is: '*My* rate of (time) discount is much more than 25 per cent per annum; my rate of discount is about 40 per cent per annum.' Then, in terms of the discounting formula, your decision to reject even £180 in two years' time in favour of having £100 now is shown by the application of your (subjective) discount rate, as follows:

$$180(1 + 0.40)^{-2} = 180 \times 0.51 = 91.80$$

So that, for you, £180 in two years' time has a (subjective) discounted present value of £91.80, and this is disadvantageous when compared with the alternative of £100 in the present.

What, then, determines the location of the 'indifference boundary'? The indifference boundary depends on your rate of discount. If your rate of discount is 25 per cent per annum, then your indifference boundary, £X, occurs where:

$$100 = £X(1 + 0.25)^{-2}$$

and, solving for £X, we get:

$$\begin{aligned} £X &= 100(1 + 0.25)^2 \\ &= 100 \times 1.5625 \\ &= 156.25 \end{aligned}$$

So that, if your rate of discount were 25 per cent per annum:

(a) you would choose £100 now in preference to any sum less than £156.25 in two years' time;

(b) you would choose any sum greater than £156.25 in two years' time in preference to £100 now; and

(c) you would be 'indifferent' between the choice of £100 now and £156.25 in two years' time.

If your rate of discount were 40 per cent per annum, then your boundary, or 'switch-over', point would be £196, computed in the same way:

$$\begin{aligned} £X' &= 100(1 + 0.40)^2 \\ &= 100 \times 1.96 \\ &= 196 \end{aligned}$$

The 'meaning' of these boundary-points is that they indicate, for the respective rates of discount, *the sum of money arising in two years' time which is equivalent to £100 in the present.* That is, for the boundary points we may write the following tabulation:

---

*Please note two things. First, this choice is assumed to be made in the entire absence of price inflation: that is, the problems obviously caused for such present/future choice by price inflation are here *not* under consideration. Second, the amount arising in the future is an amount *certain*; the problems introduced by the fact that present sums are certain and future sums may be uncertain (which is probably what the proverb about the bird in the hand is driving at) are also not under consideration here.

Discount rate, per cent per annum	Future sum arising in two years, £	Discounted present value equivalent of future sum, £
25	156.25	100
40	196	100

The businesslike, objective answer as to the significance of discounting depends on the investment opportunities open to one. Suppose you could, if you had £100 now, invest the sum at a rate of (compound) interest of 20 per cent per annum, and 20 per cent per annum is the best you can do. Then £100 now is preferable to any sum less than £144 arising in two years' time. This is so because the compound growth formula:

$$100(1 + 0.20)^2 = 144$$

tells you that you could yourself invest the £100 (now) and thereby gain £144 in two years' time. However, when the choice is between £100 now and any sum greater than £144 in two years' time, you would choose the latter (the greater the sum), because you are unable, at the best rate of interest available to you, to do any better than this greater sum. The best rate of interest available to you thus determines at least the lower limit of the discount rate, and if investing money is all that really concerns you (as is usually the case with enterprises by the time they have reached this stage), then the 'best' interest rate available to you will determine your discount rate.

Whether chosen on subjective or objective grounds, the rate of discount provides the basis for comparing sums of money arising in the future with sums of money available in the present; textbooks tend to put this rather cryptically by saying that 'discounting reduces future sums to their present values'. Having now seen something of the meaning of discounting, as providing the basis for choice between (lesser) sums in the present and (greater) sums in the future, let us now consider how all this applies to assessing the 'profitability' of an investment.

In general terms, that which we call an 'investment' is a complex transaction with two distinctive features:

(a) an outlay, in the present, of a sum of money, in the expectation of

(b) a flow of monetary benefits due to arise in the future.*

Any technique for assessing the 'profitability' of an investment – technique for 'investment appraisal', it is called – has two analytically

distinct but related problems to overcome.

The first problem is that sums of money due to arise in different future periods have to be compared with a present outlay. (The purpose of the previous remarks about choosing between £100 now and £102/£180/etc. in two years' time was partly to show that this *is* a problem in that one cannot sensibly – or 'economically meaningfully' – compare simply the face-values of these future sums with present outlays but on the contrary that one must compare only their discounted present values with present sums.)

The second problem is more subtle and tends sometimes to be confused with the first. This problem concerns the fact that the (commitment to a) present outlay is a liability – that is, a *stock* – whereas the future benefits may arise as a *flow* of receipts during many future periods. That the outlay is a liability (a stock) is clearly obvious when one borrows the money to invest. Now, although we often compare a flow with a stock, such as when we compare the *annual flow* of a company's profits with its *stock* of capital, we should be aware that such a flow/stock comparison (to give the annual rate of profit) is a complex problem simplified by taking only one year's profit flow. What do we do in such flow/stock comparisons if we have to take into account more than one year's flow, as we nearly always have to where investment appraisal is concerned?

The answer to the first problem is that we can, by discounting, reduce the face-value of the future sums arising to their 'present value' (discounted) equivalents, so that all sums become thereby comparable. The answer to the second problem is that discounting conceptually 'converts' future *flows* to a (present value) *stock* equivalent: that is, each future *flow* when discounted becomes an equivalent at-the-present-

*A few qualifications, unimportant in principle, should be mentioned. Some of the outlays may be due to take place in the future (this can readily be accommodated in the analysis). The benefits need not necessarily occur as a flow but may simply be a lump-sum future payment (again, the analysis can handle this). Although we shall confine ourselves to monetary outlays and benefits, by extension the term 'investment' may be applied to non-monetary outlays and benefits; for example, practising a musical instrument is an outlay of present (non-monetary) effort in the expectation of future (non-monetary) enjoyment and so learning to play a musical instrument competently may be called 'an investment'. Likewise, reading this book is, I hope an investment!

date *stock*. To expand on this subtle point: if we have a future stream of receipts – flows arising in more than one period – then this whole stream is, by discounting each period's flow and by summing all the discounted present values, 'converted' to an asset (*stock*) equivalent at-the-present-date; this is generally expressed by saying that discounting and summing *capitalises* the stream of future expected receipts into an equivalent capital (stock) value, and this stock is, of course, an asset.* Likewise, a stream of future obligations to pay out money is converted by discounting to a liability (stock) equivalent at-the-present-date. Future obligations can also thus be capitalised into a present liability (stock). In these two ways discounting is essential to investment appraisal: it provides (a) the *present value*, and (b) *stock* equivalents of future flows of benefits which may then be compared with the present value commitment to outlays.

Let us illustrate what all this means with a simple example which will serve also to explain the arithmetical mechanics of discounting. Suppose an enterprise intends to borrow £1,000 at 12 per cent per annum, and by investing this borrowed £1,000 it expects (with reasonable certainty) to obtain an income (after deduction of costs, which deduction includes interest charges – i.e. a cash flow of net-of-interest profits) of £300 per annum for the next four years only, after which the income (profits) cash flow ceases (without any return of the capital outlay). We now ask: is this investment 'profitable' or not?†

Now, a return of £300 a year for four years might at first sight *seem* quite a good investment on the basis of the straightforward but *incorrect* argument that a return of £1,200 in total (after meeting interest charges – already deducted before reaching the cash-flow income of £300 per annum) when matched against an outlay of £1,000 must be good business: one apparently will have £1,200 in hand to repay the borrowed £1,000, leaving one with a net gain, apparently, of £200. But this argument is incorrect because: (a) it treats each of the future £300 flows as all equivalent to one another (and so as capable of being added together at face-value); and (b) it simply aggregates the four flows of £300 into a four-year flow.

Our preceding argument about the need to discount sums arising in the future so as to reduce them to (a) a *present value* equivalent and (b) a *stock* equivalent means that the only correct procedure is to discount appropriately each of the future sums to an equivalent present value stock, and that only these present value stock equivalents can properly be added together (i.e.

it is an incorrect procedure on *two* counts to add together the *face-values* of the future *flows*). Thus, using the 12 per cent per annum borrowing rate of interest as the discount rate (this follows the objective, businesslike basis for choosing an interest rate and assumes that 12 per cent is the best rate available to the enterprise; the enterprise could choose a higher discount rate, but this would complicate the exposition in practice without contributing anything of substantial principle), we proceed to discount each of future flows as shown opposite:

*The capitalised (present value) of the stream of receipts is, theoretically, the price at which you could (or should be able to) sell the entitlement to the stream of receipts; the classic discussion of this (and much more besides) is Irving Fisher, *The Nature of Capital and Income* (1906; Augustus Kelley Reprints of Economic Classics, 1965) especially chapters XI 'Four income–capital ratios' and XIII 'Value of capital'.

†Three points should be noted here. *First*, we are not concerned with the problem of uncertainty as to the future flows, hence the parenthetical interjection about reasonable certainty, but we should note that uncertainty introduces considerable complications into the analysis. *Second*, although for ease of grasping the essentials of the problem we depict the enterprise as borrowing the money from outsiders, it makes no difference in principle if the money were its own retentions – in the case of retentions there is an 'opportunity cost' of interest forgone by using the retentions for this investment (rather than another) and this opportunity cost performs the same function as the rate of interest paid to outsiders. In practice, of course, there are important differences between borrowing and retentions which may well affect the enterprise's assessment of its 'cost of capital'. These differences relate, rather obviously, to the fact that borrowing involves a legal obligation to pay interest and to repay the principal, with the threat of liquidation if these obligations are not met, whereas use of retentions does not involve such a scenario; retentions are usually regarded as a 'cheaper' source of finance for this reason (among others). One of the expository advantages of taking a borrowed sum is that measuring the cost of capital is reasonably straightforward. *Third*, the term 'cash flow' in 'discounted cash flow' refers to the fact that this technique works on flows only as and when the flows occur (it does not work on flows *accruing*); in this way the technique takes a precise account of the *timing* of each inflow and outflow when actually received or paid. This regard to timing is obviously important when assessing net-of-tax profitability (if tax payments are deferred and investment grants are advanced).

Year, i	Discount factor, $(1 + 0.120)^{-i}$	Future flow, £	Discounted present value stock equivalent of future flow, £
1	$(1 + 0.12)^{-1} = 0.892857$	300	267.86
2	$(1 + 0.12)^{-2} = 0.797194$	300	239.16
3	$(1 + 0.12)^{-3} = 0.711780$	300	213.53
4	$(1 + 0.12)^{-4} = 0.635518$	300	190.66
Total			911.21

At a discount rate of 12 per cent per annum (0.12 per annum), the discounted present value stock equivalent of a flow of £300 arising in one year's time is £267.86 (*equals* £300 × 0.892857); the discounted present value stock equivalent of a flow of £300 arising in two years' time is £239.16 (*equals* £300 × 0.797194); and so on. Each of the future benefit flows (at face-value) must be discounted by its appropriate discount factor to give its present value stock equivalent, and only these present value stock equivalents can properly be added together to give the total 'return' from the investment, a capitalised 'return' which is now measured correctly at a present value stock equivalent – that is, as an *asset* (a stock at-the-present-date). This is, of course, only a *notional* asset – it is, we might say, the 'capitalised asset valuation' of the investment's prospective stream of returns. What exists (or will exist) in reality is the stream of future returns; but the only way in which we can properly assess this stream of future flows is to 'convert' or capitalise it (by discounting and summing) to a notional asset at-the-present-date; and this notional asset valuation is (it must be) a *stock*.

By doing this correct calculation (and not simply lumping all the £300 flows together at face-value), we see that the total of all the discounted present value stock equivalents of the future benefit flows is £911.21. By comparison with the present outlay of £1,000 – the borrowing commitment or liability – we see that we have a notional 'loss' on the investment, which 'loss' we may measure as:

$$\text{Net present value} = \frac{\text{Total of discounted present values of future benefits (asset, i.e. a } stock)}{} - \text{Total present value of outlay (liability, i.e. a } stock)$$

$$= £911.21 - £1,000$$

$$= -£88.79$$

What does this negative 'net present value' mean? It means that, by comparison with the borrowing commitment (liability) into which the enterprise entered in order to obtain the initial £1,000 outlay, the enterprise is suffering a (present value and notional) *diminution* in its 'wealth' of £88.79 (wealth being measured by the difference between the stock of assets and the stock of liabilities).

To understand this remark fully, we need also to appreciate that the enterprise's borrowing commitment should be looked at, not simply as 'borrowing £1,000 now', but as a commitment to pay interest of £120 per annum for four years (12 per cent per annum on the capital sum of £1,000) and then to repay the principal of £1,000 at the end of four years (for the sake of simplicity we keep to the simplest possible terms for the loan). The assessment of the present value stock equivalent of the borrowing commitment – the liability which the enterprise is incurring – is as follows (because we must again use discounting):

Year, i	Discount factor, $(1 + 0.12)^{-i}$	Future payment, interest and principal, £	Discounted present value stock equivalent of future payment, £
1	$(1 + 0.12)^{-1} = 0.892857$	120	107.143
2	$(1 + 0.12)^{-2} = 0.797194$	120	95.663
3	$(1 + 0.12)^{-3} = 0.711780$	120	85.414
4	$(1 + 0.12)^{-4} = 0.635518$	{ 120 {1,000	76.262 635.518
Total			1,000.000

So that the present value stock equivalent of the enterprise's borrowing commitment is a (notional) liability of £1,000 exactly equivalent to the (actual) liability of £1,000 principal outstanding.*

Accordingly, in this example, the enterprise's prospective total gain from the investment, in present value stock equivalent terms – in terms of the notional or capitalised asset valuation – is £911.21; this represents, so to speak, the present value of the asset (stock) it is acquiring by undertaking the investment. By comparison, the present value stock equivalent of the borrowing commitment into which it is entering is £1,000; this represents, so to speak, the present value of the liability (stock) it is incurring in order to undertake the investment. Thus, there is a sense in which, in terms of present value stock equivalents, the enterprise is incurring a liability (stock) greater than the asset (stock) it is acquiring, and so the enterprise can be said to be 'diminishing its wealth' by undertaking the investment. This is what the negative net present value means: the enterprise's (notional) net asset/liability (stock) position would deteriorate if it were to undertake the investment. Conversely, a positive net present value indicates that the enterprise is increasing its 'wealth' as a result of such an investment. Accordingly, only those investments with a positive net present value will be undertaken (it might be more realistic to say that only such positive net present value investments *should* – economically 'should' – be undertaken).

The net present value method is one way of assessing the 'profitability' of an investment – in terms of its impact on the notional present wealth (asset/liability position) of the enterprise. Another related way of assessing an investment is to ascertain that rate of discount which discounts the future benefits, when totalled at present value stock equivalents, back to exact equality with the present value of the outlay. In other words, if B_i represents the flow of benefits arising in year i, and C is the present value of the outlay, we ascertain that value of the discount rate per annum, to be designated as r^*, which

satisfies the following equation of a zero net present value:

$$\text{Net present value} = \Sigma \frac{B_i}{(1 + r^*)^i} - C = 0$$

(the summation being over $i = 1$ to $i = n$, assuming that the first benefit flow arises in year 1 and the last in year n – these benefit flows can, of course, include any residual 'scrap' value). Or, which comes to the same thing, we ascertain that value of r^* which makes:

$$\Sigma \frac{B_i}{(1 + r^*)^i} = C$$

Given the values for B_i and for C, the appropriate value of r^* can be ascertained by (iterative) trial and error: that is, by choosing an initial trial value for r^*, calculating $\Sigma(B_i/(1 + r^*)^i)$ and, if the result is greater (less) than C, choosing a bigger (smaller) trial value for r^*, until one gets the answer right (there is no other way to ascertain r^*, but computers will nowadays do the iterations very quickly). Proceeding in this iterative way, we may ascertain for our example shown below that applying a discount rate of 7.7 per cent (0.077) per annum gives almost exactly the right answer ('almost', because we do not have enough decimal places in the discount rate). So that (disregarding the odd 32p), a discount rate of 7.7 per cent per annum will give a total of the discounted present value stock equivalent of future benefits exactly equal to the present value borrowing commitment (or capital outlay) of £1,000. This rate of discount is variously known as the investment's 'internal rate of return', its 'yield', or simply its 'rate of return'. (The internal rate of return is the answer to the problem of ascertaining a *rate* of profit on capital invested which takes more than

*This result of an equivalence between principal initially outstanding and the capitalised liability valuation of the borrowing commitment (as represented by the payment schedule in the tabulation) will always arise if we discount the future payments at the rate of interest charged on the loan.

Year, i	Discount factor, $(1 + 0.077)^{-i}$	Future flow, £	Discounted present value stock equivalent of future flow, £
1	$(1 + 0.077)^{-1} = 0.928505$	300	278.55
2	$(1 + 0.077)^{-2} = 0.862122$	300	258.64
3	$(1 + 0.077)^{-3} = 0.800484$	300	240.15
4	$(1 + 0.077)^{-4} = 0.743254$	300	222.98
Total			1,000.32

one year's profit flow into account.)

By comparing an investment's internal rate of return with the rate of interest charged on borrowing (or, more generally, with the enterprise's 'cost of capital'), one can determine whether or not the investment is 'profitable' for the enterprise. In this example the cost of borrowing is 12 per cent per annum and the internal rate of return is 7.7 per cent per annum, so this indicates that the investment is not 'profitable' and will have a negative net present value. Therefore, an enterprise with a cost of capital of 12 per cent per annum and a proposed investment with a 7.7 per cent per annum internal rate of return should not undertake the proposed investment.

We can now see how economic policy has a bearing on investment by enterprises. Looking at all the enterprises in the economy, we can imagine each enterprise as having a list of many proposed projects for investment, with each project ranked in descending order of its internal rate of return. (Here our previous arguments about the enterprise as a forward-looking entity with a product portfolio to develop come into play.) Against this ranking of possible projects by internal rates of return will be matched the enterprise's cost of borrowing, which is determined by the rate of interest in the economy at large. Any project with an internal rate of return greater than the borrowing rate of interest (i.e. any project with a positive net present value) is likely to be undertaken.* Any investment with an internal rate of return below the cost of borrowing (i.e. any project with a negative net present value) should not be undertaken. If the cost of borrowing rises, then certain projects, whose internal rates of return were previously just above the borrowing cost 'cut-off' point, will now fall below the cut-off point and so will not be undertaken (or will be abandoned, if this is possible which it generally is not).

In this way, a rise in interest rates in the economy at large (in the cost of borrowing) should reduce the amount of investment (the number of projects) being undertaken by enterprises. This is, of course, a simplified account of the process, but it contains the basic essentials. (Note also that it introduces a further element into our previous analysis of what may cause changes in investment: namely, prospective 'profitability' as assessed by net present value.) Clearly, under the net present value method, the higher the rate of interest used for discounting, the lower will be any investment's net present value (and vice versa). Thus 'profitability' varies inversely with the rate of interest (because the latter will influence the rate of discount to be used). So that, high interest rates may adversely affect company investment, and, because the country depends for its long-run prosperity on investment (which brings about modernisation, technical progress, etc. – see Chapters 7 and 8), such an adverse impact is most undesirable. Governments should therefore seek to avoid high interest rates.

*We are here ignoring the problems raised by the availability of funds; in principle, the enterprise's cost of capital rises as it goes from (safe) internal finance to (costly) new issues of equity capital to (increasingly liquidation-dangerous) borrowed finance.

Inflation and the money supply

The cause (or causes) of inflation is a hotly disputed subject, the satisfactory settlement of which may not be possible due both to the circularity of many of the causal links and also to the multiplicity of possible original 'shocks' which may initiate inflation (see Dudley Jackson, H. A. Turner and Frank Wilkinson, *Do Trade Unions Cause Inflation?*, Cambridge University Press, 1972). It would, unfortunately, take us too far out of our way to examine these controversies and the alleged links (or alleged lack of linkage) between changes in the money supply and price inflation, though it is theoretically clear (and obvious from historical and contemporary examples) that the impact of rapid expansion in the money supply, and hence in expenditure, on various markets may well be to raise prices. This is as much to say that controlling the growth of the money supply may be a *necessary* precondition for controlling inflation; but it is not to say that such control will be *sufficient* by itself. To put a metaphor: it is a necessary condition for stopping a moving car that the driver takes his or her foot off the accelerator, but this will not always be sufficient to stop the car. (A working, but not a full, definition of 'monetarism' could be that it is the argument that controlling the expansion of the money supply is a necessary *and* sufficient condition for controlling inflation.)

If we look at the long-run data on increases in the money supply in the United Kingdom and on the annual rate of price inflation (as measured by the implied GDP price deflator), it seems that the evidence may arguably be taken as ambiguous. Diagram 14.2 (illustrating the data in Appendix 13.2) shows at first glance that there have in the United Kingdom during the postwar period been episodes of price inflation unaccompanied and accompanied by expansion of the money supply. (To standardise the change in the money supply, this is taken as a percentage of each year's GDP – we do not have a long-run series of reliable data on the actual stocks of money itself so we cannot compute, for as long a period, the percentage change in the money stock itself.)

DIAGRAM 14.2   *Change in money stock sterling M_3 (change taken as a percentage of GDP) and percentage change over previous year in implied GDP price deflator, 1952 to 1980*

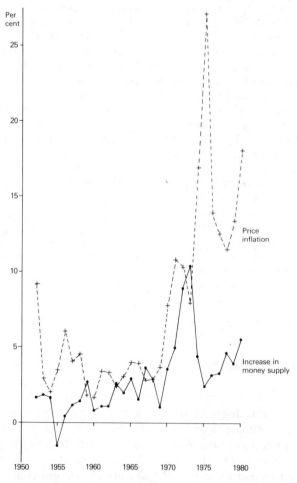

From the configuration of the curves, it is clear that the unprecedented inflation of the 1970s was accompanied by (but partly preceded) an unprecedented expansion of the money supply. In order to try and sort out what sort of relationship, if any, may exist, we have for the period 1952 to 1980 the following correlation coefficients:

Money supply increase in year *t*, and price inflation in year	Coefficient of correlation
t − 1	+0.427
t	+0.394
t + 1	+0.524
t + 2	+0.802
t + 2, peak year pair 1973/1975 omitted	+0.676

It seems that the change in the money supply (taken as a percentage of GDP) is not well correlated with the percentage rate of price inflation in the same year (nor in the previous year), though the correlation is positive. However, the correlation is stronger if we allow for a delay, or 'lag', of one year in the impact of increases in the money supply on price inflation and stronger still if we allow for a lag of two years (even allowing in the last row for the effect on the correlation coefficient of the coincidence of the respective 'peaks' which a two-year lag brings about). It seems, then, that above-average expansion of the money supply in year *t* is likely to be accompanied by above-average price inflation in years *t* + 1 and *t* + 2 – that is, after a delay or lag of one to two years.

The most that we could reasonably conclude from this evidence is that expansion of the money supply may facilitate inflation and that, therefore, if one wishes to control inflation it is probably advisable to limit the growth of the money supply (although much more than this may be required, in addition, if a country is to reduce and hold down the rate of inflation – note that in the 1960s there tended to be not much distance between the curves but that in the second half of the 1970s there is a wide gap).

With this (rather tenuous) evidence of Diagram 14.2, we could perhaps accept, even if only for the purposes of analysing monetary policy, that there is at least the possibility of some positive and probably delayed-action relationship between the increase in the money supply and the rate of price inflation and that controlling the former may well be a precondition for reducing the latter.

The general government financial deficit and the overseas sector's financial balance

The next step in the analysis of economic policy is to consider the relationship between the general government's financial deficit (which forms a large part of the PSBR) and the overseas sector's net acquisition of financial assets. We shall consider the overseas sector's financial balance with respect to imports (overseas sector's income) and exports (overseas sector's expenditure): that is, for simplicity we ignore the other elements of the current-account balance of payments (see Table 11.11).

In Table 12.7, the model economy of that chapter was near to full employment with government consumption expenditure of 4 and government investment of 6; the marginal propensity to import out of final expenditure was 0.25, and with the other parameters the multiplier was 1.2605. We now need to see what happens to the financial balances in this economy if the government increases its expenditure and at the same time the marginal propensity to import rises; the new set of accounts is shown in Table 14.1. In order to change the figures in Table 12.7 as little as possible we shall increase only government consumption expenditure from 4 to 12 and shall raise the marginal propensity to import from 0.25 to 0.3; enterprise investment, the marginal propensity to consume and the rate of taxation remain unaltered. The multiplier becomes 1.125, lower than in Table 12.7 because of the greater leakage into imports. The total 'injection' of expenditure is now $26 + 12 + 20 = 58$; given the new multiplier, GDP is $1.125 \times 58 = 65.2$ (note that the

TABLE 14.1   *National accounts when government consumption expenditure increases from 4 to 12 and the marginal propensity to import rises from 0.25 to 0.3 (see Table 12.7); multiplier is $(1 - 0.3)/[1 - 0.6(1 - 0.1) + 0.3 \times 0.6 \times (1 - 0.1)] = 1.125$*

| | £ p.a. | | | | |
| | Final sales | Imports | Domestic value added | Wages | Profits |
Category of final expenditure					
Consumers' expenditure	35.2	10.6	24.6	17.2	7.4
Investment	26	7.8	18.2	12.7	5.5
Government consumption	12	3.6	8.4	8.4	—
Exports	20	6	14	9.8	4.2
Total expenditure	93.2	28	65.2		
Imports	28				
Gross domestic product	65.2	—	65.2	48.1	17.1

| | £ p.a. | | | |
Account	Personal sector	Enterprise sector	Government sector	Overseas sector
Current account				
Income	65.2	17.1	6.5	28
Expenditure	41.7	17.1	12	20
Saving	23.5	0	−5.5	8
Capital account				
Expenditure	0	20	6	—
Financial balance	+23.5	−20	−11.5	+8

combined effect of increased government expenditure and the higher marginal propensity to import is to keep the economy near its full-employment ceiling of 65 – see discussion of Table 12.7). From the consumption function, consumers' expenditure is 0.6 of disposable income and, as the personal sector receives all profits distributed as dividend income and the rate of taxation is 0.1 of income, disposable income is $(1 - 0.1) \times 65.2$, so consumers' expenditure is 35.2. Total expenditure is accordingly 93.2, and as the propensity to import out of expenditure is 0.3, imports are $0.3 \times 93.2 = 28$. Using this uniform propensity to import, we can calculate the import component of each item of final expenditure and hence domestic value added, which latter we distribute as 0.7 of wages and 0.3 of profits, except for government consumption expenditure, which is deemed to be entirely wages.

We can now work out the sector current and capital accounts and financial balances. The personal sector gets the whole of GDP as its income; it pays one-tenth of this, i.e. 6.5, as taxes and spends 35.2 on (induced) consumers' expenditure. This leaves the personal sector with saving and a financial balance of +23.5. As in Table 12.7, the enterprise sector distributes all profits as dividend income and, as its investment remains at 20, its financial balance also remains at −20.

The government sector's accounts have altered considerably from what they were in Table 12.7. Receipts of income tax are 6.5, only a very slight increase on Table 12.7, but government current expenditure has risen, so government-sector savings have gone from a positive 2.3 to a negative 5.5, a deterioration of 7.8. With government investment at 6, the government's financial balance is −11.5, so it is clear that there has been, by comparison with Table 12.7, a substantial increase in the government's financial deficit and hence in this economy's PSBR.

The counterpart of the government's financial deficit, given that there has not been much change in the private sectors' financial balances, is the greatly increased overseas sector's financial surplus, up from +1 to +8. In other words, the economy's balance of payments has deteriorated sharply and imports now exceed exports by 8.

We could have made the deterioration in the balance of payments even worse, had we supposed that enterprise-sector investment had also risen – perhaps compounded by a fall in exports. Exactly such episodes of a deterioration of government financial balance and an increased overseas-sector financial surplus (balance-of-payments current-account deficit) have occurred in the UK economy in the postwar period. In other words, the shift from Table 12.7 to Table 14.1 is not without its application to the real world. Diagram 14.3 (illustrating data from Appendix 12.1) shows how the general government's financial deficit (expressed as a percentage of GDP) has tended to move in opposite directions from the overseas sector's financial balance as a percentage of GDP. The coefficient of correlation between the two series in Diagram 14.3 is $R = -0.574$.* So we can conclude that in the UK economy there is a tendency for above-average overseas sector financial surpluses (balance-of-payments deficits) to accompany above-average government sector financial deficits (modulus of), just as expected from the models in Tables 12.7 and 14.1.

Almost paradoxically, such increased balance-of-payments deficits may help to finance

DIAGRAM 14.3 *General government financial balance and overseas sector financial balance, both expressed as a percentage of GDP, 1948 to 1980*

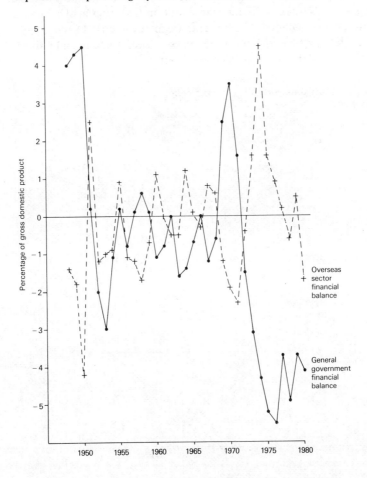

*We have $(OSFB/GDP)\% = -0.54 - 0.34\ (GGFB/GDP)\%$; conversely, there is a *positive* relationship between the overseas sector financial balance and the general government *borrowing requirement* arising from the general government financial balance.

part of the PSBR arising from the government deficit, because there will be a net inflow of sterling to the Exchange Equalisation Account (and a corresponding reduction in foreign exchange reserves). We may now try to integrate the implications of all this for economic policy, using a schematic diagram which shows how all these ingredients *may* fit together from a theoretical point of view.

The framework for economic policy

In Diagram 14.4 we measure the public sector borrowing requirement in £ million up the vertical axis. This PSBR is partly determined by the general government's financial deficit (sign reversed) and partly by the public corporation's financial deficit again, sign reversed. In what follows, we shall ignore the problem of maturing debt (i.e. we shall concentrate on net finance required); also, we shall concentrate on changes in the PSBR caused by changes in the general government financial deficit (taxation *minus* expenditure) – that is, we shall ignore net lending and the public corporations' contribution. In other words, we are forcing an equivalence between the general government financial deficit and the public sector borrowing requirement. Rightwards along the horizontal axis we measure the annual percentage rate of price inflation; leftwards along the horizontal axis we measure the overseas sector's financial balance in £ million. This financial balance is determined by the current-account balance of payments (sign reversed). In what follows we shall be concerned mainly with variations in the overseas sector's financial balance brought about by changes in the balance of imports over exports.

DIAGRAM 14.4   *The framework for economic policy*

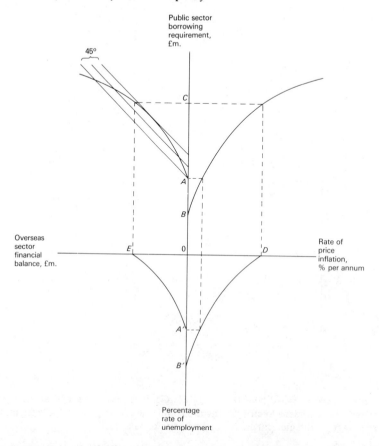

In the upper-left quadrant we may draw an upward-sloping curve expressing a positive relationship between the PSBR (government financial deficit) and the overseas sector's financial surplus (balance-of-payments deficit)*. This PSBR–overseas sector financial balance curve starts at the positive intercept A, where the distance OA represents the private sector's financial surplus. Were the private sector's financial surplus to remain unaffected by the size of the government financial deficit and by the size of the overseas sector's financial balance, then the line outwards from A would have to be at 45° upwards, indicating a one-to-one relationship between the government financial deficit (PSBR) and the overseas sector's financial surplus.† But it is likely that an increasing general government financial deficit will, at least up to a point, increase the private sector's financial surplus; if private-sector capital formation is stimulated by the increased government deficit, then the private-sector financial deficit may at some point decrease. So we must imagine a grid of 45° lines each with a different private-sector financial surplus intercept, and as movement along the PSBR-axis involves different intercepts and different 45° lines, so a path is traced out between the PSBR and the overseas sector's financial balance. Obviously, the curve tracing this path is not a very stable curve, because anything which affects the private sector's financial balance (the intercept) can, for any given PSBR, move the curve to a different 45° line. So we must not think of the curve traced out in the upper-left quadrant as being inherently stable and fixed; it may well be given to shifting around. For example, the production of previously imported fuel (North Sea oil) can shift the curve upwards and to the right (conversely, a decline in such production could shift the curve to the left).

In the upper-right quadrant we may draw a curve showing the likely positive relationship between the PSBR and the rate of price inflation brought about by the influence of the PSBR on the money supply (as per the empirical relationships of Diagrams 13.6 and 14.2 and the schematic model of Diagram 14.1). This PSBR–inflation curve has a positive intercept, B, on the vertical axis showing that it ought to be possible to fund a certain level of the PSBR, OB, without recourse to borrowing from the banks, and so without expanding the money supply, which ought in theory to produce a zero rate of price inflation (that is, assuming that only expansion of the money supply and nothing else affects price inflation). However, it is possible for this curve to be further to the right and even to intercept the price inflation axis if, for example, there are other influences bearing upon price inflation; an increase in world oil prices would be only one example of such possible other influences; devaluation of the currency which raised the prices of imports would be another; increased taxation of workers leading to demands for higher wages and so to increased unit labour costs passed on in prices would be still one more. Therefore, we must not expect this PSBR–inflation curve to be very stable either. Rather, we should expect it, in reality, to shift around inconveniently. A hard-line monetarist might, however, argue that this curve is relatively stable. But even so, we should note that if raising the PSBR increases the rate of price inflation along a given curve, this may set off forces, such as worker resistance to reduced real wages, which shifts the locus of action to a different curve. Wherever the intercept, we give this curve a twist indicating that successive increments to the PSBR may produce successively bigger increases in the proportionate rate of price inflation (which, in the light of history, seems more plausible than the converse possibilities).

We now measure the rate of unemployment (numbers unemployed as a percentage of the working population) down the vertical axis away from the origin. The 'conventional' Keynesian argument is that the rate of unemployment may be inversely connected to the government financial deficit, so a movement up the PSBR-axis should correspond to a

---

*This is the converse of the relationship seen in Diagram 14.3.
† That is, a one-to-one relationship *after* (higher up than) A.

reduced rate of unemployment. Strictly speaking, it is not so much the government deficit which affects unemployment as (a) the positive impact via the multiplier of government expenditure, and (b) the negative impact of the rate of taxation on the multiplier itself (see the impact on GDP of the transition through Tables 12.2 to 12.5 inclusive, and the government financial balances therein). However, given a relatively constant tax rate and constancy of other parameters in the multiplier together with a constant flow of exports and of private-sector investment, variations in aggregate economic activity will tend to depend upon variations in public expenditure, which in turn may lead to corresponding variations in the government's financial deficit and so in the PSBR. In Table 12.5 full employment is achieved with government spending of 10, a tax rate of 0.1, and a government financial deficit of -3.5. If private-sector investment cannot be increased and the marginal propensity to consume remains at 0.6, then unemployment will tend to vary inversely with the PSBR or government financial deficit. Metaphorically we may think of this connection as being like a length of hollow tubing which fits over the vertical axis (and which may slide up and down it); the length of the tube corresponds to that level of the government financial deficit at which (given all the other expenditures and parameters) there would be no unemployment (i.e. where the complementary effects of government activity produce an aggregate level of demand which fully utilises the economy's capacity). We shall call this the 'full-employment government deficit' and in Diagram 14.4 we shall assume that this deficit (PSBR) is equal to OC. We may then represent the full-employment government deficit by the length of the hollow tube, OC, which may be called the 'unemployment tube'. As we slide this tube downwards from C, reducing the government financial deficit (PSBR) either by cutting government expenditure or raising the rate of taxation, so we reduce the level of economic activity and so increase unemployment; this can be measured by the intersection of the bottom of the 'unemployment tube' and the unemployment axis.*

The full-employment government deficit is not an absolutely fixed constant: that is, the tube is not completely rigid in length; it may be shortened or elongated by other factors. For example, if private-sector investment or exports increase, the full-employment government deficit will be reduced and the unemployment tube will diminish in length; or if the marginal propensity to consume decreases (the propensity to save increases) or the propensity to import increases, then the tube will lengthen (this will be discussed at greater length towards the end of this chapter).

Having duly noted that both the configuration of points in the two upper quadrants and also the length of the connection between the PSBR and the rate of unemployment are liable to all sorts of 'flexibilities', so that nothing is as stable as it may seem, we may use the diagram assuming initially a sufficient rigidity to give a clear picture. We shall use the PSBR–overseas sector financial balance curve which begins at A, and likewise the PSBR–inflation curve which begins at B.

If we start at a PSBR of OC, representing the full-employment government deficit, we have, by assumption, zero unemployment, but, given this PSBR, there is fairly extensive government borrowing from the banks and so there is an expansion of the money supply which at least facilitates (many economists would argue that it 'causes') price inflation at rate OD per cent per annum. Also, given this PSBR and the underlying government financial deficit, the overseas sector has an annual financial surplus of £OE million; in other words, the balance-of-payments deficit is $-£OE$ million. There is less controversy about this connection, the underlying basis of which is quite simply that government expenditure in excess of taxation stimulates aggregate final demand in the economy, so 'sucking in' imports, via the propensity to import, and perhaps even causing a diversion of potential exports to the buoyant home market.

---

*This depends on having the appropriate scaling between the two parts of the vertical axis, but this is a technicality. The references to the financial deficit are always to the modulus thereof.

This combination of rapid price inflation and a balance-of-payments deficit will probably be unacceptable to the government: people will be grumbling about inflation; and the reserves of foreign exchange (and the ability to borrow to replenish the diminishing reserves) will be running out. Clearly, this configuration of *OC*, *OD* and *OE* is an untenable situation. Now, if the curves are (more or less) fixed – and we shall subsequently be considering policies aimed at shifting the curves – then the government has to get out of this position by cutting its financial deficit and the PSBR, say to *OA*. This has two main effects. First, it should reduce government (residual) borrowing from the banks, so reducing the growth of the money supply and so having a beneficial effect on the rate of price inflation as indicated. Second, by cutting aggregate demand (directly by cuts in government expenditure, or indirectly by the dampening effect on the multiplier of an increase in rates of taxation, or both) the reduced government deficit (PSBR) should reduce imports (and perhaps force firms to export more so as to counteract the impact of the less buoyant home market) so improving the balance of payments, i.e. reducing the overseas sector's financial surplus. In the diagram as drawn, the government reduces the overseas sector's financial balance to zero at a PSBR of *OA*.

At *OA* the government has, it is to be hoped, succeeded in reducing inflation considerably. This blandly assumes away all unpleasant realities such as the possibility that increased taxation to cut the PSBR may spark off compensating wage demands so increasing unit labour costs and shifting the PSBR–inflation curve bodily to the right.

However, the lower end of the 'unemployment tube' will now be at *A'*, where *AA'* = *OC*. Thus the 'cost' of the reduced inflation and the elimination of the balance-of-payments deficit is a considerable rise in the percentage rate of unemployment. This will be unpopular, and may prevent the government from trying to reduce the PSBR still further in the effort to eliminate inflation, and perhaps at the same time push the balance of payments into surplus (although I have refrained from complicating Diagram 14.4 by drawing this rightward extension of the PSBR–overseas sector financial balance curve).

If we continue this process of varying the PSBR and hence the intercept of the lower end of the 'unemployment tube' on the unemployment axis, we can by using the two curves in the upper quadrants trace out two 'trade-off curves' in the lower quadrants: one representing a trade-off between inflation and unemployment, the other representing a trade-off between the balance-of-payments deficit and unemployment. These trade-off curves will, by their construction, be mirror images of their originating curves in the upper quadrants. We can now use the completed diagram to analyse the main problems of economic policy. Note that an important part of this diagram is the way in which it shows the interdependence of the balance of payments (overseas sector financial balance), the rate of inflation, and unemployment – an interdependence which is mediated through the various effects of the government's financial deficit, or 'fiscal stance', as here represented by the PSBR.

Economic policy options

The history of economic policy in the United Kingdom is largely the history of movement along the trade-off curves in the lower quadrants of Diagram 14.4 combined with attempts to escape from these trade-off curves by trying to shift them in towards the origin, which shifts can be effected either if the curves in the upper quadrants can themselves be moved in the appropriate direction or if the full-employment government deficit (the length of the 'unemployment tube') can be reduced. This is a simplification of a complex reality but it helps to interpret the problems of economic policy by putting policy measures into four (but by no means unrelated) groups:

1. Policies which 'accept' the configuration of the curves and which then 'choose' points on the given trade-off curves.

2. Policies which try to shift the PSBR–overseas sector financial balance curve to the right and upwards.
3. Policies which try to shift the PSBR–inflation curve to the left and upwards.
4. Policies which try to reduce the full-employment government deficit (i.e. the length of the 'unemployment tube'); such policies try to create a state of full employment from sources other than government expenditure and the government financial deficit.

In practice, of course, policy measures may be a combination of any of these, and often protagonists of a particular policy will claim that the policy will simultaneously achieve more than one effect. For example, a policy to improve exports will not only shift the PSBR–overseas sector financial balance curve to the right but will at the same time, by providing a greater 'injection' of exports into final expenditure, permit the government to reduce its expenditure without affecting unemployment – i.e. will reduce the full-employment government deficit.

Clearly, full discussion of such policy measures would itself necessitate writing a large book (such as F. T. Blackaby (ed.), *British Economic Policy 1960–74*, Cambridge University Press, 1978), but we can briefly describe some of them.

In our description of Diagram 14.4 we have already partly discussed those policies which accept the curves as fixed and which then seek to choose some appropriate set of points. Such a set may be expansionist and inflationary, such as the set *OC*, *OE* and *OD*, with low (in this case, zero) unemployment; or the set may be deflationary, such as at *OA* with *OA'* unemployment, a zero balance-of-payments deficit and a low rate of inflation. UK governments have tended to oscillate between such sets, producing what has come to be called the 'stop–go economy'; the stop being at *OA'* unemployment; the go being at a PSBR of *OC* with (near) zero unemployment but a balance-of-payments deficit of $(-)OE$ and a high rate of inflation. Note that, if the curves are fixed, the points forming the set are all interdependent. That is, if any one point is chosen as the objective of policy, all other points are thereby determined. Inevitably, therefore, the possibility of trying to escape from this interdependence is most attractive; this may be done by shifting the PSBR–overseas sector financial balance curve, or the PSBR–inflation curve, or both.

Devaluation

There are two possible ways for the government directly to shift the position of the PSBR–overseas sector financial balance curve: one is devaluation; the other is import controls. (We may note that other factors, for example the advent of North Sea oil, may shift this curve but such factors will not be discussed here.) Devaluation occurs when, for example, the exchange rate (the rate at which foreign currency is bought or sold for sterling) alters.

A 'good' result – 'good' in terms of net foreign exchange receipts – from devaluation is obtained when the (modulus of the) foreign price elasticity of demand for UK exports is greater than 1.0, so the increase in export volume more than compensates for the fall in the dollar price; and when the (modulus of the) sterling price elasticity of demand is also greater than 1.0, so the decrease in import volume (and hence in dollar expenditure) is also considerable. (The precise rule is that the sum of (the moduli of) the two elasticities must be greater than unity – see John Robinson, 'The foreign exchanges', in *Essays in the Theory of Employment*, Macmillan, 1937 – the reactions should also be speedy otherwise a '*J*' curve will be produced on net receipts of foreign exchange: dipping at first (along the hook of the *J*), then slowly picking up as the appropriate reactions occur.)

If the foreign trade elasticities lead to a 'good' result in terms of net receipts from trade of foreign exchange then, as illustrated in Diagram 14.5, devaluation will shift the PSBR–overseas sector financial balance curve from position 1 to position 2. Suppose that

DIAGRAM 14.5   *Possible options for economic policy*

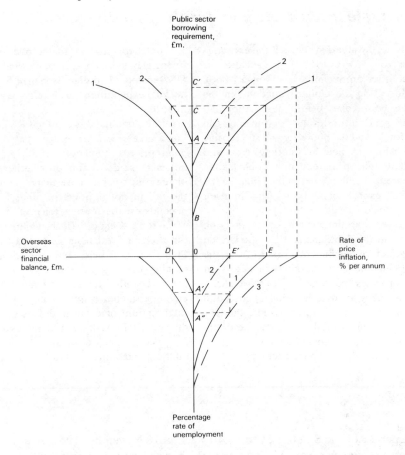

before devaluation the full-employment budget deficit was *OC* but the government were running a financial deficit which gave a PSBR of *OA*, in turn leading to unemployment of *OA'* and an overseas sector financial surplus of *OD* (a balance-of-payments deficit of −*OD*). After devaluation, the government may continue to run a financial deficit of *OA*; unemployment will remain at *OA'* but the overseas sector's financial surplus (the balance-of-payments deficit) will have been reduced to zero, as shown by the new trade-off curve. (To keep the analysis as simple as possible, we are here ignoring the fact – quite important in practice – that the full-employment budget deficit, *OC*, is likely to be reduced by devaluation because of the expansionary effect of increased exports and reduced leakage into imports – this will be considered subsequently.)

Alternatively, after devaluation the government may expand its deficit and PSBR to *OC*, so creating full employment but without worsening the balance-of-payments deficit, which will then be, as before, at (−)*OD*. (Note that this move will increase price inflation.)

Unfortunately, it may be the case that the foreign trade elasticities are not altogether favourable: both (in modulus terms) may, for the United Kingdom, be low, so devaluation may not shift the PSBR–overseas sector financial balance curve by very much. Another problem strongly militating against devaluation is that it may shift the PSBR–inflation curve to the right, because by raising the sterling price of imports (food especially) it causes wholesale and retail price indices to rise. This initial rise may then be aggravated by wage (unit labour cost) increases as employees try to defend their real wages through compensating increases in money wages. If this happens (and historical evidence from the devaluation in the United Kingdom, when the sterling–dollar exchange rate was devalued

An example to illustrate how devaluation should work

To illustrate, devaluation occurs if the exchange rate goes from $3 = £1 to $2 = £1. Take the case of a publisher producing a (paperback) book selling for £1 in the United Kingdom; in the USA the book costs, before devaluation, $3 (when $3 = £1); after devaluation the book can be sold for $2 and the publisher will still receive £1 from which to meet his (sterling) costs and profits. This dollar price reduction should lead to an increased volume of sales in the USA. So the volume of exports should rise (this in itself stimulates the domestic economy).

By converse argument, an American book costing $3 in the USA and so £1 in the United Kingdom before devaluation costs £1.50 in the United Kingdom after devaluation (£1.50 at $2 = £1 provides the American publisher with the $3 he needs to cover his (dollar) costs and profits). So the volume of imports into the United Kingdom should fall (and a decline in the propensity to import should increase the multiplier and so stimulate economic activity).

What happens now to the overseas sector's financial balance depends upon what happens to UK receipts of foreign exchange from exports net of expenditure of foreign exchange on imports.

On the one hand the United Kingdom is selling a greater *volume* of exports but at a lower *dollar* price, so total dollar receipts may or may not increase depending on whether or not the increase in volume more than compensates for the fall in dollar price. In other words, it all depends on the foreign price elasticity of demand for UK exports (if the volume reaction to the dollar price change is a delayed reaction, then there will be a temporary drop in dollar earnings).

On the other hand, the United Kingdom is buying a smaller *volume* of imports, so that the total amount paid out in dollars will decrease; the extent of this decrease depends on the sterling price elasticity of demand for imports (and on the speed of the reaction).

---

by 14.3 per cent from $2.80 = £1 to $2.40 = £1 on 18 November 1967, strongly indicates that such a sequence is very likely to ensue), then the rate of price inflation at a PSBR of *OA* may increase considerably with a (possibly considerable) rightward shift of the PSBR–inflation curve (not shown on the diagram).

Import controls

Another way to shift the PSBR–overseas sector financial balance curve to the right and upwards is by controlling (not necessarily reducing) imports either through a tariff (a tax on imports – largely non-discriminatory), or through quantitative controls, such as imposing limiting quotas (or rationing) on the amounts which may be imported (which quotas need not necessarily be discriminatory but which may well be so in practice). Such import controls have the great advantage over devaluation (if the foreign price elasticity of demand for exports is low) of not reducing the foreign price of exports and so leaving gross earnings of foreign exchange from exports unchanged (providing that other countries do not retaliate against quantitative controls on imports – their exports; this is, of course, a vitally important proviso). Import controls have an even greater advantage of not *directly* causing domestic inflation.

The proponents of import controls argue, moreover, that the purpose of import controls is *not* to reduce the overseas sector's financial balance but to increase the level of domestic economic activity (i.e. reduce unemployment). This is a very important part of the argument for import controls and it needs to be properly and fully appreciated (the most accessible statement of this argument, stemming from the Cambridge Economic Policy

Group, is Wynne Godley, 'Britain's chronic recession: can anything be done?', in Wilfred Beckerman (ed.), *Slow Growth in Britain: Causes and Consequences*, Oxford University Press, 1979; with more technical arguments in University of Cambridge Department of Applied Economics, *Cambridge Economic Policy Review*, April 1980, ch. 4).

Suppose that, to use Diagram 14.5 again, import controls are used to shift the PSBR–overseas sector financial balance curve from 1 to 2. Then, the argument goes, the government can expand its deficit (the PSBR) from *OA* to *OC*, say by cutting the rate of taxation, thus achieving full employment at home, while maintaining the overseas sector's financial surplus at *OD*, but now on the new unemployment–balance-of-payments trade-off curve. In other words, in terms of their financial balance, the overseas sector is no worse off than before – so it has no valid cause for complaint, and therefore no reasonable grounds for retaliation against import controls – while the domestic economy no longer has to suffer unemployment as the price of keeping the overseas sector's financial surplus down to *OD*. In the absence of import controls, it is quite impossible to run the economy at full employment because the balance-of-payments consequences, along curve 1, of running at *OC* are quite unacceptable.

Moreover, the imposition of quantitative import controls, unlike devaluation, may not be likely to shift the PSBR–inflation curve so directly in an adverse rightward direction as will happen under devaluation. This remark does not apply to the imposition of tariffs, unless the revenue from tariffs is used to reduce other taxes on expenditure in an offsetting way so far as retail price indices are concerned – and, proponents of import controls argue, this is exactly what should be done with tariff revenue. There may, however, be a movement along the initial PSBR–inflation curve as a result of the increase in the PSBR from *OA* to *OC*; although, as the Cambridge Economic Policy Group argue (on the basis of their empirical work on inflation), a higher level of economic activity tends to reduce unit costs of production by improving capacity utilisation and so the policy of import controls and expansion from *OA* to *OC* may, it is argued, pull the PSBR–inflation curve rather to the left, so mitigating the (alleged) inflationary effects of a higher PSBR.

Against this optimistic view of the impact on inflation of import controls there must be set the more pessimistic view that either the change via tariffs in the relative prices of imported goods and home-produced goods, or the quantitative rationing of imports, will create a situation in which prices of domestically produced goods will rise. If this happens the United Kingdom may become 'locked into' a high-cost system of production which would be permanently dependent upon import controls and, even worse, which would not be capable of selling its exports in free competition with other countries. If the prices of domestically produced goods do rise, this may increase either profits or wages. If profits are increased and thereby more investment may be financed, this 'featherbedding' of UK producers may thus provide the basis for economic expansion and improvement of efficiency. On the other hand, if wages rise, so possibly leading to higher unit labour costs, then the benefit of increased investment is unlikely to follow import controls to the requisite extent. Therefore, it is probably necessary (perhaps even essential) to combine import controls with controls on wage increases if the former are to be as effective as it is claimed they could be. Unfortunately, the history of pay controls in the United Kingdom does not create confidence in their efficacy.

Incomes policy

This brings us to those policies which try to shift the PSBR–inflation curve to the left and upwards. To use Diagram 14.5 again, if the government could operate a PSBR of *OC*, but could contrive to shift the PSBR–inflation curve from 1 to 2, then full employment on the trade-off curve 2 could be achieved with an inflation rate of *OE'*. If inflation is ascribed to increases in unit labour costs rather than to increases in the money supply (caused in turn by a large PSBR), then a policy to restrict wage increases – an 'incomes policy' – may achieve this result. Such a policy may seek also to restrict price increases themselves as well as the 'underlying' unit cost increases (for one episode of such a policy, see Allan Fels, *The British Prices and Incomes Board*, Cambridge University Press, 1972). Unfortunately, such policies usually become unpopular after a while (if not being so from the start) and the government is either forced to abandon them or is replaced by a government which disavows such policies. This may then lead to a reacting move to the right in the PSBR–inflation curve when the incomes policy is abandoned, and the government then seeks to counteract the ensuing inflation by reducing the PSBR, but at the same time this creates unemployment. Employees may thus be faced with an inescapable either/or choice between incomes policy and (fairly) full employment or no incomes policy ('free collective bargaining') and unemployment.

If the reaction of wages to a period of pay restriction is such as to decrease profits, and hence private-sector investment, then this will increase the full-employment budget deficit, i.e. it will increase the length of the 'unemployment tube' at the same time as the government is reducing the PSBR; so the combined effect is to redouble the increase in unemployment. To illustrate: if the reduction in private-sector investment (brought about by a wage 'squeeze' on profits following a rightward shift in the PSBR–inflation curve from 2 to 1) means that a counteracting rise in government expenditure, and so in the PSBR to OC', is required, then the unemployment–inflation trade-off curve shifts downwards from 1 to 3 (i.e. trade-off curve 3 corresponds to the PSBR–inflation curve 1, but with OC' as the full-employment government financial deficit). If the government reduces the PSBR to counteract inflation (having given up on direct pay controls), then it not only moves down the unemployment–inflation trade-off curve, but it also shifts on to a new and higher trade-off curve such as trade-off curve 3. (We must not forget that the position of the unemployment–inflation trade-off curve depends on the full-employment government deficit – on the length of the 'unemployment tube' – and so this trade-off curve can shift around in a quite agile manner depending on all sorts of factors such as changes in private-sector investment or in exports – the non-government final expenditure base for the multiplier process – or changes in the parameters of the multiplier itself.)

Incomes policies are not the only way in which the government may seek to shift the PSBR–inflation curve upwards and to the left. If, for any given PSBR, the government raises the rate of interest, then (see Diagram 14.1) this should reduce the increase in the money supply. This, it is argued, should in turn reduce the rate of inflation (i.e. the PSBR–inflation curve is shifted up and to the left). However, if higher interest rates adversely affect private-sector investment, then, although the PSBR–inflation curve will be shifting up and to the left (this by itself tending to produce a corresponding upwards shift in the unemployment–inflation trade-off curve), the reduction in private-sector investment will at the same time increase the length of the unemployment tube, and this by itself will tend to produce a downward shift in the unemployment–inflation trade-off curve. Thus the net effect of higher interest rates on unemployment may be adverse, i.e. unemployment may increase.

Reducing the full-employment government deficit

Thus it seems that policies to shift the curves in the upper quadrants face all sorts of obstacles. What about policies which accept that neither of the upper-quadrant curves may be readily or permanently shifted and which therefore try to reduce the full-employment government deficit? Clearly, if in Diagram 14.5 the full-employment government deficit could be reduced to B (the length of the 'unemployment tube' to OB), then the government could put the PSBR at B and enjoy zero inflation, zero unemployment, and have a balance-of-payments surplus as an added bonus. Policies to reduce the full-employment government deficit probably have to focus their attention on increasing private-sector investment. The argument is as follows.

We use the following notation:

Y = gross domestic product

Y^* = GDP at full employment

I = *private*-sector investment

G = general government *total* expenditure (final consumption expenditure *plus* investment expenditure)†

X = exports

T = general government income-tax receipts

b = marginal propensity to consume

m = marginal propensity to import

t = proportionate rate of taxation on incomes

We know from Chapter 12 that the multiplier relationship which determines gross domestic product (output having adjusted to aggregate final demand) is:

$$Y = \frac{1 - m}{1 - b(1 - t) + bm(1 - t)} \times (I + X + G)$$

If the parameters of the multiplier are fixed and I and X are (for the moment) constant, then government expenditure, G, must be set at that level which will provide full-employment GDP, Y^*; let us denote this level of government expenditure as G^*. Then we may rewrite the multiplier relationship which leads to full employment as (see Table 12.7):

$$Y^* = \frac{1 - m}{1 - b(1 - t) + mb(1 - t)} \times (I + X)$$
$$+ \frac{1 - m}{1 - b(1 - t) + mb(1 - t)} \times G^*$$

That is, government total expenditure does the necessary to produce full employment given the other variables and parameters. From this we may by algebraic manipulation derive the expression for G^*:

$$G^* = \left[Y^* - \frac{1 - m}{1 - b(1 - t) + mb(1 - t)} \times (I + X) \right] \frac{1 - b(1 - t) + mb(1 - t)}{1 - m}$$
$$= \frac{1 - b(1 - t) + mb(1 - t)}{1 - m} \times Y^* - (I + X)$$

The full-employment government financial deficit is the difference between this level of government expenditure and the total taxation which would be raised at full-employment GDP. Assuming for simplicity that there are no expenditure taxes and that all tax is income tax, full-employment tax receipts, denoted T^*, are:

$$T^* = tY^*$$

We then have the full-employment government financial deficit as:

$$G^* - T^* = \left[\frac{1 - b(1 - t) + mb(1 - t)}{1 - m} - t \right] Y^* - (I + X)$$

†Note well this new definition of G, which includes government investment, and the corresponding new definition of I, which excludes government investment. Note also that we are here ignoring the complications caused by public corporations; this would be included in G but with a corresponding (and complicated) modification to T.

So, if we want to reduce the full-employment government financial deficit, we can either increase the flow of private-sector investment or of exports, or alter the parameters of the multiplier appropriately. This latter task is difficult to accomplish; for example, it would be possible to reduce the marginal propensity to import (which by increasing the denominator reduces the multiplicand for Y^*), but this probably involves policies to restrict imports. The marginal propensity to consume is not readily alterable, and has in any case probably been decreasing secularly (see Diagram 3.5), which, for the present problem, is a move in the wrong direction as it increases the numerator and so the multiplicand for Y^*. So the hopes for decreasing the full-employment government financial deficit are likely to depend upon increasing private-sector investment or exports. Increasing the volume of exports can be achieved by devaluation, but this has adverse consequences for inflation. So we are more or less left with trying to increase private-sector investment as the means to reducing the full-employment government financial deficit to some such level as OB in Diagram 14.5 with all its delightful and simultaneous consequences for inflation, unemployment, and the balance of payments. And this conveniently brings us to the subject of our concluding chapter: investment and growth seen from a macroeconomic point of view.

Exercises

14.1 *(To practise your understanding of Diagram 14.1.)*

(i)   If OA marks the point where the government can meet its entire borrowing requirement from the UK non-bank private sector (also taking into account finance from the overseas sector), explain why offering rate of interest r_2 on new government debt entails OE increase in the money stock sterling M_3.

(ii)   What would happen to the interest rate–money supply trade-off (for the OA configuration) if the government were to call for Special Deposits of OC?

14.2 *(To practise your understanding of discounting.)*

(i)   An investment of £100 returns £30 per annum for five years (starting after one year) and the rate of discount is 12 per cent per annum. What is this investment's net present value?

(ii)   What is this investment's net present value if the rate of discount is reduced to 10 per cent per annum?

(iii)   What is this investment's internal rate of return?

14.3 *(To see the lagged relationship between inflation and the increase in the money supply.)*

(i)   Update Appendix 13.2.

(ii)   Using the data from the updated Appendix 13.2, draw the scatter diagram for the two-year lagged relationship between annual changes in the money supply and the annual rate of price inflation.

14.4 *(To practise your understanding of financial balances and financial intermediation.)* In terms of inter-sectoral flows of borrowing/ lending and financial instruments, describe a plausible scenario for financial intermediation in the economy of Table 14.1.

14.5 *(To see the relationship between the general government financial balance and the overseas sector financial balance.)*

(i)   Update Appendix 12.1.

(ii)   Using the data from the updated Appendix 12.1, draw the scatter diagram to show the relationship between the general government financial balance and the overseas sector financial balance.

(iii)   Discuss the significance for economic policy of the relationship between the general government financial balance and the overseas sector financial balance (*further reading:* J. A. Bispham, 'The New Cambridge and "Monetarist" criticisms of "conventional" economic policy-making', *National Institute Economic Review*, November 1975, pp. 39–55; Francis Cripps, Martin Fetherston and Wynne

Godley, 'What is left of "New Cambridge"?', University of Cambridge Department of Applied Economics (Cambridge Economic Policy Group), *Economic Policy Review*, No. 2 March 1976, pp. 46–9).

14.6 *(To practise your understanding of Diagram 14.4.)*

(i) In Diagram 14.4, what happens to the relationship between price inflation and the percentage rate of unemployment if the 'full-employment government deficit' is (a) larger than *OC*, (b) smaller than *OC*?

(ii) In Diagram 14.4, explain why the rate of unemployment is likely to increase as the government reduces the public sector borrowing requirement by reducing the general government financial deficit (modulus of).

(iii) Explain the diagram below used by the National Institute of Economic and Social Research to describe 'changes in the budgetary stance' (see *National Institute Economic Review:* February 1975, chart 2 and pp. 13–16; February 1977, chart 4

and pp. 18–20; May 1980, chart 2 and pp. 20–1; May 1981, chart 3 and pp. 11–13).

(iv) In the light of your answers to (ii) and (iii), and using Diagram 14.4 and the figures given below, interpret the change in 'budgetary stance' between 1975 and 1977:

	1975	*1977*
Public-sector financial balance (− deficit) as a percentage of gross domestic product (factor cost)	−8.2	−4.7
Overseas-sector financial balance (+ surplus) as a percentage of gross domestic product (factor cost)	1.6	0.2
Rate of price inflation (implied GDP price deflator), percentage change over preceding year	27.1	12.3
Rate of unemployment, wholly unemployed as a percentage of the working population	3.9	5.6

Sources: Appendices 1.2, 12.1 and 13.2.

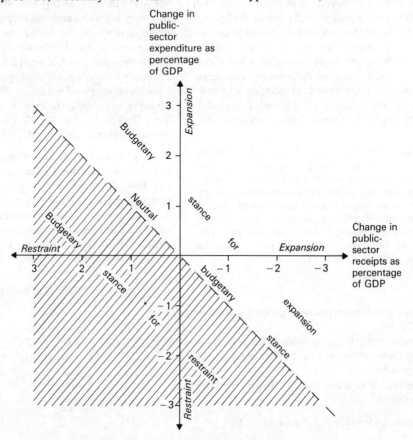

14.7   *(To develop your understanding of changes in the exchange rate in general and of devaluation in particular.)*

(i)   What effect is a devaluation of sterling likely to have on (a) the overseas sector's financial balance, and (b) the rate of domestic price inflation?

(ii)   The £ was devalued on Saturday, 18 November 1967 by 14.3 per cent from £1 = $2.80 to £1 = $2.40. Using Diagram 14.4 and the data given at the foot of this page, interpret the ensuing years' movement in the budgetary stance, in the overseas sector's financial balance, and in the rate of unemployment. What effect did the devaluation appear to have had on domestic price inflation? Comment on the 'trend' in unemployment in the three years after 1967 given the trend in the government's budgetary stance.*

14.8   *(To develop your understanding of the arguments for and against import controls.)*

Reflation sufficient to halt the rise in unemployment and enlarge the area of dynamism in industry would lead to a financial deficit on the balance of payments of the order of £10 billion after a year or so. It therefore remains our view that import controls would be necessary to sustain recovery on a scale which would bring unemployment down while at the same time keeping inflationary pressures within tolerable bounds (University of Cambridge Department of Applied Economics (Cambridge Economic Policy Group), *Cam-*

*In answering this last question you may derive some guidance from the celebrated interchange between Sherlock Holmes and Inspector Gregory in the case of the missing racehorse Silver Blaze concerning the curious incident of the dog in the night-time; see: Arthur Conan Doyle, *Memoirs of Sherlock Holmes*, 'Silver Blaze': *The Penguin Complete Sherlock Holmes*, Penguin Books, 1981, p. 347, lines 1 to 4.

bridge Economic Policy Review: Economic Policy in the UK, vol. 7, no. 1, April 1981, p. 1).

Using Diagram 14.4, explain and discuss this argument. (*Further reading:* source of quotation, pp. 1–5 and 8–24; Wynne Godley, 'Britain's chronic recession: can anything be done?' in Wilfred Beckerman (ed.), *Slow Growth in Britain: Causes and Consequences*, Oxford University Press, 1979; Christopher Allsopp and Vijay Joshi, 'Alternative strategies for the UK', *National Institute Economic Review*, February 1980, pp. 86–103; Maurice Scott and Robert Laslett, *Can We Get Back To Full Employment?*, Macmillan, 1978, chs 6 'The balance of payments constraint' and 7 'Policies to restore full employment'; University of Cambridge Department of Applied Economics (Cambridge Economic Policy Group), *Cambridge Economic Policy Review*, vol. 6, no. 1, April 1980, ch. 4 'Academic criticisms of the CEPG analysis'.)

14.9   *(To develop your understanding of the arguments for and against incomes policy.)*

Experience over the last two years has reinforced the conclusion that the attempt to get rid of inflation simply by deflating the economy leads to unacceptably high figures of unemployment at still high rates of inflation. So the search for alternative methods – and that means essentially a search for workable reforms of the wage bargaining system – will have to be renewed sooner or later. There is no other way (National Institute of Economic and Social Research, *National Institute Economic Review*, no. 96, May 1981, p. 5).

Even with current levels of unemployment one cannot therefore dismiss out of hand the risk that a revival of demand will entail a revival of inflation. There are those who argue that this prospect will always threaten until some kind of permanent incomes policy is put in place. But a major reform of the pay bargaining system is not a realistic option at the

	1967	1968	1969	1970	1971
General government financial deficit as a percentage of GDP	−1.2	−0.6	2.5	3.5	1.6
Overseas-sector financial balance as a percentage of GDP	0.8	0.6	−1.2	−1.9	−2.3
Wholly unemployed as a percentage of the working population	2.2	2.2	2.2	2.4	3.2
Percentage change in implied GDP price deflator over preceding year	2.8	2.9	3.7	7.8	10.8

Sources: Appendices 1.2, 12.1 and 13.2.

present time (National Institute of Economic and Social Research, *National Institute Economic Review*, no. 98, November 1981, p. 26).

(i) Using Diagram 14.4, explain why it is thought that a 'revival of demand will entail a revival of inflation'?

(ii) Using Diagram 14.4, explain how an 'incomes policy' is supposed to get round this difficulty.

(iii) In the light of the data given below, consider the accuracy of the National Institute's assertion about 'unacceptably high figures of unemployment at still high rates of inflation' and describe what a 'workable reform' of the pay bargaining system might comprise.

(*Further reading:* Allan Fels, *The British Prices and Incomes Board*, Cambridge University Press, 1972, esp. part I; Robert Taylor, 'The need for an incomes policy', Samuel Brittan, 'Why British incomes policies have failed', and Ken Gill, 'Incomes policy: the trade union view', all in Robin Chater, Andrew Dean and Robert Elliott (eds), *Incomes Policy*, Oxford University Press, 1981; Samuel Brittan and Peter Lilley, *The Delusion of Incomes Policy*, Temple Smith, 1977.)

14.10 (*The great lesson to be learnt in economics is that everything affects everything else. This exercise shows you one aspect of this economic truth.*)

(i) Using Diagram 14.4, explain why an increase in private-sector investment should be a relatively non-inflationary way of reducing unemployment.

(ii) In Table 4.17 we saw that the percentage change, at constant prices, in the total gross income ('profits') of industrial and commercial companies – denoted $\dot{\Pi}^*$ – between 1979 and 1980 was -13.8 per cent; in Table 4.18 we saw that the lagged relationship between the percentage change in 'profits' (at constant prices) and the percentage change in company-sector fixed capital formation ('investment'), at constant prices – denoted $\dot{I}^*$ – was:

$$\dot{I}_t^* = 2.36 + 0.453\dot{\Pi}_{t-1}^*$$

Forecast the percentage change from 1980 to 1981 in company-sector fixed capital formation at constant prices. Comment on the implications of all this for unemployment and for economic policy.

(*Further reading:* National Institute of Economic and Social Research, *National Institute Economic Review*, no. 98, November 1981, ch. I 'The British economy in the medium term'.)

	1979	1980	1981 2nd qtr–2nd qtr
Wholly unemployed as a percentage of the working population	5.4	6.8	10.5
Percentage change in implied GDP price deflator over preceding year	13.4	18.3	11.2

Sources: Department of Employment, *Employment Gazette*, January 1982, table 2.1, p. S20; Central Statistical Office, *Economic Trends*, February 1982, p. 6.

Chapter 15

Investment and Economic Growth

Contents

Chapter guide

Chapter 15, the final chapter, explains the basic theory of growth in the macro economy and looks at the international comparative record on economic growth.

The trend relationship between the aggregate gross capital stock and gross domestic product, in the form of the *incremental capital–output ratio*, is one of the key concepts in growth theory and it is explained with reference to data from the UK economy and from ten other economies. The other key concept in the theory of growth is the growth of the capital stock as determined by the *'net' investment ratio* (where 'net' means net of *retirements* from the capital stock, and where 'net' capital stock growth is taken as a ratio to GDP). We see how these two concepts were put together in the *growth equation* and we explain how the growth equation, when balanced against (multiplier) changes in aggregate demand, may create a situation of potential instability in the economy. We consider the role of exports in 'demand-led' economic growth. Data on the United Kingdom's 'net' investment ratio is examined and we consider some possible explanations for the reduction in this ratio in recent years.

Finally, we look at some international comparative data on growth and investment, and the positive relationship between the two, in eighteen economies in the period 1955 to 1978 and we consider some explanations for, and obstacles to solving, the United Kingdom's comparatively low growth rate (especially with regard to labour productivity) in the light of the 'virtuous circle' of economic growth. We consider the prospects for the UK economy and, using the growth equation, we describe the magnitude of the increase in gross investment required to raise the UK growth rate even to only the average of that obtaining in other countries. At this concluding point we see again the importance of the argument, advanced in previous chapters, that investment to expand capacity and reduce unit production costs is financed largely from retentions and so depends on (company) profits.

Introduction

In this chapter we consider the basic analysis of growth in the capacity of the economy to produce value added. This analysis is fundamentally concerned with underlying *trends* and is not so much concerned with temporary fluctuations, or 'cycles', in economic activity or in aggregate demand. For example, the analysis of growth helps us to understand the trend towards increased unemployment which the UK economy has experienced since about 1965 (see Diagram 1.5), but it is not concerned to explain the cyclical ups and downs of UK unemployment – such fluctuations are caused by the sorts of influences on aggregate demand which were described in Chapters 11, 12 and 14. However, there is an important relationship between the growth of aggregate demand and the trend growth in the capacity to produce output and, as we shall see, this interaction may well account for the 'instability' of modern industrial market economies.

The analysis of the causal factors underlying trends in the economy also helps us to understand why the United Kingdom's economic growth has been slower than that in other countries (even though postwar UK economic growth has been quite rapid relative to growth rates achieved in the past), and for this reason we look at the international comparative record on economic growth.

The gross capital stock and GDP – the incremental capital–output ratio

We saw in Diagrams 1.10 and 7.6 the relationship that apparently existed between the growth of output per worker and capital stock per worker over the long run, and we saw in Table 1.14 and Diagrams 1.11 and 7.7 that there was also a positive relationship (of a certain 'production function' sort) between output per worker and capital per worker in various branches of industry. The first step in the analysis of aggregate economic growth is to establish the relationship between the annual flow of total output produced and the total gross stock of capital used to produce that output flow (the reader whose recollection of the discussion of gross and net capital stock in Chapter 1 is a little hazy should at this juncture read that section again). We use the gross capital stock because that is the concept and measure relevant to capacity to produce: two Minis still in service (the end-1977 gross stock in Table 1.9) will provide the same productive transport services regardless of the cumulated depreciation (the end-1977 net stock in Table 1.9 is *not* relevant to production capacity, though it is relevant to wealth ownership). And, of course, we must work in constant prices, because the analysis of growth must be conducted in 'real' terms.

Diagram 15.1, which plots the data in Appendix 1.1 from 1871 to 1980, shows that there is a quite close-fitting trend relationship between the gross capital stock and gross domestic product (both measured at constant 1975 prices). For a reason which will become clear, we plot GDP – here supposed to be the 'caused' or dependent variable – on the horizontal

DIAGRAM 15.1   *The relationship between the capital stock and gross domestic product, 1871 to 1980*

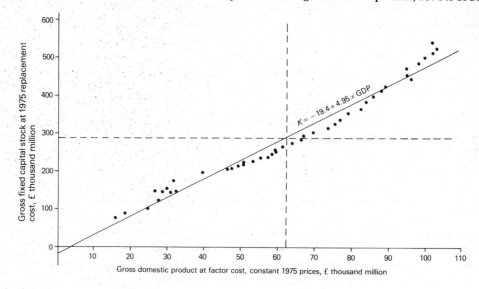

axis, and we plot the capital stock – the 'causing' or independent variable – on the vertical axis, thus reversing the conventional procedure. Note well that in Diagram 15.1, the scale of the vertical capital axis is ten times the scale of the horizontal GDP axis (this solely for the purpose of making the diagram drawable – the student should now, on a rough piece of paper, sketch out the diagram as it would appear if the same scale were used on both axes: this will show you that a 'lot' of capital has to be added in order to add a 'little' to output. (*Hint:* to do this sketch, multiply the numbers on the horizontal axis by 10 and then imagine how the points would look.)

The trend relationship, expressed as a straight line, is:

$$\text{Capital stock, year-end, 1975 prices, £ billion} = -19.38 + 4.954 \times \text{Annual flow of GDP, 1975 prices, £ billion}$$

(the decimal places have been rounded on the diagram). The coefficient of correlation is $R = +0.986$; in other words, 97 per cent of the variance in the capital stock is 'explained' by the linear relationship and the variance in GDP (or, in a more economically meaningful sense, vice versa).

The coefficient in this trend relationship is an economically important parameter. If we use the letter K to denote the gross capital stock at constant prices, and Y to denote annual flow of gross domestic product at constant prices, then from the equation above, we have in round terms:

$$\frac{\Delta K}{\Delta Y} = 4.95$$

(where Δ means 'change in'; ΔK is the change in the capital stock from one year-end to the next, and so is a flow per annum; ΔY is the change in the annual flow of GDP and this change, too, is a flow per annum). That is to say, along this trend relationship, for every increment of 1 unit added to the annual flow of output, 4.95 units would have to be added to the gross capital stock to enable the extra 1 unit of output to be produced. To illustrate using the trend relationship (but see also the data for 1938 and 1952 in Appendix 1.1):

£ billion, 1975 prices

	Gross domestic product per annum	Capital stock
	40	178.8
	50	228.3
Change	+10	49.5

We suppose that the (trend value of the) capital stock determines the (trend value of the) annual flow of output because the capacity to produce annual output depends on the amount of capital available. A trend value of annual output (GDP) of £40 billion requires, according to the long-run estimated relationship, £178.8 billion of gross capital stock (all at 1975 prices). That this is so can be determined from the estimated linear relationship:

$$178.8 = -19.38 + 4.954 \times 40$$

(One reason for estimating the relationship in the form shown in Diagram 15.1 is that we can readily ascertain, according to the trend, how much capital would be required to produce any given output flow. The other reason is that we can read the coefficient $\Delta K/\Delta Y$ straight off from this relationship.)*

Likewise we can determine that the capital stock required to produce an annual output flow of £50 billion is £228.3 billion. In other words, and most importantly, if we wished to increase the annual output flow by £10 billion from £40 billion to £50 billion, the trend linear relationship between capital stock and annual output flow tells us that we have to increase the capital stock by £49.5 billion from £178.8 billion to £228.3 billion. Or, dividing by ten, for every 1 unit (billion) to be added to the annual output flow, 4.95 units (billions) must be added to the capital stock (presuming that we can be guided by the past trend relationship between the capital stock and the annual output flow).

Clearly, this parameter $\Delta K/\Delta Y$ showing the increase in capital stock required to produce a 1-unit increase in the annual output flow is an important one. It has been given a special name, 'the incremental capital–output ratio', or ICOR for short, where the word 'incremental' indicates that it is the ratio between an increment (say of 1 unit) to the annual output flow and the requisite accompanying increment to the capital stock.

Note that in Table 8.16 we considered Denison's finding that, over the period 1950 to 1962, the growth of total factor input contributed about one-half of the UK growth in output, with about one-third coming from 'technical progress' and the remainder mostly from economies of scale. Because of the *ex post* nature of the way in which we measure the incremental capital–output ratio – the growth of actual output achieved relative to growth of actual capital stock – the ICOR incorporates also the aggregate impact of these other effects as well. In other words, the ICOR, as here measured, does not relate simply to a movement along a fixed (aggregate) production function (which perhaps in all strictness it ought to do), but it relates to movements along a *shifting* production function (shifting upwards because of technical progress: see Diagrams 7.6, 7.7 and 8.1); and, moreover, along a shifting production function which incorporates the effects of economies of scale (see Diagram 7.9). However, the fact that the aggregate ICOR incorporates all these effects is no theoretical disadvantage (a) if we assume that these effects (technical progress, economies of scale) will have more or less the same proportionate effect on the

---

*From a theoretical point of view, the technically preferable econometric procedure would be to estimate the regression as $Y = a' + b'K$, treating K as the independent variable, and then to take the incremental capital–output ratio as $1/b'$; however, with the high correlation coefficients here obtained (see Table 15.1) the difference would be negligible, so we proceed according to the less appropriate, but simpler to follow, procedure as described.

aggregate economy each year, and (b) if we argue that in any case technical progress and economies of scale are inseparable from increases to the capital stock because, in order to affect output, they both need to be 'embodied' in new capital equipment. So the ICOR as here measured incorporates the impact of technical progress and economies of scale.

In what follows we shall take the aggregate incremental capital–output ratio in the UK economy to have a value of 4.95, because this is what we are told by the trend relationship of the longest run of data which it is possible to muster (other studies covering different periods also give a very similar value: see Wilfred Beckerman *et al. The British Economy in 1975*, Cambridge University Press, 1965, table 1.7, p. 30; A. Lamfalussy, *The United Kingdom and the Six*, Macmillan, 1963, table 15, p. 72). Different branches of the economy may, of course, have their own incremental capital–output ratios. Furthermore, it is entirely possible that the aggregate incremental capital–output ratio could be affected by various changes: a change in technology which called for more capital per unit of output could raise the ICOR; more, and continually increasing, efficient use of the capital stock or a faster rate of technical progress might reduce the ICOR; and, of course, if different branches of industry have different ICORs, then the growth of one branch relative to other branches (say the extraction of North Sea oil) could affect the aggregate, over-all ICOR. It seems that the United Kingdom has, by comparison with other economies, a rather high incremental capital–output ratio (although it is by no means certain that the state of capital-stock measurement permits confident comparisons among countries – see Michael Ward, *The Measurement of Capital: The Methodology of Capital Stock Estimates in OECD Countries*, OECD, 1976).

Table 15.1 (computed from the data in Appendix 15.1) shows some estimates of the incremental capital–output ratios for various countries derived in the same way as the ICOR in Diagram 15.1. In all cases there is a high correlation between the capital stock and aggregate output, so the straight-line equation and the regression coefficient (the ICOR) is statistically well determined (note that this value of the ICOR for the United Kingdom is slightly different, because it relates to a different time period). Among the countries, Sweden has a slightly higher ICOR than the United Kingdom, but the other countries have lower ICORs.

It is an intriguing question as to why ICORs differ so much among countries. From a

TABLE 15.1   *Incremental capital–output ratios in eleven countries*

Country	Incremental capital–output ratio [a]	Correlation coefficient
Whole economy		
Sweden	4.372	0.992
United Kingdom	4.286	0.993
Norway	3.905	0.998
West Germany	3.847	0.991
Canada	2.682	0.997
Denmark	2.643	0.993
Italy	2.240	0.994
France	1.718	0.997
Enterprise sector		
USA	1.502	0.989
Japan	1.253	0.986
Manufacturing industry		
Ireland	1.990	0.988

[a] Estimated by least squares as the regression coefficient b in the equation $K = a + bY$.

Source: computed from data in Appendix 15.1.

purely theoretical point of view, one would expect a unit increment to annual output to require much the same extra capital in any comparable industrialised economy. One possible answer is, of course, that differences in measuring the gross capital stock may explain this (apparent) difference. Another possible answer is that national differences in capacity utilisation may explain the variation. For example, if three-shift working for twenty-four hours a day were the norm throughout the French economy and one-shift working for eight hours a day were the norm throughout the UK economy, then clearly the French economy should obtain three times as much (extra) output per (extra) unit of the capital stock. So differences in capacity utilisation could explain the variance in aggregate ICORs (such differences in capacity utilisation could be caused by factors other than shift-working; say in the intensity with which workers were prepared to work). Differences in aggregate ICORs could also be caused by different sectoral composition of additions to the capital stock. We can see in Table 15.1 that the ICORs for the enterprise sector (excluding government final consumption from GDP and the government capital stock) are much lower than the aggregate ICORs for the whole economy. The figures for the ICOR in Ireland's manufacturing industry is also lower. So that, if one country were to concentrate more of its investment in a part of the economy which had a lower (or higher) ICOR, the aggregate ICOR resulting would be lower (or higher) as well. We do not have sufficient data fully to test these alternative explanations ('hypotheses'), so we shall simply note this variation in ICORs among countries as a fact. It is, as we shall see, a variation with significant implications.

Growth of the capital stock

In Diagram 1.9 and Table 1.12 we saw how the gross fixed capital stock (at constant prices) grew as a result of the difference between the annual inflow, to the stock, of gross fixed capital formation and the annual outflow, from the stock, of retirements. So it is gross investment in fixed capital *less* retirements (all at constant prices) which determines the change in the capital stock. As shown in Chapter 1, working in constant prices (and omitting the adjective 'fixed'):

Gross capital stock at end of previous year	+	Gross capital formation during year	−	Retirements from capital stock during year	=	Gross capital stock at end of year

which can be rearranged to give:

Gross capital stock at end of year	−	Gross capital stock at end of previous year	=	Gross capital formation during year	−	Retirements from capital stock during year

If we denote the annual flow of gross fixed capital formation by I ('gross investment') and the annual flow of retirements by R, and using the previous notation of ΔK for the change in the gross capital stock from one year's end to the next, we can write this equation as:

$$\Delta K = I - R$$

We need now to measure the relative extent of an economy's gross investment *less* retirements. This may be done quite simply by dividing $I - R$ by the annual flow of gross domestic product Y to give the ratio:

$$\frac{I - R}{Y} = \frac{I}{Y} - \frac{R}{Y}$$

the left-hand side of which gives gross investment *less* retirements as a proportion of gross domestic product. It is a relative measure of the extent to which the annual flow of value added is being devoted to investment, qualified or adjusted by the extent to which the annual flow of retirements is counteracting that relative investment effort so far as the growth of the gross fixed capital stock is concerned. I shall call this the *'net' investment ratio*, but shall always put the word 'net' in inverted commas to remind you that we are here using the word to refer to 'net of retirements' (and not net of capital consumption or depreciation, as is usually the case). The 'net' investment ratio is equal to the gross investment ratio, defined as I/Y, *minus* the retirements ratio, R/Y. Clearly, for any given rate of retirements (R/Y), the greater is the gross investment ratio (I/Y), the higher will be the 'net' investment ratio and so the greater will be the growth of the capital stock.

The growth equation

We may now analyse the proportionate growth rate of the aggregate economy (the rate of growth of GDP at constant prices) in terms of the incremental capital–output ratio and the 'net' investment ratio. This can be done quite straightforwardly by demonstrating that the proportionate growth rate of GDP, written as $\Delta Y/Y$, is equal to the 'net' investment ratio divided by the incremental capital–output ratio:

$$\frac{(I-R)/Y}{\Delta K/\Delta Y} = \frac{\Delta K/Y}{\Delta K/\Delta Y} = \frac{\Delta Y}{Y}$$

The above equation starts with the 'net' investment ratio divided by the ICOR; the next step is to substitute ΔK for $I - R$; the final step is to cancel out the ΔK expressions and rearrange.

We shall use this growth equation – expressing the rate of growth as the ratio between the 'net' rate of investment and the ICOR – to analyse some of the main problems concerning aggregate economic growth in the United Kingdom.

History of the growth equation

We should note that this equation has appeared in various guises. If one notes the Keynesian equality between total saving and total gross capital formation, then the gross investment ratio, I/Y, is equal to the average saving ratio, S/Y, where S denotes the total flow of saving. In this form (and ignoring the complication of detail relating to the adjusting impact of the retirements ratio, R/Y) the growth rate of the economy could be expressed as:

$$\text{Proportionate growth rate of GDP} = \frac{\text{Saving ratio}}{\text{ICOR}} = \frac{S/Y}{\Delta K/\Delta Y}$$

and it was in basically this form that the equation was introduced in 1939 by Sir Roy Harrod (see the enlargement of his article in *The Economic Journal*, March 1939, in *Towards a Dynamic Economics*, Macmillan, 1948, lecture 3 'Fundamental dynamic theorems').

At about the same time, Evsey Domar pointed out that, because gross investment increased the gross capital stock and hence the economy's capacity to produce output, there then arose the Keynesian problem of ensuring that aggregate final demand expanded sufficiently to 'take up' the extra production capacity ('Capital expansion, rate of growth, and employment', *Econometrica*, April 1946, reprinted as chapter III of *Essays in the Theory of Economic Growth*, Oxford University Press, 1957). If the parameters of the multiplier were constant, Domar argued, and if other elements of the final expenditure base, such as government consumption or exports, on which the multiplier worked, were also constant, then the only source of the requisite expansion in final demand was an expansion in investment – gross capital formation – itself. In short, because the annual investment flow causes production capacity to expand (according to the ICOR), and because *increases* in the annual investment flow lead to increases in aggregate final demand (according to the multiplier relationship), if full employment of (increasing) production capacity is to be maintained, investment must grow constantly at a certain rate. This certain rate can be derived as follows. The absolute increase in production capacity, ΔY, is (ignoring retirements, or, rather, assuming zero retirements – positive retirements can be readily incorporated but they are only a complication of detail and we are here concentrating on essential basic principles):

$$\Delta Y = \frac{I}{\Delta K/\Delta Y} = \frac{\text{Gross investment}}{\text{ICOR}}$$

But the absolute *expansion* in final demand, $\Delta Y'$, is, according to the multiplier in a two-sector economy (no government, no foreign trade):

$$\Delta Y' = \frac{1}{1-b} \times \Delta I$$

where b is the marginal propensity to consume. For 'equilibrium', i.e. if there is to be just sufficient extra final demand to absorb the extra output from the additional production capacity, extra final demand must be equal to extra production capacity:

$$\Delta Y' = \Delta Y$$

or:

$$\frac{1}{1-b} \times \Delta I = \frac{I}{\Delta K/\Delta Y}$$

that is:

$$\frac{\Delta I}{I} = \frac{1-b}{\Delta K/\Delta Y}$$

Note that [1 *minus* Marginal propensity to consume] *equals* Marginal propensity to save, and the requisite growth of investment which gives 'equilibrium' can be written as:

$$\frac{\Delta I}{I} = \frac{\text{Marginal propensity to save}}{\text{ICOR}}$$

If investment does not grow at exactly this rate, then there will be a divergence between extra final demand and extra production capacity. If investment grows at a faster rate than this, then:

$$\frac{1}{1-b} \times \Delta I > \frac{I}{\Delta K/\Delta Y}$$

and so:

$$\Delta Y' > \Delta Y$$

It would appear reasonable to argue that a situation in which total final demand was increasing faster than additions were being made to production capacity is a situation which would tend to stimulate still more investment (i.e. to speed up the growth of investment). But the initial problem was that the rate of growth investment was 'too fast' (in the sense of causing final demand to outrun production capacity). So the problem makes itself worse and should, in theory, provoke a cumulative economic expansion at an increasing rate (such 'booms' tend, in the United Kingdom especially, to lead to balance-of-payments deficits as imports rise to meet the gap between aggregate demand and the capacity to produce).

Conversely, if investment grew too slowly, there would emerge a situation in which total final demand was increasing more slowly than additions were being made to production capacity. This, it could be argued, is a situation likely to lead to still less investment, so exacerbating the initial problem, and so leading to a cumulative recession. In short, it seemed that 'making Keynesian economics dynamic' led to the likelihood in theory that the growth process would be 'unstable', or 'balanced on a knife-edge', and would make economies prone either to cumulative expansion or to cumulative recession. It is clear that economic cycles of one sort or another have long been a problem, but their causes are very complex and we are here concerned with growth and not with cycles (the student who wishes to go further in this direction should read R. C. O. Matthews, *The Trade Cycle*, Cambridge University Press, 1959, and E. Lundberg, *Instability and Economic Growth*, Yale University Press, 1968).

Investment and the increase in aggregate demand

This book has, in various chapters, concentrated on a theory of investment which emphasises the supply of internal finance as a critical factor. However, we saw in Chapter 5 (especially Diagrams 5.1, 5.3 and 5.4) that enterprises tend to rely on forecasts of sales volume when undertaking their business economic planning. Such forecasts form the basis of any capital expenditure plan. It is therefore reasonable to argue that the more rapidly enterprises expect sales volume to grow the more capital expenditure they will plan (stage 5 of Diagram 5.4) and, perhaps also, they will expect or hope for a greater flow of internal finance under such conditions. Forecasts, or expectations, of faster growth in sales volume will have a considerable effect on investment because the incremental capital–output ratio cuts both ways: if 4.95 extra units of capital are required for every 1 unit added to the annual output flow, then for every 1 extra unit which is expected in terms of increased sales volume 4.95 extra units must be added to the capital stock. This 'geared-up' ratio of 1 : 4.95 in extra output to extra capital stock required is known as the 'accelerator' or the 'acceleration principle'. Consequently, many theories of what determines investment have concentrated on these 'demand' effects arising from output growth, and such theories have considerable empirical support, some even to the extent of favouring the 'demand' explanations of variations in investment over 'supply of finance' explanations, though the supply of finance usually finds a place in the explanation as well (see Edwin Kuh, *Capital Stock Growth: A Micro-Econometric Approach*, North Holland, 1963; Bert Hickman, *Investment Demand and US Economic Growth*, Brookings Institution, 1965; Alexander Jack, 'A cross-sectional model of the capital expenditure function', in P. E. Hart (ed.), *Studies in Profit, Business Saving and Investment in the United Kingdom 1920–1962*, vol. II, Allen & Unwin, 1968; or G. J. Anderson, 'Investment and profits in the industrial and commercial sector', and G. Meeks, 'Cash flow and investment', in W. E. Martin (ed.), *The Economics of the Profits Crisis*, HMSO, 1981).

Consequently, many economists have argued that aggregate economic growth may be greatly influenced by the growth of aggregate final demand: in other words, the growth of the capital stock will accommodate to whatever extra capacity is required to produce the requisite final demand. Setting aside possible influences from changes in the parameters of the multiplier, we can see that the increase in final demand, $\Delta Y'$, will be determined by the multiplier and changes in the 'exogenous injections' into the economy coming from either (or all) increased investment, ΔI, increased government expenditure, ΔG, or – most important of all – increased exports, ΔX, as follows (see p. 560):

$$\Delta Y' = \frac{1 - m}{1 - b(1 - t) + mb(1 - t)} \times (\Delta I + \Delta G + \Delta X)$$

Some economists have pointed out that the volume of UK exports has grown slowly relative to the growth in the volume of other countries' exports, and so the expansion of final demand, as per this equation, has been relatively slow in the United Kingdom, and this may then have retarded the rate of increase in the capital stock (see Wilfred Beckerman, 'Demand, exports and growth', in Wilfred Beckerman *et al.*, *The British Economy in 1975*, Cambridge University Press, 1965). In this explanation a fast growth of exports leads to a fast growth of final demand which induces a larger flow of investment and so expands the capital stock, thus raising labour productivity and reducing unit costs (see Chapters 7 and 8), which in turn makes exports more competitive and so leads to even faster growth of exports. Economic growth thus benefits from a 'virtuous circle'. Conversely, slow growth of exports retards the growth of final demand, which dampens down the flow of investment so slowing the growth of the capital stock and consequent productivity increases/unit cost decreases. Exports thus become less competitive and so expand at a slower rate, aggravating the initial situation. Economic growth is thus trapped in a 'vicious circle'.

Other economists have pointed out that fluctuations in the growth of final demand, induced perhaps by government 'stop–go' policies (see Chapter 14), have made the returns from investment more uncertain and so may have induced a cautious approach by British business towards expanding the capital stock.

As we shall see from some international comparative data, such 'demand' explanations with regard to exports may well be applicable to explaining differences in growth rates among countries and to explaining the relatively slow rate of growth in the UK economy.

But having shown that the growth equation which we first derived, expressing the aggregate growth rate as the ratio of the 'net' investment ratio to the ICOR, is capable of manipulation into a variety of interpretative forms, and that many other considerations besides the supply of capital influence economic growth, we shall first use the growth equation to examine the record of economic growth in the United Kingdom as determined by the UK incremental capital–output ratio and the UK 'net' investment ratio.

The 'net' investment ratio and the share of profits in value added

Diagram 15.2 (based on Appendix 15.2) charts the UK gross investment ratio from 1948 to 1980, and the retirements ratio and 'net' investment ratio from 1956 to 1980. It is apparent that the gross investment ratio rose fairly steadily, and quite considerably, between 1948 (12.2 per cent) and 1967 and 1968, the two peak years when it reached 22.3 per cent. Since 1968 the gross investment ratio has declined fairly steadily to 19.8 per cent

DIAGRAM 15.2 *Gross investment ratio, retirements ratio, and 'net' investment ratio in the United Kingdom, 1948 to 1980*

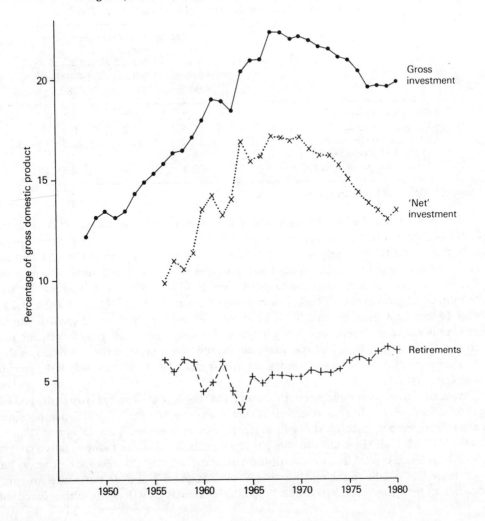

in 1980. The retirements ratio used to be about 5 per cent, but since 1970 has risen slightly to 6.4 per cent in 1980. The 'net' investment ratio more or less follows the gross investment ratio, rising considerably from 9.8 per cent in 1956 to a peak of 17.1 per cent in 1967 and 1968, and then falling quite sharply and steadily to 13.4 per cent in 1980.

If we take, in Table 15.2, three-year averages, so as to take more than simply one year, we can see that in the three years 1956 to 1958 the 'net' investment ratio was 10.4 per cent of gross domestic product, and using the incremental capital–output ratio of 4.95, the trend growth rate of the production capacity of the entire UK economy treated as a whole was therefore 10.4/4.95 = 2.1 per cent per annum during that period. That is, to use our previous notation (but working in proportions rather than percentages):

$$\frac{(I-R)/Y}{\Delta K/\Delta Y} = \frac{0.104}{4.95} = 0.021 = \frac{\Delta Y}{Y}$$

By the period 1967 to 1969 the trend growth rate of production capacity had reached 3.4 per cent per annum, but this was the peak period, and since then, due mostly to a fall of 2.5 percentage points in the gross investment ratio (from 22.2 to 19.7) but partly to a rise of 1.2 percentage points in the retirements ratio, the 'net' investment ratio has fallen by 3.7 percentage points (a decline of 22 per cent!) and the growth rate of production capacity during the three years 1978 to 1980 was 2.7 per cent per annum (13.3/4.95 = 2.7).

TABLE 15.2   *Investment and growth of production capacity in the UK economy during three contrasting periods, 1956 to 1958, 1967 to 1969, and 1978 to 1980*

	Average for three-year period		
	1956 to 1958	1967 to 1969	1978 to 1980
Gross investment ratio	16.2	22.2	19.7
Retirements ratio	5.8	5.2	6.4
'Net' investment ratio	10.4	17.0	13.3
Growth of production capacity, per cent per annum	2.1	3.4	2.7

Source: calculated from Appendix 15.2.

Over the period 1956 to 1980 as a whole the annual 'net' investment ratio averaged 14.484 per cent; divided by the ICOR of 4.95 this produces a trend growth rate in production capacity of 2.93 per cent per annum. You may recall from Table 3.24 that the trend growth rate (continuous exponential function) of real personal-sector income was 2.948 per cent per annum (over the longer period 1946 to 1980; over the period 1956 to 1980 the trend growth rate of real personal-sector incomes – first column of Table 3.23 – was 3.14 per cent per annum). So it is likely that the long-run trend growth rate in production capacity determines fairly closely the long-run trend growth rate of real incomes. But we must here add the qualification that some economists would argue that this relation went the other way round: growth of real final demand determines the growth of the capital stock.

Part of the (trend) unemployment problem is that the recent slowing down in the growth of production capacity has occurred just at that juncture when, for historical-demographic reasons, the growth rate of the labour force has accelerated (see Diagram 1.3 and Tables 1.3 and 1.4). (In addition, there is the possibility that the rising relative cost of labour has caused capital–labour substitution to take place, and that technical progress has been biased in a labour-saving direction – see Chapters 7 and 8; but these are only possibilities for speculation.) In the early 1980s the annual growth of the labour force will be reaching a peak as persons born during the 1964 peak (see Diagram 1.4) enter the labour market. At the same time as growth trends have moved adversely, economic policy moved towards deflation (see Chapter 14) – first in the mid-1970s to counteract balance-of-payments deficits, and subsequently to counteract inflation – so this has sharply worsened an already adverse trend.

The argument in Chapters 4 and 5 was that industrial and commercial companies financed a high proportion of their fixed capital formation from their own saving, or 'retentions' (see Diagram 4.3) and that the first-ranking reason for managerial interest in profitability was 'to provide finance for expansion' (see Table 4.19). The links between profits and retentions and investment form a lengthy chain (see Diagrams 5.1 and 5.3), but there does appear to be a reasonably close connection between the changes in profits of industrial and commercial companies and the changes in their fixed capital formation (see Tables 4.17 and 4.18, and Diagrams 4.4 and 4.5). Gross investment in the economy consists of more items than investment by companies (in 1980 company gross fixed capital formation was one-half of UK gross domestic fixed capital formation), but it is possible for companies to offset the effects of falling profits on investment either by reducing other payments from the appropriation account, so protecting retentions (and this appears to have happened – see Table 4.6), or by using more external finance (increasing their financial deficit). But even if we take all this into consideration, as well as the 'demand' influences on investment discussed previously, the falling gross investment ratio of Diagram 15.2 leads us to expect, in the light of the previous chapters' supply of finance arguments, that some part of the fall may be due to a decline in company profitability. Diagram 15.3 (based on Appendix 15.3) shows the considerable decline since about the

DIAGRAM 15.3   *Company profits as a percentage of gross domestic product, 1956 to 1980*

mid-1960s that has occurred in company profits (taken as a percentage of gross domestic product).

The causes of this 'squeeze' on company profits are undoubtedly manifold and complex and it would take a lengthy book to unravel the causes fully. Part of the squeeze may have originated in various governments' policies to control prices; part in increasing competition from foreign trade, which affects both prices and volume of output (this problem has been worsened by the recent rising value of the pound on foreign exchange markets); and part has originated from unit labour costs rising in excess of prices (the pressure on unit labour costs coming mainly from employees' reactions not only to rising prices but also to the increasing extent to which income-tax deductions and National Insurance contributions reduced take-home pay). In terms of Diagram 2.1, the first two tend to reduce the inflow of sales receipts for any given volume of output, while rising unit labour costs increase the outflow of wages for any given volume of output. The end-result is to reduce the flow of profits and so, if the outflow of dividends is unchanged (which has not in fact been the case in the United Kingdom), to reduce the flow of retentions from which fixed capital formation can be financed.

Working backwards along this chain, if it were wished to raise the rate of gross investment in the UK economy, then it may be necessary to increase retentions by increasing profits, but as it is both undesirable and not always possible to increase profits by raising prices (because this conflicts with the need to sell the extra output both at home and abroad), attention must concentrate on unit labour costs and the share of the total wage bill in value added. The algebra of this argument is quite straightforward:

$$\text{Sales receipts} = \text{Price} \times \text{Quantity}$$
$$= p \times Q$$
$$\text{Value added} = \text{Price} \times \text{Quantity} - \text{Materials costs}$$
$$= p \times Q - C$$
$$\text{Wage bill} = \text{Average wage} \times \text{Number of workers}$$
$$= w \times L$$
$$\text{Gross profits} = \text{Value added} - \text{Wage bill}$$
$$= p \times Q - C - w \times L$$

Then the share of gross profits in value added is:

$$\frac{\text{Gross profits}}{\text{Value added}} = \frac{p \times Q - C - w \times L}{p \times Q - C}$$
$$= 1 - \frac{w \times L}{p \times Q - C}$$
$$= 1 - \frac{(w \times L)/Q}{p - C/Q}$$

That is, the share of profits in value added is equal to 1 *minus* [unit labour costs ($w \times L/Q$) divided by the difference between price (p) and materials cost per unit of output (C/Q)].

Three important points about the above equation are worth noting. First, a reduction in materials costs per unit of output (C/Q) will increase the denominator, so reducing the ratio on the right-hand side and so raising the share of profits in value added; because unit materials costs are often quantitatively the largest part of total unit costs, this underlines the importance of using materials economically.

Second, raising prices relatively to unit materials costs will also raise the *share* of profits in value added, but by diminishing the volume of sales may cause total sales receipts and hence total profits to fall (see Chapter 6 and Diagram 6.8), which reduces the rate of profit on capital used.

Third, reducing unit labour costs ($w \times L/Q$) will also raise the share of profits in value added, and such reductions can come about if unit labour requirement (L/Q) falls – i.e. labour productivity (Q/L) rises – by more than the average wage (w) increases. Hence here is an indication of the importance to aggregate economic growth of the microeconomic processes discussed in Chapters 7 and 8 which tend to increase labour productivity.

In conclusion, it should be noted that this problem of the share of 'profits' in value added and the connection of that share to aggregate economic growth exists regardless of the institutional arrangements under which society chooses to conduct its productive economic operations. To illustrate, if all privately owned enterprises in the United Kingdom were nationalised (with or without compensation), the problem of ensuring a sufficient 'surplus' in value added to finance fixed capital formation would still remain – this we saw clearly in Chapter 10's discussion of the continuing financial deficits of the public corporations. Those who argue in favour of changing institutional arrangements often argue as though such change would somehow circumvent the problem of financing fixed capital formation. It would not, and proponents of such change have an important obligation to say exactly how they would tackle this financing problem. Likewise, those who argue that society's present institutional arrangements should be retained have a duty to address themselves to ensuring a satisfactory and acceptable solution to this problem of raising the share of profits in value added so that the gross investment ratio can be raised and a faster rate of growth of output thereby obtained. This would also depend upon obtaining the requisite steady increase in final demand, and obtaining this is likely to be very difficult (see Michael Posner (ed.), *Demand Management*, Heinemann, 1978). Without all this, unemployment in the United Kingdom is likely to remain on a rising trend (quite apart from its cyclical variation). If this problem remains unsolved (and, of course, it may be incapable of solution), I can only leave you to ponder the words of my favourite ancient Chinese curse: 'May you live in interesting times!'

Conclusion: the international comparative record and prospects

It is not pleasant to end on a dismal and cheerless note, but the record is there and deserves to be examined. Table 15.3 shows, for the period 1955 to 1978 inclusive, the trend annual rate of growth of domestic product at constant 1975 prices. We take 1955 as the starting-point because it is a reasonable argument that by then the (temporary) effects of recovery from the economic impact of the Second World War (and also of the Korean war) must have been wearing off, if not altogether a thing of the past; 1978 is the end-year because that is the latest year for which standard international comparative data were available. The period covered is twenty-four years, sufficient for long-term trends to emerge fairly clearly.

Over this period, Japan has had by far the fastest trend rate of growth of real GDP, growing at 8.9 per cent per annum (real GDP doubling every eight years). The United Kingdom has had by far the slowest trend rate of growth of real GDP, growing at 2.68 per cent per annum (real GDP doubling every twenty-six years). With its rapid growth rate and large population (117 million in 1980) Japan is now the world's third-largest industrial economy (after the USA and the USSR). *Per capita* gross domestic product (total GDP in US dollars divided by total population) in Japan was by 1978 one-half higher than in the United Kingdom: such are the rewards and penalties for fast or slow economic growth (OECD, *Main Economic Indicators*, October 1981, pp. 169–70; such comparisons are very greatly affected by movements in exchange rates – the subsequent appreciation of the pound against the dollar and depreciation of the yen against the dollar eliminated, by 1980, the Japan/UK *per capita* GDP differential (in $); however, by 1982, the £ had again depreciated and the yen appreciated).

TABLE 15.3   *Growth rates of GDP and exports and gross investment ratios in eighteen countries, 1955 to 1978*

Country [a]	Trend growth rate over period 1955 to 1978 inclusive; per cent per annum [b]		Percentage share of gross fixed capital formation in GDP (current prices), annual average for period
	Gross domestic product (1975 prices)	Exports (1975 prices)	
Japan	8.90	13.01	31.0
France	4.97	8.90	22.3
Finland	4.86	6.40	26.2
Canada	4.84	6.78	22.6
Italy	4.78	10.38	20.9
Australia	4.66	5.78	24.8
Austria	4.61	8.09	25.9
Netherlands	4.54	7.94	23.8
Denmark	4.46	6.14	21.6
West Germany	4.29	7.74	23.8
Belgium	4.25	7.82	20.6
Norway	4.15	6.13	29.7
New Zealand	3.85	4.22	22.6
Ireland	3.83	6.96	20.4
Switzerland	3.52	6.10	25.6
Sweden	3.47	6.29	22.0
USA	3.44	5.50	17.9
United Kingdom	2.68	4.62	17.8

[a] Listed in descending order of GDP trend growth rate.

[b] Trend growth rates computed as the exponential trend, b, by least squares (on the logarithmic transformation of):

$$Y = A \times e^{bt}$$

where Y is the relevant variable and t is years ($1955 = 0$, $1956 = 1$, ..., $1978 = 23$). In all cases the goodness-of-fit is very high. Data at market prices ('purchasers' values').

Source: computed from data in OECD, *National Accounts Statistics 1950–1978*, vol. I, *Main Aggregates*, OECD 1980, pp. 24–45, 50–3, 56–9, 64–7, 70–1.

In terms of the growth equation, we can see also that Japan had, over this period, much the highest gross investment ratio: 31 per cent of GDP going, on average each year, to gross fixed capital formation; while the United Kingdom had the lowest gross investment ratio, 17.8 per cent. Among these eighteen countries, the coefficient of correlation between the trend rate of growth of GDP and the long-run average gross investment ratio is $R = +0.653$, so there is a definite positive association of the sort which we would expect, given the basic growth equation: that is, countries with above-average gross investment ratios tend also to have above-average growth rates of GDP.*

The correlation coefficient indicates that the association between growth rates and gross investment ratios is rather a 'loose' one (only about 43 per cent of the inter-country

---

*If we exclude the 'extreme' observation on Japan from the sample (for no reason other than that it is extreme), the coefficient of correlation drops to 0.434, which is still statistically significant for a sample of this size. However, this then includes the 'extreme' observation on Norway (where investment was to some extent concentrated on capital-intensive hydro-electricity projects); if we then exclude the observation on Norway as well, the correlation rises to 0.544; if we exclude Norway and include Japan, the correlation coefficient rises to 0.764.

variation in growth rates is 'explained', or statistically accounted for, by the linear relationship and the variation in gross investment ratios), but this is what we should expect in the light of the variation in incremental capital–output ratios (shown for eleven countries in Table 15.1) and in the light of the fact that capital stock retirement ratios also affect the growth rate. As we have not taken these two other sources of variation into account, it is not surprising that the 'unexplained' variation is still considerable. For example, there are countries with higher gross investment ratios than France but with lower growth rates (such as West Germany), but we can see from Table 15.1 that France has a low aggregate ICOR (much lower than West Germany's) and so benefits from this in terms of her achieved growth rate.

The association between growth rates and gross investment ratios is at least a reasonable ground for arguing that if the United Kingdom wished to increase her rate of economic growth, then an increase in the gross investment ratio is likely to be a necessary condition for obtaining this result (which is not to assert that it would be a sufficient condition – as subsequent discussion will show).

In Table 15.3 we can see also that the growth rate of UK exports has been very slow by international comparative standards (only New Zealand, with her predominantly agricultural exports – battling against world-wide agricultural protectionism – has had a slower rate of growth of exports).* The unweighted average growth rate of exports among the eighteen countries was 7.16 per cent per annum, so the UK export growth rate was only two-thirds of the average. There is a strong correlation between the trend growth rate of exports and the trend growth of GDP: $R = +0.829$ for all eighteen countries (0.627 if we omit Japan). Thus the argument that 'demand' factors, such as the growth of exports, may affect economic growth receives considerable support from the international comparative data. It is certainly the case that those countries with an above-average rate of growth of exports have tended to have an above-average rate of growth of GDP (and vice versa, especially the United Kingdom).

These two statistically significant correlations (between output growth and the gross investment ratio, and output growth and export growth) support the 'virtuous circle' theory of economic growth, and its converse, the 'vicious circle', of economic stagnation. As shown in Diagram 15.4, the flow of investment does two things. On the one hand, through embodying technical progress and enabling capital–labour substitution in response to changing factor price ratios, it leads to lower unit costs of production and so to lower (relative) prices. The lower prices then lead to an expansion of demand. On the other hand, investment also increases production capacity so that the greater demand can be met by increased sales (output). Together the reduced unit costs and the greater volume of sales generate a higher flow of profits and retentions which facilitate the financing of the investment. The prospect of higher profits also acts as an inducement to investment, so the arrow of influence may also be a two-way influence. Profits and retentions are the hub of the virtuous circle of economic growth: without this hub the wheel of growth will not roll.

Success then breeds success, because the greater flow of output reaps the benefits, in terms of further reductions in unit production costs, of economies of scale and the impact of the learning curve (and Chapters 7 and 8 showed these benefits to be considerable).

The dark other side of this coin is that a low gross investment ratio leads to relative technological backwardness through the failure to adopt (as fast as competing economies) innovations in production. Because of this, unit costs, and therefore prices, remain higher than those elsewhere and the growth of demand, especially for exports, is retarded. The low rate of investment also means that production capacity is not expanded by so much,

---

*In 1980, three-quarters of New Zealand's exports (excluding re-exports) came from food, live animals, beverages and tobacco (45 per cent) and inedible crude materials such as wool, hides and forest products (29 per cent) – Department of Statistics (Wellington, New Zealand), *Monthly Abstract of Statistics*, November–December 1981, table 11.01, p. 46.

DIAGRAM 15.4   *The virtuous circle of economic growth*

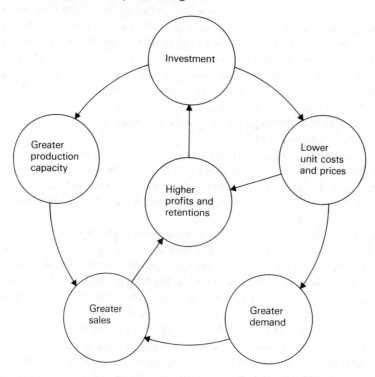

and the retarded growth of demand, together with slow expansion of production capacity, leads to a reduced or retarded increase in sales and so, combined with slow improvement in unit production costs, the flow of profits and of retentions is adversely affected. This means that there is insufficient finance and inducement to investment. Failure then breeds failure, because there is relatively little gain to unit production costs from economies of scale and the learning curve, and so the economy is trapped in a 'vicious circle' of relative economic stagnation or retarded growth.

The operation in one economy of a 'virtuous circle' and in another economy of a 'vicious circle' may then create a 'gap' in unit production costs which tends to widen as time goes by: because of economies of scale and technical progress, enterprises in the growing economy are able to move to ever-lower unit isoquants (see Diagrams 7.9 and 8.1, and Tables 7.7, 8.5 and 8.6), while their competitors in the (relatively) slowly growing economy are left on the higher unit isoquants with increasingly relatively higher unit production costs (for an excellent discussion of the implications of all this and the applicability of the analysis to the UK economy see D. K. Stout, 'De-industrialisation and industrial policy', in Frank Blackaby (ed.), *De-industrialisation*, National Institute of Economic and Social Research Economic Policy Papers No. 2, Heinemann, 1979).

We shall not pause here to discuss those arguments which assert that slow or zero growth is a desirable state of affairs (for a critique of these theories see Wilfred Beckerman, *In Defence of Economic Growth*, Jonathan Cape, 1974, and also his paper 'Does slow growth matter? Egalitarianism versus humanitarianism' in the volume edited by him, *Slow Growth in Britain: Causes and Consequences*, Oxford University Press, 1979). The implausibility of these zero-growth arguments stems partly from the demonstrable fact (for the United Kingdom and for many other countries) that slow growth, especially when set against a growing labour force, in an internationally competitive situation leads to the 'destruction' of the economy's industries, to an increase in unemployment, and to the sort of poverty and deprivation that accompany unemployment (for a discussion of which, see my book *Poverty*, Macmillan, 1972).

It may be that the United Kingdom has a stark choice – either to improve her growth rate or to continue to slide into a state of 'economic underdevelopment' characterised by:

1. Chronic inability to provide full employment (i.e. a high proportion of the labour force permanently without jobs or the hope of acquiring a job).
2. Chronic inability (once the North Sea oil boost is over) to earn sufficient from exports to pay for imports (i.e. chronic balance of trade deficits and constant policy preoccupation with that deficit – see the volume *De-industrialisation*, ed. Frank Blackaby (Heinemann, 1979) especially the paper by A. Singh, 'North Sea oil and the reconstruction of UK industry').
3. Chronic inability to balance the government finances as demands for welfare payments (unemployment benefit, retirement pensions) press against an increasingly inadequate tax-revenue base (see the paper by Walter Eltis, 'How rapid public sector growth can undermine the growth of the national product', in Wilfred Beckerman (ed.), *Slow Growth in Britain*).
4. Chronic inflation which is not only rapid but which also tends periodically to accelerate to high annual rates (say, around 100 per cent) caused partly by the general government financial deficit and its monetary consequences (Chapter 13 above) and partly by 'cost push' from employed workers who still maintain expectations of constant if not rising living standards (for a discussion of such inflation see Dudley Jackson, H. A. Turner and Frank Wilkinson, *Do Trade Unions Cause Inflation?*, Cambridge University Press, 1972).
5. A relatively poor state of industrial relations, characterised by a high and increasing incidence of strikes.
6. Increasing general poverty (without discussing the conceptual problems of defining and measuring the extent of poverty, we could note that, in 1961, 1.9 million persons in Great Britain were receiving regular supplementary benefit payments each month while by 1980 this figure had risen to 3 million).

This is an unpleasant catalogue of prospective possibilities. What could be done to prevent such a situation (already threateningly present) from worsening?

The trend growth rate of the UK gross domestic product over the period 1948 to 1980 was 2.65 per cent per annum (Appendix 15.2), and this has apparently been insufficient to satisfy people's expectations of a rising standard of living and to preserve the international competitiveness of UK industry as a whole. The incremental capital–output ratio in the UK economy may be taken to be 4.95 (Diagram 15.1). If it were wished to raise the UK growth rate to the unweighted average for all countries of 4.45 per cent per annum (Table 15.3), then, given that the UK retirements ratio was, in 1980, 6.4 per cent (Appendix 15.2), we can make the following calculation. From the growth equation:

$$\frac{\Delta Y}{Y} = \frac{(I-R)/Y}{\Delta K/\Delta Y} = \frac{I/Y}{\Delta K/\Delta Y} - \frac{R/Y}{\Delta K/\Delta Y}$$

we may derive:

$$\frac{I}{Y} = \frac{\Delta K}{\Delta Y} \left(\frac{\Delta Y}{Y} + \frac{R/Y}{\Delta K/\Delta Y} \right)$$

$$= \frac{\Delta K}{\Delta Y} \times \frac{\Delta Y}{Y} + \frac{R}{Y}$$

To put the above-mentioned numbers into this equation for the gross investment ratio:

$$\frac{I}{Y} = 4.95 \times 0.0445 + 0.064$$

$$= 0.284$$

By manipulating the growth equation into an expression giving the gross investment ratio, I/Y, on the left-hand side, we can then calculate that value of the gross investment ratio required to provide a trend growth rate of 4.45 per cent per annum, given that the ICOR is 4.95 and the retirements ratio is 0.064. This gives a required gross investment ratio of 28.4 per cent – to be contrasted with the 1980 gross investment ratio of 19.8 per cent. In other words, an increase in the gross investment ratio of 8.6 percentage points, or by 43.4 per cent(!), would be required to bring the UK growth rate up to only the average for the eighteen industrialised economies of Table 15.3. It is therefore apparent that the increase required in investment is of very considerable magnitude. (This assumes that it would be very difficult to reduce the UK incremental capital–output ratio, so that this is not a realistic option for policy.)

There are two major problems connected with raising the gross investment ratio by such a degree of magnitude. First, how could such an increase be *induced*? Second, how could such an increase be *financed*?

The empirical support for the 'demand' theory of growth would lead us to expect that increased investment could only be obtained if there were steadily increasing aggregate final demand. From what sources could such increasing final demand be obtained? It would seem arguable that increased government expenditure is not appropriate because this may lead to a greater government financial deficit, the financing of which has, through higher interest rates, an adverse impact on investment financing. Not much is to be expected from investment itself (at least initially) because the initial problem is excess capacity, which serves to dampen investment. This leaves either exports or a change in the parameters of the multiplier as sources of increased final demand. A once-for-all boost might be given if the marginal propensity to import were reduced (say, by import controls) or if the rate of taxation were reduced (although that has other adverse implications for the government's financial deficit). But it is hard to see that *continuing* increases in final demand could come in this way (although if the reduced propensity to import provided a sufficient stimulus to get investment going, this could help). This leaves exports as the source from which the United Kingdom would have to obtain the demand stimulus to growth. And the only way to ensure that exports grow is to have relatively lower unit production costs: if profits and retentions are the hub of the 'virtuous circle' of growth, then unit production costs are the oil and grease for the wheel of growth.

How could such an increase in investment be financed? The possible answers to this question are all controversial. It may be that more of the flow of life assurance and superannuation funds' net acquisition of financial assets should be, somehow, directed into fixed capital formation, especially in the enterprise sector of the economy. The inescapable corollary of this is a cutback of considerable magnitude in the general government financial deficit and borrowing requirement, because given (a) the high rate of interest on lending to the government, and (b) the low profitability of most of the enterprise sector, much of the life assurance and superannuation funds' financial asset acquisition is directed towards the government sector (although a greater part is now flowing abroad due to the abolition of foreign exchange controls – if one thinks that 'regenerating' the UK economy is a task which cannot be accomplished, then, of course, such investment abroad by these funds is the *only* way in which the commitments of the pension funds, etc., can be honoured).

There is also the further question of whether the enterprise sector in its (depressed) state of profitability would wish to accept such a directed flow of lending or new issue acquisition from the life assurance and superannuation funds.

Given the consistent record of financial deficits of the public corporations (Appendix 10.4), it is difficult to envisage nationalisation as being anything of a solution to this investment-financing problem (it is relevant to note that so sympathetic an observer of the public corporations as Richard Pryke – see his book *Public Enterprise in Practice*, MacGibbon & Kee, 1971 – should have subsequently become more critical of their performance – see his book *The Nationalised Industries: Policies and Performance since 1968*, Martin Robertson, 1981). Certainly, nationalisation (even expropriation) would of itself do nothing to solve the investment-financing problem.

It has been a consistent theme in this book that internal financing – the flow of retentions – is very important to the financing of investment. We can see this not only in all the statistics, but also in the way in which retentions appear as a key element in business affairs – pricing decisions, business economic planning, managerial attitudes.

Suppose that, against all the odds, a steady expansion of final demand could be obtained in the UK economy. It would seem then to follow that finance for the increased investment (on the scale required to put the UK economy on even the 'average' growth path) would inescapably require a considerable and sustained increase in the share of enterprise profits in the gross domestic product (including the trading surpluses of the public corporations).

At this point it must be observed that the employee population of the United Kingdom seems firmly to hold a set of opinions, beliefs and attitudes almost wholly antipathetic to profits. (One must point the finger at the entire employee population and not at 'the trade unions', which are merely the creatures of the employees they serve; it really is ludicrous to kick the monkey if you do not like the organ-grinder's tune! For excellent examples, among a multitude of works which could be cited, of this culture of employee opinion, see Huw Beynon, *Working for Ford*, Penguin, 1973; Christopher Hird, *Your Employers' Profits*, Workers' Handbook No. 2, Pluto Press, 1975; or Ken Coates and Tony Topham (eds), *Workers' Control*, Panther Modern Society, 1970.)

Such employee opinions and attitudes, and the general behaviour stemming therefrom, have been inimical to unit labour costs, as these tend to be raised both by increases in wages in excess of productivity growth and by a general difficulty in obtaining employee co-operation in the process of reducing labour requirement per unit of output (see the equation on page 682 on the share of profits in value added). It is certainly the case that the growth of labour productivity in manufacturing industry in the United Kingdom has been lower than that prevailing in manufacturing industry in other countries. Table 15.4 shows the trend growth rates between 1963 and 1980 of labour productivity in manufacturing industry as measured by the volume of output per person-hour (so that the effect of changes in hours worked is abstracted from the series). Japan has by far the fastest trend annual rate of growth in hourly labour productivity of 8.20 per cent per annum (doubling every $8\frac{1}{2}$ years), while the United Kingdom has the slowest trend annual rate of growth of 2.99 per cent per annum (doubling every $23\frac{1}{2}$ years). Japan's phenomenal productivity growth is a clear indication of the working of the 'virtuous circle' of economic growth: a high gross investment ratio leading to rapid productivity growth and to (relative) reductions in unit labour costs; reflected in product prices this then permits a rapid growth of export sales, which, in turn, helps to generate the profits required to finance investment. The converse case would appear to be true of the United Kingdom.

The record on productivity growth thus emphasises the need for investment to raise labour productivity, though, paradoxically, the United Kingdom's slow growth of labour productivity tends to aggravate the problem of raising sufficient internal finance for investment. Furthermore, the erosion of living standards in the United Kingdom arising as a consequence of the slow rate of productivity growth tends to 'harden' employees' opinions about, and attitudes towards, profits and the achievement of profitability (as measured by the share of profits in value added).

Whether this set of deeply rooted and often cherished employee opinions, beliefs and attitudes is based on an articulated ideology or ignorance of the role of profits in financing

TABLE 15.4   *Growth of labour productivity in manufacturing industry in seven countries, 1963 to 1980*

Country	Trend growth rate of labour productivity as measured by output per person-hour in manufacturing, per cent per annum [a]
Japan	8.20
France	5.62
Italy	4.86
West Germany	4.77
Canada	3.47
USA	3.31
United Kingdom	2.99

[a] Computed by fitting an exponential trend to (linked) indices on output per person-hour in manufacturing.

Source: computed from data in National Institute of Economic and Social Research, *National Institute Economic Review*: August 1972, table 18, p. 70; May 1974, table 18, p. 99; February 1979, table 18, p. 79; May 1981, table 19, p. 73.

the investment on which alone long-term full employment, job security and prosperity depend is, in this context, not a relevant question (because the advent of a 'socialist economy' would in no way circumvent the investment-financing problem – indeed, by raising employee expectations it could make that problem worse). Whatever their origins, these ingrained and usually unquestioning employee beliefs mean that the prospects for substantially increasing the share of profits in the United Kingdom's gross domestic product by lowering unit labour costs must, for the foreseeable future, be reckoned as negligible. From this it follows that a continuation of the relatively low rate of gross investment, and therefore of the slow rate of economic growth in the United Kingdom (with all the consequences thereby implied), is inevitable and inescapable. With the advent of the 'newly industrialising countries' of the Third World, some reportedly with lower unit production costs than Japan's, the international competition of the past decades seems only to foreshadow the even more severe competition still to come.

It is of course true that the United Kingdom's economic growth during the postwar period has been considerably more rapid than that which had been achieved previously (see Diagram 1.10 and Table 1.13). Judged by our own historical standards, the economy has performed remarkably well, especially with regard to the growth of fixed capital per worker and of output per worker. Unfortunately, this historically remarkable achievement has been insufficient to satisfy expectations and to safeguard UK producers from the adverse impact of more dynamic growth in other countries.

Exercises

15.1 *(To practise your understanding of the incremental capital–output ratio.)*

(i)   Using the data from Appendix 1.1, calculate by simple arithmetic the actual incremental capital–output ratio in the UK economy over the period 1953 to 1973 (use data for these two years only).

(ii)   Using data from Appendix 15.1, calculate by simple arithmetic the actual incremental capital–output ratio in the UK economy over the period 1955 to 1974 (use data for these two years only).

(iii)   Using data from Appendix 15.1, calculate by simple arithmetic the actual incremental capital–output ratio in the West German economy over the period 1955 to 1974 (use data for these two years only).

15.2 *(Further to practise calculating incremental capital–output ratios, and to make some international comparisons thereof.)*

(i)   Given the data below, calculate the incremental capital–output ratio in UK manufacturing industry over the period 1954 to 1974:

	£ billion, 1975 prices	
UK manufacturing industry	*1954*	*1974*
Gross capital stock (end-year)	39.5	91.8
Value added	16.1	28.7

Sources: Central Statistical Office, *National Income and Expenditure 1969*, table 63, p. 76; Central Statistical Office, *National Income and Expenditure 1972*, table 64, p. 76; Central Statistical Office, *National Income and Expenditure 1981 Edition*, tables 1.9 and 11.12, pp. 12 and 84; Central Statistical Office, *Economic Trends Annual Supplement 1981 Edition*, p. 80. Manufacturing capital stock for 1954 at 1975 prices calculated as: (Manufacturing capital stock for 1954 at 1963 replacement cost *divided by* Manufacturing capital stock for end-1970 at 1963 replacement cost) *multiplied by* Manufacturing capital stock for end-1970 at 1975 replacement cost. Manufacturing value added at 1975 prices cal-

culated for 1954 as: Index of manufacturing production for 1954 (1975 = 1.00) *multiplied by* Manufacturing value added in 1975 (£ million at current prices); for 1974 as: Index of manufacturing production for 1974 (1975 = 1.00) *multiplied by* Manufacturing value added in 1975 (£ million at current prices).

(ii)   Lamfalussy and Beckerman (see p. 674) and Table 15.1 give incremental capital–output ratios for the following common set of countries: United Kingdom, West Germany, Italy and France (albeit for slightly different periods and with the first two not taking account of retirements). Tabulate and compare the three sets of ICORs for these countries.

15.3 *(An important exercise to show you how to splice data together.)* Find, from the original sources, all the actual figures behind the calculations for the UK data given in Exercise 15.2(i). Explain, and illustrate, how the UK data given in 15.2(i) were calculated.

15.4 *(To develop your understanding of how the gross capital stock grows and to practise working with the relevant data.)*

(i)   Appendix 15.2 gives the flows from which 'net' investment in the whole economy is calculated, and Diagram 1.9 (p. 35) shows how these flows relate to the growth of the gross capital stock. For the most recent period of five years, show how 'net' investment at constant prices in UK manufacturing industry may be calculated and show how this relates to the growth of UK manufacturing industry's gross capital stock at constant prices (take care to obtain from *National Income and Expenditure* the appropriately dated capital stocks to give the changes in the stocks (i.e. the annual flows) which match the annual fixed capital formation and retirements flows).

(ii)   For the latest available year and using the data found for the answer to (i), draw for manufacturing the counterpart to Diagram 1.9 with all appropriate data inserted.

15.5   *(To practise your understanding of the 'net' investment ratio.)*

(i)   Using the data obtained for Exercise 15.4(i) and obtaining manufacturing value added at constant prices by the method described in Exercise 15.2(i) (see also Exercise 15.3), calculate for UK manufacturing industry: the gross investment ratio; the retirements ratio; and the 'net' investment ratio for the most recent period of five years.

(ii)   Using the data given below, compare the gross investment ratio in Japanese manufacturing industry over the period 1973 to 1975 with that for UK manufacturing industry found in (i):

Yen billion, current prices

Japanese manufacturing industry	1973	1974	1975
Total gross fixed capital formation (exc. major group 314)	5,452	6,711	5,751
Value added (exc. major group 314)	41,337	48,693	46,354

Source: United Nations, *Yearbook of Industrial Statistics 1978 Edition*, Volume I, *General Industrial Statistics*, p. 292.

(iii)   Given (at best) a similarity of manufacturing ICORs and retirements ratios between UK and Japanese manufacturing industries, what does the comparisons of (ii) imply for the trend growth rates of manufacturing industries in the two countries?

(iv)   How is your answer to (iii) affected if the Japanese manufacturing industry ICOR is lower than that in the UK?

(v)   How is your answer to (iii) affected if the retirements ratio in Japanese manufacturing industry is lower than that in the UK?

15.6   *(To practise your understanding of the growth equation.)*

(i)   Assuming that UK manufacturing industry has the ICOR which you calculated in Exercise 15.2(i) and taking the UK manufacturing industry's 'net' investment ratio as the average over the last five years (Exercise 15.5(i)), calculate the trend rate of growth of UK manufacturing industry's capacity to produce output in recent years.

(ii)   What 'net' investment ratio would be required in UK manufacturing industry if the trend rate of output growth were to be raised to 5 per cent per annum?

(iii)   Calculating the average of the retirements ratio in UK manufacturing industry over the last five years (Exercise 15.5(i)), estimate what your answer to Exercise 15.6(ii) implies for the gross investment ratio in UK manufacturing industry. How does this compare with the gross investment ratios actually achieved?

15.7   *(To see what has been happening to company profits when the profits from North Sea activities are excluded.)*

(i)   Given the figures below and using data in Appendix 15.3, calculate company profits (after deducting stock appreciation) *excluding* profits from North Sea activities, as a percentage of gross domestic product at factor cost:

(ii)   How does the exclusion of company profits from North Sea activities affect Diagram 15.3? (Did you think of this 'wrinkle' for yourself when you first looked at Diagram 15.3?!)

15.8   *(To practise working with international comparative data on economic growth.)*

(i)   Using the data in Table 15.3, draw the scatter diagram to show the international

£ million

	1976	1977	1978	1979	1980
Gross profits of companies from the exploration and extraction of petroleum and natural gas	448	1,729	2,325	4,782	7,003

Source: Central Statistical Office, *National Income and Expenditure 1981 Edition*, p. 118.

comparative relation between the growth of GDP and the growth of exports.

(ii) Using the data in Table 15.3, draw the scatter diagram to show the relationship between the growth of GDP and the gross investment ratio.

(iii) Comment on the relative position of the United Kingdom in both these scatter diagrams.

15.9 *(To see how the various arguments in this book fit together.)* Explain the rationale behind all the connecting arrows in Diagram 15.4.

15.10 *(To conclude by examining the United Kingdom's most intractable economic problem.)* Explain why lower unit labour costs are the key to raising the rate of economic growth in the United Kingdom.

APPENDIX 15.1 *Gross capital stock and gross domestic product at market prices* (a) *in eleven countries, 1955 to 1974*

Year	United Kingdom £ million, 1970 prices		Canada $C million, 1961 prices		Denmark Kroner million, 1955 prices		Germany DM billion, 1962 prices		Sweden Kroner million, 1968 prices	
	Gross capital stock	Gross domestic product	Gross capital stock	Gross national product	Gross capital stock	Gross domestic product	Gross capital stock	Gross domestic product	Gross capital stock	Gross domestic product
1955	107,400	34,198	82,019	31,788	57,770	28,732	784	225.598	365,382	84,548
1956	110,000	34,747	86,793	34,474	60,070	29,309	832	241.794	378,907	87,359
1957	112,900	35,432	92,338	35,283	62,520	30,583	881	255.399	393,011	89,424
1958	115,700	35,503	97,690	36,098	65,190	31,435	931	264.424	407,535	91,534
1959	118,900	36,918	102,696	37,470	68,440	33,590	988	284.016	422,711	96,307
1960	122,700	38,649	107,695	38,553	72,370	35,583	1,115	319.086	438,813	99,978
1961	126,900	39,945	112,553	39,646	76,770	37,853	1,189	345.630	454,217	105,690
1962	131,100	40,296	117,224	42,349	81,710	39,998	1,267	360.880	473,606	110,223
1963	135,500	41,906	121,893	44,531	86,660	40,253	1,346	371.650	492,947	115,966
1964	140,900	44,273	127,177	47,519	92,090	43,984	1,435	396.587	514,302	124,001
1965	146,600	45,289	133,504	50,685	98,300	45,987	1,527	418.918	533,423	129,098
1966	152,600	46,142	141,033	54,207	104,630	48,493	1,619	429.373	555,526	131,954
1967	159,100	47,377	149,183	56,016	111,310	52,021	1,698	428.675	577,158	136,670
1968	165,900	48,999	157,060	59,292	118,050	54,230	1,784	455.622	600,860	141,660
1969	172,600	49,660	164,937	62,448	125,280	57,967	1,881	491.284	625,723	148,411
1970	179,500	50,907	173,196	64,014	133,270	59,483	1,990	520.655	652,160	156,287
1971	186,400	52,326	182,037	67,585	141,550	60,931	1,880	537.477	682,150	155,993
1972	193,400	53,630	191,493	71,515	150,230	64,228	1,983	557.115	708,250	158,555
1973	200,600	57,153	201,572	76,345	159,690	67,596	2,085	584.392	736,665	163,894
1974	207,700	56,805	212,446	77,200	168,630	67,002	2,173	587.545	763,210	170,788

Year	Japan — Yen billion, 1970 prices		USA — $ million, 1958 prices		Italy — Lira billion, 1963 prices		France — Fr. million, 1959 prices		Norway — Kroner million, 1970 prices		Ireland — £ million, 1958 prices	
	Gross business capital stock	GDP (exc. government final consumption)	Gross business capital stock	GDP (exc. government final consumption)	Gross capital stock	Gross domestic product	Gross capital stock	Gross domestic product	Gross capital stock	Gross domestic product	Gross manufacturing capital stock	Manufacturing value added
1955	18,113	13,600	572,708	363,437	71,520	19,596	356,018	228,634	—	—	136.93	103.40
1956	18,862	14,917	595,509	370,936	74,120	20,511	368,385	242,208	—	—	145.75	101.92
1957	20,037	16,295	615,884	374,617	77,060	21,599	383,106	256,708	—	—	151.87	100.45
1958	21,608	17,293	630,255	370,011	80,550	22,646	400,625	264,211	—	—	158.56	103.40
1959	22,980	19,018	645,172	395,975	84,220	24,123	419,536	269,894	—	—	167.54	112.26
1960	24,742	21,857	663,545	404,927	88,270	26,509	438,710	286,381	234,472	57,910	175.79	121.13
1961	27,530	25,394	680,050	411,124	92,580	29,614	460,252	302,150	244,106	60,104	188.11	131.47
1962	31,095	27,126	699,872	435,387	97,450	31,451	486,617	322,309	253,705	63,116	204.37	140.33
1963	34,506	30,060	720,014	455,847	103,170	33,215	515,962	339,544	264,667	66,451	222.86	147.71
1964	38,144	34,412	745,146	482,977	108,810	34,144	547,679	361,677	276,196	68,966	245.50	159.53
1965	42,414	36,396	778,123	516,098	113,370	35,260	582,965	378,958	289,365	73,283	267.69	166.92
1966	46,330	40,975	817,822	541,762	116,950	37,370	619,642	398,718	298,841	74,937	292.94	171.35
1967	50,735	46,509	855,333	548,336	120,200	40,053	661,043	417,410	307,954	78,313	320.87	184.64
1968	56,955	53,632	894,472	574,909	123,870	42,674	705,014	435,187	321,681	79,876	347.30	203.85
1969	64,777	60,663	936,638	593,996	128,160	45,276	752,827	465,609	337,267	83,533	—	—
1970	74,336	68,205	973,369	595,028	132,980	47,681	807,371	492,293	349,464	87,852	—	—
1971	85,267	71,629	1,006,842	619,285	137,870	48,464	—	—	365,041	91,463	—	—
1972	96,360	78,498	1,045,134	660,719	—	—	—	—	—	—	—	—
1973	108,504	86,696	—	—	—	—	—	—	—	—	—	—
1974	121,044	86,082	—	—	—	—	—	—	—	—	—	—

(a) For purposes of this analysis it would be preferable to have gross domestic product at factor cost, but the market price series is the only long-run series available. The series has been calculated from the international source by: (a) dividing current-price GDP by constant-price GDP to obtain the implied GDP price deflator; (b) changing the base of the deflator to conformity with gross capital stock constant-price series; (c) deflating current-price GDP by this deflator. In the case of the United Kingdom and Canada the series have been taken from national sources which give a consistent long run of data deflated to the appropriate base. In the case of the USA and Japan government final consumption (at current and constant prices) has been excluded from GDP (again, at current and constant prices) in order to provide the nearest approximation to enterprise-sector output, in conformity with the limited coverage of the capital stock. In the case of Ireland, manufacturing value added at constant 1958 prices was calculated by multiplying the volume index of manufacturing output by 1958 value added in manufacturing. Where there is a change from the old SNA (System of National Accounts – as recommended by the United Nations) to the new SNA the two figures for GDP in the link year have been averaged.

Sources: capital stock – Michael Ward, *The Measurement of Capital: The Methodology of Capital Stock Estimates in OECD Countries* (Organisation for Economic Co-operation and Development, 1976) pp. 140–41; GDP–OECD, *National Accounts Statistics 1950–1978* (1980) pp. 26–7, 28–9, 38–9, 42–3, 44–5, 52–3, 58–9, 64–5; Ministry of Industry, Trade and Commerce, *Canada Year Book 1974*, table 21.1, p. 811; Central Statistical Office, *National Income and Expenditure 1966–76*, table 2.1, pp. 18–19; OECD, *Industrial Production: Historical Statistics 1955–1971*, p. 116; United Nations, *The Growth of World Industry 1953–1965*, p. 209.

APPENDIX 15.2 *Gross fixed capital formation, retirements, and 'net' investment in the United Kingdom, 1948 to 1980*

Year	£ million at constant 1975 prices				Percentage of gross domestic product		
	Gross domestic fixed capital formation (a)	Retirements (b)	'Net' investment (c)	Gross domestic product at factor cost (a)	Gross investment	Retirements	'Net' investment
1948	5,622	—	—	46,050	12.2	—	—
1949	6,202	—	—	47,482	13.1	—	—
1950	6,582	—	—	49,039	13.4	—	—
1951	6,639	—	—	50,813	13.1	—	—
1952	6,786	—	—	50,819	13.4	—	—
1953	7,589	—	—	53,206	14.3	—	—
1954	8,233	—	—	55,131	14.9	—	—
1955	8,724	—	—	57,155	15.3	—	—
1956	9,181	(3,481)	5,700	58,271	15.8	6.0	9.8
1957	9,694	(3,194)	6,500	59,376	16.3	5.4	10.9
1958	9,752	(3,552)	6,200	59,089	16.5	6.0	10.5
1959	10,469	(3,569)	6,900	61,090	17.1	5.8	11.3
1960	11,423	(2,823)	8,600	63,911	17.9	4.4	13.5
1961	12,597	(3,197)	9,400	66,197	19.0	4.8	14.2
1962	12,649	(3,849)	8,800	66,815	18.9	5.8	13.2
1963	12,781	(3,081)	9,700	69,532	18.4	4.4	14.0
1964	14,954	(2,554)	12,400	73,261	20.4	3.5	16.9
1965	15,739	3,809	11,930	75,234	20.9	5.1	15.9
1966	16,167	3,705	12,462	76,821	21.0	4.8	16.2
1967	17,543	4,094	13,449	78,813	22.3	5.2	17.1
1968	18,329	4,272	14,057	82,328	22.3	5.2	17.1

Year							
1969	18,428	4,295	14,133	83,760	22.0	5.1	16.9
1970	18,895	4,318	14,577	85,484	22.1	5.1	17.1
1971	19,159	4,706	14,453	87,654	21.9	5.4	16.5
1972	19,171	4,747	14,424	88,815	21.6	5.3	16.2
1973	20,557	5,022	15,535	95,635	21.5	5.3	16.2
1974	20,050	5,195	14,855	94,905	21.1	5.5	15.7
1975	19,791	5,580	14,211	94,475	20.9	5.9	15.0
1976	20,016	5,964	14,052	97,948	20.4	6.1	14.3
1977	19,500	5,777	13,723	99,240	19.6	5.8	13.8
1978	20,109	6,453	13,656	101,869	19.7	6.3	13.4
1979	20,203	6,773	13,430	102,957	19.6	6.6	13.0
1980	20,087	6,520	13,567	101,354	19.8	6.4	13.4

(a) Excluding (estimated) transfer costs of land and buildings (at 1975 prices) which do not enter into the change in the gross capital stock, but which are usually included by the CSO in gross fixed capital formation; estimates for 1966 to 1948 calculated by 'chaining' backwards according to proportionate changes in other constant-price series for transfer costs. Note that in 1972 substantial underestimates in previous years' figures were discovered and that chaining backwards has the effect also of adjusting for these underestimates (see *National Income and Expenditure 1972*, p. 110).

(b) Italicised figures in brackets are estimates based on change in (constant 1975 price) capital stock, in turn based on chaining backwards from 1967, the gross capital stock at 1975 prices for that year (£353.2 billion); chaining based on various CSO estimates of constant-price capital stock (1970 prices and 1963 prices) and Michael Ward's capital stock figures for 1955 to 1958. Italicised figures not in brackets calculated by chaining back from 1967 the retirements 1975-price figure for 1967 (£4,094 million) according to 1970-price retirements figures. Inevitably, these italicised figures are only approximations.

(c) Gross domestic fixed capital formation (adjusted to exclude transfer costs of land and buildings) *minus* Retirements.

(d) Expenditure-based figures.

Sources: Central Statistical Office, *Economic Trends Annual Supplement 1981 Edition*, pp. 5 and 14; Central Statistical Office, *National Income and Expenditure: 1959*, table 52, p. 53; *1960*, table 51, p. 52; *1961*, table 56, p. 55; *1962*, table 57, p. 61; *1964*, table 60, p. 68; *1965*, table 53, p. 65; *1966*, table 60, p. 72; *1967*, table 59, p. 74; *1969*, tables 56, 63, pp. 68, 76; *1970*, tables 55, 62, pp. 66, 74; *1971*, tables 56, 65, pp. 68, 78; *1972*, tables 55, 64, pp. 66, 76; *1973*, tables 55, 64, pp. 66, 78; *1964–74*, tables 62, 73, pp. 71, 82; *1965–75*, tables 11.7, 12.2, 12.12, pp. 73, 78, 85; *1966–76*, tables 10.7, 11.2, pp. 75, 80; *1967–77*, tables 10.7, 11.2, pp. 79, 84; *1979 Edition*, tables 10.7, 11.2, pp. 77, 82; *1980 Edition*, tables 10.7, 11.2, pp. 73, 78; *1981 Edition*, tables 2.1, 10.7 and 11.2, pp. 17, 73 and 78; Michael Ward, *The Measurement of Capital* (OECD, 1976) p. 141.

APPENDIX 15.3   *Company profits in the United Kingdom, 1956 to 1980*

Year	£ million, current prices		
	Gross trading profits of all companies, exc. stock appreciation	Gross domestic product at factor cost (income-based)	Gross trading profits as a percentage of GDP
1956	2,769	18,053	15.3
1957	2,934	19,019	15.4
1958	3,001	19,827	15.1
1959	3,240	20,935	15.5
1960	3,653	22,759	16.1
1961	3,518	24,069	14.6
1962	3,485	25,175	13.8
1963	3,992	26,842	14.9
1964	4,363	29,080	15.0
1965	4,517	31,271	14.4
1966	4,353	33,023	13.2
1967	4,540	34,610	13.1
1968	4,779	37,235	12.8
1969	5,092	39,983	12.7
1970	5,172	44,071	11.7
1971	6,065	49,058	12.4
1972	6,997	56,071	12.5
1973	8,035	65,423	12.3
1974	6,755	74,398	9.1
1975	7,678	93,755	8.2
1976	10,264	109,880	9.3
1977	15,228	126,417	12.0
1978	18,220	145,965	12.5
1979	19,779	168,663	11.7
1980	19,930	195,533	10.2

Sources: Central Statistical Office, *National Income and Expenditure: 1967–77*, table 1.2, p. 4; *1979 Edition*, table 1.2, p. 4; *1980 Edition*, table 1.2, pp. 4–5; *1981 Edition*, table 1.2, pp. 4–5.

Index of Subjects, Data,
and Exercises

References are given in the order:
page numbers;
followed by the prefixed numbers of:

T = Table;
D = Diagram;
E = Exercise;
A = Appendix.

(Note that the Chapter Guides, which merely list concepts in a descriptive narrative, are not indexed.)